This massive volume introduces readers into the foundations and the fundamentals of the missionary work of the church, written by a wide range of authors who are concerned with scriptural integrity and commitment to the gospel and its proclamation. The book is highly recommended.

—ECKHARD J. SCHNABEL, Mary F. Rockefeller Emeritus Distinguished Professor of New Testament, Gordon-Conwell Theological Seminary

Grounded in Holy Scripture, informed by history, and shaped by theological and missiological principles, this multiauthored volume offers thoughtful and practical guidance for a full-orbed vision for international evangelism, cross-cultural church planting, and global engagement. Mark Tatlock and Chris Burnett are to be congratulated for bringing together an array of talented authors to articulate principles, priorities, and practices for a holistic understanding of biblical missions. I am sure that this major resource will serve well the next generation of students, church leaders, missionaries, and missiologists for years to come.

—DAVID S. DOCKERY, president and distinguished professor of theology, Southwestern Baptist Theological Seminary; president, International Alliance for Christian Education

Drawing from the wells of systematic theology, biblical theology, and missions history, as well as hundreds of years of combined experience, a group of pastors, scholars, and missionaries joins forces in this book to provide unique perspectives from the mission field (in places as diverse as India, Italy, and Israel) to answer such questions as these: How should the example of the apostles guide missions? How does systematic theology inform missions? And how should churches support missions? Comprehensive, practical, and fascinating, this is a significant Reformed textbook on missiology. Come with questions and leave with biblical answers.

—JOEL R. BEEKE, chancellor and professor of homiletics and systematic theology, Puritan Reformed Theological Seminary

Believing the practice of missions to be extremely crucial, I was excited to discover a volume containing so many valuable insights. The biblical and historical undergirdings make it even more relevant. Here is a must-read for all who take our Lord's Great Commission seriously.

—DAVID ALAN BLACK, senior professor of New Testament and Greek (retired), Southeastern Baptist Theological Seminary; author of *Will You Join the Cause of Global Missions?*

I commend this book highly for its refreshing emphasis on theologically grounded missiology. Not all readers will agree with everything in this wide-ranging volume, but everyone will benefit from its zeal for world missions combined with careful biblical reflection.

—J. MATTHEW PINSON, president and professor of theology, Welch College

The book you hold in your hands is a veritable treasure trove of immense importance that concerns key missiological issues confronting the global church today. Rejecting the "hallowed" trends in much of the modern evangelical mindset, the authors of this book propose instead a bold, thorough, and more eminently biblical philosophy of missions, carefully articulated by some of its most prominent representatives across the globe. This book may become the standard textbook on doing missions God's way for years to come. The global church is very much indebted to Tatlock, Burnett, and all the other contributors for their courageous, clear, and comprehensive endeavor in the service of God and His church.

—MARIUS BIRGEAN, director, Timisoara Bible Baptist Seminary, Romania

God's redemptive plan is biblical, theocentric, Christ exalting, and church driven. History demonstrates that effective missions efforts have always been anchored in the Word of God, believed, lived out, and proclaimed in the power of the Spirit of God. *Biblical Missions* is an important work that argues for this kind of Great Commission work and from many different voices.

—CHOPO MWANZA, pastor, Faith Baptist Church Riverside, Kitwe, Zambia; deputy vice-chancellor of advancement, Central Africa Baptist University

Modern evangelical missiology too often attributes authority to culture and the secular sciences over Scripture. Placing the focus back on the Bible where it belongs, this valuable compendium pushes against integrationist models for global missions work and advances a conservative biblical theology of missions. I am thankful for Tatlock and Burnett—along with the many contributors—for providing this tremendous (and much needed!) resource on biblical missions that views Scripture as the ultimate authority and approaches it with a consistent literal methodology.

—CORY M. MARSH, professor of New Testament, Southern California Seminary; scholar in residence, Revolve Bible Church, San Juan Capistrano, CA

In the current missions world, mushy thinking and semibiblical, speed-driven efforts have now become the norm. This book takes us back to a Scripture-driven missiology. Tatlock and Burnett have gathered a group of solid thinkers and practitioners who shine a bright light on where the missions world is today and how we got there—a must-read for anyone serious about the Great Commission.

—BRAD BUSER, pioneer church planter; founder, Radius International

Biblical Missions is a resource we've needed for a long time: a meticulously researched and carefully reasoned missions textbook that unflinchingly turns to Scripture first as it discusses the various thorny issues that have plagued modern day missiology. I was encouraged and sharpened by what I found here.

—MATT RHODES, pioneer church planter, North Africa

This excellent new volume is both comprehensive and committed to biblical authority. Moreover, to one deeply concerned with restoring biblical leadership to local churches, this book is a great encouragement because it rightly seeks to restore missions to the local church also, from training missionaries to indigenous church planting to raising up elders in the planted church. *Biblical Missions: Principles, Priorities, and*

Practices is a clear, resounding call to every local body of believers to arise and fulfill her Lord's commission in her Lord's way. I warmly recommend it to readers everywhere.

—Alexander Strauch, author of *Biblical Eldership* and founder of Biblical Eldership
Resources; teacher and leader, Littleton Bible Chapel, Littleton, CO

For more than thirty years I have been directing missions and equipping missionaries throughout the world. I only wish this masterpiece, *Biblical Missions: Principles, Priorities, and Practices*, could have been available sooner. It is by far the most comprehensive, theologically accurate, and Christ-honoring reference book for missions I have ever seen.

—Mike Gendron, director, Proclaiming the Gospel Ministries

A profound and thorough work for anyone interested in missions or who is already serving in missions. A fascinating, enlightening, and enjoyable read. To God be the glory!

—Susan Heck, author and speaker, With the Master Ministries

Such a valuable resource! Each contributor offers biblically grounded, practical insights on key missiological issues, demonstrating how Scripture guides the mission of the church today. This is the one book to have if you are passionate about advancing the gospel with biblical clarity, theological depth, and global perspective.

—Les Lofquist, assistant professor of practical theology, Shepherds Theological
Seminary; former executive director, IFCA International

Biblical Missions is, in my opinion, the most comprehensive treatment on the subject of missions in recent decades. In bringing together some of the most brilliant theological minds in the church today, it recovers a topic that is often relegated to the ecclesiastical cellar and places it where it rightly belongs: at the forefront of what the church exists to do in the world—making disciples of all nations (Matt 28:19).

—Darrell B. Harrison, shepherding and teaching pastor, Redeemer
Bible Church, Gilbert, AZ; host, *Just Thinking Podcast*

Here is a much needed resource for the church today. It encompasses the whole of missions from the call to the care of the missionary. Here is a unique and timely tool for missionaries, missions committees, pastors, and the church at large, put together by a worldwide school of scholars involved in fulfilling the Great Commission.

—Alex Montoya, pastor, First Fundamental Bible Church, Whittier, CA

Though clouded and confused by many in the twenty-first century, the first-century work of biblical missions continues to advance worldwide by God's grace through the strategic work of faithful disciples of Christ. Participants in this vital cause must be trained and guided by seasoned leaders who have remained tenaciously faithful to God's Word. Herein you will find timeless principles, indispensable priorities, and a variety of practical insights that will aid the next generation in getting one step closer to the completion of the Lord's Great Commission.

—MIKE FABAREZ, pastor, Compass Bible Church, Aliso Viejo, CA;
president, Compass Church Planting Association

There are unique seasons in redemptive history when the Lord providentially gathers His choice servants for a very special ministry fruitfulness. Decades of missionary experience and ministry wisdom have merged in this volume, producing a remarkable blend of biblical depth, fresh practical clarity, and gospel urgency. Insightful ministry voices from around the globe leave no missionary challenge unaddressed, giving the church a comprehensive study guide for faithfully obeying our Lord's Great Commission. Pastors will love this tool for its biblical precision, and missionaries will find new boldness in its pages. Truly an extraordinary gift to God's people!

—JERRY WRAGG, senior pastor, Grace Immanuel Bible Church, Jupiter, FL; president, The Expositors Seminary

During my time in seminary, it was a missiology class that lit a fire in my heart for missions that has never gone out. Those early years shaped much of the way that our own church now prioritizes reaching the nations. Before that, I had little clue as to what biblical missions really looked like, which led to a host of well-intentioned but unbiblical ideas and efforts. Thanks to Mark Tatlock and Chris Burnett, a whole new generation can not only embrace the mission of God to the nations with zeal but also do so with biblical accuracy and experience God's blessing through their faithful labors.

—COSTI W. HINN, teaching pastor, Shepherd's House Bible Church;
founder and president, For the Gospel Ministries

Not just biblical but also practical and thorough. As a pastor concerned about fidelity and fruitfulness, I commend *Biblical Missions* as an essential training tool for years to come.

—JUSTIN HARRIS, senior pastor, Faith Bible Church, Naples, FL

Want to gain a biblical perspective on planting a God-honoring, biblically healthy and reproducing church among any people group? Read and heed this book!

—DAVE BARNHART, global outreach pastor, Grace Bible Church, Bozeman, MT

BIBLICAL MISSIONS

BIBLICAL MISSIONS

PRINCIPLES, PRIORITIES, AND PRACTICES

MARK TATLOCK AND
CHRIS BURNETT, EDS.

THOMAS NELSON®
Since 1798

THOMAS NELSON

Biblical Missions

Copyright © 2025 by The Master's Academy International

Published in Nashville, Tennessee, by Thomas Nelson. Thomas Nelson is a registered trademark of HarperCollins Christian Publishing, Inc.

Thomas Nelson titles may be purchased in bulk for educational, business, fundraising, or sales promotional use. For information, please email SpecialMarkets@ThomasNelson.com.

Library of Congress Cataloging-in-Publication Data

Names: Tatlock, Mark, 1974- editor. | Burnett, Chris (Professor of missions), editor.

Title: Biblical missions : principles, priorities, and practices / Mark Tatlock and Chris Burnett, eds.

Description: Nashville, Tennessee : Thomas Nelson, [2025] | Includes bibliographical references and index.

Identifiers: LCCN 2024023917 (print) | LCCN 2024023918 (ebook) | ISBN 9780310158172 (hardcover) | ISBN 9780310158226 (ebook)

Subjects: LCSH: Missions—Biblical teaching. | Evangelicalism. | Church history.

Classification: LCC BV2073 .B53 2024 (print) | LCC BV2073 (ebook) | DDC 266—dc23/eng/20240628

LC record available at https://lccn.loc.gov/2024023917

LC ebook record available at https://lccn.loc.gov/2024023918

Cover Design: Maffrine LaConte

Interior Design: Denise Froehlich

Printed in the United States of America

24 25 26 27 28 /TRM/ 5 4 3 2 1

Contents

PART 1: PRINCIPLES

SECTION 1: BIBLICAL FOUNDATIONS

Sub-Section 1: Missions and the Bible

SECTION 2: CHURCH PLANTING

Sub-Section 1: Biblical Parameters for Church Planting

Section 3: The Maturing and Reproducing Local Church

Sub-Section 1: Equipping Indigenous Church Leaders

Sub-Section 2: Theological Education for Church Leaders

Sub-Section 3: Music in Missions

Sub-Section 4: Bible Translation and Print Resourcing

PART 3: PRACTICES

SECTION 1: LOCAL CROSS-CULTURAL PRACTICES

SECTION 2: INTERNATIONAL PRACTICES

Sub-Section 1: Short-Term Ministry

FOREWORD

John MacArthur

When I was a student in seminary, I seriously considered going to the mission field. After reading about Martin Luther and the Protestant Reformation, I learned about the rise of theological liberalism and the subsequent decline of the German church. God used those studies to give me a heart for the church globally and especially in Germany. I began thinking that perhaps the Lord wanted me to serve as a missionary, to the extent that I went to a local college and began to study German. Though the Lord had other plans, my desire was simply to be available for what God might want me to do. Later in my life and ministry, I was blessed to make nearly a dozen trips to Russia. A similar desire arose in my heart for the church in Russia.

In God's providence, I began to be invited to preach elsewhere around the world. As I was blessed to minister in various places, an essential priority became increasingly clear to me: missions is about leadership. As the New Testament reveals, the church is effective when it has strong spiritual leadership, and conversely, churches languish under weak or corrupt leaders. Strong leadership consists of biblically trained, doctrinally sound, and elder-qualified pastors who are wholly committed to God's Word and God's work. Yet in too many churches (in both my homeland of the United States and abroad), such leadership is sorely lacking.

In my ministry travels around the world, I repeatedly saw the need for strong spiritual leadership. One experience cemented that reality in my mind. It took place in the 1980s, during a visit to Calcutta, India. One night a group of us attended a meeting of missionaries in the William Carey home in that city. A new missionary was also there who had recently arrived from a prominent evangelical seminary in the States. I was aware of the school, so I asked him in front of the group, "What is your objective in coming to India?" Without hesitation he said, "To liberate Indian women from male oppression." Incredibly, he said nothing of the gospel, nor of service to the church. That was a definitive moment for me. At the time, the seminary he had attended was a leading missionary training school for evangelicals. But here was a recent graduate deployed to the field, devoid of the gospel in terms of his ministry objectives. I left that meeting alarmed and dismayed. Moreover, I was convinced that something far different had to happen if the church was to be faithful to fulfill the Great Commission.

In spite of what some seminaries might teach, biblical missions is not driven by socioeconomic concerns, because its focus is not temporal but eternal. It is motivated by a love for the Lord Jesus, a passion for His Word, and a desire to see every soul bow in worship and submission to Him (Phil 2:9–11). True missionary work centers on the faithful proclamation of the gospel—the good news that sinners can be forgiven and reconciled to God through the person and work of Jesus Christ. Anything that distorts, dilutes, or distracts from the biblical message of salvation not only is not missions but is antithetical to the Great Commission.

For qualified spiritual leaders to be deployed to the mission field, they must be sent by churches that rightly understand and support the work of biblical missions. How is that kind of missions mindset cultivated in a local church? It is not primarily through annual missions conferences and periodic missionary reports. Rather, it is through the consistent preaching of the Word. It is the duty of every faithful pastor not only to do the work of an evangelist but to stir up a love for missions in the hearts of his congregation. This is primarily accomplished through the diligent and accurate exposition of Scripture, which reveals the purposes of God, including His heart to save the lost (1 Tim 2:3–4). As believers humbly receive the truth of God's Word, they become increasingly missions-minded as they grow in godliness and Christlikeness. As a result, they pray for the lost (2:1–2) and give sacrificially to support evangelistic work. In some cases, they will even embrace the work and become missionaries themselves.

Even now, the Lord is raising up many faithful workers to be sent into the harvest. Some will pastor domestically. Others will travel to foreign lands to serve in overseas missions. All will embrace the mandate of being a Great Commission Christian, preaching the truth of Jesus Christ and always being ready to give a defense for the hope of the gospel, with gentleness and reverence (1 Pet 3:15). Like the generations of believers who persevered before us, we have now been given the responsibility to guard the purity of the gospel and herald it boldly to the world around us.

What joy there is in knowing we belong to a cause that cannot fail. The Lord Jesus has promised to build His church (Matt 16:18). He will save sinners from every tribe, tongue, nation, and people. In His sovereign providence, He uses preachers to accomplish this global task (Rom 10:14–15). It is therefore imperative for the church to train up faithful men, locally and globally, who will study the Word as approved workmen (2 Tim 2:15) and then proclaim it boldly, in season and out of season (4:2). When the Word of the gospel is preached, the Spirit of God wields that truth to convict the heart and revive the soul (Heb 4:12). Thus, if the Great Commission is to be fulfilled, the church must raise up and send out preachers into the world.

I often hear people say, "We need to pray for a great global revival." Personally, I believe that we are living in the greatest revival of biblical truth in the history of the church. There is an immense hunger for the truth and for trained pastors who can handle the Word with precision. Nevertheless, the work is not done. The challenge is still critical, so our strategy needs to be right. That strategy is given to us in 2 Timothy 2:2: "The things which you have heard from me in the presence of many witnesses, entrust these to faithful men who will be able to teach others also." Paul's focus in this verse was on spiritual leadership—identifying, training, and deploying the next generation of faithful men. That is the biblical strategy for accomplishing the global mission. In articulating this strategy and explaining its implications, the book at hand seeks to convince its readers that biblical missions must begin with qualified pastors being trained to preach the Word and lead local churches.

If we train a generation of faithful men to shepherd the flock of God around the globe, they will be positioned to entrust the truth of the gospel to the next generation. In this way, their efforts will exalt the Lord Jesus, edify the church, and evangelize the lost. My prayer is that this book will make an enduring contribution to that end.

GENERAL EDITORS' PREFACE

The title *Biblical Missions: Principles, Priorities, and Practices* sets before the reader the core conviction that the authority under which believers commit to the Great Commission lies outside of culture, human wisdom, and pragmatic rationales. An examination of the evangelical global missions literature of the last half century reveals a preponderance of thinking, methods, and strategies primarily informed by the secular fields of sociology, anthropology, and cultural studies—which, in many cases, have replaced Scripture as the primary authorities in missiology.

The disciplines of missiology and the practices of world missions have adapted and applied these secular fields as their own, primarily within the last half century. Not all contemporary missions courses and programs are secularized, as many missions teachers and trainers have labored tirelessly to send workers into the harvest with conservative evangelical convictions. Yet a survey of the missions literature—including books, academic journals, magazines, courses, study guides, websites, and even missionary newsletters—reveals that this integrationist approach has led to dangerous compromises to biblical faithfulness over the last few generations. Many missions teachers and mentors have disproportionately relied on training resources that do not uphold the Bible as the authoritative and sufficient foundation for faithful missionary work. As a result, they have planted humanistic and extrabiblical sociocultural philosophies in the minds of their disciples. The secularizing of missions is particularly concerning, given that the students of today become tomorrow's missionaries, leaders, pastors, mentors, and teachers.

The current evangelical missionary movement is in need of reform. The *Biblical Missions* textbook and workbook are not intended to be the only voice in this effort, nor are they the only conservative evangelical tool worth commending. However, the resources here are unique. God has graciously assembled over one hundred contributors who are experienced international practitioners and leaders, originating from and serving in all global regions, representing a wide variety of backgrounds and experiences. Though the textbook and workbook are produced in North America, nearly forty of our authors originate from the regions of Africa, Ibero-America, Asia Pacific, the Middle East and North Africa (MENA), and Europe, and more than sixty currently reside and minister in these regions.

The diversity of our contributors is celebrated because of their unity: each contributor is biblically trained and writes out of conservative evangelical convictions, following a grammatical-historical hermeneutic for applying biblical texts to treat a range of missiological problems and topics affecting the mission of the global church. Though the contributions do not treat every mission topic, practice, or debate exhaustively, each author applies sound doctrine exegetically, theologically, methodologically, and practically to articulate how to let the Scriptures guide the principles, priorities, and practices for advancing the gospel among the nations today.

The *Biblical Missions* workbook is a companion volume that applies the textbook's instruction and insights, layering questions and projects across twenty-four lessons to help readers become students. These students will then translate the essential missiological ideas of the textbook into action for use in new contexts, as the Lord leads. Both volumes are designed to equip readers across academic, local church, and organizational contexts worldwide so that they carry out faithful Great Commission ministry to the glory of God.

When a local church pastor upholds the authority of Scripture in his preaching, the ministries of his church will implement a biblical philosophy of ministry and church members will be sanctified in the truth. Then the church's gospel witness will radiate with integrity—not only in its own context but across the village, township, city, or national context and beyond its borders, with far-reaching, eternal, and spiritual impact. Simply said, *mature churches become sending churches*. Therefore, it is our desire for this resource set to help believers in local churches across the world to grow spiritually, so that in time their local churches will become sending churches to new, unreached fields. Indeed, if they are to advance the Great Commission, they must reproduce.

To that end, the Lord has provided the opportunity for us, through the ministry of The Master's Academy International (TMAI), to equip national pastors in eighty-five locations worldwide to faithfully preach and teach the Word of God. TMAI's world map, which began to be drawn back in 1991, is pinned with countless local churches, by the grace of God and to His glory. This world map illustrates that faithfulness to New Testament principles produces mature churches. We have designed the *Biblical Missions* textbook and workbook specifically to emphasize the centrality of the local church in the work of global missions, that the fulfillment of the Great Commission hinges upon the priority of ministry in and through the local church in every place.

As you begin this study, consider your motivation for world missions, whether as one who goes or one who sends. Is your motivation shaped by human standards and measurements or by God's heart to redeem sinners? The question is subtler than it seems. It is easy to measure ministry success quantitatively, especially when there are Western influences, theological systems, and denominational patterns passed down through missions history and in our churches that have placed the greater emphasis on man's ability. Yet numbers-oriented strategies demonstrate an overreliance on man's abilities for bringing salvation to the lost. Ultimately, we can miss the heart of the gospel message, which is that God alone saves sinners, so that He is glorified as the Savior (Ps 115:1; Rom 11:36; 2 Cor 4:15; Phil 2:10–11).

Opposite a man-centered motive for missions is a theocentric focus—a focus on God's purpose for sending the Lord Jesus Christ into the world. In John 17, Christ emphasized that His motive for going to the cross is that sinners might be granted eternal life, "that they may know You, the only true God, and Jesus Christ whom You have sent" (v. 3). Thus, God's motive to save and sanctify sinners is so that they might find their greatest delight in the love of the Father, Son, and Holy Spirit (vv. 24–25). To glorify and enjoy God is the ultimate purpose of the cross. It is therefore the goal of God's purpose in saving men and women, and it must be the motivation for which we participate in the missions endeavor until the end of the age (Matt 28:20).

With the cross before Him, Christ prayed that the believer would go into the world sanctified in the truth, proclaiming the truth, and demonstrating the truth:

> I have given them Your word; and the world has hated them, because they are not of the world, even as I am not of the world. I do not ask You to take them out of the world, but to keep them from the evil one. They are not of the world, even as I am not of the world. Sanctify them in the truth; Your word is truth. As You sent Me into the world, I also sent them into the world. For their sake I sanctify Myself, that they themselves also may be sanctified in truth. (John 17:14–19)

May all who use the *Biblical Missions: Principles, Priorities, and Practices* textbook and workbook find the encouragement and examples needed to be faithful in their calling to bring glory to God as participants in His unfolding plan of redemption in our generation.

For the honor of Christ and the salvation of the nations,

MARK TATLOCK AND CHRIS BURNETT
Los Angeles, California, USA

ABBREVIATIONS

AB	Anchor Bible
ABD	*Anchor Bible Dictionary*. Edited by David Noel Freeman. 6 vols. New York: Doubleday, 1992.
ANF	*Ante-Nicene Fathers*. Edited by Alexander Roberts and James Donaldson. 10 vols. 1885–1887. Reprint, Peabody, MA: Hendrickson, 1994.
BDAG	Bauer, Walter, Frederick W. Danker, William F. Arndt, and F. Wilbur Gingrich. *Greek-English Lexicon of the New Testament and Other Early Christian Literature*. 3rd ed. Chicago: University of Chicago Press, 2000.
BECNT	Baker Exegetical Commentary on the New Testament
BSac	*Bibliotheca Sacra*
EEC	Evangelical Exegetical Commentary
EDNT	*Exegetical Dictionary of the New Testament*. Edited by Horst Balz and Gerhard Schneider. ET. 3 vols. Grand Rapids: Eerdmans, 1990–1993.
EMSS	Evangelical Missiological Society Series
EMQ	*Evangelical Missions Quarterly*
EBC	Expositor's Bible Commentary
HALOT	*The Hebrew and Aramaic Lexicon of the Old Testament*. Ludwig Köhler, Walter Baumgartner, and Johann J. Stamm. Translated and edited under the supervision of Mervyn E. J. Richardson. 4 vols. Leiden: Brill, 1994–99.
ICC	International Critical Commentary
IJFM	*International Journal of Frontier Missiology*
JBL	*Journal of Biblical Literature*
JETS	*Journal of the Evangelical Theological Society*
KEL	Kregel Exegetical Library
L&N	Louw, Johannes P., and Eugene A. Nida, eds. *Greek-English Lexicon of the New Testament: Based on Semantic Domains*. 2nd ed. New York: United Bible Societies, 1989.

MNTC	MacArthur New Testament Commentary
MSJ	*The Master's Seminary Journal*
NA²⁸	*Novum Testamentum Graece*. Kurt Aland, Barbara Aland, Johannes Karavidopoulos, Carlo M. Martini, and Bruce M. Metzger. 28th ed. Stuttgart: Deutsche Bibelgesellschaft, 2012.
NAC	New American Commentary
NICNT	New International Commentary on the New Testament
NICOT	New International Commentary on the Old Testament
NIDNTTE	*New International Dictionary of New Testament Theology and Exegesis*. Edited by Moisés Silva. 5 vols. Grand Rapids: Zondervan, 2014.
NIGTC	New International Greek Testament Commentary
NIVAC	New International Version Application Commentary
NPNF¹	*Nicene and Post-Nicene Fathers*, Series 1. Edited by Philip Schaff. 14 vols. New York: Christian Literature Co., 1886–1889.
NPNF²	*Nicene and Post-Nicene Fathers*, Series 2. Edited by Philip Schaff and Henry Wace. 14 vols. New York: Christian Literature Co.; Scribner, 1890–1900.
PG	Patrologia Graeca [= *Patrologia Cursus Completus*: Series Graeca]. Edited by Jacques-Paul Migne. 162 vols. Paris, 1857–1886.
PNTC	Pillar New Testament Commentary
TDNT	*Theological Dictionary of the New Testament*. Edited by Gerhard Kittel and Gerhard Friedrich. Translated by Geoffrey W. Bromiley. 10 vols. Grand Rapids: Eerdmans, 1964–1976.
Them	*Themelios*
TNTC	Tyndale New Testament Commentaries
TOTC	Tyndale Old Testament Commentaries
WBC	Word Biblical Commentary
WCF	*The Westminster Confession of Faith*. 3rd ed. Lawrenceville, GA: Committee for Christian Education and Publications, 1990.
WTJ	Westminster Theological Journal
ZECNT	Zondervan Exegetical Commentary on the New Testament
ZECOT	Zondervan Exegetical Commentary on the Old Testament

INTRODUCTION

Understanding the term *missions*, as reflected in *Biblical Missions: Principles, Priorities, and Practices*, is critical for every believer. Throughout the volume the term *missions* appears in the plural, rather than the singular form *mission*, though it is used grammatically in the singular (e.g., "Biblical missions is . . ."). There are two reasons for this nomenclature.

First, using the plural form of the noun grammatically in the singular has been standard parlance among conservative evangelicals for generations and continues to reflect common usage today. The compound term *biblical missions* adopts this usage and is defined as *the Great Commission task of proclaiming the excellencies of Christ to sinners cross-culturally and applying the authority and sufficiency of Scripture to every activity of disciple-making in all contexts.*

The apostle Paul is the paramount example of biblical missions in action, an example that begins the moment of his calling by the risen Christ, which he recounts in Acts 26:16–18:

> But rise up and stand on your feet; for this purpose I have appeared to you, to appoint you a servant and a witness not only to the things which you have seen, but also to the things in which I will appear to you; rescuing you from the Jewish people and from the Gentiles, to whom I am sending you, to open their eyes so that they may turn from darkness to light and from the authority of Satan to God, that they may receive forgiveness of sins and an inheritance among those who have been sanctified by faith in Me.

Paul's commission captures biblical missions today: going where Christ sends and preaching and teaching to people blinded by sin—so that the Holy Spirit might use His powerful Word to open their darkened spiritual eyes and place them under the sovereign authority of God, who forgives, sanctifies, and glorifies all who believe in His Son.

The apostle Peter emphasized the cross-cultural dimension of biblical missions for believers who live among people trapped in the darkness of their sin, writing in 1 Peter 2:9–12 this charge:

But you are a chosen family, a royal priesthood, a holy nation, a people for God's own possession, so that you may proclaim the excellencies of Him who has called you out of darkness into His marvelous light; for you once were not a people, but now you are the people of God; you had not received mercy, but now you have received mercy.

Beloved, I urge you as sojourners and exiles to abstain from fleshly lusts which wage war against the soul, by keeping your conduct excellent among the Gentiles, so that in the thing which they slander you as evildoers, they may because of your good works, as they observe them, glorify God in the day of visitation.

Many local church members across the world today, like Peter's recipients, have cross-cultural opportunities to bring the light of Christ into the surrounding spiritual darkness. These opportunities are present even without being sent to live, like Paul, among sinners in a different place with a different culture. In fact, believers in most locations today live in cross-cultural environments because of the increasing presence of foreign peoples in cities and towns across the world. Simply put, then, biblical missions is a reality for all believers in one way or another. The term *biblical missions* is to be read throughout the volume with this global and local cross-cultural force.

The second reason for using the plural form of the noun rather than the singular form, *mission*, is to avoid adopting or promoting the nonevangelistic concepts the term written in the singular has conveyed since the middle of the twentieth century, when the ecumenical movement became ascendant in the evangelical church. The insertion of the term *mission* into evangelical discourse served to broaden the scope of "missions" to include any activity that a believer might do in an attempt to glorify God, such as creation care and political activism.[1] *Mission* has now become so inclusive of broadly Christian endeavors that it cannot be read immediately with the evangelistic understanding that is embedded in the plural *missions*. It is unclear to what degree *mission* involves the verbal assertion of the gospel's content or the confrontational application of the truth to repudiate sin and establish growing disciples of Christ.

Therefore, the addition or removal of just one letter is hardly inconsequential—it has the power to clarify or confuse the missionary task. The believer who desires to advance the Great Commission in faithfulness to Christ and to Scripture will do well not only to use the plural form *missions* in speech but to embrace the definition of *biblical missions* in action.

---

1. The real-time development of this change in terminology was documented in Norman Goodall, ed., *The Uppsala Report 1968: Official Report of the Fourth Assembly of the World Council of Churches Uppsala July 4–20, 1968* (Geneva: World Council of Churches, 1968), especially in Arne Sorvik, "Section II: Renewal in Mission," 21–38. See also the lucid remarks in Craig Ott and Stephen J. Strauss, *Encountering Theology of Mission: Biblical Foundations, Historical Developments, and Contemporary Issues* (Grand Rapids: Baker Academic, 2010), 200–201.

Motivation for the Work

Believers can be grateful the Lord has instructed the church through His Word how to fulfill the Great Commission, according to which His disciples must "go therefore and make disciples of all the nations, baptizing them in the name of the Father and the Son and the Holy Spirit, teaching them to keep all that [He] commanded [them]" (Matt 28:19–20). Biblical clarity, however, is not always met with biblical consistency in practice by Christ's disciples. In fact, it seems as if two rival realities are simultaneously operative in world missions.

On one track, biblically faithful leaders of local churches and missions agencies are helping to plant churches that are maturing and reproducing new, doctrinally sound congregations all over the world. These leaders and their church members need a biblical framework for understanding the essential topics of missions that require their attention. For these readers, the expert contributors in the textbook offer accessible instruction and wise insights about the complex work of world missions in one go-to resource that is comprehensive and culturally diverse, making for a multifaceted and dynamic approach to understanding and practicing missions God's way.

On the other track, many training institutions, local churches, and missions organizations risk ineffectiveness in the field, despite their time, resources, and personnel, who serve with courage and sacrifice. They face at least two problems. The first can be called the "strategy-before-Scripture" problem, in which they are regularly absorbing the literature of nonconservative and nonevangelical theorists without conservative evangelical response, leaving their understanding and approach to missions unbalanced. Many missiological publications detail practices with culturally and sociologically rich examples but often have more anecdotal insights than scriptural argumentation. Readers might receive much cultural exposure, but it is questionable how much instruction they receive about how to implement biblical missions principles in tangible ways, or whether those activities being promoted are biblically and theologically grounded. This strategy-before-Scripture approach can leave readers more confused than convicted about which theories to attempt in practice.

A second problem that can lead to ineffectiveness in missions work is the opposite of the first. It might be labeled the "concept-without-context" problem, and it can stem from conservative evangelical missions literature. While conservative scholars do well to detail the exegetical and theological basis for missionary service, their writings often sorely lack cross-cultural examples that model biblical consistency in practice. This concept-without-context approach can make otherwise helpful materials seem culturally unaware and incomplete, if not irrelevant. Real-world examples of biblical missions practices often remain hidden from the readers who need them—perhaps simply for lack of documentation or due to the assumption that they are not necessary to commend to observers. As a result, missions enthusiasts look elsewhere, finding biblically incompatible or unconvincing case studies ready for their consumption.

Purpose and Scope of the Work

Biblical Missions: Principles, Priorities, and Practices is a resource set consisting of the textbook and an accompanying workbook. The objective of the textbook is to analyze and promote biblical missions from within the disciplines of biblical and theological studies and to provide a variety of cultural case studies that exemplify in faithful practice the topics discussed.

The workbook's lessons serve to guide the user to apply the textbook's biblical teaching in personal and practical ways for the advance of the Great Commission. The biblically faithful instruction of both volumes will help readers learn how to align their missions efforts under the authority of Scripture, respond to modern challenges with biblical principles, and translate sound doctrine into obedient action at home and on the mission field.

To achieve these results, the textbook and workbook aim to equip readers in two specific ways. First, readers will discern how to avoid wasteful activities that are falsely called "missions." Missions-minded believers today, who have a growing sense of urgency to fulfill the Great Commission, need to examine whether their labors contribute to disciple-making in the context of the local church, and whether their investments help to mature local churches on the mission field. Many instructions illustrated by numerous examples will help them to utilize their God-given resources to fulfill the tasks of biblical missions for the glory of God alone.

Second, readers will learn how to challenge unbiblical missions leadership in light of the Great Commission. Many well-intentioned missionaries are not living and working in alignment with a biblical approach to missions, partly because their leaders in their local churches, educational institutions, and missions organizations do not offer them the biblical direction they need to fulfill essential missionary roles and activities. For this reason, the textbook and the workbook have been designed for use by local believers, missionaries, and their leaders in these very contexts.

Readers of the Work

The textbook and workbook are designed to instruct and enable a spectrum of individuals involved in or interested in missions to engage in cross-cultural ministry more faithfully and effectively. There are three categories of readers for whom the work was designed, each equally important but in a distinct way.

First are *institution-level readers*: students in training centers, Bible colleges, universities, and seminaries who are considering becoming missionaries, are already missionary candidates, or are open to engaging in missions in the future. These readers are seeking from the textbook a solid biblical foundation and a conservative, evangelical understanding of missions theology. They desire to learn theories, concepts, and strategies that directly correlate to biblical passages, and they value reading accounts of biblical activities, historic practices, and faithful contemporary examples from a variety of cultural contexts.

Second are *organization-level readers*: missionaries and the missions agency leadership that oversees their activities. This category includes missionaries in active service on the field—at every stage of experience—as well as those in executive roles within missions organizations and sending agencies, including regional, country, and team or project leaders. These readers want the *Biblical Missions* resource set to sharpen their understanding and practice of missions so that they comprehend their work, design their programs, and operate every cross-cultural activity with biblical fidelity. Additionally, missions executives will look to the volumes to provide better guidance to their missionaries—including correcting unbiblical teaching and activities and assisting workers in a state of plateau or burnout on the field.

Third are *ecclesiastical-level readers*: believers in local churches who are members of the global church. This category encompasses a broad audience, including those who are church leaders and members who desire to be involved in missions work or already are. Some of these readers are pastor-teachers, missions committee members, Bible study leaders, congregants, and longtime missions donors. They might be exploring missions as a new and interesting topic, or they sense the need to further align their missions efforts with biblical principles and teach them more effectively so that their fellow believers have a depth of understanding about the priorities they should uphold in the local church.

Regardless of the category, each reader of the textbook shares common convictions and presuppositions. Here are several:

- They want a resource they can trust to train them in biblical missions.
- They want to be obedient to God's Word in all ways, including the Great Commission.
- They want their missions practices to be theologically aligned with Scripture and profitable to the global church.
- They want to correct any unbiblical assumptions and activities for ministries they do, follow, or support.
- They want to develop greater cross-cultural understanding and perspectives.
- They want to be able to analyze modern missions concepts and strategies biblically.
- They want to serve the Lord of the harvest with wisdom, urgency, and joy, and they want others to join them.
- They want Christ to build His church, making faithful disciples worldwide.

Structure of the Work

The *Biblical Missions: Principles, Priorities, and Practices* textbook follows the tripartite division in its title. The missions principles in part 1 are derived from the Old and New Testaments and described in missions history. These principles lead to a multifaceted discussion about missions priorities in part 2, all which center on the work of Christ in, to, and through His church. On the foundation of biblical principles and priorities, many missions practices are described in part 3, offering guidelines and corrections for many common contemporary activities so that they will be conducted according to the Great Commission and maximally useful to Christ's kingdom.

The textbook is then subdivided with sections and Sub-Sections that build from biblical knowledge to action steps. Editors' notes are supplied at the beginning of the three parts to summarize the content that follows and to provide rationales for their inclusion of topics at their given points in the overall argument of the textbook. Within each section are Sub-Sections comprised of chapters and inserts. The chapters provide the core instruction on the topic of the Sub-Section, while the inserts are global case studies or biblical and theological excursuses that generally reflect creative applications of an element from the chapter. The chapters and inserts together present a unified voice to speak positively about biblical missions as well as critically against unbiblical concepts and practices operative around the world today.

Additional components in the textbook include an abbreviations list for scholarly references throughout the volume, a glossary of key terminology with definitions that are informed by the doctrinal presuppositions and convictions of the authors, and indices to aid readers in cross-referencing topics and Scripture passages.

A Final Word

Biblical Missions: Principles, Priorities, and Practices would not be possible without the effort of many teammates and ministry partners who worked together in a spirit of unity to ensure a good and pleasant process designing and completing this project (Ps 133:1). Many more names could be added to this list, but we would like to thank the board members, directors, and special donors of The Master's Academy International; lead copy editor Joshua Sherrill; editorial project manager Josiah Sisto; editing teammates Jamie Bissmeyer, Kevin Bell, Grant Gates, Jeremy Phillips, Aaron Darlington, Daniel Gumprecht, Hillary Megee, Max Megee, Jeff Miller, Collin Vassallo, and Tony LaConte; student reviewers Will Hale, Adam Wilson, Garrett West, Bien Cedro, Tyler Williams, and Dillon Phillips; pastor reviewers Michael Chalmers, Henry Anderson, and Timothy Dinkins; cover designer, Maffrine LaConte; the supportive team of Thomas Nelson; prayer partners in many local churches around the world; and the Tatlock and Burnett families, who met longsuffering with joy throughout many stages of the process.

It is the prayer of the general editors, the authors, and the entire production team that today's church will embrace biblical missions and be faithful in accomplishing it for the glory of the Lord Jesus Christ. Christ promised to build His church, and the gates of hell will not prevail against it (Matt 16:18). Every person ministering cross-culturally is thus given two assurances by Christ: first, that He alone will accomplish the great outcome of redeeming for Himself a people, the church; second, that victory is secure as the truth advances against the enemy and his powers of darkness. Both assurances lead the missionary to the unmistakable conclusion that Christ's work done Christ's way will accomplish the goal for which He died and rose (1 Cor 15:12–22) and for which we die daily (15:31)—that Christ would be glorified in His church. Therefore, the work of biblical missions is the noblest of life's pursuits for the one who is devoted to Christ. With Christ at the center of your vision, we now invite you to apply godly zeal and passion to understanding how to "make disciples of all the nations" (Matt 28:19).

PART 1

PRINCIPLES

Editors' Note

Part 1 lays a foundation for understanding the biblical, theological, and historical principles of world missions. Scripture reveals that God has always used His supremely authoritative Word to transform sinners into citizens of His kingdom. The New Testament presents Christ's Great Commission as the foundation for disciple-making. This divine mandate, further elaborated in Acts and the Epistles, emphasizes reliance on God's Word and the Holy Spirit's power rather than human strategies. As key moments of missions history bear out, making disciples begins with confronting unbelief, verbally asserting the biblical gospel, calling for repentance and belief in the truth, and instructing new believers to become obedient to Christ at all costs in the context of the local church. The good news of the gospel for missionaries is that God's Word has always triumphed over evil, as seen in the conversion of sinners, despite extreme opposition in this dark world. With urgency and hope, all who long for Christ to reign over His earthly kingdom must proclaim His excellencies until He comes again.

SECTION 1

BIBLICAL FOUNDATIONS

Sub-Section 1: Missions and the Bible

CHAPTER 1

Fidelity to the Word of God in Missions: Scripture as the Launch, Life, and Legacy of the First Missionaries

Abner Chou

In God's plan, the apostles were the first Christian missionaries. After all, they were the ones who originally received the Great Commission (Matt 28:19–20), who took the gospel from Jerusalem to Samaria and Judea (Acts 1–8), and whom God used to break through to the Gentiles by empowering them to take the gospel from Antioch to Athens and plant churches from Colossae to Corinth. They were the ones who suffered shipwreck, beatings, persecution, and even death all for the sake of Christ. They were the ones who brought the gospel to Rome, and since all roads lead to and from Rome, they were the ones who set up for the gospel to go to the ends of the earth. In that way, the generation of the apostles was the generation of those who were not only the first missionaries but the foundational ones, those whose work inaugurated and established the work of missions after them.

By their own declaration, the cornerstone of the ministries of these first missionaries was Christ (Eph 2:20; 1 Pet 2:6), and as such, this foundational generation declared that the highest view of His Word is the foundation of all those who would follow in their footsteps (Eph 2:20; 2 Pet 1:4; Jude 3). The apostles devoted themselves to "the service of the word" (Acts 6:4), preaching Jesus from the Old Testament, and teaching His commands (1:8; 4:2; 5:42; 8:35; 10:42–43; 17:2–3; 28:31). It was the Word that repeatedly increased, multiplied, spread, and was received (6:7; 8:14; 11:1; 12:24; 13:49; 19:20). And it was the Word that Saul and Barnabas proclaimed wherever they went, after the Spirit set them apart as missionaries (13:2–5). There is a reason why the dominant storyline of the book of Acts is the spread of God's Word:[1] the apostles were fixated on it. For them, Scripture was critical in launching the church, crucial in the life of the church, and the core of their legacy for the church. The first missionaries were marked by a pure and unyielding fidelity to God's Word, and those who desire to follow in their footsteps must bear this same mantle.

The Word in Launching the Church

Scripture's self-attestation is that its words and syntax, in its original autographs, are absolutely true in all its claims.[2] The first missionaries not only believed this truth, but they were the ones, under inspiration, who wrote it and established it as foundational for the church. In Acts, Peter's proclamation at Pentecost assumed the truthfulness of Scripture, boldly declaring the reality of the fulfillment of prophecy (Acts 2:25–28). He understood that the prophetic word dealt with historical reality, emphasizing the historicity of David (2:25, 29, 34) as well as Christ's death and resurrection (2:29–36). Peter's subsequent sermon in Acts 3 also assumed the truthfulness of Scripture, affirming the historicity of Abraham, Samuel, and Moses (3:22–25). Peter grasped the Scriptures' authority, demanding repentance in light of the word preached (2:38), and since many believed his message that day (2:41), the inerrancy and authority of God's Word were part of the fundamental perspective of the church in Jerusalem.

Stephen also upheld the inerrancy of Scripture in Acts 7. Though not an apostle, he was commissioned by them and functioned in an official capacity under them (Acts 6:2–6, 8). Standing before the Sanhedrin, Stephen indicted them as having become just like their "fathers," who opposed God and His prophets. In Stephen's sermon, he quoted nineteen times from five Old Testament books, presupposing the historicity of the stories of the patriarchs, the exodus, and the time at Sinai and the wilderness wanderings.[3] Stephen affirmed the details of these biblical accounts, including people, places, and chronology.[4] Stephen was

---

1. Brian S. Rosner, "The Progress of the Word," in *Witness to the Gospel: The Theology of Acts*, ed. I. Howard Marshall and David Peterson (Grand Rapids: Eerdmans, 1998), 215–34.

2. Paul D. Feinberg, "The Meaning of Inerrancy," in *Inerrancy*, ed. Norman Geisler (Grand Rapids: Zondervan 1979), 267–304, esp. 294; International Council on Biblical Inerrancy, "The Chicago Statement on Biblical Inerrancy," accessed June 18, 2024, https://library.dts.edu/Pages/TL/Special/ICBI_1.pdf; John MacArthur and Richard Mayhue, *Biblical Doctrine: A Systematic Summary of Bible Truth* (Wheaton, IL: Crossway, 2017), 81, 107–13; Roger R. Nicole, app. 5, "Charles Hodge's View of Inerrancy," in *Inspiration*, Archibald A. Hodge and Benjamin B. Warfield (1881; repr., Grand Rapids: Baker, 1979), 93–95.

3. Barbara Aland et al., eds., "Index of Quotations," in *The Greek New Testament: Apparatus*, 5th ed. (Stuttgart: Deutsche Bibelgesellschaft, 2014).

4. In Acts 7:14, Stephen cited "seventy-five" descendants of Jacob, found in the Septuagint of Genesis 46:26 and Exodus 1:5, whereas the Masoretic Text gives "seventy" in both of these and in Deuteronomy 10:22. The larger number is the sum of all persons, including Joseph's children (I. Howard Marshall, *Acts: An Introduction and Commentary*, TNTC 5 [Downers Grove, IL: InterVarsity,

an inerrantist—unflinchingly so in the face of a hostile and learned crowd.

Paul did not deviate from the convictions of Peter and Stephen. In Acts 13, he preached the Scripture with full confidence in its truthfulness, discussing the exodus, wilderness wanderings, conquest, judges, and other events up through David chronologically (vv. 16–22). Such history serves as the backdrop for proclaiming Jesus as the final David, who fulfills God's promises (vv. 23–41). For Paul, Scripture described reality, one that grounded the very events in his day, a truth that the nascent churches embraced upon hearing his message (v. 48).

In addition to the book of Acts, the New Testament epistles attest to the great labor of the first missionaries to ground the church with convictions about God's Word. Peter wrote to scattered exiles that God's Word is inspired, more sure than experience, and that which one must cling to like a light in a dark place (2 Pet 1:19–21). Paul wrote to Timothy, reminding him that the local church and its leaders must understand that all Scripture is God-breathed, the very communication of God, and thereby should be preached with all authority (2 Tim 3:16–4:2). The same apostle reminded the Corinthians of the historicity of Scripture, that without the actual event of Christ's resurrection, one's faith is meaningless (1 Cor 15:15–19). Even in his short epistle, Jude presupposed the reality of Scripture, using the wilderness wanderings, Sodom and Gomorrah, Cain, and Balaam, as reminders of what God will do against false teachers (Jude 6–13). Battling false teachers, the apostles persistently reminded the church that they did not follow myths (1 Tim 1:4; 4:7; Titus 1:14; 2 Pet 1:16).

In recent days, some have argued that inerrancy is a recent doctrinal creation,[5] that the gospel can be divorced from its historical foundations,[6] and that the Bible may have errors in history and science though having some redemptive truths.[7] However, from the beginning of the church, the apostles labored to entrench God's people with the conviction that Scripture is inerrant, and they built their exhortations and teachings upon this truth. The first inerrantists include the first missionaries, demonstrating that inerrancy is not merely an assumption of missions but that its proclamation and inculcation are part of the very endeavor of missions.

1980], 146), and it befits Stephen's purpose of giving a historical overview. The apparent tension, however, does not challenge the inerrancy position but supports it, for that view has always affirmed the need for and legitimacy of responsible text criticism for determining the canonical text. For there would be no need to ascertain the original reading of an unreliable Bible. See art. X of International Council on Biblical Inerrancy, "The Chicago Statement on Biblical Inerrancy"; art. XVI, "The Chicago Statement on Biblical Hermeneutics," November 13, 1982, https://library.dts.edu/Pages/TL/Special/ICBI_2.pdf.

5. This was Francis Watson's appraisal in "An Evangelical Response," in *The Trustworthiness of God: Perspectives on the Nature of Scripture*, edited by Paul Helm and Carl R. Trueman (Grand Rapids: Eerdmans, 2002), 288.

6. E.g., the Jesus Seminar (1985–98); "The Jesus Seminar," Webstar Institute, n.d., accessed June 18, 2024, https://www.westarinstitute.org/projects/the-jesus-seminar/.

7. This began being articulated in the late nineteenth century, for example, in Henry B. Smith, *The Inspiration of the Holy Scriptures* (New York: John Gray, 1855), found today in Clark Pinnock, *The Scripture Principle* (San Francisco: Harper and Row, 1984); Michael Licona, *Why Are There Differences in the Gospels?* (New York: Oxford University Press, 2017).

The Word in the Life of the Church

The apostles not only grounded the church on Scripture but made Scripture central to the life of the church. This is inherently true since it is their scriptural writings that explain the principles by which the church should conduct itself (1 Tim 3:15). The commands to proclaim the gospel (Acts 1:8), to make disciples (Matt 28:19–20), to love one another (1 John 4:7–8), to baptize (Matt 28:19–20), to partake of the Lord's table (1 Cor 11:17–34), to sing (Eph 5:19), to show hospitality and humility, and to serve, pray for, and even greet one another (Jas 1:6; 1 Pet 4:9–10; 5:5, 14) all come from inspired writ. Scripture defines the gospel (1 Cor 15:1–4), the very core message of which the church testifies, and Scripture even explains and justifies the church's existence (Acts 2). The Bible is so intrinsic to the church that without it, the church would not only have no objective way to know what it should do, but it would not even have grounds for existence.

Scripture's centrality in the church is why Paul declares that biblical revelation is the foundation for the church (Eph 2:20) and the very way the saints are equipped for the work of ministry (Eph 4:11–12). It is why leadership is charged with carefully stewarding sound doctrine (2 Tim 1:13; 2:1–2). It is why the reading of God's Word is crucial in the church service (1 Tim 4:13; 2 Tim 4:1–2). It is also why preaching God's Word is a must for the ministry (1 Tim 5:17). At the beginning of the church in Acts, there were numerous sermons. The book of Hebrews is a sermon, and Paul commanded preaching (2 Tim 4:1–2). All of this accentuates that scriptural teaching and proclamation are to permeate the life of the church (Eph 4:11; Titus 2:1–9) as they drive sanctification (Col 3:16; 2 Pet 1:5). In hearing God's Word, the saint is to be a doer of it (Jas 1:19–24), and such fruitfulness in the Word provides assurance (Jas 1:25; 2 Pet 1:10). Scripture is necessary for the Christian life, and that is why God's people must pay careful attention to what God has revealed (Heb 2:1) and contend for it (Jude 3). It is the spiritual milk that the saint craves and needs (1 Pet 2:2).

Thus, the apostles labored to make Scripture central to the life of the church. This was an explicit emphasis by every author of the New Testament in their various epistles and to a wide geographic spread of churches. Scripture is not merely found at the beginning of the first missionaries' ministries, that which lays the foundation for the church, and then the church moves beyond it. Rather, the entirety of the church's life and ministry is to move further into it. For it is both that which provides all the truths for the entirety of the Christian life, as well as the power of God that convicts the soul, makes wise the simple, and compels one toward Christ (Ps 19:7–10; Heb 4:12).

"More Sure" Than Experience

In contending for the centrality of Scripture in the church, the first missionaries labored tirelessly against two major falsehoods. One was the elevation of one's own wisdom or experience. "We have as more sure," Peter wrote, "the prophetic word" (2 Pet 1:19). In context, the apostle was recalling his own immersive experience at Jesus' transfiguration (vv. 17–18; cf. Matt 17:1–8). He vividly remembered what he had seen and heard. Some thirty years later, he was still reporting it to the churches of Asia (v. 16).[8] He knew beyond any doubt that it was real. Yet he said, Scripture was "more sure."

To demonstrate the categorical difference of Scripture from any human experience or knowledge, Peter emphasized that the Scripture is "prophetic." Naturally, by this, Peter affirmed that the Old Testament was authored by the prophets. More to the point, the Word is "prophetic" because it decrees what then comes to pass (Deut 13:1–5; 18:20–22; Amos 3:7). As opposed to experience testing the validity of Scripture, Peter reminded his audience that God's decrees determine "the end from the beginning" and everything in between (Isa 46:10). Therefore, because God's words cause all experiences, they are more sure than any single experience or knowledge.

Peter therefore contends that His written Word should define God's people, not the other way around. The apostle exhorts, "To [this word] you do well to pay attention as to a lamp shining in a dark place" (2 Pet 1:19). "Pay attention" (*prosechō*) means to put high-quality focus on something until it consumes and controls the one doing so.[9] Believers must fixate on Scripture as needing a light in a dark and dangerous place (Ps 119:9–11, 105). For God's Word will guide His people to when

"the day dawns and the morning star arises in [their] hearts" (2 Pet 1:19), to the moment when Christ returns and all is fulfilled and made right. Scripture is sufficient to the end.

Life is full of experiences, and people usually know their memories of them to be true. The stronger something impresses the senses, the stronger the feeling of assurance. It is no wonder, then, that the temptation is strong to elevate experience above Scripture. When the two contradict, most people simply subordinate what they read to what they sense or feel. After all, others claim that advances in science have shown the Bible's validity needs to be qualified or that inerrancy can no longer be reconciled with collective human knowledge. However, Peter declares that the Bible is "more sure" than what one knows that he knows. It is the only true standard for life in the church.

"More Sure" Than Subjective Interpretation

Another threat to Scripture's centrality in the church is subjectivity. The Bible may not be replaced by one's experience, but it might be reinterpreted, especially since the spirit of the age proudly rejects objective moral and spiritual authority (Rom 1:21, 25, 28). Even in the times of the first missionaries, false teachers had indeed crept in and were adding their philosophies, traditions, and "knowledge" to the Bible, even as they do today. They taught heresies and

---

8. On the date and destination of the epistle, see Thomas R. Schreiner, *1, 2 Peter, Jude*, NAC 37 (Nashville: B&H, 2003), 276–77; D. A. Carson and Douglas J. Moo, "2 Peter," in *An Introduction to the New Testament*, 2nd ed. (Grand Rapids: Zondervan, 2005), 663–64.

9. "προσεχω," BDAG, 879; H. Kuhli, "προσεχω," *EDNT*, 3:171.

empty promises (2 Pet 2:1, 19), mocked some Scriptures and twisted others (1:16; 3:3–4, 16). They purposefully misinterpreted prophetic texts and then justified their interpretation by subjectivizing the texts' origins.

Thus, in his final letter, Peter reminded God's people, "Know this first of all, that no prophecy of Scripture comes by one's own interpretation" (2 Pet 1:20). The term *interpretation* has the idea of "loosing" and denotes the way God unleashed His truth.[10] The idea is that even a prophet's "interpretation" (from *epilysis*)—his understanding of the dreams, visions, auditions, and impressions he received from God—was not his own.[11] What was said, why it was said, and its intended implications were given by God in the inspiration process.

This is precisely why Peter later said that false teachers twist the Scripture to their own destruction (2 Pet 3:16). God's Word is not left to one's private creativity or personal fancy. For its original meaning was not at all in anyone's personal interpretation, but in the God-given intent of the inspired author, who was perfectly moved by God so that what he wrote was God's very revelation down to the words of

the autographs (Ps 12:6; 119:160; 2 Tim 3:16). Even while using the prophets' language and style, God's message was necessarily perfectly conveyed. Human fallibility and subjectivity never entered the equation, and the way the Scriptures came to be is the way they always will be, objective and divine.

Naturally, this allows no "personal" or "secret" meanings, and no "deeper" or "fuller" sense in Scripture. The divinely intended meaning was expressed through divinely given words, exactly equal to those of God's chosen instruments (1 Cor 2:10–13; e.g., Exod 7:1–2; 2 Sam 23:2).[12] The only acceptable interpretation thereafter is that same objective meaning. This is the approach of the grammatical-historical hermeneutic, "to determine the sense required by the laws of grammar and the facts of history."[13]

This also means that Scripture is not beyond the believer's grasp but is conveyed in terms people can understand. So, by the Spirit's illumination (1 Cor 2:14–16; 1 John 2:27), help from divinely gifted teachers (Eph 4:11–12), and one's own diligence (2 Tim 2:15),[14] Christians can sufficiently interpret the Bible

---

10. "ἐπιλύω," *NIDNTTE*, 2:224–25.

11. Richard J. Bauckham, *Jude, 2 Peter*, WBC 50 (Dallas: Word, 1983), 229–35.

12. See discussion of "concursive operation" in B. B. Warfield, *The Inspiration and Authority of the Bible*, ed. Samuel G. Craig (Phillipsburg, NJ: P&R, 1948), 94–96; and of "organic inspiration" in Herman Bavinck, *Reformed Dogmatics*, vol. 1, *Prolegomena*, 388–89, 435–39; Brad Klassen, "The Doctrine of Inspiration and Its Implications for Hermeneutics," *MSJ* 34, no. 2 (Fall 2023): 343–67.

13. Walter C. Kaiser Jr., *Toward an Exegetical Theology: Biblical Exegesis for Preaching and Teaching* (Grand Rapids: Baker, 1981), 87; cf. art. XV of International Council on Biblical Inerrancy, "The Chicago Statement on Biblical Inerrancy"; Robert L. Thomas, *Evangelical Hermeneutics: The New versus the Old* (Grand Rapids: Kregel, 2002), passim; Milton S. Terry, *Biblical Hermeneutics: A Treatise on the Interpretation of the Old and New Testaments*, 2nd ed. (1890; repr., Eugene, OR: Wipf and Stock, 2003), 173. See also the present author's discussion in *The Hermeneutics of the Biblical Writers: Learning to Interpret Scripture from the Prophets and Apostles* (Grand Rapids: Kregel Academic, 2018), 12–14, and the works cited there.

14. The Westminster Confession helpfully calls this "a due use of ordinary means" (*WCF* 1.7).

as God intended. Indeed, they must pay careful attention to the Word (2 Pet 1:19). For God has not made man to seek Him out subjectively but has given His Word objectively and propositionally to them (Deut 18:10–22).

Yet, when missionaries seek to be "culturally relevant," the temptation is again strong to wield the Bible as if its origins and meaning were "open to interpretation." This is effectively what happens when one accommodates Scripture's content to local, contemporary ways of thinking. One might think that as long as Christ is kept central and clearly proclaimed, then the "more peripheral" doctrines of Scripture can be held more loosely. But while this attitude has an appearance of piety, it neglects the apostolic warning not to permit philosophy, human tradition, or worldly principles to creep in and take anyone captive in place of Christ (Col 2:8). A reinterpreted Bible is a reinterpreted Christ and Christianity and is truly no Christianity at all.

Therefore, believers must endeavor not to subject Scripture to their own understanding but subject their understanding to Scripture. By pursuing authorial intent (literal), through the rules of language used by the author (grammar), and with the understanding of the original cultural context of the text (history), one can understand God's Word on His terms and not one's own.

The Only Foundation

The apostles fought to keep the Bible central to the life of the church because they knew that the Christian life depends on Scripture. Peter made this clear in 2 Peter 1:19–21, his "textbook definition" of inspiration, which has been expounded above. To synthesize, the definition is worth repeating in full:

> And we have as more sure the prophetic word, to which you do well to pay attention as to a lamp shining in a dark place, until the day dawns and the morning star arises in your hearts. Know this first of all, that no prophecy of Scripture comes by one's own interpretation. For no prophecy was ever made by the will of man, but men being moved by the Holy Spirit spoke from God.

The inspiration of Scripture makes it unique among all other books or knowledge, and because it is in a category by itself, it stands as the exclusive authority for the true church. As in Peter's day, there are still those who attempt to displace Scripture from its central position, but Peter, along with all the first missionaries, reinforces that this book could never be replaced by experience nor undermined by reinterpretation. Inspiration made the Bible "more sure" than anything else in this world and the only foundation for life. The first missionaries recognized that this commitment was necessary to fulfill Christ's commission, "teaching them to keep all that I commanded you" (Matt 28:20).

The Word as the Legacy for the Church

The first missionaries demonstrated their dedication to the Scriptures by what they said when they were about to die. Knowing that his execution was imminent, the apostle Paul penned the book of 2 Timothy (4:6). Every chapter of this epistle is filled with exhortations and reminders about Scripture. It charges the man of God to "hold to the standard of sound words" and to "guard" it as treasure (1:13, 14); exhorts him to be diligent, "accurately handling the word of truth" (2:15); reminds him that "all Scripture is God-breathed" (3:16); and charges him again to "preach the word" (4:2). In the face of death, Paul impressed the glory of Scripture upon his son in the faith.

In writing to Timothy, Paul not only declared these truths to the young man but demonstrated them. "When you come," the apostle wrote, "bring the cloak which I left . . . and the scrolls, especially the parchments" (2 Tim 4:13). On death row, Paul requested only two items: one, a coat for the winter, the other, some copies of Scripture.[15] Paul's requests reflect that he needed his Bible as much as clothing. Having just expressed the centrality of Scripture, the apostle lived it out as he yearned for his Bible, testifying by his example that there is nothing more sufficient and necessary than Scripture.

When Peter was about to die (2 Pet 1:13–14; cf. John 21:18–19), he, too, was consumed with Scripture and instructed his readers in the most important doctrines they would need to remember (2 Pet 1:15). Most fundamental of these was inspiration, which refuted the false teachers who undermined God's Word with their "false words" (2:1–3) and twisted Scripture to their own condemnation (3:16). Of everything this missionary could have addressed in his final days—all doctrines, practical urgencies, or missional strategies for the future—Peter wrote that God's Word was trustworthy. Its "precious and magnificent promises" (1:2–4), the Old Testament (1:19–21), the commandments of Christ (3:1–2), and even the letters of the emerging New Testament (3:14–19)[16]—were all to be held fast. What mattered most to this pastor dying far from home was the Bible.

What the apostles wrote at their death displays their deep and abiding concern for the Scriptures. The desire to pass on this message to those who followed them demonstrates that this conviction and passion were not just for the first missionaries. A high view of Scripture, a ministry that champions the Scriptures, and a labor that defends the Scriptures are not just for the first generation. This is the endeavor for any who would carry onward the apostles' legacy. They must love and trust the Bible. It must be their treasure and comfort. Confidence in it must be the dying witness to their churches, their co-laborers, and even their persecutors. For it has "words of eternal life" in Jesus Christ (John 6:68).

---

15. On "the scrolls" (*ta biblia*) and/or "the parchments" (*tas membranas*) being Scripture portions, see "βιβλίον," *TDNT*, 1:617–20; I. Howard Marshall, *A Critical and Exegetical Commentary on the Pastoral Epistles*, ICC (London: T&T Clark, 2004), 820–21; Michael J. Kruger, *Canon Revisited: Establishing the Origins and Authority of the New Testament Books* (Wheaton, IL: Crossway, 2012), 251–54.

16. Kruger, *Canon Revisited*, 204–5.

Conclusion

The apostles were the first missionaries, and as they set the pattern for all those who would follow in their footsteps, they modeled a profound love for God's Word. Scripture was the foundation they laid for every church plant as they boldly proclaimed its inerrant message. Scripture was at the heart of the Christian life, grounding the church's understanding and practice, and the apostles vigorously contended to ensure that this Word would remain central to each congregation. Scripture was also the legacy the apostles left to subsequent generations, a reminder of the supreme importance of the Bible to these first missionaries and, further, an indication that such conviction was not just for the first missionaries but for all missionaries, anyone who claims to champion the cause of Christ.

For any who yearn to follow in the footsteps of the first missionaries and engage in true missions, the secret is not new theories or methodologies. Rather than innovating, one must go back and receive the mantle of ministry that was handed off by the first missionaries and every faithful generation thereafter. One must not adopt new ideas but the convictions of the saints of old in ministry, loving and living out God's Word in life and in death. Then, and only then, will one truly work out the Great Commission.

INSERT 1.1

Trends in Global Missions Away from Biblical Fidelity

E. D. Burns

Those who were born in the 1910s and died in the early twenty-first century witnessed a tremendous amount of change. They saw common modes of travel shift from horses and buggies and steam-powered trains and ships to transcontinental jet flights, electric cars, and everything in between. The breakthrough of nuclear power and the prospect of nuclear war changed the human experience in terms of both personal comfort and national security. Lights, heat, and air-conditioning could be turned on with the flip of a switch, but life, health, and civilization could be turned off with a nuclear launch button. The internet and smartphones brought instant access to virtually any and all information the mind could imagine, but curiosity and vice gave life to both seedy lust and totalitarian control. The world as a whole has witnessed more rapid change in the last century than all centuries of world history combined.

Amid all the change, the church of Christ continues to march militantly through the dark chapters of communism, fascism, Islamic terrorism, New Ageism, evolutionary atheism, and every other "ism" man has devised to suppress the knowledge of God and His righteousness. Though while the global church has made its advances, it has also lost some ground in places. To rightly assess the missions trends away from biblical fidelity in the twenty-first century, it is prudent to reflect on the strengths and weaknesses of the past few generations and to learn from the ways conservative evangelicals have historically pushed back. Then the opportunities and threats of the foreseeable future can be assessed also.

Looking Back at Strengths

The World Missionary Conference was held in Edinburgh in 1910.[17] Afterward, mainline Protestant denominations jumped headlong into ecumenical dialogue, attempting to unite Christians around earthly causes, banking on theological minimalism and a revisionist gospel to accomplish it.[18] This appeared to be a loss for biblical missions, but the evangelical church rallied to clarify and restate its theological conviction that only in the crucified and risen Christ can sinners find eternal salvation. Christ's exclusivity as Savior and Lord regained a central focus in missions-minded churches.[19]

Evangelical churches also articulated their loyalty to the inerrancy of Scripture. It was no coincidence that the Chicago Statement on Biblical Inerrancy in 1978 grew out of a generation of evangelical missions leaders who were committed to translating and distributing the Bible around the world.[20]

Looking Back at Weaknesses

The eighteenth and nineteenth centuries were markedly different from the missions efforts that have followed. Former generations of the modern missionary movement were known for their emphasis on evangelism, preaching,

---

17. F. L. Cross and Elizabeth A. Livingstone, eds., "Edinburgh Conference," in *The Oxford Dictionary of the Christian Church* (New York: Oxford University Press, 2005), 533–34.

18. Harold H. Rowdon, "Edinburgh 1910, Evangelicals and the Ecumenical Movement," *Vox Evangelica* 5 (1967): 49–71. See also, Brian Stanley, *The World Missionary Conference, Edinburgh 1910*, Studies in the History of Christian Missions (Grand Rapids: Eerdmans, 2009).

19. Arthur Johnston, *The Battle for World Evangelism* (Wheaton, IL: Tyndale, 1978). See also, W. H. T. Gairdner, *Echoes from Edinburgh, 1910: An Account and Interpretation of the World Missionary Conference* (New York: Revell, 1910); and Bobby Jamieson, "Evangelism and Social Action: A Tale of Two Trajectories," *9Marks Journal* 7, no. 1 (January–February 2010): 51–55, https://www.9marks.org/article/evangelism-and-social-action-tale-two-trajectories/.

20. International Council on Biblical Inerrancy, "The Chicago Statement on Biblical Inerrancy."

and teaching,[21] but the generations of the twentieth and twenty-first centuries have employed a buffet style selection of missions methods, so that anyone can do missions and everything can be missions.[22] The long-term priority of translating and teaching the Bible has been replaced with short-term devotion to expediency in the name of "being the love of Christ" or "building the kingdom." Short-term causes have smothered previous efforts to make Christ known through the pastoral task of teaching and preaching the Word.

Furthermore, a pervasive focus on evangelistic zeal over theological confessions seemed to unite churches that held historically distinct theological commitments, as evidenced in Edinburgh 1910 and its later development into the World Council of Churches (1948). The surface-level cooperation, however, gave way to the burden of its long-term growth; the broadened ecumenical vision increasingly diluted its evangelistic mission in favor of social and political agendas.[23] The twentieth century's evangelical missions movement has sometimes seemed theologically inconsequential and faddish because it has prioritized methods based on the burning sentiments and "felt needs" of the ever-changing culture rather than theological confessions that emerge from Scripture and stand the test of time.

Looking Ahead at Opportunities

Scripture's use of the term *nations* has come to be understood as a reference to ethno-linguistic people groups, not just geopolitical states. This missiological clarification pricked the evangelical conscience, highlighting the fact that thousands of small, unknown language groups exist without a Bible in their heart language. This realization has spurred evangelical missionary mobilization for the sake of reaching the most resistant and least reached people groups. The opportunities are indeed vast for Bible translation and theological resource development in small, obscure language groups around the world. With ever-improving digital technology and linguistic software, the chance to engage unreached language groups is remarkable.

---

21. See E. D. Burns, *The Missionary-Theologian: Sent into the World, Sanctified by the Word* (Fearn, Ross-shire, UK: Christian Focus, 2020), 91–118; Burns, *A Supreme Desire to Please Him: The Spirituality of Adoniram Judson* (Eugene, OR: Pickwick, 2016), 18–46; Stephen Neill, *A History of Christian Missions*, 2nd ed., Penguin History of the Church 6 (Harmondsworth, UK: Penguin, 1986), 224.

22. See Denny Spitters and Matthew Ellison, *When Everything Is Missions* (Orlando, FL: Bottomline Media, 2017); Kevin DeYoung and Greg Gilbert, *What Is the Mission of the Church? Making Sense of Social Justice, Shalom, and the Great Commission* (Wheaton, IL: Crossway, 2011); Gilbert Greg and D. A Carson, *What Is the Gospel?* (Wheaton, IL: Crossway, 2010), 15–22.

23. David J. Hesselgrave, *Paradigms in Conflict: 15 Key Questions in Christian Missions Today*, ed. Keith E. Eitel, 2nd ed. (Grand Rapids: Kregel Academic, 2018), 285–95.

The general ease of international travel has likewise created increased opportunities to access the world. International college students, for instance, heavily enroll in Western universities. This gives local churches enormous opportunities to evangelize and disciple future global leaders. Similarly, Christian students have great opportunities to study abroad in hostile countries and learn foreign languages that will uniquely equip them for service in the Great Commission.

Looking Ahead at Threats

In 2020 the world changed with COVID-19, and not for the better. Not only did some people grieve the loss of family members and friends to the infectious disease, but many people around the world experienced communist global hegemonies asserting totalitarian control over their lives and livelihoods through digital surveillance, which poses a threat to freedom of information, ease of communication, and unrestricted assembly. The projected rise of a global surveillance state that could digitally harvest unlimited information about every person creates untold future challenges to God's people—people who gather to hear from the King who rules the nations.

Christian doctrine continues to experience direct opposition and hostility. Though some disparate worldviews like Islam and New Ageism do not seem to have much in common, they do share a common disdain for biblical truth and the lordship of Christ. Christians must wake up to the fact that the tolerant pluralism of the twentieth century is over. God's people have always been at war with the spirit of the age, but it seems that many Christians have compromised with the culture in recent generations in exchange for a perception of peace. The church now faces a new anti-truth campaign, one that threatens the mind, heart, and resolve of every faithful Christian.

CHAPTER 2

The Authority and the Sufficiency of the Bible for the Missionary Task

Chris Burnett

The Gospels record how a Gentile placed his trust in the Lord Jesus Christ at a time of desperate need (Matt 8:5–13; Luke 7:1–10). He was a Roman centurion with a sick and dying servant under his charge, and he sought help from the one who wields sovereign power over life itself. As an army officer, he was established as an authority over others yet was himself under authority. At the moment of greatest distress, the centurion made a profession of faith that has echoed throughout history: "Lord, I am not good enough for You to come under my roof, but just say the word, and my servant will be healed. For I also am a man placed under authority, with soldiers under me" (Matt 8:8–9; Luke 7:7–8). Jesus described the centurion's profession as an indication that he had "such great faith," and this kind of faith pleased the Lord (Matt 8:10; Luke 7:9).

Gospel proclaimers everywhere today, whether they are missionaries, church leaders, or church members, are called to exercise the great faith of the Roman centurion. For them, faith means engaging sinners with the core belief that only Jesus wields authority over spiritual death and life, because to Him alone "all authority has been given" (Matt 28:18). This chapter presents a biblical and theological rationale as to why gospel proclaimers can have a settled confidence that the Bible holds divine authority and is completely sufficient to make maturing disciples according to the Great Commission. The words of the Bible are the authority by which eternal life is proclaimed to the spiritually dead, and they are sufficient to provide everything sinners need to know to begin living out their spiritual lives now with lasting effect.

Missiological Tensions

There are many approaches to making disciples and teaching biblical truth. The range of strategies proposed by mission theorists today runs along a spectrum with two fundamental poles.

One pole is "biblical proclamation." Biblical proclamation is best understood as preaching and teaching the Scriptures in a way that affirms and applies the authority and sufficiency of Scripture in every missionary activity. Proclamation ministries aim to make the biblical and theological content of Scripture understandable to their target audience, expounding and explaining the text so hearers can believe and live with a transformed worldview and culture.

At the pole of biblical proclamation, the central missionary activity is preaching and teaching the text of the Bible, being careful not to neglect any theological concept or passage, since every word of Scripture constitutes "all that [Christ] commanded" (Matt 28:20) and is prescribed for missionary use everywhere. Proclamation activities prioritize the ministries of Bible translation, biblical exposition, theological education, and a range of practical applications to matters of local church governance, public worship, ministry, and Christian conduct.

The opposite pole of the spectrum of missionary activity is "cultural accommodation." "Cultural accommodation" refers to modifying the biblical author's intended meaning for a text and its teachings when communicating in a new context. The goal is to make Scripture "culturally relevant" to hearers with different social and cultural assumptions and values, whose spiritual concepts and language are embedded in other faiths and worldviews. To arrive at an understanding of what "cultural accommodation" is and why it is diametrically opposed to proclamation strategies, it is necessary to state a few ideas of what "cultural accommodation" is not.

First, cultural accommodation is not a function of linguistics and should not be confused with what might be called "linguistic accommodation." Linguistic accommodation specifically deals with articulating the content of biblical truth according to the rules of grammar and the implications of culturally shaped terminology, such as idioms, expressions, and certain word choices.[1] Missiologists today helpfully affirm linguistic accommodation as necessary to cross-cultural communication. Many evangelicals join nonevangelicals in using the term *contextualization* to represent the importance of making Scripture and the Christian faith understandable to the target audience.[2] However, the concepts of contextualization, which originated from nonevangelicals

---

1. For ancient discussions on the method of linguistic accommodation, see Jerome, "The Letters of St. Jerome," 57.5 (113–14); on Jerome's search for sense equivalence, see Kadhim Khalaf Al-Ali, "St. Jerome's Approach to Word-for-Word and Sense-for-Sense Translation," *Journal of the College of the Arts, University of Basrah* 74 (2015): 49–74.

2. See David J. Hesselgrave and Edward Rommen, *Contextualization: Meanings, Methods, and Models* (Pasadena: William Carey Library, 1989), 200; repeated in David J. Hesselgrave, *Communicating Christ Cross-culturally: An Introduction to Missionary Communication* (Grand Rapids: Zondervan, 1991), 143–44; Scott A. Moreau, *Contextualization in World Missions: Mapping and Assessing Evangelical Models* (Grand Rapids: Kregel Academic, 2012), 36; Timothy C. Tennent, *Invitation to World Missions: A Trinitarian Missiology for the Twenty-First Century* (Grand Rapids: Kregel Academic, 2010), 85–86, 325; Dean Flemming, *Contextualization in the New Testament: Patterns for Theology and Mission* (Downers Grove, IL: InterVarsity, 2005), 19–20; Will Brooks, "Grammatical-Historical Exegesis and World Mission," in *World Mission: Theology, Strategy, and Current Issues*, ed. Scott N.

for broad sociocultural and political ministry activity, remain unhelpfully varied and impractical for those committed to biblical exposition.[3]

Second, cultural accommodation does not refer to superficial cultural adaptations in the missionary himself. Proponents who use the term "contextualization" to describe linguistic accommodation also use the term to encompass the missionary's public persona, such as his dress, rhetorical style, artistic sensibilities, and social behaviors.[4] They suggest that a missionary's own cultural adaptations, his personal "contextualizations," facilitate understanding and believing the Christian faith. There is no question that a missionary's modifications to his lifestyle, appearance, and behavior in his new context are matters of common sense that facilitate cross-cultural communication by helping to limit distractions to the biblical message being proclaimed. Hudson Taylor (1832–1905), early missionary to China, shaved his head, grew a traditional pigtail, and donned Chinese attire, with the goal of reducing the distraction of his foreignness while he preached from the Bible.[5]

The kinds of cultural accommodation strategies that sit opposite of text-based ministries are those that look to the hearer's sociocultural context and religious beliefs and practices as the starting place for determining what Christian texts and doctrines are to be communicated and which of them might need adapting, delaying, or possibly withholding from the target population. Biblical interpretation (hermeneutics) and theological method are two main areas of discussion among proponents of cultural accommodation. Scholars have discussed whether a missionary's message is invalidated if the interpretation of Scripture is conducted according to Western principles, methods, and perspectives, while the worldview, local beliefs, and thought patterns of the target audience are non-Western.[6] Missions theorists now question whether the Bible can indeed be the starting place for evangelistic engagement if their audiences do not perceive biblical claims

Callaham and Will Brooks (Bellingham, WA: Lexham, 2019), 239–67.

3. For the original proposal of "contextualization," see Theological Education Fund, *Ministry in Context: The Third Mandate Programme of the Theological Education Fund (1970–77)* (Bromiley, UK: Theological Education Fund, 1972), 17–20; Ray Wheeler, "The Legacy of Shoki Coe," *International Bulletin of Missionary Research* 16, no. 2 (April 2002): 77–80; M. P. Joseph, Po Ho Huang, and Victor Hsu, *Wrestling with God in Context: Revisiting the Theology and Social Vision of Shoki Coe* (Minneapolis: Fortress, 2018). Concerns are noted in Hesselgrave, *Communicating Christ Cross-Culturally*, 138. On the revisionist hermeneutical methodologies and pragmatic approaches of evangelical contextualizers, see Raymond C. Hundley, "Towards an Evangelical Theology of Contextualization" (PhD diss., Trinity Evangelical Divinity School, 1993), 14–25, 84, 272; also see Steven J. Schneider, "A Hermeneutical and Exegetical Evaluation of Contextualization in Light of John 1:14" (ThM thesis, The Master's Seminary, 2009), esp. 17–19, 21–28, 64–71.

4. Paul G. Hiebert, *The Gospel in Human Contexts: Anthropological Explorations for Contemporary Missions* (Grand Rapids: Baker Academic, 2009), 19–22; Robin Dale Hadaway, *A Survey of World Missions* (Nashville: B&H Academic, 2020), 189.

5. J. Herbert Kane, "The Legacy of J. Hudson Taylor," *International Bulletin of Missionary Research* 8, no. 2 (April 1984): 74, 76; John Charles Pollock, *Hudson Taylor and Maria: A Match Made in Heaven* (1962; repr., Fearn, Ross-shire, UK: Christian Focus, 2015), 52–55.

6. For a hermeneutical proposal of cultural accommodation, see Elizabeth Yao-Hwa Sung, "Culture and Hermeneutics," in *Dictionary for Theological Interpretation of the Bible*, Kevin J. Vanhoozer, gen ed. (Grand Rapids: Baker Academic, 2005), 150–55.

as spiritually valuable.[7] Proponents of cultural accommodation also question what theological method missionaries should employ to engage target populations with cultural sensitivity and how unique Christianity is compared to other faith traditions.[8] Some scholars openly question what constitutes doctrinally sound Christianity across the global church, given that contextual forms of Christian theology have given rise to nearly limitless modes of evangelical identification.[9]

The fact that there is a spectrum of approaches for missionary engagement—from the priorities of proclamation to the strategies of accommodation—leads to at least two insights. First, positively, missionaries of all types desire to see the message of the gospel impact the dying world, even if they do not agree on how that impact will be achieved. Second, negatively, not all missionaries are convinced that the Word of God is the Holy Spirit's sufficient means for gospel transformation, even though they agree that Scripture plays a role in authentic transformation. The question for cultural accommodation proponents is ultimately whether the Bible has the divinely authoritative grounds for use as the missionary's sufficient tool for theological engagement with other cultures.

Biblical Authority and Global Proclamation

According to Scripture, the undebatable, supreme authority for all cultural engagement is Scripture itself. The reason is that God breathed out His Word for the purpose of spiritual instruction for "everything pertaining to life and godliness" (2 Pet 1:3), so that God's revealed thoughts would affect the listener's thoughts and conduct and then result in all praise and glory going to His name (Deut 29:29; 2 Tim 3:16; 2 Pet 1:3; cf. 1 Tim 4:16). With the true worship of God at stake, the Bible demands an obedient response by all people— people of all times, in all places, in all contexts, and in all ways. It is the missionary's task to call for repentance, that hearers would believe in the one true God and submit wholly to His written revelation.

The authority inherent to the Scriptures is Christ's own inherent authority, by which He empowers His disciples to proclaim His Word. The Great Commission of Matthew 28:18–20 makes this connection when Christ charged the

---

7. Jackson Wu stated provocatively that "it is possible to unwittingly 'Judaize' (i.e., 'Westernize') our listeners." Jackson Wu, *One Gospel for All Nations: A Practical Approach to Biblical Contextualization* (Pasadena, CA: William Carey Library, 2015), 6. For the perception that historic Western attempts at adapting, accommodating, and indigenizing Scripture and theology were harmfully conditioned by Western culture, see David J. Bosch, *Transforming Mission: Paradigm Shifts in Theology of Mission* (Maryknoll, NY: Orbis, 1991), 447–50.

8. For example, some Western scholars who downplay theological distinctions between the Christian triune God and Allah of Islam include Miroslav Volf, *Allah: A Christian Response* (San Francisco: HarperOne, 2011); Carl Medearis, *Speaking of Jesus: The Art of Not-Evangelism* (Colorado Springs, CO: David C. Cook, 2011); J. Dudley Woodberry, "Reflections on Christian-Muslim Dialogue," *Fuller Studio*, accessed June 18, 2024, https://fullerstudio.fuller.edu/reflections-christian-muslim-dialogue/.

9. For an ever-expanding openness to context-specific orthodoxy, consult the seminars of the working group "Method in Systematic Theology: The Search for Biblical Orthodoxy," at the National Meeting of the Evangelical Theological Society, November 21, 2019, particularly those of Veli-Matti Kärkkäinen and Kurt Anders Richardson.

first missionaries to proclaim His Word with His authority: "All authority has been given to Me in heaven and on earth. Go therefore . . . teaching them to keep all that I commanded you." As the following sections will show, the doctrine of the authority of Scripture undergirds this Great Commission expectation of authoritative proclamation. Specifically, Jesus' universal authority is communicated to His disciples, who exert derived authority when they undertake the cross-cultural task of biblical proclamation.

The Universal Authority of Jesus

The reason Jesus' disciples go to all the nations to proclaim the gospel is because they are confident that the divine author of the message is the supreme authority over the message. Jesus' authority is established in the first verse of the first Gospel, in Matthew 1:1—"The book of the genealogy of Jesus Christ, the son of David, the son of Abraham." The Lord Jesus Christ is in the seed line of Abraham, through whom all the nations will be blessed (Gen 12:3). He is from the family of King David, to whom was promised an heir over a divinely established kingdom forever (2 Sam 7:12–13, 16).[10] Jesus is Israel's Messiah, who exercises global sovereignty and mediates divine blessing across the

world spiritually now and materially in the future (Isa 11; 60).

Matthew's conclusion, then, reiterates that Jesus' supreme dominion is unlimited in scope, being "in heaven and on earth" (Matt 28:18). Because His control is supreme and universal, His followers will now reach the farthest ends of the earth with His power, starting with the "lost sheep of the house of Israel" (Matt 10:5–6; 15:24; 22:1–10; Rom 11:13; cf. Acts 26:16–18).[11] As the disciples are sent out into the world, Jesus continues to possess ultimate authority over the preaching and teaching of His Word far and wide today.

The Derived Authority of Jesus' Disciples

Christ alone is to be obeyed as the utmost ruler of a person's life. This statement has implications for both the proclaimer and the hearer. For the proclaimer, "all that [Christ] commanded" delimits the range of what the missionary should proclaim to his audience (Matt 28:20). Not just anything the missionary thinks his audience should hear will fit within the box of Christ's commands, yet the range of teachings ready to be applied is not a small box, only a well-defined one.[12] Personal testimonies alone do not save, nor do the personal

---

10. The Great Commission of Matthew 28 is a thematic *inclusio* to Matthew 1:1 because it is David's Messiah who "makes possible the fulfillment of the universal intention that the good news is brought to the nations." In Craig Ott and Stephen J. Strauss, *Encountering Theology of Mission: Biblical Foundations, Historical Developments, and Contemporary Issues* (Grand Rapids: Baker Academic, 2010), 36. Also see Eckhard J. Schnabel, *Early Christian Mission*, 2 vols. (Downers Grove, IL: InterVarsity, 2004), 1:365.

11. R. T. France, *The Gospel of Matthew*, NICNT (Grand Rapids: Eerdmans, 2007), 1079.

12. Jesus' teachings consisted of "the Law and the Prophets" (Matt 5:17–19; 7:12; Luke 16:16–17; 24:27; cf. Luke 4:16–17; Acts 13:15ff., 27). The Old Testament canon was the prophetic foundation for the person and work of the Lord Jesus Christ (Luke 24:25–27, 44–47; 1 Cor 15:3–4).

opinions of the missionary. Paul asserts, "For we do not preach ourselves but Jesus Christ as Lord" (2 Cor 4:5). To the apostle Paul, the gospel proclaimer in every place must be bound to the Word of Christ, so that the only person magnified in the eyes of the audience is the Lord, who alone reigns. God's singular instrument for transformation is God's Word proclaimed, and therefore, the singular reason to go to the nations as a missionary is to proclaim the Word, "to give the Light of the knowledge of the glory of God," which is "in the face of Christ" (2 Cor 4:6).

Likewise, the unregenerate person, who hears Jesus' commands as they are delivered by the missionary, must be careful to obey them. Only if the nonbeliever adheres to the demands of the Word, to believe in Jesus by faith in Him alone, will Jesus become his Lord (Matt 7:21–23). Therefore, obedience to Christ is marked by obedience to His commands, which the missionary must deliver patiently and regularly. When missionaries use Scripture to call unbelievers to submit their lives to the lordship of Christ, they act on Christ's behalf and wield His divine authority to proclaim either forgiveness to the sinner who repents or judgment for ongoing unbelief (Mark 16:16; Luke 24:47).

It is wonderfully helpful to missionaries and those who send them to know the power inherent in the Word they proclaim. Wherever Christ's followers enter with the Word, when they proclaim His commands, their message carries the same authority as if Jesus Himself were speaking. Jesus' sole authority over life and death thus becomes the source of comfort needed by all who desire to act by His authority in faithfulness to the Great Commission. Jesus' powerful presence becomes an amazing daily promise of divine intervention, for He has promised to be with those who proclaim His Word personally "even to the end of the age" (Matt 28:20).

The Recognition of Biblical Authority at Salvation

Not only do gospel proclaimers live by the conviction that Scripture is the ultimate authority for the message of life, but sinners also do, in the moment of their salvation. When the Holy Spirit regenerates the soul by His sovereign choosing (John 3:5–8), the person who receives the Word immediately recognizes its inherent authority and welcomes it as divine in origin.[13] To the sinner who is regenerated, the message being preached is accepted "not as the word of men, but for what it really is, the word of God, which also is at work in [those] who believe" (1 Thess 2:13). Therefore, the sinner's newfound conviction matches Scripture's witness of its inherent authority, which is that the Bible itself possesses the divine right to command what people are to believe and how they are to conduct their lives (John 10:35; 1 Thess 4:1–2).

Given that the gospel, as revealed in the Bible, "is the power of God for salvation to

---

13. For discussion, see John Calvin and his discussion of the doctrine he called the "testimony of the Spirit," in John Calvin, *Calvin: Institutes of the Christian Religion*, Library of Christian Classics 20, ed. John T. McNeill, trans. Ford Lewis Battles (Philadelphia: Westminster, 1960), 1:78–79; see also the concise description in *WCF* 1.10.

everyone who believes" (Rom 1:16), there is no place where the proclamation of the biblical text cannot achieve an effective gospel witness. Sinners who become believers understand that they must respond to the revealed grace of God by placing their faith in the Lord Jesus Christ, according to the faith "once for all handed down to the saints" (Jude 3). The authority of Scripture therefore provides a sure foundation on which gospel proclaimers can participate in the Great Commission in farther locations across the world with the promise that Christ is with them and blesses their labors for His glorious purposes of salvation. It is a great source of confidence to know that the Lord Jesus Christ Himself authorizes the gospel message that is to be proclaimed and that, when sinners are given the faith to receive it, they do so with the utmost sincerity of heart and sobriety of mind.

The Sufficiency of the Bible for the Missionary Task

The written Word of God provides hearers and readers with adequate information about the nature and will of God and the nature of spiritual and physical realities so that they might obey Him with a whole heart (Ps 119:79–80). God has not revealed everything about Himself nor brought to light everything He has created and accomplished (Dan 8:26; 12:4; Rev 10:4). Yet He has revealed in His Word all that He deems necessary to know about Him, His way of salvation, and His will for mankind and for the rest of creation (John 20:30–31; 2 Tim 3:14–15;

Titus 1:9; 2 Pet 1:3–4). God's special revelation of Himself and all spiritual reality is so sufficient that man is prohibited from adding to or subtracting from any word of the sixty-six-book canon (Deut 4:2; 12:32; Rev 22:18–19).

Three theological underpinnings to the doctrine of Scripture's sufficiency, in addition to bringing more support to the doctrine, have missiological value. These three key teachings give gospel proclaimers the confidence to assert the divinely revealed contents of Scripture in any cultural context. They assert that there is no need for cultural accommodation strategies— that the preaching and teaching of Scripture in comprehensible language is enough to save sinners, as the Lord wills (1 Cor 1:18–24; 2:1–2).

First, Scripture is sufficient for spiritual understanding because it is the divinely inspired revelation of the one true God (2 Tim 3:16). God must record His thoughts in words for imperfect, finite people to understand any truth about their perfect, infinite Creator.[14] Through the supernatural superintendence of the Holy Spirit (2 Pet 1:21), God revealed His eternal words to the biblical writers, teaching them so that they could teach all audiences (1 Cor 2:13, 16; cf. John 14:26; 15:26–27; 16:13). Through the normal means of language, the biblical writers wrote accurately every word God desired to reveal to mankind.

A second theological claim that undergirds the sufficiency of Scripture follows from the first. Because the words of the Bible are divinely inspired, they represent theological

---

14. See also Daniel Strange, *Their Rock Is Not Like Our Rock: A Theology of Religions* (Grand Rapids: Zondervan, 2015), 46.

truth perfectly. Every text originates in the mind of God, who is the source of all truth, making every word of God not only trustworthy but "truth" itself (2 Sam 7:28; Ps 119:160; John 17:17).

Third, the content of Scripture is eternal and animated by the Holy Spirit. What Scripture says in its embedded literary, historical, and cultural settings is what it was always meant to say. That is because the contents of Scripture were founded and fixed in eternity past for a future eternal duration (Pss 119:89; 152; Isa 40:8; Matt 24:35; 1 Pet 1:23–25). Readers of Scripture can be assured that every spiritual revelation that God intended them to receive, regardless of their situation, has been delivered already in the canon of Scripture, making the Bible the sufficient source for all manner of spiritual applications (2 Tim 3:16–17).

These theological supports to the doctrine of sufficiency are important for missions in at least two ways. First, the missionary has every reason—indeed, has no excuse not—to preach and teach the contents of the Bible because God has provided all of the knowledge essential for all people to understand the spiritual and physical realities of their context from God's perspective (Deut 29:29; John 20:30–31; 2 Tim 3:14–16; 2 Pet 1:3–4). Second, and consequently, a hearer's obedience to the Word does not depend on his subjective impression of how the theological concepts of Scripture correspond to local beliefs and traditions. Simply put, the sinner who hears the message has the responsibility to repent, believe, and participate

in the sanctification the Holy Spirit accomplishes through His Word, "for with the heart a person believes, leading to righteousness," and "faith comes from hearing, and hearing by the word of Christ" (Rom 10:10, 17).

Missiological Conclusions on the Authority and Sufficiency of Scripture

The doctrines of the authority and sufficiency of Scripture orient cross-cultural ministry toward the biblical proclamation pole of the missiological spectrum. Some of the theological support given can now be emphasized missiologically, to embolden missionaries to fulfill the Great Commission task of proclaiming God's Word to hostile and indifferent audiences (Rom 8:6–8; cf. Acts 17:32).

First, the Bible describes itself as the sufficient, authoritative means by which the Holy Spirit delivers sinners spiritually, both presently and for eternity. That means that the interpretation and proclamation of Scripture is the essential starting place for missions. The Holy Spirit uses His Word to convict sinners through preaching and teaching, and they must believe the message absolutely and objectively (Rom 10:8, 13–17). Therefore, disciples of Christ in all times are called to present the clear gospel to reveal the sinner's need for salvation and then call for a repentant response.

Second, God has communicated to mankind in verbal assertions that express spiritual truths that are accurate to reality. Therefore, when missionaries interpret the Scriptures according to the normal rules of grammar and syntax and expound the Scriptures accordingly in the target language, they wield the greatest tool to confront all rival theologies and call people to repent and believe the gospel (Acts 17:30). Linguistic and cultural adaptations that alter the original intent of the biblical writer compromise the gospel message and are not faithful to the Great Commission.

Third, Scripture grants audiences access to the full complement of spiritual knowledge that they must hear and believe to be conformed to the image of Christ. They must become doers of the Word (Rom 2:13; Jas 1:22–25), who "hold to the standard of sound words" of Scripture (2 Tim 1:13). This means that the missionary must preach and teach spiritual content that is free of doctrinal error, accurate to the biblical author's meaning, and affirmed by the canon of Scripture as within the framework of the true faith.[15] Once the reader understands the meaning of the content of Scripture and turns from sin to Christ, he will begin the lifelong journey of applying the Word to his life (John 17:17; 2 Pet 1:2–4) and in service to the local church (Rom 1:16; 2 Tim 4:5).

Negatively stated, if the missionary's evangelistic and discipleship activities are not saturated in the complete trust that Scripture is God's means of converting and conforming sinners to Christlikeness, then his search for cultural relevance will itself be irrelevant. His message will be little more than a moralistic appeal for a new social ethic, with no ability to curb sin, no confident call for repentance, and no demand for progress in holiness among converts. Instead, a faithful ambassador for Christ (2 Cor 5:20) proves his faithfulness by seeking to accomplish the public task of preaching God's Word at every opportune moment (2 Tim 4:2), knowing that the results belong to the Lord, who gave him the words of the message in the first place. Faithfulness in preaching and teaching the authoritative and sufficient Word of God has as its reward comfort and rest.

---

15. Otherwise known as the "rule of faith" (*regula fidei*). See Paul L. Allen, *Theological Method: A Guide for the Perplexed* (London: A&C Black, 2012), 53–56; and Adriani Milli Rodrigues, "The Rule of Faith and Biblical Interpretation in Evangelical Theological Interpretation of Scripture," *Them* 43, no. 2 (August 2018): 257–70.

Missiological Application:
God-Ordained Authority in Missions

Mark Tatlock[16]

First Authority

The most prevalent issue in missions today is the neglect of Scripture's authority in the approach to missions work and particularly the work of the local church. In a lot of international settings, authority in the church resides in a man, the pastor. For instance, in many traditional cultural settings, people are conditioned to think in terms of a tribal or patriarchal leader who holds the position of authority and speaks on behalf of the people. When you go into the church, you can find a similar mentality, the man behind the pulpit speaking as the ultimate authority. The problem is, he is fallible; he could be misinterpreting Scripture, leading to doctrinal error, confusion, and even heresy. What happens when the pastor or church leader possesses final spiritual authority is the people become vulnerable and captive to whatever doctrine

he teaches. They have no form of accountability to the Scriptures.

Our focus in missions training ought to be ensuring that men apply themselves to the rigorous effort of rightly interpreting the Scriptures in a consistent hermeneutical fashion (2 Tim 2:15). Then they ought to derive their homiletical outlines from the original author's intent, without distortion, because that is what God's people need to hear (Rom 15:4; 2 Tim 3:15–16; cf. Gal 1:6–7; 2 Pet 3:16). Such pastors explain to their congregations that they themselves submit to the authority of God's Word and are accountable to Him for the faithful, accurate teaching of His Word (2 Cor 3:17; 4:2). They then give their people the skills and permission to study God's Word and to hold them accountable to the text of Scripture (Gal 1:7–8; cf. 1 Cor 4:6). They model that their calling is to be mouthpieces

---

16. This excerpt is adapted from an interview of the author with ABWE (Association of Baptists for World Evangelism): "The Tragic Fruit of Liberalism in Missions: Mark Tatlock Explains," *The Missions Podcast*, hosted by Alex Kocman and Scott Dunford, n.d., https://missionspodcast.com/podcast/mark-tatlock-on-the-tragic-fruit-of-liberalism-in-missions/.

for God. Our aim is not just to train pastors, but to see their congregations mature, becoming Bereans, holding both their pastors and themselves accountable to the Bible (Acts 17:10–11).

False teaching, false gospels, false prophets, heresies, and cults are rampant in our world. Satan is personified as the deceiver and described as a liar in the Bible (Gen 3:13; John 8:44; 2 Cor 11:3, 14; Eph 6:11). Those who are not faithful to the right interpretation of Scripture and the preaching of the true gospel are in essence the mouthpieces of Satan, keeping multitudes under their influence in bondage to his lies (2 Cor 4:4; 2 Tim 2:24–26; 1 John 5:19). Most pastors are not effectively trained for preaching ministry, and many are not even saved themselves. In both cases, the Word of God is not accurately proclaimed. Those who are not saved use their position of authority for the exploitation of their congregations for personal and financial gain. I refer to it as "theological injustice" when false teachers and devious pastors "fleece the flock," using their platform to exploit followers for personal benefit. The New Testament is very clear that we will continue to see that until the Lord comes (Matt 7:15; Acts 20:29; 2 Thess 2:1–12; 1 Tim 4:1–2; 2 Tim 3:13).

Yet, for pastors who are sincere in their love for Christ but simply have not been afforded the training to enable them to correctly handle God's Word, most are eager to be taught because they love God and love their flocks. They acquire instructional books, listen to free lectures online, seek the mentorship of more equipped preachers, or seek formal training. When they discover that they have not taught their people faithfully, the sincerity of their hearts is evidenced in sorrow and conviction. They confess their failure to the congregation, seek forgiveness, and then share with joy the things they are learning from the Word.

What cuts through all these realities is the reestablishing of the Scriptures as the primary authority in the local church. Of course Christ is the head of the local church just as the global church (Eph 1:22; 5:23; Col 1:18), but He has left us an instruction manual, the Spirit-inspired Word, given through His apostles (John 14:25–26; 16:12–15; 17:20–21; 1 Tim 3:15; 2 Pet 3:2). When Scripture is made the authority, then the missionary has to develop a biblical philosophy of ministry consistent with the Scriptures. Then he will have a church that is able to fulfill the Great Commission, a church from which the word of Christ "sounds forth" into the world around it (1 Thess 1:8).

Second Authority

There is a second and derivative concern in missions regarding authority. This is manifest not in the national leader but in the Western missionary's attitudes about authority. For instance, the general American cultural disregard for authority, coupled with the cultural value of independence, leads some missionaries from the United States to approach missions as more of an entrepreneur than a committed churchman. This can lead them to undervaluing and not working with local church leaders in a respectful and discerning manner. But to do so is to rebel against the teaching (authority) of Scripture (1 Cor 16:15–16; 1 Thess 5:12–13; 1 Tim 5:17–18; Heb 13:17).

Many missionaries today don't begin with a love for the local church. They have their own agenda. The thing that can characterize us who are from the West, and particularly Americans, is hyper-individualism; we don't want to put ourselves under God-ordained authority, whether of the Scriptures or of church leaders. That includes not only the church in the field but the church that sends us also. I think our pride and disregard for authority in our own cultural setting leads to missionaries who do not sense their responsibility or obligation to work with or work under local churches, at home or abroad.

Overall, then, God has clearly ordained the church and called Christians to submit themselves to the authority of church leadership that He has ordained (Eph 4:11–13). And ultimately those leaders must lead under the God-ordained authority of Christ as revealed in God's Word (John 21:15–17; Acts 20:28; Titus 1:7–9; Jas 3:1; 1 Pet 5:1–4). The ministry under such authorities is the ministry God blesses.

INSERT 2.2

The Influence of African Authority Structures on Spirituality

Nathan Odede

Sources of authority are different in many African cultural contexts than in societies that follow a code of law such as a constitution. There is no objective document to consult for governance. Rather, authority lies with the elders, who are individuals, personalities. By extension, spiritual authority is derived from departed ancestors who serve as mediators between man and the supreme divine being, however it may be defined in a particular culture.

To evangelize an African is not easy because the source of content and authority for the gospel is a document, a book, the Bible. Africans historically follow oral rather than literary traditions. Missionaries, however, often neither recognize this disparity nor make attempts to bridge it. Outreach efforts are too often focused on a message that quickly transitions to and ends with Christ, without any emphasis on the source and authority of the message. For a more effective African evangelism, below are five contextual factors of which missionaries should be aware.

The Influence of African Traditional Religion

It is often assumed that Christ, especially given the commemoration of His death, is simply a white man's "ancestor," someone dead who mediates between God and man. Thus, out of appreciation and accommodation for other cultures—in a word, *Ubuntu* (Zulu for "humanness")—the African believer of traditional religion would readily acknowledge, respect, and even accept such a belief without fully comprehending it. In his mind, he does not have to understand it; it is not foundational to his own belief.

This is why syncretism is rife within indigenous African "Christian" movements. Christ is worshiped as the Mediator who gets one to heaven (the afterlife), while ancestors are venerated as the mediators who help one in the present life. Yet, because the present life matters more to the lost sinner, ancestors will always take preeminence over Christ. They remain authoritative.

It is nearly impossible to evangelize such people in a way that illuminates the pure gospel. One woman from the Zion Christian Church (South Africa) rejected our message outright because the prophet in her "church" taught that she could worship both her ancestors and Christ. To her, the only difference between the two entities was their ascribed rituals and purposes. Our message of the exclusivity of Christ was less appealing than that of her prophet-leader. Missionaries should expect this and remember that what is impossible with man is possible with God (Luke 18:27).

The Influence of Roman Catholicism

Missionaries must also contend with Roman Catholicism. It is highly influential in Africa because it resonates with oral tradition. For a start, Roman Catholics will never challenge anyone to read the Bible, a written authority. A person could be Roman Catholic for life and yet die without having read the Scriptures. In oral cultures, however, this problem goes unnoticed and even passes for normal. Speaking for myself—someone born into the Roman Catholic Church and who subscribed to it for many years—it makes perfect sense why so many African Roman Catholics never come to the conviction of sin and to salvation in Christ yet think they are heaven-bound. Catholicism confirms these preconceptions.

The other key attraction for Africans is that the pope supposedly speaks *ex cathedra*, with infallible authority. Even on a recent visit to the Congo, the pope pronounced on civil rights (by which he alluded to recent LGBTQ demonstrations) without sound scriptural backing;[17] he was the authority. But this, too, goes unnoticed, because in Africa authority is tied to individuals. A church leader presuming to speak authoritatively resonates well in that context; it is a cultural blueprint.

Finally, Rome venerates the Virgin Mary, through whom one is supposed to pray to Christ. This appeals to Africans because Mary is a type of ancestor. Plus, she is one seen as compassionate; whereas, the typical African ancestor may act unfavorably toward his people. These influences are a strong spiritual undercurrent against evangelism.

The Influence of the Prosperity Gospel

Prosperity preachers have also manipulated the oral tradition of the African context to great effect. Because the prosperity gospel's source of authority lies in the prominent charismatic individual, false teachers have used it to their advantage to deceive many. As well, because the status of the authority figure is key, it is common for those who initially designate themselves pastors to suddenly promote themselves under "divine decree" to offices such as prophet and apostle. The higher the office, the greater the authority with which they speak and the seriousness with which people listen.

Because of modernization and Western influence, it is increasingly unpopular to consult traditional African spiritists. It is frowned upon as evil because it is associated with witchcraft and the related dark arts. However, the seemingly perfect and righteous substitute to many is the prosperity preacher. He promises exactly the same things as the spiritist—a prosperous

---

17. Pope Francis, keynote address, "Meeting with Authorities, Civil Society, and the Diplomatic Corps," Kinshasa, Democratic Republic of Congo, January 31, 2023, https://www.vatican.va/content/francesco/en/speeches/2023/january/documents/20230131-autorita-repdem-congo.html; cf. Nicole Winfield, "Pope, Anglican, Presbyterian Leaders Denounce Anti-gay Laws," Associated Press, February 5, 2023, https://apnews.com/article/pope-francis-lgbtq-people-south-sudan-religion-ddd1e52de12a95216e798a9ddd103ade.

life, riches, protection, and control of future circumstances—but he promises them under the guise of Christianity, thus making himself more acceptable to modern minds. By virtue of his office, he guarantees these promises when the Bible does not. Listeners do not seek any sound scriptural backing because the supposedly prosperous "man of God" is authoritative.

The Influence of the African Theological Scholar

With changing times and the influence of modernity and globalization, significant room is being made for literary traditions in Africa. This is popularized by African theologians, the authority figures when it comes to theological education on the continent. With their increasing numbers and influence, "decolonization" has fast become a major agenda in institutions of higher learning. The idea is that curriculums in every field of study, including theology, have to be overhauled to omit Western content and influence, and have to be "contextualized" to reflect indigenous knowledge and solutions to African problems.

For theology, this means that Africans must adopt an "African hermeneutic," an interpretative method of seeing the Bible through African lenses, just as the West allegedly interprets the Bible through its Western lenses. There is therefore an emerging group of African theologians and church leaders who acknowledge the written Word but who formulate unique interpretive principles, like subjective considerations of traditional religions and cultures. This appeals to Africans because it pads pride and promises spiritual and intellectual liberation to accompany the political liberation of the mid-twentieth century.

The Lack of Influence of the Written Word

In view of the above, Africa may be described as a mission field where false teachers understand the context and manipulate it well. Yet true gospel preachers often do not understand it, and therefore either fail or accomplish little in their efforts to bring in a harvest of African souls, which today numbers over one billion. Africa needs to reckon with the one true God who communicates differently than their traditions, because His Word is true and fixedly written (Ps 19:7–11; 119:160; Matt 5:18; John 10:35). It is not subject to man's manipulation but is given by divine inspiration (2 Tim 3:16; 2 Pet 1:21). The battle for missions in Africa is a battle over authority, over the Bible itself and for its accurate interpretation.

If Christ is introduced in a vacuum, without regard for these authority factors, He will end up on the shelf as one god among many, either in the home or the seminary. He may be called upon for a specific task but not exalted and worshiped as God (John 20:28), head of the church (Col 1:18), or exclusive Savior (John 14:6). It is imperative, then, that missionaries in Africa be aware of this and be wise to hold fast "the faithful word" (Titus 1:9). It is "the word of life" (Phil 2:16).

CHAPTER 3

A Biblical View of God's Servants, Work, and the Church

David Doran

Evangelical missions is plagued by personal pietism and ministerial entrepreneurism. Because of a subjective sense of calling to missions work, there is a sense in which missionaries have been elevated above the church. As a result, missionaries are often not truly "sent" by a local assembly. Rather, they tell the church what they are going to do. Rather than missionaries serving the mission of the church, the church serves the missionaries. Further, the entrepreneurial nature of evangelicalism has produced an environment in which anyone who has a creative idea and can raise money gets a green light for their "missionary" work. In these ways, the local church has been marginalized in missions. It has become a fundraising source, either directly, through its own financial support of missionaries, or indirectly as it houses individual givers. This privatization of the Great Commission is both unbiblical and ineffective in carrying out the Lord's purpose for the church.

Weak ecclesiology produces this kind of flawed missiology. The pattern is not new. It is one that is traceable in the early church, particularly in Corinth. Paul directly addressed the way the carnal thinking of the Corinthians was producing flawed views of God's servants, the work, and the church. This chapter considers 1 Corinthians 3:5–17 in order to correct the same kind of flawed thinking about missions in the contemporary church.

Carnal Ideas regarding God's Servants

The Corinthians were using the names and status of God's servants for their own purposes (1 Cor 3:5–9). This was especially true of those who were trying to marginalize Paul's influence. They were fabricating a false divide—Paul and Apollos were on the same team. But, more dangerously, by using famous servants to advance their own agenda they were dishonoring the Lord of the church. Christians must be careful to avoid three flaws that were present in the Corinthians' thinking about God's servants.

Focusing on Servants Instead of the Master

Christians are to be teachable and should count excellent teachers and thinkers as a gift from God. But human voices must never be louder or more influential in the believer's thinking than God's. Furthermore, it must be remembered that His voice comes to His people only via Scripture. "What then is Apollos? And what is Paul? Servants through whom you believed, even as the Lord gave to each one" (3:5). Even the greatest of God's servants are just that—servants. Missions practitioners and specialists are important in helping the church think through the Great Commission at the level of application, but there is a danger of setting aside the Bible in favor of giving attention to theories of culture and contextualization. If the names Apollos and Paul are replaced by famous modern missionaries or missiologists, then the "I am of" mindset will foster a spirit of pride and will subordinate the Scriptures to the theories and traditions of men. The Bible was written as a missionary book to people who were wrestling with culture. It provides a fully sufficient foundation for missiological thinking. Churches must trust the Bible as the primary text for developing and implementing their philosophy of missions.

Thinking That Servants Are the Source of Success

The man-centeredness of the Corinthians was also evident in the way they were attributing to human instruments what truly can only be credited to God. Paul countered this kind of thinking by explaining, "I planted, Apollos watered, but God was causing the growth" (3:6). God's servants have clear responsibilities before God, but the success of their ministries is due to God's power, not their own. Christians should rejoice when God works through human instruments, but they must remember that gospel success comes from obedience to God's Word by the power of His Spirit.

The tendency to focus on successful strategies, methods, and techniques was a precise point of failure for the Corinthians. Preoccupation with immediate, visible success tends to exalt models above the Master. Love for models that supposedly work[1] can cause Christians to pursue the "success" of others. By focusing on the immediate and visible, believers adopt a standard that falls short of God's simple mandate—"It is required of stewards that one be found faithful" (1 Cor 4:2).

Forgetting That Servants Are under God's Command

Paul wanted the Corinthians to understand that servants do not call the shots. God does. Each servant is to fulfill their God-given role, and for

---

1. E.g., David Garrison, *Church Planting Movements: How God Is Redeeming a Lost World* (Richmond, VA: WIGTake Resources LLC, 2004).

that, each servant is accountable. "Now he who plants and he who waters are one; but each will receive his own reward according to his own labor" (1 Cor 3:8). Each servant has "his own labor" assigned by God because together God's servants "are God's fellow workers" (v. 9). This truth is both freeing and sobering. It is freeing because it rescues the Christian from a thousand different masters. It is sobering because it means the final assessment belongs to Jesus, and His standard is faithfulness.

Too often missions is reduced to "going somewhere to do something for Jesus." If the "somewhere" is away from home and the "something" gets enough financial support to survive, it is called "missions." In that case, the servants, not the Master, are calling the shots. Jesus left clear commands, however, about what His mission for the church is. Christians have a responsibility to obey those commands, not make up their own. Just as the Lord Jesus came to do the will of the one who sent Him, so, too, He has commissioned His church to do His will (John 4:34; 5:30; 6:38; 17:18; 20:21). Believers are commissioned by the Master to do the work He assigned, not to make up new plans or follow subjective dreams. Christians are commissioned servants, not entrepreneurs.

Carnal ideas regarding God's servants shift the focus away from the Master to the servants, mistakenly attribute success to the servants rather than the Master, and forget that the servants are not the authority but are under the authority of the Master.

Carnal Ideas regarding the Ministry

Some of the Corinthians wanted a different approach to ministry than the one modeled by Paul. They wanted a model more attractive to both the Jews and Gentiles in the culture around them. These desires, however, were built on false and fleshly assumptions about ministry.

Ministry is a stewardship from God that must be done God's way. Paul's ministry was rooted in "the grace of God" which had been "given" to him (1 Cor 3:10). It was a divine assignment that brought both a call and the capability to fulfill it. He, along with all who serve Christ in the ministry of the gospel, labor because of God's gracious work to set them apart and send them out (Matt 9:38; Acts 20:28; Rom 10:15). It is a stewardship that entrusts the servant with the deposit of the gospel. A faithful servant is focused on God's approval, not man's—"Just as we have been approved by God to be entrusted with the gospel, so we speak, not as pleasing men, but God who examines our hearts" (1 Thess 2:4; cf. Gal 1:10; 2 Cor 5:9). The Corinthians wanted to be attractive to the culture, but Paul wanted to be faithful to the Lord who called him.

Paul's statement about being a "wise master builder" is a subtle reference to the debate in 1 Corinthians 1–3 regarding human versus divine wisdom. The Corinthians were in love with human wisdom. They neglected the fact that it is God's wisdom that had converted sinners and had produced the congregation in Corinth. The message of the cross is the wisdom and power of God (1:24). Faithful ministry speaks "God's wisdom," not the wisdom of this age (2:6–7). The church at Corinth was wisely built on divine truth, and they were to build carefully on that foundation (3:11).

It is possible to do ministry in ways that will ultimately prove worthless, regardless of perceived temporal success. In verse 12, the difference between the materials Paul lists—gold, silver, precious stones, wood, hay, straw—does not focus on inherent value as much as it does the ability to withstand the test of fire. In other words, gold is not better than wood because it has greater commercial value but because it will "remain" after the fire, whereas wood will be "burned up" (vv. 13–15). The sober implication is that someone might appear very successful in this life but find that their "success" was a mirage. If Christians do not build churches according to God's design, the labor will prove fruitless. There is a coming "day" that will show the character of each Christian's work (v. 13; cf. 2 Cor 5:10). This will be a judgment of service and reward, not salvation (1 Cor 3:15). By God's grace, the believer's salvation is secure, but for a ministry that bears eternal fruit, each one must "be careful how he builds" on the foundation of Christ (v. 10).

Carnal Ideas regarding the Church

The root of the Corinthians' carnal thinking was the mistaken notion that the church in Corinth was their own. Paul pointed this out when he wrote, "You are God's field, God's building" (1 Cor 3:9). He used the field metaphor to emphasize the differing roles of the workers (i.e., planting and watering in vv. 6–9). He used the building metaphor to emphasize different types of work (i.e., gold versus wood in vv. 12–15). Both metaphors communicate the same basic truth that the church belongs to God. It is His field; it is His building.

Paul turns to address the fact of God's ownership of the church in verses 16–17. There he describes the congregation in Corinth as God's temple. He uses the second person plural ("you") to identify the local church as God's dwelling place in a community.

Just as God gave detailed instructions for temple activities in the Old Testament, the New Testament contains His will for the local church (1 Tim 3:14–15). The congregation should not be viewed as a dispenser of spiritual goods and services, existing merely to meet consumer demand and desires. God rules the church, and what the church does in missions must be regulated by His Word. The mission must follow the manual left by the Master.

Paul conveys the seriousness of the church's charge in 1 Corinthians 3:17: "If any man destroys the temple of God, God will destroy him, for the temple of God is holy, and that is what you are." The Corinthians' desire to adopt worldly wisdom was destroying the church, God's temple, and God takes that seriously. Jesus sets Himself in direct opposition to those who are destroying His temple (Rev 2–3). Believers must not miss the intensity of this warning and the seriousness of the situation. Paul was writing to the Corinthian church about a real and present danger today also. Fleshly views of ministers, ministry, and the church puts individuals in conflict with God.

The Centrality of the Word and the Church

God's Word must have active, functional control over the local church's missiology, including its view of the work and the workers. Jesus remains in charge of the mission today, just as He authorized His disciples before His ascension. The book of Acts shows how the early church understood this commission and what they did to obey it. The New Testament epistles reinforce such understanding. Christians must not undercut the sufficiency of Scripture by effectively setting it aside to develop cross-cultural ministries and methods controlled by the social sciences rather than the Bible.

Furthermore, the local church is at the center of Christ's New Testament mandate. The content of His Great Commission presumes this by its inclusion of baptism and ongoing teaching ministry (Matt 28:19–20). Acts demonstrates that the early church understood their obligation. The first converts at Pentecost believed, were baptized, and were added to the fellowship of God's people, a fellowship that was devoted to the apostles' teaching (Acts 2:41–42). The first missionaries were sent out from a local church, started local churches, and then reported back to the congregation from which they had been sent (Acts 13–14).

Paul's instruction in 1 Corinthians 3 confirms the centrality of the local assembly. Although it is common to apply what this text says about planting and watering to the task of evangelism, that is not Paul's point. Paul planted the church at Corinth. Apollos followed with a teaching ministry that "greatly helped those who had believed through grace" (Acts 18:27). The concept of sowing and reaping in evangelism is a valid one, as seen in John 4:37–38, but the point in 1 Corinthians 3 is that God builds the church as His servants play their assigned role. In Paul's agricultural metaphor, the servants plant and water (3:6). In his architectural metaphor, the servants lay a foundation and build upon it (3:10). The planting of crops and the laying of a foundation refer to the work of establishing a congregation of Christ's disciples in Corinth. That was and is the task of missionaries—to start and strengthen local assemblies. Evangelism is indispensable to missions, but it is not the sum of missions. Christ said to make disciples, baptizing and teaching them to observe His commands.

Missions springs forth from the local church, starts local churches, and is accountable to the local church. Parachurch ministries aid the local church in fulfilling its commission. However, many parachurch ministries have become hyper-church or even anti-church ministries because they place themselves above the local church or in the place of the local church. From the standpoint of sound ecclesiology, such ministries should not be labeled as parachurch. They should be hypo-church (i.e., under the church). First Timothy 3:15 teaches that the local congregation is the pillar and support of the truth. Missions must center on starting and strengthening local congregations, not the myriad other good things that Christians might be interested in doing and funding.

The Current Shift from the Biblical Pattern

In the early twentieth century, some began using the label *larger mission* to extend missions work beyond gospel proclamation and church planting.[2] The second half of the twentieth century brought the term *holistic mission* and its inclusion of social action as part of the mission of the church.[3] The Lausanne Movement, though it has done many good things to advance evangelism globally, demonstrates this negative shift away from the local church focus of the Great Commission. At its 2010 Cape Town event, the Lausanne Congress defined "the work of the gospel" as an endeavor that includes "evangelism, discipling, peace-making, social engagement, ethical transformation, bearing witness to the truth, caring for creation, overcoming evil powers, suffering and enduring under persecution, etc."[4] One of the chief voices for this viewpoint is Christopher Wright, who writes,

> So when I speak of *mission*, I am thinking of all that God is doing in his great purpose for the whole of creation and all that he calls us to do in cooperation with that purpose. . . . But when I speak of *missions*, I am thinking of the multitude of activities that God's people can engage in, by means of which they participate in God's mission. And it seems to me there are as many kinds of missions as there are kinds of sciences—probably far more in fact. And in the same way, in the variety of missions God has entrusted to his church as a whole, it is unseemly for one kind of mission to dismiss another out of a superiority complex, or to undervalue itself as "not real mission" out of an inferiority complex.[5]

Wright's argument is emblematic of the "going somewhere to do something for Jesus" approach to missions. The church must reject that approach and return to a biblical view of the mission that Jesus Christ has given. Like the Corinthians, contemporary believers need to have their carnal ideas about God's servants, God's work, and God's church challenged by New Testament truth.

Conclusion

Missionaries are servants assigned by the Master to their respective roles. They are not the source of ministerial success; God is. The work they do must be done God's way so it will have eternal value and pass the final test at the judgment

---

2. See Walter Johnston, *The Battle for World Evangelism* (Wheaton, IL: Victor, 1978), for an excellent historical accounting of this.

3. E.g., John R. W. Stott, *The Contemporary Christian* (Downers Grove, IL: InterVarsity, 1992).

4. *The Cape Town Commitment: A Confession of Faith and a Call to Action*, The Third Lausanne Congress, 2010, accessed June 18, 2024, https://lausanne.org/wp-content/uploads/2021/10/The-Cape-Town-Commitment-%E2%80%93-Pages-20-09-2021.pdf.

5. Christopher J. H. Wright, *The Mission of God's People: A Biblical Theology of the Church's Mission* (Grand Rapids: Zondervan, 2010), 25–26.

seat of Christ. All of this is true because the church is God's temple and God's temple is holy. Believers must live and serve within it with holy reverence, letting God's Word have active, functional control over every aspect of life and ministry.

CHAPTER 4

The Old Testament: God's Heart for the World

Michael A. Grisanti

This chapter focuses on the Old Testament teaching about God's heart for the world and the function God assigned to Israel before the surrounding nations. One debate in this discussion is whether there was an Old Testament Great Commission. Did God want Israel to be a missionary nation? Or did God give Israel a more passive role as a witness nation with a distinct lifestyle, through whom neighboring nations would be drawn to God?

To answer the question, this chapter considers key passages in Genesis, Exodus, Deuteronomy, the Psalms, and the Prophets that provide a glimpse of God's plan to provide Jews and Gentiles with the potential for a faith relationship with Him. That plan progressively builds through the Old and New Testaments. Understanding this divine plan enables readers of Scripture to correctly interpret numerous passages (and even biblical books like Jonah) as that plan unfolds.

Is There an Old Testament Great Commission?

As with many issues, terminology is important. "Missions" often refers to the training, preparation, and sending of willing servants of the Lord to carry out God-honoring ministry in some part of the world. "Mission" more narrowly refers to God's plan to bring to pass an eternal resolution to mankind's sin problem (Gen 3:15). That divine plan reached an initial phase of culmination with the life, death, and resurrection of Christ—providing the theological basis for forgiveness and hope for eternity in God's presence. Christ's future return to earth to vanquish the forces of Satan and establish His Millennial Kingdom will be the next phase in the culmination of God's plan. That is all part of God's mission and is something revealed in numerous Old Testament and New Testament passages (e.g., Pss 2; 110; Isa 11:1–10; 24–25; Dan 7; Zech

14; Matt 24–25; Mark 13; Luke 21; Acts 3:19–21; Rev 19:11–20:6).

Christopher Wright proposes that Israel, God's chosen nation, "had a missional role in the midst of the nations—implying that they had an identity and role connected to God's ultimate intention of blessing the nations."[1] God's bringing them into existence as a people, and then a nation, and working in and through them throughout Old Testament history laid the groundwork for "missions," the outward-moving spread of the gospel.

The key issue, however, is whether the Old Testament depicts Israel as having a divinely commissioned and active missionary role in the world or a passive one. The question is about Israel's God-given function. Scholars use two terms to describe these options: *centrifugal* and *centripetal*. The term *centrifugal* conveys the active idea, wherein the object moves away from the center; *centripetal* conveys the passive idea, wherein the object moves toward the center.

Some scholars contend that there is, in fact, an active Old Testament Great Commission. For example, Walter Kaiser writes, "The prophet Isaiah surely called his nation to function actively as a missionary to the Gentiles

and nations at large."[2] Kaiser writes elsewhere, "Rightly understood, the O.T. is a missions book *par excellence* because world missions to all the peoples of the earth is its central purpose."[3] However, Wright asserts that God did not mandate Israel to send missionaries to the nations.[4] Craig Ott and Stephen J. Strauss also point out, "The Old Testament consistently depicts the worship of the Lord as being centralized in Zion. The nations were to abandon idols, submit to God's reign, and come."[5] But that gathering of the nations to Zion is contextually placed in the distant if not eschatological future (Isa 1:27; 2:2–4; 35:10; 50:28; 51:11; 56:3–7; 66:18–24; Jer 31:6–14; 33:7–9; 50:4–5, 28; 51:10; Mic 4:1–4; Rev 14:1).

Andreas Köstenberger and T. Desmond Alexander further note that although Peter expressed his understanding of the church's mission (1 Pet 2:9) using Exodus 19:6 and Isaiah 43:20—an Old Testament conception of Israel's role—it "does not imply that God intended Israel to be 'a nation of evangelists and foreign missionaries,' engaging in 'cross-cultural' or foreign mission as we understand it today."[6] Finally, as part of his lengthy study of Isaiah 40–55, Eckhard Schnabel states

---

1. Christopher J. H. Wright, *The Mission of God: Unlocking the Bible's Grand Narrative* (Downers Grove, IL: InterVarsity, 2006), 24–25.

2. Walter C. Kaiser Jr., *Mission in the Old Testament: Israel as a Light to the Nations*, 2nd ed. (Grand Rapids: Baker, 2012), 63.

3. Walter C. Kaiser Jr., "The Great Commission in the Old Testament," *IJFM* 13, no. 1 (January–March 1996): 7.

4. Wright, *Mission of God*, 24. Drawing on the above definitions, Wright would agree that the Israelites had a *missional reason for existence*, without implying that they had had a *missionary* mandate to go to the nations (25).

5. Craig Ott and Stephen J. Strauss, *Encountering Theology of Mission: Biblical Foundations, Historical Developments, and Contemporary Issues* (Grand Rapids: Baker, 2010), 22.

6. Andreas J. Köstenberger and T. Desmond Alexander, *Salvation to the Ends of the Earth: A Biblical Theology of Mission*, New Studies in Biblical Theology 53, 2nd ed. (Downers Grove, IL: IVP, 2020), 93n100. Cf. Charles H. H. Scobie, "Israel and the

that Israel's participation in Yahweh's salvation seems to be primarily centripetal. He adds, "The prophet does not speak of Israel or individual Israelites being sent to the nations; rather, the nations congregate in Jerusalem as a result of YHWH's epiphany and as a result of the redemptive ministry of the Spirit."[7]

The following overview of passages supports the understanding that Israel had a centripetal function in the Old Testament. Israel functions as a "witness" nation, beckoning other nations to see the incomparability of Yahweh and come to Jerusalem to hear fuller truth.

God's Worldwide Intentions from the Moment of Creation

God's plan for His creation, spanning both Old Testament and New Testament, is bracketed by two creation events. Genesis 1–2 records His creation of the universe, including earth and humanity, while Revelation 21–22 describes an even more glorious creation—the new heaven and the new earth. God created "the heavens and the earth" for His own glory and purposes (Pss 8:1; 19:1; Isa 43:7; Rom 11:33–36; Eph 3:9–11; Rev 4:11). Paul attributed that creative act to Christ as well as to the Father, again indicating purpose— "For in Him all things were created, both in the heavens and on earth . . . all things have been created through Him and for Him" (Col 1:16). Central to that purpose was God's universal rule.

God's Intention to Extend His Rule throughout the World

On the sixth day of creation, God formed the crowning jewel of His created world— man. Genesis 1:26 states that the Godhead made man "in Our image, according to Our likeness." He created mankind to function as image-bearers and mediators of His dominion, setting humans apart from the animal world (1:28).[8] However, Adam's sin rebelled against Yahweh's intentions for His creation and marred God's perfect order. No longer would the earth and animal world willingly submit to His direction. After casting Adam and Eve out of the garden (Gen 3:23–24), Yahweh initiated the provision of reconciliation for fallen mankind. In the midst of God's curse on the serpent, He promised the "He" who would provide grounds for the required forgiveness of sin (Gen. 3:15).[9] It is the salvation provided by this reconciliation promise that enabled mankind to return to his role as God's vice-regent.

Man's Rebellion and God's Response

Still, man's penchant to rebel against God's sovereignty manifested itself in the abhorrent

---

Nations: An Essay in Biblical Theology," *Tyndale Bulletin* 43, no. 2 (November 1992): 283–305.

7. Eckhard J. Schnabel, *Early Christian Mission*, 2 vols. (Downers Grove, IL: InterVarsity, 2004), 1:82–83.

8. Eugene H. Merrill, "A Theology of the Pentateuch," in *A Biblical Theology of the Old Testament*, ed. Roy Zuck (Chicago: Moody, 1991), 14; Merrill, "Covenant and the Kingdom: Genesis 1–3 as Foundation for Biblical Theology," *Criswell Theological Review* 1, no. 2 (Spring 1987): 298.

9. For an explanation and defense of the messianic significance of this text, see Michael Rydelnik, *The Messianic Hope: Is the Hebrew Bible Really Messianic?*, NAC Studies in Bible and Theology (Nashville: B&H, 2010), 129–45; T. D. Alexander, "Messianic Ideology in Genesis," in *The Lord's Anointed: Interpretation of Old Testament Messianic Texts*, ed. Philip E. Satterthwaite, Richard S. Hess, and Gordan J. Wenham (Eugene, OR: Wipf and Stock, 2012), 19–39.

human conduct leading up to the flood (Gen 6:1–5) and the Tower of Babel (11:1–9). God's response to both rebellions was severe judgment. In each case, one could ask, "Does this mean the end of God's redemptive dealings with mankind?" Yahweh resolves that tension by raising up other mediators like Adam, Noah and Abram, to carry out His purposes for mankind after each judgment. In fact, the textual interwovenness of the narratives describing these rebellions and God's response, with the genealogies in Genesis 5 and 10–11, carefully delineates the significant role played by these mediatorial figures.

The rest of the Bible unfolds how God will provide ultimate reconciliation through the "He" of Genesis 3:15, the one who will bring resolution to mankind's inherent sin. The Scriptures also demonstrate the way God will transmit that message of reconciliation to the sinful world—through the death of Christ, followed by faithful disciples who pursue lives that highlight God's surpassing character and who speak the gospel message to others.

God's Covenant Plan for Israel Will Have Worldwide Impact

Genesis 12 narrows God's focus on one man and his offspring. The historical stage onto which Abraham enters is characterized by chaos and rebellion (Gen 11:1–9). Yet, in Genesis 12:1–3 Yahweh enters into a unique, covenant relationship with Abram (later renaming him Abraham) and his descendants. This passage provides the worldwide context for the way Yahweh began fulfilling His purposes for those who would become the nation of Israel.

Yahweh's Intentions for Abraham's Descendants

Yahweh promised to give Abraham a land, make his offspring into a nation, and bless the world through him (Gen 12:1–3; 13:14–17; 15:1–21; 17:1–27; 22:15–18).[10] The promises of a nation and a land were part of God's larger plan for His creation and will find ultimate fulfillment in a future millennial reign of Christ on earth (Isa 2:2–4; 11:1–16; Amos 9:11–15; Matt 19:28–29; Rev 20:1–6).[11] Yet already Yahweh intended that His chosen people would live on the land He set apart for them as a stewardship (Gen 22:17–18; 26:3–4; 28:13–15; 35:9–12; 48:3–4). He demanded that they pursue lives of loyalty, advertising His matchless character to one another and to the surrounding world (Gen 18:17–19; 21:22–24; 26:28–29; cf. Deut 4:5–9; 1 Kgs 8:41–43).

Yahweh's Intentions for the Entire Created World

Yahweh's promise that "in you all the families of the earth will be blessed" (Gen 12:3)

---

10. Together these passages comprise the Abrahamic covenant, each progressively ratifying and filling out the previous. Robert B. Chisholm Jr., "Evidence from Genesis," in *The Coming Millennial Kingdom: A Case for Premillennial Interpretation*, ed. Donald K. Campbell and Jeffrey L. Townsend (Grand Rapids: Kregel, 1997), 36–37.

11. Moses and subsequent prophets assumed the unconditional nature and literal fulfillment of these stipulations of the Abrahamic covenant. Chisholm, "Evidence from Genesis," 52–54.

involved various parts of His plan but included the preaching of the gospel, based on Christ's redemptive work, to all humanity (Matt 28:18–20; Mark 16:15; Acts 10:42; 28:23). But God's plan to provide a means of salvation for sinful humanity and to send His followers throughout the world is not just a New Testament idea. Israel had a witnessing function in the Old Testament, though this function was different than what takes shape in the New Testament. Ultimately, Yahweh intended that the fulfillment of His plan for Abraham's descendants would also bless the entire created world.

God's Purposes for Israel and the Law He Gave Them Have Worldwide Implications

As Yahweh executed the plagues against Egypt, He intended to show His sovereign power not only to Pharaoh but also to the whole earth (Exod 9:14, 16).[12] After Pharaoh released God's chosen people to depart from Egypt, Yahweh brought them across the Red Sea and guided them to Mount Sinai. His redemption of the Israelites provided the theological basis for His call for them to pursue lives of loyalty. Shortly before Moses ascended Mount Sinai to receive the Law, Yahweh reminded His people of His intervention and how He led them to their present location (Exod 19:4).

Then when Yahweh made binding demands of His people in the Israelite covenant,[13] He emphasized the potential impact. If the people obeyed the requirements of the covenant—"If you will indeed listen to My voice and keep My covenant"—they would put Yahweh's glory on display (Exod 19:5–6). By giving His servant nation His Law, Yahweh intended for His people to represent Him to one another and to the surrounding nations (Deut 4:5–8).

These verses from Exodus along with Deuteronomy 26:16–19 serve as theological bookends for the Mosaic law and its requirements. Deuteronomy 26 has Moses reminding Israel that Yahweh would put them in a place of world prominence as His representatives if they would only be loyal to Him. Neither passage refers to Israel "going" to the nations. Yahweh's mission for Israel primarily involved them being a witness nation.

The Psalms and Prophets Show That God Always Intended a Worldwide Kingdom

Numerous psalms celebrate God and His salvation being exalted throughout the world. These abundant references underscore God's intent to bring salvation to the nations. In the context of worldwide war, Psalm 46:10 says, "Cease striving and know that I am God; I will be exalted among the nations, I

---

12. Kaiser has suggested that God's actions toward Egypt and the Pharaoh (plagues) had an "evangelistic" thrust. Kaiser, *Mission in the Old Testament*, 13. No doubt His activity involved self-revelation to the Egyptians and to other nations, but also to His chosen people. The idea that evangelism by means of the plagues is a key objective seems strained.

13. Although often called the Mosaic covenant, this additional covenant was made between Yahweh and the Israelites. Participating in this covenant did not necessarily include individual salvation but did make that person a member of God's chosen *nation*.

will be exalted in the earth." As David celebrates God's deliverance from his enemies, he declares in Psalm 18:49, "Therefore I will give thanks to You among the nations, O Yahweh, and I will sing praises to Your name." Psalm 22:27–28 declares, "All the ends of the earth will remember and turn to Yahweh, and all the families of the nations will worship before You. For the kingdom is Yahweh's and He rules over the nations." The psalmist enthusiastically announced his plan to praise God among all nations in Psalm 57:9–11: "I will give thanks to You, O Lord, among the peoples; I will sing praises to You among the nations. For Your lovingkindness is great to the heavens and Your truth to the skies. Be exalted above the heavens, O God; let Your glory be above all the earth."[14]

The Psalms repeatedly proclaim what God had already revealed in other parts of the Old Testament. The entire created world—heavens and earth—are God's domain. Inhabitants of every nation will one day recognize Him as their Sovereign and sing praises to Him. The expectation of these and several other passages from the Psalter express full confidence that Yahweh will orchestrate the spread of the message of eternal forgiveness to the entire world. Proclaiming forgiveness worldwide is a key part of God's intentions for His creation. Israel is not a missionary nation, but one that paves the way for the gospel of Christ to spread throughout the earth.

Broadly—God's Future Dealings with the Nations

Many prophetic oracles depict people from the nations worshiping God. Isaiah writes that the Servant will "bring forth justice to the nations" (Isa 42:1), He will minister "until He has established justice in the earth" (Isa 42:4), and Yahweh will appoint Him to be "a light to the nations" (Isa 42:6; Acts 13:47). The prophets' international focus is clear in the following passages:[15]

> Also *the foreigners* who join themselves
>   to Yahweh,
> To minister to Him, and to love the
>   name of Yahweh,
> To be His slaves,
> every one who keeps from profaning the
>   sabbath
> And takes hold of My covenant,
> Even those I will bring to My holy
>   mountain
> And make them glad in My house of
>   prayer.
> Their burnt offerings and their sacrifices
> will be acceptable on My altar;
> For My house will be called a house of
>   prayer
> *for all the peoples.* (Isa 56:6–7)
>
> For *the earth* will be filled
> With the knowledge of the glory of
>   Yahweh,

---

14. For more passages in Psalms that express God's burden for all nations, see 66:7; 72:17–19; 86:8–9; 96:1–13; 102:15–22; 108:3–5; 117:1–2; 126:2; 138:4.

15. Emphasis added. Cf. Isa 52:10; Jer 3:17.

As the waters cover the sea. (Hab 2:14)

I will cut off the chariot from Ephraim
And the horse from Jerusalem;
And the bow of war will be cut off.
And He will speak peace *to the nations*;
And His reign will be *from sea to sea*
And *from the River*
to the ends of the earth. (Zech 9:10)

"For *from the rising of the sun even to its setting*,
My name will be great *among the nations*, and
in every place incense is going to be presented
to My name, as well as a grain offering that
is clean; for My name will be great *among the
nations*," says Yahweh of Hosts. (Mal 1:11)

Specifically—God Will Extend Salvation to the Gentiles in the *Eschaton*

In the second half of Isaiah, the prophet
announces to exiled Israel that Yahweh will
liberate them and restore them to power and
significance in the land of promise. Yahweh
certifies the credibility of His promises by highlighting His absolute uniqueness. He is the only
true God, and He is able and willing to carry
out all His promises (Isa 40–41).

Although Yahweh will bring destruction
upon the intransigent Gentiles, this passage
demonstrates His intention to save submissive
Gentiles: "Gather yourselves and come; draw
near together, you who have escaped from the
nations; they do not know, who carry about
their graven image of wood and pray to a god
who cannot save. . . . Turn to Me and be saved,
all the ends of the earth; for I am God, and

there is no other" (Isa 45:20, 22). This invitation for Gentiles to embrace salvation looks
forward to the New Testament era and beyond
when God's plan provides Gentiles with fuller
and more direct access to salvation.

Conclusion

Both Israel in the Old Testament and the
church in the New Testament received the
divine exhortation, "You are My witnesses"
(Isa 43:10–12; Luke 24:48; Acts 1:8). Both were
entrusted with the task of pointing to Yahweh
as the true God and source of salvation. But
the differences between the two Testaments
are clear, with Israel being a passive witness
and the church being both passive and active.
However, the idea of a "mission" involving
worldwide impact is a fundamental part of
biblical theology.

The Bible is permeated from beginning to
end with God's own great mission—"Salvation
belongs to our God" (Rev 7:10). He will bring
His sovereign and redemptive intentions to
pass. Whatever Old Testament believers did
to put God's character on display and whatever New Testament Christ followers do as the
outflow of their salvation represents the participation of God's people in His mission.

From the time of God's creation of the universe and earth, He intended to make Himself
known to all humanity through a redemptive
relationship. He would rule over that redeemed
world (Gen 1:26–27). He chose how He would
bring that divine plan to pass. In the Old
Testament, he chose to work through Abraham's
descendants—later Israel—and commissioned

them to bear witness to His incomparable character through their heartfelt covenant allegiance to Him. Then, after Christ's earthly ministry, he added an active missionary enterprise to His expectations of the church. Recognizing God's constant commitment to present the hope of salvation to the world throughout the Old Testament and New Testament and the distinction in the manner He commanded that to happen, enables us to correctly handle numerous Old Testament passages as well as be challenged by God's perpetual burden that the potential for a faith relationship with Him was made available to all humanity.

INSERT 4.1

Does the Old Testament Have a Great Commission?

Kyle C. Dunham

Whether the Old Testament commands Israel to carry on missionary outreach to the nations is a perennial question. Many argue in the affirmative, citing examples such as Jonah (Jonah 1:1–2, 9; 3:1–10) and Naaman's servant girl (2 Kgs 5:1–4). Others find insufficient evidence of a missionary mandate for Israel. They contend that such a task belongs uniquely to the church as commissioned by Christ. A careful reading of the biblical text suggests that the Old Testament does not provide a Great Commission. Rather, while the Old Testament promises future salvation for the nations, Israel engages primarily in a passive, intermediary, and centripetal witness. The New Testament, on the other hand, inaugurates salvation promises for the nations and transforms the task into an active, indigenous, and centrifugal outreach that culminates in the salvation of every tribe, tongue, people, and nation (Rev 5:9).

This insert aims to complement the preceding chapter by advancing and distilling the proposal that the Old Testament does not present a Great Commission but that the great mission of God reaches its apex in Christ's mandate for His church to proclaim salvation to the nations.

Israel Is a Passive Witness

From the beginning, God's design was to bless all creation (Gen 1:27–28). God would glorify himself by establishing his righteous reign over the universe and his fellowship with humanity. Despite God's good creation, mankind rebelled in the fall, and the created order was subjected to corruption, frustration, and futility (Gen 3:14–18; Eccl 1:1–11; Rom 8:20).

Against this backdrop, Abraham emerges as God's chosen means of blessing to the world (Gen 12:1–3). He begins the long process of restoring order, harmony, and fruitfulness. Yet, while Abraham is designated as God's agent, God Himself is the ultimate source and producer of blessing. The passive verb saying the nations "will be blessed" (Gen 12:3)[16] keeps the focus on God's prerogative and intention, not on any capacity in the nations themselves to find blessing, nor even on Abraham to bring the blessing to fruition. This inclusionary model by which the nations are blessed in Abraham would continue.

Israel Is a Special Mediator to the Nations

Following the exodus, Yahweh covenanted with Israel to establish them as His chosen nation and special intermediaries in the world (Exod 19:4–6; Deut 7:6; 14:2). He presented Israel with a unique and solemn challenge: by conforming to His law, they would carry a privileged position, not only in moral distinction from the surrounding nations but also as God's cherished servant and priestly royal intermediary (Exod 19:5–6). Israel was to image God as His chosen representative, both reflecting His character and mediating His presence and glory to the surrounding peoples (Exod 15:13; Lev 19:2; Deut 4:6–7; 26:19; Isa 42:6).

This focus on presence and mediation fortifies the earlier strain of inclusionary blessing: Israel centralizes God's presence so that the nations experience this blessing by coming to join with God's people in submission to Yahweh.

Israel's Mission Moves Inward Rather Than Outward

This inward theme reverberates through the Old Testament to underscore the ingathering posture for Israel's mediation. In most stages of Israel's history, provision was made for incorporating people of non-Israelite descent. Groups and persons would assimilate, such as the "foreign [or mixed] multitude" fleeing Egypt (Exod 12:38), Rahab and her family (Josh 6:25), Ruth (Ruth 4:13–22), and the

---

16. The voice of this Hebrew root (דרב) in the Niphal stem is debated as to whether it conveys the passive ("be blessed"), middle ("find blessing"), or reflexive sense ("bless themselves"). Critical scholars often take it as a reciprocal reflexive ("bless one another") and so undermine the divine agency implied, in turn undermining its corresponding literary theme that is borne out in the Old Testament, as shown in this essay. But helpful discussions by Bruce K. Waltke (*Genesis: A Commentary* [Grand Rapids: Zondervan, 2001], 206) and Gordon J. Wenham (*Genesis 1–14*, WBC 1 [Dallas: Word, 1987], 277–78) show that the meaning of the verb in this immediate context, whatever the voice's usual nuance, would necessarily, as Wenham wrote, "carry the implications of the passive."

foreigners in David's royal court (2 Sam 11:3; 15:19–23). Torah stipulations also showed special concern for the *gēr*, the sojourner who resides in Israel without fully integrating. Israel was to show exceptional kindness to such strangers (Deut 10:18).

The prophets, however, foresaw a time when the nations of their own initiative would proceed en masse to the worship of the true God by bringing tribute and submitting themselves in joy (Isa 2:2–4; 56:6–7; Zech 2:11). A special strain of these prophecies concerns the Servant of Yahweh, who would initiate an outward movement toward the nations (Isa 42:1–7; 49:6). These prophecies lay the groundwork for the New Testament transformation of mission.

The Old Testament Grounds Mission While the New Testament Transforms Mission

In the New Testament, Jesus shows concern for the nations. He heals the Syro-Phoenician woman's daughter (Matt 15:22–28) and the demoniac of the Gerasenes (Mark 5:1–15). He ministers to the Samaritans (John 4). He asserts that the temple should be a place of prayer for all nations (Mark 11:17) and that other sheep from outside the fold should come (John 10:16). With His death, resurrection, and ascension, Jesus brings His church into the last days (1 Cor 10:11; Heb 1:2; 1 John 2:18) and transforms the church's mission (Matt 28:19–20; Luke 24:47).

New Testament mission, then, is both an amplification of the Old Testament promise that the nations will experience God's salvation and a methodological reversal from a primarily inward impulse to a primarily outward impulse—from "come and see" to "go and make." God's blessing through Abraham to the nations has been set in motion by Christ, and the church must take up the task with urgency and faithfulness.

CHAPTER 5

One Holy Race: Ethnicity and the People of God

Scott Callaham

Commenting on the heavenly worship scene in Revelation 7:9–10, one urban ministry leader writes, "God does care about color and ethnicity. . . . We will maintain our ethnicity whether mixed, black, brown, yellow, red, olive, or white—our distinctions will be distinct yet unified under the eternal Lordship of Jesus. And the reason He singled you out is so that He could have representation of your people group in heaven!"[1] Ethnocentric, reader-centered interpretations such as this entirely miss the focal point of the passage, the cry of the redeemed from all peoples: "Salvation belongs to our God who sits on the throne, and to the Lamb" (cf. Rom 9:22–26).

Instead of making much of the creature at the expense of the Creator, this chapter invites a return to God-centered thinking about ethnicity and the people of God. It marshals important insights from the biblical theologies of creation, election, and judgment to reflect upon ethnicity and God's people. Finally, the chapter suggests ways that missionaries may help local churches to restore God-centered thinking on ethnicity as they obey the Great Commission.

Creation

Genesis 1:27 reads, "And God created man in His own image, in the image of God He created him; male and female He created them." Much theological reflection on the image of God centers on humans exercising dominion as His representatives.[2] Verse 27, however, particularly its third clause, "male and female He created them," typically receives far less attention.

---

1. Eric M. Mason, *Woke Church: An Urgent Call for Christians in America to Confront Racism and Injustice* (Chicago: Moody, 2018), 170.
2. See, e.g., Paul van Imschoot, *Théologie de l'Ancien Testament* (Tournai, Belgium: Desclée, 1956), 2:7–11; Wolfhart Pannenberg, *Systematische Theologie* (Göttingen: Vandenhoek and Ruprecht, 1991), 2:232–65.

According to that verse, the "image of God" in humanity is "male and female." Bearing God's image thus determines both what humans must do (exercise dominion) and who humans are (male and female). Sin and the resulting banishment from Eden alter neither what humans must do nor what they are.

"Race" is strikingly absent from biblical teaching on the nature of humanity. According to Scripture, there is only one human race. Furthermore, ethnicity is not a meaningful concept to describe the first human couple, the man made of dust (Gen 2:7) and the woman fashioned from him (2:22). Those looking for skin color "representation" in the garden of Eden will be disappointed, for the only "representation" mentioned in Scripture has to do with sin (Rom 5:12). Put plainly, ethnicity is not a fundamental element of what it means to be human.

Election

The flood of Genesis 7–8 reduced the human population of the world to eight persons: Noah and his family. Genesis 10 describes how Noah's descendants then branched into separate "nations." The rise of these "nations" marks the entry of ethnicity into the Bible.[3] Summary statements about the descendants of Ham (Gen 10:20) and Shem (10:31) bundle together "families," "languages," and "nations" with "lands."

This correspondence of ethnic groups to lands matches Paul's description of God's sovereign placement of peoples throughout the earth (Acts 17:26). Following that verse, Paul explains God's reasoning for such placement: "that they would seek God, if perhaps they might grope for Him and find Him, though He is not far from each one of us" (v. 27). According to Scripture, God's dealings with distinct ethnic groups work toward a God-centered purpose: to cause people to search for Him.

Election of the Covenant People

God's voice fell silent after He established His covenant with Noah. Generations passed until at last God broke His silence and spoke to Abram, promising, "And I will make you a great nation, and I will bless you, and make your name great; and so you shall be a blessing; and I will bless those who bless you, and the one who curses you I will curse. And in you all the families of the earth will be blessed" (Gen 12:2–3).

In this extraordinary biblical passage God directly creates an ethnic group: the Hebrews. Every other ethnic group that existed alongside the first Hebrews and all ethnic groups that would arise later through history together fall into the catchall category of "the nations," that is, the Gentiles. God's election of Abram and promise to make him a nation (*goy*), not just a people (*am*),[4] would result in blessing for all these other ethnic "nations" through one of

---

3. The Greek translation of the Hebrew *goy* ("nation" in many English Bible translations) in these verses is *ethnos*. This is the term the New Testament uses for "ethnic group," which in English Bible translations likewise often appears as "nation." Cf. "ἔθνος," BDAG, 276–77.

4. Eugene H. Merrill, "Israel according to the Torah," in *The People, the Land, and the Future of Israel: Israel and the Jewish People in the Plan of God*, ed. Darrell L. Bock and Mitch Glaser (Grand Rapids: Kregel, 2014), 28.

Abram's physical descendants (Gen 22:17–18; see also Gal 3:16).

The Gentile ethnic groups each had a land, a language, and a common genetic identity. Abram was unlike the Gentiles in each of these three respects. First, Abram did not have a land. In fact, after departing from Haran at God's command, Abram remained a sojourner the rest of his life.[5] Second, Abram would have needed to change languages, perhaps switching from Akkadian in his native Ur to proto-Aramaic (or some Northwest Semitic predecessor) in Haran, then to Canaanite in Canaan (which later developed into the Hebrew language).[6] Third, Abram did not have a genetic identity that set him apart from other members of his family. As for Abram's physical descendants, God did not include Hagar's son Ishmael within the covenant, although he was Abram's first son. Instead, God clarified that the covenant would be for Isaac alone (Gen 17:19–21). Then, among Isaac's sons, God elected Jacob and not Esau (Mal 1:2–3; see also Rom 9:6–13).[7]

Joining the Covenant People

Even after Jacob received the new name "Israel" in Genesis 32:28, genetic identity did not strictly define God's covenant people. For example, in Exodus 12:37 the "sons of Israel" departed Egypt. The following verse then states that "a foreign multitude also went up with them" (v. 38). Soon "all the people" enter into covenant with God at the foot of Mount Sinai (Exod 24:1–11). Most likely, the foreign multitude joined themselves to the descendants of Jacob as one nation in covenant relationship with God.[8]

With the passage of time the Hebrews would eventually possess a land, a language, and a genetic identity distinct from those of other peoples. God gave them specific laws to maintain separation from other ethnicities. For example, Deuteronomy 23:3 instructs, "No

---

5. Note the repeated use of the verbal root for "sojourn" (*gwr*) in relation to Abram in Genesis 12:10; 17:8; 20:1; 21:23, 34; 23:4; 26:3; 35:27.

6. See the concise introductions to Akkadian (pp. 6–7), Aramaic (pp. 18–21), and Canaanite (pp. 15–18) in Aaron D. Rubin, *A Brief Introduction to the Semitic Languages*, Gorgias Handbooks 19 (Piscataway, NJ: Gorgias, 2010), and the language distribution maps in Gideon Goldenberg, *Semitic Languages: Features, Structures, Relations, Processes* (Oxford: Oxford University Press, 2013), 21–23.

7. Genesis 17:12–14 demonstrates the primacy of covenant over genetic descent from Abraham (so named from 17:5 onward) for defining the Hebrew people. Verses 12–13 indicate that every male covenant member must receive circumcision as the sign of the covenant, including foreigners, defined as "not of [Abraham's] seed." Then verse 14 emphasizes that uncircumcised males are not only outside the covenant but also outside the Hebrew people: "An uncircumcised male who is not circumcised in the flesh of his foreskin, that person shall be cut off from his people; he has broken My covenant." It is significant that the foreigners in Abraham's household included at least Egyptians (12:15–16), Arameans (15:2–3), and eventually proto-Philistines (20:1, 14), the men alone numbering in the hundreds from early on in Abraham's sojourn (14:14). Such details are not repeated with Isaac or Jacob, and how many of these foreigners remained with the Hebrews until their migration to Egypt is not explicit. Yet for indications that the clan could have remained ethnically mixed, see Genesis 26:12–17; 27:37; 30:43; 32:5–10; 46:5–7, 26–27; 50:7–9.

8. Some of the covenant Israelites were half Egyptian (Lev 24:10), as were Joseph's two sons Manasseh and Ephraim (46:20), who fathered entire tribes of the Hebrews. Moses' sons were half Midianite (Exod 2:15–3:1; Num 12:1), and the descendants of foreigners circumcised in Abraham's entourage (see previous note) may have also been included at Sinai. Eugene E. Carpenter, *Exodus*, EEC (Bellingham, WA: Lexham, 2016), 1:469; Duane A. Garrett, *A Commentary on Exodus*, KEL (Grand Rapids: Kregel, 2014), 366.

Ammonite or Moabite shall enter the assembly of Yahweh; even to the tenth generation, none of their seed shall ever enter the assembly of Yahweh."

Yet the book of Ruth contains what may appear at first glance to be a glaring violation of Deuteronomy 23:3.[9] Ruth the Moabitess—a Gentile—abandons her former gods and people (Ruth 1:16) and swears by the name of Yahweh (1:17). Yahweh enables her to marry a Hebrew and conceive (4:13). Through this conception, Ruth even becomes an ancestor of the Messiah (4:17, 22; Matt 1:5), the savior for all peoples.[10] Hence the book of Ruth raises a key question for the formation of a biblical theology of ethnicity: how should the covenant people remain distinct from the Gentiles if one of their paradigmatic stories of covenant faithfulness is that of a Gentile woman who assimilated into Israel?[11]

Preserving the Covenant People

The answer to the arresting question posed by the book of Ruth regarding the purity of God's covenant people lies in perhaps the last place critical scholarship would look for it: the books of Ezra and Nehemiah.[12] In the books that carry their names, both leaders face the problem of the covenant people intermarrying with unbelieving foreigners. Some recent English translations of Ezra 9:2 unfortunately read similar to the ESV: "For they have taken some of their daughters to be wives for themselves and for their sons, so that the *holy race* has mixed itself with the peoples of the lands."[13] Readers of translations like this one cannot help but suspect a racial motive behind Ezra and Nehemiah's similar and seemingly harsh responses, which included the dissolution of the ethnically mixed marriages of men listed in Ezra 10:20–43.[14] But the offense of the marriages was in the foreign wives' "abominations," their other gods, which they did not abandon (Ezra 9:1; cf. Deut 7:1–6).[15] Nehemiah's lament that the children of these marriages could not speak the language of Judah (Neh 13:24) is likewise liable to modern misunderstanding

---

9. Perhaps due to the use of two masculine singular verbs and a masculine plural pronoun in Deuteronomy 23:3, the midrash *Ruth Rab.* 2.9 teaches that the law prohibits only Ammonite and Moabite men from entering the covenant people. See *Midrash Rabbah: Ruth*, trans. L. Rabinowitz (London: Socino, 1939), 30–31. However, Nehemiah 13:1–3 clearly understands Deuteronomy to refer to women as well. See Jacob M. Myers, *Ezra–Nehemiah*, AB 14 (New York: Doubleday, 1965), 207; see also p. 76.

10. While narrating the dramatic tale of Ruth's entry into the covenant people, the author belabors the point that Ruth is a Moabitess. See Ruth 1:22; 2:2, 6, 21; 4:5, 10.

11. On the one hand, it seems reasonable that ten generations could have passed between the proclamation of Deuteronomy 23:3 and "the days when the judges judged" (Ruth 1:1), the setting of the book of Ruth. On the other hand, the genealogy in Ruth 4:18–21 (cf. 1 Chr 2:5–12) places Boaz in the seventh generation from Perez. In any case, Ruth's response to Israel's God and her role in the history of redemption testify to her place among the elect people of Israel and point up the more comprehensive answer below.

12. For example, rather than finding harmony, Artur Weiser asserts that the story of Ruth is partly a protest against the "reckless practice of Ezra and Nehemiah in the issue of mixed marriages." Weiser, *Enleitung in das Alte Testament*, 4th ed. (Göttingen: Vandenhoek and Ruprecht, 1957), 245.

13. Italics added for emphasis. See also the NASB2020, NET, and NLT.

14. In grief Ezra tore out his own hair (Ezra 9:3), and Nehemiah tore out the hair of covenant breakers (Neh 13:25).

15. On the relationship of Ezra 9:1–2 to Deuteronomy 7:1–6 and 23:3–8, see Gary Edward Schnittjer, *Old Testament Use of Old Testament* (Grand Rapids: Zondervan, 2021), 655–59.

as xenophobia. Instead, it was that ignorance of the Hebrew (or possibly Aramaic) language constituted an existential threat: the next generation would no longer understand the Word of God.

Ezra and Nehemiah were concerned not about the purity of a holy "race" but about the preservation of the holy "seed" (*zera* in Ezra 9:2), the same Hebrew term God used for Abraham's offspring that, besides highlighting the covenant relationship, also specifically pointed to one physical descendant, the Messiah (Gen 12:7; 15:5; 22:17–18). Time and again since the call of Abraham, God graciously elected some people not physically descended from Abraham, such as Ruth, to join His covenant people (e.g., Esth 8:17). Now following the exile, the books of Ezra and Nehemiah continue to attest that people from other ethnicities could leave their prior ethnic identity behind and assimilate into the Hebrew people. For example, Ezra 6:21 relates, "Then the sons of Israel who returned from exile *and all those who had separated themselves from the uncleanness of the nations of the land to join them, to seek Yahweh, the God of Israel,* ate the Passover" (emphasis added). Likewise Nehemiah 10:28 lists "all those who had separated themselves from the peoples of the lands to the law of God" among those who promised not to intermarry with those same peoples (v. 30).[16] The books of Ezra and Nehemiah consistently teach that the nature of the separation

God commanded was not ethnic but covenantal. Put another way, God's gracious election of His covenant people included the Hebrews as well as some Gentiles.

Judgment

Unfortunately, most Gentiles who encountered the Hebrews did not assimilate into the covenant people. In Exodus, Egypt serves as a paradigmatic biblical example of this sad reality. The drama of Israel's deliverance from slavery in Egypt depicts Pharaoh responding to Moses' first call to let the Israelites leave: "Who is Yahweh that I should listen to His voice to let Israel go? I do not know Yahweh, and also, I will not let Israel go" (Exod 5:2). Following the promise of impending judgment in Exodus 7:4, verse 5 reads like a direct response to Pharaoh's dismissive attitude: "Then the Egyptians shall know that I am Yahweh." The book of Exodus casts God's judgment upon Egypt not primarily as retribution for enslavement of Israel but as judgment for refusal to acknowledge and then obey God.[17]

Indeed, Egypt and other ancient peoples are the target of special prophetic messages called the "Oracles against the Nations" (e.g., Isa 13–23; Jer 45–51; Ezek 25–32). These announcements of judgment generally follow common forms, though the oracles differ from one another in their content, with some of them even containing explicit prophecies of God's coming mercy through His judgment.

---

16. Peter H. W. Lau and Gregory Goswell, *Unceasing Kindness: A Biblical Theology of Ruth*, New Studies in Biblical Theology 41 (Downers Grove, IL: InterVarsity, 2016), 8–9.

17. John L. McKenzie, *A Theology of the Old Testament* (Garden City, NJ: Doubleday, 1974), 295.

For example, God's future "striking" of Egypt in Isaiah 19:22 leads to God healing Egypt from the very wounds He dealt them. By the conclusion of the oracle in verse 25, Egypt's position with respect to God has changed completely. Isaiah writes, "Blessed is Egypt My people, and Assyria the work of My hands, and Israel My inheritance."[18]

Although the Bible contains many pronouncements of judgment against Gentile nations, the audience that heard these prophecies was not those nations themselves but God's covenant people, Israel. Since Israel alone possessed God's special revelation, they alone would be able to make sense of God's acts of judgment in history. They would understand that just as all the Gentile ethnic groups stand under God's judgment for specific sins (Amos 1:3–2:3), they as the covenant people also merit judgment for their sins (2:4–9:10). Amos 9:7 makes universal judgment plain: "'Are you not as the sons of Ethiopia to Me, O sons of Israel?' declares Yahweh. 'Have I not brought up Israel from the land of Egypt, and the Philistines from Caphtor and the Arameans from Kir?'"

Readers both ancient and modern thus discover that ethnic identity contributes nothing toward averting God's judgment. Both the Old and New Testaments attest that the only hope of experiencing deliverance through God's judgment is repentance leading to forgiveness of sin in the context of covenant relationship.[19]

The Church

The Old Testament theology of ethnicity directly applies to the new covenant people of the New Testament. To review, ethnicity is not a core component of human identity. The election of God's covenant people is based not on ethnicity but on God's sovereignty in election. Consequently, membership in any particular ethnic group itself conveys no benefit toward deliverance through judgment. Ethnicity is not, and never has been, the focal point of God's dealings with humanity through history. Instead, redemptive relationship with God comes only through covenant. Such was the unique, defining characteristic of the Hebrews in the Old Testament. People of other ethnicities could enter covenant with God, but only if they joined themselves to the Hebrews, taking upon themselves the associated covenantal responsibilities. Perhaps the most basic of these responsibilities was for males to receive circumcision.

Yet, obeying the stipulations of the Mosaic law and undergoing circumcision ignited contention as Gentiles entered the early church (Gal 5:2–4). Resolving the tension between the strong affirmation of circumcision in the Old Testament and the contrasting rejection of it in the New Testament requires the interpretive

---

18. For discussion of the grammatically expressed logic of this oracle, see Scott N. Callaham, "Old Testament Theology and World Mission," in *World Mission: Theology, Strategy, and Current Issues* (Bellingham, WA: Lexham, 2019), 19. Given the history of Egyptian and Assyrian contact with Israel in the Bible, the notion that God would bless them equally with Israel would likely have been shocking, even offensive, to the original reader. Both the Septuagint (Greek) and the Targum (Aramaic) renderings of Isaiah 19:25 limit blessing to Israel alone.

19. See, e.g., Isaiah 55:7; Joel 2:12–13; Luke 24:47; Acts 3:19–20; and Romans 8:1.

key of Christ, the Mediator of the "new covenant" of Jeremiah 31:31–34 (Heb 8:8–13; 9:15; 12:24).

In the new covenant, circumcision of the flesh loses its function as a covenant sign. Instead, circumcision becomes a potent metaphor for the change of heart longed for in Leviticus 26:41 (Jer 9:26), commanded in Deuteronomy 10:16, promised in Deuteronomy 30:6, and finally performed by the Holy Spirit in Romans 2:29.[20] Peter explains to "those who were circumcised" that the Holy Spirit had fallen on Gentiles who believed in the Lord Jesus Christ (Acts 11:2–17). Regardless of ethnicity, it is the presence of the Spirit—the circumciser of the heart—that is the identifying sign of the new covenant relationship with God.[21] In line with the fact that ethnicity was not the fundamental basis of relationship with God at any prior point in redemptive history, in the new covenant the Spirit is poured out on "all flesh," ethnic Jew and ethnic Gentile alike, in the church (Joel 2:28–29; Acts 2:17–18).

Christ's disciples from among all nations (ethnicities) are one people whom Christ commands to make disciples of all ethnicities. Jesus explains how to make these disciples: go wherever the nations are, baptize them, and teach them to obey all His commands (Matt 28:18–20). This Great Commission is the mission of the church, and its result is the populating of the new heavens and new earth with people of every ethnicity—who through their redemption have become one holy race—in unending worship.[22]

The "Judaizers" ("the party of the circumcision" in Gal 2:12) were the first group in church history to attempt to split apart God's one holy race according to ethnicity. Paul characterized their error as "a different gospel" (1:6), for they regressively promoted circumcision and other distinguishing marks of Jewishness. Paul staunchly opposed them (1:8), for treating circumcision as if it had any meaning in light of the new life in Christ was to oppose the gospel itself. The "new man" in Christ, Paul argues, bears "no distinction between Greek and Jew, circumcised and uncircumcised, barbarian, Scythian, slave, and freeman, but Christ is all and in all" (Col 3:11).

One who insists on the ongoing relevance of ethnicity as an identity marker of spiritual relevance in the new covenant community commits the error of the "Judaizers" and is ironically an ethnocentric "Gentilizer." He destroys unity

---

20. The need for circumcision of the heart among those not in covenant relationship with God lies in the background of Ezekiel 44:7 and 9, which depict foreigners as "uncircumcised in heart and uncircumcised in flesh."

21. A much fuller argument that the sign of the new covenant is the Holy Spirit dwelling in all covenant members appears in Scott N. Callaham, "Blasphemy against the Holy Spirit: Rejecting the Sign of the Covenant," *Horizons in Biblical Theology* 45, no. 1 (2023): 37–58.

22. As stated at the beginning of the chapter, with Eric Mason it is right to notice whom God has saved in Revelation 7:9: the elect "from every nation and all tribes and peoples and tongues." Mason, *Woke Church*, 170. Yet it is also right to listen to their cry in the next verse, a cry undifferentiated by skin tone: "Salvation belongs to our God who sits on the throne, and to the Lamb." In this visionary scene, God the Father has brought glory to Himself through the salvation of His elect (one holy race) from all nations. God the Son has gathered His elect (one holy race) through the Great Commission, and God the Holy Spirit has empowered His elect (one holy race) through history in their Great Commission obedience. Salvation of the elect is by God and for God, and God is the focus of the adoration of His one saved people.

in the church by rebuilding "dividing walls" that Christ decisively tore down (Eph 2:14). He preaches "a different gospel" (Gal 1:6), a distorted gospel (1:7), and a new-old heresy that damns rather than the gospel that saves. Ethnocentric "Gentilizers" are to be accursed.[23]

Missionary Opposition to Ethnocentrism

Missionaries carrying out Christ's Great Commission stand at the front lines of opposition to all ethnocentric, Gentilizing, skin-color-conscious evisceration of the gospel message. Skin-color-conscious religion is human-centered instead of God-centered. Skin-color-conscious religion "looks at the outward appearance, but Yahweh looks at the heart" (1 Sam 16:7). Skin-color-conscious religion defines relationships between people of different ethnicities in terms of power dynamics, even though Jesus forbade His followers from seeking to wield power over one another (Matt 20:25–28). Skin-color-conscious religion traffics in partiality based on ethnic identity, despite Scripture's equating such partiality with blasphemy (Jas 2:7). Skin-color-conscious religion withholds forgiveness and nurses grievances,

often for generalized "systemic" sins that nobody in particular has committed. Depersonalizing sin by projecting guilt on entire ethnic groups and cultural "systems" is utterly alien to the Bible (e.g., Ezek 18:20). Skin-color-conscious religion exhibits the self-righteousness of the Pharisee in Luke 18:11–12, who decries the sins of others and congratulates himself for how good he is. Skin-color-conscious religion is an "unfruitful work of darkness." The church must not only refuse to participate in skin-color-conscious religion but must also expose it for what it is (Eph 5:11). This pagan religion attacks the image of God by pitting unbiblical "races" against one another in perpetual class struggle, and it has no place within the church.[24]

In contrast to the overt racism of skin-color-conscious religion, the body of Christ should adopt the biblical perspective of "color irrelevance" with wholehearted conviction.[25] "Color irrelevance" is a practical outpouring of the biblical theology of ethnicity in the church, and it is profoundly unifying. After all, the very meaning of the word *church* in the Bible is "assembly," a gathering together of the saints.[26] Unity is the theme of Jesus' final prayer for His

---

23. The Greek word translated "accursed" in the New Testament is *anathema*, the term the Septuagint translators selected to render the Old Testament "ban" (*herem*) of complete giving over to Yahweh, often for utter destruction. "ἀνάθεμα," *NIDNTTE*, 1:281–82.

24. Incidentally, the resolution of the problem of unequal distribution of food among the widows of the Jerusalem church (Acts 6:1–7) provides no justification whatsoever for treating people differently based on the color of their skin. The root of the problem was not racism, and the church did not solve the problem through employing race-conscious practices. See the misuse of Acts 6 to justify skin-color consciousness in Rodney M. Woo, *The Color of Church: A Biblical and Practical Paradigm for Multiracial Churches* (Nashville: B&H Academic, 2009), 166–68.

25. Promoters of skin-color consciousness vehemently reject "color irrelevance." For example, Parker tellingly labels such thinking as "White supremacist authoritarianism that stems from the doctrines of inerrancy and infallibility." Angela N. Parker, *If God Still Breathes, Why Can't I? Black Lives Matter and Biblical Authority* (Grand Rapids: Eerdmans, 2021), 55.

26. Contrary to popular belief, the New Testament Greek word for "church" (*ekklēsia*) does not mean "called-out ones." Its basic meaning of "assembly" has the opposite meaning, of calling *together*. See James Barr, *The Semantics of Biblical Language*

followers in John 17. The unity of "every nation and all tribes and peoples and tongues" (Rev 7:9) in heaven is due to the atoning work of Christ to redeem the elect of every ethnicity for the sake of the worship of Christ forever. To sing in harmony with this heavenly chorus in the present, the church should repent of the racism of skin-color-conscious religion and believe the gospel—the color-irrelevant gospel—which alone has the power to save.

In God's providence, missionaries proclaiming this color-irrelevant gospel in obedience to the Great Commission are uniquely positioned to oppose skin-color-conscious religion. Perhaps the most obvious way cross-cultural international missionaries encounter skin-color-conscious religion has to do with their own ethnic difference from—or similarity to—the people they serve. As for the case of ethnic difference, skin-color consciousness in the missionary's words and deeds will inevitably "color" reception of the missionary's message. In other words, if a missionary treats people of various ethnic groups differently based on skin color, it is only natural for a national to assume that God does too. In the case of ethnic similarity with host peoples, missionaries can take advantage of ethnicity as a point of contact with a certain culture. However, missionaries must also guard against allowing the way of life of "people who look like" them to become the basis of their

message rather than Scripture. All cultures bear evidence of human sinfulness, and all missionaries are sinful human beings. Therefore, only the color-irrelevant, biblical gospel should define missionaries' perspective on their own ethnicities and the ethnicities of the peoples they serve.

Missionaries must also soberly evaluate their partnerships on the basis of faithfulness to the color-irrelevant gospel. This evaluation is necessary because ethnocentrism corrupts the gospel message. No fellowship in the gospel (Phil 1:5) is possible with those who actively promote ethnocentrism, whether the "Gentilizers" one encounters are fellow missionaries or organizations that brand themselves as Christian. While separation from these groups may bring hardship on the mission field, separation from unrepentant, entrenched sin is necessary.

That said, missionaries may find ethnocentricity to be the default stance of those they serve, perhaps even including churches on the mission field and their sending church. In such cases, missionaries should recognize that their presence on the mission field is itself a witness against anti-gospel, anti-missional ethnocentrism. They should then point to Christ, whose Great Commission requires proclaiming and teaching the color-irrelevant gospel. Then, as people of "all the nations" repent and believe, God will draw them into his new covenant people, the church: one holy race.

(Oxford: Oxford University Press, 1961), 119–29. The unity of the church as God's assembly of his elect is clear in Ephesians 4:4–6: "There is one body and one Spirit, just as also you were called in one hope of your calling; one Lord, one faith, one baptism; one God and Father of all who is over all and through all and in all."

CHAPTER 6

A Messiah for All Peoples:
Christ's Affirmation of a Nonexclusive Gospel

Mark Tatlock

The Old Testament consistently provided God's people with the expectation that their Messiah, the Seed of the woman (Gen 3:15), would bring redemption to all mankind. Beginning with God's choosing of Abraham, the Scriptures conveyed that God's blessing of salvation would extend first to the nation fathered by Abraham and then, through that nation, to "all the families of the earth" (Gen 12:1–3). Paul unequivocally stated in Galatians 3:6–14 that the blessing spoken about to Abraham was "the gospel"—the good news of redemption— and that the Jews would be the first but not the exclusive recipients of it. This promise was ratified in the Abrahamic covenant (Gen 15:1–21).

However, because of the Jewish nation's unfaithfulness, especially through idolatry, to the later Mosaic covenant that God made with them (Exod 19:3–6), God judged and gradually sent Israel into exile in the eighth, seventh, and sixth centuries BC (2 Kgs 15:29; 17:3ff.; Jer 3:6–10; 11:9–13). Still, He promised to remember His covenant with their father Abraham, to preserve them, to judge their persecutors, and to forgive and restore them with a new covenant (Jer 31:31–37; 33:25–26). From the beginning of the return from exile (538 BC) and onward, Israel seemed to have relinquished idolatry altogether. But many also developed an exclusive perspective on the scope of God's redemptive plan toward them.[1] Hating the Gentiles who ruled over them, many in Israel could no longer

---

1. E.g., 1QM; Jub. 22:16–21; Pss. Sol. 9:8–11; 17:21–31; 2 Bar 72:1–6. Shaye J. D. Cohen states that in the sectarian ideology that arose during this time "the polarity of Jew versus gentile is accompanied, if not replaced, by the polarity of the righteous (the sect) versus the wicked (all the other Jews and apparently the gentiles as well). . . . The righteous dead would be resurrected to glory (or otherwise rewarded), and the nation of Israel would be restored to the state of preeminence that it deserves." *From the Maccabees to the Mishnah*, 3rd ed. (Louisville, KY: Westminster John Knox, 2014), 97. See also Everett Ferguson, *Backgrounds of Early Christianity*, 3rd ed. (Grand Rapids; Cambridge, UK: Eerdmans, 2003), 538–39, 546–47.

imagine God lovingly including the Gentiles in His salvation.

Under Seleucid (198–164 BC) and Roman rule (officially from 37 BC), the Jewish people of the intertestamental period came to focus primarily on their salvation and restoration in military-political terms. They had experienced war and persecution, ruthlessness and scandal in the reigns of Antiochus IV Epiphanes (175–164 BC) and Herod the Great (37–4 BC). They came to expect a Messiah who would free them from Gentile domination.[2] Thus, one of the dominant ideologies in the first century redefined the scope of God's redemption plan to be exclusively Jewish and in terms of their political autonomy under an earthly king. The Messiah would indeed be Israel's king, but just as important, He would bear their sins and the sins of many (Isa 52:13–53:12).

In this context, the Gospel of John reports, the long-awaited Messiah, Jesus Christ, "came to what was His own, and those who were His own did not receive Him" (John 1:11). For that reason, it was necessary for Christ to repeatedly, unapologetically affirm that He came to save both Jews and Gentiles from their sins,

"for God so loved the world" (John 3:16). This chapter surveys eleven episodes from the life of Christ, besides the Great Commission, which affirm that He is a Messiah for all peoples.

His Genealogy

The first references in the life of Christ to the inclusive scope of His messiahship are in His genealogy in the Gospel of Matthew (1:1–17). Thus, the entire New Testament begins with a rehearsal of Christ's kingly credentials and includes the unexpected recognition of several Gentile women in His genealogy: Tamar (Matt 1:3), Rahab (1:5), Ruth (1:5), and perhaps "the wife of Uriah," Bathsheba (1:6).[3] Rahab the Canaanite heard about Yahweh's might, recognized the coming calamity of Jericho, and so rejected the gods of her people to believe in the true God, the God of Israel (Josh 2:1–24; 6:17, 23–25). By her faith she "gained approval" from God (Heb 11:1–2, 31), just as on the basis of Abraham's faith God counted to him the righteousness of Christ (Gen 15:6; Gal 3:6–9). In a similar way, Ruth the Moabitess declared to her Jewish mother-in-law, Naomi, "Your people shall be my people, and your God, my God" (Ruth 1:16).

---

2. In the Gospels this was evident in circumstantial notes such as those in Mark 15:7; Luke 3:15; John 6:14–15; Acts 5:36–37; and 21:38. Cohen, *From the Maccabees to the Mishnah*, 99, 163–64; William A. Simmons, "The Zealots—Religious Militancy and the Sole Rule of God," in *Peoples of the New Testament World: An Illustrated Guide* (Peabody, MA: Hendrickson, 2008), 89–97.

3. Uriah was a Hittite (2 Sam 11:3, 6), a descendant of one of the nations the Lord had driven out of Canaan several generations earlier (Exod 23:23, 28). Though Israel had not been permitted to covenant with those nations (34:11–16), Uriah had joined himself to Israel and to her covenant with Yahweh (cf. 2 Sam 11:10–11), becoming one of David's mighty men (23:39; 1 Chron 11:41). His wife, Bathsheba, is alluded to but not named by Matthew. Her father is named Eliam in 2 Samuel 11:3, who, if he was the same Eliam as in 2 Samuel 23:34, was one of David's mighty men also and the son of Ahithophel, David's advisor-turned-traitor (cf. 15:12; 16:15ff.). In that case, though Bathsheba was apparently not a Gentile, the mention of her foreign husband's name instead seems to make Matthew's inclusion of Gentiles in the lineage of Jesus all the more intentional. On Bathsheba's family, see V. Philips Long, "2 Samuel," in *Zondervan Illustrated Bible Backgrounds Commentary (Old Testament)*, vol. 2, *Joshua, Judges, Ruth, 1 and 2 Samuel*, ed. John H. Walton (Grand Rapids: Zondervan, 2009), 458, 480. On the implications of the women in Matthew's genealogy, see Leon Morris, *The Gospel according to Matthew*, PNTC (Grand Rapids; Leicester, England: Eerdmans; Inter-Varsity Press, 1992), 23.

These Gentiles in the genealogy of Christ are examples of the "wild olive branches" grafted into the cultivated olive tree of the Abrahamic covenant. That was Paul's analogy for Gentiles who could be integrated into the remnant of believing Israel (Rom 11:1–24). Since it is those who are of faith that are true descendants of Abraham, it was fitting for Matthew to include believing Gentiles in the royal genealogy of Christ, the Seed of Abraham (Matt 1:1–2, 17). They stand as a testimony to all Gentiles who would read Matthew's account of the coming King of Israel.

His Birth Narratives

The narratives of Jesus' birth (Luke 2:8–20; Matt 2:1–12) demonstrate that the Messiah was anticipated by both Jews and Gentiles. In Luke 2 is given the famous account of Jewish shepherds "keeping watch over their flock by night" (v. 8). An angel appeared and said to them, "I bring you good news of great joy which will be for all the people. For today in the city of David there has been born for you a Savior, who is Christ the Lord" (vv. 10–11). Upon hearing the announcement and the subsequent *Gloria*, they went directly to the manger to see Jesus (vv. 15–16). Then they affirmed His messiahship by telling others "the statement which had been told them about this Child," in other words, the good news (v. 17). Jewish readers of this account can be thrilled to see that God fulfilled His promises to send a Savior and called humble Israelites to honor Him at His birth.

Yet it was not only Jews to whom the birth of Christ was announced. In Matthew 2, there were also wisemen, "magi from the east" (2:1), who recognized that the prophecy of a Jewish king was being fulfilled when they saw a new and extraordinary star in the east (v. 2). Likely these magi (learned men) were familiar with the prophets dating back to Daniel's time in Babylon (Dan 2:48–49; 5:29–31; 6:28; cf. 9:1–2).[4] They were Gentiles who traveled to Israel, found the child sometime after His birth, worshiped Him prostrate, and presented Him with gifts of honor (Matt 2:11). God had alerted them to their Messiah's birth and led them all the way.

His Dedication in the Temple

Following the account of the Jewish shepherds, Luke relates the scene of Christ's dedication in the temple (Luke 2:21–35). There, a prophet named Simeon had been promised by God that he would not die until he had seen the Messiah (vv. 25–26). Being providentially led by the Holy Spirit into the temple courts on the day of Jesus' dedication, it was revealed to Simeon that the infant Mary was holding in her arms, just eight days old, was the Christ that Simeon was awaiting (vv. 27–28). In response

---

4. *Magoi* (magi) is how the Greek Septuagint translates a certain class of magicians (Heb. *hartummim*), part of a collective of diviners and wise men over whom Daniel was appointed after he interpreted Nebuchadnezzar's dream (Dan 2:2, 10, 48–49). The same technical terms appear in Aramaic in Daniel 4:7–9, 18, but these verses are lacking in the Septuagint. There Daniel is referred to as "chief of the magicians" (4:9). The magi who came to Jesus' birth are perhaps owing to Daniel's legacy. Cf. D. A. Carson, "Matthew," in *EBC*, vol. 8, *Matthew, Mark, Luke*, ed. Frank E. Gaebelein (Grand Rapids: Zondervan, 1984), 84–85.

to the Spirit's revelation, Simeon prayed, "Now Master, You are releasing Your slave in peace, according to Your word. For my eyes have seen Your salvation, which You prepared in the presence of all peoples, a light for revelation to the Gentiles, and for the glory of Your people Israel" (vv. 29–32). God's appointed witness to the arrival of "the Lord's Christ" (v. 26) knew He was a Savior to the Gentiles as well as "the comfort of Israel" (v. 25), for "all peoples" as well as His chosen people (v. 31).[5]

His Sermon in Nazareth

At the start of His public ministry, Christ preached a sermon in His hometown synagogue, as recorded in Luke 4:16–30. Having revealed Himself as the Servant of Yahweh in Isaiah (vv. 17–21; cf. Isa 61:1–2), He was met with initial excitement and wonder. Those who heard Him, spoke well of Him, marveling at the gracious words falling from His lips (v. 22). One can imagine the hearers' excitement that perhaps the "favorable year of the Lord" had arrived (v. 19), perhaps this man would prove to be the Messiah. But the enthusiasm turned to hostility when Jesus confronted their unbelief at His apparent ignobility, "Is this not Joseph's son?" (vv. 22–24).

In verses 25–27, Jesus contrasted the unbelief of His Jewish hearers with the genuine faith of two Old Testament Gentiles, the starving widow of Zarephath in Phoenicia (1 Kgs 17:8–24) and the Syrian commander and leper,

Naaman (2 Kgs 5:1–19). These outsiders to whom the revered prophets Elijah and Elisha ministered were recognized by Christ as beneficiaries of God's redemptive work—and that so, when He could have sent the prophets to many widows and lepers in Israel. The sting of this statement is only discernible in view of these religious Jews' pride and prejudice.

Upon hearing Jesus' pointed words, the initial excitement over the message about the Messiah was replaced by hatred and by seeking to kill the one claiming to be Messiah (Luke 4:28–30). Though Christ frequently confronted the religious hypocrisy of the Pharisees throughout His ministry, the first hostility and attempt to kill Him was on this occasion: a jealous rage toward a Messiah who would equally save Gentiles.

His Story of the Good Samaritan

In Luke 10, a scribe tested Jesus with what he must do to inherit eternal life (v. 25). Knowing the man's self-righteousness, Jesus replied with the impossible task of keeping the Law (meant to condemn, not to justify; Rom 3:19–20). The scribe offered back the two simple but greatest commandments: to love the Lord with all his heart, soul, strength, and mind; and to love his neighbor as himself (vv. 26–27; cf. Matt 22:34–40). Jesus answered tersely, "Do this and you will live" (v. 28). Once more the scribe challenged Him, "And who is my neighbor" (v. 29)?

Christ responded with the well-known

---

5. Walter L. Liefeld, "Luke," in *EBC*, vol. 8, *Matthew, Mark, Luke*, ed. Frank E. Gaebelein (Grand Rapids: Zondervan, 1984), 849.

story of the good Samaritan (vv. 30–35). It is comprised mostly of Jewish characters: a traveler to Jerusalem, a Levite, and a rabbi. The fourth man, however, is from the region of Samaria, a half-Jew. Following Israel's exile in the eighth century BC, the Assyrian kings imported foreign peoples into the land of Galilee and Samaria (2 Kgs 17:24; Ezra 4:2, 10), according to their policy for maintaining dominance over conquered peoples. Over time, Gentiles and Jews in the region intermarried, producing an ethnically mixed population concentrated around the old northern capital Samaria and later Shechem. The monotheistic religious sect known as the Samaritans probably then arose out of this milieu in the Hellenistic period.[6] Jews despised the Samaritans, excluding them from worship in the temple because of their mixed ethnicity and because they, in fact, maintained their own aberrant tradition of worship on Mount Gerizim (John 4:20). It was unimaginable, then, for the religious elite to accept the hero of Christ's story as a Samaritan, one who was more righteous than a Levite or a rabbi. Yet Jesus once again held up as a model of saving faith—the kind that fulfills the righteous requirement of the law—a Gentile (vv. 36–37).

His Confrontation of Skepticism

As Jesus' notoriety grew, crowds began asking Him to perform miraculous signs to prove that He was the Messiah. In response, He addressed what was for some skepticism and for others sensationalism, but in both cases, unbelief. Knowing what was in their hearts, Jesus warns in Luke 11,

> The Queen of the South will rise up at the judgment with the men of this generation and condemn them, because she came from the ends of the earth to hear the wisdom of Solomon. And behold, something greater than Solomon is here. The men of Nineveh will stand up at the judgment with this generation and condemn it, because they repented at the preaching of Jonah. And behold, something greater than Jonah is here. (vv. 31–32)

In Jesus' first example, the queen of the south was a Gentile from Sheba (in Arabia), who traveled to see for herself what she had heard about Israel's God through Israel's king (1 Kgs 10:1–25). In Jesus' second example, the men of Nineveh were also Gentiles; in Jonah's day, they were the Assyrians who would soon conquer Israel! They were feared for their menacing acts and violent atrocities, yet they responded to Jonah's pronouncements of God's wrath with wholehearted repentance (Jonah 3:1–10).

The Lord's use of Nineveh in Luke 11 was also a poignant allusion to the pouting prophet's

---

6. The Samaritans' origins are debated, but see current opinion in Robert T. Anderson, "Samaritans," *ABD*, 5:947; Lidija Novakovic, "Jews and Samaritans," in *The World of the New Testament: Cultural, Social, and Historical Contexts*, ed. Joel B. Green and Lee Martin McDonald (Grand Rapids: Baker Academic, 2013), 212–13; H. G. M. Williamson and C. A. Evans, "Samaritans," *Dictionary of New Testament Background: A Compendium of Contemporary Biblical Scholarship*, ed. Stanley E. Porter and Craig A. Evans (Downers Grove, IL: InterVarsity Press, 2000), 1057–59.

response. Upon seeing the Gentiles' repentance and God's forgiveness, Jonah angrily protested, confessing his motive for originally disobeying God's call to go and preach: he knew that God was a gracious and compassionate God—and by implication, toward Gentiles no less than toward Israelites (Jonah 4:2). Jesus came to purchase that grace and mercy for all peoples.

His Cleansing of the Ten Lepers

Many followed Christ to seek miracles of healing. When this occurred, Christ often either affirmed or challenged their motives, whether authentic faith or unbelief. When He cleansed a group of ten lepers from their incurable disease in Luke 17, He did so out of mercy (vv. 11–13). The cleanse would take place on a delay, after they had departed to seek the lawful inspection of the priests, just as Jesus commanded (v. 14; cf. Lev 14:1–32). All of them obeyed and were cleansed, but nine proved to be unbelieving, having no desire to glorify God. Only one of them showed gratitude, returning to worship at Jesus' feet (vv. 15–16). That one happened to be a Samaritan (v. 16). Jesus' rhetorical question "But the nine—where are they?" highlighted the contrast between "this foreigner" and the others, His Jewish kinsmen (vv. 17–18). Then, Jesus' pronouncement that the Samaritan's faith had saved him, affirmed that His salvation is for all peoples (v. 19).

His Appointment with the Samaritan Woman

In John's dramatic account of "the woman at the well" episode (John 4:1–42), Christ's Jewish disciples might have questioned why Jesus would willingly travel through Samaria (Luke 9:52–56). The woman He met there in Sychar certainly wondered why He spoke to her, "for Jews have no dealings with Samaritans" (John 4:9). Yet Jesus "had to pass through Samaria" (v. 4); He had a divine appointment (vv. 33–35). While the disciples had gone into town to buy food, the woman had come to draw water from the well where Jesus was waiting (v. 7). He had come to give her "living water," eternal life (vv. 10, 14). When she sarcastically dismissed the offer, He exposed her life of sin, revealing His omniscience and her need for salvation (vv. 16–18). She confessed that Jesus must have been a prophet, but changed the subject, deferring repentance, it seems, until Messiah should come (vv. 19–25). Jesus replied, "I who speak to you am He" (v. 26). Something changed. The woman left, eager to tell the townsmen about Jesus (vv. 28–29, 39), and they came out to meet Him (v. 30).

In that time, Jesus' disciples had returned, confused at His refusal to eat (John 4:27, 31–34). And as the crowds were coming to Jesus, He uttered these immortal words: "Lift up your eyes and look on the fields, that they are white for harvest. Even now he who reaps is receiving wages and is gathering fruit for life eternal; so that he who sows and he who reaps may rejoice together" (vv. 35–36). This Gentile city, lost but expecting a Messiah, was coming out to meet Him in droves. John concludes,

From that city many of the Samaritans believed in Him because of the word of the woman who bore witness, "He told me all the things that I have done." So when the Samaritans came to Jesus, they were asking Him to stay with them; and He stayed there two days. And many more believed because of His word; and they were saying to the woman, "It is no longer because of what you said that we believe, for we have heard for ourselves and know that this One is truly the Savior of the world." (vv. 39–42)

Perhaps no episode shows more clearly Jesus' joy in bringing salvation to all peoples.

His Healing of the Centurion's Servant

Judea was under Roman occupation throughout Christ's ministry. A striking example of a Roman who came to faith—a military commander, no less—took place in Capernaum, as recorded in Matthew 8:5–13. While Jesus was healing many Jews on this occasion (Matt 8:1–4), the Roman centurion approached Christ and urgently requested that He heal his servant, who lay at home paralyzed with sickness (vv. 5, 6). The request demonstrated the centurion's humility and faith, for while he could have attempted to exercise his political power by commanding Christ to come, he instead simply asked for Christ to heal the servant without coming. The Roman called Jesus "Lord," confessed his own unworthiness for Jesus to enter his house, and professed his faith in Jesus' word (vv. 6–9). Before responding with a promise to

heal the servant (v. 13), Jesus marveled and said to the crowds who were following Him,

> Truly I say to you, I have not found such great faith with anyone in Israel. And I say to you that many will come from east and west, and recline at the table with Abraham, Isaac and Jacob in the kingdom of heaven; but the sons of the kingdom will be cast out into the outer darkness; in that place there will be weeping and gnashing of teeth. (vv. 10–12)

Surrounded by self-seeking Jewish throngs, Jesus affirmed that the greatest demonstration of faith was this Gentile military officer. A centurion would have been the most despised of Romans; his cohort of hundreds of troops were among the many responsible for occupying the land. For Christ to publicly affirm this man was no small offense to the crowd. Yet He added that in the coming kingdom, while Gentiles "from east and west" would come and enjoy table fellowship with the patriarchs, the "sons of the kingdom" (i.e., the expected heirs, the Jewish masses in Jesus' day)[7] would be cast out! Jesus directly confronted the crowd's ethnic pride and exclusivist mindset.

His Mercy on the Syrophoenician Woman

It is important to remember that for all Jesus' condemnation of His unbelieving countrymen, He loved them. He was sent specifically to "the lost sheep of the house of Israel" (Matt 15:24; cf. 10:5–6). With compassion, He saw them "like

---

7. R. T. France, *The Gospel of Matthew*, NICNT (Grand Rapids: Eerdmans, 2007), 318–19; Carson, "Matthew," 202–3.

sheep without a shepherd" (9:36). He wept over the judgment that would befall them for rejecting Him (Luke 19:41–44; cf. 13:33–35). Thus, while affirming that His gospel is for all people, He also affirmed the Jewish priority of the gospel's offering; as Paul would later put it: "to the Jew first and also to the Greek" (Rom 1:16). For to them are the promises and from them is the Christ (Rom 9:4–5).

The episode of the Syrophoenician woman in Mark 7:24–30 demonstrates this dual affirmation. Jesus had entered the region of Tyre and Sidon, two Gentile cities of the Phoenician coast (Mark 7:24; Matt 15:21). A local Gentile woman came falling down before Christ, pleading that He would free her daughter from demon possession (Mark 7:25–26). She received a response from Christ that surprises readers: "Let the children be satisfied first, for it is not good to take the children's bread and throw it to the dogs" (v. 27). One is obligated "first" to feed bread (the gospel) to his family (the Jews) before the dogs (the Gentiles). Referring to Gentiles as "dogs" was a test of faith. Though the word likely refers to small household pets, not mongrels,[8] it was unflattering and represented "a challenge to the woman to justify her request."[9] She passed the test by her response. She submitted to Jesus' lordship and pled only for the mercy that He had implied was possible (vv. 28–29). Christ approved of her faith, freed

her daughter from the demon, and showed that both Jews and Gentiles receive His grace.

His Clearing of the Temple

In the second of Jesus' two acts of clearing (or "cleansing") the temple (cf. John 2:13–16), the Gospel of Mark records Jesus' motivation including the Gentiles.

> Then they came to Jerusalem. And He entered the temple and began to drive out those who were buying and selling in the temple, and overturned the tables of the money changers and the seats of those who were selling doves; and He was not permitting anyone to carry merchandise through the temple. And He began to teach and say to them, "Is it not written, 'My house shall be called a house of prayer for all the nations'? But you have made it a robbers' den." (11:15–17)

It must not be overlooked in this account that the portion of the temple being desecrated by business was designated the "Court of the Gentiles." The power brokers within the religious establishment of Jerusalem, apparently having dismissed any redemptive purpose for the Gentile, had no qualms about using for profit the only space in which Gentiles could come to pray.[10] But the international scope of the Abrahamic covenant had been built into

---

8. "κυνάριον," BDAG, 575; Eckhard J. Schnabel, *Mark: An Introduction and Commentary*, TNTC 2 (London: Inter-Varsity, 2017), 173–74.

9. Morna D. Hooker, *The Gospel according to Saint Mark*, Black's New Testament Commentary (London: Continuum, 1991), 183.

10. It seems Caiaphas had recently introduced this practice, though against the wishes of some in the Sanhedrin. R. T. France, *The Gospel of Mark: A Commentary on the Greek Text*, NIGTC (Grand Rapids; Carlisle: Eerdmans; Paternoster, 2002), 443–44.

the original temple's design given by God through David and Solomon (1 Kgs 8:41–43; 1 Chr 28:11–19). Herod's temple, functionally complete by 10 BC,[11] had been designed to reflect this understanding also. Isaiah, whom Jesus quoted, also affirmed the place of the Gentile worshiper in the temple (Isa 56:7). It was likely there in that court, after its clearing, that the Greeks in John 12:20–23 sought Jesus (Luke 19:47). Jesus' bold and confrontational action had communicated to everyone in Jerusalem that they could not deny the inclusion of the Gentiles in His kingdom.

Conclusion

Jesus' gospel, though coming through God's chosen nation Israel, is nonexclusive; it is for all peoples. From Rahab to Ruth; from the Jewish shepherds to the eastern magi; from the widow of Zarephath to Naaman the Syrian; from the queen of Sheba to the men of Nineveh; from the Samaritan leper to the woman at the well; from the Roman centurion to the Syrophoenician woman; from faithful Jews, like Simeon and Anna, to the Gentile worshipers in Herod's temple, the life and teaching of Jesus show that men and women from every nation are included in redemption's scope. He, the seed of Abraham, came to bless all the families of the earth by His salvation. Anyone who believes in Him, just as Abraham did, has this abiding and powerful assurance from Christ: He is the Savior of the world, a Messiah for all peoples.

---

11. The detailing and adornment of the temple continued into and beyond Jesus' ministry (cf. John 2:20). B. Chilton, P. W. Comfort, and M. O. Wise, "Temple, Jewish," *Dictionary of New Testament Background: A Compendium of Contemporary Biblical Scholarship*, ed. Stanley E. Porter and Craig A. Evans (Downers Grove, IL: InterVarsity Press, 2000), 1168.

CHAPTER 7

God's Invincible Plan: A Structural Study of Acts

Alejandro Peluffo

Students have often approached the book of Acts as a transitional historical account. It is seen as providing a necessary historical background and literary bridge from the Gospels that precede it to the Epistles that follow it in canonical order.[1] For that purpose, a tripartite outline of the text according to the geographic expansion of the church is sufficient, which traditionally corresponds to Acts 1–7; 8–12; and 13–28.

With a view toward global missions, the present chapter desires a more comprehensive view. It revisits the structure of Acts and combines it with the perspectives of Acts' theological theme and purpose. First, the chapter examines the literary structure of Acts in detail, and then it supplements this with several recurring theological motifs that point to a unifying theme—the sovereign plan of God. The chapter then considers the purpose of Luke in writing Acts[2] and concludes that it is primarily to offer pastoral encouragement and instruction to those suffering for the sake of ministry. Finally, all of the above is synthesized into an exegetical outline. Inasmuch as Luke's contemporaries could be encouraged and instructed by God's sovereign plan, of which the church is an essential part, so, too, should Christ's witnesses today be instructed and encouraged.

The Literary Structure of Acts

Several sets of structural markers have been discerned in Acts' form. These provide alternative methods for outlining the book and thus can

---

1. This order of the New Testament has been common since the second century; for example, it appears in the Muratorian Canon fragment (ca. AD 170). By the time Acts was written in the early AD 60s, almost all other parts of the New Testament were complete but were not yet in circulation as a unified canon. Andreas Köstenberger, L. Scott Kellum, and Charles L. Quarles, *The Cradle, the Cross, and the Crown: An Introduction to the New Testament* (Nashville: B&H, 2009), 25–30, 333–34; Michael J. Kruger, *Canon Revisited: Establishing the Origins and Authority of the New Testament Books* (Wheaton, IL: Crossway, 2012), 203–10.

2. Though Acts is anonymous, both it and the third Gospel were unanimously attested in the early church as being authored by Paul's traveling companion Luke (see Col 4:14; 2 Tim 4:11; Phlm 24). D. A. Carson and Douglas J. Moo, *An Introduction to the New Testament*, 2nd ed. (Grand Rapids: Zondervan, 2005), 290–96.

indicate different, complementary designs or, if the book were a building, frameworks. The major markers are geographic expansion, key people, growth and expansion statements, and chiasm.

Geographic Expansion

Acts 1:8 is strategically placed to be the programmatic statement of the whole book. In this verse, Jesus established His Great Commission in geographic terms: the disciples would be His witnesses beginning in Jerusalem (where in vv. 4–5, He commanded them to wait for the promised Holy Spirit), expanding outward to Judea and Samaria (i.e., the land of Israel, including Galilee; cf. 9:31),[3] and finally reaching "the ends of the earth" (the farthest reaches of the known inhabited world;[4] cf. Isa 49:6). Chapters 1–7, 8–12, and 13–28 roughly correspond to the three-part geographic outline of Jesus' commission. As the book progresses, it shows how the church is spreading according to this scheme, from Jerusalem to Rome, from Jews to Gentiles, and simultaneously from infancy to maturity.

Therefore, if the purpose of Acts is primarily to be a historical transition from the Gospels, which conclude with Jesus' commission to make disciples among the nations, to the Epistles, which are written to disciples among the nations, then the geographical outline foreshadowed in Acts 1:8 is simple and sufficient. It is the overall organization that many fine commentaries have used.[5] However, other structural markers are present.

Key People

Certain people are structurally significant in Acts. Most striking is the heavy focus on Peter and Paul, while Luke says little about the other apostles. No reason is explicitly stated for this focus, but the New Testament bears out that Paul came to be recognized as foremost apostle to the Gentiles and Peter as apostle to "the circumcised" (i.e., Jews, cf. Acts 9:15; Rom 11:13; Gal 2:7–9). Thus, Luke records the ministry of Peter first, which was focused in Jerusalem, and then Paul, who was based in Antioch but lived on the mission field until eventually reaching Rome.

This contrast is further enhanced by the many parallels between the ministries of Peter and Paul. Grouped this way, the events of chapters 1–12 and of chapters 13–28 notably correspond, though not in identical order (see table 1).

The above structure overlaps with the tripartite geographical one. The general focus on Peter's ministry covers most of geographical sections one and two (Jerusalem in Acts 1–7 and Judea and Samaria in Acts 8–12, respectively), but it includes the ministries of other apostles in Jerusalem and of other believers in Israel and even Syria. Then, as the narrative spirals farther out from Israel, Paul's apostleship comes to the fore (Acts 8:1–3; 9:1–31; 11:25–30; 12:25), until

---

3. Eckhard J. Schnabel, *Acts*, ZECNT (Grand Rapids: Zondervan, 2012), 78–79.
4. Schnabel, 78–79.
5. E.g., Everett F. Harrison, *Acts: The Expanding Church* (Chicago: Moody, 1975), 11–13; John MacArthur, *Acts*, MNTC (Chicago: Moody, 1994), 1:6; Bruce Milne, *The Acts of the Apostles: Witnesses to Him*, Focus on the Bible Commentary (Fearn, Ross-shire, UK: Christian Focus, 2010), 13–15.

TABLE 1: PARALLELS OF PETER AND PAUL IN ACTS

Peter (chapters 1–12)	Paul (chapters 13–28)
Sermon in Jerusalem (2:22–36)	Sermon in Pisidian Antioch (13:26–41)
Lame man healed (3:1–10)	Lame man healed (14:8–11)
Extraordinary healings (5:15)	Extraordinary healings (19:12)
Laying on of hands to receive the Holy Spirit (8:17)	Laying on of hands to receive the Holy Spirit (19:6)
Conflict with magician (8:18–24)	Conflict with magician (13:6–11)
Tabitha raised from the dead (9:36–41)	Eutychus raised from the dead (20:9–12)
Miraculous release from jail (12:6–11)	Miraculous release from jail (16:25–40)

Table adapted from C. H. Talbert, *Literary Patterns, Theological Themes and the Genre of Luke-Acts* (Missoula, MT: Scholars Press, 1974), 23–26; cf. discussions in Richard N. Longenecker, "The Acts of the Apostles," in *The Expositor's Bible Commentary*, vol. 9, *John and Acts*, ed. Frank E. Gaebelein (Grand Rapids: Zondervan, 1981), 234. For further discussion, see Gary M. Burge, *The New Testament in Antiquity* (Grand Rapids: Zondervan, 2009), 232.

it is the general focus of the third geographic section, "the ends of the earth" (1:8).

Church Growth and Expansion Statements

Another prominent structural element in Acts is its growth and expansion statements. Luke's narratives can be viewed as collections under six of these statements, which all succinctly describe the multiplication of the church through the progress—whether implied or expressed—of God's Word (Acts 6:7; 9:31; 12:24; 16:5; 19:20; 28:31).[6] Each statement appears at the end of a series of pericopes that are "reasonably homogenous, geographically speaking."[7]

When overlaid on the above two structures, all three are easily harmonized, and these six growth and expansion statements refine the other division markers. Blomberg proposes the following outline:

I. The Christian Mission to the Jews (1:1–12:24)

  A. The Church in Jerusalem (1:1–6:7)

  B. The Church in Judea, Galilee, and Samaria (6:8–9:31)

  C. Advances in Palestine and Syria (9:32–12:24)

II. The Christian Mission to the Gentiles (12:25–28:31)

---

6. C. H. Turner, "The Chronology of the New Testament," *A Dictionary of the Bible: Dealing with Its Language, Literature, and Contents, Including the Biblical Theology*, ed. James Hastings (Edinburgh: T&T Clark, 1898), 1:421; Longenecker, "The Acts of the Apostles," in *EBC*, vol. 9, *John and Acts*, ed. Frank E. Gaebelein (Grand Rapids: Zondervan, 1981), 234, 244–47.

7. Craig L. Blomberg, *From Pentecost to Patmos: An Introduction to Acts through Revelation* (Nashville: B&H Academic, 2006), 37. Other summaries may be found in the book, but not with the same emphasis or structural capacity as these six growth and expansion statements. Cf. Darrell L. Bock, *Acts*, BECNT (Grand Rapids: Baker Academic, 2007), 13, 41, 46–48.

A. Paul's First Missionary Journey and the Apostolic Council (12:25–16:5)
B. The Second and Third Missionary Journeys (16:6–19:20)
C. Paul's Final Journeys to Jerusalem and Rome (19:21–28:31)[8]

The transitional nature of chapters 10–12 is thus confirmed. Both Peter's ministry to certain "God-fearing" Gentiles (10:1–48; note v. 22) and the planting of the mostly Gentile church in Antioch (11:19–30) show the overlap between the more overarching structural divisions—those between Peter and Paul and between Israel and the ends of the earth.

Chiasmus

Another approach is to see the whole of Luke-Acts as one masterwork that is structured in a chiasm; that is, having elements in its first half that are repeated in its second half in reverse order.[9] Luke's Gospel begins by placing the birth of Jesus in the context of world history, that is, in the Roman Empire (1:1–5; 2:1–3; 3:1–2). He then presents Jesus' ministry in Galilee (4:14–9:50) and then His travels through Samaria and Judea (9:51–19:27). Finally, Jesus is shown in Jerusalem (19:28–24:51).

Then, in reverse order, the preceding general structure of Luke is repeated in Acts. Jesus' post-resurrection appearances and ascension around Jerusalem are summarized (1:1–11). The expansion of the church is reported, in the details shown above, moving from Jerusalem to Judea, to Samaria, and to the Gentile world. Finally, the book ends with Paul at Rome (28:16–31), underscoring how the gospel is being preached throughout the Roman Empire.[10]

The chiastic form does loosely fit the text of Luke-Acts at a basic and broad level, and it is a legitimate device at the disposal of biblical authors for their use in the selection and thematic arrangement of their historical material. It is plausible for Luke to have used a chiastic model, as long as it is not misunderstood to be comprehensive. That Jesus' Galilean ministry and the ministry of His witnesses to the Gentiles are parallel elements may be defended by the biblical phrase "Galilee of the Gentiles" (Isa 9:1; cf. Matt 4:15). The literary center point of the chiasm is then effectively the climax of Luke's two-volume work: the resurrection and ascension of Jesus. Viewing Luke-Acts as a chiasm contributes little else to an understanding of Acts, but neither does it conflict with the other structural observations made above. In all, several literary designs are compatible and can be seen as a complex framework like the structure of a building.

---

8. Blomberg, 37.

9. This literary device is called chiasmus because of its resemblance to the equally opposite-angled strokes of the Greek letter *chi* (X).

10. Craig L. Blomberg, *Jesus and the Gospels: An Introduction and Survey,* 2nd ed. (Nashville: B&H Academic, 2009), 161–62; *From Pentecost to Patmos,* 37; and Kenneth Wolfe, "The Chiastic Structure of Luke-Acts and Some Implications for Worship", *Southwestern Journal of Theology* 22 (1980): 60–71.

The Unifying Theological Theme of Acts

Going further, missions-minded Christians can benefit greatly from seeing the theological emphases of Acts combined with the above structural paradigms. No outline can be exhaustive. The purpose at this juncture, rather, is simply to look beneath the above exegesis of Acts' literary structure, which is legitimate, and to see its major theological themes like a foundation. In this case, the foundation has multiple elements, like reinforced concrete threaded with steel rods; the themes or motifs run crisscross throughout the book, creating a unified whole foundation.

For one reason or another, some major motifs are noticeably absent from the above models' analyses. For example, the Spirit sent by God appears at the beginning of Jesus' ministries in both Luke and Acts (Luke 4:18; Acts 2:17),[11] but this parallel is an exception to the chiastic structure. Also, Luke frequently declared that the events he recorded are the fulfillment of Old Testament prophecies (e.g., Luke 1:1; 24:44; Acts 1:16; 3:18)[12] or that they

took place by absolute necessity.[13] The narrative is complemented by the common interventions of angels, epiphanies, and miracles.[14] All of these finer points add up to God's immanent involvement in the activities within Luke's two-volume work.

The Word of God is another motif that demands attention, and it is widely observed by exegetes.[15] Acts repeatedly highlights the power of Scripture by attributing the growth and strength of the church to the action of God's Word. Active verbs are used for the growth of the Word, but passive verbs are used for the growing of the churches. For Luke, the growth of the church is the growth of the Word (Acts 6:7). One could say, the Word is the true "hero" of Luke's narrative.[16] The Word was the decisive factor; churches were simply the agents and means for the Word to be made known worldwide.[17]

Related to the Word motif is that of suffering. For the three clearest statements about God's Word growing and multiplying (Acts 6:7; 12:24; 19:20) are at the climax of pericopes that record the resolution of some conflict or

---

11. Cf. Carson and Moo, *Introduction to the New Testament*, 324.

12. E.g., Acts 1:20; 2:16–21; 3:22–23; 4:11; 7:48–49.

13. This is indicated by the Greek terms *dei* ("it is necessary"; Luke 2:49; 4:43; 9:22; 13:33; 17:25; 21:9; 22:37; 24:7, 26, 44; Acts 1:16, 21; 3:21; 9:16; 17:3; 23:11; 27:24) and *boulē* (Luke 7:30; Acts 2:23; 4:27–28; 5:38; 20:27); John T. Squires, *The Plan of God in Luke-Acts*, Society for New Testament Studies Monograph Series 76 (Cambridge: Cambridge University Press, 1993), 1–2.

14. Squires, 1–2; e.g., Acts 1:10; 2:4; 3:7; 4:30; 5:19, 21; 8:26; 10:10–16; 11:5; 16:9; 22:13; 28:5–6.

15. Cf. the survey and analysis in Brian S. Rosner, "The Progress of the Word," in *Witness to the Gospel: The Theology of Acts*, ed. I. Howard Marshall and David Peterson (Grand Rapids: Eerdmans, 1998), 215–33.

16. Daniel Marguerat, *The First Christian Historian: Writing the "Acts of the Apostles."* Society for New Testament Studies Monograph Series 121 (Cambridge: Cambridge University Press, 2002), 37; David Peterson, "Luke's Theological Enterprise: Integration and Intent," in *Witness to the Gospel*, 541; Jerome Kodell, "'The Word of God Grew': The Ecclesial Tendency of Λογος in Acts 1,7; 12,24; 19,20," *Biblica* 55, no. 4 (1974), 518. "The word of God" is mentioned twelve times in Acts, "the word of the Lord" ten times, "the word" ten times, "the word of his grace" twice, and "the word of the gospel" and "of this salvation" once each.

17. See also C. K. Barrett, *Luke the Historian in Recent Study* (London: Epworth, 1961), 72, 74.

the cessation of some persecution.[18] In fact, throughout Acts, suffering provides the opportunity for more ministry, and it is intimately related to the growth of the Word.[19] Paul House concludes, "The gospel prospers in spite of, or because of, persecution. Nothing can stop the gospel, but its spread still causes grief and loss."[20]

When these motifs are viewed as a whole, the elements in Luke-Acts point to a fundamental concept: both volumes reveal God's sovereign, invincible plan being worked out in history.[21] This central theological idea, the plan of God, shapes Luke's presentation of the motifs he presents and underpins the historical and geographical events that he narrates. "Everything narrated by Luke comes under God's providence."[22] Thus, God's plan is the unifying theme or foundation to the literary structure resting upon it.

The Practical Purpose of Acts

A further element to combine with Acts' literary structure is Luke's goal in writing the book. To continue the illustration, if Acts' literary structure is the framework of the building and its unified theological theme is the foundation, then Acts' practical purpose is like the furnishings and fixtures. It conveys how the building is intended to be used. As others have noted, however, the purpose of Acts is not as easily discerned as those of the Epistles or Gospels.[23] Scholars have suggested several possible purposes for the book.[24] Below are the most common.

Historical and Evangelistic-Apologetic Purposes

Some argue that Luke-Acts was offering a history of the early church to provide an authoritative account of Christian origins. However, Luke leaves out too many historical details, such as the progress of the gospel in Egypt and Arabia, Paul's visit to Arabia (Gal 1:17), and the details of other characters' travels. Luke is selective, not comprehensive.[25]

Other scholars see evangelism and apologetics as one of the primary purposes of Luke-Acts. They consider that Acts' speeches and miracles were included to "awaken faith"

---

18. Peterson, "Luke's Theological Enterprise," 542.

19. E.g., Acts 4:23–37; 5:12–16, 41–42; 6:7–8; 6:15–7:53; 8:4–40; 9:31–11:26; 12:24–13:5; 13:12–43, 46–49; 13:52–14:1; 14:7–18, 21–28; 15:35; 16:1–15; 17:1–4, 10–12; 17:15–18:11; 18:18–19:12; 19:17–22; 20:1–2; 20:4–21:19; 22:1–21; 22:30–23:11; 24:1–27; 25:8–26:32; 28:7–23, 30–31.

20. Paul R. House, "Suffering and the Purpose of Acts," *JETS* 33, no. 3 (1990): 323.

21. Cf. Squires, *Plan of God in Luke-Acts*, 1–3, 186–94; however, to recognize the validity of Squires' observations one need not accept his evaluation of Luke's understanding of God's plan as essentially Stoic. Cf. also the two chapters devoted to this theme and its explication as central in Darrell L. Bock, *A Theology of Luke-Acts: God's Promised Program Realized for All Nations*, Biblical Theology of the New Testament (Grand Rapids: Zondervan, 2012), 99–148.

22. Squires, *Plan of God in Luke-Acts*, 3.

23. Walter L. Liefeld, *Interpreting the Book of Acts*, Guides to New Testament Exegesis 4 (Grand Rapids: Baker, 1995), 16.

24. For example, Robert J. Cara ("Acts," in *A Biblical-Theological Introduction to the New Testament: The Gospel Realized*, ed. Michael J. Kruger [Wheaton, IL: Crossway, 2016], 143–44), enumerated fifteen different purposes proposed for the book of Acts.

25. Simon J. Kistemaker, *Exposition of the Acts of the Apostles*, New Testament Commentary 17 (Grand Rapids: Baker, 1990), 33.

in the reader. Or, in light of its address to a Roman dignitary, Theophilus (Luke 1:3; Acts 1:1), and of the court trials that occupy roughly one-fourth of the book, they suppose that its purpose may have been to defend Christianity (or Paul individually) as contiguous with Judaism, law-abiding, or nonthreatening to Roman peace and order. Luke's opening address to Theophilus in the Gospel implies also a confirmatory purpose in Acts, concerning the teaching about Jesus that Theophilus had already heard.[26] However, much in Luke-Acts is irrelevant to evangelistic or defensive purposes.[27] Even an outsider sympathizer—such as one might assume Theophilus to have been[28]—would have found it challenging to endure Acts' repetition and detail if their only interest was political.[29]

On the contrary, the general form, content, and narrative style of Acts suggest that Christians rather than unbelievers were its primary intended readers.[30] Thus, the historical and evangelistic-apologetic approaches, though likely identifying peripheral concerns in Luke's purpose, will divert attention from his main purpose if they are made central.[31]

Theological Purposes

Undoubtedly, it is also true that Luke wrote Acts for various doctrinal reasons. But it is reductionistic to conclude, as some scholars do, that he was prompted by any particular theological controversy, such as the rise of Gnosticism or a supposed delay of the *parousia* (the "appearance" of Jesus at His return).[32] Rather, as argued above, Luke uses multiple doctrinal themes—the Holy Spirit, divine agents, miracles, prophetic fulfillment, preordained necessity—to provide a larger theological interpretation of the development of the early church.

In fact, everything that Acts relates rests upon the sovereign, invincible plan of God. Essential to that plan is His work of

---

26. Darrell L. Bock, *Luke 1:1–9:50*, BECNT 3a (Grand Rapids: Baker, 1994), 64.

27. See the helpful discussions in Carson and Moo, *Introduction to the New Testament*, 303–5; cf. John C. O'Neill, *The Theology of Acts in Its Historical Setting* (London: SPCK, 1970), 166–85; Michael Green, *Evangelism in the Early Church* (Grand Rapids: Eerdmans, 2004); F. F. Bruce, *The Acts of the Apostles: Greek Text with Introduction and Commentary*, 3rd ed. (Grand Rapids: Eerdmans, 1990), 22–27.

28. Köstenberger, Kellum, and Quarles, in *Cradle, the Cross, and the Crown*, 264–65, 334, concluded that Theophilus was most likely Luke's literary patron and possibly a Christian, while others have suggested he was a God-fearer (cf. Bock, *Acts*, 27; *Luke 1:1–9:50*, 64).

29. Barrett, *Luke the Historian in Recent Study*, 63; cf. Robert Maddox, *The Purpose of Luke-Acts* (Edinburgh: T&T Clark, 1982), 91–99.

30. Carson and Moo, *Introduction to the New Testament*, 306; Köstenberger, Kellum, and Quarles, *Cradle, the Cross, and the Crown*, 335; I. Howard Marshall, *The Acts of the Apostles*, TNTC 5 (Grand Rapids: Eerdmans, 1980), 20–21; Bock, *Luke 1:1–9:50*, 64.

31. For example, Peterson warned against one such mistaken apologetic emphasis: "When everything is interpreted so as to establish the authority and authenticity of Paul's ministry, Paul, rather than Jesus, becomes the key character in Luke-Acts." Peterson, "Luke's Theological Enterprise," 533.

32. Carson and Moo, in *Introduction to the New Testament*, 305, refuted the proposals of Talbert and Conzelmann concerning these supposed dilemmas, respectively. Charles H. Talbert, *Luke and the Gnostics: An Examination of the Lucan Purpose* (Nashville: Abingdon, 1966); Hans Conzelmann, *The Theology of St. Luke* (New York: Harper and Row, 1961).

redemption, shown to have been fulfilled in the life, death, resurrection, and ascension of Jesus the Messiah, and which continues to unfold as the Spirit-filled church takes the message of salvation from Jerusalem to the ends of the earth. As Simon Kistemaker comments, the purpose of Acts is "to convince Theophilus that no one can hinder the victorious march of the gospel of Christ."[33] This is true not only for Theophilus's reading but for all—Christians in the twenty-first century included.

Pastoral Purposes

Valid as the latter theological purpose may be, the practical question still remains as to why Luke desired to emphasize God's plan. Today a growing number of scholars are seeing the edification of wavering Christians as one of the primary purposes of Acts.[34] This pastoral purpose coheres closely with the theme of suffering as a means to the gospel's advance. And it could not be any more practical to missionaries on the field today.

It is curious that Luke culminates his work, the first volume of which concerns the content of the gospel, with Paul's imprisonment and trials on behalf of the gospel in volume two. This must be in part because Luke's interests are not in Paul as a person per se but in Paul as a model—a model of a regular, faithful

witness to Jesus Christ (Acts 1:8). Paul is more important for what he represents than for his contributions to the church, the extent and longevity of his ministry, or his martyrdom.[35] That is, Luke portrays him in persecutions and imprisonments in a didactic way. Paul's life is, in fact, the Christian life: "Through many afflictions we must enter the kingdom of God" (Acts 14:22; cf. 9:15–16). Believers in Luke and Paul's day experienced this firsthand. Still, nothing that happens to Paul can affect the advance of the church. On the contrary, Luke shows that afflictions are part of the process by which God realizes His purposes in the world. In this, Christians can not only be encouraged, they can rejoice (5:41).

As Paul House contends, "Rather than serving a polemical purpose, Paul's suffering defends him as a Christian and worthy servant of Jesus."[36] Indeed, Luke goes to great lengths to show how Paul, the imprisoned missionary, has divine approval. Such observations support the view that Luke wrote Acts to strengthen the early witness of the church in the face of opposition and persecution.[37] David Peterson concludes,

> Just as one of the chief bases of Christianity is the suffering of Christ, so a main characteristic of the early church is its own suffering. The prominence of Jesus' suffering in the

---

33. Kistemaker, *Exposition of the Acts of the Apostles*, 36–37.

34. Marshall, *Acts*, 20–21; Carson and Moo, *Introduction to the New Testament*, 305; W. C. van Unnik, "The 'Book of Acts' the Confirmation of the Gospel," *Novum Testamentum* 4, no. 1 (January 1960): 48, 58; Maddox, *Purpose of Luke-Acts*, 186–87.

35. Maddox, *Purpose of Luke-Acts*, 70. Luke would hardly have failed to report Paul's death if his interest was really in the person of Paul as such.

36. House, "Suffering and the Purpose of Acts," 328.

37. House, 320; Peterson, "Luke's Theological Enterprise," 540.

Gospel [of Luke] and the extension of that suffering to his representatives in Acts provides a profound link between the two volumes of Luke's work. Readers are encouraged to follow the example of the earliest believers, and Paul in particular, by holding fast to the same gospel and continuing to be active in its dissemination, even in the face of persecution from without and conflict from within the churches.[38]

Thus, the assurance that Acts is intended to offer is both practical and pastoral. Like the furnishings and fixtures of a building, it rests upon the underlying unifying theme of God's plan (the foundation), and it enlightens the literary structure of the book (the framework).

An Exegetical Outline of Acts

The final task of this chapter is to combine Acts' pastoral purpose and theological theme with its literary structure into one whole plan. The following is an exegetical outline or plan of the book seen through the elements of suffering, opposition, and growth according to God's sovereign plan:

I. **Opposition and suffering (1:1–6:6)**— the opposition of the priests, the Sanhedrin, and the high priest; internal hypocrisy of Ananias and Sapphira; imprisonment and prohibition from preaching in Jerusalem; internal murmuring for the daily distribution

II. **Growth and expansion (6:7)**—"And the word of God kept on spreading, and the number of the disciples continued to multiply greatly in Jerusalem, and a great many of the priests were becoming obedient to the faith."

III. **Opposition and suffering (6:8– 9:30)**—the murder of Stephen; great persecution in Jerusalem (Saul the persecutor); scattering of the believers; false conversion of Simon; Saul's threat of persecution in Damascus

IV. **Growth and expansion (9:31)**—"So the church throughout all Judea and Galilee and Samaria was having peace, being built up. And going on in the fear of the Lord and in the encouragement of the Holy Spirit, it continued to multiply."

V. **Opposition and suffering (9:32– 12:23)**—the believers scattered among Judea and the Gentiles; the persecuted church plant in Antioch; imperial persecution from Herod; murder of James and imprisonment of Peter

VI. **Growth and expansion (12:24)**—"But the word of the Lord continued to grow and to be multiplied."

VII. **Opposition and suffering (12:25– 16:4)**—the persecution in the synagogues of Asia; Paul stoned in Lystra; internal opposition of the Judaizers; sharp disagreement between Paul and Barnabas

VIII. **Growth and expansion (16:5)**—"So

---

38. Peterson, 544.

the churches were being strengthened in the faith, and were abounding in number daily."

IX. **Opposition and suffering (16:6–19:19)**—Paul and Silas imprisoned in Philippi; violent riots in Thessalonica and Berea; mockery in Athens; prosecution in Corinth; slander and charlatans in Ephesus

X. **Growth and expansion (19:20)**—"So the word of the Lord was growing mightily and prevailing."

XI. **Opposition and suffering (19:21–28:29)**—the riot in Ephesus; the arrest of Paul and the plot to kill him; incarceration in Caesarea for two years; storm and shipwreck; a venomous snake; imprisonment in Rome for two years

XII. **Growth and expansion (28:30–31)**—"[Paul] stayed . . . welcoming all who came to him, preaching the kingdom of God and teaching concerning the Lord Jesus Christ with all confidence, unhindered."

In all of this, the church grew and expanded according to God's plan by the triumph of God's Word through religious, pagan, imperial, internal, doctrinal, and natural threats of all kinds.

Conclusion

God's plan is simply invincible. Luke demonstrates this principle by tracing the gospel's advance through the lives of Jesus' witnesses, from Jerusalem through Judea and Samaria, and even to the ends of the earth. The theological emphasis in the whole of Luke-Acts, that God through His Spirit is immanently and providentially involved in history, combined with the progress that Acts reports after every opposition and persecution, was most likely aimed to pastorally encourage suffering Christians in Luke's day that God was accomplishing His plan.

God is still accomplishing His plan today. Christians are still Jesus' witnesses to the ends of the earth. The Word is still spreading, and suffering still advances it. Missionaries and their supporters should still be encouraged and instructed, just as in the first century AD. They should read Acts and come to the same firm conviction that whatever trials they encounter are not in vain, nor will they ultimately thwart the gospel. Come riots or stoning, sword or prison, "the word of God has not been chained" (2 Tim 2:9). Let Jesus' witnesses, then, follow the early church's example and finish their stories likewise: "preaching the kingdom of God and teaching concerning the Lord Jesus Christ with all confidence, unhindered" (Acts 28:31). Indeed, may God grant it to be so.

Practical Pauline Missions: Paul's Missions to Pisidian Antioch and Philippi

William D. Barrick

The impetus for Christian missions comes primarily from Jesus in the Great Commission (Matt 28:18–20). It also comes from the disciples' commission as "witnesses" (Acts 1:8). Although His mandate is clear, Jesus did not provide His disciples with an exhaustive, universal methodology for accomplishing the task. The New Testament describes a variety of successful missionary methods and practices disciples used. Modern missionaries can learn much from these biblical examples. By looking for similar and dissimilar mission practices by Paul in different localities, we can discover a good deal about the flexibility of mission methodologies. Multiple strategies bear greater fruit than treating every locality identically. Paul's work in Pisidian Antioch (Acts 13:13–52) and Philippi (16:11–40) provide excellent examples.

Missionary Motive

From Paul's example, we learn that God sometimes leads missionaries to a people group for which they have a certain God-given burden or a desire to see saved. The apostle Paul acted with his heart when he reached out to the Jewish community first (Acts 13:14; cf. Rom 10:1). In the most theologically systematic of his epistles, he declared the gospel goes first to Jews, then to Gentiles (Rom 1:16). This priority arises from the Lord's choice of Israel as His witness to the nations (Exod 19:6; Isa 43:8–13; 44:6–8; 48:20; 49:6). God never rebuked Paul for his practice of going to Jews first (Acts 9:20; 13:5, 14, 46; 17:1–2).

Strategic Variation

Paul's mission strategy eventually shifted its focus to Gentiles, in keeping with Christ's Damascus mandate (Acts 9:15; 22:21). However, the message never changed. Paul's sermon in Acts 13 repeatedly refers to Scripture. The missionary's message obtains its authority from God's written Word. Note the following ways Paul's strategy pointed to Scripture in his context and message:

- Respect for the public reading of Scripture (Acts 13:15)

- Reliance on Scripture for teaching (13:22, 33–35, 41)
- Belief in Scripture's promises (13:23, 27, 32)
- Recognition of Scripture's core message of salvation (13:26)
- Realization of Scripture's prophetic accuracy (13:29, 33, 40)
- Scripture as the object of faith (13:48)
- Scripture as the empowerment of ministry and cause of the ministry's expansion (13:49)

In verses 46 and 47, Paul based his switch to the Gentile mission on his understanding of the theological implications of Isaiah's prophecies regarding the "servant of Yahweh." In Isaiah 42:6 and 49:6, Isaiah presented a singular servant (the Messiah) as an everlasting covenant and light for the nations. Since Isaiah presented the servant both as an individual and as a corporate people, Paul interpreted the prophecies regarding the singular servant, Jesus, to apply to the church as well.[39] Thus he read Isaiah's prophecy as a command applying to his personal ministry. Paul demonstrated the reliance of his ministry on the whole of God's revealed Word in the Old Testament, producing a shift in Paul's mission strategy.[40] Modern missionaries should likewise keep their strategies flexible to remain faithful to God's Word.

Paul seems to have targeted larger towns like Philippi or Pisidian Antioch for gospel preaching, perhaps because congregations established in larger communities might more greatly influence Christianity's development. Entering a town, Paul and his companions usually visited synagogues, as they did in Pisidian Antioch. Within these synagogues they would primarily converse with male leaders (Acts 13:14–15). In Philippi, however, they chose a place of prayer along the river outside the city (16:13). Paul then began by interacting with devout Jewish women, including Lydia (16:14). Paul continued to work with Lydia and other women, perhaps because there were not enough Jewish men in the city for a synagogue (16:15–16). Not until Paul and Silas's arrest did God finally put them in contact with a man who might lead the new church plant, the Philippian jailer (16:16–34).[41]

39. I. Howard Marshall, "Acts," in *Commentary on the New Testament Use of the Old Testament*, ed. G. K. Beale and D. A. Carson (Grand Rapids; Nottingham, UK: Baker Academic; Apollos, 2007), 587–88; David G. Peterson, *The Acts of the Apostles*, PNTC (Grand Rapids; Nottingham, UK: Eerdmans, 2009), 397–99, especially 398n99; Paul R. House, *Isaiah: A Mentor Commentary*, Mentor Commentary (Ross-shire, Great Britain: Mentor, 2018), 2:427, 433; cf. Bock, *Acts*, 464.

40. The shift did not mean that Paul would never preach to Jewish audiences again nor that he had never preached to Gentiles before. Rather, it reflected his priority of Jewish evangelism in every town he visited, until its synagogue would no longer permit his preaching and teaching, at which point he would focus on Gentile audiences and venues. Schnabel, *Acts*, 588; Peterson, *The Acts of the Apostles*, 398.

41. Alternatively, Luke, who may have been from Philippi, having joined Paul at Troas, appears to have stayed behind

Missionaries through their social interactions and conduct should demonstrate responsibility and wisdom. Paul's interactions with the demon-possessed slave girl provide one example (16:16–18). He realized the gospel must not be associated with divination or demons, so he put an end to her public announcements. While that resulted in Paul and Silas being thrown into prison (16:19–24), that provided them an opportunity to model a Christlike response to persecution. After the earthquake, Paul did not lead a jailbreak (16:26–28). He showed respect for the jailer's authority and had compassion for him. When the apostle stood firm on his rights as a Roman citizen (16:35–39), he respected the laws of both city and empire. Paul displayed similar social prudence in the different situation at Pisidian Antioch. There Jews, rather than Gentiles, ultimately ran him out of town (13:50–52). Instead of asserting his Roman citizenship, Paul shook the dust off his feet and left.

Through these acts of responsibility, Paul found two highly regarded believers—Lydia and the Philippian jailer—to entrust with the development of the church (16:40). Modern missionaries must likewise resist the temptation to unduly delay turning the work over to nationals.

Lessons for Modern Missionaries

Paul's ministries in Pisidian Antioch and Philippi provide several lessons for modern missionaries. His heartfelt desire to evangelize the Jewish diaspora provided a powerful motivation throughout his ministry. Yet recognizing his call to bring the gospel to the Gentiles, Paul showed flexibility in whom and how he evangelized. In Pisidian Antioch, Paul started with the male leaders of the Jewish synagogue, but in Philippi he started on the riverbank with women. Paul made these and other changes to the target audience, place, mode, and other aspects of his ministry in response to the Word of God. For example, Jesus had directly told Paul he would be an apostle to the Gentiles and had revealed to him in a dream that he should travel to Macedonia, arriving at Philippi. This flexibility demonstrates Paul's practicality—he sought the best means of proclaiming the gospel wherever he went. Today's missionaries ought to be equally practical and flexible, being prepared to apply God's Word differently in differing real-world contexts.

---

with the church in Philippi while Paul and the rest of his company went on ahead on their journey (cf. the first "we" section in Acts 16:10–17, and the second, resuming in Philippi, in 20:5–6). Longenecker, "Acts," 458, 467.

CHAPTER 8

The Kingdom of God in the Church Age

Chris Burnett

Understanding the kingdom of God from the past to the present and to the future helps the missionary understand how to fulfill the Great Commission. The kingdom of God is the central and unifying theme of Scripture,[1] which is defined as the rule of God over His creation.[2] It is the climactic fulfillment of the story of redemption.[3] This chapter aims to provide biblical clarity on the topic of the kingdom of God, specifically to show from Scripture that it is spiritually present in and through believers today who inhabit the church age—the dispensation between Pentecost and the rapture—but will take its full, physical manifestation in the future, when the Lord Jesus Christ comes

to reign on the earth. In view of the biblical understanding of the kingdom, the task of the missionary is to proclaim repentance to the nations because the King is coming and today He offers kingdom citizenship to all who will believe in Him (Acts 2:21, 38–39; 28:30–31).

The Mandate of the Kingdom of God

The Christian's life in the fallen world today is informed by the earliest statement about how man is to live on the earth. In Genesis 1:26–28, God reveals His kingdom plan in what is considered the "kingdom mandate" or the "creation mandate."[4] The passage indicates that God's

---

1. Eugene H. Merrill, *Everlasting Dominion: A Theology of the Old Testament* (Nashville: B&H Academic, 2006), 42, 646–47; see also discussion in Stephen G. Dempster, "Chapter 2: The Beginning, Middle and Ending of the Tanakh: A Preview of the Storyline," in *Dominion and Dynasty: A Biblical Theology of the Hebrew Bible* (Downers Grove, IL: IVP Academic, 2006), 45–51.

2. This definition is adapted from Michael J. Vlach, *He Will Reign Forever* (Silverton, OR: Lampion, 2017), 5 ("Foreword" by John MacArthur), 22; also Alva J. McClain, *The Greatness of the Kingdom: An Inductive Study of the Kingdom of God* (Winona Lake, IN: BMH, 1959), 19.

3. Charles L. Feinberg, *Millennialism: The Two Major Views*, 3rd and enlarged ed. (Winona Lake, IN: BMH, 1985), 188n10.

4. Used interchangeably, the terms *kingdom mandate* and *creation mandate* follow closely with the definition and descriptions offered in Michael J. Vlach, *Dispensational Hermeneutics: Interpretation Principles That Guide Dispensationalism's Understanding of the Bible's Storyline* (n.p.: Theological Studies, 2023), 12–29. For discussion of the creation mandate as it applies to cultural engagement, see William Edgar, "The Creation Mandate," The Gospel Coalition, accessed June 18, 2024, https://www.thegospelcoalition.org/essay/the-creation-mandate/.

creation is the theater of His glory, and man is at the pinnacle of all that He has created:

> Then God said, "Let Us make man in Our image, according to Our likeness, so that they will have dominion over the fish of the sea and over the birds of the sky and over the cattle and over all the earth and over every creeping thing that creeps on the earth." And God created man in His own image, in the image of God He created him; male and female He created them. God blessed them, and God said to them, "Be fruitful and multiply, and fill the earth, and subdue it; and have dominion over the fish of the sea and over the birds of the sky and over every living thing that creeps on the earth."

Mankind was commanded to expand God's rule across the world and to reign on God's behalf as ambassadors or vice regents, as kings and queens on the earth. Adam failed that mandate, thereby plunging the world into sin and marring the image of God for all people (Gen 3:16–19). But just as the image of God in Adam was not entirely lost, only corrupted (Gen 5:1–3), neither was Adam's mandate abrogated, though it has brought devastating consequences both to man and to creation to this day.

According to God's decree, however, neither mankind nor the earth is left to fend for itself against the ravages of the curse. By divine design, the failure of man to carry out that role in righteousness was overcome in victory through God's Son, the God-man, Jesus Christ. And it is Jesus Christ, the King of kings and Lord of lords, who in the future will exercise a perfect reign in every way that Adam has failed—a reign that would be, by necessity, on the very earth that had been corrupted by sin (Ps 8:3–8; Rom 5:12–21; 1 Cor 15:21–28, 45–49; Heb 2:5–9). Unless King Jesus returns to the earth to reverse the curse, He is not the last Adam and Satan will have permanently destroyed that very good nature of God's creation from the beginning.[5] But Jesus will return and will rule over the world in perfect righteousness.

The Church and the Kingdom of God Mistaken

Believers seek practical guidance about how to serve Christ in such a way that they can be sure they are doing kingdom work. Implementation, however, depends on a proper theological framework. Two aberrant kingdom views will be discussed briefly to aid the reader in better understanding how one's theology of the kingdom shapes one's strategies for fulfilling the Great Commission.

Establishing the Kingdom of God through the Church

The theological lens of "postmillennialism" views a continuity between the creation mandate to Adam and the Great Commission to Christ's disciples. Postmillennialism identifies

---

5. Vlach, *He Will Reign Forever*, 59–70, 543–50; McClain, *Greatness of the Kingdom*, 42–44.

Christ's disciples as God's agents to bring about a sociopolitical manifestation of the kingdom of God to prepare the world for the return of Christ. According to postmillennialism, the "one thousand years" of Revelation 20:2–7 are not literal years, as would be the normal, plain-sense reading of the passage, but a representative age of Christianization and positive development in the world that establishes Christ's kingdom on earth.[6] Practically, to establish such a postmillennial kingdom of God, the church must assist King Jesus in establishing His righteousness in all sectors of all societies, culturally, socially, and politically, so that Christ can return to a God-glorifying world. One postmillennial scholar has presented a summary definition of the view:

> Postmillennialism expects the proclaiming of the Spirit-blessed gospel of Jesus Christ to win the vast majority of human beings to salvation in the present age. Increasing gospel success will gradually produce a time in history prior to Christ's return in which faith, righteousness, peace, and prosperity will prevail in the affairs of people and of nations. After an extensive era of such conditions the Lord will return visibly, bodily, and in great glory, ending history with the general resurrection and the great judgment of all humankind.[7]

This paradigm of worldwide Christianization is a form of "dominion theology," which considers the Great Commission to be the "new creation mandate." According to the dominion paradigm, the Great Commission means that disciples go out from Jerusalem in the way that Adam was to go out from Eden to hold dominion over the whole world.[8] The creation mandate and the Great Commission would in this way share the basis of God's purpose to restore the marred image of God in man in both soteriological and political ways through a covenantal framework.[9] In some postmillennial understandings, preaching the gospel to all nations with a range of sociopolitical activities most directly builds God's kingdom in fulfillment of God's eschatological plans.[10] Such proclamation of the gospel "seeks the salvation of the world, the bringing of the created order to submission to God's rule."[11]

---

6. For a scholarly treatment of postmillennialism, see Kenneth L. Gentry Jr., *He Shall Have Dominion: A Postmillennial Eschatology* (1992; repr., Chesnee, SC: Victorious Hope, 2021).

7. Kenneth L. Gentry Jr., "Postmillennialism," in *Three Views on the Millennium and Beyond*, ed. Darrell L. Bock (Grand Rapids: Zondervan, 1999), 13–14.

8. Keith A. Mathison, *Postmillennialism: An Eschatology of Hope* (Phillipsburg, NJ: P&R, 1999), 58–59, 87–88, 115–20; Loraine Boettner, "Postmillennialism," in *The Meaning of the Millennium: Four Views*, ed. Robert G. Clouse (Downers Grove, IL: IVP Academic, 1977), 117–20.

9. Kenneth L. Gentry, *The Greatness of the Great Commission: The Christian Enterprise in a Fallen World*, rev. ed. (Tyler, TX: Institute for Christian Economics, 1993), 10–14, 20–23. On the eschatological optimism of the Puritans, which accords with the later designation of postmillennialism but is more readily defined by their common historicist approach to predictive prophecy, see Joel R. Beeke and Mark Jones, *A Puritan Theology: Doctrine for Life* (Grand Rapids: Reformation Heritage, 2012), 773–75, 787–88.

10. So Paul Mumo Kisau, "Acts," in *Africa Bible Commentary: A One-Volume Commentary*, ed. Tokunboh Adeyemo (Nairobi: WordAlive, 2006), 1300.

11. Gentry, *Greatness of the Great Commission*, 128.

To be sure, missionaries proclaim the kingdom and teach Jesus' commands in such a way that believers' lives increasingly reflect the lives of kingdom citizens. However, missionary outreach cannot fulfill the kingdom mandate of Genesis 1:26–28, because the church does not subdue nations but preaches and teaches the gospel to individuals among the nations, which is what Christ commanded the church to do (Matt 28:19; Luke 24:47). Great Commission transformation is the goal at the individual level, in the soul of those who repent and believe the gospel. A nation today would benefit much if its large-scale systems of society, politics, and culture would submit (Pss 2:10–12; 33:12; 144:15; Prov 14:34). Yet such sweeping transformation is not directly indicated in the Great Commission as the missionary's objective, though it might be a by-product.

The Missio Dei *and the Kingdom of God*

In the mind of many believers, the nature and function of the kingdom of God in the church age relates in some way to the nature and function of Israel's theocratic kingdom. Given that

there are Old Testament accounts of Israel's cultural engagement with the surrounding nations,[12] the question arises as to whether those accounts in some way either inform or equate to the missionary methods of the New Testament church, at which time the global advance of the gospel is made explicit in the Great Commission. In support of a uniformly missiological reading across the entire canon, many missiologists have encouraged a "missional hermeneutic," which comes under the theological paradigm called the *missio Dei*, the "mission of God."[13]

The *missio Dei* paradigm emphasizes the triune God as the center of mission, asserting that since all of Scripture reveals God, then all of Scripture reveals His mission. According to this paradigm, readers of the Bible are supposed to understand that the church plays a part in God's mission but is itself not at the center of His purpose for mission, since the New Testament and the Great Commission (e.g., Matt 28:19–20) do not define God's mission but manifest new dimensions of it now through the Lord Jesus Christ.[14] The missional hermeneutic and the *missio Dei* framework propose that the local church must participate in the

---

12. See the examples of Old Testament "intercultural encounter" in David J. Hesselgrave and Edward Rommen, *Contextualization: Meanings, Methods, and Models* (Pasadena, CA: William Carey Library, 1989), 4–7: political (Josh 9; 1 Kgs 15:16–22), religious (Judg 6:31–32; 1 Kgs 18:1–40; Zeph 1:4–8), economic (2 Chr 8:17–18; 9:21; Ezek 27:12–25), and artistic (Ezek 23:11–21).

13. Michael Kinnamon and Brian E. Cope, *The Ecumenical Movement: An Anthology of Key Texts and Voices* (Grand Rapids: Eerdmans, 1997), 339–40. For a detailed survey of *missio Dei* theology among Roman Catholics, Eastern Orthodoxy, and mainline Protestants, see Cristian Sonea, "Missio Dei: The Contemporary Missionary Paradigm and Its Reception in the Eastern Orthodox Missionary Theology," *Review of Ecumenical Studies Sibiu* 9, no. 1 (2017): 70–91. For the *missio Dei* as held by John Stott, see *Christian Mission in the Modern World*, updated and expanded by Christopher J. H. Wright (Downers Grove, IL: InterVarsity, 2015), 22–23, 41–54; see also the paradigm developed by Lesslie Newbigin in his seminal work on the topic, *Foolishness to the Greeks: The Gospel and Western Culture* (Grand Rapids: Eerdmans, 1998).

14. For discussion of the tenets of the *missio Dei*, see David J. Bosch, *Transforming Mission: Paradigm Shifts in Theology of Mission* (Maryknoll, NY: Orbis, 1991), 10, 389–90; John G. Flett, "Missio Dei: A Trinitarian Envisioning of a Non-Trinitarian Theme," *Missiology* 37, no. 1 (2009): 5–18; Keith Whitfield, "The Triune God: The God of Mission," in *Theology and Practice of Mission:*

mission of God under the lordship of Christ, but the local church itself is not at the center of God's purpose for mission.

Thus, the missional hermeneutic has become for many the interpretive key for tracing the theological theme of missions throughout Scripture, even where the theme has no direct lexical or conceptual connection to the passage or section.[15] Because of the dynamic and varied ways the mission of God may be conceived in a cultural context, the missional hermeneutic and the *missio Dei* framework encourage every believer to actively serve God's missionary purposes in nonassertive ways that do not necessarily involve proclaiming the contents of the gospel in words or pursuing biblical disciple-making. If all of God's activity with creation is considered a part of His mission, then any activity associated with God's work in the world might constitute missionary activity, regardless of its connection to the way of salvation or local church discipleship. The *missio Dei* paradigm thus opens the door for missionary activities to move in a limitless direction.

Not only does reading the Old Testament for the unstated theme of missions misrepresent the emphases of Scripture in part and in whole,

but the missional hermeneutic leads to subjective interpretations about the implications of the biblical storyline. Looking at Israel's activities in and toward the nations through the missional hermeneutic leads to the conclusion that Israel was commanded by God to conduct proclamation activities according to an implicit Great Commission and that, due to Israel's unfaithfulness, missionary activity was taken up explicitly by the church at a later time instead.[16]

Yet a straightforward reading of Scripture leads to the conclusion that Israel's international engagement as a theocratic kingdom is not directly correspondent to the examples of global missionary outreach that characterize the evangelistic activity of the church. The question nevertheless looms as to whether accounts of Israel's cultural engagement are suitable to guide contemporary missions strategies. Reading Scripture with the kingdom of God in view as the main theme, not missions, reveals that the greatest vision of Israel's international kingdom witness in the Old Testament is not of Israel's past but of its future, at the prophesied time in which the people of Israel will gather the nations who partner with Israel for restoration in the land (Isa 19:16–25).[17]

God, the Church, and the Nations, ed. Bruce Riley Ashford (Nashville: B&H Academic, 2011), 45–47; and Michael W. Goheen, *Introducing Christian Mission Today: Scripture, History, and Issues* (Downers Grove, IL: InterVarsity, 2014), 74–84; J. D. Payne, *Theology of Mission: A Concise Biblical Theology* (Bellingham, WA: Lexham, 2021), 1–7.

15. The classic proposal of a missional hermeneutic comes from Anglican missiologist Christopher J. H. Wright, *The Mission of God: Unlocking the Bible's Grand Narrative* (Downers Grove, IL: IVP Academic, 2006). See pp. 33–69 for his rationale. A missional hermeneutic is also defended and described in Mike Barnett and Robin Martin, eds., *Discovering the Mission of God: Best Missional Practices for the 21st Century* (Downers Grove, IL: InterVarsity, 2012), 18–29, 31–47, 49–67; Arthur F. Glasser, Charles E. Van Engen, Dean S. Gilliland, and Shawn B. Redford, *Announcing the Kingdom: The Story of God's Mission in the Bible* (Grand Rapids: Baker Academic, 2003), 11, 14, 17–20; and Goheen, *Introducing Christian Mission Today*, 35–39, with survey and suggestions for a missional theology on pp. 74–111.

16. Glasser et al., *Announcing the Kingdom*, 23, 26, 105, 112, 322; Goheen, *Introducing Christian Mission Today*, 49–57.

17. Kyle C. Dunham, "Mission in the Old Testament: Israel's Role as a Precursor to Gospel Proclamation" (paper presented

The Church's Mission in View of the Kingdom of God

Global evangelism and theological training today must be done with the expectation of what Christ will accomplish after the closure of the church age. In other words, it should be a premillennial missiology. It should expect that when King Jesus returns to earth, He will establish His perfect dominion over all peoples in all places for one thousand literal years (Rev 20:2–7). Then He will hand over the kingdom to the Father, and they will reign together (1 Cor 15:24; Rev 21:22–23; 22:1, 3).

The following statements summarize select biblical evidence for a future, literal, Millennial Kingdom. Jesus Christ will sit on David's throne (Matt 19:28; 25:31), according to the Davidic covenant (2 Sam 7:13, 16; Ps 89:3–4, 35–37), in the physical city of Jerusalem (Zech 8:20–23) for a one-thousand-year reign of peace and justice (Rev 20:4–7; Zech 14:9; cf. 1 Cor 15:24–28). At the return of Christ to the earth, "all Israel" will be saved (Rom 11:25–29), so that the promise of the Abrahamic covenant will be fulfilled in the land (Gen 12:1–3). In the Millennium, the land covenant of Deuteronomy 29–30 will finally be realized, and the borders of Israel will be restored to the fullest extent for the Jewish people when they convert to serve Messiah as their rightful King. Only when the salvation of the Gentiles is complete (Rom 11:25; cf. Luke 21:24) and God's judicial act of spiritually blinding Israel is reversed will the Millennial Kingdom be established and the biblical covenants fulfilled.[18]

The coming reality of the Millennium affects the missionary's ethic today. Because the Millennium will one day come, it is important to discern the types of activities worth conducting among the nations now. If missionary activity today is to be done in light of Jesus Christ's millennial reign, then at least a few key considerations come into play.

The Church Calls Sinners into the Kingdom of God

While the church is not called to establish the kingdom of God but to wait for King Jesus to do so upon His physical return to earth, the church does have a mission to bring sinners into the kingdom by calling the nations to repentance (Luke 24:47; cf. Matt 3:2; 4:17; Mark 1:1, 14; Luke 4:43; Acts 17:30–31). Only if people are born again, with new hearts, can they repent and become kingdom citizens (John 3:3, 6; cf. John 1:12–13; 2 Tim 2:25). To the Old Testament prophets, the Spirit brings about repentance in the heart from sin (Ezek 11:17–20; 36:24–28; 37:14; Zech 12:10), which provides the first step toward entrance through the gates of the future kingdom of God (Lev 26:40–42; Deut 30:1–6; Jer 24:6–7; 50:4–5; Zech 12:10–13:1). For Israel, that necessarily

---

at E3 Pastors Conference, Detroit, MI, October 2019), 14–15; John Mark Terry, Ebbie Smith, and Justice Anderson, eds., *Missiology: An Introduction to the Foundations, History, and Strategies of World Missions* (Nashville: Broadman and Holman, 1998), 61.

18. Paul N. Benware, *Understanding End Times Prophecy: A Comprehensive Approach* (Chicago: Moody, 2006), 216; Vlach, *He Will Reign Forever*, 102–6, 561–63.

involves God's restoration of them with the King He will install to rule over them, their Messiah (Ps 2:6; Jer 3:15–18; 16:14–15; Ezek 43:1–7). With such a condition in their hearts, the King promises to sit on Israel's throne (Gen 49:10; Num 24:17–19; Zech 6:13).

The New Testament clarifies and expands these prophetic features of the Old Testament (e.g., Luke 2:25, 30–32, 36–38). Jesus proved not only to be Messiah for Israel but the Anointed One for all the world (Matt 8:5–13; 22:1–14; John 4:42). However, Israel rejected their King and did not repent.[19] Matthew details this rejection in a pivotal section (Matt 11–12).[20] Lack of belief in the Messiah during His earthly ministry in Israel meant lack of national restoration and lack of kingly rule from Jerusalem at that point in history (Matt 23:37–39; Luke 19:41–44).[21] Yet, through this rejection, God brought salvation to the Gentiles as He promised (Acts 28:28; Rom 10:11–24; cf. Isa 49:6). Belief makes a person a citizen of the future kingdom—all the while living in an age of unbelief and among a people hostile to the King. Thus, while the church today proclaims repentance to the nations, the kingdom itself will not have an earthly reign until the leaders of Israel bow their knee to Messiah.

Individual Evangelism and Faithful Disciple-Making

The missionary must engage in individual evangelism and in making faithful disciples. All missionaries are tasked with bringing individuals from all nations and worldviews to the saving knowledge of the King of kings, that they might worship Him as the only God. There is no room for a fatalism that would impede evangelism. The missionary should be motivated by God's patience in the current age (2 Pet 3:9; cf. Luke 13:6–9) to labor in any way useful for the salvation of even a few (1 Cor 9:19–23).

Conversion, however, is itself not the goal but the gateway to a God-glorifying life. Today's believer must be discipled into a mature person who will serve the King now, throughout the Millennium, and into eternity (Rev 5:10). Making biblical disciples requires great toil in the indigenous church because it involves the transformation of the believer's cultural orientation (Titus 1:12–13).

Pastoral Training and Church Equipping

The missionary must invest in training pastors for the ministry of the local church. True disciples are maturing Christians, and spiritual

---

19. Stanley D. Toussaint and Jay A. Quine, "No, Not Yet: The Contingency of God's Promised Kingdom," BSac 164 (2007): 131–147.

20. Interestingly, Fazio points out the dispensational distinction between Jesus' and the apostles' early kingdom message to Israel, which he terms the "Germinal Commission" (Matt 10) and the later, more familiar "Great Commission" in Matt 28:18–20. See James I. Fazio, *Two Commissions: Two Missionary Mandates in Matthew's Gospel* (El Cajon, CA: SCS Press, 2015), 15–61.

21. For the earliest Christian views on the kingdom to be situated in a future restored and repentant national Israel, see Paul Hartog's and Jeremiah Mutie's essays in *Discovering Dispensationalism: Tracing the Development of Dispensational Thought from the First to the Twenty-First Century*, ed. Cory M. Marsh and James I. Fazio (El Cajon, CA: SCS Press, 2023), 49–127.

growth happens, by God's design, through the godly leadership of Christ's undershepherds in the local church (1 Pet 5:1–5). Paul and his missionary delegates considered the raising up of elders for the church worth their greatest efforts (1 Tim 1:3, 5–7, 18–19; Titus 1:5). They considered it as preparing a bride to meet her coming Husband (2 Cor 11:2; Eph 5:25–27, 32).

Furthermore, certainty of the Millennial Kingdom in which Christ is physically present and the saints of the church age reign with Him (2 Tim 2:12; Rev 5:10; 20:6) enables radical sacrifice because of the confidence it engenders for a future of peace and plenty (Matt 5:5; Rev 2:26; 3:21). And beyond the blessing and prosperity of the Millennium, believers are promised the ultimate comfort of a sin-free world—in the new heaven and new earth He will wipe away every tear (Isa 25:6–8; Rev 21:4; cf. 1 Cor 15:24–28).

Strategic Priorities

The missionary must not prioritize activities that compete with or compromise the mission of the church. Faithful missionaries must discern ways in which even good activities can exceed the biblical mandate and betray the missiology that derives from their method of interpreting Scripture. Assigning environmental care a priority over church planting, for example, would show no correlation between prophecy and practice. The earth itself groans for renewal, but the renewal will come only in the Millennium (Rom 8:18–22).

A premillennial missiology also decries the problems of viewing social justice and political

restoration as the work of the church. Walking in the light of God might be the present reality of some individuals from many nations, but in the Millennium the nations, no longer under the deception of Satan (Rev 20:3), will flock to the city of Jerusalem to apply Christ's justice in their governments (Isa 2:2–5; cf. 60:3). Yet today the nations are not submitted to the lordship of Christ but to the deceiver who rules over the whole world (2 Cor 4:4; Eph 2:2; Heb 2:8; cf. Rev 12:9).

It is important therefore for the missionary to ask whether his involvement in a particular environmental, social, or political cause competes for time and resources with evangelistic and discipleship strategies that are in line with biblical eschatology. If so, the activity risks shifting the missionary's focus from urgent gospel proclamation to a pragmatic "Christianization," and he must change course quickly—the Lord could return at any time, and the missionary will have to give an account of his stewardship.

Christ's reign during His Millennial Kingdom will be a time of international peace and harmony, where earth is free from natural disasters, disease, and threats (Isa 11:6–8; 32:19–20; 35:1; 65:25). Human culture will flourish in the Millennial Kingdom, as nations will be blessed by Christ and bless Him and Jerusalem in return (Ps 72:17; Isa 60:3–17; Hag 2:7). The world today during this church age does not match this vision of the earthly reign of Messiah. But in that day, Christ will be a blessing to all the nations from Jerusalem (Gen 12:1–3; Ps 72:17; Isa 2:2–4), with His saints reigning with Him (Rev 5:9–10). Believers hold out this hope for the world and model kingdom peace in life and relationships, but the full reality of such harmony will only come about when Jesus returns.

Conclusion

This chapter has argued that the kingdom mandate will be fulfilled in a future, earthly millennium, with Christ reigning as King over a restored national Israel. It is improper to read the Bible through a missional hermeneutic or a political and theocratic lens, since the kingdom of God is for Christ to establish, not the church. The way for believers to fulfill the Great Commission is to proclaim the gospel that brings rebellious sinners into Christ's kingdom. Believers are to teach the commands of the King and to build up kingdom citizens in such a way that their King is glorified and the world takes notice. The greatest message the Christian can give is to proclaim the hope of the coming reign of Christ, in which peace, justice, and harmony will reign on the earth, a hope that is partly realized today as salvation is freely given to all who call Jesus Lord.

Sub-Section 2: The Great Commission and Biblical Evangelism

CHAPTER 9

The Composite Teaching of the Great Commission Passages

Chris Burnett

Those who participate in evangelistic outreach and church work in foreign contexts generally consider their activities to be a part of fulfilling the Great Commission; otherwise they would not do them. However, examining how exactly their ministries fulfill the Great Commission requires discernment. This chapter examines the key passages in which the Lord Jesus Christ instructs His disciples about what activities His followers must carry out to participate in His work of building His church

(Matt 16:18). These five passages, commonly referred to as Great Commission passages, were given by Christ after His resurrection: Matthew 28:18–20; Mark 16:15–20;[1] Luke 24:46–49; John 20:21; and Acts 1:8. This chapter will then synthesize the teachings of the five passages to give a composite understanding of Jesus' teaching on what the Great Commission is, so that believers who are eager to fulfill it around the world can do so faithfully and effectively.

---

1. The purpose here is not to assert the originality of Mark 16:9–20, though the discussion has an important place in textual and missiological scholarship. In support of the canonicity of the longer ending of Mark 16:9–20 is the view that since the vast majority of manuscripts have the long ending of Mark, it was most likely part of the original autograph. See Maurice A. Robinson and William G. Pierpont, *The Case for the Byzantine Priority* (Malta: Infinity, 2005), 13–46; Wilbur N. Pickering, *The Identity of the New Testament Text IV* (Bengaluru, Karnataka, India: WNP, 2014), 89–128.

In analyzing Jesus' commands in the Great Commission passages, two fundamental observations emerge that put Scripture at the center of His mission to the nations. First, the risen Christ proclaims a global mandate for missions by His divine authority, supplying His authority and spiritual power to those who preach and teach the exclusive gospel of God. Second, the risen Christ tasks those He sends with making disciples on the basis of the biblical content, by sending them to the nations to baptize and teach. The structure of the analysis will largely follow the order of phrases in the Matthean account, because in it several major themes related to missions coalesce.

The Risen Christ Ushers a Global Mandate on His Divine Authority

Matthew's Great Commission passage (Matt 28:18–20) elucidates how the Lord Jesus Christ has authorized His disciples to make new disciples didactically by teaching the truth of God's Word. It is because Christ is King that His Word is binding on every soul. The following components of the Great Commission evidence how Christ supplies His supreme authority to His witnesses, so that as they proclaim His exclusive gospel, sinners will come under His authority in obedience to the truth.

Christ Supplies His Supreme Authority to His Disciples

In Matthew 28:18 Jesus declares that His authority is comprehensive and absolute—His sovereign control is adjectivally described as "all" (*pasa*).[2] The risen Christ's authority over the Great Commission is delegated from His Father and is operative in the supreme sense because, as the eternal Son, He is of equal divine essence to the Father (John 1:1; 10:30; 12:41; 17:5, 10, 21–24). Because Jesus is God, His authority is limitlessly transdimensional, being "in heaven and on earth" (Matt 28:18). The term "all" in verse 18 is couched in the immediate context of Jesus' post-resurrection appearance to His disciples in verses 16–17. Jesus' resurrection to an eternally glorified life means that His commanding role will continue into the future without end.

With His unlimited authority, Christ mandates the mission of His followers (28:19).[3] Furthermore, He grants them to wield His unassailable authority as they preach and teach His Word.[4] According to the subsequent Great Commission statement in Acts 1:8, because the Son's reign is universal, His followers now take up His preaching and teaching ministry with His power beyond Judea and Samaria to the "ends of the earth," which is as far as His followers can go.

---

2. "ἐξουσία," BDAG, 352–53; "πᾶς," BDAG, 782; Leon Morris, *The Gospel according to Matthew*, PNTC (Grand Rapids: Eerdmans, 1992), 745.

3. So noted in Eckhard J. Schnabel, *Early Christian Mission*, 2 vols. (Downers Grove, IL: InterVarsity, 2004), 1:371; Craig L. Blomberg, *Matthew*, NAC 22 (Nashville: Broadman and Holman, 1992), 431; David L. Turner, *Matthew*, BECNT (Grand Rapids: Baker Academic, 2008), 689.

4. R. T. France, *The Gospel of Matthew*, NICNT (Grand Rapids: Eerdmans, 2007), 1083–84; Donald Alfred Hagner, *Matthew 14–28*, WBC 33B (Dallas: Word, 1995), 889.

Christ Empowers an Exclusive Mission

The Great Commission demonstrates that preaching and teaching can only be accomplished by Christ's inexhaustible power. He promises to be present with His disciples so that they will persevere by His power in His exclusive mission. The following sections will show how Christ gives power to His disciples to proclaim God's wrath upon sinners and the reward of eternal life for those who become God's Son's disciples.

CHRIST PROMISES POWER FOR PROCLAMATION

Two affirmations of divine enablement arise from the final phrase of Matthew 28:20—"and behold, I am with you always, even to the end of the age." In the first phrase, "I am with you always," Christ asserts the legitimacy and viability of biblical proclamation ministry in every generation. Christ promises to perpetually support His envoys as they proclaim the gospel and disciple believers in the truth of Scripture.[5] In the sense of Christ's active presence, those who "labor at preaching the word and teaching" can be confident that their efforts are fully approved by Christ (1 Tim 5:17).

In the second phrase of Matthew 28:20, "even to the end of the age," Christ promises to sustain proclamation activities in every generation by His Holy Spirit (Acts 6:10; 8:29, 39; 10:44; 11:15; 13:2, 4; 16:6). Jesus' ongoing presence as Immanuel—the God who is with His people (Isa 7:14; Matt 1:23)[6]—comes with His power,[7] so that the work of building His church will continue until His work is complete.[8] The divine presence and activity of the risen Christ that empowered the earliest missionaries remains the reality today because Christ is faithful to His promise and His will is immutable (Rom 11:29; Titus 1:2; Heb 6:17), as He Himself is eternally unchanging (Heb 13:8; Jas 1:17). The Great Commission thus constitutes the continuous pattern for all disciples of Christ to preach and teach from the Scriptures and pass it down as a stewardship to their disciples. The strategies of the apostles and their disciples will never be obsolete as long as Christ's Great Commission is in force.

CHRIST CALLS MISSIONARIES TO PROCLAIM WRATH AND REWARD

Although there are many ways that the Great Commission task of preaching and teaching might be conducted (depending on the context, situation, and audience), the undeniable reality is that to proclaim the gospel is to pronounce divine wrath and reward. Preaching and teaching is not obedient to the Great Commission unless it is grounded on the fact that Christ alone is "the

---

5. Affirmed by Morris, *Gospel according to Matthew*, 749; Grant R. Osborne, *Matthew*, ZECNT (Grand Rapids: Zondervan, 2010), 1085; and Schnabel, *Early Christian Mission*, 1:367.

6. So recognized by Hagner, *Matthew 14–28*, 888; Turner, *Matthew*, 690; and Ben Witherington III, *Matthew*, Smyth and Helwys Bible Commentary (Macon, GA: Smyth and Helwys, 2006), 534.

7. For defining power as successful accomplishment of intergenerational discipleship, see Osborne, *Matthew*, 1107.

8. See Turner, *Matthew*, 690; Hagner, *Matthew 14–28*, 889; and Craig Ott and Stephen J. Strauss, *Encountering Theology of Mission: Biblical Foundations, Historical Developments, and Contemporary Issues* (Grand Rapids: Baker, 2010), 37.

way, and the truth, and the life. No one comes to the Father but through [Him]" (John 14:6).

The Great Commission in Mark 16:16 gives the solemn warning that unbelief will incur God's judgment: "He who has believed and has been baptized shall be saved; but he who has disbelieved shall be condemned." In a similar vein, John 20:23 highlights the spiritual seriousness of sending the disciples to new territories: "If you forgive the sins of any, their sins have been forgiven them; if you retain the sins of any, they have been retained." Missionaries are sent by the Lord to deal powerfully with sin, either by communicating His forgiveness to those who repent or His condemnation to those who do not. By repentance and belief the sinner will come to possess "life in His name" (v. 31), whereas unbelief signals the retention of sins (v. 23)—which, if left unconfessed by grace through faith, will lead to final condemnation (Rom 11:20; Heb 3:19).

Belief in the proclaimed gospel is central to the success of the Great Commission, but the unique message of the gospel is a hard message to hear (John 6:60–66). Christ provides His power in the moment of preaching, both for the missionary who proclaims the truth and also for the hearer to perceive it as true when it is preached (Rom 1:16–17; 1 Cor 1:18, 24; 2:1–5). In the case of certain Gentiles whom Paul and his companions approached, 1 Thessalonians 1:5 records that the missionaries' gospel came to the pagan audience not only in word, "but also in power and in the Holy Spirit and with full assurance." The language of "power" and "full assurance" denotes that the Spirit mediated both the gospel proclamation and its reception by the hearers. The Holy Spirit caused the missionaries to grow in the total conviction that as they were preaching they were pronouncing the very oracles of God. This confidence further emboldened them to continue proclaiming the gospel to their audience.[9]

From the audience's perspective, 1 Thessalonians 2:13 describes that those whom God called into His kingdom (v. 12) "accepted" the gospel when it was preached to them, so that they approved of the truths being proclaimed. Such genuine conversion resulted from regeneration. The sinners were previously spiritually blinded to the truth, but in the moment Christ was preached, they understood that the gospel was the other-worldly, divine power of God poured out for their salvation. The example of the Thessalonian preaching event is itself not prescriptive, but it is descriptive of Christ's Great Commission promise to send His witnesses to preach by His divine enablement. The Lord's powerful presence brings comfort and confidence to all of Christ's witnesses who engage in biblical proclamation to make disciples.

The Risen Christ Tasks His Witnesses to Make Disciples on the Basis of the Biblical Content

According to the Great Commission in Matthew 28:19, the risen Christ sends His

---

9. From the term *plerophoría* ("full assurance"), as treated in "πληροφορία," BDAG, 827; Gerhard Delling, "πληροφορία," *TDNT*, 6:310–11; L&N, 1:371, §31.45.

witnesses to all nations to carry out cross-cultural biblical proclamation, with the goal being to "make disciples of all the nations." Grammatically, "make disciples" (*mathēteusate*) is the finite verb of the verse and is stated in the imperative form. This reveals that making disciples is Jesus' main command for His followers to obey.[10]

The distinction between making a convert and making a disciple is an important one: the conversion of the sinner is only the beginning of spiritual life, whereas being a disciple is a lifelong process of pursuing Christlikeness (Rom 8:29; 2 Cor 3:18; Col 3:10). Once the writings of Scripture make one "wise unto salvation through faith which is in Christ Jesus" (2 Tim 3:15), they become beneficial throughout life "for training in righteousness, so that the man of God may be equipped, having been thoroughly equipped for every good work" (3:16–17).

Three participles in Matthew 28:19–20 clarify how "making disciples" is to be done in order to fulfill the Great Commission: by going (*poreuthentes*, v. 19), by baptizing (*baptizontes*, v. 19), and by teaching (*didaskontes*, v. 20). Scholars have rightly understood that "the last participles [baptizing and teaching] are a pair that explain how or by what means

the disciples will fulfill their commission," and that "the chief means of making disciples is teaching."[11] Each participle will be treated in turn to show how Christ commands missionaries to prioritize the preaching and teaching of His Word above all other activities and, in so doing, to make disciples according to the Great Commission.

Christ Commands His Disciples to "Go" to "All the Nations"

Not only does Jesus consider the entire world the sphere of His mission, but He sends His disciples as message-bearers to "go" to "all the nations" (Matt 28:19). Care must be taken to understand the terms and concepts related to the command to "go" to "all the nations."

CHRIST'S DISCIPLES MUST "GO"

Christ's use of the passive participle "go" (*poreuthentes*) in Matthew 28:19 is best translated as a command connected with the command to "make disciples."[12] John 20:21 brings in the idea of sending to the Matthean command to "go": "As the Father has sent Me, I also send you." The sending motif in John's Gospel[13] highlights Jesus' authority to dispatch a messenger for a specific purpose. In the Great Commission as recorded in John 20:23, Jesus'

---

10. Daniel M. Doriani, *Matthew* (Phillipsburg, NJ: P&R, 2008), 2:532; Ott and Strauss, *Encountering Theology of Mission*, 36.

11. Quoted from Doriani, *Matthew,* 2:532, who cites Daniel Wallace, *Greek Grammar beyond the Basics* (Grand Rapids: Zondervan, 1996), 642–45; followed by Witherington, *Matthew*, 534.

12. The participle *poreuthentes* is translated imperatively as "go" (cf. "πορεύω," BDAG, 853) and correlates as an introductory circumstantial participle with the main imperative, "make disciples" (*mathēteusate*; "μαθητεύω," BDAG, 609).

13. See John 3:17 (cf. v. 16); 3:34 (cf. v. 31); 4:34; 8:42; 10:36; 11:42; 17:3, 8. For a detailed discussion of the sending motif in the Gospel of John, see Andreas J. Köstenberger, *The Missions of Jesus and the Disciples according to the Fourth Gospel: With Implications for the Fourth Gospel's Purpose and the Mission of the Contemporary Church* (Grand Rapids: Eerdmans, 1998), 180–98.

disciples are instructed to carry out the express work of forgiveness and judgment in new global contexts. It is unmistakable, then, that Christ sends His disciples into the world on a divine errand. The general meaning of "go" and Matthew's repeated connection of it to the main verb "make disciples" should caution the reader from placing too great an emphasis on the "going," as if the combined imperative "go and make" requires transnational movement in every case.[14]

Nevertheless, according to Luke 24:47, Jesus commanded His disciples to testify of the gospel first in Jerusalem and move outward "to all the nations." Even the earliest ministry in Jerusalem involved cross-cultural proclamation, given the birth of the church on the day of Pentecost, when "every nation under heaven" was assembled to hear Peter preach the gospel (Acts 2:5, 14–41). The Great Commission command to "go" is depicted likewise in Acts 1:8, in a general sense, as outward-going toward the farthest reaches of the inhabited Gentile world. The apostle Paul delineates those outward locations as places "where Christ was [not] already named," where a pioneering work was still needed because the foundation of the gospel had not yet been built there (Rom 15:20–21).[15]

Since Luke is the author of both the Great Commission passages of Luke 24:46–49 and Acts 1:8, it is reasonable to read the latter of Jesus' depictions, "ends of the earth" in light of the former, "all the nations."[16] Biblical history records how the farthest nations were the target of gospel spread. After witnessing in Jerusalem (Acts 1–7), the disciples moved outward into Judea and Samaria (chs. 8–9), and to the "ends of the earth" (chs. 10–28),[17] experiencing a series of culture shifts as they moved from a heavily Jewish context (chs. 1–12) to a range of Gentile environments (chs. 13–28).

THE "NATIONS" ARE FOREIGN TO THE MISSIONARY

The phrase "of all nations" in Matthew 28:19 is also basic to the Scripture-centered emphasis of the Great Commission. In its plainest sense, the term *nation* (*ethnos*) refers to geopolitical nation-states.[18] A sociological dimension of the term *nations* accompanies the geopolitical one to highlight that a nation is an ethnic group of people united by family heritage, culture, and traditions.[19] Together the qualities of a nation accentuate the foreignness of missionary activity. Christ's disciples must "go" to the foreign environment of "the nations," where the commonalities enjoyed within the local ethnic group (the nation) will be perceived in some

---

14. France, *Gospel of Matthew*, 1080.

15. C. E. B. Cranfield, *Romans*, ICC (London: T&T Clark, 1979), 2:762; Robert H. Mounce, *Romans*, NAC 27 (Nashville: Broadman and Holman, 1995), 267.

16. Thomas S. Moore, "'To the End of the Earth': The Geographical and Ethnic Universalism of Acts 1:8 in Light of Isaianic Influence on Luke," *JETS* 40, no. 3 (1997): 396.

17. The general geographical breakdown of Acts outlined here is reproduced from Ott and Strauss, *Encountering Theology of Mission*, 41.

18. Schnabel, *Early Christian Mission*, 1:361–65.

19. "ἔθνος," BDAG, 276.

way as foreign to those outside of the group (the missionary).[20]

The corollary Great Commission passage of Luke 24:47 expresses the command to go "to all the nations," which includes both Jews and non-Jews across the world.[21] In John 20:21–23, the geopolitical destination of "nations" or "world" is not explicit, yet the universal scope of the mandate is unmistakably both Jews and Gentiles. Christ's emissaries are authorized to take to nonbelievers everywhere His peace (*eirēnē*; cf. John 14:27), which is at the soteriological core of the gospel (Eph 2:14–18).[22] For the gospel of peace (Eph 6:15) to reach "the nations," a member of one nation must directly engage a member of another nation with the goal of disciple-making.[23]

From the sociological vantage point, the physical location of the hearer is not critical. Those who do not enter new time zones but instead go next door to proclaim the gospel to a neighbor who has come from a foreign location participate in the inherently foreign task of discipling the "nations." The goal of being sent as an ambassador of Christ to the nations need not change for one who goes less distance than another, as long as the goal remains to see the gospel extend out in concentric rings to and through the hearer from "the nations." With the objective of reaching the "nations" in mind, however near or far the believer travels, he must be faithful to go where he is sent. He must enter into the local culture of the foreign individual as the Lord leads, and he must preach and teach God's Word with the firm trust that the Lord will raise up new disciples among "the nations."

THE "NATIONS" ARE INDIVIDUALS WITHIN A POPULATION

According to the Great Commission passage of Mark 16:15, the gospel must be proclaimed far and wide: "Go into all the world and preach the gospel to all creation." The individuals who comprise "all creation" in "all the world" are the target audience of the missionary outreach, because it is individuals who are called to faith: "He who has believed" (vv. 16–18). The focus of evangelism and disciple-making therefore is not on the sociocultural or political macrostructures of the nations themselves but on the conversion and growth of individual believers within a target population (Matt 10:18; Acts 11:18; 14:27; 15:3–7; 26:17; Rom 3:29; 9:24; 15:10; 16:4; Rev 7:9).[24]

In terms of Great Commission strategy, viewing the individual within the ethnic whole

---

20. "ἔθνος," BDAG, 276.

21. For reasons to include the Jews in "all the nations" see Schnabel, *Early Christian Mission*, 1:361–64. On the Gentile-Jewish distinctions of "nations," see Peter T. Lee and James Sung-Hwan Park, "Beyond People Group Thinking: A Critical Reevaluation of Unreached People Groups," *Missiology: An International Review* 46, no. 3 (2018): 215.

22. Schnabel, *Early Christian Mission*, 1:378–80.

23. Turner, *Matthew*, 690.

24. Affirmed by Robert Garrett, "The Gospels and Acts: Jesus the Missionary and His Missionary Followers," in *Missiology: An Introduction to the Foundations, History, and Strategies of World Missions*, ed. John Mark Terry, Ebbie Smith, and Justice Anderson (Nashville: Broadman and Holman, 1998), 72 and n4; *contra* Kenneth L. Gentry Jr., "Postmillennialism," in *Three Views on the Millennium and Beyond*, ed. Darrell L. Bock, Counterpoints: Bible and Theology (Grand Rapids: Zondervan, 1999), 46–47.

of a nation is also legitimized by the immediate context of the phrase "make disciples of all the nations" in Matthew 28:19. The command to "make disciples" limits the scope of discipleship to individual people, since discipleship requires evangelizing person by person and directly baptizing and teaching new local converts so that they continually adhere to the divine truths proclaimed by the discipler.[25]

Luke 24:47 provides another reason why individual transformation is Christ's objective, not societal or geopolitical structural transformation. The phrase "to all the nations" connects with the proclamation of "repentance for forgiveness of sins . . . in His name," revealing that the focus of Great Commission proclamation is spiritual and personal to the listener. The intention of missionary witness to the nations is thus the spiritual transformation of all hearers, Gentiles or Jews, "beginning from Jerusalem." All nonbelievers are inherently unfit for spiritual partnership until they enter into the family of God (3 John 5–8). Nonbelievers among the Jewish people are "far off" from God until they are saved by faith in the Lord Jesus Christ (Acts 2:39), and nonbelievers from among the Gentiles are decidedly worldly and immoral (Matt 18:17). No matter the background, identity, or context of the sinner, they all need the same redemption by Christ, who alone establishes and strengthens the bond of unity in the family of God (Gal 3:28; Col 3:11).

Therefore, interethnic spiritual fellowship hinges on the proclamation of the gospel and the repentance of individual hearers, concentrically moving out from Jerusalem "to all the nations" where there are new individual hearers. Such a spiritual emphasis in the Great Commission reinforces that the reason to go to the nations, more than any other purpose, is to make individual disciples of Christ, who will bear His image in continually God-glorifying ways (2 Cor 3:18).

Christ's Disciples Must "Baptize"

The second participle in Matthew 28:19, "baptizing" (*baptizontes*), characterizes the activity of the discipler with new believers. The practice of baptism in the New Testament is understood as an individual's full immersion into water. Jesus commanded water baptism within the context of the established practice in the Jordan River that John the Baptist modeled in his preaching ministry (Matt 3:1–12; Mark 1:4–8; Luke 3:3; 7:29; John 3:23; cf. Acts 11:16; 13:24; 19:1–7), which Jesus Himself fulfilled (Matt 3:13–17). Post-resurrection, the early church made full-immersion water baptism a standard activity of new converts, who were self-conscious adults or maturing adolescents (Acts 2:38, 41; 1 Cor 1:10–17; Rom 6:3; Gal 3:27; Col 2:12).[26]

The command to baptize in the Matthean Great Commission shows that it is a unique

---

25. In Matthew 28:19, whereas *ta ethnē* ("the nations") is neuter, the object of baptizing and teaching, *autous* ("them"), is masculine and "refers to the implied direct object of the main verb," making disciples (Charles L. Quarles, *Exegetical Guide to the Greek New Testament: Matthew* [Nashville: B&H Academic, 2017], 352). In other words, it is not all nations that are being discipled as such but individuals from all nations. See also Schnabel, *Early Christian Mission*, 1:536.

26. Matt Waymeyer, *A Biblical Critique of Infant Baptism* (The Woodlands, TX: Kress, 2008), 11–15; Schnabel, *Early Christian Mission*, 1:358 (iv); G. R. Beasley-Murray, *Baptism in the New Testament* (1962; repr., Grand Rapids: Eerdmans, 1994), 359.

feature of discipleship for it is separated from the teaching content identified in verse 20 as "all that I have commanded you."[27] The Markan Great Commission passage identifies the act of being baptized as following one's belief in the gospel (Mark 16:16), wherever the believer is in the world (v. 15). Water baptism is not for salvation but serves as a public testimony of saving grace that has already been accomplished by faith in the Lord Jesus Christ.[28] Thus, in terms of baptism's logical and chronological placement in the conversion story of the new believer, "baptism is the initiatory step, to be taken at the beginnings of discipleship."[29]

The event of full-immersion water baptism transitions missionary outreach from evangelizing sinners to discipling saints in the context of the local church worldwide. The event itself requires at least a basic understanding that the God of the Bible is triune. The distinct reference to the one name of the Father, Son, and Holy Spirit in Matthew 28:19 is a reference to the essential unity of the divine persons, to whom the disciple must commit.[30] No other god nor any other concept or identification of God is acceptable for one who is now identified

with the death, burial, resurrection, and glorified life of the Son of God (Rom 6:3–11). The expression "in the name" indicates the spiritual relationship as one of possession, where the convert has come under the ownership and authority of God and publicly declares so in word and act. Therefore, the missionary task of baptizing into the Trinitarian name is a physical act that is critical for all true believers to perform because it is designed to demonstrate the spiritual fellowship that the disciple has with the three persons of God Himself.[31]

Christ Sends "Witnesses" to "Teach"

The third participle in Matthew's Great Commission account is "teaching" (*didaskontes*) in Matthew 28:20, which Christ explains as "teaching them to keep all that I commanded you." Jesus' commands in the Gospels now become the commands of His students, who must teach them to future students. The transference of authority from Christ to His disciples is expressed by the verb "command" (*entellō*), which refers to giving orders or instructions of all kinds.[32] In context, the referent "all that" is the content of Jesus' speech and righteous

27. Jack Cottrell, *Baptism: A Biblical Study* (Joplin, MO: College Press, 1989), 11, with discussion on 12, 15. On the distorted applications of the ordinance of full-immersion water baptism in insider movements, see John Massey and Scott N. Callaham, "Baptism as Integral Component of World Mission Strategy," in *World Mission: Theology, Strategy, and Current Issues*, ed. Scott N. Callaham and Will Brooks (Bellingham, WA: Lexham, 2019), 168–74.

28. John Calvin and William Pringle, *Commentary on a Harmony of the Evangelists Matthew, Mark, and Luke* (Bellingham, WA: Logos Bible Software, 2010), 3:387–88.

29. Joe Kapolyo, "Matthew," in *Africa Bible Commentary: A One-Volume Commentary*, Tokunboh Adeyemo, gen ed. (Nairobi: WordAlive, 2006), 1170. Also emphasized in Waymeyer, *Biblical Critique of Infant Baptism*, 93; Massey and Callaham, "Baptism as Integral Component of World Mission Strategy," 152–53.

30. Morris, *Gospel according to Matthew*, 748; John Nolland, *The Gospel of Matthew*, NIGTC (Grand Rapids: Eerdmans, 2005), 1269; France, *Gospel of Matthew*, 1117.

31. Cottrell, *Baptism*, 16.

32. "ἐντέλλω," BDAG, 339.

conduct in the Gospels—everything he taught on the foundation of the Old Testament and everything that can be observed about his obedient life.[33] New disciples need to be trained to be obedient to "every last thing Jesus says" (cf. Matt 5:19).[34]

In Luke 24:48, Jesus uses the term "witnesses" (*martyres*) as the earliest description of those who undertake the Great Commission challenge to assert biblical truth "to all the nations."[35] He calls His disciples to bear testimony of "these things" (*toutōn*), which is a demonstrative pronoun that covers the written predictions of the suffering, death, and resurrection of Christ (v. 46). These teachings link back to the Old Testament (v. 44) and reach forward to the proclamation of repentance and forgiveness for sins that will usher from Jerusalem through the disciples (v. 47). The range of scriptural content that constitutes "these things" in Luke 24:48 corresponds to "all that" in Matthew 28:20, simply showing that Jesus' authority lay behind the commands of the Old Testament also. New Testament scholar Eckhard Schnabel has listed some of the biblical themes that the earliest disciples were careful to proclaim:

Jesus' life and ministry (Acts 1:21–22), his death and resurrection, his vindication and his exaltation (Acts 1:22), the salvation "from this corrupt generation" (Acts 2:40), the

word of the Lord (Acts 8:25), the necessity of conversion and faith in the Lord Jesus Christ (Acts 20:21), the gospel of the grace of God (Acts 20:24), the message of Jesus (Acts 23:11), the kingdom of God (Acts 28:23).[36]

Disciples of Jesus in every generation must themselves adhere to the full range of biblical content as a way of life and they must continue to teach the biblical way of life to new disciples.[37] Christ's witnesses must understand Scripture well enough to teach it where it has not been taught in the world. Thus, teaching is a discipling activity from Christ to His disciples and, through them, to the next disciples. Teaching as Christ's "witnesses" reflects the importance of imparting the full content of Jesus' teachings in His Word to new converts, with the goal that the next generation of believers will likewise be obedient to all that Jesus commands and again pass down the faith (Ps 145:4).

Conclusion

Viewing the Great Commission across its five key passages helps all who desire to be faithful in their witness for Christ in the world to focus their efforts on the ministry of the Word. What is most striking from the analysis is how indispensable a role Scripture itself plays in accomplishing the Great Commission. The Word of God is the Holy Spirit's instrument in

---

33. Nolland, *Gospel of Matthew*, 1270; France, *Gospel of Matthew*, 1118–19.
34. Doriani, *Matthew*, 2:532; Schnabel, *Early Christian Mission*, 1:368–70.
35. Schnabel, 1:368–69.
36. Schnabel, 1:370.
37. Hagner, *Matthew 14–28*, 888; Morris, *Gospel according to Matthew*, 749.

the hands of His servants to make disciples of the risen Christ and to give them the transformative theology He taught so that they might preach and teach the content of Scripture where Christ has not yet been named (Rom 15:20).

Because Christ is powerful to save sinners, no matter the cultural context or the circumstances, it is with hope and humility that His disciples undertake His mission. They will do even "greater works" than the apostles, as the Holy Spirit sends them out to bring in a global harvest for the glory of the Son (John 14:12). Christ prayed that the Father would providentially guide and protect His disciples as they attempt to glorify God (John 17). His prayer continues to be answered on the human stage as He spiritually empowers generations of disciples to preach and teach from the Scriptures everywhere they go. It is both an inspiring vision and a glorious reality that every day, as new believers mature in their faith, they go out as Christ's witnesses to make new disciples in farther reaches of the world. All glory belongs to the risen Christ, who will continue to build His church through His messengers until the end of the church age.

INSERT 9.1

Examples of Less-Than-Great Commissions in Latin America

Josué Pineda Dale

One who departs from God's Word is bound to fail. This is a general principle in theology and in life, but the same applies to missions. Though Jesus' power undergirds the simple Great Commission to preach the gospel and make disciples, Latin America has seen the rise of many "less-than-great commissions." Many people in the Spanish-speaking world are influenced by preachers who add to the Lord's mandate, altering it to make it more appealing to the people they want to please. So that churches might understand the greatness of the biblical Great Commission, this survey provides examples of current problematic Great Commission substitutes found in Latin America. Although the less-than-great commissions are many and varied and some of them even intersect at points, below are highlighted three of the most influential ones circulating in Latin American churches today.

Kingdom Expansion

The Honduran-American self-styled "apostle" Guillermo Maldonado is the founder and pastor of the Ministerio internacional el Rey Jesús (King Jesus International Ministry) in Miami, Florida. Through it he has a wide network of churches under his "apostleship" in the United States, Latin America, and Europe. In his book *Cómo caminar en el poder sobrenatural de Dios* (*How to Walk in the Supernatural Power of God*),[38] Maldonado speaks of the power of God in the believer as a tool for advancing the kingdom. Even though he understands the kingdom as being already present, he wants to see it more and more on earth. In his viewpoint, the supernatural power of God through signs and wonders serves to achieve more work in less time, helping believers to be effective witnesses for God.[39] Maldonado argues that people need to witness miracles today to avoid turning back to idols.[40] He also describes healing as "a legal right of the believer for himself and to impart it to others"[41] and describes casting out demons as "a visible manifestation that the kingdom of God is present."[42] The "apostle" sums it up with the following statement: "Healing, miracles, signs, wonders and casting out demons, are key to expanding the kingdom on earth."[43] At the same time, in his book *El reino de poder* (*The Kingdom of Power*), he speaks of bringing the kingdom from heaven down to earth by bringing "health, liberation, peace, joy, forgiveness, miracles, healing, prosperity and much more!"[44] In other words, again, he seeks to make the kingdom more visible.

Spiritual Warfare Liberation

The famous Argentinian evangelist and international speaker Carlos Annacondia speaks of liberation from demons as one of the five facets of the Great Commission.[45] For him, it's a conquest, a military operation. In his recent book, *¡Oíme bien, Satanás!* (*Listen Well, Satan!*), Annacondia includes a chapter,

---

38. Guillermo Maldonado, *Cómo caminar en el poder sobrenatural de Dios: Experimente hoy señales, maravillas y milagros* (New Kensington, PA: Whitaker House, 2011).

39. Maldonado, *Cómo caminar en el poder sobrenatural de Dios*, 55–58.

40. Maldonado, *Cómo caminar en el poder sobrenatural de Dios*, 170.

41. Maldonado, *Cómo caminar en el poder sobrenatural de Dios*, 174. This and all other English translations of Spanish works provided in this essay are mine.

42. Maldonado, *Cómo caminar en el poder sobrenatural de Dios*, 182.

43. Maldonado, *Cómo caminar en el poder sobrenatural de Dios*, 183. See also Maldonado, *Evangelismo sobrenatural* (Miami, FL: GM Ministries, 2003); *La muerte al yo, el camino al cambio y al poder de Dios* (Miami, FL: Ministerio Internacional El Rey Jesús, 2015); and Eleuterio Uribe Villegas, *Pentecostés el nuevo Sinaí: La revelación que marcó la teología del Nuevo Testamento* (Salem, OR: Publicaciones Kerigma, 2020).

44. Guillermo Maldonado, *El reino de poder: Cómo demostrarlo aquí y ahora* (New Kensington, PA: Whitaker House, 2013), 30–31.

45. Carlos Annacondia, *¡Oíme bien, Satanás!* (Miami, FL: Casa Creación, 2021), 190.

"Manual de liberación spiritual" ("Spiritual Freedom Manual"), which provides keys for spiritual warfare, including signs to discern when demons leave a person (for example, by vomiting them out), as well as procedures to follow. For Annacondia, the battle also includes healing, among other things, which is another facet of the Great Commission. Healing is "one of the signs because of which persons come to Christian meetings,"[46] so they need to be pursued and encouraged for the sake of reaching out to people.[47] In addition, the very popular preacher and pastor Carlos "Cash" Luna from Guatemala speaks in terms of spiritual warfare. For him, the gospel and God's power become visible when believers "lay hands to heal and liberate."[48] Also, Pastor Roger D. Muñoz, founder of Ministerio de Liberación (Ministry of Liberation), who trains pastors and leaders in spiritual warfare, casting out demons, healing the diseased, and setting captives free, believes that casting out demons was essential to Jesus' plan to make people truly free.[49]

Social and Political Liberation

Professors Robert W. Pazmiño and Octavio Esqueda, both with Hispanic heritage in their veins (Ecuadorean and Mexican, respectively), highlight Peruvian Gustavo Gutiérrez, a prominent Catholic philosopher-theologian, when they speak about social and political liberation as part of the Great Commission, in addition to the necessary liberation from sin.[50] Pazmiño and Esqueda place evangelization and social action side by side, affirming that salvation must include transformation of the person and society.[51] Jesús Adrián Romero, a captivating Mexican religious leader, singer, composer, and president of Vástago Producciones, also upholds a more social approach to the Great Commission, affirming that there are people "waiting to be valued, defended, rescued, redeemed,"[52] and that "to understand the redemptive work in its totality implies helping people in their different problems and giving them hope, not helping at a distance, but being friends of the poor and the weak."[53]

---

46. Annacondia, 190–91.

47. Annacondia, 62.

48. Cash Luna, *No es por vista* (Nashville: Editorial Vida, 2018), 62.

49. Roger de Jesús Muños Caballero, *La verdad en la Gran Comisión: Echad fuera demonios* (Seattle: Cristo Libera, 2019). See also Guillermo Maldonado, *Poder y autoridad para destruir las obras del diablo* (Miami, FL: Ministerio Internacional El Rey Jesús, 2015); and Maldonado, *Liberación sobrenatural: Libertad para su alma, mente y emociones* (New Kensington, PA: Whitaker House, 2016).

50. Robert W. Pazmiño and Octavio J. Esqueda, *Enseñando con unción: Colaborando con el Espíritu Santo* (Salem, OR: Publicaciones Kerigma, 2019), 33–34.

51. Pazmiño and Esqueda, *Enseñando con unción*, 34–35.

52. Jesús Adrián Romero, *Besando mis rodillas: La belleza de una espiritualidad añeja y actual* (Miami, FL: Editorial Vida, 2014), 165.

53. Romero, 165.

A Response

The problem with these three less-than-great commissions is that they go beyond what Jesus instructed, contradict the Great Commission, or fall short of it. First, most of the kingdom expansion commission's key "selling points" and conclusions are not grounded in Scripture. The position leads believers to assume for themselves the role of the Holy Spirit when witnessing to others, for example. Also, the view presupposes the continuity of signs and wonders according to Third Wave, power-encounter theology,[54] and the inauguration of the kingdom on earth, while at the same time urging for more of the kingdom to be brought from heaven to earth.

Second, the spiritual warfare liberation commission makes much more of demonic forces than Scripture does.[55] For them, the gospel is more about casting out demons from people, to set them free from their oppression, than praying that the Lord set them free from their bondage to sin. Although it is hardly ever either/or in their literature—because sin is always mentioned at least—still the big emphasis on liberation puts sin effectively on a subordinate tier.

Finally, the social and political liberation commission puts this kind of freedom on par with the gospel, which, in practice, pushes the pendulum more toward the former. In this approach, the Great Commission is predominantly work conducted among the poor and the oppressed, so much that it appears to be a "gospel" exclusive to the marginalized. The view does not consider that all people alike, being dead in sin, need the gospel. The gospel "is the power of God for salvation to everyone who believes" (Rom 1:16).

---

54. For an introduction to the theological position as presented for evangelistic use, see John Wimber and Kevin Springer, *Power Evangelism*, rev. ed. (San Francisco: Harper, 1992), 203–5.

55. More balanced biblical surveys, though at points differing from the present author's theology, can be found in C. Fed Dickason, *Angels: Elect and Evil* (Chicago: Moody, 1995); Graham A. Cole, *Against the Darkness: The Doctrine of Angels, Satan, and Demons*, Foundations of Biblical Theology (Wheaton, IL: Crossway, 2019).

CHAPTER 10

Make Disciples: What the Great Commission Means and What We Must Do

Scott Callaham

What is the mission of the church? There are an infinite number of initiatives that churches can undertake, but they must all serve the church's one mission. This singular mission of the church comes from Christ: His Great Commission. In Luke 24:49, Jesus directs His disciples to stay in Jerusalem to await the Holy Spirit. In John 20:22, Jesus commands them to receive the Holy Spirit. Then in Acts 1:8, Jesus reveals what will happen after the Spirit comes. These passages anticipated the coming of the Spirit at Pentecost, the birth of the church (Acts 2:17–18, 33). Once born and filled with the Spirit of the living God, the church could commence its Great Commission task.

The classic expression of the Great Commission is Matthew 28:18–20, and careful attention to this passage is vital for understanding what the Great Commission means and

what Christians must do. This chapter complements the preceding chapter by drawing out pointed missiological application from the exegetical details of Matthew's account.

What the Great Commission Means

In his earthly ministry, Jesus exercised direct authority in word and deed. Jesus explains the origin of his authority in Matthew 28:18: "All authority has been given to Me." Two literary aspects of this expression merit immediate attention. First, Jesus' mention of heaven and earth is a merism. A merism defines a composite idea by listing a range of its component parts.[1] When Jesus evokes the merism of heaven and earth, He underscores the totality of his authority. Second, the only one who could grant such absolute authority is the Creator of heaven and

---

1. A. M. Honeyman, "Merismus in Biblical Hebrew," *JBL* 71 (1952): 11–18. See p. 16 for specific treatment of "heaven and earth."

earth. "Has been given," therefore, is a "divine passive."[2] This passive voice expression not only identifies the source of Jesus' authority, but it also closely ties the Great Commission to the apocalyptic vision of Daniel 7:13–14. Daniel sees one "like a Son of Man" approaching the Ancient of Days in heaven and receiving from Him "dominion, glory, and a kingdom." The term for "dominion" in the Septuagint is the same word Jesus used for "authority" in Matthew 28:18.

Selecting terms clearly alluding to Daniel 7:14, Jesus identified Himself as its heavenly Son of Man figure. Therefore, if Jesus' disciples understood his scriptural citation, Daniel's apocalyptic vision would impress upon them that the resurrected Jesus claimed to speak to them with the authority of the Ancient of Days. Furthermore, Daniel 7:14 provides the reason the Ancient of Days granted his own authority to Jesus: "That all the peoples, nations, and men of every tongue might serve Him." The Great Commission drives toward a foreordained, glorious end: the worship of Jesus Christ among all peoples of the world.

The Command

Most English Bible translations front the word "go" in Matthew 28:19, making it appear as the central action of the Great Commission.[3] In the original text, however, the verse contains only one command: "make disciples." Obedience to the Great Commission—the mission of the church—entails making disciples of Jesus, a process that continues "even to the end of the age" (v. 20).

Though "make disciples" stands at the center of the Great Commission, much missiological literature lacks biblical grounding on disciple-making. For example, it is possible to write hundreds of pages about world evangelization without once mentioning the discipleship that must follow.[4] Further, in at least one prominent theory of missiology, "discipleship" is simply a catchall term for whatever a missionary does in contact with host nation people—"teaching others to love Jesus as much as you do."[5]

Ignoring or altering Jesus' definition of discipleship inevitably leads to disobeying the Great Commission. According to Matthew 28:19–20, Jesus' disciples must disciple "all the nations" through three core actions: going, baptizing, and teaching.

The Necessity of Going

"Going" is the first of three actions expressed with participles rather than commands. In Matthew 28:19, "go" is a participle of attendant circumstance that depends on the command

---

2. Joachim Jeremias, *New Testament Theology: The Proclamation of Jesus*, trans. John Bowden (New York: Scribner, 1971), 9–14.

3. A few English Bibles (among them NET, NIV, NLT, and CEB) begin with "therefore," which better highlights the transition from the premise of v. 18 to its logical result in vv. 19–20.

4. See, e.g., Edward R. Dayton and David A. Fraser, *Planning Strategies for World Evangelization* (Grand Rapids: Eerdmans, 1980).

5. V. David Garrison, *Church Planting Movements: How God Is Redeeming a Lost World* (Bangalore, India: WIGTake Resources, 2004), 265. Garrison's missiological theory advocates for "an *improved* definition of discipleship." Emphasis in original.

"make disciples" for its imperative sense. Since there are no English grammatical expressions like "attendant circumstance" participles in biblical Greek, modern English Bible translations must translate the participle as if it were a command. Even so, Greek grammar and syntax require that "going" not be the primary point of the Great Commission.[6]

That said, in practical terms, reduced emphasis on "going" in the proclamation of the Great Commission risks rationalizing and justifying the natural human urge not to go. Clichés such as "every Christian is a missionary" cannot help but vitiate evangelical fervor toward the arduous task of cross-cultural missions. Therefore, it is crucial that individual Christians and churches grasp the implications of Great Commission "going" rightly. Attendant circumstance participles have an ingressive force, which means that "going" has to happen first in order for the main activity of making disciples to take place.[7] Hence the Great Commission is clear; the church must physically go to all peoples of the earth. Put another way: no going, no making disciples.

The First Step of Disciple-Making

"Baptizing" has suffered a fate like that of "making disciples," in that the church has largely untethered "baptizing" from its biblical-theological meaning. Pragmatism drives a wide range of mutually contradictory baptism practices on the mission field, such as encouraging the immediate baptism of converts, discouraging the immediate baptism of converts, and baptizing converts more than once.[8] Some missionaries even advocate abandoning baptism altogether.[9] Beyond pragmatism, another challenge facing the practice of baptism on the mission field is denominationalism. Each major denominational movement maintains distinctive, mutually contradictory theologies and practices of baptism that have developed through the centuries.[10]

Missionaries should derive their theology of baptism neither from pragmatism nor from denominational distinctives, but instead from the Bible alone. That said, surveying the biblical theology of baptism is well beyond the scope of this chapter. Even so, gaining footing

---

6. Daniel B. Wallace, *Greek Grammar beyond the Basics: An Exegetical Syntax of the New Testament* (Grand Rapids: Zondervan, 1996), 640–45; Andreas Köstenberger, Benjamin L. Merkle, and Robert Plummer, *Going Deeper with New Testament Greek: An Intermediate Study of the Grammar and Syntax of the New Testament* (Nashville: B&H, 2020), 338–39.

7. Wallace, 642.

8. Missionaries advocate these disparate viewpoints within the same volume: Ralph D. Winter and Steven C. Hawthorne, eds., *Perspectives on the World Christian Movement: A Reader*, 4th ed. (Pasadena, CA: William Carey Library, 2009). For immediate baptism upon conversion, see George Patterson, "The Spontaneous Multiplication of Churches," 633–42, esp. 636. For delaying baptism, see Rick Brown, "A Movement to Jesus among Muslims," 706–7, esp. 707. For baptizing more than once, see Ken Harkin and Ted Moore, "The Zaraban Breakthrough," 687–90, esp. 689.

9. Richard Taylor, "On Acknowledging the Lordship of Jesus Christ without Shifting Tents," *Religion and Society* 19 (1972): 59–68. Note this assessment by the author, a Methodist missionary in India: "In our cultural context baptism has tended to become a social rite which in a fundamentally Christian sense is as objectionable as it is unnecessary" (59).

10. Incidentally, the notion that churches, missionaries, and mission agencies should accommodate multiple baptism theologies and practices is not a "neutral" position that is preferable to denominationalism. To the contrary, it is more rigidly sectarian than any denominational doctrine. In "agree to disagree" settings, "neutrality" becomes an inviolable article of faith, thus flatly denying the truth claims of every other position.

in the biblical theology of baptism is necessary for rightly understanding and obeying the Great Commission.

To begin, "baptizing" (Matt 28:19) and "teaching" (Matt 28:20) are participles of means, explaining how to make disciples.[11] Baptism is for those who have begun following Jesus and are seeking to learn from Him. This insight explains Peter's proclamation at Pentecost: "And Peter said to them, 'Repent, and each of you be baptized in the name of Jesus Christ for the forgiveness of your sins'" (Acts 2:38). In the New Testament, repentance and faith in Christ come before baptism. Baptizing those who are unconverted, including infants, has no biblical warrant. Baptisms conducted upon those who are not disciples of Jesus not only violates biblical teaching but also contradicts every biblical account of the practice of baptism.

Discussions of what constitutes a valid, biblical baptism often raise the issue of "mode," which implies that there are various methods of application of water in baptism such as sprinkling, pouring, or immersing. However, the word for "baptize" in the Bible simply means "immerse."[12] Hence the "mode" of baptism is inseparable from the definition of the act, and since nonimmersions are by definition not immersions, they are not baptisms at all. Biblical baptism—immersion in water in the name of, and importantly, under the authority of the Father, the Son, and the Holy Spirit—is a single event intended for the beginning of one's journey as Jesus' disciple. Biblical baptism is a necessary step of obedience to Jesus for the church, the baptizer, and the disciple receiving baptism.

A Lifelong Process of Disciple-Making

"Teaching" is the second participle of means, which together with "baptizing" explains how the church makes disciples. The teaching Jesus requires His disciples to pass on in obedience to the Great Commission is comprehensive. Just as "all" peoples are those who become disciples, "all" of Jesus' commands are what those disciples must learn.

Jesus commands repentance and belief in the gospel (Mark 1:15). The gospel is the message Scripture reveals of man's reconciliation to God through the Holy Spirit's regenerating work upon the human heart (Ezek 36:26–27), bringing repentance of sin and faith in Jesus Christ (Acts 20:21) as Savior and Lord (2 Pet 1:11; 2:20; 3:18). Jesus' perfect obedience means that He can redeem those who were under the law (Gal 4:4–5) and unable to fulfill its demands (Jas 2:10). Absent atonement, guilt from sin brings separation between humanity and God (Isa 59:1–2). Therefore, there is no law to keep nor work to do that will make a person right in God's eyes (Rom 3:28). Christ Jesus is the only hope (1 Tim 1:1).

While baptism marks the beginning of following Jesus, learning to obey all that Jesus

---

11. Wallace, *Greek Grammar beyond the Basics*, 628–29.
12. "βαπτίζω," *BDAG*, 164.

commands takes place through the rest of one's life. Obedience entails submitting to the authority of Scripture just as Jesus did.[13] For God's new covenant people, the Old Testament is authoritative and ultimately points to Jesus (Luke 24:27; John 5:46). The New Testament is authoritative as well, in that it unfolds the Old Testament in light of the coming of the Messiah.[14] Thus the whole Bible is the textbook for disciples of Jesus.

Christ with His Church

In Matthew 28:20 Jesus assures his disciples that He is with them as they make disciples among all peoples. Since Jesus was preparing to leave them, His promise of being with them is all the more striking. Jesus' word choices such as "I am" in "I am with you always," call to mind previous passages in the Gospel of Matthew. In Matthew 14:27 Jesus walked to His disciples on the surface of the stormy Sea of Galilee and called out, "Take courage, it is I ("I am" in the original language); do not be afraid." Jesus' presence brought a calming of the winds (v. 32) and prompted His disciples' worship (v. 33).

Furthermore, "I am with you always" forms a fitting bookend to the Gospel of Matthew, recalling the angel's instruction to Joseph about naming Jesus (Matt 1:21–23). The name "Jesus" would constitute fulfillment of the prophetic sign of Isaiah 7:14. There an integral component of Isaiah's message is the name "Immanuel,"

which means "God is with us." Hence the One whose very identity proclaimed "God is with us" assured His disciples that He would continue to be with them as they obey His Great Commission, "even to the end of the age."

To review, the Great Commission is a command: make disciples. The church's disciple-making of "all the nations" takes place through going to them, immersing them in the name of the Father, Son, and Holy Spirit, and teaching them to obey all that Jesus commands. This Great Commission demands action from Christ's church; therefore, the final section of this chapter draws guidance from the Great Commission itself on what the church must do.

What We Must Do

"Make disciples" is a plural imperative, and the "going," "baptizing," and "teaching" actions of disciple-making are plural participles. Jesus used these plural forms as He issued the mission of the church to His disciples. No individual disciple bore singular responsibility for disciple-making; Jesus entrusts disciple-making to the church. Indeed, the Great Commission is the mission of the church—the local church, the future church, and the global church.

The Church on Mission

First and foremost, as emphasized above, responsibility for Great Commission obedience falls to the local church. Parachurch

---

13. In Matthew 5:17–19, Jesus teaches submission to the Law and the Prophets (Old Testament Scripture) along with His fulfillment of them.

14. Note the premise-bearing title of G. K. Beale, *A New Testament Biblical Theology: The Unfolding of the Old Testament in the New* (Grand Rapids: Baker Academic, 2011).

ministries—whether denominational, inter-denominational, or nondenominational—can help churches send missionaries, but these organizations do not appear in the Bible and are not the body of Christ. Missionary sending organizations should remember that Jesus promised to build his church, not mission agencies (Matt 16:18). Furthermore, missionaries should not view the churches they plant as if they are primarily missionary sending organizations. Rather, they are full-orbed churches: truly the body of Christ. Embracing Great Commission obedience, local churches should pray for more laborers for the mission field (Matt 9:37–38) and be willing to be the answer to their own prayers. That is to say, churches should actively assess who among them should go to, baptize, and teach the nations to obey Jesus. Churches should support their missionaries financially as they go and maintain relational connection with them as they serve.

Second, the Great Commission also belongs to the future churches that missionaries will start on the mission field as they make disciples. Where there are no churches, missionaries must start new ones. In places with already existing churches, missionaries should prayerfully decide whether to plant still more.[15] These new churches should intentionally nurture God's missionary call among their members and, when ready, become missionary sending churches themselves.

Third, the Great Commission belongs to the global church. Admittedly, staying mostly within one's own cultural sphere while doing missionary work can be one way that God leads, as would be the case with a North American leading an English-speaking church in East Asia, or with a South Korean missionary starting a Korean church in California. Yet even these culturally bound churches bear responsibility to participate in mission among all the peoples of the world, including the people of the lands that host them.

Some people groups live in nation-states that actively bar missionary work and persecute Christians. Neither the local church nor the future church nor the global church should passively accept that citizens of these countries should live in societies devoid of Christian witness. Whenever governments make a mockery of their God-appointed role (Rom 13:1–7), Christ's churches "must obey God rather than men" (Acts 5:29) and find a way to obey the Great Commission among all the peoples of the earth.

Discipleship within the Local Church

Discipleship is a function of the local church. With the passage of time, however, churches tend to turn inward. When faithfulness to God and Scripture fades away, culturally sourced human wisdom fills the vacuum left by the Bible's absence. When a church mirrors the surrounding culture's worldview, distinguishing between the supposedly regenerate within the

---

15. Missionaries who plant and raise up these "future" churches should meet the qualifications of elders in 1 Timothy 3:1–7 and Titus 1:6–9, for they will perform the church leadership duties of elders in the early life of newly planted churches. Elder qualification is also essential to train and mentor elder-qualified men to assume leadership as churches continue to mature.

church and the unregenerate without becomes increasingly difficult. The church may even attempt to justify its growing worldliness by mixing religious-sounding language with the trending terminology of prevailing political and social movements.

Hence missionaries live in tension, for they sense the call for evangelistic preaching and Bible studies to call the lost to repentance on one hand, and the nonnegotiable need for deep discipleship and theological training for indigenous church members and leaders on the other. In these common situations, missionaries do well to remember the Great Commission. Discipleship within the local church entails baptism and teaching everything Jesus commands. "Everything Jesus commands" includes the gospel, and the gospel is for everyone. Indeed, missionaries proclaim the gospel message that sets people "free from the law of sin and of death" (Rom 8:2). The message of the gospel is most at home in churches that evidence trust in the authority and sufficiency of Scripture and embrace their part in the Great Commission.

Discipleship outside the Local Church

Great Commission "going" naturally entails discipleship outside missionaries' sending churches. However, in the technologically saturated way of life of many missionaries, electronic means of communication provide an attractive alternative to actual cross-cultural "going." Yet even as more and more people across the world connect to the internet each year, hundreds of millions of people live in countries that vigilantly monitor and censor

electronic communications. Furthermore, there are many people in the world who have no access to electronic devices. Also, just as gathering online for "virtual church" entails not gathering at all, "going" via online methods means not going at all. Obeying Jesus' call to make disciples requires physical going when it is humanly possible to do so.

The physicality of "going," when possible, is necessary on the mission field as well. While electronic means of communication can indeed multiply an individual missionary's connections, screens often "screen out" areas of life from the reach of discipleship. Put another way, a person can easily hide sin from a camera or microphone that he or she controls. There is simply no substitute for in-person disciple-making.

Conclusion

Great Commission discipleship requires going, baptizing, and teaching. These are not optional actions that missionaries, churches, and sending agencies are free to redefine. Baptizing and teaching are disciple-making tasks that take place after the Holy Spirit regenerates a new believer and he or she experiences salvation by grace alone through faith alone in Christ alone (Eph 2:8). Now, since it is God who grants repentance (2 Tim 2:25), it is possible that some missionaries who obey the call to "go" will never have the opportunity to baptize and teach. They may faithfully labor in obscurity, "holding fast the word of life" (Phil 2:16), but never see conversions to Christ.

However, those whose ministries God uses

to bring people to faith in Christ must baptize them as Jesus commands. Refusal to immerse, whether for reasons of persecution (whether religious, political, or from within one's family), practicality (perhaps due to frigid temperatures or lack of convenient access to water), cultural considerations (such as superstitions that stoke fear of getting wet as a source of sickness), or traditional practices (like sprinkling following supposed deathbed conversions) means disobedience to the Great Commission. Perhaps the most sobering temptation to abandon immersion may arise in reaction to experiencing hostility from other Christians. Under conviction, these fellow believers may view biblical baptism as an indictment of their own faith and practices rather than a joyous celebration of a disciple's new creation in Christ.

Despite all opposition, missionaries must baptize, and they must baptize under the authority of their church. Baptizing outside of the context of serving a church signals that obeying the Great Commission is for individuals rather than churches, which discourages newly baptized disciples from viewing themselves as being under the authority of a church.

Missionaries must also teach new disciples to obey all that Jesus commands. Truly teaching all that Jesus commands tests the patience of missionaries who have imbibed the missiological spirit of the age, which prizes rapid reproduction and shallow personal investment. Missionaries will need a solid grasp on the gospel and biblical theology to guide new believers in Scripture, as well as a humble heart to restrain themselves from teaching their personal opinions as if they were also authoritative. Missionaries must resist the paternalistic impulse to "dumb down" "all the treasures of wisdom and knowledge" (Col 2:3) in Christ. If they indeed treat new disciples as more important than themselves (Phil 2:3), they will rejoice when new disciples' capacity for training and potential in ministry exceeds their own. If missionaries are passionate expositors of God's Word, they will likewise train church leaders in expository preaching. Finally, despite whatever challenges may come, missionaries can rest in the assurance that Jesus will always be with them (Matt 28:20) as they carry out the mission—the Great Commission—of His church.

Essentials to Discipleship Strategies

Phillip F. Foley

To understand specific discipleship strategies, one must first know the aim of discipleship. Jesus clearly articulated the aim in His commissioning of the Twelve: "It is enough for the disciple that he become like his teacher" (Matt 10:25). He also described the means of discipleship when he said in the Great Commission, "Go . . . baptizing them . . . teaching them to keep all that I commanded you" (28:20). Biblical discipleship in any context thus contains the essential components of teaching, shepherding, and accountability (John 8:31; 13:35; 15:8).

Yet there are also context-specific aspects to the above that may vary from culture to culture. Discipleship strategies therefore must be broad enough to help learners grow in the following areas: (1) convictions, (2) character, (3) competence, and (4) care for others. Then, as the learners grow in these areas, (5) reproduction (or further disciple-making) follows. Gleaning from the work of missionaries on four different continents, this essay offers insights into these five essentials to successful discipleship strategies.

Developing Convictions

If disciples are to develop biblical convictions, they must be taught the truth and then shown its relevance for life and ministry (Eph 4:11–16). In American culture, this is typically done by taking followers through various written materials. In some cultures, however, the average person has a high school degree or less and likely struggles with reading. In that context, using a book study to foster convictions may not be realistic. Instead, a sermon or teaching review with the goal of application may be a more practical tool.

In any case, the aim in creating convictions is not simply that disciples learn the truth. They must also know how that truth relates to life. It is critical that they have mentors who can help them apply what they are learning in specific situations. Much of Jesus' teaching to His disciples was informal, stemming from the circumstances in which they found themselves (Matt 17:18–20; Mark 9:33ff.; Luke 9:57ff.). In many cultures, discipleship is almost completely informal; mentors instruct, encourage, and counsel from life-on-life circumstances. Yet, in every culture, this is essential to some degree. For instance, one missionary always took a younger man with him when he went on ministry trips. That strategy meant the opportunity for hours of informal, one-on-one, question-and-answer instruction while traveling.

Developing Character

Developing Christlike character may be the biggest challenge for the teacher. This area has the built-in requirement that teachers be present with their students. Mentors must observe how their followers relate to their families and how they respond to troubles and adversity. Learners must also see how their teachers model living for Christ (1 Cor 11:1). Hence, teachers must prioritize finding ways to spend time with learners. Serving in ministry together is an ideal way to achieve this goal. By being with Paul in ministry, Timothy learned to imitate both his Christlikeness and his teaching, which he was then able to pass on to others (1 Cor 4:16–17).

Spending extended time together provides the teacher opportunities to observe the disciple's life and to identify points of immaturity or weakness. In a culture more heavily oriented to honor and shame, challenges arise because people do not open up about their sins and frailties. In such cultures, the act of receiving counsel itself indicates something is wrong. That kind of perception of weakness is considered shameful, so people hide their problems. Discipleship in that context takes much patience. One way mentors can overcome this challenge is by acknowledging their own sin and failure, along with their testimony of the Lord's grace in bringing victory (e.g., 1 Tim 1:15).

Developing Competence

For disciples to be useful in the kingdom, they must work to exercise their gifts with competence. A good initial strategy in this regard is to focus on faithfulness in small things, so that more important responsibilities can follow (Luke 16:10). If a mentor and disciple regularly meet to study a book together, the mentor could ask the learner to take a turn leading their meeting, as this will prepare that learner to disciple others. If the two serve together in a ministry, the teacher can give the student various tasks that would further reveal the latter's giftedness. In assigning duties, the mentor should give clear instructions and then follow up with a constructive critique so the disciple can learn and improve (Luke 10:1–24).

Developing Care

The best strategy for developing care in disciples is to let them see such care in action. Paul, Silas, and Timothy cared for the Thessalonians by having a fond affection for them, imparting their lives because they had become beloved to them (1 Thess 2:8). Timothy watched his mentors do this. Then, as mentors ask learners themselves personal questions concerning various areas of their lives, learners discover how they can do likewise to care for others, including their teachers (Matt 10:25). Mutual love is a mark of true discipleship to Christ (John 13:35).

Reproduction

An essential goal of any discipleship strategy is to help disciples become disciple-makers; that is, to lead others to follow Christ the Teacher. This goal should be communicated from the outset and repeated often (Matt 28:19; John 20:21; 2 Tim 2:2). In many cultures, young age is often a

hindrance to taking initiative in discipling others. Timothy faced this problem, but he overcame it through his godly example. His progress in sanctification was evident to all (1 Tim 4:12–16). Whatever the ages, biblical discipleship involves mature believers coming alongside younger believers, caring for them, and helping them grow toward spiritual maturity.

All the strategies explored here require the mentor to be willing to forgo his own interests to serve the interests of others, so that they are built up in Christ (Phil 2:3–4). This outcome will result in the furtherance of the gospel of Christ to the next generation. But it will also assist every believer in Christ today to become more like Him, our Teacher, to the glory of God.

CHAPTER 11

The Message of Our Mission

Michael Riccardi

The cornerstone of the Great Commission is the proclamation of the gospel. That repentance for the forgiveness of sins should be proclaimed in the name of the Christ who suffered and rose on the third day is the great business of the church's mission (Luke 24:46–47). As such, any resource on missions ought to include an explicit explanation of that message that Christians are charged to proclaim to the world. It is a message that proclaims the holiness of God, the sinfulness of man, and the salvation accomplished in Christ, and then calls sinners to respond in repentant faith in Him.

God Is Holy

The Bible teaches that the entire universe was created by God, that the Creator has spoken to humanity in the Bible, and that He is fundamentally holy. First John 1:5 says, "God is Light, and in Him there is no darkness at all." That is a way of saying that God is entirely pure. His character is one of perfect moral uprightness.

He is the essence of all that is good, so much so that He can have absolutely no fellowship with that which is not perfectly holy, righteous, and pure.

God's righteous character was expressed in the law He gave Israel on Mount Sinai, and the Ten Commandments summarized the perfection of God's character. These laws were directives for how people who are in a proper relationship with God must act. God is to be worshiped above all else (Exod 20:3–6) for He is the most glorious being that can be. Accordingly, His name is to be treated with reverence and never blasphemed (Exod 20:7). Further, God's image-bearers must not commit murder (Exod 20:13) for God is the giver of all life. They may not commit adultery (Exod 20:14) for God is unfailingly faithful. They are forbidden from stealing what belongs to others (Exod 20:15) for God never steals but gives freely to all. They are not to bear false witness (Exod 20:16) for God is the embodiment of truth itself and cannot lie.

Man Is Sinful

The problem is that all mankind is sinful. We have all broken God's law. Isaiah 53:6 tells us that all humanity has "like sheep . . . gone astray. Each of us has turned to his own way." We have not loved the Lord our God with all our heart, soul, mind, and strength. We have stolen. We have told lies. We have been angry with one another in our hearts, which Jesus says is committing murder of the heart (Matt 5:21–22). We have looked upon others with lust, which Jesus says is committing adultery in our hearts (Matt 5:27–28). We are sinful.

We have tried to live our lives without God, according to our own standards, in our own ways. Whether drug addicts and murderers, or well-to-do, upstanding citizens, in our natural, sinful state, we do what we do because we want to do it, with no consideration for God and what He would have us do. The Bible calls that sin—missing the mark, falling short of God's standard of perfect righteousness.

And people seem to understand that. Though many fool themselves into thinking that they are "good persons," very few people believe they are perfect persons. In all cultures, people tend to acknowledge that they fall short of even their own moral standards. And yet "good" is not the standard; "perfect" is, as Ecclesiastes 7:20 shows: "Indeed, there is not a righteous man on earth who continually does good and who never sins." "All have sinned and fall short of the glory of God," says Romans 3:23.

And therein lies the problem. If God is Light, and in Him there is no darkness at all (1 John 1:5), and if every one of us is stained by the "darkness" of our sin (John 3:19; 12:46), we are cut off from Him. Man becomes absolutely incapable of doing the very thing he was created and designed to do: to enjoy a relationship with his Creator.

There Is a Penalty for Sin

But it is not just that man and God cannot be friends. There is a penalty to be paid for sin. And the Bible tells us that that penalty is death (Rom 6:23). But the death that Paul talks about in this verse is not just physical death. It is not as if we pay for our sins by departing from this earthly existence. The death that is the wages of sin is a spiritual death—the eternal conscious torment of hell. Jesus Himself calls it a "fiery furnace," where there will be "weeping and gnashing of teeth" (Matt 13:50).

The idea of hell grates against the sensibilities of westerners, because hardly anyone believes they are bad enough to deserve something like eternal torment. "Maybe I have done some things I am not proud of, but how could all of my finite sins ever merit eternal punishment?" The reasoning is plausible but skewed. The punishment for sin is not measured merely by the act considered in a vacuum, but by the dignity of the one sinned against. All sin is fundamentally sin against God, and He is infinitely holy. Therefore, it is right that sin against an infinitely holy God should demand an infinite punishment. The punishment for sin is so serious because God is so righteous. So the bad news is that, in our natural state, mankind is sinful, separated from God, and doomed to spend eternity in hell. And there is nothing we can do about it. God is a perfectly just and righteous Judge. His justice demands that sin be punished. But the only payment answerable to the crime is eternal spiritual death.

God Became Man

The good news is that God pitied the miserable condition of humanity. He knew that we humans could never pay for our sins—that there was no way to earn our way back to fellowship with Him, and that we were all doomed to spend eternity in hell. But "while we were still weak, at the right time Christ died for the ungodly" (Rom 5:6). In the midst of our hopelessness, God the Father sent His Son to the earth on a mission (1 John 4:9–10). The eternal Word, God the Son, became flesh and dwelt among us (John 1:14). The one existing from eternity in the nature of God assumed the nature of man (Phil 2:6–7).

The Holy Spirit miraculously conceived Jesus in the womb of a virgin (Luke 1:34–35). Though the Son was God from all eternity, He assumed a full and true human nature into union with His divine nature. This is the greatest mystery in the universe. As finite creatures, we cannot entirely comprehend the incarnation, but it is true: Jesus was fully God and fully man.

And He lived for thirty-three years on the earth. He grew up just like every other child. He learned the family trade and became a carpenter. The great difference between Jesus and every other human being, though, was that He never sinned (2 Cor 5:21; Heb 4:15; 7:26). Never once did Jesus ever break God's law. He

always loved God with all His heart, soul, mind, and strength—in everything He did. He never sought satisfaction apart from the Father's will. He never disobeyed His parents, lusted, stole, lied, or coveted. He was never selfish. He never spoke sinful words. He never even had sinful thoughts. In a word, Jesus Christ lived the life that every man and woman was commanded to live but failed to live. He lived a life that was purely "Light," with "no darkness at all."

Jesus Paid the Penalty

And because He was perfectly righteous, He was fit to be the substitute for sinners. The religious leaders of Israel plotted to kill Jesus because they saw Him as a threat to their religious establishment (John 11:47–48). But because they could not carry out capital punishment (John 18:31), the Jews sought help from the Romans. Because the governor, Pontius Pilate, feared that the people would riot if he did not give them what they wanted, he agreed to have Jesus crucified (John 19:4, 6; cf. Mark 15:15).

At the same time, Scripture also tells us that God sent His Son to die this way (1 John 4:9–10). This was part of God's plan. God used the sinful desires of the Jews and the Romans to accomplish His own good purpose (Acts 2:23; 4:28). On the cross, Jesus suffered for sins, but not for His own; He had no sins of His own! But on the cross, the Father "caused the iniquity of us all to fall on Him" (Isa 53:6). He had partaken of flesh and blood to be the propitiation for the sins of His people (Heb 2:14–18). "He was pierced through for our transgressions, He was crushed for our iniquities; the chastening for our peace fell upon Him, and by His wounds we are healed" (Isa 53:5).

On the cross, the Father was carrying out upon Jesus the punishment that rightly belonged to His people: "He made Him who knew no sin to be sin on our behalf, so that we might become the righteousness of God in Him" (2 Cor 5:21). On that cross, Jesus was receiving in His own person the full exercise of the righteous wrath of His Father against the sins of His people. He Himself "bore our sins in His body on the tree . . . [for] by His wounds you were healed" (1 Pet 2:24). The judgment, the condemnation, the punishment—all the bitterness of hell itself, everything that sinners deserved because of our sin—the Father poured out on Jesus.

God treated Jesus as if He lived the sinner's life of sin, and therefore, through faith in Christ alone, God can justly treat the sinner as if he lived Jesus' life of perfect obedience. Because God is perfectly righteous, the only way to get to heaven is to be perfectly righteous (Matt 5:20, 48); however, if someone has already failed at being perfectly righteous, that person has no hope in himself to bring himself to heaven. But because Jesus was perfectly righteous, and because He took the sinner's place on the cross, the sinner can take Jesus' place in the courtroom of God. The perfect righteousness needed to go to heaven is Christ's righteousness—applied to the sinner's account as a free gift of God's grace.

After Jesus died, God raised Him from the dead on the third day in order to show that He was satisfied with His Son's sacrifice (Acts 2:24). The bodily resurrection of Christ now "furnish[es] proof to all men" that this message is true and trustworthy (Acts 17:30–31). The empty tomb of Joseph of Arimathea stands throughout the ages as the sure guarantee of the truth of the gospel and the certainty of the coming day of judgment (v. 31).

Man's Necessary Response

And now the Lord God commissions His ministers of reconciliation to preach this message of reconciliation (2 Cor 5:18–20). Disciples of Jesus throughout the world are to proclaim to all the nations that if (a) sinners confess their sin that they have broken God's law; (b) they admit that there is no way to earn His favor and His forgiveness; (c) they purpose to turn away from their life of sin and commit their life to following after Him; (d) they turn away even from their "good" works as a ground of confidence for heaven; (e) and they trust in Jesus' righteousness alone for their acceptance before this holy God—then He will have treated Jesus as if He lived their lives, and He will treat them as if they lived Jesus' life. Such believing sinners will be saved from the penalty of sin and possess the sure hope of fellowship with the triune God forever in heaven. They will even possess the great blessing of fellowship with Him now in this life, the sweetest of all earthly joys.

In other words, preachers of the gospel proclaim to sinners this message:

If you confess that you are a sinner and deserve God's punishment because of your sin, but you believe that the Father sent Jesus to endure that punishment in your place and that His sacrifice is perfectly sufficient to purchase your pardon and your righteousness, then God promises that He will forgive you and you will be saved. Dear friend, would you receive Christ? Would you acknowledge your sinfulness before God and admit you cannot do a thing about it? Would you turn from your sin and purpose to live your life in submission to Jesus Christ? Would you trust in Jesus alone for your righteousness before God? "Behold, now is 'the acceptable time,' behold, now is 'the day of salvation'" (2 Cor 6:2). Repent and trust in Jesus.

The Power of God unto Salvation

This is the message that is the lifeblood of the church's mission. This is the message believers have been left on earth to proclaim. This is the message that conquers lusts, that subdues sins, that breaks the bondage of iniquity, that melts hearts of stone, that opens blind eyes to the glory of God revealed in the face of Christ—in every culture under heaven. This message—so despised by the world—is the power of God for salvation to everyone who believes. May God give grace, that His people would proclaim His gospel by His power unto His glory.

INSERT 11.1

The Missionary Must Call for Repentance

Bill Shannon

Most sinners are not aware of the depth of their sinful condition, and if they do not understand the condemnation they are under (Rom 3:23; 6:23; Ps 5:5), how can they know they need to repent? For the natural man it is impossible to see that the fundamental human problem is a spiritual one (1 Cor 2:14). Therefore, repentance must be a top-priority message on the mission field. Sometimes people who come to a new house church, evangelistic Bible study, or community outreach event will think that they just need to get something spiritually adjusted and then life will be better. They do not realize their true need is to repent of their sins and be forgiven by God. Jesus came to call sinners to repentance (Luke 5:32) and the missionary must continue that mission (Matt 28:18–20).

Calling the Lost to Repent

Jesus began His ministry by calling for repentance from everyone He encountered. Matthew recounts, "From that time Jesus began to preach and say, 'Repent, for the kingdom of heaven is at hand'" (Matt 4:17). Repentance is a call to salvation, and salvation is the free gift of God (Rom 3:24; 6:23). Because of the work of Jesus Christ, an individual responds in faith and receives new life. The message of repentance must be proclaimed to individual sinners.[1]

What Is Repentance?

The Greek word for repentance is *metanoia*, which means a change of mind.[2] A sinner's thinking about sin, the Savior, the Bible, and God must all change. Being sorry for sin does not constitute true repentance. Lots of things can make someone feel sorry. There has to be sorrow over sin, a genuine turning to Jesus, and an ongoing, growing relationship with Him (2 Cor 7:10–11). Therefore, the kind of change of mind involved in repentance is really a change of heart that leads to salvation. Recognizing oneself as a sinner is the first step to getting saved. People need to realize that they are separated from God and that their sin is not simply a mistake but a volitional act (Rom 1:32). Sinners are blessed only when they recognize their spiritual bankruptcy (Matt 5:3) and deal with their sin before the Lord at the cross. They must not play with or entertain sin (Rom 13:14) but instead mortify that sin in themselves (Rom 8:13). Repentance means forsaking sin and embracing Jesus Christ as Lord and Savior (Rom 10:9–10).

What Does Repentance Look Like?

Those who respond to the gospel with genuine repentance have a wholesale desire to forsake sin. But if they commit the same sin habitually, it is as if they are controlled by it and not by their Savior—they are dominated by sin. Yet, when sinners truly repent, they make a 180-degree turn and say, "I am not going to do that today." They turn from their previous life of sin toward what had once disinterested them—the gospel (1 Thess 1:9–10). The God-honoring life that he once neglected, he now embraces (Luke 19:8–9). Jesus' counsel to metaphorically cut off hands, eyes, and feet if they lead to sin underscores the seriousness of sin and repentance (Matt 5:29–30). Repentance consists in going from the kingdom of darkness to the kingdom of light (Col 1:12–13).

When the missionary considers the

---

1. For discussion of how to address the need for repentance in one-on-one meetings from a biblical counseling perspective, see Heath Lambert, *A Theology of Biblical Counseling: The Doctrinal Foundations of Counseling Ministry* (Grand Rapids: Zondervan, 2016), 228–35.

2. "μετάνοια," BDAG, 640.

people he is evangelizing and those who received the gospel and are now under his care, he must ask himself important questions: "Do I see a converted heart that loves Jesus? Is there evidence this person understands the weight of their sin and has turned from it to Christ? Is there growth in the fruit of the Spirit in this person's life?" (Gal 5:22–23; cf. Matt 7:17–20).

The Missionary Requirement to Preach Repentance

When Jesus was going to send His disciples as His apostles, He told them that they were to go out and call others to repent (Mark 6:12). Luke 24:46–47 records the last act of Jesus Christ's earthly ministry. "And He said to them, 'Thus it is written, that the Christ would suffer and rise again from the dead the third day, and that repentance for forgiveness of sins would be proclaimed in His name to all the nations, beginning from Jerusalem.'" The apostles were to preach repentance. His disciples bear the same responsibility (Matt 28:19–20). The missionary's message comes from Jesus—it is a message of repentance.

Missionaries today need to be like Christ's men of old. They should not want just to make friends in another culture and to invite them to come to church. Going to church itself without repentance does the person no ultimate good. The person should be worshiping in church because they love Christ. There are those who are self-deceived in every church. These false professors may attend regularly, establish genuine friendships, and even serve faithfully. But what a tragedy that on the last day they would hear not affirmation but rejection by Christ (Matt 7:22–23).

Although repentance is what Jesus preached from the beginning of his ministry, some missionaries might question the need to preach repentance to the unsaved, given that there are many other, more seemingly practical needs that occupy the missionary's time and resources. The missionary who sees repentance as only a change of mind or actions and not a change of heart might ask, "Must we be in the business of changing external behavior?" Considering sin as the root problem, a sinner's other needs, even the most practical and material, are less important than his need to repent of his sin. Nevertheless, lifestyle modifications exhibit the fruit of true repentance (Matt 7:15–23) when the sinner's heart and mind have been turned from what has enslaved him.

To know if someone is repentant, then, the missionary must look at his fruit. If there is none, he must call the person to repentance again. If someone is not demonstrating the fruit of righteousness but predominantly the fruit of wickedness, he is in a fearful position. So, it is of utmost importance to the person's life that the missionary preaches repentance like Christ.

Conclusion

From the beginning of Jesus' ministry to the sending of His apostles and all disciples thereafter, Jesus has been calling sinners to repentance. Missionaries therefore must labor with both the lost and their own people to show them what God's Word has to say about the sinner's predicament. They must look for spiritual fruit, call for spiritual fruit, and cultivate spiritual fruit. Such is the mandate of the Chief Shepherd, and such is the ministry that meets the people's greatest need.

INSERT 11.2

Decisions and Discipleship: The Relationship between Conversion and Obedience

Rodney Andersen

Most missionaries who are sent from evangelical churches desire to see the lost come to a saving knowledge of Christ, to believe in Him and be saved (John 17:3). But what it means to possess that knowledge and the process by which it comes about both need clarification. Asking such fundamental questions today might seem unnecessary over two thousand years after the Great Commission. Yet clear, biblical answers must be restated due to missions tendencies and fads that have jettisoned doctrine in the pursuit of "results." Two misguided, unbiblical answers as to how to obtain saving faith—so-called decisionism and obedience-based discipleship—are prominent missions trends that stand in contrast to the biblical model of gospel proclamation and disciple-making.

Decisionism

Believers who give financial resources to missions want to know that their donations are put to good use. This is reasonable, as each believer is commanded to steward well the money God has provided them. Missionaries also know that many donors are interested in their "return on investment," and can therefore be under unspoken pressure—or sometimes clearly stated pressure—to demonstrate that souls are being added to the kingdom.

This pressure results in some missionaries pursuing individuals to make "decisions for Christ." It might mean conducting altar calls or leading people to recite the "sinner's prayer," in the hopes that many will respond to their need for a Savior and decide by these means to follow Christ. Others who prayed such a prayer in the past might be encouraged to "rededicate their lives." All of these decisions are then counted up and reported back to supporters as how the Lord used the missionary to save souls.

What is often lost, however, is genuine regeneration or the discipleship of those individuals who made the decisions. The work is assumed to be accomplished, with the next wave of decision-makers already in view. "Deciders" are given assurance that they are saved and are basically left to fend for themselves. Sustained obedience to all that Christ commanded is left wayside. What inevitably happens is that many hearts behind such "conversions" turn out to be the rocky or weedy soils of Jesus' parable; they receive the gospel but then fall away (Matt 13:1–9, 18–23). The true saving work of the gospel never occurs in them.

Obedience-Based Discipleship

A more recent trend in missions takes a different tact. Instead of downplaying discipleship and Christ's commands, obedience is emphasized from the beginning, even before conversion. Rather than preaching the gospel of grace and teaching obedience as a result of the new birth (John 15:8; Eph 2:8–10; Col 1:9–11), the latter is placed up front, conversion coming later. The new "disciple" is encouraged to continue in obedience-based discipleship until a time of decision comes and he or she is converted.

The problem with this method is that it defines faith as obedience. Those who advocate for it can still claim to teach that salvation comes by faith alone, but this is only made possible by a sleight of hand, by redefining faith in such a way that includes good works. One book advocating the method states, "Faith is defined as the continuous act of choosing to be obedient to God's Word regardless of what it may cost, even our lives."[3] However, faith defined this way is no longer faith but works (Rom 4:1–5; 11:6; cf. Heb 11:1). While obedience-based discipleship avoids the shallow decision-based approach, it swings the pendulum so far that it loses the gospel of grace.

---

3. David L. Watson and Paul D. Watson, *Contagious Disciple-Making* (Nashville: Thomas Nelson, 2014), 37.

Biblical Conversion and Obedience

At salvation's core is a proper understanding of the relationship between conversion and obedience. Conversion occurs at the moment of faith and repentance, when God regenerates the sinner's heart, bringing conviction of sin and a turning toward Christ (2 Cor 3:12–4:6; cf. Acts 26:18; Phil 3:8; 1 Thess 1:9). It is part of the salvation package made possible only through Christ's atonement, His payment of sin's penalty and His righteousness credited to the sinner's account (Ps 32:1–2; Isa 52:13–53:12; Rom 3:23–26; 2 Cor 5:21; 1 Pet 2:24). The whole package is the gift of God, and one is saved by faith alone, not by one's works of obedience (Gen 15:6; Eph 2:8–9; Titus 3:5–6).

Still, saving faith includes God's work in the sinner's life to make the spiritually dead person alive, and therefore it always produces a changed life (Eph 2:5, 10; Jas 1:17–18)—the evidence of repentance (Matt 3:8; Acts 26:20). Most missionaries who pursue "decisions" on the field would not deny the need for repentance in conversion (Mark 1:14–15; cf. Acts 20:21), but customarily conversions are counted and reported before there is any practical evidence of repentance. True conversion will be apparent over time by good works (Matt 13:3–23; 2 Cor 5:17; Eph 4:1–3).

This does not mean that good works are equivalent to faith. Rather, when Scripture explains conversion, faith is often contrasted to good works (John 6:28–29; Rom 3:28; Eph 2:8–9; Titus 3:5; cf. Ps 51:16–17; Hos 6:6). Nor are good works combined with faith to yield salvation; they are simply the result of saving faith (Eph 2:10; Titus 3:8; Jas 2:26). When a person puts their faith in Christ, salvation is secured instantaneously, but through the Spirit's ongoing work of sanctification the believer puts off the sinful deeds of the old self and puts on the righteous deeds of "the new man" (cf. 2 Cor 5:17; Eph 4:17ff.; Col 3:8ff.). The ability to stop sinning and to do righteousness in any way that pleases God is only possible when one has been freed from sin's power and given a new heart (John 8:34–36; Rom 6:1–23; 8:6–8; Heb 11:6; cf. Ezek 36:25–26).

Whether in pursuit of impressive conversion reports or following the latest missions fads, many missionaries are involved in promoting an unbiblical soteriology. Decisionism and obedience-based discipleship are two of the ways. Yet God will not judge a missionary's life by his number of conversions, but by faithfulness in life and teaching (1 Cor 4:1–5; 1 Tim 4:6, 16). Let missionaries then watch closely their doctrines of faith and obedience, and so be found as good and faithful servants (Matt 25:21).

The Commercialization of Christianity in South Africa

Nathan Odede

A Glimpse into Christianity in Africa

A few years ago in Kenya, a documentary aired on national TV covering the evil practices of a false preacher. It included explicit footage from hidden cameras of ways the pastor had executed his con game during live services, on television, and on radio, while raking in millions of shillings from gullible followers. Despite the exposure, his church service was full the following Sunday. Instead of shame and indictment, he received fame and praise. He was even invited onto a popular national TV show to rehash his deception, much to the excitement of a live audience. More recently, he was also among other religious leaders invited for an interdenominational service held by the Kenyan president after the 2022 national elections.

In South Africa, a well-known televangelist of Congolese descent was also featured in a documentary exposing his deception, complete with eye-witness accounts from his previous associates. Despite the damning report, his followers persisted and termed the documentary an attack from the devil. Undeterred by the revelations of his pretense, the pastor went on to fake the resurrection of an allegedly dead man during one of his services, and his following grew stronger. These and countless other examples may tempt one to conclude that the apostle Paul had today's Africa in mind when he prophesied in 2 Timothy 4:3–4: "For the time will come when they will not endure sound doctrine, but wanting to have their ears tickled, they will accumulate for themselves teachers in accordance to their own desires, and will turn away their ears from the truth and will turn aside to myths."

The South African Government's Response

In mid-2017, South Africa's Commission for the Promotion and Protection of the Rights of Cultural, Religious and Linguistic Communities (the CRL Rights Commission) published a report in response to the above alarming practices in the country, mainly around the Christian community.[4] The Pentecostal and charismatic churches comprised the largest number of religious institutions summoned to participate in the research. The report observed that the number and size of churches, among other religious organizations, had increased rapidly in recent years and that they had changed "the face of the religious community and practice irreversibly" in mostly negative ways.

The CRL Rights Commission decried certain unorthodox practices in the churches. It cited both local and international media reports where, for example, pastors instructed congregants to eat grass and snakes, to drink petrol, and to part with significant amounts of money in exchange for miracles or blessings. Other ill practices included the exploitation of the poor and vulnerable, a lack of formal registration for nonprofit organizations, hero worship of church leaders, practices that potentially violated human rights and ethics, "extremism" (such as forbidding children to attend school), and providing unqualified recommendations for health-related issues. While gathering their findings, the commission also cited intimidation and a lack of cooperation from certain religious institutions.

As a response, the commission mainly recommended that the government amend the current "CRL Act"[5] to establish religion-specific peer review committees in order to enforce accountability, yet without infringing upon religious freedom. The report further stated that "professionalizing the religious sector cannot be deemed to be unconstitutional" because regulating religious practitioners as professionals is in line with South Africa's constitution and bill of rights.[6] Professionalizing the sector would also demand that practitioners be trained. Rwanda has already legalized the requirement for a degree qualification for pastors.

In South Africa, the Minister of Home Affairs terminated the issuance of work permits on religious grounds in 2022.[7] This locked out foreign pastors and missionaries

---

4. Commission for the Promotion and Protection of the Rights of Cultural, Religious, and Linguistic Communities, *Report of the Hearings on the Commercialisation of Religion and Abuse of People's Belief System*, Johannesburg, South Africa, 2017, accessed June 18, 2024, https://crlcommission.org.za/wp-content/uploads/2023/02/Report-On-Commecialization--of-Religion-and-Abuse-of-Peoples-Believe-Systems-final.pdf.

5. Commission for the Promotion and Protection of the Rights of Cultural, Religious and Linguistic Communities Act, No. 19 of 2002, Parliament of the Republic of South Africa, *Government Gazette* 23676 (July 30, 2002): 2–24, https://www.gov.za/documents/commission-promotion-and-protection-rights-cultural-religious-and-linguistic-communities-3.

6. *Report of the Hearings*, 41.

7. Aphiwe Ngwenya, "Foreign National Religious Workers No Longer Eligible for Work Permits or Permanent Residency," SABC News, September 18, 2022, https://www.sabcnews.com/sabcnews/foreign-national-religious-workers-no-longer-eligible-for-work-permits-or-permanent-residency/.

as what it considered to be a vital first step in curbing religious malpractice. One may therefore conclude that the church in South Africa has been left embarrassed. The world, which lies in darkness, is seeking ways to shine its "light" (by way of law) into a seemingly very dark church. For that church has failed to be the light of the world (Matt 5:14–16; Phil 2:15). What used to be the Dark Continent is now home to a dark church.

The Starving Pastor's Response

Evangelical pastors and churches in South Africa seem to adopt an outreach strategy that requires the lost to look for them and not the reverse. Personally, I have both an extensive Roman Catholic and Pentecostal heritage spanning decades. I only heard about other theological perspectives when a friend stumbled upon a conservative evangelical institution and urged me to drop my theological studies elsewhere and transfer. I was surprised that I had never come across an exegetically grounded theology in my decades of identifying with the Christian faith. Given the false prosperity gospel taught at my local Pentecostal church, I had often felt hungry for the Word, but I never knew where to turn. All the religious billboards on the streets were labeled with charismatic theology, advertising miracles and healings, giving the impression that there were no other options.

This is the experience and feeling of many pastors on the continent. I recently attended two pastors' conferences with pastors from all over sub-Saharan Africa in attendance, some of them national bishops with thousands of churches under their oversight. The pastors were Protestants, but none were from conservative evangelical circles. They lamented the lack of sound theological training available to address contextual issues such as the inroads of the prosperity gospel and of African religions. A lack of resources was also cited as a major issue, with many once-thriving denominational and nondenominational institutions closed due to funding shortages. However, rarely are they invited to attend conferences of more conservative denominations and churches, where they would encounter resources, be confronted and challenged with the truth in love, and find satisfaction for their souls.

The Evangelical Pastor and Missionary's Response

There needs to be a deliberate shift in focus from the reached 1 percent to the unreached 99 percent. Conservative, evangelical theology needs to be put on wheels to roll into charismatic and syncretistic churches. If a missionary in Africa is not consistently interacting with pastors who make him uncomfortable because of those pastors' theological stances, then he has yet to encounter the real context in which he ministers. For example, the Zion Christian

Church (ZCC) is a syncretistic movement that appeals to African religious beliefs and is one of the largest Christian movements in Southern Africa, with about twelve million members. Yet many reformed or conservative pastors and missionaries in South Africa will never have a testimony of evangelizing a ZCC adherent.

Africa is not necessarily virgin ground where the gospel has not been preached, but rather is polluted ground where the false commercialized gospel has spread like wildfire and continues to be fanned into flames. Therefore, the mission field includes the charismatic and syncretistic church movements. Jesus likewise found Himself in a highly religious but deceived context and proceeded to train twelve men to proclaim the gospel into that context. The evangelical pastor and missionary should likewise seek to evangelize leaders of these charismatic and syncretistic movements and then train them, who would in turn cause a ripple effect across the continent. Given the extensive networks and followings of such movements, these leaders could reach thousands and some millions. Therefore, shifting focus to engaging these individuals and their denominations may help meet the challenge of having only a few laborers for a potentially great harvest.

If we do not reckon with and embrace this challenge, then we must contend with another reality, the indictment that after all the missionary efforts into South Africa over decades, we find ourselves here, where the government believes it can do a better job at reforming the church.

CHAPTER 12

One Gospel for All Contexts:
Paul's Cross-Cultural Communication

Chris Burnett

Should local churches in the Pacific Islands sing worship songs to Jesus the "Pig of God" as they read in their Bibles: "Behold, the Pig of God that takes away the sins of the world"? For decades, scholars have debated over contextual theologies of a "Pacific Jesus" in the Oceania region.[1] It is indeed critical to ask whether the search for a "Pacific Jesus" misrepresents the historical, biblical Jesus and whether the worship of the true Jesus by Pacific Island believers falls short. Many missionaries and church leaders face the temptation to alter the content of Scripture to incorporate aspects of the target culture that

are considered significant or valuable from the perspective of a reader's life experiences, as seemingly benign as a change of animal, like from a Palestinian lamb to a Melanesian pig. Some assume that if the missionary and Bible translator cannot overcome the foreignness of biblical terms and concepts by someone from a different cultural context and worldview than theirs, then the importance of the message might be lost.[2] Consequently, attempts are made to limit the perceived obstacle of foreignness. Yet missionaries and church leaders who encourage local people to read their local context into the text of Scripture

---

1. See the corpus of biblical critique by Melanesian theologian Ma'Afu Palu, including Ma'Afu'a Tu'itonga Palu, "Pacific Theology," *Pacific Journal of Theology* 2, no. 28 (2002): 21–53. For more recent documentation and discussion that seems to support such contextual theologies in Oceania, see Matt Tomlinson, *God Is Samoan: Dialogues between Culture and Theology in the Pacific* (Honolulu: University of Hawaii, 2020), 84–87.

2. This is the proposal of the Sapir-Whorf hypothesis for linguistic and cultural relativism, well represented in the volume by Benjamin Lee Whorf, *Language, Thought, and Reality: Selected Writings of Benjamin Lee Whorf*, ed. John B. Carroll, Stephen C. Levinson, and Penny Lee, 2nd ed. (Cambridge, MA: MIT Press, 2012). Some missiologists who support the proposal include Randolph E. Richards and Brandon J. O'Brien, *Misreading Scripture with Western Eyes: Removing Cultural Blinders to Better Understand the Bible* (Downers Grove, IL: InterVarsity, 2012), 70–90; Boubakar Sanou, "Exegeting the Bible and the Social Location of the Gospel Recipients: A Case for Worldview Transformation," *Andrews University Seminary Studies* 57, no. 2 (2020): 375, 379. See the well-reasoned rejection by evangelical scholar Karen H. Jobes, "Relevance Theory and the Translation of Scripture," *JETS* 50, no. 4 (December 2007): 775–76.

should ask whether altering the terms and concepts of the Word of God is necessary or profitable for facilitating faith and discipling believers to biblical literacy and theological maturity.

"Cultural engagement" represents a range of activities concerning a missionary's identification with his hearers in order to deliver the gospel to new audiences, and "cross-cultural communication" is central and paramount to those activities. The goal of cultural engagement in missions is to communicate the Word so that local people might understand and respond in faith. Therefore, the proclamation ministries of the missionary—preaching, teaching, and Bible translation—must be done cross-culturally in a way that does not accommodate false worldviews or dilute the Word's objective meaning.

This chapter will first analyze three passages from Paul's letters (Rom 10:8–17; 1 Cor 1–2; 2 Cor 2:12–17) to delineate Pauline principles for cross-cultural communication. It will then consider two examples of evangelism from the apostle Paul's missionary journeys, in Lystra (Acts 14:8–20) and in Athens (Acts 17), which provide insights into the kind of cross-cultural communication that the missionary should attempt when bringing the gospel to new audiences.

Paul's Principles for Cross-Cultural Communication

The following New Testament selections, Romans 10:8–17; 1 Corinthians 1–2; and 2 Corinthians 2:12–17, offer principles to help missionaries in every age to proclaim the truths of the Bible like Paul did. They are useful reminders not to attempt to steer the inclinations of the audience through terms and concepts that might be more agreeable with their pagan worldview and beliefs.

The Missionary Must Preach for People to Believe (Rom 10:8–17)

Romans 10:8–17 instructs that the proclamation of Scripture is God's means of granting saving faith. The passage presents a chain argument that connects saving faith to gospel proclamation. There is an inextricable link between the preaching of "the word of faith" (v. 8), and righteousness and salvation by faith (vv. 9–10) to "whoever calls on the name of the Lord" (v. 13). For Paul, salvation depends on the listener's adherence to the doctrines that the apostles teach about righteousness in Christ. Whoever publicly confesses Jesus Christ, once he has believed the facts of the gospel in his heart, demonstrates that the word of faith is now a personal, transformative faith (vv. 9–10).[3]

Scripture affirms that the kind of faith that leads to the public declaration of Jesus' lordship is trustworthy because the Lord, who is generous to save all who believe, is Himself trustworthy (Rom 10:11–13). Confessing the name of Jesus comes when the sinner completely trusts in Him for righteousness, a righteousness he has heard about from a preacher (v. 14).[4]

---

3. Thomas R. Schreiner, *Romans*, BECNT (Grand Rapids: Baker, 1998), 560.
4. Robert H. Mounce, *Romans*, NAC 27 (Nashville: Broadman and Holman, 1995), 211.

Gospel proclamation is therefore paramount for cross-cultural missionary activity, so that the good news of salvation, which is the "word of Christ," will go "into all the earth . . . to the ends of the world," to be heard and believed by faith (vv. 15–18).

Since "faith comes from hearing" the Word of Christ (Rom 10:17), the words of Scripture must be held as true, and the message of those words must be delivered verbally (1 Cor 11:23; 15:1, 3; Gal 1:9, 12; Phil 4:9). The sinner must hear the message, understand it, and respond by faith in order to be in the true faith. The Spirit will utilize the preaching and teaching of the biblical content of the Scripture as the means to save all whom He is calling (Rom 10:10). Therefore, Romans 10:8–17 asserts that the missionary must preach for people to believe.

Those Being Saved Find Scripture Culturally Relevant (1 Cor 1–2)

In 1 Corinthians 1–2, Paul explains to the Corinthians the power of the gospel to break through the spiritual limitations of a Christless culture and transform the sinner into a disciple of the Lord. Spiritual fellowship is "in every place" where sinners are saved and sanctified by the Lord Jesus Christ, according to the will of God (1:1–2).[5] No matter the context or the culture, Paul made it his goal to keep the propositions of the gospel and theology clear and free from manipulative techniques (1:17).[6] Through the gospel the Corinthians were given grace from the triune God (1:3–4), by which the Spirit allowed them to develop manifold spiritual gifts "in all word and all knowledge" (1:5–7).[7] As a result of receiving the straightforward propositions of Scripture from Paul, the believers themselves received gifts of speech and knowledge. The missionary's faithfulness to the Great Commission led to the equipping of the saints for Great Commission service to new hearers.

In 1 Corinthians 1:17–2:16, Paul instructed that a gospel of straightforward truths is not simplistic, even though the message of the cross appears as foolish to the learned Gentiles (1:17–18, 21–23). When God reveals Christ to those whom He calls to salvation, He reveals His power and wisdom (1:24–31). Paul's learning surpassed that of the philosophers.[8] Yet he strategically opposed any rhetorical method that could lead listeners to think that his gospel proclamation was simply worldly wisdom akin to that which they heard from pagan rhetors (2:1–5).[9] True wisdom rises from the text of Scripture, and by its very words, worldly wisdom is spiritually discerned to be foolishness (1:19–21). Only the knowledge of the Word of God gives access to spiritual salvation and, with it, a true spiritual appraisal of what is wise and foolish in God's eyes (1:21). Through the

---

5. Mark Taylor, *1 Corinthians*, NAC 28 (Nashville: B&H, 2014), 35–36.

6. Taylor, 43.

7. So understood by David E. Garland, *1 Corinthians*, BECNT (Grand Rapids: Baker Academic, 2003), 33–34.

8. Craig S. Keener, *Acts: An Exegetical Commentary*, vol. 2, *3:1–14:28* (Grand Rapids: Baker Academic, 2013), 41–42.

9. Garland, *1 Corinthians*, 33.

Spirit's power, true spiritual wisdom flows from the preacher to the listener (2:4) and persuades the listener to believe and so by faith be saved (2:5; cf. 1:17).[10] Therefore, the persuasion that saves is not the art of man but the work of the Spirit.

Paul nevertheless did not denigrate his own preaching as actual foolishness. To the contrary, he considered his message to be wisdom—a timeless, divine wisdom that is transmitted verbally and received by all who are enabled by the Spirit to receive it (1 Cor 2:6–9). The one who proclaims the message of Scripture must himself accept the entirety of the Word as having been revealed by God through His Spirit (2:10). Furthermore, the preacher must be confident, like Paul, that the "things" that "God has prepared for those who love Him" (2:9) are revelations of His perfect plan of redemption (2:7).[11] Such revelations emanate from the deep thoughts of God and are delivered by the Spirit (2:10–12). The Spirit has communicated in humanly understandable words the revelations that God has chosen to give freely to believers (2:12). The role of the missionary is therefore to proclaim what the Spirit has disposed, proclaiming it with full conviction of its message and its effectiveness to save sinners, so that those prepared by God to receive His words will be enriched by their wisdom (2:13).

Once Paul has clarified the divine origin of the message that the preacher must proclaim, he returns to the matter of audience reception (1 Cor 2:14). In his natural, unregenerate state, the hearer will not be able to accept or understand the words of Scripture as coming from God (2:14) unless he is divinely granted a spiritual nature.[12] With a regenerated soul, though, the believer has access to all learning in the text of Scripture. This is because the biblical writers were given the "mind of Christ," so that by the Holy Spirit all the hidden wisdom of God has been revealed (2:15–16; cf. 2:4, 7).[13]

In the moment of proclaiming and receiving the Word of God, the Spirit will actively transform the sinner to accept and understand what he formerly considered foolish from his cultural vantage point (1 Cor 2:14). He has been transformed into a disciple who receives his instruction from Christ (2:16). Therefore, the missionary who makes it his goal to deliver the message of Scripture to a target audience is conscious that he, like Paul, is sent by God to proclaim what has been divinely revealed, and he must trust that God will use it in the soul of the listener who is being divinely enlightened according to the will of God.

First Corinthians 1 and 2 clarify that the Word will do the work by the power of the Holy Spirit, not by any rhetorical contrivance. Cultural accommodation strategies that attempt to add artificial significance to the

---

10. Roy E. Ciampa and Brian S. Rosner, *The First Letter to the Corinthians*, PNTC (Grand Rapids: Eerdmans, 2010), 118.

11. Taylor, *1 Corinthians*, 91.

12. Garland, *1 Corinthians*, 100–101.

13. Walter C. Kaiser Jr., "A Neglected Text in Bibliology Discussions: 1 Corinthians 2:6–16," *WTJ* 43 no. 2 (Spring 1981): 315, 319.

Word of God are of no benefit to the missionary, the audience, or God. Only those being saved find Scripture culturally relevant.

God Empowers Faithful Preaching for Salvation (2 Cor 2:12–17)

Second Corinthians 2:12–17 serves as a primary example of the divine empowerment that Christ promised in Matthew 28:20 to undergird the activity of biblical proclamation and lead sinners to salvation. The specific phrases and descriptions in the passage reveal three steps Paul was empowered to do to make disciples among the Gentiles in Troas and Macedonia.

First, evangelism was Paul's initial step in fulfilling the Great Commission in a new region (in Acts 4:3–4; cf. Rom 10:14–15). He described God's favor on his efforts in Troas with a passive construction: "a door was opened" for him "in the Lord" (2 Cor 2:12).[14] Through this open door, the apostle expressed thankfulness that here, as in "every place," God "always leads [him] in triumphal procession in Christ" so that the knowledge of Christ will diffuse like an aroma (v. 14). Paul was confident that the open door he sought would, by divine favor, lead to the positive reception of the gospel by those who found his biblical message to be "an aroma from life to life" (v. 16). This perception proved that they were being saved unto spiritual life, given that "those who are perishing" instead sense "an aroma from death to death" (vv. 15–16).

Second, Paul employed a straightforward evangelistic strategy: he spoke "as from sincerity" (2 Cor 2:17). He proclaimed the truth he had received, which is the Word that is "as from God" (v. 17). Paul believed that the successful, triumphal march of his evangelistic activities depended on proclaiming God's Word (v. 14). Though he did not recount the particular aspects of his cross-cultural preaching and teaching activities in the region, his triumphant proclamation stood in contrast to that of the false teachers, who were "peddling the word of God" (v. 17). He was not like other so-called evangelists who tried to trick their audience into believing a culturally accommodated message for a price.[15]

Third, Paul's evangelistic strategy was to preach "in Christ" and "in the sight of God" (2 Cor 2:17). He operated with the understanding that God would grant to the spiritually darkened sinners "the Light of the knowledge of the glory of God in the face of Christ" (4:6). He was conscious of conducting his cross-cultural activities on the authority of Christ, with the words of Christ, and in the favorable presence of the Trinity (4:2; 12:19; 13:3). Paul exhibited humility in his ministry, asking, "Who is sufficient for these things?" (2:16). He was humbled to consider that the "open door" to gospel proclamation would result in spiritual eyes being divinely opened to all who believe (4:3–6), where spiritually dead sinners become disciples of Christ who are being sanctified by God's good hand.

To Paul, the opening of the door referred

---

14. Cf. "ἀνοίγω," BDAG, 84.
15. "καπηλεύω," BDAG, 508.

to the divine enablement to proclaim the gospel with the promise that the Holy Spirit would use it to save sinners by His sovereign choice. Simply put, God empowers faithful preaching for salvation. The missionary today can be confident that God will use the straightforward preaching and teaching of the Scriptures to call sinners to repent and believe what they have heard (Acts 12:24; Rom 1:16; 1 Cor 1:18; 1 Thess 2:13). Missionaries need to be convinced like Paul that the Word of God is the key to propagating the biblical faith, as new believers, from the moment of their salvation, participate in God's saving grace "spreading to more and more people" (2 Cor 4:15).

Examples of Paul's Cross-Cultural Communication

Two examples of Paul's cross-cultural communication with pagan idolaters are particularly instructive. The focus of the engagement in the passages is evangelistic and, subsequently, local church elders were established to ensure the new converts' ongoing transformation.

Paul's Proclamation in Lystra (Acts 14:8–20)

The preaching ministry of Paul and Barnabas to the Lycaonians in Acts 14:8–20 captures the first recorded speech to an entirely pagan Gentile audience with no prior knowledge of biblical truth. The Lycaonians most likely represented a primitive, uneducated population that had little interaction with or influence from either Greek philosophy or Jewish literature but instead practiced the local mystery religion.[16] Thus, evangelizing the people would require laying a new and seemingly foreign foundation for spiritual truth, from a source of authority of which they had no prior exposure.

After Paul had performed a miracle that caused the Lycaonians to think he and Barnabas were gods (Acts 14:8–14), Paul preached a gospel message to the Lycaonians with four main points. First, he reminded his audience of their shared humanity—he and Barnabas preached the gospel as men like them, not as the gods the pagans supposed them to be (v. 15). Second, Paul called them to repent from their idolatrous worship and instead believe in the living God (v. 15). Third, Paul informed them about the person and work of God the living Creator, using terms derived from the Hebrew Scriptures (v. 15).[17] Finally, Paul described the patient provision of the one true God, who extends common kindness by providing all that is necessary for their satisfaction in life, since He is both the living Creator and the gracious Sustainer (v. 17).

The proclamation of the gospel in Paul's sermon is confrontational, with deliberate urgency—the words utilized by him are those gospel truths that directly refuted and demolished the

---

16. Dean Flemming, *Contextualization in the New Testament: Patterns for Theology and Mission* (Downers Grove, IL: InterVarsity, 2005), 67; David G. Peterson, *The Acts of the Apostles*, PNTC (Grand Rapids: Eerdmans, 2009), 406.

17. Exod 20:11 (LXX); Ps 146:6 (LXX). So recognized in F. F. Bruce, *The Defense of the Gospel in the New Testament*, rev. ed. (Leicester, UK: Inter-Varsity, 1977), 38; also considered "echoes" of Scripture in Flemming, *Contextualization in the New Testament*, 69; conceded as possible references in Marion L. Soards, *The Speeches in Acts: Their Content, Context, and Concerns* (Louisville, KY: Westminster John Knox, 1994), 89.

Lycaonians' worldviews and practices. In addition, Paul's sermon was a confrontational application of the gospel preached earlier (Acts 14:6–7). Though life-threatening persecution ensued (vv. 18–19), the gospel proclamation in Lystra was effective, for disciples were made and local churches with elders were established (vv. 20–23).

Paul's Proclamation in Athens (Acts 17)[18]

Acts 17 describes Paul's itinerant mission through Macedonia (vv. 1–14) and Athens to the south (vv. 15–34). Greco-Roman cult practices littered the regions, and Judaism was also present in Macedonia.[19] In Athens the citizens held high regard for novel, intellectual presentations (v. 21), which facilitated Paul's open-air evangelism. Yet, given the proliferation of idolatrous imagery in Athens, Paul became "provoked" with a mix of anger and desire for the conversion of the people (v. 16),[20] among whom were the Stoics, the Epicureans, and the Skeptics. Because Paul's worldview and propositions shared no doctrinal affiliation with the intellectual cohorts, the Athenian philosophers saw Paul as bringing "strange things" that did not make sense to them (vv. 20–21). To his audience, the apostle was regarded as no more than a "babbler," a scavenger of philosophical scraps with an oddly cobbled worldview.[21]

The philosophers brought Paul up to the Areopagus, the cultural center of Athens that valued roundtable dialogue above all, and he had one opportunity to proclaim the gospel to the religiously pluralistic audience. Paul's message and doctrines, which he delivered as the "preacher" or "proclaimer" (Acts:17:18), would not have differed from the regular messages that he consistently proclaimed up till then (Acts 13:5; 15:36; 16:14; 17:13). Indeed, He proclaimed the knowability of the Creator (v. 24), His active, providential relationship to His creation both universally and personally (vv. 24–28), and His patience toward the ignorant idolaters (vv. 29–30).

Paul's speech contradicted every belief system of the Areopagites and would have been cause for offense. However, he did not shy away from drawing upon the incompatible nature of the gospel with their pagan worldviews nor from delivering a divine warning that required immediate action: "God is now commanding men that everyone everywhere should repent, because He has fixed a day in which He will judge the world in righteousness through a Man whom He determined" (Acts 17:30–31).

Paul's gospel message to the Athenians was indeed offensive to some of his hearers, because by the end of it they mocked him (Acts 17:32; cf. 2:13). Yet, in this pagan context, Paul modeled biblical cross-cultural communication in three steps worth following in any foreign

---

18. Portions of this section are adapted and expanded from Chris Burnett, "How Would Paul Engage Today's Secularizing Society? An Exegetical Revisiting of Acts 17," *MSJ* 30, no. 1 (Spring 2019): 147–67. Used by permission.

19. Markus Bockmuehl, *The Epistle to the Philippians* (London: A&C Black, 2006), 7–14.

20. "παροξύνω," BDAG, 780. Cf. Acts 15:39; LXX usage: Deuteronomy 9:18; Psalm 106:29; Isaiah 65:3; Hosea 8:5.

21. "σπερμολόγος," BDAG, 937; John B. Polhill, *Acts*, NAC (Nashville: Broadman, 1992), 367.

context. First, he observed the local culture to find points of contact for interaction.[22] These included their philosophies, worldviews, literature, beliefs, and religious symbols (vv. 16, 23, 28). Second, he addressed the audience in a winsome way, utilizing a rhetorical element of respect,[23] acknowledging their fervor, however misguided it actually was (vv. 22–23). It is important to recognize that neither Paul's cultural observations nor his introductory comments constituted the proclamation of a gospel message but were designed to draw the attention of the hearer for the message that followed. Third, Paul proclaimed the gospel with assertive force. His message left no room for pluralism or relativism, but he confrontationally applied biblical language and concepts with the pronouncement of judgment for all who would not repent (vv. 30–31). Though some listeners mocked Paul, some believed his message and were saved (v. 34). As Paul departed, the new believers left their idolatry behind, joined Paul, and followed Christ.

Conclusions about Paul's Cross-Cultural Communication

The principles and examples of biblical cross-cultural communication by Paul affirm that the missionary's greatest tool for reaching the people of new and disparate cultures is the Bible in his hands. All who engage today in preaching and teaching activities should follow Paul and "do the work of an evangelist" (2 Tim 4:5), trusting in the Holy Spirit to facilitate the message of His Word in the heart and mind of the hearer. Paul's direct evangelistic speeches to pagans were confrontational and decisive—a fitting indictment of the audience of their sin and a refutation of their predominant pagan worldviews. The straightforward words and concepts of the gospel, expressed in a linguistically understandable way with assertive force, are the Holy Spirit's weapons to disrupt all that is false in the belief system of the audience. Yet preaching reveals the life-giving truth by which sinners can be saved, and so it is as beautifully inspiring to those being saved as it is offensively putrid to those still dead in their sins. By committing to faithfully follow the example of the apostle Paul, the missionary already marches triumphantly in ministry and, if God desires, will see many sinners sanctified "in every place" (1 Cor 1:2).

As to evangelistic strategy, then, sinners need to hear that God commands them to repent or face eternal judgment (Acts 17:30–31). The Holy Spirit will be pleased to use the message as He sees fit, to transform the souls of those whom He draws to Christ and to expand His glory where He has not yet been made

---

22. For the term "points of contact," see F. F. Bruce, *The Defense of the Gospel in the New Testament*, rev. ed. (Leicester, UK: InterVarsity, 1977), 41, 48.

23. For treatments of the often-misunderstood rhetorical element, see Francis P. Donnelly, "A Function of the Classical Exordium," *The Classical Weekly* 5, no. 26 (May 11, 1912): 204–7; P. Amedeo Cracco, *La "Captatio Benevolentiae" nella Evangelizzazione dei Gentili* (Roma: Centro Nazionale di Propaganda Missionaria Francescana, 1951); Craig S. Keener, *Acts: An Exegetical Commentary. Volume 3: 15:1–23:35* (Grand Rapids: Baker Academic, 2014), 2626–29. So recognized in Flemming, *Contextualization in the New Testament*, 75; Ben Witherington III, *The Acts of the Apostles: A Socio-Rhetorical Commentary* (Grand Rapids; Carlisle: Eerdmans; Paternoster, 1998), 518.

known. When believers faithfully preach and teach the reality of sin and the offer of forgiveness, God's strategy becomes manifest, for He directly and actively communicates His power to save sinners at the perfect time and in the perfect way (Rom 10:17; Jas 1:21; 2 Pet 1:4).

Therefore, knowing the biblical content of the gospel message and being able to communicate the foundational doctrines that "are able to make [one] wise unto salvation" (2 Tim 3:15) is the most effective outreach strategy a missionary could ever develop. One gospel is sufficient to reach the lost in any place at any time. The divinely revealed Word of God, which "stands firm in heaven" (Ps 119:89), is exactly what local people need to join in eternal praise, where they will forever proclaim, "Worthy is the Lamb that was slain to receive power and riches and wisdom and strength and honor and glory and blessing" (Rev 5:12).

INSERT 12.1

Birth of a Church: The Taliabo of Southeast Asia

Stephen Lonetti

Scattered among the rainforests of the Indonesian archipelago live hundreds of unreached tribes, each possessing a unique language and lifestyle. Hidden away and often small in number, Indonesia's indigenous peoples have been largely forgotten by both the world and the church. But God has not forgotten them, for He has sent and continues to send heralds of His Word into the darkest places.

Such was the case when God sent two young families—mine and one other—to a primitive tribal village on Taliabo Island to begin a thirteen-year pioneer church-planting mission. During the first difficult years, as we struggled to learn an unwritten language, God planted a growing affection between us and the people we came to serve. The Taliabo loved us by building our homes and bringing us food. We loved them by caring for their sick and dying. Lacking the ability to speak, this became our means to reflect the love of Christ.

The Taliabo had no knowledge of the God of the Bible, nor had they heard the name of Jesus Christ. Centuries of spiritual darkness had enslaved them through bondage to demonic appeasement, sorcery, and an overwhelming fear of death. In the words of an old grandfather:

> We had heard from the old stories that there was a river of life. Whoever found that river and drank from it would live forever. We searched and searched, but no one found it. So, eternal life was lost, and we died. We feared death. It was our greatest fear. We groped in darkness, like blind men, looking for a way to escape. For this reason, we called out to the spirits. We used black medicines of all kinds to guard our bodies, so that we would not die. But when we least expected it, death would swoop down and carry us away.

Hebrews 2:14–15 teaches that it was Christ's death that would "render powerless him who had the power of death, that is, the devil, and might free those who through fear of death were subject to slavery all their lives." The Taliabo's fear of death had prepared them for the gospel of grace.

After four years of language study, the responsibility to clearly communicate the gospel hit home. Scripture would be spoken for the first time in the Taliabo language, and we were concerned that its message would be misunderstood or mixed with their animistic beliefs. The Taliabo had to be taught foundational truth, so that the gospel would make sense to them.

Beginning in Genesis, we invested six months in teaching through Old Testament narratives with redemptive themes from creation to Christ, each showing God in life-related action.[24] We knew we had gotten through to the Taliabo when they identified themselves with those left outside the ark, for example, or when they began calling their two villages Sodom and Gomorrah. Every minute spent laying Old Testament groundwork was worth the effort. In the end, Scripture alone convinced them of their sin and need for deliverance.

As we taught through the Gospels the Taliabo were introduced to Jesus Christ and loved Him from the start. The grandfather continued:

> So, God had come to live with us men, as a man. I'll never forget the story of John the Baptist as he pointed at Jesus and said, "Look, the Lamb of God that takes away the sin of the world." When I heard that, I thought, "The lamb! The Passover lamb! The sacrificial lamb!" My mind opened! It had to be: this Jesus is the Promised One. It would be Jesus who would deliver us from sin.

---

24. For an excellent example of redemptive narratives used for evangelism, see "The Chronicles of Redemption," available through lifegateworldwide.org.

The teaching climaxed with the crucifixion and resurrection of Jesus. Finally, an audience of several hundred Taliabo men and women heard the gospel proclaimed in their own language. Then God put His amazing saving power on display and moved Taliabo souls from darkness into light (Acts 26:18; 2 Cor 4:6; 1 Pet 2:9). In the words of a former shaman:

You taught and taught, and I thought and thought. I was confused, and I said, "If this Promised One is dead, who is there left to save us?" Then I heard that death could not hold him. I cried, "Jesus is alive to rescue us. Thank you, thank you, God! Jesus has paid my sin debt."

The grandfather recounted:

For a long time we had looked for power so we would not die. That way of living bound us. We did not find life. Our ancestors were deceived, greatly deceived in this. We lived on this island like people in a black room. There was not one light to be found. We sat alone in the darkness—and then you came. We said, "Those two have a light!"

And so my heart pulled me. I wanted to hurry and hear the story. I wanted it.

I cried for this story like a child cries for food. I listened and said, "Now I know. Oh, the wall of death, the wall that stands between us and God, Jesus has torn down."

When I think back on our old ways, I repent. I regret what we did, because we worshiped vain things. Then I had no way out, but now I'm on the path. Now dying doesn't frighten me because I finally understand why we live and why we die. I know now, because of these words you brought. Otherwise, there's no way I would have known about living, dying, or this journey we are on. You brought the words—and the words gave us life.

Hundreds of Taliabo came to saving faith in Christ over the following months. Believers were discipled and taught through the New Testament. Indigenous leadership was ordained and, twelve years after arriving, the missionaries moved off site. Today, decades later, the Taliabo church remains strong, manifesting the fruit of genuine salvation and reproducing themselves on their island and beyond.

The moving testimony of the Taliabo has been video documented.[25] But the story of the grace granted to them recurs over and over throughout the world, as God calls out "a people for His name" (Acts 15:14). Truly,

---

25. *The Taliabo Story*, written by Mary and Stephen Lonetti, directed by John R. Cross (New Tribes Mission, 1997); *Delivered from the Power of Darkness*, written by Mary and Stephen Lonetti, directed by John R. Cross (New Tribes Mission, 1997).

there is no greater privilege or joy than to share in gospel ministry and the advance of Christ's church. For us and for the beloved Taliabo, all glory be to God.

INSERT 12.2

Evangelizing in the Shadow of the Vatican

Massimo Mollica

The title "graveyard of missionaries" has been applied to various countries, but perhaps none more frequently than the nation of Italy.[26] A tiny fraction of Italians are evangelical Christians, while Roman Catholicism dominates the landscape. The seeming impossibility of lasting gospel fruit in a people plagued by their idolatrous religion leads many missionaries to return to their sending country after one term on the field. Those who minister under the ubiquitous pressures of Italian Roman Catholicism are keenly aware of the patience required to see one person come to Christ in saving faith. It is not uncommon to hear stories of missionaries in the shadow of the Vatican who labor five to ten years for one convert. There are three major barriers to evangelism in Italy that stem from the influence of the Vatican: Roman Catholic heritage, Roman Catholic assumptions, and Roman Catholic modernization.

Roman Catholic Heritage

The unique role of the Roman Catholic Church due to the Vatican's location in Rome gives Italy a Roman Catholic heritage that hinders the gospel to this day. Considering another "form" of Christianity is unsettling for a Roman Catholic; to them the Roman Catholic Church is the historic church, and to be Italian is to be at least nominally Roman Catholic. The Roman Catholic heritage creates the social fabric in which most Italians live from cradle to grave. Most family gatherings and life events

---

26. Jason Manryk, *Operation World: The Definitive Prayer Guide to Every Nation*, 7th ed. (Colorado Springs, CO: Biblica, 2010), 485.

center around Roman Catholic events, holidays, and sacraments, including baptism at birth, first communion and confirmation in childhood, weddings in adulthood, and last rites and funerals at death. Conversion out of Roman Catholicism is often seen socially as a denial of Italian identity and a full betrayal of family, friends, and society.

The Reformation backlash by Roman Catholic authorities, in which the true gospel was anathematized, continues to impact how evangelicals are viewed and treated in Italy. Protestants continue to be stigmatized as heretics, which reinforces the social barriers to the gospel that were constructed long ago. Despite freedom of religion in contemporary Italy, many Italians instinctively reject the full dignity of any faith other than Roman Catholicism. Evangelicals therefore are often considered members of cults.

Roman Catholic Assumptions

Italy's Roman Catholic heritage is the cause of the second major barrier to evangelism in Italy: Roman Catholic assumptions. Italians trapped in the Vatican system of thought and practice view Christianity, the Bible, the gospel, and the church within the framework of Roman Catholicism. This means that they generally assume the pope is head of the church, that the Bible is not for personal reading, that they themselves are inherently good people, that they should participate in the sacrifices of the Mass, and that they

should venerate Mary and the saints in their heart and in practice. Although belief and adherence can vary regionally and generationally, basic gospel truths get confused with Roman Catholic dogmas, which further complicates the advancement of gospel ministry.

Effective evangelistic dialogue with a Roman Catholic requires careful definition of various terms like *sin, salvation, Jesus, justification, sanctification, baptism, conversion,* and *prayer*. One effective method is for the evangelist to explain how the Roman Catholic Church arrived at its official teachings today and how their teachings diverge from biblical and historical Christianity. Leveraging shared history prior to the Reformation reduces the barriers created by Roman Catholic assumptions.

Roman Catholic Modernization

The modernization of the Roman Catholic Church presents a third barrier to evangelism in Italy. While Italians are proud of their Roman Catholic heritage and hold dogmatic views innately, the Roman Catholic Church broadened its interests in religious ecumenism. The Second Vatican Council (1962–1965) led many Italians to assume that there is no meaningful difference between Roman Catholic and evangelical Christianity, even though many would still consider evangelicals to somehow be heretics. This minimization of differences over foundational gospel truths creates further confusion and can lead to a general disinterest by many to understand their own faith system or the beliefs of others, like evangelicals. In a positive way, ecumenism has reduced some social barriers, for example, by allowing personal Bible reading among the laity, which has opened doors for evangelicals to read from the Scriptures with their contacts. Moreover, any opportunity to dialogue about truth is profitable for evangelism, especially if people show interest in interacting about faith and theology.

Negatively, however, the modernization of the Roman Catholic Church has not successfully resisted the secularization of Italian culture, especially with regard to the education of young people. For decades, Italians have grown up with both a religious and secular education, relegating religious beliefs to the realm of "culture" or "faith" and philosophical or scientific beliefs to the realm of "reality." For example, school-aged children are taught that God created the world and that Adam and Eve sinned in the garden of Eden during religion class, but that man is the result of millions of years of evolutionary processes in their history and science classes. The Bible is taught to be mythical in the face of scientific theory. For many, this creates a great dissonance between faith and theology on one hand and the perception of reality on the other.

In conversation with evangelicals, the barrier to accepting the truth of Scripture is massive, because the Italian may not see a gospel conversation as a conversation about reality.

Roman Catholic Evangelism in Italy

Considering the many obstacles to evangelizing Italians, one must give thought as to how to strategically spread the gospel. Most conversations about biblical truth will be met with resistance because of Roman Catholic heritage, confusion because of Roman Catholic assumptions, or indifference because of Roman Catholic modernization. These obstacles are deeply rooted and are further exacerbated by the sinful heart of the unregenerate person. This means that evangelism must be viewed more as a process than an event in a church or a onetime conversation. Various evangelistic events and literature distributions rarely produce any immediate fruit but are useful to give visibility to the evangelical faith within the community. This does not mean that events or onetime conversations are to be avoided, but rather that they should be used to create contact with people who might be ready to take the next step, like to attend an evangelical church or to have further dialogue about faith and theology or to read and study the Scriptures with an evangelical.

Evangelism requires gaining the trust of individuals. Sincere relationships with people in which the love of Christ is lived out goes a long way toward bringing down barriers, preconceptions, and the cultural stigma of being evangelical. The best way to arrive at the point of meaningful dialogue and interactive personal study is through relationships. Acquaintances often become friendships through hospitality in the home. Regularly inviting people to events can create an atmosphere of openness and participation.

The Vatican casts a long shadow that no evangelical believer or missionary in Italy can escape, given the Italian pride of identity, prejudice, and apathy. Yet far worse is the reality lived by unsaved Italians, because for them the shadow of the Vatican signifies a darkness from which they can never escape unless they are exposed to the powerful and living Word of God. Believers should pray that over time the Holy Spirit might draw more Italians out of the darkness of the Vatican's shadow through Scripture alone into the light of the full assurance of hope in Christ alone.

CHAPTER 13

Sharing the Gospel with Jewish Friends

Marty Wolf

The Lord Jesus Christ commands His followers to "make disciples of all the nations" (Matt 28:19). That includes the unreached 15.3 million Jewish people in the world today. "God has not rejected His people, has He?" asks the apostle Paul. His emphatic answer is, "May it never be!" (Rom 11:1). Because of their unbelief in Jesus the Messiah, Paul's heart was broken for his lost Jewish brothers (Rom 9:1–5). Yet he says, "At the present time, a remnant according to God's gracious choice has also come to be" (Rom 11:5). Thus, there is a remnant even today waiting to know the love of its Messiah, our Lord Jesus!

However, Christians find it hard to share the gospel with their Jewish friends. Many feel they do not know enough about what practicing Jews believe. Jewish people are not unique in their need to be won to Christ, but they must be won uniquely. That requires knowing how they understand Judaism and how they view Christianity. This chapter therefore summarizes key information regarding Jewish perceptions,

beliefs, misconceptions, denominations, and the "How to" of approaching Jewish people with the gospel in order for Christians to fulfill Jesus' command "to make disciples of all nations" and to reach their Jewish friends for Christ.

Jewish Perceptions and Misconceptions

When Jewish people think of Christianity, they think of persecution. They experienced persecution in and even prior to the Crusader period (1095–1291). The Spanish and Portuguese Inquisitions drove Jewish people from the Iberian Peninsula to Brazil and, in 1654, when inquisition expanded, many Jews fled to North America. The anti-Jewish pogroms in Russia beginning in 1821 also caused many Jews from central and eastern Europe to flee to North America. Worst of all, the persecution and murder of six million Jews in Europe during the Nazi Holocaust (1933–1945) is seen by many Jewish people as partly the fault of Christianity.

Conversely, modern Judaism is a unique religion because it does not even require one to believe in God. Those adherents who do claim belief in God do not all believe the same thing about God. Nor do they all observe the same rituals or customs. Yet some basic misconceptions about Jewish people should be corrected foremost:

- Not all Jewish people are rich.
- Not all Jewish people know their Bible, nor even have a copy of the Holy Scriptures.
- Not all Jewish people reject Jesus as Messiah; the first Christians were all Jewish.

Regrettably, Jewish people have also been called "Christ killers" and even worse. It should be remembered, however, that Jesus died for both Jews and Gentiles on the cross (Acts 2:23–24). It is because of the sins of both Jews and Gentiles (1 Cor 15:3)—those of every believer—that Jesus went to the cross!

Many Jewish people have one major misconception when it comes to religious affiliation: they are Jewish because they were born into a Jewish family. Likewise, non-Jews (Gentiles) born into a Gentile family are seen as automatically Christian. In other words, most Jewish people make no distinction between an unsaved Gentile and a born-again Christian, unless of course someone claims Hinduism or Islam.

Jewish Denominations

Within Judaism there are several denominations that differ in beliefs, observances, and practices. Within each denomination, groups have also adapted some variant beliefs. Below are the major groupings and their tenets.

Orthodox Judaism

Orthodox Jews believe that only the five books of Moses, the Torah, are divinely inspired.[1] However, the Talmud and its commentaries are the real basis of faith and practice. As Rabbi Adin Steinsaltz writes, "In many ways, the Talmud is the most important book in Jewish culture. . . . No other work has had a comparable influence on the theory and practice of Jewish life, shaping spiritual content and serving as a guide to conduct."[2] Orthodox Jews are zealous to preserve the traditions and rituals of "the Oral Law" (derived from the Mishnah and the Talmud, not the Scriptures). They consider themselves to be the true Judaism and view Messiah as a nationalistic redeemer-emancipator, not a spiritual one.

Reform Judaism

The Reform Judaism movement began in nineteenth-century Germany as an attempt to adapt Judaism to the demands of modern life. It abandons many traditional laws, rituals, and observances. For example, unlike the orthodox denomination's reserving of leadership in the synagogue to men only, Reform Judaism

---

1. The closest document to a catechism that Judaism has is "The Thirteen Articles of Faith." Article 6 affirms "faith that all the words of the prophets are true." However, for Orthodox Jews the Torah is in a category of its own.
2. Adin Steinsaltz, *The Essential Talmud*, 30th anniversary ed. (New York: Basic Books, 2006), 3.

ordained its first female rabbis beginning in 1972. It does not view the Holy Scriptures (Tanak) as the inspired Word of God but teaches an ethical monotheism. Belief in a personal Messiah is abandoned. Jesus is seen as a great teacher and reformer, somewhat similar to the view of modern liberal Protestantism.

Conservative Judaism

The conservative branch of Judaism developed in twentieth-century America, advocating for the existence of a "spiritual Jewish nation." Though not abandoning traditional liturgy and practices, it allows for modifications to them. The denomination tends to be a compromise between Orthodox and Reform branches. Thus, a synagogue may lean more toward one or the other, depending on its rabbi.

Sharing the Gospel with Jewish People

History confirms that as a people Jews have experienced hatred and persecution from Gentile nations, groups, and individuals for millennia. Even now we see anti-Semitism around the world. Therefore, when a Christian shows sincere love and interest in a Jewish person, he or she should not be surprised by a skeptical response. God will honor that Christian's persistent efforts. Some basic steps include the following:

- Developing a sincere friendship
- Expecting that friendship to be tested
- Sharing the spiritual blessings received from the Jews (the Bible, forgiveness of

sins, peace with God; John 4:22; Rom 5:1; 9:4–5; 11:18; 15:27)
- Knowing that most Jewish people come to Messiah through a loving Christian friend

With these basics in mind, below are also some practical ways to engage one's Jewish friends.

1. **Christians can extend an invitation to lunch or dinner.** Because their friend may have dietary restrictions, pork or shellfish, like shrimp, must be avoided. Then, if discussion warrants, they can share Scriptures such as Isaiah 53.
2. **Christians can attend a synagogue.** This can be done either with their friend or alone. If alone, they should call ahead and express their interest as a Christian in knowing about Jewish worship. They must not go to hand out tracts, but go as a guest. However, they should feel free to engage in conversation and to ask questions after the service. Note-taking, however, should not be done, since writing on the Sabbath is not allowed in synagogues.
3. **Christians can invite the friend to their church, especially if the pastor is speaking on an Old Testament passage.**

When sharing the gospel with Jewish people, Christians must also be sensitive to their language. They must avoid telling jokes about Jewish people. It is often helpful to use "Messiah Jesus" instead of "Christ," since Jews have been persecuted in the name of "Christ." Even "Christian" should be defined: one who is both a believer in and a follower of Jesus as Messiah. They must also explain that they were not born a Christian but became one when they repented and believed that Jesus' death, burial, and resurrection provided forgiveness for their personal sins (1 Cor 15:3–7). Biblical terms used in conversation must also be explained. Here are some probing questions to ask a Jewish friend:

- "Do you attend a local synagogue?" and then, "What branch is it?"
- "How do you observe the high holidays [New Year, Day of Atonement, and Sukkot]?"
- "If you believed in the Messiah, how would you recognize Him if He came?"
- "Do you know what the Jewish Scriptures say about the Messiah?"
- "Do you mind if I take a few minutes and show you what they say about Him?"
- "Can you think of any person in history who has fulfilled these prophecies?"

Here are some key messianic prophecies from the Old Testament to know:

- The Messiah's identity as the God-man—Isaiah 9:6
- The Messiah's birthplace in Bethlehem—Micah 5:2
- The Messiah's being scorned—Isaiah 53:3
- The Messiah's suffering and submission to it—Isaiah 53:4–9; Zechariah 12:10
- The Messiah's sacrifice for sin—Isaiah 53:10
- The Messiah's satisfaction—Isaiah 53:11–12

Christians should encourage their Jewish friends to read these and the Scriptures in general.

Conclusion

The Christian's Jewish friends may not be reading the Bible, but they are "reading" the Christian's attitudes and actions. Jesus' disciples must remember, then, that they are also His ambassadors (2 Cor 5:20). As such, they should be themselves, ask questions, share their testimonies. But most of all, they should pray for the Jewish people in their area, and encourage their church members to pray for those they know.[3]

---

3. For literature, tracts, videos, and other resources, visit the Friends of Israel Gospel Ministries website (www.foi.org).

The Importance of Israel and Jewish Evangelism

David Zadok

God is doing amazing work in Israel and among the Jewish people in the world. Our God is faithful to His promises, covenants, and His people. God, in His divine wisdom, determined to use the Jewish people as an instrument to showcase His grace and judgment. Through Abraham and his descendants, the triune God gave us the prophets and His Word. Through the seed of Abraham, He gave us the Messiah, the Lamb, who takes away the sin of the world (John 1:29). However, God's redemption of the Jewish people, the descendants of Jacob, did not end with the coming of Messiah and the completion of the canon of Scripture.

The apostle Paul, in his three crucial chapters of Romans 9–11, succinctly argues that God has not forsaken nor will He ever forsake His people Israel, and that one day "all Israel will be saved" (11:26). Paul, as a trained rabbi, builds his case by showing the sovereignty of God in all things, including His plan of salvation for the world. Church history teaches that there have always been Jewish people and even prominent rabbis who believed in Jesus as their Lord and Savior. However, in the last century, we have seen a shift as, once again, the church among the Jewish people has been reestablished, particularly since the establishment of the State of Israel in 1948. The God of history has paved the way through the work of restoration. Three particular restorations evidence God's hand of protection and deliverance for Israel, which will result in a very great salvation when Messiah returns to Jerusalem.

A Restored Language

The significance and influence of biblical Hebrew are evident from the days of the Reformation and in the work of Martin Luther in the German language. Even though I have ambivalent feelings toward him, particularly because of his later writings about the Jewish people, we cannot deny that his German translation of the Bible from Hebrew manuscripts not only called out the false teachings of Roman Catholicism but unified the German language from many dialects, effectively birthing the German people.[4] Later, in the nineteenth century, God again used biblical Hebrew and a Lithuanian Jew, Eliezer Ben Yehuda (1858–1922), to initiate and ignite the Jewish people's own restoration process.[5] Eventually, Modern Hebrew was developed using many of the Hebrew Bible words with new meanings. The restoration of Hebrew as a vernacular language has brought the Jewish people together.

A Restored Land

In 1948, some years after the consolidating of the Modern Hebrew language, God also restored the land of Israel, bringing back the Jews from the four corners of the world to its historical location of Canaan, promised to Abraham, Isaac, and Jacob and to their descendants. Though biblical prophecy sees ultimate restoration of the land at the return of Messiah (Isa 19:23–25; Zech 12:8), the presence of the people in the land today is a kind of restoration that gives hope for the future. The dual restoration of the language and the land paved the way for the restoration of the people with a fuller sense of their national identity. Paradoxically, through the ashes of Auschwitz and other death camps, God reestablished a state for the Jewish people—the Israelite people.

In recent years, Israel has been a significant contributor on the world stage through its innovations in many areas, including agriculture, medicine, water distillation, solar energy, security, and hi-tech business, becoming a "start-up" nation. Ironically, seventy-five years after its establishment as a state, Israel sold the Arrow 3 defense system to Germany, enabling the land from which the Holocaust arose to protect itself from exo-atmospheric threats like ballistic missiles.[6] The State of Israel, in many similar ways, is a light to the nations—but not yet spiritually. In God's timing, that will come as well.

A Restored Population

The significance of the restoration experienced in the last century is deeper than the language and the land. It is related to the very essence of the gospel and the church. Regathering the Jewish people into a small, confined piece of land, speaking one common language, has enabled the expeditious spread of the gospel. Without these two restorations, to evangelize the Jewish people

---

4. Roland H. Bainton, *Here I Stand: A Life of Martin Luther* (Peabody, MA: Hendrickson, 1950), 398–400; cf. Eric Metaxas, *Bonhoeffer: Pastor, Martyr, Prophet, Spy* (Nashville: Thomas Nelson, 2010), 20.

5. See Angel Sáenz-Badillos, "Modern Hebrew," in *A History of the Hebrew Language*, trans., J. Elwolde, 267–88 (Cambridge: Cambridge University Press, 1993).

6. Seth J. Frantzman, "Israel Finalizes Arrow 3 Deal with Germany, Aims for Late 2025 Delivery," Breaking Defense News, November 27, 2023, https://breakingdefense.com/2023/11/israel-finalizes-arrow-3-deal-with-germany-aims-for--late-2025-delivery/.

required reaching out to them in various countries and speaking innumerable local languages. However, God, in His great wisdom, gathered us into a tiny land and has caused us to speak the same, unified language, albeit with different accents. As a result, we can all understand the gospel as it is proclaimed throughout Israel by believers in Yeshua (Jesus).

To grasp the momentous work of God among the Jewish people in the last seven and a half decades, one needs to look at some statistics. Today, seventy-five years since the rebirth of the State of Israel, more Jewish people live in Israel than any other country, and in fact, the majority of the Jewish population worldwide lives in Israel. In 1948 the Jewish population of Israel was about 650,000.[7] On December 31, 2021, the Jewish population of Israel was approximately 7 million.[8] So, between 1948 and 2021 the Jewish population grew almost eleven times.

In terms of Jewish Christians, growth has also been significant. In 1948 there were a recorded 23 Jewish Christians in Israel, but today there are approximately 30,000 Jewish believers in the land.[9] What the statistics suggest is an amazing phenomenon: while the Jewish population in the land since 1948 has grown to eleven times larger, the number of messianic Jews has grown to more than 1,100 times larger. God is at work among the Jewish people in Israel and throughout the whole world. "For who has known the mind of the Lord, or who became His counselor?" (Rom 11:34).

A Call for a Restored Commitment to Jewish Evangelism

For almost two thousand years, the church either diminished or dismissed its call to evangelize the Jewish people. For many reasons, Jewish evangelism was not a prominent activity among the nations. Throughout history, the church seemed to reject its Jewish roots, ignoring the reality that Gentile faith was based on the Jewish Bible and the Jewish Messiah, going out from the Jewish people. It was only in the nineteenth century that small missionary organizations were established with the goal of reaching out to the Jews.[10] Yet believers of

---

7. State of Israel Central Bureau of Statistics, "On the Occasion of Holocaust Remembrance Day, 2023," April 16, 2023, https://www.cbs.gov.il/en/mediarelease/Pages/2023/On-the-Occasion-of-the-Holocaust-Day-2023.aspx.

8. State of Israel Central Bureau of Statistics, "Population of Israel on the Eve of 2022," December 30, 2021, https://www.cbs.gov.il/en/mediarelease/pages/2021/population-of-israel-on-the-eve-of-2022.aspx.

9. Joel Rosenberg, "Studies Reveal There Are Now 1 Million Followers of Jesus Worldwide of Jewish Descent," *All Israel News*, November 28, 2022, https://allisrael.com/studies-reveal-there-are-now-1-million-followers-of-jesus-worldwide-of-jewish-descent.

10. For example, the Anglican diocese founded in 1841 at Christ Church Jerusalem by the Messianic Jewish bishop Michael Solomon Alexander. See "The Enduring Legacy of Michael Solomon Alexander," January 21, 2022, https://

all time have the responsibility to evangelize the lost, which includes the Jewish people. In fact, the gospel is "the power of God for salvation to everyone who believes, to the Jew first and also to the Greek" (Rom 1:16).

God has not forgotten nor forsaken His covenant with Israel and His detailed promises that the prophets proclaimed. The apostle Paul wants us today to be sure that "For as many as are the promises of God, in Him they are yes" (2 Cor 1:20). Furthermore, "the gifts and the calling of God are irrevocable" (Rom 11:29). Yet, in His kindness, He uses people and means to accomplish the task of evangelizing the Jewish people. May the church in our times arise to evangelize the people who are "the apple of His eye" (Zech 2:8).

---

christchurchjerusalem.org/2022/01/the-enduring-legacy-of-michael-solomon-alexander/. See also the study by Erez Soref, "The Messianic Jewish Movement in Modern Israel," in *Israel, the Church, and the Middle East: A Biblical Response to the Current Conflict*, ed. Darrell L. Bock and Mitch Glaser (Grand Rapids: Kregel, 2018), 137–50—the findings of which are summarized in the web article "Findings of New Research on the Messianic Movement in Israel," One for Israel, n.d., accessed June 18, 2024, https://www.oneforisrael.org/bible-based-teaching-from-israel/findings-of-new-research-on-the-messianic-movement-in-israel/.

SECTION 2

THE HISTORY OF EVANGELISM

CHAPTER 14

Biblical Proclamation in Missions History:
A Concise Reference Guide

Chris Burnett

This concise reference guide for believers today highlights the most momentous periods, trends, and events of missionary activity throughout church history. "Missions history" is evaluated through the lens of proclamation ministry, namely, preaching and teaching, Bible translation, Christian literature publication, pastoral training, and theological education. Through this lens, the greatest attention is given to people and events in the early centuries of Christian expansion, since many of them epitomized the apostolic perspective and activities of biblical missions. The treatments of other periods are more synthetic, either because they were less punctuated by specific developments or because the developments coalesce between a vast range of theories and movements. Also, in some eras, there is little missions history to study, especially when the trend of the church was to eschew the Great Commission altogether.

In each era of Christianity, the activities of proclamation can be characterized as moving along a spectrum of cultural engagement in the direction of one of two poles. In missions history, the pole of "biblical proclamation," represents the activities of asserting the expressions and concepts of Scripture to nonbelievers and new believers. The opposite pole of "cultural accommodation" represents historic activities of cultural engagement that do not consider Scripture to be the primary, foundational means for evangelism and spiritual transformation. Depending on the historical era, missionary practices tend to be situated toward one or the other pole. A select bibliography for each section is footnoted.

The Subapostolic Age and the Early Patristic Period (AD 95–165)[1]

In the late first century the missionary practices of cultural engagement by believers were

---

1. Select bibliography: Michael W. Holmes, *The Apostolic Fathers: Greek Texts and English Translations*, 3rd ed. (Grand Rapids:

grounded in the gospel and accomplished in strict adherence to the Great Commission. Christian witness grew from Jerusalem to farther reaches as the Roman Empire expanded among a multitude of ethnic peoples, cultures, languages, philosophies, and religious beliefs. The expansion of the church into distant Roman territories was thus the activity of foreign missions, as many patristic sources demonstrate.

The earliest apostolic fathers, those of the subapostolic period (AD 70–110), directly succeeded the leadership of the twelve apostles. Their commitment to activities of biblical proclamation within the church served as the foundation on which the second-century fathers would develop cross-cultural methods of biblical proclamation. Writings from the subapostolic period include *1* and *2 Clement*. Both writings demonstrate the desire to impart scriptural teaching to the local congregations and instill a lifestyle of faith in adherence to Scripture. *First Clement* quotes directly and extensively from the Old Testament in order to persuade for peace in a season of great dissent in the Corinthian church. In *2 Clement*, the presbyter quotes directly from the Old and New Testaments, attesting to the authority of Scripture for transformative living. As men who held positions of ecclesial influence, they directly appealed to the authority of Scripture to shepherd God's people during turbulent times.

By mid-second century, persecution mounted against the Christians as the gospel became more prominent in the Roman Empire. The early apologists employed Scripture to evangelize their pagan audiences, to defend the Christian faith, to attack false religion, and to point their audience to true divine revelation. They quoted, echoed, and illustrated Scripture, and formulated theological tenets from the content of Scripture. The ethos and activities of biblical proclamation are observed in the following examples: *The Apology of Aristides* (ca. AD 125–133); *The Epistle to Diognetus* (ca. AD 150–225); *Martyrdom of Polycarp* (ca. AD 155–160); Theophilus of Antioch, *Apology to Autolycus*; and Irenaeus, *Against Heresies*. On the contrary, the apologetic writings of Justin Martyr (ca. AD 100–165) exemplify his desire to defend the faith by using the language and concepts of Greek philosophy (Middle Platonism and Stoicism) to make Christian concepts relevant to his audience.

In summary, the subapostolic fathers and most of the second-century apologists expressed their commitment to delivering the sufficient and authoritative Word of God to defend the Christian faith before their pagan audiences. Their missiological practices involved countering the central religious convictions of their recipients through varying degrees of biblical exposition. The tendency toward cultural accommodation with Greek philosophy, however, became more pronounced in the ethos and practice of the third-century fathers.

Baker Academic, 2007); William Varner, *The Apostolic Fathers: An Introduction and Translation* (London: T&T Clark, 2023); Nick R. Needham, *2000 Years of Christ's Power*, vol. 1., *The Age of the Early Church Fathers* (Fearn, Ross-shire, UK: Christian Focus, 2016).

Third-Century Fathers[2]

The apologists stand out as the key missionaries of the third century, although there is significant variation to their communication styles and methods. The method of biblical interpretation practiced in Alexandria, Egypt, like that of Antioch, had an evangelistic emphasis. Yet the Alexandrian method was compromised by the practice of Philo's nonliteral, multiple-meaning hermeneutic, leading to heavily allegorizing the text. Three proponents of cultural accommodation arise in this century, with one outlier.

Clement of Alexandria (ca. AD 150–215)

Clement of Alexandria was committed to Hellenistic interpretive methodologies and searched for common ground between Greek history and Christianity. He leveraged Greek (Stoic) phrasing, logic, and a Greek literary approach (in his *Stromata*) to represent Christ as the reasonable fulfillment of all human desire and virtue and to set the biblical God above all philosophy in the minds of those who might otherwise disregard Christian doctrine. Ultimately, his desire to win pagans to Christ through their own methods of reasoning and interpretation hampered his ability to accurately communicate theology to them.

Origen of Alexandria (AD 185–254)

Origen read Scripture for a Gnostic-type, spiritual meaning, which he believed to be in line with the practices of the apostles. His use of Stoic and Platonic language and concepts led him to present confused expressions of Trinitarian doctrine. Even though his theological formulations employed Scripture, his philosophically oriented allegorical reading of Scripture led to a largely ineffective, culturally accommodated theology.

Minucius Felix (ca. AD 210/230)

Minucius Felix's dialogue *Octavius* brought the cultural accommodation ideals and practices of the Alexandrians into the Latin-speaking world. His winsome evangelistic work followed a Greek dialectic form to demonstrate the superiority of Christianity to paganism and to call for personal belief. However, he engaged his audience from natural reason rather than from Scripture and argued for the authority of the Christian faith without using the authoritative propositions of Scripture. At best, his work possessed the quality of an evangelistic tract that could serve as a "pre-evangelistic" bridge from the pagan worldview toward the gospel, but it did not contain a gospel presentation.

---

2. Select bibliography: Wolfram Kinzig, "Apologists, Christian," in *The Oxford Classical Dictionary*, ed. Simon Hornblower and Antony J. S. Spawforth (Oxford: Oxford University Press, 1996), 128–29; C. Gordon Olson, *What in the World Is God Doing? The Essentials of Global Missions*, 7th ed., updated and rev. (Lynchburg, VA: Global Gospel, 2013); John Mark Terry, "The History of Missions in the Early Church," in *Missiology: An Introduction to the Foundations, History, and Strategies of World Missions*, ed. John Mark Terry, Ebbie Smith, and Justice Anderson (Nashville: Broadman and Holman, 1998), 171–74.

Tertullian (ca. AD 155–240)

Tertullian is the "Father of Western Christianity" and could be considered the "Father of Contextual Theology." His many Latin writings model exegetically based theology in line with the proclamation ministries of the apostles and subapostolic fathers. In nearly every chapter of his writings, he cited Scripture, recognizing it as the church's authoritative source for spiritual tradition and godly conduct in a world of false beliefs and pagan traditions. Tertullian taught that for Christians to live out biblical truth in society, they must affirm the "rule of faith"— the formulaic, creedal affirmations that define the gospel and serve as the standard for evaluating which sociocultural customs may be retained by believers.

For Tertullian, to separate spiritual truth from error requires pursuing a consistently literal hermeneutic that upholds the plain sense of the biblical literature. In the face of the Alexandrian methods of philosophical theology, Tertullian explained that only when the original author's meaning for the text is understood can the interpretation be considered biblically faithful. To express the plain sense of passages and their doctrines, he engaged in what might be called "linguistic accommodation." He appropriated some philosophical language to explain central Christian doctrines in Latin, such as to explain the Trinity in the face of the heresies of his day. He achieved theological precision through language and concepts common to his opponents yet did not compromise the meaning of the Scriptures, nor did he adopt the pagan concepts into his theological formulations in a kind of interreligious dialogue.

Synthesis of Third-Century Cultural Engagement

There was a growing tension in missionary methods among the third-century fathers as the most formidable leaders of the church conducted cultural engagement from opposing poles. At the pole of "cultural accommodation," Clement, Origen, and Felix acted on their belief that through allegory and natural, philosophical reasoning they could win pagans to true faith. At the biblical proclamation pole, Tertullian exemplified the biblical proclamation of the apostles with the nuance of linguistic accommodation, which he found necessary to clarify the "rule of faith" in the target language and culture.

Biblical Proclamation in the Fourth Century[3]

By the fourth century, missionary outreach was characterized by a dynamic range of attempts to propagate the faith. Emperor Constantine's Edict of Milan in AD 313 moved Christianity from social hostility to prominence, paving the way for the peaceful expansion of the faith

---

3. Select bibliography: Paul L. Allen, *Theological Method: A Guide for the Perplexed* (London: A&C Black, 2012); Justo L. González, *The Story of Christianity, Volume I: The Early Church to the Dawn of the Reformation*, rev. and updated (New York: HarperCollins, 2010); Adolf von Harnack, *The Expansion of Christianity in the First Three Centuries*, vol. 2., trans. and ed. James Moffatt (New York: G. P. Putnam's Sons, 1905); Stephen Neill, *A History of Christian Missions* (Baltimore: Penguin, 1964).

throughout the Roman Empire. Practical outreach ministries became well established in the churches, but the newfound peace afforded by official state Christianity quickly brought with it a sense of complacency and secularism. Some concerned believers moved out of the social sphere and into the ascetic lifestyle of monasticism. Learned scholars Jerome, John Chrysostom, Ambrose of Milan, and Augustine represent a range of lifestyles and vocations with a variety of cultural engagement activities that significantly advanced Christian theology in the church. While Jerome and John Chrysostom represent the biblical proclamation pole of cultural engagement, Ambrose and Augustine represent proclamation ministries that were compromised by practices of cultural accommodation.

Jerome (AD 342/348–420)

The extreme ascetic Jerome produced the Latin Vulgate translation of the Bible for the common people so they could read the Scriptures for themselves. He opposed any speculative theology that risked syncretizing with pagan philosophy and maintained the importance of preserving the syntax and grammar of the original biblical languages in Bible translation and interpretation. He proposed a methodology for linguistic accommodation, asserting that the communication of a text might be word for word or sense for sense, depending on what is needed to accurately preserve the text's meaning for a new audience. Any alteration to a text was solely for the purpose of making its meaning clear and maximally useful for the task of evangelism and disciple-making.

John Chrysostom (AD 347–407)

John Chrysostom was an avid biblical expositor in the Antiochene line of interpreters, known for his preaching and his writing. He expounded a text in order to draw out a situation-specific exhortation from it, and he called for real spiritual response by listeners from all walks of life. He advocated for personal Bible reading as a means of spiritual transformation, and he upheld the ideals of biblical proclamation by sending missionaries among pagan regions and people groups, including sending evangelists to the Goths.

Ambrose of Milan (AD 340–397)

With professional rhetorical skill, Ambrose practiced regular expositional preaching and confrontational evangelism against paganism, clericalism, and elements of Roman culture and politics. However, he practiced an allegorical hermeneutic that produced certain untenable expositions, particularly in his *Hexaemeron*, which capitulated biblical authority to philosophical constructs found in the Greek poets.

Augustine (AD 354–430)

Augustine, who grew up in North Africa, identified with both Berber and Roman culture. Before his conversion to Christ, while living an immoral lifestyle, he considered the biblical text stylistically low and unfit for intellectual pursuit. Yet, to post-conversion Augustine, only the writers of Scripture combined eloquence with wisdom, illuminating the path to true spiritual knowledge for people everywhere. Consequently, he preached the biblical text with passion and was active in evangelism, urging his hearers to study and apply the Scripture for themselves. His *De doctrina christiana* developed interpretive rules for expositors to draw out application, yet he followed his allegorical inclinations where a straightforward reading of a passage would prove difficult to understand. His tendency toward allegorization compromised his exposition and led to doctrinal inconsistencies by the theologians who followed him in the centuries thereafter.

The Missiological Paradigm Shift (AD 500–1500)[4]

Missionary outreach by the medieval church was characteristically lethargic and can be described as having shifted away from the ethos and practices of the biblical proclamation that characterized the earlier centuries. There are at least four reasons to conclude that a paradigm shift in cultural engagement had occurred during the Middle Ages—the so-called Dark Ages.

The first reason was the demand for imperial conformity. Rome, now an unholy marriage between church and state, attempted to institute and stabilize its form of worship across the expansive empire. The goal of spiritual and cultural compliance with the Latin-speaking Roman Church[5] was to counterbalance the transnational movements of pagan people groups, cultures, and languages throughout the centuries. By standardizing the Christian practices of worship and using the imperial Latin language as the vernacular in society, citizens across disparate, foreign environments were assimilated into the now-ubiquitous faith of the capital.[6] This sociopolitical objective replaced the early church's goal of spiritual conversion according to the biblical gospel and the Great Commission.

A second reason to conclude that there was a missiological paradigm shift was the lack of proclamation ministries to the farther reaches of the empire. Persuasive, Scripture-oriented proclamation largely disappeared and was replaced by instruction on moral (and often monastic) living. There are only a few extant records that document overseas missionaries acquiring the languages of the people, undertaking Bible translation, or expounding Scripture for evangelism and disciple-making. Some notable missionaries include sixth-century Patrick to Ireland, seventh-century A-lo-pen (Olopun) to China, eighth-century Boniface to Germany

---

4. Select bibliography: Paul L. Allen, *Theological Method: A Guide for the Perplexed* (London: A&C Black, 2012); Justice Anderson, "Medieval and Renaissance Missions (500–1792)," in *Missiology: An Introduction to the Foundations, History, and Strategies of World Missions*, ed. John Mark Terry, Ebbie Smith, and Justice Anderson (Nashville: Broadman and Holman, 1998), 185–87; Kenneth Scott Latourette, *A History of the Expansion of Christianity*, vol. 1, *The First Five Centuries* (1937; repr. Grand Rapids: Zondervan, 1970); Latourette, *A History of the Expansion of Christianity*, vol. 2, *The Thousand Years of Uncertainty* (1938; repr. Grand Rapids: Zondervan, 1970); Steven Ozment, *The Age of Reform, 1250–1550: An Intellectual and Religious History of Late Medieval and Reformation Europe* (New Haven, CT: Yale University Press, 1980).

5. So designated here for its gradual evolution into the Roman Catholic Church from the fall of Rome to the Great Schism of 1054. See Nick Needham, *2000 Years of Christ's Power*, vol. 2, *The Middle Ages* (Fearn, Ross-shire UK: Christian Focus, 2016), 131–37.

6. Latourette, *The First Five Centuries*, 204–5.

and John of Damascus to adherents of early Islam, and ninth-century Cyril and Methodius to the Slavic people.

A third reason to view biblical missions as shifted, nearly untraceable during the Middle Ages, is due to the syncretism inherent to the Roman Church's form and practice of worship. With the diffusion of the Roman Church into the Germanic kingdoms and Byzantine Empire, the local, pagan beliefs were often absorbed into its cultic practices, as demonstrated in the growing emphasis on the role of miracles, the perceived divine capacity of relics, the multifaceted veneration of the saints, and the art forms and liturgical aids that replaced scriptural teaching to catechize the laity. While parishioners across the empire could espouse the Christian faith according to the established practices of the church, there was no sufficient means of ensuring that their worldview was either biblically accurate or spiritually transformed. Imperial Christianity was both ubiquitous and uncompelling, providing no persuasive contrast to the magic practices and superstitious beliefs that were already central to many local cultures.

A fourth reason to conclude that there was a missiological paradigm shift was the rise of scholastic theology. In the High Middle Ages, namely, the eleventh century onward, ivory-tower universities became the seedbed for myopic theological inquiries and nuanced metaphysical reasoning. The laity benefited little from the novel solutions to philosophical and social problems that were achieved apart from the grammatical-historical hermeneutic and exegetical method of the early church. Thomas Aquinas, who denied the biblical gospel of salvation by grace through faith in Christ alone, expressed doctrine in extrabiblical, philosophically derived ways in his *Summa Theologica* and proposed in his apologetic missionary manual, *Summa Contra Gentiles*, that human reasoning and the natural observation of the world are the proper starting place for evangelism and Christian teaching. In diametric opposition to Thomistic natural theology, Anselm of Canterbury promoted that divinely revealed theology is the basis of true spiritual knowledge and that a Christian will mature in understanding as he builds on the foundation of Scripture with a God-given "faith seeking understanding."

Early Reversals toward Biblical Proclamation (1170–1500)[7]

In contrast with the culturally accommodating practices of the Roman Church and its

7. Select bibliography: Gabriel Audisio, *The Waldensian Dissent: Persecution and Survival c. 1170–c. 1570* (Cambridge, UK: Cambridge University Press, 1999); Justo L. González, *The Story of Christianity, Volume I: The Early Church to the Dawn of the Reformation*, rev. and updated (New York: HarperCollins, 2010); B. K. Kuiper, *The Church in History* (Grand Rapids: Christian Schools International, 1964); Stephen E. Lahey, *John Wyclif* (Oxford: Oxford University Press, 2009); Heiko Oberman, *The Dawn of the Reformation: Essays in Late Medieval and Early Reformation Thought* (Edinburgh, T&T Clark, 1986); Steven Ozment, *The Age of Reform, 1250–1550: An Intellectual and Religious History of Late Medieval and Reformation Europe* (New Haven, CT: Yale University Press, 1980); Lorenzo Polizzotto, *The Elect Nation: The Savonarolan Movement in Florence, 1494–1545* (Oxford: Clarendon, 1994); John Mark Terry and Robert L. Gallagher, *Encountering the History of Missions: From the Early Church to Today* (Grand Rapids: Baker, 2017).

ivory towers during the High Middle Ages, a series of local "renewal movements"[8] attempted to call the Roman Church back to the Great Commission activities of biblical proclamation. These attempts constitute the Pre-Reformation period of dissent over a series of centuries. Specifically, four movements shared the attitudes and approaches to biblical proclamation of the early church, most involving Bible translation, expository preaching, evangelism, discipleship, and pastoral training for the next generation.

First, Peter Waldo (1140–1205) and the Waldensians of Lyons, France, and later in northern Italy, emphasized the public reading of Scripture, which they translated into the vernacular language. They promoted disciplined Bible study and extensive memorization as they cared for the material needs of their poor countrymen.

Second, John Wycliffe (1330–1384) and the Lollards of England translated Jerome's Latin Vulgate into their contemporary form of English. They espoused a literal hermeneutic and a highly intellectual theological method that both opposed the philosophical theology of the Scholastics (Wycliffe was himself an Oxford professor) and applied scriptural principles to the local lifestyle of both clergy and laity.

Third, Jan Hus (1372/75–1415) and the Hussites of the modern-day Czech Republic engaged in the vernacular translation of the Bible and the free preaching of the gospel, which brought biblical literacy to the laity and, with it, a growing concern for biblical doctrine to shape society and government.

Fourth, Girolamo Savonarola (1452–1498) of Florence, Italy, placed a high value on text-based proclamation with pointed application to his hearers. Yet his message was often unbalanced by philosophical constructs, political entanglements, and strange divine visions, which led him to nearly convert the Renaissance city to a theocratic municipality. However, elevating the Great Commission to a political movement to Christianize the government and society failed to reach the spiritually purifying effect he intended.

Reformation-Era Cultural Engagement (1500–1650)[9]

European missionaries recaptured the activities of biblical proclamation lost since the patristic fathers, principally through the invention of the printing press and the upswell of classical literary studies. A high value was placed on recovering and publishing original ancient texts of all kinds, to retrieve their literary sense. To the Reformers, the goal of literary discovery was first and foremost the study of the

---

8. So termed in Terry and Gallagher, *Encountering the History of Missions*, 110.

9. Select bibliography: Nathan A. Busenitz, "Does *Sola Fide* Represent a Sixteenth-Century Theological *Novum*? Examining Alister E. McGrath's *Iustitia Dei* in Light of More Complete Evidence" (PhD diss., The Master's Seminary, 2015); Alister McGrath, *Reformation Thought: An Introduction* (Oxford: Blackwell, 1993); John Knox and David Buchanan, *The Historie of the Reformation of the Church of Scotland, Containing Five Books: Together with Some Treatises Conducing to the History* (London: John Raworth, 1644); Robert Bireley, *The Refashioning of Catholicism, 1450–1700: A Reassessment of the Counter Reformation* (Washington, DC: Catholic University of America Press, 1999); Oberman, *The Dawn of the Reformation*; Allen, *Theological Method*.

canonical text of Scripture for its supernatural, and thus superior, meaning, so that its transformative message could be placed in the hands of laypeople.

Sola Scriptura, the Latin expression that the Bible is the sole authority for receiving sound doctrine and practicing the true faith, became the foundational principle for the biblical proclamation of the Reformation-era Protestants. The Reformers—from the Magisterial (including Luther and Melanchthon) to the Reformed (including Zwingli, Bucer, Calvin, and Knox), to the Anglican (including Cranmer, Cromwell, and Tyndale)—operated by the principle of *sola Scriptura* in their multifaceted ministries of the Word, which resulted in lay-level biblical expositions, biblical commentaries, and Bible translations.

Sola Scriptura fueled global missionary outreach as well, including the Calvinistic French Huguenots to Brazil, Hungarian Venceslaus Budovetz to the Muslims in Istanbul, and certain European pastors who wrote treatises encouraging foreign missions and themselves went overseas. However, the clerical missionary forces of the Counter-Reformation, including the Roman Catholic Jesuits, Franciscans, and Dominicans and the Eastern Orthodox proselytizers, were commissioned after the Council of Trent (which anathematized belief in the biblical gospel) to supplant the propagation of Protestant missionary biblical proclamation in and outside of Europe. The Counter-Reformation missionary orders employed strategic, culturally accommodating activities that were successful in advancing their false gospel.

Modern Era Missiological Developments (1650–1910)[10]

The modern era (1650–1910) is composed of two opposing directions that run simultaneously along the spectrum of cultural engagement: text-driven ministries by theologically conservative missionaries at the biblical proclamation pole and the cultural relativism of the liberal Protestants at the cultural accommodation pole.

The early expansion of biblically faithful post-Reformation missions was most recognized in the following missionaries, whose cross-cultural communication practices included learning the local native language, translating Scripture, preaching the text evangelistically, training disciples, and raising up

---

10. For more expanded treatment and bibliographic sources, see also chapter 16. Select bibliography: Ernst Cassirer, *The Philosophy of the Enlightenment*, trans. Fritz C. A. Koelln and James P. Pettegrove (Princeton, NJ: Princeton University Press, 1951); Justo L. González, *The Story of Christianity, Volume II: The Reformation to the Present Day*, rev. and updated (New York: HarperCollins, 2010); S. G. Hefelbower, "Deism Historically Defined," *American Journal of Theology* 24, no. 2 (April 1920): 217–23; Kenneth Scott Latourette, *A History of the Expansion of Christianity*, vol. 4, *The Great Century: Europe and the United States* (1941, repr.; Grand Rapids: Zondervan, 1970); Latourette, *A History of the Expansion of Christianity*, vol. 5, *The Great Century: The Americas, Austral-Asia, and Africa* (1943, repr.; Grand Rapids: Zondervan, 1970); Latourette, *A History of the Expansion of Christianity*, vol. 6, *The Great Century: Northern Africa and Asia* (1944, repr.; Grand Rapids: Zondervan, 1970); James C. Livingston, *The Enlightenment and the Nineteenth Century*, 2nd ed. Modern Christian Thought 1 (Minneapolis: Fortress, 2006); Nick R. Needham, *2000 Years of Christ's Power, Volume 4: The Age of Religious Conflict* (Fearn, Ross-shire, UK: Christian Focus, 2016); C. Gordon Olson, *What in the World Is God Doing? The Essentials of Global Missions*, 7th ed., updated and rev. (Lynchburg, VA: Global Gospel, 2013).

local church leaders: John Eliot (1604–1690) to New England Native Americans; Philipp Jakob Spener (1635–1705) and the Pietists (from ca. 1675) to northern Europe and later through Count Ludwig von Zinzendorf (1700–1765) and the Moravians (from ca. 1735) to North America, the Caribbean, and South America; and David Brainerd (1718–1747) to New England Native Americans. The ensuing "Great Century" (1786–1910) was an energetic period for strategizing new and lasting ways to bring the gospel to the nations and reflected even farther global reach by men like the following: William Carey (1761–1834) to India, Robert Morrison (1782–1834) to China, Robert Moffat (1789–1883) to South Africa, Adoniram Judson (1788–1850) to Burma (modern-day Myanmar), and Hudson Taylor (1832–1905) to China.

The fruit of ministry at the biblical proposition pole continued through the modern era among those who also recognized the centrality of Scripture in advancing the Great Commission. In the 1880s, zealous young people began training for future missionary service at Bible institutes, where they received a theological education that did not intermingle the secular sciences and the higher critical methodologies of the liberal Protestants. Students understood that by studying Scripture they were participating in kingdom work, laying a foundation for their foray into cross-cultural evangelism and disciple-making.

Concurrent with the Great Century of missions was the rise of modern-era liberal Protestantism by the middle of the eighteenth century, which introduced medieval philosophical theology and Jesuit methodologies into mainline Protestant universities, beginning with the Lutherans, the Deists, the Romantic philosophers of the Counter-Enlightenment, and those theologians who urged missionaries to operate on the grounds of cultural relativity. The merger of philosophy and cultural relativism within Protestantism led scholars to publicly critique those overseas modern-era missionaries who were preaching, teaching, and planting churches with Scripture as their primary authority.

The Rise and Reality of Missiological Ecumenism (1910–2020)[11]

Only a brief summary of missiological ecumenism in the twentieth century is presented here. Two concurrent streams of missiological theory and activity merged in the second half of the twentieth century to espouse an ecumenical, multiconfessional understanding of the mission of the church, with Roman Catholic, Eastern Orthodox, and mainline Protestant partners. Liberal missiology spread across the world through joint assemblies, conferences, and councils, most notably between 1910 and 1961, unhinged from the bibliological, soteriological, and ecclesiological exclusivity of the Great Commission. The ecumenical movement, undergirded primarily by the Protestant-led

---

11. For more expanded treatment and bibliographic sources, see also chapter 16.

Edinburgh World Missionary Conference of 1910 and the later Roman Catholic Vatican II council documents *Lumen Gentium* (1964) and *Gaudium et Spes* (1965), grew into a platform of political, social, and cultural activity, which largely ignored the bibliological and soteriological doctrines central to the missionary task.

By the 1970s, many evangelicals who would not agree with liberal theology engaged in practical global ministries with ecumenical partners who did. Today many contemporary theories and practices that affect the cultural engagement of evangelicals are theologically inconsistent, promoting cultural accommodation practices to varying degrees above biblical proclamation. For example, since the 1980s, many evangelical missionaries have developed interest in applying sociocultural studies, such as "contextualization" theories, that involve the strategies of Roman Catholic contextualizers, termed *inculturists*, who have modernized the Counter-Reformation cultural accommodation practices of the Jesuits.[12] It is questionable whether missionary training in institutions of Christian higher education today balance the sociocultural and missiological theories with the exegetical and theological preparation

necessary to conduct biblical proclamation on the field. Perhaps the balance question is no longer even asked.

Conclusion of the Historical Survey

The poles of the cultural engagement spectrum have been well traveled in the two millennia since the Lord Jesus Christ declared the Great Commission to His disciples. The cross-cultural activities of the early generations represent conscious efforts to evangelize and disciple new converts according to the model of biblical proclamation practiced by Christ's eyewitnesses. However, it did not take long for cultural engagement to steer in a philosophical, culturally accommodating direction toward the language and concepts of pagan religion. While the practice of "linguistic accommodation" helped to preserve the meaning of the text in new contexts, ancient philosophy eventually overtook the hermeneutical practices of church leaders and kept the light of Scripture hidden from common view throughout the Dark Ages.

Unsurprisingly, by the High Middle Ages the missiological orientation of the church had undergone a paradigm shift away from biblical authority toward anti-proclamational Roman

---

12. Roman Catholic inculturation strategies began in 1534 with Jesuit founder Ignatius de Loyola (1491–1556). Evangelical missiologists today tend to noncritically appreciate Roman Catholic inculturation from a cultural-anthropological perspective, considering inculturists to have struck a balance between being authentically cultural and authentically "Christian," though they do not comment on the damning soteriology of Roman Catholic dogma that the inculturists brought to the mission field. For examples of evangelical appreciation for inculturation, see Alice T. Ott, "Accommodating Christianity to Confucian Culture: Matteo Ricci and the Early Jesuit Mission to China, 1582–1610," in *Sixteenth Century Mission*, ed. Edward L. Smither and Robert L. Gallagher (Bellingham, WA: Lexham, 2021); Harold A. Netland, *Encountering Religious Pluralism: The Challenge to Christian Faith and Mission* (Downers Grove, IL: InterVarsity, 2001), 254–56; Todd M. Johnson and Cindy M. Wu, *Our Global Families: Embracing Common Identity in a Changing World* (Grand Rapids: Baker Academic, 2015), 87–88. Contemporary inculturists with an authoritative presence in evangelical missiological circles include Robert Schreiter and Stephen Bevans. See the influential works of Robert J. Schreiter, *Constructing Local Theologies* (Maryknoll, NY: Orbis, 1985); and Stephen B. Bevans, *Models of Contextual Theology*, rev. ed. (Maryknoll, NY: Orbis, 2002).

Catholicism, a shift that was only undone by the pre-Reformation dissidents at the end of the era within limited circles. However, by the sixteenth century, true believers regained personal contact with Scripture and propelled the preaching and teaching of Scripture into the public square as the operative paradigm for cross-cultural communication and local church life. The Reformers and their disciples were God's agents for the global expansion of the gospel, despite fiery opposition by Counter-Reformation missionary orders that attempted to uproot the Great Commission wherever it spread.

It was not long before the Protestant advancements in theological education exchanged pastoral training for unbiblical intellectual pursuits, akin to pre-Reformation scholasticism. Liberal Protestantism eventually leveled anti-Christian teachings against those who practiced biblical proclamation, yet, concurrently, God was pleased to birth the "Great Century" of biblical missions. Faithful missionaries spent themselves to expand the reach of Scripture across the world through Bible translation, preaching, teaching, and pastoral training. Yet, the liberal efforts at interconfessional unity in the last century quickly became a far-reaching ecumenical movement between Protestants, Roman Catholics, and Eastern Orthodoxy, which many evangelical churches and educational institutions have tolerated.

It is unclear after two millennia of missionary activity whether the evangelical church of the next generation will follow this trend or reform once again. Therefore, it is of utmost importance that missionaries today raise up believers to lead the church of tomorrow back to the biblical proclamation pole of the missions spectrum, where the Word of God is valued as the sufficient and authoritative means for accomplishing the Great Commission. If new generations of disciples will remain steadfast in hope that the Word will do its work (Ps 119:74, 81, 114), then they will witness the Lord Jesus Christ fulfill His promise to build His church in their day (Matt 16:18) until the end of the age (28:20). If today's missionaries and church leaders do not advocate the convictions of the earliest disciples, then future missions activities might cease to involve Scripture at all and enter into another Dark Age.

The Origins and Growth of the Church in India

Sammy Williams

The church in India is one of the oldest in Southeast Asia. It demonstrates the power of the gospel. Yet a weakness lay in its early inclination toward higher caste communities, coupled with later alliances with Western social movements.

The earliest historical traditions indicate the Indian church originated with the work of Thomas, one of the twelve disciples.[13] Tradition holds that Thomas landed in southern India at Cranganore (Kodangaluru) in about AD 52. Similar to Paul in the book of Acts, he is said to have first preached to the Jewish colony there, seeing many come to faith in Christ. It is believed that the first elders Thomas ordained were from four Brahmin high-caste families (as they would be labeled today).[14] These early converts were not particularly evangelistic, in part because people of their high-caste status viewed the lower castes as "untouchable." They nevertheless stand as evidence of the apostles' obedience to the Great Commission, and they demonstrate Christianity's presence in India long before the Western world knew of the gospel.

Christianity remained a minority influence in India for centuries. The arrival of the Portuguese in the late 1400s brought the first significant Western influence to India. The initial motive of the Portuguese was to capitalize on the lucrative spice market of India, so they set up trading posts across

---

13. Some debate still exists on whether Thomas actually came to India. Documents from his actual visit may have been destroyed. But early records of Christianity in Kerala and the evidence of churches there are strong indications of his missionary activity in India. A good survey of his ministry according to the traditions can be found in Roger E. Hedlund, *Christianity Made in India: From Apostle Thomas to Mother Teresa* (Minneapolis: Fortress, 2017), 11–20.

14. On Thomas' founding of churches with Kerala Brahmins, see James Puriulumpil, "The Tradition of Seven Churches," in *St. Thomas and India: Recent Research*, ed. K. S. Matthew, Joseph Chacko Chennattuserry, and Antony Bungalowparambil (Minneapolis: Fortress, 2020), 149–60. It is believed that the caste system in India dates back to the Vedic period, as early as mid-second millennium BC, though the first significant treatment of the term and topic was by Bhimrao Ramji Ambedkar's 1916 paper, "Castes in India. Their Mechanism, Genesis and Development," reproduced in Bhimrao Ramji Ambedkar and Vasant Moon, *Dr. Babasaheb Ambedkar, Writings and Speeches*, vol. 1 (1989, repr. 2014, Bombay: Education Department, Government of Maharashtra), 3–22.

the western coasts. These commercial ventures, however, quickly took on a religious component. In 1534 the Roman Catholic Church assigned the new Portuguese colony of Goa to be the base of their Indian efforts. With Portuguese government support, the Church labored to Christianize India. Under Francis Xavier, the Church established the Goa Inquisition, implementing directives issued by the Council of Trent's Counter-Reformation mandates. Authorities also destroyed non-Christian religious sites and outlawed public worship by Hindus and Muslims. This dark period of history resulted in the forced conversion of many Hindus and still produces indigenous bitterness toward Christianity.

Protestant missions in India began with German Lutherans in 1706. Bartholomäus Ziegenbalg first translated the Bible into Tamil and saw several hundred converts turn to Christ from that culture. William Carey, known as the father of the modern missionary movement, later arrived in Calcutta in 1793, having been sent by the Baptist Missionary Society in England. Other mission societies, British and American, followed the Baptist Missionary Society into India, thereby ushering in a "golden age" of missions. As a result, most Indian groups gained access to the Bible, and the full New Testament was translated into thirty-five different Indian languages.

Despite these Western efforts, an inherent weakness remained. National Indians were not being trained as church leaders. Indeed, indigenous missions were all but nonexistent until the 1950s. Foreign missionaries dominated leadership roles until the Indian government began pushing them out of the country. In 1977 the Indian Supreme Court declared evangelical Christian mission work to be a "threat to the freedom of conscience" of the Indian citizens. This development forced missionaries to turn the ministry over to nationals. The Indian Christians responded, flourishing through their own indigenous missions organizations, such as the Indian Evangelical Mission and the Friends Missionary Prayer Band.

As in the West, the twentieth century saw Indian missions struggle with the push for ecumenical ministry alliances. Western influence led Indian leaders to form the National Christian Council, unifying their congregations and joining along with the World Council of Churches. The Lausanne conference of 1974 was a similar catalyst for ecumenical unification across India. Other ecumenical movements, such as Discipling a Whole Nation (DAWN) and AD 2000 and Beyond followed. These groups had goals of unifying missions work, nation by nation, to speed up world evangelism. The pursuit of numerical success, however, contributed to anemic doctrine and discipleship.

There is much to be grateful for in the story of the church in India, including the abundance of laborers who have invested their lives in translating the Scriptures and proclaiming Christ. In addition, at least three points emerge from this short survey: God's Word is powerful when it is proclaimed faithfully, indigenous believers still need equipping for the work of the ministry, and Christ's church must remain vigilant to be faithful to His commission in this generation.

Recent Slavic Christian History

Robert Provost

The fall of the Berlin Wall on the night of November 9, 1989, marked the beginning of the collapse of the atheistic, militant Soviet Union and the end of the Cold War. On December 8, 1991, the elected officials of Russia, Ukraine, and Belarus signed an agreement forming a new association to replace the crumbling Union of Soviet Socialist Republics (USSR). It was established as the Sodruzhestvo Nezavisimykh Gosudarstv (Commonwealth of Independent States or CIS). The initial three Slavic republics were joined by five in Central Asia and three in the Caucasus region—totaling twelve now sovereign states and almost all of the former USSR republics. The role of the CIS is to coordinate the policies of its member states in matters of economics, foreign relations, defense, and—notably for missions—police and immigration.

Though religious freedom has not been without some challenges, particularly in today's political and religious climate in Ukraine and Russia, the situation drastically changed overnight in 1989. Two ministry organizations that have thrived since that time are the Union of Evangelical Christian Baptists (UECB) and the Slavic Gospel Association (SGA). The churches in the former republics of the USSR easily continued in their association under the CIS, and since it had always been the mission of the SGA to serve the evangelical Baptist churches of the USSR, their ministry continued through the change. In Ukraine, missionary translator Sergei Omelchenko supplied this update prior to Russia's invasion of the country in 2022:

> Ever since the fall of the Soviet Union there has been a wide open door for the gospel. There have been so many opportunities to preach the gospel that we have not had enough workers to seize them all. In recent years, we have even received opportunities to establish Christian kindergartens and Christian schools. Today there are very few, if any, restrictions to restrain the preaching of the gospel in Ukraine. Ukraine may have more freedom to preach the gospel than any other country in the world. In the words of Jesus, the fields in the CIS are simply "white for harvest" (John 4:35).

However, politics in this vast geographic region continue to be tumultuous, especially in the face of a devastating war and recent conflicts. Yet the church has been a light in the darkness for many souls. During the Second Chechen War for independence, on September 1, 2004, the first day of the local school year, Chechen terrorists attacked the large public school in Beslan, southern Russia, killing 335 students and teachers, and injuring many more.[15] News of the horrendous Beslan School massacre was trumpeted throughout the globe. Tragically, some of the children of the pastors and deacons of the Beslan Baptist Church were among the perished or injured. I traveled to Beslan to offer SGA's ministry assistance. I encouraged the devastated pastors as they ministered to their own affected families and to the other survivors in their congregations and neighborhoods.

Despite this devastation, the gospel continues to advance in the Slavic nations. In Russia and Belarus, from 2017 to 2022, SGA's total number of supported missionary pastors grew slightly, and due to the war in Ukraine the number in Ukraine shrank slightly; yet, altogether across the CIS, the total number of SGA-supported missionary pastors grew from 287 to 308. It was a remarkable 7 percent growth during a time of war. All the praise goes to Jesus Christ. Since then the churches continue to serve all those in need. They help them in every way possible, from taking food to the hungry to helping the homeless find a place to live. Above all, they continue their worship services and outreach, with numerous people repenting and trusting Christ as Savior.

Hearing personal testimonies from the Slavic nations is always a joy. They have a

---

15. "2004: Russian School Siege Ends in Violence," *BBC On This Day*, accessed June 18, 2024, http://news.bbc.co .uk/onthisday/hi/dates/stories/september/3/newsid_4652000/4652213.stm; "Attackers Storm Russian School," *BBC News*, September 1, 2004, http://news.bbc.co.uk/1/hi/world/europe/3616868.stm.

characteristic and biblical way of describing salvation. Luke 24:45–47 relates well the success of the gospel's progress in recent times:

> Then He opened their minds to understand the Scriptures, and He said to them, "Thus it is written, that the Christ would suffer and rise again from the dead the third day, and that repentance for forgiveness of sins would be proclaimed in His name to all the nations, beginning from Jerusalem."

As Jesus spoke here, "repentance" is also the word the pastors and member churches of UECB use most frequently to refer to their salvation experience. When believers are asked how long they have been a Christian, their usual reply is framed as the time when they "repented," the date that they turned from their sins and trusted only in Christ's death on the cross for salvation. According to the Word of God, true conversion requires both repentance of sins and faith in Christ's finished work on the cross of Calvary (Mark 1:15; Acts 20:21). Let us pray, then, that God continues this Slavic Christian history, that He sends more workers into the fields white for harvest, and that many more souls be granted repentance unto life (Acts 11:18).

CHAPTER 15

Reformation Power: God's Word, a Light in Darkness

Nathan Busenitz[1]

In the greatest reformations of biblical and church history, a common theme emerges. God draws sinners to Himself through the proclamation of His Word. Thus, missions (featuring the declaration of God's saving message to sinners) and reformation (the response of sinners to God's saving message) are tightly bound. From Nineveh's repentance at Jonah's simple sermon (Jonah 3:4–9) to the thousands who repented at Pentecost in response to Peter's preaching (Acts 2:37–42), the supernatural power behind spiritual awakening and revival is always the same: the Word of God. Where God's Word is absent, spiritual darkness abounds. But where His truth is faithfully proclaimed through the power of the Holy Spirit (Eph 6:17), the light of the Word pierces the darkness and transforms lives (Ps 119:105). This was profoundly evident in two of the most significant reformations in redemptive history, the

Protestant Reformation of sixteenth-century Europe and the reforms under King Josiah of Judah, recorded in the Old Testament.

Scripture in the Protestant Reformation

The Protestant Reformation was one of the greatest spiritual awakenings in church history. Countless souls embraced the gospel of grace through faith in Jesus Christ, being rescued from the clutches of religious ritualism and self-righteous legalism. But given the penchant for personality-driven church growth strategies today, one might wonder what power fueled and propelled the Reformation. Some might suggest it was the courage or cleverness of the Reformers, or, more specifically, of Martin Luther (1483–1546) and his Ninety-Five Theses. Yet, if one were to ask Luther whether this was so, his answer would be a

---

1. Portions of this chapter are adapted from Nathan Busenitz's editorial in *MSJ* 30, no. 2 (Fall 2019): 181–83. Used by permission.

resounding no. The other Reformers would respond the same.

Luther refused to credit himself or his writings for the widespread impact of the Reformation. Instead, he gave all the credit to God and His Word. Near the end of Luther's life, he declared, "All I have done is put forth, preach and write the Word of God, and apart from this I have done nothing. . . . It is the Word that has done great things. . . . I have done nothing; the Word has done and achieved everything."[2] Elsewhere he exclaimed, "It was by the Word the world was overcome, by the Word the Church has been saved, and by the Word will she be reestablished."[3] Then, noting Scripture's importance in his own heart, Luther wrote, "No matter what happens, you should say: There is God's Word. This is my rock and anchor. On it I rely, and it remains. Where it remains, I, too, remain; where it goes, I, too, go."[4]

Luther understood what truly caused the Reformation. It was the Word of God, empowered by the Holy Spirit, preached in the common languages of Europe, so that all people could understand it. When ears were exposed to the truth of God's Word, hearts were pierced by it and transformed. Such power is summarized in the familiar words of Hebrews 4:12: "The word of God is living and active and sharper than any two-edged sword."

During the late Middle Ages, the Roman Catholic Church had imprisoned God's Word in the Latin language, a language the common people of Europe no longer spoke. The Reformers unlocked the Scriptures by translating them and preaching them in the common tongue. Then, once the people had access to the Word of God, the Reformation became inevitable.

Forerunners to the Reformation

When Luther and his fellow Reformers took this bold stand to uphold Scripture, they were standing on the shoulders of those who had come before them. In the twelfth century, the Waldensians—so named for the leader of their movement, Peter Waldo (1140–1205)—began translating the New Testament from Latin into the regional dialects of France. It was said that the Waldensians were so committed to Scripture that they memorized large sections of the Bible.[5] When Roman Catholic authorities confiscated their handwritten Bibles, the Word of God was hidden in their hearts.

In the fourteenth century, John Wycliffe (1330–1384) and his associates at Oxford translated the Bible from Latin into English. Then Wycliffe's followers, known as the Lollards, went throughout the countryside preaching and reading passages of Scripture aloud in English.[6]

---

2. Martin Luther, cited in Gerhard Ebeling, *Luther: An Introduction to His Thought* (Minneapolis: Fortress, 1970), 66–67.

3. Martin Luther, cited in Jean Henri Merle d'Aubigné, *History of the Reformation of the Sixteenth Century*, trans. Henry Beveridge and H. White (New York: Robert Carter and Bros., 1862), 2:89–90.

4. Martin Luther, *What Luther Says: An Anthology*, ed. Ewald Plass (St. Louis, MO: Concordia, 1959), 1:68 (emphasis mine).

5. Philip Schaff and David Schley Schaff, *History of the Christian Church* (1907; repr., Grand Rapids: Eerdmans, 1994), 5:502.

6. Johann Heinrich Kurtz, *Church History*, ed. W. Robertson Nicoll, trans. John Macpherson, The Foreign Biblical Library (New York: Funk and Wagnalls, 1889–94), 2:204–5.

A generation later, Jan Huss (1372/75–1415) preached in the language of the people, not in Latin, making him the most popular preacher in Prague. Yet, because he insisted that Christ alone was head of the church, not the pope, the Roman Catholic Council of Constance (1415) condemned him for heresy and burned him at the stake.[7]

The sixteenth century saw scholars in western Europe recover the study of Hebrew and Greek. This enabled Luther (in 1521–1522) to make a new translation of the New Testament into German. In 1525 William Tyndale (1490/94–1536) completed his translation of the Greek New Testament in English. A few years later, he translated the Pentateuch from Hebrew. Shortly thereafter he was arrested and executed as a heretic, being strangled and then burned at the stake. According to *Foxe's Book of Martyrs*, Tyndale's last words were, "Lord, open the eyes of the king of England."[8] It was only a couple years later that King Henry VIII commissioned what became known as "the Great Bible," an English translation to be installed in every church in England (1538)—a Bible that was, incidentally, largely based on Tyndale's translation work.[9]

The common thread, from the pre-Reformers to Reformers, was an undying commitment to the authority and necessity of Scripture. They were willing to sacrifice everything, including their lives, to get the Bible into the hands and hearts of their countrymen. They knew the power for spiritual reformation was not in them but in the gospel (Rom 1:16–17). Their conviction regarding biblical truth was aptly summarized by the Latin phrase *sola Scriptura* ("Scripture alone"). They recognized the supernatural power and ultimate authority of God's Word.[10] It was the ignorance of Scripture that made the Reformation necessary. It was the recovery of Scripture that made the Reformation possible. And it was the power of Scripture that gave the Reformation its enduring impact.

Long before the Reformation

Fifteen hundred years before the Reformation, this same reality unfolded at the beginning of the church age. In Acts 2, 3, and 4, it was as Peter preached the truth of God's Word that the Spirit convicted the hearts of the hearers, and many were added to the faith. Throughout the book of Acts, Luke emphasizes the role of the Word in the growth of the church. In Acts 6:7, he writes, "The word of God kept on spreading; and the number of the disciples continued to multiply greatly in Jerusalem." In Acts 12:24, in contrast to the death of the persecutor Herod, Luke again notes, "But the word of the Lord continued to grow and to be multiplied."

---

7. Kurtz, 2:209–10.

8. John Foxe, *Foxe's Book of Martyrs*, ed. J. Milner and Ingram Cobbin (London: Knight and Son, 1856), 488.

9. Michael Mullett, "Bible," *Historical Dictionary of the Reformation and Counter-Reformation*, Historical Dictionaries of Religions, Philosophies, and Movements 100 (Lanham, MD: Scarecrow, 2010), 33; Jack P. Lewis, "Great Bible, The," *ABD*, 2:1090; Norman L. Geisler and William E. Nix, *A General Introduction to the Bible*, rev. and exp. ed. (Chicago: Moody, 1986), 553.

10. Mark D. Thompson, "Sola Scriptura," in *Reformation Theology: A Systematic Summary*, ed. Matthew Barrett (Wheaton, IL: Crossway, 2017), 153–61; cf. esp. Luther's defense at the Diet of Worms (1521) quoted therein.

In Acts 19:20, he describes the awakening that broke out in Ephesus, where many former idolaters turned to Christ, "So the word of the Lord was growing mightily and prevailing."

Repeatedly in Acts, the work of regeneration is connected to the dissemination of the Word of God. This fits what the apostle Paul expressed to the Romans, that "faith comes from hearing, and hearing by the word of Christ" (Rom 10:17; cf. 1 Thess 2:13). The power of God's Word explains the rapid expansion of the early church. It was the catalyst that produced the Protestant Reformation also. And today it is still the truth of Scripture, empowered by the Spirit, that regenerates, revives, and reforms (Jas 1:21; 1 Pet 2:1–3). It instructs and encourages, convicts and admonishes—converting hearts and molding minds into the image of the Lord Jesus (2 Tim 3:14–17).

Scripture in Josiah's Reformation

A classic example of this reformation power is found in 2 Chronicles 33–35. There, in an episode from seven centuries before Pentecost and more than two millennia before the Protestant Reformation, the events of another reformation are recorded. Again, God's Word was central. This reformation took place during a dark period in Israel's history. Power in the ancient Near East was shifting from the Assyrians to the Babylonians, and the floundering nation of Judah was in desperate need

of spiritual revival. Against such a backdrop, the power of God's Word shone like a bright light. Three simple principles can be drawn from this episode as a case study of true spiritual reformation: its need, its catalyst, and its effects.

The Need for Reformation

In 695 BC Manasseh ascended the throne of Judah. Scripture's chronological data suggest he was made co-regent with his ailing father, Hezekiah (2 Kgs 20:1–7; 2 Chr 33:1), who had been fully devoted to the Lord (2 Kgs 18:1–6; 2 Chr 29:2).[11] But when the throne became Manasseh's alone, he proved to be a wicked king. In fact, according to tradition, he was the despot who killed the prophet Isaiah, having him sawn in two.[12] The Chronicler describes Manasseh this way:

> He did what was evil in the sight of Yahweh, according to the abominations of the nations whom Yahweh dispossessed before the sons of Israel. Indeed, he rebuilt the high places which Hezekiah his father had torn down; and he erected altars for the Baals and made Asherim, and worshiped all the host of heaven and served them. And he built altars in the house of Yahweh. . . . Indeed, he built altars for all the host of heaven in the two courts of the house of Yahweh. He even made his sons pass through the fire in

---

11. Eugene H. Merrill, *Kingdom of Priests: A History of Old Testament Israel*, 2nd ed. (Grand Rapids: Baker, 2008), 446; Edwin R. Thiele, *The Mysterious Numbers of the Hebrew Kings*, new rev. ed. (Grand Rapids: Kregel, 1983), 173–74.

12. *Ascension of Isaiah* 5.1; *The Lives of the Prophets* 1.1; cf. the likely allusion to this in Hebrews 11:37 and the Jewish affirmation that Manasseh was responsible in Talmud b. Yebamot 49b, y. Sanhedrin 10:28c, 37.

the valley of Ben-hinnom; and he practiced soothsaying, interpreted omens, practiced sorcery, and dealt with mediums and spiritists. He did much that was evil in the sight of Yahweh, provoking Him to anger. . . . Thus Manasseh led Judah and the inhabitants of Jerusalem astray in order to do more evil than the nations whom Yahweh destroyed before the sons of Israel. (2 Chr 33:2–9)

This unprecedented season of evil was the result of Manasseh's wicked heart. The people of Judah joined him in his rebellion against the Lord, as the author of Chronicles notes in verse 10, "Yahweh spoke to Manasseh and his people, but they paid no attention." Through prophets, God sent His word to Judah, but the people refused to listen. They ignored and suppressed His word. Consequently, the Lord brought judgment on Manasseh and pledged that Judah would go into captivity (2 Kgs 21:10–15). Manasseh's capture and subsequent bondage are recorded in 2 Chronicles 33:11–14. Incredibly, while in captivity, Manasseh finally turned from his evil ways. Still, the damage he had inflicted on Judah was not easily overcome.

Manasseh's son Amon succeeded him (2 Chr 33:21). Scripture says of Amon, "He did what was evil in the sight of Yahweh, as Manasseh his father had done, and Amon sacrificed to all the graven images which his father

Manasseh had made, and he served them. . . . Amon multiplied guilt" (vv. 22–23). So intolerable was his reign that his own servants conspired together and murdered him (v. 24). After these two successive reigns, Judah was in desperate need of reform.

Though not an exact parallel, the spiritual darkness that characterized western Europe in the late Middle Ages was likewise caused by a suppression of God's Word. The Roman Catholic Church banned the translation of the Bible in the late twelfth century under Pope Innocent III, largely in response to the Waldensians.[13] In 1229 the Synod of Toulouse declared, "We prohibit also that the laity should be permitted to have the books of the Old or the New Testament . . . [and] we most strictly forbid their having any translation of these books."[14] The Council of Tarragona in 1234 stated, "No one may possess the books of the Old and New Testaments in the Romance [common] language, and if anyone possesses them he must turn them over to the local bishop . . . so that they may be burned."[15] After John Wycliffe and his colleagues at Oxford finished their translation of the Bible, the Third Synod of Oxford (1408) condemned him for it, saying, "We therefore command and ordain that henceforth no one translate any text of Holy Scripture into English or any other language in a book (*per viam libri*), booklet or tract. . . . He who shall

---

13. Kurtz, *Church History*, 2:133–34.

14. Canon XIV, cited in Edward Peters, *Heresy and Authority in Medieval Europe* (Philadelphia: University of Pennsylvania Press, 1980), 195.

15. Canon II, cited in E. Christopher Reyes, *In His Name* (Bloomington, IN: AuthorHouse, 2010), 246.

act otherwise let him be punished as an abettor of heresy and error."[16]

With church services conducted in Latin and the Scriptures imprisoned in the Latin language, the laity of Europe were kept in a perpetual state of spiritual darkness, purposefully shielded from the Bible by a corrupt religious system. In that sense, the dark days of the Middle Ages were like those of Judah's history. Yet the power of Scripture could not be suppressed indefinitely.

The Catalyst for Reformation

In the episode of 2 Chronicles, reformation came in the next chapter, with a new king, a boy named Josiah (34:1–2). Verse 3 reads, "Now in the eighth year of his reign while he was still a youth, he began to seek the God of his father David; and in the twelfth year he began to cleanse Judah and Jerusalem of the high places, the Asherim, the graven images and the molten images"—those set up by his father and grandfather. Josiah came to the throne at age eight, around the year 640 BC.[17] He committed himself to following Yahweh at age sixteen, and four years later, at age twenty, he embarked on an expansive, kingdom-wide campaign to remove idolatry. But the climax of his reforms took place in the eighteenth year of his reign, about the year 622.

Josiah initiated a renovation of the temple, which had fallen into disrepair and syncretism (2 Chr 34:8). During the renovation, the crew discovered a most unexpected treasure: "Hilkiah the priest found the book of the law of Yahweh given by the hand of Moses" (v. 14). Evidently, since the reign of Hezekiah some seventy years earlier, God's Law had been lost, and ironically, lost inside the temple. When a scribe brought the newfound book to the king and read it aloud, Josiah tore his clothes to demonstrate his repentance (vv. 18–19).

Josiah responded to the recovery of God's Word as any true believer would: he was cut to the heart and grief-stricken with repentant remorse (Acts 2:37). He recognized that Judah had fallen into spiritual darkness and rebellion against the Lord; for, they had disregarded His Word (2 Chr 34:20–21). Yet, now that God's Word had been found, spiritual renewal could begin to take place.

Two millennia later, the same reality was vivid in the Protestant Reformation. Despite Rome's attempt to keep the Scriptures hidden—hidden within church walls, no less— the Word of God could not be permanently concealed. God raised up human instruments, scholars to recover the study of biblical Hebrew and Greek. In the 1500s, men with this knowledge, such as Martin Luther, William Tyndale, Miles Coverdale, John Rogers, Jacque Lefevre, and others, began translating Scripture from its original languages into the languages of Europe, such as German, English, and French. Gutenberg's printing press, invented just decades earlier, made it possible for copies to be

---

16. Francis Aidan Gasquet. "The Pre-Reformation English Bible (1)," in *The Old English Bible and Other Essays* (London: John C. Nimmo, 1897), 122–23.

17. Merrill, *Kingdom of Priests*, 454ff.; Thiele, *Mysterious Numbers*, 180–82.

printed en masse, paving the way for the laity to access the Bible. It was then that the Reformation became inevitable, as the Holy Spirit used His Word to transform millions of hearts by revealing the gospel of God's grace to them.

The Effects of Reformation

Second Chronicles 35 shows what happens when Scripture is rediscovered by those with ears to hear. Having found God's Word and then having grieved over their ignorance and neglect, Josiah and his people immediately put Scripture into practice. Besides guiding their reforms by Scripture, they also worshiped the Lord through the proper observance of a Passover meal. The Word of God informed both their obedience and their worship.

The Chronicler recorded that exuberant feast in 35:1–15. This highest of holy convocations was finally celebrated after seven decades of neglect. According to 35:16–18, Josiah oversaw the affair with such diligence and enthusiasm that "there had not been celebrated a Passover like it in Israel from the days of Samuel the prophet." No king of Israel had ever celebrated a Passover that was its equal.

Though it may seem incidental to modern readers, there is real significance to this feast being the first major response to Scripture's rediscovery. The Passover celebration, instituted by God in Exodus 12, was a memorial to teach the Israelites how the Lord had miraculously rescued them from slavery in Egypt. It highlighted His mercy for causing "the destroyer" to pass over the houses of those whose doorposts

were covered by the blood of a lamb (vv. 13, 23). It emphasized His grace for showing His people unmerited favor by redeeming them from slavery (vv. 24–27). They could not deliver themselves; they needed a miracle from God. Josiah's reformation brought sinful Judah to consider again the reality of God's grace in the redemption of His people.

This, too, finds a parallel in the Protestant Reformation. For the Passover feast not only pointed back in redemptive history; it pointed forward to the coming of the Messiah, who is the final Passover Lamb (1 Cor 5:7). His once-for-all sacrifice on a cross would appease the wrath of God, causing divine justice to pass over all who are covered by His blood (1 Pet 1:18–19). This gospel of salvation was at the very heart of the Reformation.

That central truth is expressed in the "five *solas*" of the Reformation, a later summary of its theology. The Reformers understood that if Scripture alone (*sola Scriptura*) is the final authority in the church, then the gospel of Scripture must be proclaimed by the church: the good news of salvation by grace alone (*sola gratia*) through faith alone (*sola fide*) in Christ alone (*solus Christus*). This salvation, being all of God's doing, means that He alone deserves the glory (*soli Deo gloria*). Just as the Israelites were slaves in Egypt, so every person is born enslaved to sin. As the Israelites could do nothing to liberate themselves, neither can any sinner. All are helpless, hopeless, and bound for hell. No penance, indulgence, or self-righteous work can save them—only the grace of God in Jesus Christ (Eph 2:4–8). Sinners can be forgiven and justified not on the basis of their good works but solely through faith in Christ who paid the penalty for the sins of His people at the cross and clothes them in His perfect righteousness (2 Cor 5:21). That is the good news of the gospel. It was the rediscovery of God's Word that made the recovery of the biblical gospel possible; and it was the recovery of the gospel that resulted in revival.

Reformation Power for Evangelism Today

The Reformers in Geneva had a Latin saying, *post tenebras lux*, "after darkness, light." The darkness they fought was spiritual ignorance and religious corruption; the light they held out was the truth of Scripture. Its light shone forth with piercing brilliance, reviving hearts by the working of God's Spirit (2 Cor 4:6). The theme of "after darkness, light" also captures well the preaching of the apostles in the book of Acts, and every other genuine revival in history. As both the reformation in 2 Chronicles and its counterpart in sixteenth-century Europe illustrate, the need for reformation is caused by a lack of biblical truth; the catalyst for reformation is the faithful proclamation of Scripture; and the result of reformation is the recovery of worshipful obedience and sound doctrine, starting with the truth of the gospel.

It is this same gospel that the church is charged to take to the nations in the Great Commission (Matt 28:18–20). When it was let loose from its medieval shackles, it turned Europe upside down. The reason for this is simple: the gospel is the power of God for salvation (Rom 1:16). The Word is still the way the Lord works in the world today. If missionaries would see any genuine spiritual awakening among the unbelievers to whom they go, or any lasting revival in the weak or unhealthy churches to which they are called, it will not come through market-driven techniques or man-centered strategies. It will only come through the faithful preaching and teaching of Scripture as the Spirit uses His Word to do a supernatural work in the hearts of people.

Reformation power is not only corporate; it is profoundly personal. The Word of God does its work in the hearts of individuals. Its purpose is to direct sinners to the Savior so that they might be reconciled to their Creator. Then, after darkness, there is light. For "the god of this age has blinded the minds of the unbelieving so that they might not see the light of the gospel of the glory of Christ" (2 Cor 4:4). But the God who called the light out of darkness uses the simple proclamation of His Word to give sight to the spiritually blind. Knowing that God is the only One who can impart life to dead hearts, evangelists need only to preach His Word, trust His Spirit, and then look back at the end of their ministries and say with Luther, "The Word has done everything."

William Carey and the Spark of Modern Missions

Brad Klassen[18]

Most Christians today would agree in principle that obedience to Christ entails involvement in global missions. Yet such an understanding was not always widely held. William Carey was a man used by God almost single-handedly to bring the Great Commission back to the fore of Christian thinking. Recognized today as the father of modern missions, he came on the scene in a period of evangelical lethargy. Paralyzed by hyper-Calvinism and apathy toward the lost, most English churches in the eighteenth century believed that if God wanted to save sinners, He would do so without their participation. Carey's life sparked a dramatic change.

Early Life and Ministry

Carey was born in England in 1761. The village school he attended was adequate for the basics, but advancement came through his own curiosity. He loved reading exploration journals, which at the time were charting the Western and Southern hemispheres. His intelligence, self-discipline, and working-class upbringing produced in him a strong sense of self-sufficiency. He learned the unglamorous trade of shoemaking. But as God would have it, another young cobbler presented the gospel to him, and in 1779, at age seventeen, Carey cast himself on God's mercy. His wretched self-righteousness was exchanged for the righteousness of Christ.

As a new Christian, Carey struggled with assurance. This served him well, however, for it drove him to the Bible. He resolved to become "a man of the Book,"[19] and become that he did. A love for languages grew alongside that of the Bible. He taught himself biblical Hebrew and Greek, and he continued reading the journals of

---

18. Adapted from "William Carey and the Spark of Modern Missions," *The Master's Seminary Blog*, February 21, 2018, https://blog.tms.edu/william-carey. Used by permission.

19. S. Pearce Carey, *William Carey, D.D., Fellow of Linnaean Society (1761–1834)*, 5th ed. (London: Hodder and Stoughton, 1924), 9.

the explorers. It was the famous Captain James Cook, describing the tribes of the South Pacific, that opened Carey's eyes to the sin and misery of the unevangelized.

In 1785 Carey began pastoring the Baptist church of Moulton. He ministered diligently, being ordained in 1787. He also studied the lives of John Eliot and David Brainerd, missionaries to the Native Americans. They and the apostle Paul served as his role models as he compiled detailed statistics of the countries and tribes unreached by the gospel. It was said that the atlas became his "other Bible," and that simply by looking at it he could be moved to tears.[20]

Inquiry and Appeal

Carey was called in 1789 to pastor in Leicester, and there his passion for missions flamed into an unquenchable fire. He drafted a booklet in 1792 titled *An Inquiry into the Obligation of Christians to Use Means for the Conversion of the Heathen*. With this eighty-seven-page treatise, he intended to rouse churches from their apathy and convince them that God's sovereignty was not diminished by using human means. The work presented a detailed exposition of Matthew 28:19–20 and a thorough response to the hyper-Calvinist objections toward missions

in his day. It was revolutionary—the first known published theology of missions.

In May of that year, Carey followed the booklet with a sermon to a fellowship of Baptist pastors in Nottingham. It was later nicknamed "The Deathless Sermon" for the immortal motto that Carey coined: "Expect great things from God; attempt great things [for God]."[21] In October that fellowship finally formed the first English mission organization: The Particular Baptist Society for the Propagation of the Gospel amongst the Heathen. It started with a meager £13, or approximately $1,120 in today's US currency. Outside observers laughed, but the society never looked back.

Ministry in India

As one of the society's first missionaries, Carey and his young family voyaged to India in 1793. He would never see his homeland again. In India his commitment to God's Word drove him to learn the languages of people who needed it. By 1795 he could preach in Bengali. By 1796 he was able to converse in Hindi and Hindustani as well.[22]

Although he made tremendous linguistic progress early on, discouragement threatened him all the way. Illness, loneliness, opposition, and the absence of conversions were

---

20. Carey, 51.
21. Carey, 78.
22. Carey, 243.

constant thorns in his flesh. Still, Carey's convictions in the sovereignty of God and the obligation of His commission would not let him concede.

In 1801 Carey received the firstfruits of his labor: the first edition of the New Testament ever printed in Bengali. He had initially hoped to translate the Bible before he died, but at age forty he had already completed the New Testament. Now, Scripture in just one of India's languages was not enough. There were dozens of others and millions of people who spoke them, all having never heard the gospel. It was then that Carey determined to establish a translation and missions training center.

By 1812 his home station had grown to house a print shop that produced Bibles, tracts, and Christian books. Eleven Indian churches had been planted, and twenty Indian evangelists and pastors had been trained. God's Word was not returning void.

Death and Legacy

Forty years after Carey first set foot in India, eighteen missionary posts like the one he first established had been founded. Half of those trained in those centers were Indian natives, and the New Testament was being printed in more than thirty Indian languages. Yet Carey's impact continued to be felt in his home country. Fourteen other missions societies had been established in Britain since he left.

Carey knew the key to this success. It was the Word of God—faithfully exposited in Britain to awaken lethargic churches, translated and proclaimed in India to awaken perishing souls. If success had to be attributed to any human quality in an instrumental sense, Carey believed it was diligence. Of himself he said, "I can plod. That is my only genius. I can persevere in any definite pursuit. To this I owe everything."[23]

In 1834 Carey died peacefully at seventy-two years of age—in India. He insisted his gravestone contain only his name, dates of birth and death, and these simple hymn lyrics:

A guilty, weak and helpless worm,
    On thy kind arms I fall;
Be thou my strength and righteousness,
    My Jesus and my all.[24]

This was indeed William Carey's legacy. God reignited global missions through this man who expected great things and attempted great things for God's glory.

---

23. Carey, 23.
24. Carey, 385.

Adoniram Judson: Reasons for a Lasting Impact on Myanmar Churches Today

Silas Van Duh Hmung

The deep love that pioneering missionary Adoniram Judson (1788–1850) had for Myanmar (Burma), my home country, has powerfully impacted me personally. After graduating from seminary, I returned home and became a church planter in rural southern Myanmar. My wife and I named our son Judson to serve as an ongoing reminder that we want to follow in the footsteps of Adoniram Judson. Foreign missionaries have been excluded from Myanmar since the 1960s. Yet there remains a growing church in Myanmar today. Let's examine why the work of this American missionary left such a lasting impact on my family and the people of Myanmar in general.

First, Judson was well prepared before going into ministry. Before the Lord chose Judson to be his vessel for the proclamation of the gospel in Myanmar, Judson had committed himself to a high level of education.[25]

At the age of nineteen, after graduating from Brown University, he opened the Plymouth Independent Academy in Massachusetts and authored two textbooks.[26] His school did not remain open, but in the year of his conversion he began studies at Andover Theological Seminary. Altogether, besides Greek, Hebrew, and Latin, he studied ancient literature.[27] God used these skills on the mission field for teaching, translating, and producing much literature.

When Judson converted at age twenty,[28] he carefully counted the cost of following Jesus, and especially the cost of working in a foreign land. His famous letter two years later to Ann "Nancy" Hasseltine's father, in which he requested her hand in marriage, reveals the possible hardships and sufferings of a missionary life that Judson fully, willingly anticipated encountering.[29] None of these things, when they actually

---

25. Courtney Anderson, *To the Golden Shore: The Life of Adoniram Judson* (Valley Forge, PA: Judson, 1987), 31–32.
26. Anderson, 36.
27. Anderson, 49.
28. Anderson, 42–45, 50.
29. Anderson, 83.

occurred—illness, imprisonment, or even death—did in fact deter Adoniram or Nancy from following the Lord. Their life purpose was purely to please Jesus Christ.[30] The church today needs to learn from the Judsons that missionaries must be well prepared. The gospel and commission of Christ are worthy of it.

Second, Judson submitted himself to the authority of Scripture. His submission to and love for God's Word are displayed throughout his life and ministry. For example, he and his wife had been christened as children in Congregationalist churches of New England, but after a careful, prayerful, months-long examination of Scripture—while en route to the mission field—they chose to be rebaptized by immersion as believers. He would write, "Thus, my dear Nancy, we are confirmed Baptists, not because we wished to be, but because truth compelled us to be."[31]

Judson's commitment to the authority of Scripture was also demonstrated in evangelism. Judson was always hesitant to recognize anyone as a Christian who might be merely superficially interested in Christ, and this turned out for the genuine salvation of many who had made false professions. For instance, U Shwe Ngong, a highly intellectual Buddhist who later became a Christian in 1820, once told Judson that he believed in Jesus Christ. Judson asked him,

> "Do you believe all that is contained in the book of Matthew that I have given you? In particular, do you believe that the Son of God died on the cross?" "Ah," he replied, "you have caught me now. I believe that he suffered death, but I cannot admit that he suffered the shameful death of the cross." "Therefore," replied Judson, "you are not a disciple of Christ. A true disciple inquires not whether a fact is agreeable to his reason, but whether it is in the book. Teacher, your pride is still unbroken. Break down your pride, and yield to the word of God."[32]

Judson's commitment to Scripture is also seen in his translation of the Bible into the Burmese language. He reasoned that winning people to Christ would require "distributing Bibles and tracts in every possible way, and in every language under heaven."[33] He finished translating the New

---

30. Edward Judson, *The Life of Adoniram Judson* (1883; repr., New York: Anson D. F. Randolph, 1996), 474.

31. Judson, 39.

32. Maung Shwe Wa, *Burma Baptist Chronicle*, ed. Genevieve Sowards and Erville Sowards (Rangoon: University Press, Burma Baptist Convention, 1963), 24.

33. Robert T. Middleditch, *Burmah's Great Missionary: Records of the Life, Character, and Achievements of Adoniram Judson* (New York: Fletcher, 1854), 312; E. D. Burns, *A Supreme Desire to Please Him: The Spirituality of Adoniram Judson* (Eugene, OR: Pickwick, 2016), 81.

Testament in 1823 and the whole Bible in 1834. Judson's commitment to Scripture should stimulate churches to take a stand on Scripture's authority alone in preaching the gospel of Jesus Christ.

Finally, Judson poured his heart into reaching the Burmese people. The country of Burma got its name from the largest people group living there, the Bama. Though the Bama had proven to be among the hardest people to reach, Judson tried every possible way to win them to Christ. Besides preaching and teaching at the regular *zayat* (a bamboo hut) and distributing gospel tracts, Judson courageously approached the Burmese king in Innwa (the capital city then) to formally request official tolerance of the Christian religion.[34]

After Nancy died from malaria (1826),[35] Judson traveled to Prome. Yet, because of the government's opposition, he and his local team had to leave the city. He wrote tearfully that he wished he could have re-mained in that very city.[36] Judson's heart was so captured by Christ's love that he relentlessly preached the gospel to Burmese people despite temptations to harbor resentment against them or to reason that other people groups would be easier to reach. His approach set a strong example for churches in Myanmar today that are tempted to harbor resentment due to political or cultural oppression brought on by the majority people group.

Thus, Adoniram Judson's commitment to preparation, to the authority of Scripture, and to the people to whom he was sent surpassed the weaknesses and desires of the flesh. All of this—and especially his love for God's Word—resulted in the production of a Burmese Bible that remains the most widely used translation two hundred years later. Every missionary in Myanmar today stands on Judson's shoulders. His goal in life was to please the Lord, and the Lord continues to use his life to impact Myanmar today.

---

34. Maung Shwe Wa, *Burma Baptist Chronicle*, 25, 41–52.

35. Maung Shwe Wa, 54–55; see also Sharon James, *My Heart in His Hands, Ann Judson of Burma: A Life with Selections from Her Memoir and Letters* (England: Evangelical Press, 2012), 190–93.

36. Maung Shwe Wa, *Burma Baptist Chronicle*, 84.

CHAPTER 16

The Consequences of a Compromised Commission: A Historical Analysis of Twentieth-Century Mission Theory

Chris Burnett

Today many missiologists downplay the need for missionaries to clearly present the biblical gospel or lead converts into active disciple-making programs. They propose that cultural accommodation strategies are necessary to make the Christian faith relevant to new audiences. Some contemporary theories and trends in missions, like many approaches to social action, do not seem doctrinally coherent or compatible with the types of proclamation ministries that conservative evangelicals consider central to the missionary task. Cultural accommodation strategies with a questionable connection to the Great Commission are symptoms of the widespread disease of ecumenism that has its roots in the modern era. This chapter will briefly describe the tenets of ecumenism, survey its historical developments

as a movement, and identify how evangelical churches today have drifted away from the attitudes and practices of biblical missions. The goal is to reassert the basics of the Great Commission for practice by well-meaning believers who love and serve God but are surrounded by the darkness of the world.

Ecumenism Defined and Described

Ecumenism is the term that represents formal or informal alliances between distinct Christian traditions and denominations in order to cooperate practically in political, social, and cultural engagement activities.[1] Ecumenism has led to organized, structured fellowship that conservative evangelicals find troubling. Unity as a concept is not the problem, for faithful evangelicals prize cooperation as

---

1. D. H. K. Hilborn, "Ecumenical Movement," in *New Dictionary of Theology: Historical and Systematic*, ed. Martin Davie et al. (Downers Grove, IL: InterVarsity, 2016), 283–86; J. Briggs, "Ecumenical Theology," in *New Dictionary of Theology*, 286–87.

long as it promotes the biblical gospel and the advancing of the Great Commission in doctrinal like-mindedness (John 17:20–21).[2] The problem is that unity, in the ecumenical frame, requires participants to put aside at least some of their theological convictions and doctrinal priorities.[3] For example, joint action in evangelization (a common ecumenical term that adds to biblical evangelism the idea of transforming societal structures)[4] by Protestants, Roman Catholics, and Eastern Orthodox adherents means that diverse partners must be ready to disregard their philosophies of ministry and possibly some of their moral positions when teaming up on matters of mutual political and social concern.

Despite its inherent incongruity with the Great Commission, ecumenism has moved from a goal to a reality for many missions organizations and activities across the world today. In light of the necessary compromises that are needed to achieve ecumenical unity, no missionary can be assured that an ecumenical partnership will lead to the true gospel being proclaimed through a joint evangelistic event or program, or to disciple-making being achieved through biblically faithful local churches.

Post-Reformation Missions Emphases

The Reformers left the strong theological foundation of *sola Scriptura* as an enduring legacy for successive generations. They also fostered an ever-deepening understanding of the biblical teachings that distanced their beliefs and practices from those of Roman Catholicism and distinguished the theological frameworks emerging among fellow Reformers.[5] Protestant missions history would bear out the Reformation-era focus of putting the Bible into indigenous hands so that through missionaries, local elders would be raised up in local churches. Such was the goal of the Calvinistic French Huguenots, for example, who in 1557 attempted to establish self-propagating gospel-centered communities in Brazil.[6]

However, by the middle of the eighteenth century, liberal Protestant theologians, particularly those of the Counter-Enlightenment Romantic movement, began to actively propose that foreign ministry move in a culturally accommodating direction, straying far from the *sola Scriptura* conviction of the Reformation era. During the upswing of foreign missionary endeavors, such as that of William Carey

---

2. T. P. Weber, "Ecumenism," in *Evangelical Dictionary of Theology*, ed. Walter A. Elwell (Grand Rapids: Baker, 1984), 340–42.

3. Ecumenism, as it downplays theological clarity, is expressed as a satanic strategy in John MacArthur and Richard Mayhue, *Biblical Doctrine: A Systematic Summary of Bible Truth* (Wheaton, IL: Crossway, 2017), 688.

4. See the usage of the term in the Lausanne Covenant, initially published by John Stott, *The Lausanne Covenant: An Exposition and Commentary* (Minneapolis: World Wide, 1975), https://lausanne.org.

5. Justo L. González, *The Story of Christianity, Volume II: The Reformation to the Present Day*, rev. and updated (New York: HarperOne, 2010), 224–25.

6. The French Huguenots' Guanabara Confession of 1558 was written by four missionary church planters in Brazil, three of whom were martyred by Roman Catholic captors shortly after composing the document as a defense of their doctrinal convictions. A recent English-language translation is provided in James T. Dennison, *Reformed Confessions of the 16th and 17th Centuries in English Translation: Volume 2, 1552–1566* (Grand Rapids: Reformation Heritage, 2010), 117–24.

to India, liberal Protestant scholars circulated the progressive idea of cultural relativism. They urged foreigners to focus on empathizing with the pagan worldviews of indigenous populations rather than engage them with the theology of the biblical text, because, to them, to assertively confront sin with Scripture was to commit violence against a local culture and worldview.[7]

Appeals for cultural empathy eventually led the liberal Protestants to adopt the scholastic methods of the Counter-Reformation Jesuits.[8] Since the sixteenth century, the Jesuit missionaries had been promoting syncretism between their Roman Catholic dogmas and local pagan beliefs, moving beyond cultural relativism into religious pluralism, adopting contradictory local traditions and concepts into Christian theology and worship.[9] Throughout the modern era, the scholarly focus of the Jesuit-leaning liberal Protestants had the effect of locking theology and ministry strategy within the theoretical confines of ivory-tower academia.

Theological developments in the later years of the modern era, from approximately 1850 to 1910, continued to build on the missiological compromises of the liberal Protestants, opening the door for more Protestant adherents to publicly criticize biblical missions on the foreign field. The transcendentalism of American Horace Bushnell pushed European Romanticism further toward ecumenism by rejecting doctrinal absolutes and any intellectual, exegetical method to arrive at biblical truth, and by instead promoting dialogue by diverse faith participants.[10] In the first half of the twentieth century, many missionaries continued in the ethos and practices of the conservative, Scripture-oriented missionaries of earlier generations. Yet, simultaneously, new generations of missionaries and missiologists began to unite with the culturally relativistic strategies of liberal theologians.[11] The result was a united, multi-confessional understanding of the mission of the church that included not only Protestant, but Roman Catholic and Eastern Orthodox confessions. Such missiological unity did not result in the rediscovery of biblical missions but in the further expansion of cultural relativity across the world.

Ecumenism from 1910 to 1970

The goal of modern ecumenism for most of the twentieth century was to bring together

---

7. Herder captured the sentiment of his age well in his "First Dialogue Concerning National Religions," in Johann Gottfried Herder, *Against Pure Reason: Writings on Religion, Language, and History*, trans. and ed. Marcia Bunge (Eugene, OR: Wipf and Stock, 2005), 101–3.

8. González, *Reformation to the Present Day*, 225.

9. An early example is that of Matteo Ricci's controversial adoption of Confucian rites and concepts for describing the triune God and conducting worship. For brief treatment and analysis, see Paul A. Rule, "The Chinese Rites Controversy: A Long Lasting Controversy in Sino-Western Cultural History," *Pacific Rim Report* 32 (February 2004): 2–8.

10. See Horace Bushnell, "Preliminary Dissertation on the Nature of Language as Related to Thought and Spirit," preface, *God in Christ: Three Discourses, Delivered at New Haven, Cambridge, and Andover, with a Preliminary Dissertation on Language*, 3rd ed. (Hartford, CT: John Chapman, 1850).

11. On their eventual cooperation with ecumenical partners, see William Richey Hogg, *Ecumenical Foundations: A History of the International Missionary Council and Its Nineteenth-Century Background* (1952; repr., Eugene, OR: Wipf and Stock, 2002), 1–14.

theologically diverse Christians under the common cause of spiritual fellowship and social presence, in an attempt to demonstrate a unified global representation of Christ's church. Key historical events turned the principle of ecumenism into a platform for social action to become the center of many believers' Great Commission consciousness.

The ecumenical movement began with the founding of the Evangelical Alliance in England in 1846, with branches becoming established across Europe, North America, and Turkey in the following decade.[12] However, the most influential of the early assemblies was the Edinburgh Conference of 1910, which brought global missionary leaders together to strategize for worldwide evangelization, yet without establishing a doctrinal basis for partnership.[13] Avoiding theological discussions about the gospel and the role of Scripture in achieving the Great Commission left a vacuum that was filled by the pragmatism of modern-era liberal theologians.[14] No longer was it the biblically faithful church and missions leaders who would promote popular cultural engagement strategies but theologically distanced partners who would work together to overcome social problems apart from a common biblical understanding.

In 1921 the International Missionary Council (IMC) was established to perpetuate Edinburgh's goal of cooperation among mission organizations. The World Council of Churches (WCC), which was established in 1948, existed to consolidate denominationally separated Christians toward a wide range of social actions, with the goal of witnessing to the gospel in the needy world, yet without explicit biblical or doctrinal direction. Following the ecumenical flow, the IMC eventually merged with the WCC in 1961, unifying their missionary focus to an expansive set of churches, denominations, and faith systems, from mainline Protestantism to Eastern Orthodoxy.[15] The ecumenical movement thus developed into a platform of social representation, in which worldwide missionary outreach could be achieved only at the cost of ignoring the fundamental question of what doctrines are central to the missionary task.[16] Therefore, ecumenism by the mid-twentieth century, as a principle, expressed Christian goals for missions but, in practice, avoided defining the biblical doctrines that bound missionary partners or their activities.

By mid-twentieth century, the Roman Catholic Church was one of the principal anti-evangelical voices that articulated the goals of ecumenism. Roman Catholic instruction on

---

12. World Evangelical Alliance, "Our History," *World Evangelical Alliance*, accessed June 18, 2024, https://worldea.org/who-we-are/our-history/.

13. Discussed for its pivotal role in ecumenical thought and action in Craig Ott, "Introduction," *The Mission of the Church: Five Views in Conversation*, ed. Craig Ott (Grand Rapids: Baker, 2016), xi.

14. For detailed critique from a conservative missiological perspective, see David J. Hesselgrave, "Will We Correct the Edinburgh Error? Future Mission in Historical Perspective," *Southwestern Journal of Theology* 49, no. 2 (Spring 2007): 121–49.

15. Ott, *Mission of the Church*, xiii, xv; Hesselgrave, "Will We Correct the Edinburgh Error?"

16. For the WCC statement on doctrinal autonomy, see World Council of Churches, "Self-Understanding and Vision," accessed June 18, 2024, https://www.oikoumene.org/about-the-wcc/self-understanding-and-vision.

cross-cultural ministry became more deliberate and public-facing after Pope John XXIII declared in 1961 that the Church's Second Ecumenical Council (informally referred to as Vatican II), would be principally tasked with *aggiornamento*—updating or modernizing longstanding dogma about cross-cultural ministry. In the later language of Pope John Paul II in 1990, cultural accommodation was "not a matter of purely external adaptation [of the gospel]," but "the on-going dialogue between faith and culture," in which the Church reciprocally "transmits to them her own values, at the same time taking the good elements that already exist in them and renewing them from within."[17] The updated approach to evangelization by the Roman Catholic Church nevertheless retained the expectation of primacy over all other faith traditions, for while expressing the desire for joint evangelization from "brothers" previously separated due to differences of belief and practice, salvation was clarified as only possible through adherence to Roman Catholic dogma and sacraments.[18]

By the 1970s, the WCC established the Theological Education Fund (TEF), in line with its vision of social justice through missionary outreach. Practically linking the gospel message to international matters of social and civil development was deemed a "theological necessity demanded by the incarnational nature of the Word."[19] American evangelist Billy Graham's 1966 Berlin World Congress on Evangelism was pivotal in advancing an ecumenical reach among largely nonecumenical churches, furthering the aims of Edinburgh 1910. Historians consider that Billy Graham by that time was seeking "a larger, more representative, and more expansive approach to framing the Christian message and its evangelistic mandate in relation to current problems."[20] Graham had "come to accept the primary idea of ecumenism that there is a shared experience of salvation in Christ which makes all differences of belief a very secondary matter."[21]

The most prominent ecumenical development among evangelical churches and missions organizations was the 1974 International Congress on World Evangelization in Lausanne, Switzerland, which Billy Graham spearheaded with Anglican theologian John Stott.[22] The first Lausanne event was intended to offer a

---

17. See Pope John Paul II, "Redemptoris Missio: On the Permanent Validity of the Church's Missionary Mandate," §52, accessed June 18, 2024, https://www.vatican.va/content/john-paul-ii/en/encyclicals/documents/hf_jp-ii_enc_07121990_redemptoris-missio .html.

18. *Catechism of the Catholic Church* (Rome: Libreria Editrice Vaticana, 1992), §§813–22.

19. Hwa Yung, *Mangoes or Bananas? The Quest for an Authentic Asian Christian Theology* (Oxford: Regnum International, 1997), 11. See also Theological Education Fund, *Ministry in Context: The Third Mandate Programme of the Theological Education Fund (1970–77)* (Bromiley, UK: Theological Education Fund, 1972), 17–18; David J. Hesselgrave and Edward Rommen, *Contextualization: Meanings, Methods, and Models* (Pasadena, CA: William Carey Library, 1989), 48–52.

20. In Robert A. Hunt, "The History of the Lausanne Movement, 1974–2011," *International Bulletin of Missionary Research* 35, no. 2 (April 2011): 81–84, with quote on 82.

21. Iain H. Murray, *Evangelicalism Divided: A Record of Crucial Change in the Years 1950 to 2000* (Edinburgh: Banner of Truth, 2000), 69, with detailed tracing of Graham's growing ecumenism from 51–78.

22. For an early description of the event, see "Religion: A Challenge from Evangelicals," *Time*, August 5, 1974, https://content

more doctrinally conservative alternative for participants who desired to engage in common sociopolitical action without the theological liberalism of the WCC, yet a large number of participants were already WCC members, Roman Catholics, and Eastern Orthodox leaders.[23] Stott regarded social action as an implicit component of the Great Commission, reasoning that "the actual commission itself must be understood to include social as well as evangelistic responsibility."[24] While he considered social action a "partner of evangelism," he was careful to specify that they should not be totally enmeshed, for "men without Christ are perishing" and transformation through accepting the gospel is always the highest goal.[25]

The Lausanne Congress became a movement of its own, leading to the 1989 Lausanne II Congress in Manila, Philippines, and the 2010 Lausanne III Congress in Cape Town, South Africa. Thousands of missions leader participants have united at these events under common evangelistic convictions, with increasing attention to sociocultural needs, particularly in developing countries. By the time of Cape Town 2010, the Lausanne Movement wedded proclamation and social engagement with the term *integral mission*, defined as "social consequences" and "evangelistic consequences" that occur from "the proclamation and demonstration of the gospel. It is not simply that evangelism and social involvement are to be done alongside each other."[26] The 2010 concept of *integral mission* has thus brought the original 1974 definition of *evangelization* into a more practical focus than when it was first presented as a somewhat vague axiom: "World evangelization requires the whole Church to take the whole gospel to the whole world."[27]

For evangelical missionaries and church leaders, the Lausanne Movement remains a more appealing option than the WCC, which defines "transformational discipleship" as holistic living: "a Christ-connected way of life"[28] for the purpose of personal and communal renewal, actively changing the political, cultural, and societal infrastructures most in need of social, economic, and gender justice.[29] The WCC end goal is to achieve "God's mission of transformation toward justice, peace, and fullness of

.time.com/time/subscriber/article/0,33009,879423-1,00.html. On Stott's important role in asserting doctrinal fidelity alongside social action, see Tim Chester, *Stott on the Christian Life: Between Two Worlds* (Wheaton, IL: Crossway, 2020), 30, 180–82.

23. "Religion: A Challenge from Evangelicals." See the Lausanne Covenant, para. 5, for an expression of distancing from the common commitments of ecumenism: "Although reconciliation with other people is not reconciliation with God, nor is social action evangelism, nor is political liberation salvation, nevertheless we affirm that evangelism and socio-political involvement are both part of our Christian duty."

24. John R. W. Stott, *Christian Mission in the Modern World* (Downers Grove, IL: InterVarsity, 1975), 23–24.

25. Stott, *Christian Mission in the Modern World*, 28; also the thrust of the Lausanne Covenant, para. 5.

26. *The Cape Town Commitment: A Confession of Faith and a Call to Action*, The Third Lausanne Congress, 2010, accessed June 18, 2024, https://lausanne.org/wp-content/uploads/2021/10/The-Cape-Town-Commitment---Pages-20-09-2021.pdf.

27. Lausanne Covenant, para. 6.

28. Risto Jukko, Jooseop Keum, and (Kay) Kyeong-Ah Woo, eds., *Called to Transforming Discipleship: Devotions from the World Council of Churches Conference on World Mission and Evangelism* (Arusha, Tanzania, March 8–13, 2018), 53.

29. Social, economic, and gender justice are some of the areas of investment presented on the WCC website at https://www.oikoumene.org/.

life for the entire world."[30] Yet the concern with Lausanne remains how to safeguard "integral mission" from becoming full-blown holism in practice, so that political and social activities done in the name of Christ do not consume the making of local church disciples in the name of Christ (Matt 28:19).

The Missiological Results of the Ecumenical Movement after 1970

Many contemporary theories and practices that affect cultural engagement are entrenched in ecumenism and therefore promote cultural accommodation rather than proclamation ministry to varying degrees. The following section categorizes some of the major theories and practices, namely, the influence of sociocultural studies on missions and the worldwide effect on church-planting (growth) strategy.

The Sociocultural Framing of the Gospel and Theology

The first major category of theory and practice that has influenced missionary outreach in the ecumenical movement is the "social gospel." In terms of overseas missionary service involving

the social gospel, the so-called "Hocking Report" in 1932 advocated for Asian missions to change from evangelistic proclamation to social welfare and educational programs due to increasing resistance to evangelistic efforts in India, Burma, China, and Japan.[31]

By the second half of the twentieth century, ecumenical partnerships provided the platform for Christians from diverse backgrounds, locations, and confessions to engage global cultures with increasing interconnectedness. As intercultural interest grew among newly networked Christians, so grew the connections between the secular social sciences and theology. In 1950 the Christianized discipline of cultural anthropology became a popular option for university-level study in preparation for cross-cultural ministry.[32]

By the late 1960s, Latin American socioeconomic inequalities became the focus of Roman Catholic and ecumenical political theology, named "liberation theology." By the mid-1970s, the liberation framework had become an organized front for Marxist ideologies in the public sphere of ecumenical activity.[33] Liberation theology was soon adapted to non-Latin situations

---

30. Jukko, Keum, and Woo, *Called to Transforming Discipleship*, 90.

31. William Ernest Hocking, *Re-Thinking Missions: A Laymen's Inquiry After One Hundred Years* (New York: Harper and Brothers, 1932), 325–29. For criticisms, see Leroy S. Rouner, "Hocking, William Ernest," in *Biographical Dictionary of Christian Missions*, ed. Gerald H. Anderson (New York: Macmillan, 1998), 295.

32. Secular cultural anthropology traces to the functionalist school of Bronislaw Malinowski. See Bronislaw Malinowski, *A Scientific Theory of Culture* (Chapel Hill, NC: University of Chapel Hill, 1960). For a historical summary of the secular field of cultural anthropology, as it developed in evangelicalism, and its relation to cultural studies in missions today, see Bruce Riley Ashford, "The Gospel and Culture," in *Theology and Practice of Mission: God, the Church, and the Nations*, ed. Bruce Riley Ashford (Nashville: B&H Academic, 2011), 215–18. On the variety of schools of cultural anthropology within the secular and Christian institutions, see Abraham Rosman and Paula G. Rubel, *The Tapestry of Culture*, 8th ed. (New York: McGraw Hill, 2004), 1–26; Paul G. Hiebert, *Cultural Anthropology*, 2nd ed. (Grand Rapids: Baker, 1983), 69–86.

33. Gustavo Gutiérrez, *A Theology of Liberation: History, Politics and Salvation* (Maryknoll, NY: Orbis), 3–62; noted with concern by the Congregation for the Doctrine of the Faith, "Instruction on Certain Aspects of the 'Theology of Liberation,'" the *Holy*

and quickly grew to represent all global regions.[34] It now encompasses a range of sociopolitical contextual theologies worldwide, including feminist theology, queer theology, and critical race theory, among other contextual theologies.[35] Not all of the contextual theologies have developed strategies for missionary outreach, but they have already trumpeted the ecumenical desire for Christianity to exist within the bounds of preexisting religious and cultural frameworks worldwide.[36]

As cultural awareness and a growing recognition of political and socioeconomic problems has increased on a global scale, over the last two decades missions scholars have been articulating tangible theologies of culture. Their aim is to provide biblical, conceptual bases for cross-cultural communication and strategies of theological "contextualization."[37] While contextualization theorists generally seek to articulate and appropriate the content of truth found in the Bible in a way that can be perceived with some degree of local, cultural significance, no proposal of how to do it has satisfied all who attempt it.[38] Indeed, there are few evangelical proposals identifying how to make the Bible "culturally relevant" to target audiences practically.[39]

See, accessed June 18, 2024, https://www.vatican.va/roman_curia/congregations/cfaith/documents/rc_con_cfaith_doc_19840806_theology-liberation_en.html; Mary Veeneman, *Introducing Theological Method: A Survey of Contemporary Theologians and Approaches* (Grand Rapids: Baker Academic, 2017), 124–26.

34. Prime examples include the 1976 Ecumenical Association of Third World Theologians, documented in John Parratt, ed., *An Introduction to Third World Theologies* (New York: Cambridge University Press, 2004), 11; and Pan-Africanism, a South African political ideology that has expanded to North America. See Josiah Ulysses Young III, *A Pan-African Theology: Providence and the Legacies of the Ancestors* (Trenton, NJ: Africa World, 1992); Faustin Ntamushobora, "African Theology in Quest for Alternatives to the Hegemony of Western Theology," *Common Ground Journal* 6, no. 2 (Spring 2009): 49–50.

35. A sampling of resources for those mentioned includes Delores S. Williams, "Womanist Theology: Black Women's Voices," in *Feminist Theology from the Third World: A Reader*, ed. Ursula King (Maryknoll, NY: Orbis, 1994), 77–87; Patrick S. Cheng, *Radical Love: An Introduction to Queer Theology* (New York: Seabury, 2011); Marcella Althaus-Reid, *Indecent Theology* (London: Routledge, 2002); Love L. Sechrest, Johnny Ramírez-Johnson, and Amos Yong, eds., *Can "White" People Be Saved? Triangulating Race, Theology, and Mission* (Downers Grove, IL: IVP Academic, 2018); Eric Mason, *Woke Church: An Urgent Call for Christians in America to Confront Racism and Injustice* (Chicago: Moody, 2018).

36. For an introduction to the analytical framework of postcolonialism from the understanding of ecumenical theologians, see Marèque Steele Ireland, "Postcolonial Theology," in *Global Dictionary of Theology*, ed. William A. Dyrness and Veli-Matti Kärkkäinen (Downers Grove, IL: InterVarsity, 2008), 683–87.

37. See, e.g., Michael S. Horton, *Where in the World Is the Church?* (Phillipsburg, NJ: P&R, 2002); Albert M. Wolters, *Creation Regained*, 2nd ed. (Grand Rapids: Eerdmans, 2005); T. M. Moore, *Culture Matters* (Grand Rapids: Brazos, 2007); David Bruce Hegeman, *Plowing in Hope*, 2nd ed. (Moscow, ID: Canon, 2007); Andy Crouch, *Culture Making* (Downers Grove, IL: InterVarsity, 2008); David VanDrunen, *Living in God's Two Kingdoms* (Wheaton, IL: Crossway, 2010); Ashford, *Theology and Practice of Mission*, 215–51.

38. Some prominent conservative evangelical contextualization statements and studies include Bruce J. Nicholls, "Theological Education and Evangelization," in *Let the Earth Hear His Voice: Official Reference Volume—Papers and Responses*, ed. J. D. Douglas (Minneapolis: World Wide, 1975), 634–48; David J. Hesselgrave and Edward Rommen, *Contextualization: Meanings, Methods, and Models* (Pasadena, CA: William Carey Library, 1989); Dean Flemming, *Contextualization in the New Testament: Patterns for Theology and Mission* (Downers Grove, IL: InterVarsity, 2005); Scott A. Moreau, *Contextualization in World Missions: Mapping and Assessing Evangelical Models* (Grand Rapids: Kregel Academic, 2012).

39. On the problem of insufficient practical direction by evangelical contextualizers, see Chris Burnett, "Contemporary Contextualization Theory through the Lens of Conservative Bibliology" (ThM thesis, The Master's Seminary, 2017). For one notable proposal for discipling local believers to conform their personal, cultural value system to the Scriptures, see E. D. Burns, *The*

Church Growth Movements

The church growth movement of the 1970s rose up to aid believers in the "missional" lifestyle of faith, facilitating nonproclamational methods of evangelization that were already evident in ecumenical circles. Church growth theorists offered strategic formulas that drew from the best practices of secular organizational management in order to experience numerical increase in local churches.[40] The doctrinally incomplete or nonspecific theological core of many church growth strategies, coupled with their cultural accommodation strategies, have been found to produce little spiritual fruit.[41]

Outside of the North American context, ecumenically favorable church growth principles evolved into controversial strategies, such as insider movements, many of which encourage converts to remain within the contextual community of their origins, primarily to practice faith in Christ inwardly.[42] The disciple making movement (DMM), also called the church planting movement (CPM), is a strategic growth model that is designed for use in unreached foreign contexts.[43] The engagement strategy of DMM/CPM seems to hold evangelism and church planting as its ultimate objectives, yet it is highly developed in the nonproclamational and ecumenical direction and seems to have little to no exegetical or theological basis.[44]

Other features and developments that steer missionaries in a nonproclamational direction could be added to the treatment here, but the point has been made: the ecumenical movement, particularly over the last sixty years, has left indelible consequences on global missions. Many well-meaning missiologists and organization leaders that influence evangelicals have become swept up into the compromises of mainline liberal Protestants and the Roman and Eastern churches. As a result, despite their appeals to do Great Commission work in the world, they do not insist on the ancient activities of confronting false faith and presenting the true gospel through preaching and teaching

Transcultural Gospel: Jesus Is Enough for Sinners in Cultures of Shame, Fear, Bondage, and Weakness (Cape Coral, FL: Founders, 2021).

40. See the early proposal by Donald A. McGavran, *The Bridges of God: A Study in the Strategy of Missions* (New York: Friendship, 1955); Gary McIntosh, ed., *Evaluating the Church Growth Movement*, Counterpoints (Grand Rapids: Zondervan, 2004).

41. Greg L. Hawkins et al., *Reveal: Where Are You?* (Barrington, IL: Willow Creek Resources, 2007); one such church growth strategy book was by Mark Mittelberg, *Building a Contagious Church: Revolutionizing the Way We View and Do Evangelism* (Grand Rapids: Zondervan, 2000).

42. Kevin Higgins, "The Key to Insider Movements: The 'Devoted's' of Acts," *IJFM* 21, no. 4 (Winter 2004): 155–65; Rebecca Lewis, "Promoting Movements to Christ within Natural Communities," *IJFM* 24, no. 2 (Summer 2007): 75–76. For an introduction to insider movements and the "C-Scale" spectrum of contextualization within insider communities, see Phil Parshall, *Muslim Evangelism: Contemporary Approaches to Contextualization* (Grand Rapids: Baker, 1980).

43. For description and training support in DMM strategy, see Jerry Trousdale, *Miraculous Movements: How Hundreds of Thousands of Muslims Are Falling in Love with Jesus* (Nashville: Thomas Nelson, 2012). On the interchangeability of DMM and CPM nomenclature, see Ted Esler, "Two Church Planting Paradigms," *IJFM* 30, no. 2 (Summer 2013): 67–73. For an early espousal of CPM, see V. David Garrison, *Church Planting Movements* (Richmond, VA: Office of Overseas Operations, International Mission Board of the Southern Baptist Convention, 1999).

44. For critique of DMM, see Gerald L. Sittser and Carlos Calderon, "Discipleship in Christendom . . . and Beyond," EMQ 54, no. 1 (January 2018): 25–30. For technical analysis and critique of CPM, see Robert Christopher Abner, "An Embryonic Ecclesiology Enabling Church Planting Movements to Flourish" (PhD diss., The Southern Baptist Theological Seminary, 2019), 65–96.

God's Word assertively. Rather than boldly hold out the light of the gospel in a world of spiritual darkness, in varying degrees they shroud it (2 Cor 4:4, 6).

Conclusion

Ecumenism has won many evangelicals to ministry causes and outreach programs that ring a shallow message of love and faith. Whether today's missions leaders actively promote ecumenism or passively cooperate in outreach-oriented activities with theologically contradictory partners, over time there are consequences. Neglecting to proclaim the biblical gospel message or teaching shallow and incomplete doctrine can lead new converts to a state worse than compromise. What can seem to be spiritual acceptance and growth among new audiences can prove to be spiritual stagnation, the failure to transition into the growth pattern of a true disciple. Worse yet, belief in an incomplete gospel will often reveal itself in apostasy, the return to previously held convictions, even after a time of seeming agreement with the truth.

Well-intentioned church and missions leaders must recognize the dangers that ecumenism poses to the indigenization goal of the Great Commission. The concern is that genuine converts, who persist in the faith despite insufficient preaching and teaching, will remain confused as to the convictions they should hold and may struggle to overcome sin, persisting in a continual state of spiritual immaturity. If believers remain ill-equipped for local church ministry, they will be unfit for leadership where they can most impact individual lives for Christ.

Missions agencies, missiological societies, pastoral training centers, theological institutions, and sending churches must reject outright any cultural accommodation strategies and partnerships that encumber gospel workers to the point of distraction from their divine mandate of biblical missions. Disentangling missionaries and those who support them from the ecumenical movement may require churches and missions leaders to end partnerships, remove affiliations, and even dissociate from the mainstream evangelical flow they have upheld for generations. It is good to pray for God's hand of providence to empower the global church in the face of ecumenism. Yet it would be better to pray for God to restore a vision in sending churches and missions leaders for the highest, most excellent form of unity the world can ever know: "the unity of the faith" and of "the full knowledge of the Son of God" (Eph 4:13).

CHAPTER 17

A Witness to the End: The Church's Mission in the Last Days

John MacArthur

In every generation, wild-eyed doomsday prophets and feverish conspiracy theorists have deceived the gullible by proclaiming that they were in "the last days." According to Scripture, however, the last days began with the first coming of the Lord Jesus Christ, when He died and rose again before ascending to the right hand of His Father (Acts 2:16–17; 1 Cor 10:11; 1 John 2:18). And the last days will end with the return of Christ, when He comes again to conquer His enemies and establish His earthly kingdom in Jerusalem (Rev. 20:4–6). In the time between those two comings of the Lord, the church has been given a specific mission: to go into the world and preach the gospel to all nations, calling every person to embrace the Lord Jesus in saving faith (Matt 28:18–20; Luke 24:44–49; Acts 1:6–8).

The apostle Paul warned Timothy that ministry in the last days would be difficult (2 Tim 3). That reality has proved to be true, not just for Timothy, but for every faithful

follower of Christ. The church has always faced significant threats, both from within (from false teachers) and from without (from a hostile world). Despite the challenges, the Lord has called His people to persevere in fulfilling the Great Commission.

But just because these "last days" have lasted for nearly two thousand years, the mandate for worldwide gospel proclamation is no less urgent. The apostles called the church age "the last days" precisely in order to heighten our urgency in fulfilling our commission. While no one knows the day or the hour of Christ's return, there is no question that we are closer to the end of the age than we ever have been. The Lord Jesus may come to rapture His church at any moment (1 Thess 4:13–18). Once the church is caught up to heaven, the Tribulation will commence on earth (Rev 6–18), culminating in the Lord's conquering return (Rev 19) and millennial reign (Rev 20). The recognition that the end is at hand and the coming of Christ is imminent ought to fuel a greater evangelistic zeal in the hearts of God's people as they recognize that God will not indefinitely delay His punishment of the wicked (2 Pet 3:14–15). These truths have practical implications for how believers think about missions. The reality of Christ's imminent return and the coming of the end of the age ought to heighten our fortitude, increase our fervency, clarify our focus, and motivate our faithfulness. This kind of intensified approach to fulfilling the Great Commission becomes inevitable when our theology of missions is consistent with what Scripture reveals about the future.

Fortitude

If our approach to missions is consistent with a biblical eschatology, we will be bold and courageous—knowing that the Lord whom we serve will soon return. In 2 Timothy 4:1, Paul invoked the presence of God and of Christ Jesus, "who is to judge the living and the dead," and the gravity of "His appearing and His kingdom," to deliver a final, solemn charge to Timothy. Paul's son in the faith faced serious opposition in ministry, and his resolve to press on may have been waning (1:6–7; 2:3). But Paul reminded him that the One who will judge his ministry is the Lord who sees, who is present, and who is coming. Christ will judge each man's ministry by the criteria revealed in Scripture, not by what other people say or think (Rom 14:10; 2 Cor 5:10). In light of this, Paul's charge was, "Preach the word" (2 Tim 4:2). How important this charge is for all who live in the last days, for that is when "difficult times

will come" (3:1), when "evil men and imposters will proceed from bad to worse" (3:13).

The minister of God must not compromise or capitulate in difficult times. As part of his charge, Paul warns Timothy that the time will come when people no longer endure sound doctrine, but wanting to have their ears tickled, will accumulate for themselves teachers in accordance with their own desires (2 Tim 4:3–4). The church, however, does not acquiesce to such people, whether their assaults come from outside pressures or from within their own ranks. When such opposition increases, fearless preaching is all the more necessary. When people do not tolerate the truth, that is when faithful preachers most need to speak the truth with unwavering fortitude.

Thus, Paul says, "Endure hardship, do the work of an evangelist" (2 Tim 4:5). At first glance, it might seem an abrupt change of direction to insert a call to evangelism (and by extension missions) here. But Paul is not calling Timothy to leave his flock and go out as a missionary. Rather, he is calling Timothy to be faithful in the work of boldly proclaiming the gospel. This includes announcing God's standard of holiness, which condemns everyone (Rom 3:20), along with the good news of forgiveness through faith in Christ alone (3:21–26). This is a work the pastor must not neglect, even when it raises the world's ire. Paul wanted Timothy to face the world and fearlessly preach the *evangel*, the *good news* of Christ crucified. Timothy was charged to proclaim the realities of God's law (Rom 5:20–21; Gal 3:19; 1 Tim 1:8–11), sin (Luke 24:47; John 16:8; Acts 13:38;

Gal 3:22), righteousness (Matt 5:20, 48; Rom 10:9–10; 2 Cor 5:21), and judgment (Acts 10:42; 17:30–31; Rom 2:16). He was called to magnify the glory of the cross (1 Cor 1:23; 2:2; 15:3), the hope of the resurrection (Acts 4:33; 17:18; 1 Cor 15:4, 12), and the wonder of salvation by grace alone through faith in Christ (Rom 3:24; 6:23; Eph 2:8–9). He was to proclaim these truths with clarity and conviction, no matter the consequences.

Timothy's evangelistic ministry took place in a difficult context, a world that was only growing in its hatred for Christ and His followers. "If the world hates you," Jesus said, "know that it has hated Me before it hated you. . . . 'A slave is not greater than his master.' If they persecuted Me, they will also persecute you" (John 15:18, 20). He said again, "An hour is coming for everyone who kills you to think that he is offering service to God" (John 16:2). In fact, "All who desire to live godly in Christ Jesus will be persecuted" (2 Tim 3:12). To do the work of an evangelist, then, requires courageous endurance to the end.

Scripture declares that, in spite of the world's hatred and resistance, the gospel will reach the ends of the earth before Christ's return (Matt 24:14; cf. Acts 1:8). There will be persecution, yes, but the command and the promise are presented together—the command to make disciples of all nations and the promise that heaven will include redeemed people from every tribe, tongue, nation, and people. As believers seek to fulfill the Great Commission, they must press on with this assurance that, while fulfilling the work of an evangelist

means enduring hardship, God will certainly accomplish His redemptive purposes, so that every one of His elect is saved.

Fervency

The return of Christ is the culmination of all Scripture (Rev 19:11–19) and of all Christian hope, the hope of every saint from every age. Paul typified this, writing at the end of his life, "In the future there is laid up for me the crown of righteousness, which the Lord, the righteous Judge, will award to me on that day, and not only to me, but also to all who have loved His appearing" (2 Tim 4:8). A Christian is one who loves and looks for Christ's return (Titus 2:13). In fact, the closing prayer of Scripture voices this longing on behalf of the universal church, saying, "Come, Lord Jesus" (Rev 22:17, 20).

Knowing that Christ may return at any moment adds a sense of urgency to the church's mission. The days are evil, the time is short, and Jesus is coming quickly (Rom 13:11; Eph 5:16; Col 4:5; Rev 22:20). Though the day and the hour are not given in Scripture, the next major eschatological event to take place will be the rapture of the church (2 Thess 2:2). The Lord Jesus has gone to prepare a place for believers, and He will come to take them there to be with Him until the end of the tribulation period (John 14:2–3; 1 Thess 5:9; Rev 3:10). When He does, Christians will be "caught up . . . to meet the Lord in the air," and then will return with Him to heaven (1 Cor 15:51–52; 1 Thess 4:15–17; 1 John 3:2). That is why the church has always believed that Christ's "appearing" (*parousia*) is imminent (Heb

10:24–25, 36–38; Jas 5:7; 1 Pet 4:7; 1 John 2:18; Rev 1:1).[1]

The nearness of Christ's return is a great motivation for the church. Living every moment knowing that Jesus might come in the next—this moves those who love Him to joyful obedience in such things as evangelism, or even martyrdom for His name. Nothing shows this better than the book of Revelation, since it speaks more than any other New Testament book about the events surrounding Christ's return (1:7; 2:5, 16; 3:3, 11; 12:10; 16:15; 19:11–19; 22:7, 12, 20). The initial letters to the seven churches of Asia are filled with exhortations, warnings, comforts, and promises (2:1–3:22). Revelation was not given so that the church could draw up complicated eschatological charts or interpret current political events. The Lord revealed these future realities to encourage His people with the sure hope of His soon return and to give them the strength and grace to live in light of it.

To be faithful in fulfilling the Great Commission, the church must grasp the very themes the book of Revelation proclaims. Believers must remember the awesome majesty of Jesus, their Savior and the glorious Lord of the church. They must consider the terrors of hell and let such sobering meditations spark a compassion in their hearts that produces fervent evangelism. At the same time, they must peer into the courts of heaven, see the streets of gold, hear the songs of worship, and taste the joy of sinless fellowship with the triune God who is their supreme delight.

The book of Revelation also assures the church that going to "the nations" will bear fruit for eternity to the praise of God (5:9; 7:9; 14:6; 15:3–4; 21:24–26; 22:2). Neither persecution nor death itself can stop the progress of the church's testimony to Christ, nor outweigh the value of His reward (1:9; 2:10, 13; 6:9; 12:11; 20:4). The sure hope of guaranteed success allows Christ's people to labor with the kind of unyielding fervency that bespeaks the glory and seriousness of our task.

Focus

The hope of Christ's return also sharpens believers' focus on the priority of the Great Commission. Rather than becoming distracted with activities that have no eternal value, living in light of eternity fixes our eyes on the things that truly matter, giving believers the most purposeful and fulfilled life there is to live. Paul called the Corinthian believers to that very life in 2 Corinthians 5:18–21:

Now all these things are from God, who reconciled us to Himself through Christ and gave us the ministry of reconciliation, namely, that God was in Christ reconciling the world to Himself, not counting their transgressions against them, and He has committed to us the word of reconciliation. So then, we are ambassadors for Christ, as God is pleading through us. We beg you on behalf of Christ, be reconciled to God. He made Him who knew no sin to be sin on our

---

1. "παρουσία," *NIDNTTE*, 3:649–50.

behalf, so that we might become the righteousness of God in Him.

Christians have been entrusted with "the ministry of reconciliation"—announcing to sinners that they must be reconciled to God through the substitutionary death of His Son. Because believers have been saved by the message of reconciliation, they are entrusted with the ministry of reconciliation. In fact, one might say that the one reason the redeemed remain on earth after conversion is to beg sinners to be reconciled to God just as they have been. Everything else the church does can be done better in heaven: worship will be purified, service will be perfected, love and fellowship will be consummated. Indeed, it is far better to depart and be with Christ (Phil 1:23). But evangelism requires that there be unbelievers to whom to preach the gospel, and there will be no unbelievers in heaven. So, to remain on in the flesh is more necessary for the sake of those elect sinners who have yet to come into Christ's fold (Phil 1:22–24; cf. John 10:15–16). Evangelism is what the church has been left on earth to do.

The Bible makes clear that all people are sinners by nature and by action, and thus are condemned by and alienated from holy God (Rom 3:9–20). All judgment has been given to the Son (John 5:22–27; Acts 17:31), and He will execute this judgment when He returns to earth. He will send out His angels to gather the nations before His throne and then will judge the nations (Matt 13:41, 49; 25:31ff.). To the unrepentant and unbelieving, Jesus will speak these sobering words: "Depart from Me, accursed ones, into the eternal fire which has been prepared for the devil and his angels" (Matt 25:41). Then "these will go away into eternal punishment, but the righteous into eternal life" (v. 46). The time for repentance will have passed, and the cost for rejecting the gospel could not be greater (Matt 7:21–23).

But the church has the good news: "the word of reconciliation" (2 Cor 5:19). By "word" (or *logos*) Paul meant "what is true and trustworthy, as opposed to the term 'myth' (*mythos*) which is descriptive of what is fictitious and spurious."[2] The wondrous truth the church proclaims is that the enmity between hopeless, wicked people and a holy God can be ended.

The lie of every false religious system is that somehow man can satisfy the wrath of God through good works and self-effort. But it is impossible for sinners to save themselves—or even to contribute to their salvation. That is why Paul says, "All these things [the things regarding becoming a new creation, 2 Cor 5:17] are from God, who reconciled us to Himself" (2 Cor 5:18; cf. vv. 14–17). Salvation is entirely God's doing. It is given by Him as a gift of His marvelous grace (Eph 2:8–9).

The logical conclusion of this is Paul's burden for missionary preachers in Romans 10:5–17. Since lost sinners must hear the

---

2. Philip E. Hughes, *The Second Epistle to the Corinthians*, NICNT (Grand Rapids: Eerdmans, 1997), 207; cf. "μῦθος," BDAG, 660; cf. 2 Tim 4:4; 2 Pet 1:16.

message of reconciliation to be saved, Christians must preach that message! Paul asks, "How will they hear without a preacher? And how will they preach unless they are sent?" (10:14–15). The answer is that they will not hear without a preacher, and so preachers must be deployed. They must warn sinners of their present alienation and future judgment, and earnestly plead with them to be reconciled to God. The church's sure hope of heaven and God's absolute sovereignty are no excuses for complacency. Instead, believers must stay focused on the task at hand. Knowing that the return of Christ is near and the end of the age is at hand, they must not become distracted from what God has called them to do through the ministry of reconciliation.

Faithfulness

The reality of Christ's imminent return also defines the true standard for faithfulness in fulfilling the Great Commission. It reminds us that we have been commanded not merely to make converts but to make disciples.

In other words, the Great Commission is not merely to preach the gospel to the lost. It is to gather those sinners who respond in repentant faith into the membership of sound local churches ("baptizing them") where they will be instructed in the depth and breadth of the Word of God ("teaching them to keep all that I commanded you," Matt 28:20). As followers of Jesus, new believers are to be taught to obey all their Master commanded in every aspect of their lives. The content for such instruction is the entirety of Scripture (John 17:17; 1 Pet

2:2)—both the Old Testament, which Jesus affirmed and perfectly fulfilled (e.g., Matt 5:17–19; John 10:35) and the New Testament, which Jesus revealed through His apostles (John 14:26; 16:12–14).

Paul and Barnabas exemplified this kind of faithful approach to missions (e.g., Acts 15:35; 18:11). Acts 14:21–22 records their start toward home at the end of their first missionary journey: "After they had proclaimed the gospel to that city [Derbe] and had made many disciples, they returned to Lystra and to Iconium and to Antioch, strengthening the souls of the disciples, encouraging them to continue in the faith."

As they carried the gospel to new territories, they invested in strengthening the people already won to Christ. They were not satisfied with saved sinners; they labored to produce sanctified saints, presenting "every man complete in Christ" (Col 1:28). Biblical missions, then, is didactic and pastoral. Paul would look back on his ministry in Ephesus—spanning two years of his third missionary journey (Acts 19:1–10)—and say that he taught the church there everything that was profitable, declaring to them the whole purpose of God (Acts 20:20, 27). Necessarily, that would mean that Paul taught them the truth found in all of Scripture (2 Tim 3:16).

The goal of teaching in missions is to see new converts become spiritually mature believers who have grown in Christlikeness and sound doctrine. When sinners are converted, the Holy Spirit immediately begins conforming them into the image of Christ, until He glorifies them in heaven (Rom 8:29–30; Eph 4:13; Col 3:10–11). The church is then sanctified and "prepared" as a spotless bride (2 Cor 11:2; Eph 5:23–32; Rev 19:7–8). This is the long-term goal of missions: that Christ would have His bride "in all her glory, having no spot or wrinkle or any such thing," but that she would be holy, blameless, and fit for her Savior (Eph 5:27). A faithful approach to missions must include teaching the Bible, then, because the church cannot be prepared for her Bridegroom without it. God will complete His sanctifying work on that final day (Phil 1:6), but in the meantime Christ washes His bride in the Word (Eph 5:26).

The Great Commission requires the teaching of Scripture for evangelism and discipleship. But it also orients that teaching magnificently toward the coming "end of the age" (Matt 28:20). All of redemptive history pivots around the two comings of Jesus Christ, so that His cross cannot fully be preached without pointing to His crown (e.g., Acts 3:19–21; 17:31). Moreover, the Spirit uses the entire canon of Scripture to sanctify the church and prepare her

to meet her Savior. Since that is so, the church must teach all the Lord commands to all whom He saves. This is what allegiance to Christ requires, and this is the kind of faithfulness He promises to reward (Matt 25:21, 23).

Persevering in the Last Days

Christians stand on the shoulders of the apostles and disciples who first received the Great Commission. The baton has been passed down to every generation, and it carries the same demand for faithful obedience that it did in the first century. The only difference is that "the end of the age," when Christ will return, is nearer now by some two thousand years (Matt 28:20; Rom 13:11). Because the future is certain and the time is short, believers ought to pursue the mission Christ has given us with fortitude, fervency, focus, and faithfulness.

As these final days grow darker and shorter, let the church hear her call once again and advance with blessed assurance. Christ will have the bride for whom He died. May God enable His people to be faithful until Jesus comes. Maranatha!

INSERT 17.1

Endpoints Determine Midpoints

Abner Chou

The world lives with a sense of anticipation, one that affects how people conduct their lives. To put it simply, endpoints determine midpoints. One's end goal determines his present strategy. We see this in businesses—the company has a "vision" and plans its operations accordingly. In athletics, an athlete has the goal of winning the game, so every play he makes is intended to get him closer to victory. Even in academia, undergraduate students choose majors because they hope for the end goal of some occupation or specialization. Endpoints determine midpoints.

The Christian's final cosmic endpoints influence his present earthly choices. Eschatology matters, because what a person believes about the end determines how they live today—what he invests in, strives toward, and focuses on. There should be no wonder, then, that a missionary's mindset, motives, and methods are directly or indirectly determined by his eschatology. If the missionary believes the world is moving in a certain way—for example, getting better and better—that belief will dictate how he expresses care for others and what activities he will undertake to carry out the Great Commission. Or, if the missionary believes that the world is his home, then he is going to make it more like home for him, and he will seek to get comfortable and more entrenched in the matters of this world that directly affect his lifestyle and sense of purpose. However, when the world becomes increasingly hostile, such missionaries may become afraid and angry because circumstances do not look like they are going according to plan.

Take, for example, postmillennial theology, which espouses that Christ will come after the kingdom is established on the earth.[3] The view is growing exponentially among young people worldwide, who are

---

3. For scholarly defenses of postmillennialism, see Kenneth L. Gentry Jr., *He Shall Have Dominion: A Postmillennial Eschatology* (1992; repr. Chesnee, SC: Victorious Hope, 2021); Gentry, "Postmillennialism," in *Three Views on the Millennium and Beyond*, ed. Darrell L. Bock (Grand Rapids: Zondervan, 1999), 11–57; Greg L. Bahnsen, *Victory in Jesus: The Bright Hope of Postmillennialism*, ed. Robert R. Booth (Texarkana, AR: Covenant Media, 1999); and Keith A. Mathison, *Postmillennialism: An Eschatology of Hope* (Phillipsburg, NJ: P&R, 1999).

seeing the fall of Western civilization, are witnessing the degradation of the morality of their parents' generation, and do not want to sit by and let paganism take over. In light of the moral, social, cultural, and political collapse they perceive around them, they want to stand up in opposition and appreciate the idea that Christ will use everyday people to establish his physical, perfect reign on this planet. Postmillennialism is the eschatological system that seems to give them the best justification to fight. But "the anger of man does not achieve the righteousness of God" (Jas 1:20). One does not select an eschatological view simply because of his circumstances. That can lead to a range of faulty applications, from frustration to militancy.

Scripture presents a different eschatological view that is intended to conform the believer's midpoints to godliness. In Daniel 2, God revealed the progression of history to the very end. After the nations of Babylon, Medo-Persia, Greece, Rome, and even a revived Roman Empire[4] appear, a stone, not made with hands, would come, strike these nations, making them nothing, and become a great mountain filling the earth with His dominion (Dan 2:38–45). This stone, as attested by Scripture (Ps 118:22; Eph 2:20; 1 Pet 2:7), is none other than the Lord Jesus

Christ. Just like every kingdom mentioned in Daniel's prophecy, Jesus' kingdom will be one that is physical in space and time (Dan 2:44). Just as Daniel's prophecy outlines, Jesus' coming will precede His kingdom, the mountain that fills the earth (2:34). Just as Daniel's prophecy describes, Jesus' coming will destroy all the nations, a feat that is reserved for His second coming (2:35). This progression becomes the paradigm for the rest of Scripture, both Old (Dan 7:1–14; 11:35–12:2; Zech 11–14) and New Testaments (Matt 24:15–31; 2 Thess 2:8–11; Rev 19–20). This is a premillennial eschatology.

Yet Daniel not only revealed the prophetic outline of world history but also what God would do throughout this time and how the saints should respond. Daniel prophesied that times would be hard for God's people as nations would be taken over by increasingly vicious empires (Dan 8:1–14), that even mirror the time of the Antichrist at the end (Dan 8:17; 11:35–45). As the rest of Scripture affirms, times will go from bad to worse (2 Tim 3:13). Global difficulties will mount until the Lord Jesus Christ returns to reign on the earth (Matt 24–25; Acts 20:29–30; 2 Pet 2:1–2; Jude 3–4; Rev 6–18). Nevertheless, God is sovereign over the nations; He cannot be rivaled,

---

4. J. Paul Tanner, *Daniel*, EEC (Bellingham, WA: Lexham, 2020), 202–5; Stephen R. Miller, *Daniel*, NAC 18 (Nashville: Broadman and Holman, 1994), 97–99.

and He cannot be challenged. Kingdoms might stand against him now, but He laughs at their future (Ps 2). The Lord is bringing history to its climax in the final Adam (Dan 7:9–13; Rev 19:11–21).

That the days go from bad to worse and that God alone brings in His kingdom sharpens the necessity of the Great Commission. The church cannot make the world paradise regained, and the church's role is not to bring in God's kingdom. Rather, the church is to be the witness of Christ, the One who will achieve that victory. The issue at this stage of history is not the betterment of society but to be on the right side when He returns, judges the earth, and makes all things right. That is what the church must focus on.

Endpoints determine midpoints. And God's strategy for the end highlights why God gave the church its role at present. Believers everywhere are commanded to preach the gospel so that the world hears that the Christ who offers salvation today will rule and subdue the world in righteous judgment tomorrow. Christians do not get themselves to the end, and they themselves do not achieve the kind of victory that only He can achieve. Missionaries must not set out in their activities and programs thinking that it is in some way up to them to make the world better, so that the kingdom conditions are suitable for Christ to return. God will set the world right when the last Adam comes to subdue all evil and reign over the earth in righteousness (1 Cor 15:24–26, 45; cf. Gen 1:26–28). The church's role, then, is to declare Him until He comes.

CHAPTER 18

Missions Today in Light of Christ's Imminent Return

Chris Burnett

The missionary activity of the apostles and the first-century church was motivated in large part by predictive prophecy concerning the return of Christ. However, in debates over the nature and location of Christ's return and millennial reign, an often-overlooked aspect is the timing of the return of Christ. This chapter will look at select New Testament passages and show how they teach believers to view the return of Christ as imminent—the next stage in God's redemptive plan that could happen at any moment. These passages encourage Christians everywhere to conduct themselves in godly ways and advance the Great Commission with an urgency and focus because the next stage of God's redemptive plan is the soon return of Christ.

Matthew 24–25

The first passage that teaches about the imminent return of Christ is Matthew 24–25. There Jesus did not reveal a clear time frame for the "end of the age" as the disciples asked (24:3). However, by focusing on tribulation events that awaited a future generation (v. 34), Jesus taught on imminency—His signless, sudden return—to urge the present-age believers to remain faithful regardless of what may appear to be end-time events.[1] The fruit of expectancy, that patient anticipation of the Lord's imminent return, is an all-encompassing tension in the life of the Christian. To this end, believers should be alert at all times, watching for His return (Mark 13:33–37) and ministering boldly until He comes (1 Cor 16:13; 1 Thess 5:6; 1 Pet 5:8; Rev 3:2). In Matthew 24:45–51, Jesus called his disciples to holy living and to prioritize servanthood. In 25:1–13, He demanded urgent expectation for His return in all godliness, and in 25:14–30 He taught on the importance of responsible labor for the kingdom.

In light of Jesus' prophetic content and

---

1. See Robert L. Thomas, "The Rapture and the Biblical Teaching of Imminency," in *Evidence for the Rapture: A Biblical Case for Pretribulationism*, ed. John F. Hart (Chicago: Moody, 2015), 23–24, 31.

exhortations, the missionary must reinforce the expectancy of Christ's sudden return with local disciples: serve the Master with all diligence and haste until the *parousia* (the "coming" of Christ; see Matt 24:3, 27, 37, 39).[2] Every believer must be characterized by moral living, eager preparedness to be with Him in glory, and faithfulness in ministry. As Jesus taught, failure to appreciate the imminence of Christ's return opens the door to folly and peril (24:42; 25:13).

1 Corinthians 15

In his letter to the Corinthians, Paul delineates the doctrine of bodily resurrection and rapture to offer a transcendent hope that will buttress the church in the face of false teaching. In our secularized twenty-first century, Paul's message resonates strongly, especially to those who suffer opposition to the gospel: living faithfully before a faithless world is in part shaped by a biblical view of the future. For, "if we have hoped in Christ in this life only, we are of all men most to be pitied" (1 Cor 15:19).

The illogical claim that believers would not be raised from the dead (1 Cor 15:12) is countered by the reality that Jesus Christ was raised as the "first fruits" of all who die in the faith (vv. 13–23, esp. 20, 23). Were there no resurrected Christ, there would be no redemption in Christ, nor would there be any resurrection or rapture in Him. And if, in the end, death rather than Christ held authority over the believer, then there would be no motivation to serve Him during times of suffering (vv. 30–32).

When missionaries teach national believers to expect the rapture and the bodily resurrection with the imminent return of Christ, they will have been faithful to the work and will stand confidently before Christ in the day of glorification and reward (Phil 2:16; cf. 1:6; 1 Cor 3:10–15; 4:5; 2 Cor 5:9–10). Eschatologically informed believers will live above the evils of this world and will be more ready to proclaim the gospel to their people. The stronger their convictions about the truth the more confident their ministry to their people—eschatological hope is a key motivator to being a light in this crooked and perverse generation (Phil 2:15).

Conversely, the missionary who denies the global church the rich exhortations that arise from eschatology is guilty of theological ignorance both for himself and for those he serves. Considering eschatology to be a minor topic to be sidelined, or even an advanced topic kept at bay from young believers, leaves the believer exposed to worldliness rather than a mind set on heaven (1 Cor 15:33–34). What is more, beyond implicitly hindering one from living heaven-bound, the national church will not be sufficiently motivated to defend the truth of God that Paul affirmed. Quelling the kinds of eschatological heresies that plague the church, as was the case in Corinth, becomes all the more difficult to the theologically dull and undiscerning.

---

2. "παρουσία," BDAG, 780.

Titus 2

Paul's message to his missionary delegate Titus in the overseas context of Crete outlines the godly behavior required of both the missionary and the indigenous believer, and it does so on exegetical grounds. The missionary must authoritatively proclaim how saving grace powerfully intervened in the world at Jesus Christ's first coming (Titus 2:11) and now provides spiritual redemption and purification to all who will believe in Him today (v. 12). But the proclamation of the gospel (v. 15) is not complete unless it points to the final redemption promised at Christ's future physical appearance. The hope that Christ will soon be revealed in His unfading glory provides the motivation for boldness in proclaiming the gospel now (v. 15; cf. 2 Cor 3:10–12).

Additionally, it is that longing for the realization of the future hope, that expectancy, that fuels today's church to live in righteousness (Titus 2:12). The renunciation of sin, the practice of righteousness, and eager service today are zealously lived out under the looming shadow of Christ's appearing (v. 14).

Therefore, keeping a focus on the "blessed hope" strengthens the missionary's resolve to instruct nationals on the importance of godly conduct now. The expectancy of Christ's imminent physical return is the context whereby the faithful missionary must rebuke believers who are not living "sensibly, righteously, and godly in the present age" (Titus 2:12).

1 Thessalonians 1, 4, 5

More eschatological teaching is found in 1 Thessalonians (1:10; 2:12; 2:19; 3:13). According to 1 Thessalonians 1:9–10, all believers are commanded to uphold the doctrines of the rapture, bodily resurrection, and the physical return of Christ. Paul's recap of the Thessalonian conversions provides a clear example of how evangelization and a precise eschatology pair together in a missionary context. The passage indicates that a successful gospel witness must lead to a successful discipleship in which eschatology is incorporated into the early theological instruction of new converts from an unchurched setting.

Missionaries ought to find Paul's model of evangelization and eschatological instruction among the Thessalonian believers useful. In the narrative, the new converts received the gospel with full assurance (1 Thess 1:5) and renounced their idolatry, demonstrating sincere repentance by serving the true and living God (1:9). They continued to live out their Christian hope by eagerly awaiting the return of the resurrected Christ who saved them. The missionary who girds the national believer with eschatology actually bolster's the believer's Christology—the believer now lives a life of expectancy, permeated by service to the Savior who will return.[3]

Yet emotional and intellectual challenges arise as a disciple grows in the knowledge of doctrine and love for God and others.

---

3. Similarly expressed in R. C. H. Lenski, *The Interpretation of St. Paul's Epistles to the Colossians, to the Thessalonians, to Timothy, to Titus and to Philemon* (Columbus, OH: Lutheran Book Concern, 1937), 234–35.

The Thessalonian believers, who had been instructed on the return of Christ by Paul (2 Thess 2:5), raised troubling questions about those in the church who died or would die before the rapture (1 Thess 4:13). Despite Timothy's efforts to root them in doctrine (3:2), they apparently needed follow-up from Paul to resolve tensions about the timing of the resurrection of the saints and their uncertainty about whether those they mourned would participate in the glorious return of Christ.[4] In light of this deeply emotional question, Paul instructs on the future bodily resurrection. The doctrine was Paul's remedy for grief, especially in the face of the hopelessness common to nonbelievers in the local culture (4:13). For the believer, death must not generate hopeless sorrow but rather an abiding hope because of the teaching on life after physical death. Death is an inherently eschatological topic, for death as sleep (as in John 11:11) implies the promise of an awakening (1 Thess 4:16).

There are world events today that look "tribulational" from the vantage point of history. Persecuted global Christians might tend, like the Thessalonian believers, to wonder if their fiery trials constitute *parousia* events. To address such concerns about end-time events, Paul opens 1 Thessalonians 5 with the new topic of the day of the Lord. Instruction about the terrifying, wrathful event is meant as an encouragement to keep doing the important reciprocal work of edifying the saints—those

experiencing a fearful anxiety about the future should encourage one another (5:11). The sincere faith of believers can only be strengthened when recognizing that the terrifying, cataclysmic events are not for their destruction but for the wicked (5:3). The thought that the dead in Christ will be resurrected when the living believers will be snatched away, all before the day of the Lord, is designed to be a great comfort to the church.

The prophetic content ought to lead to clearheaded thought and action in the work of the ministry (1 Thess 5:6–8). Christ is even now sanctifying all who are identified with Him now with faith, hope, and love, and His sanctifying work will be made complete at the rapture or bodily resurrection of the dead in Christ. Furthermore, the fact that Christ's return will bring swift and severe punishment on unbelievers serves to motivate the church to evangelize the lost while time permits—the coming wrath necessitates urgent Christian witness (Luke 13:6–9).

The question is not whether Christ will fulfill His promise to rapture the church and raise dead church-age believers, but whether believers will pursue the completion of their sanctification with integrity and marked growth in holiness during their earthly years. Such an eschatologically aware believer will become mature. Such a believer will be emotionally grounded and positioned well to counsel and lead others to live sanctified lives in the hope of

---

4. Lenski, *Colossians, Thessalonians, Timothy, Titus, Philemon*, 323. For helpful discussion of the timing and participation view in light of problematic proposals, see Kevin D. Zuber, "Paul and the Rapture: 1 Thessalonians 4–5," in *Evidence for the Rapture*, 151–55.

the soon coming Christ. Blamelessness of spirit, soul, and body are not just ultimate goals but real desires that should tangibly mark every Christian. For a missionary to neglect teaching this eschatological content to persecuted global Christians is, on a very real and practical level, unconscionable.

2 Thessalonians 1:1–2:12

The severity of the affliction suffered by the church caused the Thessalonians once again to fear they were living in the vengeful day of the Lord (2 Thess 1:4). Though they were maturing in faith and love since Paul's first letter (1:3), they apparently waned in eschatological hope due to their pressing difficulties. Paul's second letter addresses the believers' debilitating concern that they had somehow missed the gathering of the saints at the rapture (2:1–2). Yet, as bad as the suffering may have been, there was still little correlation with the ultimate day of the Lord because specific events would need to take place before Christ would come to rule (2:3–4). Ultimate relief from suffering and persecution must wait for an unknown future time when Christ in his wrath metes out all due vengeance against the wicked (1:6–10; 2:8, 12).

Having a right view of the end of the wicked is necessary so that the suffering Christian might understand both the full extent of God's justice and the present call to personal righteousness. A correct eschatological framework is essential for reinforcing the believer's steadfast pursuit of a worthy walk full of deeds commensurate with true faith, all done to the glory of the Lord (2 Thess 1:11–12; cf. Phil 1:9–11).

Once again, it is the missionary's task to adopt these doctrines, live in the light of them, and teach them in the very difficult circumstances in which the global church suffers.

Notice how practical the theological instruction is. Paul's letter indicates that the Thessalonian disciples believed the doctrine of the rapture. What they needed now was pastoral care so that they could live godly lives in light of the prophecies. Paul, in his wisdom, actually addressed their concerns with a more detailed doctrine of eschatology. The missionary would do well to utilize doctrine to instill a Christian hope, and to do so pastorally, especially as the global church faces increasing persecution.

2 Peter 3:1–18

Peter reminds his readers to be attentive to the eschatological teaching that they receive because the predictive prophecy he proclaims comes from the Old Testament prophets, and also from Jesus and the other apostles (2 Pet 3:1–2). No Christian should disparage the doctrine of the return of Christ with some feigned "pan-millennialism," the idea that everything will work out in the end, so it doesn't matter what people believe, which is no better than false teaching. In fact, Peter does not record the prophecy lesson simply to fill out his readers' eschatology. Rather, he does so to help the maturing believers grow stronger in discernment and fight more astutely against the false teachers who preyed on them with twisted theology (3:16).

Peter's eschatology, as a weapon for the fight, covers the following aspects. First, Christ's return is imminent (2 Pet 3:10) and will come when His patience—which should be considered a gracious opportunity for salvation (v. 15; cf. Acts 2:40; 2 Cor 6:2)—runs out (2 Pet 3:9; Phil 4:5; James 5:8–9; Rev 3:11; 22:7, 12, 20). The timing of the return of Christ is sovereignly determined based on when Christ completes His saving work in this epoch. Second, the events of the *parousia* will ultimately usher in drastic cosmic changes, and such knowledge is the motive for believers in the interim to remain immovable in their faith and exhibit the fruit of holiness and godliness in all their affairs (2 Pet 3:11–12).

The missionary is tasked with proclaiming the predictions from the Old Testament and New Testament prophets, for knowing the future is designed to impact the present. Precisely because the Lord has promised that the new heavens and a new earth will be inhabited in righteousness (2 Pet 3:13), the believer must now practice righteousness (v. 14). Despite the fiery trials now being faced (1 Pet 4:12) and no matter the global upheaval to come (2 Pet 3:10, 12), true believers must live in peace (v. 14). Peace now, in view of the coming cosmic chaos, is true stability of heart and mind (vv. 16–17). The missionary must stave off the perversion that comes from biblical ignorance (v. 16). Peter sees eternal fruit in the proper understanding of eschatology: believing and applying the truths of the *parousia* lead to growth "in the grace and knowledge of our Lord and Savior Jesus Christ" and ultimately the ascription of more glory to Him "both now and to the day of eternity" (v. 18). Such is the hope for believers in all cultures of all generations, until the Lord has accomplished the fullness of His salvation.

Conclusion

Accordingly, there are good reasons to teach dispensational eschatology in the foreign context. The biblical teachings on the future are not vague, esoteric, or sideline matters that the missionary can take or leave when making indigenous disciples. Understanding the prophetic hermeneutic is significant for the Christian's convictions today in at least three ways. First, the believer has a sure future upon which to fix his or her thoughts, so that during the fiercest of earthly trials he or she may hold an unwavering hope in the ultimate rescue of Christ. Second, biblical clarity on the future of those who are not caught up in the air with Christ demands a level of urgency in evangelism and ethical conduct among unbelievers, so that they might be won to Christ and saved from His targeted wrath. Third, Christ's delay in returning has thus far given believers more opportunity to follow Him in His virtues, namely, by cultivating patience and steadfast faith, and a richer sanctification during this time of exile on the earth.

A New Creation Model for Today

Michael Vlach

Differing views of eschatology often result from contrasting assumptions people have regarding God's purposes. Prior beliefs about how God works can influence how one approaches prophetic texts and the Bible's storyline. Wrong assumptions distort what God has revealed. Christians, then, need to make sure their understanding of God's purposes stems from the Bible and not from other worldviews or philosophies. That includes their understanding of how eschatology informs missiology and the Christian life.

Two Models of Eschatology

On the spectrum of how Christians view God's purposes, there are two models—the Spiritual Vision Model and the New Creation Model.[5] The Spiritual Vision Model elevates spiritual realities over physical matters and adopts influences stemming from Plato.[6] Most early Christians were not Platonists, but these ideas often infiltrated the church. For example, Origen (AD 185–254) denied or came close to denying bodily resurrection.[7] The influential theologian Augustine (AD 354–430) thought the idea of an earthly kingdom of Jesus was carnal and opted to view the kingdom of God as a spiritual entity, the church, a view that came to be known as amillennialism.[8] The Roman Catholic Church of the Middle Ages likewise operated according to overspiritualized assumptions about God's kingdom.

The New Creation Model is a better paradigm for grasping all of God's purposes revealed in Scripture. It recognizes that God's creation, kingdom, covenant, and

---

5. This language is borrowed from Craig Blaising, "Premillennialism," in *Three Views on the Millennium and Beyond*, ed. Darrell Bock (Grand Rapids: Zondervan, 1999), 161; cf. Howard A. Snyder, *Models of the Kingdom* (Eugene, OR: Wipf and Stock, 1991), 42.

6. Cf. Blaising, 161; Randy Alcorn, "Christoplatonism's False Assumptions," in *Heaven* (Wheaton, IL: Tyndale, 2004), 459–66.

7. Alister E. McGrath, *A Brief History of Heaven* (Malden, MA: Blackwell, 2003), 33–34; Benedict T. Viviano, *The Kingdom of God in History* (Eugene, OR: Wipf and Stock, 1988), 39–40.

8. Diogenes Allen, *Philosophy for Understanding Theology* (Atlanta: John Knox, 1985), 82, 91; Viviano, *Kingdom of God in History*, 52–54.

salvation purposes in Jesus are multidimensional. These purposes involve the salvation of sinners, and they include spiritual, material, individual, national, and international elements. God's plans involve the earth, the promised land, Israel, geopolitical nations, the church, animals, the inanimate creation, and social-cultural-political realities.

All areas of creation have been marred and distorted because of sin and the fall, as described in Genesis 3 and Romans 8. But God does not give up on either humanity or creation. Jesus is working to restore everything damaged by the fall. Peter stated that the sending of Jesus will bring the "restoration of all things" (Acts 3:21), and elsewhere Jesus' return is promised to bring a "regeneration" of everything (Matt 19:28; cf. Isa 65–66; Rev 21). Resurrected believers will live on a new earth where they enjoy the direct presence of God and fellowship with other people with social and cultural interactions (Rev 21:23–22:4). All death, disease, and any remnants of the curse will be removed (Rev 22:3).

The New Creation's Implications

Through His two comings to the earth, Jesus saves people, and He will rule the nations, restore all creation, and defeat all of God's enemies. While much of church history has emphasized the spiritual and the individual, the New Creation Model challenges believers to grasp the fullness of the "restoration of all things" that God is accomplishing through Jesus. What does this mean for Christians and their role in Jesus' kingdom program? There are at least four elements to the answer.

First, the New Creation Model helps us understand and appreciate the broad scope of what God is accomplishing through Jesus. As Colossians 1:20 states, Jesus is reconciling "all things to Himself . . . through the blood of His cross." In Him all things were created (Col 1:16); in Him all things will be recreated (2 Cor 5:17; Heb 1:10–12; Rev 21:5).

Second, the hope of this model helps believers to overcome this present evil age. Jesus' followers are on the right side of history. With Revelation 2:26–27, Jesus tells the church that, for them, overcoming the world now will mean ruling the nations with Him when He returns. As the line from the hymn says, "Though the wrong seems oft so strong, God is the Ruler yet" (1 John 4:4).[9]

Jesus' followers belong to the One who will fix everything. Our labor for Him truly is not in vain (1 Cor 15:58). This age will give way to a righteous kingdom of Jesus

---

9. Maltbie Davenport Babcock, "This Is My Father's World," tune by Franklin L. Sheppard, *Alleluia: A Hymnal* (Philadelphia: Westminster, 1915).

on earth (Pss 2; 110; Zech 14:9). The trials, tribulations, and injustices will not continue forever. And when Jesus reigns, His saints will reign with Him. Revelation 5:9–10 says that people "from every tribe and tongue and people and nation . . . will reign upon the earth," meaning that our destiny is tangible. The reality of that promise gives strength to God's people in conflict with the world (Rev 2:7, 11, 26; 3:21).

Third, as salt and light in a decaying and dark world, Christians should bring their Christian worldview to all areas of their existence and environment (Matt 5:13–16). The restoration of creation and of the social, cultural, and political realms that awaits the return of Jesus shows that those areas matter. We should be motivated therefore to take our Christian worldview into every area of life.

Fourth, the New Creation Model brings focus and a sharpened understanding of why we are here and for what we are working. We are not laboring for a nebulous, mystical destiny beyond the universe. We are looking for "new heavens and a new earth, in which righteousness dwells" (2 Pet 3:13; cf. Heb 11:10). We serve the Creator God who is working to fix the world He made, and we are living among and working with people who will spend eternity either on the new earth or in the lake of fire (Rev 20:14–15). The stakes could not be higher.

The Church's Part Today

The stakes underscore the urgency and eternal value of missions. God is establishing a kingdom for Himself out of every nation through the gospel of His Son. That kingdom, reflecting a multitude of cultures, languages, and ethnicities, will take part in glorifying the Son and the Father. It will glorify God's creative goodness (Gen 1:31; Rev 5:9–10; 7:9–10). The church's mission now is to take the gospel to the nations, confident that God will accomplish this purpose. It is in these ways that the New Creation Model gives perspective, strength, motivation, and focus to all that Christians do now, including the church's mission.

PART 2

PRIORITIES

Editors' Note

Part 2 addresses priorities of biblical missions that revolve around the priority that Jesus Christ be glorified as He builds His church. Three practical, strategic areas of focus are essential for fulfilling the mission of Christ's church. When these areas are accomplished according to God's design, they result in reproducible indigenous churches that are grounded in God's Word to the glory of Christ. The first major priority of the church is to invest in developing missionaries through the local church, who will be faithful to replace themselves with local leaders in new local churches. The second priority, then, is to plant churches according to the strategies given in Scripture so that the authoritative and sufficient Word of God brings disciples in their contexts to spiritual unity and maturity in Christ. The third priority is to ensure that indigenous church leaders are theologically trained and provided the resources—starting with a faithful Bible translation—that are needed to exercise godly authority as they preach, teach, and lead the congregation in worship to God.

THE MISSIONARY DEVELOPMENT PROCESS

SUB-SECTION 1: SELECTING MISSIONARIES: IDENTIFYING AND EQUIPPING

CHAPTER 19

Igniting Passion for Missions in the Local Church

Rodney Andersen

In the busyness of day-to-day life and weekly ministry activities, churches can lose sight of the urgency of Christian missions. But as Charles Spurgeon once said, "If there be any one point in which the Christian Church ought to keep its fervour at a white heat, it is concerning missions to the heathens. If there be anything about which we cannot tolerate lukewarmness, it is the matter of sending the gospel to a dying world."[1]

It is incumbent upon pastors to ask whether their churches are marked by a white heat for missions or by the lukewarm condition Spurgeon warns against. Pastors and elders can foster this kind of passion in their churches by prioritizing missions, both privately and publicly, preaching on the theological necessity of missions, leading forth in prayer for missions, and taking practical steps to promote specific missionaries and their ministries.

Prioritize Missions

Igniting the local church's passion for missions starts with the church's own leadership. If leaders view missions support as just another side program of equal importance with the

---

1. C. H. Spurgeon, "A Young Man's Vision," in *The Metropolitan Tabernacle Pulpit Sermons*, vol. 14 (London: Passmore and Alabaster, 1868), 220.

decorating committee, for example, the congregation's view of missions will be small as well. Church leaders must make missions a priority on several fronts.

Prioritize Missions Personally

When zeal for missions in the church is low, the pastor must first examine his own heart. If he lacks genuine passion for Christ's glory among the nations, any attempt to feign excitement about missions will ultimately ring hollow. The pastor simply cannot call a congregation to have a desire for the expansion of God's kingdom if he does not possess it himself.

Of all the words a pastor can use to promote excitement for missions, his personal example will always speak the loudest. Paul wrote to the Corinthian congregation, "Be imitators of me, just as I also am of Christ" (1 Cor 11:1). If the pastor has a heart for God's glory in the nations, that conviction will leak out to the congregation, and they will develop the same heart as well. Moreover, pastors and elders who are personally passionate about missions will naturally undertake to lead their congregation's efforts. They will desire to give hands-on, godly direction, and their flock will see it.

Prioritize Financial Support of Missions

The church's support of missions is multifaceted. Financial support, however, is a real and undeniable need. Failing to commit money to gospel efforts to reach the nations effectively announces that missions is not a priority for the church. Priorities and funding are inextricably linked; to argue otherwise is disingenuous. There may be a concern that money raised toward missions will necessarily reduce the congregation's giving toward the church's other needs. Experience has shown this assumption is almost always proven false. When the congregation joyfully gives toward missions, regular church giving grows as well. The pattern is a biblical one: God loves cheerful givers and often provides them with abundant resources with which to faithfully minister (Prov 11:24; 2 Cor 9:7).

Preach Missions

The preaching of God's Word is essential in the church's weekly service. Corporate worship involves the people of God gathering together both to sing praises to Him and to hear from His Word (Eph 5:19; 1 Tim 4:13). Faithful preaching of the Scriptures declares gospel truths that lead the congregation to a passion for missions (e.g., Acts 11:19–30; 13:1–3). As Eric Wright observes, "Wherever the Scriptures are faithfully preached God's people should find missionary passion bubbling up within them. Unless the pastor deliberately avoids certain Scriptures, a careful attention to the message of the Bible will underline God's missionary vision."[2] Indeed, the clear preaching of God's Word will expose the church to God's

---

2. Eric E. Wright, *A Practical Theology of Missions: Dispelling the Mystery; Recovering the Passion* (Leominster, UK: Day One Publications, 2010), 227.

glory, man's sinfulness, and how they are to obey God's commands (2 Cor 4:1–5; 1 Tim 4:6–11).

Preach That God's Glory Demands Missions

God's desire is for His own glory to be known, and rightly so, because He is worthy of all glory. God has created all people for His glory (Isa 43:6–7), has chosen believers for His glory (Eph 1:4–6), and will bring His children to heaven for His own glory (John 17:24). God pursues His own glory because glory given to anyone or anything else would be exalting what should not be exalted. To that end, God commands His people to bring Him glory in all things (1 Cor 10:31). Those who truly know and love the Lord will have the compelling desire to glorify Him in all things—to see Him receive the glory that He alone deserves. And yet it is not enough for Christians to worship God personally and give Him glory. He should be receiving glory, receiving worship from all people in all places. As John Piper famously and accurately wrote, "Missions is not the ultimate goal of the church. Worship is. Missions exist because worship doesn't."[3] The missionary task is to bring the knowledge of God's glory to the ends of the earth.

To ignite the church's passion for missions, pastors must preach boldly and clearly about the majesty and the glory of God. The more the congregation comprehends the greatness of God, the more they will passionately desire to see Him praised among all peoples. Craig Ott and Stephen Strauss comment on this connection, "The highest motive [for missions] must remain rooted in the person of God himself: his love for the world, his redemptive work in Christ, and his promise that all the nations will hear and that his glory will fill the earth."[4] In contrast, a small view of missions, whether from the pastor or the people, is traceable to a small view of God. There will be no lasting passion for the lost if the Christian's heart is detached from the glory of God.[5]

Preach That Man's Fallenness Demands Missions

Faithful preaching exalts God, but it also explains the sinfulness of man. Although people have real needs, whether physical, emotional, relational, or social, such temporal needs pale in comparison with those that are spiritual and eternal. Humanity's temporal needs must be viewed in light of their greatest need, forgiveness from a holy God against whom they have rebelled. As Jesus taught, it ultimately amounts to nothing if the church labors to meet humanity's material needs, even with great temporal success, but neglects matters of eternal judgment and salvation (Matt 16:26).

Pastors must preach the plight of man as revealed in Scripture. They must preach the

---

3. John Piper, *Let the Nations Be Glad! The Supremacy of God in Missions* (Grand Rapids: Baker, 2003), 17.

4. Craig Ott, and Stephen J. Strauss, *Encountering Theology of Mission: Biblical Foundations, Historical Developments, and Contemporary Issues* (Grand Rapids: Baker Academic, 2010), 191.

5. Piper, *Let the Nations Be Glad!*, 41.

realities of hell (Matt 10:28; Mark 9:43). They must not neglect what Scripture has made abundantly clear. When preaching passages that speak of the individual's need to repent and follow Christ, the pastor is to remind the people of their obligation in both personal evangelism as well as the support of ministries that take the gospel to every nation, tribe, and tongue (Rev 5:9). The nations will die in their sins apart from the saving knowledge of Christ (Matt 25:41; Rev 20:11–15). Understanding man's greatest need, salvation from God's righteous wrath, will stimulate the church's passion for missions.

Preach That the Church's Obedience Demands Missions

Scripture contains many commands for Christ's followers, and each one of them is important. But in His last words before ascending to heaven, Christ gave only one command, the command to make disciples of all the nations (Matt 18:18–20; Luke 24:45–48; Acts 1:7–8). The book of Acts and the epistles that follow describe the disciples' obedience to this command and detail the spread of the gospel from Jerusalem to Judea and Samaria and to the rest of the world.

Preaching through the book of Acts should emphasize the direct link between the Great Commission, the first years of the New Testament church, and how the work remains unfinished. Several other passages compel believers to continue to evangelize (Rom 1:16–17; 2 Cor 5:18–21; 1 Thess 1:8–10; 2 Tim 4:5). New Testament passages that speak to

the reality of heaven and hell likewise require believers to proclaim the good news to the lost (Rom 2:6–8; 2 Thess 1:6–12). As pastors preach truth from God's Word and its power to save, they are to remind the church that they are responsible before God to be part of that same proclamation to the nations.

Pray for Missions

God has instituted prayer as a means for His children to give Him praise, express thanksgiving, confess sin, and bring their requests before Him. God answers the prayers of His people, simultaneously accomplishing His purposes through those prayers (James 5:16). Even as the Lord hears and answers prayer, the act of prayer itself has a profound effect on the hearts and minds of those who pray, including when they pray for Christian missions. The pastor gets the opportunity to model this vital aspect of the Christian life through his public prayers and to lead his church members to pray both corporately and individually.

Pray for Missions from the Pulpit

Prayers from the pulpit should be marked by a passion for missions. The pastor's heart for God's work among the nations is an example for the congregation, demonstrating what should be on their hearts as well. These prayers must not be performances but should accurately reflect the pastor's desire to see more worshipers of Christ around the globe, to see the missionaries thrive in their gospel ministry, and to see God raise up more workers for the harvest (Matt 9:37–38; Luke 10:2; John 17:20–21).

Pray for Missions as a Congregation

Pastors should encourage the congregation by reminding them that God works through the prayers of His people. This is a spiritual reality that holds as true in missions as in any other area. He should organize times for the church to come together to pray for the missionaries the church supports or to focus on a few countries at a time and their need for biblical churches. If the pastor provides the congregation with abundant details, giving them the most accurate representation possible of the difficulties the missionaries face, the people will begin to develop a love and compassion for the work of missions.

American Samuel Zwemer (1867–1952), was perhaps the most effective missionary to the Muslim world in the twentieth century. He was a passionate evangelist, writer, and speaker who influenced many Christians to go to the mission field.[6] He spent most of his life in Egypt and Arabia seeking to win sinners for Christ. Despite his tireless work, Zwemer never believed that his labors would change the hearts of the lost. Rather, he trusted only in God's saving power to work in the hearts of people. With this understanding, Zwemer could say with conviction, "The history of missions is the history of answered prayer."[7]

Pray for Missions as Individuals

Prayer for missions must not be isolated to corporate gatherings only. Each believer has the responsibility and opportunity to pray for cross-cultural ministries. But calling on church members to pray for missions without providing details will only discourage them, as their prayers will quickly become repetitive. The church leaders need to supply them with the information they need to understand and pray specifically for God's work among the nations.

One way pastors can encourage individual members to pray for missionaries is by providing information about the ongoing work overseas. Some churches produce calendars that highlight a different missionary each month for prayer. The church can post missionary prayer requests in the weekly bulletin to guide members in their personal prayers throughout the week. They can forward copies of missionary prayer letters so members can get better acquainted with individual ministries and needs around the world.

Promote Missions

"Out of sight, out of mind" is often the case with missionaries the church supports. When they are not around, they are often forgotten. Although it takes effort to keep the congregation informed of what is happening in the lives and ministries of missionaries, this effort is essential if the pastor wants the congregation's love for missions and its missionaries to keep going strong. Pastors can do this by strategically highlighting church-supported missionaries, encouraging members to learn more about

---

6. J. Christy Wilson Jr. *Apostle to Islam: A Biography of Samuel M. Zwemer* (Grand Rapids: Baker, 1952), 13–14.

7. Samuel M. Zwemer, *Taking Hold of God: Studies in Prayer* (London: Marshall, Morgan and Scott, 1936), 113.

missions, and calling the church's attention to the vast scope and eternal weight of the Great Commission task.

Promote the Church's Missionaries

Churches best promote their missionaries by providing stories of the lives that have been changed as a result of the missionary's labors. The plight of the church in places like Burundi is difficult to imagine for most Western Christians, so it can be understandably difficult to feel connected to what is happening there. Yet, when a believer reads of a young Burundian woman whom the Lord brought from suicidal self-neglect and turned into a joyful young believer, it is much easier to pray, both for this new sister in Christ and the church that is ministering to her.

Promoting the work of missionaries can include special events that feature missionaries, whether through a videoconferencing interview or a live speaking opportunity if the missionary is in town. Churches can also highlight missionaries by giving them a prominent place on the church website or in the weekly bulletin.

When missionaries come for furloughs, churches should make sure that there are numerous opportunities for them to build relationships with members. This should include time for sharing on Sunday mornings and in Bible studies. It is perhaps even more important to show the missionaries hospitality in the homes of church members. When members of the church build personal relationships with missionaries, they will stay engaged with the ministry overseas and share that excitement with others.

Children's ministry is another critical way for churches to promote missions. Leaders of children's programs can designate individual missionaries to feature. They can then help the children learn about the missionary, pray for them, and even collect offerings toward their ministry. Leaders must remember that there may be future missionaries in the room. The Lord often uses such experiences to draw individuals to the field. Children who learn missionary stories in Sunday school often develop the desire to go themselves one day.

Promote Missionary Biographies

Reading the biographies of missionaries who answered Christ's charge to take the gospel to the nations is a common way that Christians have developed a heart for missions. Biographies reveal both the difficulties of missions and the great joys of seeing God's saving work. Many in the church may hesitate to read a doctrinal treatment of missions, but a captivated real-life story can teach those same principles. God often uses the reading of missionary biographies to raise up others who are willing and eager to go to the nations.

Promote Visits to Missionaries

As the church prays for and gets to know the missionaries it supports, there will be natural opportunities to give more than finances. A young missionary wife may benefit from spending some quality time with a like-minded sister in Christ. A missionary in India may need help cataloging books for his seminary library. A small church in Croatia might want to run a children's summer outreach in their community. A church in Ukraine may need help repairing their bombed-out building. These needs and many more can be filled by church members who are willing to invest their time, skills, and resources.

When church members visit a missionary, the missionary receives not only a short-term benefit but a long-term connection to the supporting church as well. Additionally, the church members who go catch an even greater vision for the work the missionary is doing. They have now seen with their own eyes what the missionary is doing, they have talked to the nationals who are part of the local church, and they have seen what the missionary's daily life entails. They have learned how to pray more fervently, support more practically, and love more sincerely.

Promote the Needs of the Lost World

The busyness of life and the current "age of entertainment" in the West are two of the greatest hindrances of enthusiasm for missions in the church. Families can become so absorbed in children's activities and aspirations that there is hardly time to consider the plight of the lost. Furthermore, even well-intentioned believers can fill what little free time they have with entertainment, such as with streaming shows and movies, endlessly scrolling on social media, or becoming absorbed in video games.

Pastors must call the church to look beyond the things of earth and seek the things above (Col 3:1–2). Countless people are still without a gospel witness in their town, having no local church where the Bible is preached. Conversion to Christ is a crime in many countries and leads to the government persecution of Christians. Pastors must remind the church of the reality that there are millions of souls that will face God's wrath unless they hear the gospel and follow Jesus Christ.

Conclusion

Christ is worthy of the praise of all peoples, and He has commanded His followers to make His glory known throughout the world. Pastors therefore have the distinct responsibility of leading and equipping their people to obey this mandate. To that end, they must prioritize, preach, pray, and promote missions in the church so that more Christians will join the effort to see multitudes come to know and worship Him. Andy Johnson captures the result that this kind of pastoral effort will ideally render:

> Elders guide the congregation toward strategic missions. Missions is held up as a concern for all Christians, not just the niche "missions club." The tyranny of new trends and demands for immediate, visible results holds no sway. Members see missions as the work of the church together rather than the personal, private activity of the individual. In this church, members see missions as a core ministry of the church, not an occasional short-term project. Relationships with missionaries are deep, serious, and lasting. Joyful giving to missions is a basic part of the church's budget, not merely the fruit of occasional and desperate appeals. And members

actually value missions enough that some want to uproot their lives and be sent out long-term by the church.[8]

May such churches abound as pastors take up their high calling and privilege to promote gospel missions in their congregations.

8. Andy Johnson, *Missions: How the Local Church Goes Global* (Wheaton, IL: Crossway, 2017), 19.

Priorities a Missions-Minded Pastor Needs to Have

Paul Washer

Local church pastors deserve deep respect for their "invisible work." They get up early and go to bed late for their flocks. They carry great burdens and sometimes have little reward in this life. Such work never receives applause. Yet, without diminishing their efforts, it must be said that there is no excuse for stepping back from the Great Commission. The pastor's task is to look not only unto his own sheep but also unto the world—and not just to look, but to involve himself in global missions. Being missions-minded means that he prioritizes the activities of his local church accordingly. What follows are brief considerations about the commitments a local church pastor must make so that he does his part to advance the Great Commission.

The Pastor Must Personally Obey the Great Commission

In the charge "Go therefore and make disciples of all the nations" (Matt 28:19), "go" allows only two responses from the man of God: going to the nations himself or training and sending those who go. In some cases, "Go" has been given too much emphasis, and in others, too little.[9] When "Go" is underemphasized, it is not viewed as a necessity for the church (John 20:21; Acts 1:8); only "make disciples" is. According to this view, one might say, "I will simply bloom where I am planted." But that is wrong. It is true, the combined command "go and make" does not require transnational movement for every missions endeavor. Yet the Lord commanded His

9. Craig Blomberg, *Matthew*, NAC 22 (Nashville: Broadman and Holman, 1992), 431.

disciples to look out over the fields that are ready for harvest, the places where someone still needs to take the gospel, and still today that includes many "nations," that is, ethnic groups (John 4:35; cf. Rom 15:20–21). Those whom God calls to pastor at home are given the Great Commission like everybody else, so they must be involved in the "going." Perhaps this is directly through their church or through some intermediary with which their church can partner, but they must be involved in going to the nations, and they must involve their flock.

What is more, church members imitate their pastors. A pastor can preach evangelism all day long, but if he is not evangelistic, his church will not be either. He can talk about missions all day long, but if he is not risking his life, his finances, and everything else for missions, then his church will not either. This is why pastors should take their own ministry trips to foreign churches and overseas pastoral training sites. For two weeks, one man can pour himself into twenty-five others and see with his own eyes at least part of the story there on the mission field. He will return home exhausted but encouraged. He will have personally modeled for his people the kind of sacrificial commitment to the Great Commission they should make. More importantly, those he taught will be encouraged and equipped. Pastors must prioritize this kind of personal commitment.

On the other hand, when "Go" is overemphasized, some think that because the world is so needy, the church must send people out whether or not they are trained or qualified. A missionary half trained is better than none at all, they reason. This also is not true. The command is not, "Go, send anyone," but, "Go . . . and make disciples . . . teaching them to observe all that I commanded you" (Matt 28:20). Missions is therefore a doctrinal endeavor. It is didactic in nature. It is not even about sending missionaries as such but about sending God's truth through missionaries. This means that the local church pastor must prioritize the doctrinal training of missionaries as much as he does their sending so that they will go and make disciples on the field.

The Pastor Must Follow Paul's Missions Strategy

Strategically, missions should be simple. In the New Testament, the missionary Paul and his co-laborers employed one fundamental strategy: to plant biblical, autonomous, local churches. Missions therefore means church planting, and a church is planted in the same way it is pastored back at home. In 2 Timothy 4:5, Paul instructed Timothy, who shepherded the planted church, "Be sober in all things, endure hardship, do the work of an evangelist, fulfill your ministry." Pastors must evangelize while also pastoring the converted by teaching and discipling. In the process, they also set their sights on men to train as elders—elders in the very church they lead, who will in turn become the local pastors to teach and disciple the flock. Paul instructed Timothy, "The things which you have heard from me in the presence of many witnesses, entrust these to faithful men who will be able to teach others also" (2:2).

The result of planting and pastoring a local church is that some who are trained by the missionary will become the pastors and others will go out to plant new churches. They will evangelize, disciple, and raise up elders elsewhere among their people and beyond. This is the cycle of biblical missions—the outworking of the Great Commission. It is neither fancy nor clever, nor can it be done in the flesh. It is hard. It requires bloody knees. It requires the death of the flesh. But if a local church pastor is missions-minded, instilling the model of local, maturing, reproducing churches everywhere is his priority.

The Pastor Must Preach the Gospel Authoritatively

Too many missions organizations reduce their doctrinal statements to the lowest common denominator among self-identified Christians—and pastors are asleep to it. The reduction allows agencies to enlist as many laborers as possible. The people they send may be sincere, and the organizations themselves are sincere in wanting to fulfill the Great Commission. Yet sending out a minimally united team—for example, four men having different ecclesiologies—is a recipe for doctrinal apathy and mission drift wherever they go. The teammates cannot exposit the whole Word with authority; if they do not, both they and the pastors who send them are failing in missions again. Pastors must preach, and they must send men to preach on the authority of Jesus Christ (Matt 28:18; Rom 10:14–15).

This problematic mixture of sincerity and unbiblical authority is not marginal, for the gospel message inevitably suffers in it. Modern Christianity has reduced the majestic, powerful declaration of Calvary down to a handful of "spiritual laws," a few "things God wants you to know," or a simple, repeated prayer. And where the gospel is reduced, its power is lost. Yet, when a man understands that the pure gospel is the power of God (Rom 1:16), he stands in the pulpit as Ezekiel in a valley of dry bones (Ezek 37:1–10). When he preaches faithfully, men will be raised from the dead by the supernatural working of the Holy Spirit just as God promised they would.

The latter preaching is precisely what missionary Paul did. He said to the Thessalonians, "Our gospel did not come to you in word only, but also in power and in the Holy Spirit and with full assurance" (1 Thess 1:5). He renounced every method and metric of success besides fully preaching Christ and trusting the Spirit to work through his preaching (1 Cor 2:7; 2 Cor 4:1–10). For, his message stood not on the authority of its worldly wisdom or cultural acceptability, but on the authority of its Source, the only wise, all-powerful God (1 Cor 2:1–8). So, too, pastors absolutely must prioritize authoritative preaching and gospel purity in their pulpits, their missions training, and their missions partnerships. It is their responsibility to guide missions teams into the same confidence and faithfulness in every place.

Pastors indeed have much to carry. Praise God, He sustains them for it. But by His command, these essential priorities of the Great Commission must be carried too. If pastors do not embrace personal obedience in missions, following Paul's strategy and preaching or sending preachers with authority, then they are not truly missions minded. What is more, if pastors do not embrace these commitments their churches will not either. There is no excuse for disobedience.

CHAPTER 20

Mobilizing and Mentoring for Missions: Ten Key Considerations for Every Church

Cecil Stalnaker

Biblical missions aims to make disciples of all nations, disciples who worship God in spirit and in truth (John 4:23). Making disciples is also the primary responsibility of the local church (Eph 4:11–16). Therefore, to accomplish its God-ordained goal, the local church must mobilize its people for missions and mentor its potential missionaries. That means the church's missions intelligence must be high. This chapter offers ten key principles, related to these two categories of mobilization and mentoring, to equip the local church with knowledge so that it can faithfully and effectively carry out its Great Commission priority.

Mobilizing for Missions

Mobilizing for missions refers to the general preparatory activities of enabling and organizing someone for action. Below are the key ways that biblical missionaries are mobilized.

Churches Are Responsible for Mobilizing Missionaries

Contrary to what many think, missions agencies are not the primary mobilizers of missionaries. That responsibility belongs to the local church (e.g., Acts 13:1–4). Agencies are valuable facilitators of this biblical pattern, but they do not bear primary responsibility. Both church and agency need a proper understanding of their respective roles in order to work together effectively.

The missions-minded church may serve in two roles: sending and supporting. Biblically, Paul and Barnabas were mobilized, sent, and supported by the Antiochene church. However, they were assisted on their missionary journeys by other churches, such as the believers in Philippi (Phil 4:14–16). A sending church selects, affirms, trains, supports, and sends its own missionaries across cultures to make disciples. Supporting churches are those that assist cross-cultural missionaries who do not originate from their own congregation.[1]

Churches Need Strategic and Intentional Missions Programs

Local churches must think strategically and intentionally about how they will accomplish the mission that Jesus has given. Church leaders must be more than responders, waiting for missionary candidates to tell them where they want to go. Some African church leaders, for example, have implored, "Please do not send us missionaries who plant churches and do evangelism. We are doing that. The strategic need is the equipping of church leaders." In other words, the sending of missionaries must be strategic, meeting objective needs.

Many local churches fail to guide their potential missionaries to places where there is a need. A candidate might come to the missions agency claiming, "God has called me to Spain." When asked for clarity about what he plans to do in Spain, the candidate replies that he does not really know. Pushing further, the interviewer asks, "What is it that you would like to do?" The response: "I haven't figured that out yet." This was a real-life interchange in the author's experience, and it reflects the necessity of churches to help their potential missionaries think critically about the ministry. They need to ask such questions so as to discern what the candidate's giftedness is or

whether it makes sense to send him or her to a place where nationals are sufficiently doing the work already. Churches need to lead by proactively and strategically asking these kinds of questions.

Churches Must Send Only Those Who Are Biblically Qualified

Someone has said, "It takes hundreds of nuts to hold a car together, but it takes only one of them to scatter it all over the highway." The same is true for missions. One faulty missionary has the potential to bring havoc to a ministry. Many people who would like to serve in a cross-cultural context are not qualified to do so. Of course, missionaries are not perfect; they bring both strengths and weaknesses to the field. However, specific weaknesses make certain people unfit for cross-cultural missions. For example, traveling to a foreign country will not change a person's character. For this reason, churches must be diligent in selecting and sending only those fit for the missionary task.

In sending missionaries out, the church must look at the lists of qualifications for church leaders found in 1 Timothy 3 and Acts 6. From these two passages, it is apparent that good missionaries are above reproach, sober-minded, self-controlled, respectable, hospitable, and gentle. Stated negatively, the passages show that people who have problems with alcohol, become violent, are quarrelsome, and are

---

1. Cf. Steve Beirn, *Well Sent: Reimagining the Church's Missionary-Sending Process* (Fort Washington, PA: CLC International, 2015), 164.

attached to financial gain are not qualified leaders. Additionally, the candidate must not be a new convert. They must be well thought of by outsiders. Those who are married must be faithful and manage their homes well, including their children.

Character is foundational to missions work because it lends the missionary credibility and the ability to positively influence others toward God's truth. If a church would not hire the candidate to their own staff in good conscience, then they should not entertain sending that person to the mission field. Simply put, not every Christian can be a missionary, for many do not qualify from a character perspective.

Churches Must Assess and Test Potential Missionaries

Paul instructed Timothy to test deacons before appointing them: "And these men must also first be tested; then let them serve as deacons if they are beyond reproach" (1 Tim 3:10). The verb for "tested" is in the present tense and refers to the ongoing "general assessment of a believer's service by the church."[2] Potential missionaries should be tested as part of their missionary qualifications before being sent out by a local church.

The Great Commission is urgent. The workers are few and the harvest is plentiful. But having more workers is not necessarily better, for a church's failure to carefully evaluate missionary candidates can cause significant damage to the cause of Christ. Testing and

approval are critical because life and ministry become more complex and stressful in cross-cultural contexts. Marriages will be under greater stress. Interpersonal relationships with fellow missionaries and national workers will be tried. In these circumstances, the sins of one missionary have the potential to undo years of foundation work laid by others.

When assessing a potential missionary, a helpful framework is to examine that person regarding their caliber, competency, and compatibility:

- Missionary Caliber
  - » Faithfulness
  - » Teachability
  - » Flexibility
  - » Initiative
  - » Submissiveness to authority
  - » Flexibility and adaptability
- Missionary Competency
  - » Does the candidate have the necessary spiritual gifts and skills to do the job?
  - » Can the candidate defend and explain doctrine?
  - » Can the candidate evangelize appropriately in light of the cultural context?
  - » Is the candidate competent in disciple-making?
- Missionary Compatibility
  - » Is the candidate compatible with the church and missions agency on doctrine?

---

2. John MacArthur, *1 Timothy*, MNTC (Chicago: Moody, 1995), 129.

» Is the candidate compatible with the church's vision and goals for missions?

» Is the candidate compatible with other team members?

» Is the candidate compatible with the national church and its leaders?

Only missionaries who pass these tests should be mobilized for the field.

Churches Must Examine the "Call" of the Candidate

It is critical for a missionary to have a firm understanding of their calling. In other words, those going to the field must be convinced that God wants them in cross-cultural missions work. This is important, because an articulable call will carry the missionary through many difficulties, such as constant encounters with people who are resistant to the gospel, immature believers, conflict with other missionaries, or incompetency of mission organizations.

There is no cookie-cutter way to discern a missionary's calling. In making an evaluation, however, both the individual and the church should look for two essential elements: internal and external calling. The internal call involves the leading of the Holy Spirit. It is often identified as a personal drive to fulfill the Great Commission. The Holy Spirit will profoundly move the people He is calling into the field. Charles Spurgeon said that the Spirit will create

"an intense, all-absorbing desire for the work."[3] Often this subjective aspect of the call is so intense that a person will not want to do anything else in life, feeling as if they have been created to make disciples in a cross-cultural context.

The external element of the call is an affirmation by the local church. It includes the local church's objective evaluation of the person's life, character, spiritual giftedness, and general fitness for ministry. In essence, the church is to provide the external confirmation of the missionary's internal desire.

Churches Do More Than Affirm Missionaries; They Send Them

Missiologist Steve Beirn says, "Missionaries don't just go to the lost; they are sent to the lost."[4] They are not sent because they volunteer but because they have been selected and sent by the Holy Spirit through the local church. Being sent was the experience of Paul and Barnabas in this same way: "The Holy Spirit said, 'Set apart for Me Barnabas and Saul for the work to which I have called them.' Then when they had fasted and prayed and laid their hands on them, they sent them away" (Acts 13:2–3). The church at Antioch was entirely behind them.

The apostle John was of the same mind, writing to another church, "You will do well to send them [certain others] on their way in a manner worthy of God. For they went out for the sake of the Name. . . . Therefore, we ought

---

3. Charles H. Spurgeon, *Lectures to My Students* (1875; repr., Grand Rapids: Zondervan, 1954), 26.
4. Beirn, *Well Sent*, 45.

to support such men, so that we may be fellow workers with the truth" (3 John 6–8). The church's job is to send people, not merely let them go. They should be sending missionaries as if God Himself were sending them out. It involves diligent prayer and help—financially, spiritually, and emotionally—just as in the New Testament.

Churches Must Be Selective When Choosing Agency Partnerships

Churches need a list of agencies that have been vetted and evaluated with whom they can partner. A preferred missions organization should be compatible with the church's doctrine, missions vision, values, and goals. For any missionary team to succeed, compatibility will be necessary. Having the same fundamental theology and vision is a necessity. This does not mean that every theological "jot and tittle" must be agreed upon, but the foundational issues must be settled. Otherwise, there will be no staying power with the team.

Doctrinal issues such as the role of women in ministry or the use of spiritual gifts have been volatile, and they have caused splits within Christianity. It is essential, then, to know a missions agency's position regarding these issues. Along with doctrine, the church needs to evaluate the agency's philosophy of ministry, its approach to evangelism, how it views discipleship, and its strategy for planting churches. Additionally, the agency should have a good track record of missionary care and accountability. Finally, it should promote proper partnership and collaborative decision-making between the local church, the missionary, and the agency.

Mentoring for Missions

When churches have done their duty to mobilize qualified missionary candidates, their job is then to mentor them—to train, equip, and advise them—until they reach the field and then continually thereafter.

Churches Are Responsible for Mentoring and Equipping Their Missionaries

Churches should apply Proverbs 19:2 as they consider sending out missionaries: "It is not good for a person to be without knowledge, and he who hurries his footsteps sins." Although there is an urgent need to make disciples, the church and its missionaries must not be hasty. Too many missionaries rush to the field without proper equipping. They may arrive at their target field in record speed, but they may experience a rapid departure as well.

Although cross-cultural ministry is complex, the local church, no matter its size, can provide the core of what a missionary needs for effective ministry in another culture. Potential missionaries should build godly character and learn the pastoral skills needed for the field in their home church. It is here they should learn how to study and interpret the Bible, lead a Bible study, share the gospel, disciple others, exercise oversight, counsel, and preach and teach God's Word. A proper ecclesiology is also a critical part of equipping. The missionary needs to know what a church is and how it is to function.

More and more churches, however, are taking shortcuts to get workers to the field. Permitting missionaries to take shortcuts is harmful because it stunts their spiritual formation and limits their acquisition of much-needed cross-cultural ministry skills. Desire without knowledge will eventually lead to discouragement and problems on the mission field.

It is striking that Paul did not begin his missionary journeys in Acts until some ten years after his conversion. Although he knew at his conversion that God had called him to reach the Gentiles (Acts 9:15–16), it was a long time before he was sent by any church. He spent three years in Arabia and Damascus, probably in preaching ministry of some sort (Gal 1:17–18),[5] and several years in his hometown of Tarsus, Cilicia (Acts 9:26–30; Gal 1:21). Then he ministered in the church plant at Antioch (Acts 11:25–30; 12:25), all before taking his first missionary journey (13:1–4). Churches should not insist that a person wait ten years before they go to the field, but they do need to ensure that the missionary candidate gets local church mentoring and equipping before being sent.

Effective mentoring has three key elements:

- Reading—deep and extensive reading of the Bible, along with rich theological and ministry-oriented books
- Ministry experiences—leading Bible studies, evangelism, disciple-making, counseling, organizing, and planning
- Dialogue—intentional interaction and discussion with seasoned mentors in ministry

Mentors guide missionary candidates in their spiritual growth and can help them understand God's heart for the nations. Mentors help candidates discover their giftedness and consider particular ministries for future work.

Churches Must Assist with Cross-Cultural Skills Training

Cross-cultural ministry is complex and challenging. Though indispensable, the missionary needs more than faithfulness, availability, and teachability. Depending on the individual ministry plan, the missionary may need deeper biblical and theological knowledge than they might receive in the local church. Every missionary needs cross-cultural skills. Matt Rhodes puts it this way:

> Christian doctors, Christian firefighters, and Christian math teachers must master a set of professional skills before they can expect God to bless others through their work period. It is no different for missionaries. The Spirit works in unique ways in each vocation, but—and this is critically important—he does not bypass our humanity when he works through us.[6]

Without the proper cross-cultural training, Christian workers can commit missionary

---

5. F. F. Bruce, *Paul: Apostle of the Free Spirit* (Milton Keynes, UK: Paternoster, 1977), 80–82.
6. Matt Rhodes, *No Shortcut to Success: A Manifesto for Modern Missions*, 9Marks (Wheaton, IL: Crossway, 2022), 19.

malpractice. One well-intentioned missionary was sent by his local church in Asia to Belgium without being culturally prepared. He did not recognize the cultural distance between the Belgian culture and his own. He then created enormous problems when he attempted to impose his own cultural values on a Belgian church. He mistakenly equated his home church culture with the way that every biblical church should look. As a result, his ministry was cut short at four years.

In another case, a young American couple was sent to the Netherlands without any cross-cultural training. Both were ill-equipped to handle the complexities of their new context. They were overwhelmed by their Dutch hosts' worldview, communication patterns, family dynamics, concept of time, and more. In both of these examples, local churches had sent committed, faithful, and available believers. Yet they were ignorant of how to approach ministry in a foreign culture. They lacked crucial missionary professional skills.

In most cases, local churches are not equipped to train their missionary prospects in advanced skills like acculturation, culture shock, and understanding worldviews. However, good missions agencies are able to provide the expertise needed to help missionaries handle the cultural barriers they will encounter. This is one reason why churches should have a list of compatible agencies to which they can point their missionaries. Such training should occur pre-field but should also continue once they have arrived on the field.

Churches Must Beware of "Mission Drift"

The world of ministry, including missions, is sadly known for individuals and institutions drifting away from their founding values, doctrine, and goals. In launching a missions program, churches normally set goals and values in precise, straightforward language built on Jesus' mandate that His followers make disciples of all nations. Gospel proclamation is the central focus. Churches that fall to mission drift are the churches that lose this focus, turning instead to other pursuits, such as social ministries.

Talk of missions is prevalent in the contemporary church. In the minds of many, there are unlimited forms of missions and every believer is a missionary, whether baking cakes for a neighbor, selling paintings in Paris, or cleaning graffiti off city walls. For some churches, agencies, and missionaries, this kind of social benevolence is the essence of missions. Each of these activities, of course, can lead to opportunities to preach Christ. Typically, however, gospel conversations rarely, if ever, happen. That is because mission drift has set in.

Mission drift is evident when the preaching of the gospel is absent or obscured, when the call to belief and repentance disappears, and when there is no thought of making biblical disciples. Mission drift is evident when the church and its missionaries cross cultures to help people with physical, social, and emotional needs without addressing their greatest need—their need for Christ. That kind of work is no longer Christian missions. Churches must be alert to this.

Conclusion

The local church carries the primary responsibility for mobilizing and mentoring missionaries to proclaim the gospel. Therefore, churches need strategic, intentional programs so that they will send only qualified, tested, and affirmed missionaries, and send them in a manner worthy of God with biblical partnerships. Churches must also take responsibility to train, equip, and advise their missionaries for cross-cultural contexts and to guard against mission drift.

To fulfill this commission well, churches must know both their role and the many pitfalls to avoid. By adhering to the biblical parameters of the task and availing themselves of the accumulated wisdom of those who have faithfully gone before, churches can effectively carry out their calling by the Lord's grace and for His glory.

INSERT 20.1

Psalm 67: Pray to Be a Blessing to the World

Chris Burnett

Psalm 67 is a familiar psalm focused on the topic of missions with a global reach. In the psalm, Israel focuses not on itself, not on local concerns, and not even on its own call to praise and worship God. Instead, it has an outward focus of worldwide praise and worship. God will receive praise from the nations, and He wants believers to pray toward that end. The psalm reads as follows:

For the choir director. With stringed instruments. A Psalm. A Song.

[1]God be gracious to us and bless us,
And cause His face to shine upon
    us—*Selah*.
[2]That Your way may be known on the
    earth,
Your salvation among all nations.
[3]Let the peoples praise You, O God;
Let all the peoples praise You.
[4]Let the nations be glad and sing for joy;
For You will judge the peoples with
    uprightness
And lead the nations on the earth. *Selah*.
[5]Let the peoples praise You, O God;
Let all the peoples praise You.
[6]The earth has yielded its produce;

God, our God, blesses us.

⁷God blesses us,

That all the ends of the earth may
fear Him.

Psalm 67 serves as a model of prayer for global missions. Believers who understand God's missionary purposes for the nations are taught to pray that they might participate in missions in a way that pleases God. The psalm reveals three priorities for prayer based on God's plan for receiving praise across the world. First, believers need to pray that the nations would be blessed with salvation (vv. 1–2). Second, they need to pray that the nations would praise God (vv. 3–5). Third, they need to pray that God would use believers to reach the world (vv. 6–7).

That God Would Bless the Nations with Salvation

In verses 1–2, God's missionary plan is revealed: He desires to bless the nations with salvation. Verse 1 records the words of a personal prayer for divine favor made by a faithful Jewish person, borrowed from the well-known Aaronic blessing of Numbers 6:22–27.[7] Verse 2 of the psalm quickly moves the inward desire outward, because believers are called to prioritize praying for God to bless the nations. Specifically, they must ask God to cause His face and joy to shine upon individuals of all family origins across the world. Such a goal reflects a heart set on fulfilling God's ancient promise in Genesis 12:1–3 to bless the nations through Abraham's descendants. The church partakes in this promise of spiritual blessing through faith in Yahweh, the God of Abraham.

It is interesting, however, that Psalm 67 uses "God" (Elohim) instead of "Yahweh," which is God's personal, covenant name revealed to Israel (Exod 3:14) and the source of Israel's blessing in both the Abrahamic Covenant in Genesis 12:1–3 and the Aaronic blessing of Numbers 6:22–27. By combining the name of "God" (cf. Elohim in Gen 1:1) with the references to the Abrahamic Covenant and the Aaronic blessing, the psalmist is showing that the spiritual blessings that Israel experienced in salvation are not just for Israel but for all believers of all time and all nations.[8]

---

7. Ross understands that for God to "cause His face to shine upon us" is an anthropomorphism referencing saving grace, given the use of "gracious" in Num 6:25 as well as "save" in Ps 31:16—"Make Your face to shine upon Your slave; Save me in Your lovingkindness." Allen P. Ross, *A Commentary on the Psalms, Volume 2 (42–89)* (Grand Rapids: Kregel Academic, 2013), 446.

8. John Piper, *Let the Nations Be Glad! The Supremacy of God in Missions* (Grand Rapids: Baker, 1993), 188. Merrill helpfully distinguishes that the name Elohim "is used most commonly in contexts where his transcendent apartness or otherness is in view as opposed to his immanence or closeness, a relationship better described by the name *Yahweh*." Eugene H. Merrill, *Everlasting Dominion: A Theology of the Old Testament* (Nashville: B&H, 2006), 39, emphasis in original.

The request for world blessing that God wants believers to make is no generic "world peace." He desires for nonbelievers scattered across the earth to receive salvation. The word order in verse 1, "gracious" before "bless," emphasizes God's gift of saving grace as the key to the spiritual reality of blessing. Believers are like Abraham, who received God's unmerited favor while he was a pagan idolater from the nations, so that he was justified by faith and transferred into a state of spiritual blessing (Gen 15:6; cf. Gal 3:6–9). According to verse 2, saving grace is the "way" that pagans from the nations need to know. The highest priority in prayer is that God would make a clear path toward saving grace for those on the earth who currently walk in the way of spiritual deadness (Eph 2:1). The path toward true restoration and stability, indeed any long-lasting peace and happiness, begins when a person enters into the spiritual blessing of salvation.

That God Would Allow the Nations to Praise Him

Verses 3–5 reveal the second missionary purpose the believer must prioritize in prayer: God's praise among the nations. If the God of heaven will answer the first request for the salvation of far-off individuals, then the second request is subsequent. Verses 3 and 5 are identical, petitioning God to cause the nations to praise Him

("let the peoples," "let all the peoples"), and the language of petition begins verse 4 as well ("let the nations").

Verse 4 is the center of this second missionary purpose of God and the center of the song. Believers are called to pray that sinners everywhere would be saved and live out the dynamics of a Spirit-filled life by praising God, rejoicing in their salvation, and singing a new song to God (Pss 40:3; 98:1; Isa 42:10; Rev 5:9). The glad rejoicing of believers in the nations today is not because of the present world conditions in which they live, for they face many hardships and conflicts for the sake of Christ (John 15:18–21; Phil 2:15; 1 Pet 1:6–7). Gladness and songs of joy recollect the grace God has accomplished for them (Ps 23:3) and are rooted in the hope of Christ's return, when He will come to judge the nations, to bring his sovereign rule to bear on the earth, and to lead the peoples of the world in the paths of righteousness (Isa 2:3–4).

That God Would Use Believers to Reach the World

The final verses of Psalm 67 (vv. 6–7) build toward the conclusion that God uses everyday believers to reach the world. The prayer priority is that God would use them to achieve His global purposes. Verse 6 begins by stating that the whole world enjoys material resources that sustain life.

The second line of verse 6 and the first part of verse 7 emphasize that it is God and no one else who brings the yield, since it is a common grace of the Provider (Acts 14:17). Believers consider what they receive to be a blessing, because by faith they see the invisible hand of God at work to supply their needs. They have reason to thank God that their needs are abundantly met (Ps 37:25–26) and to pray that they can meet the physical needs of others (2 Cor 9:8–11).

Material resources, however, are God's gift for a much greater purpose than supplying material need. Psalm 67:7 ends with a purpose clause ("that") to highlight that the resources given to Israel are to have a multiplying effect for the worldwide worship of God. Material blessing is designed to lead to spiritual blessing, to usher in the "fear" of God as far as "the ends of the earth." Here "fear" refers to the awe-struck worship of the Creator. The prayer is that God will redeem sinners everywhere from pagan idolatry with its empty chanting so that they will be released from the shackles of sin and enter a state of wonder and humility, to praise God forever with gladness and joyful singing. For a believer to pray for worldwide blessing like this is to pray to be a blessing to the world in some practical way. It is right for faithful believers to ask God how they might participate materially in global missions. They are to pray, like the faithful believers in the psalm, that God would extend the blessing of His sovereign grace to the nations, in part by using their resources, time, money, talent, or other "produce" to make a return on investment in God's global harvest (Matt 25:14–30; Luke 19:11–27).

In conclusion, Psalm 67 shows that God's heart for the world spans all generations. Praying for the nations, then, is a whole-person endeavor, moving from thought to action as the Lord provides opportunity. Believers who understand God's missionary purposes of redemption through Christ need to press into His purposes for them, so that they understand how to pray for and participate in global missions today, whether that is as sent missionaries or missionary senders.

CHAPTER 21

Courage to Carry Out the Great Commission: Missionary Calling, Competence, and Character

E. D. Burns

In Christ's service, some of His saints are conscripted into frontline truth warfare in the darkest, most unreached, and undiscipled corners of the earth. Defining the identity and the work of the missionary is essential to participating obediently in Christ's commission to the church. Church leaders evaluating potential missionaries must consider the individual in light of the biblical qualifications for elders and deacons,[1] the giftedness of the prospective missionary, the presence or absence of an enduring desire for the work, and an observable track record of evangelistic ministry through and with the local church. In other words, church leaders must evaluate each candidate's calling, competence, and character.[2]

The Calling of the Missionary

Missions work involves two things that last forever—the Word of God and the souls of mankind. The weightiness of the missionary role deserves to be guarded. Since missions is a work of the church, the missionary must be more than an altruistic volunteer. The Bible gives no indication that a missionary can be less qualified than a deacon or elder, depending on the sphere of service. If a missionary would not be welcomed as a spiritual leader in his home church, what should be expected of him in a pre-Christian or undiscipled context, where there is minimal accountability and insufficient theological resources? Sending someone across cultural and language barriers does not suddenly transform him into a church planter, Bible translator, or

---

1. This should not discourage or demean godly women from participating in the Great Commission. In cultures where men work only with men, many ministries that evangelize and disciple women and children require women missionaries. Nevertheless, this chapter focuses on the ordained missionary as a church leader, which underscores the role of men in missions.

2. For a more theologically thorough explanation of the missionary, missions work, and the biblical missionary call, see E. D. Burns, *The Missionary-Theologian: Sent into the World, Sanctified by the Word* (Fearn, Ross-shire, UK: Christian Focus, 2020), 53–67.

trainer of pastors.[3] Missions is not a hobby or vacation. It is a blood-earnest conviction that one must plant a flag for Christ, even if that means ministering in obscurity and dying on post.

When a Christian leader is ministering in a culture with multiple Bible translations and a history of Christian witness, not every error produces severe damage. But in a pre-Christian culture where there is no local church, or merely a fledgling church with a roughshod Bible translation and no theological resources in the local language, the impact of every influence—good, neutral, or bad—can last for generations. A lay elder in an established church might commit a theological error, receive pastoral rebuke, and step back from ministry for a season. But on the mission field, small theological compromises in the name of "cultural sensitivity" and "missional creativity" can create massive theological and practical problems for the indigenous people. A missionary must be theologically sound and demonstrably articulate, but he must also be able to defend the truth in a way that is honest, unambiguous, humble, consistent, and courageous. He must be confident to proclaim all that Scripture teaches and content to say no more.

Paul could have argued for his missionary calling by highlighting his desire, visions, and apostolic experiences, but instead he argued that the promises of Scripture were the driving force

of his missionary impulse: "But as it is written, 'They who had no declaration of him shall see, and they who have not heard shall understand'" (Rom 15:21). Paul appeals to the sacred text of Isaiah's scroll as the ground for his missionary burden. Likewise, the text should both drive and direct the missionary's labor today.

To plant a church and train pastors, to wage war for the truth against an onslaught of demonic doctrines that blind the minds of pre-evangelized people, the missionary must be a polemicist with the mind of a theologian—not a bureaucrat or diplomat. To rightly proclaim Scripture in the heart language of the target people, communicating biblical truth in the grammatical and syntactical systems of that people, the missionary must be a linguist with the dedication of a scholar—not a Christian tourist or a social activist.

The Competence of the Missionary

When training indigenous pastors and missionaries, the main goal must be to convince them of the centrality of the Word. If they identify their source of authority and truth in the Bible alone, many challenges to maturity and ministry are avoided, or are at least short-lived. The Holy Spirit is pleased to work in His people through the Word rightly divided.

It is important to impress upon indigenous pastors the qualifications of elders and deacons.

---

3. The logic of this assertion reflects that of 1 Timothy 1:7–8. One's desire to teach the law does not indicate that they understand what they are teaching. "The Law is good, if one uses it lawfully" (v. 8). The same principle applies to missions. Just because someone wants to be a church planter or to train pastors in a foreign country, that radical desire to teach the Word does not itself qualify them to do so any more than one who stays home in their passport country. To be sure, passion for the work is necessary (1 Tim 3:1) but is not an exclusive or even primary qualification. For the man of God must be competent to teach the Word (3:2), which necessitates study and hard work that is proven through rightly handling the Word (2 Tim 2:15).

Before hearing instructions on how they should discharge their duties, they need to understand the mindset and heart required for the Lord's service. Scripture is perhaps nowhere more instructive on this point than in 2 Timothy. This text serves as a memorable and reproducible case study, as Paul, the illustrious church planter, trains Timothy:

> You therefore, my child, be strong in the grace that is in Christ Jesus. And the things which you have heard from me in the presence of many witnesses, entrust these to faithful men who will be able to teach others also. Suffer hardship with me, as a good soldier of Christ Jesus. No soldier in active service entangles himself in the affairs of everyday life, so that he may please the one who enlisted him as a soldier. And also if anyone competes as an athlete, he is not crowned unless he competes according to the rules. The hard-working farmer ought to be the first to receive his share of the crops. (2 Tim 2:1–6)

Paul begins his instructions with a pastoral call to derive strength not from oneself but from grace in Christ. He calls Timothy to rest in his union with Christ and in how the grace of the gospel can supernaturally enable him to do and be what can be explained only by the power of the resurrected Christ. Paul then pictures the missionary's competence in eight roles.

Teacher

Paul instructs Timothy to have the mindset of a teacher (2 Tim 2:2). He wants Timothy to entrust the doctrines he has learned to faithful men. This trust is significant because Christ builds and purifies His church through the proclamation of the Word, which requires faithful teachers. Feeding and leading the lambs of God is a heavy task—metaphorically, fighting off wolves, searching out lost sheep, and obeying the Chief Shepherd's instructions in the face of fear and hardship. These are the tasks of a shepherd-teacher who rightly handles the Word. Paul's description of the men to be entrusted as "faithful" suggests that they must be proven and qualified.

Moreover, these taught men must likewise teach those under their charge. A missionary has the opportunity to do many good things in his target culture—things like starting a business, helping in an orphanage, or teaching English. Though he may do those things to the glory of God, if he does not prioritize translating the Bible and teaching it to indigenous disciples, he is not doing the work of a missionary. He might be a Christianized philanthropist, a bighearted businessman, or a selfless educator. But he is no biblical missionary.

Soldier

Paul also charges Timothy to have the mindset of a soldier (2 Tim 2:3–4). What kind of soldier? He must be a Great Commission soldier who is content to suffer. He must be ready to forsake the pleasures and privileges of civilian life in order to remain loyal to his King. Many good opportunities distract missionaries from their service, but it takes heavenly-minded tenacity and grit to say no, press on, and imitate the priorities of the apostle: "But I do not make my life of any account nor dear to myself, so that I may finish my course and the ministry which I received from the Lord Jesus, to testify solemnly of the gospel of the grace of God" (Acts 20:24).

Athlete

Paul encourages Timothy to develop the mindset of an athlete (2 Tim 2:5). He sternly warns Timothy that there is a right way and a wrong way to compete as an Olympian. One might seem to win the contest, but if he does not compete according to the rules, he receives no victor's crown. Considering an athlete's exertion in the games, it would be a shame to lose it all and be disqualified for not abiding by the rules. Many missionaries fall to the lure of innovative methods that manufacture observable results. Such approaches may indeed help meet physical needs. But if good works like teaching dental hygiene, digging wells, building orphanages, or launching fair-trade coffee companies take priority over translation, evangelism, and discipleship, the work falls short of Christ's commission to the church. There are many opportunities for compassionate Christians to adorn the gospel with their good deeds, but those deeds do not fulfill Christ's instructions to the church to disciple the nations.

Farmer

Paul calls Timothy to view Great Commission service like a farmer (2 Tim 2:6). As the Lord's servant, he must work hard. Many good distractions litter the mission field, and numerous excuses persuade a missionary to do the bare minimum. After all, many of their superiors repeatedly tell them not to work so hard, to focus on "being" and not "doing," to focus on the family, to stay in sync with their Enneagram type, and to monitor their self-care. J. C. Ryle compared the distaste for doctrine among young missionaries in his day to a spineless, lifeless "jellyfish Christianity."

> A jellyfish . . . is a pretty and graceful object when it floats in the sea, contracting and expanding like a little delicate, transparent umbrella. Yet the same jellyfish, when cast on the shore, is a mere helpless lump, without capacity for movement, self-defence, or self-preservation. Alas! It is a vivid type of much of the religion of this day, of which the leading principle is, "No dogma, no distinct tenets, no positive doctrine." . . . They have no definite opinions. . . . They are so afraid of "extreme views" that they have no views at all. We have thousands of "jellyfish" sermons preached every year, sermons without an edge, or a point, or corner, smooth as billiard balls, awakening no sinner, and edifying no saint.[4]

That problem continues today also. But biblical missionaries must work hard.

---

4. J. C. Ryle, *Principles for Churchmen: A Manual of Positive Statements on Some Subjects of Controversy* (London: Forgotten Books, 2012), 97–98.

Student

Later on in the chapter, Paul presses Timothy to labor as a student (2 Tim 2:15). The King James Version translates Paul's command, "Study to shew thyself approved unto God, a workman that needeth not to be ashamed, rightly dividing the word of truth." Although many no longer look at the act of "study" as a mark of diligence or of doing one's best (as it is translated in modern English versions), the metaphor of a hardworking student still applies. Paul contrasts two kinds of students here: those approved who have no need to be ashamed before God and those disapproved who should be ashamed before Him. What is the difference? The former works hard at rightly handling the Scripture; the latter either inaccurately handles Scripture or does not handle Scripture at all. In other words, a shameful missionary is one who is not a serious student of God's Word.

Fighter

Paul wraps up his instructions to Timothy in the letter by reflecting on his life's service as a missionary. He writes, "I have fought the good fight, I have finished the course, I have kept the faith" (2 Tim 4:7). Three more pictures of the missionary's competence are found here. A missionary, like Paul, must have the mindset of a fighter. He is not a boxer. A boxer fights for the sake of sport, seeking the romance of a big tournament. But a fighter must fight. His fight is not a mere competition; it is a commission. The missionary is a truth fighter who does not battle against flesh and blood but against

deceptive ideologies and demonic doctrines. He does not battle with a contentious spirit but with a compassionate spirit. A seasoned fighter knows when to walk away and when to engage. He does not fight dirty but struggles to win according to the rules.

Runner

A Pauline missionary must also have the mindset of a runner: "I have finished the course" (2 Tim 4:7). Great Commission service is a long-distance race. The work demands marathon-hardened runners—those who train dutifully, prepare themselves for the long haul, and focus more on steadily reaching the finish line than on their speed. A marathon requires focused endurance, while a sprint demands fast exertion. Some innovative missionary methods that guarantee rapid church-planting success may offer initial excitement, but the fruit of such methods is unripe and sour. The fruit of the biblically faithful method may seem to come slowly, but it is fruit that is rooted for generations.

Sentinel

Finally, being a missionary like Paul requires the mindset of a sentinel: "I have kept the faith" (2 Tim 4:7). Paul uses Roman military language, explaining that he had kept, guarded, and protected the gospel faith. Sentinels were known for loyally keeping their post in honor of Rome. Paul's claim was not that he kept his faith (his abiding trust in Christ) but that he had guarded the faith (the doctrine concerning Christ).

The missionary is not a Christianized UN worker, sent to pacify regional strife and maintain cultural civility. The missionary is an ambassador sent by the King of kings, through the church and with church support. He is sent to announce that because of what happened on a bloody Roman cross two thousand years ago, peace has been made possible between God and sinful man. The free offer of reconciliation is for all who would bow the knee before Christ alone through faith alone.

The Character of the Missionary

In addition to a biblical mindset to courageously contend for the truth, the missionary must also have the character of Christ. Though the context of 2 Timothy 2 refers to people under Timothy's direct teaching ministry, the principle extends to unreached people as well. Paul instructs, "And the Lord's slave must not be quarrelsome, but be kind to all, able to teach, patient when wronged, with gentleness correcting those who are in opposition, if perhaps God may give them repentance leading to the full knowledge of the truth" (2:24–25). Here four character qualities of the missionary are required.

Kindness

Missionaries should seek to discover how people in their target culture understand genuine kindness. Understanding his host culture's norms for hospitality and interpersonal interactions is not enough. True Christian kindness goes beyond mere civility. The Bible says that the kindness of God leads people to repentance

(Rom 2:4). Yes, kindness, the benevolence of God's heart, overflows with goodwill for ill-deserving souls. It calls them away from the dominion of darkness and toward the kingdom of light.

Being sent out to proclaim the grace of God in the gospel, missionaries have the opportunity to spend themselves in a way that draws attention to something otherworldly. They communicate a powerful message when they explain that they uprooted their lives, not for the preference of different cultures or the joy of traveling, but because they are compelled by the kindness God has displayed in the gospel. A Spirit-filled life of genuine benevolence transcends all languages and touches people in a way that makes them want to know why a foreigner would actively treat them so kindly.

Patience

Many missions methods offer guarantees for unlocking a resistant culture by God's power. Missionaries have worked to the point of exhaustion, trying to decode the Spirit's secret formula for pouring out blessings. These efforts may come from good intentions and zealous hearts, but they never truly produce fundamental transformation. No one can manufacture what God has promised to do by Himself. God's promises must dominate the missionary's mind so that no matter how enemies attack the gospel, the missionary can persevere with patience when wronged (2 Tim 2:24). He must be fully convinced of the unbreakable promises of God, the power of the written Word, and his own inability apart from God's working. The road of patience in the face of evil is the only way through the Great Commission.

Teaching and Correcting

The Bible does not describe the Lord's servant as one who merely teaches but as one who is "able to teach" (2 Tim 2:24). Paul points out in 1 Timothy that some indeed desire to teach who should not teach, because they do not know what they are asserting (1:7). He identifies others openly as false teachers (1:3; cf. 2 Tim 4:3). In contrast, the missionary must have a proven ability to rightly handle the Word.

Competence to teach presupposes the ability to correct others. The missionary must correct more than just false ideas. He must correct people. Because the missionary is often dealing with undiscipled people whose cultures highly revere their teachers, the missionary's teaching and correction must be manifestly gentle, humble, and approachable. He must teach people with patience, kindness, and gentleness, just as the Lord tenderly teaches His own.

Steadiness

Finally, applying these biblical principles to Great Commission service is dependent on God's power and help. Contemplating the truth that God alone grants repentance (2 Tim 2:25) is a marvelous assurance to a road-weary missionary. The missionary does not need to create emotional experiences wherein people feel compelled to repent. Nor should he believe that repentance is unnecessary. He must, however,

remember that repentance is a gift from God (Acts 11:18). Despite his kindness, patience with evil, competent teaching, and gentle correction, the missionary should never presume credit for people coming to the knowledge of the truth. Salvation is all of God.

Consider Ryle's charge to ministers and missionaries to wage the truth war with doctrinal courage, faithful endurance, and unflinching hope in the triumph of Christ's gospel:

> For your own soul's sake, dare to make up your mind what you believe, and dare to have positive distinct views of truth and error. Never, never be afraid to hold decided doctrinal opinions; and let no fear of man and no morbid dread of being thought party-spirited, narrow or controversial, make you rest contented with a bloodless, boneless, tasteless, colorless, lukewarm, undogmatic Christianity. Mark what I say. If you want to do good in these times you must throw aside indecision, and take up a distinct, sharply cut, doctrinal religion. If you believe little, those to whom you try to do good will believe nothing. The victories of Christianity, wherever they have been won, have been won by distinct doctrinal theology, by telling men roundly of Christ's vicarious death and sacrifice, by showing them Christ's substitution on the cross and His precious blood, by teaching them justification by faith and bidding them believe on a crucified Savior by preaching ruin by sin, redemption by Christ, regeneration by the Spirit, by lifting up the

bronze serpent, by telling men to look and live, to believe, repent and be converted. This, this is the only teaching which for eighteen centuries God has honored with success. . . . But, depend on it, if we want to "do good" and shake the world, we must fight with the old apostolic weapons, and stick to sound doctrine.[5]

---

5. J. C. Ryle, *Holiness: Its Nature, Hindrances, Difficulties, and Roots* (Apollo, PA: Icthus, 2017), 328–29.

INSERT 21.1

Living on the Brink of Eternity: The Life of David Brainerd

Brad Klassen[6]

Jonathan Edwards introduced the biography of his dear friend David Brainerd with these words: "There are two ways of representing and recommending true religion and virtue to the world. . . . The one is by doctrine and precept, the other is by instance and example. Such an instance we have in the excellent person whose life is published in the following pages."[7]

Today we know Brainerd primarily through his personal diary, which Edwards used to compose his biography. Brainerd kept the diary exclusively for himself, to be used as a thermometer for his soul. At the end of his life, he insisted that it be destroyed, but his friends prevailed upon him to preserve these writings and allow others to benefit from them. In due course, God would use Brainerd's entries as fuel for the flames of the modern missions movement, influencing individuals like John Newton, William Carey, and Jim Elliot.

Reading the entries of this diary in Edwards' biography, one quickly learns that Brainerd ministered in unimaginably difficult circumstances while exhibiting extraordinary humility and self-denial. His love for God's glory and sinners' souls

---

6. Adapted from Brad Klassen, "Living on the Brink of Eternity: The Life of David Brainerd," *The Master's Seminary Blog*, April 30, 2019, https://blog.tms.edu/living-on-the-brink-of-eternity-the-life-of-david-brainerd. Used by permission.

7. Jonathan Edwards, *The Diary and Journal of David Brainerd* (1902; repr., Edinburgh: Banner of Truth, 2014), xli, xliii.

is captivating. He died at age twenty-nine, having lived only eight years as a believer. Although some consider Brainerd too radical and reckless, a closer look at his life proves him to be a faithful servant worthy of admiration.

Overwhelmed by the Surpassing Majesty of Jesus

David Brainerd was born on April 20, 1718, in Haddam, Connecticut. He grew up in the Puritan tradition but was unconcerned about his own spiritual state. At age twenty, still not saved, he decided to follow his older brother's example and enter the ministry. According to the strength of his own love for study and reading, Brainerd began to devote himself to religious disciplines. He would later say of this period of life that he was a very good Pharisee.

But in July of 1739, when Brainerd was twenty-one years old, he experienced overwhelming conviction. He saw the world's insufficiency to bring satisfaction and his inability to produce anything truly good. He was overwhelmed by the surpassing majesty of Jesus Christ and was saved.

Serving alongside an Experienced Missionary

Now a believer, Brainerd continued to pursue ministry. In November 1742, a Scottish mission society learned about David and proposed that he should serve among the Native Americans, first serving alongside an experienced missionary before traveling to more remote and dangerous frontier regions. Brainerd agreed. Arriving in Stockbridge, Massachusetts, early in 1743, Brainerd would study the Algonquin language, minister, and learn under the oversight of John Sargent.

The circumstances of this internship were anything but easy, and he often struggled with feelings of doubt and inadequacy. Yet his journal entries at this time record repeated references to the conviction that he felt unworthy even of these difficult circumstances. In fact, as he reflected on his hardships, he recorded repeated expressions of gratitude to the Lord as they weaned him from this world and cultivated a longing for heaven.

Later that summer, he left his hosts and decided to live among the nearby native population. He moved into a wigwam in Count Amick, New York. This was not ideal lodging, but it eliminated the need for daily travel. It also allowed him to live directly with the people he sought to evangelize and to learn their language in context.

Ministry on the Frontier

After spending almost a year in Count Amick, it was time for David to move to the frontier—to the forks of the Delaware River, northeast of Bethlehem, Pennsylvania—where he would now be on his own. He needed to find a translator until he could learn the language, a different regional dialect. He soon found one—Moses Tatamy, who would eventually become the first convert of his ministry and a dear friend.

Brainerd had contracted tuberculosis some time earlier, and the hardships of frontier ministry caused recurring bouts. He began taking trips to the surrounding regions to seek new opportunities to spread the gospel. On these journeys, he was frequently exposed to the elements, which aggravated his tuberculosis and left him writhing in pain, even praying for death. Perhaps worst of all, Brainerd was left to suffer these pains in isolation, void of Christian fellowship.

But encouragement came when he began to witness the fruit of his labors. On one trip, Brainerd preached in a village where there was a twenty-year-old Native American, the daughter of a notable chief. Her family had been horribly mistreated by white settlers. Yet upon hearing David hold out the promise of the gospel, the Holy Spirit gave her ears to hear, and she responded by placing faith in Jesus Christ. Later she would recall to her children that Brainerd was the first white person for whom she ever cared. The conversion of this woman marked a turning point in David's ministry. Within days, he observed a spiritual sensitivity and conviction as many Native Americans came to Christ, eager for spiritual growth and counsel.

The Final Days of Brainerd

However, in 1746 David's health declined dramatically. His diary recorded growing anticipations for heaven as he realized the inevitable was approaching. On September 21, he wrote, "Oh how blessed it is to be habitually prepared for death." March 20, 1747, was the last day Brainerd would spend with his precious Indian believers, as his illness forced him to leave the frontier. He headed east and stopped at Jonathan Edwards' home in Northampton, Massachusetts, where a doctor gave him the news—there would be no recovery. Still, he mustered up the strength to travel yet another hundred miles to Boston to report on his work among the Native Americans.

David returned to the home of Jonathan Edwards for the final months of his life. Edwards would gather his entire family at Brainerd's bedside. He would later recount how Brainerd spoke about his dear congregation with such tenderness that his speech was interrupted with tears. Then, on Friday, October 9, 1747, the minister's suffering ended, as he was called home to his Savior at age twenty-nine.

Jonathan Edwards was so impacted by this young man that he took Brainerd's diary and had it published, adding his own commentary of what he had gleaned from their friendship. One of the first missionary biographies ever written, it became the most popular of Edwards' works. And little wonder that is. While other missionaries have known similar adversity and even lost their lives on the field, few have tasted of these things so soon after being awakened to Christ's majesty and commission. Brainerd's life shows by "instance and example" just how worthy Jesus Christ is of our lives and our deaths.

Two hundred years later, a young missionary-in-training by the name of Jim Elliot (1927–1956) would get a copy of Edwards' biography of Brainerd. Captivated by what he read, he wrote in his own diary a motto that captured the essence of Brainerd's example: "He is no fool who gives what he cannot keep to gain that which he cannot lose."[8] Seven years later, while making first contact with those he sought to evangelize, Elliot's life was also cut short as he was martyred on the banks of an Ecuadorian river.

May God grant that Christians today learn to grasp eternity's nearness, to understand the fleetingness of the pleasures of this world, and to recognize the worthiness of Christ in life and death.

---

8. Elisabeth Elliot, ed., *The Journals of Jim Elliot: An Ordinary Man on an Extraordinary Mission*, repackaged ed. (Grand Rapids: Revell, 2023), 174.

Where Are You on the Spectrum of "Suffering for Jesus"? Brief Examples from the Field

Kevin Edwards

As followers of Jesus, we are called to take up our cross and follow Him (Matt 16:24). The Bible tells us that all who desire to live a godly life in Christ Jesus will be persecuted (2 Tim 3:12). Throughout history, countless believers have suffered for their faith in Jesus. From being martyred in ancient Rome to being imprisoned in Communist countries, the followers of Jesus have faced persecution for their belief in Him.

Dietrich Bonhoeffer was a German pastor and theologian who actively resisted the Nazi regime during World War II. He was arrested and eventually executed for his involvement in a plot to assassinate Adolf Hitler. Bonhoeffer's willingness to suffer for his faith in Jesus cost him his life, but his legacy and teachings continue to inspire believers today.[9]

Another example of suffering for Christ is the Chinese believers who meet in house churches. Despite facing persecution from the Chinese government, these underground churches continue to thrive and grow. Believers in China risk imprisonment, torture, and even death for their faith in Jesus, yet they remain steadfast in their belief and continue to boldly share the gospel with others.

In the Middle East, Christian minorities have been persecuted for their faith by various empires and governments throughout history. Today Christians throughout the Middle East continue to face sponsored persecution, which can lead to Christians being displaced from their homes and countries for their faith.

In India, Hindu nationalists have targeted Christians—particularly converts from Hinduism—with violence and intimidation. Christian pastors have been beaten, churches have been burned down, and believers have been falsely accused of forced conversions. Despite this persecution, the church in India continues to grow.

Believers all over the world continue to face persecution for their faith in Jesus. In some African countries, believers are targeted for their faith by Muslim extremist groups. In addition, in many Muslim-majority countries around the world, converts to Christianity face excommunication and violence from their families and communities.

From verbal abuse and discrimination to imprisonment and even death, the persecution that believers face around the world takes many different forms. But we must remember that Jesus Himself suffered and died for us, and He promises to be with us always (Matt 28:20).

As we consider where we are on the spectrum of suffering for Jesus, it is important to keep in mind that suffering is not our goal. Our ultimate goal is to be faithful to Jesus Christ, to proclaim the gospel, and to bring glory to God. As Paul wrote in 2 Corinthians 4:17, "For our momentary, light affliction is working out for us an eternal weight of glory far beyond all comparison."

Those who are called to follow Jesus will face persecution (John 15:20). The

---

9. Eric Metaxas, *Bonhoeffer: Pastor, Martyr, Prophet, Spy: A Righteous Gentile vs. the Third Reich* (Nashville: Thomas Nelson, 2010).

question is not if we will suffer for Jesus but how we will respond to persecution. When we hear of those who are persecuted, we can pray. We can support and encourage those who are suffering (1 Thess 5:11).

When we suffer for the sake of Christ, we can remain faithful because God is faithful (1 Cor 10:13), and He has promised to protect and strengthen those whose hope is in Him (2 Thess 3:3).

INSERT 21.3

The Accumulation of Small Sufferings

Brooks Buser[10]

The Measure of a Missionary

Early in my work of consulting overseas church planting, I visited a missionary team on a remote island eighty miles offshore the island of Papua New Guinea to help their church plant kickoff. On our way to the island, the seas picked up, and I found myself in one of the scariest situations of my life. The storm grew so large that our eighteen-foot skiff would motor up one wave, clear the water, then have to motor down the other side to maintain control. At one point, the waves were breaking over the boat so strongly that one of the children brought by a fellow consultant was swept down the length of the boat and just barely saved by her father as he caught the straps of her life jacket. After seven hours, we finally reached the island. I have rarely known such thankful joy and complete exhaustion.

Paul knew this kind of life. After my boat encounter, I read Acts 28:2–3: "The natives showed us extraordinary affection; for because of the rain that had set in and because of the cold, they kindled a fire and received us all. But when Paul had gathered a bundle of sticks and laid them on the fire, a viper came out because of the heat and fastened itself on his hand." The outcome of the snake bite is well known. But I had never

---

10. This insert is adapted from Brooks Buser, "The Accumulation of Small Sufferings," *Radius Report*, October 7, 2019, https://radiusinternational.org/the-accumulation-of-small-sufferings/.

before understood the magnitude of those two sentences. Paul, after many days of being driven across the Adriatic Sea, being shipwrecked, swimming to shore on driftwood, and being rained upon (Acts 27:39–44), still was part of the group that gathered firewood. Paul did not see what he had gone through as a reason to do less or to cease leading the men that God had given him. He could easily have given the job of firewood collecting to someone else, but he kept going, even when he was surely weary and fatigued.

One of the aspects that I love so dearly about the training program that I lead is that it gives each student the opportunity to see how they do when they are tired, occasionally hungry, out of their home environment, and still part of a team that needs them. Nearly everyone does well when their bellies are full and they are well rested, unafraid, and in a comfortable environment. The measure of a missionary is when one or all of these things is taken away. It is in how they respond, where they go, and whether they can be counted on.

The Many Forms of Sacrifice

While on one trip to a Muslim country to visit missionaries, local churches, and church-planting teams "in the trenches" of life, one brother told us of three coworkers who had lost their lives and of his heartache when their bodies were brought back for burial. Another spoke of missing one son's college graduation and another's wedding back in his home country because his country visa would most likely be revoked if he left. Sacrifice comes in many forms. It is usually not at the end of a weapon, but rather in the simple things where a follower of the King lays down his life in ways that are never printed in a support letter.

Jesus repeatedly warned those who followed Him that they must deny themselves, take up their crosses daily, and follow Him (Luke 9:23). Jesus never offered an easy life, but one of physical and emotional sacrifices that often come in small ways (9:24–27; 14:25–33). Those disciples who looked for a less painful way of following Jesus were routinely exposed to the actual costs: the Son of Man had no home, no security in this earthly life (9:57–62); He was harassed regularly by those who hated Him (7:32–34); and He laid down His life for His enemies (23:33–34). This is what He told His followers to expect for themselves as well.

Ann Hasseltine Judson, the wife of missionary Adoniram Judson, reflected on the hardships of her family: "Had it not been for . . . an assured conviction that every additional trial was ordered by infinite love and mercy, I must have sunk under my accumulated sufferings."[11] One of the

---

11. Cecil B. Hartley, *The Three Mrs. Judsons* (1880; repr., Wilmore, KY: First Fruits, 2019), 160.

more heartbreaking aspects of my trip was hearing from the missionary teams whose coworkers had returned home because of the accumulation of pressure, tensions, and unfulfilled expectations. The tension of the government looking for ways to remove them, the two-to-four-year battle of becoming proficient in a hard language, the struggle to establish an authentic business, the constant challenge of living in a Muslim country—it all takes a toll. Weariness can come over a person when these difficulties come in regular, daily doses.

Comfort amid the Cost

Two passages of Scripture bring me much comfort when I think of the life that so many gospel ambassadors are living out today. Luke 22:45 recounts how Jesus, having requested prayer in Gethsemane, found Peter exhausted, "sleeping from sorrow." Peter was unsure of what was coming, and though he wanted to stay awake, he was unable when necessary. But the other side is found in Acts 12:6. Peter was in jail, chained with a guard on either side, unsure of what the following day would bring, though death was most likely. And he slept. He slept so deeply that he was unaware when an angel showed up in his cell and, even after waking, thought he was seeing a vision (12:9). Peter slept in the confidence that the One who sees all, knows all, and controls all was watching over every detail of his life.

Missionary candidates need to be shaped and molded for a life that will be filled with regular, daily cost. If tomorrow they cross that great chasm of death or have to say no to a major life event back at home, they will rest in a God who counts each tear and has ordained each sacrifice. No hardship great or small is overlooked by the Master (Heb 6:10). Each will have its just reward in the age to come (Luke 18:28–30; Rev 22:12).

Missions Includes Missionaries with Disabling Conditions

Dave Deuel

Missions is God's theater before a watching world. On this global stage, weakness often tells His story of power and sufficiency. That is, God displays His power through the weakness of His messengers, some of whom have disabling conditions. In so doing, He shows us our dependency and reveals His perfect and complete sufficiency. Our part demands that we not distort God's story with our misunderstandings of His mission power and our weakness.

The Wrong Questions

George Stott (1835–1889) from Aberdeen, Scotland, lost his leg in a farming accident at age twenty-one. During his long recovery, he embraced the gospel and became convinced that God had called him to missions. When a doubter asked why he, having only one leg, had the audacity to go to China, Stott's response was, "I do not see those with two legs going, so I must."[12] Stott's answer points up the false assumptions of his inquirer.

When thinking about sending people with disabilities on missions, Christians tend to immediately run to the challenges that might overwhelm such people due to their perceived inabilities. Christians tend to focus on whether those people will be safe or whether they will fail. These honest questions are rooted in genuine concern, but they miss the point. After all, anyone's safety can be risked on missions, and anyone can fail. Three better questions should help clarify the calling of people with disabilities to the mission field.

Has God Not Called and Gifted All of His People?

God reminds His people in Scripture that all believers have gifts (Rom 12:3; 1 Cor 7:7; 12:7; 12:11; Eph 4:7; 1 Pet 4:10). Therefore, if God gifts those with disabling conditions to do "the work of service" (Eph 4:12), how could they not also be called to that work? To reject the calling of these believers would

---

12. "George and Grace Stott," Asia Harvest, accessed June 18, 2024, https://www.asiaharvest.org/china-resources/zhejiang/george-stott.

be to directly contradict Paul's teaching regarding the diverse gifts of the different members of the body. Paul taught that the gifts God gives people are intended for the church's growth, not for the possession of the individual. And since people with disabilities are gifted, they must support the church and its work like anyone else. To put it succinctly, the church needs its people with disabilities.

Has Jesus Not Commissioned All of His Followers to the Mission?

When Jesus gave the Great Commission to His disciples—and by extension, to the forthcoming church—He did not limit that call to only some people. Rather, He introduced the commission with the universal declaration, "All authority has been given to Me in heaven and on earth," and He ends it with the perpetual proclamation that, "I am with you always, even to the end of the age" (Matt 28:18, 20). Thus, Jesus sandwiched the Great Commission with assurances of His power and presence, assuming His disciples' weakness and inability without Him. For it is in the knowledge of their weakness that Jesus' messengers possess both Jesus' power and Jesus' presence through His Spirit for fulfilling His mission (Luke 24:48–49; John 20:21–22; Acts 1:8). He conscripted all people for service, including people with disabilities.

Has God Not Displayed His Power and Glory in Weakness?

People with disabilities are specially prepared for missions, because in their dependency on the Lord, they have learned greater spiritual resilience, that their sufficiency is from God (2 Cor 3:5–6), that His grace is sufficient for and His power is shown perfect in their weaknesses (12:9–10). A profound example is God's calling of Moses to be His messenger to Israel and Egypt. This must have happened through God's own mission power and presence, for Moses suffered from a disability in the one faculty that he needed for performing the task that God gave him: a disability of speech (Exod 4:10). However, Scripture says that Moses was the godliest and most impactful prophet in Israel's history (Deut 34:10–12), and it was God who had sovereignly made Moses' mouth as it was (Exod 4:11–12).

Similarly, veteran missionary Tom Brewster (1939–1985) captured the paradox of losing power and control due to his suffering from quadriplegia. Paralyzed from a diving accident as a teenager, Brewster's insights about disability in missions are invaluable:

> In many ways this accident has been a great blessing in my life. In fact, apart from the privilege of knowing Christ as Lord and Savior and the wonderful family that He has given me, this injury and

the paralysis over these years have been the biggest blessing in my life. That may sound a bit strange and I'm sure that it's nothing that any of us would ever wish for, but God has used this in a way in my life to give me a sense of His leading and of His power.[13]

God had called and gifted Brewster in full use of his paralysis. He became a missions leader, traveling all over the world to teach and consult on missions. His gifts and calling did not require the use of arms or legs. Rather, disability even prepared him for missions, giving him a greater desire for God's power to work through his weakness. Brewster succeeded not in spite of his disability but through it and even because of it. Weakened messengers do God's work in their humility and dependency on the Lord of the mission, and God is glorified.

Conclusion

Giving affirmative answers to the right questions above, the church must accept the role of people with disabilities in missions. For missions is God's story of power and sufficiency. The church is to display dependency on His power so that He will be glorified in its weaknesses. This means that people with disabilities must pursue their missions calling and deliver their gifts to Jesus and His church like anyone else. John MacArthur put it well: "There are many people in ministry too strong to be useful. There are no people in ministry too weak to be useful."[14]

---

13. Dan Brewster, *Only Paralyzed from the Neck Down: The Life and Ministry of Tom Brewster* (Pasadena, CA: William Carey Library, 1997), xiii.

14. John MacArthur, plenary session speech, Together for the Gospel 2018, Louisville, KY, April 12, 2018.

CHAPTER 22

The Elder-Qualified Missionary:
Preparing Missionaries to Plant Churches and Train Others on the Field

Tom Pennington

Churches, their leaders, and missionary candidates feel the weight and urgency for workers to enter the fields now ready for harvest. However, that urgency has often meant that churches send missionaries to the field unprepared for the rigors and demands of cross-cultural ministry. In many cases, missionaries are sent to the field to perform duties requisite of an elder but are wholly unable to exhort with sound doctrine, refute those who contradict, shepherd the flock, or train future elders on the field (Titus 1:5–9; 1 Pet 5:1–3).[1] But the urgency of missions is not justification for taking unbiblical shortcuts; the church must hold fast to the biblical pattern of sending out elder-qualified missionaries to serve in elder or elder-like roles. Practically, this means that missionaries who plant churches or strengthen churches by training leaders must themselves be biblically qualified and trained as elders before they are sent out.

First, the common terms *church planting* and *church strengthening* need clarification. Church planting is the gathering of disciples into a newly formed body that is self-governing, self-propagating, and self-supporting.[2] Since

---

1. Chad Vegas writes, "It was the Apostle Paul, the most urgent gospel minister in Christian history, who warned us to avoid being 'hasty in the laying on of hands' (1 Tim. 5:22). Rather, he exhorted us to qualify and train faithful men who could carry the gospel to the nations." Quoted from private correspondence (July 27, 2022). Shared with permission. I am indebted to Rocky Wyatt and Bryan Murphy with *XL Ministries* for sharing this correspondence. Furthermore, Brooks Buser, president of Radius International, writes, "Missions in the twenty-first century is in sore need of qualified well-trained men. Missionaries are typically more poorly screened and more poorly trained than their counterparts in domestic pastoral ministry. . . . Much of the blame lies with sending churches having a generally low bar for missionaries to be qualified to be sent." Quoted from private correspondence (July 26, 2022). Shared with permission. I am indebted to Rocky Wyatt and Bryan Murphy with *XL Ministries* for sharing this correspondence also.

2. See the widely accepted "three-self formula" for defining an indigenous church, as cited in A. Scott Moreau, "Missiology," *Evangelical Dictionary of Theology*, 3rd ed., ed. Daniel J. Treier and Walter A. Elwell (Grand Rapids: Baker, 2017), 553.

this necessarily includes appointing elders in the new church, the church planter must himself be elder qualified, even if he is not an elder in the new congregation.

Church strengthening, though it is biblical in origin (Acts 15:41; 16:5; cf. 14:21–23), is a broader term, and its tasks may or may not require elder qualification.[3] Seminary professors and administrators are two examples of this type that require elder qualification, given that they are training church leaders. Supporting roles such as Bible translators, pilots, school educators, and mercy ministries, though strengthening the church in varying degrees, do not biblically require elder-qualified individuals. Missionaries—men or women—who serve in these supporting roles should be spiritually mature, manifesting the character qualities of a mature believer; in other words, they should be deacon qualified.

Those definitions and distinctions serve as the framework for this chapter. The concern is that the church of Jesus Christ sends out missionaries that are elder qualified for elder-like roles. The chapter sets forth, first, the New Testament pattern of sending out elder-qualified missionaries and, second, a practical process for training elders in the church, whether they remain at home or are sent to the field.

The New Testament Pattern

The local church is the center of New Testament missions. Yet many missiologists and church leaders downplay or even ignore the essential role of the church in missions and thus relegate the church to two supporting roles: a pool for potential applicants and a purse for financing the missionary enterprise. But the ecclesiology and missiology of the New Testament emphasize that Christ has assigned to every local church the primary role in world missions and, thus, in raising up elders in the field.

Local Churches and the Great Commission

The church of the Lord Jesus Christ is at the heart of the Great Commission. The monumental text of Matthew 16:18 records Jesus' promise of the coming church and of His priority to build it: "I will build My church; and the gates of Hades will not overpower it." Eleven months later, Jesus met with all of His disciples on a mountain in Galilee and gave them the mandate known as the Great Commission (Matt 28:18–20). While in Matthew 16:18, Jesus simply stated, "I will build My church," in the Great Commission He revealed how local churches are to send out missionaries to make disciples, to teach those disciples to obey all that Christ commanded them, and thus to plant indigenous churches. These churches, in turn, make new disciples, who continue the Great Commission mandate to baptize, instruct, and plant other churches.

The role of the local church in missions is reflected throughout the book of Acts and the

---

3. The word group related to "strengthen" (*stērizō, stereoō*, their derivative forms, and synonyms) should be considered in their usage across Acts and the New Testament at large. It is not reserved for only the work of a church planter or an elder (Luke 22:32; Acts 15:32; 2 Thess 2:17; Jas 5:8).

New Testament, starting with the birth of the universal church on the day of Pentecost. Acts 2:41–42 records that "those who had received [Peter's] word were baptized; and that day there were added about three thousand souls. They were continually devoting themselves to the apostles' teaching and to fellowship, to the breaking of bread and to prayer." At the Jerusalem church's beginning, the threefold pattern of the Great Commission is evident: evangelism (some "received his word"), incorporation of new believers into the church (they "were baptized; and . . . were added [to the church]"), followed by ongoing instruction ("to the apostles teaching").[4] Therefore, the church's worldwide mission to make disciples is only accomplished when a new church has been planted, disciples have been added to it, and when they are baptized, taught the Scripture, and trained to obey it through the ministry of the local church leaders.

The Appointment of Elders in the Local Church[5]

A key point that is often missed in the Great Commission is that Jesus' inclusion of baptism and instruction makes the local church central in its fulfillment, since both tasks are typically carried out under the authority of elders in a local church.[6] The Great Commission is accomplished when true disciples are made, those disciples are added to the church (or a new church has been planted), and those disciples are baptized and instructed in Scripture in the church under the elders.

On the day of Jesus' ascension, He restated this priority for His disciples' ministry once again. To make disciples, they were to bear witness about Him, starting in Jerusalem and radiating out from there across the world (Acts 1:8–9). But this command did not change Jesus' earlier commission—it only restated and specifically applied it. The apostles' ongoing priority was to make disciples and establish churches.

Not surprisingly, the original church in Jerusalem reflects that very plan. It began on Pentecost when three thousand individuals became Jesus' disciples and were baptized (Acts 2:41). The "church in Jerusalem" was thus established (5:11; 8:1), and it immediately began functioning as a church (2:42). Likely, the apostles functioned as the first elders in it (6:1–6) but eventually installed other qualified elders (11:30; 15:2).

When the church in Jerusalem was forced to scatter through the persecution of Saul,

---

4. A helpful resource on the Great Commission and the primary role of the local church is David M. Doran, *For the Sake of His Name* (Detroit: Detroit Baptist Theological Seminary, 2018).

5. For a thorough review of the biblical arguments for a plurality of elders in each church, see Alexander Strauch, *Biblical Eldership: An Urgent Call to Restore Biblical Church Leadership*, rev. and exp. ed. (Colorado Springs, CO: Lewis and Roth, 1995); Tom Pennington, *A Biblical Case for Elder Rule* (Southlake, TX: The Word Unleashed, 2022); Pennington, "The Biblical Case for Elder Rule," plenary session speech, XL Ministries' Becoming Biblical Elders Conference, Southlake, TX, February, 11, 2022, https://xlministries.org/videos/.

6. The New Testament delegates responsibility for instruction to the elders of the church (e.g., Eph 4:11; 1 Tim 3:2; 2 Tim 4:1–5). Baptism is consistently administered by spiritually qualified leaders, either the apostles and their companions (Acts 2:41; 8:12–13, 38; 10:48; 16:15, 33) or the elders in each church who were also tasked with instruction (Matt 28:19; 1 Cor 1:14–15).

these Christians preached the gospel and made disciples elsewhere (Acts 8:3–5, 12). Once the Jerusalem elders discovered these new disciples nearby, they sent leaders who taught them and established churches with their own qualified leadership (8:14; 9:31). The same pattern marked the church in Antioch (11:19–26), which eventually sent out others to plant additional churches (13:1–4).

Luke explicitly says that Paul and Barnabas appointed a plurality of elders in every church they planted on their first missionary journey (Acts 14:21–23), just as there was a plurality of elders in the church in Ephesus where Timothy ministered (1 Tim 5:17, 19–20; cf. Acts 20:17), and just as Paul demanded that the young pastor who received the other pastoral epistle, Titus, also establish elders in every church on Crete (Titus 1:5).[7] The implication is that a plurality of elders was the requirement everywhere, whether in established churches, sending churches, or new missionary plants.

The Training of Elders Appointed

In the New Testament, those who served as church-planting missionaries were leaders in their sending churches, were sent out on behalf of their churches, and then trained and installed elders in the churches they planted. For instance, the Jerusalem church sent Peter and John to Samaria (Acts 8:14) and Barnabas to Antioch (11:22). The former were two of the twelve apostles, and Barnabas was known among the apostles for his ministry of exhortation to the Jerusalem believers and his leadership by example in the church (4:36–37). When the church in Antioch grew large, Barnabas recruited the apostle Paul (then, still called Saul) to join him (11:24–26). Then, the church in Antioch commissioned Paul and Barnabas—who were serving as leaders in Antioch—to plant and strengthen churches elsewhere (13:1–3; 14:21–23). Later Paul left their trainee and companion Titus (Gal 2:1) to appoint elders on Crete in the churches planted there (Titus 1:5). Titus, like Timothy—who was also instructed for the appointing of elders (1 Tim 3:1; 2 Tim 2:2)—had also likely served in and been qualified by a church before he appointed leaders in any other (Acts 16:1–3; 1 Tim 4:14).

That pattern proves that the biblical qualifications for elders are not superfluous for church-planting missionaries—they are essential. Moreover, Christ holds local church elders responsible, not seminaries or missions agencies, for vetting and training their elders and the missionaries they send out. If the leaders of a local church fail to personally train men for ministry, they have disobeyed the Lord's mandate in 2 Timothy 2:2: "The things which you have heard from me in the presence of many witnesses, entrust these to faithful men who will be able to teach others also." Paul addressed this command to Timothy and to the lay and

---

7. The cities on Crete were too small to require multiple churches, so each city had one church and each church had multiple elders. See discussions in I. Howard Marshall and Philip H. Towner, *A Critical and Exegetical Commentary on the Pastoral Epistles*, ICC (London; New York: T&T Clark, 2004), 152–53; and Eckhard J. Schnabel, *Paul the Missionary: Realities, Strategies and Methods* (Downers Grove, IL: InterVarsity, 2008), 120–21.

staff elders who served with him in Ephesus (1 Tim 5:17), which means it is a call to the *leaders* of every church.

Incidentally, the essential nature of elder qualifications for the mission field can also be seen in that several of them link directly to the most common reasons missionaries fail on the field. For example, missionaries who fail often do so because they struggle to function well on a team. The underlying problem is frequently being self-willed, quick-tempered, or pugnacious, all of which disqualify an elder (Titus 1:7; 1 Tim 3:3). Others struggle to shepherd their families in ministry transitions to or between fields and in difficult circumstances on the field. This potential problem, too, can be identified and potentially avoided if the sending church ensures that the candidate meets the elder qualification of managing his household well (1 Tim 3:4–5).

More broadly, the character qualifications for an elder are applicable even if the missionary candidate is not church planting or is a woman. For instance, although Scripture forbids a woman from being an elder (Titus 1:6; 1 Tim 3:2)[8] or from teaching or exercising authority over men in the context of the church (1 Cor 14:34–35; 1 Tim 2:11–12),[9] missionary women should demonstrate not only the character qualities that mark a godly woman (1 Tim 2:9–10; 5:5–10; Titus 2:3–5; 1 Pet 3:3–4) but also those that mark a godly elder. For apart from the skills of teaching and managing, the qualifications in 1 Timothy 3 and Titus 1 are not intended to be unique to elders but rather marks of spiritual maturity for every Christian. Therefore, any missionary serving in support roles, such as Bible translators, pilots, school educators, and mercy ministries should also consistently manifest the character qualities demanded of an elder. But the church-planting or elder-training missionary needs to be elder qualified, biblically equipped, and affirmed as such by his sending church.

Thus, sending out biblically qualified elders to plant churches and then to raise up and train indigenous elders was not tangential but essential in the recorded missionary journeys in Acts. This must be the ongoing missions priority of every faithful church today.

A Practical Process for Raising Up Elders

Ideally missionaries should learn from their sending churches specifically (not other supporting churches) how to equip elders. When each church has systematic leadership training, the sending church, the missionary candidate,

---

8. Scripture requires that elders be men. In 1 Timothy 3:2 and Titus 1:6, the "husband of one wife" is literally "a one-woman man." The Greek word for "man" is not the generic word (*anthropos*) but the word for male (*aner*) as opposed to female.

9. Elders must also be male since Scripture explicitly forbids women from teaching or leading men in the church (1 Cor 11:3–16; 14:34–35; 1 Tim 2:9–16). Scripture allows women to teach other women (Titus 2:3–5) and children, including male children (2 Tim 3:14–15). And a woman, serving with her husband, can privately instruct a man in a personal, informal context (Acts 18:26). See the treatment in John Piper and Wayne Grudem, eds., *Recovering Biblical Manhood and Womanhood: A Response to Evangelical Feminism*, rev. ed. (Wheaton, IL: Crossway, 2021), passim, but esp. D. A. Carson, "'Silent in the Churches': On the Role of Women in 1 Corinthians 14:33b–35," 179–98; and Douglas Moo, "What Does It Mean Not to Teach or Have Authority over Men? 1 Timothy 2:11–15," 233–52. See also John MacArthur, *1 Timothy*, MNTC (Chicago: Moody, 1995), 82–87.

and the churches planted or strengthened by the missionary all benefit. A systematic, practical, and biblical process for raising up elders involves at least four components: identifying, training, evaluating, and confirming a man.

Identifying Potential Elders

Christ is the head of His church (Eph 1:22–23; 5:23; Col 1:18; 2:19), and He gives gifted men to His church (Eph 4:10–12). The Lord through His Spirit gifts and calls a man, but it is the role of the elders, working in concert with the members, to identify those men whom Christ has gifted and called.

There are two primary ways to identify potential elders. A man who is already serving faithfully in a teaching, shepherding role in the church may approach the elders and express a desire to serve. First Timothy 3:1 uses two words to describe an appropriate desire.[10] His desire should not only be for the office of elder but also for the work of an elder. He must long to invest his life in studying and teaching God's Word and in caring for, protecting, and shepherding God's people. A missionary candidate who desires to plant churches is necessarily also expressing a desire to be an elder.

A second way to identify potential elders is for the existing elders to regularly review a comprehensive list of all the men already serving in a teaching, shepherding role in the church.[11] It is helpful to sort any potential elders into one of two groups: those who could become elders in the short term (e.g., one to two years) and those who could in the longer term (e.g., three to five years). Men in the long-term group can be added to a watch list and given more opportunities to teach in adult settings as appropriate, without telling them they are being considered as future elders.

For a man in the short-term group, a first step is to have all the elders review a recording of his teaching to determine if he is gifted to teach. If the elders agree on his gifting, they can designate an elder (often, the one with the closest relationship with the candidate) to approach the man with three goals: explain the role of elder, determine if he desires to serve and believes he is potentially elder qualified, and then become his mentor through the rest of the process. If the candidate desires to move forward, it is helpful at this stage for him to fill out an application and to have a preliminary interview with the elders regarding his testimony, spiritual disciplines, biblical qualifications, and essential agreement with the church's doctrine. Once the elders have identified a man as a potential elder and confirmed the man's own desire, the next step is training.

Training Potential Elders

To assist in training, it is helpful if the elders designate a specific elder who will mentor the

---

10. "Aspires" (from *oregō*) means "to stretch one's self out in order to touch or to grasp something, to reach after or desire something." Joseph Henry Thayer, "ὀρέγω," *Thayer's Greek-English Lexicon of the New Testament* (1896; repr., Peabody, MA: Hendrickson, 2021), 452. "Desires" (from *epithymeō*) means "to set one's heart upon, to have a desire for, long for." Thayer, "ἐπιθυμέω," 238.

11. At the church where I serve, twice a year the elders review a comprehensive list of all men who teach regularly at the middle school level and above for this very purpose. Since the qualification that distinguishes elders from deacons is the ability to teach, it is best to consider only those already demonstrating a teaching gift.

candidate. For a training curriculum, the elders may choose from existing materials or create their own. With men in the long-term group, the training should focus on being biblical leaders in their marriages, families, and the church, and on strengthening their teaching gift. For those in the short-term group, the elders will want to begin more specific elder training immediately.

Specific elder training should focus on helping the candidate prepare for the evaluation stage and for his future ministry. Using 2 Timothy 2:2 as a grid, his training should focus on the following:

1. A thorough, working knowledge of the content of Scripture
2. A thorough understanding of systematic theology that includes defining and biblically defending all important theological terms and concepts, as well as defining and biblically refuting common errors in doctrine
3. A thorough knowledge of and growing maturity in the character qualities required of an elder in 1 Timothy 3 and Titus 1
4. A thorough preparation in the skills regularly required of elders, such as teaching, counseling, making hospital visits, and wisely participating in elder meeting discussions

It is especially helpful if the elders provide the candidate with a complete list of the questions he may be asked in his evaluation. As the elders determine their training program, they must keep in mind two goals: preparing the candidate for his evaluation as a potential elder and equipping him to serve as an elder if he is confirmed.

Evaluating Potential Elders

First Timothy 3:10 says that deacons "must also first be tested." The implication is that potential elders, whose qualifications are listed in the paragraph preceding those for deacons, are also to be carefully tested or evaluated. Part of that testing is the confirmation of the congregation that the man meets the biblical qualifications. This does not mean that the congregation should vote on making a man an elder—there is no biblical warrant for that.[12] However, the elders should inform the congregation that they are considering a man as a potential elder so that if anyone knows a reason the man is not qualified, it can be brought to the attention of the elders.[13]

---

12. Although the apostles directed the congregation in the Jerusalem church to select men to lead in serving daily food to the widows (Acts 6:3–6), there is no New Testament example of a congregation selecting and installing elders. Instead, elders select and install elders (Acts 14:21–23; 1 Tim 4:14; 5:22; 2 Tim 1:6; Titus 1:5).

13. Here is an example of how the membership may interact with a potential candidate: once the elder candidate is approved by the elder board, he may be presented to the church at a regular morning worship service, at which point he and his wife are introduced and he shares his testimony. The members may then be encouraged to seek out the candidate to encourage him. Additionally, if any member has a concern regarding the candidate serving in this office, he or she may be encouraged to approach the candidate with those concerns and then to share them with an elder. After a period of thirty days, if no disqualifying concerns are raised and confirmed, the elder board then installs the candidate as an elder.

Assuming the elders have already evaluated the man's faithfulness, character, and gifting to teach at the outset of the process, in this stage they will primarily evaluate his understanding of the content, theology, and application of Scripture. The standard is Titus 1:9: "holding fast the faithful word which is in accordance with the teaching, so that he will be able both to exhort in sound doctrine and to refute those who contradict."

After adequate preparation, the candidate should appear before the elder board (or a subcommittee) for an in-depth evaluation of Bible knowledge, systematic theology, and practical or applied theology,[14] concentrating on questions from the materials they provided the candidate and in which he has been mentored.[15] After the evaluation, the elders must determine whether he demonstrated accurate and sufficient knowledge. If he did not, they should explain to the candidate the areas where he was not adequately prepared so that he can prepare for a follow-up examination in the areas of weakness. If the candidate passes the evaluation, the elders should then formally vote to install the man as an elder.

Confirming Elders

Once a candidate has been affirmed by the congregation (they raise no disqualifying concerns) and has been approved by the elder board (via thorough evaluation of his knowledge and doctrine), the elder board officially confirms him as an elder by their unanimous vote in a regularly scheduled elder meeting. Subsequently, the new elder is publicly installed as an elder during a regular worship service, with the elders laying on hands (1 Tim 4:14; 5:22).

The elders of the sending church may choose to make the prospective missionary an elder in their church and publicly install him at this point if they expect a significant delay in his departure for the field and think the church would benefit from his service in the interim. More often the elders will choose to confirm the man as a biblically qualified elder and announce their plan not to make him an elder of the sending church but to send him out as a missionary once he completes further missions training and has raised the necessary support.

Conclusion

The Great Commission dictates that New Testament missions be centered in the local church and carried out under the authority of its elders. Therefore, church planting and strengthening must not only be the priority of faithful churches but must also be done in a way that follows the New Testament pattern. Practically, this means that every missionary involved in planting churches or training elders must be biblically qualified as an elder, trained to serve as an elder, and know how to train other biblically qualified elders on the field.

---

14. It is helpful to establish a time frame to devote to each of the three sections.

15. The Bible knowledge and theology sections of a candidate packet can include more material than that of which the elders plan to examine a candidate's knowledge, included simply for his information. If so, highlight either what the elders expect the man to know or what they do not expect him to know.

Despite their zeal to obey the Lord's command in the Great Commission, churches must never compromise on the qualification and preparation of the ones they send to fulfill it.

Thus, every church needs a plan for equipping and testing elders. The process outlined above for identifying, training, evaluating, and confirming elders can be used to install lay elders, staff elders, missionaries, and elder candidates in the churches planted by those missionaries. When the elders of a local church follow a process that is faithful to Scripture, they can affirm a man to be biblically elder qualified, gifted, and approved with confidence and can send such men as missionaries to the field with the same confidence.

CHAPTER 23

Nonoptional Pre-Field Training: Biblical Doctrine

Chris Burnett

Every day many well-intentioned gospel workers penetrate farther reaches of the map with burning enthusiasm and copious resources but with limited understanding of the core theology that buttresses the missionary task. They are like those who have "a zeal for God, but not according to knowledge" (Rom 10:2). Faithful missionaries, on the other hand, rely on the theology of Scripture to inform their evangelistic convictions and to bolster their assurance that they are God's kingdom ambassadors, no matter how tough the season or the circumstances they must endure. The teachings of the Bible are sufficient to understand and implement missions God's way.

The following sections consider how each major area of biblical teaching, arranged under the categories of systematic theology, connects to the task of making disciples across the world until "the end of the age" (Matt 28:20). This bridge between theology and practice aims to give all Christians greater confidence about their role as God's ambassadors in their local contexts. Of all the guidance that a missionary candidate can receive from their church leadership, program, institution, or agency, biblical doctrine is the most foundational and therefore must be regarded as nonoptional pre-field training. The sections are laid out as a reference guide for missionaries and church leaders to understand and teach.

Prolegomena

The term *prolegomena* refers to a range of biblical teachings that are preliminary to the traditional categories of systematic theology. Prolegomena covers epistemology (the nature of knowledge and belief), clarifies what the biblical worldview is, and shows how to safeguard it as a believer. Prolegomena teaches about the proper sources for the task of theology, which include God's general revelation of Himself in the natural world (Rom 1:20), and, supremely, God's special revelation of Himself in the infallible and inerrant Scriptures (Pss 119:160; 138:2). Prolegomena indicates how to harness theology from the Bible by laying out the principles of interpretation ("hermeneutics") for analyzing the grammar and syntax ("exegesis") of the biblical text.

The missionary who approaches these preliminary topics (and every doctrine) in the humble fear of the Lord (Prov 1:7) is laying a biblically faithful foundation for evangelizing sinners with the teachings of the revealed Word of God. The missionary must personally uphold and publicly promote the standard and pattern of the sound words of Scripture in Christlike faith and love (2 Tim 1:13). The best way to cultivate the missionary's assurance that God is sovereign in this dark world of unbelief is to adhere to biblical teaching in lifestyle and activity. Such faithfulness fuels the conviction that God's Word is God's weapon for tearing down the false beliefs of nonbelievers everywhere (2 Cor 10:5) so that they, too, can believe the truth about the Creator and about themselves.

Bibliology

God, through His Holy Spirit, has directly and verbally revealed the full extent of spiritual truth that all people everywhere must believe, regardless of their cultural context and background. The doctrines of bibliology reinforce that the sixty-six books of the Bible are the authoritative and sufficient source of divine spiritual knowledge by which sinners obey God, are saved, and grow as disciples in every place (Acts 6:7; 10:44; 12:24; 13:49; 19:20). The doctrines include the revelation, inspiration, illumination, clarity, authority, inerrancy, sufficiency, canonicity, and preservation of Scripture.

Every word of the biblical text, in its original manuscripts, was penned by men with their distinct personalities, styles, intellects, and wills, through the supernatural moving of the Holy Spirit, who is Himself the divine author of Scripture (2 Pet 1:19–21; cf. 2 Sam 23:2). The Bible, now translated into many languages, is just as living and active as it ever was (Heb 4:12), since God's Word is fixed forever in heaven and historically preserved on earth (Ps 119:89; Isa 40:8; cf. Matt 5:18). A Bible translation is sufficient for salvation and sanctification when it delivers, in its new context, the original meaning that the biblical writer delivered to the original audience (Neh 8:1–8).[1] Scripture will thus continue to serve as God's authoritative source of sound doctrine for saving faith and true spiritual growth (Ps 19:7–11; 2 Tim 3:15), no matter the distance of millennia, continents, and languages from the original manuscripts.

Closely related to the doctrines of inspiration, revelation, and preservation is the biblical concept of inerrancy. It describes how the words and syntax of the Bible in the original

---

1. Nehemiah 8:8 describes reading for understanding to involve "explaining and giving insight," though the phrase has been defended as retaining the idea of "translating," given that "the Jews who spoke Aramaic needed someone to translate the Hebrew of the law for them in their own vernacular." In F. Charles Fensham, *The Books of Ezra and Nehemiah* (Grand Rapids: Eerdmans, 1982), 217. For bibliographic support of translation activity in the context of reading the Law in Neh 8:1–8, see Philip Y. Yoo, "On Nehemiah 8,8a," *Zeitschrift für die alttestamentliche Wissenschaft* 127, no. 3 (2015): 503n6.

manuscripts are absolutely true in all their content when interpreted in their historical, grammatical, literary, and moral settings—not only on matters of faith and practice, but on any topic or concept therein (Pss 12:6; 119:160; Prov 30:5–6; John 10:35; 17:17). Missionaries who affirm the necessity of the Great Commission must affirm the full inerrancy of Scripture; otherwise they cannot trust in Jesus' assertion that He holds "all authority" in missions (Matt 28:18) nor His promise that He will be present with His disciples "even to the end of the age" (v. 20).

Scripture's teachings on the bibliological doctrines help the gospel proclaimer brace against all opposition to the truth with all preparation (Eph 6:14). Such doctrines remind missionaries not to accommodate difficult or offensive concepts in the Bible to the spiritual felt needs of their pagan audiences in the hopes of winning them to the truth through the falsehood of local beliefs. Instead, they must boldly proclaim the excellencies of Christ (1 Pet 2:9) and trust the Holy Spirit to effectually illuminate and enable the hearer to appraise Scripture subjectively and spiritually as what it really is—the wisdom and power of God (Rom 1:16; 1 Cor 1:18–2:16). The completed canon is therefore the divinely revealed standard for all matters to which it speaks, so that any claim to "truth" that arises from the ground of the local culture—whether of pagan or professing Christian origin—is tested for consistency with the total biblical content. Any compromised, sub-biblical truths are nothing less than syncretistic and harmful philosophies and must be rejected by the local church leadership and their people.

Such a conservative understanding of the doctrines of bibliology assures the missionary of the sufficiency of Scripture to bring light and life to the darkened and dead soul, because "all Scripture is God-breathed and profitable for teaching, for reproof, for correction, for training in righteousness" (2 Tim 3:16). Scripture promises to accomplish its goal, that all who are saved by the Holy Spirit through the faithful proclamation of the Word "may be equipped, having been thoroughly equipped for every good work" (3:17). Missionary success today is therefore singularly measured by one's conviction that God, through His Word, is to be glorified above all else (Acts 13:48).

Theology Proper

Theology proper is the doctrine of God. As a category it covers the biblical content about the existence and perfections (attributes) of God, who is one absolute and eternal divine essence, eternally subsisting in three distinct, coequal, and consubstantial persons—Father, Son, and Holy Spirit (Matt 28:19; 2 Cor 13:14). All believers, out of faithfulness to the truth of God, must unequivocally assert that God is one in triunity, according to the perfections predicated of Him in Scripture (Deut 6:4; cf. Isa 46:9; John 1:1; Acts 5:3–4).

In many contexts around the world, the missionary's target population is ignorant and even hostile to the mysterious reality of the triune God, especially where they proclaim a monotheism devoid of the coessential equality of the Father, Son, and Holy Spirit. However, biblical disciple-making begins with affirming the God of the Bible and being baptized "in the [one] name of the Father and the Son and the Holy Spirit" (Matt 28:19). Such a proclamation of the "one name" of the triune God asserts His identity and power and is fundamental to a God-pleasing faith, for God is a "rewarder of those who seek Him" as He is revealed in Scripture (Heb 11:1, 6).

All false belief and nonbiblical worldviews, customs, and traditions that distort the biblical teaching about God or attempt to ascribe glory to any other being than the one true God are therefore idolatrous, speculative strongholds that must be demolished in obedience to God through Christ (2 Cor 10:5). Any reticence on the part of the missionary to confront the cherished beliefs of sinners in their contexts is not winsome but wicked. Withholding the full teaching about God's existence and perfections out of a fear of local misunderstanding or disbelief is itself cause for the missionary to repent. Where an evangelistic strategy is found to be compromised or corrupted, the solution is always to return to the biblical teachings of theology proper, from where all evangelistic conviction and zeal usher forth, "for God so loved the world, that He gave His only begotten Son, that whoever believes in Him shall not perish, but have eternal life" (John 3:16).

Christology

The Lord Jesus Christ is the glorious, preexistent Son of God, coeternal and coequal to the Father and the Holy Spirit (John 1:1). Jesus was conceived and born of a virgin by the power of the Holy Spirit in the fullness of time, such that He is truly God and truly man (Gal 4:4). Unlike the first Adam, whose disobedience brought condemnation to all who were united to him, Jesus' life of perfect obedience completely pleased God. His obedience thus becomes the ground of righteousness for all who are united to Him by faith (Rom 5:15–19), and His sin-bearing death completely satisfies the wrath of God against the sins of His people (Rom 3:25; Heb 2:17; 1 Pet 2:24). As the Mediator of the new covenant in His blood (Luke 22:20; cf. Exod 24:8), He accomplished exactly what the name Jesus means: "Yahweh saves" (Matt 1:21).

While Jesus' favorite title for Himself, "Son of Man," references that He is the ideal human and worthy of emulation by all people of all cultures (cf. its messianic use in Dan 7:13), He is more than a moral example to follow. He is the King of kings and Lord of lords, and He alone will exercise perfect dominion over all the earth when He returns to rule in righteousness (1 Cor 15:24–25; 1 Tim 6:15; Heb 2:5–8; Rev 1:5; 17:14; 19:15–16). At His name, every knee will bow, every tongue will confess in truth, either in eternal enjoyment of His glory and kingship or by force of judgment, at which time all unbelief will be revealed as eternally damnable wickedness (Phil 2:10–11; cf. Isa 45:23–24; Rev 20:11–15).

Missionaries are ambassadors of spiritual reconciliation to God through the Lord Jesus Christ (2 Cor 5:20). They must prioritize preaching to sin-cursed people everywhere that Jesus, as revealed in the Bible, is the exclusive and sufficient way to God (John 14:6). Because the Son has truthfully revealed the Father, faith in Jesus as Lord is God's requirement to receive eternal life and live with God forever (1:12–13). The missionary must not be surprised that the glorious message of hope that centers on the person and work of the Lord Jesus Christ is an offense to all people, because all people nurture the practices of sin and reject the Son (3:18–19; Rom 2:14–15; 3:10–20; Eph 2:1–3).

The missionary must therefore be bold in proclaiming the obligation to worship and obey Jesus as Lord and Savior, for He is the greatest expression of the kindness of God to those who believe. The reason for the severity of God, on the other hand, is the rejection of Christ, the eternal Deliverer, which will result ultimately in the unbeliever's eternal destruction (Rom 11:22).

Pneumatology

Pneumatology is the doctrine of God the Holy Spirit, who is coeternal and coequal to the Father and the Son. The biblical revelation of the Spirit presents His person and work in such a way as to keep believers from any thoughts, impressions, or experiences that might contaminate the truth of the Spirit and distort their understanding of their real relationship to Him. A biblical understanding of the Spirit leads believers to be more controlled by Him, increasingly separated from sin, and further consecrated to Christ, so that through His active ministry in the believers' lives, the Son would be more glorified in them in practical, daily ways.

The Spirit of God is the Spirit of Christ (Rom 8:9), the Spirit of holiness (Rom 1:4), of glory (1 Pet 4:14), of wisdom (Isa 11:2; Eph 1:17), of truth (John 14:17), of grace (Zech 12:10; Heb 10:29), of adoption (Rom 8:15), and of life (Rom 8:2). Such divine titles reveal the Spirit's perfections and activities, which are transcendently superior to all earthly powers and all evil spirits that pervade the lives of countless people across the world and attempt to supplant His authority.

In the face of powerful wickedness, believers will "overwhelmingly conquer" by the power of the Spirit (Rom 8:37), not because the believer is inherently powerful but because the Spirit inseparably works with the Father and the Son to accomplish His glorious ministries in the world. His activities include creating and sustaining the world and everything in it (Gen 1:2; Job 34:14–15); revealing the will of God in Scripture by supernaturally directing the biblical writers ("breathing out" upon them in the process of inspiration, 2 Tim 3:16; 2 Pet 1:20–21); granting saving grace (Rom 8:7–11; Eph 2:3–5) by regenerating the spiritually dead soul (John 3:5–6, 9, 10; cf. Deut 30:6; Ezek 37:12–14); permanently indwelling the believer (John 7:38–39; Rom 8:9), a provision of the new covenant (Isa 59:21; Ezek 11:19–20; 36:26–27; cf. Jer 31:31–34); granting assurance of salvation (Rom 5:5; 8:11); enabling sanctification (Rom 8:5–9; 1 Cor 6:19); and providing gifts for spiritual service to edify the church (Rom 12:3–8; 1 Cor 12; Eph 4:7–16; 1 Pet 4:10–11).

Angelology

The doctrine of spiritual beings covers what can be known from Scripture about angels, demons, and Satan. Given their nearly three hundred references across the Old and New Testaments, the missionary must not ignore teaching on their nature and activities. All spiritual beings are God's creation during the creative week in the beginning (Job 38:4–7). Angels and demons work along organizational hierarchies, such that they are described as powers, authorities, rulers, and princes (Dan 10:13, 20–21; Eph 6:12), and either serve God's righteous purposes in holiness or Satan from an evil nature. Satan is "the ruler of the power of the air" (Eph 2:2) and "the god of this age" (2 Cor 4:4) who spiritually blinds (2 Cor 4:4) and enslaves all people (Heb 2:15) with murderous schemes (John 8:44; 2 Cor 2:11; Eph 6:11). His demons can indwell nonbelievers (Mark 5:1–16), physically afflict and terrorize people (Mark 9:17, 22; 2 Cor 12:7), and promote false teaching and false worship (Deut 32:17; 1 Cor 10:20–21; 1 Tim 4:1).

Missionaries in regions dominated by spiritual darkness might tend to emphasize teaching on the power of evil spirits and Satan, but it is ill-advised to place emphasis on topics that Scripture does not. While Satan is exceedingly intelligent, powerful, and crafty (Gen 3:1; Isa 14:12–14; Ezek 28:12–17), he is not all-knowing, all-powerful, or omnipresent, and he does not sovereignly control any situation. He does not share God's nature, and therefore he must not be thought of as a divine being.

Believers everywhere must understand that they have been triumphantly delivered from Satan's power by the Lord Jesus Christ (Acts 26:18; Col 1:13; 2:15). God sends His holy angels to provide swift and effective service to believers (Heb 1:7, 14), and they are exceptionally strong to do battle with demons (Dan 10:13, 20–21). Indeed, Satan and his demons are already defeated (Gen 3:14–15; John 12:31; 16:11) and will be eternally destroyed at the appointed time (Matt 25:41; Rev 20:10). No matter the spiritual attacks believers will face in the meantime, they are equipped with the spiritual weaponry to "overwhelmingly conquer" (Rom 8:37) "in the might of His strength" (Eph 6:10, 11–20), for "greater is He that is in you than he that is in the world" (1 John 4:4).

Furthermore, missionaries do not need to perform "signs and wonders" to display the power of the Holy Spirit over evil spirits as they evangelize. Instead, they need to preach and teach from the Word of God, trusting that the Holy Spirit will use the message to initiate saving faith and establish a confident foundation in the spiritual power of God "far above all rule and authority and power and dominion" (Eph 1:21).

Anthropology

The doctrine of anthropology relates mankind—the pinnacle of God's creation—to the Creator and to the created order. Every human possesses the image of God (*imago Dei*) and bears the spiritual responsibility of representing Him as His ambassadors on the earth (Gen 1:26–28; Ps 8:4–8; Jas 3:9). The Lord Jesus Christ, who is the final Adam, is the perfect image of God (Heb 1:3; cf. 1 Cor 11:1). It is because of the resurrection of the ultimate Adam that regenerate believers will also receive glorified bodies that are modeled after Jesus' own resurrection body, so that they are fit for life as rulers on a new earth (1 Cor 15:22–23, 42–50; 1 Thess 4:13–17; 1 John 3:2; Rev 20:4–5; 21:24; 22:5).

The image of God in man is most visible in regenerate believers because they are being conformed to the image of God's Son (Rom 8:29; 12:1–2; 2 Cor 3:18). By being in God's family as sons and daughters, regenerate believers are commanded to model the Son of God's perfect ethic toward other people and creation. Believers strive to represent Jesus' authority and love in their relationships and activities, upholding the rights and dignity of all people, including the unborn, the disabled, the elderly, and the marginalized. God's earthly image bearers also understand the importance of treating animals and the environment in a respectful manner, exercising their biblical stewardship, so that the needs and welfare of animals are maintained as they submit fruitfully to man for the good of all people (Prov 12:10; Luke 14:5).

God's kingly sons and daughters live in a world of ethno-linguistic cultures. Cultures operate according to established social norms that reflect the complex contextual and generational worldviews, values, and ways of living of dynamic people groups in their societies. While the customs and expressions of cultures can be significant and beautiful from the human standpoint, "culture" is not a morally neutral concept. All image-bearers suffer the fall of the first Adam into a nature and life of sin (Gen 3:6–7, 10–12, 16–20; cf. 2:16–17; Rom 5:12). As sinners from ideological communities, their cultural customs and expressions reflect the universal effects of sin.

Missionaries must instruct local believers to shine "as lights in the world," blamelessly living out their faith "in the midst of a crooked and perverse generation" (Phil 2:15). Believers everywhere must aim to be God-glorifying mediators of God's rule in their contexts. Gospel proclamation activities include actively engaging the local culture in order to plead with the people to be conformed to the image of God's Son, the Lord Jesus Christ (2 Cor 5:18–20; cf. Acts 17:30). Out of concern for the glory of God to be manifest in society and culture, believers must expose any local beliefs, traditions, customs, and practices that conflict with the exclusive gospel of the one true God and conform themselves to the exclusive commands of Scripture for godly image-bearing. Yet, societal transformation will be successfully accomplished only when the Lord Jesus Christ returns to the earth to rule as the ultimate Davidic King from Jerusalem (Hag 2:7–9; Zech 14:9–21). At that time, He will transform every sector of society across the face of the earth beautifully, establishing global peace and prosperity for all people (Isa 2:2–4; Mic 4:1–8).

Hamartiology

Also known as the biblical doctrine of sin, hamartiology is foundational to biblical anthropology, as every aspect of unregenerate man's being is totally contaminated by sin (1 Kgs 8:46; Prov 20:9; Jer 17:9; Rom 3:23; Eph 4:22; Titus 1:15). The guilt of Adam's sin has been reckoned to all people (Rom 5:12–14), and the corruption of sin continues to evidence itself in death and destruction throughout the world (Gen

3:23–24; Rom 6:23). Consistent with their inherited depravity, all people walk in rebellion against God and His law, and thus they are accountable to His justice without excuse (Rom 1:18–20; 2:14–15; 3:20; 4:15; 5:15, 20; 7:7).

All people, prior to receiving salvation, are sinners alienated from God because of their hard and darkened hearts (Gen 6:5; 8:21; Ps 14:1–3; Rom 1:21; Eph 4:18). They are hostile toward God (Rom 8:7) and unwilling to ascribe glory to Him with their lives (Rom 1:21). They instead use their bodies and lives to do and promote evil (Rom 1:18–32; 3:9–20). By extension of man's sin nature, all societies and cultures operate with sinful intent under the control of Satan (Eph 2:1–3), even though they do not express evil to the fullest measure and can still project some goodness, beauty, and benefit individually and collectively (Gen 4:20–22; Matt 7:11; Titus 1:12–13; Heb 12:10).

Believers are not like the world but are children of light, who are called to expose the evil deeds of darkness (Eph 5:11). It is both unbiblical and unproductive to consider sinners as "pre-Christians," or by any term or description that euphemizes the reality that they are pagan. Local believers and gospel workers who fail to understand the widespread effects of sin on individuals and their cultures run several risks in an attempt to draw upon the supposed sensibilities of their pagan audiences. Some of these risks include supporting sinful aspects of a culture by uncritically engaging in certain local practices; accommodating the communication of Christian doctrine to pagan worldviews by using sub- or nonbiblical expressions; expressing undue appreciation for local, pagan theology as a supposed bridge to Christian concepts; and hybridizing (syncretizing) pagan and Christian teachings and practices into a new, localized form of faith.

Soteriology

The doctrine of salvation, termed soteriology, teaches the core of the gospel message that must be verbally proclaimed (Rom 10:8, 17) and details the incalculable riches of redemption by the triune God. The most important emphasis Scripture places on salvation is that God the Father, who has set His love from eternity past on the sinner (Rom 8:29–30), must receive all the glory for the accomplishment of salvation through the Son and for its application by the Spirit (Eph 1:3–14). God's chief concern in saving sinners is to exalt His name as glorious above all else (Exod 9:16; Ps 106:8; Isa 42:8; 48:9–11; Eph 1:6; 1 John 2:12), which is why salvation is granted by the sovereign will and activity of God alone (John 1:12–13; 3:5–8; 1 Pet 1:3; 1 John 3:9).

At a moment of God's choosing, though invisible to the human eye, God regenerates the soul through the work of the Holy Spirit by means of the proclaimed Word (1 Pet 1:23–25; cf. Ps 19:7). He makes the one who is spiritually dead alive together with Christ (Eph 2:1, 4–5) by granting him spiritual birth (Rom 5:8; 2 Cor 5:17; Gal 2:20; Eph 2:1, 5). Now, with a soul made to understand the condemning reality of sin against a holy God, the sinner instantaneously repents and trusts in Christ for salvation (Rom 10:13–17; 2 Cor 4:3–6;

1 Pet 1:23; cf. Gen 15:6). Such faith is a gift of God's grace (Eph 2:8–9; cf. Acts 18:27; Phil 1:29). God is faithful to deliver the new believer from sin and Satan (Pss 32:1–2; 103:10–12; Isa 1:18; Col 1:13; Rev 1:5), so he can live in such a way as to glorify God, both presently and for eternity (Rom 6:23; 11:36; 15:5–9; 1 Cor 6:20; 1 Pet 2:12).

The missionary must not soften the reality of the wrath of God against sinners (Pss 5:5; 7:11; Rom 1:18; 2:5; Eph 2:1–3; Col 3:6); otherwise there is no good news to proclaim (1 Thess 1:10). The sinner is a criminal in God's court, yet, through faith in the person and work of Christ, he is legally acquitted of all crimes against God and declared fully righteous by the holy Judge (Isa 53:10–11; Rom 3:26; 5:9). The forgiveness of sins means that the sinner, on the merits of Christ's righteousness alone (Rom 3:27–28; 4:5; 5:16–19), now relates to God as Father. The unworthy person is permanently adopted into God's family and becomes a child of God (John 8:35; Eph 1:4–5; Heb 2:10–13) who is being progressively sanctified for holy service to the Father (1 Cor 1:2; 2 Cor 3:18; Phil 1:6; cf. Prov 4:18). Perseverance in holiness will have its perfect reward (Heb 12:14) when the divinely preserved believer enters into the pleasures of paradise to be with the triune God forever (Rom 8:17, 30; 2 Thess 2:13–14). Therefore, the missionary is sent on behalf of God Himself to proclaim the gospel and call all people everywhere to repent (Acts 17:30) so that they might live as good and faithful slaves of righteousness (Rom 6:16–23; cf. Matt 25:21–23) according to the faith the Righteous One alone gives.

Ecclesiology

Jesus Christ died to build His church (Gk. *ekklēsia*; Eph 5:25–27; cf. Matt 16:18), which is the universal assembly of the redeemed, who are now citizens of heaven, united to Christ by faith as the people of God (Phil 3:20; 1 Pet 2:9–10). Christ is the cornerstone and foundation of the household of faith (Acts 4:11–12; 1 Cor 3:11; Eph 2:20; 1 Pet 2:4–8), the "head" of the church (Eph 5:23; Col 1:18), whose "body" is constructed by faith in His redemptive work on the cross (1 Cor 3:9–10; Eph 2:19–22; Heb 3:4–6; 1 Pet 2:4–8). The church exists in fellowship with Christ (1 Cor 1:9) and, with each new member, expands to take the gospel farther across the world (cf. Rom 15:20–27).

The church age commenced on the day of Pentecost in Jerusalem with the pouring out of God's Spirit on new covenant believers (Acts 2; cf. Joel 2:28–29). The church is God's spiritual kingdom, albeit in a temporary form that will reach completion at "the end of the age" (Matt 28:20). Since its inception, the church grew numerically and geographically from Jerusalem, according to the Great Commission (Mark 16:15; Luke 24:47; Acts 1:8), and it continues to spread regionally, as it did in its earliest years (Acts 8:1; 11:22; Rom 16:5; 1 Cor 1:2; 2 Cor 1:1; Gal 1:2; 1 Thess 1:1). The church age will end when the Lord Jesus Christ returns to rapture all living believers from the earth, immediately after the "dead in Christ" are resurrected to join Christ in the clouds (1 Cor 15:51–53; 1 Thess 4:13–18; cf. John 14:1–3; 1 Thess 1:10; Rev 3:10).

Preachers and teachers should take care to

distinguish the spiritual entity of the church from ethnic, national Israel. Israel is described in the Old and New Testaments as God's chosen people and His holy nation forever (Exod 19:6; Deut 10:15; Isa 43:20; Rom 11:1–7). In this age, however, the church is God's chosen people through adoption (Rom 8:14–17; 9:26; 2 Cor 6:16–18; Heb 4:9; 1 Pet 2:9–10), so that those in the family of God receive spiritual blessings from Israel's Messiah (Acts 8:12; Rom 15:27; cf. Mark 1:14–15; Luke 17:20–21). God bestows spiritual blessings on believing Jews who become members of His church (Rom 9:1–8; Gal 6:15–16), yet He will still fulfill every ancient promise made to the nation of Israel tangibly and materially in the future, according to prophecy (Jer 33:19–26; Rom 9:4; 11:1–2, 25–29).

Missionaries must encourage and aid disciples of Christ in every place to participate in regular meetings in local congregations. Assembling together for the corporate worship of God is expected of true believers everywhere (Heb 10:24–25), so that they are equipped to minister to one another with their spiritual gifts (Rom 12:4–13; 1 Cor 12:4–7, 11, 18; 14:12, 26; Eph 4:11–16; 1 Pet 4:10–11) and thus mature in Christlikeness (1 Thess 5:14). The body of Christ grows under the shepherding protection of godly leaders (1 Thess 5:12–13; Heb 13:7, 17).

By Christ's design, church leadership is reserved for spiritually mature men (1 Tim 2:11–12) who are appointed by other spiritually mature men (Acts 14:23; 1 Tim 4:14). Male leaders may hold the role of "elder" if they are above reproach in every aspect of life and relationships and are able to edify the church through preaching and teaching sound doctrine (1 Tim 3:1–7; 2 Tim 4:2; Titus 1:6–9). Elders hold a position of kind and wise rulership in the church (Rom 12:8; 1 Thess 5:12; 1 Tim 3:4–5, 12; 5:17), which is intended to be conducted in a plurality (e.g., Acts 11:30; 14:23; 15:2; 20:17; Titus 1:5; Jas 5:14). Spiritual rulership entails setting up the shepherding network in the church (Acts 15:22; 1 Tim 4:14), guiding and protecting the flock (Acts 20:28–30; 1 Pet 5:1–2), and serving as an example for the sheep to follow (Heb 13:7; 1 Pet 5:3).

As the gospel spreads geographically through missionary instruction (Matt 28:20), regenerate believers everywhere are commanded to practice the ordinances of full-immersion water baptism (Acts 2:38; cf. Matt 28:19) and the Lord's Supper (1 Cor 11:20–34; cf. Luke 22:19). As disciples adopt the biblical worldview of Scripture and exercise spiritual disciplines in their local church settings, they express their newfound faith in culturally distinct ways. Yet, to mature in obedience to Christ they must be careful to purge any sinful cultural beliefs, customs, and practices (Col 2:16–23; 1 Thess 1:6–10; Titus 1:10–14) so that they express worship to God and loving service to the saints—just as believers before them have done across their cultures and generations (John 14:21; 17:14–17; 1 John 2:15).

Eschatology

The doctrine of the end-time events, or the "last things" (Gk. *eschaton*), is the study of how God will bring history to completion through the Lord Jesus Christ—who will reign over a restored earth as the last Adam and the ultimate Davidic King (Ps 110:1–3; 1 Cor 15:22–28, 42–50; Heb 1:13; 2:5–8; Rev 1:5–8)—and then usher in the eternal state of His kingdom on the new earth (Isa 65:17; 66:22; 2 Pet 3:13; Rev 21:1). Eschatology was revealed through the prophets and apostles to bolster the faith of their readers during some of the hardest years of life. These teachings fuel the race of faith today as believers perceive the end drawing nearer (2 Tim 4:3–4; Heb 10:25). Missionaries and church leaders should not consider eschatology the "last things" to teach but rather entry-level information to instill Christian virtue in the new believer (1 Thess 1:9–10; 2 Thess 2:5, 15–17).

Eschatological instruction will help servant-hearted believers to evaluate which activities please the Lord during the church age. Not all of the good goals of missionaries and church leaders are the mission of the church, such as many activities attempting societal transformation and economic prosperity. God has promised to fulfill His biblical promises literally (Matt 5:17–18; Luke 16:17; cf. Ps 119:89; 1 Pet 1:25), including global restoration and liberation, but the realization of these goals will come after the church age, when Messiah will return to reign from Jerusalem (Isa 2:2–4; Mic 4:1–5). Nevertheless, some prophecies have already been fulfilled partially but await completion when the Lord Jesus Christ returns to the earth (cf. Ps 118:26 with Matt 21:9 and 23:39). The tension for local churches is to focus their time and resources on proclaiming the gospel to the lost, edifying believers,

and maturing personally in faith, hope, and love, while eagerly awaiting for King Jesus to complete their sojourn in this dark world (Heb 11:13; 1 Pet 1:1; 2:11) and finally accomplish global transformation to the glory of God (Rom 8:18, 23–25; 1 Cor 1:7; Phil 1:6; 4:5; Jas 5:8; 2 Pet 3:11–13; Jude 21).

Some of the eschatological events taught in Scripture that are recommended to teach believers for their equipping include the following: the imminent rapture of the church (1 Cor 15:50–53; 1 Thess 1:10; 4:13–18; Rev 3:10; cf. John 14:1–3; 1 Cor 1:7; Phil 3:20–21; Titus 2:13); the bodily resurrection of the righteous, first, for New Testament saints (1 Cor 15:22–26; 1 Thess 4:14–17), second, for the martyrs of the tribulation period (Dan 12:2–3; Rev 6:9–11; 20:4) and Old Testament believers (Dan 12:13; cf. Ezek 37:12–14), and finally, for the wicked from all time to receive judgment (John 5:28–29; Rev 20:5, 11–15; cf. 21:8); the "bema seat" tribunal of Christ to reward church age believers (Rom 14:10; 2 Cor 5:10; cf. Matt 16:27; 1 Cor 3:12–15; 4:1–5; 2 Tim 4:6–8), followed by the "marriage supper of the Lamb" in heaven (Matt 26:29; Rev 19:7–9; cf. John 14:2–3); a seven-year tribulation period on the earth for nonbelievers, to accomplish worldwide evangelism, judgment, and the humbling of Israel (Deut 4:30; Isa 24:1; Jer 30:7; Dan 9:24–27; 12:7; Matt 24–25; Rev 3:10; 6–19); the rise and fall of the Antichrist and his renewed Roman Empire during the tribulation (Dan 2:33, 41; 7:7–8, 21–26; 9:26–27; 2 Thess 2:3–12; Rev 6:2; 13:1–2; 17–18); the visible, physical return of the Lord Jesus Christ to Jerusalem (Joel

3:1–17; Zech 14:4; Matt 24:29–31; 25:31–46; Luke 21:25–28) and His reign for one thousand years with all believers in a restored world (Isa 2:2–4; 11–12; 19:22–25; 32:12–20; 35:1; 60:1–18; 65:19–25; Mic 4:1–5; Hag 2:6–9; Zech 8:4–5; Matt 19:28; 1 Cor 15:24–28; Rev 2:26–28; 5:9–10; 20:1–6); the final overthrow of evildoers and death itself, the dissolution of the present universe, and the institution of the eternal state of the new heavens and new earth (Isa 25:8–9; 34:4; 1 Cor 15:24–26; 2 Pet 3: 3:7, 11–13; Rev 20:7–15; 21–22).

Conclusion

The goal of understanding biblical doctrine is to understand all that God has revealed and be obedient to it. Missionaries and church leaders must be the first among all to understand, believe, and inculcate the sound teaching of Scripture in the local church context. They are called to model for everyone the conviction that Scripture is sufficient to equip the saints to live out the love of God excellently and to proclaim it to the outside world authentically (1 John 4:11–12). The missionary or church leader who neglects the study of theology because he finds the doctrinal propositions of Scripture in some way irrelevant to life in his context has an immature mindset and a disobedient spirit that risks deviating from the faith (Eph 4:14; Col 2:8; 1 Tim 4:1; 6:3–5; 2 Tim 4:3–4). Anything less than the eager pursuit of doctrinal clarity is the wanton disregard of the truth and is unfitting for service to God.

May the Master send more workers to the harvest (Matt 9:37–38). May they not only believe all that God has revealed in the Scriptures but seek to be obedient to it all by passing it along to the next generation. And may they live with conviction that, although "the secret things belong to Yahweh our God . . . the things revealed belong to us and to our sons forever, that we may do all the words of this law" (Deut 29:29).

SUB-SECTION 2: SENDING AND SUPPORTING MISSIONARIES

CHAPTER 24

Church Elders and Missions: Evaluating and Planning a Missions Program in the Local Church

Tom Pennington

The Lord Jesus Christ established the local church as the command center for world missions. Seminaries and mission agencies provide crucial support in the advance of the gospel, but the Great Commission is to be carried out through the local church. Therefore, the elders of every church must personally shoulder this duty.

The New Testament refers to elders as overseers (Acts 20:28; Phil 1:1; 1 Tim 3:1, 2; Titus 1:7). In 1 Timothy 5:17, Paul explains the nature of an elder's oversight when he uses the synonym "rule," which means "to exercise a position of leadership" or "to direct."[1] Elders are not called to do everything in the church but they are called to shepherd people and to oversee, manage, or supervise everything that happens in the life of the church.[2]

According to this divine job description, elders are also called to oversee or manage their local church's part in the Great Commission. Managing well the local church's missions

---

1. The participle *proestōtes* is from the verb *proistēmi*; also translated "leads" in Romans 12:8, and "manages" in 1 Timothy 3:4–5. "προΐστημι," BDAG, 870.
2. "Overseer" (*episkopos*), one of the three New Testament words for the office of elder, identifies "oversight" as the elder's responsibility (Acts 20:28; 1 Pet 5:1–2). The Septuagint uses the term for local officials, including tabernacle administrators (Num 4:16), supervisors of the temple repair (2 Chr 24:12, 17), temple guardians (2 Kgs 11:18), army officers (Num 31:14), and city supervisors or mayors (Neh 11:9).

program requires two duties inherent in oversight: first, evaluating the current missions program and missionaries, and second, planning the church's future missions strategy.

Evaluating the Current Missions Program and Missionaries

Whether a pastor-elder is new and still learning the church's missions program or has served for years, biblical oversight demands that he know the state of the ministry—not only within his local church but also the church's ministry to the world. Some elders mistakenly believe that their duty as elders lies solely in the study and pulpit, but the New Testament requires elders to ensure that every aspect of church life functions in a careful, orderly way. In 1 Corinthians 14, Paul makes this sweeping demand: "All things must be done properly and in an orderly manner" (v. 40). In context, this deals specifically with use of the gift of tongues in the first-century church, but it is also a basic principle for the church's overall ministry. Everything in the church must be done in an orderly way. First Corinthians 14:33 presents the ultimate reason: "for God is not a God of confusion but of peace."

A crucial part of managing or overseeing is planning. Scripture describes God Himself as making and carrying out His plans.[3] In the context of weighing the demands of discipleship, Christ praises human planning and implies that a wise person will try to make plans in every situation (Luke 14:28–32).[4] Planning is therefore a spiritual endeavor and a function of biblical leadership in the church today.[5] Christ gave a plurality of elders to every local church because their collective wisdom is greater than their individual wisdom—there is wisdom in many counselors (Prov 11:14; 15:22; 24:6).

Practically, then, Scripture demands that elders wisely oversee the church's missions program, administrating it today and planning for its future. The elders collectively are called to make overarching decisions about the church's missions program. For an elder board to oversee or administer its missions program, it must begin, first, with a careful evaluation of the church's missionaries and, second, an evaluation of the missions leadership and structure.

A Practical Process for Evaluating Missionaries

The best way for the sending church to begin the process of evaluating the supported missionaries is by reviewing the key information they have about them: who they are, how they are connected to the church (e.g., homegrown, referred by a sister church, etc.), where they serve, the nature of their ministry (e.g., church planting, Bible translation, missionary pilot,

---

3. E.g., 2 Kings 19:25; Psalm 33:11; Proverbs 19:21; Isaiah 14:24, 27; 25:1; Jeremiah 18:11; 29:11; 49:20; 50:45; Acts 2:23; Ephesians 1:11.

4. Israel's sages call for human planning, even as they acknowledge God's sovereignty over those plans (Prov 16:1, 3, 9; 19:21; 20:18; 21:5; 24:8).

5. Strauch stresses this responsibility: "Since shepherd elders must lead and manage a congregation of people, the New Testament requires that all elder candidates evidence management ability by the proper management of their own households." Alexander Strauch, *Biblical Eldership: An Urgent Call to Restore Biblical Church Leadership*, rev. ed. (Littleton, CO: Lewis and Roth, 1995), 26.

etc.), how long the church has supported them, and the amount of their financial support.[6]

In evaluating current missionaries, it is helpful to group them into one of three categories. First are those missionaries who are biblically and philosophically like-minded, faithful, and warrant the church's continued support in every sense. Second are missionaries who have been supported for some time but whom the elders would not begin supporting today because of minor biblical, theological, or methodological differences with the sending church, or a ministry focus that does not fit the current missions emphasis of the elders. In such cases, because the differences are minor and the relationships well established, there is warrant to continue the financial support, rather than remove it, though the elders might determine not to increase it.

Third are missionaries whom the church needs to transition off all support. There are several reasons a missionary might fall into this category. There might be troubling biblical or theological differences, significant ministry philosophy differences, or damaging practical issues, like a poor work ethic or unresolved relational conflicts. Unless major doctrines are at stake, it is important to be gracious and patient in making these transitions since it will take time for the missionary to replace the funding that the church withdraws. If he is near retirement, it might be best to graciously continue providing support until he leaves the field.

A Practical Process for Evaluating Missions Leadership and Structure

A crucial part of evaluating a church's missions program is considering how well the leadership structure fits the church's current circumstances and priorities. The leadership and structure required for an effective missions program changes with the size and complexity of the church. If the church is small, with only two or three elders and a few missionaries, the elders may choose to function as the missions leadership.

However, as a church grows in membership, elders, and missionaries, it may be wise to have a separate missions committee, missions counsel, or what might be called a "missions leadership team" (MLT), that reports to the elders (1 Tim 3:8–13; cf. Phil 1:1; Acts 6:1–6); although team members may not necessarily be deacons, as many churches would define them. The biblical warrant for the delegation of such a crucial ministry comes from the examples of Moses (Exod 18:13–27) and the apostles (Acts 6:1–6), who established patterns of healthy leadership in response to the great needs of their people. Elders who fail to delegate will either find themselves working day and night or discover that they have neglected legitimate needs. That is especially tragic if they are the needs of the church's missionaries, who struggle at a distance. Before creating a missions leadership team, the elders will have to decide what authority and decisions to retain and what to delegate to the team.

---

6. Many local churches with technological capabilities record pertinent information on a chart or spreadsheet that can be easily accessed by and kept private to the leadership.

The elders will need to carefully evaluate if the MLT members are qualified to serve, if they have been assigned the most fitting duties, if they are effectively fulfilling those duties, and if they are appropriately reporting and submitting to the elder board. After completing their review, the elders might choose to make specific changes to strengthen a team that is functioning well. If the current team is not functioning well, the elders might choose to change some or all of its members, or to transition to a new leadership structure entirely.

Selection Criteria for the Missions Leadership Team

The elders will determine who will be part of this committee, counsel, or leadership team. They will need to weigh such practical issues as the size of the team, the ratio of elders to deacons, whether it will include both men and women, if there will be a term of service, and who will serve as chairman. Many churches with an MLT advise including several elders and several deacon-qualified leaders, and recommend that the chairman be either an elder or recognized deacon.

The criteria the apostles used to select ministry leaders in Acts 6 provide a helpful guide for choosing members for the MLT. The apostles delegated leadership to those with the right character. According to verse 3, leaders in the church must have a good reputation, be truly spiritual people, and consistently demonstrate biblical wisdom. The apostles also delegated authority to people who had a passion and affinity for that specific ministry;

they chose seven men with Greek names to care for the Hellenistic widows who had assimilated into Greek culture and might have experienced particular linguistic and cultural barriers from their Aramaic-speaking counterparts, the Hebrews. By delegating leadership to Greeks, they enabled men with the right gifts and skills to serve in a much-needed ministry.

By implication of the text, each person chosen to serve on the MLT should be passionate about missions and either have or be willing to develop a robust understanding of biblical missions. The elders should select leaders for the MLT whom the Holy Spirit has gifted to serve in that role. They should be able to lead because they have the gift of administration (Rom 12:8) and biblical discernment. The apostles ensured that the congregation affirmed the leaders they placed in this role. Acts 6:5–6 describes how "the whole congregation . . . chose" specific men. "And these they stood before the apostles, and after praying, they laid their hands on them." With the MLT, the elders should likewise choose those whom the church would affirm. This does not mean just those excited about missions; they can serve in other ways, such as caring for and praying for missionaries. Rather, the MLT should include only those with both the necessary abilities and the maturity for leadership in this crucial area.

The Practical Function of the Missions Leadership Team

The elders will need to determine and document the issues and decisions that will be handled by the MLT and the ones that will need to come to the elders for information, discussion, or decisions. There are responsibilities that are typically delegated to the MLT and responsibilities that are typically retained by the elders.

The elders will often delegate the following responsibilities to the oversight of the MLT: determining the financial and practical support to provide to current missionaries, comprehensively evaluating potential missionaries to recommend to the elders for support, promoting missions throughout the ministries of the church, ensuring the missionaries' continued agreement with the church's doctrinal statement, and initiating, administrating, and reporting on short-term ministry trips to serve them on the field.

The elders usually retain responsibility for the following: approving new missionaries, removing existing missionaries, approving the overall missions budget, setting the budget support levels for the missionary categories they have identified, approving the MLT's recommendations for the support level for new missionaries, and making other decisions as they determine necessary or when asked by the MLT. The elders may choose to divide these duties differently, but the specific responsibilities of the elders and the MLT should be clearly delineated and documented.

Planning the Future Missions Strategy

The elders are responsible not only to evaluate and manage the current missions program and missionaries but also to set a course for the future. Without a defined strategy, the elders will tend to perpetuate the status quo and react to requests for support without proper criteria. The result is a missions program that lacks direction and unity and fails to capitalize on the church's strengths. A strong missions strategy will include developing a biblical missions philosophy and operating from a practical missions grid.

Developing a Biblical Missions Philosophy

World missions is a biblical goal, but not all missions philosophies and methodologies are biblical. It is important for the elders, a subcommittee of the elders, or other qualified, appointed leaders to write out a shared understanding of what constitutes biblical missions. This shared understanding or philosophy must be based on the New Testament priorities and pattern of making disciples, planting new churches where the gospel is not known, and strengthening existing churches internationally. The heart of a biblical missions philosophy is the fulfillment of the Great Commission, namely, making disciples by proclaiming the gospel to the unreached, planting churches among those who believe, and strengthening those churches to become self-supporting and self-reproducing.

A missions philosophy may also include priorities unique to the sending church, such as specific kinds of ministry focus or global emphases, exact mission fields, and decisions about various levels of support by category. It is worth the time and effort for the elders to work through these decisions, to document them, and to ensure they agree on the future direction of the church's missions program.

Creating a Practical Missions Grid

An extraordinarily helpful tool for the sending church to use is a missions grid. This grid is useful as a template to identify how the elders and the MLT prioritize the kinds of ministries and missionaries they support and how they establish the support level they apply for each category. Such a grid promotes objective decisions about which missionaries to support rather than subjective or emotional decisions. An effective missions grid will be based on three key criteria.

CRITERION 1: NEW TESTAMENT MISSION PRIORITIES

The New Testament priorities enumerated in the church's missions philosophy serve as the primary criterion. The grid needs to reflect as top priority those missionaries whose activities are closest to the New Testament model of evangelizing and planting new churches or strengthening existing churches, primarily through pastoral leadership training. An important but lesser priority are those missionaries whose ministries support church planting and strengthening, including those engaged in transportation (e.g., aviation), Bible translation and resource publication, and discipleship of local believers. The grid is best designed with the top-priority ministries and missionaries in the most prominent position, perhaps at the top of a quadrant or list.

CRITERION 2: THE MISSIONARY'S RELATIONSHIP TO THE SUPPORTING CHURCH

The second criterion for a practical missions grid focuses on the missionary's relationship to the supporting church, to reflect the degree of influence and discipleship the church has on the supported missionary. The highest or most prominent relationship to support should be that of the missionary who grew up in this church and was sent out from it. An easily identifiable label for this relationship is "homegrown, home church." Next in order of relationship are the following:

- "Home church," reflecting missionaries who joined this church at some point and are now sent out from the church
- "Homegrown, related home church," reflecting missionaries who grew up in the supporting church but moved away and are sent out from another like-minded church
- "Related home church," reflecting missionaries who were sent out from a like-minded church with whom this church has a relationship or connection, and who therefore come under the primary authority and accountability of that church. The relationship between churches allows the supporting church to have greater confidence in the missionary
- "Unrelated home church," reflecting missionaries who are sent from churches with which this church does not have a relationship. Since most churches have limited

missions funds, the elders may choose not to support a missionary in this category

The intersection of these first two criteria forms the primary matrix of a missions grid and forms the basis for the elders and the MLT to ensure that their unique missions plan is implemented. However, other criteria that are important to the church and its leadership should also be considered for the allocation of support, including greater need in a specific region or field as identified by the church leadership in consultation with their missionaries or a deliberate choice to focus on a specific country or region.

CRITERION 3: THE MISSIONARY'S LEVEL OF FINANCIAL SUPPORT

It is essential that the missions grid include the level of financial and material support for the different categories of missionaries. Based on the rank assigned by category, leadership can then prioritize the missionaries they will support financially and materially at the highest level. Depending on how the elders and the MLT have structured their priorities and represented them on the grid, it might be that the most prominent category for financing would be the homegrown missionary sent from their church, whose ministry involves church planting and pastoral training in a region significantly devoid of evangelism. On the other hand, for example, the same church might provide the lowest-level support to a missionary sent from an unrelated church serving in a support role in an area with a well-established missions history.

In establishing levels of financial and material support, it is helpful to create a beginning support level, the baseline monetary figure the church would supply consistent with the missions budget and God's provision. Each level of financial support should also have a cap or limit that the leaders believe accords with the wise stewardship of available funds. Nevertheless, the leadership will still want to allow some flexibility to respond to changes in the missionary's need, changes in the relationship, and other factors that might warrant additional support regardless of the missionary's position in the grid.

As a church considers levels of support, it should avoid extremes. In a desire to support a larger number of missionaries, some churches contribute only a small fraction of each missionary's support. This approach, although well intentioned, presents difficulties for missionaries. It lengthens the deputation (support-raising or partnership development) phase interminably and spreads their furlough time impossibly thin, as they try to visit all their supporting churches. Other churches generously provide a missionary's entire support, making his ability to remain on the field completely dependent on the health of a single sending church. A healthy, balanced approach is to have fewer missionaries who are supported well but not entirely. The elders may also choose occasionally to provide a onetime gift (e.g., toward initial relocation expenses) for a potential missionary who is like-minded but not one they would consider for long-term ongoing support based on their missions grid or current financial limitations.

A carefully constructed missions grid serves as an invaluable tool that enables the missions leadership of the sending church to decide which missionaries to support and with what financial commitment, and to do so objectively, based on their own established missions philosophy and priorities.

Conclusion

The members and elders of every sending church must shoulder the responsibility not only for personal evangelism but also for world missions as assigned in the Great Commission. As the overseers of the church, the elders are called to manage their church's part in proclaiming Christ to the world. To ensure that the church's missions program is biblical and healthy, the elders should carefully evaluate the current missions program and missionaries and strategically plan the church's missions strategy so that the church faithfully supports its missionaries into the future.

CHAPTER 25

Don't Hand Them Off: The Ongoing Role of the Home Church in the Life of a Missionary

Rodney Andersen

The work of missions is frontline ministry. Missionaries often serve in locations without a gospel witness, places with widespread doctrinal confusion, or places that lack faithful biblical preaching. They go out in obedience to the command given by the Lord Jesus Christ to "go . . . and make disciples of all the nations" (Matt 28:19). As they go, their effectiveness depends on those who send them. In other words, the work of missions is not only the work of the one who goes. Those who send and support have a great responsibility as well.

Just as soldiers on the frontlines depend on those serving on the home front, missionaries depend on an array of faithful believers to provide vital services for their ministries abroad.

The home-front support of missionaries comprises administrative, strategic, and spiritual support. Numerous missions agencies have been created worldwide over the past two centuries with the intent of providing the administrative and strategic support missionaries need to successfully transition to and live long term in a foreign land or an unevangelized area.[1]

Many sending churches lack the expertise needed to handle such support on their own. Therefore, they look to missions agencies to provide these services.[2] Churches, however, while benefiting from the administrative and strategic support of missions agencies, must not abdicate their role of spiritual support for their missionaries. Missions agencies are parachurch

---

1. Administrative support for many Western agencies includes processing donations given to the missionary through the banking system, providing publicity opportunities that encourage further support, and assisting with other considerations like medical insurance and retirement accounts.

2. Missions agencies often excel at certain types of strategic support as well, including but not limited to keeping the most current information on how people can legally enter and remain in their host countries and providing hands-on training in areas such as language learning and cultural acclimation. Through sending organizations, missionaries often make connections with like-minded teammates and can attend conferences and workshops for encouragement and further training.

organizations and, by that definition, are instituted to come alongside the local church to support their missionaries. They must never usurp the role of the local church in fulfilling its responsibility to identify, train, and support their missionaries.

The biblical model of sending missionaries demonstrates that a relationship with the sending church must be maintained not only for the benefit of the missionary but for the good of the sending church as well. This chapter will examine select New Testament passages to show how God's design for accomplishing the Great Commission involves the local church commissioning missionaries, remaining connected to them, and caring for them.

The Local Church Commissions Missionaries (Acts 13:1–3)

While recognizing that narrative portions of Scripture are not always normative for believers, the historical account of the beginning and expansion of the early church described by Luke in Acts is not merely history but is inspired by the Holy Spirit for the benefit of every reader.[3] Acts 13:1–3 reads as follows:

> Now there were at Antioch, in the church that was there, prophets and teachers: Barnabas, and Simeon who was called Niger,

and Lucius of Cyrene, and Manaen who had been brought up with Herod the tetrarch, and Saul. While they were ministering to the Lord and fasting, the Holy Spirit said, "Set apart for Me Barnabas and Saul for the work to which I have called them." Then, when they had fasted and prayed and laid their hands on them, they sent them away.

The Church Must Evaluate an Individual's Suitability for Missions

From Acts 13:1–3, it is possible to draw several implications for missions today. The first verse identifies Barnabas and Saul (later called Paul) as two of the five prophets and teachers in the church of Antioch. From this context the Holy Spirit directed the church to set apart Barnabas and Saul for a particular ministry. These men who were called by the Holy Spirit to be missionaries were already active leaders in the church.[4] The church did not just send the willing; they sent two of their best—men who were qualified to be leaders in the church and thus strong in Christian character and doctrine. Though the qualifications for elders were not recorded in Scripture until years later (1 Tim 3:1–7; Titus 1:5–9), it is reasonable to assume that the early church in Antioch would have had similar character and ability requirements for men to take the role of prophet or teacher (Acts 6:3).

---

3. "It is impossible but that the account so carefully given by St. Luke of the planting of the Churches in the Four Provinces should have something more than a mere archaeological and historical interest. Like the rest of the Holy Scriptures it was certainly 'written for our learning.' . . . It was really intended to throw light on the path of those who should come after." Roland Allen, *Missionary Methods: St. Paul's or Ours? A Study of the Church in the Four Provinces* (Grand Rapids: Eerdmans, 1983), 1.

4. This was not Barnabas and Saul's first ministry trip, but this was a new missionary journey and one that would be commissioned by the church in Antioch. See Eckhard J. Schnabel, *Paul the Missionary: Realities, Strategies and Methods* (Westmont, IL: IVP Academic, 2008), 74–75.

According to verse 2, Barnabas and Saul were ministering to the Lord and fasting when the Holy Spirit called upon them for the work of the ministry. While this passage does not explicitly state how the Holy Spirit spoke this command, the fact that there were prophets among them (v. 1), seems to indicate that the Holy Spirit spoke through a prophetic statement of one of those leaders.[5] The Holy Spirit called them to the "work" of proclaiming the gospel and planting churches in Cyprus and the Galatia region, as described in chapters 13 and 14.

Having been instructed by the Holy Spirit, the church in Antioch dutifully fasted, prayed, and then laid their hands on Barnabas and Saul and sent them out. While fasting and prayer would have been regular practices in the early church, the laying on of hands was only done at special times when church leadership commissioned individuals to a specific ministry work (Acts 6:1–6; 1 Tim 4:14; 2 Tim 1:6). The point of the text is that the Holy Spirit sent out two highly qualified churchmen for missionary work. They were leaders of their home church before being sent to minister in other places.

The implication of the text, when considering those who go out as missionaries today, is that their qualifications should not be anything less than those required of a church elder if they are going out to plant churches. For a missionary to establish elders or provide instruction to elders while not being qualified himself is a sure guide to disaster. Those sent to serve in other capacities than church planting should likewise meet the criterion for deacons, who are already faithfully serving in their local churches (1 Tim 3:8–13).

Who is to determine if a person who desires to be sent as a missionary meets biblical qualifications for the task? Only the local church can adequately identify and confirm the character and spiritual giftedness of a missionary candidate. Is this person striving for holiness? How does this person conduct himself or herself in ministry? Is the individual trustworthy and responsible? How does the missionary candidate respond to pressures and trials? Does he or she solve problems and interact with others biblically? These are not questions a missions agency can or should be responsible to answer. Only the local church leadership, by looking to the Lord in prayer and acting wisely, based on a close relationship with the missionary candidate, can rightly determine if that person is called to missionary service, and to what range of ministries.

The Church Trains Individuals for Missions

If the church leadership determines through prayer and practical evaluation that a person meets the moral and objective requirements to be considered as a missionary, the church must take responsibility to equip the candidate for what lies ahead. In some cases, the missionary candidate has been serving for years and has already been proven faithful. They are ready to go. In other

---

5. Eckhard J. Schnabel, *Acts*, ZECNT (Grand Rapids: Zondervan, 2012), 555.

cases, a person may have great zeal for missions but be lacking in experience, spiritual maturity, Bible knowledge, or a sound philosophy of missions. Such a person may need more time in purposeful discipleship under the elders of the church before approval can be given.

The local church can also assist the missionary candidate in determining what kind of ministry the candidate would be well suited to undertake. For example, does the candidate have the qualities needed to plant churches, train pastors, teach missionary children, or provide technical and administrative support to an existing ministry? The local church elders should help identify these gifts. Additionally, the church should consider its ministry connections and determine if there is an existing team that the individual would be well suited to join.

Provided that the local church has taken the lead role in preparing the individual in terms of personal character, biblical and theological accuracy, and the ability to proclaim the gospel effectively, outside agencies can come alongside the church and provide the candidate with more instruction on missions principles and practices.

The Sending Church Remains Connected to Missionaries (Acts 14:26–28)

It is plain from Acts 13 that the church at Antioch knew well the men they sent out for the Lord's work. Paul and Barnabas went out to distant locations to proclaim the same gospel they had taught at the church in Antioch. But the Antioch church did not view Paul

and Barnabas's departure as the end of their relationship. Acts 14:26–28 records that when Paul and Barnabas returned from their missionary journey, the church in Antioch gladly welcomed them back "to report all things that God had done" (v. 27). The full account is detailed as follows:

> And from there they sailed to Antioch, from where they had been committed to the grace of God for the work that they had fulfilled. And when they had arrived and gathered the church together, they began to report all things that God had done with them and how He had opened a door of faith to the Gentiles. And they spent not a little time with the disciples. (Acts 14:26–28)

The Antiochian church's response to their returning missionaries is not surprising in light of the integral ministry roles Paul and Barnabas played before their departure. The remaining leaders of the church in Antioch, as well as the congregation as a whole, certainly continued to pray for their missionaries in their absence. Now they were eager to hear of the ways God had answered their prayers. When Paul and Barnabas returned and reported on their ministry, they were careful to give all glory to God as they reported what God had accomplished and how God opened a door of faith to the Gentiles. It was truly a worship service! Furthermore, Paul and Barnabas did not just share a brief update. They settled back into the life of the church and "spent not a little time with the disciples" (v. 28).

Missionaries Report Back to the Sending Church

The church in Antioch illustrates how to establish relationships that will endure across the miles and over time. The sending church took the necessary time and care to evaluate, disciple, and train their missionaries. The same principle applies today. When missionary candidates are confirmed, assisted, and mentored by local church elders, they will see themselves as part of a team with joint interests and goals. They will know of the investments and prayers their elders and fellow church members have made. Their hearts therefore will be knit together for the sake of the gospel.

With the relational foundation in place, the missionary will have confidence that their home congregation is praying and ready to help. Such knowledge makes the missionary more inclined to convey their personal and ministry needs on the field. In turn, the church receives joy and encouragement by seeing the Lord work through their missionary's labors on the field. The church is also able to participate in the trials of missionary life, lending wisdom, counsel, and encouragement in times of opposition and suffering. While employees of faithful missions agencies also pray for and support their missionaries, the rich personal connections that come from the church body are irreplaceable.

Philippians contains an example of missionaries maintaining communication with churches back at home. While Philippi was not Paul's sending church, it was a church that supported him spiritually and financially. In Paul's letter to the Philippians, he frequently referred to his high regard for their partnership in ministry, not only for himself but also for the benefit it brought to them. He wrote, "I thank my God in all my remembrance of you, always offering prayer with joy in my every prayer for you all, because of your fellowship in the gospel from the first day until now" (Phil 1:3–5).

Paul's letter to the Philippians exemplifies how he cherished the communication between himself and the supporting church.[6]

- Paul prayed for them, thanked God for them, and communicated that to them (1:3).
- Paul expressed gratitude to them for their "fellowship in the gospel" (1:5).
- Paul recognized that their partnership worked two ways: he was blessed by them and was a blessing to them (1:5; 4:15).
- Paul's love for them was genuine, and he repeatedly expressed it to them (1:8; 4:1).
- Paul shared about his ministry and its challenges with the church (1:12–26).
- Although Paul was imprisoned, he did not focus on his difficult circumstances but expressed joy at the spread of the gospel (1:12–18; 2:17–18).
- Paul encouraged them that God would reward them for their partnership in ministry (4:19).

---

6. List adapted from Kenneth Williams, "A New Way to Look at Missionary Support," International Training Partners, 2020, https://itpartners.org/resources/A-New-Look-At-Support.pdf.

- Paul was thankful for their financial contribution to the ministry (4:15–18)

The Philippians' support of Paul serves to remind believers today that no missions agency, no matter how robust and diligent its staff, can replace the church's support of the missionary. Likewise, Paul's missionary impact on the Philippian believers, who were personally invested in the work of the ministry, is a reminder of the kind of personal impact a missionary can have on believers in the supporting church.

Missionaries Are Resent by the Local Church

After recounting Paul and Barnabas's reception by the church in Antioch at the end of Acts 14, Luke describes the events of the apostles' council in Jerusalem (Acts 15:1–29).[7] At the conclusion of the council, Paul and Barnabas returned to Antioch to report to the church the apostles' decision. They also spent time there teaching and preaching (15:35). Acts 15:36 records that after Paul and Barnabas spent a profitable time with the church, they were sent out once again. This recommissioning was not without conflict, as Barnabas and Mark went one way and Paul and Silas another. The local church, however, sent out these men as representatives, who were "committed by the brothers to the grace of the Lord" (15:40).

There are times in every missionary's service when it becomes necessary to reevaluate the team's strategy or to make decisions about the next field of service. A division could arise within the team, as happened between Paul and Barnabas, necessitating a new team formation. Perhaps the objective of a particular ministry comes to fruition and it is time for the missionary to move on. In any case, the support and guidance of the local church in making these decisions and resending the missionary is invaluable.

Supporting Churches Care for Missionaries (3 John 5–8)

Finally, 3 John 5–8 is instructive about how supporting churches are to care practically for those they send to the mission field. Here the apostle John writes to his friend Gaius to commend him and encourage him to continue in his service to the Lord.

> Beloved, you are acting faithfully in whatever work you do for the brothers, and are doing this though they are strangers; and they bore witness to your love before the church. You will do well to send them on their way in a manner worthy of God. For they went out for the sake of the Name, receiving nothing from the Gentiles. Therefore we ought to support such men, so that we may be fellow workers with the truth.

John heard a report that Gaius had done well in showing hospitality to some visiting missionaries. A missionary traveling in those days would have been particularly dependent on such hospitality, and Gaius was commended

---

7. An analysis on whether this was an official church council or not is outside of the scope of the discussion here.

by John for his warm welcome, receiving missionaries with whom he had not been previously acquainted.

John goes on to encourage Gaius to excel still more by sending the missionaries off in the same way he had received them, providing for their needs to please and honor the Lord. John's reason that Gaius should treat missionaries with this kind of care is, "For they went out for the sake of the Name" (3 John 7). The "Name" refers to the Lord Jesus Christ, and so the missionaries were messengers of Christ, sent by the church to preach the gospel. As such, they were to be welcomed and aided by churches along the way.

Third John 7 also says that the missionaries were to receive help, not from the pagans they encountered, but from believers, "so that we may be fellow workers with the truth" (v. 8). The church is obligated to help missionaries. In doing so, the supporting church shows itself in partnership with the truth as the latter changes people's lives. This role is given to believers in the churches so that churches and missionaries together might work for the common goal of advancing the truth of the gospel of Christ. Supporting churches are not just spectators to what God is doing; they are active participants!

Such care for missionaries should demonstrate care for them "in a manner worthy of God" (3 John 6). This phrase could mean providing care in a manner that God would approve, or treating them in a way appropriate for a minister of God, or caring for them as if caring for the Lord Himself (Matt 25:31–46).[8] While the third interpretation is most likely,[9] they all set a high standard for how missionaries should be cared for by supporting churches. We are called to provide for missionaries with more than just our leftovers and castoffs. They have left much for the name of Jesus. They should be treated accordingly.

Supporting churches that come alongside missionaries sent from other churches have no reason to view themselves as unimportant or second class. When they demonstrate love and care for missionaries, they prove to be vital partners in the advancement of the kingdom of God.

Conclusion

The pattern of the relationship between early New Testament churches and their missionaries is apparent. From beginning to end, there is an integral and ongoing link between the two. The church identifies, develops, and sends its missionaries. But those are only the initial steps. The relationship between the church and the missionary is a spiritual partnership, one that persists throughout the life of the ministry, on and off the field, from commissioning missionaries to keeping an active connection with them and caring for their needs. Churches and missionaries alike should see this relationship as a great privilege and as an essential component of success as they strive for the glory of Christ's kingdom.

---

8. Cf. Robert Yarbrough, *1–3 John*, BECNT (Grand Rapids: Baker Academic, 2008), 372n5; Gary W. Derickson, *First, Second, and Third John*, EEC (Bellingham, WA: Lexham, 2012), 674; Karen H. Jobes, *1, 2, and 3 John*, ZECNT (Grand Rapids: Zondervan, 2014), 303.

9. Cf. *Didache* 11:4–6.

Supporting Your Church's Missionaries

Tom Pennington

The Particular Baptist Missionary Society was formed on October 2, 1792, in Kettering, England. Andrew Fuller became the secretary of this new society, created to direct and maintain the work at home, and William Carey became its first missionary. Fuller later famously described the duty of all those who send out missionaries:

> Our undertaking to India really appeared at its beginning to me somewhat like a few men, who were deliberating about the importance of penetrating a deep mine which had never before been explored. . . . Carey, *as it were*, said, "I will go down, if you will hold the rope." But, before he descended, he, *as it seemed to me*, took an oath from each of us at the mouth of the pit, to this effect that "whilst we lived, we should never let go the rope."[10]

The churches and elders who send out missionaries have a profound duty to them and to Christ: to support them in every way possible, holding the rope as they go down.

Jesus' command to His disciples to "make disciples of all the nations" (Matt 28:19) makes this same point. He was not demanding that every disciple leave the nation of his birth and travel abroad (though He calls some to that). Rather, in addition to the duty of personal evangelism, Jesus was demanding that every disciple shoulder responsibility for and actively support His international mission for the church. Every member and leader, whether he goes or stays, is personally responsible for the nations. Every believer in the church needs to hold the rope.

The Elders

Elders can serve and support their missionaries in at least six ways. First, be available to provide counsel. Missionaries are often faced with difficult decisions and need a multitude of wise counselors. Some are hesitant to approach the elders of their sending or supporting churches unless the elders express an eagerness to help, maintain ongoing communication, and keep open relationships.

---

10. S. Pearce Carey, *William Carey* (London: Wakeman Trust, 2008), 108, italics original.

Second, visit the field. Missionaries love to introduce their leaders to their world, and visits allow elders to know firsthand the state of the missionary, the ministry, and how best to serve them. Some elder visits may be with a short-term team or a specific ministry focus, but it is also beneficial to visit for the sole purpose of spending time with the missionary and becoming familiar with his daily life, family, and ministry. By sharing brief updates about their visits, the elders can also keep the congregation connected.

Third, encourage church members to engage with their missionaries in ways that are genuinely supportive. One especially helpful way is for the missions leadership team to form missionary support teams (described below).

Fourth, regularly pray for the church's missionaries. One of the chief duties of spiritual leaders is to pray for those under their charge (1 Sam 12:23; Acts 6:4). Elders should pray for the spiritual health and growth of their missionaries and their families,[11] for the success of the gospel they proclaim (Eph 6:19; Col 4:3; 1 Thess 5:25; 2 Thess 3:1), and for more frontline workers, including from their own church (Matt 9:38). Their prayer should echo that of Charles Spurgeon: "that God would pour out on this church a missionary spirit."[12]

Fifth, provide opportunities for members to get to know the church's missionaries. This means opportunities for new and existing missionaries to share about their ministries in person (e.g., when visiting on furlough or for a missions emphasis Sunday) and electronically (e.g., via videoconferencing or a prerecorded video update).

Sixth, constantly emphasize a biblical ministry philosophy rather than a numbers- or results-based one. Elders can help to free missionaries from the man-centered performance trap of pressure to "produce" by encouraging and reminding them of the biblical standard of faithfulness (1 Cor 4:1–5).

The Lead Pastor-Teacher or Elder

While all elders need to engage in missions, the lead pastor-teacher or elder plays a crucial part in supporting the church's missionaries. He can do this in three key ways.

First, by establishing meaningful relationships with the church's missionaries for

---

11. See Matthew 6:13. Christ uses the plural pronoun "us" to remind us to pray these requests faithfully for one another. This sixth and final petition in the Lord's Prayer is for sanctification and growth in holiness, a prayer that our Lord prays with us (John 17:17).

12. C. H. Spurgeon, "Marah; or, The Bitter Waters Sweetened," *Metropolitan Tabernacle Pulpit*, vol. 17 (1871; repr., Pasadena, TX: Pilgrim, 1971); available online at *The Spurgeon Center for Biblical Preaching at Midwestern Seminary*, accessed June 18, 2024, https://www.spurgeon.org/resource-library/sermons/marah-or-the-bitter-waters-sweetened/#flipbook/.

the sake of love, encouragement, counsel, and help. When they return from the field for any reason, the pastor should seize every opportunity to reconnect and deepen his relationship with them.

Second, by visiting missionaries on the field. The pastor-teacher or primary teaching pastor has a unique opportunity to encourage by his visits. Because when he makes the effort, it underscores the church's support in a heightened way. Often the pastor can support the missionary's ministry by preaching in his church or at a related conference or by intensively teaching the men whom the missionary is training for ministry.

Third, by preaching on missions and reporting on his trips to the field. The pastor-teacher, through his teaching ministry, needs to keep the church's focus on the international mission Christ assigned. He can accomplish this by having missions-emphasis Sundays and by taking opportunities in his regular exposition and application of Scripture to focus on Christ's heart for the nations. Likewise, he can emphasize every believer's duty to obey the Great Commission by supporting those who go.

The Missionary Support Teams

The missions leadership team (MLT) is responsible for the entire missions program under the authority of the elders. But it is impossible for the MLT to carry out that duty alone, nor should they. They need to motivate and engage church members to come alongside them to support the church's missionaries. Two uniquely valuable tools for that purpose are missionary care teams and missionary prayer teams.

Missionary care teams help, especially when churches and their missions programs grow, by providing a missionary with a smaller group of close, personal relationships. Care teams provide a structure for intentional, proactive care tailored to missionaries' unique needs in ministry, location, life stage, family, and other factors. They might send care packages, care for family affairs back home, or prepare for their missionary's furlough before arrival.

Missionary prayer teams are composed of members who have indicated a commitment to pray regularly—preferably daily—for the missionary (or missionaries) they choose. The team's primary purpose is to provide missionaries with constant and fervent prayer for them and their families as they minister. Members should therefore receive missionary newsletters so they are aware of their missionaries' needs.

The Members

Elders should encourage members to support their missionaries in a variety of ways. Members should pray regularly for one or more missionaries and consider joining a prayer team or care team. The elders should also encourage members to give regularly through the church, not only so the needs of the church and its members are met, but also so that the missionaries can be well supported financially (3 John 5–8).

Members can also be encouraged to consider joining short-term ministry trips. Because of the many benefits of these trips, the elders and MLT should consider providing regular church sponsorship to short-term ministry teams.

CHAPTER 26

Gospel-Centered Prayer:
Paul's Priorities in Colossians 4:2–6

Mark Tatlock

Churches and missionaries alike need to ensure that their prayers for missions align with biblical priorities. The evangelism of the lost is ineffective unless entrusted to God in prayer; yet the prayer of a faithful servant is effective (Jas 5:16) and should be unceasing (1 Thess 5:17). Missionary Hudson Taylor (1832–1905) is credited with saying, "You can work without praying, [though] it is a bad plan . . . but you cannot pray in earnest without working. Do not be so busy with work for Christ that you have no strength left for praying."[1] Work without prayer will be frustrated, even anti-productive.

To be sure, there is personal responsibility in evangelism from a human perspective; that is, Christians must open their mouths to proclaim the good news (Eph 6:19). Yet evangelism is impotent apart from divine power.

Missionaries must not be guilty of presuming that they can, by their best efforts, bring anyone into the kingdom of God. As no man can save himself, neither is he able to save another. God must be at work opening hearts to receive the gospel (Titus 3:5; cf. Acts 16:14) and opening doors for the missionary to proclaim it (1 Cor 16:9; 2 Cor 2:12). The way missionaries entrust their gospel work to the sovereign plans of God is through prayer. It should be the starting point of the missions enterprise, permeate the work, and, once answered, credit back to God all glory with thanksgiving and praise (Rom 11:36; Phil 4:6).

Paul, the greatest of missionaries, the apostle to the Gentiles, understood this truth. He expresses his reliance on God's power to do the work of missions in his call to prayer in Colossians 4:2–6. The context of that prayer

---

1. Dr. and Mrs. Howard Taylor, *Hudson Taylor and the China Inland Mission*, vol. 2, *The Growth of a Work of God*, 5th impression (London: China Inland Mission, 1921), 444.

is below, followed by four opportunities that gospel-centered prayer affords. Missionaries and churches do well to pray likewise.

The Context of Paul's Prayer in Colossians

Colossians emphasizes the supremacy of Christ (Col 1:18; 3:11).[2] In the letter, Paul exalts and affirms the person of Christ who is the cornerstone, the foundation, the cause, and the reason that Christians are alive spiritually. Many points in the book show how the Christian is to honor Christ in light of His supremacy:

- 1:10—"Walk in a manner worthy of the Lord, to please Him in all respects."
- 1:16—"All things have been created through Him and for Him."
- 1:28—"Him we proclaim, admonishing every man and teaching every man with all wisdom, so that we may present every man complete in Christ."
- 2:6—"Therefore as you received Christ Jesus the Lord, so walk in Him."
- 2:13—"He made you alive with Him, having graciously forgiven us all our transgressions."
- 3:3—"For you died and your life has been hidden with Christ in God."
- 3:10—"And [you] have put on the new man who is being renewed to a full knowledge according to the image of the One who created him."
- 3:17—"And whatever you do in word

or deed, do all in the name of the Lord Jesus."

Then, in Colossians 3:18–4:1, Paul described how all relationships should be affected by Christ's supremacy:

- Wives are to "be subject to [their] husbands, as is fitting in the Lord" (3:18).
- Husbands are to "love [their] wives" as the Lord loves the church (3:19; cf. Eph 5:25).
- Children are to "obey [their] parents . . . for this is pleasing to the Lord" (3:20).
- Parents are to bring up their children in the Lord's way of instruction (3:21; cf. Eph 6:4).
- Employees/slaves are to "work heartily, as for the Lord rather than for men" (3:22–25).
- Employers/masters are to do what is right and fair before their Master in heaven (4:1).

Finally, after all that Paul conveys about the supremacy of Christ, he urges the Colossians to pray:

Devote yourselves to prayer, being watchful in it with thanksgiving; praying at the same time for us as well, that God will open up to us a door for the word, so that we may speak the mystery of Christ, for which I have also

---

2. John F. MacArthur Jr., *Colossians*, MNTC (Chicago: Moody, 1992), 9.

been bound, that I may make it manifest in the way I ought to speak. Walk in wisdom toward outsiders, redeeming the time. Let your words always be with grace, seasoned with salt, so that you will know how you should answer each person. (Col 4:2–6)

Unsurprisingly, the four specific opportunities for which Paul urges prayer revolve around Christ being honored and the advancement of His gospel.[3] Such urging shows that even if a missionary is equipped with as robust a doctrine of the person and work of Christ as Paul had, he must still devote himself to prayer and ask others for it if he wants to be effective on the field.

Gospel-Centered Prayer Is an Opportunity to Delight in Christ (Col 4:2)

The first opportunity for gospel-centered prayer comes in light of what Christ has done for believers. The imperative in verse 2 is, "Devote yourselves to prayer." Paul exhorts the Colossians to be courageously persistent, to hold fast and not let go of prayer, which is a common charge in his letters: praying at all times (Eph 6:18), praying without ceasing (1 Thess 5:17), being devoted to prayer (Rom 12:12). The Lord Jesus also gives examples of persistent prayer in Luke 11:5–10 (the neighbor seeking bread at midnight for his unexpected

guests) and 18:1–8 (the "persistent widow" seeking justice from an unjust judge).

However, here in Colossians persistence in prayer is characterized not by what is needed but by what has been provided already, redemption through the atoning work of Christ (Col 1:21–22)—the gospel! For the manner of prayer that Paul commands is "being watchful . . . with thanksgiving" (4:2). First, being watchful (*grēgorountes*), which means "being alert,"[4] amounts to being intentional, purposeful, and specific in the things for which one prays. It means being "alert to specific needs" or answered needs without becoming vague.[5]

Second, alert prayer is to be done with thanksgiving (Col 1:12). Thanks is given to the Father, because it is in Christ that the believer has reconciliation and forgiveness of sins. For missionaries or supporting churches, persistent and alert prayer will inevitably be grateful for the work of Christ graciously applied to them. Thus, the first opportunity that gospel-centered prayer affords is to delight in the grace of God.

Gospel-Centered Prayer Requests the Opportunity to Declare Christ (Col 4:3–4)

Persistent, alert, and grateful prayer leads to praying that God's grace be applied to others. Thankful prayer turns to intercessory prayer. Thus, the second opportunity of

---

3. Compare the similar three-point outline for this passage titled "Eschatological Mission to the World" in David W. Pao, *Colossians and Philemon*, ZECNT (Grand Rapids: Zondervan, 2012), 290.

4. "γρηγορέω," BDAG, 207.

5. MacArthur, *Colossians*, 182.

gospel-centered prayer concerns what Christ can do for others. It requests an opportunity to declare Christ. Notice three specifics about this opportunity requested in Colossians 4:3–4.

For Open Doors

In verse 3, Paul describes the kind of prayer he commanded: "praying at the same time for us [Paul, Timothy, and their company] as well, that God will open to us a door for the word, so that we may speak the mystery of Christ." The open door imagery is an affirmation of the doctrine of election. If God has called individuals to Himself, then any effort at evangelism must recognize His sovereignty in the event and should be preceded (or accompanied) by requests that God prepare the heart (Acts 16:14) and the occasion (14:27) for one to respond to the gospel message.[6]

Another use of the open door illustration is in 1 Corinthians 16:8–9, "But I will remain in Ephesus until Pentecost, for a wide and effective door has opened to me." In 2 Corinthians 2:12, Paul states that at Troas "a door was opened for me in the Lord." These passages use the so-called "divine passive," the biblical author's way of implicitly noting God's agency.[7] But in Acts 14:27, God's agency is explicit; at the close of Paul's first missionary journey, he and Barnabas reported to their sending church at Antioch "all things that God had done with them and how He had opened a door of faith to the Gentiles." So, too, in Revelation 3:7–8, Jesus is the One who holds the key and who opens and closes the door to His kingdom,[8] which is to imply by necessity that Jesus Himself directs all effective evangelism, whether the hearer is saved or not (Rev 1:18). Thus, it is God whom Paul desires would open a door for the gospel to be heard and received, and it is the Colossian church whom he requests to pray for it.

Churches and missionaries cannot afford to pray for open doors only once, whenever the missionary is sent. Doors close, and sometimes missionaries are forced to leave. However, Stephen Gaukroger put it this way: "Prayer needs no passport, visa or work permit. There is no such thing as a 'closed country' as far as prayer is concerned. . . . Much of the history of missions could be written in terms of God moving in response to persistent prayer."[9] Let Christians, then, pray like Paul that God would open new doors, open alternate doors, and hold wide the doors He has already opened.

For Grace to Speak

Another important doctrinal affirmation can be seen in Colossians 4:3: the missionary must

---

6. Cf. William Hendriksen, *Exposition of Colossians and Philemon*, New Testament Commentary 6, ed. Simon J. Kistemaker (Grand Rapids: Baker, 1964), 180–81.

7. However, this is probably so either because God's agency was obvious or because Paul's focus was on the verb's subject (a door) not the agent (God). It was not an aversion to using the divine name, which is sometimes meant by the term *divine passive*. Daniel B. Wallace, *Greek Grammar beyond the Basics* (Grand Rapids: Zondervan, 1996), 435–38.

8. Robert L. Thomas, *Revelation 1–7: An Exegetical Commentary*, ed. Kenneth Barker (Chicago: Moody, 1992), 275, 277–78; Buist M. Fanning, *Revelation*, CECNT (Grand Rapids: Zondervan, 2020), 172–73.

9. Stephen Gaukroger, *Why Bother with Mission?* (Leicester, UK; Inter-Varsity, 1996), 19–20.

"speak" the word. His evangelistic method must not consist of slick marketing strategies, creative bait-and-hook programs, or charismatic personalities. It must consist of Scripture, spoken, read aloud, explained, and applied. The methodology Paul affirms relies on Scripture as what the Spirit uses to pierce and regenerate hearts (Acts 2:37; 16:14; Heb 4:12). The sovereignty of God and the sufficiency of the proclaimed Word in salvation should be a comfort and an encouragement to every believer in gospel-centered prayer, for the gospel's effect is not contingent upon individual efforts or eloquence but upon God's election and effectual calling through His Word.

When God opens doors, faithful Christians, still relying on grace, must walk through them. Evangelism cannot occur without the Word being somehow communicated through a human instrument. Elsewhere Paul asks, "How then will [the lost] call on Him in whom they have not believed? How will they believe in Him whom they have not heard? And how will they hear without a preacher? . . . So faith comes from hearing, and hearing by the word of Christ" (Rom 10:14, 17). Therefore, Paul asks the Colossians to pray that he would be that very preacher, thus confessing that he needs God's grace to open his mouth boldly as he ought (Eph 6:20). It is only the ministry of proclamation empowered by God Himself that leads to the obedience of faith (Rom 16:25–26). In sum, God is at work both in the proclaimer

and in the hearer of the gospel. Churches and missionaries ought to pray thus for themselves and for one another.

To Speak as One Ought

Paul elaborates on the word to be spoken by calling it "the mystery of Christ." Mystery (*mysterion*) is used in Paul's writings to explain truths that were hidden until Christ came—especially Christ Himself "and Him crucified" (1 Cor 2:1–10; Col 2:2–3)—but which were then being revealed to those being saved (Rom 11:25; 1 Cor 4:1; Eph 3:2–3, 8–9; Col 1:26–27).[10] The mystery did not indicate a discovery of isolated, esoteric, or magical facts, but an understanding of Christ latently revealed in Scripture and finally manifest in the flesh (John 1:9, 14, 17–18; 1 Pet 1:10–12). Earlier in Paul's letter, he summarized it: "Christ in you, the hope of glory" (Col 1:27). The application of Christ's atonement to the believer, Jew or Gentile, through union with Him by faith, resulting in eternal life—that was the gospel, the word Paul had to speak.

In light of this full and final revelation of the gospel at long last, Paul expressed in Colossians 4:4 an urgency to "make it manifest in the way [he] ought to speak." It was for the sake of the gospel that Paul the missionary had been imprisoned (v. 3). While in prison, however, his mission continued; he wrote four New Testament epistles as well as testified of Christ to kings, governors, guards, and the household of Caesar (Acts

---

10. "μυστήριον," *NIDNTTE*, 3:354–56.

25:10–12, 22ff.; Eph 3:1; Phil 1:12–13; 4:22; Phlm 1, 9; cf. Acts 9:15).[11] Still, he requested prayer to speak in the way he ought. Not being hindered by timidity, confusion, indifference, or fatigue—all things which can tempt missionaries on the field—Paul wished to be bold with clarity, completeness, and conviction. He had done just that in Ephesus, "solemnly testifying" of "the whole purpose of God" (Acts 20:21, 27). Gospel-centered prayer from churches today seeks the same for their missionaries and for their local evangelism. It seeks open doors, grace to speak, and to speak as one ought.

Gospel-Centered Prayer Results in the Opportunity to Demonstrate Christ (Col 4:5)

Paul's prayer request turns to consequent exhortation in Colossians 4:5. If the Colossians pray in a gospel-centered way for Paul, then certain applications of that prayer should also be true in their lives. So, as a third opportunity, they should demonstrate the truth of Christ they confess. Paul's first and main application is a command: "Walk in wisdom toward outsiders." Elsewhere Paul gives instructions for how believers are to walk:

- Walk in the Spirit, bearing the fruit of new life in Christ (Gal 5:16–25).
- Walk properly, as in the day; in righteousness, not in sin (Rom 13:13; cf. 1 John 1:7).

- Walk in a manner worthy of the gospel, a life consistent with gospel truths (Phil 1:27).

In Colossians all of the above are captured in the phrase "wisdom toward outsiders." Wisdom used throughout the Old and New Testaments simply means knowledge applied to life, or truth put into practice. It describes the Christian's walk in all aspects, progressing toward becoming "complete in Christ" (Col 1:28; cf. Jas 3:13–18). But in 4:5, Paul makes the application of wisdom toward "outsiders," that is, unbelievers. His point is that Christians must practice what they preach; they must be self-aware, circumspect, discerning in their behavior, because the unbelievers for whom they are praying in gospel-centered ways are observing their behavior. How Christians live before the world will either affirm or invalidate the gospel they proclaim (Titus 2:5, 8, 10). It should never be that a Christian gives unbelievers, through sinful and unwise actions, an easy excuse to reject the gospel, as if it is powerless to transform a life (Rom 2:24; 1 Pet 2:12).

On the contrary, Paul applies the urgency he feels to the Colossians' gospel witness too: "Walk . . . redeeming the time" (Col 4:5). The days are "evil," he says elsewhere (Eph 5:16), evil men go from bad to worse (2 Tim 3:13), and the return of Christ is imminent, making the time that missionaries and churches have to proclaim Him a precious commodity (Rom

---

11. P. T. O'Brien, "Colossians, Letter to the," *Dictionary of Paul and His Letters*, ed. Gerald F. Hawthorne, Ralph P. Martin, and Daniel G. Reid (Downers Grove, IL: InterVarsity, 1993), 148, 152; Andreas J. Köstenberger, L. Scott Kellum, and Charles L. Quarles, *The Cradle, the Cross, and the Crown: An Introduction to the New Testament*, 2nd ed. (Nashville: B&H Academic, 2016), 465–66.

13:11–14). All Christians, then, must make the most of the time that God has allotted them by praying gospel-centrically, speaking the gospel, and then affirming the gospel with wise living.

Gospel-Centered Prayer Anticipates an Opportunity to Defend Christ (Col 4:6)

The second application of Paul's prayer request comes in Colossians 4:6 and serves as the fourth opportunity for the Colossians: "Let your words always be with grace [i.e., gracious], seasoned with salt." The injunction toward gracious speech is in various New Testament texts. Christians are to speak only truthful, loving, wholesome, edifying, and grace-giving words (Eph 4:15, 29) and to avoid speech that is inconsistent with a pure heart (Matt 12:34–35; Jas 3:8–12). The need for speech that extends grace to others is especially strong in evangelism. Opening one's mouth to speak the gospel is sometimes met with personal attacks, criticisms, or false accusations. Missionaries, pastors, and evangelists are not to respond in argumentative, defensive, self-promoting manners, but with grace—kindly, gently, patiently insisting on the truth (2 Tim 2:24–25).

Speech "seasoned with salt" has a dual effect. Salt in the ancient world was used, among other things, as a purifying, cleansing agent (e.g., 2 Kgs 2:19–22; Ezek 16:4) and to enhance the taste of food (Job 6:6–7; Matt 5:13). In a general sense, then, Christians' speech should exude the flavor of the gospel by being gracious, defined in the ways listed above.[12] But at the same time, speech could have no greater purifying effect than to apply the word of God's grace to the impurity of sin (Ps 19:7; John 17:17; Eph 5:26; cf. Jas 5:19–20).

The latter is indicated by Paul's purpose clause to end verse 6: "so that you will know how you should answer each person." The command for speech to "always" be with grace now comes full circle. The constant practice of gracious speech, besides honoring the Lord, makes the Christian ready to proclaim Christ and "answer" the unbelieving response in manifold forms. A similar exhortation is found in 1 Peter 3:15–18. There Peter uses the word *apologia*, from which is derived the English word "apologetics," meaning the reasoned defense of the faith (Acts 17:2–3; 18:28; 2 Cor 10:5; Phil 1:7; Jude 3).[13] Apologetics are useful in evangelism in several ways, such as in showing the error of false religions and worldviews (2 Cor 10:3–6), or in demonstrating the unbeliever's awareness of and responsibility toward general revelation (the truth about God revealed in creation, conscience, and history; see Acts 14:16–17; Rom 1:19; 2:14). Yet, as the evangelist gives a defense for the faith, he is to remain gracious and wise

---

12. Curtis Vaughan, "Colossians," in *EBC*, vol. 11, *Ephesians through Philemon*, ed. Frank E. Gaebelein (Grand Rapids: Zondervan, 1981), 222.

13. See the helpful overview of apologetics in light of these Scriptures in Norman L. Geisler, "Apologetics, Need for," *Baker Encyclopedia of Christian Apologetics* (Grand Rapids: Baker, 1999), 37–38. As Geisler also shows from Titus 1:9 and 2 Timothy 2:24–25, facility with apologetics is required of Christian leadership.

in how he answers. That must be predicated upon a practice of gracious speech always and upon the gospel-centered prayer for such opportunities.

Conclusion

Paul's letter to the Colossians exalts Christ. It also shows that one who trusts and obeys Christ is steadfastly intent on seeing others come to know their beloved Lord. Colossians 4:2–6 shows that believers can, with a heart of gratitude, pray that the Lord would give them opportunities to delight in, declare, demonstrate, and defend His gospel. This brief text also gives Paul's affirmation of human responsibility and divine election and power at work simultaneously to win the lost. Missionaries have a responsibility to proclaim the gospel, but it is only God's power that can initiate the work and make it effective.

These are priorities to which missionaries and churches must align their praying if they would be effective in biblical missions. Believers must make sure that—as they go and send others into the Lord's harvest fields, whether around the corner or around the world—prayer permeates their efforts. Those who have gone before, whose hearts were as committed and zealous as any missionary today, had to learn this same lesson in their missionary careers. For example, Samuel Zwemer (1867–1952), the missionary nicknamed "The Apostle to Islam," summed up that "[prayer] is the key to the whole missions problem."[14] Let the global church hear the words of Colossians 4:2 once again: "Devote yourselves to prayer."

---

14. Samuel M. Zwemer, *Taking Hold of God: Studies in Prayer* (London: Marshall, Morgan and Scott, 1936), 115, 122.

CHAPTER 27

Seven Ways to Pray for Missionaries

John Glass

A Personal Account of Prayer

Never will I forget that day in 1995. It was the day a team of elders in one of our supporting churches prayed for us. It became one of the most vivid prayer memories of my life. My wife and I had been serving as church-planting missionaries in France for nine years. We were in our home country on furlough, recovering from a brutal time on the field. Some in the church had attempted a takeover the Sunday before we began our travels home. The church's leadership reacted by threatening to discipline the agitators out of the church if they did not repent. By God's grace, they did repent, publicly, in the church service the day before we left. The church was saved, but the battle was debilitating. We were tired, discouraged, and partly disgusted by the ministry. We almost quit.

A couple of weeks later we were visiting one of our supporting churches. I was asked to be in attendance first thing in the morning. The sixteen elders of this large church were all there with one objective: to pray. It was my first time joining their prayer meeting, but it was how they started each Lord's Day together. After greeting me warmly, they asked me to share any prayer requests. I briefly explained to them that our family had just gone through a very difficult time over the last four months on the field, and I gave them a few details. The elders thanked me for sharing, and then each of them, in turn, prayed for my wife and me. I never prayed; they prayed. And wow, did they pray!

The entire focus of their prayer meeting turned to us. One after another, these men prayed and interceded intensely for us and our situation. They prayed for my wounded heart. They prayed for my wife, and asked that God would renew and refresh her. They prayed for our children by name. They prayed for our church in France and for its new pastor, whom I had led to Christ ten years prior, trained, and then left behind in this difficult place. They even prayed for those who had hurt us so badly—and on and on they went. I cannot remember how long it lasted, but it felt like standing under a waterfall of intercession.

I was overwhelmed by a sense of God's presence and by deep emotion. I began to weep uncontrollably as these men, one after another, some laying their hands on me, continued to intercede on my behalf. I slowly began to feel the burden on my heart lift. It was as if those pastors, through their prayers, asked me to give them my burden so that they could then in turn offer that burden to the Lord, knowing that I was too weak and distraught to offer it myself. As this long prayer ended, I felt a total sense of relief. I knew the Lord had heard them. I knew that God was going to heal us and that our missionary future was not compromised.

God did indeed answer those prayers. We returned to France a few months later. We have served there now for almost forty years, and we are still planting churches. That prayer meeting so long ago is carved in my memory as a memorial to the power of prayer. How often I have thought back to that moment and been encouraged.

Some might respond to this experience by saying, "I thought missionaries were the giants of the faith, that they were autonomous ministry machines. I thought missionaries were trained, ordained, and tested for endurance, that they were naturals at suffering. Should they really need this kind of prayer?" Allow me to dispel the myth. There is nothing special about missionaries. They are people like any other, saved by grace and called by grace to the task of reaching the world for Christ. We are simply weak sinners attempting to the best of our abilities to obediently fulfill our Lord's commission. But there are many bumps in the road, and being prayed for is a vital need along the journey, something that missionaries crave.

Paul's Request for Prayer

The greatest missionary of all times was incontestably Paul. He could be considered "the perfect missionary" for several reasons: he was bicultural (Jewish and Roman), tri- to quadrilingual (Greek, Hebrew, probably Aramaic, and maybe Latin), biblically brilliant (he actually wrote inspired Scripture), single and thus economical, a tentmaker and thus self-supported, a natural leader, a preacher, a teacher, an evangelist, a church planter, a pastor, an author, willing to suffer, bold, dedicated, motivated, and more.

Yet even Paul wrote in his letters, "Brothers, pray for us" (1 Thess 5:25). By using the term "brothers," the apostle speaks intimately and specifically with his recipients in the Thessalonian church. His consummate request from them—that they "pray"—is from the Greek verb *proseuchomai*, a compound word from *pros-* ("toward") and *euchomai* ("pray"), meaning to petition or to make requests of God.[1] It is the general New Testament word for prayer, including thanksgivings, praises, and pleas, indicating that Paul simply wanted prayer of all and any kinds (Eph 6:18–19). Plus, he issued the imperative in the present

---

1. "προσεύχομαι," BDAG, 879.

tense, implying that he did not want a once-for-all prayer, but a continual, habitual prayer on his behalf.[2] By using the phrase "for us," Paul included his partners Silas and Timothy (1 Thess 1:1). What is more, the church he was asking for prayer was quite young—at most, six months old (Acts 17:2).[3] Paul simply knew he had needs that only the Lord could meet, and that the Lord listened to His children.

The New Testament exemplifies how Paul asked for prayer in seven areas. These Pauline prayer requests give missionaries practical pointers on the kinds of requests to make so that their supporters and friends will know how to intercede for them.

Partners

Missionaries need people who will commit to partnering with them in prayer. Paul not only asked the Thessalonian church to pray for him, but he asked other churches to do the same. In Romans 15:30–31, for example, Paul asked the church in Rome "to strive together with [him] in [their] prayers to God for [him]," and specifically in this case, to deliver him from evil men. In Philippians 1:19 he asked the Philippians to pray for him that he might be delivered from jail.

With regard to partnership in prayer, I recall one Lord's Day when I was visiting our home church. After the service concluded, a man sitting behind me whom I did not know leaned toward me and said that every morning

at four o'clock he prayed for me, for my wife, my children, and my ministry activities. I was floored. These are the kind of partnerships that allow ministries to flourish.

Possibilities

In 2 Thessalonians 3:1, Paul asked that the church pray for opportunities to proclaim the gospel. Paul wrote the Thessalonians from Corinth as he thought back on the fruitful ministry he had just had with them. He wrote, "Finally, brothers, pray for us that the word of the Lord will spread rapidly and be glorified, just as it did also with you." Paul requested that they beg the Lord to do what was not humanly possible—to cause the Word to advance in Corinth as quickly as it did in Thessalonica.

In Colossians 4:2–3, writing from a prison cell in Rome, Paul sent the Colossian believers the following request: "Devote yourselves to prayer, being watchful in it with thanksgiving; praying at the same time for us as well, that God will open up to us a door for the word, so that we may speak the mystery of Christ, for which I have also been bound." Here Paul simply asked the believers to pray for gospel possibilities in prison and the matching boldness to proclaim Christ even while wearing chains. Paul was totally dependent on the prayers of his friends, knowing that unless the Lord opens doors and gives the missionary the possibility of proclaiming the Word, nothing will happen.

When the Second Gulf War, the Iraq War,

---

2. D. Edmond Hiebert, *1 and 2 Thessalonians*, rev. ed. (Winona Lake, IN: BMH Books, 1996), 275.

3. Cf. Gary Steven Shogren, *1 and 2 Thessalonians*, ZECNT (Grand Rapids: Zondervan, 2012), 17; F. F. Bruce, *1 and 2 Thessalonians*, WBC 45 (Dallas: Word, 1982), xxxiv–xxxv, 8.

broke out in 2003, our church in Geneva was divided about who was right and who was wrong in the war. To reduce the tension, I decided to do a series on war from the Bible to bring God's perspective on the matter to our people. A French publisher heard about the series and asked to turn my sermons into a book on the biblical perspective on war. Then one day I got a call from a French navy officer explaining that he had just read my book. He invited me to come and speak about war to the top brass and soldiers in Toulon, France, which is a large French naval base. The conference was organized in a church off base, and it was packed. I not only spoke about war, but I articulated the gospel, explaining that ultimately the Prince of Peace is the key to peace.

These are the kinds of amazing opportunities that a missionary could never have created on his own. Knowing that many people pray for their missionaries daily, it is reasonable to perceive that gospel opportunities are the direct result of an army of saints praying for open doors of ministry.

Power

Note what Paul writes to the Ephesian church in Ephesians 6:18–20:

> Praying at all times with all prayer and petition in the Spirit, and to this end, being on the alert with all perseverance and petition for all the saints, as well as on my behalf, that words may be given to me in the opening of my mouth, to make known with boldness the mystery of the gospel—for which I am an ambassador in chains—so that in proclaiming it I may speak boldly, as I ought to speak.

Once God opens a door for ministry, the believer must seize the opportunity and proclaim the gospel message. This is truly a startling prayer request because of who Paul was. Though Paul was an evangelistic machine, it would be wrong to assume he was "a natural" at evangelism. Proclaiming the gospel was not necessarily a carefree, easy endeavor for him, just as it is never really easy for anyone. Jesus said that believers would be hated, insulted, and even persecuted for proclaiming His message (John 15:18–20). It is a lot easier to stay quiet and say nothing than to confront sinners with their sinfulness and the truth of the gospel. John the Baptist was brutally decapitated by Herod because he dared confront him for his adultery (Matt 14:3–12). Had he remained quiet, John could have saved his neck easily. But he didn't.

Two of Paul's requests stand out in Ephesians 6:19. First, Paul asks the congregation to pray that he would speak with boldness (*parrēsia*), "outspokenness, frankness, plainness."[4] Second, Paul asks them to pray that he would be courageous enough to open his mouth. Here then, is the bottom line. The local church is to pray that missionaries would boldly open their mouths and preach the gospel, and not falter at the primary task. Romans

---

4. "παρρησία," BDAG, 781.

1:16 suggests that believers could tend to be "ashamed of the gospel," so brothers and sisters are to pray that missionaries would not be ashamed of the gospel.

Protection

In 2 Thessalonians 3:1–2, Paul requests, "Finally, brothers, pray for us that the word of the Lord will spread rapidly and be glorified, just as it did also with you; and that we will be rescued from perverse and evil men, for not all have faith." In the work of gospel proclamation, a celestial battle is raging between Jesus Christ and Satan. The world is under Satan's influence today (Eph 2:2–3). He is the god of this world (2 Cor 4:4), and as Ephesians 6:12 recounts, "For our struggle is not against flesh and blood, but against the rulers, against the authorities, against the world forces of this darkness, against the spiritual forces of wickedness in the heavenly places."

As the spiritual battle rages, those who have embraced the gospel are called to snatch people away from Satan's powerful grip by using their mouths to communicate the life-giving message (Rom 10:7, 17). It sounds like a suicide mission—like walking into a lion cage, for "your adversary, the devil, prowls around like a roaring lion, seeking someone to devour" (1 Pet 5:8). Satan hates when believers evangelize the lost. Particularly appetizing are pastors and missionaries. This is because the downfall of one pastor or of one missionary can mean the fall of an entire ministry. Satan therefore does everything in his power to make church leaders fail.

Attacks by the evil one, though sovereignly allowed by a loving Father, can come in multiple forms: persecution by evil men, conflicts in the church, basic discouragement, sickness, accidents and tragedies, death of spouses or children, lack of fruit, conflict with teammates, temptation and sin, depression, and family problems. The list of potential problems in which Satan delights to harm church leaders is almost endless. Though not all problems can be attributed to Satan, he certainly tries to use any and all circumstances to discourage leaders and make them ineffective in the ministry of the Word.

Provision

In Philippians 4:10–18, Paul thanked the local church and the Lord for the financial gifts they gave him. Though this passage is not a prayer request per se, Paul's public thankfulness for the Lord's provision indicates that he frequently prayed for his physical needs, asked others to do the same, and did not hesitate to thank them for their generosity on his behalf.

First Corinthians 9:14 (and passages like 2 Thess 3:7–10 and 1 Tim 5:17) suggests that some people are called to the ministry and should receive remuneration for their service: "So also the Lord directed those who proclaim the gospel to get their living from the gospel." Many missionaries fall into that category of servants needing financial support, being dependent in one way or another on other people to be able to serve on the mission field. Some missionaries never mention financial support needs as they prepare to depart for the field, and others don't hesitate to mention their needs to potential supporters and churches. Whatever the case may be, most missionaries are dependent on others to meet their material needs, and so asking believers to pray that God might provide through their churches is understandable and important.

Purity

The writer of Hebrews[5] makes a prayer request for purity in Hebrews 13:18: "Pray for us, for we are convinced that we have a good conscience, desiring to conduct ourselves well in all things." The writer is honest and transparent, effectively stating that life is tough in ministry; temptations are great; he is weak; he could fall into sin at any time. Because of these difficulties, the brethren should pray to God that his conscience would never get accustomed to sin, that it would continually react violently at the inevitable sight of sin, and that he would remain holy and pure, a child of God "without blemish in the midst of a crooked and perverse generation" (Phil 2:15). The writer of Hebrews knew that nothing discredits a ministry more quickly than sin.

For churches to pray for the moral purity of their missionaries is particularly important because in the work of the ministry, missionaries are often alone, living in a different culture and language than that of their original home. They have less accountability, they can dry up emotionally and spiritually, and they often live in pagan cultures that bombard them with enormous amounts of sin daily. Therefore, missionaries can be more susceptible to sin and defeat. Many missionaries leave the field due to disqualifying sin. Believers must ask the Lord to help missionaries resist temptation and preserve them from disqualification from ministry.

Pauses

Defying the image most people have constructed of the apostle Paul, he expressed in Romans 15:30–32 that he needed refreshment. The need emerged in his prayer request:

> Now I urge you, brothers, by our Lord Jesus Christ and by the love of the Spirit, to strive together with me in your prayers to God for me, that I may be rescued from those who are disobedient in Judea, and that my service for Jerusalem may prove acceptable to the saints; so that I may come to you in joy by the will of God and find rest in your company.

Paul's prayer request is not puzzling but sensible. Paul was tired. Expending himself to boldly reach the lost, being incessantly battered by spiritual rebels while striving to live a holy and pure life in a series of foreign cultures had left the apostle exhausted. With this glimpse into his human heart, Paul revealed that he longed to rest (*synanapauomai*) in the Romans' company.[6]

Missionaries need occasional breaks and sabbaticals after periods of service. Paul

---

5. Though no one knows who wrote the book of Hebrews, the verse holds value for this study.

6. "συναναπαύομαι," BDAG, 965; cf. Thomas R. Schreiner, *Romans*, BECNT (Grand Rapids: Baker Academic, 2018), 736–37.

returned to his home church in Antioch when he had completed his first missionary journey. Acts 14:27–28 describes his return: "And when they had arrived and gathered the church together, they began to report all things that God had done with them and how He had opened a door of faith to the Gentiles. And they spent not a little time with the disciples." It appears that Paul's ministry break in his home church with his friends in a safe and secure environment was truly refreshing and reposing.

Rest is a big problem for many missionaries. Many don't know how to stop, rest, or enjoy leisure time with their families. Many missionaries are "workaholics." Their predicament is understandable. There is tremendous pressure to produce a quantifiable return on investment, especially if they are sent out from a result-oriented society full of result-oriented churches. Such missionaries feel great pressure to send prayer letters that represent gospel success, and so they work and don't stop until the results are secured. Sooner or later, however, they can succumb to physical and emotional stress. So praying that missionaries would schedule regular times of refreshing is important. And for supporters not only to allow them to rest but to provide for them to retreat restoratively is a godly goal.

Conclusion

It is critical for believers to pray for missionaries. The prayers of supporting churches for their missionaries can have an immediate impact on them and those they serve in the work of the gospel. If the apostle Paul, the greatest missionary who ever lived, needed prayer, so, too, do missionaries today. Therefore, missionaries should follow Paul's example and openly admit their need for prayer, asking the churches to pray for their partnerships, possibilities, power, protection, provision, purity, and pauses. Neither the missionaries nor those who support them should ever underestimate the need for nor the power of prayer for ministers of the Word.

CHAPTER 28

Shrewdly Investing in the Great Commission: The Parable in Luke 16:1–13

Eric Weathers

God brings financial gain to believers through their marketplace labors and investment successes. Each of these blessings comes with opportunities for the Lord's people to creatively steward resources toward the Great Commission. The reward for faithfulness in doing so is shown in Luke 16, where Jesus teaches His followers an important point: many souls who are led to Christ will one day heartily welcome into eternal dwellings those who used their resources to advance the gospel. The lesson is conveyed through Jesus' ironic parable of the shrewd manager, which, being directed to Jesus' disciples, is applicable to them still today. This chapter will examine Jesus' parable and apply its principle to investing in the Great Commission today.

The Parable of the Shrewd Manager

Jesus' parable of the shrewd manager from Luke 16:1–13 is ironic for the purpose of teaching a principle. It consists of a rich man and his unrighteous manager or "steward" who administers his business affairs. The irony is found in the way the steward's wicked strategies had laudable characteristics that even his manager could recognize. The story is designed to encourage believers to wisely steward their resources on earth for righteous purposes by illustrating the tact with which unbelievers do the same for unrighteous purposes. Let's look at the four elements in the story: the problem, the plan, the praise, and the principle.

The Problem

Jesus' description of the unrighteous manager was not of a low-level employee who made a onetime mistake. I. Howard Marshall comments on the rich man's perspective, that of an absentee landlord: "His affairs were therefore in the hands of an οἰκονόμος [*oikonomos*; Luke 12:42], here an estate-manager . . . who acted as his agent with considerable legal powers."[1] The steward was likely responsible for his boss's entire enterprise.

Yet someone reported to the rich man that the manager had been "squandering [his] possessions" (Luke 16:1), which could imply embezzlement or simply neglect (15:13).[2] This was a serious accusation, deserving investigation into the alleged mismanagement. In this particular case, the owner's inquiry began with the conclusion already in mind: he was going to fire his steward because he was incapable of managing the business. Yet before terminating him, the rich man demanded an accounting.

The parable does not convey anything about the manager's defense, which, in context, allows the reader to safely assume that the accusations were true.[3] Jesus simply portrays the manager's thoughts via soliloquy. He silently asks himself, "What shall I do, since my master is taking the stewardship away from me? I am not strong enough to dig; I am ashamed to beg" (Luke 16:3). John MacArthur comments, "The business evidently provided him with housing because that was one of his main concerns (v. 4). Once he was released from this job, he would literally have no income and no place to live."[4] For the steward, this is a crisis.

But it seems at least that the rich man gave him time to make appropriate arrangements before his official separation. That time, allotted for gathering the necessary accounting records and surrendering them to his master,[5] allowed the steward to formulate a plan.

The Plan

The wicked manager quickly analyzed his precarious situation and decided to focus first on shelter (Luke 16:4). Consulting only himself, he determined to leverage his master's debtors to secure a place to live. Before they caught wind of his termination, the manager "summoned each one," asking them, "How much do you owe my master?" (v. 5). The debtors were oblivious that this man was manipulating them, because he presented the landlord as his "master" as though he was performing his administrative duties.[6]

Though the steward summoned all of the debtors one by one, Jesus summarized his shrewd strategy with only two specific examples.[7] The first debtor owed one hundred measures of oil, which was no small debt (Luke 16:6). By today's standards, that would equal nearly nine hundred gallons.[8] The manager told the man to falsify the "bill" or promissory note

---

1. I. Howard Marshall, *The Gospel of Luke: A Commentary on the Greek Text*, NIGTC (Exeter, UK: Paternoster, 1978), 617.

2. Marshall, 617.

3. Marshall, 617; William Hendriksen and Simon J. Kistemaker, *Exposition of the Gospel according to Luke*, New Testament Commentary 11 (Grand Rapids: Baker, 1978), 768.

4. John MacArthur, *Parables: The Mysteries of God's Kingdom Revealed through the Stories Jesus Told* (Nashville: Thomas Nelson, 2016), 146.

5. Hendriksen and Kistemaker, *Exposition of the Gospel according to Luke*, 768.

6. Hendriksen and Kistemaker, 769.

7. Leon Morris, *Luke: An Introduction and Commentary*, TNTC 3 (Downers Grove, IL: InterVarsity, 1988), 265.

8. A measure of oil equals roughly 8.75 gallons. The total oil in this example, then, was about 875 gallons, an amount that would

and cut the amount owed in half. By changing the debt outstanding from one hundred to fifty measures of oil, the debtor received more than four hundred gallons of oil at no cost. But nothing is ever free; someone must cover the associated cost. In this case, it was the seller, the landlord, who paid for the surplus oil—unwittingly. The second customer's case was much like the first, except that he was given a 20 percent discount on a hundred measures of wheat (v. 7), perhaps erasing all interest from the promissory note.[9] Whatever the logic, the debt written off was equivalent to approximately eight to ten years of a working man's income.[10]

In both examples, the callous manager defrauded his master of a significant amount of money. Jesus did not need to continue the parable with all the master's debtors; the reader should conclude that the amount the steward defrauded from his master totaled a fortune. The text never indicates that the debtors knew that they were being scammed either. They relished the opportunity to have a portion of their debts forgiven. But the move would cost them.

In exchange for a reduced debt load, the customers fell victim to an obligation of open-ended reciprocity. MacArthur again comments, "Reciprocation was an integral part of Jewish society; if someone did a person a favor, that person was obligated to do one for him."[11]

Thus, the debtors remained indebted; the manager simply redirected their obligation away from his master to himself. They received extreme discounts at the rich man's expense but would be obliged to give the ingratiated steward such things as free room and board, or perhaps even a job,[12] with basically no limitation. The rich man effectively became the financier of his fired steward's retirement plan.

Jesus' illustration of the shrewd manager is a notorious example of unfaithfulness with someone else's riches (Luke 16:1, 11–12). In that sense, Jesus set him up as a bad example, which Christians are not to emulate. They are to be faithful in what is little if they would be entrusted with what is much (v. 10). The irony of the parable, however, is that the defrauded master still praises the manager's genius.

The Praise

Luke records that the Pharisees, who were searching for reasons to undermine Jesus' teaching, listened to all of these things (16:14). One might therefore wonder why the Lord would tell His disciples a story about theft and deceit, and then, of all things, conclude it with praise for the deceiver and thief. After all, God emphatically declared to His people, "I am Yahweh your God. . . . You shall not steal. . . . You shall not covet . . . anything that belongs to your neighbor" (Exod 20:2, 15, 17). But Jeus

---

have been drawn from about 146 olive trees. Morris, 264–65; cf. Marshall, *Gospel of Luke*, 618–19.

9. Marshall, *Gospel of Luke*, 619.

10. John MacArthur, *Luke 11–17*, MNTC (Chicago: Moody, 2013), 337.

11. MacArthur, *Luke 11–17*, 336.

12. John A. Martin, "Luke," in *The Bible Knowledge Commentary: An Exposition of the Scriptures*, ed., John F. Walvoord and Roy B. Zuck (Wheaton, IL: Victor, 1983), 2:246.

unequivocally called the manager "unrighteous" (v. 8). His point, which the Pharisees missed, was that the steward's plan was so well implemented that even the swindled rich man—the one from whom the manager had stolen—praised him.

Preempting the question of why the master praised the unrighteous manager, Jesus said, "because he had acted shrewdly." That adverb "shrewdly" (*phronimōs*) can be positive or negative.[13] Here the master applauded his steward's craftiness and intelligence. He did not praise the steward for being dishonest, but, as Hendriksen writes, "for being so clever, so astute, so shrewd. In other words, for 'feathering his nest,' seeing to it that his physical needs would be supplied for a long time, perhaps for the rest of his life."[14] The rich man's focus was on the manager's creativity, his ability to manipulate his personal monetary crisis into a retirement windfall at the expense of his boss and the boss's debtors.

Then Jesus' commentary begins to apply to His disciples: "For the sons of this age are more shrewd in relation to their own kind than the sons of light" (Luke 16:8). He places the wicked manager and the rich man in His parable in the same category; they were "sons of this age," not "sons of light" as the disciples were (John 12:36). These unbelievers were shrewder and more innovative with their wealth to achieve temporal goals than believers were with their resources to advance eternal goals. Both the manager and the wealthy man were captivated by money (v. 13)—just as the Pharisees themselves were "lovers of money" (v. 14). They would look admiringly upon devious strategies that manipulate financial success, even if they were harmed by the strategy. Yet their shrewdness was instructive for the believer, because while the "sons of this age" gain temporary friends by their intelligence, believers could gain eternal friends by way of wise investments.

The Principle

The principle of this parable must be applied in accord with Jesus' intent, as revealed in Luke 16:8–13. Interpreters, however, have not always done so. For instance, while Jesus referred to the manager as unrighteous, John Maxwell portrays the manager as merely a "lousy leader."[15] Maxwell, a pastor in Florida, is well known among evangelicals, being regarded by many in the business world as the foremost leadership and management expert in the world today.[16] He lauds the unrighteous manager for his ability to proactively face his problems because "good leaders aren't afraid to face reality."[17] He describes the manager as a leader who, though lousy, "understood the value of relationships," and through these connections

---

13. "φρονέω," *NIDNTTE*, 4:616–17.

14. Hendriksen and Kistemaker, *Exposition of the Gospel according to Luke*, 769–70.

15. John C. Maxwell, ed., *The Maxwell Leadership Bible*, 2nd ed., New International Version (Nashville: Thomas Nelson, 2014), 1232.

16. Jeff Haden, "Top 50 Leaders and Management Experts," *Inc.*, May 12, 2014, https://www.inc.com/jeff-haden/the-top-50-leadership-and-management-experts-mon.html.

17. Maxwell, *Maxwell Leadership Bible*, 1232.

received "a return on his investment."[18] Thus, Maxwell compliments the man's influence over those who are actually his victims but does not address Jesus' own purpose statement in verse 9.

On the other hand, the Lord desires disciples to use their resources in such a way that, like the wicked manager, they make friends—but not for their own financial gain or leadership success. Rather, they are to make friends who will receive them after wealth and temporal dwellings have "failed" or passed away, friends who will receive them "into eternal dwellings." Jesus' earlier teaching precludes such "friends" from meaning subjugated debtors (6:32–35).[19] Nor should the friends here be considered angels, or an indirect reference to God, as though the righteous use of money could purchase heaven.[20] They should, rather, be understood as those who benefited from the disciple's giving while on earth[21]— and no one could benefit more than those who were led to saving faith. In other words, Jesus' parable teaches believers to steward their wealth for eternal purposes and, one could surmise, toward proclaiming eternal life, the very life the disciples already possessed. When the disciples then entered into eternity, some whom they befriended by use of their wealth would be there waiting to greet them.

This teaching anticipates Jesus' Great Commission (Luke 24:45–49; cf. Matt 28:16–20). In Luke 16, however, Jesus explained further about wealth management from an eternal perspective:

> He who is faithful in a very little thing is faithful also in much, and he who is unrighteous in a very little thing is unrighteous also in much. Therefore if you have not been faithful in the use of unrighteous wealth, who will entrust the true riches to you? And if you have not been faithful in the use of that which is another's, who will give you that which is your own? No servant can serve two masters. . . . You cannot serve God and wealth. (16:10–13)

Jesus regularly compared and contrasted temporal wealth with heavenly riches (Matt 6:19–21; 13:44–46; Luke 18:22). In this case, the "unrighteous wealth" that belongs to someone else is worldly goods, and the "true riches" are heavenly goods,[22] or what Jesus elsewhere calls "unfailing treasure in heaven" (Luke 12:33). That treasure means eternal life and all its benefits, yes, including the tangible rewards of God's grace. However, for Christians the treasure in heaven *par excellence* is not any crown or mansion, but God Himself and being present with Him (Pss 16:11; 73:25; Rev 21:3–4).

---

18. Maxwell, 1232.

19. Joel B. Green, *The Gospel of Luke*, NICNT (Grand Rapids: Eerdmans, 1997), 594.

20. Marshall (*Gospel of Luke*, 622) interpreted "friends" as "a circumlocution for the name of God," though he stresses that the giving of alms is a testimony to the reality of discipleship, not the means of salvation. However, the more straightforward implication of the text is that those who welcome the giver are those who benefited from the giving.

21. Hendriksen and Kistemaker, *Exposition of the Gospel according to Luke*, 770–71.

22. Trent C. Butler, *Luke*, Holman New Testament Commentary 3 (Nashville: Broadman and Holman, 2000), 263.

Added to that, Jesus says, will be the other souls saved by grace (Matt 19:29; Luke 18:29–30). The principle in His parable therefore is His command to His disciples to be wise stewards, using their resources for eternal purposes, none of which is greater than proclaiming the message of eternal life.

The Application to Global Investment

The above biblical principles are timeless and transcultural. But Jesus did not give specific examples for how the Christian is to shrewdly invest the resources that God gives. Christ's followers must prayerfully decide how they can best honor him with their money from an eternal perspective. There is perhaps no better way to do this than by investing in the advancement of expositional preaching in both local and global contexts, so that individual congregations are equipped by their pastors to do the work of the ministry for generations. However, many other ministries are designed to support the local church and its proclamation too, and these should be considered accordingly. Some specific investment examples below are from my context in the United States. Yet, regardless of cultural differences, believers should strive to find creative ways to utilize finances to advance the gospel so that people of all nations may become Jesus' disciples.

Innovative ways to support gospel ministry include but also go beyond cash offerings.

Individuals, for instance, can donate noncash assets directly to a nonprofit ministry. In some cultures, the tax advantages for the ministry or the donor can be significantly more attractive than first selling the asset and then donating cash from the sale. This might include appreciated shares of stock, agricultural commodities, life insurance policies, or retirement funds.

Donor-advised funds (or the equivalent) are a means of wisely donating cash. These are funds that are managed by nonprofit organizations, to which donors can give tax-deductible gifts, which are then invested in instruments of the donor's choice and distributed over time to a ministry the donor designates. Organizations such as the Barnabas Foundation[23] and the National Christian Foundation[24] also work directly with estate-planning attorneys for gifts left in wills and family trusts. The same holds true for real estate gifts, whether personal or business.

Two examples of Christians wisely managing their money for eternal purposes are encouraging. One is a married couple I know who found themselves with significant financial resources upon retirement. They considered giving a onetime cash donation to their favorite ministry, but instead they orchestrated a plan to reinvest their wealth into a real estate business, generating even greater revenue. They now work to grow this business, anticipating that profits will support grants to ensure future pastors are trained to exposit God's Word all over the world. By giving scholarships to these men, they

---

23. The Barnabas Foundation, accessed June 18, 2024, https://barnabasfoundation.org.
24. The National Christian Foundation, accessed June 18, 2024, https://www.ncfgiving.com/.

are supporting multiple pastors who will equip the saints to do the work of the ministry. They are simultaneously enabling local churches in small villages and major cities all over the world to bring the gospel to unreached communities in their indigenous languages. Profits from the couple's business also support publishing works, such as Bible translations and the writing of exegetical commentaries in national languages so that future expositors have biblically sound resources for generations to come.

Another example is a corporate management team leading a well-known multimillion dollar company. The company prominently displays the full text of John 3:16 on its website. Whether toward customers or suppliers, employees at this company are encouraged to be clear about the gospel. Some former employees have been granted seminary scholarships by the company so that they were trained to teach God's Word. One such worker, who received generous company scholarships, ultimately earned a PhD in theology and has been a seminary professor and theological writer for several years. This man's former students are now all over the world pastoring local congregations, leading overseas seminaries, and training up the next generation of expositors so that a people yet to be created may praise the Lord (Ps 102:18).

Conclusion

Jesus' parable of the shrewd manager is an ironic but powerful lesson in the wise use of money in God's economy. Jesus did not specify in the parable the means by which His disciples must give or steward their resources. Nor had He even yet declared the Great Commission to go to the nations and make disciples. Yet He powerfully taught the principle of investing shrewdly for eternity. He left the responsibility of implementing that principle to the disciples themselves.

This side of the Great Commission, a Christian must see that investing God's bounty in missions pays dividends long after the donation. There is no more profitable strategy to be found before the Lord returns. Let "the sons of light," then, not be outdone by "the sons of this age" in the clever use of their worldly wealth. The latter use wealth for unrighteous purposes and are even enslaved by their love for it, though it passes away and leads only to ultimate poverty. But Christians can make friends for eternity with their God-given wealth. They can bless the nations with the message of eternal life by funding and sustaining missionaries, preachers, and churches to make disciples of all nations. They can be faithful in little or in much. If they are, what joy they will share when they meet these friends in heaven.

The Place of Paul's Letters in His Missions Efforts

Dave Deuel

Paul wrote his epistles strategically. Scripture canonized some of his letters, but he wrote many more. In Paul's time, a letter was one part of a mission. As a missionary, Paul used his letters to support the work of missions around the world of his day. This insert examines how Paul's writings relate to practical considerations in fulfilling his mission. For Paul, the essence of raising support was relationship building. Paul used letters and their messengers to close the relational gap created by the geographical distance between them.

The Purpose of Paul's Letters

When someone like Paul sent a letter—one in which the sender held a position of authority in relation to the recipients—the sender intended the letter to support him personally in his efforts. Paul's letters were no different; he expected them to have the effect of supporting his mission.

The apostle argues for support worthiness based on his plan to go to named places like Spain (Rom 15:24), which is an overt response to Jesus' command to go to the "end of the earth" (Acts 1:8). Paul even commends others whom he considers worthy of the Roman church's support. The Romans must "receive" them, a term of relational and financial engagement (Rom 16:1–2). Sometimes Paul must even address challenges to his apostolic credentials when his support worthiness is called into question (2 Cor 12:14–17). Paul's amazing argument in his defense? He is weak!

The purpose was typically more than the letter itself, although delivering or reading the letter may have been central to Paul's intentions. He hoped to accomplish significant ministry through his letters. The apostle intended for letters to instruct, encourage, challenge, rebuke—in short, just about anything the apostle accomplished in face-to-face ministry. For example, 1 Corinthians involves much of the rebuke and instruction one might normally associate with only face-to-face ministry.

The Role of the Messenger

Paul wanted his messengers to conduct ministry conducive to the message of the letter. Many of his messengers were also his trainees, as will be seen in some of the examples below.

Paul chose gifted messengers. The messenger not only carried the letter but supported its message. The recipients of Paul's letters likely asked the messengers questions about Paul's intentions. And the messengers brought back reports to Paul about the letter's impact (feedback critical to the mission) and to prepare for the next message. It is no wonder that some of Paul's messengers—Timothy and Titus, for example—became pastors. They built relationships with the people to whom they delivered Paul's letters by reading them to the recipients. Since Paul's letters were the Word of God, the messenger's work is that of the expositor today; that is, Paul's messengers implicitly had pulpit ministry. The indicators are in the letters themselves, particularly when Paul instructs the recipients that they should respond to the messenger and his message, such as "receive him" (e.g., Phil 2:25, 29; Phlm 17).

Interestingly, this applies to gathering support for Paul's ministries, like the support of other churches. Second Corinthians 8:22–24 is an example:

And we have sent with them our brother, whom we have often tested and found earnest in many things, but now even more earnest because of his great confidence in you. As for Titus, he is my partner and fellow worker among you; as for our brothers, they are messengers of the churches, a glory to Christ. Therefore openly before the churches, show them the proof of your love and of our reason for boasting about you.

Titus was not just Paul's letter reader but also his "partner and fellow worker." The clause "show them the proof" is an admonition to give the messenger the previously promised financial support (2 Cor 8:23–24).

Christian teachers today, when delivering Paul's message in training center lectures, evangelism work, or Sunday sermons, serve similar roles to Paul's first messengers. In a paraphrase of Paul's affirming words to Timothy, "You must read Scripture, and teach and preach it" (1 Tim 4:13). Perhaps the role in delivering Paul's messages was ultimately used to train and affirm Timothy, Titus, and others as future pastors. The church today would do well to do the same. Missionaries must deliver every message of Scripture faithfully as Paul's messengers delivered his letters. In truth, they come from God through the pen of Paul. That means making sure the recipients of the message can both understand the reading and how to apply it to their lives.

Conclusion

Whether through the instructive and exhortative content of the letters, the deliverers of the letters, or the support requests made in the letters, Paul's epistles all served aims within his broader ministry goals. They provided strategic instructions for missionaries regarding the power of ministry even without personal presence. Ongoing relationships and modern communication allow missionaries today to exhort their siblings in Christ around the world. Entrusting messages and tasks to developing leaders can serve vital roles in establishing the future leaders of local churches. Furthermore, ministry letters to believers serve to instruct and inspire about the ongoing need for the gospel in new locations and contexts, for which readers can become prayer supporters and financial donors. These simple techniques were modeled for missionaries in Scripture through the examples of Paul's preserved letters.

INSERT 28.2

Best Practices for Effective Support-Raising Letters

Santiago Armel

Acts 8 contains the story of Philip, one of the first missionaries in church history, as well as one of the first missionary updates: "When the apostles in Jerusalem heard that Samaria had received the word of God, they sent them Peter and John" (8:14). Missionary reports that convey what God is doing in other regions have motivated the church from the beginning. They move the hearts of believers to commit prayerfully, personally, and financially for the advancement of the gospel. They help the missionary build and maintain relationships for the ministry.

Not all reports are created equal. Some are good, and some are bad. Some encourage, strengthen faith, and incite action. Others are ignored after reading the title. Below are fifteen best practices that honor God and can make communications more effective. The aim is not to manipulate readers for financial gain but to communicate and solicit partnership in the ongoing work of God.

1. **Pray, asking God to provide the necessary resources (Neh 2:4–8; Isa 41:10; Phil 4:11–19; 1 Tim 5:18).** The first thing a missionary should recognize is that those who support him are the means God uses to provide. Because God is the only source of all provision, it is to Him that the missionary should turn first in prayer, asking Him to guide him in forming a budget and in petitioning others for the funds needed. In this way, the missionary will remember that God is his boss and benefactor, and it is Him whom missionaries should please above any human supporter (Prov 29:25).

2. **Focus on the main need: prayer support (Eph 6:18–19; Col 4:2–3).** Missionaries may have thousands of dollars in monthly resources, but if churches are not praying for them, they really have no support. They must attempt to involve people spiritually in the mission through prayer. It is important to remind partners that they are part of what God is doing from afar. Ask them to commit to praying regularly, and provide specific requests concerning the missionary and the country or city.

3. **Work hard in ministry (Prov 6:6–11; 1 Cor 15:10; 2 Cor 11:21–33; 1 Thess 2:1–12).** If a missionary desires to communicate what he is doing, then he must do his work diligently. Results do not depend on him, but faithfulness does. The missionary of integrity manages his time and gifts well to put them into service for the church in the best way possible. Then he is also able to tell his supporters everything that is being done with the resources they send.

4. **Present a clear, biblical, and Great Commission–oriented project (Matt 28:19–20; Rom 1:13–17; cf. Gal 1:6–9).** Missionaries without a clear plan will not be able to communicate clearly why they need support. Their plans ought to align with the establishment of a new church or with the strengthening of an already established congregation. Gospel proclamation should always be connected to the service of a local church. If something does not help in that proclamation, it should be discarded. Social action, aid for the needy, or education, for example, if they are not connected to the proclamation of the gospel, should be readjusted.

5. **Begin with a short devotional thought (Pss 1:1–3; 119:15–16).** Whether giving an oral report, sending an email, or sending a printed ministry report, the missionary should begin with a short biblical reflection. This allows recipients to know that they will always receive

edifying content when reading the missionary's updates. The reflection should be short and connected to the rest of the content.

6. **Use clear, eye-catching headings and subheadings.** Many recipients of newsletters will read only the subtitles that appear in them. An effective tip, then, is to write titles and subtitles that are so clear the supporter could be informed by reading those alone. In terms of formatting, headings can be highlighted with differing font sizes and styles.

7. **Use photos and videos whenever possible.** Some recipients will ignore text, but all supporters appreciate pictures. For this reason, it is important to be attentive in the ministry and, from time to time, to take pictures and videos of what is happening. These graphic materials support what is said in writing. If God provides people in the mission with media skills, encourage them to help in the process.

8. **Write short, compelling paragraphs (Prov 10:19).** A lot can be said with a few words. This is important when explaining visual aids or making specific prayer requests. Only the main details are needed, and this will ensure that the reader does not get distracted from the point.

9. **Present testimonies of God's grace (Acts 22:1–21).** One of the best ways to communicate God's work is to ask people impacted by the ministry to give testimonies. Besides allowing supporters to see the impact on living souls, it also ensures that the focus of attention is not on the missionary but on God. Regarding future projects, one could even use testimonies of the people who are waiting for the missionary and their expectations of the ministry desired.

10. **Present letters of recommendation (Acts 15:22–35).** During initial support-raising, it is best for the elders of the missionary's sending church to provide letters of recommendation. This gives testimony of the character and suitability of the missionary to carry out the ministry, that he or she is someone proven and faithful.

11. **Do not focus on asking for money (Prov 23:4–5; Matt 6:19–21, 25–34; 1 Tim 3:2–3; 6:9–10).** The main content of the report should not be asking for money. Information should be clear about existing financial needs, but one should never resort to manipulation or pressuring people to send support. It is best to state the needs and then request that readers prayerfully consider how they might participate.

12. **Be clear on how readers can support financially.** A common problem in missionary communications is making the process of giving financial support

too complicated. It is best to be specific in how people can help, at the end of the letter, with sparing text and clear titles. In the case of emails, buttons or links can be created that lead directly to giving sites. For those partnering with a missions agency to manage their resources, informing supporters that donations are tax deductible can encourage support also.

13. **Use an online design platform.** Nowadays there are many platforms for designing newsletters, freely accessible online. These allow missionaries to design clean, visually appealing emails, PDFs, and printed brochures with great efficiency.

14. **Send printed material without neglecting the electronic.** A physical prayer card or annual report will always be a more effective reminder than electronic equivalents. People throw away advertisements they receive at home, but they will not throw away something sent to them by a missionary they love. This type of printed material is commonly kept in a special place and serves as a constant reminder to pray for and support the missionary.

15. **Exalt Jesus Christ (1 Cor 10:31).** God can do great things through a faithful missionary, but the missionary must keep focus on who the real hero is. All communications from beginning to end should emphasize that nothing could be possible if God's grace and favor were not at work. Everything must be done for the glory of God.

Sub-Section 3: Shepherding Missionaries

CHAPTER 29

It's More Than Money: How to Support Missionaries on the Field

Rodney Andersen

The work of missions is not accomplished by the missionary alone, but in partnership with supporting churches. The apostle Paul recognized that supporting churches, such as the one in Philippi, played an important role as participants in the gospel (Phil 1:5). The Philippian believers counted it a privilege to participate in the work of ministry, and therefore joyfully supported Paul, even out of their poverty (2 Cor 8:1–5).

The Philippians' giving allowed Paul to occasionally forgo the physical labors necessary to meet his needs. There were times that he determined to work rather than to live off of gifts (Acts 18:1–3; 1 Cor 4:12; 9:12–18), so that there would be no accusation of his preaching

as being from selfish motives—both a common problem of false teachers and a sure hindrance to the gospel. But the support that the Philippians sent did more than meet needs; it brought Paul great encouragement. Paul rejoiced not only because of the benefits he received from that church's generosity but because of the blessings he knew that the church itself would receive in return (Phil 4:10–20).

The Philippian believers also provided nonfinancial support. They helped by sending Epaphroditus, who cared for Paul and even risked his life for him (Phil 2:25–30). The church prayed that Paul would be delivered from harm (1:19), and they expressed their love by rejoicing with him in the progress of the gospel (1:26). As a supporting church, the believers demonstrated exemplary and multifaceted care for their missionary.

Some churches fall short in caring for gospel workers because they view their missionary partnership in terms of finances alone. Financial support is only one facet of the care that supporting churches should provide. The many other areas of missionary care for which every church is responsible broadly fall under two categories: shepherding missionaries and encouraging missionaries. This chapter looks at these areas of service and exhorts the church to rise and fulfill them out of love for Christ and for His servants.

Shepherding Missionaries

Before missionaries arrive on the mission field, the sending churches evaluate, train, and commission them to ministry. Therefore, it is the elders of the sending churches who have the best understanding of the spiritual character, history, and weaknesses of missionaries who have arisen from their congregations. These same elders therefore are best suited to provide their missionaries with ongoing shepherding care. While other churches can and should come alongside sending churches as supporting churches, the sending churches fulfill the primary responsibility of shepherding the ones they have sent.

Those who have been involved in missions know that unexpected issues requiring pastoral care arise. Adjusting to the culture, rearing children in a foreign setting, caring for aging parents from afar, as well as points of conflict within churches and team members on the field, are common points of difficulty. Because of such challenges, missionaries can get discouraged, misguided, and confused. They need to know that they can turn to their sending churches for help when such issues arise.

For some problems, the missionary can get help from believers in his target context. Many issues, however, are not easily understood by those who have never left their home culture or may not comprehend the particular needs of a foreigner in their midst. Additionally, missionaries are often serving in churches whose leaders are still maturing spiritually. Missionaries in these settings may perceive that raising certain concerns will only lead to confusion and unintended schisms. For these reasons also, sending churches are best suited to address missionaries' needs, and they must keep several important aspects of pastoral care in mind when considering how to shepherd their missionaries.

Clarifying Roles

The first important aspect is to clarify the roles of the missions agency and the sending church with regard to the activities of the missionary. For most churches, a missions agency can be a helpful partner in both the initial and ongoing administrative support of its missionaries. In a variety of tasks, including logistics, financial matters, and international adaptation, a parachurch agency can come alongside the church. While providing these services, the agency builds a relationship with the missionary and often learns about the missionary's difficulties. Some agencies wrongly assume that they have the primary responsibility for spiritually shepherding missionaries in such circumstances.

Therefore, both the missions agency and the sending church must understand and agree on their respective roles before those circumstances arise. Role clarity will prevent the missionary from receiving conflicting counsel.

The best way for ministry partners to achieve and articulate such clarity is by drafting a written agreement. That agreement should state that the sending church has the primary role in shepherding the missionary's character and doctrinal fidelity, areas in which the church originally evaluated and confirmed the missionary before the sending. The agency should always voice any concerns regarding personal holiness and doctrine, but the sending church will take the lead role in overseeing those areas.

On the other hand, missions agencies often exercise key guidance of the missionary's ministry plan. The agency may have other missionaries in the region and can coordinate efforts between family units on the field. Furthermore, missions agencies sometimes have a greater understanding of specific needs in the target country and can provide helpful counsel as to ministry direction. Any deviation from the initial ministry plan, however, should be agreed upon by both the agency and the sending church. At no point should a missionary's ministry plan fall outside of the sending church's or missions agency's convictions of biblical ministry. For that reason, biblical discernment is needed for the elders to choose the agencies with which they are willing to cooperate. When the missionary, sending church, and missions agency are working in harmony, the ministry will benefit greatly.

Communicating Often

Part of shepherding a missionary includes regular contact, which nowadays means phone calls, emails, and videoconferencing. Current technology allows for frequent communication at little or no cost to either party. Regular interactions between the church and the missionary promote unity, prevent misunderstandings, and strengthen relationships among the ministry partners.

Ideally, the church will identify an elder or group of elders who bears responsibility for communicating with each missionary. This leader will read each of the missionary's newsletters, respond whenever possible, and regularly pray for the missionary. The elder should promote interaction and make sure the missionary feels free to reach out whenever questions or concerns arise. Likewise, the church elders must know the missionary well enough to provide natural input and wise counsel as the ministry develops.

Making Personal Visits

Personal presence communicates much more than an email or video call. Visits demonstrate much about the church's estimation of the missionary and his work. When the church therefore makes the investment of sending an elder or another key leader to visit the missionary family, it communicates its commitment and love in more than words. Moreover, it is a true ministry of elders exemplified in the New Testament (1 Cor 16:15–18).

A visit during the missionary's first year on the field can be especially valuable. Missionaries are often lonely in their initial months and can easily become discouraged as the task of integrating into a new culture takes time and patience. A visit from those who love and support the missionary, however, provides a much-needed boost, a refreshing of spirit (1 Cor 16:18). The missionary gets the chance to show his visitors what daily life is like, introduce them to the people he has met, explain what he has learned about the culture, and demonstrate the progress he has made in the local language.

Additionally, the missionary's context comes to life for the visiting church leader. Through the visit, the church itself becomes keenly aware of the sacrifices, joys, and challenges the missionary encounters on the field. When returning leaders report about the visit, they can intimately describe how the church can be praying for and encouraging the missionary.

Another benefit of visiting a missionary on the field is the opportunity to speak to those with whom the missionary is ministering. Many difficulties that missionaries face are relational. Therefore, getting to know these other saints and witnessing their mutual interactions can provide valuable understanding for current or future issues.

Finally, visits allow for time with the missionary's family. The church leader should take note of how each family member is adapting to the culture and building relationships, and observe their overall spiritual and physical condition. A missionary must first care for the needs of his family. This care can be evaluated and encouraged by the visiting church leader.

Caring for Women

Leaders from sending churches must not neglect the care and shepherding of women on the mission field. Whether the woman is single or married, whether she plays a direct or supporting role, the demands of ministry life are burdensome. Those demands necessitate significant support from the sending church.

The care of missionary wives in particular is an often overlooked but important aspect of shepherding missionaries. Wives play vital roles on the mission field as they facilitate ministry and practice hospitality. They bear their husbands' burdens and share in making sacrifices to serve the Lord. They teach other women by both word and example. They evangelize the lost, counsel their family and others, and selflessly extend themselves daily. For these reasons and many more, missionary wives need pastoral care.

Missionary women may receive wise counsel and care from godly national women, but these kinds of relationships are often difficult to find on the mission field, especially early on. Furthermore, such relationships may be complicated due to cultural dissonance, as well as the unique demands involved with being a missionary wife. For missionaries who are married, then, the sending church should consider having not only an elder visit but his wife as well. If the missionary is a single woman, having the elder's wife visit along with her husband would not only bring great encouragement, but it would also allow her to lend insight from a woman's perspective. It is important therefore that women receive field visits as well.

Encouraging Missionaries

Elders and other church leaders take the primary role in shepherding their missionaries, but the support of missionaries is the responsibility of the whole church. Church leaders need to help their people know how they can best pray for and partner with the missionaries whom they are supporting. This includes pastors informing the church and church members keeping themselves informed of their missionaries' needs, the church making short-term ministry trips, leaders delegating and members taking ownership of missionary support, caring for missionary furloughs, and caring for missionary families.

Keeping Informed

A pin on a map and a stack of prayer cards in the church foyer are a good start, but these efforts alone are not enough to build a connection between the church body and those who are sent out for the sake of the gospel. Churches must be purposeful and creative in finding ways to introduce their missionaries to the congregation and to invite them to actively support the ministry work abroad.

The broader church will not love and care for the missionaries if the elders do not. Elders who are in touch with the missionaries and their ministries will not be able to stop sharing about what is taking place on the mission field. Their love for missions will come through in their sermons, their prayers, their pulpit announcements, and even in the choice of corporate worship songs. When pastors love their missionaries and talk about them, church members follow.

Publicity can happen informally, but churches should consider purposeful missions events and prayer meetings, wherein the leaders highlight the supported missionaries and inform the congregation of prayer needs for their gospel ministries overseas. Many churches designate missionary support groups. Often these are groups of women who gather for the purpose of praying for missions and undertake practical projects to raise funds or provide tangible gifts to those serving overseas (e.g., Luke 2:36–37; 1 Tim 5:5, 9–10). Sunday school classes and youth groups can also easily be involved with regular prayer time and updates given in their announcements. As an additional and priceless benefit, God frequently uses the experience of hearing missionary stories, participating in special offerings, and praying for missionaries as a means to inspire young people to become missionaries themselves. But whatever the event or the age of the believer, the church's members should prioritize keeping themselves informed of their missionaries. Their ministries are not to be dismissed.

Missionaries need to likewise understand that if the church rarely or never hears from its missionaries, the members' love and care for them will be stunted. Churches should prompt missionaries to faithfully send updates to their supporting churches and to visit when they are in town. In turn, churches must make sure the congregation has access to missionary updates, and that they give their missionaries appropriate time to stand before their congregations during visits. Though pastors love to preach to their congregations, the one who loves his missionaries will gladly give the needed time for a report to the church about what the Lord is doing on the field.

Making Short-Term Ministry Trips

Short-term ministry trips (STMs) are another helpful way for a sending or supporting church to encourage missionaries. Missionaries often have projects or special events that are perfectly suited for an STM team to accomplish. Examples of STMs that lend support and encouragement to missionaries are evangelistic outreach events, such as vacation Bible schools and English camps, building projects, or helping with evangelistic concerts and pastoral conferences.

Short-term ministry teams can be a great encouragement to missionary families as they connect with and serve alongside like-minded believers. Missionaries left behind family, friends, and much they were familiar with to serve the Lord in a foreign land. The fellowship, advice, prayer, resources, babysitting, and familiar foods an STM brings is a great encouragement. Most of all, the STM visit encourages missionaries by reminding them that they are not alone in their desire to reach the world for Christ. In this way, STM teams improve the partnership between missionaries and their sending and supporting churches.

Taking Ownership

Churches that send out many missionaries face the challenge of keeping track of and appropriately caring for each one. Therefore, they must carefully determine how many missionaries to

support. A church should only take on additional missionaries if it is equipped to give ongoing support, both financially and with encouragement and prayer.

One way to address this challenge is by giving smaller groups "ownership" of missionary families. For example, a home Bible study group can be chosen to receive updates from, pray for, and communicate with a specific missionary family or two in particular. This provides the Bible study and the missionary family with an intimate connection, and it encourages a greater sense of responsibility for the former to provide support. They will be conscientious of the Great Commission's fulfillment and will be challenged to evangelize the lost in their own corner of the world as well. Delegating ownership this way also increases STM visibility and participation.

Caring for Furloughs

Furlough (Dutch for "permission," which is to say, a leave of absence) is one of the most misunderstood aspects of missionary life. Outsiders view the furlough as an extended vacation. In reality, most missionaries describe the furlough as one of the most hectic facets of the ministry. These trips to the missionary's native land involve extensive travel, meeting with many people, speaking in churches, and completing countless errands—all without a place to call home. Churches therefore have opportunities to serve their missionaries in key ways during furloughs.

Individual church members, for example, can care for missionaries by picking them up from the airport, providing a welcome basket, saving seats at their first Sunday back at the church, scheduling a time for them to speak at a Bible study, inviting them over for a meal, planning a fun activity to do with them, or providing babysitting or childcare so that missionary couples can go on a date. These are simple and practical ways church members can bless their missionaries.

Corporately, churches can also bless their missionaries by giving forethought to their furloughs. The logistics and costs involved in renting transportation and housing are a great challenge for missionaries. Thus, in addition to having Bible study groups care for missionaries, churches can also provide a vehicle for them to use at little or no cost or a place to live while they are in town (with a well-stocked refrigerator upon arrival). The church that strives to meet these kinds of common needs demonstrates true love and care, and greatly blesses its missionaries (Titus 3:13; 3 John 6–8).

Caring for Families

One of the greatest sacrifices missionaries make involves being away from their relatives, including their immediate families. Churches therefore must consider the indirect ministry needs of their missionaries' family members who are nearer in proximity to them than to the missionaries.

Depending on the context, many missionaries face a day when they will send their children back to their home country for college or to work, while they themselves remain on the field. This can be one of the most difficult phases of life for that parent abroad, and when it happens, their sending church has an excellent opportunity to minister to them. The son or daughter coming home may need a place to live while going to college. They may need transportation, or even need to learn how to drive a vehicle or how to use the services of a bank. They may need someone to disciple or to counsel them. Though the missionaries desire to be there for their children and to teach them such things, it is not always possible. Thus, a genuine need for the missionaries' own support and encouragement is that the church love their returning children.

Another challenge involves caring for elderly parents. There will be times when the missionary needs to come back and personally provide this care. A missionary's need for extended time with aging parents or for ordering their affairs should be treated by the church with kindness, prayer, and understanding. For the supporting church to visit the parents and assist in meeting their spiritual and physical needs—as any elder would those of his own flock—is part of honoring "in a manner worthy of God" those who "went out for the sake of the Name" (3 John 6–7).

Conclusion

The Great Commission is not fulfilled by missionaries alone, but in partnership with supporting churches. By necessity, this means that churches must financially support their missionaries even as the Philippian church did Paul. Such support is basic to the missionary going on behalf of the church, often with his family, to do the work of the ministry full-time abroad. But the Philippian church also shows that every church's responsibility to their missionaries is much more than money.

A sending church must partner with its missionaries by shepherding them, just as the elders shepherd their own flock. Elders and, when appropriate, their delegated leaders can do this by clarifying roles with the missionary's agency, by communicating often with the missionary, by personally visiting the missionary, and by remembering the needs of missionary wives and single women. The congregation as a whole and its members individually can also encourage their missionaries by keeping informed of their work and needs, by making short-term ministry trips to assist them, by taking ownership to pray on their behalf, by caring for their furloughs, and by caring for their families in their home country.

Such support is true participation in the gospel (Phil 1:5), in a manner worthy of God (3 John 6). Therefore, as faithful churches everywhere supply the needs of their missionaries in this way, let them remember the words of missionary Paul in response to their giving and serving: "And my God will fulfill all your needs according to His riches in glory in Christ Jesus" (Phil 4:19).

INSERT 29.1

Creating a Missionary Care Team in the Supporting Church

Tom Pennington

What a Care Team Is

A care team is a small group (four to eight members) of committed people or couples who come together to care for their missionary, including but extending beyond prayer. It is a group with whom the missionary can be open and honest, sharing their needs, successes, and failures. Each care team has a team leader selected by the missionary and approved by the church's missions leadership team (MLT). The care team leader is responsible for recruiting team members to fulfill various roles as needed and is assigned a member of the MLT as a direct contact and a resource to them and to their team.

What a Care Team Does

A care team represents the church in caring for the missionary and represents the missionary to the church by discharging the following duties:

1. *Communicating with the church*: The care team is responsible to serve as the missionary's advocate and representative to the church. To fulfill this role, each care team makes a commitment to communicate the following:

   - Specific needs of its missionary— such as financial or prayer needs—to the MLT
   - General information about its missionary's ministry with church members and other ministries

2. *Caring for the missionary*: A care team works together to care for its missionary, striving to meet his or her spiritual, physical, and emotional needs. The missionary is encouraged to communicate his or her needs to the team.

   The specific ways in which a care team goes about meeting their missionary's needs will vary depending on the personality and needs of the missionary as well as the personality of the care team. The team should ask how it can best assist the missionary, learn from the example of other teams, be creative, and pray for wisdom. At a minimum, each care team makes a commitment to do the following:

- Meet quarterly to pray for (and if possible with), communicate with, and/ or discuss how to care for its missionary in the coming months.
- Pray for its missionary individually.
- Correspond regularly with its missionary (e.g., via email, phone, or video chat), working to create an atmosphere where the missionary feels safe and comfortable sharing personal items that may need to be kept confidential.
- Be available to provide practical care for its missionary.

Care teams should also actively seek to do these things:

- Work with the missionary to create and maintain a distribution list for newsletters, prayer requests, and occasional announcements to their broader prayer team.
- Find creative ways to share the missionary's ministry with church members, such as through youth and adult Sunday school classes, women's ministries, men's ministries, and home fellowship groups, starting with those ministries with which the team's members are already involved.
- Organize necessary housing, transportation, and schedules for its missionary while he is on furlough.

- Organize church receptions for its missionary while he is visiting or on furlough.
- Host a fellowship luncheon or dinner for its missionary and the care team members.
- Recognize birthdays and anniversaries in the missionary's family by sending cards or care packages.
- Visit and assist the missionary's aging parents or children living nearby.
- Make the missionary feel loved and cared for by the church family in any way.
- Accept requests for new members to join the missionary's prayer team.
- Recruit members to serve on the care team as needed.

INSERT 29.2

What Local Church Missions Leadership Needs

Rodney Andersen

Not every church has a missions pastor, but every church must have pastors who are committed to missions. For the ones with the privilege of focusing all or part of their ministry on the work of missions, there is reason for both rejoicing and trembling. Playing a role in the Lord's work of making disciples from every tribe, nation, and tongue is a great honor. It is also a weighty responsibility. Those charged with leading the church's missions endeavors must have these four essentials: a passion for missions, a pastor's heart, a passport, and a plan for the year.

A Passion for Missions

Leading the church in missions requires a passion for the work of Christ around the world. A lack of excitement about the work of missions will quickly become evident to others. Leaders without zeal will, by example, quench the congregation's enthusiasm about the global advance of the church. Pastors and leaders must stir their own hearts toward missions by reading missionary biographies, communicating with missionaries, and spending personal time in the Word and in prayer about missions.

In developing a passion for missions, a robust understanding of missiology is necessary. Zeal without knowledge is always dangerous, but never more than in spiritual matters (Rom 10:1–2). Leaders must hone their understanding of biblical missions theology to better promote and support God's agenda for reaching the lost world.

This passion for missions, and the biblical theology of missions it is built on, needs to be proclaimed to the church. The harvest is still plentiful, and the workers are still few (Matt 9:37–38). The church must be busy supporting those who have already gone out but must simultaneously seek to bring more missionaries into active service from the congregation as well. The passion of missions leaders who foster missions will overflow onto those around them.

A Pastor's Heart

The leaders of a church's missions efforts must also have a pastor's heart. Missionaries on the field need spiritual care just the same as every other member of the congregation. They go through trials and have times of discouragement and uncertainty. The sending church has the responsibility to continue to pastor the missionary and his family, and supporting churches have the responsibility to encourage them. They have sacrificed much to serve the Lord in difficult areas, but they have not reached perfect sanctification. Thus, the home church must remain vigilant

to admonish, encourage, help, and be patient with them in all things (1 Thess 5:14). This kind of shepherding is necessary for the entire family—they all need pastoral care.

A Passport

Proper care for a missionary family requires more than an occasional email or phone call. Furthermore, spending time with missionaries while they are stateside on furlough is no substitute for visiting them in their country of service. Personally experiencing the culture, joys, and difficulties of the missionary's life is important for church missions pastors. Doing so provides encouragement to the missionary and strengthens the link with the home church in a more tangible way. Meeting the people the missionaries are serving will also inspire the leader's prayers as he is able to put faces with names, and will enable him to better represent the ministry to those at home.

Churches should consider having their missions leadership take their families along for the visits as well. Or perhaps there are other church members with deep relationships with the missionaries who might go along and offer encouragement and help. It is worthwhile to consider what would be most uplifting to the missionary family and what the church might do to further develop relationships between the church and its missionaries. Of course there is a high cost and time commitment to visiting the missionaries in person. The missionaries know that, and that is why it means so much to them.

A Plan for the Year

Church missions leadership should consider their missionaries as they set out the year's ministry calendar. A few key questions need to be asked in this regard.

When Are the Missionaries at Home?

Missions leaders should check in with their missionaries at the beginning of the year to see if they are planning for any home visits. Consider making use of their planned visit to have them give a presentation to the church. If there is a time when it would be important for them to leave the mission field for a church event, be sure to reimburse them for their expenses.

Missionaries have many priorities during return trips that missions leaders must keep in mind. They often need to obtain medical care, visit family, take care of financial matters, attend to the schooling needs of their children, or handle visa issues. Churches must be considerate of the missionary's responsibilities and the demands that are put on them when scheduling events.

When Are the Missions Events during the Church Year?

Most churches have a special Sunday each year with a missions emphasis. Scheduling these kinds of events should be a top priority as pastors plan their ministry year. When selecting dates, leaders need to consider when most of the congregation will be in town and when their missionaries are planning to be stateside. It may be fitting to hold more than one missions Sunday. Having multiple missions events will better help the congregation know how to pray for and support their missionaries.

When Is a Good Time for a Missionary Visit?

Visiting missionary families on the field is an essential responsibility of the church's missions leadership. The pastors should involve the missionary families from the beginning of the planning process. They need to take into account the ministry schedule of the missionaries and what would serve them the best. The missionaries will also provide helpful information as to when the weather is most conducive to visitors, and particular times to be avoided for various other reasons. Church visits should not be a burden to the missionaries or their ministry efforts.

Conclusion

Those who have the great privilege of providing leadership to the missions efforts of their churches should do so "in a manner worthy of God" (3 John 6). A passion for Christ's glory will be evidenced by caring for the missionaries who have gone out for the sake of Christ's name.

CHAPTER 30

Holding the Rope: 3 John for Missions Donors

Eric Weathers

In the late eighteenth century, William Carey heeded the call to take the gospel outside England's borders. His famous response to the call—"I will go down, but remember that you must hold the ropes"[1]—was his first utterance of the need all missionaries have to enlist supporters and donors to participate in every gospel venture. God does not call or equip every Christian with the needed skill set for preaching His Word, for planting churches, or for training indigenous leaders on the mission field. But He does equip every Christian for ministry. In particular He equips some to "hold the rope." He gifts them with marketplace abilities to generate income—income that can be used for international missions. This chapter is primarily geared toward such Christians.

The apostle John's third epistle is largely about holding the rope. This short letter is written to a certain Gaius, about whom likely nothing else is known.[2] But he is a prime example of a faithful Christian using his resources to support the work of missions. In writing to him, John highlights three requirements for faithful rope holders of every era. They are to pray for missions (vv. 2–4), sustain missions (vv. 5–8), and be discerning about missions (vv. 9–12).

Pray for Missions

The opening verses of 3 John display the apostle's heart of prayer and give an exemplary picture of how ministry supporters are to pray. Though John's opening prayer may be considered a standard component of first-century greetings, the seriousness of his petition for his beloved friend must not be lost. John continually prayed for two specific items. First, he

---

1. John Brown Myers, ed., *The Centenary Volume of the Baptist Missionary Society 1792–1892* (London: The Baptist Missionary Society, 1892), 8.

2. John R. W. Stott, *The Letters of John: An Introduction and Commentary*, TNTC 19 (Downers Grove, IL: 1988), 226; Robert W. Yarbrough, *1–3 John*, BECNT (Grand Rapids: Baker Academic, 2008), 363.

prayed that Gaius would prosper in all things, and second, he prayed that his health would remain strong.

John prayed that Gaius would thrive physically: "I pray that in all respects you may prosper and be in good health, just as your soul prospers" (v. 2). The Greek word for "prosper" (*euodoō*) appears four times in the New Testament, twice in this verse, and always in the passive voice.[3] The word means to "be led along a good road," or to have a "good journey."[4] In 1 Corinthians 16:2, Paul wanted each believer to set aside money as he or she may "prosper" (*euodōtai*), so that they might advance the Great Commission in Jerusalem. In a similar way, John prayed for God to continually cause Gaius to thrive. He pled for the Lord to prosper Gaius so that Gaius could be a more effective missionary supporter. James Rosscup pointed out that by using the present tense, John wanted Gaius to thrive continually, and that his use of the passive voice indicated the expectation that only God could bring about such prosperity.[5]

Moreover, John emphatically prefaced this prayer with "in all respects" at the beginning of verse 2.[6] Gaius was a man who practiced truth, so it makes sense that John prayed for him to receive prosperity from God in all things that advance the truth. If he was to continue acting faithfully (v. 5), if he was to continue accomplishing remarkable things for missionaries whom he did not know (v. 5), if he was to send them off in the same way that God Himself would send them off (v. 6), then he would need resources. Prospering "in all respects," therefore, would include God's bringing to Gaius financial success from the marketplace so that he could meet Great Commission expenses.[7] Gaius's God-given prosperity would allow him to underwrite efforts to spread the word of truth (v. 8).

John also explained the reason for his twofold prayer. He linked verse 3 with the conjunction "for" (*gar*), introducing the purpose of his prayer for Gaius's prosperity.[8] John remained exceedingly joyful because other Christians told him about how Gaius's actions testified to the truth. John's terminology indicates that there were many occasions when

---

3. "εὐοδόω," BDAG, 410.

4. "εὐοδόω," BDAG, 410; Spiros Zodhiates, "εὐοδόω," *The Complete Word Study Dictionary: New Testament* (Iowa Falls, IA: World Bible Publishers, 1992), 1148. In Romans 1:10, referencing a successful journey to Rome, the same word is similarly rendered "succeed" by English versions.

5. James E. Rosscup, *An Exposition on Prayer in the Bible: Igniting the Fuel to Flame Our Communication with God* (Bellingham, WA: Lexham, 2008), 2693.

6. Daniel Akin, *1, 2, 3 John*, NAC 38 (Nashville: Broadman and Holman, 2001), 240.

7. Rosscup, *Exposition on Prayer in the Bible*, 2694. Rosscup cautioned that "some have used 3 John 2 to insist on material, monetary wealth as a boon that all Christians should expect as a part of prospering. However, the word for 'prosper' does not convey a monetary emphasis." Rosscup's caution has merit in that Christians ought not to use this passage as a proof text to further their wealth for selfish purposes. Notwithstanding, John's prayer for prosperity in all respects includes financial gain which is further explained in the remaining verses, so that Gaius may continue caring for missionaries.

8. The explanatory "for" (γὰρ, *gar*) "gives the reason for his confidence in Gaius's spiritual progress." I. Howard Marshall, *The Epistles of John*, NICNT (Grand Rapids: Eerdmans, 1978), 83.

Christians told him about Gaius's love and truth in action.[9] They testified about how he lived his life, always behaving in harmony with the word of truth.[10]

Finally, in verse 4, John described the intense joy he received from hearing about how people under Gaius's care consistently walked in the truth. As Daniel Akin comments, John rejoiced over those who "know it, believe it, and live it."[11] All this considered, John was holding the rope with Gaius. His prayers for him honored the Lord and resulted in a significant advancement toward Great Commission success. In the same way, each Christian today should consider how fervently and regularly they are praying for those who are "fellow workers with the truth" (3 John 8), those who sacrificially and tangibly give for gospel ministry.

Sustain Missions

Getting into the heart of the letter, John's encouragement to Gaius lays out three aspects of missionary support that are still applicable today: the nature, the manner, and the reasons for sustaining missionaries for Christ.

The Nature of Sustaining Missionaries

First, John commended Gaius for how faithfully he worked to accomplish much for the brethren, even when they were strangers (3 John 5). He maintained a reputation of consistent manifestation of the truth in all he accomplished. The verb rendered by some English versions as "accomplish" (ergazomai) in verse 5 is the same verb employed by the Septuagint translators to render God's command for man to cultivate the ground (Gen 2:5, 15; 3:23). Paul used the verb in 1 Corinthians 4:12 when he wrote, "We toil, working (ergazomenoi) with our own hands." He likewise used this verb in exhorting the Thessalonians to "make it your ambition to lead a quiet life and attend to your own business and work (ergazesthai) with your hands, just as we commanded you, so that you will behave properly toward outsiders and not be in any need" (1 Thess 4:11–12; see also 2 Thess 3:10). In all these cases, the verb conveys activity that requires real effort[12] and physical labor that is apparent to others.

With such a life of work, Gaius fulfilled Jesus' mandate to let his light shine before men so that they might see his good works and glorify the Father in heaven (Matt 5:16). He worked and toiled on behalf of strangers, of missionaries and gospel preachers who gave up everything to declare God's Word. These, then, in turn, preached so as to equip the local church "for the work (ergon) of service," for the work of fulfilling the Great Commission (Eph 4:11–12; Matt 28:16–20).

The brothers that Gaius encountered had

---

9. Simon J. Kistemaker, *Exposition of James and the Epistles of John*, New Testament Commentary 14 (Grand Rapids: Baker, 1986), 391.

10. Kistemaker explained about John's reference to Gaius's "truth" in verse 3: "σου τῇ ἀληθείᾳ [*sou te aletheia*]—the genitive case σου (your) is objective (the truth that affects you), not subjective (the truth that belongs to you)." Kistemaker, 391.

11. Akin, *1, 2, 3 John*, 241.

12. "ἐργάζομαι," BDAG, 389.

gone out "for the sake of the Name, receiving nothing from the Gentiles" (3 John 7). He received them, as if receiving the Lord. Had they been hungry, he gave them something to eat. Had they been thirsty, he gave them something to drink. He welcomed them, very likely inviting them into his home for shelter (vv. 6, 10). For Gaius knew that everyone who called upon "the Name," the name of the Lord, would be saved, as the Scripture says (Joel 2:32). Therefore, holding the rope, Gaius sustained those who proclaimed the gospel, and he thereby enabled the lost to hear the truth. That is the nature of sustaining missions: faithful work for the sake of Jesus' name.

The Manner of Sustaining Missionaries

Second, John elaborated on the manner in which churches ought to sustain missionaries. The "they" to whom John referred in verse 6 are missionaries, pastors, and evangelists who were originally strangers to Gaius. They were the ones who testified of his love before the church in John's hearing (3 John 6). They affirmed him publicly and spoke well of him as one who walked in truth. As missionaries, they were sent out by their home churches (Acts 13:1–3), perhaps by the very church that John himself pastored in Ephesus, and they seem to have been directed to Gaius for help along the way. Akin

describes the active involvement of the church, saying, "It was natural, perhaps obligatory, for the itinerant teachers to report back to the home base their reception and treatment by Gaius. They provided a glowing report worthy of the elders' earlier accolades. John informs Gaius that before the church they gave witness of his love."[13]

Thus, John encouraged Gaius to continue his love for the missionaries. He told him that he would "do well to send them on their way in a manner worthy of God" (3 John 6). The same is true in the global church today. While a local church is responsible to appoint missionaries, other individuals like Gaius do well to send them on their way in a manner consistent with how Jesus Himself would send them. "Well" (*kalōs*) describes the "high standard of excellence" John was calling for.[14] Jesus used the same word in adjective form twice in John 10:11, saying, "I am the good (*kalos*) shepherd; the good (*kalos*) shepherd lays down His life for the sheep."

Furthermore, the root of the word "send" in 3 John 6, *propempō*, includes helping one journey toward a destination.[15] Missionary supporters therefore are to outfit those who go with the resources necessary for their ministry.[16] I. Howard Marshall writes that "sending the missionaries on their way involved providing for their journey—supplying them with food and money to pay for their expenses, washing

---

13. Akin, *1, 2, 3 John*, 243.

14. "καλῶς," BDAG, 505.

15. "προπέμπω," BDAG, 873; Kistemaker, *Exposition of James and the Epistles of John*, 394.

16. Joseph Henry Thayer, "προπέμπω," *Thayer's Greek-English Lexicon of the New Testament* (1896; repr., Peabody, MA: Hendrickson, 2021), 541. Louw and Nida additionally define "send" as "to send someone on in the direction in which he has already been moving, with the probable implication of providing help." "προπέμπω," L&N, 190.

their clothes, and generally helping them to travel as comfortably as possible."[17] This kind of sending expresses a high standard of quality, not secondhand, tattered leftovers that leave missionaries feeling like beggars. The latter treatment would insult God's name under the guise of "support."[18] Supporting churches today should never settle for it.

On the contrary, Christians whom God has gifted with marketplace abilities and whom God has prospered, must use their incomes as a means to hold the rope for their brothers and sisters in the trenches. They must sustain their efforts with aid. The following table shows how the lessons of 3 John can be applied for donors in particular.

Sustaining missions means more than financial giving—but not less. Financially prosperous believers must give financially to the work of missions if they, like Gaius, would walk in the truth, love the brethren, and be fellow workers in the Great Commission.

The Reasons for Sustaining Missionaries

Finally, John provided three reasons for donors to sustain missionaries. First, donors should sustain them because they go out "for the sake of the Name" (3 John 7). The brothers who came to Gaius were busy making and baptizing disciples for the sake of Christ. They were not serving their own fame. Rather, they devoted

Donors Holding the Rope for Missionaries	Passage
Christians must pray like the apostle John for the Lord to prosper donors who labor in support of missions.	3 John 1–4
Believers, like Gaius, must sustain the work of the Great Commission.	3 John 5–8
A portion of the believer's hard-earned resources should be stewarded toward the Great Commission.	3 John 5
It is okay for others to testify of a donor's love for missions and missionaries.	3 John 6
Christians must support missionaries in a way that is worthy of God Himself.	3 John 6
Marketplace Christians are morally obligated to help fund the Great Commission.	3 John 8
Marketplace income producers who donate toward the Great Commission are known as, "fellow workers with the truth."	3 John 8
All Christians must heed warnings about missions.	3 John 9–12
Believers must not imitate men like Diotrephes who refused to support missionaries.	3 John 9–11
Demetrius is a reminder to manifest the truth with a reputation for doing good.	3 John 11–12

17. Marshall, *The Epistles of John*, 85–86.
18. Marshall, 86.

themselves to obeying Jesus' charge and making His name known. This alone is sufficient reason for their fellow workers to fund their Great Commission expenses.

Second, the brothers refused to receive donations from "the Gentiles," from those they sought to reach with the gospel (3 John 7). The missionaries were targeting people who, in the words of Ephesians, were dead in their transgressions and sins (Eph 2:1). Such people cannot purchase salvation. They must never be given an opportunity to boast in their own merit; they have no merit (2:1–3). Rather, they receive salvation when they come to the place of complete dependence on grace alone, through faith alone, in Christ alone (2:4–10).

Third, Christians should sustain missionaries because by doing so, they become "fellow workers with the truth" (3 John 8). John uses the present tense verb "ought" (*opheilō*) to describe the continual moral obligation Christians have to support missionaries.[19] By way of comparison, one might consider how Jesus told His disciples that they "ought" to care for one another (John 13:14). Paul says believers "ought" to bear the weaknesses of those without strength (Rom 15:1), and that husbands "ought" to love their wives as their own bodies (Eph 5:28). In 3 John 7–8, since

the missionaries did not receive donations from unbelievers, the believers "ought to support such men" by giving them assistance.

Unbelievers cannot be fellow workers in a gospel they repudiate. The funding for gospel ministry must come from Christ's followers.[20] Simon Kistemaker offers helpful insight on this point:

> But if we say that John exhorts us to work together with missionaries for the truth, then biblical evidence supports us in this interpretation. For instance, Paul sends the greetings of three companions (Aristarchus, Mark, and Jesus called Justus) to the church in Colossae. He says, "These are the only Jews among my fellow workers *for* the kingdom of God" (Col. 4:11, italics added; also see 2 Cor. 8:23). John, then, is asking us to help missionaries in the work by spreading the truth, that is, the gospel of Christ.[21]

Thus, John held the rope by praying for Gaius to be prosperous in all respects so that he could continue serving as a faithful fellow worker. Gaius held the rope by diligently laboring for his fellow workers in order to send them forth onto subsequent legs of their journeys. Then, John had one final aspect of missions to teach.

---

19. "ὀφείλω," BDAG, 743.

20. Paul said that the "Lord directed those who proclaim the gospel to get their living from the gospel" (1 Cor 9:14, cf. Luke 10:7), and in 1 Timothy 5:18 he wrote, "For the Scripture says, 'You shall not muzzle the ox while he is threshing,' and 'The laborer is worthy of his wages.'"

21. Kistemaker, *Exposition of James and the Epistles of John*, 395. James Boice's comments are likewise helpful. He noted that those who long to be actively involved in missionary work but cannot be because of physical or circumstantial limitations still serve as fellow workers by way of support in terms of gifts, interest, and prayer, which play a vital role in making disciples. James Montgomery Boice, *The Epistles of John: An Expositional Commentary* (Grand Rapids: Baker, 2004), 169.

Be Discerning about Missions

John followed his exhortation for Gaius with some unexpected remarks. In addition to his affirmation and encouragement, he delivered a sobering warning about a man named Diotrephes in 3 John 9–11, and then mentioned a friend and "reinforcement," Demetrius, in verse 12.[22] Diotrephes stood in sharp contrast to Gaius's selfless benevolence. For, John said, "I wrote something to the church; but Diotrephes, who loves to be first among them, does not accept what we say" (v. 9). Rope holders must be constantly vigilant against men like Diotrephes (e.g., Acts 20:28–31; 2 Tim. 4:1–5). Decided enemies of the gospel are not to be entertained (2 John 9–11).

Diotrephes was mining in a different trench, so to speak, than were John and Gaius. While the latter were actively engaged in gospel ministry to others, Diotrephes was a man struggling for his own preeminence.[23]

Unlike Gaius, Diotrephes was not a fellow worker with the truth. He did not pray for, receive, or support disciple makers. Rather, John leveled four charges against him in verse 10:

1. He was a slandering gossiper.
2. He refused to receive or support the missionaries.
3. He prevented people in his church from supporting the missionaries.
4. He expelled from the church those who attempted to support the missionaries.

Thus, John writes, "If I come, I will bring to remembrance his deeds which he does" (3 John 10). The apostle promised to confront the man authoritatively, and so, was warning Gaius to take heed (v. 11). Diotrephes was not a man who practiced the truth. His actions were, in fact, a denial of the truth. He willfully obstructed those fulfilling the Great Commission by withholding their needs and throwing those who met their needs out of the church. In short, Diotrephes was not a rope holder but a rope cutter.

Just as John was emphatic that Gaius must heed the warning against men like Diotrephes, so the church today must heed the warning. Faithful fellow workers for the truth must not imitate this man's evil. They must not seek to promote their own name—not even when they give to missions—but Christ's only. They must "imitate . . . what is good."

On that note, John commended Demetrius to Gaius as one having a "good witness" (3 John 12). Perhaps it was he who bore the letter of 3 John to its recipient, but he was certainly sent out by his elders.[24] Thus, John encouraged Gaius with the means by which he could discern between friends and foes of the mission, and those means are still applicable today: the one who continually does what is good is from God, while the one who is continually doing evil does not know God (1 John 3:6).[25] In other words, those "doing good" outwardly display characteristics of being saved by grace through faith in the Name.

---

22. Akin, *1, 2, 3 John*, 238.
23. Stott, *Letters of John*, 234.
24. Akin, *1, 2, 3 John*, 249–50.
25. Kistemaker, *Exposition of James and the Epistles of John*, 399–400.

Those who "do good" will pray that the Lord would prosper their fellow workers, and they will faithfully care for those workers themselves, whether pastors, missionaries, missions support teams, or seminarians. Anyone who is sent out to preach the gospel and make disciples will be loved by them.

Conclusion

Christians must hold the rope for one another. Missionaries who advance the gospel of Jesus Christ ought not to be dropped or left to their own devices, whether in life-threatening dangers or in need of basic provisions. In the first century AD, Gaius held fast to the rope for certain brethren on the other end. He knew there were gospel preachers on the other end of the rope, so he held on faithfully by receiving them and helping them on their way, as if they were Christ Himself. Each Christian should so consider the ones in the trenches for whom they are laboring. A missionary, a pastor, or a student halfway around the world is on the other end of the proverbial rope, but he is the Lord's own emissary.

Not all Christians are gifted to go down in the trench; many are gifted to hold the rope. If Christ's followers apply the lessons of 3 John to missions today, they will serve both Him and their fellow workers well. Like John and Gaius, they will pray, sustain, and be discerning about missions, and together they will reach more people "for the sake of the Name" (v. 7).

CHAPTER 31

Shepherding the Family on the Mission Field

Mark Borisuk

There must not be an incongruity in the disciples raised up outside and inside the home. The spiritual lives of people on the other side of the world do not trump those in the missionary's family. In fact, faithfulness to the Great Commission in the missionary's home is a prerequisite to being sent out from the church to fulfill the Great Commission worldwide (1 Tim 3:4–5; Titus 1:6).[1] Fulfilling the Great Commission in the home is not only a necessary qualification for a missionary to be sent; it also gives the missionary a biblical platform to fulfill the Great Commission in others. The importance of a biblically centered Christ-honoring home cannot be overstated. The marriage and parent-child relationships within missionary families always either obscure or amplify both the gospel message to unbelievers and the preaching of the Word to believers.

Understanding the Biblical Roles in the Family

In the context of worship and ministry within the church, Paul told the Corinthian believers that God "is not a God of confusion [or disorder] but of peace" (1 Cor 14:33). God has designed roles in the church and in the family to promote order in a sin-cursed world full of disorder (Jas 3:16). Going to the mission field or accepting the title of missionary does not spiritually transform a family into one that is ready to face the challenges of missionary life. On the contrary, perhaps nothing so quickly reveals the continued need for sanctification than being placed in a foreign culture. Going to the mission field is like applying fertilizer to the field of one's sins. The sinful nature chafes at the roles God defined for husband and wife, parent and child. God defines these roles within the family to bring stability and, ultimately, to bring glory

---

1. This encouragement is applicable to missionaries: "Pastors who pastor their family well usually pastor the church well. The two go hand in hand. Care for your smaller flock, and the larger flock will reap the benefits." Jason Helopoulos, *The New Pastor's Handbook: Help and Encouragement for the First Years of Ministry* (Grand Rapids: Baker, 2015), 72.

to Himself. No matter the culture in which the missionary family serves, the people will need to see how a family functions according to the biblical roles God has defined in Scripture.

The Marriage Relationship: Leadership, Love, and Honor

Scripture presents the husband as the wife's leader and head of the home (Eph 5:25–33; Col 3:19; 1 Pet 3:7). Wives are to submit to their husbands because the husband is the head of the wife (Eph 5:22–23; Col 3:18; 1 Pet 3:1–6; cf. 1 Cor 11:3). Therefore, the relationship of the husband to the wife is that of leading her by loving and serving. The relationship of the wife to the husband is that of honoring him by submitting and helping. How a man manages his family will qualify or disqualify him from serving as a missionary (1 Tim 3:4–5). To that end, the husband has been given the authority and thus the mandate from God to lead and manage the family.

In Ephesians 5:22–33, the husband is instructed twice in the imperative (vv. 25, 33), commanded to love his wife. He is given the sobering reality that his love for his wife needs to imitate Christ and His love for the church: Christ gave Himself up for the church (v. 25). A husband is to emulate Christ by giving himself in love and service to his wife. The husband needs to be a sanctifying influence in the home through sharing the Word of God with his wife and his children (vv. 26–27; 6:4). Practically, the missionary husband must love his wife

and desire for her to find fulfillment and satisfaction in the ministry as much as he himself does. As he leaves his current and oftentimes fulfilling ministries in their home country for a range of ambitious ministry activities in a new country, he must ask himself if he is willing to sacrifice some of his own goals and desires to meet the needs of his wife.

Knowing the needs of one's wife is vital to living with her, as 1 Peter 3:7 says, in an understanding way. If she is seeking to obey the Lord by living in submission to her husband (vv. 1–6), then there is a sense that she is weaker positionally, though this is a blessed position, according to the design of God for marriage.[2] Missionary husbands should therefore honor their wives' submission. The husband must seek to understand and honor his wife, knowing her strengths and weaknesses, and, in turn, he must protect, encourage, and help her. Otherwise, the consequences are profound—his prayers are hindered (v. 7). The missionary husband must ask himself if he desires God to hear and answer his prayers! In the times of greatest duress in ministry, a hindered fellowship with his wife is a hindered fellowship with God.

As to the role of the wife, she is to honor her husband by submitting to him and helping him. As with other God-ordained institutions like the church and government, the family unit involves both authority and submission (Rom 13:1ff.; Eph 6:5–6; Heb 13:17; 1 Pet 5:1–5). The wife submits to God in everything, which includes submitting to the God-ordained

---

2. D. Edmond Hiebert, *1 Peter* (Winona Lake, IN: BMH, 1997), 206.

leadership of her husband. Such submission is God-glorifying and draws others to glorify God (Matt 5:16).

The marriage relationship is at a level much grander than any other earthly relationship, as the union of the husband and wife (Gen 2:24) pictures the glorious union of Christ and the church (Eph 5:23–27, 31–32). As a picture of union with Christ, a Christlike marriage will make one of the most significant impacts on the mission field. It is an image that transcends cultural differences and immediately speaks of both the message of the gospel and of the life-change wrought by the gospel.

Parental Relationship: Loving Instruction and Discipline

While honoring one's parents is a responsibility of young and old children alike (Exod 20:12; Eph 6:2; 1 Tim 5:4), the Scriptures command, "Children, obey your parents in the Lord, for this is right" (Eph 6:1; cf. Col 3:20). A child's role while still in the home is to submit to the God-ordained leadership of parents "in the Lord." The parent's responsibility is best summed up in the command: "Fathers, do not provoke your children to anger, but bring them up in the discipline and instruction of the Lord" (Eph 6:4).

The book of Proverbs gives critical instruction for the wise parent. It says that a child's life flows out from his or her heart (Prov 4:23) and that "folly is bound up in the heart of a child" (22:15). A changed environment may become an instrument for revealing what was already in a child's heart. The challenges that come to the child who moves to a new context provide parents an incredible opportunity to come alongside that child with the truth of God's Word for dealing with foolishness and gaining the wisdom they need from Him (Prov 1:7; 9:10; cf. Jas 3:13–17).

Parenting on the mission field, as in any context, requires discipline, which God ordained to include physical discipline (Prov 13:24; 19:18; 22:15; 23:13–14; 29:15). But it is never to be carried out in anger or vengefulness, which is blatantly unbiblical. A man is unqualified if he is pugnacious (aggressive, violent; 1 Tim 3:3). The correction of his children, as with any church member, must be "in a spirit of gentleness" (Gal 6:1). Then, always following discipline, comes instruction (Prov 1:8; 4:1–2; 23:12; Eph 6:4), because with consistent biblical discipline the parent will be afforded more time with the child to instruct the child, affirming, exhorting, and encouraging him or her with love (Prov 3:12; 1 Thess 2:11; cf. 1 Cor 4:14). When correctly accomplished, the process reminds the child that he or she cannot meet the standard of a holy God and points to the only One who can—Jesus Christ, who bore sinners' penalty to give them His righteousness (2 Cor 5:21). Thus, the parent-child relationship is reconciling and evangelistic.

Such biblical discipline and instruction of children inevitably goes against cultural norms. Therefore, it speaks immediately to those whom the missionary serves regarding his dependence on and submission to God's directives for the family. The missionary's belief in the power and sufficiency of the living Word of

God reveals itself in the instruction he gives in the home, and it will amplify or obscure what he teaches outside the home.

As the missionary shepherds people who have often only seen unresolved conflict in relationships, his family becomes a living illustration of the transforming power of the gospel. The missionary's family is not perfect or conflict-free, but it is a real-life testimony of the missionary practicing what he preaches.

A year after arriving in China, our family started a home Bible study, and a man named Victor started attending. Today he faithfully preaches God's Word as a leader in his local church in Beijing. Victor recently shared some of the influences the Lord used to bring him from atheism to Christianity:

> Mark would be the person who was most influential in breaking the wall of my disinterest in religion, as I was not only an unbeliever but also quite antagonistic toward Christianity. I regarded religion as "the opium of the masses" due to the communist way of educating us, considering it something that only the weak believe. However, he and his family, along with his friends, played different roles in God's purpose. First and foremost, the aroma of the marital love that he and his wife showed naturally attracted me to what they believed, since I grew up with parents who fought a lot, and so I had embraced the prevalent view that marriage was the graveyard of love. In addition, Mark and his wife extended their great hospitality and love toward my friends and me by inviting us for meals and by showing sincere concern toward my parents and me, asking about and praying for us. Last but not least, his children displayed respect toward others and obedience toward their parents, qualities I would not have expected from intelligent and sociable children. These are some of the things the Lord used to soften my heart toward belief in Christianity.

God graciously used a marriage and a home that, though far from perfect, was attempting to live out God's roles and design for the family to give Victor an illustration of the power of the gospel to transform lives and families.

Understanding How to Prepare the Family for the Mission Field

The most important thing a family preparing for the mission field can do is to understand and fulfill God's design for the family to the best of their ability. By cultivating unity and knowing the needs of each person, the family can be the "aroma from life to life" to a world in need of God's grace (2 Cor 2:16).

The Need for Unity

Often each family member is not on the same page in their desire to begin a new ministry in a new country or culture. Whether the desire originated from the husband or the wife, it is paramount that both be unified in the decision and together shepherd the children as the decision becomes practical. The husband needs to lead in getting the family together not only to study what the country will be like but to appreciate the biblical motives for making this life-changing decision. Eventually all members should be involved in learning the language, studying facts about the country, reading missionary biographies, and engaging in other activities that will prepare them to act upon this decision effectively when it comes time.

Upon arrival it is important to find simple, fun things to do to help the family to thrive together in the new culture, like biking as a family to and through the Olympic park in Beijing. However, even more important, shepherding must continue through the many challenges on the field, difficult days, and discouragement. The missionary's children can be a key part of ministry, and making this happen is a significant aspect of their spiritual growth. For us, this meant things like my wife bringing our girls to shop at the local fruit and vegetable stand, building a relationship with the owner, and praying for her as a family. I looked for ways the family could be part of the ministry at the translation office and be involved in the lives of the staff. When we started our home Bible study after being in China for a year, the girls were a key part of welcoming, playing games with, and sitting alongside the college-age students who came to study the Bible. As the Lord began to save different ones in this group, these began to be part of the discipleship process in our children's lives. Through all this, the family did not lose sight of the wonder of being in Christ and sharing it with others. They saw the Lord transform lives and then saw these new believers begin to make a spiritual impact in the family.

The Wife's Needs

Before arriving in country, the husband should make sure his wife has adequate information regarding what life will be like, which can be at least partially accomplished by taking a survey trip together. Upon arrival, the wife often takes the brunt of shopping and setting up the home. The husband must understand the areas in which his wife excels and those in which she struggles (1 Pet 3:7). Part of encouraging her might be to initiate contact with missionaries or expatriated families (expats) living in the country, both before arriving and as the family settles in. He may need to adjust his language and ministry plans to make sure his family is thriving, because ministry success depends on the family's spiritual and emotional health in the new culture.

The Children's Needs

Preparing the children for a move to a foreign environment requires prayerful and thoughtful guidance from the church elders, and then very proactive help for the children. It is important that older children especially are included in the early discussions and that their opinions or concerns gain a hearing, even though the votes that ultimately count in the decision to move overseas for ministry are those of the parents.

Our family started attending monthly missionary board meetings at the church seven years before leaving for the field. Missionaries stayed with us or came over for a meal whenever possible. We ministered with our kids at church, at nursing homes, and during the travel period to raise support. The desire was to help the children serve the Lord and be a part of the parents' activities pre-field. Once a year, at Christmastime, the children would write an update on their lives to build relationships with prayer supporters and financial donors, many of whom still ask about and pray for the children many years later. Also, it was important to find and bring Christian books that were enjoyable for the children but, most importantly, taught timeless biblical truths by which to face the challenges of life.

Understanding the Temptations for Husbands and Wives on the Mission Field

The struggles faced by a husband and wife on the mission field are often the same spiritual struggles of a typical married couple in ministry. However, there are some temptations unique to those on the mission field, and the purpose of this brief section is to raise awareness to them, though many other kinds of temptations could be listed.

Temptations Not to Prefer Each Other in Language Acquisition

Both the husband and the wife must take the opportunity to study the language. In some contexts of language study, it might be preferable to arrange for other believers to help with the schooling of the children for the first couple of years or arrange for them to be part of a local school that will greatly enhance their language acquisition. This encourages the wife with the time needed for language acquisition, such as morning language classes, free of some of the distractions that come with being at home.

With such early dedication, the husband might find his wife learning the language faster than he does. Thus, the temptation can be twofold: the risk of jealousy for the advancing spouse, or the desire to neglect language study due to the daily demands of the household.

Temptations to Neglect Close Fellowship with Believers

The couple must make sure they have fellowship, encouragement, and accountability on the field or through believers back at their sending church. Life can get lonely on the mission field, and it is easy to begin to feel isolated. God designed people for fellowship, and so fellow believers need to be in the lives of the husband and wife, both individually and as a couple.

Temptations Not to Interact with Nationals

Husbands and wives should encourage each other and the children toward ministry opportunities and interaction with nationals. Hopefully this will happen through involvement in an established national church or as a church is being planted. However, if the missionary family decides to attend an international church, where the local language is not spoken or few of the national believers attend, there must be even more intentional interaction with the people whom the missionary is called to serve.

Temptations in Becoming an Expat Family

For those who live in larger metropolitan areas with international schools, international churches, and possibly an embassy or consulate to which businesses cater, there is a great temptation to become immersed in the international community rather than with the local people. The default pattern of all people is to move toward that which is comfortable. Perhaps even without realizing it, the missionary family can transform into just another expat family, albeit one that witnesses for Christ in the international community. Therefore, it is crucial to be intentional about spending as much time as possible with nationals, especially during the first few years on the field. Hopefully there will come a day when the missionary realizes that spending time with national brothers and sisters in Christ is as comfortable or even more so than with people from one's own country or culture.

Understanding the Hard Decisions the Family Will Face on the Mission Field

Although it will be field dependent, typically there will be several hard decisions that directly impact missionary children. These decisions will affect the family as a whole and will either curtail or advance the ministry for which the missionary was sent. These decisions need to be made after prayer and counsel from the elders of the sending church and other missionaries on the field.

Where to Worship Corporately

For many missionary families, where to go to church will be one of the most complex decisions they face. The decision must be based on the individual family's spiritual and ministry goals. The opportunity to get involved with a national church should be prioritized and understood as a blessing for the missionary family—giving an opportunity to serve and not just be served. In the first few years, the family might not understand much of the sermon, so it can be useful to overcome that lack by listening to a message in the family's native language, perhaps on Sunday afternoon upon returning home.

Ultimately, ministry flows out from involvement in and firsthand knowledge of the local church. As local people come to faith in the Lord Jesus Christ through a home Bible study, they are channeled into national churches, some into the same church as the missionary family. Coming alongside pastors in national churches is a fruitful ministry and a blessing to the family.

How to Educate and Shepherd Children

Educationally, many options are available today for missionary families. It is best to consider options and determine what is ideal for the family before relocating, if possible. In many contexts, it may be beneficial to send children to the public school to help with language learning and to build relationships with local families. In other cases, homeschooling remains an option, which can allow for a hybrid approach with a local school or with online dual enrollment programs in the language of origin, where the internet is available.

Children may eventually head back to the family's country of origin for university study or for work. Three principles for shepherding adult children are helpful in such cases. First, the missionary parents should remain approachable. Hopefully the parents have cultivated a level of approachability in the home since the children were young so that when they are grown they know the value of sharing their concerns with their parents. Second, the missionary parents must continue to be available. Availability to grown children springs from thankfulness that the children still want their parents involved in their lives. It is therefore important to be reachable when they are reaching out, corresponding with them and responding to them with little delay, even if they are in a different time zone. Finally, missionary parents need to be aware. The children might be half a world away, but they should be aware of the basic aspects of their lives, such as study and work schedules. Such knowledge might lead to opportunities for visits that coincide with visits to supporting churches without taking prolonged time away from the field. Most importantly, staying connected means that fellowship and shepherding will continue to whatever degree the Lord reveals as profitable to the children in their varying seasons of adulthood.

Conclusion

Although life on the mission field is not without challenges and sacrifices, a missionary has many reasons to thank the Lord for the opportunity to bring his family to the mission field. His marriage is God's chosen illustration of Christ and the church, and his children can be a tremendous help in building relationships with other families. The interrelationships of the family can be the first exposure others have to the power of the gospel to bring peace to all who believe (Isa 52:7). As the missionary family embarks on this journey to bring good news to another people, they would do well to remember that they are not alone. God has given them His perfect instruction to follow. No matter what the issues at hand may be, the missionary family can be blessed by the knowledge that their God reigns in every place and in every moment of their lives.

Sociocultural Challenges to the Missionary Family in Colombia

Santiago Armel

Colombia is full of beautiful landscapes and magnificent cultural expressions. The best thing about Colombia, however, is its spiritual awakening. This present display of God's kingdom advancement is the thrust for more missionary workers to come to this nation in recent years. Even though these missionaries come to beautiful lands to minister, not everything is easy for them. Colombia is a country with multiple social complications and a history where the true gospel was absent. While precise preaching is essential, the holy example of missionary families is fundamental.

The Dominant Culture

The cultural association most people have regarding Colombia is drug trafficking. This comes as no surprise. For several decades Colombia's cocaine production was the highest in the world. In 2021 coca leaf plants made up approximately 504,100 acres of its land, enough to produce 1,400 metric tons of cocaine per year.[3] These numbers are discouraging since cocaine cultivation is on the rise.

The side effects of this drug problem are often overlooked. The mafia or the more colloquially termed "narco" culture has been a powerful influence, proliferating Colombia's national evil, producing many other sinful norms, and its collective imagery has been propagated globally through television series. Thus, parallel to the proliferation of the drugs themselves, there are the narco standards. Many young Colombians grow up with the ideals of obtaining quick, easy money and living a debauched life, governed by lust, in which women are treated as trophies.

The problem of man's total depravity is manifest in all kinds of sins everywhere

---

3. United Nations Office on Drugs and Crime (UNODC)—Sistema Integrado de Monitoreo de Cultivos Ilícitos (SIMCI), *Monitoreo de territorios afectados por cultivos ilícitos 2021* (Bogotá: UNODC-SIMCI, 2022), 13, https://www .unodc.org/documents/colombia/2022/Octubre/Otros/Informe_de_Monitoreo_de_Territorios_Afectados_por_Cultivos _Ilicitos_2021.pdf.

(Gen 6:5; Jer 17:9; Rom 3:10–18). But it cannot be ignored that certain environments are conducive to certain sins. Particular iniquities can become characteristic of a nation, and this is the case with Colombia. Over five decades of mafia culture has sown a crop of national sins that can only be combated with the Word of God and exemplary family models.

What Families Must Fight

The gospel of Jesus Christ is the only solution to the problem of sin, and the family is the fundamental entity for establishing values in a society. Thus, pastoral and missionary families must rise up as moral beacons and reflections of the gospel they proclaim. This is especially true in the areas of life where sinful norms dominate society. In Colombia, ministers must fight on three combat fronts.

Against Corruption and Lies

Lying and corruption are predominant sins in many countries. From the highest spheres of economic power to the poorest citizens, dishonesty is the evidence of a corrupt society. Politicians steal millions from the nation, while thousands of ordinary citizens skirt the ticket systems on public transportation, robbing their nation daily. This epitomizes the popular Colombian belief that the most skillful one in breaking the law is the wisest. Lies and corruption have fully metastasized.

Because of this, pastoral families must radically commit to the truth. This calls for an unashamed faith and proclamation of Jesus Christ and His gospel (Rom 1:16). This must then be accompanied by a consistent testimony of life (Jas 2:17). The family's culture must be one where they speak the truth to one another in love (Eph 4:15; Col 3:9–10); the truth is nonnegotiable as lying is detestable (Pss 15:2–3; 120:2; Prov 12:22). The father must establish a pattern of integrity, demonstrating that one's word is meaningful (Matt 5:33–37; Jas 5:12). Any commitment he makes to his wife, children, or church, however small, must be kept. He must faithfully represent God, who always keeps His Word (Num 23:19; Deut 7:9; Titus 1:2). Families must also submit to the government in their cities (Rom 13:1ff.; 1 Pet 2:13–14). For, he who lies and breaks the law is not clever or shrewd but foolish. Above all, his behavior is incompatible with a true disciple of Christ.

Against Physical Vanity

Colombia is one of the world's leaders in medical tourism. For many years, drug traffickers offered women plastic surgeries to modify their bodies as the traffickers liked. The result was that many women in the country modified their bodies after a voluptuous ideal. Nowadays hundreds of plastic and cosmetic surgery clinics are open to Colombians and to foreigners for low-cost surgeries, especially in cities like Medellin and Cali. It would be false to cast all Colombian women in this light. But, in general, they are under continuous pressure to reach given standards of beauty and weight. The vanity of physical appearance is a national idol for which the gospel of Jesus Christ alone is the solution.

Families must cultivate values to combat such vanity in their homes. First, they need an awareness that one's value comes from being created in God's image (Gen 1:26–27) and that fullness is found only in Christ (Eph 3:19; Col 2:8–12). Second, a value for inner beauty must be cultivated, where godliness is praised instead of appearance (Prov 31:30; 1 Tim 2:9–10; 4:7–8; 1 Pet 3:3–4). The pastor-missionary should openly converse with his wife about whether they incidentally promote, by their lives and speech, the dominant idol of vanity (Eph 4:17–20).

Against Covetousness and "Easy Money"

"Narcos" in Colombia are known as "the new rich," people who become millionaires at a moment's notice. Their outlandish and imprudent lifestyles give them away. Many in Colombia, though not entering illicit businesses, still dream of a stroke of luck to make them millionaires overnight, of quick money and no effort. Those who think this way are simply fools according to the Bible (Prov 13:11; Luke 12:15–21).

Pastoral families must be industrious. No member of the congregation should doubt whether the pastor-missionary truly works at his job. His diligence in preaching preparation, time-intensive counseling, and planning for future ministry should be "evident to all" (1 Tim 4:15). So, too, must be his motivation, that he ministers before God and not before men, nor for dishonest gain (1 Thess 2:4–12; Titus 1:7). In the home, the family must work heartily to please the Lord and be content (Col 3:23–24; 1 Tim 5:4; 6:6–8; Titus 2:5). Their lives as well as the pulpit should emphasize that work is a blessing from God and that hastily pursuing wealth is foolish.

Foundational to all this, every pastor-missionary who would impact the nation where he serves must be an exegete of the people. It is there that he must apply the eternal truths of God and His gospel to particular sins and sociocultural norms. He must guard and shepherd his family accordingly also. Precise preaching and personal application in conjunction with a holy testimony in the missionary family are two catalysts for a nation's transformation.

Survey of Top On-Field Family Shepherding Issues

Chris Burnett

Regional directors of a missions agency that oversees more than a hundred missionary families met in Los Angeles in March 2023. They shared the most significant areas of struggle that the families in their charge were experiencing. They offered one another counsel and prayed together about how to shepherd the families well as regional leaders, country leaders, and team leaders. The top concerns centered around marriages, child-rearing, extended family, and the balance between home life and the outside world. Some takeaways from the meeting are reported below.

1. Marriage
   - *Unspoken problems:* Many couples are unsure who to talk to when marital struggles arise. Young wives need older women on the field to mentor them, who are gracious, understanding, and patient. Husbands need other men to whom they can be vulnerable and accountable about their marriage problems, and to whom they can con-

fess sin. Team leaders would do well to provide intentional opportunities for marital check-ins and biblical counseling without leaving the field.
   - *Workaholism:* Because missionaries long to serve effectively and gospel opportunities abound on the field, ministry demands can easily eclipse the needs of the family. Team leaders need to affirm the importance of setting aside time, energy, and resources to meet the needs of the family, starting with the spouse. In practice, supervisors need to remind practitioners, "If anyone does not provide for his own, and especially for those of his household, he has denied the faith and is worse than an unbeliever" (1 Tim 5:8).
2. Children
   - *Developmental disorders:* All children have sinful tendencies and some children continue to practice sin due to unbelief. However, learning disabilities do not indicate sin and unbe-

lief but they do create problems in children's lives that are outside of the parents' control. For a variety of reasons, adopted children sometimes have particular needs for discipline and training that are different from biological children. Team leaders need to encourage parents to make every effort to follow biblical parenting principles and support parents as practically as possible as they confront problems that surface due to the weaknesses of their children (Eph 6:4; Col 3:21; 1 Thess 2:11; 5:14). Attentiveness to the father's spiritual leadership in the home is also important, because a lack of discipline in the home is a contributing factor to a child's problems, and rebellion might signal a disqualifying problem for the missionary.

- *Support needs:* Every cultural context offers different resources and networking opportunities for parents and children, such as for education and extracurricular activities. Some missionaries have little to no support system on the field, leaving them largely unaided during challenging seasons of child development. It is critical for team leaders to be mindful of parents' needs for a support system as they educate and guide the learning and skills development

of their children. It is never too late to connect people and resources that can help a growing family.

3. Aging Parents
   - *Where to provide care:* At some point, most missionaries must decide how to provide logistical help to their aging parents, especially when they live far away. Relying too heavily on siblings at home can lead to resentment by the extended family, while regular trips for active care can limit ministry time and energy on the field. Some families bring their parents to the field to use their retirement to serve in ministry. Team leaders should listen well and pray much before presenting their opinions about another missionary's family dynamics.
   - *How to provide care:* From a sending church or agency perspective, if a missionary family needs increased funding to care for parents, team leaders should be willing to advocate by asking if the family's budget can be increased to help feed, clothe, or care for them. Leadership teams should attempt to be flexible with their funding, to help their field workers honor their parents.

4. Isolation on the Field
   - *Living in a virtual world:* Some missionaries have prioritized videoconferencing with family, friends, and sup-

porters back in their home culture, sometimes for several hours per day, over actively engaging with people on the field. Screens and devices are the social vehicles for many children, leaving them socially uninvolved with the locals. Team leaders need to recognize symptoms of escapism and the seclusion that can come with living behind a screen, and encourage direct, active involvement in church life and with their evangelistic contacts.

- *Never embracing the culture:* Not every member of a missionary family or team reaches language fluency or facility with the culture and society around them. Team leaders would do well to encourage missionaries to participate in local festivities and cultural events, provided they will not inadvertently participate in a sinful activity or religious ceremony. However, team leaders should help teammates to recognize that they each have different language aptitudes, personalities, and preferences.

INSERT 31.3

Women Caring for Missionary Women and Families

Lauren Brown

The Lord has given His people a unique opportunity for gospel partnerships as Christ builds His church (Matt 16:18). Believers at home have a special privilege to support missionaries on the field, and that includes support by women for women as those at home care for their sisters on the field. This begins with a shared understanding of foundational ministry principles and can be done in several practical ways.

Principles of Ministry

The first ministry priority is recognizing that all Christians are called to support those who take the gospel to the world. John made this point when he emphasized to Gaius, "You will do well to send them on their way in a manner worthy of God. For they went out for the sake of the Name. . . . We ought to support such men, so that we may be fellow workers with the truth" (3 John 6–8). This by no means excludes women, for Paul asked the Corinthians, "Do we not have authority to take along a believing wife?" (1 Cor 9:5; e.g., Priscilla in Acts 18:2, 18; Rom 16:3).[4] Moreover, Phoebe traveled from her home church in Cenchrea to Rome, probably delivering the letter of Romans, and Paul urged the church to support her in the service she was rendering to many.[5] Both single women and wives on the mission field need support as they glorify God through evangelism to unbelievers and through encouragement, discipleship, and service to believers. They have gone out for the sake of the Name, and Christians at home ought to support them appropriately.

The second priority is recognizing that in the work of the Great Commission, God alone causes success, according to His perfect plan and for His glory. Missionaries labor and plant seeds, but it is God who brings the increase (1 Cor 3:5–9). Serving faithfully for many years and not seeing fruit can be discouraging for missionaries. Women on the field experience this discouragement, whether from their own ministry trials or, if they are married, those they bear alongside their husbands. But remembering that gospel work is God's work, and that He is the One who determines the fruitfulness of any ministry, is encouraging.

Both of these ministry principles are foundational to women at home committing to faithfully pray for the personal and ministry needs of missionary women on the field.

Practical Care for Missionaries

Perhaps the greatest challenge in caring for missionaries is a lack of relationships between those on the field and those in the church at home. When people do not know one another, they cannot care for one another well. Several simple yet profoundly effective opportunities are available for those at home to get to know their missionaries and to minister to them in the process.

Such opportunities require active and ongoing relationships where specific personal and ministry needs can be shared in confidence. Scripture instructs women to care for and counsel one another (Titus 2:3–5), and woman-to-woman relationships are especially helpful in areas such as the practical commitment to study Scripture,

4. John F. MacArthur Jr., *1 Corinthians*, MNTC (Chicago: Moody, 1984), 201.

5. John F. MacArthur Jr., *Romans 9–16*, MNTC (Chicago: Moody, 1991), 359–62.

submission to authority at church and at home, prioritizing care and respect for one's husband (for those who are married), raising children in the fear and admonition of the Lord (for those who have children), and serving and discipling women in the church. All of these can be more challenging for our sisters who are living in a different culture and often speaking a second language.

The most important variable in practical care for our missionaries is time. Relationships with other women can only be nurtured through a commitment to spend regular, consistent time together, whether on the phone or video chats or through emails or text messaging. God has given the blessing of digital platforms that allow real-time international conversations that allow supporters to know where and how their missionaries live, where they have devotions, what the view is from their kitchen window, and what their children's rooms are like. These are all details that give a sense of the missionaries' daily lives as they serve thousands of miles from their families.

Such relationships do not replace the relationships with nationals who are sisters in Christ, but godly women at home, whether family members or supporters, are in an extraordinary position to provide confidential counsel, wisdom, encouragement, and prayer.

Prayer is the next variable in practical care for our sisters on the field. It is the primary way Christians at home can support missionaries, so we must make it our priority to find out about their specific needs and then bring those requests before the Lord. To just think about praying is not enough. Each woman at home must make a commitment to actually pray, keeping track of missionaries' personal and family needs as well as ministry opportunities and concerns.

Such tracking can be done in many ways, but it is perhaps best accomplished through a prayer journal, so that those on the field know they are remembered and loved. This journal can be written by hand or in a private document on one's phone or computer. It allows women at home to be accountable as they pray for their sisters on the field, to follow up specific requests, and then to thank God as He answers these prayers.

A third objective as we care for our missionary sisters is also to care for their children. Missionary kids (MKs) are often the ones whose adjustment is the most difficult. They are not the ones who made the choice to uproot to the other side of the world, distancing themselves from family and friends. MKs often no longer feel American, but neither do they fit in well with the country of ministry, even if they have grown up there. Many of these children have no youth ministry to attend or other opportunity to be around peers, so the mission field can be far more isolating for them than for their parents. Supporting women can pray for MKs, send cards for their birthdays, and help them to connect with other MKs or to stay connected with their own children. It is worthwhile to consider sponsoring a special group for older children, perhaps ages eleven and up, who utilize video calls or video messaging like their parents. This allows young people to get to know others who are in similar situations and seasons of life, share from their own experiences, ask questions of one another, and understand that their parents' choice of ministry in a different culture can also be their ministry. It is helpful to involve the pastor and adult volunteer staff from the home church, since they already serve in a similar capacity and are familiar with the dynamics of communicating with and caring for teenagers.

Finally, missionary furloughs are also an excellent opportunity for women in the sending churches to show support. When missionaries are in town, supporters should invite them to stay in their homes or share a meal together. They might also volunteer to babysit their little ones or plan excursions for their older children. These tangible reflections of care are acts that will bless not only the missionaries but the hosts as well, as they get to know the missionary families personally.

Conclusion

The missionaries' sacrifice of leaving their homes to go to countries with differing languages and cultures is a worthy sacrifice for the sake of Christ. For believers at home, it is a distinct privilege to serve the Lord by partnering in His work with those who serve in nations around the globe. Women are in a special position to encourage and strengthen their missionary sisters through faithful prayer and a commitment to share their resources, just as with those at home (Titus 2:3–5). One of women's scarcest and yet most precious commodities is time, and being available to listen to those who are serving around the world is a practical way to show that we care for them and to assure them that they are not forgotten. The Bible calls believers to be generous with their time and resources to support those on the field (3 John 6–9), and prioritizing relationships with our missionaries is a sweet opportunity for those at home to give from the abundance with which God has blessed them.

CHAPTER 32

A Deadly Enemy of Faithful Missionaries: Love of Material Comfort

Luis Contreras

Second Kings 5 introduces a deadly enemy in ministry: the love of money. The passage records how Elisha's servant Gehazi had seen the Lord perform miracles through his master Elisha. He saw Elisha raise the Shunammite's son (2 Kgs 4:18–37). He saw Elisha heal Naaman's leprosy (5:1–14). He saw how the Lord transformed Naaman's heart (5:15). And he saw how Elisha refused to accept Naaman's gift (5:16–19). In Elisha, Gehazi had a clear example of a man of God who was not motivated by greed. Even so, Gehazi himself gave in to the love of money (5:20–27).

The same enemy that defeated Gehazi threatens to defeat faithful missionaries today. This chapter assesses this deadly enemy through the negative example of Gehazi and the wise counsel of Solomon in Proverbs in order to help missionaries biblically define, describe, and deflect the love of money.

The Enemy Defined

God is not opposed to money. He commands His people to provide for their families (1 Tim 5:8). And in His grace, He often bestows believers with wealth (1 Tim 6:17). Paul himself enjoyed a measure of earthly comfort at times. He explained that he knew how to live in abundance (Phil 4:12). The problem arises when believers are not content with what God has given them. Ingratitude comes along with discontentment, and the two subsequently bring a failure to trust in God's provision. Hebrews 13:5 warns about this very attitude: "Make sure that your way of life is free from the love of money, being content with what you have; for He Himself has said, 'I will never desert you, nor will I ever forsake you.'"

For those on the mission field, the sinful love of money means placing comfort and possessions above diligent study, personal obedience, and faithful preaching of the Scriptures. In other words, missionaries must not make material gain the preliminary consideration when making ministry decisions. They should always ask, "How can I best obey and preach the Word, serve the church, and evangelize the lost?" Instead, the mind set on comfort asks, "Where can I preach and serve the church and be in the best situation financially?" This kind of thinking will corrupt ministry and limit usefulness to the Lord. As men called to serve Christ's sheep, missionary pastors are warned against ministering with money as a goal (1 Pet 5:2).

The Enemy Described

The book of Proverbs describes the love of money in a unique manner. Solomon wrote most of the book to instruct his children in the ways of wisdom (Prov 1:8). Wisdom in Proverbs means the ability to understand and apply the Scriptures to life (Prov 2:6–8; 13:13; 16:20; 22:17–21; 28:4, 7, 9; 29:18; 30:5–6).[1] This kind of wisdom comes only to those who are true children of God (Prov 1:7; 9:10; Col 2:2–3).

Before looking at several passages in Proverbs, it is important to remember two important principles of application. First, Proverbs gives general principles, not absolute laws. And second, the moral principles Proverbs teaches are repeated in the epistles of the New Testament. Therefore, they apply to Christians today. This section describes the love of money in two parts: its destructive nature and its inferiority to wisdom.

The Destructive Nature of the Enemy

After Proverbs' introductory verses (1:1–7), Solomon warns his son about the danger of loving money and the danger of associating with those who love money. Love of money is one of the first themes Solomon writes about and one he revisits often throughout the book. Solomon knew firsthand how much the human heart longs for wealth. He, along with his family, was surrounded by abundant comforts (1 Kgs 10:23).

From that context he writes, "Hear, my son, your father's discipline and do not abandon your mother's instruction" (Prov 1:8). Solomon's teaching was based on biblical principles, as the rest of the passage shows. If the son obeyed biblical instruction, his life would be blessed. He describes the teaching therefore as "a garland of grace for your head and ornaments about your neck" (1:9).

Solomon then gives his son more specific instructions: "My son, if sinners entice you, do not be willing" (Prov 1:10). From verses 13 and 19, he describes these sinners as those who were characterized by loving money, so much that they would kill for it. These forbidden friends explicitly give their motive: "We will find all

---

1. Derek Kidner commented on Proverbs 13:13 that, there, "*word* and *commandment* are a reminder that *revealed* religion is presupposed in Proverbs." Derek Kidner, *Proverbs: An Introduction and Commentary*, TOTC 17 (Downers Grove, IL: InterVarsity, 1964), 97. See also the comments on Proverbs 28:9 and 29:18 in Allen P. Ross, "Proverbs," in *EBC*, vol. 5, *Psalms, Proverbs, Ecclesiastes, Song of Songs*, ed. Frank E. Gaebelein (Grand Rapids: Zondervan, 1991), 1104, 1115, respectively.

kinds of precious wealth, we will fill our houses with spoil" (1:13). To make this proposal more attractive, the sinners entice him, saying, "Cast in your lot with us, we shall all have one purse" (1:14). In other words, "Not only are we going to find a lot of wealth, but we are also going to share it with you. We'll have a common fund. We are going to share what we all collect from killing the innocent so easily."

Not everyone, of course, reaches the point of saying, "Let's kill to get money." But the willingness to kill is reflective of the attitude that willingly and coldly minimizes sin to gain a profit. The same attitude is present in the corrupt politician, the gang member, the drug lord, or the petty criminal. And in a subtler but equally sinful way, the missionary who sees a ministry opportunity as a means to material gain is operating from the same premise.

Those who seek to gain from ministry act like wretched mercenaries. God wants true servants in His church, not those who use it as a vehicle for self-service (Acts 20:33–35; Titus 1:7). Missionaries must not let themselves be driven by the pursuit of wealth. They must resist the world's incessant drive toward acquiring money. Instead, they must heed Solomon's counsel: "My son, do not walk in the way with them. Withhold your feet from their pathway, for their feet run to evil and they hasten to shed blood" (Prov 1:15–16).

Solomon then adds these words: "For it is no use that a net is spread in the sight of any bird" (Prov 1:17). Why is it useless to place a net in front of a bird if you are trying to catch it? Because the bird sees the net and does not fly toward it, but rather flees from it. In contrast to the bird that avoids death, these lovers of money "lie in wait for their own blood; they ambush their own lives" (1:18). In other words, with its God-given instinct, a bird is more intelligent than these people who love money. This is so because a bird flees from danger. These lovers of money, however, do not flee from the deadly consequences of their sin.

Solomon concludes this exhortation by identifying who these men are: "So are the paths of everyone who is greedy for gain; it takes away the life of its possessors" (Prov 1:19). These men who follow the path of quick wealth are actually on a path of self-destruction. Missionaries must be careful about who they are surrounding themselves with. Lovers of money may appear godly on the outside, but like the false teachers of 2 Timothy 3:4–5, they may be men who are "lovers of pleasure rather than lovers of God, holding to a form of godliness, but having denied its power."

The love of money is immensely destructive. Missionaries who heed Solomon's counsel and mortify this deadly sin will avoid prostituting their ministry and dishonoring the Lord. Furthermore, they will avoid much heartache and squandered opportunities.

The Inferiority of the Enemy

Throughout Proverbs, the Holy Spirit compares the value of money with the value of wisdom. By doing so, God shows how money and the love of money are worthless in comparison to faithful obedience to His Word. Proverbs 3:13–15 says, "How blessed is the man who finds wisdom and the man who obtains discernment. For her profit is better than the profit of silver and her produce better than fine gold. She is more precious than pearls; and nothing you desire compares with her." In these verses, Solomon effectively says, "The value of wisdom, of understanding and applying the Word of God faithfully, exceeds the value of all riches." Wisdom's value is supreme, beyond comparison with any earthly wealth.

Later in Proverbs 8:10–11, Solomon personifies wisdom. Wisdom calls out, "Take my discipline and not silver, and knowledge rather than choicest fine gold. For wisdom is better than pearls; and all desirable things cannot compare with her." Solomon had already given instruction in chapter 3 about the value and superiority of wisdom compared to material riches. Why does he do it again? He wanted his son to be strengthened against the sinful human tendency of loving money. His words came from a context of extreme wealth. When Solomon wrote Proverbs, he was the king of Israel and the richest man in the world. He enjoyed the best comforts and luxuries available in his time, and his son was raised in this atmosphere of abundance. Solomon therefore wanted to emphasize to his son the importance of not living for the kind of luxury he was surrounded with.

In chapter 8, the personification of wisdom goes on to say, "My fruit is better than fine gold, even pure gold, and my produce better than choice silver" (v. 19). Solomon repeats the idea of verses 10–11—wisdom is superior to gold and silver of the highest quality. Why does he repeat the thought? He knew how tempting it would be to value money over wisdom. The drive for wealth could lure his son from the more profitable pursuit of understanding and obeying God's Word.

A few chapters later, Solomon returns to the same idea. In Proverbs 15:16–17, he writes, "Better is a little with the fear of Yahweh than great treasure and turmoil with it. Better is a dish of vegetables where there is love than a fattened ox and hatred in it." According to Solomon, it is better to have a reverential awe and healthy fear of the Lord with a small amount of money than to have great wealth and face the pain involved with sin. Obeying the Lord is more important than having money, regardless of the temporary comforts money can provide. In verse 17, Solomon emphasizes the same truth with different words. In Old Testament Israel, the ox was considered the largest and strongest of domesticated animals.[2] When someone had an ox that was fattened, therefore, they had money. But as Solomon teaches, it is better to have a small and humble meal of vegetables if it is enjoyed with love than it is to feast on delicacies in an atmosphere marked by hatred. He makes the same point in Proverbs 16:8: "Better is a little with righteousness than great produce with injustice." In other words, it is better to be an obedient poor person than to be a rich sinner.

One must not evaluate obedience to the Lord by the amount of money or material comforts that someone enjoys. As these proverbs make clear, there are people who live in relative poverty but are faithful to the Lord. This

---

2. Bruce K. Waltke, *The Book of Proverbs, Chapters 1–15*, NICOT (Grand Rapids: Eerdmans, 2004), 383.

should encourage every Christian, especially missionaries, to focus on obeying the Lord above the pursuit of wealth (Matt 6:32–33).

Proverbs 16:16 is another verse in which Solomon extols the value of wisdom over possessions: "How much better it is to acquire wisdom than fine gold! And to acquire understanding is to be chosen above silver." This verse teaches what has already been seen: the value of understanding and applying Scripture surpasses the value of money and material comfort. When believers understand the value of understanding and obeying the Word of God, they will value it above money and material comfort (Ps 119:72, 127).

The Enemy Deflected

In 2 Kings 5, Elisha's servant Gehazi did not heed wisdom but yielded to the temptation of loving money. Below are four principles gleaned from Gehazi's sinful example that help missionaries avoid the love of money.

Do Not Forget Godly Examples

"Then Gehazi, the young man of Elisha the man of God, said to himself, 'Behold, my master has spared this Naaman the Aramean, by not receiving from his hands what he brought. As Yahweh lives, I will run after him and take something from him'" (2 Kgs 5:20). Gehazi turned his back on the godly example that he saw in Elisha. In contrast, Paul commended Timothy centuries later for his success in standing against the same temptation: "But you followed my teaching, conduct, purpose, faith, patience, love, perseverance" (2 Tim 3:10).

Both Gehazi and Timothy received solid examples from their mentors. Gehazi disregarded Elisha's example, but Timothy was faithful to observe Paul, emulate him, and consequently become an example to others. Missionaries must take advantage of the gift of godly examples, whether from Scripture or those they know personally. God provides these kinds of mentors, professors, and disciplers as gracious guides for His servants, that they might avoid the love of material comfort.

That is why it would be helpful for younger missionaries to spend time with or listen to missionaries who have been on the field for a number of years. Their experience and insights and even their advice in this area could be very helpful as they seek to avoid prioritizing material comfort over faithfulness in ministry. On one occasion, one former missionary told a group of men involved in ministry, "The natives in your mission field know that you have more money than they do. So don't pretend that you don't. Be simple in the way you live, but recognize that they expect you to enjoy things that they cannot enjoy." This is a sample of the blessing of learning from godly examples on the mission field.

Do Not Forget the Lord's Supremacy

In 2 Kings 5:16, Naaman urged Elisha to take something, but he did not. Elisha was concerned with the Lord's reputation before Naaman and the Syrians. He was more concerned with honoring the Lord than seeking his own benefit. Gehazi, however, acted out of a desire for personal gain. The contrast between Gehazi and Elisha is a stark one:

> So Gehazi pursued Naaman. And Naaman saw one running after him, so he came down from the chariot to meet him and said, "Is all at peace?" And he said, "All is at peace. My master has sent me, saying, 'Behold, just now two young men of the sons of the prophets have come to me from the hill country of Ephraim. Please give them a talent of silver and two changes of clothes.'" Then Naaman said, "Be pleased to take two talents." And he urged him and bound two talents of silver in two bags with two changes of clothes and gave them to two of his young men; and they carried them before him. (2 Kgs 5:21–23)

The contrast between Gehazi and Naaman is remarkable as well. In verses 17–18 of the same chapter, there is evidence of Naaman's confession, generosity, conscience, and worship of God. It is a shame that Naaman, the new convert from Syria, showed more concern to honor God than did Gehazi, the personal assistant of Elisha.

The missionary who wants to avoid the love of material comfort must think about pleasing God before pleasing his own desires. The Bible makes it plain that indulging selfish desires amounts to idolatry (Col 3:5).

Do Not Forget Sin's Deceitfulness

Gehazi's sin affected his ability to reason clearly. He of all people should have considered the supernatural ability God had given his master to perform miracles. Yet the text shows where his true concern was and how that concern blinded him from what was self-evident.

> So he came to the hill, and he took them from their hand and deposited them in the house. Then he sent the men away, and they departed. But he came in and stood before his master. And Elisha said to him, "Where have you been, Gehazi?" And he said, "Your servant went nowhere."
>
> Then he said to him, "Did not my heart go with you, when the man turned from his chariot to meet you? Is it a time to receive money and to receive clothes and olive groves and vineyards and sheep and oxen and male and female slaves?" (2 Kgs 5:24–26)

Gehazi gave no thought to Elisha's track record as God's prophet, a track record he had personally witnessed. It did not occur to him that God might supernaturally reveal his sin to Elisha. The concern for satisfying his base greed eclipsed any notion of faithfulness to the Lord or to Elisha's example.

Sin always affects one's ability to reason. It distorts and deceives (Heb 3:13). It makes people think illogically and act irrationally, just as it did to Gehazi. Missionaries must never underestimate the deceitful nature of sin.

One way in which a missionary can be protected in this area is by seeking advice from spiritually mature national leaders, as the missionary determines at which financial level he must live. Where to live, what to wear, what to drive—these decisions are often clouded by our desire to be comfortable. And the counsel of native, faithful men on the mission field, can help him protect his heart.

Do Not Forget the Lord's Discipline

God acted miraculously in 2 Kings 5. He healed Naaman through a miracle and likewise miraculously revealed Gehazi's sin and judged him: "'Thus the leprosy of Naaman shall cling to you and to your seed forever.' So he went out from his presence a leper as white as snow" (v. 27). This kind of supernatural intervention was a unique occurrence. Nevertheless, it reflects a timeless principle for contemporary Christians. When people sin by loving money, they expose themselves to the Lord's discipline (1 Tim 6:9–10; Heb 12:5–11). Missionaries should think deeply on this truth and let it serve as a powerful and needed deterrent against the love of material comfort.

Conclusion

The love of money will destroy a Christian minister's faithfulness. Each one must think of how he can best honor the Lord in life and ministry, not of how to maximize the enjoyment of temporal benefits. A wrong outlook here can easily cause men who are ideal for overseas ministry to stay in America. It can also cause international students who study in Christian universities and seminaries in America not to return to their home country to serve.

Missionaries must not serve on the basis of comfort. Rather, their prime consideration must be how they can best contribute to the Lord's kingdom. May the Lord use His Word to expose this sin and keep His undershepherds from corrupting their ministry and detracting from the glory of the Chief Shepherd in this way.

INSERT 32.1

Living in the Joy of Missions: An Antidote to Burnout

Rick Kress

Why do many who intend to be lifelong missionaries burn out on the field and return home earlier than expected?[3] Though every believer becomes an alien in

---

3. Perhaps correlated, the 2019 "Field Attrition Study Research Report" by Missio Nexus documented that between 2016 and 2018 across eleven organizations almost as many missionaries left their organizations and/or fields (974 units) as were sent to the field (1014 units). Presented by Karl Dahlfred, "Missionaries Get Lonely Too and It's Contributing to Missionary Attrition," August 17, 2021, https://omf.org/us/missionaries-get-lonely-too-its-contributing-to-missionary

this fallen world at the moment of salvation, missionaries quite literally experience alien status when they embrace the privileged weight of proclaiming Christ's glory as their vocation. They face not only the pilgrim condition common to every believer but also visa requirements and fundraising responsibilities, not to mention language and culture challenges along with a multitude of miscellaneous trials that can lead to missionary burnout.[4]

In his first epistle, the apostle Peter wrote to believers as elect aliens—foreigners living in a land no longer theirs (1 Pet 1:1). He said believers have one overarching mission—to represent Christ and proclaim His excellencies to those around them (2:9–10). Thus, Peter's purpose in writing was to encourage followers of Christ to stand firm in the grace of God, no matter the suffering they would inevitably experience (5:10–12). In 1 Peter 1:1–9, the apostle gives believers and missionaries alike three vital encouragements for living in supernatural joy that overcomes every trial.

The Plan of Sovereign Grace

Plainly stated in the opening two verses of 1 Peter, being an alien in a hostile world is part of God's eternal plan and purpose for His people, which is "according to the foreknowledge of God the Father, by the sanctifying work of the Spirit, to the obedience of Jesus Christ and the sprinkling of His blood" (1:2). Believers may give assent to the eternal decree of God, but the question is whether they truly believe it and fully embrace it. This world is not the believers' home. They are strangers here. The Father's sovereign plan, the Spirit's sanctifying work, and Christ's saving blood not only call for obedience but also supply the Christian with divine grace and peace—no matter the circumstances they may face. Living in the supernatural joy that overcomes the world means truly embracing one's status as an alien and stranger on the earth.

The Praise for Saving Mercy

In 1 Peter 1:3–5, Peter models the pilgrim saint's intentional, believing praise for the

---

-attrition/. According to a 1994 survey of fourteen sending countries by the World Evangelical Fellowship Missions Commission, 5.1 percent of the mission force leaves the field every year, and 71 percent of those leave for preventable reasons. Findings and analysis were published in Peter W. Brierley, "Missionary Attrition: The ReMAP Research Report," in *Too Valuable to Lose: Exploring the Causes and Cures of Missionary Attrition*, ed. William D. Taylor, Globalization of Mission Series (Pasadena, CA: William Carey Library, 1996), 85–87. See the broader discussion of unplanned reasons missionaries leave the field in Tom Steffen and Lois McKinney Douglas, *Encountering Missionary Life and Work: Preparing for Intercultural Ministry*, Encountering Mission (Grand Rapids: Baker, 2008), 329–31.

4. Recent trends in burnout as the cause of attrition are observed in Billy L. Drum, "Burnout among Cross Cultural Workers: An Analysis of Systemic Issues That Lead to Burnout within Medium Sized North American Mission Organizations" (MA diss., Redcliffe College, 2021); Geoff and Kristina Whiteman, "Supporting Today's Global Workers toward Missional Resilience," *EMQ* 58, no. 2 (April–June 2022): 27–29.

Father's mercy in initiating and sustaining the new birth in Christ, which includes the unwavering conviction of one's own unworthiness: "Blessed be the God and Father of our Lord Jesus Christ, who according to His great mercy has caused us to be born again to a living hope through the resurrection of Jesus Christ from the dead" (v. 3).

The believer's hopelessly dead condition is conquered by a living hope, through the resurrection of Jesus Christ from the dead. Christ's sinless life, substitutionary death, and saving resurrection is the believer's eternal, all-sufficient hope. Whatever one may face—whatever failure, whatever sin, whatever victory, whatever success, whatever disappointment—the Christian's ultimate confidence is the saving mercy of God in Christ—nothing more and nothing less. Praise God for the basis of the sinner's salvation—sovereign, saving mercy through the person and work of Jesus Christ!

This merciful salvation in Christ includes an everlasting inheritance, as asserted in 1 Peter 1:4–5: "to obtain an inheritance incorruptible and undefiled and unfading, having been kept in heaven for you, who are protected by the power of God through faith for a salvation ready to be revealed in the last time." The eternal Son of God is Himself the fount and fullness of all that is ever-living, ever-pure, and ever-beautiful. Our inheritance in Him is both reserved and preserved, not by our own faithfulness, fruitfulness, or piety (past, present, or future), but rather by the unbreakable promise and power of God.

The eternal plan of God includes our alienation from this world. Believers need to expect it and embrace it without seeking to be either detached or eccentric, but genuinely living for the Lord in everyday life. Additionally, the praise of God's saving mercy is vital to supernatural joy that overcomes adversity.

The Pleasure of Trusting in Jesus Christ

In 1 Peter 1:6–9, Peter expresses the pleasure that elect aliens experience when they trust in Jesus Christ:

> In this you greatly rejoice, even though now for a little while, if necessary, you have been grieved by various trials. . . . And though you have not seen Him, you love Him, and though you do not see Him now, but believe in Him, you rejoice with joy inexpressible and full of glory, receiving as the outcome of your faith the salvation of your souls.

Trusting in Jesus Christ and rejoicing in God's saving promises in Him is the only antidote to a believer's multifaceted distresses. He must actually believe that his trials are only now for "a little while" in the face of eternity, no matter how they may currently feel. He must genuinely trust that he is going through them only if our loving Savior has deemed them "necessary." Furthermore, he must be convinced that after the testing is over and his faith is refined—when the Lord appears—his reward of praise will be from Christ Himself, so that all praise will return to Him and He Himself will be the greatest reward.

This pleasure—this supernatural joy—is apprehended by faith. And this faith is not to be merely intellectual but must be intensely personal (1 Pet 1:9). Though believers today have not seen Christ with their eyes, they really do love Him. Though they do not see Him now, they genuinely do trust in Christ personally and intimately. The joy of loving and trusting Jesus as He reveals Himself in the Scriptures is ultimately undefeatable. Even if these sojourners must fight in faith at times to hold on to their love, they trust that His love for them is unfailing. Thus, they continue to love and trust Him—even amid times of dryness, doubts, fears, sins, and weaknesses.

The Final Word

Peter's three encouragements can provide joy and serve as an antidote to prevent ministry burnout, and ought to be considered often, particularly by missionaries who live in difficult contexts far from home. In fact, Peter himself returns to these same encouragements in the final chapter of his first epistle, in 5:5–12. If Peter dwells on these encouragements, so ought all servants of Christ:

God is opposed to the proud, but gives grace to the humble. Therefore humble yourselves under the mighty hand of God, that He may exalt you at the proper time, casting all your anxiety on Him, because He cares for you. . . . And after you have suffered for a little while, the God of all grace, who called you to His eternal glory in Christ, will Himself restore, strengthen, confirm, and ground you. To Him be might forever and ever. Amen. . . . I have written to you briefly, exhorting and bearing witness that this is the true grace of God. Stand firm in it!

Ministering the Word in a Time of Crisis: A Pastor's Report from Ukraine

Oleg Kalyn

Paul told Timothy to "preach the word; be ready in season and out of season" (2 Tim 4:2). But what does that look like in a time of war, when a pastor's city is blown to pieces? How does he "reprove, rebuke, [and] exhort" when his church family is losing loved ones daily? The ivory tower theologian can only speculate, but for the church in Ukraine, darkness showed up on its doorstep in the late winter of February 2022. Below is a report from a local church pastor on ministry during those dark days in Kyiv, Ukraine. It is replete with advice for the global church.

QUESTION: *How did you respond to the crisis?*

We had a Bible study the night before the invasion. That evening our church assumed nothing would happen. But when it did, there were three decisions a pastor could make: simply leave—like many pastors did, lead some of your people to a safer place, or stay where you are and minister. John 10:11–13 was running through my mind constantly, where Jesus says, "I am the good shepherd; the good shepherd lays down His life for the sheep. He who is a hired hand, and not a shepherd, who is not the owner of the sheep, sees the wolf coming, and leaves the sheep and flees—and the wolf snatches and scatters them—because he is a hired hand and is not concerned about the sheep."

The Lord was bringing theology to practice. For His Word to inform my life meant staying with my people even if I must lay down my life for them. Such a time could be "out of season" for the Word (2 Tim 4:2), in terms of the convenience of preaching, but it is a time when the people need their pastors the most.

The people of Kyiv also needed light during this very dark time. Enemy soldiers used rape as a means of warfare. They shot and killed male civilians for simply being of a potential age to become soldiers. Rockets were shot into civilian buildings, including a maternity hospital. These atrocities are only a glimpse into the dark depravity of man without Christ.

The church is a light in this darkness

(Matt 5:14; Phil 2:15–16). It is quite different than a charitable organization. Yes, many of my brothers in ministry and I have done "social action" in Ukraine; we have had many practical opportunities to give the needy food, drink, shelter, and clothing (Matt 25:35–36). But Christ's church has a duty to bring the gospel to suffering people, not just physical aid. Food, clothing, shelter, and medicine do not solve the ultimate problem of each person. On one occasion, a woman came up to me and said, "Just give me a pill, something that will make me sleep." What she really needed was peace in her soul amid suffering and danger—the kind that comes only from a saving relationship with the Prince of Peace (Isa 9:6), the Lord of peace (2 Thess 3:16), Jesus Christ (John 14:27).

We pastors have the honor of bringing God's Word into people's lives and thus bringing His peace to them when they need it most. My brothers and I have given many people Bibles and biblical literature, counseled them with Scripture, and witnessed the gospel to them. We have reminded them that God is sovereign and that His plan and purposes are still at work. In this way, when crisis comes, pastors need to be ready and available to minister the Word. It will bear fruit, by God's design (cf. Isa 55:10–11; 2 Tim 3:16–17).

QUESTION: *What does preaching look like when your world is turned "upside down"?*

The normal format we follow for preaching in our church service is verse-by-verse, book-by-book through the Bible. When the war came, people asked us whether we would change our message format. But we did not, and we could never have anticipated how God would make the expository sermon applicable and encouraging to our people. Many times during the crisis, I found myself saying, "I could not think of a better text for today." I always encourage preachers and teachers to likewise continue doing what they are doing when crisis strikes. God uses this ordinary means of grace to accomplish His will, in war or otherwise.

In reality, the war has helped each verse I have preached to come alive for me and also for our church. Every passage has been relevant to our situation. Actually, due to my regular and sequential exposition of Scripture during the first few months of war, I believe I became a better pastor in and out of the pulpit. When one holds an orphan in his arms, he feels the pain of the orphan in Scripture (cf. Ps 27:10; Jas 1:27). Sometimes we pastors do not grasp the implications or appreciate the weight of our texts until we have lived the hardships to which they refer. But God's Word is always relevant (Rom 15:4), and our people's eyes are opened to see this also. Crisis does not call for a drastic change in ministry—we simply read the Word, live the Word, and teach the Word as we ought always to do.

Ultimately, we minister in times of crisis because Christ is the Chief Shepherd of "the flock of God" (Pss 23; 100:3; 1 Pet 2:25; 5:2–4). He is shepherding, feeding, and tending His lambs through undershepherds, which we are (John 10:11; 21:15–17; 1 Pet 5:4). We are simply called to be faithful, administering His words of eternal life (John 6:63, 68). This does not remove the pastor's personal responsibility to labor in the Word. In fact, church members and nonbelievers will bring their pastor many personal matters during seasons of greatest need (like war has been for our people). He therefore needs to know Scripture well so he is able to pray, meditate, and think biblically about the crisis and how to address the problems of the people. Really, though, the only thing that brings lasting comfort and change is contact with the Word of God, which has better words than the preacher. Ultimately, peace and life come from the Chief Shepherd, not the undershepherd.

QUESTION: *How did the war affect your spiritual growth?*

When a pastor experiences war, all of a sudden he has the opportunity to live out his theology as never before. If he has weak theology, it will come out quickly. We found that the crisis intensified our focus on right living and faithful ministering. We grasped more and more that every moment counts—day by day, minute by minute, we are on the cusp of eternity. For me, personally, I became more spiritually disciplined. Quality time with the Lord was not optional for me. My discipleship ties to other pastors and churches deepened. My desire for Bible study grew to new levels. Second Timothy became an especially sweet epistle to me, teaching me how I should be as a pastor during the worst of times. I began reading through the New Testament monthly because I wanted to have its full breadth of understanding in my life and have it fuel my daily encounters.

So, these were some of the manifestations of God's grace in my life during the hard days of war. Crisis should drive pastors deeper into the Bible and into fellowship with like-minded pastors. Living and ministering the Word of God is not optional for us. We cannot back down when crisis comes but must entrust our souls to God and keep doing what He has called us to do: "preach the word; be ready in season and out of season" (2 Tim 4:2).

SECTION 2

CHURCH PLANTING

SUB-SECTION 1: BIBLICAL PARAMETERS FOR CHURCH PLANTING

CHAPTER 33

Church Planting by the Book

Stephen Lonetti

The Great Commission of the Lord Jesus Christ has burned in the hearts of His people through two millennia. Today the gospel advances swiftly when God's people invest in the task. Yet apathy, distraction, and theological weakness in the church are great hindrances. Weak churches send weak missionaries, who then plant weak churches on the field.

One example of the latter is the disciple making movement (DMM),[1] also known as the church planting movement (CPM),[2] a child of the pragmatic church growth focus of the late 1950s.[3] Boasting exponential growth with

---

1. Primary sources on DMM include Jerry Trousdale, *Miraculous Movements: How Hundreds of Thousands of Muslims Are Falling in Love with Jesus* (Nashville: Thomas Nelson, 2012); David Watson and Paul Watson, *Contagious Disciple Making: Leading Others on a Journey of Discovery* (Nashville: Thomas Nelson, 2014).

2. For descriptions of CPM and connections to DMM, see Ted Esler, "Two Church Planting Paradigms," *IJFM* 30, no. 2 (Summer 2013): 67–73; V. David Garrison, *Church Planting Movements* (Richmond, VA: Office of Overseas Operations, International Mission Board of the Southern Baptist Convention, 1999); Garrison, *Church Planting Movements: How God Is Redeeming a Lost World* (Midlothian, VA: WIGTake, 2004); Garrison, *A Wind in the House of Islam: How God Is Drawing Muslims around the World to Faith in Jesus Christ* (Monument, CO: WIGTake, 2014).

3. For the foundations of the church growth movement, see Donald A. McGavran, *Understanding Church Growth*, 3rd ed., rev. and ed. C. Peter Wagner (Grand Rapids: Eerdmans, 1990). See the missiological emphases of the church growth movement by one of its greatest advocates, Wilbert R. Shenk, ed. *Exploring Church Growth* (Grand Rapids, Eerdmans, 1983); Wilbert R. Shenk, "Can These Dry Bones Live Again? The Priority of Renewal," in *Converting Witness: The Future of Christian Mission in the New Millennium*, ed. John G. Flett and David W. Congdon (Lanham, MD: Fortress Academic, 2019), 213–30.

hundreds of thousands of converts and thousands of churches planted, DMM has garnered phenomenal influence with churches, missions agencies, and church planters alike. In the world of DMM, "The disciple-maker [church planter] does not do any of the traditional things required by traditional disciple-making. He does not preach or teach."[4] They claim that Bible preachers and teachers obstruct the gospel: "When working with lost people, we have to avoid falling into the role of explaining Scripture."[5]

However, the Bible certainly does not suggest that Christians discard preaching and teaching.[6] That error leads to false conversions and underlies much of the weakness within church planting today. This chapter will not dwell on the errors inherent within DMM or any other derivative approach. Rather, it looks at church planting in light of Scripture, church planting "by the Book," in order to recover biblical foundations that have been lost and to encourage reconformity to them. These foundations are essentially two doctrines with two spheres of application: first, disciple-making and the local church, and second, the gospel message and the church planter.

Disciple-Making and the Local Church

The Great Commission is the mission of the church. Its central command to be obeyed is: make disciples. Disciples are made by mature believers going into all the world, proclaiming the gospel, baptizing those who have responded in faith, and teaching them all that Christ commanded (Matt 28:18–20) in the context of the local church (16:18; 18:17). This is the basis for all church planting. Yet this foundation—disciple-making in the church—must be laid in order: defining the church first, then church planting second.

Defining the Local Church

The apostles put Christ's commission into action shortly after His ascension. Acts 2 records Peter's first sermon on the day of Pentecost. His clear, Spirit-enabled proclamation of the gospel and call for repentance resulted in the conversion of three thousand souls. This ingathering of disciples in Jerusalem, then, marked the birth of the first New Testament church plant. The marks of transformation in the lives of the new disciples in Acts 2:41–42, 44–47 are instructive for church planters today:

> So then, those who had received his word were baptized; and that day there were added about three thousand souls. And they were continually devoting themselves to the apostles' teaching and to the fellowship, to the breaking of bread and to the prayers. . . . And all those who had believed were together and had

---

4. Garrison, *Wind in the House of Islam*, 127.

5. The authors further comment, "Did you know lost people can evangelize? Well, they can if you keep it simple enough." Watson and Watson, *Contagious Disciple Making*, 146–50.

6. To the contrary, see Matt 28:20; Mark 16:15; Acts 5:42; 10:42; 15:35; 28:31; Rom 15:20; 1 Cor 1:17; Eph 3:8; 1 Tim 3:2; 5:17; 6:2; 2 Tim 2:2; 4:2.

all things in common; and they began selling their property and possessions and were dividing them up with all, as anyone might have need. And daily devoting themselves with one accord in the temple and breaking bread from house to house, they were taking their meals together with gladness and sincerity of heart, praising God and having favor with all the people. And the Lord was adding to their number daily those who were being saved.

After the believers heard and received the gospel—that is, after they were regenerated by the Holy Spirit—they gathered together and devoted themselves to Christ, to the apostles' teaching, and to prayer. They lived in fellowship, deliberately caring for one another. They joyfully served Christ in unity. These marks of life flowed from hearts filled with gratitude and a spiritual hunger that only regeneration can create.

Regenerate, transformed believers will cultivate discipleship relationships in the context of the local church like the one just described. Some today who read Matthew 18:20 out of context might assume that a church exists "where two or three have gathered" in the name of Jesus. Others might believe that a church is born when a father teaches his family the Bible or when a group of "seekers" study the Bible to grow closer to God. But the Bible itself authoritatively defines and depicts the local church,

providing a clear and consistent model to follow, one that began here in Acts 2 in Jerusalem and was repeated in other regions, as recorded throughout the New Testament.

That biblical model defines the local church as an assembly of redeemed individuals indwelt by the Holy Spirit (John 14:17), whom He has baptized into the body of Christ (1 Cor 12:13). It means a local assembly in a specific city or region (cf. 1 Thess 1:1; 1 Pet 1:1),[7] where believers gather regularly for worship, prayer, and instruction (1 Tim 2:1; 4:13; Heb 10:25). They are led and nurtured by biblically qualified male leadership (1 Tim 3:1–10; Titus 1:5–9), participate in the ordinances of baptism and the Lord's Supper (Matt 28:19; Luke 22:19), and hold one another accountable as Christ commanded (Matt 18:15–20).

Such a local church is also "the pillar and support of the truth" in its environment (1 Tim 3:15; cf. Matt 5:13–14; Eph 4:15–16). Thus, it links to the Great Commission in an organic way as its members commit to proclaiming the gospel, both individually and corporately, and then to applying the gospel in discipleship. Rolland McCune highlighted the local assembly's role in making disciples by stating that it is "the only God-appointed institution authorized to carry out His program of witness and service on earth during this present age. . . . The local church becomes the base of operations for these converts to go out and win [other] converts to Christ."[8]

---

7. The use of the word *church* in this chapter generally refers to the local or visible church, not the universal or invisible church comprised of all who have been baptized into the body of Christ beginning at Pentecost (1 Cor 12:13; cf. Eph 1:22–23; Col 1:18).

8. Rolland McCune, *A Systematic Theology of Biblical Christianity*, vol. 3 (Detroit: Detroit Baptist Theological Seminary, 2010), 195.

Planting the Local Church

According to the New Testament model, church planting is the founding of an assembly of believers in a new location. The objective of the church planter is to establish and organize a self-governing, self-supporting, and self-propagating church that will live out the discipleship model of the Great Commission. A church planter then often goes on to repeat the process of church planting elsewhere. When targeting unreached people groups, this is called *pioneer missions* or *frontier missions*.[9] According to the biblical pattern, there are five steps in the birth and development of a church plant.

LOCAL CHURCHES COMMISSION DISCIPLE-MAKERS

The role of the sending church in assessing potential church planters cannot be overstated. The immensity of the church planter's task requires they first be tested and approved (2 Tim 2:15). Personal desire to serve Christ as a missionary is not sufficient. The book of Acts does not record a single case of a missionary acting on his own initiative or because of subjective compulsion.

Churches must uphold the nonnegotiable, biblical qualifications described in 1 Timothy 3:1–7 and Titus 1:5–9. They must look for men who are committed to sound doctrine, are elder qualified, and are not novices. If a man is to be an effective leader, he must lead through his mature Christian character. Furthermore, churches must ensure the potential church planter is prepared for a long-term commitment, especially if language learning is necessary. It will take a significant portion of his life to evangelize and establish a church that is able to stand on its own. The task of church planting is an intense and demanding ministry endeavor. The planter needs both the affirmation of his church leaders and a clear understanding of his task.

DISCIPLE-MAKERS PROCLAIM THE GOSPEL

Evangelism involves proclaiming the gospel of Jesus Christ in a clear way to unbelievers. "It is a work of communication in which Christians make themselves mouthpieces for God's message of mercy to sinners."[10] It includes a call to turn and trust, a summons to repentance and faith in the work of Jesus Christ for the forgiveness of sins and the gift of eternal life.

BELIEVERS ARE GATHERED AND TAUGHT (DISCIPLED) AS A CHURCH

Luke writes that the believers in the Jerusalem church "were continually devoting themselves

---

9. However, A. Scott Moreau distinguishes frontier missions, which "are focused on crossing significant cultural barriers to plant churches," as a subset of pioneer missions, which do not necessarily have such a focus. Moreau, "Pioneer Mission Work," *Evangelical Dictionary of World Missions*, ed. A. Scott Moreau (Grand Rapids: Baker, 2000), 759–60. John Piper also refers to pioneer or frontier missions as a "Paul-type missionary," one who continually goes to new cultures to plant churches where Christ has not been named (Rom 15:20–21). This he contrasts with the "Timothy-type missionary," who goes cross-culturally to minister but remains long after a church has been planted with its own elders and outreach (e.g., Ephesus, Acts 19:10; 20:17). John Piper, *Brothers, We Are Not Professionals: A Plea to Pastors for Radical Ministry* (Nashville: Broadman and Holman, 2002), 192–93; John Piper, *Let the Nations Be Glad! The Supremacy of God in Missions* (Grand Rapids: Baker, 1993), 192–96.

10. J. I. Packer, *Evangelism and the Sovereignty of God* (Downers Grove, IL: InterVarsity, 2001), 45.

to the apostles' teaching" (Acts 2:42). The apostles taught them to observe all Christ had commanded (Matt 28:20). Teaching simply means giving a thorough explanation of the Word of God. It links the Word of God to Christian living, and this application is itself sound doctrine. It includes correcting error and explaining how to live and think rightly. God's Word, faithfully taught, will result in a life that follows God and is "equipped for every good work" (2 Tim 3:16–17).

As in first-century Jerusalem, so today a spiritually healthy church grows from spiritually healthy Christians—Christians devoted to biblical priorities. Thus, Christians who are sustained and nurtured by "the apostles' teaching" do not see their church as an appendage to life. Rather, the church is their life.

CHURCH LEADERSHIP IS CULTIVATED AND CONFIRMED

The Holy Spirit guides the church planter in cultivating leadership from within the church plant itself (Acts 20:28). Potential elders will need to meet the same biblical qualifications (1 Tim 3:1–7; Titus 1:5–9; 1 Pet 5:1–3). They need to receive training that is not merely academic but that involves real-life ministry experience with the church planter (2 Tim 3:10).

THE CHURCH MATURES AND SENDS OUT MORE DISCIPLE-MAKERS

Mature churches are marked by a few key hallmarks. First, they are filled with a growing numbers of believers who are progressing in Christian character and serving faithfully in the church. Second, the mature church is governed by unified and confirmed elders within the assembly who lead, feed, and protect the church. Third, the mature church is sustained by the members of the church, who work together to support the needs of their pastors and the ministry itself. Fourth, the mature church plants new churches. In the biblical pattern, disciples become disciple-makers who reproduce themselves by planting new churches.

The Gospel Message and the Church Planter

If the mission of the church is to make disciples of all nations, then accurately proclaiming the gospel is foundational too. Gospel proclamation precedes and is essential to the making of disciples in a new place, that is, planting a church. Moreover, Jesus commanded that one gospel be proclaimed to all the nations where disciples were to be made (Luke 24:45–49). Neither the gospel itself nor the biblical pattern for proclaiming it changes based on one's context. In fact, whether evangelizing an "unchurched" (pagan) audience, where biblical knowledge never existed, or a so-called post-church (also pagan) audience, where that knowledge has been lost and rejected, the unredeemed have no foundation for the absolute truth that the gospel is. Preaching and teaching it therefore presents a series of challenges for the church planter. Below are three such challenges and biblical solutions for how the church planter should navigate his mission field with an accurate presentation of the gospel.

The Loss of Truth in Westernized Societies

Moral relativism has been the prevailing worldview in the West for decades, coinciding with the secularization of society in the postmodern age, and understanding this trend helps to explain the challenges of communicating biblical truth in many parts of the world that have experienced Western influence.[11] Underlying moral relativism is the rejection of any truth claim to be valid for all people groups, cultures, and traditions—or even for all of the individuals who make up such a group. Thus, in abandoning the biblical worldview—once generally adopted on an intellectual and moral level in the West—many people have abandoned objective truth. By abandoning objective truth, they have detached themselves from reality. Such thinking has trickled down from academia to popular culture, permeating song lyrics, films, and mass media, creating a devastating effect on younger generations who know nothing else. The resulting social disintegration and moral decline in many westernized societies can be traced directly to the wholesale rejection of God's authority and design for humanity, irrespective of time or place.

Evangelists and pastors face that rejection when communicating the gospel to everyday people. Because moral relativists disdain the authoritative claims of Scripture, the veracity of God's Word, evangelists and pastors continue to encounter new forms of an old phenomenon, namely, Lucifer's deceitful question to the woman in Genesis 3:1, "Indeed, has God said . . . ?" and Pilate's question to Jesus in John 18:38, "What is truth?"

The Lack of Authority in the Church

Pastors influenced by the West's loss of truth often succumb to the tendency to preach "in conversation" with the congregation, as if the audience were an equal participant in the process of preaching, acting as the co-interpreter and decision-maker of a text.[12] Such an "inductive preaching" method advances the idea that authority shifts away from the Scriptures, as delivered by pastors and missionaries, and given, at least in part, to the listeners in the congregation.[13] This approach of downplaying authoritative biblical proclamation has likewise been exported across the globe through DMM and other missions models that prefer a preacher-audience dialogue method to authoritative preaching.

What necessarily follows is biblical illiteracy in the churches. The inevitable outcome of weak preaching that lacks the authority of

---

11. Some evangelicals have appealed to the postmodern thinker when expressing biblical truth but have compromised absolute truth in the process. E.g., Alister McGrath, *A Passion for Truth: The Intellectual Coherence of Evangelicalism* (Downers Grove, IL: InterVarsity, 1996); Stanley J. Grenz and John R. Franke, *Beyond Foundationalism: Shaping Theology in a Postmodern Context* (Louisville, KY: Westminster John Knox, 2001); John R. Franke, "Reforming Theology: Toward a Postmodern Reformed Dogmatics," *WTJ* 65, no. 1 (Spring 2003): 1–26.

12. Fred B. Craddock, *As One without Authority*, 4th ed., revised and with new sermons (St. Louis, MO: Chalice, 2001), viii.

13. For a conservative critique of the effects of truth loss on biblical proclamation, see R. Albert Mohler Jr., *He Is Not Silent: Preaching in a Postmodern World* (Chicago: Moody, 2008).

Scripture is both a lack of confidence in the Bible and a growing unwillingness by church members to read it for themselves. The missiological problem is most evident when churches that are influenced by truth loss commission church planters to "make disciples." The question is whether such church planters even understand the authority of Scripture in their own lives, to then know how to bring it to bear in the lives of new believers.

The Lack of Connection to the Worldview of the Audience

The communication of biblical truth is not complete without considering the listener's worldview—the cluster of beliefs he holds about the most significant concepts of life, such as God, values, and morality. A person's worldview undergirds his presuppositions and informs the whole of his life. If church planters fail to understand that they are speaking an alien message to an alien culture, they risk talking only to themselves or worse.

For example, using foreign-born terminology to communicate biblical concepts is dangerous because it might conflict with the local usage of such words and because the meanings of those words might connect to a different, inappropriate set of presuppositions. In this way, an evangelist might unintentionally plant an unbiblical understanding of gospel vocabulary into his audience—such as with the terms *sin, judgment, substitutionary atonement,* and *justification by faith.* The evangelists themselves might understand the biblical gospel, the meaning of the words they use, and the

biblical concepts the words represent, but the locals might assign a false meaning to them. Assuming that essential biblical concepts can be understood by merely speaking biblical words to the target audience is therefore unrealistic.

Furthermore, huge communication gaps happen when evangelists assume a biblical foundation that does not exist. The need for a Savior is not perceived as necessary where sin is not understood. Sin cannot be understood where the greatness and holiness of God is not understood. Biblically illiterate nonbelievers must acquire this body of knowledge for their worldview to be challenged and replaced. Whether confronting the worldview of a moral relativist, an animist, or any other view that is antithetical to the truth of the Bible, the newly planted church can expect it to take much time and effort to lay the necessary foundation. To put it simply, the gospel must be taught from start to finish, and teaching through select redemptive narratives in the Old Testament and Gospels is a proven way to do this.

Redemptive Narratives and the Gospel Message

A God-given, ready-made solution to the above challenges is to teach the gospel by the Book. Old Testament and gospel narratives provide the foundation and chronology necessary to understand the Bible's greater storyline of the redemptive plan of God. This is basic pedagogy. Students learn the Bible's metanarrative sequentially, story by story, concept by concept. Biblical narratives impart theological content through historical actions and relationships.

For, in Scripture, God reveals His character as He relates to people in real life, not by recording His attributes in a systematic list. Then, as God's moral perfections, such as His truthfulness, holiness, justice, mercy, and grace, are expressed in life-related actions, so are His moral commands.

Redemptive narratives also include several vital biblical-theological concepts. Theological terms are infused by biblical history with their accurate meanings in a way that people can understand, regardless of their worldview. When these concepts and divine attributes are exposited from scriptural narratives, they also stand on God's authority, not the missionary's.

The approach unfolds quite simply. First, redemptive narratives teach that God is a sovereign Creator and that mankind is fallen and needs redemption. Genesis 1–11 establishes God's creative work, beneficence, and sovereign reign; the entrance and spread of sin; the origin of judgment and death; the continued rebellion of man; and the meaning of the atonement. Second, redemptive narratives teach that God is a holy Lawgiver who called and preserved Israel to be His chosen channel for redemption to all peoples. Genesis 12 through the rest of the Old Testament narrates how the Law reveals God's holiness and righteous standard, how it exposes sin, and how it is a tutor that leads to salvation by faith. Third, redemptive narratives teach that God is a loving Redeemer who purchased salvation for all whom He called by grace through faith. The Gospels narrate the incarnation of God's Son, the promised Messiah; His sinless life; His substitutionary, atoning death; His resurrection; and the way of salvation through repentance and faith alone in Him.

It is important to understand that the above manner of gospel proclamation through teaching redemptive narratives is not "storying" the gospel. The latter is a recent, popular approach to evangelism, whereby the storyteller communicates biblical narratives in his own words, bypassing the process of translation and exposition, for fear that the written Word would not be effective in a culture of orally based traditions.[14] No, the preacher must do the work of an expositor in every scriptural

14. Some uses of this terminology do encourage Scripture memorization and recitation, even of entire narrative passages. At other times, *storying* seems intended to describe simply a chronological Bible-teaching approach, as advocated here. Still, at other times, the term means "the discipler's own experience with God," and often, Bible teaching that crafts the narrative for "cultural relevance" and the audience's "felt needs." For most users, it is intended to be nonconfrontational and "not preaching," and some even continue to use it within established congregations of believers, downplaying the written Word. This not only subverts the Bible's authority and apologizes for God's method of communication to His church, but it deprives believers of the means He has provided to fully equip them individually and together: "Scripture" (*graphē*, literally "what is written;" 2 Tim 3:16–17). See, for example, the mixed analysis and sources gathered in the following: Lausanne Committee for World Evangelism, Issue Group on Making Disciples of Oral Learners, "Making Disciples of Oral Learners," Lausanne Occasional Paper 54, ed. David Claydon (a paper produced at the 2004 Forum for World Evangelization, Pattaya, Thailand, September 29–October 5, 2004), https://www.lausanne.org/docs/2004forum/LOP54_IG25.pdf; Rick Brown, "Communicating God's Message in an Oral Culture," *IJFM* 12, no. 3 (Fall 2004): 122–28; Robin Hadaway, *A Survey of World Missions* (Nashville: B&H Academic, 2020), 250–51.

narrative he presents. He is to exegete the truth, deliver it with clarity and authority, and apply it against the worldview of his audience. As the exemplary British expositor D. Martyn Lloyd-Jones cautions, "He [the preacher] is a man who is there to declare certain things; he is a man under commission and under authority. He is an ambassador, and he should be aware of his authority."[15] Namely, a preacher's only authority is the Bible, the God-given message he declares. His personal opinions, advice, experiences, and exhortations carry no authority whatsoever in any context. As soon as he strays from the biblical text, all authority evaporates.

Scripture itself is the Holy Spirit's powerful tool for preparing unbelievers to hear the gospel. Through reading and explaining biblical passages, the teacher educates the conscience of the hearers through direct contact with the inspired text. All the while, the teacher is praying that the truth will penetrate the listener's mind as the Spirit begins His convicting, affirming, and transforming work. Because truth is by nature authoritative, it is naturally antagonistic to the unbeliever (1 Cor 2:14; Titus 3:3). Teachers should expect resistance as the content of the gospel is proclaimed, even through narratives. Still, some listeners will be drawn toward God. They will become convinced of the truth as the Holy Spirit reveals it and prepares them to respond to the gospel, and then they will respond to the grace of God by faith in the Lord Jesus Christ (Rom 10:17; cf. Acts 17:34).

Conclusion

Church planting by the Book requires preaching and teaching. This means discipleship in local, healthy churches that are defined by Scripture, and it means faithful, expository gospel proclamation from Scripture by church planters. As J. I. Packer notes, the gospel must be "learned before it can be lived, and understood before it can be applied. . . . Hence Paul, as a preacher of it, had to become a teacher. He saw this as part of his calling: he speaks of 'the gospel, for which I was appointed a preacher . . . *and teacher*' (2 Tim 1:10–11)."[16] When missionaries and their sending churches realize the centrality of teaching biblically, they will recover and reconform to the biblical foundations for the entire church-planting enterprise.

Finally, church planters should remember that the work of redemption belongs to God. Evangelists are tasked with telling the truth as accurately and boldly as possible. But they are not responsible for regenerating their audiences. Their confidence must be in the power of the gospel (Rom 1:16). No godless philosophy is able to stand against the unadulterated Word, which clearly presents the gospel of God. As Charles Spurgeon eloquently said, the faithful evangelist is to trust the message:

---

15. D. Martyn Lloyd-Jones, *Preaching and Preachers* (Grand Rapids: Zondervan, 1971), 83.
16. Packer, *Evangelism and the Sovereignty of God*, 50–51, emphasis in original.

A great many learned men are defending the gospel; no doubt it is a very proper and right thing to do, yet I always notice that . . . it is because the gospel itself is not being preached. . . . The best "apology" for the gospel is to let the gospel out. . . . Preach Jesus Christ and Him crucified. Let the Lion out, and see who will dare to approach Him. The Lion of the tribe of Judah will soon drive away all His adversaries.[17]

---

17. C. H. Spurgeon, "Christ and His Co-Workers," *Metropolitan Tabernacle Pulpit*, vol. 42 (1896; repr. Pasadena, TX: Pilgrim, 1976), 253–64; online at The Spurgeon Center for Biblical Preaching at Midwestern Seminary, https://www.spurgeon.org/resource-library/sermons/christ-and-his-co-workers/#flipbook/12.

INSERT 33.1

Partnering in Church Planting: The Benefits of a Shared Ministry

Eduardo Izquierdo and David Perez

During the last days of March 2020 the first pandemic-related deaths were announced in Mexico. Undoubtedly, that spring was a time of great anguish for the world's population. Fear led to the closure of hundreds of businesses, offices, schools, and churches. As stress and anxiety began to invade the minds of people around the world, these words of Jesus became a comfort for thousands: "Come to me, all who are weary and heavy-laden, and I will give you rest" (Matt 11:28).

Years beforehand, the Lord in His grace had brought the two of us, Eduardo and David, to The Master's Seminary to prepare for the work of ministry. Both of us came from the city of Monterrey, Mexico, but it was in California that we met. Along with our families, we arrived on the campus, shared with Grace Community Church, without yet having concrete plans for our future. That friendship plus the COVID-19 pandemic, in God's providence, led to a church-planting partnership with many inherent blessings for which we will always be grateful.

A Common Burden

If there was one thing the Lord had placed upon the hearts of both of us, it was the need for biblical churches in our home city. Truthfully, neither of us had ever attended a biblical church before our years at seminary. We had never before known the kind of pastoral care we received from men who faithfully expounded the Scriptures at Grace. Nevertheless, while we rejoiced and thanked God for such a great privilege, we always felt a burden pointing us back home. We continually prayed that the Lord would guide our steps to serve in our city. Without our realizing it, those difficult days in March 2020 were the opening of a door.

Hearing about closed churches and learning about the spiritual needs of family and friends back home in Monterrey was common that spring. There seemed to be no more appropriate time to start an online Bible study to share hope and life than in such need. From our combined network of relationships, our Bible study began with four or five families on a group call every Thursday. Eventually it served as the seed and preparation for the planting of Iglesia Bíblica de Monterrey.

Plurality of Leadership

Scripture is clear regarding the principle of a plurality of leaders in churches and of pastors entrusting the work of the ministry to still others (Acts 14:23; 2 Tim 2:2; Titus 1:5). The Lord placed in the hearts of both of us the desire to serve in pastoral ministry, and we prioritized that any church plant we attempted would follow the biblical model. Again, because of our partnership, there were months of prayer for one another when, despite the discouragements that arose, we found hope in the Lord, who guards and sustains us until the final day (Phil 1:6; 1 Thess 5:24). Then, by God's grace, we were ordained to pastoral ministry by the elders at Grace before moving our families back to Mexico in 2022.

Partners in Preparation

What came prior to planting the church was not easy, but because we were partners, we bore the burden together (Eccl 4:9–10). We met once a week to plan and serve the Spanish ministry of Grace Community Church. We also trained our Monterrey planting team remotely from California. We thank God for granting us the wisdom and strength to coordinate during those nearly two busy years. We ended the Bible study at the beginning of 2022, and on Sunday, February 13, of that year, Iglesia Bíblica de Monterrey gathered as a local church for the first time in person, one week after the Izquierdo family arrived home.

During the planning stage, we prayed and considered locations for Sunday meetings, taking into account factors and costs. Initially we thought a home would be ideal, but we soon realized that more people would arrive that first Sunday than a home would accommodate. After visiting several sites, the good hand of the Lord granted us favor and a place at a lower price than the one initially offered (Ezra 7:9).

Sharing of Labors

Membership is a biblical doctrine (Acts 2:41–42; 16:5; Rom 16:1; Col 4:12; 1 Tim 5:9), but it has not been understood or practiced in our city. Therefore, it took time to establish it in the church. After a year and six months, we officially had our first right hand of fellowship (Gal 2:9), which is our final stage of the membership process. The process consists of four membership classes, reading our doctrinal statement, filling out an application, and, finally, an interview with the pastors. Throughout the process, each of us played important roles that included teaching and interviewing membership candidates.

The Word of God teaches that spiritual leadership within society and the family rests with men (Gen 2:23–24; Eph 5:23–28, cf. Isa 3:1–12). So we decided to prioritize and start Bible studies with the men in the congregation. The Lord had prepared their hearts for this moment, for attendance was greater than we expected. Nine months passed, and then, by God's grace, we began other meetings with various groups, such as servants (ushers or volunteers), women, youth, and married couples, all centered on the exposition of God's Word (1 Tim 4:13 and 2 Tim 4:2). In addition to the various teaching opportunities during the week, prior to weekly worship we hold a Sunday school class. This gives each of us opportunities to preach. We thank God for the opportunity to serve together in this way.

Conclusion

Planting Iglesia Bíblica de Monterrey would have been an almost impossible load for one person to carry. Despite trials and discouragements, mutual encouragement sustained us. The Lord always showed and continues to show His grace, upon which we are depending day by day. The final benefit to our partnership is that the two of us can look back and remind one another poignantly that each of these developments—and many more—have all been "according to the good hand of our God upon us" (Ezra 8:18).

CHAPTER 34

Essential Principles for Church Planting

Carl A. Hargrove

This chapter outlines the essential principles for planting churches. They are essential, that is, if God is to be honored in the process, leaders are to be developed, gospel proclamation is to be extended into communities lacking local churches, and churches are to be established for long-term gospel witness. However, this outline is limited. What follows are merely the essentials, whether in the domestic or international harvest fields.

Because some view church planting as extracurricular in terms of ministry vision and preparation, it does not receive the treatment of the fundamental facet of Great Commission work that it actually is. Teaching the essentials to students and missionaries needs to be prioritized in theological training and Christian resourcing. Since church planting is essential to the church's call to evangelize the world (Acts 1:8; 13:1–3; 14:21–23), every minister should have some level of training and exposure to it. In fact, no legitimate reason can be offered for not directly or indirectly supporting

church planting. Either a church will directly plant churches, or it must financially support others that do. In either case, this work requires biblical guidance.

In the same way that a missionary defines his philosophy of ministry by understanding biblical texts and the principles derived from those texts, the missions-oriented pastor must develop a "ministry philosophy" for planting churches. That said, this chapter offers nine essential principles for planting churches biblically.

A High View of God

First, every church plant must make it their supreme motivation to operate with a high view of God from the very start. In reality, every aspect of Christian ministry is beholden to proclaim the greatness of God's character, His redemptive plan, and the response that is due Him (Acts 9:15; 28:31; Rom 2:1–16; 15:20–21; Eph 3:8–10). In planting churches in particular, starting with a high view of God establishes the proper motivation and authority for decision-making in the church. The Father, after all, gave the Son to be head of the church, and it belongs to Him (Eph 1:22; Col 1:18, 24). The local church with a high view of God, then, will have as a consistent objective the presentation of the Savior as a God of holiness, righteousness, and justice (Isa 6:1–4; Rom 3:21–26; 1 Pet 1:15). This will motivate congregants to live lives of practical holiness and to avoid sin (1 Pet 1:15), but also to avoid man-centered ministry, which fails to exalt God and instead comforts sinful man.

A high view of God will also help the church planter personally. It will move him to resilience in proclaiming truth and avoiding the temptation of pleasing men (Acts 5:29; Gal 1:10; 1 Thess 2:4). With a high view of God, sin will be addressed faithfully, that is, using the language of Scripture and not the trending, accommodating vocabulary of the culture. The excellencies of Christ will be preached, at once, as the authority and spiritual food for those in the church; as the minister does so, he himself will be drawn to the person of Christ, and his faith will be nurtured and will be capable of sustaining him through his journey (1 Tim 4:6).

A High View of Scripture

Second, every church plant must begin with a high view of Scripture. Church planting that is not ordered by Scripture is not merely extra-biblical but unbiblical and will not glorify God despite any numerical growth it may see (2 Tim 4:3). The church planter's authority must be the divinely inspired Word of God. This is important since he enters a spiritual battle with only one weapon, the sword of the Spirit (Eph 6:17). The church-planting pastor will encounter opposition to the gospel message he carries (Matt 24:9–10; Acts 20:28–31; 1 Cor 16:9; Eph 6:10–18), but he must accept the Scriptures for everything they are: besides his weapon, nourishment for his own soul (Job 23:12; Pss 19:7; 119; Jer 15:16), the wisdom Christ's disciples need (Ps 19:7; Prov 2:6–7; John 6:68), and the spiritual compass for leading the church (1 Tim 3:14–15; 2 Tim 2:15; 4:1–5; Titus 1:9).

One church plant that began on the westside of Inglewood, California, had this motto: "Where the Bible is the authority."[1] This was more than a tagline. The leadership made an intentional statement in contrast to the norms of authority in other area churches, such as the pastor himself or personal revelations. In this simple, summary approach, the Scriptures were presented to the people as inherently authoritative, as demanding absolute obedience, and as relevant, addressing every life challenge. For, though Scripture does not specifically address every question that arises in life, its principles are sufficient for guiding the church to live in a manner that will glorify God (2 Pet 1:3). Church planters must live as if God's Word is absolutely sufficient and authoritative, because it is.

---

1. I planted Westside Bible Church in 1993 and resigned in 2006. It remains a beacon of hope in a community in need, having merged with another biblical church six years later and being known now as Community of Faith Bible Church.

A Qualified Leader

Third, every church plant must start with a qualified leader. This is to say that not every missionary is a candidate for planting churches. Just as every pastor is not gifted to be a lead pastor, so not every missionary is gifted to be a founding pastor. Even if a man possesses some practical attributes key to the church-planting enterprise—he is a self-starter, can communicate a biblical vision, has a passion for the lost, is capable of developing leaders, and thrives on preaching the gospel—he must first be a biblically qualified elder.

The church planter is a man who meets the demands of God's clear expectations in Scripture found in 1 Timothy 3:1–7 and Titus 1:5–9. He is a man who demonstrates humble reliability on the Savior's grace. He has experienced the saving call of God in his life as one calling others to faith in the Lord. Church planters are men who, like every genuinely called minister of the gospel, possess a resiliency for the cause of Christ—he is not a man to be deterred. He is a man called from above and from among; that is, he has a divine call complemented by a call of peers and church leaders who recognize that the Lord has set him apart for the work. An element of their recognition stems from observing his spiritual and natural abilities to fulfill the work faithfully. The church planter is a man with a heart for the people of God. He strongly desires to care for the sheepfold (1 Pet 5:2).

Thus, a church planter should be observed, vetted, and nominated for planting a church before he takes on this privilege and responsibility for the Father's house. The spiritual qualifications of a pastor are simply unbending requirements for this honorable and challenging work.

A Biblical Burden (Vision)

A fourth essential is that every church plant must arise from a biblical burden or vision. The hearts of all genuine missionaries have a burden for a particular people—they have a passion for proclaiming Christ to that people for His glory (Rom 15:20–21; 1 Cor 9:16). Whether as translators, administrators, educators, church planters, or pastors strengthening a church, such men and women have left family and all that is familiar to them to honor Christ in the harvest fields, domestic and foreign (cf. 3 John 7). They, like Paul, are a people driven by the glory of God and the love of Christ (2 Cor 5:14). This is a biblical burden. The church planter in particular has a vision for the people in need of gospel representation, that is, for people in whose proximity there is no faithful, gospel-witnessing church (Rom 15:20–21).

Despite the negative connotations of the word *vision* today, as in something ethereal, a term used to promote aspiration in the business world, or a means to promote personal goals, it is nonetheless an acceptable way to capture the burden any mature Christian, particularly the minister-missionary, has for gospel ministry. It is merely something like John Knox's burden for Scotland, William Carey's for India, David Brainard's for Native Americans, and Hudson Taylor's for China, to name only a few. Paul had a burden for his fellow Israelites, which informed his prayer for them and made him willing even to die for the proclamation of Christ to them (Rom 9:1–5). Church planters are not simply men fulfilling an administrative directive to reach a particular area. They have a heart for its people, a prayer, and a passion for proclaiming the saving knowledge of Christ to them.

Of course, burdens for a people group may grow over time. History is full of men who never thought they would minister to certain people but ended up with an undeniable passion for them. Yet a church must never commission a man who needs to be convinced that he is the right person to meet some need. A man may need encouragement for the task ahead, as it may seem overwhelming to him, but a burden for the people must reside deeply within him.

Core Values

A fifth essential is that every church plant must establish its core values. Core values are biblical anchors for body life and outreach. Though the phrase is modern, the concept of articulating what is of "first importance," in doctrine and in ministry practice, is scriptural (cf. 1 Cor 15:3; Gal 2:9–10). By articulating core values, the church plant says to itself and to its surrounding community, "These truths are dear to us, we want to understand them deeper, and it is our prayer that you will adopt them too." For example, the core values of one church plant serve as excellent examples of biblical values for internal and external use:

We value God's Word, the Bible, as solely authoritative and sufficient in all matters of belief and behavior for every believer's enjoyment of God and for the ministry of the church (Ps 119; 2 Tim 3:16, 17; 1 Pet 2:2; 2 Pet 1:24).

We value prayer as the visible engine of all our efforts in ministry and worship (Acts 2:42; Eph 6:18–20; Phil 4:6; Col 4:2; 1 Thess 5:16–18). Fully relying on the Holy Spirit (1 Cor 2:14–16; Zech 4:6; Eph 3:16; 1 Pet 4:10–11).

We value personal and corporate worship of God, which engages both the mind and the heart (John 4:23–24; Jam 4:8; Ps 16:11; 2 Tim 4:1–4).

We value Christ-centered relationships, especially through the regular gathering of small groups focused on God's Word, prayer, and mutual love (John 13:34; Eph 5:1–2; 1 Thess 5:11; Heb 10:23–25; Jas 5:16).

We value husbands, wives, and children fulfilling their biblical roles in the family and in the church (Deut 6:4–9; Ps 78:1–9; Eph 6:4; 2 Tim 3:14–15).

We value every believer faithfully serving in the body of Christ (Rom 12:9–13; 1 Pet 4:11–12; 1 Cor 12:7; Eph 4:11–13).

We value corporately developing biblical knowledge, character, and actions that imitate Christ (Eph 4:12; Col 1:28).

We value reaching those who do not know Christ in our communities and throughout the world (Matt 28:19–20; Acts 1:8; Rom 10:1; Col 4:2–4).

We value the submission to Christ's leadership, which is carried out by a biblically qualified team of elders (Acts 20:28; 1 Tim 3:1–7; Titus 1:5–9; 1 Pet 5:1–3; Heb 13:17).

We value equipping leaders in the context of the local church (Eph 4:11–12; 1 Tim 5:17).[2]

A Core Team

Sixth, every church plant must begin with building a core team. Having co-laborers with a similar passion as that of the founding pastor is essential to the plant's development. Indeed, the church planters in Scripture went out in teams. Paul did so with at least Barnabas, John Mark, Timothy, Luke, Sopater, Aristarchus, Secundus, Gaius, Tychicus, and Trophimus (Acts 13:1–3; 20:4; Phlm 24). These co-laborers then appointed multiple elders (other teams) in the churches they planted (Acts 14:23; cf. Titus 1:5). Jesus set the precedent for this plurality of elders by calling and commissioning a team of men to reach the world with His good news (Matt 28:16–20; cf. 10:1–42), and, in fact, several of those men pastored the Jerusalem church together as a team (Acts 15:4, 7, 13; 1 Pet 5:1). Besides following these New Testament examples, a core team will afford accountability (Eph 5:21), mutual encouragement (e.g., Acts 16:25), and the advantage of the Spirit's diverse spiritual giftings (Rom 12:4–8; 1 Cor 12:4–31.; 1 Pet 4:10–11; cf. 1 Tim 5:17).

Paul always ministered for a time in the newly planted churches before moving on, and for some of them, he later wrote letters of organization and instruction (e.g., Ephesians, Colossians, 1 and 2 Timothy, Titus). It is noteworthy that when he wrote to key people in those churches, he expressed expectations of them as any modern church planter would of his core team: prayer requests, encouragements, and instructions for the work (e.g., Rom 16, esp. vv. 1–2, 17–20). Of course, Paul had enduring apostolic authority over these churches long after he left. But church planters should emulate Paul at least by developing deep and abiding relationships in ministry leadership (core teams) and motivating the churches to follow the examples of those leaders, even as the leaders follow the example of Christ (1 Cor 11:1; Phil 3:17).

An Indigenous End Goal

Seventh, missionaries must strive to plant indigenous churches. Missionaries sometimes go, plant, build, and stay on as a pastor somewhere, having adopted the new country as their home and place of death. However, the leadership and future of the planted church must be in the hands of the people that comprise it—a mature local church is an indigenous-led church.

Reaching maturity is why, for instance, the modern concept of multisite megachurches is not theologically sound. From the onset, it is unsound because the clear and necessary call to shepherd the flock in an intimate manner is lost for the governing elders (1 Pet 5:2). Streaming services into multisites and treating them as if they are

---

2. "What We Teach," City Bible Church Sacramento, accessed June 18, 2024, https://www.citybiblesacramento.com/what-we-teach. Used with permission of City Bible Church of Sacramento, California, with pastor Vlad Burlaka.

no different than a multiservice congregation is a disservice. Even multiservice congregations have challenges, yet the shepherding leaders can at least interface with the members on a given Sunday and make themselves readily available any other day of the week. The multisite model places a noticeable if not extreme strain on local church fellowship (which is beyond obvious, then, with multicity sites).[3]

The planted church must be a self-governing assembly according to the New Testament model for biblical eldership (Titus 1:5–9). This will occur only if the church planter invests in developing indigenous leadership from within it and in continual training for the growing body. Here the pattern of Paul's church-planting strategy should be emulated again. The church at Ephesus is a prime example, from which missiologist David Hesselgrave draws the following eight strategic steps:[4]

1. Audience contacted (Acts 18:19; 19:1, 8–9)
2. Gospel communicated (Acts 19:4, 9–10)
3. Hearers converted (Acts 19:5, 18)
4. Believers congregated (Acts 19:9–10)
5. Faith confirmed (Acts 20:20, 27)
6. Leadership consecrated (Acts 20:17, 28; 1 Tim 1:3–4; 2:2)
7. Believers commended (Acts 20:1, 25, 32)
8. Relationships continued (Acts 20:17; Eph 1:1–3, 15–16)

A church matured on sound doctrine will naturally be self-propagating and self-supporting. This does not mean that other local churches or missionaries cannot help a church grow to this point. Just as the churches of Macedonia helped believers in Jerusalem (2 Cor 8–9), so congregations and parachurch organizations can help a young church grow without stifling its potential future growth. However, it is a disservice to any local body if those helpers never expect the church to support itself.

One of the common significant errors of church planting in the mission field is a failure to prepare churches for a transition to indigenous leadership when the missionary departs. But biblical ecclesiology will naturally correct this shortsightedness so that church plants mature and reproduce long after the founding pastor leaves. Biblical ecclesiology may be divided into nine subjects: its definition, purpose, spiritual authority, biblical dynamics, means of grace in church life, unity and purity, membership, spiritual gifts, and preview to heaven.[5] When studied properly, it will produce a desire to support church planting.

---

3. Johnathan Leeman, "Theological Critique of Multi-Site: What Exactly Is a 'Church'?," *9Marks Journal* (May–June 2009), archived at 9Marks.org, September 30, 2010, https://www.9marks.org/article/theological-critique-multi-site-what-exactly-church/; Leeman, "The Alternative: Why Don't We Plant?," *9Marks Journal* (May–June 2009), archived at 9Marks.org, February 26, 2010, https://www.9marks.org/article/alternative-why-dont-we-plant/.

4. List reproduced from David Hesselgrave, *Planting Churches Cross-Culturally: North America and Beyond*, 2nd ed. (Grand Rapids: Baker, 2000), 49.

5. John MacArthur and Richard Mayhue, eds., *Biblical Doctrine: A Systematic Summary of Bible Truth* (Wheaton, IL: Crossway, 2017), 739–820.

Cross-Cultural Adaptation

An eighth principle is that every church planter must prepare for cross-cultural adaptation. One of the beauties of the body of Christ is the church's natural diversity brought about by God's expansive plan of redemption in a world of varying cultures, social statuses, and backgrounds (1 Cor 1:26; Rev 5:9). Today, like no other time in history, as people migrate and the nations meet in cities worldwide, most missions training recognizes that cultural adaptation is expected of nonindigenous students, so curriculum is appropriately developed. The missionary knows he will submerge himself in a culture that is, in most cases, unlike his own. This does not change any of the principles presented here, but it may call for adjustments in how they are communicated and applied.

One model of preparing for this adjustment in culture can be found at Grace Advance, a Los Angeles–based ministry aimed at supplying trained pastors both to churches in need of revitalization and to groups of believers wanting to plant biblical churches.[6] In their training program, men are assessed as to their "cultural adjustability" even when being considered for pastorates in the United States, for there are real cultural differences in the diverse regions of America, even though it is one nation. So, too, for example, when a man is born in rural Wisconsin (a farming culture not densely populated), trained for ministry in metropolitan Los Angeles, and has a burden for the Swahili and English-speaking people of Kenya, he must prepare for cultural adjustments (e.g., learning the language, becoming familiar with cultural nuances in social interactions, grasping the importance of key religious terms, understanding family values) though fiercely maintaining his doctrinal convictions.

Fervent Prayer

Finally, church plants must be sustained by fervent prayer. This principle is not presented last as an activity to be done after all else is accomplished. It is placed last because it is a spiritual anchor for planted churches in tandem with a high view of God. Everyone knows that many tasks can be accomplished without prayerful consideration; however, without prayer as primary in ministry, nothing can be done that honors the One who called the church planter into ministry. Thus, it is impossible to find any lasting missionary effort that did not include men and women committed to prayer.

This principle is exemplified in Scripture whenever faithful ministries are seen. For instance, the early church was dedicated to two life-giving elements: to preaching and to prayer (Acts 6:4). Christ prepared for His public ministry through prayer ("fasting"; Matt 4:1–2; Luke 4:1), and He continued regular communion with the Father on earth until His final breath (Matt 27:46; Luke 3:21; 5:16; 23:46). Paul's missions were saturated in prayer—of thankfulness for God's grace among the saints (Eph 1:15–16; Phil 1:3–5; Col 1:3–8; 1 Thess 1:2; 2 Thess 1:3) and of petitions for open doors

---

6. "About," Grace Advance, accessed June 18, 2024, http://graceadvance.org/about.html.

(Col 4:3), for the spiritual growth of the flock (2 Cor 13:9; Eph 1:18–19; 3:14–16), for unity within the body (Rom 15:5–6), for spiritual illumination (Eph 1:18; 3:17–19), for divine help against gospel opposers (Rom 15:30–31), and of course, for the salvation of the lost (Rom 9:1–5; 1 Tim 2:1–4). If the apostle Paul so recognized his need for prayer (Eph 6:18–20; Col 4:3–4; 1 Thess 5:25), how much more ought the contemporary church planter! Any minister who is not a man of prayer is practically resting his confidence not in God's grace but in his own chosen methodology, organizational support, and talents.[7] Such an exchange undermines the first principle of church planting: a high view of God.

Key subjects for a church planter's prayer on behalf of the body he helps to form will be the following: a praying church (Matt 21:13; Acts 6:4, 6; Eph 6:18–20; 1 Tim 2:1–2), an evangelistic church (Matt 28:19–20; Col 4:5–6), a hospitable church (Rom 12:13; Titus 1:8; Heb 13:2; 1 Pet 4:9), an influential church (Matt 5:16; 1 Pet 2:12), a Bible teaching church (2 Tim 4:1–5), a gossip-free church (2 Cor 12:20; Titus 2:3), a financially responsible church (2 Cor 8–9), a praising church (Eph 5:19; Col 3:16), a morally pure church (Eph 5:3–4; 1 Thess 4:3), a doctrinally sound church (Eph 4:14; 2 Tim 4:3; Titus 2:1), and a Christ-honoring church (1 Cor 10:31). If a man cannot commit to praying in this manner, it is questionable whether he is suited for church leadership. Prayer is the great reminder that the success of the work is dependent on the intervening grace of God!

Conclusion

These nine principles of church planting are not optional for the church-planting pastor. They are not optional, that is, if the work is to be carried out biblically, if God is to be the acknowledged source of the church's success, and if the church is to have an unshakable foundation for sustained global impact. Church planting is essential to the Great Commission of Jesus Christ. Therefore, let churches do away with the business, consumerism, and sociologically driven church growth and multiplication models trending in the churched cultures of the West. Rather, ministry training for pastors and missionaries must bring the study of planting churches back under the high views of God and of Scripture and under the other biblical principles that unfold from them: a qualified leader, a biblical burden, core values, a core team, an indigenous end goal, cross-cultural adaptation, and fervent prayer. This is how the missionary builds a ministry philosophy of church planting while submitting to the head of the church also. To God, then, "be the glory in the church and in Christ Jesus to all generations forever and ever. Amen" (Eph 3:21).

---

7. "A clear indication of the core trust of an individual or church is their prayer life. If we are praying about something, we are ultimately dependent on God for it. If we are not praying about something, we are ultimately depending on some other resource." Craig Ott and Stephen J. Strauss, *Encountering Theology of Mission: Biblical Foundations, Historical Developments, and Contemporary Issues*, Encountering Mission (Grand Rapids: Baker, 2010), 250.

Doing the Work of an Evangelist

John MacArthur

Every local church pastor is called to be an evangelist. He fulfills the Great Commission by preaching the gospel to the lost. As Paul told Timothy, "But you, be sober in all things, endure hardship, do the work of an evangelist, fulfill your ministry" (2 Tim 4:5).

Timothy was a pastor in the church at Ephesus when Paul charged him with these words, exhorting him to do the work of an evangelist. But Paul was not calling Timothy to leave his flock and go out as a missionary. Rather, he was underscoring the fact that evangelism is an essential part of the work of pastoral ministry. Paul's emphasis was intended to encourage Timothy not to shrink back from this duty in the face of growing hostility against the gospel. Rather than giving up and throwing in the towel, Timothy was to stand strong and stir up the gift of God within him (2 Tim 1:6).

Timothy's discouragement must have been serious, given the nature of Paul's admonitions throughout his final epistle. The apostle recognized that faithfulness in ministry would not be easy, as evil men grew worse and worse (2 Tim 3:13).

But Timothy, by contrast, was to follow the faithful example of Paul—an example that included resolute perseverance despite facing arrest, imprisonment, persecutions, and even martyrdom (3:10–12). All of this was for the sake of the Lord Jesus and the advancement of His gospel.

The work of evangelism constitutes one of the most challenging aspects of ministry. The evangel, the good news of salvation through Jesus Christ, is a polarizing message. It confronts sin, pierces the conscience, and calls sinners to repent. As a result, it is often met with resistance and antagonism. That is why some preachers try to win over the lost with an ear-tickling message in a misguided attempt to remove the offense of the gospel. But Paul exhorted Timothy to press on, not by tickling ears but by preaching the truth without compromise, in season and out of season. The responsibility to do so was fundamental to Timothy's pastoral ministry.

When I came to Grace Community Church, I had three main objectives. The first was to preach the Scriptures to God's people each week. This was foundational, as Paul indicated to Timothy (2 Tim 4:1–2). The second objective was to train men to lead in the church. Paul expressed this principle in 2 Timothy 2:2—"The things which you have heard from me," Paul said, "entrust these to faithful men who will be able to teach others also." Preaching the Word and training spiritual leaders represented a twofold discipleship focus in my pastoral ministry.

The third ministry objective was to spread the truth of the gospel to the ends of the earth. Though we were just one congregation in Southern California, we recognized that "the work of an evangelist" has no geographic limits. The Great Commission is a call to take the gospel to every creature, meaning that—as the Lord enables each local church—the goal should be to reach the surrounding world with the good news of Jesus Christ. Given our ministry objectives, our strategy was simple: preach the Word, train leaders, and proclaim the gospel to the lost. In pursuing these goals, we entrusted the results to the Lord, resting in Him to do the work through the power of His Word. Fifty years later, the fruit of

God's blessing on those ministry objectives has been far greater than we could ever have asked or imagined (cf. Eph. 3:20).

As Paul reiterated to Timothy, pastoral ministry is challenging work. Yet the key to ministry success is not found in eloquence or cleverness, but in faithfulness. The Lord is looking for those who will prove to be faithful, even in the face of hostility and hardship. A ministry that honors the Master is marked by fidelity to Him, His Word, and the ministry objectives laid out in Scripture. Like Paul, the faithful pastor is one who—at the end of his ministry—has fought the good fight, finished the course, and run the race with endurance (2 Tim 4:6–8).

My prayer for this generation of pastors and church leaders is that they will be found faithful in all that Christ has called them to do, including the work of evangelism. You will undoubtedly face trials like Timothy faced, and even share his tears (2 Tim 1:4). But press on. Paul's charge to Timothy applies to you too: "Be sober in all things, endure hardship, do the work of an evangelist, fulfill your ministry" (4:5). May that be true of you as you serve with humble diligence for the glory of Christ.

CHAPTER 35

The Joys of Planting a Church

Conrad Mbewe

Paul planted the church in Philippi during his second missionary journey (Acts 15:36–18:22). He later testified that he remembered his time with the people there fondly and with great joy (Phil 1:3–5, 7; 4:1). The church at Philippi began as Paul tried to enter the Roman province of Asia to continue his church-planting efforts. The Holy Spirit, however, prevented him from doing so (Acts 16:6–7). It was not until Paul reached the edge of the land, with nothing in front of him but water, that he saw a vision. A man beckoned him and his coworkers across the Aegean Sea to Macedonia (16:9). They concluded that God was leading them into Europe. The missionaries crossed over, and the very first city they entered was Philippi (16:12). Through their evangelistic efforts, a church was born in that city (16:11–40).

The first three converts in Philippi were not the most obvious choice for a new church plant. They included Lydia, a businesswoman (Acts 16:14–15), an abused slave girl (16:16–18), and a civil servant, a jailer (16:30). For Paul, planting this church was not the end goal. Rather, it was the start of greater ministry. The little church that started with these unlikely few became the launch pad for several other churches that Paul and his team would plant in Europe during their missionary journey. Because of this, the Philippian church was a particular source of pleasure for Paul. More importantly, as young as the people were in faith, they were active participants in the work of missions, giving even when no others were (Phil 4:15).

The Philippian believers brought Paul so much joy, one might miss that he wrote his letter to them while in prison. Indeed, of all his letters, Philippians is the most joyful. In Philippians 1:3–4 he writes, "I thank my God in all my remembrance of you, always offering prayer with joy in my every prayer for you all." He states from the beginning that he is so joyful because of "your participation in the gospel from the first day until now" (1:5).[1] Paul doubtless found pleasure in the "stickability" of this church, hanging on to him despite all the difficulties. Even while he was in prison, they were still sending him help (2:25).

The Pauline church-planting model, though beautiful and effective, does not come without cost. As in Paul's time, the church today faces significant obstacles to its multiplication efforts. This chapter aims to help pastors and missionaries by assessing three of those obstacles, specifically as they relate to congregations in the Global South,[2] along with church-planting realities that motivated the apostle personally.

Obstacles That Hinder Church Planting

All missionaries should look forward to partnering with churches like the one in Philippi. Likewise, churches established on the mission field should exemplify the same pattern— namely, a steadfast commitment to missions. Unfortunately, however, churches fail to mimic the Philippian church because of three particular obstacles, examined below.

Lack of Models

The church in Philippi had an excellent example to follow; they could look to the church in Antioch. Certainly Paul would have shared with the Philippians how after he had helped to plant that church, they sent him out to preach the gospel and to plant churches across Asia in places like Iconium and Lystra (Acts 14). Paul likely shared his ministry experience with the Philippian church, which challenged them to continue the mission others had started. Thus, they would have emulated the Antioch church, supporting Paul and Silas's missionary endeavors in the rest of Europe.

Most churches in the Global South, however, have no such role models. New churches start, but they are often break-offs from other churches. They consist of individuals who are frustrated by what is (or is not) taking place at their respective churches, who leave and start their own churches across the city, or even across the street. Other churches begin because people move into new residential areas and want a church nearby. Still others are started by graduates of Bible colleges and seminaries who are not content simply to remain as church members but want to start their own congregations.

Thus, church planting does happen in the South, but very little of it is marked by biblical intentionality. Still less is done by existing churches. Unlike those in Acts, very few contemporary church plants have roots in another indigenous church, and very few have church planting as part of their missions philosophy. In other words, most churches see themselves as the end of the chain, rather than as runners in the middle of a relay—runners who must pass the baton on to others. The lack of churches

---

1. About the words, "until now," John Calvin comments that Paul is referring to the way the Philippian church persevered alongside him in his work of missions. John Calvin, *Commentaries on the Epistles of Paul the Apostle to Philippians, Colossians, and Thessalonians*, trans. John Pringle (Edinburgh: T. Constable, 1851), 25.

2. "Global South" refers to Latin America, Africa, and much of Asia.

that plant churches in the twenty-first century should bother all believers.

Lack of Missions Focus in Bible Colleges

The second reason churches are not planting churches is that Bible colleges are not emphasizing missions. Those who train pastors, including well-known African theologians, often miss the opportunity to instill church planting as a priority in their students. Ask one to preach on missions and he will excel; ask him to describe his church-planting work and he can only blush. This is because church planting has largely existed as a mere academic theory. It has not been a reality within the professor's or preacher's personal ministry.

The disconnect between theory and practice must change. New pastors must be shown the place of church planting in God's commission for His people. Indeed, God has commanded anew, "Be fruitful, and multiply, and fill the earth and subdue it" (Gen 1:28). For He calls the church with this order as well. It is not enough for a church to be a "happy clappy" congregation, always enjoying a nice time among themselves. The church is to multiply. As it does, there will be greater light in the midst of the world's darkness.

Therefore, pastors need to be trained with excellence in both hermeneutics and homiletics. They need to know how to provide oversight and counseling to God's people. They need to be equipped to handle the various administrative tasks they will face. But they also must be trained to promote and lead church expansion through church planting.

Lack of Financial Resources

The context of the Global South is largely marked by a lack of financial resources. Even so, the response to the church-planting need cannot be "We just do not have the resources." God is not awaiting the provision of resources as the missing ingredient for church planting. It is true that when reading church history we see that the economic and political power of nations and kingdoms played an important role in the spread of Christianity. The Greco-Roman world, for example, facilitated the spread of the gospel among the Gentiles in the days of Paul. Paul understood the cultural landscape. He saw and took advantage of unique opportunities that his Roman citizenship provided. Likewise, in the British Empire of the eighteenth and nineteenth centuries, the gospel was sent wherever the monarch of England desired. Missionaries enjoyed governmental protection and broad cultural and financial support, factors that aided them in their ministries.

Currently, however, Christianity is multiplying fastest in parts of the world where there is little political or economic backing. Theologians anticipate that by 2050, one-third of the world's professing Christians will be in Africa.[3] But without resources, sustaining

---

3. Gina A. Zurlo and Todd M. Johnson, eds., *World Christian Database* (Leiden: Brill, 2024), www.worldchristiandatabase.org /wcd; Philip Jenkins, *The Next Christendom: The Coming of Global Christianity*, 3rd ed. (Oxford: Oxford University Press, 2011), 3.

growth will require partnerships with healthy churches in more affluent parts of the world. Thankfully, Christians and churches in the West gladly help finance the training of pastors, the provision of literature, and sometimes even capital projects. But faithful, supporting ministries must also partner with national churches, helping them identify and send out their own indigenous missionaries to plant national churches. A vital component of deliberately and purposefully joining hands with global churches must be to see more indigenous churches established.

Moreover, useful partnerships with the West should not stop the churches in poorer parts of the world, like Africa, from also contributing financially. Jesus clearly taught, "Where your treasure is, there your heart will be also" (Matt 6:21). Correspondingly, one's financial spending will reveal one's treasure. If one has a true heart for missions, he will lift every stone to find the needed money. Saying, "We don't have money" is not an excuse before God. For most Christians, funding is a matter of priority and not strictly a question of lack. Therefore, recipients in poorer contexts must understand the nature of gospel partnerships and not be content to always be the beneficiary. That is, those who have little are to contribute the little they have so that they are working alongside those who can contribute more.

Reciprocity is key to a biblical church-planting partnership. Paul did not thank the Philippians for their spiritual partnership alone, but for their material partnership. They gave, not out of abundance, but out of poverty (2 Cor 8:1–4). In effect, Paul acknowledged that his church planting happened only because the Philippians gave. Therefore, even when help is available from more affluent quarters, the poorer church is to contribute financially what they have to offer as well.

The Global South is uniquely poised to participate in missions through "tent making." Continents like Africa send out many information technology professionals, for example. Those workers go to America, Europe, Australia, and South America. Such a dispersion marks a significant missionary opportunity. But instead of church planting, many are merely transplanting the church of their home culture to their new home. Hence, Zambian churches, Nigerian churches, and Ghanaian churches are showing up on other continents. The result is that they are failing to bring the gospel effectively to the local populations where God has brought them. The needed change will start when the national pastors get their young professionals to use their opportunities to be intentional for the gospel. God is spreading professional Christians from the Global South around the world. It is time for them to recognize God's hand in moving them, and to realize that this alleviates much of the need for funding as they are already earning money. They must take advantage of this opportunity for the sake of the Great Commission.

Biblical Motivations for Church Planting

When thinking of what would ignite the passion of local churches for church planting, it is helpful to consider Paul's own ministry perspective. Using the Philippian church plant as a case study, we can see that Paul was committed to church planting as the greatest vehicle for glorifying the Savior and edifying the saints.

Healthy Church Plants Produce Love for the Gospel

Paul saw healthy churches as indispensable for believers to grow in their knowledge of and love for the gospel (Eph 4:15–16). Therefore, he wanted the Philippians to continue contending for the gospel as a unified church: "Only live your lives in a manner worthy of the gospel of Christ . . . standing firm in one spirit, with one mind contending together for the faith of the gospel" (Phil 1:27). Their contention was not against those outside of their body who proclaimed the true gospel, even if from false motives (1:15–18), but against those coming into their body who undermined the gospel, the Judaizers (3:2). Paul knew that once one begins undermining the gospel of grace, a death knell is rung upon the church.

Paul was unmistakably concerned that the church in Philippi not only knew the true gospel but loved it. He wanted them to cherish the gospel as much as he did personally. When addressing his conflict with the Judaizers, he spoke of his own "righteous" works—many of which a Judaizer would be proud (3:4–6). But in his eyes, these deeds were filthy dung compared to the righteousness imputed to him in Jesus Christ (3:7–9). According to Paul, having a distinct experiential knowledge of Christ is of more value than ten thousand words of commendation (3:10–11). That is essentially what

Paul was exhorting the Philippian church to do (3:15–17), and because of his own example, these individuals ended up loving the gospel too. When a church loves the gospel and grows in its appreciation of it, the believers will want the world to know (1 Thess 1:6–8).

Healthy Church Plants Reproduce Themselves

Paul was also ambitious to establish healthy, well-fed, local churches because those are the churches that reproduce their like. For example, the model church at Antioch was healthy and well-fed (Acts 11:19–30) before the missionaries it sent out planted other churches, including Philippi (13:1–3). At the beginning of Paul's letter to the Philippians, he wrote, "And this I pray, that your love may abound still more and more in full knowledge and all discernment, so that you may approve the things that are excellent, in order to be sincere and without fault until the day of Christ; having been filled with the fruit of righteousness which comes through Jesus Christ, to the glory and praise of God" (1:9–11). If church members, even after many years of being in the same church, are still in a state of spiritual infancy, that church will likely not have a significant missionary force (Heb 5:11–14). If the people are still self-centered, worldly, and are given to fighting with one another over trivial matters, that church is not legitimately concerned with exporting the gospel to the world nor with contending alongside one another in the gospel (Phil 4:2–3). Therefore, it is not enough for pastors to want to preach the gospel and see souls converted.

Pastors must labor to see individual believers grow in Christ within the local church.

Paul further reflects this desire for believers' growth when he writes of how each Christian ought to be looking not to his own interests, but to the interests of others (Phil 2:4), which extends to one's concern for gospel proclamation. For, he continues, "Have this way of thinking in yourselves which was also in Christ Jesus" (2:5), and he tells the Philippians something of the mind of Christ. Though being God, Jesus accepted humiliation in order to redeem a world to Himself and to glorify God the Father (2:10–11). The Son underwent such humiliation because He knew the Father's agenda and knew that He could trust His Father to the end. Jesus Christ thus displayed more than anyone the missionary spirit that He commands in the church. There is nothing more capable of producing such a missionary spirit than when God's people grow to be more like His Son, grow to see God's agenda, grow to trust Him, and grow to serve one another locally. These are the churches that send out preachers of the gospel.

Healthy Church Plants Produce Partners in Joy and Prayer

Finally, Paul demonstrates the joy that comes to any church from receiving news from other churches afield. He writes, "Now, I want you to know, brothers, that my circumstances have turned out for the greater progress of the gospel" (Phil 1:12). Elsewhere he wrote of how he was sending others—such as Timothy (2:19), Epaphroditus (2:25), or Tychicus (Eph 6:21;

Col 4:7–9)—so that his supporting churches might know how things were going among the church plants and then have joy with him. The sending also included progress reports to Paul from the church plants themselves. Exposure to what is happening on the mission field motivates God's people.

Sharing also fuels both their prayers and their desires to go. Many prayer meetings in churches lack the focus and substance that will engender God's people for missions work. Typical prayer meetings revolve around relatives who are hospitalized, friends who need traveling mercies, or acquaintances who are getting married. God becomes a mere servant of man who needs to be informed about temporal needs. Those prayers do not fit the pattern Jesus gave. He taught His disciples to pray, "Our Father who is in heaven, hallowed be Your name. Your kingdom come. Your will be done, on earth as it is in heaven" (Matt 6:9–10). It is only afterward that He said, "Give us this day our daily bread" (6:11). Pastors must lead so that the church knows what it is to pray for on behalf of God's kingdom, on behalf of real, live missionaries. This requires deliberate effort. Most people do not have ready access to the current ministry needs on the mission field. Their minds are consumed with what they see and read from secular news sources. They do not hear about the soldiers of Christ who serve the Lord in anonymity. Pastors must trace Paul's approach and seek to know current needs and developments. Then, when church plants, like Philippi, send their members with reports of their progress and needs to other churches, all become partners in both joy and prayer.

Conclusion

The early believers in the church plant of Philippi are a paradigm for modern missions to follow. Their story is one that exemplifies the constant need for faithful church-establishing missionaries, as well as the blessings that come along with that important ministry. The story highlights contemporary obstacles that stand between churches and this urgent need, particularly in the Global South. There are at times a lack of model churches to plant others, a lack of appropriate focus in missions training, and a lack of resources. This chapter issues a challenge to rise above the obstacles.

Moreover, the Philippian case study also uncovers the joy of participating in the work of establishing new churches on the mission field. There is great motivation to this task when one sees that healthy church plants produce love for the gospel, reproduce themselves through growing believers, and produce partners in joy and prayer. By these means, among others, church planting is shown to be the greatest vehicle for the glory of the Savior and the edification of believers. Let pastors around the world, then, rise up and lay hold of this opportunity, indeed this obligation, to follow the example of Paul and the Philippians for God's sake.

INSERT 35.1

Church Planting in Post-Calvin Geneva: A Personal History

John Glass

Geneva, on the westernmost tip of Switzerland, is in many ways the epicenter of Europe. One million people live in the greater Geneva area, sprawling into France. The number of staff at the United Nations—in hundreds of international organizations, nongovernment agencies, and diplomatic missions—is tens of thousands. Every year Geneva hosts thousands of conferences with hundreds of thousands of participants. It is one of the most international cities in the world.

Geneva is also very secular, radically different from the city of five centuries ago. When it officially joined the Reformation in 1536, all existing churches became Protestant. As the surrounding villages were won over to the Reformation, under the leadership of Reformer John Calvin (1509–1564), Protestant pastors were placed in their churches also. Today, however, secularism has significantly replaced this heritage. The percentage of Geneva that is evangelical is negligible. The city of John Calvin is in critical need of church planting.

Coming to Geneva

I was born to American parents in Paris and raised as an unbeliever in Geneva. My father was a businessman, and my mother, a journalist at the United Nations. At age nineteen, while backpacking from Geneva to India, I was led to Christ by a Dutch missionary on a street in New Delhi. My life completely changed.

After college I met my wife Meg, and one year later I went off to seminary. I began to wonder, *How could I have been raised in the city of John Calvin for fifteen years without ever hearing the gospel?* I asked God if I could go back someday and plant churches. Then, in 1986, the Lord led Meg and me to France as church planters for ten years. When the first man I led to Christ became the pastor there, it was time to move to Geneva.

In God's providence, we landed in 1997 at La Servette, church home of the small Action Biblique evangelical denomination, in downtown Geneva. La Servette had already financially sustained a pastor for over forty years. But since I could continue receiving missionary support from our sending churches, we all decided to put aside La Servette's pastoral salary every month for future church-planting efforts.

Planting Churches around Geneva

Prior to my arrival, La Servette had already spawned two daughter churches in the Geneva area. About two years afterward, a third church was hoped for in neighboring France. A children's Bible club was running in Annemasse, France, where a significant number of La Servette members lived. From this group launched our church plant, meeting in a local hotel. A young elder from La Servette was sent as the pastor, with financial support phasing out over five years. Twenty years later, the church is thriving.

Several families were also living in Annecy, France. They were traveling about an hour to come to La Servette. In God's providence, a missionary colleague in France had just given closure to a successful ministry. I called him, and within another year, he and two other missionary couples moved to Annecy to plant a church there. Today it is thriving also, fully supporting a native pastor.

The challenges for us as the mother church in both cases was that we lost almost all of our elders, who wanted to be part of the new churches, and the departure of several families hit our finances hard. But we kept trusting the Lord, because church planting is God's will. We pulled through, and it was well worth it. Between all of these daughter churches, three of them have planted another four!

After serving twelve years at La Servette, it was my turn to plant a new church also. Meg and I left in 2007 and started the Eglise Evangélique Internationale de Genève. Thirteen years later, I turned it over to a French pastor. Today it is mature and vibrant. What a thrill to see!

Four Lessons Learned

I have long pondered the lessons I have learned from my time and experience in church planting. I would distill it into four practical lessons.

Church-Planting Costs

One of the biggest challenges with sending out church plants, especially in Europe, is that the mother church pastor is relegating himself to small-church ministry. Oftentimes, so many members leave to help the new church that he is in perpetual "reboot mode." If that pastor is looking to grow his own ministry, he will quickly be discouraged; it will not grow as much as others that are not planting churches. This requires humility and a kingdom perspective. We are here to see the kingdom of God grow—not our own ministries.

Church Planting Works

Discouragement will be short-lived if one has a kingdom perspective. Periodically I updated a chart that tracked the membership of La Servette and its daughter and granddaughter churches. It kept me encouraged, especially when La Servette shrank. The number of people now attending all of them combined is nearly three times that of the largest church in Geneva. Church planting works because it grows the kingdom. Every plant represents more people who will come to Christ through its ministry.

Church Planting Motivates

By planting churches, mother churches lose gifted people—usually those excited about evangelism. They are motivated to see the plant grow and to give it momentum. In fact, just about everyone attending a church plant must be actively serving. Even people who might be more passive in a large church become more involved. Hence, the mother church loses people but ministries overall multiply—a net positive outcome!

Church Planting Distresses

Still, church planting is not for the fainthearted. Many battles must be fought to plant a church in hostile environs. And

Satan has found an effective way to slow down our efforts: internal conflicts. They sap energy from the church-planting vision. Through the years, many battles arose in the churches above. Some churches were "splants"—churches planted due to church splits. The reality is sometimes messy and brutal. But when all is done, the missionary can look back and say with Paul, "I have fought the good fight [2 Tim 4:7]. Churches have been planted. Thank You, Lord." Yes, thank You, Lord.

Sub-Section 2: The Goal of Unity and Maturity in the Planted Church

CHAPTER 36

Unity in Holiness: A Biblical Theology of Race and the Church

David Beakley

Perhaps no other word in human history has carried as much emotional charge as *race*. Today, *race* is commonly used to refer to a group sharing some outward physical characteristics and history. *Ethnicity* commonly refers to cultural, traditional, and familial bonds among a geographically located people.[1] Discussion of race has become a point of destructive division and is misplaced. God did not divide humanity into "races" of people but made them male and female (Gen 1:27), and "He made from one man every nation of mankind to inhabit all the face of the earth" (Acts 17:26). But because of

man's sin and Satan's active opposition, there is a continued push to destroy God's creation and intended harmony through division and strife (Gen 3:15).

After the flood, men united in their rebellion against God (Gen 11:3–4). Their sin against Him grew to the point that He dispersed humanity by introducing divergent languages (Gen 11:8–9). The people moved from Babel, settling in places with differing climates and challenges, which brought about differing physical adaptations. To this day, Satan has been using God's judgment at Babel

---

1. "The Difference between 'Race' and 'Ethnicity': How They Differ and Overlap," Merriam-Webster, accessed June 18, 2024, https://www.merriam-webster.com/grammar/difference-between-race-and-ethnicity.

as a tool to destroy humanity. Because of God's promise in Genesis 3:15, however, there is hope for true unity. A "seed" would come, redeem God's people, and destroy the works of Satan. God provides the way for all His children—those from every language and ethnic group who are united with His "seed"—to be in harmony and unity.

This chapter traces God's program for establishing unity among His people and the way this program is to be applied in the church.

"You Shall Be My People"

After the dispersion of humanity in Genesis 11, God chose Abraham, a former pagan idolater, to begin this great journey of hope. He promised him a special land and added that He would make him the father of a great nation and would bless the entire world through his lineage (Gen 12:1–3; 15:4–5). His seed would become God's servant nation, Israel (Exod 19:5–6). Later, under Moses' leadership, God brought Israel out of slavery in Egypt and taught them His ways so that He would be their God and they would be His people (Exod 20:2; Deut 4:20). God was very explicit: on the basis of their identity as His people, He also commanded them, "You shall be holy, for I, Yahweh your God am holy" (Lev 19:2). The path to peace and unity came through Him, and this unity was rooted in holiness.

Yet, in contrast to this holy standard, Numbers 12 presents how jealousy toward Moses by his siblings led them to make the ethnicity of Moses' foreign wife a visible point of contention (v. 1). God continued to demonstrate His holiness and taught Israel how to be a holy people, yet their ongoing sinfulness demonstrated that the holiness to which they were called could only be initiated by God. Though He commanded them to "circumcise" their hearts (Deut 10:16; 30:1–3), this was a work that only He could do (29:4; 30:6).

Abolishing the Hostility

By the time of the New Testament, hostility on the basis of nationality had become a sustained problem between Jews and Gentiles (Eph 2:15). The heart problem of national hostility is "partiality," no matter the context (Jas 2:9). Partiality on the basis of any external, superficial feature has always been sinful in God's eyes (Lev 19:34; Deut 1:17; 10:19; Rom 11:2; Gal 2:6).

God's plans for restoration and peace, however, were not thwarted. He did not abandon Israel because of this sin. Rather, He faithfully executed the plan He promised from the beginning (Gal 4:4). He sent His Son, Jesus Christ, to save a people for Himself (1 Pet 2:9–10) and bring unity, breaking down "the dividing wall of the partition by abolishing in His flesh the enmity" (Eph 2:14–15). He came to circumcise the hearts of all people who trust in Him, reconciling them and making peace with the Father (2:15–18). He did this by becoming the perfect sacrificial Lamb and fulfilling the requirements of the law (1 Cor 5:7; Heb 9:11–26). On the merits of Jesus' atoning sacrifice, even God's enemies can receive new hearts and experience unity with God and men (1 Cor 6:11).

Paul, a former "Hebrew of Hebrews" (Phil

3:3–7), celebrated how Jews and Gentiles have a common identity in Christ that abolishes all hostility between them (Gal 3:28–29; Eph 2:14–15). For Jesus Christ died to fulfill the righteous requirements of the law (Matt 5:17), including Israel's former separation ordinances (Eph 2:15; cf. Lev 20:25–26; Deut 7:1–6), "by removing believers from the law's condemnation" (Rom 8:1).[2] He brings perfect peace. And when one has true peace with God (Rom 5:1), he can have true peace with all people. The true unity in holiness experienced in the church between formerly hostile groups is "the mystery" that has now been made known in Christ (Eph 3:4–10; cf. Col 3:11).[3] Jews and Gentiles now enjoy unified fellowship in Christ as "one new man" (Eph 2:15).

Seeking Ethnic Unity in the Church

Despite being united with Christ, having a circumcised heart, and being a new creation, Christians find breaking with their old nature difficult. The presence of a multiplicity of ethnicities in the local church, especially when there is a history of hostility, threatens the biblical harmony of the believers. For the earliest example, the Jerusalem church in Acts 6 faced a dispute over the ethnicity of the members. It appeared that Hebrew widows were getting more than their share of food compared to their Hellenistic counterparts (6:1). Both groups were Jews, but because the Hellenistic widows were from the Greek culture of the Diaspora, not natives of the Hebrew culture in Israel, prejudices began to develop.

In the contemporary church, missionaries find that many countries contain pockets of ethnic identities and cultures that do not assimilate. South Africa, for example, has eleven official languages. Kenya has more than forty tribes. In India a caste system divides the people into fixed categories. In the Baltic states, people are divided by language, history, and religion. Missionaries and church leaders are nevertheless called to plant churches that thrive in such environments. The remainder of this chapter considers the assumption of cultural superiority as a major obstacle to ethnic unity in the early church and today that Christ's people must strive to overcome with the Holy Spirit's power and the faithful guidance of their elders.

The Problem: Assuming Cultural Superiority

An invisible obstacle to establishing unity in the local church is the assumption of superiority of one's own culture, training, and upbringing—starting with the leadership. The apostles' plan for table service in the Jerusalem church in Acts 6 did not eradicate the problem of favoritism among believers in the early church. While at

---

2. S. M. Baugh, *Ephesians*, EEC (Bellingham, WA: Lexham, 2015), 193.

3. Harold W. Hoener writes, "The mystery is not that Gentiles would be saved, because the OT gives evidence for their salvation, but rather that believing Jews and Gentiles are together in Christ. This concept was revolutionary for Jews and Gentiles alike. The only way this information can be obtained is through the gospel." Harold W. Hoener, *Ephesians: An Exegetical Commentary* (Grand Rapids: Baker Academic, 2002), 327.

Antioch, Peter seemed to slip back into a pattern of ethnic prejudice (Gal 2:11–14) even after he had come to realize God's intent to save Gentiles by grace and welcome them into the church on equal footing with Jews (Acts 10:34–35).[4] He succumbed to pressure from influential Jewish leaders and began to exhibit his old tendencies of maintaining table separation from Gentiles (Acts 10:28). James, brother of Jesus, later called the church to avoid prejudice (James 2:1–9; cf. Acts 15:19).[5] He discerned that the distinctions that lead to this sin do not always follow ethnic or cultural lines. People view wealth, age, education, and a host of other differences as a basis for disparaging and despising others.

The inability to break from one's home culture is a natural flaw that many Western missionaries from strong churches in developed countries bring to the field. They leave nations with an established history of gospel advance and with theologically sound churches to go to undeveloped countries where they meet economic, social, political, and theological challenges with which they cannot readily identify. In such settings, missionaries labor on several levels to help people to understand the need to turn from their cultural worldview to a biblical worldview.

Missionary John G. Paton,[6] for example, brought conviction to the people of the New Hebrides islands in the South Pacific that their practices of cannibalism and slavery were unacceptable to God and to their fellow men. He did not infer that the indigenous people needed to be "cultured" or "civilized," but rather that they were called by God to be new creatures in Christ. Because of the vast differences between Paton and the indigenous people, Paton had to take great pains to communicate that he was not trying to convert them to be Western. In essence, the people needed to forsake their pagan identity for a Christian identity.

Because Western missionaries often come with more resources, freedom, and power than the people in their target contexts, they can come across as authoritarian, superior, and even colonial. Paul's words in 1 Corinthians 4:7 are particularly important for missionaries to remember: "For who regards you as superior? What do you have that you did not receive? And if you did receive it, why do you boast as if you had not received it?" Spiritual immaturity led the Corinthian believers to infighting, jealousy, and improper alignment under celebrity preachers, all to gain recognition by others for what they perceived would make them superior.

---

4. Or possibly his "hypocrisy" lay in not having "the courage of his real convictions" when faced by the ethnic prejudice of others, real or imagined. Ronald Y. K. Fung, *The Epistle to the Galatians*, NICNT (Grand Rapids: Eerdmans, 1988), 106–11, esp. 107n14.

5. In light of this, we should be cautious; the "men from James" in Galatians 2:12 may not have represented him in any attempt to break the Jew-Gentile table fellowship necessarily. In fact, they may not have intended to influence Peter at all, for Paul's letter criticizes neither them nor James but only Peter. Scripture simply does not give the details of that event. Baugh, *Ephesians*, 146–47; Thomas R. Schreiner, *Galatians*, ZECNT (Grand Rapids: Zondervan, 2010), 139–40.

6. See *John G. Paton: The Autobiography of the Pioneer Missionary to the New Hebrides (Vanuatu)* (1889; repr., Edinburgh: Banner of Truth, 2013).

In response, Paul asked three questions that level the field and crush any thought of superiority, cultural, ethnic, or otherwise: Does God see you as superior? Did you accomplish anything without help? If you did receive help, why are you boasting as if you did not?

Every missionary is from somewhere. Paul was born a Jew, but he was not from Jerusalem; he was born in Tarsus as a Roman citizen. Paul did not think he was superior but acknowledged that he had nothing to do with his place of birth or what people group he was born into. That is why he wrote, "But by the grace of God I am what I am, and His grace toward me did not prove vain; but I labored even more than all of them, yet not I, but the grace of God with me" (1 Cor 15:10).

The Solution: Growing Local Leadership

The church in Jerusalem in Acts 6 did not ultimately solve the problem of ethnic conflicts; they managed it. Policies and procedures can never transform hearts. Churches are composed of elders and pastors, mature believers, new believers, false believers, unbelievers, and even some scoffers. Not all of these are members, but part of the wider, visible church community, even if only through family relationships.

In the church mix, the Hebraic-Hellenistic divide still exists in quality. The divide might be based on language, family standing, wealth and influence, politics, and even ethnicity. The solution the apostles found is instructive and

vital for the church today. To the undiscerning, Acts 6:2–4 can make it seem as if the apostles simply avoided getting involved:

> So the twelve summoned the congregation of the disciples and said, "It is not pleasing to God for us to neglect the word of God in order to serve tables. Therefore, brothers, select from among you seven men of good reputation, full of the Spirit and of wisdom, whom we may put in charge of this need. But we will devote ourselves to prayer and to the service of the word."

The apostles were not looking to avoid the problem—their primary concern was that they not neglect the Word of God and prayer as they dealt with thousands of new church members and an administrative crisis. They responded by making a commonsense plan so that their ministry focus remained on point. It involved a vetting process to ensure the spiritual maturity of those who would implement the work. In addition, the apostles were so eager to express their love for the Hellenistic widows that the men they chose to deal with the matter were Grecian Jews.[7]

Later in the expansion of the church, when Paul sent Titus to the island of Crete, he gave him specific instructions. He wrote in Titus 1:5, "For this reason I left you in Crete, that you would set in order what remains and appoint elders in every city as I directed you." Titus was to "set in order" those things that were not yet

---

7. John F. MacArthur Jr., *Acts*, MNTC (Chicago: Moody, 1994), 1:183.

completed. Paul wanted Titus neither to leave early nor to assume control of the churches there. Titus had a mandate to appoint elders in every city. There would not be a legitimate self-sustained church until there were elders leading the local churches.

Local leadership is vitally important for handling the many multiethnic challenges on the mission field. No matter how long a missionary has been working in a particular church or ministry, he will still be deficient in discerning all the nuances at play with the local people. When there are intersecting cultures, specifically cultures with a history of conflict, it is crucial to have elders who know the people.

It is also important for the missionary to understand the cultural demographics of the church and its surrounding area. This can be a difficult challenge to navigate. While it is critical to maintain the highest level of scrutiny in selecting men for training and eldership, it is also important to have local input. Missionaries who are starting out need to find other men, whether seasoned missionaries or mature local Christians, to assist them in decision making. The goal of a church is not to have diversity in its leadership—that kind of social engineering is worldly. Rather, the goal is to have qualified men that have insight into the people of the church. In a multiethnic church, this goal will challenge the leadership to make sure they are raising up men who can provide the best understanding of the true needs and concerns of all the people.

Local churches in which a variety of ethnicities are present often have the additional struggle of language. Favoring one group over others will create a sense of rejection. Even in countries with multiple common majority languages, such as English, French, or Spanish, churches will struggle when the "language of best fit" is chosen. In South Africa, many churches conduct their services in English, even though the majority of the congregation speak English as their second or third language. Sometimes, having songs in different languages, and having greetings in multiple languages is just enough to provide a signal that the Christian culture is one that desires all people to know their Creator and Lord.

Conclusion

Crises of ethnic disunity in the church continue today across the world, with each one bringing its own unique details and context. In response, missionaries and church leaders must always remember that it is the ministry of the Word of God and prayer that changes the lives, thinking, and prejudices of the people in the church, starting with themselves.

Sanctification: Essential for the Integrity of the Missionary's Witness

Mark Tatlock

While the Holy Spirit is responsible to save sinners, it is undeniable that the holiness of the messenger is critical for establishing the viability and integrity of the gospel. Nowhere is this more acutely felt than on unreached mission fields and in fledgling church plants, where every word and action face scrutiny in cultures that are skeptical or hostile to the claims of Christ. Even small hypocrisies provide reasons to dismiss the life-giving truths of the gospel. As pioneers carrying the truth in their hands, missionaries and church planters must make every effort to pursue their own spiritual growth in the grace of Christ. Their walk of faith fuels their outward approach to their target audience. In the darkness, even a dim light shines brightly. The implications of one's Christlikeness therefore move beyond the personal realm and very much have to do with the advance of the kingdom.

Sanctification reflects the steady progression in holiness that ushers from the heart into real life conduct by the sovereign working of "the Spirit of holiness" (Rom 1:4) in each believer (Rom 8:9; 2 Cor 3:17–18; Phil 2:12–13). It is as a holy people that the church, made up of individually sanctifying believers, will witness to the world that God is holy (1 Pet 1:15–16). Such holiness is possible only because the Lord Jesus Christ "loved the church and gave Himself up for her, so that He might sanctify her, having cleansed her by the washing of water with the word, that He might present to Himself the church in all her glory, having no spot or wrinkle or any such thing, but that she would be holy and blameless" (Eph 5:25–27).

Missionaries and local church leaders everywhere in the world today have the distinct honor of proclaiming the wondrous reality that Christ sacrificed Himself to display His eternal glory through His glorious church. It is with this exalted view of the church that gospel proclaimers should also have a heightened awareness of their own need to live increasingly holy lives like Christ. Scripture's call to witness to the world about God's holiness requires that the gospel message be unstained by hypocrisy and dishonor by someone who pays lip service to the truth but is himself disinterested in continually transforming into the image of Christ, the glorious image of the Father (2 Cor 4:4; Heb 1:3). An unholy messenger truncates the vision of God's glory that the world so desperately needs to behold.

Some brief highlights primarily from Colossians 3 are useful for reminding believers in their local churches that the sanctifying work of Christ through His Holy Spirit is essential for participating as ambassadors in God's plan of redemption in the world.

The apostle Paul's letter to the Colossians celebrates the supremacy of Christ as God. It expresses God's desire for all who have been made new in Christ to live in the true and glorious knowledge revealed about Him in Scripture. True knowledge leads to transformed living. Because the glory and honor of Christ holds primacy over all things and all people, believers must "keep seeking the things above, where Christ is, seated at the right hand of God" (Col 3:1). The believer no longer lives according to "self-made religion" (2:23) but has died to himself (3:3) and has been raised in newness of life (3:1). He now lives a resurrected life with his mind set "on the things above, not on the things that are on earth" (3:2). Living a resurrected life is in contradiction to how the believer used to live, in "immorality, impurity, passion, evil

desire, and greed, which amounts to idolatry . . . wrath, anger, malice, slander, and abusive speech" (3:5–8). If he keeps pursuing Christ, these characteristics will not be part of his conduct or character, nor be expressed in his relationships.

Contrary to his thoughts and deeds before Christ, the new believer is continually "being renewed to a full knowledge according to the image of the One who created him—a renewal in which there is no distinction between Greek and Jew, circumcised and uncircumcised, barbarian, Scythian, slave, and freeman, but Christ is all and in all" (Col 3:10–11). The result of the new nature is to bear out the perfections of God in as of yet imperfect ways on the earth, including "put[ting] on a heart of compassion, kindness, humility, gentleness, and patience; bearing with one another, and graciously forgiving each other . . . put[ting] on love, which is the perfect bond of unity. . . and let[ting] the peace of Christ rule" in the believer's heart (3:12–15).

The believer's primary identity is no longer his ethnicity, culture, nor language; neither is it about past religious affiliation or even his previous rebellion against God. But it is that he is a child of God and minister of reconciliation to the Father (2 Cor 5:17–18). More than just preaching, Christians must live consistently with God's nature, displaying His character before others in tangible ways so that through the combined effect of godly words, actions, and relationships, they will "be blameless and innocent, children of God without blemish in the midst of a crooked and perverse generation, among whom [they] shine as lights in the world" (Phil 2:15).

The demonstrable result of a sanctifying life will fulfill Paul's command in Colossians 3:17: "And whatever you do in word or deed, do all in the name of the Lord Jesus, giving thanks to God the Father through Him." The follower of Christ now models his life after the One who modeled selfless sacrifice in every way on the earth toward those in the faith and those who yet reject it (1 Pet 2:17). Sanctification therefore is missions-oriented in real, tangible expressions of faith in thought, word, and action. Believers who are being perfected in the image of the Holy God reflect the image of the Son of Man, who "has come to seek and to save the lost" (Luke 19:10).

In summary, Scripture calls believers to grow in Christlike holiness so that as God's set-apart people they give credible gospel witness to the lost world. Striving for holiness should manifest not just inwardly but outwardly in real, relationship-building ways—in compassionate words and selfless actions, bridging man-made divides in dark places with the light of Christ. The believer's spiritual growth verifies the reconciling message of the church to the unbelieving world with such force that while the believer is pursuing the upward call of Christ for holiness, he is compelled to fulfill the outward call to seek and save the lost near and far.

Division has always been a scourge on the church. While doctrinal boundaries are a critical reality for a biblical church, the Lord hates division (Rom 16:17–18; 1 Tim 5:21; Titus 3:10), especially over external differences (Acts 10:34; Rom 2:11; Eph 6:9; Jas 2:1, 9; cf. Lev 19:15). The concept of "race," as in grouping people by external physical or biogenetic traits, is a foothold people continue to use to their own advantage. But internal heart issues are at play. Whether it is ethnicity, wealth, age, education, class, or politics, missionaries and elders must be on guard to shepherd the people to grow biblically according to God's program for unity among His people.

The Deconversion Stories That Go Unnoticed

Brooks Buser[8]

Recently there has been a spate of "deconversion" stories from high-profile individuals walking away from the Christian faith.[9] Each time a "celebrity Christian" walks away from the faith, there is the usual outpouring of thoughts from those in the media, sermons delivered on the dangers that led to the fall, and general reviews of how we arrived at this point in Christian history. Without delving into speculations about the reasons for such celebrity deconversions, what is striking is that for every high-profile professed Christian who turns their back on the faith, there are hundreds overseas who likewise walk away from the faith—and go largely unnoticed.

Christians revel in the statistics of baptisms and churches planted annually overseas. But for true accuracy, there should be a third and fourth category of statistics reported: professed converts who turned back to their original, non-Christian beliefs, and churches that did not survive their first years of ministry. These figures paint a more accurate picture of the overseas reality and bring some much-needed scrutiny to the role of Protestant missionaries to capitulate to apostasy and failure. There are three major reasons why such deconversions are happening: missionaries are too quick to baptize, too limited in language, and too concerned with numbers.

---

8. This essay is adapted from my previously published article "The Deconversion Stories That Go Unnoticed," Radius International blog, September 13, 2021, https://radiusinternational.org/the-deconversion-stories-that-go-unnoticed/. I have borrowed this term from Michael J. Kruger, "The De-conversion of Saruman: Five Lessons to Learn," *Canon Fodder*, May 4, 2020, https://www.michaeljkruger.com/the-de-conversion-of-saruman-five-lessons-to-learn/.

9. The popular YouTube comedians Rhett McLaughlin and Link Neal came out in 2020 with a series of videos about why they had "deconstructed" their Christianity. See summary with web links by Alisa Childers, "Let's Deconstruct a Deconversion Story: The Case of Rhett and Link," *The Gospel Coalition*, February 29, 2020, https://www.thegospelcoalition.org/article/rhett-link-deconversion/. In 2019 respected evangelical author Josh Harris (*I Kissed Dating Goodbye* [Colorado Springs, CO: Multnomah, 1997]), announced that he was walking away from the Christian faith and put out a five-part course to help reverse the damage that his former teachings had caused. See the insightful analysis by Carl R. Trueman, "Josh Harris's Message Remains the Same," First Things web exclusive, August 12, 2021, https://www.firstthings.com/web-exclusives/2021/08/josh-harriss-message-remains-the-same.

Too Quick to Baptize

Too often there is an unhealthy speed in declaring someone a Christian, baptizing them, and adding them to the church. Second-century church father Justin Martyr would stress that the effectiveness of the Christian witness was only as good as how Christians themselves lived. Only those who had a proven record of living out the Christian faith were to be admitted for baptism, the Lord's Supper, and church membership.[10] In fact, it was common in the early church to have those who professed belief undergo discipleship and evaluation for three years before admitting them for baptism.[11] Still, the emphasis was not on time but "the character only is what shall be judged."[12] If the character of the disciple (the "catechumen") was not changed in a way that was evident, it was judged better to wait on baptism than to rush it.

By hurrying baptism, two negative outcomes become potential realities: an individual unbeliever is given false confidence that he is made right with God, and unbelievers generally now make up part of the church membership. The latter concern is not that unbelievers attend the church's meetings. That is, in fact, a good thing. The concern, rather, is that they are now seen as believers by other church members and the community as a whole.

Only saved people should be admitted for baptism and church membership (Matt 28:19; Acts 2:38–41; cf. Rom 6:1–4). Spurgeon, commenting on Acts 2:47 ("And the Lord was adding to their number daily those who were being saved"), said, "Saved persons were added to the church, and only the saved were fit to be added. We are not authorized to receive into our number those who desire to be saved, as certain churches do: I commend their plan in doing so, but I am sure they have no scriptural warrant for it."[13] By hurrying the process, domestically or overseas, unbelievers may be brought into churches to be assured of something they do not have: salvation. The resulting fruit of this rapid approach is ripe for deconversion.

Too Limited in Language

Being fluent in the target language is not a high enough priority for many missionaries.[14]

---

10. Justin Martyr, *Apologia i* 61.2; 66.1.

11. Hippolytus, *Traditio Apostolica* 17.1–2; cf. Alan Kreider, *The Patient Ferment of the Early Church* (Grand Rapids: Baker Academic, 2016), 177.

12. Hippolytus, 17.1–2.

13. Charles H. Spurgeon, "Building the Church (Additions to the Church)," ed. Tony Capoccia (sermon preached on April 5, 1874; updated and rev. manuscript, 2000), https://www.biblebb.com/files/spurgeon/1167.htm.

14. The missions training ministry that I am privileged to serve as president, Radius International, has spilled much ink in trying to bring true language and culture fluency back into prominence in missions. This essay is another attempt. "About," Radius International, accessed June 18, 2024, https://radiusinternational.org/.

Many missionaries claim to be fluent but actually possess what might be labeled "market fluency." That is, they are proficient enough in the language to buy groceries, have brief conversations in coffee shops, give elaborate greetings or farewells, and do all manner of necessary daily tasks. But if the subject matter of conversation turned to the abstract, to spontaneous question-and-answer by earnest listeners, or to weightier matters like justification, substitutionary atonement, or the Trinity, the missionary would not be equipped to communicate clearly.

The rationale most missionaries give for not achieving what might be called "worldview fluency," the ability to communicate at a worldview level, is a lack of time, being already fully involved in ministry, and, most commonly, that they minister regularly through translators. Translators, however, can be a dangerous handicap when working with the message of life. Missionaries typically put a high level of confidence in what is communicated by their translators, not all of which is unwarranted, especially when working with gateway language translators (e.g., Mandarin, Bahasa, Arabic). Yet, when working within an unreached people group, speaking to and through unbelievers as translators runs the unfavorably high risk that what is assumed to be communicated is not accurate to the biblical message. When missionaries are not fluent, the gospel is unclear. When the gospel is unclear, false converts arise and eventually fall away. The level of "worldview fluency" takes longer and is more painful for the missionary to achieve, but the weightiness of the message demands it.

Too Concerned with Numbers

The seduction of numbers can be strong. Quite often today missionary agencies will send progress reports to churches and donors from missionaries on the ground. The main thrust of these reports is often in two categories: the number of baptisms and the number of churches planted. Those areas, countries, and ministries that are "producing" more of these numbers will be highlighted, the missionaries will be platformed, their support will increase, and eventually they will be moved into leadership positions. Yet the Lord Jesus is the missionary's example of One who never fell prey to the overwhelming power of producing "good numbers" (John 2:23–25; 6:60, 66). For this, too, produces false converts.

John G. Paton, nineteenth-century missionary to the South Pacific,[15] resisted sending back such numeric reports to his supporters. Paton was well steeped in the healthy skepticism that his contemporary,

---

15. See the autobiography of John G. Paton, *The Autobiography of the Pioneer Missionary to the New Hebrides (Vanuatu)* (Edinburgh: Banner of Truth Trust, 1965); also see the shorter biography by Paul Schlehlein, *John G. Paton: Missionary to the Cannibals of the South Seas* (Edinburgh: Banner of Truth Trust, 2017).

Pastor Charles Spurgeon, harbored for the revivalism of their time. Spurgeon, reflecting on the big numbers being produced at evangelistic revival meetings throughout England, with their heavy-handed altar calls, rightly surmised,

> I am weary of the public braggings, the counting of unhatched chickens, this exhibition of doubtful spoils. Lay aside such numberings of the people, such idle pretense of certifying in half a minute that which will need the testing of a lifetime. Hope for the best, but in your highest excitements be reasonable. Enquiry-rooms are all very well; but if they lead to idle boastings, they will grieve the Holy Spirit, and work abounding evil.[16]

The missionary pressure for numbers is worth noting. Paton's contemporary biographer, Paul Shlehlein highlights the concern:

"If Paton faced the pressure of quick conversions several generations ago, how much more the missionaries and evangelists of the contemporary church!"[17]

The rush to baptism and church membership, the lack of true fluency, and the allure of numbers are not new in today's missions milieu. All three missionary problems have undoubtedly been blights on the cause of Christ at one time or another in many cultural and linguistic contexts. The tragedy today is that these problems are all at once so prevalent in missions, and yet there are few who perceive the danger or are willing to address it systemically with missions agencies, their practitioners, and their churches. The problems must no longer persist. May sending churches be unenticed by numerical results, may they value faithfulness over speed, and may they require true language fluency for the sake of gospel clarity.

---

16. Charles H. Spurgeon, "What Is It to Win a Soul?" *The Soul-Winner: Or How to Lead Sinners to the Saviour* (New York: Fleming H. Revell, 1895), 13.

17. Schlehlein, *John G. Paton*, 162.

CHAPTER 37

Resolving Conflict in Cross-Cultural Settings

Brian Biedebach

One of the privileges of living in a cross-cultural setting is gaining a greater appreciation for people who grew up in a different environment. It is an especially sweet blessing for missionaries to see God's redemption of people from cultures that are different from their own, to see sinners from different cultures united in love for their common Savior. At times, however, cultural differences can cause confusion and offense.

For example, in South African Afrikaans culture, men are expected to allow women to go through a doorway first as a sign of respect. Yet, in the Zulu culture, which is also present in South Africa, the man is often expected to go first through the doorway, as a gesture of protection—he makes certain that no danger lurks on the other side before the women come through. One can imagine what happens when an Afrikaans woman and a Zulu man both exit the elevator on the same floor: they bump into one another. She looks at him as if to say, *How rude! Ladies should go first.* He looks at

her perplexed, *Why is she offended when I seek to protect? I was trying to be a gentleman.* This is a somewhat trivial example, but experienced missionaries know how easy it is to offend one another on the field, how easy it is to offend the people to whom they minister, and, admittedly, how easy it is to be offended. Besides this, like all Christians, missionaries are also called to be peacemakers.

Though it may seem like some cross-cultural conflicts may never be resolved, there is hope. God's Word is able to supersede culture so that whether a conflict arises from innocent misunderstandings or is intended to cause harm, biblical principles can help to resolve the conflict. In addition to resolution, the goal should be to reconcile the offended parties.

To understand the biblical principles of conflict resolution, it is essential to define key terms. Four biblical terms, which are also distinct actions, are essential: the harboring of bitterness, the willingness to forgive, the granting of forgiveness, and reconciliation. Many

Christians use one term, *forgiveness*, believing that it somehow encompasses all four actions. But when terms are used in ill-defined ways, expectations regarding the results often remain unmet and conflict continues. Below, then, are explanations of the four terms and their differences followed by a case study of how all four terms apply to a specific situation.

The Harboring of Bitterness

Harboring bitterness is always a sin and never beneficial for the believer. Missionaries who harbor bitterness themselves model sin to their national partners and local believers. In Hebrews 12:14–15, believers are admonished, "Pursue peace with all men, and the sanctification without which no one will see the Lord, seeing to it that no one falls short of the grace of God; that no root of bitterness springing up causes trouble, and by it many be defiled." The term *bitterness* (*pikria*) was originally used to describe something "pointed, sharp," and by extension, the taste one has in his mouth when he eats something sour or unpleasant.[1] It was also used for people who had intense resentment, presumably because, when their offender's name was mentioned, the resentful person's face would express sharp displeasure— like a child who just tasted his first lemon. In the context of Hebrews 12, the "root of bitterness" is a person who is apostate, who was "superficially identified with God's people, and

who falls back into paganism."[2] Thus, the warning is that bitterness is dangerous; it spreads throughout the church and causes doubt and dissension, such that "many be defiled." And because bitterness is both destructive and contagious, all Christians need to be careful not to harbor it (Eph 4:31–32).

One of the keys to getting rid of bitterness is for the Christian to remind himself that he has already sinned against God much more than anyone could possibly ever sin against him. For a believer to harbor bitterness against someone who has wronged him, when the believer has offended the infinitely holy God much more, portrays a skewed view of mercy (Matt 18:23–35). Jonathan Edwards understood this well when he penned his eighth resolution: "Resolved, to act, in all respects, both speaking and doing, as if nobody had been so vile as I, and as if I had committed the same sins, or had the same infirmities or failings as others; and that I will let the knowledge of their failings promote nothing but shame in myself, and prove only an occasion of my confessing my own sins and misery to God."[3]

The Willingness to Forgive

A willingness to forgive is always required of every believer in Christ (Luke 6:27–36). The parable of the unmerciful servant (Matt 18:23–35) highlights the fact that believers have been forgiven an unpayable debt, and

---

1. "πικρός," *NIDNTTE*, 3:744.
2. John F. MacArthur Jr., *Hebrews*, MNTC (Chicago: Moody, 1983), 407.
3. Jonathan Edwards, *The Works of Jonathan Edwards*, ed. Edward Hickman (1834; repr., Edinburgh: Banner of Truth, 1974), 1:lxii.

so they ought to be willing to forgive others their much smaller debts. As one commentator has noted, "A believer in Christ should be occupied with how graciously God has forgiven his wrongs rather than how the world or the church recognizes his rights. Emotionally, we should be occupied with the love of God and should be seeking to express our love for Him in obedient service."[4] But it is important to make a distinction between a willingness to forgive and actually granting forgiveness. A willingness "from the heart," as Jesus says, must always precede the bestowal, but at times there may never be an occasion to actually grant forgiveness.

For example, if a missionary has a conflict with a national and the national is unaware or unconvinced that he sinned against the missionary, it would be pointless for the missionary to transactionally grant forgiveness and say, "I forgive you." The national would likely respond by saying, "You forgive me for what? I never sinned against you." The national does not feel that he needs forgiveness for that offense. He may, in fact, never be persuaded that he does. Even still, the missionary—like every believer—must always have a heart that is willing to forgive. Otherwise, bitterness will come in and interfere with the missionary's witness and work, and he will likely receive the Lord's discipline, as the unmerciful emissary Jonah once did (Jonah 4; cf. Prov 3:12; Heb 12:5–11). Ultimately, one who is unwilling to forgive others betrays the fact that he himself may never have experienced the life-changing forgiveness of God (Rom 1:31).

The Granting of Forgiveness

Biblically speaking, when God forgives sins, He removes them from the sinner such that He remembers them no more (Ps 103:12; Isa 43:25; Mic 7:19). That is the wonderful message that missionaries are privileged to proclaim in Jesus' name to all nations (Luke 24:47). The interpersonal forgiveness, then, that they must exemplify is patterned after God's forgiveness: a conscious choice never to bring up the sin again nor to use it against the offender. In other words, forgiveness simply defined is actively choosing not to remember someone's offenses. This doesn't necessarily mean that the offense is never spoken of again, but it is never brought up in a way to make them feel the sting of their sin. Psalm 32:1 says, "How blessed is he whose transgression is forgiven, whose sin is covered!" Because the essence of forgiveness is covering over the offenses of another, at times forgiveness can be granted unconditionally. Other times forgiveness might only be granted after the offender repents.[5]

---

4. John F. Walvoord, *Matthew: Thy Kingdom Come* (Chicago, Moody, 1974), 140.

5. Some would say that forgiveness is always conditional (e.g., Jay Adams, *From Forgiven to Forgiving* [Amityville, NY: Calvary, 1994], 36). Those who believe that forgiveness is always conditional typically consider "covering over with love" as a different activity, not to be equated with forgiveness. However, since Psalm 32:1 (cited above) indicates that "covering over" is synonymous with forgiveness, there must be times when forgiveness can be unconditional and even unilateral. See also John MacArthur, *The Freedom and Power of Forgiveness* (Wheaton, IL: Crossway, 1998), 121. Essentially, both Jay Adams and John MacArthur end up with similar positions. MacArthur recognizes that forgiveness at times must be conditional; other times it can be practiced unconditionally.

While maintaining a willingness to forgive an offender is a nonnegotiable for a believer, there is another choice that can be very difficult to make. Every time a believer is offended, he or she needs to decide whether to confront the offender. The following guidelines are helpful.

When Not to Confront (Unconditional Forgiveness)

In Mark 11:25–26, Jesus commands forgiveness to take place while the offended party stands praying. No condition of confrontation is involved. This kind of forgiveness is especially needed for petty or unintentional offenses (cf. 1 Cor 13:4–5). In such cases the sinner is called to pardon unilaterally and unconditionally. Love does cover over a multitude of sins (Prov. 10:12; 1 Pet 4:8).

Thus, on a personal level, whenever possible, it is best to overlook an offense by extending forgiveness unilaterally. After all, if believers confronted others every time we were personally offended, we would be some of the most painful people on earth. Ephesians 4:1–3 calls believers unto "bearing with one another in love," while 1 Corinthians 13:5 says that love is not easily angered. The underlying principle that should be kept at the forefront of the offended person's mind is to do what is best for the offender: "doing nothing from selfish ambition or vain glory, but with humility of mind regarding one another as more important than yourselves" (Phil 2:3). If an offense was petty, if significant time has passed by, or if bringing it up might cause more damage than leaving it be, the offended person should do what is best for the offender and unconditionally forgive them.

When to Confront (Conditional Forgiveness)

There are times when a person in sin should be confronted (Matt 18:15–17; Luke 17:3)—and missionaries must be willing to confront sin. When a sin must be confronted, the offender's best interests must still be at heart. It is not about the offended person's satisfaction. If confrontation will help the offender or help others, then the missionary needs to confront the offender with the goal of obtaining conditional forgiveness. That is to say, he seeks a granting of forgiveness based on the sinner's repentance. This includes offenses observed against someone other than the missionary and even against those outside the church (Matt 18:15–17; Luke 17:3–10; Gal 6:1).

Moreover, missionaries in a pastoral role are responsible to protect the churches they shepherd by confronting sin in the churches' members. They are charged to protect the flock from the inroads of immoral behavior (1 Cor 5:6–13; Gal 6:1), from factions and false teachings (Titus 1:10–14; 3:10–11; 2 John 10–11), and from losing their witness in the midst of a watching world (1 Cor 5:1; 1 Pet 2:12). Even still, in every case, confronting a sinning brother or sister is aimed at that person's benefit, their restoration to God and to the flock (Matt 18:12–14; 1 Cor 5:5; 2 Cor 2:6–8; Gal 6:1; 2 Thess 3:15; Jas 5:19–20). It is aimed at forgiveness, and therefore, when the person repents, Jesus says, "you have won your brother" (Matt 18:15).

Luke 17:3–10 gives three steps to this kind of conditional forgiveness. The first step is to confront the offender. The verb "rebuke" (*epi-timaō*) used in verse 3 has to do with warning another person in order to prevent an action.[6] It can mean a strong rebuke, but the idea in this context is to help the sinning person. When someone insults, harms, or offends the missionary, his or her natural response might be anger, retaliation, or self-justification and withdrawal. But according to Luke 17, an appropriate response is a cautious, loving confrontation with the goal of bringing about reconciliation. The obligation lies on the offended person to go quietly to the one who has sinned. However, this does not relieve the offender from his obligation to go and repent if he knows he has wronged someone (Matt 5:23–24). Simply put, there is never an excuse for a Christian on either side of a broken relationship to refuse to pursue forgiveness and ultimately reconciliation.

The second step in conditional forgiveness is to forgive the offender if he or she repents (Luke 17:3). As described above, it means deciding not to bring up the sin again, whether to the sinner or to anyone else. This does not preclude other biblical responsibilities, such as legal reporting, accountability, or biblical counseling when the sin requires such responses. Yet forgiveness means laying the personal injury of the offense to rest.

The third step is to repeat the first two steps as often as necessary. Jesus said in Matthew 18:21 that His disciples are to forgive repentant offenders seventy times seven times, which is to say, without limit in terms of quantity.[7] Neither is forgiveness limited by the variety or consistency of offenses committed. Luke 17:4 says, "And if he sins against you seven times a day"—which could be seven different sins or the same sin seven times—"forgive him."

When to Withhold Forgiveness

The only time a Christian could withhold forgiveness from someone, biblically speaking, is when confrontation is necessary and the offender does not repent. The willingness to forgive must still be present, only the granting of forgiveness is withheld. In other words, for the sinner's own good or for the good of others, his sin must be remembered and addressed until he repents; it cannot be swept away (3 John 9–10).

When unrepentance occurs within a congregation, the pastor must then be involved. Jesus guides that confrontation process with four specific steps in Matthew 18:15–17: (1) the offended person privately confronts the sinning brother one-on-one (in the manner described above); (2) he privately confronts the brother again, with one or two witnesses, who either arbitrate between parties or collectively plead for repentance from the brother; (3) they tell the church (via its leaders), which then confronts the sinning brother privately as a congregation; and finally, (4) the sinning "brother" is put out of the church. At this final stage, he is no

---

6. "ἐπιτιμάω," BDAG, 384.
7. R. T. France, *The Gospel of Matthew*, NICNT (Grand Rapids: Eerdmans, 2007), 704–5.

longer assumed to be a Christian brother but an unbeliever who needs faith in Jesus (Matt 18:17; 1 Cor 5:5). He should be considered part of the mission field, not the church.

Church planting or leading missionaries may have to exercise church discipline for the protection of the church or of Christ's name. This should never be the escalated response to mere cross-cultural differences or unintended offenses that could be overlooked with grace. It is reserved for spiritual dangers; sins that must be confronted. When syncretism is introduced by a member, or when sinful cultural customs are not relinquished, or when one member harmfully sins against another without amends, the missionary must do his duty to lovingly confront the sinning member, seek their repentance, and ultimately obtain their forgiveness from the offended party. As with the unnamed brother in Corinth, such confrontation can and does lead to repentance, forgiveness, and full restoration (2 Cor 2:5–11; cf. 1 Cor 5:1–13). But even when it does not, Jesus has commanded it, and missionaries must obey.

Reconciliation

The fourth and final key term in conflict resolution is reconciliation, which goes beyond the willingness to forgive or the granting of forgiveness. The New Testament term *katallassō* ("reconcile") refers to more than just restoring something to some previous standard; rather, it refers to the concept of exchange.[8] For example,

when believers are reconciled to God, they exchange a bad relationship for a good relationship (Rom 5:10; 2 Cor 5:18–21). The same is true when two sinners are reconciled.

In fact, when sinners have been reconciled to God, a natural consequence is that they live reconciled to one another also (Eph 2:13–18). Missionaries, in this respect, ought to be peacemakers (Matt 5:9; 2 Cor 13:11). Since they are ambassadors for Christ, as if God were making His appeal to sinners through them, "be reconciled to God" (2 Cor 5:20), then the missionaries themselves must be eager to reconcile with those who have wronged them.

Moreover, God commands brothers to seek reconciliation, not merely forgiveness (Matt 5:23–24). This means that the offended person reaffirms his love for and brotherhood with the repentant sinner. Second Corinthians 2:8 gives that very command for the Corinthian church, that they reaffirm their love for the brother who had greatly offended them. That is the essence of reconciliation—forgiveness that produces love and the exchange of a bad relationship for a good one.

The process of reconciliation might look different for each person. One party might be restored to a good relationship with the offender quickly, but someone else might need more time, even years, depending on the severity of the sin. Certain sins require more remediation than others, such as where abuse or illegal crimes are involved. In such cases, the relationship between parties may never look the

---

8. "καταλλάσσω," BDAG, 521.

same again, but that does not mean that reconciliation cannot occur incrementally or that a bad relationship cannot be exchanged for a good relationship. Essential elements of genuine repentance include restitution, accepting the consequences of one's wrongdoing, and a desire to rebuild trust (2 Cor 7:10–11). Regaining that trust may take time. Yet, regardless of how long reconciliation may take, the whole conflict resolution process needs to be accomplished in a timely manner that guards oneself from harboring bitterness.

A Case Study: When Your Disciple Steals from You

One of the most challenging tasks for a missionary is to develop leadership for taking over ministry responsibilities after he completes his mission. It is not uncommon for offenses to take place between the missionary and the national whom they have trusted the most. If, for example, the national were to steal money from the missionary, and if it were to be discovered, how should the national be dealt with?

The first step would be for the missionary to examine his own heart and ensure that he is not harboring any bitterness or pride. Galatians 6:1 makes it clear that spiritual leaders are to examine their own lives first before trying to help those who are caught in transgressions. It would be easy for a missionary from a Western country to be overcritical of a national from a non-Western country when it comes to stealing. While in no way trying to diminish the seriousness of breaking the eighth commandment, different cultures often look at this sin with varying levels of contempt. The fact should be faced that it is often not easy for nationals to work with missionaries. Besides the cultural differences, the economic gap can cause great pressure on the national. If he is employed by the missionary, many of his family members and friends are likely to believe that he must be making more money than he actually is. In a culture where extended family members are expected to share goods equally, the pressure on those who work for missionaries might be more daunting than the missionary would imagine. Although the missionary might be hurt and feel violated, he must recognize that his offenses to God have been much greater than any offense anyone could commit against him personally. It is important to fight against feelings of bitterness and resentment and to determine what the most Christlike response to betrayal would be.

The desire of the missionary should also include a willingness to forgive. But more difficult than manifesting that desire internally could be the manifestation of it outwardly. Should he confront the national who steals from him, or should he overlook it? This can be even more challenging if he is not 100 percent sure that the person he suspects is, in fact, the thief. Suspicion kills relationships, and therefore missionaries should avoid false accusations. Having been robbed on numerous occasions, my advice is not to chase after suspected thieves when the evidence is absent.

It is also easy for a missionary to lose his focus and act more like a detective than a missionary—a practice that can distract everyone from productive ministry. If he has reason to suspect someone, it is enough to ask them if they have any idea what happened to the property that had been stolen, and then, in love, he should believe them (1 Cor 13:7). First Corinthians 6:7 warns that sometimes conflicts can get so out of hand that it is better just to be wronged. In that case, 1 Peter 2:23 says that the believer's greatest example "kept entrusting Himself to Him who judges righteously," when He experienced injustice—and there has never been a greater injustice.

On some occasions, it is best for missionaries to confront individuals, especially when the offense might not have been against them personally. On one such occasion, a disciple of mine had stolen something from the church. The evidence was clear. When we confronted the individual, he admitted to the theft and confessed it openly with what I believed was heartfelt repentance. The church elders were eager to grant him forgiveness, but we also recognized that we needed to serve this individual by presenting him with a plan of reconciliation.

Churches and missionaries sometimes do a disservice to a national by not dealing with a sin completely. They may confront it, they may even grant forgiveness, but sometimes they neglect to set out a clearly defined path toward reconciliation. The result can be that the forgiven person continues to feel unnecessary shame and/or guilt. In the situation of the theft in the church, the elders asked the individual to do the following: make restitution, repent before the congregation, write a letter explaining the situation, and complete some discipleship training.

Restitution not only is important for those who have had a loss but also is beneficial for those who desire to break a habit of sin (Rom 13:8–10; Eph 4:28). While public repentance is not always necessary for every sin, genuine repentance is evidenced by a willingness to confess before all offended parties. In the case of stealing, the offense was against the entire congregation. The request of the elders for this person to confess publicly was not meant to shame or punish the offender but to give him the opportunity to seek forgiveness from all offended parties. Gratefully, the individual was eager to confess before all. Writing a letter to explain the situation was also a way to serve those in the future who might have questions about this situation.

The goal of a reconciliation plan should always be to help the individual be granted forgiveness and be reconciled with the entire congregation, with the hope that one day he can be above reproach and qualified to serve in any role in the church. Depending on the offense, the time frame for continued discipleship may vary, but it should be spelled out with measurable goals.

Conclusion

Conflict resolution will look different from case to case, but the common theme is always that Christians have been forgiven a debt far greater than the sins of anyone against them. Since that truth disallows the sin of bitterness, Christians need to be willing to forgive whether or not the offender shows repentance. When forgiveness is granted, the offended should commit not to bring up the offense in any way that makes the offender relive or remember the sting of their sin. Finally, Christians must take tangible, measurable steps toward a reconciled relationship, with both parties desiring to exchange a bad relationship for a good one.

Missionaries in particular are called to be agents of forgiveness. They proclaim repentance for the forgiveness of sins in Jesus' name (Luke 24:47). They announce the good news of peace with God and salvation (Isa 52:7; Rom 5:1; 10:14–15). They plead with men to be reconciled to God through the blood of His Son (2 Cor 5:18–20). And if that is their message in word, then they, of all people, should be ready to forgive and to seek forgiveness from others. They must recognize that a cross-cultural life is likely to encounter conflict and to complicate the task of making peace. But participating in God's cross-cultural work of redemption is well worth it, and His Word is sufficient to guide them in reconciliation.

INSERT 37.1

Impacts of the Shame-Honor Culture on the Local Church: A Case Study from the Philippines

Sean Ransom

Everyone is influenced by the culture they live in, whether they realize it or not. Culture shapes one's values, thinking, actions, and worldview. For the Christian, the influence of culture can be so powerful that it even impacts the way one views and submits to Scripture. In the context of the local church, culture's pervasive influence is evident in the way shame-honor societies approach the matter of church discipline, the public admonition and restorative rebuke of a sinning brother (Matt 18:15–17). In Asia the dominant worldview that permeates the mindset is known as shame-honor culture. This cultural value drives people to do everything necessary to maintain a good reputation or standing by one's family and community, and it avoids anything that threatens them, such as correction, confrontation, and confession. The community finds behaviors that harm relationships or demean the standing of someone in the community to be shocking. This cultural value and its practice stand as an impediment to obeying Scripture's clear instructions for dealing with unrepentant sinful and divisive people in the church.

Conflict and the Consequences of Nonconfrontation

A certain Filipino church contained a small but influential group of people who disagreed with their church's form of governance. The disgruntled members met with the elders and expressed their concerns, then asked them to change the church's doctrinal statement, which clarified the church's leadership structure. After hearing the objectors, the elders held to their convictions and denied the group's request. Not willing to accept or submit to the decision of the elders, the group began grumbling against them and maligning them, both privately and publicly through email and social media. The group became bitter and increasingly unkind in their words to the elders. They even began accusing them of sin.

The elders decided to ignore the complaints and slander. They did this for several reasons. First, they hoped to win them over by patiently shepherding them through the teaching of the Word of God. Second, they did not want to hurt relationships in the church by fighting or shaming anyone. Third, they feared confrontation and potential consequences, such as angry members, a church split, or the loss of church property.

Because of these concerns, the elders kept quiet while their opposition spread rumors, assigned wrong motives, and spun false narratives. The pattern dragged on for several years in this Filipino church.

Most of the congregation was unaware of the group's sinful behavior because the elders kept the matter quiet, in hope of restoration. However, because they did not correct or confront the dissenters, division began to grow within the church. The longer the elders avoided rebuking their sinful behavior and publicly addressing their errant views, the more the complaints and lies grew. Additionally, because of the elders' silence, the only side of the narrative anyone in the church heard was that of the accusers. The consequence was that some church members were persuaded by the unverified charges of the vocal minority and, with time, the once small circle became a large group that eventually split the church.

God's Timeless Word on Dealing with Sin in the Church

Sad situations like the one in this church can be prevented. Foundationally, believers in shame-honor cultures should strive to recognize where cultural values can hinder them from upholding God's values. While church leaders are commanded to preserve relationships, protect reputations, exhibit patience when wronged, and instruct the unruly, the forbearance of corrupting sin is not a godly virtue and must be short lived (1 Cor 5:6–13). When offenders hurt the church, are not teachable, and remain unrepentant, they must be directly rebuked (Titus 1:10–13). Failure to obey God's Word in this area can do severe damage to the church and its witness. In the end, more relationships are hurt by inaction and the fear of man than by practicing loving, restorative church discipline.

Paul's instructions on dealing with rebellious people in the church are obligatory for church leaders in all cultures. In Titus 1:9, Paul explained that elders must be devoted to Scripture, "so that [they] will be able both to exhort in sound doctrine and to reprove those who contradict." To reprove means to rebuke or correct.[9] Faithful elders therefore are required to lovingly confront those who have a pattern of arguing against sound teaching.

Just as in Asian culture, Jewish culture in the New Testament was averse to causing shame. But that did not stop Paul from saying that elders are duty-bound to "silence" rebellious men and women in the church. He instructed Titus to "reprove them severely" (Titus 1:13). While this may be difficult to do, and seemingly scandalous in churches that have a shame-honor culture, all elders today must "reprove with all authority" and "let no one disregard" them, insofar as they represent the truth (Titus 2:15).

Finally, in Titus 3:10–11, Paul revealed God's command to elders on dealing with those who attempt to divide the church. They are to "reject a factious man after a first and second warning, knowing that such a man is perverted and is sinning, being self-condemned." While cutting off fellowship is difficult, especially in a culture that values harmonious relationships and community, failing to do so can result in ravenous wolves being free to run loose among God's sheep (1 Pet 5:2, 8; cf. Acts 20:29).

In Matthew 18:15–17, Jesus Himself taught in four steps how to deal with sinful people who claim to be believers. First, He commanded that sinners must be confronted for their sins with the hope of restoring damaged relationships (v. 15). Second, if there is no repentance, witnesses are to confirm and confront the sin (v. 16). Third, if repentance still does not come, the elders must tell the church so that they can join in confronting the sinners and urging them to repentance (v. 17). Finally, if the sinners reject the pleas of the church family, the church is to call them to turn to Christ for salvation (v. 17).

---

9. Similarly, "to bring a person to the point of recognizing wrongdoing." "ἐλέγχω," BDAG, 315.

Conclusion

In whatever culture Christians find themselves, they must reject all values and practices that prevent faithfulness to Christ, such as was the case in the shame-honor culture in which the Filipino church trapped themselves. While public admonition may bring shame and dishonor to Filipinos, when rightly done, it shows reverence and honor to God. It is on account of love for God and His church that Christians must confront sin.

When a Plurality of Elders Is Countercultural

Jung-Ui Cho

In South Korea, the first thing someone asks a person they meet for the first time is their age. This is because it is considered convenient to rank seniority before conversing and possibly establishing a relationship. In Korean society, where Confucianism has deep roots, younger people are expected to respect older people. The vocabulary used and the attitude conveyed differs based on the age of the person being addressed. Social status is also considered just as important as age. There are many unspoken rules about how to speak and behave toward superiors. Sometimes unnecessary conflicts or problems arise between young bosses and older subordinates because the cultures of honor and shame are intricately intertwined. This honor-shame aspect of Korean culture also has a great influence on how churches establish elders and work together according to the Bible. This insert examines Korean culture, examines the present state of eldership in its midst, and sets an agenda for biblical correction.

Cultural Norms Competing with Plural Eldership

The system of eldership in New Testament churches is that of plurality, where two or more male overseers share spiritual leadership responsibilities in the local church (cf. 1 Tim 4:14; Titus 1:5; Heb 13:7, 17, 24). The apostle Paul exhorted Timothy, who served as the leader of the church in Ephesus while yet a young man, "Let no one look down on your youthfulness, but show yourself as a model to those who believe in word, conduct, love, faith, and purity" (1 Tim 4:12). In Korea a young age is considered synonymous with lack of experience and wisdom. So Korean believers tend to look down on, or at least patronize, young church elders. I myself started working as a senior pastor at the young age of thirty-five in the church where I was born and raised. After my first sermon, many elderly members of the church came up to me and said, "I am so proud of you, my son."

Even church elders themselves can despise youth and youthfulness. Unless people are of the exact same age, a hierarchy is created even among church leaders. When a new young elder is elected for the future of the church, the age gap between him and the existing elder is almost like that between a father and a son. Where the plurality of eldership is marked by age differences, it is not easy for two elders of different ages to discuss freely on equal footing or even express their opinions comfortably. It is almost impossible for the younger elder to advise the older and correct mistakes, even when unbiblical error surfaces. I attend a meeting of thirty to forty church elders from several local congregations monthly, and most of them are over seventy years old. Although they do not intend to create an age hierarchy or an atmosphere of superiority, it is generally a virtue for young elders like me to remain silent when older men are present. Speaking one's thoughts boldly is easily judged as arrogance.

Backgrounds such as social status, wealth, education, and origin can also become obstacles to the plural elder system. If an elder has a prominent job that is lucrative or graduated from a prestigious school, he will often be favored by the church members and treated with more respect than his peers. If an elder lacks biblical quality, he may try to use his titles and successes to his advantage to gain power and influence. It is not easy for elders to respect one another and serve with one mind when elders assert themselves over others.

Present Status of Plural Eldership

The plural elder system depicted in the Bible is where order and equality coexist. At the Jerusalem council in Acts 15, Barnabas and Paul were given the opportunity to defend the gospel and make a full argument in front of "James and Cephas and John, who were reputed to be pillars" (Gal 2:9; cf. Acts 15:7, 13). Peter concluded the discussion and confirmed, "We believe that we are saved through the grace of the Lord Jesus, in the same way as [the Gentiles] also are" (Acts 15:11). To unite with other saints, James added, "But . . . we write to them that they abstain from things contaminated by idols and from sexual immorality and from what is strangled and from blood" (15:20), confirming the authority of the apostle to all Gentile churches. A letter containing their affirmation was then sent to the churches (15:22–31).

Acts 13 is another passage that describes the plural leadership of the Antioch church, identifying prophets and teachers specifically (v. 1). According to the command of the Holy Spirit, the church set apart Barnabas and Saul, laid hands on them, and sent them away. The passage highlights that the church did not make important decisions based on the single leadership of Barnabas or Saul, but rather made decisions based on the fasting and prayers of multiple people in leadership (13:1–3).

The advantage of plural leadership is that the church is not placed under the leadership of one person but under the united leadership of many people. The direction and operation of the entire church is not determined by the wisdom and gifts of one person, but the church moves by the wisdom and gifts of many people. Elders can respect one another's gifts and freely share their opinions with the wisdom given by God, for "without consultation, plans are frustrated, but with many counselors they succeed" (Prov 15:22). At the same time, the plurality model of leadership recognizes the nature of order established by God, since those elders with more influence and responsibility must serve and lead fellow elders humbly and gently, while other elders must support the leadership of their fellow elders, each taking responsibility in their own roles.

Most Korean churches have a one-man ministry, that is, a church government in which the senior pastor alone exercises leadership. Of course, there are other members of the leadership, such as elders and assistant pastors, but since the senior pastor has tremendous authority and influence, it is for all intents and purposes a one-man ministry. Because of the insurmountable differences in status (and among pastors, the senior pastor is generally the oldest), it is difficult for members in leadership positions to freely share their wisdom and gifts. It is difficult to demonstrate one's spiritual gifts and capacities without the permission of the senior pastor. You may be ignored because you are young, or you may be treated poorly because you are an assistant pastor or "evangelist" (in Korea, before completing theological studies, a person is called an evangelist). This leadership style, while it is suppressive and socially stifling, is the status quo of many churches in South Korea.

Biblical Agenda for Plural Eldership

The power to destroy this unhealthy hierarchical structure in the church is found in the advice of the apostle Paul in 1 Timothy 4, which follows his command that the younger leader, appointed by God and the elders, "let no one look down on [his] youthfulness" (v. 12). The young man must "take pains" (v. 15) to maintain an exemplary public and private life (v. 12), and "be absorbed" (v. 15) in carrying out the work of exposition, application, and instruction (v. 13). To the end of being an example of saving grace that might draw others to salvation and sanctification, he must "pay close attention to [himself] and to [his] teaching" (v. 16).

Leadership that transcends age, status, origin, and background is revealed through everyday life by the power of the Holy Spirit. Exceptional love, faith, and fidelity are shown through words and actions (Jas 1:22–27) and can powerfully lead the church to receive biblical teaching and exhortation even from a younger man. In the face of structural problems that can persist in one's local church leadership context, God calls all men to pursue their own spiritual growth in character and ministry competence on a daily basis. Therefore, no matter the ministry position God has permitted to a younger leader, he can exercise powerful biblical leadership in the church. Through the power of the Holy Spirit, he can set a clear example of maturing biblical responsibility that can influence the functional relationships among the elders and the people. It is comforting to look out from any cultural context back to Scripture's portrayal of plural eldership and trust that as God's men follow the biblical examples of the greatest of men, God will be pleased to use them today to build His church.

CHAPTER 38

Women's Ministries in Cross-Cultural Settings

Betty Price

All believers in a local church are valuable and important in that church's life and ministry. All of them have gifts to be used in edifying and building one another up for the glory of God. All of them are responsible to make disciples and to proclaim the gospel. Women's ministry in a church is one way these things must happen. Women serving will look different from church to church, depending on factors such as congregation size and cultural setting. The common factors, however, are the love Christian women have for one another and their need for service, mutual fellowship, and prayer. With that in mind, this chapter looks at the biblical foundation, examples, and end goal of women's ministries in cross-cultural settings.

A Biblical Foundation for Women's Ministries

The Bible is the believer's starting point for all learning of how to serve in one's church family. God has ordained certain roles for women, and churches must consider how to apply those roles in varying cultural settings. Still, while cultural influence must be considered with sensitivity, ultimate authority rests with God's Word (Rom 12:2). Three biblical texts are instructive: Titus 2:3–5; 1 Timothy 3:11; and Philippians 4:2–3.

Women Ministering to Other Women

In Paul's pastoral letter to Titus, he explains what it means to live with godly character in the midst of a pagan culture. When he instructs Titus in chapter 2 on establishing church order, he includes specific instructions for the church's older men and older women. Of the latter he writes,

> Older women likewise are to be reverent in their behavior, not malicious gossips nor enslaved to much wine, teaching what is good, so that they may instruct the young women in sensibility: to love their husbands, to love their children, to be sensible, pure, workers at home, kind, being subject to their own husbands, so that the word of God will not be slandered. (Titus 2:3–5)

This passage gives four descriptions of godly older women. They should first be reverent, marked by a sobriety about the things of God, rather than silliness or superficiality (v. 3). Second, they must be able to control their tongues (v. 3), for as mentors or counselors, they will learn personal information about others' lives, and they must be able to refrain from sharing it inappropriately. Third, they must not be controlled by alcohol or other substances that impact clear thinking (v. 3). Fourth, they are to teach and train younger women in wise behavior and good judgment (vv. 3–5).

The content of the older women's teaching includes godly character (sensibility, purity, kindness), unselfish love for husbands and children, respect for their husbands' leadership, and a strong work ethic in the home. While the focus is mainly on women as wives and mothers, single women can also learn much from an older woman. Younger women are to humbly desire this kind of training for their own benefit and spiritual growth but also for the sake of the gospel and how it is viewed by those outside the church. Older women need to be faithful to give this kind of training for the benefit of the church and for the reputation of Christ's gospel. Paul views the ministry of older women to younger ones as vital. Without it, God's Word and reputation will be dishonored among unbelievers (v. 5).

Titus 2:3–5 is one of the clearest guides to discipleship in the New Testament. *Discipleship* is often used by Christians to mean one-on-one mentorship, and that is an effective way to fulfill the instructions in Titus 2. Yet Paul does not limit the method to one-on-one mentoring. Women can teach more than one woman at a time. Besides this, women are also equipped for the Christian life by their pastor's preaching of this text to the church, through intergenerational women's Bible studies and discussions, through small group sharing and prayer, and through reading biblically sound Christian books on the topic. Regardless of how the truths of Titus 2 are passed on, a church body is always blessed to have older women who are eager to engage younger women and to lead them to the fruit of spiritual maturity. The godly homes and families that come as a result point others to Christ.

Missionaries face challenges when they seek to implement Titus 2 in their ministry to the women of their target culture. One older woman, serving faithfully in her native region in Japan, reported that women are not interested in hearing other women teach the Bible. They want to listen to their pastor. Thus, in a culture where women are not inclined to value a Titus 2 ministry—discipleship led by women—it is essential for pastors to teach the passage clearly while leaving time for the church to mature. The leaders need to take measured steps, prayerfully seeking steady spiritual growth from their congregations in this area. The pastors' support of women-to-women ministry is essential.

On the other hand, some missionary wives report that in their target cultures local pastors do not value women's ministries or, in some instances, even view them negatively. In those scenarios, women who read Scripture and desire biblical fellowship with other women should submit to their pastor's leadership and patiently pray for him. They could meet one-on-one in each other's homes to pray for and encourage each other yet without going against their pastor's leadership.

Women Meeting Qualifications

First Timothy 3 is useful for identifying when a woman is qualified to lead in discipleship ministry. Paul specifically states that his purpose in writing 1 Timothy is to give instructions about the way the church should function (3:14–15). Then, while listing the qualifications for elders and deacons, he specifically mentions women: "Women *gynaikas*) must likewise be dignified, not malicious gossips, but temperate, faithful in all things" (3:11).

Several translations alternately render the Greek word *gynaikas* as either "women" or "wives." The former term takes Paul to be referring to the wives of deacons, but the latter, to women serving in the formal role of deacon (or deaconess).[1] Either way, Paul notes that these women should be qualified in their character before they (or their husbands) are recognized for leadership. Also, though the qualities he lists should be the goal of all women in the church (cf. Gal 5:22–23), they should especially be true of those discipling younger women in the manner of Titus 2. They should be "dignified" (worthy of respect) by way of their speech, temperance, and faithfulness.

For a woman to be qualified for discipling others, self-control in speech is vital. Malicious speech and gossip are excluded (cf. Titus 2:3). Cultures have differing norms for what is regarded as appropriate speech. For example, one missionary wife who serves with her husband in Central Europe is surrounded by people who speak very bluntly. If they disagree about something, they feel no inhibition about speaking their minds. The missionary wife has had to learn that this is the culture's communication pattern, and that people mean no lack of love by their speech. She adds that something shared with another woman as a prayer request, regardless of how personal, will likely be shared with other church members in short order. In such cultures where people do not prize confidentiality, it takes time to teach biblical truth and then to shepherd women (and men) into becoming trustworthy leaders whose speech edifies others (Col 4:6). It is, however, essential.

"Temperate" is likewise an expression of self-control, indicating balance, levelheadedness, and restraint from excess (Titus 2:2).[2] Then, for a woman to be "faithful (*pistas*) in all things" (1 Tim 3:11) implies her trustworthiness,[3] which should also be understood in light of the New Testament's teaching that all believers are duty-bound to conform their lives to the whole truth of Scripture (Rom 12:1–2). That is to say, they must be obedient and submissive to Scripture. Jesus teaches that the foremost commandment is to love God with

---

1. See the discussion in Robert W. Yarbrough, *The Letters to Timothy and Titus*, PNTC (Grand Rapids: Eerdmans, 2018), 210.
2. Yarbrough, 508.
3. "πιστός," BDAG, 820.

all one's heart, soul, and mind, and the second is to love one's neighbor as oneself (Matt 22:37–39). Both commands are about relationships. The relationship with God comes first, and the relationships with others flow out from it. The woman in church leadership therefore must be committed to her own relationship with God as the main priority. Along with that, her godly love should be reflected in the way she seeks to fulfill the biblical "one anothers" (e.g., John 13:34–35; Rom 12:15–16; Eph 4:32; Phil 2:3; Col 3:16; 1 Thess 5:11; Heb 3:13; 1 Pet 4:9–10).

Women Leading in Harmony

Regarding relationships, two women in the New Testament provide both a positive and a negative example. In Philippians 4:2–3, Paul directly addresses Euodia and Syntyche, prominent women in the church who were capable servants but locked in some conflict. Though he saw them as "fellow workers" and partners in the gospel proclamation (v. 3), he also needed to urge them to live in harmony, "to think the same way in the Lord" (v. 2; cf. 1 Cor 1:10). Their conflict was apparently affecting the whole church, or Paul would not have named them publicly.[4] He respected these women and their ministries, and so sought their reconciliation.

Both men and women can have conflicts that negatively impact the church, and sometimes they need help in making things right. Several years ago, I was speaking at a women's luncheon at a church. While there, the pastor's wife invited me to come along to a meeting of their women's ministry leadership team, about six women, plus her husband, the pastor. I asked if the pastor had something special to communicate to the women, but his wife sheepishly said no. Rather, two of the women could not get along with each other, and the only way to prevent the meeting from continual conflict was for the pastor to attend. His presence motivated them to conduct themselves more appropriately. How frustrating it would be to the ministry, however, if these women never resolved their conflict.

Like Euodia and Syntyche, conflict will arise between women of leadership and influence in a church. No two people agree on everything, and cross-cultural ministry presents even more opportunity for differences of preference or opinion. Yet any leader must consider the example she or he sets for others when disagreements arise. Leaders must, on the basis of their relationship with the Lord, live in harmony with others. The character qualification of being "temperate [and] faithful" requires being self-controlled and persuadable, and taking steps to resolve conflict biblically. Whether for good or for bad, the leadership of women will affect the whole church.

Examples of Women's Ministries

All believers are called to exercise spiritual gifts for the building up of the body of Christ (Rom 12:3–8; 1 Cor 12:1–11; 1 Peter 4:10–11). These spiritual gifts are not gender specific but may be

---

4. See Mark J. Keown, *Philippians*, EEC (Bellingham, WA: Lexham, 2017), 2:310–11.

shared by men and women in varying degrees.[5] Women's ministries are excellent platforms for women to discover and exercise their giftedness. They will love doing what God has equipped them to do as they see spiritual fruit and as they are affirmed in their service by other members of the church.

New Testament Examples

There are many New Testament examples of women serving in accord with their individual circumstances and giftedness. Dorcas, for instance, displayed her compassion ministry by making garments for widows (Acts 9:36–42). Anna the prophetess served at the temple by worshiping in prayer and fasting. When she saw the baby Jesus, she proclaimed the arrival of the Messiah to those in Jerusalem who were awaiting His coming (Luke 2:36–38). Many scholars believe that Phoebe was entrusted by Paul with the book of Romans to deliver it to the church in Rome (Rom 16:1–2).[6]

With her husband Aquila, the woman Priscilla made tents alongside Paul. Paul referred to them both as fellow workers, "who for my life risked their own necks, to whom not only do I give thanks, but also all the churches of the Gentiles" (Rom 16:3–4).[7] He obviously had great respect and appreciation for this husband-wife team. When they were in Ephesus, God used them in a private conversation to bring theological correction to the eloquent preaching of Apollos (Acts 18:24–28).

Many women also served by hosting missionaries and churches in their homes. Such was the case with Mary and Martha (Luke 10:38–42); Lydia (Acts 16:11–15, 40); Apphia, who was likely Philemon's wife (Phlm 1–2);[8] and Nympha (Col 4:15). There were also women who proclaimed the good news of the Messiah's arrival, such as the Samaritan woman who told the people in her town about her meeting with Jesus, with the result that "many of the Samaritans believed in Him because of the word of the woman who bore witness" (John 4:39–42). Some women traveled at times with Jesus and the disciples and provided for them financially as well (Luke 8:1–3). Some of these women were not married, at least not at the time they are mentioned in the New Testament. In that regard, it is important to understand that though formal women's ministries in the church often focus on marriage and parenting in their teaching, single women should not be neglected.

---

5. This excludes the offices of apostle and pastor, which are called gifts to the church in Ephesians 4:11, for example, and are elsewhere shown to have been only filled by men or prescribed only for men. See John F. MacArthur Jr., *Ephesians*, MNTC (Chicago: Moody, 1986), 140–49.

6. "It is highly probable that Phoebe was the bearer of this epistle to the church at Rome." John Murray, *The Epistle to the Romans* (Grand Rapids: Eerdmans, 1975), 226.

7. Priscilla and Aquila's names are mentioned six times in the New Testament, with her name mentioned first in four of those instances. Since her name is mentioned first in the text about the conversation with Apollos, it is reasonable to believe that she was an active participant in the discussion, not a silent listener. That would mean that she had theological knowledge and understanding with which she could serve others, including Apollos. Simon J. Kistemaker, *Exposition of the Acts of the Apostles*, New Testament Commentary 17 (Grand Rapids: Baker, 1990), 668–69; John Calvin, *Commentary upon the Acts of the Apostles*, ed. Henry Beveridge, (Bellingham, WA: Logos Bible Software, 2010), 2:202–3.

8. J. B. Lightfoot, *Saint Paul's Epistles to the Colossians and to Philemon* (1879; repr., Grand Rapids: Zondervan, 1982), 306.

They, too, have needs and should be cared for. Furthermore, when they are taught and trained, they typically have more time for serving in the church than women with families do.

Modern-Day Examples

The specific opportunities for women in ministry will vary depending on individual circumstances and culture. But the church everywhere needs women who are gifted in teaching women and children, mentoring women, biblical counseling, prayer, music, writing and publishing, serving as missionaries, caring for missionaries, evangelism and outreach, hospitality, fostering children, skills teaching, administration, and event planning.

Modern-day examples of women doing these things abound. Many pertain directly to the family. For instance, one missionary wife in a majority Muslim country is conducting marriage counseling with her husband for a young local couple who were planning to divorce but are willing to seek reconciliation—and there is the hope that this couple will come to faith in Christ through the process.

Many examples pertain to children's ministry specifically, which is highly valued by Christ (Matt 10:42; 19:13–15). A Christian couple in Central Europe has developed a ministry caring for refugee children from Africa. A missionary couple in southern Asia has started a local school for children, where they share the gospel and include many locals, especially women, to help them in the ministry. In another Asian country, a local believing couple cares for orphans abandoned by their parents,

enlisting local Christian women to help. One single woman I know has served as a missionary in Eastern Europe for about ten years, and she has impacted hundreds of children for the gospel through summer camps, vacation Bible schools, and Sunday school. As well, a missionary couple in Africa attended a church in their early years with preaching services that lasted two to three hours—yet without a program to teach the children. The wife started a children's class, teaching the Bible at a level the children could understand, and thereby granting the parents the ability to gain more from their pastors' teaching also. Eventually this missionary wife led women's Bible studies and also trained women how to teach.

Other examples pertain to young and adult women. A single woman who is a former student of mine had a longtime desire to be able to teach and train women biblically in a cross-cultural setting. After finishing university, she completed a master's degree in biblical counseling, then a doctorate at a biblical seminary. She was invited to join the faculty at a seminary in the Middle East where students attend from many countries. She is an associate dean and teaches classes for the women students who expect to return to their own countries and teach women there.

Other women have gone into restricted-access countries as English teachers, after earning degrees in education or certificates in TESOL (Teaching English to Speakers of Other Languages). Some go as registered nurses, which allows them to reach where pastors or missionaries cannot. All of these women are following in the footsteps of the biblical examples for women's ministry and the Great Commission.

The Goal of Women's Ministries

Finally, women's ministries must exist as a support to the ministry of the pastor-elders of the local church. Scripture teaches that the office of elder is exclusively reserved for men. First Timothy 2:11–12 identifies the two main responsibilities of elders: to be the congregation's doctrinal teachers and to exercise godly authority over the congregation. Holding to this view today is called complementarianism because of the complementary designs God gave men and women (Gen 2:18). Men and women are ontologically equal in value, in bearing God's image, and in salvation (Gen 1:26–28; Gal 3:28; 1 Pet 3:7) yet have distinct roles in the church (1 Tim 3:1–2; Titus 1:5–6) and family (Eph 5:22–33; Titus 2:5; 1 Pet 3:1–7).[9]

Those promoting egalitarianism commonly point to culture when rejecting the exclusivity of male leadership in the church. Paul, some argue, taught that women could not be pastors in his context because in his culture women were not well educated. Today, however, women have access to the highest levels of education, even theological and biblical studies. Others contend that women were not highly valued in the first century, but with social progress, women are now properly respected for their intelligence and skills. But Paul does not cite cultural issues as his reasons for insisting

upon male pastorship. Instead, he points back to creation (1 Tim 2:13–15; cf. 1 Cor 11:3–12). The truths of God's design for men and women have not changed from the beginning, regardless of cultural factors like chauvinism, feminism, or gender fluidity.

This does not mean that all women are called to submit to all men. Nor does it mean that submission is only for women. Only a few men in the church are elders, and all other believers, both men and women, are called to submit to their leaders (Heb 13:17). All believers, including the pastor-elders, are called to submit to Christ (1 Cor 11:3; Eph 5:23–24). Complementarians believe there are kinds of leadership that women can and sometimes should fulfill in the church without violating Paul's teaching in the New Testament, such as director of women's ministries, director of children's ministries, missionaries (single or married), or other roles that the pastors may designate. Women have many outlets in which they can support the local church's leaders.

Conclusion

Pastor and Bible teacher Philip De Courcy, in his small book *You Go, Girl*, gives timely encouragement for women:

> Ladies, do what you can for Christ, through Christ (Phil. 4:13). What God allows you to do is broad, bold, and beautiful. . . . I pray that you will think through this

---

9. See the excellent representation in John Piper and Wayne Grudem, *Recovering Biblical Manhood and Womanhood: A Response to Evangelical Feminism*, rev. ed. (Wheaton, IL: Crossway, 2020); and "The Danvers Statement" and other resources from The Council on Biblical Manhood and Womanhood, accessed June 18, 2024, cbmw.org/about/danvers-statement.

wide-ranging menu of ministries that are open to you and get busy serving in your local body of believers (Rom. 12:1). Join the endless line of women parading across the Bible and redemptive history who enhanced the life of the church, won people to Christ, proclaimed Jesus' name, blessed the saints, and supported the spread of the gospel. Now you go, girl![10]

In God's infinitely wise plan, women have tremendous opportunities to glorify God, impact the church, and shape lives for God's kingdom. Cross-cultural ministries need them as much as domestic ministries do, so let women be encouraged to prayerfully and humbly use their spiritual gifts and abilities to serve in many capacities that honor Christ and point others to him.

---

10. Philip De Courcy, *You Go, Girl: How Women Build Up the Church* (Anaheim, CA: Know the Truth, 2021), 33.

INSERT 38.1

Should We Send Single Female Missionaries to the Field?

Lisa LaGeorge

Yes, the church must send single female missionaries to the field. Single women can and must serve in their churches. For women who know Christ as Savior are coheirs of the gospel of Jesus along with their brothers (Gal 3:27–28). As such, they have been equipped with gifting through the power of the Spirit of God for the purpose of the building up of the body of Christ (1 Tim 5:9–10, Titus 2:3–5; cf. 1 Cor 11:5; 14:31). And just as single women serve in their local church— discipling, fulfilling the commands of the New Testament, or providing support for

their leaders—the Lord also uses single women to serve in cross-cultural contexts for the sake of His gospel work (Col 4:15; Rom 16:1–2, 12–13; Phil 4:3).

Sometimes churches have discouraged single women (and men) from going to the mission field. However, Jesus in Matthew 19 and Paul in 1 Corinthians 7 said that those who are single are less distracted by the cares of the world and therefore have the potential of being more dedicated to the work of Christ. Indeed, church history has demonstrated how God has used single women on the field throughout the centuries. Three women, Amy Carmichael, Lilias Trotter, and Mary Nemire, provide significant examples of single women whose faithfulness continues to ripple throughout God's world today.

Amy Carmichael

Amy Carmichael (1867–1951) may be one of the most familiar names in missions. While still a teenager in Northern Ireland, Amy worked among child laborers, helping to plant the Welcome Hall, a still-thriving church near the linen mills in Belfast. After a short stint as a missionary in Japan, although frail in health, Amy moved to Southern India where her heart was broken by children trapped in Hindu worship practices. She became known as *Amma*, "mother," as she began to rescue children who were enslaved as temple prostitutes. As rescued orphans, church workers, medical personnel, and evangelists began to gather around Amy, the gospel was dispersed throughout India in a ministry that continues to this day.[11]

Lilias Trotter

Lilias Trotter (1853–1928) was a Victorian heiress who believed she was called to proclaim the gospel of Jesus cross-culturally. Though a gifted painter, she gave up a promising career to move to Algeria, a hard posting where few Christians dared to venture. Lilias was a missions pioneer. She employed the ministry of hospitality, sharing the gospel with men and women who stopped at her wayside home for a rest from their desert travels. She invited short-term, financially independent, single female workers to serve with her. Lilias wrote and illustrated gospel tracts. She studied the writings of the Sufi mystics and wrote an apologetic demonstrating the truth and beauty of Jesus through His seven "I Am" statements in the Gospel of John. In her lifetime, more than three dozen missionaries, both singles and couples, were mobilized to a vigorous ministry across North Africa. Thousands more joined in the decades after Lilias's death.[12]

Mary Nemire

Unlike Amy and Lilias, Mary Nemire (1923–2013) is known to relatively few. She dedicated her life to serving the Lord at the age of thirteen. She graduated at age twenty-one from Bible college in New York and began immediately to work among the Dine (Navajo) in Arizona and New Mexico. She made home visits on horseback, taught the Navajo language, supported young pastors, and was beloved by all who knew her.

---

11. Elisabeth Elliot, *A Chance to Die: The Life and Legacy of Amy Carmichael* (Grand Rapids: Revell, 2005).

12. Miriam Huffman Rockness, *A Passion for the Impossible: The Life of Lilias Trotter* (Grand Rapids: Discovery House, 2003).

In fact, Dine believers credit Mary with preserving their language when outside forces were discouraging its use. She collected blankets for the poor in her community each Christmas and always provided the warmth and hope of the gospel of Jesus. After fifty years of playing basketball with young women, Mary took up rollerblading because it was easier on her knees. For more than sixty-five years, Mary's service demonstrated that she loved Jesus, loved the Dine, and loved the church.

A Common Legacy

Amy, Lilias, and Mary all died on the field, surrounded by local believers. Sixty or more years of faithfulness from each of these women resulted in churches pastored by local men where none had existed before. They did not presume to fill the pastor's role, but God used their faithful, obedient, courageous use of His gifts to pave the way for the pastors who would follow. Yes, there were days of loneliness, challenges to their security, and misunderstandings among their coworkers. They each suffered a broken heart, significant illnesses, and discouraging betrayal. But they used their flexibility and lack of distraction to go where others could not.

In the last two centuries, thousands of single women have served in such roles as "Bible women" in China, nurses of Christian hospitals in Bangladesh, missionary educators in South America, Bible translators in Papua New Guinea, and missionary pilots in Alaska. In Afghanistan, single women have trained literacy workers, provided physical therapy to children with disabilities, and taught English, all the while pointing to Jesus, and many of them giving the last full measure of devotion for their faithfulness. This faithfulness, which is repeated in virtually every country of the globe, is the very fulfillment of Jesus' description of singles remaining so "for the sake of the kingdom" (Matt 19:12). Therefore, the answer to "Should we send single women as missionaries?" must be, "For the sake of Jesus and His church, yes, we will send them!"

CHAPTER 39

Lessons from the Field: Wisdom for Missionary Wives

Shelbi Cullen

This chapter contains responses to interviews from missionary wives and mothers with diverse backgrounds and mission fields who are in different stages of life and ministry and have wisdom to share from their experiences. They candidly discuss topics such as pre-field training, the raising of financial support, relationships with sending churches, early life on the field, and various personal issues they faced over the years. The purpose of this chapter is to strengthen and equip future missionary wives by gleaning from the godly wisdom of faithful women gained through many joys and challenges. Meet the missionary wives and consider the lessons they have learned as they have attempted to serve the Lord faithfully so far.

Ava in Southeast Asia. Ava and her husband met through an internship program run by their university and a church in the inner city of a major North American city. The program involved students in a poor neighborhood working with at-risk youth. After marrying, they felt called to pioneer gospel work among unreached Muslims. About ten years into marriage, they moved overseas to a Muslim city in Southeast Asia with their four children and had their fifth child on the field. They focus on church planting among unreached people groups in the city and strengthening churches to evangelize the surrounding Muslim peoples.

Sandi in Southeast Asia. Sandi was a faithful member of her sending church for two decades before her husband undertook seminary studies so they could be sent out as missionaries to a bustling metropolis in Southeast Asia. Though she received a graduate degree in biblical counseling specifically to aid in her overseas ministry, she credits her local church of origin for fostering her knowledge and use of Scripture as she counsels women and supports her husband in his work of church planting.

Glenna, formerly in Asia. Glenna moved with her family to the mission field when her oldest children were already teenagers and her husband was thriving in a desirable career. They moved to a society that accentuated their foreignness in every way. She now supports her husband as he serves in a different range of pastoral ministries back in their home city, primarily in missions leadership for a sending agency established through their local church.

Amanda in Southern Africa. Amanda is a missionary in Sub-Saharan Africa with her husband, who is from a similar culture to where they serve. Her kids are adjusting well, helped by her outgoing oldest daughter who has easily made friends. Amanda's youngest, her only son, was born in the field hospital, which was a very different experience from the other births.

Rachel in Southern Africa. Most of Rachel's married and parenting life has been spent overseas, first in a rural location and then in a well-serviced city. They have two daughters, both born on the field, and they have moved countries twice in under fifteen years. Rachel and her husband are involved primarily in discipleship and leadership training through their local church as well as teaching others how to do biblical counseling.

Nina in Eastern Europe. Nina and her husband served in a post-Communist European country for twenty-five years after seminary. They focused on church planting and starting a pastoral training center. Nina led women's groups, teaching basic Christian living since most were first-generation believers. They recently left their country of service, a difficult but necessary process to hand off the ministry to local leadership.

Meg in Western Europe. For nearly forty years, Meg and her husband have been church-planting missionaries in Western Europe. After her husband received pastoral ministry training, they spent one year on the field as a short-term project to determine the scope of ministry and their suitability. The Lord has graciously used them and their now adult children in cities large and small to plant churches and train many missionaries in French-speaking regions of the world.

Pre-Field Experiences

QUESTION: *What did you and your husband consider a top priority for training to become missionaries?*

When preparing for overseas ministry, missionary wives tend to benefit greatly from hands-on training about balancing family needs with ministry demands, especially if they can be taught by current and former missionary wives. They most want to understand how to live out proper priorities on the field, with God first, then balancing attention for the spouse, children, home, ministry, and self. Finding an order isn't easy because God has built in limitations to each person. Meg received early guidance that she reported helped her "know when to say no." Sandi, on the other hand, stated that she wrongly equated being a missionary and the concept of "dying to self" with denying all personal preferences, which led to skewed priorities and unforeseen frustrations.

Many of the parents of young children wished they could have received more firsthand tips from veteran missionary parents on teaching and caring for children in another culture. Meg recalled the many challenges of training the children while balancing different languages, and Amanda considered that wise guidance can reinforce "the nuts and bolts of missionary family life" and help the family start off well in a new lifestyle.

Looking back, most of the women also wished they had received pre-field training in biblical counseling to help them apply Scripture practically in ministry and in their own marriages and families as well. Along those lines, Rachel responded that preemptive, ongoing marriage counseling of their own— when pursued with godly elders and biblical counselors—can be useful to equip missionary couples for the kinds of challenges they will no doubt face when they dive into their new context.

The wives also prioritized developing an organized ministry plan and strategies for team building, though not all of them had that help before entering the field. Glenna said that developing a ministry plan, written and agreed upon by all involved, would have been "extremely helpful," and Ava noted that she has seen many teams fall apart because they are not united in their vision for service. Finally, anything that a missionary wife can do pre-field to cultivate gratitude and avoid the temptation to complain will serve her and her household well to persevere through difficulties. With thorough practical preparation like this, missionary wives can be better equipped for balancing family and ministry priorities and serving joyfully long term with their husbands.

QUESTION: *What ministries would you encourage missionary candidate wives to invest in, in their sending church?*

Missionary wives should take full advantage of opportunities to gain hands-on ministry experience at their sending church in areas they foresee serving in overseas, even though God will open many new ministry doors impossible to predict. For example, Amanda and her husband used to host game nights for singles and young adults at their sending church, which became useful for ministering to that demographic on the field when opportunity arose. Regardless of the specific ministry experience pre-field, wives should use their spiritual gifts freely, whether planning to serve long term or not. Glenna reflected on how the Lord allowed her to build relationships pre-field through hospitality, letter writing, speaking to children in the Sunday school program, and joining women's groups and Bible studies. Rachel added the benefit of serving in ministries "with people who are not like you," in order to see the Lord work through you when you are outside of your comfort zone and dependent on Him to serve His people when it doesn't come naturally.

God matures people through the fellowship and accountability of the body of Christ, when His Word is at the center of their ministries. Glenna and Meg encourage missionary candidates to seek to invest deeply in their sending church community, knowing they'll need that foundation when joining a still-growing congregation abroad. Sandi reflected that if you come from a healthy, biblical church to serve believers needing a lot of spiritual guidance, you learn pretty quickly that your own spiritual walk needs to grow more than you thought when you were in fellowship with other strong believers. With this balanced mindset, wives should evaluate how to make the most of pre-field ministry opportunities.

QUESTION: *What kind of pre-field training do you think would be useful for children?*

Missionary parents play a key role in shaping the attitudes of their children by modeling sacrifice and spiritual consistency inside and outside of the home. Rachel identified that parents powerfully instill a missions heart in their children when they demonstrate joy and trust during challenges that have no immediately positive outcome. Ava involved her children in selling the family's possessions, including most of their toys, as part of the uprooting process.

From an early age, missionary kids can develop a sense of being on mission as a family

unit. To that end, Amanda found it useful to help her children call their future field "home" before arriving there, giving them a sense of belonging and helping reduce comparisons between the field and their passport country. Beginning language and cultural lessons can begin the field adjustment before moving. Letting kids store some special possessions with relatives back home gives comfort too.

Nevertheless, Glenna emphasized that missionary parents should avoid burdening children with unrealistic expectations that they, too, are missionaries. While involved in the family's overseas calling, kids should be allowed to be kids.

Transitions are difficult at any age for parents and children, so perhaps the greatest pre-field training is modeling walking by faith, praying as a family through future hopes and looming uncertainties, so that the children witness bold reliance on God who looks after His people anywhere.

Sending Church Relations

QUESTION: *Before leaving for the field, did you face any challenges when it came to raising support?*

Asking people for financial support was a huge mental hurdle for all of the women to overcome, each one recognizing that requesting money and resources from others can be perceived negatively. On one occasion, Amanda overheard a pastor's family complain about missionary fundraising and wondered if her very presence in their home for such a conversation was felt to be an imposition. Glenna recognized that churches and individuals don't always have a high interest level for each ministry plan but prefer to support certain kinds of activities or even specific countries.

Nevertheless, each of the wives recounted the Lord's kindness to help them reframe the fundraising task as a ministry itself. On the one hand, missionaries can minister to those with whom they share about their plans, using the conversation to reveal God's heart for His harvest and demonstrate His unfolding kindness to their families. On the other hand, missionaries can play a part in instilling a vision for sacrificial giving in local churches, raising up supporters to joyfully take part in God's work as missionary senders, whether for their families or for other outreach ministries. Glenna expressed that this partnership perspective transformed the daunting experience of asking for money into a blessing. When considered as a ministry, fundraising meetings help everyone in the conversation to visualize how to support one another to fulfill the Great Commission as a team.

The Lord never ceases to use support-raising seasons to mature missionaries spiritually. Sandi recalled having to learn to depend on the Lord in a new way when attempting to balance fundraising with managing the children's schooling and having a husband with a full-time job already. Ava gained compassion for believers who might not have previously realized the role they play in missions, and Rachel was continually humbled by the gifts she received from caring people.

They recounted some commitments and strategies as being particularly helpful to using the fundraising season efficiently. Nina shared that from the moment she and her husband decided to go to the mission field, they began networking with like-minded pastors at conferences and events—years before actually leaving. They concentrated their efforts on churches in regions where they had relatives, which allowed them to keep their furlough travels more centralized, so they avoided exhausting nationwide trips and had more time to spend with long-unseen family members. Some missionary families sought to speak to groups that were otherwise unable to give financially, such as children's Sunday classes and disabilities ministries. Making the choice not to speak primarily with professional adults helped some missionaries to remain committed to the ministry aspect of support-raising and to grow in trust that the Lord would provide. Amazingly, in each of the women's situations, the Lord provided their outgoing expenses and monthly needs in a relatively short support-raising season.

QUESTION: *What are some ways that your sending church served you well or could have aided you more effectively?*

Sending churches serve their missionaries well in a variety of ways, which the women interviewed were quick to appreciate. Prayer support is a great resource from home. Some of their churches have set up women's prayer groups to focus on learning about overseas ministry and to pray through specific challenges. Amanda and Sandi shared how they participate in regular video conferences with fellow missionary wives across fields through their supporting churches, which they consider an "international community of like-minded women." The group provides fellowship and a lifeline when facing difficulties that church members might not fully grasp.

Rachel has always appreciated when specific elders from the sending churches reach out on a regular basis to provide biblical counseling through calls, since field visits aren't always possible and aren't very regular. Yet field visits make an almost incalculable impact. The women have been encouraged when church leaders personally visit the field and bring letters from church members back home, and Ava stated that such visits "have been life-giving to our family." Glenna recognized that regional missionary conferences are key opportunities for face-to-face input from visiting elders, often providing important biblical counseling to the missionary couple. When the sending church's missionary leadership team values long-term relationships, they tend to structure their programs in such a way that has made the women feel cared for like family.

The women didn't hide some of the pressure points they have felt throughout the years by their sending churches. Some women desired more explicit missions training, though the biblical preparation they reported having received gave them a strong foundation for ministry. In some cases, sending churches have required intensive reporting from the field that has eaten up precious ministry time and has felt more like a bureaucratic task than a relational activity with the sending church. Also, some churches that provide small donations require home visits but do not cover the large expenses involved, creating budget strains for the already frugal missionaries.

Certain pressures can also come from churches that prioritize relationship over bureaucracy. One woman identified that when the primary sending church gives so much freedom to the missionaries to determine their own ministry action plans, then it can seem that the missions leadership team is absent from field decisions. Sometimes a little more direction would at least give more confidence to the missionary at the outset of a plan. One wife recalled that as she and her husband were considering their field placement options, "everyone seemed to have their own plans for our lives." Sometimes well-intentioned friends and leaders can insert confusion early in the process of discerning God's plan. Finally, another woman expressed the disorienting feeling that comes when home leadership teams change while the family is serving abroad. Sometimes missionaries feel the strain of developing new working relationships at home while already struggling to cultivate relationships on the field.

QUESTION: *Have you experienced furlough challenges?*

The missionary wives reported having experienced many kind expressions of care during their trips back to their sending and supporting churches. Furlough care included free or reduced-cost housing, use of transportation, gift cards for groceries, and attentiveness to their spiritual health, often by receiving regular marital counseling and prayer partners. The genuine interest they received communicated love and helped ease the homesickness they suffered for their congregations on the field.

Nevertheless, furlough challenges can be real. Even a short time overseas significantly changes relationships back home, making reentry unexpectedly uncomfortable for some of the women interviewed. Fitting into new rhythms and relationships formed in their absence can lead to a lonely transition. More than one woman shared the strains her family has felt trying to fit into a home church filled with new faces, reconnecting kids in youth programs, and attempting to reestablish evolved friendships.

One might assume that home visits are like being on vacation, but to missionaries, furloughs can be exhausting physically and emotionally. With so much travel and shifting locations, coordinating logistics becomes overwhelming. Communicating daily concerns like dietary restrictions, time constraints, and budget limitations takes wisdom and grace, so as not to offend their eager hosts. Additionally, while hoping to edify their audiences, some of the women have felt that constantly having to share about themselves to churches teeters on self-promotion. They have struggled with how to avoid sounding like they are bragging about God's accomplishments through them as they seek to share their adventures of faith.

The women expressed the importance of seeking spiritual rejuvenation during home visits, since ministry abroad can be emotionally isolating and a perpetual source of spiritual testing. Remaining in one place for even a few successive weeks has helped many of the families forge deeper connections with supporting churches and also to connect meaningfully with key individuals. And spending extended furloughs near relatives, when possible, has helped the missionaries to enjoy concentrated time with their families, since it can be difficult to shepherd their children with the fast pace of appointments and events. Intentional communication and teamwork as couples aids in combating the chaos. By embracing the furlough as a unique and temporary season that brings new challenges and many blessings, missionaries can thrive on furlough.

Initial Entry Issues

QUESTION: *What would you say were some of your hardest challenges in the early days?*

Many of the first challenges on the field involve language acquisition. Many of the women were surprised by how difficult it was to enter new language groups. Despite studying some of the language and culture before departing, many missionaries soon realized they knew far too little to engage in real-life communication. Some of the women's biggest language-related fears were answering a ringing phone without a language-fluent person present, buying the wrong ingredients at the grocery store, and missing out on ministry opportunities due to the time commitment required for language school in the first few years. To many of the women, the upside of language struggles was that they were forced to build local friendships to help navigate their new lives. While some cultural dynamics could be researched beforehand, living immersed day-to-day prepared them at a deeper level for ministry.

In addition to language struggles, practical cultural challenges overwhelmed many of the women at first. In one Southern African context, it was impossible to secure stable housing until residency could be established with the local government. In one Asian context, it was difficult to understand what appliances or household goods would be useful for attempting to adapt to the local lifestyle in the home. For many, weather differences proved challenging, such as being relatively unprepared for a fiercely cold winter or suffocating humidity. Their children were not exempt from struggle, as many had no local church peers their age and no easy entrance into the activities of the young people in their locations.

For a variety of reasons, the early years required a stringent commitment by the women to push forward and not seek an exit strategy. They chose to consider their hardships necessary for their fitness in ministry and tried to thank God amid their trials. The missionaries navigated their early struggles by embracing the adventure as being crafted by the Lord for their sanctification, for the good of their families, and for the expansion of God's kingdom.

QUESTION: *Were there any expectations you had when first entering the field that had to shift once you encountered real life on the field? How did you navigate unmet expectations?*

For these missionary wives, adjusting cross-culturally has meant accepting the perpetual label of "outsider," no matter how connected they might become to the culture through language fluency and a local lifestyle. They acknowledged how easy it was at first to compare almost everything in the new culture to home, whether differences seemed small or large. An attitude of "this isn't how we do it" can breed discontentment and complaining, even over minimal inconveniences.

In some cases, like the social and cultural evils of bribery, neglect, pollution, and mockery, there can be no "fitting in" for the believer. But Glenna recognized the importance of endurance and humility in the face of lifestyle matters that are "not wrong, just different, like slower processes, more steps, or less convenience. No one will change those things for me just because they bother me. Who do I think I am?" She added, "We need to make sure we don't worship our way of doing things; otherwise we will become bitter and discontent. I had to strive to think rightly, giving up my 'rights' and cultivating a heavenly mindset to realize I am not so special that I deserve anything good."

Safety and health risks are not small matters, and they can arise suddenly, especially when living among or near volatile populations. Ava recounted a difficult experience: "Where we live, ambulances don't come for emergencies. When my daughter was stung over forty times by hornets, we were far away from a hospital, and we did everything we could to get to a hospital as the poison spread throughout her little body. We have had to learn practically to rely on God to be our Deliverer and Great Physician."

Whatever expectations missionary families may have brought to their unfamiliar, new contexts, God never fails to remind them to trust in His care when their ideals meet the messy realities of life and ministry.

Missionaries, especially wives, must check assumptions and avoid verbalizing feelings that can discourage their family and ministry participants. Amanda revealed that "trying to root out negative comments from my mouth and from my heart has been an important discipline for me." One woman compared missionaries pushing through inconveniences and discomfort to "military members deployed to war zones, who have to accept that they may die to do their job well." Avoiding comparisons is a part of dying to self on the mission field. To Rachel and Sandi, the goal has become finding gratitude for what God is allowing them to do by His strength, rather than mourning "missing" elements from home.

Ministry and Personal Matters

QUESTION: *Can you speak to the struggle with loneliness or homesickness that is so common for missionary women? How is it unique on the field?*

Sandi identified that for her and many others, homesickness is a form of grief. Loneliness exists because no one fully understands the missionary experience at home or on the field.

Missionary women often feel caught between worlds, experiencing isolation no matter where they are. Sometimes loneliness results from difficulty relating to others. Rachel recognized that in some African cultures, the missionary's wife is put on a pedestal, so relationships with local women can lack an emotional connection that allows for vulnerability and counsel. Ava has found friendships with nationals to be warm, but in her context none of her local friends are believers, so spiritual fellowship is lacking in these new relationships.

Nina believes loneliness is the number one struggle of missionary wives, often because they suffer traumatic events away from trusted friends. She opened up about her early time of bitter isolation: "That first brutal winter here, I experienced a miscarriage, which plunged me into profound loneliness—we were about to share the news of the pregnancy with family over Christmas." Meg shared the jarring experiences of having her house burglarized three times, and Glenna expressed, "There were seasons when I just didn't want to leave the house and put forth the effort that it took to do everything, including meeting with people." No matter the complexity of the trial, the wives expressed the importance of finding a friend somewhere for counsel and encouragement, whether another missionary wife, a local woman, or friends from the sending churches.

Loneliness can also affect the family in different ways. Missionaries live with constant concerns for how their children are affected by the dark world around them and what they're missing from home. Through social media, the kids can see old friends and reconnect with relatives, but often what they see is people at a great distance, living full lives with perhaps few of the same challenges they face regularly. Loneliness can manifest itself in feeling like lifelong visitors among the local people, unsure of how to act or relate in certain situations, no matter how strongly a bond is forged throughout the years. Yet by embracing the perception of solitude as part of the journey to which the missionaries are called, daily clinging to Christ, the women were confident that missionaries can adapt well to all circumstances.

QUESTION: *Are there any marriage challenges you experienced that you can share to advise a young married couple heading toward the field?*

The missionary's redeemed yet sinful heart comes with her to the field. The pressures of life on foreign soil tend to squeeze out hidden problems in the marriage. Because of this reality, Ava and Rachel suggest seeking preemptive, pre-field pastoral counseling individually and as a couple to improve communication before tensions mount on the field.

Some pressures come as a surprise, such as when one spouse achieves language proficiency before the other and begins developing friendships, while the spouse struggles to connect with the locals. When it comes to learning the language and culture, Glenna's advice is to acclimate as a team: "Don't leave anyone behind! If you're the fast one, slow down and help or patiently wait for the other to come along.

Don't leave your spouse in the dust to figure out what to do on their own." Amanda felt at times that because her husband was from a culture similar to where they serve, she had to navigate unfamiliarity alone. She learned to express her need for overt compassion from him through the process so she wouldn't feel like a foreigner in her own home.

Nina addressed that when husbands ask their wives to undertake many ministries outside the home, they might add an undue burden that sometimes causes the wives to crumble into despondency or physical illness. In reality, wives face certain limitations and can experience fragile adjustment periods that, if not treated with concern, can be a reason to leave the field without fulfilling the ministry for which they came.

On the other hand, wives must adjust their expectations and actively avoid resentment when their husbands' demanding schedules change, sometimes requiring lengthy trips away from the family. When the husband's absence might seem like a threat to the family's safety, stresses run high for the couple. Some of the wives indicated that occasionally they have to work extra hard to encourage their husbands to press on in their ministry activities. They desire to embrace eternal priorities in the midst of trials so that they can reinforce to their husbands that they are their husbands' greatest earthly champions and partners and that their families are their husbands' most unconditional earthly source of comfort and joy. Wives hold great power either to model contentment and dependence on God or to be suffocating burdens that add more pressure to their husbands' already stress-filled worlds.

A missionary couple's highest aim on the field is not marriage contentment but satisfaction in Christ. But with realistic expectations, dependence on God's grace, and a commitment to selfless love, a couple can thrive through inevitable trials wherever the Lord sends them.

Interview Wrap-Up

These honest conversations with missionary wives from a wide variety of global contexts have explored topics relevant to life on and off the mission field. Despite their diversity, these women faced many similar joys and challenges adjusting to overseas living and ministry with growing families. Each family's journey has involved unexpected challenges that reveal their continued need for the strength and wisdom that only God can provide.

There is no single formula for fruitful service overseas. The missionary wives gained much wisdom as they learned to depend on God's sovereignty in everyday life. By embracing a mindset of adaptability, the wives have found contentment in a variety of circumstances. They have learned to cling to Christ and their true home with Him, rather than idealizing their passport countries. While still works in progress, these wives aim to leave a legacy of godly wisdom for the next generation. Their lives communicate that with realistic goals, a grace-filled marriage, and biblical priorities, the Lord can use willing families mightily for His global harvest. It is hoped that women who are preparing for the field or are immersed in a foreign ministry context will follow in the faithful footsteps of these missionary wives so that they, too, might flourish in their high calling wherever the Lord leads.

SECTION 3

THE MATURING
AND REPRODUCING
LOCAL CHURCH

Sub-Section 1: Equipping Indigenous Church Leaders

CHAPTER 40

Indigenous Missions in Scripture and in Practice

Paul Washer

When people speak of "missions," most have in mind the cross-cultural kind of missions. They mean the sending of a man from one country and culture to proclaim the gospel and plant churches in a foreign country and culture. But there is another kind, one of utmost importance: indigenous missions—the recognition of men, native and local in another country, who are qualified to preach and to shepherd churches, followed by the equipping and commissioning of them for ministry. What qualifies this recognition and equipping of indigenous leadership as "missions," as opposed simply to pastoral training in general, is the sending element. First, men are sent to equip other men for ministry, and then the newly equipped men are sent to their own countrymen. But this sending, and what it requires, is the only difference; it is essentially pastoral training abroad.

Both kinds of missions, cross-cultural and indigenous, fulfill the Great Commission. Of course, there are many benefits to equipping nationals as missionaries to their homelands. They do not have to learn the language or the culture, and no one will superficially attend their churches simply because they are, for example, "rich Americans." Indigenous missions avoids many such problems inherent in cross-cultural missions. It cannot be employed everywhere, for in some places there are not yet local men of integrity and sound theology to be put into ministry. But there is nowhere that indigenous missions should not be desired, at least because of its advantages.

More importantly, however, sending churches should desire to do indigenous missions because it is modeled in Scripture. It is shown in the New Testament's first missionaries, and it is assumed in the Great Commission. Seeing it in Scripture, then, can teach the church some practical lessons for equipping leaders in the same way.

The First Missionaries' Practice

The New Testament shows that the task of missions requires the eventual handing off of the ministry to local believers. But this was not simply a final, undesirable obligation. Nor was it a strategy simply employed when the original missionaries got too old to continue. It was a strategy from the start, practiced by the first missionaries.

An indigenous missions strategy is seen every time elders were appointed by missionaries in the book of Acts. For example, on their first missionary journey Paul and Barnabas made many disciples in the cities they visited. They pastored those disciples in each city for a time before moving on to proclaim the gospel elsewhere. Then, on their journey home, they stopped along the way at each city to strengthen the churches they had planted. Luke writes, "And when they had appointed elders for them in every church, having prayed with fasting, they commended them to the Lord in whom they had believed" (Acts 14:23). The surrounding text makes clear that this appointment followed discipleship (vv. 21–22). The discipleship effort had matured certain men to the point that they were then handed the ministry with "no strings attached." Paul and Barnabas did not stay on as permanent pastors.

They entrusted the men they had trained as shepherds into the care of their Chief Shepherd, Jesus (cf. 1 Pet 5:4).

The result was that the elders in those cities continued the work faithfully. On Paul's second missionary journey, he returned to them and found there a local disciple named Timothy (Acts 16:1–3). Paul had evidently led him to Christ by the preaching of his previous visit (1 Tim 1:2; 1 Cor 4:17).[1] Now older and matured in the faith, Timothy became Paul's missionary partner. But he was appointed to this ministry by "the laying on of hands"— the hands of the very elders who were earlier discipled and appointed by Paul and Barnabas (1 Tim 4:14; 2 Tim 1:6). These local leaders were multiplying themselves through local churches. Then they sent out their own men to multiply churches in their region also.

The same activity is seen in the Pastoral Epistles, 1–2 Timothy and Titus. Paul wrote to Titus that he left him behind in Crete to "set in order what remains and appoint elders in every city" (Titus 1:5). Then he laid out the qualifications for such elders (vv. 6–9). To Timothy also, Paul wrote that he had left him behind in Ephesus to teach sound doctrine (1 Tim 1:3–4), and again, he gave him qualifications for appointing elders from among the Ephesian brethren (3:1–7). In his subsequent letter, Paul reminded Timothy once more to be passing on the baton, saying, "The things which you have heard from me in the presence

---

1. Ralph Earle, "1 Timothy," in *EBC*, vol. 11, *Ephesians through Philemon*, ed. Frank E. Gaebelein (Grand Rapids: Zondervan, 1981), 348.

of many witnesses, entrust these to faithful men who will be able to teach others also" (2 Tim 2:2). Timothy's task was to train up more "Timothys." This was an indigenous mission.

The Great Commission's Assumption

While cross-cultural missions strategy is the obvious and immediate fulfillment of Jesus' Great Commission to "go" to "all the nations" (Matt 28:19), indigenous missions is the eventual and inevitable goal of Jesus' charge. Wherever His disciples went, they were to raise up other preachers and church planters, "domestic missionaries," so to speak. A contextual look at Matthew's Great Commission account in Matthew 28:16–20 reveals that the eleven disciples were the first indigenous missionaries. Prior to this sendoff, they had been sent out to preach the kingdom twice during Christ's ministry (Matt 10:1ff.; Luke 10:1ff.). Their target country had been Israel exclusively, for while Jesus evangelized Samaritans and Gentiles when He encountered them (e.g., Mark 7:24–30; John 4:39ff.; 12:20ff.), still He and His disciples were sent only "to the lost sheep of the house of Israel" (Matt 10:5–6; 15:24). The theological priority of Israel is unique,[2] and it has no direct analogy to indigenous missions per se, except for Jewish believers or those going to the Jewish people. But even in the Great Commission, once the disciples were commanded to preach the gospel to the uttermost parts of the earth, they were still sent out beginning with their own countrymen (Acts 1:8). Those converted to Christ by their preaching were expected to be missionaries to their own kinsmen too (Matt 10:23). This is certainly to be imitated in missions today.

Since the preeminent task of the Great Commission is to "make disciples," not merely converts, it fundamentally requires lifelong instruction. It requires the lifelong labor of teachers with the full counsel of God's Word (Acts 20:27), unto full sanctification, until every believer attains "to the measure of the stature which belongs to the fullness of Christ" (Eph 4:13). The work of raising up indigenous churchmen around the world is precisely that kind of discipleship (Acts 14:21–23). Only it is discipleship to the maximum, the discipleship most equipped for further discipleship in local churches: an elder entrusting the truth to "faithful men who will be able to teach others also" (2 Tim 2:2; cf. Titus 1:5). It is gospel ministry handed off to local, reproducing believers, to shepherd their churches under the Chief Shepherd (1 Pet 5:4). Ultimately, every cross-cultural mission, if it is biblical, is designed to end here. Every time a missionary is sent out to a foreign field, this is his mission: to make disciples that make disciples, to proclaim the gospel in some place until it sounds forth from there into neighboring places also. Indigenous missions, then, is really the eventual and inevitable goal of the Great

---

2. Cf. David L. Turner, *Matthew*, BECNT (Grand Rapids: Baker, 2008), 268–69; Craig L. Blomberg, *Matthew*, NAC 22 (Nashville: Broadman and Holman, 1992), 170–71.

Commission, and it is assumed in Jesus' command to make disciples.

Practical Lessons for Equipping Leaders

If the church is going to follow the Scripture's example in practice, then it needs to establish the same kind of indigenous missions just described. In practical terms, this means the church will establish training centers alongside and based in the churches it plants all over the globe. These are locations used to teach and supply elders in neighboring cities; not commandeering authority from preexisting churches but partnering with them. In these sites, men will be taught exegesis, theology, preaching, and counseling in their own language, provided books in their own language, and discipled in the context of their own churches. Some may have to travel long distances to reach their training site, and some will inevitably endure lean times while they balance studying the Scriptures, serving their churches, and possibly working jobs to provide for their families. These especially need the support and prayer of the body of Christ.

Indigenous missions also means that the church will send qualified men to lead and teach in these centers. Such men are often difficult to part with because of their gifts and effective ministries. But they must be sent. In the internet age, by God's grace, churches can send money and resources anywhere in the world, even into closed countries. Yet the Great Commission cannot be fulfilled online. When God saved sinners, He sent His Son to dwell among men (John 1:14; Rom 8:3; Gal 4:4; Phil 2:7), and now He is calling the church to do the same, to dwell among men (John 20:21; 2 Cor 5:19–20; cf. Matt 10:16; Luke 10:3; John 17:18). It must send flesh-and-blood preachers to flesh-and-blood sinners and, in the case of indigenous missions, to flesh-and-blood pastors and church planters. Churches must boldly express faith by sending their best into missions. And about those they send, three lessons can be learned from Scripture.

Dedicated Men

First, indigenous missions requires deeply dedicated men, men who have devoted their lives to equipping other men. This is a special task and gifting, not for everyone. It is not at all divorced from pastoral ministry. Rather, the training pastor must teach and model what an elder must be to his trainees. It is a whole-life discipleship, not an "ivory tower" seminary post. These men are in the trenches doing hard work.

Certainly it is hard work to raise up theologically solid leaders and hold them accountable. To see results may take decades. It is frankly impossible without the Lord's power and blessing. That is why missionaries signing up for this task must be biblically qualified elders, just as Paul and Barnabas, Timothy and Titus were. If such a missionary is commissioned by his sending church with anything less than an ordination and all of its expectations, then it is unbiblical and destined for trouble. A high standard this may be, but it is the pattern set by the New Testament church. A man's dedication must be shown by his willingness to "first be tested" and prepared, as any elder must be (1 Tim 3:10; 5:22; e.g., Acts 13:1–4).

The dedication to do this hard work must arise from a compelling love. True, missions in general are a labor of love. Missionaries have to love God and therefore love what God loves and desire what God desires: that the knowledge of His glory covers the earth (Hab 2:14; cf. Isa 11:9), that His name be great among the nations (Mal 1:11; cf. Ps 113:3), and that sinners escape His judgment and be saved for His glory (Ps 79:9; Rom 9:23; 1 Tim 2:4; 2 Pet 3:9). Yet indigenous missions is a particularly loving labor, for it means a lifelong training of future leaders, one handful at a time, over years at a time, in churches belonging to a country and culture foreign to the missionary. It is a labor of love to persevere in the more ordinary tasks of ministry training, like teaching biblical languages or models of ecclesiology, like critiquing students' work or finding sound resources to give them (sometimes translating them oneself), like the daily concern not only for a church but also for the administration and financial support of a training center. These are ordinary tasks, for which there is little immediate reward outside the work itself. That means indigenous missions is not a ministry for the faint of heart, nor for the one who loves little. It requires dedicated men.

Scriptural Men

Second, leaders in indigenous missions must be scriptural men. The Great Commission is a theological and doctrinal endeavor. For making disciples means teaching the followers of Christ everything that Christ commanded (Matt 28:20). Missionaries must be like Apollos, "mighty in the Scriptures" (Acts 18:24), men who know their theology and can teach it to others. In indigenous missions, training pastors must be gifted to teach at an even higher level, since they teach other teachers, that is, other pastors (1 Tim 3:2; 2 Tim 2:2, 24; Titus 1:9).

According to current popular opinion, Christians ought to lay aside their doctrines and rally around a common confession of Jesus. Missions agencies are commonly reducing their doctrinal statements to so-called essentials, and in the last few decades, more and more doctrine is being relegated to the "nonessentials" category. The result is that serious errors are being taught in the field, even in soteriology, the very doctrine of salvation that missionaries are sent to proclaim (Luke 24:47).

In stark contrast, the Pastoral Epistles— the New Testament texts that expressly instruct missionaries to raise up faithful local men—are bursting at the seams with the importance of doctrine. In those three brief letters, the Greek words *didachē* and *didaskalia* appear seventeen times for "teaching" (as in content) or "doctrine," respectively.[3] These epistles also use the common term *logos* ("word")[4] for doctrinal purposes in such phrases as "sound words" (1 Tim 6:3; 2 Tim 1:13), "the faithful word" (Titus 1:9), "the word of God" (1 Tim 4:5; cf. 2 Tim

---

3. Cf. "διδαχή," BDAG, 241; "διδασκαλία," BDAG, 240.
4. "λόγος," BDAG, 598–99.

4:2), "words of the faith" (1 Tim 4:6), and "the word of truth" (2 Tim 2:15). And when Paul speaks of that which is "in accordance with the teaching" (*kata tēn didachēn*; Titus 1:9), he speaks summarily of the whole body of apostolic instruction in both doctrine and precept.[5]

The only conclusion that a faithful reading of these letters can draw is that leaders in the Lord's church must be pastor-theologians, steeped in the entirety of Scripture. This accords precisely with the Great Commission, for as Paul put it, the doctrine those leaders must defend and teach is nothing less than the "sound words . . . of our Lord Jesus Christ" (1 Tim 6:3; cf. Matt 28:20); that is to say, He is the ultimate source of all sound doctrine.[6] If the church's leaders are to be pastor-theologians, so much the more ought their trainers to be scriptural, doctrinal men.

Churchmen

Practically speaking, ivory-tower theologians who only sit around and argue can afford all kinds of doctrinal ambiguity. But when a man goes out to teach in the field and he deals with real people and real problems, defining the "small stuff" becomes critical. He cannot afford to be merely an "armchair theologian" but must be a precise exegete with conviction in his doctrine's power. For inasmuch as planting churches, evangelizing, preaching, or counseling requires embracing the scriptural weapons of warfare (2 Cor 6:7; 10:4–6; Eph 6:10–18), so much more does the raising up of elders to go out and do the same. If ministry is spiritual warfare, then the ministry that plants other ministries must be expected to be warfare of greater intensity.

A prime example of the practical need for doctrine in an area that is presently being surrendered is ecclesiology, the doctrine of the church. Ecclesiology may seem impractical to someone convinced that the Great Commission's goal is simply to record the greatest number of converts. But the missionary is not called to leave in his wake a bunch of disconnected individual disciples; he is called to bring them together in a church. For the local church is the God-ordained context of discipleship the Great Commission requires (Eph 4:11–16; cf. Matt 16:18; 18:15–20).

Even more basic, the church is fundamentally doxological; that is, in God's wisdom, it is bound up together with His plan for His glory, which includes gospel proclamation.[7] The church is appointed by God to be "the pillar and support of the truth" (1 Tim 3:15), the primary means of exalting His Son in this present world (Eph 1:19–23), and a unique means of revealing His glory in the universe (Eph 3:10,

---

5. Robert W. Yarbrough, *The Letters to Timothy and Titus*, PNTC (Grand Rapids: Eerdmans; 2018), 489; I. Howard Marshall and Philip H. Towner, *A Critical and Exegetical Commentary on the Pastoral Epistles*, ICC (London: T&T Clark, 2004), 166–67.

6. Thomas D. Lea and Hayne P. Griffin, *1, 2 Timothy, Titus*, NAC 34 (Nashville: Broadman and Holman, 1992), 166; cf. Yarbrough, *Letters to Timothy and Titus*, 308.

7. Gregg R. Allison, *Sojourners and Strangers: The Doctrine of the Church*, Foundations of Evangelical Theology (Wheaton, IL: Crossway, 2012), 106ff.

21).[8] A weak church, then, results in a weak doxology in the lives of any new converts and a weak gospel proclamation beyond them. The finer points of ecclesiology—like a church's offices, ordinances, membership, discipline, mutual service, and corporate worship—while they require a high level of knowledge in the Scriptures, they are not incidental to missions. They are essential.

That said, the ecclesiology of the indigenous missions trainer has long-lasting, far-reaching implications. For, based on whatever convictions he passes on, the leaders he produces will raise up churches that pass on the same, becoming the centers of future ministries and missions in their countries, and so on the cycle goes. The trainer has to raise up leaders with his exact same convictions thoroughly formulated from exegesis, systematic theology, and church history. Anything less is not worthy of the gospel or of God. The same is true of other doctrines besides ecclesiology, but for indigenous missions, this doctrine is crucial and yet neglected today. The point is this: indigenous missions requires churchmen through and through.

Conclusion

At bottom, indigenous missions is simply biblical pastoral ministry, only it is aimed at strengthening and growing the church in a foreign target nation. It is not the only way to fulfill the Great Commission. But it is explicitly modeled in the New Testament church via the book of Acts and the Pastoral Epistles. It is also assumed in the Great Commission, being essentially its eventual and ultimate goal.

The manner in which indigenous missions is done must imitate the New Testament's example by training men in local churches or training sites connected with them. Those sites must equip and supply church planters and pastors all around them, in partnership with their churches. The men sent into the training sites must themselves be qualified, equipped, and ordained. They must be dedicated to a lifelong labor of love, thoroughly scriptural pastor-theologians, and men of the church and of its doctrine. The men being trained must have the support and prayers of the body of Christ abroad.

The work of this high calling is impossible without the Lord's power and blessing. But the assurance Christ gave to His disciples two thousand years ago extends to today just the same. He is with them always, and He will build His church (Matt 16:18; 28:20). The church must entrust what it has received to faithful men who will be able to teach others also, both at home and across cultures. Therefore, the church must go and make disciples of all nations, and as often as it can, do it through indigenous leaders.

---

8. Allison, 57–58.

How Can Mission Churches Be Self-Supporting?

William D. Barrick

In the mid-nineteenth century, Henry Venn, an Anglican clergyman, articulated three guidelines for indigenous missions.[9] Having independently come to the same basic conclusions, Rufus Anderson, an administrator of the American Board of Commissioners for Foreign Missions, concurred and added his voice to these principles.[10] The guidelines came to be known as the "three-self" formula.[11] Each is drawn from the New Testament. Put succinctly, they are self-government, self-propagation, and self-support.

1. A local church must be led by men drawn from among its own members. A church cannot be independent and autonomous without such leadership (Acts 14:23; Titus 1:5).
2. A local church must spread the good news of the gospel (Matt 28:18–20; Acts 5:42; Eph 6:15; 1 Thess 1:8; 2 Tim 4:1–5).
3. A local church must bear the primary burden of its own financial needs (Acts 4:32–37).

Affirming the third principle is the subject of this brief study from the six angles below.

The New Testament Model for Church Finances

In the book of Acts, a pattern begins to appear in the practices of the early church. First, the church proclaimed the gospel to unbelievers (Acts 1–2). Second, the church provided teaching and fellowship to believers (Acts 3–4). Third, churches contributed to meet the financial needs of others (Acts 4:32–5:11) and to spread the gospel (Phil 4:14–19). Finally, churches commissioned

---

9. Wilbert R. Shenk, "Henry Venn's Instructions to Missionaries," *Missiology* 5, no. 4 (October 1977): 467–85.

10. Rufus Anderson and R. Pierce Beaver, *To Advance the Gospel: Selections from the Writings of Rufus Anderson* (Grand Rapids: Eerdmans, 1967).

11. A. S. Moreau, "Missiology," *Evangelical Dictionary of Theology*, 2nd ed., ed. Walter A. Elwell (Grand Rapids: Baker, 2001), 781.

individuals for God's service (Acts 6–7; 13:1–3).

Regarding the church's third practice, meeting financial needs, the New Testament shows that the lack of giving in any church may indicate a lack of sacrifice (Mark 12:41–44), love (2 Cor 8:8, 24), joy (8:2), obedience (9:13), and thus blessing (Acts 20:35). An absence of giving might also be a symptom of laziness (Eph 4:28; 2 Thess 3:6–15). When church members do not practice New Testament giving, they rob their church of grace (2 Cor 9:8), thanksgiving (9:11–12), praise to God (9:13), and the prayers of others (9:13–14). They must, rather, bear the primary burden of their congregation's needs, even as they recognize that everything they have comes from the Lord (2 Cor 9:10; Phil 4:19).

The New Testament Times of Financial Need

Historians explain the presence of the needy people in Acts 11:27–30 by pointing to their migration from agriculture-based villages because of famine and political unrest.[12] From that perspective, the apostle Paul teaches churches to be prepared to send aid to other churches experiencing famine and subsequent poverty (1 Cor 16:1–4; 2 Cor 8–9). In such times of need, local churches should rise to the challenge and give generously to help fellow believers, both within their own number and in other assemblies.

The Old Testament Pattern's Confirmation

The Old Testament provides a number of examples of believers giving to the Lord's work: (1) for the building of the tabernacle (Exod 35:20–29); (2) for sustaining the priesthood and services of the tabernacle and temple (Num 5:9–10; 2 Chr 31:3–21; Neh 12:44–47); (3) for the repair and remodeling of the temple (2 Kgs 12:4–16; 22:3–7); and (4) for the care of the needy (Lev 19:9–10; 25:35–43; Deut 15:11; Prov 31:20). This same pattern for spontaneous giving to meet a recognized need continues into the New Testament (equivalent to 2 Cor 8–9, see previous section) with its transition to churches as the assemblies for believers.

The Scriptural Precedent of Buildings and Meeting Places

According to the New Testament, the early churches met in a variety of locations: the temple (Luke 24:52–53; Acts 2:46; 3:1; 5:21, 42), synagogues (Acts 9:20; 13:5; 14:1; 17:1–2, 10, 17; 18:4, 19, 26), a lecture hall (Acts 19:9–10), an extra room in a house (Acts 1:12–14; 20:8), a public place of prayer

---

12. See discussion in Craig S. Keener, *Acts: An Exegetical Commentary: Volume 2: 3:1–14:28* (Grand Rapids: Baker Academic, 2013), 1853–59.

by a river (Acts 16:13–15), and private homes (Acts 5:42; 12:12; 16:40; 18:7; 20:20; 28:23, 30–31; Rom 16:5, 23; 1 Cor 16:19; Col 4:15). The care and upkeep of these locations entail expenses besides ownership or rent. Scripture is silent on those expenses, however, so there is no way of knowing exactly how the early believers handled such matters. Still, it is safe to assume they bore the expenses themselves collectively.

The Need for Wisdom in Mission Churches

When it comes to the matter of church planting and the need for a meeting place, the New Testament pattern points to the use of private homes and public buildings, at least in the beginning. When an assembly of believers decides that their growth requires a building, they must ask themselves how to make certain the church does not over-extend itself financially or allow a building to hinder the progress of the gospel. The following are some suggestions:

1. A local church should carefully consider whether to spend more money on its building than on its outreach programs.
2. If a local church decides to build, it should consider a building design requiring minimal expense to build or maintain.
3. A local church should put to wise use the natural assets of church property. Such options will vary from location to location and culture to culture. For example, a church might plant coconut palms or mango trees to provide support for its pastor or funds for building repairs and utilities via their fruit. Or a church might make a baptismal pond large enough to stock fish for sale and for pastoral support.

The Need for Faithfulness in Self-Support

Finally, no church or individual believer could ever outgive God. He has promised to bless the giver. Furthermore, God will never lead His people to a place where He will not provide for and preserve them. However, His biblical program of giving always includes a work ethic for His people. God rewards neither laziness nor a beggar mentality. Rather, individual church members must keep these things in mind:

1. They are the people of Christ, the church. As they obey the Word of God personally, the church itself will be in obedience to the Word of God.
2. A believer is no more spiritual than his or her attitude toward money, and a church is no more spiritual than its blameless handling of money.

Self-support means just that, and nothing less—the people of God supporting the work of God.

Brazilians Sending Brazilians

Jenuan Lira

To conservative churches in Brazil, world missions did not seem possible. We heard, prayed, and read about missions "both here and beyond," as we have heard it said. Yet we dared not go "beyond," to the nations, with the gospel. We felt burdened for this ministry, but it seemed far above our capacity. Expertise, money, credibility—we had none of these things, and for decades we remained convinced of our inability.

We thank God, however, that He changed us and our situation. Nearly twenty years ago our conservative evangelical churches sent our first missionary family to the Cape Verde Islands in West Africa. Today missionaries with sound theology are going out from Brazil to the world. This insert is a short history of how God empowered us to build our sending agency.

Laying the Foundation

Biblical conviction leads to biblical obedience. It is foundational. As Jesus said at the conclusion of His Sermon on the Mount, if anyone wants to build a firm house—a metaphor for all of life—its foundation

must be laid by listening to and obeying His words (Matt 7:24–27). In our case, as conservative Brazilian Christians thought about becoming bolder to obey Him, we simply said to ourselves, "World missions is God's will, so let's do it." From then on, we sought to establish our path accordingly, in obedience to God's Word and without fearing our apparent obstacles. Everything we envisioned in our endeavors was traced back to what we understood to be biblical directions. We finally decided to go "beyond" because we were convinced that world missions was obedience to God.

We were not pioneers in terms of sending missions from Brazil, however. For years Brazilian missionaries had been sent out under the guidance of certain agencies. We felt it would have been unwise, however, to cooperate with these organizations since they operate from different convictions. Many of these agencies do not prioritize the local church as the sender. Some also are not strongly attached to the doctrine of the sufficiency of Scripture and embrace a Pentecostal and charismatic viewpoint about pneumatology and angelology, in particular. For us, a lack of agreement on such foundational issues was a major impediment. Many conservative Brazilian churches were in the same position; they could not participate with those mission agencies, which limited their involvement in world missions once they became excited for it.

For these churches to succeed in crossing borders with the gospel, we had to begin something new, so we did: we called it Maranatha Multicultural Ministries. In 2004 directors of the Association of Baptists for World Evangelism (ABWE), based in the United States, observed that because of certain geopolitical issues, many parts of the world were being closed to American missionaries. ABWE had been in Brazil for many decades, and its leaders wisely perceived that Brazilians could easily go into any country. For, in general, Brazil has had a peaceful history and has thereby maintained good international relations. In view of these points, the directors held a special summit in São Paulo, to which they invited local leaders. The directors addressed the group, saying that after decades of work in Brazil, it was evident that God had raised up a strong and mature body of believers who could go into places where many Westerners could not. If the Brazilian churches wanted to send missionaries overseas and if they desired a hand in the project, these experienced directors would serve as their partners.

The willingness of our American brothers to help us kindled the fire of our dream—praise be to God! With their help, we gained the confidence to venture beyond our own limitations. As promised, those brothers assisted our efforts. Even today they are still committed to working alongside us. Rather than imposing their own methods or ideas, they support our development as an authentic Brazilian mission with our own biblically informed convictions guiding the direction of our organization. Our foundation thus laid, we began building the house.

Building the House

Our motto has always been, "If a door opens, we enter gladly. If God closes it, we gladly return home" (cf. 1 Cor 16:8–9). That applied even to the ministry's founding. For after much prayer and many strategic considerations, we decided to enter the door of sending our first missionary. We knew our journey would be hard and occasionally dangerous. However, founded by God's Word and encouraged by seasoned brothers, we understood it was time to mobilize and send Brazilian believers to the nations.

Yet motivation and passion are not a magic formula for overcoming limitations. Initially, we had problems because of our lack of experience. We had to humbly persevere, learning from our mistakes without becoming discouraged. God helped us through close contact with mature missionaries serving in our region. Some of them were willing to be members on our board of directors, and we benefited from their counsel.

We also had limited material resources. But we had firmly decided to follow God's commands, and as a result, He Himself multiplied our small resources. Our sending agency was born in the northeast of Brazil, where churches are generally small and poor. Thus, the board needed to be creative and bold in raising support. As we advanced, we could see God's hand upon us, providing for each need. By faithfulness over time, we gained the credibility we needed among our sister churches and their leaders. Today we have about fifty missionaries living and serving in thirteen countries across four continents. God has supplied all human and material resources (Phil 4:19).

Maranatha Multicultural Ministries is a testimony to God's grace. He turned our vision into action. Our participation in Jesus' Great Commission is no longer only a desire; it is a blessed reality, founded on biblical convictions and providential partnerships. Our experience has convinced us that the Lord can do the same in any place where His people decide to obey. They indeed can take the gospel from the nations to the nations.

INSERT 40.3

Equipping Laypeople for Service in the South African Church

Mark Christopher

Upon my arrival in South Africa twenty-eight years ago, it became evident that one of the pressing needs within the churches was "equipping of the saints for the work of service" (Eph 4:12). There was an unspoken cultural idiosyncrasy of a clergy-lay distinction fostered by historically "high church" denominations residing in the country, like Dutch Reformed and Anglican. Combined with the apartheid culture, many local churches viewed the pastor as the trained professional, while the laity maintained an uninvolved posture.

South Africa has undergone monumental changes since I arrived, but this cultural anomaly unconsciously and stubbornly remains in the church there. As a church planter in Cape Town, I was well aware of the need to equip the saints for ministry alongside presenting every man mature in Christ (Col 1:28). The question was how to do it. I have found the answer to include three simple principles, which, if missionaries apply, will faithfully build up the body of Christ where it is marked by unbiblical divisions.

Communicate a Biblical Vision for Ministry

Pastors should communicate a vision or goal to their churches for what they are to be in Christ. Ephesians 4:11–16 provides it. It is a vision where the pastor is not just some "hired gun" or professional servant. Rather, he is a leader, facilitating the work of ministry, which is carried out by all the redeemed who make up the church in one locality. Such a vision must be taught before it is caught. The faithful teaching and preaching of God's Word is the first means to the end of an engaged, serving church. Then, as a regular outflow of that teaching, the pastor should consistently model and apply it. What I have often told my flock is poignant here: "The majority of my ministry begins when I pronounce the benediction and step away from the pulpit." It is vital for the pastor to lead as a servant.

Recruit Able Believers

Pastors must not minister alone. An essential part of applying the biblical vision is recruiting spiritually able believers. Here Christ is the exemplar when He called the disciples to "Follow Me" (Matt 4:19). At a basic level, all believers are divinely enabled to serve the body (Eph 4:7; 1 Pet 4:10). But given a long history as "pew-sitters," many South African believers need to be called out into participation in body life. In many cases, recruitment means simply asking someone to do a given task for a short time.

On the other hand, when it comes to training long-term leaders, it is important to select and invite participants based on their spiritual hunger, zeal, faithfulness, and teachability. Training for specific service should have as its goal raising up men and women as deacons and some men to lead and teach Bible studies and to eventually serve as elders.

Beyond eldership, my fellow leaders have desired to equip men for vocational ministry, leading us to increase our church-based training and even partner with a government-accredited seminary elsewhere in the country. Through our seminary partnership, we have helped several South African men enter into full-time ministry with formal theological degrees.

The missionary and church leader's training approach is therefore layered by necessity. Every local church needs believers who are called upon for regular tasks that do not require specialized training, while other ministries require some believers at various levels of biblical, theological, and pastoral training. Thus, while not every church member is called to vocational ministry, all are called to be equipped to serve in some God-designed capacity.

Delegate the Work of Service

In close connection to recruitment is the vital art of delegation; the former is people-oriented, the latter is task-oriented. To be a good delegator requires the pastor to carve off any task that can be done by another. The pastor who tenaciously clutches shareable duties—like setting up for Sunday worship—is robbing a blessing from himself and from the others who could do them. It sends the false message that "if you want anything done right, you have to do it yourself."

Delegating presupposes adequate training and instruction, which takes time. If, however, people are not adequately equipped for the role delegated to them, the result will ultimately be a dearth of servants just as before. Once believers are equipped to serve, they will need generous appreciation and encouragement, and soon they will provide the training, guidance, and follow-up for the next servants (Heb 10:24). The church in South Africa still has a long way to go to erase the clergy-lay distinction that is limiting its growth. But as our local churches follow these principles of communicating a biblical vision, recruiting able believers, and delegating the work of service to all the saints, they will be salt and light and will influence others to follow suit, "to the building up of the body of Christ" (Eph 4:12).

A Testimony of Biblical Counseling in Latin America

Juan Moncayo

October 6, 2020, was a special day for our small church in Quito, Ecuador. After a long and thorough process, we became home to the first non-English-speaking training center to be certified by an international association of biblical counselors. Being recognized as an official training center has opened doors for us to provide training to churches not only in Ecuador but across Latin America. This opportunity allows us to share our knowledge and expertise in biblical counseling with a wider audience, empowering churches to enhance their skills as part of the Great Commission's charge to make disciples (Matt 28:16–20). Our focus comes from the two following phrases of Jesus' Commission.

"All Authority Has Been Given to Me"

The Great Commission starts with the words, "All authority has been given to Me." The risen Christ who defeated humanity's greatest enemy, death (John 11:25; Acts 2:24; 1 Cor 15:54–57), here unequivocally states that He has full jurisdiction over the whole world. He is Lord. However, other forces around this broken world try to compete for His authority. Among other things, Latin America is plagued by poverty, political instability, teen pregnancy, and pornography—not to mention machismo culture, drunkenness, cartels, and corruption. The common responses to these issues are either man-centered models of counseling that miss the source of true change or ineffective unbiblical solutions that find people grasping for spiritual help through syncretism, shamans, and varying shades of charismatic theology.

Yet God has preserved for His people His sufficient, authoritative, inerrant Word, and His Word is effective (Ps 19:7–14; Isa 55:10–11; 2 Tim 3:16; Heb 4:12). The counseling center at La Fuente has heard people say that though they had tried everything, only God's Word made a difference. That is because Jesus has all authority, including over every competing, enslaving power (2 Cor 10:3–6; Col 2:13–15). Churches that practice biblical counseling are beacons of light revealing that truth. He has given humanity a Bible that is sufficient and powerful to give true gospel hope in the midst of a broken world.

"Teaching Them to Keep All That I Commanded You"

Still, it is possible to hold a high view of Scripture, to teach biblical inerrancy and authority, and yet fail to grasp the Bible's sufficiency for addressing daily life. Many true disciples in Latin America experience this. For example, several years before becoming a training center, Iglesia La Fuente began translating thirty hours of biblical counseling videos. The footage featured the basis of true Christian change, as well as biblical answers to such common life issues as anger and anxiety. In God's providence, a remarkable translator had joined the team. She had experience working with theological texts, had received theological training at Bible institutes in the region, and was capable of translating the videos with the appropriate cultural nuance needed for the project. But as the project progressed, the translator started to fall behind. When asked why, she shared through her tears, "It is so hard to translate.

As I try to translate, the Lord brings conviction to my heart. I have to stop. I have to pray and confess. I have never translated anything like this!"

It is not uncommon for theologically informed, doctrine-loving, exposition-listening brothers and sisters—some even in ministry—to limit the Great Commission's obligation to intellectual content transfer. In other words, the church's focus is on teaching what Jesus commands but not on teaching His disciples to obey it. It is not on the heart transformation that leads to keeping all that He has commanded (Matt 28:20). But when Jesus' disciples obey His commands from a changed heart, it is whole-life changing (Matt 7:24; Luke 11:28; John 13:17).

The Great Commission is not completed by merely teaching good doctrine or loving expository sermons. It is a commission that includes helping people wholeheartedly submit to Christ's teaching. That is what biblical counseling seeks to do. It is nothing more than intensive Christian discipleship. It is what is universally needed to close the gap between the head and heart, and to lead to obedient implementation with the hands. For, Jesus says, "If you abide in My word, then you are truly My disciples" (John 8:31).

CHAPTER 41

Removing the Scaffolding: The Missionary's Final Phase of Church Planting

Rodney Andersen

Scaffolding serves an important purpose in both the construction and refurbishment of buildings. Its intended purpose is to remain in place for a time and then to be removed once the necessary work is finished. A time always comes when the scaffolding is no longer needed. When one observes a building that has been hidden under scaffolds for years on end, he rightly assumes that some problem or neglect has occurred.

In the same way, Hudson Taylor describes foreign missionaries as scaffolding that should be removed as soon as possible: "I look on foreign missionaries as the scaffolding round a rising building; the sooner it can be dispensed with the better—or the sooner, rather, that it can be transferred to serve the same temporary purpose elsewhere."[1]

Some might wonder if comparing missionaries to scaffolding diminishes the missionary role, or, more importantly, whether such a comparison is biblically accurate. This chapter proposes that the scaffolding motif is accurate to a proper understanding of the missionary role as transitional in the formation of a local church. This temporary but vital role was first demonstrated through the ministry of the apostle Paul and has been recognized and carried out by many faithful ministers throughout the history of modern missions. The study begins with a brief recap of the Great Commission's connection to local church leadership, leading, second, to a rationale for the scaffolding principle and, third, to key steps the missionary must take to complete the final phase of the biblical task of church planting.

---

1. Dr. and Mrs. Howard Taylor, *Hudson Taylor's Spiritual Secret* (Chicago: Moody, 2009), 197.

Why Is the Church Essential to Missions?

The church is at the center of Jesus' last instructions to His disciples.[2] The Great Commission constitutes the final marching orders of all believers, which will direct the course of the rest of their lives on earth. The Great Commission assumes the church's importance, because the focus of the command is to make disciples of all the nations (Matt 28:18–20). The method of disciple-making necessarily includes baptizing and teaching, which are activities carried out in the context of the local church. Baptism is the outward act of identification with Christ by a new convert. It is the initiation point into discipleship and is therefore representative of the moment of salvation. At the point of salvation, a believer joins the body of Christ, which is the church, and enters into regular, active fellowship with believers (Col 4:1–13; Heb 10:24–25). From the point of conversion forward, the believer grows in sanctification and is taught to obey all that Christ has commanded under the guidance of local church leadership (1 Tim 5:17; Heb 13:17; 1 Pet 5:5). The church therefore is created by God for the fulfillment of the Great Commission to make disciples.

God designed the church to be led by elders. As the gospel spread, according to the Great Commission, the book of Acts and the epistles describe how local churches were planted and elders were installed, who would actively disciple local believers toward spiritual maturity (Acts 14:21–23; Titus 1:5). As Paul went from city to city proclaiming Christ, many became disciples and were encouraged to continue in the faith (Acts 14:21–22). But rather than stay long term with the young believers, Paul and Barnabas, "when they had appointed elders for them in every church, having prayed with fasting, they commended them to the Lord in whom they had believed" (14:23).

The establishment of elders in every church was shown to be the pattern set by the apostles for fulfilling Christ's global disciple-making mandate. Paul's letter to his missionary delegate Titus includes the instruction to, "set in order what remains and appoint elders in every city as I directed you" (Titus 1:5). This directive is followed by the qualifications each elder must meet—qualifications closely mirrored by Paul's letter to Timothy regarding the teaching and leadership structure in the church (Titus 1:6–9; 1 Tim 3:1–7). As long as the Great Commission is in effect, the God-given model for discipleship through the local church is establishing elders.

Why Must Missionaries Function as Scaffolding?

The church is essential to missions, and elders are essential to the church, but where do missionaries fit into the picture? Missionaries are not simply pastors or elders who live in different countries, nor are they simply evangelists with a

---

2. Craig Ott and Stephen J. Strauss, *Encountering Theology of Mission: Biblical Foundations, Historical Developments, and Contemporary Issues*, Encountering Mission (Grand Rapids: Baker, 2010), 119.

passport. Furthermore, not just any believer who goes overseas to do good works is a missionary. The primary and vital role of missionaries in the Great Commission is to raise up worshipers of God (Rom 10:14–15; Rev 7:9–10)[3] and to teach them obedience to all that Christ commanded. Thus, biblical missionaries are sent out with the mandate to make disciples and worshipers of God, and to plant and strengthen local churches to the glory of God. There are two important reasons why missionaries must function as scaffolding to the indigenous church: first, it was the apostle Paul's missionary model, and second, it follows the God-given pattern for a healthy local church.

Missionary Scaffolding Follows Paul's Model

The work modeled by the apostle Paul and his companions in the book of Acts demonstrates how a missionary is to act as a temporary worker for the stability of the local church. Paul's pattern of Great Commission ministry was to proclaim Christ and encourage and teach the new disciples in the local churches he planted, but he stopped short of becoming their leader. He did not become the pastor but appointed elders and commended them to service (Acts 14:23). He did not set up a missions organization or a denomination of churches. His desire was to "proclaim the gospel, not where Christ was already named, so that [he] would not build on another man's foundation" (Rom 15:20). He evangelized, put elders in place, then left to plant new churches. The ongoing shepherding of the planted church was placed in the hands of the elders (Acts 20:28),[4] though he would write back to the congregations to remind them of his teachings and to exhort them to live in accordance with all that he commanded on behalf of Christ (20:31).

Paul's ministry to a given church was transitory by design. His ministry model was what might be considered a planned retirement—not from ministry but from the newly established local church. Because he did not view himself as God's long-term instrument to lead the local church, he never stayed more than three years in any city (Acts 11:26; 17:2; 18:11; 19:8, 10; 20:3, 31).[5] Certain factors unique to Paul's ministry contributed to the rapid planting of churches, such as his apostolic gifting and his knowledge of the common language and culture of the people, not to mention the providence of God that led to great gospel expansion in the apostolic age. Language fluency and cultural understanding are essential to cross-cultural ministry, so missionaries who cross language and cultural barriers today will necessarily require additional time before they can plant churches with local leadership. Challenges and time frames aside, the trajectory in missionary

---

3. See also John Piper, *Let the Nations Be Glad! The Supremacy of God in Missions* (Grand Rapids: Baker, 2003), 208.

4. See also Benjamin L. Merkle, "Paul's Mission as the Mission of the Church," in *Paul's Missionary Methods: In His Time and Ours*, ed. Robert L. Plummer and John Mark Terry (Downers Grove, IL: IVP Academic, 2012), 67.

5. L. C. A. Alexander, "Chronology of Paul," *Dictionary of Paul and His Letters*, ed. G. F. Hawthorne, Ralph P. Martin, and Daniel G. Reid (Downers Grove, IL: InterVarsity, 1993), 122–23.

ministry today must be the same as it was for Paul—to build up local men for leadership in the local churches (cf. 2 Tim 2:2).

While indigenous leadership should be the typical pattern for missionary church planting and strengthening, at times a missionary may fully overcome the cultural and linguistic barriers and commit to adopting all aspects of the new country, becoming, "all things to all men" (1 Cor 9:21–22). In such cases, the local church might invite the missionary to change roles from missionary to pastor, committing to fully support him as a local church, such that he no longer needs primary support from his sending church. In such a case, however, the long-term goal remains the same: a biblical local church that will continue until the coming of Christ.

Missionary Scaffolding Follows the God-Given Pattern for a Healthy Local Church

The second reason why missionaries must function as scaffolding to a church plant is that it allows for the local church to function as God designed. Many missiologists have studied the example of Paul and have advocated for his missionary practice of entrusting church leadership to local men.[6] Rufus Anderson (1796–1880), senior secretary of the American Board of Commissioners for Foreign Missions, oversaw the appointment of missionaries for thirty-five years. He, along with Henry Venn, was the first to articulate that the goal of missions was to plant local churches that were "self-governing," "self-supporting," and "self-propagating," now known as the "three-self principles."[7] Anderson argued, "Missions are instituted for the spread of a scriptural, self-propagating Christianity. This is their only aim."[8]

Roland Allen (1868–1947) was sent by the Society for the Propagation of the Gospel to its North China Mission. He would spend less than ten years in China due to illness before returning to England to serve in the church. Yet he was convinced of the three-self principles of church planting, having understood them from Scripture and verified them on the mission field.[9] Allen wrote strongly against missionaries remaining as leaders in local churches. He saw this as a result of sinful pride and failure to trust the Lord.[10] Instead, he strongly advocated for the transitory nature of the missionary, in view of the permanence of the local church:

---

6. See, e.g., Henry Venn and Max Warren, *To Apply the Gospel: Selections from the Writings of Henry Venn* (Grand Rapids: Eerdmans, 1971), 63; John L. Nevius, *The Planting and Development of Missionary Churches* (New York: Foreign Missionary Library, 2015), 9; Melvin L. Hodges, *The Indigenous Church: Including the Indigenous Church and the Missionary* (Springfield, MO: Gospel Publishing House, 2009), 31–32.

7. Cf. Wilbert R. Shenk, "Henry Venn's Instructions to Missionaries," *Missiology* 5, no. 4 (October 1977): 467–85; Rufus Anderson and R. Pierce Beaver, *To Advance the Gospel: Selections from the Writings of Rufus Anderson* (Grand Rapids: Eerdmans, 1967).

8. Anderson and Beaver, *To Advance the Gospel*, 27–28.

9. Roland Allen, *Missionary Methods: The Apostle Paul's or Ours?* (London: Robert Scott, 1912). This book defended the earlier-formulated three-self principles, and it continues to be an influential work in missiology today.

10. Allen, 189–90.

He [the missionary] should remember that he is the least permanent element in the Church. He may fall sick and go home, or he may die, or he may be called elsewhere. He disappears, the Church remains. The native Christians are the permanent element. The permanence of the Church depends upon them. Therefore, it is of vital importance that if he is removed they should be able to carry on the work, as if he were present.[11]

To Allen, when the missionary retains control of the church leadership, the members develop an unhealthy dependence on the missionary instead of the Holy Spirit.[12] They develop a pattern of looking to the missionary rather than to Scripture to answer their questions.[13] By placing the leadership of the church under the authority of locally raised elders as soon as practicable, the members recognize their responsibility to carry out their God-given responsibilities in the church.

Throughout missions history and today, church-planting missionaries have recognized the need for planted churches to be self-governing. Many faithful men have labored toward that end, upholding the biblical role of the elder and establishing local leadership according to the apostle Paul's methodology. To make such a commitment on the mission field requires recognizing that failing to remove the missionary scaffolding will lead to serious problems in young churches. Yet the goal of local church self-governance is a source of hope during the difficult seasons of missionary service, because the promise is a disciple-making church that will continue far past the lifespan of the missionary.[14]

How Can Missionaries Function as Scaffolding?

Understanding and embracing the concept that the missionary must function as removable scaffolding for the sake of a permanent indigenous church is necessary. Yet it is not enough. The missionary must also determine how to apply these principles to his active ministry in the local church. The following seven steps will aid the missionary in entrusting local church leadership to indigenous men.

Plan for the Future

To successfully entrust the leadership of the church to local elders, the missionary must begin the first day on the field with this end goal driving his ministry. While there are many priorities for a missionary entering a new field, including learning the language and the culture, the eventual goal of seeing a local church established and elders appointed must be in focus from day one, clearly identified as the goal of his ministry action plan.

---

11. Allen, 203.

12. Allen, 109–11, 149–61.

13. Allen, 73.

14. The principles explained here are not in any way an endorsement of recent missions methodologies such as the church planting movement or the disciple making movement, but categorically deny their presuppositions and strategies. For a more thorough evaluation of these methodologies, see Matt Rhodes, *No Shortcut to Success: A Manifesto for Modern Missions*, 9Marks (Wheaton, IL: Crossway, 2022), and the other contributions in this volume that address modern methods.

Build for Independence

The missionary must guard against creating a ministry structure that can only be sustained by missionaries and outside funding. Once this dependence on outside help is created, it will be hard for the missionary to leave because the ministry may collapse without that support. Instead, it is important to keep the structure of the ministry simple and allow it to grow only under the following conditions: when it is initiated by those inside the church, when it can be led by local men, and when local funds can support the ministry.

Teach toward Reliance on God Alone

As individuals come to the truth of the gospel, the missionary must train each person to turn to God's Word for the answers, rather than to the missionary. Instruction in the consistent, literal, grammatical-historical hermeneutic and in sound exegesis will be the keys to the long-term health of the church. Missionaries must teach a robust theology, but they should not expect the church leaders or the congregation to necessarily reach their level of understanding, as missionaries have been cultivating their biblical knowledge since they were formally trained for ministry. It is important to allow for the church's future growth in sanctification and theological understanding.

Train Elders

As the missionary teaches the believers how to study God's Word and apply it in the church and in their lives, he must train them to serve one another and give them opportunities to do so. As they begin to serve, the missionary will start identifying those men who are diligent in their pursuit of God and submission to His commands. Investment of additional time into these men is necessary to train them in biblical wisdom and discernment. Not every man identified at this point will grow into an elder of the church, but some of them will continue to grow to give leadership to the church. Teaching men to handle God's Word accurately and communicate it faithfully is one of the responsibilities of the missionary (2 Tim 2:15), so opportunities to preach and teach need to become available to these men.

Work toward Departure

The missionary should relinquish decision-making in the church as much as possible to the men of the church. Even the earliest practices and decisions made by the missionary can sometimes continue to be implemented by future local leadership on the basis that "that's how the missionary did it," rather than on a settled conviction of instruction from God's Word. Refusal to make decisions or to refrain from heavily influencing the decision-makers requires great discipline and humility on the part of the missionary since he has much more experience, biblical knowledge, and wisdom than the young church. Guiding the local, faithful men to make decisions based on biblical principles early in the development of the leadership team will give the up-and-coming elders the confidence to make wise future decisions based on God's Word.

Aim toward Self-Supporting Local Churches

In the early stages of a church, many needs become evident, such as where the church will meet and how the lights will be kept on. While needs like these can easily be met with funding from the United States or other developed countries, the missionary must resist the urge to "solve" these and other problems by continually seeking outside funds. An unhealthy dependence on outside sources to establish churches teaches the leadership that church planting cannot be accomplished without foreign help; doing so will cripple their confidence that they can also plant churches without outside resources. It is far better, if possible, to call upon the church members to find the resources to meet the needs. In this way, they will take responsibility for their own needs and will not overextend themselves financially. If the missionary must leave for some reason, they will still have what is needed for the church doors to remain open.

Implement the Plan

Perhaps the hardest part for the missionary will be departing from the planted church after so much love and care have been put into the leadership and the people. Leaving the church under the leadership of the elders, however, is not a matter of putting faith in them, but in the God who can sustain them and empower them. The missionary must trust that the Holy Spirit can do a superior job than he can of protecting Christ's church. Leaving the church under indigenous leadership does not mean the missionary leaves the church completely on its own. Just like the apostle Paul, the missionary can and should continue to remain in contact with the church, even visiting them at times, to encourage them and to exhort them in ministry.

Conclusion

Like scaffolding on a building, the missionary is sent by his local church elders to make disciples and then to come alongside the new believers for a time. The Great Commission goal of a faithful missionary is to establish churches that, after his departure, are prepared to do the work of the ministry independent of the foreign helper. May each missionary, like the apostle Paul, be able to say to the elders of the church that he has helped establish,

> And now, behold, I know that all of you, among whom I went about preaching the kingdom, will no longer see my face. Therefore, I testify to you this day that I am innocent of the blood of all. For I did not shrink from declaring to you the whole purpose of God. Be on guard for yourselves and for all the flock, among which the Holy Spirit has made you overseers, to shepherd the church of God which He purchased with His own blood. (Acts 20:25–28)

Successful Missionary Transitions: Two Examples

Luis Contreras

Bill and Anthony started serving in their respective missionary fields in the same year.[15] Bill served in Sub-Saharan Africa for more than eighteen years. For five of those years, he pastored a church, though his main responsibility was in a local seminary where he trained others to pastor. Anthony pastored a church in Latin America for more than fifteen years, and he also trained men at a local seminary. At the end of these terms, both men handed over their local churches and pastoral training ministries to nationals.

The decisions Bill and Anthony made about when to hand over their ministries varied in each case. As Bill ministered in the African church, he began the process of transition as soon as it was determined that one of the men he had trained was biblically qualified and ready to replace him as the church's pastor-teacher. At the same time, it became clear in Bill's mind that the seminary was well equipped and no

longer needed the influence of a missionary. Anthony was born and raised in the Latin American context in which he served, so given that no ministry years were spent overcoming cultural and language barriers, his desire from the beginning was to have men ready to replace him as soon as possible.

There were times when the two missionaries doubted that a ministry transition to national leadership could or would ever happen. At those times, the men they were training seemed to be marked by spiritual immaturity or a lack of biblical wisdom. By God's grace, the missionaries persevered in preaching, teaching, and training, and they focused on meeting their responsibilities to the people while trusting in the Lord's sovereign work. With time they identified potential men to replace them in church and seminary, men with whom they had worked for several years and who demonstrated faithfulness to Scripture (1 Tim

---

15. For security and privacy purposes, the names of the missionaries have been changed, and certain details of their ministries have been omitted.

4:16), the ability to teach Scripture (1 Tim 3:2; Titus 1:9), and the ability to shepherd the flock of God (1 Pet 5:1–3).

Bill and Anthony trained their replacements formally in the classroom and informally by having the men shadow them generally and in all kinds of meetings. Two key elements were sharing the load of responsibility with them and treating them respectfully in private and in public. The men—and everyone else—knew that they were valuable to God, to the missionaries, and for the work of the Lord in their context.

Some of the men whom the missionaries trained did not end up in positions of leadership. This happened because of their lack of experience or ability, or sometimes even because of sin. In at least one case, a man started well but then left his wife and was disciplined out of the church. On the other hand, some men rose up as key leaders, much to the missionaries' surprise. One surprise for Bill was a man who initially had not wanted to be in ministry but then experienced a change of heart and committed to the role of pastor-teacher. Others, from a human standpoint, did not seem capable in terms of social or economic background. Yet they were equipped by the Lord and became faithful stewards of their churches and seminaries.

As the missionaries stepped aside, they faced some personal challenges too. Bill felt in danger of giving the false impression that he was abandoning the people whom he had loved and served for nearly two decades. Yet he felt that he would be interfering with the indigenous development of the ministry if he stayed in his role any longer. Anthony contemplated how stepping aside changed all of his relationships. Ministry transitions can create tension on the field, especially when the relationships most affected are those that played critical roles in the missionary's life and long-term work. One of the missionaries had hoped to lessen this tension by continuing to counsel and assist the men whom he had trained, since after the transition he continued to live in the area for a period of time. In the end, however, he reasoned that he ought not to, in order to respect the authority God had given to this next generation of leaders. As a part of showing the native church leaders respect, the time came for both Bill and Anthony to stop attending ministry leadership meetings and to resist giving their opinions. The new leaders needed to develop their own voices and approaches in accordance with the Word of God, for the sake of their churches' long-term strength within their cultures and societies (cf. Acts 14:23; 20:27–32; Titus 1:5).

How to know when to finally step out of a ministry is a question that all missionaries should consider before setting foot on the field. They must enter with an exit strategy. For Anthony, when strong disagreements arose between himself and the men he had trained, he knew the time had come to depart from his role and eventually from the area; otherwise, he would become an obstacle to the maturation of their own convictions and direction. Anthony realized that the Lord was not going to allow the ministry to move forward according to his plans. For Bill, an indication that the time was right came when he saw that the men had developed a consistent pattern of ministering and making decisions with Scripture as their authority. He then commended them to "the Chief Shepherd" (1 Pet 5:4).

Based on the reports that Bill and Anthony continue to receive from the field, their transitions to a fully indigenous leadership have gone smoothly. By God's grace, the missionaries' faithfulness in ministry, though not without its strains and struggles, was evident from beginning to end. May their examples and lessons learned serve the next generation of missionaries to do likewise.

INSERT 41.2

Gauging Successful Church-Based Training in a Minority Faith European Context

Kristian Brackett

Cross-cultural church ministry is demanding, but cross-cultural church ministry in a minority faith context is daunting. In one real sense, biblical Christianity is a minority faith in every country. "The gate is narrow . . . and there are few who find it" (Matt 7:14). However, the focus here is on mission contexts where evangelical Christianity makes up less than 1 percent of the population. In contexts like these, the church has limited resources, its growth is stunted, and its momentum is rare. Consequently, the church remains underdeveloped. Furthermore, common methods of measuring success by numerical growth or the multiplication of programs are unreliable when the church is not accepted in society. In regions where the adage "One step forward, two steps back" characterizes church growth and development, the typical metrics discourage and burden faithful workers. Such challenges lead to the legitimate question, "How should the church measure success in cross-cultural church-based training?"

Thankfully, there are better metrics to use than conversions, multiplication of programs, training center enrollment, or the number of degrees awarded. More accurate measures of success include the multiplication of disciples, the placement of graduates in the local church, and the personal maturity and spiritual growth in the lives of the graduates. These metrics mirror the explicit and implicit expectations in the Great Commission (Matt 28:19–20), the commitment of Jesus Christ to build His church (Matt 16:18; Eph 5:25–27), God's plan to manifest His wisdom and glorify Christ in the church (Eph 3:10; Col 1:18), and the duties of the man of God who leads the local church (1 Tim 3:1–7; 3:15; Titus 1:5–9). Though not as flashy, such metrics provide a more reliable biblical analysis of the ministry's foundation, especially in the modest, struggling congregations that dot the European context.

The Metric of Discipleship

The goal of missions is not just preaching the gospel and mass conversions. The proper goal of missions is making disciples (Matt 28:19) who worship the Father (John 4:23) and who imitate their mentor or leader as he imitates Christ (1 Cor 4:16; 11:1; Eph 5:1; Heb 13:7). This kind of multiplication has a multigenerational impact (2 Tim 2:1–2).

Since theological and pastoral training has such a specific goal, it must aim for more than content delivery. Faithful training ministries produce men who are teachable and who are on a lifelong trajectory of growth and maturity. Furthermore, graduates need to be committed to continuing the process of discipleship as they take up the mantle given to them and go on to disciple and entrust to others what they have received. We might ask concerning our students, "Are they pursuing others? Are they drawn to mature men, and are they drawing others along with them?"

The Metric of Local Church Commitment

The disciple-making pastor must do his work in the context of the local church. The goal of any gospel-centered, Christ-honoring mission movement must be the creation of strong local churches. The local church serves as the incubator where disciples are made, nurtured, and reproduced. They are educational institutions where disciples receive instruction, clinics where disciples receive care, and workshops where disciples develop skills. Moreover, churches generate other churches by sending out qualified and tested men who take the gospel into new communities. Pose these questions: "Are worship and Bible study priorities in the life of the disciple? Is there an observable commitment to involvement? Has he moved from attendance to participation and contribution?"

The Metric of Maturity and Growth

The final and perhaps clearest measure of a training ministry's success is its ability to produce mature and growing spiritual leaders. When the church is underdeveloped and has but few resources, it is essential that graduates have the strength of character to face hardship and discouragement as they grow and mature in ministry. They must be well prepared and tested in their personal lives as well as their academic abilities. Many will have to support themselves bivocationally. Often, they will not have the benefit of a strong team around them.

The metric of maturity and growth may draw distinctions between true ministry candidates and those who merely graduated from a program of study. Measuring this way will also identify graduates who need further development in the form of internships or lay responsibilities in the church. Not every graduate is ready for significant pastoral responsibilities. In minority faith contexts, however, graduates are often pressed into service prematurely. In such cases there is an especially acute need for teachability, maturity, and godly character. As seasons of momentum in Europe are rare among the numerous smaller congregations, it is essential to ask, "Does this potential leader have the persistence and backbone to serve in the face of opposition, apathy, and pastoral isolation?"

Measuring Success in Croatia

Croatia is one of several former Communist countries where evangelical Christianity is now a tiny minority faith. As with similar countries, Croatia's churches are small, the pastors are few, and there is not a steady flow of candidates for training. Additional factors complicate the preparation of men for church leadership. Since Croatia is still developing, academic fluidity—that is, changing careers through nontraditional forms of education—is rare, and free-market economic opportunities are limited. Pastors therefore typically need secular training as well as theological training to support themselves. Yet secular employment leaves little room for active ministry involvement.

For these and other reasons, one evangelical training center has designed a robust full-time program that emphasizes discipleship of its candidates. Due to lack of discipleship in the church, most students that enroll have never been discipled prior to study. And due to the lack of support of pastors by the local church, many students are discouraged from even seeking theological training or pursuing a call to ministry prior to enrollment. Since churches are small, have limited resources, and rarely support their pastors, training depends on funding from the West. To be good stewards and in pursuit of reproducibility, the training program strives to be simple. By God's grace, this training center has been able to supply about half of the Baptist church pastors in Croatia. Additionally, graduates and faculty are involved in numerous church-planting efforts both in Croatia and in other surrounding countries.

Conclusion

Ministry in minority faith contexts is hard enough without the burdensome and discouraging focus on tangible success. Nevertheless, by measuring its success from a biblical perspective, the church in that context can better recognize the mighty hand of God. Christ slowly but steadily builds His church through self-reproducing disciples who are committed to local churches. Though modest and often unassuming, the beauty and preciousness of the church are evident, even in difficult and hostile contexts.

SUB-SECTION 2:
THEOLOGICAL EDUCATION FOR CHURCH LEADERS

CHAPTER 42

The First Seminary: A Biblical Case for Pastoral Training

Nathan Busenitz[1]

On June 5, 1559, John Calvin dedicated a new building in Geneva for the purpose of housing a school. That academy would include both a college to educate young people and a seminary to train pastors. As aspiring church leaders from across Europe came to Geneva, the seminary equipped them for gospel ministry before sending them back home to preach and pastor. Significantly, the academy was only a short distance from Calvin's church. The relationship between the two institutions was evident to all. Students attending the seminary were taught hermeneutics,

biblical languages, theology, and homiletics. Recognizing the critical need for healthy churches throughout Europe, Calvin and his colleagues carefully invested in the next generation of spiritual leaders. The establishment of a pastoral training center in Geneva was pivotal in accomplishing that goal.

Three centuries later, in 1855, Charles Spurgeon began meeting weekly with a man named Thomas Medhurst to teach him theology. That meeting grew to include additional students. By 1864 more than a hundred men were eager to be taught and mentored by their

---

1. Portions of this chapter are adapted from Nathan Busenitz's editorial in *MSJ* 31, no. 1 (Spring 2020): 1–4. Used by permission.

pastor. The need for a training school became apparent. Consequently, Spurgeon started an institution simply known as the Pastor's College. By 1892, the year Spurgeon died, more than nine hundred men had completed their training at the Pastor's College. Though Spurgeon himself never pastored outside of Europe, graduates from his training school were sent to numerous places around the world, including China, South Africa, Australia, and parts of South America.

A Biblical Case for Pastoral Training

These historical examples provide a precedent for the necessity and value of pastoral training and seminary education. But what about a precedent from Scripture? A biblical justification for seminary education can be made from a number of New Testament passages. Matthew 28:19 prioritizes the teaching of disciples; 2 Timothy 2:2 emphasizes leadership training; Titus 1:9 requires elders to be equipped to articulate and defend the faith. Other familiar passages could also be cited. But a somewhat obscure passage in Acts 19 provides a precedent for seminary education in a particularly insightful way. These verses, which may initially seem insignificant, describe the apostle Paul starting a theological training school in the city of Ephesus.

The setting was Paul's third missionary journey (AD 52/53–56). After leaving Antioch and traveling through the churches of southern Galatia, the missionary-apostle made his way to Ephesus. There he encountered roughly a dozen disciples of John the Baptist and introduced them to the Lord Jesus, the one to whom John pointed (Acts 19:1–7). Picking up the narrative at that point, we read,

> And after he entered the synagogue, he continued speaking out boldly for three months, reasoning and persuading them about the kingdom of God. But when some were becoming hardened and were not believing, speaking evil of the Way before the multitude, he left them and took away the disciples, reasoning daily in the school of Tyrannus. This took place for two years, so that all who lived in Asia heard the word of the Lord, both Jews and Greeks. (Acts 19:8–10)

As Luke explains in verses 9–10, Paul met with a group of believers in a school for two years, reasoning about theology from the Word of God. Therein lies a basic paradigm for seminary education.

From this short passage (Acts 19:8–10), three features of the first seminary might be derived: the imperative, the investment, and the impact of theological education. These features provide helpful parallels for both students and teachers engaged in seminary education today.

A Courageous Commitment to the Gospel

Acts 19:8 describes the content of Paul's message—a message he no doubt continued to deliver even after he left the synagogue. An analysis of verse 8 demonstrates that Paul's message was continuous ("continued"), courageous ("boldly"), careful ("reasoning"), full of conviction ("persuading"), and Christ-centered ("about the kingdom of God"). In keeping with His God-given mandate to preach the gospel, evidencing his commitment to the imperative of the Great Commission, Paul faithfully discharged the truth of salvation in the synagogue in Ephesus for a period of three months.

As inevitably happens to those faithful to biblical truth, Paul encountered hostility. His message proved controversial (Acts 19:9), not because the apostle was pugnacious but because biblical truth is always polarizing. Commenting on this verse, Donald Barnhouse notes the parallel to modern ministry: "Notice the reaction Paul received to his preaching. It is always the same; some respond favorably, but the vast majority are hardened and disobedient in their outlook. . . . This is always the response any preacher of the Word receives. This is the response any Christian receives to his faithful witness to the truth of God."[2]

Paul's unwavering commitment to the truth, in the face of hostility, sets a bold precedent for those in ministry today (whether in a church or seminary). Far too many Christian institutions are quick to soften the message for the sake of popular appeal. But the God-given imperative of any pastor or seminary professor is to champion the truth, no matter how foolish or unwelcome it may seem to the surrounding society.

A Concerted Concentration on Training

Unable to continue teaching in the synagogue, Paul withdrew and began meeting with the disciples in a nearby school, which was probably a hall used by a local philosopher named Tyrannus. Everett Harrison sheds more light on the time Paul spent in this lecture hall:

> An illuminating addition in the Western text [Codex Bezae] at this point states that Paul's daily activity in this place went on from the fifth to the tenth hour, i.e., from 11:00 A.M. to 4:00 P.M. This was siesta time for the inhabitants. It has been conjectured that Paul was able to rent the hall at a nominal figure because it was not used at this time of day.[3]

That Paul met daily for a period of two years shows the level of personal investment he made in training these believers. If the marginal note in the Western text is correct, Paul's theology classes met during the city's normal naptime. The apostle gladly sacrificed his personal rest to instruct the disciples, likely through a form of dialogue teaching.

Interestingly, if Paul met with the disciples for five hours a day six days a week, his total time with them would have been approximately three thousand hours over two years. As his later testimony in Acts 20 implies, Paul taught his students "the whole purpose of God" (Acts 20:27), addressing topics such as soteriology

---

2. Donald Grey Barnhouse, *Acts: An Expositional Commentary* (Grand Rapids: Zondervan, 1982), 176.
3. Everett F. Harrison, *Acts: The Expanding Church* (Chicago: Moody, 1975), 291.

(Acts 20:21, 24), Christology (v. 21), pneumatology (vv. 22–23), ecclesiology (v. 28), apologetics and polemics (vv. 28–31), personal integrity (vv. 33–34), pastoral diligence (v. 35), Christian charity (v. 35), and prayer (v. 36). It is also noteworthy that Paul supported himself financially during this time as a tentmaker. As F. F. Bruce explains, "We may picture Paul spending the early morning at his manual labor (cf. 20:34; 1 Cor. 4:12), and then devoting the next five hours to the still more exhausting business of Christian dialectic. His hearers must have been infected with his keenness and energy."[4]

One final observation comes from "Tyrannus," whom most commentators think was the lecturer from whom Paul rented (or was given use of) the lecture hall. Simon Kistemaker notes the significance of his name: "We have no further knowledge of Tyrannus, whose name meant Tyrant. Probably this was a nickname given to him by his pupils."[5] Apparently Tyrannus was a taskmaster of a professor. What a contrast Paul's gracious and loving approach to instruction and encouragement must have been (cf. Acts 20:18–19, 36–38). Again, Paul sets a compelling example for contemporary seminary instructors to consider. The apostle made real sacrifices to train up the next generation of Christian leadership. Two millennia later, it remains a sacred privilege to do the same for the glory of Christ.

A Christ-Honoring Contribution to the World

Luke concludes this small section by commenting on the impact resulting from Paul's training school in Ephesus: "so that all who lived in Asia heard the word of the Lord, both Jews and Greeks" (Acts 19:10). Paul focused his attention on training, and the results were explosive. In fact, one commentator notes that "this venue, with its daily discussions over the course of two years, enabled Paul to have the most extensive influence so far recorded in Acts."[6]

As a result of this training school, pastors were trained and churches were planted. Bruce notes that the area around Ephesus "became one of the chief centers of Christianity. Probably all seven of the churches of Asia addressed in the Apocalypse were founded during those years, and others too."[7] He continues, "The planting of the churches of the Lycus valley, at Colossae, Hierapolis, and Laodicea, must be dated in this period: these cities were evangelized not by Paul personally but by his fellow workers."[8] From this school in Ephesus the gospel rapidly advanced into the surrounding regions. As Kistemaker observes "We assume that the students trained by Paul became pastors in developing congregations in western Asia Minor. . . . These disciples were instrumental in preaching Christ's gospel, that is the word of the Lord, to both the Jews and the Greeks."[9]

---

4. F. F. Bruce, *The Acts of the Apostles*, rev. ed., NICNT (Grand Rapids: Eerdmans, 1988), 408.
5. Simon J. Kistemaker, *Exposition of the Acts of the Apostles*, New Testament Commentary 17 (Grand Rapids: Baker, 1990), 684.
6. David G. Peterson, *The Acts of the Apostles*, PNTC (Grand Rapids: Eerdmans, 2009), 536.
7. Bruce, *Acts of the Apostles*, 409.
8. Bruce, 409.
9. Kistemaker, *Exposition of the Acts of the Apostles*, 685.

Paul's two-year training school, by God's grace, had a far-reaching impact for the advancement of the gospel and the cause of Christ. R. C. H. Lenski writes: "Paul used Ephesus as a radiating center. While he remained in this metropolis and political center he reached out as far as possible by means of his assistants; how many he employed we cannot estimate. Congregation after congregation was formed."[10] The opportunity for gospel influence expanded exponentially as more and more students were trained.

Again, Paul's example provides a compelling model to consider. If seminaries are faithful to their God-given imperative and fully committed to the investment they are called to make in the lives of their students, they can rejoice in watching God bless their work as He uses His Word to impact the world.

Imparting the Truth to the Next Generation

Acts 19 provides an important description, albeit brief, of the pastoral training school that Paul established in Ephesus. His example provides a biblical precedent for theological education today. The imperative for any faithful seminary or training center must be to proclaim the truth of the gospel boldly and to equip the next generation of church leaders to do the same. The investment of time, energy, and resources is significant. It certainly was for Paul. Yet he never grew weary of instructing and admonishing his students day and night. When seminaries are faithful to uphold that imperative and maintain that investment, they position themselves to make a great impact for the advance of the gospel throughout the world.

These considerations provide an important backdrop to Paul's words in 2 Timothy. At the time Paul penned this letter, he was incarcerated in a Roman dungeon. Within a few months, he would be led to a place of execution, where he would be beheaded. As for Timothy, he was pastoring in Ephesus (1 Tim 1:3). It had been more than a decade since Paul's third missionary journey, when he spent three years in Ephesus. Now Timothy was leading the church there.

In 2 Timothy 2:2, Paul writes, "The things which you have heard from me in the presence of many witnesses, entrust these to faithful men who will be able to teach others also." Timothy was Paul' spiritual protégé. He had spent many years with his mentor in many different contexts, including the apostle's ministry in Ephesus. Acts 19:22 implies that Timothy was with Paul during the time Paul taught in the school of Tyrannus, before being sent to minister in Macedonia and Achaia.

When he read these words about entrusting the truth to faithful men, Timothy would have undoubtedly remembered the training he had observed Paul conducting in that same city. Perhaps he recalled those warm afternoons—day after day in the school of Tyrannus—listening to Paul teach about the whole purpose of God. Now the mantle had

---

10. R. C. H. Lenski, *The Interpretation of the Acts of the Apostles* (Minneapolis: Augsburg, 1961), 790.

passed to Timothy. It was his turn to train the next generation, just as he had been trained by Paul.

For two thousand years, it has been the duty and privilege of every generation of believers to equip the next generation of faithful men who will lead the church by teaching others also. That was what motivated Paul at his training school in Ephesus. It motivated Calvin at his academy in Geneva. It motivated Spurgeon at his Pastor's College in London. And it ought to motivate pastors and church leaders today, as they seek to be found faithful by God's grace and for His glory.

INSERT 42.1

Intentional Discipleship in Lebanon

Maurice Boutros and Mark Jeffries

Below is an interview with missionary Mark Jeffries and his former student, friend, and now ministry partner Maurice Boutros. The two met at a local church in Lebanon after Mark arrived in 2011 with a goal of strengthening churches and establishing a pastoral training center. A group of missionary candidates asked the following questions about intentional, enduring discipleship relationships.

QUESTION: *To begin, please introduce us to your ministry and friendship.*

Maurice: I was born into a church in Lebanon that saw a lot of missionaries come through. They would be there for a year or two, maybe five, and then go away. They would come, see us as a "third world" country, give us some money, do some training for two years, and then go. But Mark's perspective and vision were different.

Mark: Well, we do not get credit for the vision. I love 2 Timothy 2:2 because I consider myself the third link in a chain. There was a gentleman who trained my youth pastor, who then trained me, and then I got to pass that training on. I am convinced that the best training for ministry cannot be divorced from the church; so, while my desire to have a pastoral training center was strong, it was driven by a vision to see churches mature. Even before we had formal training centers in the modern age, the pattern of discipleship was there in the church. I have received the fruit of it, so it was simply my desire to pass it on to faithful men.

Now, the Lord put some limitations on me, namely, the language, so when I arrived

I could not teach. But discipleship is not only speaking; it is sharing life. We were able to be a part of peoples' lives and to engage in other levels of discipleship before the formal training ever arrived.

QUESTION: *What are some problems you have seen with discipleship in missions, in broader evangelicalism or in your region?*

Mark: The problem with discipleship in our region is probably not unique. It is probably a lack of understanding of what biblical discipleship is. The word *discipleship* is common in the churches we know and love, but it is not producing the kind of disciples we see in the New Testament. Biblical discipleship is spending time with people; it is teaching people, being available to them, being an example to them, and confronting sin. But the lack of this full-orbed perspective keeps churches from accomplishing what I think they really want. Some people say that we need more discipleship curriculum. I do not think it is that at all. Maurice and I do not use a lot of formal curriculum, but we see a lot of biblical discipleship.

Maurice: I can add to that. When a missionary leaves after a year or two, he does not share our problems. But with Mark, I saw what he would do in hard times. I saw him during a revolution in Lebanon, during an explosion in Lebanon, and when

there was no money in Lebanon. I saw him in all these cases with his family. Discipleship is not only about one man; it is about his relationship with his wife and with his kids, how they are adapting.

The first week I came to America with my family, I called Mark and I said, "Thank you." To all the team that left America to live in the Middle East, I said, "Guys, you were living in 'Disneyland.' Why did you go to Lebanon and Egypt? Thank you." I could see that they left a place where there is power twenty-four hours a day, gasoline for the car is always available, and stable internet. And, most importantly, they left mature churches, pastors, elders—so to come and serve us for a long period, for me, this is key.

QUESTION: *Mark, you chose to attend an Arabic-speaking church rather than an English-speaking church. How would you view this as a strategic choice as a missionary?*

Mark: If all I hope to do is distribute aid, then I do not need a language. But if I hope to impact people over the long term, I have to follow the biblical model. The verse I think of is: "I have become all things to all men" (1 Cor 9:22). There is absolutely no way in my mind that I could do that while living here but in my own culture. Not every missionary has to do that, but our desire was to impact local churches, and that goal required my wife and me to be in discipleship. English would have put up too many barriers.

Maurice: Let me give one example. Mark put six years into learning Arabic. Then he was able to disciple my father, who is reaching biblical maturity, and Mark's wife is discipling my mother. The two of them are serving together. Knowing the local language is key to long-term discipleship, and they opened a big door once they decided to learn Arabic.

Mark: I would add that, for the missionary, there has to be a giving up of a part of who you came as, or you do not have enough room to add something else. That means adapting to the culture in ways that are hard. Even some missionaries can make fairly decent progress in the language but are not able to go very far in the culture. I do not get everything right, but I ask Maurice and I ask his father for help in understanding the culture.

QUESTION: *What biblical or practical advice would you give to missionaries for longevity in their mission field?*

Mark: You have to be willing to cut yourself off to a certain degree. Technology is both a huge blessing and a huge curse in this arena. It used to be, centuries ago, that when you got on the boat, you probably never saw your home country again. These days you can talk to your mom in your home country every day for an hour, and it is no big deal. Except it is a big deal. The very thing we are blessed by can be the thing that keeps us from being effective. You have to accept a certain amount of loss in your life to gain the ministry impact in people's lives that you say you want. It is not that you cut people off, but no one has emotional capacity for limitless good relationships. You have to be willing to make your closest relationships the people in your local church.

QUESTION: *What are some of the risks or benefits of seeking someone you are discipling to become a friend whom you trust with your struggles?*

Mark: The risks are betrayal, loss of time, even the potential of upending everything you came to do. If you trust the wrong person as a foreigner, they have the ability to destroy everything you have invested in. But the benefits are just as great because you are discipling someone at a deep level, life on life. You cannot be open and vulnerable with everyone, but that is how people both learn from you and are allowed opportunities to encourage you. When they encourage us and love us back, the relationship deepens, the risks outweigh the benefits, and there is a foundation upon which ministry can be built. Down the road, that has a massive, massive payoff if the Lord blesses it.

Maurice: We started our friendship because Mark was my youth pastor. He saw a lot of mistakes. But he built up this kind of friendship with me and said, "Let's have a coffee together. Let's have breakfast." He started asking me questions just to make me think. He pushed me to think a lot, because I trusted him, which brought me to the Bible, and I learned how to have a biblical balance in ministry.

Discipleship is this balance of friendship, mentorship, accountability, and confrontation all mixed together for a long time. For me, then, I think it is important not to make quick decisions or to judge too early about a person, but to invest in many people on a small level. Then you can see who is able to walk with you and who will go with you on this journey of discipleship.

CHAPTER 43

Training Pastors Theologically:
A *Sine Qua Non* of Biblical Missions

Brad Klassen

One of the failures of the church in the modern missions era has been its neglect of training indigenous pastors. Part of this neglect springs from an anti-intellectual mysticism prevalent in segments of Western evangelicalism. If the training of church leaders at home depreciates serious training in biblical Hebrew and Greek, or a deep understanding of the principles of biblical exposition, or a familiarity with church history, or a facility in systematic or practical theology, then the theological training of church leaders elsewhere around the world will be de-emphasized also. This mentality is even manifested in the kind of missionaries who are often sent to the field—missionaries who lack theological training and any aspiration to it.

Part of this neglect can also be attributed to deep-rooted partiality. The mature, sophisticated churches in the West "need" the theological meat prepared by highly trained pastor-teachers with advanced degrees and large libraries. On the other hand, newly planted churches on the mission field—especially where those churches are comprised of the less educated—should be indefinitely content with simple gospel milk, it is assumed.

Pragmatics is also to blame for the neglect of training indigenous pastors. The cost of educating a small number of pastoral candidates for ministry—not to mention the expense of sending the missionary educators to train those men—does not sell well. The time needed to equip these candidates in exegesis, history, systematics, expository preaching, and pastoral ministry exceeds what is required for short-term mission trips and evangelistic outreaches. And the stories of training a small number of believers in a classroom for two to three years just do not compare with those of conducting evangelistic crusades, erecting church buildings, distributing food and personal hygiene products, or holding summer youth camps. David Sills recognized the harmful influence of such pragmatism on the church's faithfulness to the Great Commission when he wrote, "As missionaries have joined the race to reach the unreached people groups of the world as quickly as possible, they have strategized to increase speed. The need for speed has influenced missionary efforts so much that many traditional missions tasks have been jettisoned in order to enable it."[1]

Admittedly, it would be irresponsible to respond to one area of neglect by creating a new one—to downplay the work of gospel proclamation and church planting and to make the mission all about the equipping of indigenous church leadership. The proper approach is to find the biblical balance—to take a careful approach to the mandates and models given in Scripture so as to ensure that all of what is described therein captures the church's focus. When this is done, the training of indigenous pastors will be recognized as a *sine qua non*, an essential task, of the church's mission and a duty to be honored and fulfilled with as much zeal as evangelism. This chapter, then, attempts to strike that balance by observing the mandates and models of Jesus and Paul, by considering the consequences of neglect, and then by drawing from them a final appeal.

The Mandate and Model of Jesus Christ

Of first importance is the mission given by the Lord of the church. When His mandate is examined, evangelization and training are shown to be equally foundational to the church's mission to the world. The most succinct summary of Jesus' marching orders comes at the close of Matthew's Gospel in Matthew 28:18–20.

Central to this mandate is the making of disciples (Matt 28:19). As the Greek verb *mathēteuō* indicates, this effort is not just about achieving affirmative responses to gospel presentations and integrating such individuals into church membership. Rather, it is about the formation of a particular kind of convert—one who is specifically identified as a *learner* due to his or her reception of a quantitative body of knowledge and application of that knowledge to personal life.[2] This is further emphasized by the means Jesus prescribes for accomplishing this mandate. Not only is disciple-making achieved through the act of baptism (a solemn identification with the triune God, v. 19), but also through the ongoing process of teaching so as to obey all that Jesus taught (v. 20). In other words, the mandate of disciple-making requires the explicit act of comprehensive instruction that aims toward wholesale obedience.

Thus, Jesus' own Great Commission mandate demands theological education. This fact, coupled with an awareness of the immediate audience to whom Jesus addressed these words, underscores the importance of educating indigenous church leaders in particular. Those who stood in Jesus' presence to receive this mandate were those whom Jesus had selected and

---

1. M. David Sills, *Reaching and Teaching: A Call to Great Commission Obedience* (Chicago: Moody, 2010), 15.
2. "μαθητεύω," BDAG, 609.

trained for this mission. It was no coincidence that Jesus had called these men to be His first disciples—to hear all that He taught and to apply it to all of their lives. They were specifically equipped by the Master in order that they could make more disciples, reproducing the process Jesus Himself began.[3] In other words, the Lord of the church has not only articulated its mandate, to make disciples, but He has also provided the model for it, dedicated preparation of the disciple-makers. Sunny Tan and Will Brooks sum it up well: "Purposeful training of church leaders is rooted in the New Testament and founded on Jesus' words: 'teaching them to obey everything I have commanded you' (Matt 28:20). . . . Thus, theological education and mission are intricately woven together since the burden for training leaders grows out of the Great Commission itself."[4]

The Mandate and Model of the Apostle Paul

If Jesus' Great Commission mandate and model includes the training of indigenous church leadership, one should expect to see it implemented among those directly sent by Him. When moving from the Gospels to the rest of the New Testament, that is precisely what is seen.

Among this group of apostles, Saul (Paul) of Tarsus stands head and shoulders above the rest—largely due to the far-reaching nature of his commission. As Jesus explained to Ananias, "He [Paul] is a chosen instrument of Mine, to bear My name before the Gentiles and kings and the sons of Israel" (Acts 9:15). By the time Paul writes to the Romans just two decades after he was radically changed and commissioned by Jesus on the road to Damascus, he is able to report that "from Jerusalem and all around as far as Illyricum I have fully preached the gospel of Christ" (Rom 15:19). Noting the astounding nature of this comment, Roland Allen writes,

> In little more than ten years St. Paul established the Church in four provinces of the Empire, Galatia, Macedonia, Achaia and Asia. Before AD 47 there were no Churches in these provinces; in AD 57 St. Paul could speak as if his work there was done and could plan extensive tours into the far West without anxiety lest the Churches which he had founded might perish in his absence for want of his guidance and support.[5]

Paul articulates what was the strategy behind this success in various places throughout his writings, but two texts stand out: Titus 1:5–9 and 2 Timothy 2:2. The application of his strategy is then clearly seen in Acts 19:8–10.

---

3. A classic resource on Jesus' disciple-making approach is A. B. Bruce, *The Training of the Twelve* (Grand Rapids: Kregel, 1971).

4. Sunny Tan and Will Brooks, "Theological Education as Integral Component of World Mission Strategy," in *World Mission: Theology, Strategy, and Current Issues*, ed. Scott N. Callaham and Will Brooks (Bellingham, WA: Lexham, 2019), 177.

5. Roland Allen, *Missionary Methods: St. Paul's or Ours?* (Grand Rapids: Eerdmans, 1962), 3. Summing up the entirety of Paul's ministry, F. F. Bruce writes, "Paul was not the only preacher of Christianity in the Gentile world of that day . . . but he outstripped all others as a pioneer missionary and planter of churches, and nothing can detract from his achievement as the Gentiles' apostle par excellence." F. F. Bruce, *Paul: Apostle of the Heart Set Free* (Grand Rapids: Eerdmans, 2000), 18.

Titus 1:5–9

Regarding his instruction to Titus, it is noteworthy that Paul and his apostolic assistant arrived on the unevangelized island of Crete at some point after Paul's first Roman imprisonment (AD 60–62). For some reason, Paul was unable to continue the church-planting effort on the island, thus entrusting Titus with the remaining duties. Writing to Titus a short time after he had departed, Paul reminds his assistant of his task: "For this reason I left you in Crete, that you would set in order what remains and appoint elders in every city as I directed you" (Titus 1:5).

The church context on Crete was primitive; there remained much Great Commission work to be done to bring the congregations of new believers scattered across the island to the point of self-governance and self-reproduction. Integral to this work was the installation of a plurality of elders for each congregation. Titus was charged with the responsibility of choosing candidates for this position not only on the basis of transformed character (Titus 1:5–8), but also on the basis of theological aptitude. These candidates were to be men dedicated to "holding fast the faithful word which is in accordance with the teaching, so that [they] will be able both to exhort in sound doctrine and to reprove those who contradict" (v. 9). In fact, this requirement was not for a task that would be necessary at some point down the road. The need was urgent in light of the threat of gospel perversion and apostasy even among these new congregations (cf. vv. 10–16).

Thus, integral to the fulfillment of the Great Commission on the island of Crete was the establishment of local pastoral leadership, and this leadership required both integrity of character and theological acumen. John Chrysostom summarized the necessity of this latter requirement well:

> There is need not of pomp of words, but of strong minds, of skill in the Scriptures, and of powerful thoughts. Do you not see that Paul put to flight the whole world, that he was more powerful than Plato and all the rest? . . . He who knows not how to combat the adversaries, and to "bring every thought into captivity to the obedience of Christ," and to beat down reasonings, he who knows not what he ought to teach with regard to right doctrine, far from him be the Teacher's throne.[6]

This strong-mindedness, this skill in the Scriptures, this profound understanding of doctrine so crucial for the health of the church, is not innate to any believer. It comes only through training and preparation.

2 Timothy 2:2

How Paul envisioned elder candidates to be prepared is described in his mandate of 2 Timothy 2:2: "The things which you have heard from me in the presence of many witnesses, entrust these to faithful men who will be able to teach others also." Addressed to

---

6. John Chrysostom, *Homilies on the Epistle of St. Paul to Titus* 2 (*NPNF*¹ 13:525).

Paul's other apostolic assistant, Timothy, the letter of 2 Timothy provides insight into Paul's priorities as he contemplated imminent death. As many were abandoning him out of fear (1:15) and as false versions of Christianity were spreading (2:16–18), Paul exhorts Timothy to "guard the treasure" that had been entrusted to him (1:14). Ultimately this guarding of the gospel would be accomplished by its faithful transmission to others committed to the same end. Paul calls upon Timothy to "entrust" (2:2), an action that implies the transfer of something invaluable—in this case, the propositions of the gospel taught by Paul (v. 2)—for the purpose of safekeeping.[7] Those who could achieve this responsibility were known as "faithful men" (v. 2), and their faithfulness would be measured by whether they "teach others also" (v. 2)—an action that echoes the mandate of Jesus Himself ("teaching them to keep all that I commanded you," Matt 28:20).

Consequently, we find in Paul's mandate of 2 Timothy 2:2 an essential component for the success of the Great Commission: the manifold truths of Christ's teaching must be faithfully transmitted to qualified men committed both to the objective content of the teaching and to the subjective act of teaching.

This is the divine plan for the spread of Christ's witness to the ends of the earth, and it presumes the theological preparation of those who are to lead the charge. To put it in the words of the aphorism expressed by Jesus, "Can a blind man guide a blind man? Will they not both fall into a pit? A student is not above his teacher; but everyone, after he has been fully trained, will be like his teacher" (Luke 6:39–40). Great Commission success is dependent upon pupils being taught by skilled teachers.

Acts 19:8–10

One does not need to look hard to find how Paul's strategy, mandated for Titus and Timothy, looks in practice. The most vivid example comes from Paul's church-planting effort in Ephesus during his third missionary journey (AD 52–55):

> And after he entered the synagogue, he continued speaking out boldly for three months, reasoning and persuading them about the kingdom of God. But when some were becoming hardened and were not believing, speaking evil of the Way before the multitude, he left them and took away the disciples, reasoning daily in the school of Tyrannus. This took place for two years, so that all who lived in Asia heard the word of the Lord, both Jews and Greeks. (Acts 19:8–10)

Several observations can be drawn from Paul's implementation of the mandate to train indigenous church leaders.

First, Paul's mission was concentrated in focus. At a point early in the ministry in Ephesus, Paul transitioned from public ministry to one predominantly aimed at a smaller, select audience. He "took away" (*aphōrisen,*

---

7. "παρατίθημι," BDAG, 772.

Acts 19:9) the Ephesians who had believed in the gospel. He removed them from the unbelieving crowds so that he could concentrate on their doctrinal instruction. Luke specifically calls this group "disciples" or "learners" (v. 9; cf. Matt 28:19).

Second, Paul's mission was intensive in nature. Paul took them to "the school of Tyrannus" and was "reasoning daily" with them (Acts 19:9). The nature of this reasoning is best understood as "engaging in speech interchange" or "instructing" on a particular topic.[8] It is a term commonly used in Acts to describe Paul's method of teaching. This form of instruction occurred daily, suggesting that Paul implemented a curriculum designed to transmit a quantity of theological knowledge and to develop a set of intellectual skills.[9] And this took place, as Luke notes, in the "hall" or "school" (*skolē*) of Tyrannus—a building conducive to education.[10]

Third, Paul's mission was lengthy in duration. Paul engaged in this training "for two years" (Acts 19:10), which was no insignificant amount of time. If Paul met five days a week on average for four hours a day, he would have taught approximately twenty hours a week. If he met for fifty weeks a year for two years, his total hours of instruction would be around two thousand. Although it is impossible to know definitively, Luke's description nonetheless suggests a significant number of hours devoted to theological training.

Fourth, Paul's mission was fruitful in outcome. Luke directly links the nature of Paul's instruction to the enormous consequence it had for the region around Ephesus: "so that all who lived in Asia heard the word of the Lord" (Acts 19:10). Believers trained by Paul in Ephesus became missionaries to many other cities in the Roman administrative province of Asia. One of these disciples was undoubtedly Epaphras, who brought the gospel to the Lycus valley cities of Colossae, Laodicea, and Hierapolis (cf. Col 1:6–7; 2:1; 4:12–13). It was likely a result of Paul's training in Ephesus that disciples also went on to plant the churches of Smyrna, Pergamum, Thyatira, Sardis, and Philadelphia (cf. Rev 2–3). Most certainly, Paul equipped a generation of elders for the church in Ephesus itself, enabling this church to become one of the great centers of Christianity for decades to follow (cf. Acts 20:18–35).

This proliferation of true churches was made possible because of Paul's commitment to train pastors. By concentrating on indigenous leaders and training them well, Paul was able not only to reduplicate his own efforts but also to ensure that the efforts of those he trained would be multiplied by entrusting the

---

8. "διαλέγομαι," BDAG, 232.

9. Cf. Craig S. Keener, *Acts: An Exegetical Commentary* (Grand Rapids: Baker Academic, 2012), 3:2830–33.

10. The Western text (Codex Bezae) of Acts 19:9 adds that this instruction took place "from the fifth hour until the tenth," which would be from 11:00 a.m. until 4:00 p.m. This would place Paul's instruction during the heat of the day, when residents of the city—including those who would have normally occupied the hall—rested from their daily occupations. This siesta time would have provided an opportunity for Paul to rent the space and use it for the training of the disciples. See discussions in Keener, *Acts*, 3:2829–30; I. Howard Marshall, *Acts: An Introduction and Commentary*, TNTC 5 (Downers Grove, IL: InterVarsity, 1980), 327–28.

things they had learned to faithful men, able to teach others again (cf. 2 Tim 2:2). This was not merely a flash of practical genius on his part. It represented obedience to Jesus' mandate and model.

In light of these and other texts throughout Acts and Paul's letters, Wendel Sun was correct to conclude the following: "The missionary task is incomplete without advanced theological training. The Pauline paradigm clearly reflects a deep concern that churches and leaders are adequately equipped theologically."[11]

The Consequences of Neglect

It is necessary also to consider what happens when pastoral training is missing from the church's effort to fulfill the Great Commission. Thanks be to God that the success of Christ's church is not dependent on human effort. Jesus' promise to Peter is just as applicable today as when He first made it: "I will build My church; and the gates of Hades will not overpower it" (Matt 16:18). Despite its misplaced priorities and imperfect strategies, Christ will continue to build His church. If the gates of Hades cannot thwart His effort, neither will the church's failures. On the other hand, there is yet a price to pay. There are negative consequences that Christians and those to whom they bring the gospel will experience when they neglect the whole of Jesus' mandate. Here are three:

First, by neglecting the training of indigenous pastors as a fundamental component of the global mission, the full reward that comes from obedience to all of Jesus' mandate will be forfeited. Involvement in the Great Commission is not mandatory because God is shorthanded. Rather, the people of God are invited to partner in the great mission of God in order that they might experience the goodness and power of God working through them (2 Cor 4:7). Conversely, failure to implement Jesus' mission in the manner that Jesus intended—whether by ignorance, carelessness, or pride—will lead to disappointment in the day of Christ. The apostle Paul warns about missional infidelity:

> According to the grace of God which was given to me, like a wise master builder I laid a foundation, and another is building on it. But each man must be careful how he builds on it. For no man can lay a foundation other than the one which is laid, which is Jesus Christ. Now if any man builds on the foundation with gold, silver, precious stones, wood, hay, straw, each man's work will become evident, for the day will indicate it because it is revealed with fire, and the fire itself will test the quality of each man's work. If any man's work which he has built on it remains, he will receive a reward. If any man's work is burned up, he will suffer loss; but he himself will be saved, yet so as through fire. (1 Cor 3:10–15)

Christ's work must be implemented in Christ's way. It must because He is worthy; He

---

11. Wendel Sun, "Biblical Theology and Cross-Cultural Theological Education: The Epistle to the Romans as a Model," *Global Missiology* 4, no. 12 (2015), 1.

is worthy of obedience to the smallest detail of His mandate.

Second, to neglect the training of indigenous pastors will only work against the broader efforts of evangelism. As the saying goes, "showing up is half the battle." But the other half is found in ending well. Modern missions is too frequently plagued by a failure to achieve the second half. The church has been good at whittling away at the list of languages that still need a Bible translation and at reducing the number of communities where the gospel has never been preached. But too often the effort ends there. The baton is dropped. New believers are left without the resources to grow—without adequate translations for Bible study, without doctrinal helps to defend against heresies, and without the skilled leadership needed to shepherd the saints and equip them for ministry. These anemic churches flounder, fail to reproduce, and then fall out of existence. In a generation's time, a new evangelistic work is needed; the initial resources and opportunity have been squandered.[12]

Third, the neglect of training indigenous pastors has been one of the major causes of the spread of unorthodox teaching around the world. Indeed, some would call this unorthodoxy a natural expression of a "global theology," an inalienable right to interpret the truth according to a community's own customs. But the apostle Paul himself would have nothing to do with this, as is illustrated in his own response to departures from the apostolic standard. For example, in the primitive Christian context of Crete, Paul and Titus had to battle against those who were teaching contrary to the doctrines delivered by Paul, who sought to syncretize the gospel he preached with other religious streams (Titus 1:10–16). Paul's response was commanding the preparation of elders for each church, overseers who would be able "both to exhort in sound doctrine and to refute those who contradict" (1:9). If this was Paul's antidote, one can assume what will happen when its model is not followed. The failure to prepare leadership is to leave the door open to the propagation of lies.

A Final Plea

Crucial in the plan to correct what has often been neglected is to send missionaries who themselves have been well-trained. If training indigenous pastors is indeed a *sine qua non* of biblical missions, then the missionaries themselves must be trained as pastors. Tan and Brooks capture this need well:

If missionaries are going to be able to plant healthy churches that practice biblical modes of preaching, stewardship, worship, and so on, they need rigorous theological preparation. If they want to train church leaders to know the gospel well, and if they are going to equip church leaders to interpret and apply

---

12. That new churches require ongoing care is nothing new. Consider how much attention Paul needed to devote to the churches he planted in places like Galatia and Corinth.

Scripture to the local context, then they need to be equipped with such knowledge and skill themselves. Otherwise, how will they train others for future ministry when they have not been trained? How will they encourage others to prepare for the work to which God is calling them when they have not personally set aside the time for preparation?[13]

Today's church must recover this commitment. In the same way that the great apostle Paul was the one sent from the Antiochene church when he could have stayed to benefit the Antiochene believers, so also churches today need to send their best prepared, most qualified pastor-theologians to the field. Edward Judson, the son of Adoniram Judson, when reflecting on the responsibility of the church in his own nation, rightly said,

It is a mistake to suppose that a dull and second-rate man is good enough for the heathen. The worst-off need the very best we have. God gave His best, even His only begotten Son, in order to redeem a lost world. The most darkened and degraded souls need the best thinking. . . . It would be a sad day for . . . Christians if they should ever deserve Nehemiah's reproach: "Their nobles put not their necks to the work of the Lord." Christianity will advance over the earth with long, swift strides when the churches are ready to send their best men, and the best men are ready to go.[14]

---

13. Tan and Brooks, "Theological Education," 192.
14. Edward Judson, *Adoniram Judson, D.D.: His Life and Labours* (London: Hodder and Stoughton, 1883), 19.

INSERT 43.1

The Legacy of Pastoral Training in South Africa: A Case Study from the Limpopo Region

David Beakley and Charlie Rampfumedzi

In 1997, three years after a dramatic shift from apartheid to democracy in the political landscape of South Africa, the Lord decided to move. Following a century in which most indigenous people did not have access to theological training, the Lord saw fit to strengthen His church in that country. A small group of men from North America, specifically from The Master's Seminary and The Believer's Foundation, made a long flight to Polokwane, Limpopo, the northernmost region of South Africa, to meet with the staff of Christ Baptist Church (CBC) to discuss the need for training African pastors.

During those few days, the Americans were disturbed by the weak preaching they heard—preaching that was marked by a lack of biblical understanding and a focus on miracles and prosperity. On the final day of the trip, as the visitors resigned to look for a different place with more potential, the local pastor told them that if they walked away, they would be like everyone else. He pleaded, "This is why we asked you to come! Our men have had no training. They have had no help. We need pastoral training!" With the Lord's conviction and mercy, the visiting group returned and developed a plan to establish a pastoral training center in Polokwane. The center began in 1997 as Northern Province Baptist Theological Institute, and eventually became Christ Seminary. The purpose of this insert article is to demonstrate that long-term pastoral training does not only happen through sending missionaries; rather, it requires understanding of the need for various foundation blocks: partnership, leadership, discipleship, ambassadorship, and sponsorship.

The Need for Partnership

To reach more African pastors, the newly planted school partnered not only with the host church, CBC, but also with the Baptist Union of South Africa. As a result, Christ Seminary was tasked with training many of the African pastors in the Northern Province, most of whom had been denied entrance into Baptist seminaries prior to 1994 because of the apartheid government. Ten men from South Africa as well as Mozambique enrolled in 1997. After a few years, admittance had increased to about twenty-five men each year. Along with South Africans, students from surrounding African countries were coming to Christ Seminary and experiencing life-changing training focused on expository preaching.

The Need for Leadership

The training center began with two faculty members. Two years later, a South African pastor was added. Most of the students were not theologically grounded, but the Lord had his hand on one specific student. Charlie Rampfumedzi was a young man who had just earned a law degree from the University of Venda, in the extreme northeast of South Africa, below Zimbabwe.[15]

---

15. Venda was traditionally called a "homeland" in the Old Apartheid South Africa—it had its own government and

Charlie was on his way to becoming a state prosecutor when the Lord led him to become a student of the law of God at the training center in Polokwane.

Although he was South African, Charlie's main language was Tshivenda, the main language of the people who live in the Venda region. Attending Christ Seminary meant living and studying in a province where the main language was Sepedi (Northern Sotho), a language spoken by a different tribal group with almost no linguistic similarities. The seminary classes were taught in English, but the students mostly conversed in Sepedi. Regardless, Charlie graduated in 2000, and in 2001 he was invited to join the faculty of Christ Seminary as a lecturer.

The Need for Discipleship

Over the next few years, Charlie got married, became an elder at CBC, and grew in his quality of teaching and preaching. As Charlie grew in his lecturing at Christ Seminary, the necessity of theology—particularly Christology in the African context—became a stark reality. Charlie poured himself into the study of Christ, determined to learn how to convey the reality of the person and work of the Savior to men who had been raised in traditional African religious contexts that embraced ancestor worship and other demonic practices.

What began, prior to Charlie's involvement, as a series of "Western" systematic theology courses quickly turned into a course that was custom fit for the African worldview. Only a national lecturer could make these connections. Charlie was not just developing content; he was initiating continuous and intense discipleship with his students. He started lecturer-student relationships in the classroom, led mentoring groups, and then cemented relationships that continued to flourish even after the students graduated.

In the years that followed, Christ Seminary began to add national faculty. In 2012 Charlie Rampfumedzi was called to be the principal of Christ Seminary (which in other contexts would be called the president). Charlie began to direct the faculty. Since Christ Seminary is church-based, all faculty members were pastors and elders at CBC, and CBC continued to be the host church for the seminary and was therefore in the closest partnering relationship with the faculty and students. The nationalization of a pastoral training center was moving ahead full speed. As national faculty began to take the helm, classes were full of conversations including rich theological content and the complex realities of godless African cultural practices. Christ Seminary was meeting the students' needs by going beyond teaching

---

municipalities, even though it was considered to be part of the country. The University of Venda is well-known and well-established as a credible South African University—especially in the medical fields.

theology—the faculty was teaching pastoral discernment through discipleship.

The Need for Ambassadorship

Over the past three decades, Christ Seminary has graduated more than two hundred fifty men trained in expository preaching and pastoral ministry. Many are leading solid churches across Southern Africa, and even as far north as Kenya, Uganda, and Ghana. Others are associate pastors, professors at seminaries, or serving on the mission field, on the continent, and abroad.

From 1997 to 2006, the Baptist Union of South Africa was happy with the ministry at Christ Seminary. But when the school's popularity began to rival and even exceed that of the denominational seminaries, conflict arose. Almost overnight the relationship between Christ Seminary and the denomination began to strain. The Baptist Union began to criticize the seminary's course content and academic hours, as well as points of doctrine.

It was clear that Christ Seminary needed to pursue accreditation and gain independence from the denomination. Previously, the school could rely on the Baptist Union for support and recommendations. Now Christ Seminary needed to strengthen and maintain strong relationships with the local churches directly. School leaders sought to do this through the help of their graduates. They organized a graduate network and created alumni conferences. Graduates saw that Christ Seminary had now migrated from missionary lecturers to more and more former students qualified to teach, and their attraction to Christ Seminary grew exponentially. With this increase in trust, graduate-led churches and missionary endeavors became the main source of incoming students. Christ Seminary graduates became the school's ambassadors, resulting in increased opportunities to train more faithful pastors across the continent.

The Need for Sponsorship

Christ Seminary's need for financial support grew along with its enrollment. A full national faculty, facility, library, books, and IT support was costly to maintain. Over the years, CBC remained a strong supporter of the seminary, but the Lord also raised up faithful members to help meet the needs as well. Those believers saw the need for solid pastoral training as they regularly heard their elders, who were also Christ Seminary faculty, faithfully preach Scripture.

As Christ Seminary continues to train men in sound doctrine and the skill of expositional preaching, the receiving churches, beyond the Limpopo region, as far as there are graduates, shine brighter with the gospel and bring increasing biblical literacy and conviction to their people. For, as the pulpits go, so goes South Africa—with the capacity to reach other continents and the world!

Training Preachers in East Asia

Jimmy Tan

For many East Asian countries, access to Christianity is impeded by the official religious allegiance of various kingdoms and nations, and in some political systems the state governs Christianity. In these systems, state churches big and small dot the land along the famed shores that once welcomed the great pioneer missionaries Adoniram Judson, Hudson Taylor, and Robert Morrison. The past decade has seen the rise of new political strongmen in the Asian region, with new social and national policies and a renewed desire for control over the church and Christianity.

For state churches to exist in a communist system is a paradox, a contradiction at best. Churches there often serve as a brewing pot for diluted theology, with messages high on political flavor and low on biblical density. In these countries, Christian literature and Bibles that were once publicly available on e-commerce platforms have now been delisted. It is common to find sanctioned churches pandering to the state, while faithful congregations are placed under monitoring and their leaders are visited by state officials.

These recent developments have em-broiled both state-sanctioned churches and the free gatherings of believers, leading the faithful to continue their fellowship in the face of mounting opposition, often in secret. Restrictions in meetings directly impact formal theological training and the operations of conventional Bible institutes, colleges, and seminaries. Consequently, throughout the Asian region, pastorally trained men shoulder the responsibilities of providing for their families and leading the churches. The twin needs to train qualified men for ministry and to maintain their livelihood makes it necessary to consider skills-based approaches to missionary service, wherein qualified ministry workers possess the professional ability to earn their own keep.

The Support Needed in East Asia

Paul's own example of "working night and day so as not to be a burden" (1 Thess 2:9) points to the fact that faithful leaders, particularly in communistic contexts, ought to be willing to work and earn their keep, so as to participate in the ministry of the gospel and, where possible, even support their teammates' needs (Acts 20:34). But they should not be alone. The connectivity of today's churches worldwide means that global church partners have many opportunities to provide advice, support, and resources to emerging churches in developing lands.

There are an estimated five hundred million Christians in East Asia alone. It is approximated that in that region there is one trained church leader for every sixty thousand believers, compared to the ratio of 1:70 in the United States. To equalize the ratio, upward of seven million trained men would be needed for ministry to and through the local church. There are at least three practical ways the global church can support the training of men in Asia and chip away at the massive need for pastors in the local churches.

First, churches can fund students. Men need pastoral training, and resources are needed to provide the platform for training them faithfully. Supporting an Asian student is best done through in-country, formal training, in partnership with the local church that has sent the man to the program. It is ill-advised to send a man away to study, because when he leaves his country, he leaves his church and his pulpit remains empty!

Second, churches can send teachers to Asia. Paul was sent to train indigenous pastors, and when he could not, he sent Timothy, Titus, and others. Imagine the impact in Asia if the global church would send their best pastors and teachers to developing fields to train men for a weekend, a month, a year, or a lifetime!

Third, churches can send international students back to their home countries. From my perspective as an Asian minister, "brain drain" and "sheep stealing" are two apt metaphors for what happens when Western countries train up Asian men and women who never return to the East. Western churches that host international students from Asia to attend Western institutions would do well to remember their Asian brethren in need on the other side of the world. The churches in Asia would be blessed if Western churches would disciple international students and send them back to serve the flocks to which they first belonged. To do so would mean that the Western churches would need to raise up local faithful men from their congregations to serve their flocks, including the ethnic ministries they desire to start. An international East Asian seminary student who takes over a Western church's ethnic outreach ministry will no doubt be effective, but imagine the impact he could make if he were sent back with material support to spearhead leadership for multitudes of believers in his home country!

Conclusion

Persecution and challenges are the furnace that flames the zeal of the true church. The challenges faced by the church of East Asia are not unique from those faced by Western missionaries from generations past. In 1938 the circumstances that led to World War II significantly impacted the German state church and inflicted considerable challenges for genuine believers and church leaders in Germany. The encroachment of national politics, the institutionalization of the church, and the systematized training of governmental workers in clerical garb led to dismay for many faithful believers who were attempting to train pastors for the ministry of the gospel.

In that environment, Dietrich Bonhoeffer, German pastor, seminary founder, and ultimately a martyr, offered an alternative model for seminary education and the provision of sound theological training—training men in small bands.[16] His model was tuned for quality of attention and depth of relationship with a minimal number of trainees at a time. Bonhoeffer's seminary vision was both farsighted and practical in view of its application beyond his time and geography. It is a hopeful prospect for churches in East Asia still today.

The question remains how men in the developing fields will see their roles as pastors, trainers of pastors, and supporters of pastors. Yet much can be accomplished for God's glory through a few faithful men at a time. With our help and by God's grace, let us pray that they leave a bold and faithful legacy in their countries, no matter the obstacles.

---

16. For a curated examination of Bonhoeffer's view and practice of theological education, see Paul R. House, *Bonhoeffer's Seminary Vision* (Wheaton, IL: Crossway, 2015).

CHAPTER 44

Drafting the Distinctives of a Philosophy of Global Theological Education

Rubén Videira-Soengas

If Christians are disciples of Christ (Matt 28:19), always learning to obey Him (10:24–25; 28:20; John 8:31; 13:13), then theological education, whether formal or informal,[1] is a necessity for all men and women in the local church. Such education prioritizes passing on life-transforming doctrine to the next generation (2 Tim 2:2).[2] But church leaders need to be equipped themselves to train their people so they become biblically literate, enabled to "learn Christ" (Eph 4:15, 20; 2 Pet 3:18). There are many kinds of biblically faithful formal and informal theological education programs that train up men and women for service to the church, such as in the areas of biblical counseling and discipleship, biblical studies, or target-specific ministries of the Word.

For this reason, local church leaders need to ask themselves how they will both equip their congregations and raise up from among the flock new pastors to effectively teach in their local church and beyond. Training up men as pastors is a specific work of formal theological education that is highly prioritized in the Great Commission. Accomplishing this subset of training must be guided by a clear rationale or philosophy of education. This chapter aims to establish the biblical framework for a philosophy of formal theological education for the training of men for local church ministry and to offer practical principles to develop it.

The Doctrine behind Theological Education

A philosophy of education should not start with what to teach but with why to teach and what

---

1. Throughout this volume, the use of *informal education* includes the category of *nonformal learning* without specifying a distinction between them. In this chapter, informal education is limited to learning in the context of the church, whether from the pulpit, Bible studies, Sunday school classes, discipleship, or, at times, structured learning at a certificate-granting level. The term *formal education* refers to structured learning in a school setting resulting in a degree.

2. See Lois E. Lebar, *Education That Is Christian* (Colorado Springs, CO.: David C. Cook, 1995), 27.

to expect. Also, since it is Christian education, it needs to identify its differences from secular formal education. The Word of God provides the answers to these questions, laying the foundation to develop a philosophy of formal theological education thereafter.[3]

Why It Matters

The nature of the church makes theological education indispensable. The church is the "pillar and support of the truth" (1 Tim 3:15), and therefore the church must teach the truth. Even though this language conveys a passive role in that the church is not truth's origin but its last line of defense, it does not take away the church's active responsibility to hand over truth's baton to new generations. The truth, as Jude 3 implies, is axiomatic, meaning that it is a set of doctrinal propositions delivered to all the saints and, as such, must be explained and taught to its recipients. This is the very reason why the apostles' ministry revolved around teaching the truth (Acts 6:4), and the first Christians continually devoted themselves to it (Acts 2:42). They could not conceive a church without theological instruction, so they gave attention to education in their midst (1 Tim 4:13).

Another reason why theological education must be a priority for the church is that the leaders are required to be "able to teach" (1 Tim 3:2; 2 Tim 2:24). This phrase translates the Greek word *didaktios*, meaning "skillful in teaching,"[4] which emphasizes two aspects. First, to be able to teach is to be someone who by his own virtue is apt to instruct other people on how to become virtuous,[5] and second, it refers to a person who has been trained in the truth and therefore is qualified to teach it to others.[6] Hence, the main responsibility of Christian leaders is to be examples of godliness, and to teach theology to their people, for which they need to be equipped. The apostle Paul understood this, so setting himself as a model in training others was at the heart of his ministry. For instance, he told the Corinthians to imitate him as he imitated Christ (1 Cor 11:1), and he even taught theology in rented school space to the Ephesian disciples, including future church leaders (Acts 19:9–10; 20:31).

Theological education should also be a priority because of the Great Commission (Matt 28:19–20). Jesus, before ascending to the Father, commissioned believers to "make disciples of all the nations." This phrase means to "develop learners,"[7] and it is grounded on

---

3. Michael S. Lawson "Biblical Foundations for a Philosophy of Teaching," in *The Christian Educator's Handbook on Teaching*, ed. Kenneth O. Gangel, and Howard G. Hendricks (Grand Rapids: Baker, 1998), 61.

4. "διδακτικός," BDAG, 240.

5. For example, Philo used this word regularly in the context of someone who teaches moral virtue because he has first acquired it. See Philo, *Congr.* 35; *Mut.* 83, 88, 255; and *Praem.* 27.

6. Origen's defense against Celsus, who claimed that Christians were unwise and uneducated, was that Paul required church leaders to be trained, and therefore they were theologically educated. Origen quotes 1 Timothy 3:3 and says that "able to teach" means "able to convince gainsayers" and "to be instructed." Origen, *Against Celsus* 3.48 (PG 11:984c).

7. A. T. Robertson, *Word Pictures in the New Testament* (Nashville: Broadman, 1930), 1:245. It is presupposed that these "learners" have been regenerated by the Holy Spirit. Thus, they have repented and surrendered to Him, becoming His learners.

Christ's supreme authority (Matt 28:18–19). Hence, the church ought always to seek to turn unbelievers into believers who are students of Jesus, teaching them to observe all that He commanded (Matt 28:20). Consequently, Paul, when writing to the Colossians, speaks of the gospel as something they learned (Col 1:7). He also tells the Ephesians that they learned Christ (Eph 4:20) and the Philippians that they must obey the truth they had learned (Phil 4:8–9). Time and again, the language of the New Testament assumes that a Christian has been taught how to become a disciple. This process includes learning life-transforming theological truth. Accordingly, a congregation that neglects such teaching is neither following in the footsteps of the New Testament church[8] nor fulfilling the Great Commission[9] and, thus, "has forfeited its biblical right to exist."[10]

The basic tenet of the Great Commission, then, is to plant local churches among the nations filled with disciples of Christ. A healthy church cannot be established without local leadership that is equipped "to implement biblical forms of preaching, giving, worship, leadership, fellowship, prayer, and of course, evangelism and missions."[11] All these tasks are profoundly theological and do not happen intuitively. They need to be taught and nurtured to execute them skillfully and to fulfill the church's mission. To this end, theological education must course through the church's veins, because the Great Commission portrays Christians as life-long learners entrusted with the goal of making more Christians, whose commitment to keep on learning Christ should persist until their last breath.

As a brief word of caution: this does not mean that every local church should start its own seminary, nor that there cannot be leaders without a formal theological degree.[12] Nor does it mean that formal theological education excludes women. Scripture prizes the biblical and theological instruction of women, such as Mary's learning from Jesus, Lydia's learning from Paul, Priscilla engaging theologically with Apollos alongside her husband, Aquila, and the expectation that women teach other women in Proverbs, Romans 15:14, and Titus 2:3–4. The need for theological education for the thriving of the global church involves multiple levels and all believers.[13]

---

8. Howard G. Hendricks, "Introduction to Christian Teaching: Appointed from God," in *The Christian Educator's Handbook on Teaching*, ed. Kenneth O. Gangel and Howard G. Hendricks (Grand Rapids: Baker, 1998), 8.

9. Sunny Tan and Will Brooks, "Theological Education as Integral Component of World Mission Strategy," in *World Mission: Theology, Strategy, and Current Issues*, ed. Scott N. Callaham and Will Brooks (Bellingham, WA: Lexham, 2019), 177.

10. Oswald Smith (1889–1986), quote cited in *40 Questions about the Great Commission*, ed. Daniel L. Akin, Benjamin L. Merkle, and George G. Robinson, 40 Questions Series (Grand Rapids: Kregel Academic, 2020), 108.

11. Tan and Brooks, "Theological Education," 179.

12. See Lawson, "Biblical Foundations," 62.

13. The Ephesian church, for instance, became the tip of Christianity's spear in the region of Asia Minor after Paul established his school of theology there. See Simon J. Kistemaker, *Exposition of the Acts of the Apostles*, New Testament Commentary 17 (Grand Rapids: Baker, 1990), 684. Some of Paul's students founded the churches in Colossae, Laodicea, and Lycus. See F. F. Bruce, *The Acts of the Apostles: The Greek Text with Introduction and Commentary*, 3rd. rev. and enlarged ed. (Grand Rapids: Eerdmans, 1990), 409.

What It Produces

If theological education is necessary for the church, then its product should benefit the church as well. It needs to result in mature students "who think clearly about God and how His truth relates to their world."[14] Maturity in Christians, according to 1 Timothy 1:5, ensues love, which means that the teacher's real success is not only the growth of his students' knowledge but of their love for Christ too. Another aspect of maturity is practical holiness. The author of Hebrews, speaking of mature believers, says that they have trained their senses "to discern both good and evil" (Heb 5:14). Thus, theological education must help learners to submit their own presuppositions to Scripture and to morally transform their lives. Also, according to Ephesians 4:13–14, a mature student is immune to false doctrine and doctrinal deceit.[15] Therefore, if the goal is maturity, then theological training is more than imparting knowledge, it is also giving skills and building character.[16]

Students, without these three maturity traits—love for Christ, practical holiness, and doctrinal discernment—do not qualify for pastoral ministry.[17] They will fail to feed and protect the flock. Thus, in the end, maturity becomes the triggering agent necessary to produce pastors above reproach (1 Tim 3:2), trained to handle the Word of God accurately (2 Tim 2:15), and to fulfill the work of the ministry (Eph 4:12). Such pastors, however, should also be capable of discerning the times, defending the truth, and contributing to global theological conversations.[18] But above all, they must love Christ and His church.

Maturity is not theoretical but practical. It manifests itself in a student's ability to apply biblical truth to the demands and needs of his context. Because of this, theological education cannot be reduced to a "copy-and-paste" curriculum translated from another language and developed for a different setting. Instead, it must formulate a program specific to the student's setting that provides him with the knowledge and skills required to conceptualize biblical truth in his context.[19] If the Great Commission orders the church to go to all nations and teach them to obey Christ, then the church must be deeply rooted and established in every new context that it reaches. This means that the training of the church's leaders must be tailored to those contexts.

---

14. Tan and Brooks, "Theological Education," 181.

15. Lawson, "Biblical Foundations," 66.

16. William "Rick" Yount, "Learning Theory for Christian Teachers," in *Introducing Christian Education: Foundations for the Twenty-First Century*, ed. Michael J. Anthony (Grand Rapids: Baker, 2001), 101.

17. The New Testament asserts that pastors (see 1 Tim 3:1–7; Titus 1:5–9), must pursue love—the first maturity trait (Phil 1:8; 1 Thess 2:8; 1 Tim 6:11; Titus 1:8); godliness—the second maturity trait (1 Tim 6:11; Titus 1:7; 1 Pet 5:1–4); and be able to exhort in sound doctrine and refute those who contradict—the third maturity trait (Acts 20:28–31; Titus 1:9), among other requirements.

18. See Tan and Brooks, "Theological Education," 192.

19. *Conceptualization* means to turn a truthful proposition from a definition into a presupposition that conditions the learner's will, mind, and heart. It results in the ability to apply a globally valid conceptual truth concretely and practically in a unique setting. Conceptualization's goal, by definition, has in mind the setting of the person going through the learning process. Therefore, it would be unattainable through a cookie-cutter theological training model.

The apostle Paul followed this model. He left Titus in Crete to appoint elders, whom Titus would need to train. The instruction that Paul wrote for Titus to pass on to those elders (Titus 1:10ff.), though it falls under the category of "all that [Christ] commanded" for believers, still was expressed in response to specific challenges that arose in the Cretan culture (e.g., 1:10–12; 3:10–11).

In view of this, there could be a temptation to limit the goal of formal theological education to "training pastors and preachers." Theological education, however, is broader than training pastors, for there are many fields of formal training that support pastoral ministry that are not necessarily oriented toward filling the pastorate. Some examples include training in subspecialties that assist the church in its context to do theology, like the biblical languages or biblical counseling.

In sum, the overall expectation of theological education is to produce spiritually and theologically mature graduates who will support and advance pastoral ministry in their local context either as pastors or as those who equip the pastors and their people by fulfilling critical roles. Even the most technical nonpastoral degree must serve the church—by resourcing pastors and by protecting the truth pastors need to defend their congregations from worldly academic attacks (Titus 1:9–11; Jude 3).

How It Differs

Theological education is not simply secular education with some Bible courses added onto it. Despite any similarities in methodology, the differences set them distinctly apart. If the distinction is blurred, the final product of Christian education becomes a Christianized humanism; it may be "religious studies," but it is not theology.[20] Three key theological distinctives distinguish theological education from any other form of education.[21]

The first is that Scripture is the final authority. If Scripture is the result of God's own activity, then it is based on His character. "It is on this foundation . . . that all the high attributes of Scripture are built."[22] Therefore, if God is true (Rom 3:4) and cannot lie (Heb 6:18, 1 Pet 2:22), then His written revelation must also be true (Ps 119:160; John 17:17). The divine origin of the Scriptures (2 Tim 3:16; 2 Pet 1:21) necessitates its inerrancy.[23] Consequently, the Scriptures' original manuscripts are infallible;

---

20. See Rousas John Rushdoony, *The Philosophy of the Christian Curriculum* (Vallecito, CA: Ross House, 2001), 149.

21. These distinctives are a combination of those suggested by Robert W. Pazmiño and Dennis E. Williams. See Robert W. Pazmiño, *Foundational Issues in Christian Education* (Grand Rapids: Baker, 1988), 49–59; and Dennis E. Williams, Marlene D. LeFever, Lillian Breckenridge, and Julie Gorman, "Christian Education," in *The Portable Seminary*, ed. David Horton, 2nd. ed. (Bloomington, MN: Bethany House, 2018), 623, 651–52.

22. B. B. Warfield, *Revelation and Inspiration* (Grand Rapids: Baker, 2000), 280.

23. Paul Feinberg defines inerrancy as being that "when all facts are known, the Scriptures in their original autographs and properly interpreted will be shown to be wholly true in everything they teach, whether that teaching has to do with doctrine, history, science, geography, geology, or other disciplines or knowledge." Paul D. Feinberg, "The Meaning of Inerrancy," in *Inerrancy*, ed. Norman L. Geisler (Grand Rapids: Zondervan, 1980), 294.

that is, if properly interpreted, they cannot lead to error.[24]

As a result of the Bible's inerrancy, it is sufficient in all matters related to what it teaches.[25] There is no truth external to Scripture—nothing revealed or preserved outside of the Holy Writings—that is necessary for the believer's salvation or sanctification (2 Pet 1:2–4). Hence, it is always the final authority. When any other authoritative truth, such as philosophy, psychology, or the natural sciences, clashes with Scripture, the Bible always wins. This reality sets theological education apart from the secular because the former system requires all its contents and worldview to submit to Scripture's authority, not man's. It points the student not to his own understanding but to God's Word as the source for true knowledge (2 Pet 1:19).[26]

The second distinctive is the necessity of conversion. Since formal theological education seeks to equip church leaders, it is essential that theological training be aimed not only at those called to the ministry but more basically at genuine Christians. This means that there should be some safeguards that confirm the spiritual state of the student and affirm the desire and spiritual integrity to serve in a local church. To theologically educate is more than to inform the mind; it is to renew it as well—conversion leads to transformation. Pastoral training should motivate the student to rise above the world instead of fitting into it, and to move "beyond information and beyond desire into the realm of life-changing transformation."[27] It must aim to increasingly conform him to the image of Christ.[28] Such spiritual development will never take place in a life that has not been converted. Thus, it is imperative to invest in Christlike people—in true believers.

The final distinctive that separates Christian education from the secular is the role of

---

24. Infallibility is closely related to "epistemic meaning," which is the discernible intent conveyed by the words. Thus, the term *infallibility* here means that copies of Scripture "reliably and authoritatively communicate the specially revealed truth and purposes of God to mankind. The copies or transcripts of the original writings retain the epistemic consequences of divine inspiration of the inerrant prophetic-apostolic autographs in such a way that they authoritatively communicate the truth about God and his purposes. They and the translations faithful to them are so continuous with the original autographs that they cannot deceive men or lead them astray." Carl F. H. Henry, *God, Revelation, and Authority*, vol. 4, *God Who Speaks and Shows* (Wheaton, IL.: Crossway, 1999), 246.

25. Wayne Grudem defines the sufficiency of Scripture like this: "The sufficiency of Scripture means that Scripture contained all the words of God he intended his people to have at each stage of redemptive history, and that it now contains everything we need God to tell us for salvation, for trusting him perfectly, and for obeying him perfectly." Wayne Grudem, *Systematic Theology* (Grand Rapids: Zondervan, 1994), 127. This concept flows out of several biblical passages: Deuteronomy 4:2; 12:32; Psalms 19:7–11; 119:1; Proverbs 30:5–6; Isaiah 8:19–20; John 17:17; 2 Timothy 3:15–17; James 1:18; 1 Peter 1:23; Revelation 22:18–19. Sufficiency extends to matters not only of the faith but also of morality, history, geography, and numbers. See William Webster, *Roman Catholic Tradition: Claims and Contradictions* (Battle Ground, WA: Christian Resources, 1994), 8.

26. This conclusion follows from the premise that not all truth is "God's truth"; that is, not all that is claimed or observed to be true is divinely authoritative. Some authors would argue the opposite, and thus suggest looking at truth outside of the sacred text to come to a genuine Christian learning experience (e.g., Warren S. Benson, "Philosophical Foundations of Christian Education," in *Introducing Christian Education: Foundations for the Twenty-First Century*, ed. Michael J. Anthony [Grand Rapids: Baker, 2001], 28). However, the fact that God is the source of truth does not mean that all true observations are of equal authority.

27. Williams et al., "Christian Education," 650.

28. See Howard Hendricks, "What Makes Christian Education Distinct," in Earl Palmer, Roberta Hestenes, and Howard Hendricks, *Mastering Teaching* (Portland, OR: Multnomah, 1991), 19.

the Holy Spirit.[29] He is the agent who "works on the written Word to internalize it in students' lives."[30] This means that to understand and apply Scripture the student needs more than definitions and logical explanations.[31] Although these are necessary, in the end, the Spirit must illuminate them.[32] Therefore, the educator needs to create an environment that facilitates the work of the Spirit. Hence, Christian education is Christian when both the teacher and the student depend on the Spirit to approach the biblical text with the purpose of a transformation that honors Christ and furthers His kingdom.[33]

Theological training ensures the continuity of the church by enabling all Christians to think theologically for the sake of local churches. It prepares them to answer spiritual questions unique to their context and to better know God. Finally, it guarantees the stability and longevity of the gospel's movement because church leaders are equipped to proclaim and defend it.[34]

The Method of Theological Education

The question remains as to how missionaries and church leaders should develop a philosophy of theological education practically. Only an introduction can be offered here, but it includes a definition, a description of educational layers, and a method for evaluation. These are given below to aid readers in developing their own pedagogical method.

Basic Definition

In a broad sense, education is "the deliberate, systematic, and sustained effort to transmit, evoke, or acquire knowledge, attitudes, values, skills, or sensibilities, as well as any learning that results from that effort, direct or indirect, intended or unintended."[35] This means that education is not limited to reciting a lesson to students. Instead, it seeks to inspire them to appropriate newly taught content and to turn it into their own conviction. Theological education goes beyond instructing the mind and seeks to build character, warm the heart toward Christ, and sharpen skills necessary for theological and ministerial work.

An educational program's goal must be clear and quantifiable to ensure its outcome, especially since the ultimate goal of a theological program is to advance the Great Commission through its graduates. Four questions should be asked and answered concerning program learning outcomes for the students: What contents and skills should be learned? How should the

---

29. See Rachel Henderlite, *The Holy Spirit in Christian Education* (Philadelphia: Westminster, 1964), 15; and Roy B. Zuck, *The Holy Spirit in Your Teaching* (Wheaton, IL: Victor, 1984), 35–46.

30. Edward L. Hayes, "Theological Foundations for Adult Education," in *The Christian Educator's Handbook on Adult Education*, ed. Kenneth O. Gangel and James C. Wilhoit (Grand Rapids: Baker, 1993), 44.

31. Allan Hart Jahsmann, *Power beyond Words* (St. Louis: Concordia, 1969), 113.

32. Zuck, *Holy Spirit in Your Teaching*, 35–46.

33. Williams et al., "Christian Education," 623.

34. See Tan and Brooks, "Theological Education," 184–90.

35. Benson, "Philosophical Foundations," 27.

contents and skills be taught? At what point in the curriculum should they be taught? How should the students be evaluated to demonstrate that they have learned the content and can implement the skills? Answering these questions leads to developing educational layers so that the program will lead students to the stated goals and most effectively impact the church.

Educational Layers

An effective formal educational plan has three layers, which should be well detailed in a philosophy document: the academic, program, and curricular. First, the academic layer sets the vision for the school's existence: What does the school aim to accomplish and in whom? The academic layer of the plan focuses on overall objectives and its main target group. The academic purposes for the students must drive the school's planning in such a way that every program and every course becomes a piece of the same puzzle. The general content, skills, and qualities necessary to train preachers must be established at this level of the plan.

Second, the program layer of the philosophy of theological education sets the path to follow for the academic vision to succeed. Here the school decides what degrees to offer (e.g., certificate, undergraduate, graduate). These designations set a framework for the school's instructors to develop courses by allowing them to see how they would contribute to the kinds of learning their students need and by specifying what content, skills, and qualities each program and each instructor must

instill. Program selection includes determining a sub-target group (e.g., pastors and pastors in training with secondary-school education), a sub-purpose (e.g., to produce biblical expositors), and a training modality (residential classes, modular sessions occasionally on campus, online study, a hybrid combination of residential and online students together in a live session, purely independent study, or directed study under an approved off-site mentor). The program layer needs to establish learning outcomes that specify how the group will reach the program's purposes in precise and measurable ways, according to the training modality. At that point, the school leadership is ready to quantify and structure the needed courses according to the outcomes. Departments will be created for the cohesiveness of courses that aim to deliver similar content and impart a range of connected skills, team leads will be selected for department oversight, and course catalogs will be produced.

Finally, the curricular layer of education brings the academic vision for the specific training programs into tangible learning strategy at the course level. Building curriculum includes instructors defining their course-specific learning outcomes that will guide students to learn the content and build sequential skills throughout the course. It also includes delimiting the student workload and providing practical instructions in syllabus documents, and determining their mix of learning tools to help students reach the stated goals (e.g., lectures, assignments, research, rubrics).

Conclusion

This chapter does not pretend to be an exhaustive guide to developing a philosophy of theological education, but it does overview the process and sets a clear path for venturing out. Not every missionary or church leader will be involved in the kind of formal theological education that will result in drafting all the components and considerations in this chapter. However, the doctrine behind theological education must be remembered by every leader: *Christians should always be learning Christ.* Since church leaders must be equipped to teach them, education in the church must take place, and local church leaders are the ones to provide it. Moreover, the Great Commission's charge to multiply disciples and plant churches explicitly requires teaching. The goal of theological education, then, is to produce Christian maturity in every believer, recognizing the role that Christ has given to some in the church as pastors and teachers.

It is important to recognize that not all pastors or preachers have access to solid biblical theological programs for developing their skills. Thus, an opportunity exists for missionaries and church leaders to develop a theological education plan that could benefit them. The opportunity to participate in training men for ministry may seem like a daunting task, but the solution is always to take it one step at a time. It takes time to develop formal educational institutions, especially since informal training in the local church will be done simultaneously. Yet equipping qualified leaders for the building up of the body of Christ is the utmost goal of theological education and a God-given means for helping Christians to fully glorify God. Disciples of Jesus are lifelong learners of His ways.

CHAPTER 45

Foundation Blocks for Faithful Pastoral Training

Marco Bartholomae

The training of nationals for the work of the ministry is a biblical priority, as Paul said in 2 Timothy 2:2: "And the things which you have heard from me in the presence of many witnesses, entrust these to faithful men who will be able to teach others also." Any consideration of having a long-term impact and influence on the mission field must necessarily include a commitment to training tomorrow's indigenous church leaders. With God's help, the next generation of the pastors and teachers of God's people will replicate the biblical character qualities, theological convictions, and ministry competency of the apostles and the leaders who came before them. This chapter provides essential components, or what will be called foundation blocks, that, if in place and in operation, heartily encourage and promote the successful training of nationals. Foundation blocks are a way to describe ministry efforts that have proven to help establish formal training centers in various countries.

Core Values of Indigenous Pastoral Training

Trainers of indigenous pastors are most faithful to the Lord when they operate by and impart at least five core biblical values. First, they must instill the conviction that Scripture is the supreme authority for all areas of life and ministry (2 Tim 3:16). The inerrant and sufficient Word of God demands total submission from the trainer, from their disciples, and from the local people to whom they minister in their local churches.

Second, trainers of pastors must uphold the centrality of the local church in concept and in practice. The church is the pillar and support of the truth (1 Tim 3:15), the institution that Christ promised to build (Matt 16:18), and therefore all training for ministry has as its goal the strengthening of Christ's church.

Third, trainers of indigenous leaders must prioritize the gospel and the instruction of proclamation ministries of the gospel, since it alone is the power of God unto salvation to everyone who believes (Rom 1:16). That means they must promote the expository preaching of God's inerrant, sufficient Word that leads to salvation (2 Tim 3:15–16).

Fourth, trainers of indigenous church leaders must convey the importance of integrity, upholding God's high standard of holiness (1 Tim 3) in all matters, whether doctrinal, financial, or in the training itself. Finally, the trainers must model respect for God's work and God's people by approaching cross-cultural ministry with a commitment to honoring their co-laborers on the field, whether nationals or missionaries.

By living out and transferring these core values to their disciples, missionaries have every reason to expect God to raise up local churches with indigenous leadership to perpetuate the work of training others in new contexts for future generations. Therefore, the biblical ideal is to establish a pastoral training center that is directly connected to the local churches themselves, to accomplish the kind of training that will benefit the local churches of a given country rather than moving the training outside of and away from the indigenous body of believers. With these values and principles in mind, it is now opportune to delineate the foundation blocks that will lead to the faithful training of indigenous pastors to meet the needs of the local church in its context.

The Foundation Blocks of Indigenous Pastoral Training

The ministry efforts of the training center may be managed by the training center team or by any other partner in that country that wants to join in the effort to spread sound teaching. When conversations begin with local churches in a particular country and a main, healthy church and training center elsewhere that local churches are looking to for help and support, there may already be one or more foundation blocks in place, but all are key components for a formal training center to exist.

Importantly, the foundation blocks must have solid ground to stand on if they are to uphold an entire training center. This solid ground includes the first four foundation blocks like cornerstones: the invitation of nationals, the existence of a model church, the presence of a church network, and a training center team. Without each of these four components, it will be challenging for a training center to exist. However, with these four foundation blocks in place, the remaining six (radio/TV, publications, conferences/seminars, basic-level training, Web presence, and ministry network) can continue and further the ministry of a training center.

Invitation from Nationals

The first foundation block is an invitation and affirmation from nationals. It is the foundation for all other blocks, since it expresses the desire of nationals to train their people in sound theology. The invitation and affirmation from nationals are critical, although they may be prompted by church leaders from another context who help nationals understand their need to request assistance for training. From this perspective, one can provide assistance in response to an invitation from foreign nationals who live and serve in their country. When an invitation is made, one should not have the desire to replace the work of nationals but rather to assist and undergird them in their desire to bring biblical teaching to their people.

An invitation to train normally comes from one (or more) of the following examples. A foreign church leader who has no previous contact with a training ministry yet learns of the existing ministry through its publications or preaching ministry may initiate an invitation for training. An international seminary student who returns back home to his origin country and shares the need for training could extend an invitation. A missionary or team of missionaries who serve alongside foreign nationals might share the idea of nationals inviting other church leaders to assist with training. Or a partnering Christian organization that ministers in the country and is in close connection with a network of churches might express an interest in advancing toward formal theological training.

Model Churches

If there is a conviction and commitment to train current and future church leaders, it is essential that the training center be connected to and located at the local, model churches that are practicing the principles taught in the training center. This is another critical foundation block since a training center does not exist for itself but rather to strengthen and support the local church as "the pillar and support of the truth" (1 Tim 3:15). This must be the goal and desire of any sound training ministry, to promote and elevate the local church.

Therefore, a training center will be most

effective when it is anchored in model churches since these congregations can support the training efforts, send their members through the programs, and provide openings for students to serve in the church during their education. Additionally, the leaders of these maturing churches could become part of the training center's leadership, advisory council, or adjunct faculty. This does not need to be the case, but these church leaders will nonetheless need to be committed to the training center as a crucial ministry to support the maturing process of local churches.

"Model church" does not mean a "perfect church." Rather, it indicates that the leadership of a local church has determined to establish its ministry according to the guidelines and principles of God's Word, which includes maintaining commitments to biblical authority and sufficiency, expository preaching, and biblical qualifications for spiritual church leaders.

Connecting with the previous foundation block, the invitation to establish a training center could come first from one model church or from a multitude of like-minded churches seeking to become model churches in collaboration with the training center. While both are legitimate, it is recommended and encouraged that the training center and its leadership come out of a joint effort of like-minded churches (and preferably not just from one church, even if that is the case in the beginning phase of the invitation).

Network of Churches

While the model church or model churches serve as the hosting churches of the training center, it is crucial for a training center to establish a network of churches that are committed to training people in sound theology. These churches can collaborate and strategize with one another about the best way to engage churches across their country in theological training. In addition, this network of churches can provide crucial support to the training efforts through prayer, financial support, and recommendations to potential students. Even if there might exist some differences in (minor) theological and philosophical areas (often arising because of the lack of available serious theological training), such as the minute details of their eschatology, the specific model of their plural eldership, or whether they have women deacons (or deaconesses), a common commitment to biblical training should unite these churches in their effort to establish formal theological training in their country.

An invitation and affirmation from foreign nationals for training commonly comes from a church leadership that already has a network of church relationships in the country. If a network of churches has not yet been established, it will be challenging for a training center to expand beyond its church borders because the establishment and expansion of a network of churches drives the effort of becoming a nationwide training center and not just a training ministry of one church.

Training Center Team

Every training center needs a team of like-minded men and women who maintain and advance the administrative tasks of the school.

Even if a training center team consists of only one or (preferably) two people at the beginning, the main operations of a training center must be established over time by adding more personnel.

One of the essential components of a training center leadership team is its director(s). This initial leadership consists of one or two like-minded men who helped launch the training center, who consider it their primary ministry, and who demonstrate commitment to overseeing the school's operations (the initial directors are trained men at a sound theological institution who fully agree on the same doctrinal statement). These initial director(s) will establish the school's vision, cultivate sound leadership over all the different operations of a maturing training center, manage its training programs, and move the training center forward according to its mission.

Team members are the ones who maintain and advance the operations of a training center, which can encompass academics, student relations, admissions, registrar, general operations, accounting and finances, human resources, information technology, development, and communication and marketing. Each of these areas will ideally become its own department, led by distinct leadership personnel. For this kind of growth to occur, it must be understood that the tasks and roles of the initial team members (such as the director) may change over time to accommodate these developments. Team members operate under and serve the leadership of the training center director(s) as supported by the advisory board.

Another critical team that supports the training center director(s) and other administrative team members is an advisory board, depending on each context and situation. The advisory board members are to be selected from the in-country network of churches and other connected partner ministries that support the establishment of the training center. Upon selection, the board is expected to assist the training center leadership team by providing counsel regarding the efforts of the training center.

A deeper dive into the characteristics of team members, a training center director, and an advisory board will assist in understanding their roles and responsibilities. Training center directors should share similar academic credentials and a philosophy of education. Preferably, they should not be related to one another, and at least one national should be on the leadership team. Directors should be part of the model churches and connected with the training center's network of churches. Directors need to be confirmed in their roles by leadership from the network of churches, and as recommended by the church leaders originally invited to assist the foreign national church leaders. Once the training center is established and growing, the initial director(s) may transition into other leadership or administrative roles. Directors must understand they are to work in unity with the advisory board in establishing the training center.

The advisory board, depending on each ministry context and situation, should either be present at the launch of a training center or established over time. The advisory board ought to be formed from individuals in the network of churches and key partners, and is crucial for the growth and longevity of a training center. Like the director(s), the advisory board should be a group of like-minded men regarding doctrine and practice. They should share similar academic degrees and should preferably be comprised of marketplace specialists. The board may grow over time or change into an executive board depending on the needs of the training center, but like the director team, its membership should be balanced between nationals and foreigners.

Moving from the four cornerstone foundation blocks, six others have been identified that contribute to the establishment and strengthening of a training center.

Radio/TV

Biblical truth has spread globally through radio and television, which are effective means for establishing training centers that emphasize and promote expository preaching. Through radio and television, church leaders in a foreign context can be introduced to sound preaching, laypeople can have their appetites stimulated to hear sound preaching, and the church can be served an ongoing stream of sound theology. Additionally, when preachers hear expository preaching, desire for their own training is stimulated.

Biblically sound and model expository sermons can be broadcast regularly over radio or on television channels (including satellite), even internationally, depending on the capabilities of each country and the strategy for reaching each context.

Especially at the beginning phase of a training center, this foundation block can help not only to promote sound preaching but also to connect it with the training center, as an institution where believers can receive such preaching and where leaders learn to preach in such a way.

Publications

Everything starts with the written Word, the Bible, so this foundation block is crucial and must be an essential ministry of every training center. Much like translated sermons, translated books strengthen local churches, spread sound theology, stimulate an appetite for sound teaching, and provide opportunities for the training center to strengthen its presence in the country.

Translation and publication work is also a critical foundation block because it supports the full spectrum of training efforts, especially in providing course materials. A long-term goal of this publishing ministry is to enable training center graduates to write sound books in their own language to better shepherd their people in their own context.

Initially, it is recommended that books be published on topics such as preaching, theology, and Christian living.[1] Once a broad base of books exists, publishing efforts can expand into more technical textbooks or different genres. Regardless, each book should help readers better understand the purpose of the training center and the value it brings to their local church context. Books can be distributed through various channels, including partnering local churches, the network of churches, conferences, and training centers.

Conferences/Seminars

Conferences and seminars serve many purposes simultaneously and are to be viewed as a key foundation block in establishing a formal training center. They promote and exemplify expository preaching and sound teaching, create an environment for fellowship and ministry networking, provide an outlet for the distribution of sound books, create a platform for theologically sound worship music, facilitate the recruitment of future students, and provide a preview of what can be gained from the training center.

Conferences and seminars give laypeople an appetite for expository preaching and develop in them a greater appreciation for the authority and sufficiency of God's Word. The difference between conferences and seminars is that seminars consist of a smaller group of people, sometimes over a longer period than a conference, with more interaction while working together through a topic. The lecturer may teach on more than one topic.

When coordinating a conference, one should remember that the target audience includes pastors, teachers, lay leaders, and local church members. Conferences can cover topics relating to theological, practical, technical, and

---

1. The initial publication efforts should focus on a sound Bible translation, if one is not available. Additionally, a systematic theology, sound commentaries, and books on Christian living are crucial for the establishment of a training center and to strengthen the local church.

ministerial subjects, depending on intention and audience. No matter the topic, conferences should always model expository preaching. Yet more should take place during a conference— there ought always to be an emphasis on fellowship by means of breakout sessions, Q&A sessions, and meals. Conferences should feature all recommended reading and resources available in that language—and, if possible, a resource should be given to all who attend. An ideal conference lasts two to three days and is intended for those living throughout the whole country.

When coordinating a seminar, the following factors should be kept in mind. Seminars can be hosted in local churches around the country and present an opportunity to invite like-minded pastors as well as new churches and their leaders to partner in ministry. A possible length for a seminar is one to three days, ideally held on a weekend. Seminar topics can vary, but organizers should consider what will be most helpful for the local church and its leaders. Yet, if a significant number of potential students already exist, the first seminars offered could focus on biblical studies classes. Future seminars could address topics from other potential training center classes, to give students a stronger preview of what training would look like in the training center. Seminars also provide opportunities to contact other churches who may be able to help establish and support the training center.

Basic-Level Training

The main focus of a training center next to all ministry efforts is sound theological training.

Here it is called basic-level training (BLT), since the focus is on a global context in which men need to be trained at a foundational level.

Basic-level training is a formal way of equipping believers in the essential aspects of the Bible and theology, such as lay training on a certificate level, and is thus an appropriate foundation block for any training center. Next to conferences and seminars, BLT is a systematic and intentional approach to training a congregation and others in the areas of basic Bible knowledge and practical theology. BLT is a proven foundation block for it often serves as the early stage of formal training before a training center is established out of the church network.

Basic-level training can be established through a model church, a particular church in the network of churches aligned with the model church, or a joint effort of several churches in the network. This foundation block is focused on offering courses or programs at a fundamental level to help the church body learn and apply the Bible. BLT is primarily intended for laypeople who are interested in a more formal theological education that serves them in their day-to-day lives. BLT can be made available for a cohort of believers or set up as an individual study. There is an opportunity for flexibility at this stage and level; the key is simply the teaching of essential biblical and theological topics as a foundation.

Web Presence

An internet presence provides any training center with another way to disseminate sound teaching, rally like-minded believers, promote formal training, and serve local churches both in-country and around the world. A website and/or social media profile also provides better exposure for the training center in the region, which strengthens its reputation as a trustworthy parachurch organization. This foundation block provides clear identity of the training center as a place where one can find all the different information and ministries of a training center itself. Hence, it is strategic and ought to be pursued.

Websites provide a place to post articles (translated or national), sermons (translated or national), conference announcements, links to sound blogs and books, recordings of prior seminars and/or conferences, interviews, and other useful tools. A website target audience can range from laypeople to pastors, offering an assortment of resources for the audience spectrum. Websites generally require basic elements such as a logo, ministry name, and contact information. Other school-related platforms or training center offerings can be promoted through this outlet, all in order to strengthen the understanding that the training center is geared toward formal theological training.

Ministry Network

The final foundation block is the ministry network, something latent throughout this chapter yet now made patent. In most countries, there are a variety of like-minded Christian ministries serving to reach the lost and support the church. Because of their existing relationships and reputations in the country, these Christian ministries can be vital partners in establishing a training center. For example, these ministries have access to church networks whose pastors may want to be trained by a like-minded ministry. So it is important to reach out to these like-minded ministries in the effort to establish a training center with their support. If such national support can be secured, the effort to establish a training center will be greatly helped.

Identifying partners in the ministry network involves reaching out to like-minded missions organizations, mercy ministries, radio ministries, seminaries, theological training organizations, and any other Christian ministry in the country that serves the church. Like-minded means that these ministries clearly demonstrate that they have a shared commitment to the same doctrinal beliefs and the working out of those beliefs in their philosophy of ministry—a shared theology and practice.

A Strong Foundation

This chapter has described ten foundation blocks—four that serve as the cornerstones and six that complete the foundation—that are indispensable for the establishment of training centers. The goal toward which each foundation block contributes is a healthy and active training center, wherein national church leaders can train their people to rightly interpret, practice, and proclaim God's Word (2 Tim 2:15). As this training occurs, biblical character, conviction, and competency are embedded within those trained and solidified in those doing the training. The church is strengthened, and another generation of Christian leaders is prepared.

How to Be a Paul to Your National Timothy

Todd Dick

Theological education on the foreign field must include ongoing discipleship to prepare nationals thoroughly and biblically to effectively plant, pastor, and revive national churches. This education includes both the formal aspect of training in a Bible institute and the regular life-on-life discipleship that nurtures godliness in all relationships.

Jesus commands all believers in the Great Commission to disciple others so that they are grounded in His teachings to live fruitful lives of obedience for the glory of God. The apostles modeled this command. Paul had Timothy, Titus, Luke, and others who traveled with him, watched him, and had many conversations of how Scripture can transform lives. In Philippians 4:9, Paul told the believers, "The things you have learned and received and heard and seen in me, practice these things, and the God of peace will be with you." In 1 Corinthians 11:1, Paul proclaims, "Be imitators of me, just as I also am of Christ." Paul gave his life to the preaching and teaching of all that Christ taught him. However, Paul also

understood the importance of life-on-life modeling of these biblical truths. Godly relationships of iron sharpening iron (Prov 27:17) solidify classroom teaching in every practical situation of life.

Paul saw younger believers as his children, and as a loving parent, Paul raised them in godliness through regular discipleship. For example, he ministered to the Thessalonian believers as a parent should. These first-generation believers did not have godly parents that would lead them in godly application of biblical truth, so Paul was to them like a spiritual "mother," tenderly caring for their spiritual needs with fond affection (1 Thess 2:7–8). He was also to them a spiritual "father," exhorting, encouraging, and testifying of the Lord devoutly, righteously, and blamelessly (1 Thess 2:10–12). Believers who desire to fulfill the disciple-making mandate of the Lord Jesus Christ would do well to follow the biblical standard of spiritual parenting modeled by Paul.

Many missionaries become acutely aware

of the believers' need for personal mentorship on the foreign field when they begin to train students theologically. Young men require regular meetings that foster open conversations concerning daily battles with sin in pursuit of godliness. There are at least three realities in missions contexts that emphasize the importance of ongoing personal discipleship when training students, particularly men called to pastoral leadership.

The first reality is the personal background of the candidate. Many of our students in the former Yugoslavia are young believers who have lived many more years in the world than in Christ. They are just beginning the process of renewing their minds and becoming transformed into the image of Christ (Rom 12:1–2). Their spiritual battles against sin are just beginning. Their sinful habits are at their height, and mortifying sin is a new concept. Men like these need spiritual fathers who can wisely guide them in lives of godliness and repentance.

The second reality of the average pastoral candidate that must be confronted through loving mentorship is their religious background. Many of our students are first-generation converts from Roman Catholicism, a false religion that has infiltrated the lives of the adherents in their worldviews, rituals, daily practices, and cherished memories. Our students' understandings of God, Christ, the Spirit, salvation, sin, works, grace, faith, and life in general are all grounded in the teachings and sacraments of Catholicism. Virtually every good memory of their lives is associated with their old religious system, from the celebration of holidays to their schooling, family life, and community involvement. For them, life is inseparable from the Catholic religion prior to salvation. Therefore, the spiritual growth that accompanies their salvation is not only slow, but it is a lifelong battle to think outside of the external and hypocritical pragmatism of religion. Marriage, parenting, work relationships, friendships, and church life are all seen through the lens of their former religious life. Because of the underlying reality of an ever-present false religious system, every area of the students' lives requires regular and active discipleship so that they progress in true, biblical sanctification.

The third pressing reality of the theological student that requires close discipleship is the cultural background of their lives. In our country of service, whose population is around 90 percent Roman Catholic, there are few resources to stimulate godliness according to the Word of God. Sound preaching, good books, and Christlike examples are not easily found. Family and friends do not provide godly examples. The culture is godless and does not provide avenues for spiritual growth. All cultures are marked by more ungodly influences than godly ones, so those who train pastors quickly face the reality that they themselves might be among the trusted few who model Christ to their students.

When one considers the personal, religious, and cultural background of the average pastoral candidate, it is easy to understand why theological education must include consistent and continual mentorship. Men who train for the ministry need spiritual nurturing from older and wiser leaders who can help them navigate every aspect of life, grow spiritually, and more fully glorify God in their lives and ministries.

Meeting the need for fruitful and ongoing discipleship begins with developing intentional relationships. From the classroom, students gain the academic disciplines related to theology, Bible knowledge, church history, and the science and art of preaching. But such learning can never be divorced from personal relationships and personal application of the truths that are taught. The effective teacher must utilize classroom time to challenge the students to live out the theology they are learning. He must also help them to see practically how this will look in the church, family, and the workplace. The professor must be a spiritual father, brother, mentor, example, and friend inside and outside the classroom. All time spent, whether before, during, or after a class session, over meals, on walks, or in any shared activity—should be purposeful to develop a deep relationship of discipleship and friendship that will endure for the years that will follow a student's time of training.

In reality, after graduation, true education begins. As much as possible, professors and trainers should visit students for intentional times of spiritual discussion about their ministry, family, and personal walk with Christ since the last time they met. This may mean spending a weekend at the student's home, interacting with him and his family. The earlier shared experiences of talking over meals or on walks, or doing activities later become the instructor's "classroom" with his graduates. The teacher who desires to become the lifelong spiritual father of the student and his family will seek intentional, excellent ways to reach this biblical goal year after year. If the training efforts in foreign contexts are to fulfill the will of the Lord and make committed disciples of Christ, then the instructors must commit to lifelong relationships with their students. May Christ be glorified as professor and student walk together in progressive sanctification.

Theological Education, Worldview, and the Church's Mission: A Case Study from Kitwe, Zambia

Philip S. Hunt, Billy C. Sichone, and Benjamin Straub

Theological education, as a parachurch ministry,[2] exists to supply trained laborers to local churches in order to strengthen their hands and fill their ranks.[3] However, theological education done wrong has just as much potential to weaken local churches as it has to strengthen them.[4] In the context of global missions, both formal and informal[5] theological education models have become essential tools to equip local believers to become church leaders and church planters.[6] The prevailing question is how missions organizations and missions-sending churches can partner effectively with majority world[7] churches to establish training programs that will produce healthy, well-equipped leaders for the longevity of the mission.

---

2. Dieumene Noelliste, "Handmaiden to God's Economy: Biblical Foundations for Theological Education," in *Leadership in Theological Education: Foundations for Academic Leadership*, vol. 1, ed. Fritz Deininger and Orbelina Eguizabal (Carlisle, UK: Langham Global Library, 2017), 7–32.

3. Third Lausanne Congress, "The Cape Town Commitment," §IIF.4, The Lausanne Movement 2011, accessed June 18, 2024, https://lausanne.org/content/ctc/ctcommitment#p2-6.

4. Perry Shaw, *Transforming Theological Education: A Practical Handbook for Integrative Learning* (Carlisle, UK: Langham Global Library, 2014).

5. Throughout this volume, the use of *informal education* includes the category of *nonformal learning* without specifying a distinction between them.

6. Re-Forma, "Outcomes," accessed June 18, 2024, https://www.re-forma.global/outcomes; David Burke, Richard Brown, and Qaiser Julius, eds., *TEE for the 21st Century: Tools to Equip and Empower God's People for His Mission* (Carlisle, UK: Langham Global Library, 2021).

7. Used missiologically, "majority world" is a broad term used synonymously with *third world, two-thirds world, Global South*, and *developing world*. It reflects the historic demographic shift in the global church population predominantly from Europe and North America to the regions of Latin America, Africa, the Middle East, and Asia. See C. Douglas McConnell, "Third World," in *Evangelical Dictionary of World Missions*, ed. A. Scott Moreau, Harold Netland, and Charles Van Engen (Grand Rapids: Baker, 2000), 955–56.

How Could Theological Education Weaken Churches?

Consider three typical program partnership missteps that occasionally occur and unintentionally weaken the churches of the majority world. First, sometimes churches or missionaries who have identified promising local leaders have sent them to Western countries for higher education. When graduates remain in the West, they contribute to their home community's "brain drain," or they become so extracted from their home cultures that when they return home they struggle to connect locally.[8]

Second, some missions organizations or individuals have launched small-scale theological education programs on the field and make do with limited resources. Yet sometimes they oversell these informal programs with misleading academic terminology, making false promises by misrepresenting the level of education they offer, though they may be substandard compared to how they promote their programs.[9]

Third, mission organizations that have poured resources into local contexts to establish the highest levels of theological education have sometimes imported Western theological curricula wholesale into non-Western contexts. They churn out graduates who can argue the finer points of historic Western theological and philosophical debates but cannot effectively address the challenges of their communities biblically and pastorally.[10]

The Key to Strengthening Local Churches: Balance

One theological training institution, Central Africa Baptist University (CABU) in Kitwe, Zambia, serves as an example of seeking to maintain several critical balances in theological education, with the goal of strengthening local churches rather than weakening them. The first critical balance that CABU seeks in its education goals is walking a careful line between academic rigor and mission formation. A school that offers formal theological credentials might be required to maintain local government accreditation requirements, yet the leadership must remain constantly aware of the risk of mission drift.[11] Numbers

8. Christopher Wright, "The Challenge of the Brain Drain within Global Theological Education," *Journal of Global Christianity* 1, no. 2 (2015): 11–18, https://trainingleadersinternational.org/jgc/26/the-challenge-of-the-brain-drain-within-global-theological-education.

9. H. Jurgens Hendriks, "Theological Education in Africa: Messages from the Fringes," *Nederuitse Gereformeerde Teologiese Tydskrif* 55, no. 1 (2014): 61–80.

10. Pieter H. J. Labuschagne, "Towards a Missional Hermeneutic Informing Missional Ecclesiology and Transformative Theological Education in Africa," *Missionalia* 47, no. 2 (2019): 212–27, https://missionalia.journals.ac.za/pub/article/view/326.

11. Harriet A. C. Kintu, "Effects of the Transition of Theological Seminaries in Kenya to Universities on Their Evangelical Christian Identity," in *Governance and Christian Higher Education in the African Context*, ed. David Ngaruiya

of graduates or greater prestige in academia can never become the end goal; the focus must always remain on producing servants for the local church.

The second crucial balance is the area of educational means. Schools like CABU that offer high quality education aim to employ best practices in teaching and learning methodologies. Yet pedagogical excellence must be carefully balanced with efforts to preserve the school's discipleship ethos. Similarly, educational excellence and cultural relevance must always be balanced with a curricular commitment to the centrality of Scripture and the primacy of local churches.[12]

Finally, balance must be maintained in the development of the educational team. Schools like CABU that are committed to modeling the balance between instruction and spiritual mentorship carefully select and develop their faculty members so that they are brought into the institutional vision.[13] Furthermore, the faculty should be drawn from the membership of healthy local churches in the cultural context or, if not, should demonstrate a readiness to learn the local context; no "all Western" institution will deliver a contextually relevant curriculum.[14]

A Curriculum for Stronger Churches: Worldview Formation

For theological education to strengthen local churches, its curriculum must target prevailing cultural worldviews and provide students with tools for engagement.[15] In CABU's context, the traditional African worldview assumes that spiritual forces shape one's destiny.[16] When Christianized, this thinking partly explains why the prosperity gospel thrives in Africa;

and Rodney Reed (Carlisle, UK: Langham Global Library, 2019), 159–86; and Semeon Mulatu, *Transitioning from a Theological College to a Christian University: A Multi-Case Study in the East African Context*, ICETE (Carlisle, UK: Langham Global Library, 2017).

12. Richard E. Seed, *The Mission of God and the Teaching Church: A Biblical Model for Theological Training in Africa* (Nairobi: TEDS Africa, 2018); and Conrad Mbewe, *God's Design for the Church: A Guide for African Pastors and Ministry Leaders* (Wheaton, IL: Crossway, 2020).

13. Rupen Das, *Connecting Curriculum with Context: A Handbook for Context Relevant Curriculum Development in Theological Education*, ICETE (Carlisle, UK: Langham Global Library, 2015).

14. Perry Shaw, César Lopes, Joanna Feliciano-Soberano, and Bob Heaton, eds. *Teaching across Cultures: A Global Christian Perspective* (Carlisle, UK: Langham Global Library, 2021); and Craig Ott, *Teaching and Learning across Cultures: A Guide to Theory and Practice* (Grand Rapids: Baker Academic, 2021).

15. Jack Chalk, *Making Disciples in Africa: Engaging Syncretism in the African Church through Philosophical Analysis of Worldviews* (Carlisle, UK: Langham Global Library, 2013); and Christopher Wright, "Effectiveness and Impact in Theological Education from a Biblical Perspective," in *Is It Working? Researching Context to Improve Curriculum*, ed. Stuart Brooking (Carlisle, UK: Langham Global Library, 2018), 7–28.

16. Yusufu Turaki, *Engaging Religions and Worldviews in Africa: A Christian Theological Method* (Carlisle, UK: Langham Global Library, 2020).

people believe that the community's spiritual mediators hold one's destiny in their hands.[17] Theological educators must therefore prepare their graduates to engage at the worldview level.

African culture's collective hierarchy requires unquestioning respect for chiefs or traditional leaders who hold absolute authority.[18] Often this hierarchy is applied in local churches. This creates a "man of God" style of pastor who presumes to own all church property, commands respect and obedience, and promises his followers spiritual power and access to God.[19] So, if theological education in Africa fails to challenge the pervasive, unbiblical worldview dynamics with a gospel-informed worldview, it will weaken rather than strengthen the churches. Theological education in service to churches should ensure that unbiblical worldviews are rooted out while entrenching students in a biblical worldview.

To engage in theological education that strengthens churches, CABU is endeavoring to develop a curriculum that shapes worldview and measures student worldview growth.[20] Students are taught a biblical view of life and ministry through a contextually sensitive yet scripturally focused curriculum and through a campus environment of intentional discipleship. But worldview formation requires more than mere education reduced to philosophical worldview commitments. Therefore, CABU also emphasizes comprehensive discipleship training, which seeks to educate the mind, motivate the heart, and equip the hands for faithful service to Christ and his church.[21] The curriculum is shaped by core biblical values of honesty, obedience, wisdom, and service. These values challenge students to live authentically, love selflessly, think biblically, and serve humbly wherever they go.

Shaping worldview at CABU extends beyond classroom lectures and assignments to encompass an environment of one-on-one

---

17. Ezron Musonda, "Spirit-Power People," in *The Abandoned Gospel: Confronting Neo-Pentecostalism and the Prosperity Gospel in Sub-Saharan Africa*, ed. Philip W. Barnes et al. (Lusaka: AB316, 2021), 131–40.

18. Choolwe Mbetwa, *Why Africa Is Poor* (Secunderabad, India: G.S.Media, 2018).

19. Conrad Mbewe, "Are We Preachers or Witchdoctors?" A Letter from Kabwata, May 30, 2012, http://www .conradmbewe.com/2012/05/are-we-preachers-or-witchdoctors.html. This material was further developed and presented by Dr. Mbewe as "Are We Preachers or Witch Doctors," plenary session sermon, Strange Fire Conference, Grace Community Church, Sun Valley, CA, October 18, 2013, https://www.gty.org/library/sermons-library/TM13-13/are-we-preachers-or -witch-doctors-conrad-mbewe.

20. CABU, like many majority world schools, began with largely Western curricula, but over the years has labored to refine its curricula to better respond to African worldviews. It remains committed to that journey. Cf. Ray Motsi and Bob Heaton, "A Zimbabwean Experience: Journey to Maturity," in *Is It Working? Researching Context to Improve Curriculum*, ed. Stuart Brooking (Carlisle, UK: Langham Global Library, 2018), 75–85.

21. Bernhard Ott, "Integrating Theory and Practice in Theological Education," in Ott, *Understanding and Developing Theological Education*, ICETE (Carlisle, UK: Langham Global Library, 2016), 199–268.

mentoring relationships between university staff, students, and peers.[22] Faculty and staff mentors are trained in biblical worldview engagement and equipped to assess student worldview change.[23] Most importantly, students become local church members, where they use their growing skills to serve others. Local church leaders serve on CABU's leadership team and governing boards. They speak into the curriculum to ensure that students are trained in ways that connect the gospel to their communities and address the needs of their congregations. Theological education must actively position itself as a servant of the local churches in their context if it is to successfully strengthen churches rather than weaken them.

22. John Jusu, "Developing Transformational Leaders–Curricular Implications from the Africa Leadership Study," in *African Christian Leadership: Realities, Opportunities, and Impact*, ed. Robert J. Priest and Kirimi Barine (Carlisle, UK: Langham Global Library, 2019), 199–214.

23. On CABU's Coram Deo Initiative, see Timothy Murdoch, "A Curriculum for Developing a Biblical Worldview in Students Attending Central Africa Baptist University" (DMin thesis, Liberty University, 2020).

Sub-Section 3: Music in Missions

CHAPTER 46

Embracing Theologically Sound Music in a Theologically Unsound World

Scott Callaham

The mission field is a battlefield. Missionaries do not take the field alone, for Jesus sends missionaries to the ends of the earth in the empowerment of the Holy Spirit (Acts 1:8), and God's victory is sure before the battle begins (Prov 21:31). Yet from a human perspective, any victories that may come are hard fought, and missionaries constantly receive incoming fire from the enemy. "Friendly fire," attack from within one's own camp, is perhaps even more wounding and may arise from insufficient attention to the worship of the gathered church on the mission field. As for the church's worship through music, missionaries must exercise vigilant discernment to ensure its biblical faithfulness.

To promote such discernment, this chapter first lays out a foundational biblical-theological ethos regarding musical worship. Second, it provides recommendations for evaluating worship songs and songwriters. Finally, it touches on important ethical issues in worship music of which every Christian should be aware.

Biblical-Theological Principles for Worship through Music

Rethinking worship practices inherited from the Roman Catholic Church, the Reformers of the sixteenth century sought to establish a theology and practice of worship that would cohere with the doctrine of *sola Scriptura* ("Scripture alone"). In the wake of the Reformation, two broad approaches to worship arose: the normative and regulative principles.[1] These opposing principles grew out of different points of emphasis in biblical interpretation: what Scripture explicitly prohibits versus what it explicitly ordains. The normative principle entailed taking care to stay within the bounds of biblical prohibitions regarding worship. In other words, whatever Scripture did not prohibit was generally acceptable. In contrast, worship according to the regulative principle permitted only that which Scripture positively ordained.

The normative principle implies that human innovation and creativity are fundamental characteristics of Christian worship, thus biblical teaching on worship may be authoritative but not sufficient. In contrast, advocacy of the regulative principle derives from a stance of trust in biblical authority that extends to its sufficiency.[2] Trust in biblical authority and sufficiency entails that other factors in the process of forming theology or the practices of the faith—especially tradition, reason, and experience—hold no authority.[3] Thus,

for worship through music and all other realms of life, Scripture is the sole and sufficient standard. Accordingly, the following sections take cues from Scripture to shape a biblical theology of worship.

Scripture as Music

Many song texts appear in the Old Testament, such as the "Song of the Sea" in Exodus 15:1–18 and the "Song of Moses" in Deuteronomy 32:1–47.[4] In the New Testament, Philippians 2:5–11 and Colossians 1:15–20 may be christological hymns of the early church.[5] Yet the most well-known musical texts in the Bible are its collections of Hebrew poetry, especially the book of Psalms. As poetry, the Psalms have a musical quality to them even without being sung. Furthermore, some psalms explicitly urge listeners to break out into singing. For example, Psalm 149:1 reads, "Praise Yah! Sing to Yahweh a new song, His praise in the assembly of the holy ones." It is little wonder that the Psalms have stimulated all manner of music-making throughout history.[6] Such an

---

1. Rhyne Putman, "Does an Affirmation of *Sola Scriptura* Entail the Regulative Principle of Worship?" *Journal for Baptist Theology and Ministry* 19, no. 2 (2022): 229–43.

2. For reflection on the regulative principle of worship and *The Westminster Confession of Faith* (1646), see John Allen Delivuk, "Biblical Authority and the Proof of the Regulative Principle of Worship in *The Westminster Confession*," *WTJ* 58 (1996): 237–56. For the applicable section of the Second London Baptist Confession (1689), see William L. Lumpkin, *Baptist Confessions of Faith*, rev. ed. (Valley Forge, PA: Judson, 1969), 280.

3. Contrast the "Wesleyan Quadrilateral" (which places tradition, reason, and experience alongside Scripture as authorities for theological reflection) in Donald Thorsen, "*Sola Scriptura* and the Wesleyan Quadrilateral," *Wesleyan Theological Journal* 42, no. 2 (2006): 7–27. See treatment of the sufficiency of Scripture in John MacArthur and Richard Mayhue, eds., *Biblical Doctrine: A Systematic Summary of Bible Truth* (Wheaton, IL: Crossway, 2017), 104–6.

4. Daniel Block designates the "Song of Moses" as the "national anthem" of Israel. Daniel I. Block, *For the Glory of God: Recovering a Biblical Theology of Worship* (Grand Rapids: Baker Academic, 2014), 225–26.

5. Matthew E. Gordley, *New Testament Christological Hymns: Exploring Texts, Contexts, and Significance* (Downers Grove, IL: IVP Academic, 2018), 79–143.

6. For singing of the Psalms in Judaism before the establishment of synagogues, see Alfred Sendrey, *Music in Ancient Israel* (New York: Philosophical Library, 1969), 172–79. For perspective on the postbiblical reception of the Psalms in music, see Max Stern,

organic connection between the Word of God and music should naturally inspire the Lord's people to worship Him through song.

Scripture's Urgings toward Musical Worship

The command of Psalm 149 to "sing to Yahweh a new song," is participational and invitational, itself a command issued through song and in the act of worship. While Psalm 149 addresses God's covenant people, the concern of Psalm 67 expands to all nations, exhorting that they sing to the Savior with the melody of Scripture. Echoes of the Aaronic blessing of Numbers 6:24–26 are palpable in the first verse of the psalm: "God be gracious to us and bless us, and cause his face to shine upon us." Next, verse 2 chants the reason why the nations should desire encounter with God: "That your way may be known on the earth, Your salvation among all nations." Finally, the rest of the psalm's verses urge the nations in "all the ends of the earth" (v. 7) to worship.

Similarly, the New Testament also frames singing as a congregational, Godward, and even reciprocal act, carried out by believers toward one another. For example, Colossians 3:16 expresses, "Let the word of Christ dwell in you richly, with all wisdom teaching and admonishing one another with psalms and hymns and spiritual songs, singing with gratefulness in your hearts to God." Likewise, Ephesians 5:18–19 says, "Be filled with the Spirit, speaking to one another in psalms and hymns and spiritual songs, singing and making melody with your heart to the Lord." The words for "singing" and "making melody" appear in a list of several participles that communicate the result of being filled with the Spirit.[7] Thus, Paul frames musical worship as something that naturally takes place when the Spirit most fully guides a Christian.

Furthermore, James 5:13 records, "Is anyone among you suffering? Then he must pray. Is anyone cheerful? He is to sing praises." The phrase "sing praises" is a third-person singular imperative, meaning that James is not merely commending the singing of praise as an action that befits cheerfulness. Rather, he is commanding it of each person. Just as the suffering Christian must pray, so also the cheerful Christian must sing praise.

The New Testament also reports hymn singing as a part of the faith-filled rhythm of life. In Matthew 26:30 (cf. Mark 14:26), Jesus and His disciples sang as they concluded their Passover observance, probably from the Psalms.[8] Furthermore, Paul and Silas sang while in prison (Acts 16:25). In short, Christians must sing. They must sing with one another and to one another in an array of life circumstances. Since one of the results of salvation among the nations is singing, missionaries

---

Psalms and Music: Influences of the Psalms on Western Music (Brooklyn, NY: KTAV, 2013).

7. Daniel B. Wallace, *Greek Grammar beyond the Basics: An Exegetical Syntax of the New Testament* (Grand Rapids: Zondervan, 1996), 639, 651.

8. See R. T. France, *The Gospel of Mark: A Commentary on the Greek Text,* NIGTC (Grand Rapids: Eerdmans, 2002), 574. For a differing perspective, see Clemens Leonhard, *The Jewish Pesach and the Origins of the Christian Easter: Open Questions in Current Research,* Studia Judaica 35 (New York: Walter de Gruyter, 2006), 100n65.

and pastors must also apply biblically grounded discernment to the music of the church for the worship of God. Profiling this discernment is the task of the next section.

Evaluating the Theology in Worship Music

Missionaries and pastors should consider at least two aspects of the theology in worship music as they evaluate songs for use in worship: the theology of song lyrics and the theology of the songwriter.

The Theology of Song Lyrics

Lyrics convey theology. Accordingly, one historic approach for ensuring theological faithfulness in worship music is to sing Scripture only, notably the Psalms. In this approach, since the Psalms are both songs and Scripture, singing them is theoretically always appropriate.[9] Still, while singing the Psalms is a commendable practice, singing only the Psalms does not seem to be in accord with the message of the Psalms themselves. As mentioned above, the Psalms urge that God's people "Sing to Yahweh a new song" (Ps 149:1). "A new song" alludes to the unleashing of artistic creativity in music, generating new tunes and new lyrics.[10]

Of course, since "new songs" do not necessarily come from Scripture, their lyrics are prone to drift into theological imprecision and error. Popular songs with emotional and perhaps vaguely encouraging lyrics can easily incite theological error through ambiguity.[11] In such cases, singers construct their own meaning through a song text, a meaning unlikely to reflect biblical teaching. Scripture warns that misdirected religious singing by God's people can serve the worship of idols (cf. Exod 32:17–19).

To steer away from the ever-present threat of paganization of worship through music, churches must use Scripture as their authoritative and sufficient standard to judge song lyrics. Especially if "Christian" music already exists in a certain language and culture, the standard of Scripture will likely screen out popular emotive but theologically questionable songs. However, the task of selecting music according to biblical standards need not restrict the church to single-style, single-message songs. The example of the Psalms is instructive at precisely this point. The Psalms plumb the depths of biblical theology and the breadth of human emotions. As for the amount of theology a given psalm may express, as the shortest chapter in the Bible, Psalm 117

---

9. Nevertheless, planning to sing certain psalms would be a bold choice that would benefit from explanation, or better yet, an accompanying expository sermon on the text. One example is Psalm 137, which begins with a melancholy tone and then jarringly transforms into a plea for God's vengeance. A rhymed setting for Psalm 137 appears in *The Book of Psalms for Singing* (Pittsburgh: The Board of Education and Publication, Reformed Presbyterian Church of North America, 1973), hymn #137.

10. Since "all Scripture is God-breathed" (2 Tim 3:16), all Scripture, not only the Psalms, is amenable to singing back to God in worship.

11. For example, consider the song by Brendan Graham, "You Raise Me Up," on the Secret Garden album *Once in a Red Moon* (2001), performed by the evangelical Christian music group Selah on their album *Hiding Place* (2004). Some of the ambiguous lyrics, which nowhere specify God as the addressee, include "You raise me up, so I can stand on mountains / You raise me up to walk on stormy seas / I am strong when I am on your shoulders / You raise me up to more than I can be."

contains only a handful of words. On the other extreme of length is Psalm 119, with 176 verses! All this is to say that selecting songs with biblically faithful lyrics is not only entirely possible but is essential in Christian education, evangelism, ministry, and fellowship on the mission field.[12]

The Theology of Songwriters

In evaluating worship songs for biblical faithfulness, it is appropriate to consider the theology of the songwriter. When the religious convictions of a songwriter conflict with the lyrics he or she has composed for congregational singing, some church leaders choose to cover up or ignore the embarrassment of the theologically unsound composer.[13] Another way some leaders choose to manage the issue of a heretical lyricist is to set aside the problem altogether, allowing for the possibility that at least some orthodox lyrics can flow from the pen of a heterodox author. According to this strategy, only the lyrics themselves require evaluation, not the life of the one who produced them.[14]

In contrast, upon discovering the erroneous theology of a songwriter or music group, however popular they may be in the global church, missionaries and pastors should neither attempt to cover up nor to ignore the real theological problems before them. Biblically faithful leaders should reject unfaithful songs and would do well to offer a pastoral warning to the flock concerning the errant composer or music group's theology. Furthermore, they should consider excluding their songs altogether from use in worship. A more ambiguous and nuanced stance risks communicating tacit approval. Furthermore, in an age when payment automatically flows to songwriters every time their music is played on an electronic device, listening to songs that convey heterodox doctrine also financially supports leading the global church astray.

Especially in cultural and linguistic settings that lack preexisting Christian music, missionaries should cultivate faithful songwriting. When God begins prompting the creation of new worship music, missionaries can help budding songwriters acquire quality musical training. That said, far more important than technical expertise in music is spiritual formation through Scripture and the gathered

---

12. William J. Reynolds and Milburn Price, *A Survey of Christian Hymnody*, 5th ed., rev. by David W. Music and Milburn Price (Carol Stream, IL: Hope Publishing, 2020), xvii–xx.

13. John Bowring and his hymn "In the Cross of Christ I Glory" pose the theological dilemma of a heterodox composer who wrote orthodox lyrics. While the hymn is theologically rich and commended for singing in biblically faithful congregations, Bowring was a Unitarian who denied the fundamental Christian doctrine of the Trinity. One early attempt to mitigate the offense of Bowring's Unitarianism appears in Samuel Willoughby Duffield, *English Hymns: Their Authors and History* (New York: Funk and Wagnalls, 1886), 262. For a firsthand account of Bowring's erroneous beliefs, see John Bowring, *A Memorial Volume of Sacred Poetry, to Which Is Prefixed a Memoir of the Author, by Lady Bowring* (London: Longmans, Green, Reader, and Dyer, 1873), xlv.

14. Recent popular works more often ignite controversy in the contemporary church worldwide than older music that has stood the test of time. Songs by Hillsong Music, for example, evince a wide range of theological convictions, ranging from the sound biblical theology in Darlene Zschech's "Shout to the Lord," which became a global, evangelical worship standard, to Joel Houston, Benjamin Hastings, and Michael Fatkin's 2017 song "So Will I (100 Billion X)," which appears to espouse theistic evolution: a direct contradiction to the theology of creation in the Bible.

worship of the church.[15] The Holy Spirit then deductively and inductively trains the new songwriters to think biblically.[16] It should not be surprising when some newly composed songs emphasize themes that are especially significant to the songwriters' cultural context. Moreover, missionaries should welcome songs whose lyrics treat theological themes treated sparingly in international Christian music, for example baptism, creation, election, missions, judgment, and the resurrection in the new creation. In addition, missionaries should encourage the creation of new worship music with an eye toward encouraging new songwriters to serve the world church. At present, the worship music of the world church is suffering from the attack of the "universal acid" of theological liberalism. Faithful songs from the church on the mission field can call Christians of all people groups back to the wholehearted praise of God that overflows from his Word.[17]

Ethical Considerations

Beyond theological problems raised above, the faithful use of music in worship can pose a number of ethical challenges. For the mission field, perhaps the two most significant ethical challenges relate to issues of copyright and emotional manipulation.

Copyright

Faced with popular songs that contain objectionable theology in their lyrics, some worship leaders resort to rewriting problematic words. Yet editing an artistic work requires caution, for song lyrics are the intellectual property of the songwriter. For musical works under the protection of copyright law, altering lyrics requires the approval of the copyright holder, who is often the original artist.[18]

Of course, rather than "improve" a song, modifications to its lyrics can instead damage the song in some way. For example, one American denomination's hymnal committee attempted to change the lyrics of "In Christ Alone" from "Till on that cross as Jesus died, the wrath of God was satisfied" to ". . . the love of God was magnified." The copyright holders refused permission for this change of lyrics.[19] In another notable case, a theologically

---

15. Minds marinated in certain genres of music and certain kinds of song lyrics are those that are most likely to generate similar songs in creative, new ways. There is a significant environmental component to inspiration. See Joseph Bennett, "Inspiration in Music," *The Musical Times* 36 (1895): 221–24, esp. 221.

16. Thinking biblically is essential for the faithful composing and singing of Christian worship music. Contrastingly, Krissy Nordhoff writes, "Simple, memorable melody and lyrics are important. You want people to be able to sing and worship more than they have to think." Krissy Nordhoff, *Writing Worship: How to Craft Heartfelt Songs for the Church* (Colorado Springs, CO: David C Cook, 2020), 39.

17. For perspective on the threat liberalism poses to the worship music for the world church, see Bryan J. Sirchio, *The 6 Marks of Progressive Christian Worship Music* (Bloomington, IN: AuthorHouse, 2023), 27–32. Sirchio lists basic gospel themes that categorically do not appear in "progressive Christian" music: "penal substitutionary atonement," "blood sacrifice theology," "escaping from this world," "being saved from hell," and "Jesus being the 'only way' to God." On the final point, Sirchio writes, "To be very straightforward, there will be no references in Progressive Christian Worship Music to Jesus being the only way to God."

18. See the copyright law of the United States regarding musical works in *US Code* 17 (2010), §§ 106 (2), 110 (3), Copyright.gov, U.S. Copyright Office, accessed June 18, 2024, https://www.copyright.gov/title17/92chap1.html.

19. The original lyrics are from Stuart Townend and Keith Getty, "In Christ Alone," Thankyou Music, 2001. The adaptation

well-intended edit resulted in both lyrical awkwardness and further theological problems when another American denomination adapted "And Can It Be?" for its hymnal. The theological review committee changed "Emptied Himself of all but love, and bled for Adam's helpless race" to "Humbled himself (so great his love!), and bled for all his chosen race."[20] This attempt to express a more Chalcedonian Christology (so as not to imply that Jesus surrendered His divine nature in the incarnation) inserts an intrusive parenthetical expression. In addition, the attempt to clarify support for limited atonement through the phrase "all his chosen race" could in fact communicate the precisely opposite view of unlimited atonement, implying that the entire human race is God's chosen people. Since "And Can It Be?" has long fallen out of copyright, these edits are legal but musically and theologically problematic.

The two examples above illustrate that editing song lyrics is an ethical and theological minefield. Beyond these issues lie the difficulties of translating songs from one language to another, which will seldom allow ease of rhyme with lyrics that express similar theological concepts. Although the world church has benefited greatly from translated hymns such as "A Mighty Fortress Is Our God," the challenges treated above commend all the more the composition of new songs on the mission field for the glory of God.

Emotional Manipulation

As poetry, song lyrics communicate both cognitively and emotionally when recited. Adding to them melody, harmony, and other elements of music amplifies their emotional character. This heightened emotive power of music is open to manipulation.[21] In the "praise and worship" services of many churches across the world, worship leaders employ set strategies to manipulate audience emotions. In contemporary "praise and worship" services, emotional manipulation typically begins with twenty to forty minutes of continuous music. Placed first in the "worship set" are "praise" songs with "upbeat tempos, major harmonies, lively rhythms, and communally oriented lyrics." Next are "worship" songs with "slower tempos, more poignant contrasts between major and minor harmonies, and intimate lyrics expressing devotion, love, and desire for God."[22]

There may also be planned shifts—violations of listener expectation of volume, tempo, or harmony—within individual songs

---

proposed by the Presbyterian Church (U.S.A.) signals rejection of the doctrine of the satisfaction of God's wrath against sin through Christ's death on the cross, which is the historic teaching of Presbyterianism as in *WCF* §11.3.

20. Personal communication with John Frame, who led the theological review committee for the *Trinity Hymnal* (Philadelphia: Great Commission Publications, 1990), hymn #455, on May 17, 2022. Frame does not personally consider these edits to be theologically mandatory.

21. Jeremy S. Begbie, "Faithful Feelings: Music and Emotion in Worship," in *Resonant Witness: Conversations between Music and Theology*, ed. Jeremy S. Begbie and Steven R. Guthrie (Grand Rapids: Eerdmans, 2011), 353.

22. Monique M. Ingalls, "Introduction: Interconnection, Interface, and Identification in Pentecostal-Charismatic Music and Worship," in *The Spirit of Praise: Music and Worship in Global Pentecostal-Charismatic Christianity*, ed. Monique M. Ingalls and Amos Yong (University Park: Pennsylvania State University Press, 2015), 7.

that prompt psychological "surprise" in an audience. These jolts of surprise in music often generate a physical response of chills.[23] If a congregant has ever had goose bumps during a meaningful spiritual encounter, such as in times of prayer or conviction under the "living and active" Word of God (Heb 4:12; cf. Luke 24:32), it is natural for that person to correlate such music-prompted chills with spiritual experience.

Further manipulation techniques may include maintaining low room temperatures and dim ambient lighting punctuated by multi-colored moving spotlights turned into beams of light by fog machines; swooping overhead video cameras and projections of constantly shifting, larger-than-life quick cuts of the worship team or audience onscreen; and professional singing of a series of "power ballads."[24] The "praise and worship formula" essentially becomes an incantation for conjuring the presence of the Holy Spirit, a paganization of God's gift of music to the church. Manipulated emotions are real and feel personal, but stage-crafted stimulation of the emotions is actually impersonal on a mass scale.[25] When the music stops, having been whipped into a frenzy through waves of whole-body sensations, then the congregation sinks into their seats to receive a low-key spiritual talk that does not at all resemble an exposition of the Bible.[26] The earlier musical performance constituted the main spiritual experience, and as such it stole the rightful place of the preaching of the Bible in the worship of the church (Acts 2:42; 1 Tim 4:13).[27]

While missionaries will not likely found megachurches on the mission field and therefore will unlikely face the temptation to copy the Western megachurch "praise and worship" formula point for point, they should take stock of the pervasive influence of this model of worship in the world church. They should guard against artificially manipulating the emotions of people through music. Instead, they should faithfully worship through music themselves, and encourage others to use Bible-centered music in worship in the midst of the otherwise "dry and weary land" (Ps 63:1) of the mission field.

Embracing Theologically Sound Music in a Theologically Unsound World

In an upside-down world in which many who call themselves Christians deny the clear teachings of Jesus Christ, to worship "in spirit and

---

23. David Huron, *Sweet Anticipation: Music and the Psychology of Expression* (Cambridge, MA: MIT Press, 2006), 281–83.

24. See David Metzer, "The Power Ballad," *Popular Music* 31 (2012): 437–59, esp. 439–40.

25. William Forde Thompson, *Music, Thought, and Feeling: Understanding the Psychology of Music* (New York: Oxford University Press, 2009), 146–50.

26. See advocacy of the eighteen-minute TED Talk–style of sermon in Ramona Hayes, "Digital and Analog Preaching in a Multi-media World" (DMin diss., Luther Seminary, 2018), 63–66, 78–79.

27. "It is true, there is something that creates worship—this will shock people—it's preaching the Word, or reading the Word, so that when you know the truth, your heart reaches forward to God to express praise and gratitude." John MacArthur, "Is Music Worship?," sermon recorded at Grace Community Church on December 27, 2015, https://www.gty.org/library/sermons-library/80 -428/is-music-worship.

in truth," the church must apply biblically grounded discernment. As Jesus coined this expression in John 4:23–24, He taught in simple terms with great theological depth: a characteristic of the poetry of great worship music.

Jesus (God the Son) taught that the Father (God the Father) seeks worshipers who must worship "in spirit" (pointing to God the Holy Spirit). Hence Jesus Himself inaugurated Trinitarian—in other words, Christian—worship.[28] Jesus also taught worship "in truth." The word of God is truth (Ps 119:160).

Through careful consideration of the issues raised in this chapter, may missionaries and those they lead to faith all use scripturally soaked music to worship the Father for the glorification of Christ through the power of the Spirit both now and forever. Amen!

---

28. For an in-depth study of explicitly Trinitarian hymns, see Lee C. Hansard, "Trinitarian Structure in Hymnody: An Historical and Analytical Study of Hymns Which in Form and Content Address the Three Persons of the Godhead, and of the Hymn Tunes with Which They are Associated" (MM thesis, Southwestern Baptist Theological Seminary, 1982).

INSERT 46.1

The Role of the Arts in Evangelism

Paul T. Plew

Art is a universal phenomenon conceived by God and manifested in creation. Psalm 19 says, "The heavens are telling of the glory of God; and their expanse is declaring the work of His hands. . . . Their line has gone out through all the earth, and their utterances to the end of the world" (vv. 1, 4). In a real sense, then, the art of the heavens is evangelistic; it declares who God is. Humankind also exhibits God's excellent design, that is, His handiwork and nature (Ps 8:3–8), and that includes the human ability to appreciate and create art. In fact, human beings express themselves nowhere more fully than in the arts—whether literary, graphic, decorative, performing, or other categories of art—and this, too, can be a bridge to the gospel.

That is not to say that all people share the same creative gifts or tastes. But all do appreciate art somehow. For art to be "great," as it is commonly said, it must be unique and have a "stand-out" quality; it should evoke emotion in the beholder; it must show intelligence, knowledge, and truth; it should be original; and it should be relatable to people in many countries.[29] Such art crosses borders, because art is the common heritage of all people created in God's image (Gen 1:26–28).

God Himself is the source of art and beauty (cf. Pss 27:4; 71:8; 96:5–6; Eccl 3:11; Isa 33:17; 43:7; 49:3). Job argues, "By His breath the heavens are made beautiful. . . . Behold, these are the fringes of His ways; and how only with a whisper of a word do we hear of Him!" (Job 26:13–14). God also commands that His worship reflect His beauty and creativity (e.g., Exod 28:2, 40; Pss 29:2; 33:3; 96:9; 144:9; Eph 5:19; Col 3:16). In Exodus 31:1–11, He called two men, Bezalel and Oholiab, to be His official tabernacle artists, filling them with His Spirit and endowing them with gifts of skill and knowledge in all kinds of craftsmanship, to build and beautify the place of worship. This tent was an earthly copy or "shadow" of God's heavenly dwelling (Exod 25:8–9, 40; Heb 8:2, 5), so the tent, along with its furniture and decor, had to be a great work of art. Almighty God, who dwelt there, embodies greatness and excellence.

Gifted believers today must likewise create with excellence. Mediocrity must never be allowed; we do not serve a mediocre God. God's name is at stake for believing artists are His representatives (1 Cor 10:31). Consequently, Christian artists often need to devote more time to their work than they expected, separate from distractions, seek out others who help them flourish, and practice, practice, practice. Believers must strive to create above the level of those who do not know Christ. For, if the creativity of the Christian is to be appreciated as such—as the imagination that Christ has redeemed and set free[30]—then it must rise above whatever is the "standard" in a world weighed down and enslaved by sin.

Moreover, the Christian artist wants to reflect—not only in quality but also in content—the beauty and the glory of the Creator, in order to reflect His love and compassion toward sinners too. The Christian wants to "adorn the doctrine of God our Savior in everything" (Titus 2:10). This is not to say that "Christian art" must always have an overtly religious or gospel subject, but rather, that the worldview it expresses must be the Christian worldview, no less than in all other aspects of life. Honest art like this, whatever its form, opens doors to share Christ with an audience. For

---

29. Compare the "four standards of judgment" proposed by the beloved Christian apologist, philosopher, and amateur art critic Francis Schaeffer: (1) technical excellence, (2) validity (i.e., whether the artist is honest to himself and to his worldview), (3) intellectual content (i.e., the worldview that comes through), and (4) integration of content and vehicle (i.e., how well the artist suited the medium to the message). Francis A. Schaeffer, *Art and the Bible: Two Essays* (1973; repr., Downers Grove, IL: InterVarsity, 2006), 62–71.

30. Schaeffer, 14–15, 91.

example, while the works of secular painters reflect unbiblical worldviews to varying degrees, a believer's paintings appreciate the testimony of God's good design in creation (Rom 1:19–20).[31] Whether performing with evangelistic purposes or writing biblically sound poetry that moves the mind and spirit,[32] art forms provide persuasive vehicles to gather an audience and share the truth of Christ in His beauty.

Music, in particular, enables the gospel to be shared in places often considered impossible, for it is wrapped in the beauty of excellent art and shared from the heart. One can sing—or direct, as I have been privileged to do—all over the world in government buildings, performing arts centers, parks, museums, festivals, schools, senior centers, and nearly any event where there is a crowd. Open-air music attracts people quickly, which then gives both singers and conductors the opportunity to open their mouths and proclaim the good news of Jesus Christ.

Music is also an accessible way for amateurs or those who simply enjoy the arts for leisure to use the arts for evangelism. For example, missionaries on the field can build relationships and establish a faithful witness through joining their community choir. I know of one missionary couple in Italy who has done just that for fifty years, and of another missionary in Madrid who has done the same. Missionaries can also invite Christian choirs to join them on short-term ministry trips and host concerts including such elements as these:

- Familiar songs in the local language
- Songs from renowned local composers
- The national anthem of the host country
- Songs of Scripture and hope in Christ

Whether by music, theater, photography, painting, poetry, or any other medium, the arts can open doors in areas that are closed to evangelism. The arts offer a way to present our God's glory and excellence, His love and compassion. Then, through that open door, Jesus' disciples can "go into all the world and preach the gospel" (Mark 16:15).

---

31. For examples of one Christian painter's work, see SteveForster.net, accessed June 18, 2024, https://steveforster.net/home.html.

32. For example, see the writings of Malcolm Guite, *Sounding the Seasons: Poetry for the Christian Year* (Norwich, UK: Canterbury, 2012); *Faith, Hope and Poetry: Theology and Poetic Imagination*, Routledge Studies in Theology, Imagination, and the Arts (Abingdon, UK: Routledge, 2012).

Music Ministry to Families in France

Philippe Viguier

This insert presents a model of outreach through music writing and recording, especially outreach to children, by recounting the experience of recording a Christian children's music album during the COVID-19 quarantines imposed by the French government. Religion in many places, like in France where this model was developed, is a private matter. Thick walls often need to be brought down to speak deeply and freely about faith. It may even take years. Music can be an excellent tool to witness to the unreached and strengthen young believers. Music opens doors to hearts, and children open doors to families. The combination of music and children is a powerful tool to bring the gospel into people's homes.

Evangelism usually requires going from person to person. In God's design, the children's music album we created reached directly into homes across France. For example, one time I accompanied my daughter and her friend in the car, and the friend asked, "Can we please listen to Christian music as we drive?" It turned out that not only had this unchurched girl listened nonstop to the album, but she also memorized many of the songs and shared them with her friends and family. Today, after making a profession of faith, she looks forward to all the Sundays when her parents allow her to come with us. She comes straight to the front row and sings her heart out to the Lord. What follows is the story of how the album was created and some of its early impact for the gospel.

An Unexpected Album

Covid lockdowns in France meant that our local church had to prepare all the music sets for online church services from home. To keep the live-streamed church service music clean, we recorded the music—instruments and vocals—in a home office and just lip-synced live in front of a camera. Eventually the music recordings started including my children as well. These children proved to be musically gifted. Not only did they have crystal-clear voices, but they put themselves into the music with heart and soul. In that time of fear and sorrow, the little family worship sessions brought joy and hope to thousands of homes.

An Album for the Whole Family

The family worship sessions grew within a year to a YouTube channel that surpassed a hundred thousand views, providing a platform for the next project, a professionally produced children's album. The goal from the start was to make an album for the whole family, one that parents would look forward to listening to as much as their kids. Even children's music can profoundly stimulate and encourage believing adults, and there are many examples of such music throughout history. For example, Fanny Crosby originally penned "Blessed Assurance" as a children's hymn. It was important that the level of performance, craftsmanship, and production on the album would accomplish that vision. To achieve this objective while remaining accessible within the culture, the genres of the songs were based on the styles of popular songs for children.

Songs were written to answer questions that came up during interaction with children, some to be sung in Sunday school or church, and others just for listening. The first song for the album, "Il me tient par la main" ("He Holds Me by the Hand") was based on Isaiah 41:13. It was especially intended for my son, as he was often bullied and lonely at school. His solo of the track was picked up right away by the local radio station. On the radio, a tender duet with my four-year-old child, "Papa, c'est quoi une âme?" ("Papa, What Is a Soul?") became the most popular song of the album.

An Album to Give Freely

Initially the album was distributed exclusively as a free internet download and for free on streaming platforms. However, online streaming is very impersonal. There is no connection to the listener, and after people have listened, they move on and forget what they have heard. Physical objects—like records and CDs—engage listeners in a more lasting way. To get the best of both worlds, this album was distributed on CDs with QR codes on them for online streaming options, either given away for free or sold for a nominal price. Within a month the first order ran out. Christian camps, schools, churches, and individuals took the opportunity to acquire the music, and all the copies disappeared. The album has had ongoing impact. Instead of just becoming a deleted email or forgotten link, the object stays in the home as a visible household item.

The album accomplished in a few days a degree of gospel work that I have not accomplished in years of ministry, simply because the music entered the houses of so many families through its musical presentation of the gospel. Unbelieving and unchurched families regularly listen to the albums with their kids. I have been able to share the album with doctors, teachers, piano instructors, tennis coaches, and barbers. Through the album, they have now heard about hope, heaven, Jesus' sacrifice for their sins, the beauty of the gift of life, Christian identity in Christ, and the power of the gospel. We pray that the seed will grow.

Conclusion

Music has been a powerful instrument for sharing the gospel by missionaries of all time. It is an outstanding means of communicating the gospel with local, cultural expression. The invitation from Psalm 96:1 stands: "Sing to Yahweh a new song; sing to Yahweh, all the earth." The gospel and music go hand in hand. The good news is spread among the nations by writing and singing new songs in every language and culture that celebrates God's great work. His goal is for the gospel to reach to the ends of the earth, and yet it often starts and flourishes humbly in the home. From my home to the listeners' homes, a little album allowed me to begin a gospel-centered relationship that will bear fruit in its season.

CHAPTER 47

Teaching Music in the Global Church

Thomas Hochstetter and Kellie Cunningham

Worship leaders have the responsibility of equipping musicians to strive for excellence as they serve the Lord with their art. In so doing, they help produce lifelong worshipers in their churches. Those entrusted with the task of building a music ministry must rightly understand the biblical principles regarding music and worship—principles that transcend generational and cultural divides. They must know what the Bible says about music, how music functions, what it can and cannot do, and how to honor God through the mastery of elements such as harmony, rhythm, intervals, mood, and speed.

Cultivating individuals within a church community who can practice God's timeless music principles with excellence is the crux of the faithful music minister's calling. This chapter will benefit men and women involved in music ministry in the local church, though several sections are written for those male leaders who are called to exercise spiritual responsibility over the ministry. The aim is to help them think biblically and practically about the basis for their

ministry, how they might best raise up future music leaders, and how to instill a proper culture of musical worship in local congregations.

Defining the Role of Music in the Church

The biblical pattern of music was in place long before the church came into existence. God created the rules for music at the beginning and enabled His creation to understand them. The Bible presents music as a constant component of worship, from the angels singing for joy at creation (Job 38:7) to the saints singing a new song at the end of the ages (Rev 5:9; 14:3; 15:3); from the equipping of Jubal, the "father of all those who play the lyre and pipe" (Gen 4:21) to the training of temple musicians in Chronicles (1 Chr 6:31–48; 25:1–31); from the song of Moses following the crossing of the Red Sea (Exod 15:1–21) to the psalmists composing God's hymnal for Israel; from Jesus singing with the disciples in the upper room (Matt 26:30) to Paul's instructions about music in churches (Eph 5:19; Col 3:16).

The Central Role of Music

In Colossians 3:16, Paul gives a straightforward command to Christians: "Let the word of Christ dwell in you richly, with all wisdom teaching and admonishing one another with psalms and hymns and spiritual songs, singing with gratefulness in your hearts to God." Paul uses three participles: teaching (*didaskontes*), admonishing (*nouthetountes*), and singing (*adontes*), to show how the objective is to be achieved. "Teaching" simply refers to the preaching and teaching of God's Word, "admonishing" (*nutheteo*) relates to walking alongside someone in order to correct their path, and then comes "singing" in all its various forms. The goal is that the Word of Christ will dwell richly in the believer by means of these elements, thus affecting the necessary spiritual change.

Music as Teacher and Counselor

Ephesians 5 contains another vital aspect of musical worship: "speaking to one another in psalms and hymns and spiritual songs, singing and making melody with your heart to the Lord" (Eph 5:19). The wording in Colossians 3:16 and Ephesians 5:19 is very similar, though in Ephesians, Paul identifies singing as part of the Christian's duty to "one another." When believers worship in song, therefore, they also sing to the person next to and in front of them. This creates a whole new level of responsibility, as they are to express the Word of Christ in song to one another, thereby bringing encouragement and admonishment.

As with a sermon, both the didactic and devotional elements of music equip believers

with the Word of Christ for life's daily spiritual battles. Christians can use music to strengthen a broken spirit, encourage the fainthearted, admonish a straying brother or sister, and teach children about God and the Christian life.

Striving for Excellence in Music

In Colossians 3, Paul further reveals that Christians are to pursue teaching, admonishing, and singing in the church with excellence. The word of Christ is to dwell "richly" (Col 3:16). In other words, worship music should contain a full and well-rounded expression of biblical content. Paul then expands on that sentiment in the subsequent verse: "And whatever you do in word or deed, do all in the name of the Lord Jesus, giving thanks to God the Father through him" (Col 3:17). In other words, ministry through song is to be done "in the name of the Lord." How Christians play and sing music therefore will reflect what they think about Christ. Because humans communicate with more than words, a half-hearted approach will convey that Jesus is not worthy of one's best.

Each believer has received natural and spiritual abilities that fuel the works for which God created them (Eph 2:10). Furthermore, the church body will mature only as its individual members mature, when each part is working properly (Eph 4:16). This maturation includes striving to do one's best. Striving for excellence serves as a proper example to others. Paul called Titus to exemplify such excellence when he told him, "In all things show yourself to be a model of good works" (Titus 2:7). In music, as in the rest of the Christian life, believers are to be full of integrity, dignity, and sound speech so that others will be motivated to follow.

Training Worship Leaders

Regardless of the cultural context, individual churches need musicians to be worship leaders who are committed to biblically rich and excellent music if they expect to train musicians from among their own members. However, such qualified leaders are not easy to find. It is often most effective to identify them within the context of the local church itself and then disciple them into this role.

The Qualifications of Music Worship Leaders

To train congregations to worship through music, churches need designated leaders who faithfully provide oversight of the ministry. The leader's tasks often include formal teaching. But in other contexts, the music leader may serve under an elder or pastor. Regardless, the worship leader must meet specific qualifications, both musical and spiritual. Musical skill alone is insufficient. Because music in the church serves as a vital means of teaching and counseling, it must be grounded in theological truth and overseen with purpose and integrity. Music worship leaders need a strong grasp of musical fundamentals. Ideally, they will be able to read notation, have a working knowledge of various instruments, understand rules of harmony, know how to arrange music, and be able to lead vocally and instrumentally. Not only that, but leaders ought to impart these abilities to others in their congregation.

Specific musical qualifications may differ depending on location and preferences, but the spiritual qualifications are universal. Their responsibilities are bound up in the qualifications for deacons (1 Tim 3:8–12). Music leaders do not necessarily need to be formal deacons, but their lives must be exemplary because they stand as representatives of Christ before the congregation and a watching world.

First, the leader needs to be able to discern between theological truth and error. He has not only the opportunity but the responsibility to select songs that convey profound and timeless biblical doctrine. The leader may have opportunities to explain to the congregation why a particular song is being sung, or may need to respond with a biblical framework to questions and complaints regarding the musical style and the musicians used.

Second, the music worship leader should be prepared to disciple the musicians. This responsibility goes beyond routine administrative tasks of organizing rehearsals and assigning musicians to services. The leader must communicate and adhere to the church's philosophy of music ministry, encourage and admonish the musicians, and regularly pray for them.

Typical Approaches to Finding Such a Leader

There is no single method for finding qualified music worship leaders apart from biblical discipleship. Church leaders must invest themselves in the life of a potential candidate. The candidate might come from within the congregation or might be hired or brought in through an internship. Whatever the initial process, patience is essential. Churches must give potential leaders enough room to make mistakes, but they must also manage them well so as not to breed discouragement.

Formal education might also be considered, whether musical or theological. Many Christian institutions offer courses that combine musical and theological coursework into a single program, such as a degree in worship music. Such classes provide an excellent foundation for future music leaders of the church.

Cultivating Musicians for the Church

The church has a unique role to play in raising up both worship leaders and church musicians. No one leader can disciple and train an entire congregation to participate actively in musically excellent worship. A worship leader must duplicate a heart of worship in other musicians, who can then "teach others also" (2 Tim 2:2).

Training Church Musicians

To have excellent, Christ-centered musical worship, churches need musicians with a strong foundation. To that end, music worship leaders have several options to consider. They must decide whether to use a choir for leading worship or perhaps have an individual lead from the front, possibly with support from additional vocalists. They might consider employing a modern worship band or a more traditional ensemble.

The cultivation of singers and soloists within the church is another important facet of musical

training. Each singer must gain knowledge of a proper approach to vocal health, the changes that come with maturing voices, the selection of age-appropriate songs, and the ability to hear and sing harmony. The music worship leader may also be called on to assist in developing the skills of instrumentalists. Depending on the church's context, the leader will need the appropriate knowledge and skill for overseeing the use of specific instruments, along with the nuances of synthesizing instrumental sounds into a cohesive whole.

Music worship leaders need to think like educators as they train musicians. They should be adept at building sequential lessons, spiraling learning so that easier topics build to more complex explanations as understanding grows. From the beginning stages of teaching a song to the complex preparation that leads to developing a musical training curriculum, a music worship leader must be cognizant of the best means to equip a skillful team. Learning is best accomplished in terms of both short- and long-term goals. With planning and forethought, music worship leaders can lead their people to more excellent musical results.

Nurturing Children

The music worship leader must also carefully consider the cultivation of musical knowledge in children. Churches are to come alongside families as they shepherd and train their children "in the nurture and admonition of the Lord" (Eph 6:4 KJV). In no way is the church to supplant this God-given responsibility; rather, it supports this entrustment. Children can participate meaningfully in church life. As they receive training, they can express musicianship with ever-increasing excellence. For example, leaders can begin by teaching children to match pitch and identify a steady beat, and then introduce them to singing in parts through simple rounds, or "canons." Partner songs, in which two tunes are woven together to create harmony are the next step. Modeling basic solfège (a system of learning to hear and sing musical pitches) can assist in understanding how music is constructed and provide a stepping stone for learning to read notation. In addition, guidance in finding one's singing voice (as opposed to singing with one's speaking voice) is invaluable for children, enabling their voices to mature in a healthy way. Beginning with teaching children practical singing skills is foundational for training a congregation of singing worshipers.[1]

In addition to singing, leaders can also encourage children to play musical instruments, either through group instruction within the church or by playing alongside members of the church band. Individual instruction and practice time at home are crucial in developing a higher level of instrumental skill. Leaders and parents alike must remember that the goal is to encourage musical growth and excellence, not perfection.

As children grow in their musical skill, they must also be grounded in a proper theology of worship. They must know that musical participation in church is not a performance. They are singing for an audience of One, exalting the Lord through heartfelt praise. They are also contributing to the edification of the saints. Proper training allows them to develop a practical knowledge of the role of music in worship in this way.[2]

Considering Musical Style

In developing a particular worship music style, the dynamic of congregational participation may be encouraged or stifled, depending on style and cultural expectations. Learning to cultivate a thriving, worshiping congregation is crucial to fulfilling the biblical mandate to sing to one another in "psalms and hymns and spiritual songs" (Eph 5:19). Ministers must consider how to engage rightly with the broader culture of their congregations.

In cross-cultural settings, Western missionaries must be aware of the legacy of Western hymnody and its traditions as well as the influence of popular music styles. A more recent movement called ethnodoxology (the inclusion of non-Western, indigenous music in the worship of a particular congregation or people group) is one means of addressing this need.[3] In

---

1. For further study on this topic, see Mary Delaine Allcock and Madeline Bridges, *How to Lead Children's Choirs* (Nashville: Convention, 1991); Vivian Sharp Morsch, *The Use of Music in Christian Education* (Philadelphia: Westminster, 1956).

2. Helpful theologies of worship include Matt Merker, *Corporate Worship: How the Church Gathers as God's People*, 9Marks: Building Healthy Churches (Wheaton, IL: Crossway, 2021); John MacArthur, *Worship: The Ultimate Priority* (Chicago: Moody, 2012); Bryan Chapell, *Christ-Centered Worship: Letting the Gospel Shape Our Practice* (Grand Rapids: Baker, 2009).

3. Ethnodoxology represents a movement in worship music that sees the need to reflect the creativity of individual cultures in worship music. The term was first utilized by David Hall, founder of Worship for the Nations, of Pioneers ministries (www

non-Western traditions, it would be important to know if and how the music of the culture, perhaps with a unique tuning system or different instruments, influences the church's experience of Western contemporary music. Musical ties to religion can be inextricable. Music leaders must consider such ties carefully when they begin training musicians in the church. Countless influences will play into how musicians within the church context perceive their role in the learning process and the nature of their musical contribution to the church.

When it comes to addressing matters of style in worship, the music worship leader must approach such training with a heart that is open to consider others' preferences. Discipling a church toward the singular goal of worshiping Christ through music requires patience, as individual members may hold strong opinions. Leading within the context of various cultures and musical styles takes humility, discernment, and wisdom.

Music among the Congregation and Community

Music as ministry, whether corporately or privately, whether for edification or for evangelism, is something music leaders must faithfully model and teach.

Training the Congregation

Music leaders have the opportunity to build lifetime worshipers as they cultivate an increasing level of musical aptitude and ability in the church. Members of all ages can participate in the worship service—whether from the front or within the congregation—with ministry by children as well as adults, allowing for intergenerational worship within the service. But worship through music, as has been clearly shown, is not limited to the Sunday services.

Encouraging Family Worship

Training the church about music corporately encourages them to implement music privately in family worship. Making music a part of daily life will add a tremendous richness to the family's worship. As families sing and play music together, they create a stronger bond between individual members, building spiritually beneficial traditions. This facilitates informal vocal and aural training, contributes to the rediscovery of multipart singing, and imprints each family member with timeless truths they will carry into life. By focusing on music in the home, families can move toward a brighter future for church music. Families who are not musically trained may not feel comfortable including music in their home worship, but bringing music into homes, even through recordings, further develops music as a means of worship.

Promoting the Gospel with Music

Promoting musical knowledge in a congregation facilitates outreach within the

---

.worldofworship.org). The term continues to be expanded and developed while increasingly missionaries and local songwriters are collaborating to weave the gospel into songs for personal and congregational worship and incorporating the musical idioms of individual cultures.

broader community, giving testimony to both believers and unbelievers. Music ministries, and specifically the teaching of music, can be a profound means of extending the gospel beyond church doors. For example, in Cambodia a couple worked together to bring the gospel into their tribal community through translating the Bible and setting some of it to music. When the husband translated a Bible verse particularly full of theological truth, his wife wrote a memorable tune to go with it. Bringing together biblical truth and musical excellence, she then taught the new song to the children of the community. She found one of her greatest joys in hearing the truth of the Bible sung along the streets of their village.

Conclusion

As those who desire to "sing praises" to God and "make known His acts among the peoples" (Ps 105:1–2), Christians have the profound responsibility to provide their congregations with the tools to worship through music "in spirit and truth" (John 4:24). There is a historical precedent and a current pressing need. Music cannot be marginalized. Believers must reestablish a proper, ecclesiastical doxology. It is the responsibility of today's church musicians to train those of the next generation to cherish theology along with musical excellence, and to facilitate worship in a way uniquely fitting each congregation. Christians must share the heart of the psalmist: "Let all the peoples praise You. Let the nations be glad and sing for joy" (Ps 67:3–4).

INSERT 47.1

Music Education as Discipleship in Uganda

Kellie Cunningham

In the village of Kubamitwe, in the Luweero District of Uganda, Christians gather weekly to worship at Community Bible Church of Kubamitwe. In the usual scene there, youth banter enthusiastically, singing with fervor, playing guitars, keyboards, and drums. In this community, they are dedicated to learning, clamoring for practice time, and faithfully attending classes, rehearsals, and lessons almost daily. Cultivating a heart of worship with music education is a discipleship ministry here, and it is especially the work of one local educator, Bosco Andama.

Background and Opportunity

Andama grew up with a passion for making music in a village in Uganda. He first learned to play on local traditional instruments but eventually was drawn to the guitar. Then, after a famous guitarist whom Andama admired refused to teach him, he determined that if he ever owned his own instrument, he would use it to teach others. Eventually he did learn guitar. He attended college in Africa and went on to receive a master of arts in worship leadership from the Southern Baptist Theological Seminary in Louisville, Kentucky. Finally, he returned to Africa in 2017 to teach others also.

The opportunity to teach came where Anadama had hoped. Sufficiency of Scripture (SOS) Ministries had a growing pastoral training center, primary school, and outreach based in Community Bible Church in Kubamitwe.[4] They also provided Andama a place to start a music training program. He later reflected, "I had a talent, but I didn't have the opportunity. Now I feel like it's the time for me to give that opportunity to those who need it." In Andama's eyes, it was his God-given discipleship ministry.

Ministry Basis

Music is indeed a ministry given by God for discipleship as well as worship. In Scripture, believers are not just described as singing,

they are commanded to sing. This is true privately, as a personal expression of joy and Godward gratitude (Ps 30:4; James 5:13), as well as corporately in gathered worship (Ps 149:1). Besides vocals, worship music is also prescribed by means of instruments (Ps 150:3–5). It is prescribed with the use of creativity, producing more music (a "new song"; Ps 98:1) and in a variety of styles (Eph 5:19; Col 3:16).

Moreover, music is commanded for the church as a means of mutual "teaching and admonishing" in the congregation (Eph 5:19; Col 3:16). Thus, it is one expression of the gift of "exhortation" (Rom 12:8); singers and hearers alike receive and affirm instruction by it. This aspect is especially poignant for missionaries, since their commission is to make disciples of all the nations, teaching them to keep all that Christ commanded (Matt 28:19–20). Music is a powerful means of rehearsing the doctrines of the nature and works of God, confessing one's faith in them, exalting Christ as head of the church, and even using these truths to evangelize the listening unbeliever (Acts 16:25). It ought not to be overlooked in the missionary's church planting, pastoring, and outreach strategies.

Discipleship Goals

With this scriptural basis, Andama's vision of discipleship through music has held three

---

4. Sufficiency of Scripture Ministries, accessed June 18, 2024, https://www.sosministries.com/.

goals in particular. First was to build up Community Bible Church in unity, depth of knowledge, and theological accountability. By promoting musical literacy in the congregation, worship would become a more frequent part of everyday life for its members and a natural outpouring of their hearts in praise. But to make the community "a singing community," people needed training, so Andama got to work. He set up a structured program at the SOS training center and gave individual instrument and music theory classes. He put together multiple worship bands, able to lead in rotation or at various church locations. And he established children and youth choirs. Students came to the center every weekday in preparation for Sunday services. The idea was, in his words, that "our community should not be hiring musicians from different places. It should be recycling them within." Those gifted in music were being taught to use their gifts to edify their church (1 Pet 4:10–11).

A second goal was to pass on the music ministry by training worship leaders. Andama had organized this training program as a volunteer, and he knew his limitations. He saw the need to duplicate himself in others and realized that training more advanced musicians would extend his capacity. Thus, he developed a short-term worship leaders' course. He took the few musicians in it further

into the disciplines of song leading, like diction, energy, vocal breath, how to communicate with a congregation, and how to engage them with the voice. By strengthening these leaders with excellence, the entire community would be blessed and strengthened. Indeed, Andama can now look back and see the confidence these leaders have gained, teaching beginners and making their community even more self-edifying in the Lord.

A third and final goal has been to fuse worship styles, which Andama hopes will become a broader movement in the African church. It is often true that when building a music program in a non-Western culture, the style of music and kinds of instruments taught are issues to consider. The youth are largely interested in popular styles, keyboards, guitars, and basses. But Andama sought to incorporate traditional instruments too. The latter are often being left behind, heard only in remote villages that cannot afford modern instruments. Yet, having grown up playing the traditional, he wanted the youth to learn both. This dispels the idea that worship is limited, even in degree, by wealth or by any particular music style, origin, or trend. It also teaches students to appreciate their cultural heritage as gifted by God (Acts 17:26) and as a thread in the tapestry of tribes that will forever sing around His throne (Rev 5:9–10; 7:9–12).

Conclusion

This music ministry in East Africa is a model and encouragement to missionaries and pastors everywhere. It is a compelling example of the profound influence one man's faithfulness can have to impact the church and of the effective use of spiritual gifts in a gospel-centered, disciple-making ministry. May it resound to the praise of Jesus Christ for generations.

SUB-SECTION 4: BIBLE TRANSLATION AND PRINT RESOURCING

CHAPTER 48

Why Bible Translation Is Critical in God's Plan of Redemption

Mark Tatlock

The fulfillment of the Great Commission cannot be considered apart from the work of Bible translation, since the very proclamation and progress of the gospel message require the overcoming of linguistic barriers. This reality demands that Christians called to "preach Christ" and "make disciples" by teaching all that Christ has commanded—found explicitly in the Scriptures—must contend with the dilemma language presents when doing ministry cross-culturally.

Today though, there is a dilemma in Bible translation, often due to a disconnection from the broader biblical scope of missions and failing to ensure that translators have strong

biblical, theological, pastoral, and missiological training. To be sure, many Bible translators do their best to overcome this dilemma and produce translations that faithfully represent the authorial intent of the Scriptures in the target language. Still, the dilemma is prevalent and will most certainly produce translations that do not serve the church in its mission.

In other words, while it is an admirable goal to get the Bible into every language in the world, it does little to further the Great Commission if a Bible translation is poorly done and given to a people group with no intention of planting a church and training disciples among that group. This chapter will address the current imbalance in translation efforts by arguing for an intimate connection between languages and the broader scope of missionary work. It will do so by first tracing a biblical theology of languages and missions, and then by showing the practical pastoral-missiological impacts of connecting languages to church planting.

The Biblical Connections between Languages and Missions

Why the language barrier exists and how it relates to the progress of God's redemptive plan are two important questions to understanding Bible translation. The biblical-theological rationale for these is traced below to show that God has always planned to overcome the barrier and redeem a people from every tongue, tribe, and nation.

Genesis 11 and the Introduction of Languages

The first connections between languages and mission are found in Genesis 11. Following the near-total destruction of the human race in the flood, Noah's sons began to repopulate the earth, just as God had created man and woman to do (Gen 1:27–28). This reset to the human race led to the table of nations in Genesis 10 and anticipated the fulfillment of God's assignment to man in the creation mandate—to subdue the earth and rule over it (Gen 1:26).

The construction of the Tower of Babel was an act of rebellion against God. Instead of spreading out over the world, mankind was congregating in one place. And instead of glorifying God through their work, they were attempting to glorify themselves by making for themselves a name (Gen 11:4), indicating the presence of the same heart that led to rebellion in the garden and before the flood.

The text indicates that the primary external factor that enabled mankind's collective act of rebellion against God was the use of one common language. Genesis 11:1 begins with the statement, "Now the whole earth used the same language and the same words." Having no barrier to communication, man was unhindered in sharing and persuading his fellow man to participate in the rebellion in building the tower. Therefore, to prevent mankind from following his sinful inclination to elevate himself, God intervened in history and introduced a new, permanent reality into the human experience: diversity of language (11:6–9). God's response to mankind's rebellion was to confuse their language and thereby scatter them abroad on the earth.

Genesis 11, then, presents the "table of nations," which would proliferate while scattering over and across the planet. Thus, unique language was the genesis of unique and distinct people groups and cultures.[1] Today it is estimated that more than seven thousand

---

1. Moisés Silva writes that, while the event described in Genesis 11 "cannot explain every instance of language variation," still "it may well be that . . . [it] could account for the origin of language *families* (such as the difference between the Indo-European family and the Afro-Asiatic family) and that a memory of the event is reflected in similar stories around the world" (emphasis original). Moisés Silva, *God Language and Scripture: Reading the Bible in the Light of General Linguistics*, Foundations of Contemporary

language groups exist.[2] A global map will show that the farthest reaches of the world have been populated and that the diversity of languages defines the world not only ethnically but geographically.

God could have simply toppled the Tower of Babel to stop mankind's rebellion. However, confusing mankind's language was much more effective. One of the most common traits of those who speak a common language is to cluster together and to isolate from those whose language they do not share. This trait is demonstrated today, whether in a rural, animistic, tribal context, or within a multicultural, Western local church. Language is essential to community relationships and to fellowship. God's decision to respond to the rebellion in Genesis 11 by confusing mankind's language and creating new and different ones presents a direct challenge to the missionary and pastor as they seek to reach different cultures. As John Goldingay notes, "At the end of the history of the world's origins, the Bible opens up the problem of language."[3] Linguistic diversity is thus the very context in which the nations are birthed and then acknowledged in the next chapter of Genesis.

Genesis 12: Languages and the Beginning of Missions

Genesis 12 has direct implications for God's plan of redemption regarding how distinct language and culture groups would be reconciled to Him. The chapter begins with the recognition that there now existed multiple linguistic and cultural people groups organized as nations. From these nations, God calls out one man from one nation and declares to Him that from him He would make a "great nation" (v. 2).[4]

Moreover, unlike those at Babel who sought to make for themselves a great name, here God would bless Abraham and make his name great (Gen 12:2). God's promise to bless Abraham and his descendants is not exclusive but includes "all the families of the earth" (v. 3).[5] In that phrase, all nations are represented along with God's pursuit to call out and select one specific linguistic, cultural group to first be blessed and then extend that blessing to all groups.[6]

The term *bless* in Genesis often has to do with progeny and material blessing.[7] However, in its fullest sense, Scripture makes clear in Galatians 3:8–9 that the primary blessing God intended for the nations is one of redemption

---

Interpretation 4 (Grand Rapids: Zondervan, 1990), 28.

2. Progress Bible, accessed June 18, 2024, https://progress.bible/data/.

3. John Goldingay, *Genesis*, Baker Commentary on the Old Testament: Pentateuch (Grand Rapids: Baker Academic, 2020), 192.

4. Allen Ross notes that the dispersion of the peoples in Genesis 11 is what sets up for the call of Abraham in Genesis 12. Allen Paul Ross, "The Table of Nations in Genesis" (ThD diss., Dallas Theological Seminary, 1976), 2. Kenneth Mathews notes that it is from these scattered peoples that Abraham is called. Kenneth A. Mathews, *Genesis 1–11:26*, NAC 1A (Nashville: B&H, 1996), 85.

5. Kaiser connects the judgment in Genesis 11 to God's blessing in Genesis 12 and God's call to use Abraham to bless the nations: "What the nations could not attain on their own organization and goals would now be given to them in grace." Walter C. Kaiser Jr., *Toward an Old Testament Theology* (Grand Rapids: Zondervan, 1978), 83.

6. The term *family* is more specific than a nation; it refers to extended blood families or clan groups ("הַמִּשְׁפָּחֹת," *HALOT*, 651). Cf. Genesis 36:40; Deuteronomy 29:18; Joshua 6:23; 7:14. See also John H. Sailhamer, *The Pentateuch as Narrative: A Biblical-Theological Commentary* (Grand Rapids: Zondervan, 1992), 146.

7. E.g., Genesis 17:16, 20; 22:17; 26:12. So also Kenneth A. Mathews, *Genesis 11:27–50:26*, NAC 1B (Nashville: B&H, 2005), 113–14.

and the reversal of the effects of the fall. Thus, in Genesis 12, God is calling out and setting apart what would become the nation of Israel for a particular role in advancing His plan of redemption and reveals that the scope of His redemption extends to "all the families of the earth" (v. 3).

Languages and Pentecost in Acts 2

The most important point in the Scriptures where God demonstrates the inclusivity of the gospel message and its importance in being understood across linguistic barriers is at the inauguration of the church in Acts 2. Because of the celebration of Passover, there were Jews and Jewish proselytes who had traveled back to Jerusalem from every known linguistic and cultural group that existed within the Roman Empire. Because the Jews had suffered persecution and exile both before and during the intertestamental period, they had been scattered by God, and when they took up residency in another land, they built synagogues for the purpose of maintaining their religious practices. Living among these other culture groups, the Jews had come to speak their local languages, which the apostles, being from Galilee, would not have been expected to know.[8] People were often prejudiced against Galileans (Acts 2:7). When therefore the apostles were filled with the Holy Spirit and began speaking in different tongues (v. 4), it amazed the other Jews present (v. 7).

The apostles' languages were heard by those from every language group represented in the Roman Empire, and this illustrated two things. First, God had promised that the blessing of salvation would first be presented to the Jews but that through the Jews the blessing of salvation would be communicated to the other linguistic people groups of the earth.[9] And second, the giving of the gifts of tongues, both here in Acts 2 and elsewhere in the New Testament, was the speaking of another known language (cf. vv. 8, 11).[10] Clearly used in the apostolic period, this gift was to be employed so that the gospel could begin to advance to all the families of the earth. The ability of the disciples to speak in foreign languages, and for all who were present to understand them, represented a preliminary "reversal of the curse of Babel" (until believers are glorified in heaven; Rev 5:9–10; 7:9–10).[11] Acts 2 thus shows that God's missionary heart has always been to overcome the divisions in peoples brought about by the fall and the confusion of languages at Babel.[12]

---

8. See Eckhard J. Schnabel, *Acts*, ZECNT (Grand Rapids: Zondervan, 2012), 115.

9. There is debate as to whether Luke's primary referent in "every nation under heaven" (Acts 2:5) is the different parts of the Roman Empire, or whether it is the Jewish Diaspora. See the discussion in Ajith Fernando, *Acts*, NIVAC (Grand Rapids: Zondervan, 1998), 88. Either way, Luke's narrative puts Jerusalem as the worship center of the world, with people from all around the world there to worship God.

10. Schnabel, *Acts*, 115 and 115n15. See also John MacArthur, *Strange Fire: The Danger of Offending the Holy Spirit with Counterfeit Worship* (Nashville: Thomas Nelson, 2013), 136–42; Robert L. Thomas, *Understanding Spiritual Gifts: A Verse-by-Verse Study of 1 Corinthians 12–14*, rev. ed. (Grand Rapids: Kregel, 1999), 35–37, 222–23n5.

11. So noted by F. F. Bruce, *The Book of Acts*, rev. ed., NICNT (Grand Rapids: Eerdmans, 1988), 59; recognized but not held as the preferred view by John R. W. Stott, *The Message of Acts*, 2nd ed. (Leicester, UK: Inter-Varsity Press: 1990), 68.

12. Fernando concurs and notes that from now on people will not have to come to one place (Jerusalem) to worship but could go to the far corners of the world and worship God in their own tongue. See Fernando, *Acts*, 90–91. For further parallels between

Darrell Bock further points out that the word for "dialect" in Acts 2:8 (from *dialektos*) in context most likely refers to each person's own native language. He concludes, "God is using for each group the most familiar linguistic means possible to make sure the message reaches the audience in a form they can appreciate."[13] In other words, at the very beginning of the church's founding, God showed a concern to reach people groups in their heart language, to press home the message of the gospel.

Languages and the Fulfillment of Missions in Revelation 5 and 7

The conclusion of the grand biblical storyline of the redemption of the nations was prophesied and revealed to the apostle John on Patmos, recorded in the book of Revelation. In Revelation 5 and 7, the distinctions between people groups shows that God is still concerned with the Gentiles from all over the world— even down to particular languages.

The first picture of the redeemed nations in the end is in Revelation 5:9–10. Craig Koester notes about verse 9 that unlike world empires and the beast who conquered peoples (Rev 13:7), the Lamb purchases people from the world, not through battle but through His own blood.[14] Those the Lamb purchases then have an elevated status of membership in God's kingdom as priests (5:10), just like the Israelite slaves God saved out of Egypt (Exod 19:1–6; Isa 61:6).[15]

In Revelation 7, the same pattern of Jews being reached first will continue during the tribulation period. The 144,000 Jews saved during the tribulation (Rev 7:4–8), will also be counted along with those from every tribe, tongue, and nation crying, "Salvation belongs to our God who sits on the throne, and to the Lamb" (7:10).[16] This shift from the 144,000 to a multitude emphasizes both the broad scope of God's purposes for redemption[17] and the distinction of the multitude from the Jews and one another—emphasizing the extent to which the gospel has gone throughout the entire earth.[18] This multitude that cannot be counted is the fulfillment of God's promise to Abraham to bless the families of the earth through him (Gen 12:1–3; cf. 15:5; 32:12).[19]

Now, after the apostolic period and with the completion of the canon, the church possesses the full revelation of the Scriptures. The task of translating the Scriptures into the multitude of languages is therefore a paramount task

---

Pentecost in Acts 2 and Babel in Genesis 11, see Schnabel, *Acts*, 116 and 116n23.

13. Darrell L. Bock, *Acts*, BECNT (Grand Rapids: Baker Academic, 2007), 102.

14. Craig R. Koester, *Revelation: A New Translation with Introduction and Commentary*, AB 38A (New Haven, CT: Yale University Press, 2014), 388.

15. G. K. Beale, *The Book of Revelation*, NIGTC (Grand Rapids: Eerdmans, 1999), 389.

16. For discussion on the distinctions between the 144,000 and the multitude from every tribe, tongue, and nation, as well as their setting in the seven-year tribulation period, see Robert L. Thomas, *Revelation 1–7: An Exegetical Commentary*, ed. Kenneth Barker, Wycliffe Exegetical Commentary (Chicago: Moody, 1992), 483–89.

17. Koester, *Revelation*, 428.

18. Paige Patterson, *Revelation*, NAC 39 (Nashville: B&H, 2012), 200.

19. So Beale, *Book of Revelation*, 426.

for the church. Only by doing so effectively can it extend the knowledge of Christ to those linguistic groups not yet able to read and hear the good news of the gospel in their own language, pointing toward the salvation of the multitude in Revelation.

The Urgent Need to Reconnect Pastoral Training to Bible Translation

The following statistics on Bible translation worldwide in 2022 portray the global need for Bible translation today:[20]

- 7,388 languages are spoken in the world.
- 724 languages have a full Bible.
- 1,617 languages have the complete New Testament.
- 1,248 languages have some portion of the Bible.
- 3,266 languages have work in progress.

The same year of these statistics, translation work progressed at a remarkable pace:[21]

- The largest ever annual increase of 367 new languages with work begun was recorded.
- A new translated Bible or New Testament launched almost every week.
- Scripture portions were published at the rate of almost two new languages per week.

Producing a translation is considered by many organizations today a first step to long-term missions goals. Thus, a common pathway to Bible translation is to send linguists and specialized workers to indigenous locations with minimal biblical, theological, and pastoral training. Such Bible translation as a work unto itself, regardless of its application, is the tendency of ecumenical organizations, but this can lead to unintended consequences in the global church.

The Ecumenical Direction of Bible Translation

While the upward trajectory of Bible translation projects appears encouraging, other numbers tell a different story. In 1982 the United Bible Societies listed 574 translation projects underway, which were conducted by translators from two hundred different denominational groups, of which 133 projects involved Roman Catholics.[22] Such an ecumenical approach to translation invites compromises to textual accuracy because interpretive biases are inserted, which are driven by denominational doctrines and a low view of Scripture—especially by those denominations that have abandoned Scripture's inerrancy and the Roman Catholic

---

20. Jeremy Weightman, "Record-Breaking Year for Bible Translation!" March 30, 2022, https://wycliffe.org.uk/story/record-breaking-year.

21. Weightman, "Record-Breaking Year."

22. George M. Cowan, "Bible Translation Since John Wycliffe," *Christian History* 2, no. 3 (1983): 27–30; https://christianhistoryinstitute.org/magazine/article/bible-translation-since-john-wycliffe.

Church, which considers its interpretations equally authoritative to Scripture.

Furthermore, many Bible translators take a "hands-off" approach that separates translation work from church planting, evangelism, and discipleship.[23] Training people to focus only on linguistics has the advantage of speeding up the language and translation skill acquisition process. However, such an effort marks a separation of translation efforts from the goal of transforming the reader and the believing community through the text-oriented activities of evangelism, discipleship, church planting, local elder training, and pastoral training. Waiting until the biblical text is in hand to begin the ministry of the Word risks leaving many places with a project that has stalled, failed, or has never been released from the publisher, and—as the ultimate consequence—with no gospel witness.

However, an effective Bible translation assumes there will be a church ready to use it when it becomes available. A translation process that is conducted simultaneously with evangelistic and church-planting efforts is a more biblical approach.

The Necessity of Pastoral Training for Translation Work

Bible translators must be reconnected to theological and seminary training, specifically at a level of preparation that provides the missionary candidate with the biblical, exegetical, theological, and pastoral tool kit to be equipped for pastoral ministry anywhere.

Students who have embraced their responsibility to accurately know and interpret the biblical languages for careful sermon preparation are on their way to becoming pastor-theologians and pastor-translators who will spend their lives giving the utmost attention to biblical interpretation so that they translate and explain the text with clarity and accuracy.[24]

Many pastors recognize Bible translation as an essential task for discipleship on the mission field. Yet pragmatism has now begun to overtake the philosophies of many translation agencies. Completing a Bible for every spoken language is a noble goal. But pragmatism, such as valuing quantity over quality, makes that goal a slave to haste. Leaders' passionate statements, such as "We can complete the work of Bible translation in our lifetime," are compelling, but their expediency begins to inform method. Translation requires painstaking diligence to understand unwritten languages and cultural meaning. When accuracy is sacrificed, it often leads to misinterpretations of key biblical doctrines.

Part of this threat is that today's missionary Bible translators usually hold degrees in linguistics but rarely in theological studies, and few possess graduate training in the biblical

---

23. Paul Edwards of Wycliffe Bible Translators stated, "Wycliffe missionaries don't evangelize, teach theology, hold Bible studies, or start churches. They give (preliterate people) a written language. . . . They teach them to read and write in their mother tongue." Electa Draper, "Bible Translators Hope to Have Every Language Covered in 15 Years," *Denver Post*, June 21, 2010, updated May 6, 2016, https://www.denverpost.com/2010/06/21/bible-translators-hope-to-have-every-language-covered-in-15-years/.

24. I am indebted to Kyle Davis of Bible Translation Fellowship for coining and developing the apt title "pastor-translator."

languages in particular. D. A. Carson observes this reality in his friendly critiques of SIL (formerly Summer Institute of Linguistics) and Wycliffe Bible Translators:

> I am a huge admirer of their work, some of it undertaken in highly challenging circumstances. Some of [the translators] are linguistically well trained. But I have to say that rather few of them are trained in exegesis, biblical theology, or systematic theology. Very few of them have an MDiv, let alone more advanced training. With rare exceptions, I have not found them to be deep readers of Scripture, with the result that their approaches to translation challenges tend to be atomistic. No one can be an expert in everything, of course—but if I have any hope for this book [i.e., *Jesus: The Son of God*], it is that some of these diligent and learned workers will begin to see the importance for Bible translation of the considerations I am advancing here, and that more of them will pursue advanced theological training as part of their preparation for a life in translation.[25]

Since many contemporary translators have little to no theological education and are instead only trained as experts in linguistics, their consideration is given more to the technicalities of the local language than to the biblical languages. Their focus can allow for less priority given to biblical authorial intent in the process of cross-cultural translation.[26] However, well-trained pastors are most concerned and careful to see where cultural accommodations can lead to misinterpreting the Bible, which can cause confusion and even discredit the Bible. Thus, there is a need for those trained in doctrine and pastoral ministry to move into translation, and for translators to be involved in training nationals for the work of translation, evangelism, and discipleship.

It is simply not enough to be a linguist and Bible translator. Either the translator must work in tandem with church planters, or, ideally, the church planter must himself be an indigenous Bible translator who has a strong, biblical, theological, and pastoral foundation. Then he will have the necessary training to ensure a translation that is both accurate to the original intent and serves as part of a broader Great Commission effort.

Pastors, professors, and translators must stop and examine the collective influences of the last forty years in missiology. In reality, church leaders, entrusted with the responsibility to raise up and send out missionaries, are often illiterate when it comes to knowing the internal battle for translation work. Instead, they are

---

25. D. A. Carson, *Jesus the Son of God: A Title Often Overlooked, Sometimes Misunderstood, and Currently Disputed* (Wheaton, IL: Crossway, 2012), 107–8.

26. Biblical accuracy is sacrificed when haste is coupled with the increasing desire to contextualize the Bible and not offend a religious group. See, for example, the insider movement among Muslims and their offense at the translations of "the Son of God" and "the Father." In these cases, translators wrongfully opt to intentionally avoid translating the Scriptures accurately in the name of better reaching the lost. For further discussion, see David Garner, "Inside the Insider Movement," Westminster Theological Seminary Faculty Resources, July 2, 2013, https://faculty.wts.edu/posts/inside-the-insider-movement/.

enamored with the urgent call to complete the task in their lifetime, and they unintentionally send their best missionary prospects through agencies and translation training programs only to then learn that their own convictions about translations are downplayed by those with whom their missionaries work. This can lead not only to poor translation but to discouragement, division, and ultimately reassignment of the missionary, either back home or to another field. Therefore, pastors should carefully investigate the issues of translation that those whom they send out will encounter, to ensure the care, protection, and stewardship of lives and financial resources of their church.

The Future of Bible Translation

Modern Bible translation proponents tend to espouse the motto "Bring the Bible to unreached people groups," which can disconnect from the church-planting focus of biblical missions. However, those that see translations as essentially linked to disciple-making operate with a different motto: "Mature churches become sending churches become translating churches." They hold the long view of Bible translation, that the Word of God must penetrate further and further dialect groups, and

that dialect translations are ultimately the work of local believers rather than missionaries.

Ultimately, the most accurate and effective Bible translation will be one that is done by nationals, who themselves are pastorally and theologically trained. These are pastors who not only know their culture well but are trained to understand theology, hermeneutics, and original languages. They will not supplant the accuracy and authority of the Scriptures in their culture. This is the most effective and faithful way to mature believers in a church, from which the next generation of pastor-translators can arise.

The church, wherever it is located and whatever cultural context it is in, needs an accurate Bible translation. It is a matter of getting the gospel right, as well as aiding the sanctification of believers and giving them confidence to study the Scriptures for themselves. Bridging the gap between pastoral ministry and translation will correct the drift in philosophy of recent decades, and it will ensure that national pastors can preach from an accurate Bible version, which will instill confidence in their congregation and will be used by God to raise up the next generation of church leaders. These will then become the Bible translators and church planters of tomorrow.

CHAPTER 49

The Rationale for Bible Translation

Aaron Shryock

The Scriptures have been translated for over two millennia, beginning with Jewish scholars in Alexandria, Egypt, in approximately 250 BC and extending to modern work ongoing around the globe, involving thousands of translators, church leaders, and common Christians eager to be a part of having the Bible in their own languages.[1] There have been periods in the history of the church when translation was forbidden but also periods of intense work. Through these distinct periods, translators, missionaries, and theologians have written about the rationales for their work and the broader importance of having the Scriptures in their own language.

This chapter surveys the most significant rationales for Bible translation, classifying them into five groups. An early and recurring argument is based on historical precedence. Second, translators have often referred to the benefits of having the Scriptures as part of their reason for translation. Third, the proclamation of the gospel message to the nations has been a rationale for translation, often based on the Great Commission (Matt 28:18–20). Fourth, following the Reformation, translators and theologians have viewed the scriptural injunctions to read and study the Scriptures as the reasons for translation. Finally, some translators have suggested that translation is an act of obedience to God, who wills that Scripture be preserved and transmitted to His people in every generation and every language group.

After surveying these rationales, the chapter concludes with an evaluation of the relative importance of these rationales. Translators must attribute the appropriate importance to each and ultimately engage in this strategic ministry with a sure conviction that their endeavors glorify the triune God.

---

1. Philip A. Noss, "History of Bible Translation," in *A Guide to Bible Translation: People, Languages, and Topics*, ed. Philip A. Noss and Charles S. Houser (Maitland, FL: Xulon, 2019), 494–98.

Historical Precedence

One of the earliest and most enduring rationales for Bible translation is historical precedence. That is, translators have mentioned earlier works of translation as grounds for their own. Furthermore, the miraculous work of the Holy Spirit at Pentecost has been cited as a precedent for translation over the centuries. More recently the incarnation and earthly ministry of Jesus Christ has been cited for the same in a missionary context. In each case, the accepted appropriateness of some prior event is the rationale for translation.

An early appeal to precedence appears in a preface written by King Alfred of Wessex. During the later years of his reign (AD 871–899), he instituted religious reform and a program of translation into Anglo-Saxon (Old English).[2] In the preface to his translation of Pope Gregory I's book *Pastoral Care*, he justifies translation this way:

> Then I remembered how the law was first known in Hebrew, and again, when the Greeks had learnt it, they translated the whole of it into their own language, and all other books besides. And again the Romans, when they had learnt it, they translated the whole of it through learned interpreters into their own language. And also all other Christian nations translated a part of them into their own language. Therefore it seems better to me, if ye think so, for us also to translate.[3]

Alfred went on to summarize major events in Bible translation, even noting that other Christian nations of his time apparently had at least a portion of Scripture in their own language. Based on the appropriateness of these prior translations, he proposed that more translating be undertaken in his kingdom.

Several centuries later, John Wycliffe (ca. 1329–1384) and his associates at Oxford University translated the first complete English Bible, working from the Latin texts available at that time.[4] In the general prologue to that translation, the anonymous writer defends the project by referring to the prior works of Bede (ca. 673–735) and King Alfred in English, as well as alluding to translations in other contemporary languages such as French and Czech.[5] Given the past and present works of translation, the author reasoned, there was no legitimate case for opposing an English Bible.

Another argument based on historical precedence focuses on the work of the Holy Spirit in the early church. After the publication of the Wycliffe Bible, a pamphlet titled

---

2. Lynn Long, "Alfred," in *A Guide to Bible Translation: People, Languages, and Topics*, ed. Philip A. Noss and Charles S. Houser (Maitland, FL: Xulon, 2019), 7.

3. Henry Sweet, *King Alfred's West Saxon Version of Gregory's Pastoral Care* (London: Trubner and Co. for Early English Text Society, 1871), 5–6.

4. Paul Ellingworth, "Wycliffe, John," in *A Guide to Bible Translation: People, Languages, and Topics*, ed. Philip A. Noss and Charles S. Houser (Maitland, FL: Xulon, 2019), 63–64.

5. John Wycliffe et al., "Prologue," *The Holy Bible Containing the Old and New Testaments with the Apocryphal Books in the Earliest English Versions Made from the Latin Vulgate by John Wycliffe and His Followers*, ed. Josiah Forshall and Sir Frederic Madden (Oxford: Oxford University Press, 1850), 59–60.

Wycliffe's Wyckett was published.[6] It defended Bible translation against detractors by appealing to the miraculous manner in which the Holy Spirit empowered believers to speak in other languages at Pentecost and on subsequent occasions:

> They say it is heresy to speak of the holy Scripture in English, and so they would condemn the Holy Ghost that gave it [the Word of God] in tongues to the apostles of Christ, as it is written to speak the Word of God in all languages that were ordained of God under heaven, as it is written.
>
> And the Holy Ghost descended upon the heathen, as he did upon the apostles in Jerusalem, as it is written (Joel ii.); and Christ were so merciful to send the Holy Ghost to the heathen men (Acts viii.x), and he made them partakers of his blessed word; why should it then be taken from us in this land that be Christian men?[7]

The pamphlet's writer also noted that the Holy Spirit empowered the apostles as well as Gentile believers to speak in various languages. He argued that the Holy Spirit established a precedent for preaching in "all languages," which would eventually include English.

It should be assumed that translating the Scriptures is appropriate because it is part of the larger task of making known the Word of God to every language community. Instead of translation being an act of heresy, the writer charged those who opposed translation as condemning the Holy Spirit who established the precedent.

Pentecost remains a significant event for Bible translators. In a recent work on the theology and mission of translation, Stephen Watters and Zachary Watters write, "Pentecost set in motion one of the unique characteristics of Christianity as a world religion, and this is its penchant for translation. . . . The Hebrew and Aramaic spoken by Jesus was translated into Greek; Greek was translated into a host of contemporary languages of that time: Syriac, Arabic, Coptic, and Latin."[8]

Finally, the incarnation of Jesus Christ has been argued to be a precedent for translation. In a work on the history of Christian missions, historian Andrew Walls proposes that the incarnation was an act of "divine translation."[9] He suggests, "There is a history of translation of the Bible because there was a translation of the Word into flesh" (cf. John 1:14).[10] Walls's proposals have been widely received, and the incarnation is possibly the most common rationale related to historical precedence cited today.

---

6. Robert Vaughan, ed., *The Tracts and Treatises of John De Wycliffe* (London: Blackburn and Pardon, 1845), 273–84.

7. Vaughan, 275.

8. This is not to say, however, that Jesus did not also speak Greek. Stephen Watters and Zachary Watters, "Language Diversity: A 'Happy Fault' for the Church," in *God and Language: Exploring the Role of Language in the Mission of God*, ed. Michael Greed and Dawn Kruger (Victoria, CA: Lean, 2022), 365.

9. Andrew F. Walls, *The Missionary Movement in Christian History: Studies in the Transmission of Faith* (Maryknoll, NY: Orbis, 1996), 26.

10. Walls, 26.

Referring to Walls's view on translation as the incarnation model, Carlo Buzzetti wrote, "The incarnation model must continue: it is the great model of the relationship between God and the world. The Word always becomes incarnate in the human words of its receptors; to translate it is to enable it to go forward embodied."[11]

Benefits for the Readers of Scripture

A second rationale for Bible translation focuses on the reader and the benefits that come from reading the Scriptures. From the Wycliffe Bible of 1380 until today, translators have engaged in their task with the hope that readers might come to faith in Jesus Christ (Acts 8:25–40; Rom 10:17; 16:25–27; 2 Tim 3:15; 1 Pet 1:23). Another rationale is that Christian readers would have the opportunity to grow in their faith (John 17:17; 1 Pet 2:2) and find comfort and hope (Rom 15:4; 1 Thess 4:18; Rev 1:3; 22:7). In each case, the reason for translation focuses on the positive impact of the translation on the readers.

Regarding salvation for the reader, in the prologue to the Wycliffe Bible, the writer provides several reasons for the translation, including his desire that everyone in the English realm be saved.[12] Another case is the German missionary Bartholomäus Ziegenbalg (1682–1719), who translated the New Testament and portions of the Old Testament into Tamil. In 1714 he wrote to the king of Denmark, "We believe that God's word in mother tongue is the surest means of converting non-Christians and making them members of God's Kingdom."[13]

Over a century later, the English missionary William Carey (1761–1834) and his colleagues highlighted the importance of Bible translation for salvation. In 1819 they wrote, "Unless heathen nations can obtain the oracles of God, they must perish without any knowledge of the way of salvation. On the translation, therefore, of the Sacred Scriptures into their languages is suspended, in a great measure, the eternal destiny of unborn millions of our fellow-creatures."[14]

In terms of the believing reader's growth and comfort, William Tyndale (ca. 1490/94–1536) is exemplary. In 1526 he translated the New Testament into English, and in 1530 he published the book *A Pathway into the Holy Scripture*. In the latter, he explained to his readers that he had translated the Bible "for your spiritual edifying, consolation, and solace."[15] Likewise, the Reformer Juan Pérez de Pineda (ca. 1500–1567),

---

11. Carlo Buzzetti, "Churches and Scripture Translation," in *A Guide to Bible Translation: People, Languages, and Topics*, ed. Philip A. Noss and Charles S. Houser (Maitland, FL: Xulon, 2019), 348.

12. Wycliffe et al., "Prologue," 57.

13. Daniel Jeyaraj, *Bartholomäus Ziegenbalg: The Father of Modern Protestant Mission: An Indian Assessment* (New Delhi; Chennai, India: Indian Society for Promoting Christian Knowledge; Gurukul Lutheran Theological College and Research Institute, 2006), 218.

14. William Carey, Joshua Marshman, and William Ward, *College for the Instruction of Asiatic Christian and Other Youth in Eastern Literature and European Science, at Serampore, Bengal* (London: Black, Kingsbury, Parbury, and Allen, 1819), 28.

15. William Tyndale, *The Works of William Tyndale*, vol. 1, *Doctrinal Treatises and Introductions to Different Portions of the Holy Scriptures*, ed. Henry Walter (Cambridge: Cambridge University Press, 1848), 7.

in the preface to his New Testament in Spanish, emphasized the importance of translation for truly understanding Jesus Christ and what he accomplished, as well as for guarding believers from error and false teaching (cf. Acts 17:11; Gal 1:9; 1 Tim 6:3–4; Titus 1:9).[16]

Especially noteworthy is *The Westminster Confession of Faith*, published in England in 1646. The confession includes several arguments for Bible translation, especially noting that believers have a "right unto" as well as an "interest in" the Scriptures in translation.[17] The expression "interest in" refers to the spiritual benefits of having Scripture; the confession then refers to two such benefits. First, it notes that believers are able to offer acceptable worship because they have the Word of God and it can dwell plentifully in them. Second, believers have hope because of the patience and comfort that come through the Scriptures.[18] In this context, it appears that the "right" also includes personal ownership for reading and studying, so that the people of God receive the fullest spiritual benefit intended for them through the Word.

Christ's Command to Proclaim the Gospel

A third rationale for Bible translation focuses on Christ's commands to proclaim the gospel and make disciples of all nations. From the Reformation until today, translators have viewed their task as an act of obedience to Jesus Christ, as part of equipping others to be obedient and, ultimately fulfilling the Great Commission. For example, during the Reformation, the French humanist Jacques Lefèvre d'Étaples (ca. 1460–1536) translated the Bible into French. In response to his critics, he wrote in the preface in 1524,

> And doesn't he also say through Saint Mark "go through the world and preach the gospel to all creatures"? And through Saint Matthew "teaching them to keep all that I have commanded you"? And how will they teach them to keep Christ's commandments if they don't want the people to see and read the gospel of God in his own language?[19]

In 1535 John Calvin (1509–1564) also wrote in defense of Bible translation.[20] Following Lefèvre, Calvin noted that Jesus sent His apostles and disciples throughout the world to preach to every creature in every language (Matt 28:19ff.; Acts 2:4, 8; cf. Mark 16:15). He then drew the implication that Christians should preach and teach the gospel to every ethnicity (Rom 1:14) and, further, that if every

---

16. Peter Hasbrouk, "Enzinas to Valera: Motives, Methods, and Sources in Sixteenth-Century Spanish Bible Translation" (PhD diss., Boston University, 2015), 120–21.

17. *WCF* 1.8.

18. *WCF*; cf. 1.1.

19. Stéphane Simonnin, "Humanism and the Bible: The Contribution of Jacques Lefèvre d'Étaples," *Unio cum Christo* 2, no. 1 (April 2016): 112.

20. W. H. Neuser, "The First Outline of Calvin's Theology—The Preface to the New Testament in the Olivetan Bible of 1535," *Koers* 66, no. 1, 2 (2001): 38–39.

ethnic group should hear the gospel, they should also read and study the Scriptures, which contain the gospel and which provide the means for them to grow in their faith (2 Tim 3:16). Thus, Calvin regarded the translation of Scripture as nothing less than a command of Jesus Christ.

Bible translators continue to view their task as an act of obedience to the Great Commission. More recently, George Cowan wrote in his book *The Word That Kindles*,

> Christ's command to his followers to make disciples of all nations included "teaching them to obey everything I have commanded you" (Matt. 28:20). The Bible alone preserves what Christ commanded his disciples. . . . Implicit is the assumption that the biblical text would be available. Translation of the Bible is part of our obedience to his command.[21]

William Barrick likewise underscored the importance of Bible translation for evangelization in obedience to the Great Commission when he wrote,

> If Christians are going to be obedient to the Scriptures (Matt. 28:19–20), they must involve themselves in spreading the message about Christ. The Scriptures themselves carry

that message best. . . . Evangelization necessitates translating the Bible into the common language of common people. A significant corollary to this truth notes that churches must place a priority on the ministry of Bible translation for the world's mission fields.[22]

Scriptural Commands for Believers to Read Scripture

The fourth rationale for Bible translation is based on the scriptural injunctions for the people of God to read the Scriptures (e.g., Deut 11:18; 31:11; Josh 1:8; Isa 34:16; Jer 36:6; 1 Tim 4:13; cf. Matt 12:3; 19:4; 22:31). During the Protestant Reformation, several theologians articulated the view that all believers should have access to Scripture so that they could read them for themselves—a response to the Roman Catholic position that only clergy (or other Latin readers) could read the Scriptures. For example, the French Reformer Theodore Beza (1519–1605) wrote in his systematic theology, "Now that the unlearned and unskillful may with fruit be conversant in the reading hereof, it is needful that the Bible be translated into the mother tongue of all Christian people. Therefore we do also condemn the said Papists, who will not allow of such translations."[23] Thus, for the Reformers, though they did not

---

21. George M. Cowan, *The Word That Kindles* (Chappaqua, New York: Christian Herald Books, 1979), 26–27.

22. William D. Barrick, *Understanding Bible Translation: Bringing God's Word into New Contexts* (Grand Rapids: Kregel, 2019), 56.

23. Theodore Beza, *Propositions and principles of diuinitie propounded and disputed in the vniuersitie of Geneua, by certaine students of diuinitie there, vnder M. Theod. Beza, and M. Anthonie Faius . . . Wherein is contained a methodicall summarie, or epitome of the common places of diuinitie. Translated out of Latine into English, to the end that the causes, both of the present dangers of that Church, and also of the troubles of those that are hardlie dealt vvith els-vvhere, may appeare in the English tongue* (Edinburgh, 1591; reproduced, Ann Arbor: Text Creation Partnership, 2011), §52.11, accessed June 18, 2024, https://quod.lib.umich.edu/cgi/t/text/text-idx?c=eebo2;idno=A10250.0001.001.

dismiss the importance of historical precedence nor the implications of the Great Commission, it was imperative to provide a rationale based on the explicit commands of Scripture.

For instance, in 1588 the Cambridge theologian William Whitaker (1548–1595) published *Disputations on Holy Scripture*, an influential defense of the Reformed doctrines of Scripture. Whitaker wrote, "The scriptures are to be set forth before all Christians in their vernacular tongues, so as that every individual may be enabled to read them."[24] He supported this with several passages from Deuteronomy that show that God revealed the Scriptures to His people for them to read and obey (6:6–9; 17:19, 20; 31:11, 12).[25] Then, turning to the New Testament, he argued that Jesus' words in John 5:39 to "search the Scriptures" were an invitation to educated and uneducated alike to read and study the Bible.[26]

Likewise, the Italian theologian Francis Turretin (1623–1687) provided an in-depth discussion of the need for Bible translations.[27] His first rationale for translation was the explicit obligation to read the Scriptures, followed by the proclamation of the gospel and then a lengthy discussion of historical precedence. *The Westminster Confession*, besides the rationales above, also affirmed translation on the basis of God's command to "read and search" the Scriptures, incorporating the argumentation of William Whitaker.[28]

God's Will for Scripture in All Ages

The final reason for translation focuses on God and His relationship to the Scriptures and the church. Given that God is the author of Scripture and is providentially working to ensure that the Scriptures are preserved and accessible to His people, translators have a responsibility to transmit divine revelation on behalf of the people of God in obedience to His will.

In 1535 John Calvin wrote in the preface to the French New Testament that Bible translation was God's will, for it was God's will for His truth to reign over all humanity by the work of the Holy Spirit and through the comprehension of the gospel of Jesus Christ.[29] *The Westminster Confession* affirms the same insofar

---

24. William Whitaker, *A Disputation on Holy Scripture against the Papists, Especially Bellarmine and Stapleton* (Cambridge: The University Press, 1779), 235.

25. Whitaker, 235–36.

26. Whitaker, 236, 240. The verb "search" here was understood by many faithful believers as an imperative because the Greek text of John 5:39 read as such (*ereunate*) in the first printed Greek New Testaments published in the sixteenth century. But with the advance of text critical studies by faithful churchmen, Greek testaments from the nineteenth century onward have usually rendered this verb in the indicative, "You (do) search" (*eraunate*), based on the available manuscript evidence, which is now much fuller and better in quality. Let it be noted, however, that this textual variant does not affect Jesus' argument in John 5, which can be understood with either reading, and that the command to read the Scriptures, whatever one's station, is found throughout the Scriptures besides being implied in John 5 also.

27. Francis Turretin, *The Doctrine of Scripture: Locus 2 of Institutio of Theologiae Elencticae*, John Beardslee, ed. and trans. (Grand Rapids: Baker, 1981), 147–50.

28. *WCF* 1.8; John Valero Fesko, *The Theology of the Westminster Standards: Historical Context and Theological Insights* (Wheaton, IL: Crossway, 2014), 91.

29. Neuser, "First Outline of Calvin's Theology," 38–39.

as its article that exhorts Bible translation[30] is a consequence of the first article of that chapter (and of the entire confession), which explains that it was God's will to reveal Himself to His people in writing (cf. Heb 1:1–2) and so to make that Scripture necessary for all mankind (cf. Matt 4:4; Rom 15:4).[31] Therefore, Scripture propagated in the language of every man is God's will.

Some translators view the translation and dissemination of the Bible as one part of God's preservation of divine revelation for His people. The Haitian Bible translator Hantz Bernard wrote, "God has been providentially using men for millennia in order to transmit His Word in the form of translations. That is why today we can use many translations, whether those of the past or those of today, whether in English or in Creole, for personal devotions, teaching, or preaching."[32] It follows that individual believers and the corporate church have a right to Scripture as well as a responsibility to ensure that others have access to God's revelation. By translating Scripture, the church fulfills God's will for it by taking part in His preserving work and by propagating His will for mankind.

Evaluation

Over the centuries, Bible translators, theologians, and missionaries have offered different rationales for translating the Scriptures. It falls now to this chapter to review and evaluate them. As noted above, appeals to historical precedence may be the earliest and most prevalent rationale. It can be very persuasive because it builds on a past event that is accepted as appropriate, if not exemplary. However, appeals to some precedent do not necessarily recognize God as the author of divine revelation, nor do they necessarily recognize the authoritative commands of Scripture. Consequently, historical precedence should be strengthened with rationales derived explicitly from the Scriptures.

From the time of John Wycliffe through the Reformation and until today, translators have argued for their work from the blessings that the Scripture imparts to readers. Translators should indeed reflect on the potential benefits of Scripture in a given language and, when the work is completed, rejoice in how the Spirit works through the Bible to change lives. The focus on the benefits of Scripture, though, should also be strengthened by a more basic appeal to the manner by which the Holy Spirit works in people's lives through the Scriptures. Anyone can affirm the reading of the Bible for various benefits without assenting to its authority or divine origin.[33] But the Bible translator is interested particularly in the Holy Spirit's work through the reading, preaching, teaching,

---

30. *WCF* 1.8.

31. *WCF* 1.1.

32. Hantz Bernard, "The Autograph Though Dead Yet Speaketh: On the Translation of the Copies," in *God's Word in Our Hands: The Bible Preserved for Us*, ed. James Williams and Randolph Shaylor (Greenville, SC: Ambassador Emerald International, 2003), 323.

33. E.g., Mortimer J. Adler and Charles van Doren, *How to Read a Book: The Classic Guide to Intelligent Reading* (New York: Touchstone, 2014), 218, 287–88.

and singing of the Bible as the truths of God are comprehended (Pss 19:7–8; 119:18; John 6:63; 14:26; 1 Cor 2:4, 12–16; 2 Cor 3:14–18; Eph 1:13; 6:17; Col 3:16; 1 Thess 1:5; 1 John 2:26–27).

During the Reformation, the Reformers argued for the authority of Scripture over the traditions of the Roman Catholic Church. Translators such as Jacques Lefèvre d'Étaples argued for translation based on Jesus Christ's commands to proclaim the gospel and teach believers the rest of His commands. Reformers such as Theodore Beza and William Whitaker focused on the biblical command to read the Scriptures. These rationales are more compelling than the previous, given that they are based on the authority of the Bible for the church. Furthermore, they focus on the primary activity through which the Holy Spirit works, that is, comprehension of biblical truth by reading or hearing the Bible read aloud. Thus, both of these reasons should be in sharp focus for translators today.

Finally, some translators have suggested that the rationale for Bible translation be found in God's will for Scripture and His people. From this perspective, translation is not a task that is simply a prerequisite for obedience to a specific command, such as the Great Commission (Matt 28:18–20; Luke 24:44–49; John 20:19–23) or "the public reading of Scripture" (1 Tim 4:13; cf. Deut 31:9–13; Acts 15:21). The act of translation, in and of itself, is an act of obedience to God, who wills that His divine revelation be preserved and transmitted to His people in every generation and every language group. Thus, translators glorify the triune God through a task not explicitly commanded in Scripture but which is, nonetheless, an integral part of God's will.

These rationales contribute to a fuller understanding of the importance of translation and should be an encouragement to those doing the work or considering it in their path. An evaluation has been offered here, but regardless of the relative importance that translators ascribe to these five rationales, it is essential to recognize their collective weight. Namely, it is that translation is an act of obedience to Christ that accomplishes the will of God the Father by the power of the Holy Spirit. It is a work that glorifies the triune God as the translator ministers on behalf of His people. The final doxology of Romans 16 is therefore a fitting end to this chapter. That is, since the mystery of the gospel has been revealed by the Scriptures according to the commandment of the eternal God to all the nations (v. 26), "to the only wise God, through Jesus Christ, be the glory forever. Amen" (v. 27).

CHAPTER 50

The Word of God and Translation Faithfulness

Chris Burnett

Scripture is the sufficient authority for cross-cultural gospel engagement. The words of the Bible in their original sentence structures, paragraphs, and contexts are true, authoritative, and universal in scope. Yet the words were historically and culturally shaped by the Holy Spirit and the human authors in the process of divine inspiration (2 Tim 3:16; 2 Pet 1:21). Faithful disciples who translate the Scriptures for new language groups strive to accurately convey the fixed meaning of the original words in their syntactical arrangements in new contexts that might not have similar words or sentence structures.

These theological assertions are not foregone conclusions for many Bible interpreters and translators today. Secular linguistic philosophy often posits that words and the arrangement of words are historically, linguistically, and culturally relative, making them subject to a variety of contextual meanings rather than one fixed, original meaning.[1] Scholars have argued that it is impossible to verify a factual idea or truth represented by a word or sentence if the meaning of the word or sentence is linked to the speaker's cultural, familial, and societal context[2] or if it cannot be corroborated by observable data and proven to actually mean something, whether true or not.[3]

Contrarily, scholars who believe that every word of the Bible accurately represents God's intended meaning affirm that the meaning of the words can be portrayed accurately in new contexts, even though the biblical writers wrote

1. See the cultural-linguistic expressivism ("language-game") of Ludwig Wittgenstein (1889–1951) in his *Philosophical Investigations*, trans. G. E. M. Anscombe, P. M. S. Hacker, and Joachim Schulte, ed. P. M. S. Hacker and Joachim Schulte, 4th ed. (Oxford: Wiley-Blackwell, 2009).

2. See Donald Davidson's "Truth and Meaning" (1967), "True to Facts" (1969), and "Reply to Foster" (1976), in Donald Davidson, *Inquiries into Truth and Interpretation*, 2nd ed. (Oxford: Clarendon, 2001), 17–54.

3. See the "logical positivism" theory in Michael Dummett and John Crossley, eds., *Formal Systems and Recursive Functions: Proceedings of the Eighth Logic Colloquium, Oxford 1963* (Amsterdam: North-Holland, 1965).

those words in subjective historical, literary, and cultural contexts to original audiences. Bible translation and biblical exposition rely on the words and arrangements of words in Scripture to mean today what they have always meant, rich with life-giving, spiritual significance. The goal of this brief chapter is to provide theological, hermeneutical, and linguistic support for Bible translators, so they pursue accuracy at the word level with the expectation that an accurate translation in any receptor language can be accomplished. The chapter begins with two theological statements about Scripture's reliability and universal applicability and then considers the value of the words of the Bible from hermeneutical and linguistic vantage points.

The Theology of Scripture as God's Truth for All Peoples

Scripture does not shy away from bold claims about its own divine origination and absolute veracity for all people. The following discussions outline Scripture's transcendence and its universal relevance. Scripture's witness about itself sets the imperative for Bible translators and expositors: to declare God's words as the living voice of God, bound to no single cultural experience but intended to redeem people from every tribe and tongue.

Scripture Self-Attests to Its Veracity

The evangelical reads Scripture with the theological expectation that it delivers true spiritual knowledge. Scripture must be read with divinely enlightened eyes of faith in the person and work of the triune God in order to be spiritually understood, for faith grants the regenerate believer "the assurance of things hoped for, the conviction of things not seen" (Heb 11:1; cf. v. 6). To the regenerate reader, Scripture captures the overarching reality of all things, beyond the sentence, external to the mind of the human author, and outside of the perceptible world. It does this in expressions the reader can understand grammatically.

Because Scripture is "breathed out" by God (2 Tim 3:16), the propositions, which are His own words, must transmit the meaning He intended by using them. By His own words, He created all things and enabled the human capacity to communicate His truth with other people. This means that Scripture provides the "controlling beliefs about language and translation," because all people utilize human forms of language that flow from God as the source of all language.[4]

Additionally, Scripture exhibits an internal consistency of meaning throughout the canon, though its authorship spans fifteen centuries, three continents, and three languages, thus providing an implicit rationale for rooting spiritual knowledge in the words of Scripture: God consistently means what He says whenever and wherever He says it.[5] The terms for "truth" in the Old and New Testaments (Heb. *emeth*; Gk. *alētheia*) portray "that which is conformed to

---

4. Karen H. Jobes, "Relevance Theory and the Translation of Scripture," *JETS* 50, no. 4 (December 2007): 777.

5. According to traditional evangelical theologian Paul Helm, "If the Scriptures are the Word of God, then, properly interpreted, the sentences of Scripture will be at least logically consistent with each other. This follows from the fact that if the Scriptures are the

reality in contrast to anything that would be erroneous or deceitful."[6] Scripture bears witness to its true and faithful nature as God's truth (Ps 119:160; John 17:17) and, in the face of deceit, is "worthy of confidence."[7]

The composite picture that emerges from Scripture's statements as to its own veracity is that "the full Bible concept of truth involves factuality, faithfulness, and completeness"[8] because the truths of Scripture are expressed by words in complete, definitive, and full-orbed ways. Scripture witnesses to its truthfulness because it is indeed true, and Scripture is true because it reflects who God is.

Scripture Is Both Transcendent and Culture-Bound

Scripture does not deny that differences in human languages and cultures challenge the accurate communication of objective biblical truth. Thus, it is important to study the historical, linguistic, and cultural contexts to understand their role in shaping the overall form of life that affects the receptor audience.[9] Because truth is objective and language is subjective, the divinely revealed propositions are both universal in scope and capable of being accurately translated into any receptor language. Thus, no matter how great the contextual differences might appear between the original and receptor languages and cultures, the biblical text can be appropriately understood and, as a result, fully obeyed.

The evangelical can affirm the transcendent and absolute truth of Scripture while also recognizing that it was recorded in culture-bound language by human authors. Through their historical setting and in specific literary genres, the prophets and apostles communicated truth in full to their socially, culturally, and generationally diverse receptor audiences. The biblical writers were responsive to their audiences and adjusted the communicative process in order to be fully understood, just as any missionary must do in a new culture.[10] There is no reason to suggest that any change to the message is necessary when delivering the divine propositions of Scripture to a foreign audience. Therefore, the objective truth of Scripture is of utmost importance to understand and convey, no matter the cultural or linguistic constraints of the original words and

Word of God, then, properly interpreted, the sentences are true. And if a set of propositions is true, the propositions must be consistent with each other." Paul Helm, "Faith, Evidence, and the Scriptures," in *Scripture and Truth*, ed. D. A. Carson and John D. Woodbridge (Grand Rapids: Baker, 1992), 316.

6. Roger Nicole, "The Biblical Concept of Truth," in *Scripture and Truth*, ed. D. A. Carson and John D. Woodbridge (Grand Rapids: Baker, 1992), 287–302, with definition on 290. The term *alētheia* represents both the quality and the content of that which conforms to reality. So delineated in "ἀλήθεια," BDAG, 42.

7. As recognized in Nicole, 293–94, with support from Romans 1:25; 3:7; 15:8.

8. Nicole, 296.

9. According to Jobes' relevance theory, "God is responsible for the diversity of languages in the world and therefore can use that diversity to his purposes. . . . Because God created the rules by which language works, human language offers no barrier to his purposes nor can it frustrate his ability to communicate." Jobes, "Relevance Theory and the Translation of Scripture," 779.

10. Philip Edgcumbe Hughes, "The Problem of Historical Relativity," in *Scripture and Truth*, ed. D. A. Carson and John D. Woodbridge (Grand Rapids: Baker, 1992), 174.

arrangements of words themselves or of the cultural environment in which the missionary will communicate the message.

The Hermeneutics of Biblical Propositions as Vehicles of Truth

To conservative evangelicals, biblical interpretation is not solely a literary matter but a theological conviction that traces back to the definition of a biblical "proposition." The term *proposition* refers to words arranged syntactically to provide meaning. The propositions of Scripture are not simply words placed in a sequence by a human author to mean something potentially true. They are words delivered by the eternal, triune God that constitute the basis of all truth; God reveals His message in meaningful words.[11] Some scholars understand the biblical propositions to be limited to declarative sentences, those indicative statements that most directly state a truth.[12] However, other written forms in Scripture reflect truth, whether or not they make direct spiritual assertions, such as imperatives, exclamations, or any text that describes the pathos of its subject.[13] In the more expanded sense, then, biblical propositions are best understood as a wide variety of biblical texts from all genres, such as narrative, history, poetry, prophecy, and apocalyptic

literature.[14] It is the capacity of the form of a proposition to accurately reveal a truth claim to a reader from any context that sets evangelical hermeneutics squarely against secular linguistic philosophy and most affects cross-cultural proclamation ministry.

The grammatical-historical method of biblical interpretation is the fitting solution to secular linguistic theories that have unnecessarily introduced problems into texts, specifically the denial of authorial intent, meaning, and truthfulness. The grammatical-historical method is an exegetical approach that objectively examines a biblical proposition utilizing grammar, syntax, literary genre, historical context, and theological analysis to determine the original author's intended meaning.[15] It seeks to interpret propositions on their own terms, being careful not to impose external ideas but drawing meaning from the text in its form and context. The goal is to accurately retrieve the sense of what the biblical writer sought to communicate for proper contemporary application by readers in new situations.

Therefore, the grammatical-historical method offers the reader a straightforward, objective process for determining the biblical author's intention for his words and ultimately for affirming the truthfulness of the

---

11. Carl F. H. Henry, *God, Revelation and Authority*, 3:455–57.

12. Gordon H. Clark, *Karl Barth's Theological Method* (Philadelphia: Presbyterian and Reformed, 1963), 150; Gordon R. Lewis, "Is Propositional Revelation Essential to Evangelical Spiritual Formation?" *JETS* 46, no. 2 (June 2003): 269–98, esp. 270.

13. Daniel Hill, "Proposition," *Dictionary for Theological Interpretation*, Kevin J. Vanhoozer, gen. ed. (Grand Rapids: Baker Academic, 2005), 632–33.

14. Branson L. Woodard Jr. and Michael E. Travers, "Literary Forms and Interpretation," in *Cracking Old Testament Codes: A Guide to Interpreting Old Testament Literary Forms*, ed. D. Brent Sandy and Ronald L. Giese Jr., 38.

15. See the definition in Robert L. Thomas, *Evangelical Hermeneutics: The New versus the Old* (Grand Rapids: Kregel, 2002), 13.

concept that he has relayed by the proposition. Original meaning is fixed semantically in the proposition but with a multiplicity of possible applications.[16] Evangelicals consider an "application" to be "the use or practice of God's message in personal life."[17] Ancient propositions can be applied to contemporary contexts because they are rich with "significance" to the contemporary reader.[18] Thus, the meaning of the Scriptures, equally timeless and historic, possesses a fresh quality for audiences of every context and generation.[19]

The Linguistics of the Biblical Propositions and Meaning

Theologically and hermeneutically, the Word of God is suited for foreign language translation and cross-cultural application. However, there is a yet-unanswered question that is linguistic in nature: What safeguards are there to help the translator convert the lexical and syntactical form of a word or phrase without altering its meaning? The question concerns how the form of a proposition might retain its function to deliver transcendent truth in a locally understandable way if its form changes not only lexically but syntactically. The answer, at its most foundational level, hinges on describing a proposition's form.

To understand the form of a proposition conceptually it is useful to employ the biblical term for "form," *morphē*, which denotes the external manifestation of the true internal reality of something.[20] Discussion of the text's *morphē* is helpful for bridging the text's objective meaning with the reading of a context-specific translation. In linguistic terms, the *morphē* refers to the lexical and syntactical expression of the proposition, which is superficially observable by the words themselves, and it also identifies the internal essence of the proposition, which is its meaning.[21] The external,

---

16. On meaning governing the significance and therefore the range of possible applications, see J. Robertson McQuilkin, "Problems of Normativeness in Scripture: Culture Versus Permanent," in *Hermeneutics, Inerrancy, and the Bible*, ed. E. D. Radmacher and R. D. Preus (Grand Rapids: Zondervan, 1984), 230–40; Brian A. Shealy, "Redrawing the Line between Hermeneutics and Application," in Robert L. Thomas, *Evangelical Hermeneutics: The New versus the Old* (Grand Rapids: Kregel, 2002), 186–87. Abner Chou cautions, "Application that does not coincide with the intention of the author is really misapplication." See Abner Chou, *The Hermeneutics of the Biblical Writers: Learning to Interpret Scripture from the Prophets and Apostles* (Grand Rapids: Kregel, 2018), 221. He diagrams and details an approach to meaning-derived application on pp. 221–25 and helps the evangelical reader avoid the false applications of "trajectory hermeneutics" on pp. 226–28.

17. Shealy, "Redrawing the Line," 187.

18. E. D. Hirsch argued that the reader can retrieve the author's intention for a text and gain the knowledge that the author has asserted to be true. The reader's goal is therefore to believe the text to state the meaning that the author had in mind when writing it. To Hirsch, "significance" is consequent to "meaning": "It is not the meaning of the text which changes, but its significance. . . . *Significance* . . . names a relationship between that meaning and a person, or a conception, or a situation, or indeed anything imaginable." E. D. Hirsch Jr., *Validity in Interpretation* (New Haven, CT: Yale University Press), 8 (emphasis in original). Hirsch's view is also discussed in Kevin J. Vanhoozer, *Is There a Meaning in This Text? The Bible, the Reader, and the Morality of Literary Knowledge* (Grand Rapids: Zondervan, 1998), 26.

19. Traditional evangelical hermeneutician Bernard Ramm concluded that "interpretation is one, application is many." Ramm, *Protestant Biblical Interpretation*, 113.

20. Cf. Philippians 2:6–8, referring to the fleshly manifestation of the divine essence of the Lord Jesus Christ, who took on a human *morphē* externally.

21. See discussion of the inextricable connection between the outer form of the proposition and its internal meaning by Ramm,

superficial layer of the *morphē* changes between languages, most notably when the languages operate by a variety of differing grammatical, syntactical, and contextual rules. In Bible translations, while the external expression of a text is subject to variation due to the linguistic rules for its use, the text's internal essence is fixed—the meaning of a proposition will not change. The work of the translator is to find the *morphē* in the target language (external and internal) that most accurately represents the meaning (internal essence) of the *morphē* in the original language.

While it is the case that the biblical propositions will undergo some form change from the biblical languages, it is never the case that the external, adapted form of a proposition can be detached from its internal, fixed meaning and deliver an accurate meaning in the new language. Yet some well-meaning translators intentionally substitute terms that unwittingly betray the internal *morphē*. Bible translator William Barrick recounts a troublesome episode in which a translation partner for his Bengali Bible project attempted certain term substitutions out of a concern that local readers might struggle to imagine the force of the terms in question. In one gospel narrative, the local translator proposed converting the natural phenomenon of "rain," in the context of the arid land of Israel, to "monsoon," according to a more recognizable tropical Bengali context.

Only through pointed discussion did the translator come to "understand the need to preserve the integrity of the text in its own particular setting." Though the team leader did not question the spiritual status of the translator, he did question his faithfulness to the propositional form and content of Scripture.[22]

Contextual term choices must be made, but particular care must be taken not to dichotomize the proposition into two functionally independent parts, as if the internal essence will remain intact no matter how the *morphē* is expressed. The interrelatedness of the meaning to its form must be upheld at all costs, because meaning derives from the purposeful, fixed order of the biblical writer's words. The words of the propositions in the original languages perfectly portray the meaning God intended, and not just any change to the outer form will accurately express the author's meaning. The specific terms and syntax of the original proposition must be both accurately interpreted and represented according to the grammatical constraints of the original language and the target language.[23] Therefore, the ability to discern meaning through the new *morphē* in the target language depends on a sound exegetical process of translation.

The difficulties to overcome are many in accurately understanding the internal essence of a proposition and adequately communicating it in a new context, given that the writer of

---

who employs the terms *graphē* and *forma* as the basis for the ongoing work of Bible translation. Ramm, *Special Revelation*, 194–97.

22. William D. Barrick, *Understanding Bible Translation: Bringing God's Word into New Contexts* (Grand Rapids: Kregel Academic, 2019), 74.

23. Jobes, "Relevance Theory," 775–76.

the text used culturally based linguistic tools specific to his context. Yet it is possible for the author's meaning to be not only accurately expressed in translation but faithfully applied in the new reader's context, because the internal essence and the external *morphē* of a proposition are inseparably linked. When the translation's inner sense is true to the original in its new language and context, then the regenerate reader can uncover the meaning of the text and subjectively discern and approve God's message as true (1 Cor 2:6–7, 10–13).

Conclusion

This chapter has established critical theological, hermeneutical, and linguistic foundations for why Bible translators can have full confidence in Scripture's capacity to authoritatively convey God's immutable truths across cultures. Scripture self-attests to being God's Word, the definitive revelation of reality. Scripture's teachings eternally transcend contexts, though they are expressed using culture-bound words. Faithful interpretation and translation can accurately transfer these stable meanings to new audiences. Linguistically, while a text's form may be adapted, its essence remains unaltered. Once the author's meaning is understood from the translated proposition, the regenerate reader is well on his way to understanding how God wants him to apply it to his life and context.

Bible translators must operate from a profound conviction that Scripture transmits objective, divinely given meanings without regard to linguistic or cultural limitations. Conviction, however, must meet practice. Translators need to employ meticulous exegetical and translation methodologies that preserve the meaning of the changeless text and convey the meaning authoritatively, as the very Word of God. There is no reason to feel any need to modify the text or reorient its text forms in search of contemporary "relevance," only to labor for the most effective portrayal of the form in the new language. Scripture exudes a fixed authority and universal applicability that needs no cultural accommodation, only patient precision in the process of translating it. Ultimately, the translator's goal is the same as the reader's goal: faithful representation of the ancient texts that leads to faithful adoption by the hearers. The Bible translator's mind and heart must ring with the promise of real meaning transfer, so that he labors steadfastly with the certainty that the end product, after countless revisions for exegetical accuracy, confirms a "derived inerrancy."[24]

---

24. This term was first presented by Bible translation expert and missionary Aaron Shryock in a personal conversation in Los Angeles in September 2019. The term finds implicit support in *WCF* 1.8.

CHAPTER 51

Bible Translation: Concepts and Models

William D. Barrick

The Lord Himself established the importance of linguistic communication by providing names for some of His creations (Gen 1:5, 8, 10). He also provided human beings with language they could use to describe those creations (2:19, 23; 3:20). The transition from divine concept to human speech is a form of translation. Adam demonstrated his God-given capacity for language by his short poem in Genesis 2:23: "This one finally is bone of my bones, and flesh of my flesh; this one shall be called Woman, because this one was taken out of Man."

Indeed, all humans received the capacity for speaking and hearing language, as is revealed in Eve's conversation with the serpent (3:1–5). That very early conversation shows that the fall involved language used for deception and skewing truth. Sadly, the Bible does not report Adam or Eve verbalizing any form of confession or repentance (3:6–13).[1] God pronounced a curse on the serpent (3:14) and the ground (3:17–19) but promised hope to Adam and Eve (3:14–16). Cain verbalized his anger with God, and God sentenced him to exile for murdering his brother Abel (4:1–15). Lamech used his power of speech to boast about his sin (4:23–24), and mankind "began to call upon the name of the LORD" in spoken prayer (4:26).

Biblical history continues with humans speaking one language through which God also communicated with them. By that one language, people initiated the rebellion that built the Tower of Babel (11:1–4). Then God judged the rebels by dividing them into many language groups so that their unity to do ill could be disrupted and, like Cain, they would face

---

1. Though, some have suggested that Adam's naming of his wife Eve (meaning "life") in Genesis 3:20, which came after the Fall, indicates Adam's regeneration, since the name he chose was a hopeful statement in the face of death predicated upon the first gospel promise in 3:15; cf. Joel Beeke, "Adam, Eve, and God: Confirming the First Gospel Promise," sermon recorded at Grace Community Church, January 29, 2023, https://www.gracechurch.org/sermons/20681.

an exile from their original homeland (11:5–9). God sovereignly initiated different languages and people groups. He controlled the diversification of languages. Yet, regardless of their languages, God continued to communicate with all peoples—linguistic diversity provides no barrier to God speaking with people or providing revelation (e.g., Gen 12:1; 14:18–20; 41:25; Num 22:12, 32, 35; Deut 4:5–8; 1 Kgs 10:1–9; 2 Kgs 5:8, 15; Isa 45:1–7; Jonah 3:2; Obad 1; Dan 2:28; 5:24–25; Acts 2:5–11; 14:16–17; 17:26–28; Rom 1:18–20; Rev 14:6).

The task of Bible translation recognizes God's desire and intent to communicate His words to all language groups (Rev 5:9–10). Communication from one person to another with differing experiences and worldviews continues throughout human history. Thus, God's people have translated the Bible from its original languages into other languages for the same purpose: to convey divine history and revelation into the language of someone whose experience and worldview differ from that of the original text as well as from those of the translators themselves. This chapter explores what translation is, its current theories or models, and its practice in the field.

Defining Bible Translation

Words and definitions matter. Without agreeing on the meaning of terms, communication breaks down. To work well together, a team of Bible translators need to know exactly what they have set as their task. They need to work

at reaching a common goal. A team must be able to define what it is they are doing. Before a philosophy of translation can be established and a method for translation adopted, the very task of translation itself must be defined. At its most basic level, "to translate" means "to express in another language, systematically retaining the original sense."[2] However, this basic definition leaves some things undefined: (1) how someone might "express [something] in another language"; (2) the meaning of "systematically"; and, (3) how to identify "the original sense."

An example should help to clarify why these three aspects require explanation. Bob Creson describes an exchange that took place while translating the Bible into the language of the Hdi of northern Cameroon. Hdi verbs characteristically end in the vowels *i*, *a*, and *u*. However, the verb for "love" seemed to the translators to occur with only *i* and *a*. When Hdi leaders were asked if they could *dvi* their wives, they responded that it could be used and that it would mean the love had gone. What about *dva* their wives? Yes, that could be said, as long as their wives were faithful and cared well for their husbands. What about *dvu* their wives? "Of course not! . . . If you said that, you would have to keep on loving your wife no matter what she did, even if she never got you water and never made you meals. Even if she committed adultery, you would be compelled just to keep loving her. No, we would never say *dvu*. It just doesn't exist." When the translator asked

---

2. William Morris, ed., *The American Heritage Dictionary of the English Language* (Boston: Houghton Mifflin, 1979), 1364.

if God could *dvu* people, they sat silently for a while and, with tears, spoke of how amazing that love would be.[3]

For translating John 3:16 or even Ephesians 5:25 ("Husbands, love your wives"), *dvu* in Hdi expresses not just the word *love*, but the intended implications contextually in both biblical texts. Finding a viable translation required exploring the meaning with care for both the original language (Greek) and the receptor language (Hdi). That kind of research must systematically ask the necessary questions and evaluate responses to arrive at the best translation. The original sense of both texts does not rest solely on a word-for-word translation or a word study of the Greek term *agapaō* ("love"). The original sense can be discovered only by paying attention to the overall context in both the Gospel of John and Ephesians, taking into consideration the implications involved in each text and its context. Thus, the task of Bible translation demands more than creating word lists and replacing one word with another (which is essentially what machine translation does). Just as the exegete pays close attention to each grammatical detail and every contextual nuance to understand the biblical text, so the translator must pay equal attention to the details and nuances of the receptor language. No one outside that receptor language and its culture will ever be able to understand fully what the native speakers themselves bring to the process of translation.

Not every translation problem finds such a marvelous solution as the one among the Hdi. During the course of translating the Bible into any language, questions arise with no easy answer. Time and time again, the best of biblical language scholars must admit that the meaning of a biblical text remains hard to understand and even more difficult to translate with confidence.[4] This is when the topic of translation theory occupies a translator's thinking. As Anthony Pym says,

> All translators theorize, not just the ones who can express their theories in technical terms. In fact, untrained translators may work faster and more efficiently because they know *less* about complex theories—they have fewer doubts and do not waste time reflecting on the obvious. On the other hand, awareness of different theories might be of practical benefit when confronting problems for which there are no established solutions, where significant creativity is required. The theories can pose

---

3. Bob Creson and Carol Schatz, *The Finish Line: Stories of Hope through Bible Translation* (Orlando, FL: Wycliffe Bible Translators, 2014), 33–35.

4. For example, Ecclesiastes 11:1, as noted in *ESV Study Bible: English Standard Version* (Wheaton, IL: Crossway Bibles, 2008), 1208 ("To cast . . . bread upon the waters is a metaphor without any contemporary parallels, so interpreters are uncertain about its meaning"); Jeremiah 51:3 in *ESV Study Bible*, 1467 ("The meaning of this verse is uncertain. It refers either to the futility of Babylon resisting the invasion or the ease with which the invader will succeed"); Exodus 17:16 in John MacArthur Jr., ed., *The MacArthur Study Bible* (Nashville: Word, 1997), 121 ("The difficulty of the Heb. text permits an alternative translation"); and alternative translation suggestions like *Legacy Standard Bible* (Irvine, CA: Three Sixteen Publishing, 2022), 1 Samuel 13:1 ("The Heb is difficult; lit *Saul was one year old when he began to reign. Now he reigned for two years over Israel*"); Nehemiah 8:8, "explaining and giving insight" ("Or *translating*" and "Or *giving the sense*"); and Psalm 84:6 "Baca" ("Probably *Weeping*; or *Balsam* trees").

productive questions, and sometimes suggest novel answers.[5]

Even though a lack of awareness regarding translation theories might give the translator a certain amount of freedom, translators should study the theories. Translation theories reveal how experienced translators face translation problems and find viable solutions.

Evaluating Translation Theories

Translation and hermeneutics are two very closely entwined operations. Both deal with interpreting language and texts, then communicating one's understanding of the text. Languages differ one from another in how they are structured, how they are used, and how they change through time. Languages can be highly sophisticated and extremely flexible. Those two characteristics alone make the process of interpretation and translation a challenge. Seldom is there only one correct way of translating a text from its source language into a target language. Attempting to understand a text requires careful consideration of grammar, lexicography, semantics, textual (internal) context, cultural (external) context, and historical context.

Disagreements occur between members of a translation team about how to translate a particular text, because one member focuses on factors that the other members might have missed or ignored.[6] Individual approaches to the task might reflect their individual translation theories. For example, one translator may decide to retain "tenth" in his translation of "to the tenth generation" in Deuteronomy 23:2–3. However, another might decide to substitute "forever" or "never" for the entire phrase (perhaps due to verse 3's last clause). Yet another, however, substitutes "fourteenth" for "tenth" because the target language and culture use "fourteenth generation" in the same way the Hebrew language and culture used "tenth generation." Each of the three translation choices represent good translation choices in that each remains faithful to the text and its meaning. It is possible that they resulted merely from differences in the translators' theories of translation. That said, although many theories for translation work have been proposed, most theories fit under two categories, which are considered below alongside a synthetic theory.

Text-Oriented or Author-Oriented Theories

Formal correspondence (or formal equivalence) theory[7] attempts to preserve the words and form (textual pattern) of the text as much as

---

5. Anthony Pym, *Exploring Translation Theories*, 2nd ed. (New York: Routledge, 2014), 4 (emphasis his). Translators should not indulge in novelty without substantial evidence to support a newer, more accurate way to translate a particular biblical text.

6. See William D. Barrick, "Turning Babel on Its Head: Translating for Understanding" (Presidential Address, ETS Far West Region Annual Meeting, April 23, 2004), 8, https://drbarrick.org/files/papers/translation/2004TurningBabel.pdf. Care must be taken to avoid word-for-word translation of a source language idiom into the receiving language, since the receiving language may give a totally different meaning. For example, "are seen eye to eye" (Num 14:14) can be misunderstood in English as "agreeing" instead of the actual meaning of the Hebrew idiom, "face to face."

7. Leland Ryken, *The Word of God in English: Criteria for Excellence in Bible Translation* (Wheaton, IL: Crossway, 2002).

possible. This theory recognizes that languages differ to such an extent that replicating the source text's form might not preserve the best meaning in the receiving text. Structuralism as translation theory[8] focuses more on the differences between languages than on the similarities, viewing equivalence as nearly impossible.[9] For example, French does not possess a word for "shallow" (as in "shallow water"). However, by using *peu profound* ("not very deep"), the concept can be expressed making formal equivalence still possible, though with different structures.[10]

Formal equivalence is what many refer to as "literal translation." It normally refers to a process approximating word for word. Between cognate languages (e.g., Latin and Italian, or Hebrew and Aramaic) literal translation might be possible. However, strict equivalency is not always possible. Just because a word, phrase, or syntactical form are similar does not mean they possess identical meaning or function. Nida and Taber argue that a translation of the biblical text can possess natural equivalence so that "the best translation does not sound like a translation."[11] Therefore, "a conscientious translator will want the closest natural equivalent"[12] while sticking closely to the text. There are limits, however, to how "natural" a translation should sound. For example, "demon-possessed" might sound more natural to some readers if "mentally distressed" were used. But that translation fails to consider the biblical reality of demons. Scripture does not present the existence of demons and their attacks on humans as a reality limited to Bible times but as an ongoing peril.[13]

Reader-Oriented Theories

Any element of uncertainty or indeterminacy in the biblical text can cause translators to investigate and experiment with other types of equivalence. Nida and Taber champion dynamic equivalence (or functional equivalence) over formal correspondence. They define dynamic equivalence

> in terms of the degree to which the receptors of the message in the receptor language respond to it in substantially the same manner as the receptors in the source language. This response can never be identical, for the cultural and historical settings are too different, but there should be a high degree of equivalence of response, or the translation will have failed to accomplish its purposes.[14]

---

8. For a superb description of structuralism, see Vern S. Poythress, "Structuralism and Biblical Studies," *JETS* 21, no. 3 (September 1978): 221–37. For the theory, see Daniel Patte, *What Is Structural Exegesis?* (Eugene, OR: Wipf and Stock, 2015).

9. Pym, *Exploring Translation Theories*, 9.

10. Pym, 10.

11. Eugene A. Nida and Charles R. Taber, *The Theory and Practice of Translation*, Helps for Translators 8 (Leiden, The Netherlands: Brill, 1974), 12.

12. Nida and Taber, 13.

13. Nida and Taber, unfortunately, failed to see the theological implications and noted only that "mentally distressed" fails to consider the biblical people's "cultural outlook." Nida and Taber, 13.

14. Nida and Tabor, 24.

Dynamic equivalence tends to focus on the readers' response, rather than on the text itself. Emphasis on reader response often argues that equivalence can be achieved only if the receiving text's understood purpose replicates the source text's purpose. *Skopos* theory (*skopos*, in Greek, can mean "aim, end, object"), as a subcategory of dynamic equivalence, specifically attempts to address the text's goal or purpose, especially in the receptor language. While different translations of the source text might express different functions based on a translator's theory, *skopos* theory eliminates all variable translations except the one that results in expressing the same function as the source—in other words, the functional equivalence. Bible translators, according to this theory, must translate what the biblical text ought to do, not what the words say.[15]

According to Pope John Paul II, Bible translation involves "the incarnation of the Gospel in autonomous cultures and at the same time the introduction of these cultures into the life of the Church."[16] He adds, "Through inculturation the Church makes the Gospel incarnate in different cultures and at the same time introduces peoples, together with their cultures, into her own community."[17] This vision of Bible translation can focus on one institution's singular interpretation with the purpose of becoming more ecumenical on the one hand and of converting readers to Catholicism on the other hand. Reader-oriented translation theories like *skopos* lend themselves well to sociologically driven Bible translation, like that proposed by the Roman Catholic Church or any other religious or sociopolitical group.

Sociologically driven Bible translation today has begun to utilize technology in new ways. Computer software localization and internationalization (or globalism) converts a text to basic wording and transfers it easily into multiple languages simultaneously. Hollywood films use this method to prepare a film for dubbing or subtitling. The process does not rely on direct translation of the original screen version or its script. Instead, the film industry produces a special script "which incorporates glosses on culturally specific items, on necessary cross-references within the film text, and indeed any other kind of note that can avoid translation mistakes before they happen."[18] Bible translation software accomplishes basically the same purpose, bringing together the biblical language texts, translations into multiple languages, "explanatory glosses, and sophisticated concordancing tools."[19] Pym suggests that the "presence and function of the 'consultant' might also be seen as a humanized instance of internationalization."[20]

Such computer technologies applied to Bible translation carry inherent dangers. For

---

15. Pym, *Exploring Translation Theories*, 55.
16. John Paul II, *Slavorum Apostoli*, encyclical epistle, June 2, 1985 (Rome: Libreria Editrice Vaticana, 1985), 21.
17. John Paul II, 52.
18. Pym, *Exploring Translation Theories*, 122.
19. Pym, 122.
20. Pym, 123.

example, when examining alternatives available within the software for translating a portion of the text, the limited focus interrupts the syntactical and contextual flow of the text. Without stringent guidelines for making the best choice out of a list of alternatives, the resulting translation can stand at odds with the intended meaning and the intended purpose of the text within its greater context. In other words, the "technology imposes the paradigmatic on the syntagmatic"[21] (meaning that a range of cultural equivalents are offered as replacements potentially interrupting the text's grammatical flow). No matter how well-intended, computerized Bible translation programs[22] can draw the attention of translators to a list or a glossary of terms and phrases that draw them away from considering the greater context of the biblical text as a whole.

Another problem arises when translators select an alternative translation presented by the software, fail to perform adequate post-translation editing, and feed their ill-chosen translation choice back into the system for fellow translators working in cognate languages.

Software translation systems, community translation, user-generated translation, or collaborative translation all carry these perils.

Current translation theories attempt either to leave equivalence behind (as unattainable due to uncertainty or indeterminacy) or to broaden equivalency to make it more dynamic and adaptable to cultural and sociological factors. However, translators beware: "Once its moorings to equivalence are severed, 'translation' easily becomes a drunken boat."[23]

Synthesis of Text- and Reader-Oriented Elements

A translation model works only within its predetermined parameters based on frank discussion about translation theories.[24] A team must develop parameters to guide the translators to their intended product. The question of equivalence normally assumes that the source text determines whether the translator has found true or natural equivalence. In other words, most theories of equivalence assume the superiority of the source text. For instance, relevance theory[25] suggests the recovery of the

---

21. Pym, 124.

22. Such as XML (eXtensible Markup Language) which retrieves previously tagged texts for the purpose of exchanging the original text with reusable content. See Pym, *Exploring Translation Theories*, 125–26. See also Dennis Drescher, "XSEM: XML Scripture Encoding Model," SIL Computer and Writing Systems, September 6, 2001, https://scripts.sil.org/xsem, for SIL's explanation of XML in their XSEM markup standard for Scripture translation.

23. Pym, *Exploring Translation Theories*, 153.

24. Before choosing a model for a project, it would be beneficial for an English-speaking team to read and discuss translators' prefaces to some of the better English Bible versions, for example. The team should keep in mind that some modification will be required due to the differences between English and the language of a foreign Bible translation project, but the basic concepts remain the same. Recommended English-Bible reading for Bible translators embarking on a new project include: "Foreword to the Legacy Standard Bible," in *The Legacy Standard Bible* (Irvine, CA: Three Sixteen Publishing, 2022); "Preface to the English Standard Version," in *The Holy Bible: English Standard Version* (Wheaton, IL: Crossway, 2016); and, E. Ray Clendenen and David K. Stabnow, *HCSB: Navigating the Horizons in Bible Translation* (Nashville: B&H, 2012).

25. Jeannine K. Brown, *Scripture as Communication*, 2nd ed. (Grand Rapids: Baker Academic, 2021), 306, defines relevance theory as "a theory of communication that claims that assumed context and inference are essential for comprehending meaning." See

contextual information within the biblical text in order to rightly comprehend any utterance, since it consists of both the linguistic expression and an assumed context. This theory seeks to discover authorial intent, demanding awareness of what the writer or speaker implies. Thus, translators must pay adequate attention to cultural contexts for both the source and the target texts.[26] Relevance theory involves the following concepts: (1) "an utterance requires hearers to infer more than is provided in the linguistic features of the utterance itself (i.e., the words used)"[27] and (2) "hearers will select from among a host of contextual inputs those that are most relevant for understanding a particular utterance (for inferring meaning)."[28] Such concepts commend relevance theory as a valuable tool for Bible translators committed to biblical inspiration, inerrancy, and clarity.

Doing Bible Translation

Talking and planning alone do not complete any Bible translation project. Work must begin and translation must proceed in a systematic fashion. The following is a bare-bones outline of what a Bible translation project entails:

1. Training for translation: Acquire good seminary training in biblical languages, exegesis, and theology, which provide the most valuable skills. Linguistic training is helpful as well, but it need not involve a large number of courses.

2. Team translation: Avoid minority opinions and idiosyncratic translations by not working alone. Team members can provide a fuller variety of skill sets that will prove of great value. Cluster projects (neighboring Bible translation projects in cognate languages) can also provide opportunities for expanding interaction with other translators.

3. Tools for translation: Travel light; depend on a well-stocked digital library. Logos Bible Software offers one of the best libraries for biblical language studies, theological studies, Bible translation handbooks, and journal databases needed in a foreign field.

4. Translating the text:
   » Identify the text's meaning by exegeting the text as given in the biblical language.
   » Locate equivalences in the target language. This process can be more difficult than even a well-trained theologian and linguist might think possible. For example, the Greek *theopneustos* in 2 Timothy 3:16 has quite often been translated as "inspired." However, as Benjamin B. Warfield long ago demonstrated, too

---

also Karen H. Jobes, "Relevance Theory and the Translation of Scripture," *JETS* 50, no. 4 (December 2007): 773–97.

26. Umberto Eco, "Two Problems in Textual Interpretation," in *Reading Eco: An Anthology*, ed. Rocco Capozzi, (Bloomington: Indiana University Press, 1997), 43–44, refers to common cultural information as the "cultural encyclopedia."

27. Brown, *Scripture as Communication*, 24.

28. Brown, 24.

many readers understand "inspired" in the sense of God breathing into the text—which is "a distinct and even misleading translation"[29]—rather than God breathing out the text. English carries an additional problem in that "inspire" generally carries the meaning of stimulating someone to action or producing a work of literature.

» Evaluate choices from among multiple equivalents. Always compare with the meaning of the biblical text itself and its implications.

» Pay close attention to the multiple levels of context in both the source text and the target text. Do not neglect careful discourse analysis—it helps to see the macro-context as opposed to focusing only on the micro-context.[30]

» Beware of unintended meanings occurring when the text is heard with the ear as compared to read with the eye.[31]

» Test the ultimate choice linguistically, culturally, biblically, and theologically. This order is important—allow the Bible itself and its teachings to make the final determination. For the language and culture, use multiple outside readers for quality control in the realm of understandability.

» Be aware that back translation can hold perils of its own. Translating language A into language B does not imply that translating language B back into language A will possess or reflect the same equivalence. Traditionally, Bible translators have used back translation for checking a translation or helping a translation consultant understand how well the translation team has achieved equivalence. However, each translation direction is one step removed from the source text, making back translation in Bible translation potentially three steps removed (e.g., Hebrew into English, English into Quechua, and Quechua into English). Such linguistic distance might unintentionally codify a poor translation or even affirm error.

» Prayerfully finalize the translation choice in the target language and culture.

5. Tracking translation: Record decisions and their reasons for future reference.

---

29. Benjamin B. Warfield, "The Biblical Idea of Inspiration," in *The Works of Benjamin B. Warfield: Revelation and Inspiration*, 1:75–112 (New York: Oxford University Press, 1932; repr., Grand Rapids: Baker, 2000), 78–79.

30. Commentaries often give good examples of discourse analysis; e.g., Daniel I. Block, *Ruth*, ZECOT (Grand Rapids: Zondervan, 2015). William Varner, *The Book of James, a New Perspective: A Linguistic Commentary Applying Discourse Analysis*, 2nd ed. (Scotts Valley, CA: CreateSpace, 2017).

31. See the example "Very Short Introductions" in Matthew Reynolds, *Translation: A Very Short Introduction* (Oxford: Oxford University Press, 2016), 6.

6. Publishing and dissemination: Bring the final translation to its intended recipients, whether within the local indigenous congregation or among those being evangelized.

7. Planning for the future: Recognize that fallen humans do make mistakes in translation, even those who have been superbly trained and very watchful over their project. Improvements will take place in the knowledge of the biblical text and its background, and the target language and culture will change.

On a final practical note, keeping Bible translators knowledgeable and prepared for their task requires refreshing their skills through either formal or informal[32] programs of biblical studies (including biblical languages), hermeneutics, apologetics, and theology. Missionary translators must maintain a trajectory of increased learning about their target language and culture as well as about the process of Bible translation.[33]

Conclusion

When I first presented my Bible translation ministry to a group of church leaders during a Bible conference, they explained that their financial support would be unlikely since they supported only church-planting missionaries. After thanking them for their gracious meeting and their clarity of purpose as a church for missions, I asked them two questions: "What do your missionaries use for proclaiming the gospel?" and "What does the planted church use for preaching and teaching?" They answered, "The Bible, of course." Then I asked, "Where did they get the Bible in the language of those people to use for evangelism, preaching, and teaching?" No decision was made that night, but a few weeks later the pastor phoned to say that they had agreed to financially support my Bible translation ministry.

Fundamentally, some Bible translation must take place in order to take the gospel to another people in a different language group and culture. Furthermore, if believers establish churches, they will need the full Bible to fulfill the ministry of a biblical assembly. Missions cannot take place without Bible translation. It is essential. Therefore, translators must have a clear understanding of what the translation task is, what theory or model to adopt, and how to put it into practice in their particular mission field.

---

32. Throughout this volume, the use of *informal education* includes the category of *nonformal learning* without specifying a distinction between them.

33. Helpful resources include those posted by Aaron Shryock at https://aaronandsusanshryock.com/; Dave Brunn, *One Bible, Many Versions: Are All Translations Created Equal?* (Downers Grove, IL: IVP Academic, 2013); and William D. Barrick, *Understanding Bible Translation: Bringing God's Word into New Contexts* (Grand Rapids: Kregel Academic, 2019).

Bible Translation in Albania, Yesterday and Today

Astrit Allushi

A brief survey of Bible translation in Albania illustrates from one language what is true and needed for all—Bible translations that are accurate and faithful to the original biblical languages.

Albanian Bible Translation Prior to 1991

The history of Albanian Bible translation is varied and rich. The first known translation of selected Scriptures into Albanian dates back to the mid-sixteenth century. However, official Bible translation efforts did not begin until 1816, with the New Testament completed in 1827.[34] In the late 1870s, the Old Testament books of Genesis, Exodus, Deuteronomy, Psalms, Proverbs, and Isaiah were finished. From then until the end of World War II, more portions of the Old Testament were published, along with updated versions of existing translations, but tragically the entire Bible remained unfinished. With the rise and rule of communism from 1945 to 1991, dictator Enver Hoxha directed all Albanian Bible translations to be destroyed.[35]

Primary Modern Translations

With the fall of communism in 1991, Bible translation work resumed, the first full translation of the Bible being completed in 1994.[36] This version, undertaken by the Albanian Bible Society (ABS), was translated directly from the 1991 Italian Bible, the Nuova Diodati Revisione (itself based on the Textus Receptus).[37] Since then, this popular and foundational Albanian version has undergone some minor changes and

---

34. Reverend R. Pinkerton wrote the British and Foreign Bible Society in 1816, urging the society to pursue translating the New Testament into Albanian. James Clark, *1912 dhe Ungjilli* (Gjirokastër, Albania: AEM-Misioni Ungjillor, 2012), 11. The title translated means "1912 and the Gospel."

35. Clark, 157.

36. The European Christian Mission produced a full Bible version in 1993. However, this version never saw wide use.

37. *Bibla* (Tirana: Albanian Bible Society, 1995), vi.

one major revision.[38] Unfortunately, the 1994 version was not a translation from the original biblical languages, and various passages evince this shortcoming.

The most recent Bible translation was completed by the Interconfessional Bible Society of Albania (IBSA), a division of the United Bible Societies.[39] This IBSA version follows a dynamic equivalent translation philosophy and is the first Albanian Bible that claims to be translated from the originals. However, along with the ABS version, the accuracy of translation is questionable in various places, as evidenced in two passages addressed below.

A Sample Translation Error from the Old Testament

One example of a translation error in the dynamic equivalent IBSA is Genesis 20:6, theologically an important passage that speaks to the interplay of human responsibility and divine sovereignty. The 1995 New American Standard (NASB) translation, which is a formal equivalent English translation, accurately conveys the meaning in the original Hebrew: "Yes, I know that in the integrity of your heart you have done this, and I also kept you from sinning against Me; therefore I did not let you touch her." The NASB1995 (and other formal equivalent English translations) translates the Hebrew conjunction *waw* as "and." This communicates the synchronistic nature of the human and divine in decision-making. The ABS 1994, 2002, and IBSA all translate the *waw* with "therefore," thus conveying God's activity as if conditioned upon Abimelech's activity.[40] The Nuova Diodati also translates the *waw* this way, which could be why the subsequent Albanian translations follow suit.[41]

A Sample Translation Error from the New Testament

An example of an erroneous Bible translation in the IBSA from the New Testament is Philippians 2:12: "work out your salvation with fear and trembling."[42] This important passage, when translated correctly,

---

38. The first generation of Albanian believers and church leaders only had this version. Much like the King James Version in the English-speaking world, the ABS 1994 established much of the phraseology used in the Albanian church.

39. This team is composed of translators from Orthodox, Catholic, and Protestant churches. Therefore, its aim is to produce a text that will be approved by each of these communities among Albanians.

40. ABS 1994: "Po, unë e di që e ke bërë këtë me ndershmërinë e zemrës sate, *ndaj* të ndalova të kryesh një mëkat kundër meje." ABS 2002: "Po, unë e di që e ke bërë këtë gjë me ndershmërinë e zemrës sata, *ndaj* të ndalova të kryesh një mëkat kundër meje." IBSA: "Unë e di që veprove me ndërgjegje të pastër, *prandaj* të ruajta që të mos mëkatosh kundër meje" (italics mine—*ndaj* and *prandaj* mean "therefore").

41. "Si, lo so che hai fatto questo nell'integrità del tuo cuore e ti ho quindi impedito dal peccare contro di me; *per questo* non ti ho permesso di toccarla" (italics mine—*per questo* means "therefore").

42. Cited from the NASB1995. In the Greek text of the NA[28], there is no preposition, only the verb κατεργάζεσθε

commands believers to progress in the salvation that is already theirs. If this phrase were translated "work for your salvation," it would convey a concept of doing good deeds to obtain salvation—in other words, it would communicate that an individual can be saved by their own works. Yet all of the Albanian translations to date (ABS 1994, 2002, and IBSA) do translate the phrase as "work for your salvation," inserting the preposition meaning "for."[43] In this case the additional preposition is not found in the Nuova Diodati.[44] This small translation error results in major doctrinal error, undermining the doctrine of justification by faith alone. The message that salvation is by grace alone through faith alone in Christ alone—apart from one's works—is tragically missed by the addition of one word.

Conclusion

All Albanian translations have been used by God for salvation and sanctification. However, because current translations and versions either lack accuracy or include the translators' viewpoints (due to dynamic equivalence), Albanian speakers are often unable to know whether a passage accurately conveys the original, biblical author's language and intent. Two tools would help many Albanian speakers around the world to rightly discern God's truth. First, there must be a new formal equivalent Bible translation based on the original language. Second, a Bible study site and app in the Albanian language with access to original language tools, Bible book introductions, and doctrinal resources would assist many in seeking to rightly interpret God's Word. The Southeastern Europe Theological Seminary is currently involved in producing both of these tools. Praise be to God! May it also be remembered that this brief reflection on Albanian Bible translations serves to illustrate what is needed globally: faithful Bible translations in every language.

(*katergazesthe*; "work") and the direct object σωτηρίαν (*sōtērian*; "salvation"). This could be translated "work your salvation," which is not clear in English. Therefore "work out" is used, conveying the idea of "exercise." Further, this phrase from Philippians 2:12 in the Textus Receptus is identical with the NA[28], so the difference is not due to textual issues: μετὰ φόβου καὶ τρόμου τὴν ἑαυτῶν σωτηρίαν κατεργάζεσθε (*meta phobou kai tromou tēn heautōn sōtērian katergazesthe*), *The New Testament in the Original Greek: Byzantine Textform*, ed. Maurice A. Robinson and William G. Pierpont (Southborough, MA: Chilton, 2005), 472.

43. ABS 1994: "punoni *për* shpëtimin tuaj me frikë e me dridhje." ABS 2002: "veproni *për* shpëtimin tuaj me frikë e me dridhje." IBSA: "punoni *për* shpëtimin tuaj me frikë e me dridhje" (italics mine; *për* means "for").

44. The phrase is "compite la vostra salvezza con timore e tremore," meaning "accomplish your salvation with fear and trembling."

CHAPTER 52

Missions and the Pastor-Translator: Bible Translation "Best Practices"

Kyle Davis

In the following interview, Bible translation consultant Kyle Davis advocates for raising up "pastor-translators" for the work of Bible translation. He argues that pastor-translators play a crucial role in the Great Commission by providing churches with accurate and intelligible translations of Scripture. He begins by supplying a historical background for the term and role of pastor-translator. He then outlines the key reasons, mindset, and strategies for pastor-translators to engage in translation ministries by, for, and through the local church on the field. Overall, he makes a compelling case for sending churches and their missionaries to integrate Bible translation with church planting and church strengthening.

QUESTION: *Could you explain the roots,*

rationale, and role of what you are calling "pastor-translators"?

The title "pastor-translator" is a term I have been using to articulate the need for qualified pastors and teachers to serve at the intersection of Bible translation and church planting or church strengthening, the latter of which includes theological education. It captures the fact that translation teams need the gifts, skills, and involvement of church pastors, teachers, and theologians to help with drafting, testing, reviewing, checking, approving, distributing, and using the translated Scriptures.

The idea has deep roots in the Protestant Reformation and borrows from what has been recovered in recent years in books and articles about the need for "pastor-theologians," "generalists," and "pastor-scholars."[1] Men who

---

1. See, e.g., Gerald Hiestand and Todd A. Wilson, *The Pastor Theologian: Resurrecting an Ancient Vision* (Grand Rapids: Zondervan, 2015); John Piper and D. A. Carson, *The Pastor as Scholar and the Scholar as Pastor: Reflections on Life and Ministry* (Wheaton, IL: Crossway, 2011); S. Manestch, *Calvin's Company of Pastors: Pastoral Care and the Emerging Reformed Church, 1536–1609* (New York: Oxford University Press, 2013); Carl R. Trueman, "In Praise of the Generalist," a three-part blog post,

hold these dual titles wed together, on the one hand, theological accuracy and depth of instruction with, on the other hand, shepherding and teaching gifts that serve to equip local churches. During the Reformation, such men were trained in the biblical languages, exegesis, and theology in order to serve in churches as shepherds, preachers, teachers, and disciplers. Martin Luther, John Calvin, Theodore Beza, and many other Reformers who were pastor-theologians themselves worked to put accurate texts of Scripture in the original languages into the hands of godly men who would also preach, teach, and train up the next generation of churchmen with orthodox theology and a conviction to exposit the entirety of Scripture.

Digging a little beneath the pastor-theologian level, many Reformers also served on teams to help draft, edit, or revise Bible translations—for example, Luther in German and Calvin in French. Through their rigorous efforts, Scripture was translated into many new languages. The Reformers' commitments to pastoral training, to *sola Scriptura* ("Scripture alone"), and to *ad fontes* ("[back] to the sources," i.e., the original languages) bore much fruit, not only in seeing men minister God's Word but also in seeing God's Word put into the many languages that His people spoke.[2] With pastors skilled to exposit the Scriptures and with translations being read, preached, prayed,

and sung in the congregations, churches began to thrive.

The Reformers as pastor-theologian-translators served a pivotal role in the spiritual health of the global church and in the progress of the Great Commission in church history. But that Reformation work is still needed today.[3] Ninety percent of the world's languages do not have a full translation of the Bible.[4] Churches in these language groups need God's Word in the language they understand best, and godly men in these language groups need training to translate, preach, teach, and shepherd God's people.

As for the rationale of the idea, understanding the need for pastor-translators—or for teams of pastors and translators—in modern missions is not only an academic exploration for me. It has been pressed upon me through two decades of travel to thirty different countries. I have visited with missionaries, missions agency leaders, Bible translators, church planters, local pastors, and theological educators. Understandably, the needs are many and varied, and specialists like linguist-translators are of great value. But the mission field and especially its churches need well-rounded "generalist" pastor-theologians and pastor-translators.

The church leaders I have interacted with in Central and South America, Asia, and Africa have all emphasized a desire to receive more

---

Reformation21, September 9–13, 2010, https://www.reformation21.org/in_praise_of_the_generalist_i.

2. See Philip A. Noss, ed., *A History of Bible Translation* (Manchester, UK: St. Jerome, 2011).

3. See Carl R. Trueman, *The Reformation: Yesterday, Today, and Tomorrow* (Fearn, Ross-shire, UK: Christian Focus, 2000).

4. Find more at "Resources on Bible Translation," Bible Translation Fellowship, accessed June 18, 2024, https://www.bibletranslationfellowship.org/bt-resources.

training in exegesis, theology, and biblical languages. To them, these elements would help them establish healthier churches and are fundamental to the training they desire in a host of other areas of pastoral ministry—to name a few, church membership, discipleship, biblical correction, biblical counseling, and identifying and training leaders. Thus, I have seen that church leaders are the primary users of Scripture, as they are charged by God to minister His Word to others and to model its handling (2 Tim 2:15; 4:1–2).

Another incident that influenced me to emphasize the need for Bible translation teams to have pastors and theologians serving alongside linguist-translators was the matter of Muslim idiom translations (MITs) that were being produced in an attempt to evangelize Muslims.[5] The issue of MITs—along with other religious idiom translations—raises many questions about how to accurately and faithfully translate the Bible, especially for those who are evangelizing in religious contexts that are hostile to Christians. Instead of translating God's Word for God's people, many have followed Eugene Nida's premise that "non-Christians have priority over Christians" when it comes to making translations "intelligible."[6] That is backward. Teams need pastors and theologically trained translators who will prioritize God's people as the target audience for the translation project. It is believers and churches who are the foremost addressees of God's Word. Therefore, translation teams are well served when the shepherds of God's flock work to sharpen the translation.

QUESTION: *Why is it important for pastor-translators to help apply Scripture to the life of the church?*

An accurate Bible translation in the people's language is foundational for the orthodoxy and orthopraxy of the church in every language group. The ultimate goal in missions is not itself the distribution of more Scripture products but healthy churches that faithfully use translated Scripture in their life, worship, and ministry. The Bible must be translated so that people can preach it, teach it, counsel with it, sing it, read it aloud, pray it, and visibly demonstrate it through fellowship, baptism, and the Lord's Supper.

When much of the work in Bible translation has shifted to specialized parachurch organizations, it can be difficult to connect the work of translation with the ministry of the Word in local churches. Even with the best intentions in place, parachurch organizations can create situations where translations do

---

5. See D. A. Carson, *Jesus the Son of God: A Christological Title Often Overlooked, Sometimes Misunderstood, and Currently Disputed* (Wheaton, IL: Crossway, 2012); A. Ibrahim and A. Greenham, eds., *Muslim Conversions to Christ: A Critique of Insider Movements in Islamic Contexts* (New York: Peter Lang, 2018); A. Ibrahim and A. Greenham, eds., *Islam and the Bible: Questioning Muslim Idiom Translations* (Nashville: B&H Academic, 2023).

6. See Eugene A. Nida and Charles R. Taber, *The Theory and Practice of Translation* (Leiden: Brill, 1974), 31–32, and note their comment on page 1: "Even the old question: Is this a correct translation? must be answered in terms of another question, namely: For whom?" The most commonly used translation manual today is probably the one by Katharine Barnwell, who identifies four qualities in a good translation: clear, accurate, natural, and acceptable; see Katharine Barnwell, *Bible Translation: An Introductory Course in Translation Principles*, 4th ed. (Dallas, TX: SIL International, 2020), 29–37.

not serve local churches well. The translations might be untrusted and their manufactured copies unused or underused.

We need to return the responsibility of Bible translation, church planting, and church strengthening—including theological education—to local churches. The apostles understood the Great Commission to be about planting and strengthening churches (cf. Acts 14:21–23; 15:41; 16:5). Following their example, if we train believers who are fluent in a language that needs a Bible translation or revision to both translate and minister God's Word, it could yield decades and centuries of fruit. Therefore, the missionary-translation team needs both "general practitioners" (e.g., evangelists, pastors, theologians) and "specialists" (e.g., linguists, translators).

Not everyone who is gifted in scholarship, linguistics, translation, or theology is going to be gifted in pastoral ministry, preaching, discipleship, and training—or vice versa. But translators need qualified, well-trained leaders who put the Bible translation to immediate use, testing and applying it, allowing for the revision process to be conducted in the context of the proper target audience—the believers in the local churches of that language. Such testing and use by competent ministers of the Word will lead to local churches approving the translation upon completion and receiving it gladly.[7]

For those in contexts that lack a faithful, local Bible translation, the missionary church planter or theologian can study Scripture in the original languages and in other good translations and compile exegetical-theological notes as he prepares his sermons or teaching material. He can then use these notes to train local believers in exegesis, theology, and translation principles, so that together they produce resources that can be used for eventually translating Scripture. Beyond that, such notes can be used for producing a study Bible, commentaries, or other resources that help believers in the same language group to love, trust, worship, obey, and serve the Lord. Thus, Bible translation is not merely about linguistics and translation principles; it is a full-orbed ministry of the Word, where learning to interpret, translate, apply, and minister the text produces and sustains spiritual life in the hearts and minds of people. It must be done under the loving guidance, care, and ministry of biblically qualified shepherds.

QUESTION: *What should be the mindset of a pastor-translator, and how should he approach his task?*

The pastor-translator will be helped to consider a few key concepts. First, the Bible's primary target audience is believers and, thus, churches; the Scriptures were not primarily written for the unbeliever (Rom 15:4; 1 Cor 10:11; 2 Tim 3:16–17).[8] The Bible is a covenant

---

7. See Tim Jore, "Trustworthy and Trusted: Equipping the Global Church for Excellence in Bible Translation," paper, unfoldingWord, August 16, 2017, https://www.unfoldingword.org/publications/trustworthy-and-trusted.

8. See K. Davis, "Bible Translation by and for the Church," in *Islam and the Bible: Questioning Muslim Idiom Translations*, ed. A. Ibrahim and A. Greenham (Nashville: B&H Academic, 2023), 319–38.

document for God's covenant people. Thus, Bible translation should aim to instruct the local church first and foremost. It should help believers to maintain orthodoxy and orthopraxy in life and worship, to disciple one another with the words of their Lord, and to evangelize their neighbors with the biblical gospel. Christians need all of God's Word translated into the language they know best.

Second and consequently, the pastor-translator needs to have clear in his mind and in the project objectives that the goal is not primarily evangelistic. The impulse to go and preach the gospel where Christ is not known is, of course, established by biblical precedent and command (Matt 28:18–20; Rom 10:13–17; 15:20). And, yes, the gospel is contained in the Bible, but the Bible contains much more. It is not simply an evangelistic tract to be handed to a non-Christian with the expectation that they will read and understand it on their own (cf. 1 Cor 2:14). Evangelistic work comes, rather, through faithful Christians opening their mouths (Rom 10:13–17; Eph 6:19; Col 4:3). Therefore, Bible translations made primarily for unbelievers are measured according to the wrong audience.

Third, then, regarding the role of Bible translation in discipleship, the translation team needs to think about how pastors and teachers will exposit the translated Word in their ministries. Historically, the Bible has traveled much more frequently through the pulpit than it has through private study; it has more often been heard than read. God's people gather for corporate worship and are instructed as they hear the Scriptures read aloud, preached,

prayed, and sung in the language they know best. The translator's concern should include a sensitivity to how God has ordered each church to have pastors and teachers who shepherd His people (Eph 4:11–12; Titus 1:5, 9). Their shepherding responsibility includes the public ministry of the Word (1 Tim 4:13; 2 Tim 4:2; 1 Thess 5:27). This means that the translator will be thinking of a target audience of not only believers but also pastors and teachers who are charged by God with explaining the translated text to everyone who will listen.

As a practical example, coining words should not be at great hesitation when translating for the church, since accuracy is primary and pastors will explain them. Nor should the use of paratextual material (e.g., technical footnotes, alternate renderings, cross-references) be seen as unnecessary or distracting for the reader. However, even when the translation is intended primarily for the church, the same translation can still be produced with paratextual notes aimed at unbelievers. The translator could produce and distribute the same translation of the Gospel of John as used by the churches but modify the notes to target non-Christian readers. The same procedure can produce paratextual footnotes, commentaries, study Bible notes, and other helps aimed directly at training local pastors and teachers to interpret and minister the Word (cf. 2 Tim 2:15). In all of these ways, as the Lord draws unbelievers to the church and as He sends believers out of the church proclaiming the truth they have learned, unbelievers will hear not only Scripture but its explanation, and they will interact with the holy lives of the very people who have been transformed by God's Word (John 13:34–35; 14:15; 15:10–12; 17:17).

The ministry applications for local Bible translation by the church, for the church, and through the church are manifold and deserve much further research and reflection.[9] Indeed, the church's theology, worship, godliness, discipleship, fellowship, and witness to the world all depend on Scripture being accurately translated for Christians.

QUESTION: *How can the average missionary practically implement Bible translation on the field?*

This is an important question for every missionary and local pastor who is serving in an area that needs a Bible translation or revision. They will want to cultivate a translation ministry in connection with local churches. For starters, those who preach and teach God's Word must continue developing their own skills in exegeting God's Word from the text in the biblical languages and then work at translation while growing in systematic, biblical, and historical theology. They may even begin studying the fundamentals of linguistics or of translation program management as they develop relationships with others and seek to find the roles they can best serve in. They must not only maintain their doctrine but also live godly lives, devoting themselves to praying for the work (Matt 9:38; 2 Thess 3:1) and investing

in others if a translation ministry is going to develop (1 Tim 4:16; 2 Tim 2:2). The more immediate fruit from their studies will be in their pastoral ministry, but out of these labors and relationships, God may raise up more laborers for the work of Bible translation.

One practical way that Bible translation can immediately serve local believers is through music. The Psalms should be translated and put to music as early as possible, so that congregations can sing and pray Scripture (cf. Deut 31:22; Pss 105:2; 119:171–172; Eph 5:19; Col 3:16; Rev 15:3). Singing Scripture is a wonderful gift from God that aids believers in learning to read, interpret, pray, and meditate on the truths of God's Word, thereby benefiting their evangelism and discipleship as well.

Another way to bring the translation into immediate use in the church is by compiling the notes, already mentioned, which preachers and teachers make as they prepare sermons and lessons. By sharing these notes, they can build up a body of exegetical and theological tools that can be used in the church, such as in creating Bible studies, evangelistic tracts, and discipleship materials.

Even the most "average" missionary—if he has been well-trained for pastoral ministry—ought to see himself as an asset to Bible translation. For the missionary just setting out on the long road of church planting in a new location, he should ask around to see if there is any translation work already happening.[10]

---

9. See K. Davis, "A Theology of Bible Translation" (PhD diss., Potchefstroom, North-West University, forthcoming).

10. For help and resources on developing a translation ministry, including videos, articles, reading lists, and a repository of ongoing projects, see www.bibletranslationfellowship.org.

If there is, he could ask the team what needs they have and possibly serve in the role of exegetical adviser, or offer to help with testing, review, management, donor development, and the many other needs. If he knows the biblical languages, he can offer to teach the team Greek, Aramaic, and Hebrew, or teach workshops on how to interpret the various genres of Scripture. He might also help determine if a translation in the language in which he ministers needs to be revised, even if his checking against the biblical languages requires someone to produce a back translation. He could also start teaching what he learned in seminary, from exegesis to theology, thereby equipping local believers to serve as future translators, revisers, pastors, and theologians. Perhaps in ten or twenty years, God will have raised up a group of men who are the most effective pastors, translators, teachers, and theologians for their language group and its associated dialects.

QUESTION: *How can healthy churches support pastor-translators globally?*

Believers in healthy churches should keep doing what they are already doing— identifying, affirming, sending, and supporting missionaries who fulfill the early evangelistic and discipleship needs of church plants and who strengthen maturing churches by providing theological education. Sending churches who are actively involved in these activities of biblical missions already understand the importance of their missionaries being involved in Bible translation. The more eager the sending church leadership and members are to participate in the Great Commission through those they send, the more they will pray and publicly advocate for Bible translation. Pastors should be encouraged to pray publicly in the corporate gathering for Bible translation and revision projects so that believers are reminded to call upon the Lord to cause His Word to "spread rapidly and be glorified" (2 Thess 3:1).

Conclusion

The unique role of the pastor-translator carries important historical precedents and contemporary relevance. Pastor-translators play an irreplaceable part in furthering the Great Commission work of establishing and strengthening churches. They integrate exegetical and theological training with pastoral ministry in the church and in the church's partnership with other churches, so that believers are discipled in the context of local churches and translation teams can apply their study of God's Word to developing new projects in other languages. The exegetical, pastoral, and theological contributions of the pastor to the translation team thus goes hand-in-hand with Bible accessibility for both believers and unbelievers.

By learning from those who have modeled the pastor-translator role throughout church history, churches who send and support pastor-translators will be rewarded with the joy of seeing God's Word "spread rapidly and be glorified" in and through the church (2 Thess 3:1). They will have the joy of seeing God call, save, and sanctify a people in His truth (John 17:17; Rom 8:30). The tools for excelling as pastor-translators are available, but churches on the field need more laborers for Bible translation and the development of theological resources that serve them. Let us pray together that the Lord would raise up more laborers for His harvest, and especially the kinds of laborers that integrate the work of Bible translation with the Great Commission work of planting and strengthening healthy churches among every tribe, language, people, and nation. God is glorious and worthy to be known, loved, worshiped, obeyed, and served by every tribe, language, and people.

CHAPTER 53

Resourcing the Global Church

Rick Kress

Christ shed His blood to purchase and redeem the people of God, not a printing press. So, it is important to ask if there is a biblical basis for publishing and resourcing in world missions. Should publishing be considered a primary aspect of missions? The purpose of this chapter is to introduce the biblical reality that resourcing God's people through publishing is an intrinsic part of proclaiming the excellencies of Christ as Savior and fulfilling the Great Commission. It is helpful to survey the biblical mandate, some biblical examples, and the biblical priorities relating to resourcing the global church.

The Biblical Mandate for Resourcing God's People

From beginning to end, the Bible either implicitly or explicitly calls mankind to behold and worship God as Life-giver, Lord, and King (Gen 1:1; Rev 22:20–21). In fact, Scripture itself is the resource *par excellence* that God has graciously given the world to reveal His Son as Lord and Savior (2 Tim 3:15). In turn, salvation in Christ results in God being glorified (Eph 1:6, 12, 14). Thus, resourcing the global church is a vital part of the mission of His people. At least three aspects of our mission combine to highlight the biblical mandate for publishing and resourcing God's people.

Proclaiming the Excellencies of Christ

One of the primary reasons the Lord sovereignly chose to save sinners is so that they would "proclaim the excellencies of Him who has called [them] out of darkness into His marvelous light" (1 Pet 2:9–10). To "proclaim" or "declare" the virtue of Christ, the believer must have the resource that reveals Him—the Word of God. Thus, when God's people are resourced with God's Word, they proclaim the saving beauty and intrinsic excellence of their Savior. Declaring the praises of Christ before the lost is called evangelism; before the church it is called edification; and directly to God it is called exaltation. Resourcing the global church is vital to worship, fellowship, and evangelism. Hence, it is vital to the Christian life.

Teaching, Exhorting, and Applying the Scripture

Jesus called the church to "make disciples of all the nations . . . teaching them to keep all" that He commanded (Matt 28:18–20). Going to all nations necessitates a global ministry, and teaching necessitates resources that reveal "all" that Christ commanded. God has gifted teachers who are to expound the supreme resource—the Scriptures—to build up and mature the church (Eph 4:11–15; 1 Pet 4:10).

Paul called Timothy not only to publicly read the Scripture, but also to exhort and teach (1 Tim 4:13, 16). Hence, extrabiblical resources that properly explain and apply the Scriptures are also a gift from God to His church. Second Timothy 2:2 calls for a cycle of discipleship, which necessitates the biblical global resourcing of the church—faithful men teaching faithful men the things Paul taught in the presence of many witnesses. The Word of God and resources that explain and apply it are an integral part of ministry.

Every Tribe, Tongue, and Ethnicity

The book of Revelation gives a glimpse of the fruit of global resourcing in missions. A redeemed people from every tribe, language, and ethnicity will gather in perfect harmony to worship God through Christ (Rev 7:9–10; 21:22–27). This side of heaven, language translation is a necessary component of resourcing God's people globally. Gospel proclamation in a global context therefore mandates translation, publishing, and resources.

Biblical Examples of Resourcing God's People

In addition to the theological mandate for resourcing God's people, the Bible contains several illustrations of this same ministry in action. Adam and Eve were resourced by God's Word—as were Noah, Abraham, Moses, the prophets, and the apostles and their associates. The nation of Israel was resourced through Moses and the prophets. In fact, Moses was not only the human instrument God used to produce a foundational resource for His people (the Torah), but Moses also received an original, first printing (and later, second printing), hard-copy edition of the Ten Commandments, published by the very finger of God Himself (Exod 31:18; Deut 9:10).

The church continues to be resourced not only through the Old Testament, but through the apostolic witness of the New Testament as well. Paul expected his letters to resource the church and be circulated among the local congregations (Col 4:16; 1 Thess 5:27). Additionally, Paul quoted Jesus alongside the Old Testament and classified both as the Word of God (1 Tim 5:18). Peter cited Paul's writings as Scripture and implied that they needed to be rightly interpreted (2 Pet 3:15–16).

The testimonies of the Old and New Testaments affirm that God expects His people to publish His glory and resource the world with His revelation. Israel was to reveal Yahweh's glory through His Word and their actions.

The church is to demonstrate and declare the glory of Christ. The Word of God and teaching that accurately explains and exhorts from His Word are meant to resource the global people of God. Publishing and distribution thus are vital to missions. Note just a few picturesque examples of biblical resourcing found in the Word of God, starting with the Old Testament scribe, Ezra.

Ezra and the Levites

Nehemiah records a remarkable scene that illustrates the equipping of God's people with His Word and the explanation of it. After the remnant returned from Babylon, the repairs taking place in Jerusalem had stalled out. Ezra the scribe had set his heart to study, live out, and teach God's Word to God's people (Ezra 7:10). The Lord had put it in Nehemiah's heart as territorial governor to restore Jerusalem (Neh 1–2). Both men were walking in faith concerning the coming of the promised Messiah.

In Nehemiah 8, Ezra and a select group of Levites read from the book of the Law of God, then translated and explained the Scriptures to the people of God (vv. 1–8).[1] God's Word had a profound effect, as the people mourned over sin and then experienced joy in the Lord (vv. 9–12). They declared a holy day and then celebrated the weeklong Feast of Booths—something that had not been done since the days of Joshua (vv. 13–18). All this was in obedience to God's Word.

The people of God heard the Word of God read, translated, and explained—and it changed lives. That's global resourcing done in a Jewish Old Testament context.

The Ethiopian Eunuch

In Acts 8, an Ethiopian governmental official was in possession of an Isaiah scroll. Thus, it is evident that God's written Word had been copied and published, in order to equip God's people, along with those interested in knowing Him. But there was also a need for resources that explain and expound the meaning of God's Word. As the Ethiopian read the words of Isaiah 53, he confessed that he needed help (Acts 8:30–36). God provided Philip's commentary on that passage and his summary of its connection to Christ in the rest of the Scriptures. By way of the written and copied Word of God, the Ethiopian official came to faith and presumably became the first Christian witness to Ethiopia. But an attendant resource that God used was the biblical commentary of another believer.[2]

Paul's Parchments

Paul's last epistle contains another intriguing illustration of written resources in the early church. As his final days on earth were

---

1. Cf. 2 Chron 17:7–9. On the related activities of translating and explaining in Nehemiah 8:8, see F. Charles Fensham, *The Books of Ezra and Nehemiah*, NICOT (Grand Rapids: Eerdmans, 1982), 217–18; Israel Loken, *Ezra and Nehemiah*, EEC (Bellingham, WA: Lexham Press, 2011), Neh 8:8.

2. Consider the implications of Exodus 24:7; 2 Chronicles 15:3; Matthew 4:23; Luke 4:14–20, 31, 44; John 18:20; Acts 2:42; 6:4; 13:5, 15; 15:21; 20:1–38; 1 Timothy 4:1–16; 5:17; 2 Timothy 4:2–5.

approaching, Paul requested "the scrolls, especially the parchments" (2 Tim 4:13). He knew that his life on earth was almost over. He rejoiced knowing that he had kept the faith and that God would safely deliver him to his eternal home. But he still wanted his books and papers.

It is impossible to know for certain what those scrolls and parchments contained, since the text does not say.[3] But Paul makes it clear that his lifelong passion and pursuit since becoming a believer was to know Christ and to make Him known. Paul wanted either to study or to produce resources that focused on Christ as revealed in the Word of God. The church's ministry and mission focus should reflect this same passion. But with the abundance of resources available to the church and individuals today, the primary focus of a biblically responsible resourcing ministry should be considered also.

Biblical Priorities for Resourcing God's People: The Preeminence of God's Word

In Psalm 19 David proclaims that Scripture restores the soul, makes wise the simple, rejoices the heart, enlightens the eyes, endures eternally, and is wholly right in every way. Peter confirms that it is through God's Word that His Spirit gives believers life (1 Pet 1:23). The Word of God is the means of the believer's growth in holiness as well (John 17:17). In addition to its salvific and sanctifying power, the Bible is the only resource that is God-breathed and sufficient to adequately equip the man of God for every good work (2 Tim 3:15–17; 2 Pet 1:19–21). Everything a believer needs to live a godly life is found in the true knowledge of Christ, as revealed in the Word of God (2 Pet. 1:3–4). Furthermore, the Bible reveals Jesus, the Word of God incarnate, who is Himself eternal life (John 1:1–4; 17:3). For this reason, Scripture is the preeminent resource for every believer, church, and missionary. In the current age, there are many opportunities to resource God's people with His preserved revelation, and these entail using various media, choosing works to promote, and recognizing works to avoid and refute.

Using Various Media

As this chapter has emphasized, the Bible itself in written form is the ultimate missionary resource. The Scriptures have been formally published at least since the days of Moses. In addition to this, both Jewish and Christian literature have been published and used to benefit God's people throughout the centuries. Current resources included in the print genre encompass traditional paper books, as well as eBooks, Bible software, and digital apps.

The Word of God has been proclaimed audibly since the beginning of creation (Gen 1:1). Audio Bibles are now available in a multitude of languages, and the numbers are growing almost daily. Countless have heard of

---

3. "Only Paul, Carpus, and perhaps Timothy knew what they contained." William D. Mounce, *Pastoral Epistles*, WBC 46 (Dallas, TX: Word, 2000), 592.

Christ for the first time through these recordings. Audiobooks that explain and apply the Scriptures can also be appropriate resources to both evangelize the lost and equip God's people. The expanded use of cell phones has increased availability. God continues to use radio to bring the gospel and biblical training to multitudes all over the world, including ministries in countries and regions where believers are persecuted and biblical Christianity is outlawed.

With film and video, the church has another platform for resourcing.[4] Notably, videos of Bible classes, biblical teaching, and sermons have flooded media markets since the advent of television. With the near universal use of the internet, podcasts, sermons, and classes have found a place on video media channels online. As with audiobooks and print resources, video can be used to proclaim the excellencies of Christ. To the degree that these differing forms of media conform to an accurate explanation and application of Holy Writ, they are God-blessed means for resourcing disciples and disciple-makers.

Choosing Works to Promote

Paul calls for close attention to right doctrine and faithful application of biblical truth. There is therefore a constant need for works that help with the teaching and personal application of the Scriptures—works that rightly divide, explain, and apply the Word of God (1 Tim 4:16). Biblically resourcing God's people in this way requires certain foundational convictions, which will help determine the foundational resources to produce, and further resources to help in given contexts for application.

FOUNDATIONAL CONVICTIONS

Any resource that rightly explains the Bible must necessarily share the foundational convictions that the Scripture has revealed of itself. Those foundational convictions include divine inspiration, inerrancy, infallibility, and sufficiency. As Paul wrote in 2 Timothy 3:16–17, "All Scripture is God-breathed and profitable for teaching, for reproof, for correction, for training in righteousness, so that the man of God may be equipped, having been thoroughly equipped for every good work." Thus, any resource used to explain God's Holy Word should hold the same view.[5]

FOUNDATIONAL RESOURCES
FOR INTERPRETATION

After a good Bible translation, attendant foundational resources would include lexicons, dictionaries, grammars, and concordances. Exegetical and expositional commentaries that focus on the text and its original context will be fruitful for interpretation as well (Acts 8:25–38). In addition to textual resources, biblical

---

4. Video is a debatable resourcing form. Though it seems evident that the Lord has used this means to evangelize the lost and edify His church, it must be remembered that it is the gospel that is the power of God unto salvation. Israel was constantly warned against idolatry yet still turned to false images and visual representations of God.

5. Interaction with critical resources that do not hold to these convictions may be helpful, but such resources certainly necessitate biblical discretion.

and systematic theologies can be helpful for building up leaders and the church.

FURTHER RESOURCES FOR APPLICATION

Because Paul exhorted Timothy to give attention to his personal holiness as well as his teaching, works that focus on the application of the Scripture are helpful tools in resourcing the church. Applicational resources could include works on worship, devotion, hymnody, prayer, discipleship, admonition, and refutation. Application at these points is vital as the church seeks to teach the next generation of believers to obey all that Jesus taught (Matt 28:18–20).

Recognizing Works to Avoid and Refute

Paul warned the Ephesian elders about wolves who would arise from the congregation to draw disciples away after themselves and their own self-styled doctrines (Acts 20:28–30). Thus, we can safely infer that there will be resources that must be avoided and refuted because they misuse and misapply the Word of God. Faithful ministry therefore demands the publishing of resources that refute such opponents.

In Colossians 2 Paul similarly cautions that there will be those who seek to influence the church to adopt worldly philosophies and even demonic deceptions (v. 8). He then outlines the Christian's completeness in Christ (vv. 10–15), warning specifically about some of the deceptive and worldly philosophies that will seek to undermine that completeness (vv. 16–23). Therefore, publishing works that exalt the sufficiency of Christ as revealed in the Word of

God is essential. Likewise, resources that refute false teaching are needed.

CORRUPTION AND CAPTIVITY IN TRADITIONALISM AND CEREMONIALISM

Colossians 2:16–23 reveals some overarching categories of vain philosophies and deceptive teachings that are common to Christian communities, which lead to corruption and captivity rather than fullness in Christ. Paul writes, "Therefore, no one is to judge you in regard to food and drink, or in respect to a festival or a new moon or a Sabbath day—things which are only a shadow of what is to come; but the substance belongs to Christ" (Col 2:16–17). Paul's original context was Jewish legalism, but similar mixtures of traditionalism and ceremonialism are present today in Catholic and Orthodox traditions, Seventh-day Adventism, and liberal Protestantism. Publishing works that refute such error is a necessary part of the larger mission of God's church.

CORRUPTION AND CAPTIVITY IN MYSTICISM, EMOTIONALISM, AND EXPERIENTIALISM

Paul continues, "Let no one keep defrauding you of your prize by delighting in self-abasement and the worship of angels, going into detail about visions he has seen, being puffed up for nothing by his fleshly mind, and not holding fast to the head" (Col 2:18–19). He thereby warns against mysticism, emotionalism, and experientialism. Modern manifestations of such errors include the prosperity gospel, a movement that has become prominent in many places throughout the world. Again, resources that refute this error are necessary for healthy missions.

Corruption and Captivity in Legalism

Paul goes on to condemn religions that are built on rules of men, such as "Do not handle, do not taste, do not touch!" Though these have the appearance of wisdom they ultimately are of "no value against fleshly indulgence" (Col 2:21–23). This error is currently promoted by pseudo-Christian cults like the Watchtower Society (Jehovah's Witnesses), the Latter-day Saints (Mormonism), and hyper-fundamentalistic Protestantism. The church must find a place in its mission to refute such error.

Corruption and Captivity in Libertinism

The book of Jude exposes yet another error that must be addressed—libertinism. Jude 4 says, "Certain persons have crept in unnoticed, those who were long beforehand marked out for this condemnation, ungodly persons who turn the grace of our God into sensuality and deny our only Master and Lord, Jesus Christ." *Sensuality* (Gk. *aselgeia*) refers to "behavior completely lacking in moral restraint."[6] Because of an unbiblical misunderstanding or distortion of the free grace of God, many in evangelicalism in

the United States have fallen prey to this error. And because of the affluence and influence of American evangelicalism, that error is marketed and propagated by Christian publishing houses and bookstores and in churches throughout the world. As in Jude's day, there is a pressing need for resources that refute the idea that grace is a license for sin.

The Wise Preacher's Caution and Conclusion

Publishing plays a vital role in missions. God has made it clear in His Word that the Father designed it so, for the glory of the Son, based in the ministry of the Spirit. God does, however, give those who are dedicated to Christian resourcing a clear caution and conclusion. Relationship and reverent worship are to be the ultimate priority. Ecclesiastes 12:11–13 records the caution and conclusion memorably:

> The words of wise men are like goads, and masters of these collections are like well-driven nails; they are given by one Shepherd. But in addition to this, my son, be warned: the making of many books is endless, and much devotion to books is wearying to the flesh. The end of the matter, all that has been heard: fear God and keep His commandments, because this is the end of the matter for all mankind.

---

6. "ἀσέλγεια," LN 88.272 (1:770); see also the discussion of possible etymology in Joseph Henry Thayer, "ἀσέλγεια," *Thayer's Greek-English Lexicon of the New Testament* (1896; repr., Peabody, MA: Hendrickson, 2021), 79–80.

How to Assess the Needs and Goals of International Publishing

Mark Borisuk

Resourcing the church with print materials is part of the biblical mandate of proclaiming the excellencies of Christ and fulfilling the Great Commission. To be faithful to preach and teach through print media, the church needs to think through how best to steward globally the written resources God has given it. Specifically, the church needs to understand how to assess the current needs, where to find the existing resources, when to begin a publishing company, and what to publish. Some practical examples from Mainland China will help to bring further clarity to these issues.

Understanding How to Assess the Current Needs

Three points of view need to be considered to evaluate the current needs of the national church in a country or language group: the national, theological, and practical perspectives.

A National Point of View

Sitting down with national pastors, Bible teachers, or well-read believers is invaluable for understanding what resources are needed in the church. One translation company in Mainland China regularly surveys Bible teachers, national pastors, and church leaders to determine what written resources are available and what the local church lacks. These surveys were started before the company was even founded and have proven invaluable to give insight and direction to translators. By maintaining a teaching presence and strong connections with church leaders, those in publishing can learn to better serve the churches in their communities.

A Theological Point of View

English-speaking pastors have a nearly unlimited number of biblical resources at their disposal. Chinese pastors have comparatively very few. This is a fundamental difference between them. A major missions goal is to close the gap in this area. The lack of resources has tangible practical effects. In many Chinese churches, topical preaching that reads a text but does not reference it again has become the status quo. Some pastors think they would lose the interest of their audiences if their sermons focused on explaining the Bible. This is a practical outworking of the lack of resources about the authority and sufficiency of Scripture, expository preaching, and interpretation of the Word of God. Such written resources could change the culture of these local churches.

A Practical Point of View

Similarly, practical resources (marriage, family, biblical counseling, discipleship, etc.) are essential. Unbiblical mindsets prevalent in the culture manifest themselves in the lives of pastors and their congregants. One example of an unbiblical mindset from the Chinese church is that some pastors think God will shepherd their families in return for the pastor's work in shepherding the church. For this reason, pastors may not ask for materials to help with marriage or parenting despite their need. Experienced missionaries can help churches assess practical needs for written resources.

Understanding Where to Find the Existing Resources

Good stewardship requires researching what resources are already available. Along with conversations with national partners, the following are ways to help you find what is presently available or what might be already translated but out of print.

Bookstores

Local Christian bookstores or religious sections in secular bookstores are great places to find resources. Newly published books are usually in the front of the bookstore; older or out-of-print books are sometimes on random shelves. Taking pictures with a cell phone helps record what is available.

Seminaries

Bible college and seminary libraries house thousands of Christian resources. Usually, libraries are organized better than bookstores and are more likely to have out-of-print books. Commentary sections are particularly helpful. Translators can often find resources already translated in these libraries; working to acquire the rights to reprint these works saves much time and money as opposed to retranslating.

Publishers

It is always good to foster relationships with publishers. In Mainland China, large publishers are state sanctioned. Smaller Christian translation companies translate books and seek to have a larger publishing company publish them. It is helpful to understand what publishers are working on to avoid overlap. Sharing identified needs for resourcing and encouraging them to publish works to meet those needs can be profitable. One can also gift English copies of books to encourage publishers to translate and publish these to meet specific church needs.

Digital Content

Biblical resources in digital format are increasingly common and can be very useful. For example, the Chinese Bible Study Toolbox[7] grew out of a spreadsheet of different types of resources available through online study tools (which today would include smartphone applications as well). This table confirmed the need for a comprehensive online study tool for Chinese pastors: about half of the twenty-five thousand pages of pastoral resources in the Chinese Bible Study Toolbox were already translated into Chinese but were largely unavailable in Mainland China.

Understanding When to Begin a Publishing Company

The decision to start a publishing company should not be taken lightly. Owning the company provides some level of publishing freedom, but it is also a huge time investment that can take away from other ministry opportunities. The following are some questions to consider: (1) Are there existing publishers who have a similar vision and theology and are willing to cooperate? (2) Are there identified qualified national staff to partner with the company? (3) Is there adequate long-term financial support? (4) Will national partnerships in the publishing industry help with marketing and distribution? (5) Could the same goals be accomplished through simpler means like e-books or posting translated materials online?

Starting a translation company in China took a considerable amount of time and effort. Once started, this time and effort only increased with raising funds, meeting and establishing relationships with publishers (both Chinese and English), getting licenses, finding and managing qualified translators, and dealing with banking and accounting issues, to name a few. This has often curtailed getting involved in other desired ministries. However, the freedom and ability to translate and come alongside the local church with needed articles, books, and pastoral resources has been a great blessing. The translation office has also been a place to disciple believers and encourage young men toward the ministry. One couple who came to Christ and were a key part of the translation office for many years have recently become involved in planting a church in another province in China.

Understanding What to Publish

Understanding the current needs is important to understanding what to publish. One

---

7. Chinese Bible Study Toolbox, accessed June 18, 2024, https://home.yanjinggongju.com/CBST/index.html.

must keep in mind that one cannot do everything. Each missionary should focus on one key area, including pastoral ministry and preaching, biblical counseling, family strengthening, or church strengthening. Participating in publishing should be kept in line with a missionary's overall focus because biblical resources will support that focus. Keep in mind, the more biblical a resource, the easier it is to translate; it is not as culturally focused, and yet it will powerfully speak to the culture you are trying to reach.

Above everything else, the key to publishing choices must be driven by a mindset that is biblically and ecclesiastically centered. All of missions must be driven by meeting the needs of a present, or yet future, local church with the living and powerful Word of God. Publishing decisions are not made based on a presupposition that Scripture is deficient and must be supplemented—nowhere does Scripture present itself as deficient for the spiritual needs of people. Publishing decisions must be made out of the truth that knowledge of Christ through His Word is all that is needed for life and godliness. Scripture does not need to be supplemented, it needs to be exalted, emphasized, and explained. It is His divine power by which He grants us an increasingly godly life (2 Pet 1:3–4). Does the article, book, or commentary in question do that? A resource worth publishing leads people to understand the necessity and sufficiency of the Word of God.

INSERT 53.2

Translating and Publishing for Training

Mark Tatlock

While the primary focus of Bible translation is to bring the Word of God to the world's remaining language groups, another important work requires some attention: the consideration of what biblical resources are most useful to the global church for spiritual growth. Specifically, in today's world of Christian content creation and global accessibility, now more than ever translation teams and publishers need to increase production of materials to train lay church members, church leaders, and pastors along all levels of education.

Missions leaders, local church leaders, national publishers, and translation teams need to have a ready answer to the question "Which genres of publishing and resources relate to the kinds of training you desire to advance?" To answer this question, these leaders must know the relationship between publishing and training. As local churches on the field mature, biblical missions activities will begin to focus more predominantly on training indigenous pastors and church leaders. Publishing complements their training focus and, for some, becomes an important component early in raising up indigenous leaders. As training programs get their footing, publishing becomes a much sought-after initiative. On the other hand, for those who have a publishing ministry already, training pastors and leaders becomes the natural next step, since teaching tools have been made available and are ready for implementation. So, depending on one's primary mission, the starting point might be different, but ultimately the relationship between pastoral training and Christian publishing is the same. Whatever the starting point, the question to ask is "What are the essential needs of pastors and churches?" It is not good stewardship to spend time translating, writing, and publishing resources that are not perceived by church leaders as necessary for the work of the ministry, that might simply remain on the bookstore shelf. It is in no way commendable to produce many publishing projects with minimal effect toward advancing the gospel or seeing the local church mature. Good stewardship of one's financial resources, time, and effort demands that missionaries and publishers develop the kinds of resources that will train pastors and contribute to feeding the flock.

To assess the need for publishing initiatives in the global church, it is helpful to consider that Christian education runs along a spectrum with three categories. At one end of the spectrum, a pastor or leader will need resources of a higher academic quality than will a church member. Yet the resources that train the leader will equip him to better instruct the people. All three categories work in concert to educate the local church, and so they all are important to a publishing ministry to one degree or another, depending on the needs of a field or a language group.

1. **Informal learning.**[8] This category of Christian education is church-based or lay-level training. Church members will

---

8. Throughout this volume, the use of *informal education* includes the category of *nonformal learning* without specifying a distinction between them.

benefit greatly from Bible survey-style resources and tools related to Christian living and discipleship on critical topics such as counseling, marriage and family, parenting, spiritual growth, and biblical doctrine. Training with such materials might be conducted in small groups, church classes, seminars, or conference formats. Generally, at this level, assignments might be required, but they do not result in the kind of certification that can be evaluated by an outside agency such as an educational accreditation organization or by an institution for entrance into a formal academic program.

2. **Formal learning**. This category of training is more academic in quality, entailing a classroom component. Assignments are required to varying degrees of difficulty and are necessary for assessing the student's mastery of the learning outcomes designed by the instructor and the program. Successful completion of the coursework will result in a certificate, degree, or diploma that should meet recognized standards in the country if reviewed by some kind of accreditation body. Because formal education requires a structured curriculum with required resources to read, it is critical that resources that meet the academic criteria are written or translated and published. However, not just any course book will serve the student well, but only those that respect the theological convictions of the ministry. For those academic programs that must meet national or regional accreditation standards, it is imperative that translators and publishers help to fill library shelves with theological and biblical resources, such as textbooks, language tools, and exegetical and expositional commentaries. Most seminaries and pastoral training schools around the world rely on English resources to meet their accreditation requirements and provide study tools for students. But a library with limited local language resources will stunt formal learning because many of the theological resources in English sit largely unused. Christian publishers should give more attention and effort to funding local language materials, even if the audience is meager and there will be no profit margin from the sales. In the end, formal learning is intended to equip church leaders so that the churches will mature.

3. **Advanced learning**. Within the category of formal learning, effort must be made to provide scholarly and theological resources to the highest levels of students—graduate students in research-based degrees, who will serve their communities, nations, and language groups as pastor-theologians. These qualified church leaders are being equipped to address specific matters of concern in their cultural context with biblical skill

and theological precision. The resources needed for such advanced learning—such as academic journals, reference works, theses, and dissertations—will have the most limited audience. However, these works could, over time through the men who use them, shape the theological integrity of seminary faculty, elder councils, denominations, and many ministry efforts nationwide.

These learning categories on the spectrum of Christian education are crucial for determining what gets published when, for the sake of the local churches in a country or language group. By funding projects and purchasing books, those who cannot publish can support those who do. Publishing is a sort of litmus test for the spiritual maturity of the global church. It indicates the desire of believers to deepen their knowledge on godly topics, it identifies the readiness of pastors and church leaders to shepherd the flock more intentionally, and it reveals the hearts of writers, translators, and publishers to labor at all costs "for the equipping of the saints for the work of service, to the building up of the body of Christ" (Eph 4:12).

INSERT 53.3

Practical Early Steps for Global Translation and Publishing

Walter Heaton

Apart from one's personal influence in the lives of others, translation and publication is arguably the most enduring ministry one could have on the mission field. The now two-thousand-year-old church is rich in good literature, but in many parts of the globe it lacks literature in the native tongue. Thus, thousands of Christians (and non-Christians) can be helped by the books, pamphlets, and tracts that missionaries leave behind. Yet, since most of us involved in this ministry have access only to limited resources, it is important to think carefully about two issues: what titles to translate and who should be involved in translation. Below are some suggestions.

What Titles to Translate

Ecclesiastes 12:12 warns that there is no end to the writing of books. Indeed, far more are published each year than anyone could read. Thus, missionaries and their supporters must give thought to what titles they translate and publish so that they are, in fact, read with the most benefit to the church in a given context. This often means alternating between solid literature for church members and useful material for training and shaping church leaders.

As for church members, titles to assist the greatest number in the target country should be chosen. Evangelistic and apologetic literature dealing with the dominant religion or worldview in that country is often devoured by members, as are books dealing with marriage, family, and Christian finances. Another helpful category is issues that frequently divide Christians in the target country. The missionary-publisher could produce books that help Christians think through issues of charismatic theology, eschatology, roles in society, or Christian counseling.

Such titles often end up marking a ministry and will doubtless be read by large numbers both inside and outside the missionary-publisher's denomination. They may also open doors for future publications in circles with whom he or she currently does not have much contact. For instance, one method to help in selecting book categories and titles would be to enlist the opinions of the target country's pastors. Reaching out to these men may also help with later distribution and marketing.

When it comes to leaders, one of the best ways to help train and shape the thinking of future pastors and teachers is to put good books in their hands. Those who occupy the pulpit have the greatest influence in neighborhoods, societies, and countries. Missionary-publishers, then, should consider which books would exert the greatest influence on these men.

Systematic theologies profoundly shape the pastor's thoughts on all matters of doctrine. The more accessible, single-volume works are especially practical early on. Titles on hermeneutics and exegesis go hand-in-hand with these. Books on church history should also be translated, both histories that provide a large overview as well as those with more detailed background and development. These can help explain what shaped whole denominations and theological traditions, especially those dominant in one's place of ministry. Finally, commentaries should be translated, choosing authors and titles that provide a balance of academic rigor and pastoral care.

Tools for leaders may not see a high volume of sales. Likewise, many people own bicycles, but fewer own a set of wrenches. When a bicycle breaks, however, the owner looks for someone with wrenches to help fix it. Publishers also must produce tools that help leaders put bike chains back on their sprockets, so to speak—that is, books rich in exegesis and biblical theology to help them maintain the health of their congregations. Not everyone will understand the value of these titles, but they are important nonetheless.

Who Should Translate

Finding translators for hire is easy in most languages. But good translators are rare. When one is found, especially if skilled in theological material, it is worth the effort and financial incentive to secure his or her services. This assumes some standards in evaluation, like the following.

In most languages, it is not safe to assume that an oral translator, even an excellent one, is skilled to produce manuscripts suitable for publication. Before signing any publishers' contracts, then, it is imperative first to have a vetted team in place for every project: a translator, an editor, and a proofreader. This is especially important if one is working in a little-spoken language unsupported by any online artificial intelligence translation engines, whether free (e.g., Google Translate) or by fee (e.g., SmartCAT, DeepL, Amazon Translate).

It is not necessary to limit oneself to Christian translators or editors only. But it should be understood that, invariably, problems will arise without them. Unbelievers will not be as motivated to find the most advantageous solutions. It is, however, imperative that proofreaders be Christians of the highest moral character and, preferably, share the theological perspective of the missionary-publisher employing them.

One way to screen candidates for a project is to create test translation packets. Each packet could contain six pages of text, comprising two random pages from three different levels of text difficulty: popular, expositional or theological, and technical. If translating from an English base text, for example, the packet might include, respectively, two pages from a contemporary book on the Christian life, two from a Puritan treatise, and two from a theological journal or exegetical commentary (something that uses technical jargon, grammatical expressions, footnotes, and Hebrew and Greek fonts). Candidates will translate these pages as if submitting them for publication, which will demonstrate their grasp of both languages, their knowledge of literary standards, and their ability to work with biblical texts and fonts. Their translations should then be evaluated by native—not secondary—speakers of the target language for both technical precision and smoothness.

After screening, successful candidates should be interviewed for their moral character, academic training, and professional experience. At this stage, contracts that clearly communicate the terms of the working relationship should be reviewed, including details of pay, deadlines, methods of payment, and financial penalties. Multiple candidates may be hired for especially large projects or when the ministry can commission multiple projects simultaneously. Those hired should meet all of their publishing teammates and should meet and interact with the missions team using the project. Such meetings are the ideal time to sign contracts.

Long after we leave the mission field—and probably long after we leave this world—Christians in the countries we serve will be reading the literature that God allows us to publish. Such projects require large funding, and we need to be faithful stewards of those resources for the sake of those who give them, those who send us, and Jesus Christ. The above suggestions are intended to help missionaries do just that. May God use them both to strengthen church members and to train the next generation of pastors globally.

INSERT 53.4

Publishing for the "Nonreading," Spanish-Speaking, Latin American Church

Josué Pineda Dale

The Recent Growth of the Church

The Spanish-speaking church within the Latin American church has consistently grown in the last century.[9] In 2021 almost 496 million people worldwide spoke Spanish as their mother tongue.[10] Of these, writes

---

9. "Latin America" is usually considered to mean Mexico, Central America, South America, and those inhabitants of the Caribbean archipelago that speak Romance languages. The "Latin" label arose because of Spanish and Portuguese being such Romance languages (i.e., developed from Latin). Though their appearance in the Americas was a product of the European colonial era, today "Latin America" represents the vast majority of speakers of Spanish and Portuguese. Still, indigenous languages remain to be spoken in these regions, which, along with ethnic diversity across this vast geographic area, should remind foreign readers that Latin America is not monolithic.

10. David Fernández Vítores, *El español: Una lengua viva*, Informe 2021 del Instituto Cervantes (Madrid: Instituto Cervantes, 2021), 5, accessed June 18, 2024, https://cvc.cervantes.es/lengua/espanol_lengua_viva/pdf/espanol_lengua _viva_2021.pdf.

Miguel Núñez, "it is estimated that between 50 to 150 million people are Protestants. . . . Those numbers are important when we consider that a little more than a century ago there were only 50 thousand Protestants in Latin America."[11]

Migration played a significant part in expanding the Spanish-speaking church outside of Latin America and Spain. Spanish ministries and church plants are thriving, for example, in North America.[12] At the same time, the Lord is using migration to bring the gospel to many Latin American places that need to be re-evangelized, such as those dominated by the Pentecostal movement or the prosperity gospel.[13] In fact, in 2006 the *National Catholic Reporter* said that growth of evangelicals within Latin America was "dramatic."[14] Yet the Great Commission remains as urgent as ever, since approximately 90 percent of the population there remains Roman Catholic.[15]

As the Spanish-speaking church grows, so, too, does the need to publish more and better resources in Spanish. A complicating factor is that, according to the United Nations, "on average, 9% of those aged 15 and over are completely illiterate in Latin American and Caribbean countries (about 38 million people)."[16] Many others are literacy deficient without any reading habits, which earns for these nations the traditional label of "nonreading."[17] The governments have recognized the social and economic impact this detriment is having on their nations and are working internationally to remediate it.

For the missions-minded publisher, this

---

11. Miguel Núñez, *El poder de la Palabra para transformar una nación: Un llamada bíblico e histórico a la iglesia latino-americana* (Medellín, Colombia: Poiema Publicaciones, 2016), 27; David B. Barrett, ed., *World Christian Encyclopedia: A Comparative Survey of Churches and Religions in the Modern World* (Oxford: Oxford University Press, 2021), 186.

12. See Aaron Earls, "U.S. Protestant Hispanic Churches Are Finding Success in Building Community within Their Congregations and Reaching Those Outside Their Walls," Lifeway Research, accessed June 18, 2024, https://research.lifeway.com/2023/01/24/u-s-hispanic-protestant-landscape-full-of-growing-vibrant-churches/?fbclid=IwAR1kVpKEv7-FRrSUc_kCL3o3l4ZznlOoB6CY-8-n1mYYCWrnGtjQTh4PXiE&mibextid=Zxz2cZ.

13. See Núñez, *El poder de la Palabra para transformar una nación*, 15–37.

14. John L. Allen Jr., "The Dramatic Growth of Evangelicals in Latin America," *National Catholic Reporter*, August 18, 2006, https://www.ncronline.org/blogs/all-things-catholic/dramatic-growth-evangelicals-latin-america.

15. Núñez, *El poder de la Palabra para transformar una nación*, 24.

16. Economic Commission for Latin America and the Caribbean (ECLAC), "Illiteracy Affects Almost 38 Million People in Latin America and the Caribbean," ECLAC, December 2, 2013, https://www.cepal.org/en/news/illiteracy-affects-almost-38-million-people-latin-america-and-caribbean.

17. Cf. Richard Uribe, "Indicadores para el libro en seis países de América Latina," *Cultura y Dessarrollo* 7 (2012): 18–22. Some see this as an opportunity for the church. David Riaño, "Menos del 50% de los adultos latinos tienen hábitos de lectura, y eso podría representar una oportunidad para la iglesia," BITE Project, July 25, 2022, https://biteproject.com/menos-del-50-de-los-adultos-latinos-tienen-habitos-de-lectura-y-eso-podria-representar-una-oportunidad-para-la-iglesia/. See also "Latinoamericanos leen poco y lo hacen más por obligación," *La Nación*, April 11, 2012, https://www.nacion.com/viva/cultura/latinoamericanos-leen-poco-y-lo-hacen-mas-por-obligacion/JUJDZRHE4VEHRMZXH56L2ZDQL4/story/.

weakness in literacy is a unique challenge. However, it is no reason to despair of edifying the church with biblical and theological resources. Increasing demand indicates that the Spanish-speaking church is leaving behind the "nonreading" culture. Resourcing ministries, then, must assess these advancements and needs, and then rise to the challenge if they would steward their part in publishing God's good news (cf. Isa 52:7; Mark 13:10).

The Advancements and Needs of Publishing

Excluding Bible translations,[18] Christian resources in Spanish only recently became widely available.[19] In the nineteenth century, Protestantism had barely reached locals in their own language,[20] and because of that, publishing was practically nonexistent. That is corroborated by the fact that even three decades into the twentieth century, Protestants amounted to only 1 percent of the Latin American population.[21]

The growth of Protestantism in the Spanish-speaking world is considerable. However, the quality of materials available have missed the mark. For example, John Piper's book *Finally Alive: What Happens When We Are Born Again*[22] was originally translated into Spanish with the title *¡Más vivo que nunca!*,[23] which translated means "More alive than ever." That translation misses the author's entire point, drawn from Ephesians 2:1, that formerly the believer

18. Through James "Diego" Thomson and the Lancasterian method of education, which "used the Bible as its main text," Spanish Bibles were sent by the British and Foreign Bible Society to Buenos Aires, Argentina, around 1818, and later to other countries. Ondina E. González and Justo L. González, *Christianity in Latin America: A History* (New York: Cambridge University Press, 2008), 208–16. Before that the Sociedad Bíblica Británica (British Bible Society), founded in 1804, and the Sociedad Bíblica Americana (American Bible Society), founded in 1816, distributed "Bibles, tracts, and other Christian literature" for the purpose of evangelizing Latin America. Sociedad Bíblica de El Salvador, *Cien años de presencia evangélica en el Salvador: 1896–1996* (San Salvador, El Salvador: Sociedad Bíblica de El Salvador, 1996), 11; Wilton Nelson, *El protestantismo en Centro América* (Miami, FL: Editorial Caribe, 1982), 45.

19. In 1905 Casa Bautista de Publicaciones—now Editorial Mundo Hispano—started publishing in Spanish. A few years later, in 1924, Editorial CLIE was founded and published its first book. "Nosotros," Editorial Mundo Hispano, accessed June 18, 2024, https://www.editorialmh.org/nosotros/; "Conoce nuestra historia," CLIE, accessed June 18, 2024, https://www.clie.es/nosotros/conoce-nuestra-historia/.

20. According to González and González, one of the first reasons why Protestantism arrived in Latin America is immigration, and it stayed with them. González and González, *Christianity in Latin America*, 203. For example, "since 1825 there was Evangelical presence in Central America which was felt only within foreign groups. . . . Although geographically there was Evangelical presence, this was still isolated from Latin population and culture." Sociedad Bíblica de El Salvador, *Cien años de presencia evangélica en el Salvador*, 9.

21. Allen, "The Dramatic Growth of Evangelicals in Latin America." A few years earlier, in 1916 the "Primer Congreso de Acción Cristiana en América Latina (First Congress of Christian Action in Latin America) was clearly dominated by foreign missionary personnel and interests—out of 304 delegates, 28 were born in Latin America." González and González, *Christianity in Latin America*, 236.

22. John Piper, *Finally Alive*, rev. ed. (Fearn, Ross-shire, UK: Christian Focus, 2009).

23. John Piper, *¡Más vivo que nunca!* (Grand Rapids: Editorial Portavoz, 2010). The title of the book has since been corrected to *¡Por fin vivos!* (Grand Rapids: Editorial Portavoz, 2022), which translates exactly what the author is trying to convey.

was spiritually dead. In addition to translation issues, there are considerable delays in the distribution of resources to the furthest parts of South America, like Argentina, because of the complexities of the distribution chain, or even import regulations, among other reasons.[24]

The good news is that in recent years, the number of publishing houses in the Spanish-speaking world has grown, so that believers have more access to these resources than ever before, and many of them include contributions from indigenous voices.[25]

Generally speaking, sound Christian resources published in Spanish have been translated from English. The Lord has used the sacrifices of many scholars who have invested precious time and resources to translate Bible dictionaries, devotional commentaries, atlases, biographies, and Christian-living resources. But a gap still exists regarding books of the best theology, biblical counseling, historical theology, exegetical Bible commentaries, research tools, and works of more scholarly interaction. Similarly, apologetic books are needed that refute Christian heresies common in Latin America. The demands and needs of the Spanish-speaking church are greater than what has been translated so far.

Moreover, mere translation is sometimes not enough to adequately edify the church. Sometimes resources need to be edited and adapted. Spanish-speaking Christians in Paraguay and Chile are faced with different discipleship and apologetic issues than English-speaking Christians in North America or Australia. But adaptation requires translators with mature wisdom, and it takes time.

The Challenges and Opportunities for Missions

Some challenges are associated with the growing Spanish-speaking church. But in the Lord's hands, these are opportunities to set God's Word apart as precious and worthy of all our efforts to proclaim and obey it. A few may be considered here.

First, Latin American pastors, church planters, and publishers alike must cultivate a love for the reading of God's Word among His people. The social and economic benefits of literacy are good, but they profit nothing for eternity. Only God's Word saves and sanctifies. The main goal of Christian publishing, then, is to exposit, apply, or adorn the Scriptures. Biblical literacy is the Christian publisher's highest priority.

---

24. TecEx, experts in global import compliance, considers Argentina to be in their "5 Most Challenging Import Destinations," *TecEx*, August 11, 2021, https://tecex.com/the-5-most-challenging-import-destinations-in-the-world/.

25. See the list of current publishing houses that are members of the Spanish Evangelical Publishers Association, "Editoriales–Miembros Plenos," SEPA, accessed June 18, 2024, https://www.sepaweb.org/enlaces/editoriales-miembros-plenos/.

Publishers must invest in resources that promote the faithful reading of Scripture for the current and next generation.

Second, though translated literature comprises the majority of sound Spanish resources, it simply does not abound. More translated titles are becoming available today, but there are still great limitations to making more advanced materials available. To help overcome these limitations, capable, bilingual, missions-minded believers could always reach out to Spanish publishers, missionaries, or missions agencies to volunteer their involvement with translation and editing projects.

Third, the quality of resources published needs to improve. This does not apply equally in every setting; many publishers are producing high-quality materials. But Spanish readers often find low-quality products printed on bad paper or books with numerous typos and grammar mistakes. Spanish readers perceive this negatively, which deters them from buying books and, thus, from reading altogether. Therefore, quality work should matter to Christian publishers; it commends the value of the message they publish.

A fourth challenge is that the farther a country is from the United States—the publications "center of gravity"—the greater the problems. Latin America is geographically expansive, and countries farther south suffer delays, as much as several months. This is exacerbated by import tariffs, internal distribution problems, and bureaucracy, among other things. Translators and publishing ministries would be wise to make use of digital resources or to explore unconventional distribution options.

Finally, because Spanish-speaking churches have widely differing cultural backgrounds, much more must be done by indigenous Christians to address the unique needs and problems that arise locally. Local pastors and theologians need training to publish Christian resources in local languages. Churches in Latin America need the faithful teachers among them to put pen to paper, and to begin accumulating for their people the longer-term, multigenerational benefits of ministry in that context.

The Spanish-speaking Latin American church is growing rapidly and is emerging from a "nonreading" culture. Naturally, the reality of this characterization varies by country, church, and individual, and government-run progress will likely continue in the wider environment. But the church cannot wait. There is an urgent need to distribute God's Word and to promote its reading, study, and application through sound literature.

Trusting the Lord Step-by-Step: Lessons from a Kazakh Translator

Talgat Dossayev

There were no evangelical churches in Kazakhstan before the collapse of the Soviet Union. Imagine living in a nation where believers have gathered for only the last three decades! When you combine a young church with an uncommon language, you get a malnourished, untrained church. I once witnessed a small-town Kazakh pastor at a conference stand up to respond to a speaker who was fired up, calling believers to read good books on theology and pastoral ministry. The pastor replied that he could read only one book that year, a small one, because that was all that was newly available in the language.

When I was a teenager, as I learned about the sufficiency of Scripture, it hit me that for believers to grow, they need to study the Bible; to study the Bible, believers need tools, and those tools are books. In my youth, twenty years ago, most theological books I could obtain were in English, so I started learning English to read sound theology and translate good teaching into my native language of Kazakh. My aims have been much the same ever since, so I devoted my studies at university to earn a degree that would help me translate accurately, which I have applied to translating small, accessible Bible study and preaching books. While my translation work with a team is only scratching the surface of the need, I have struggled enough to have learned many lessons about how to choose resources to translate and become more efficient.

Lesson 1: Trust the Lord with Small Steps

Although I was starting to see the need for sound resources, few Christians in Kazakhstan were interested in having strong theology, saying that they didn't need Christian books. It didn't take long to realize that spiritual apathy toward the milk of the Word was endemic to all places, including Central Asia. Reading about biblical doctrine, especially translated from foreign authors, generally lacks appeal, but over time I noticed some changes in the Kazakh church, where people started recognizing the benefits they received from those pastors who preached expository sermons and expressed sound theology. Soon other pastors began to seek out more training resources. God worked not in my time but in His.

I learned during that period that I couldn't just start translating the grand theological treatises of church history. The believers needed resources to whet their appetites for more—books that are theologically sound but primarily devotional in quality. They needed books written by pastors who have proven faithful to the Scriptures and faithful as shepherds. They needed these brothers to explain Scripture in print and expand on its implications in a way that they would desire to apply to their own contexts. So when it came time to decide what works to translate and publish, I sought to find resources that were written on a level that is not too difficult for an average person to understand but is also deep enough to thoroughly explain the Scriptures and make that person hungry for deeper discussions. Later on will come other projects to build the library for higher education programs, such as university-level and postgraduate curriculum.

Lesson 2: Trust the Lord with Strenuous Steps

Another lesson I learned was that after I had a resource translation plan, I still had to deal with the political and corporate red tape. In Kazakhstan, religious literature has to be approved by the government, to confirm that you are not promoting some kind of negative activity toward the government, such as terrorism. The government must review the book and give approval, without which permission there is no going further in the process of assigning an international book number or printing the resource. Gaining state approval doesn't mean the resource will move through the full process. The fact that Kazakh is nowhere near one of the major world languages often means that missions agencies and Christian publishers do not print and distribute resources for such a small linguistics group. Organizations tend to focus on larger language demographics to reach more people.

Ironically, for our relatively minuscule target readership, there is a struggle to obtain the rights from the original publishers to translate their books into Kazakh. I often cannot get approval by myself, no matter how I try. Thankfully, there are organizations that have the capacity and interest to help people like me get through the copyright process by working through legal contracts; otherwise perhaps nothing would get translated for my people! Faithful translation thus requires knowing the laws of the country of ministry and praying for doors to be opened with the government, the original publishers, and distribution ministries.

Lesson 3: Trust the Lord with Scrupulous Steps

Another key lesson I have had to learn might be very obvious: after all the logistics align favorably on a project, no matter how fatiguing, I have to put excellent effort into translating. One of the most demanding tasks is translating theological terms. The slightest theological misunderstanding could cause significant confusion in the translated version. Two examples are helpful for grasping the importance of rigor and caution in translation.

The first example relates to Bible translation. The complete Kazakh Bible was first published in 2010, fixing biblical vocabulary to represent the biblical concepts in their literary contexts. But a pastor will soon realize that he needs to have terminology to express the theological concepts that emerge as one reads the Kazakh Bible. He must use new terminology to explain Scripture and hedge the biblical concepts and vocabulary; however, theological concepts in Kazakh are not yet all well-defined and readily translatable. To translate a biblical concept into Kazakh, my translation team and I must go to the original Greek and Hebrew languages, then Latin and English, long before we can look for corresponding words in Kazakh.

The second example relates to translating systematic theology works. Theology is so precise a discipline that biblically faithful translators need to spend considerable time and effort to contemplate the doctrines they are translating, consult faithful teammates and affiliates, and sometimes devise new words and phrases. For instance, just recently our translation team found out that for almost two decades the term that has been used for "counseling" also means "to survive." So to print "I am counseling" might cause some readers to think "I am surviving." Word choices in theology and ministry works, for a new field like ours, depend largely on translators taking the time to learn theology for themselves. The more the translator knows about the material under scrutiny, the more accurate the translation will be.

Lesson 4: Trust the Lord for Successful Steps

Translation work is one book at a time, and over time the work pays off. I hope that in the next twenty years we will have enough books in Kazakh for a seminary-level pastoral training program. I pray that in twenty-five years my people will be able to study the Scriptures for themselves with the tools they need, that pastors will be able to proclaim it from the pulpit faithfully, and that there will be at least one healthy church in each major city. I hope that thirty years from now there will be a pastor's conference where a speaker challenges the church to study theology faithfully and that not one pastor's library is lacking the tools needed to accurately handle the word of truth (2 Tim 2:15).

Translators struggling to get a project off the ground need to take one step at a time, as God leads. He will give the victory in His time. He will provide the necessary permissions, resources, and people. He will change the circumstances according to His will, including the theological appetites of His people. He can always be trusted to deliver His Word and the tools to understand it.

INSERT 53.6

A Lending Library and Bookstore in a Malawian Church

Newton Chilingulo

Lending Library

The idea to create a lending library first occurred to me when I reflected on the theological convictions that had the greatest impact on my life. I noted that much of my theological shaping came through reading books. I also realized that as a pastor I might not be able to reach everyone and disciple them with the depth I would like. It seemed fitting, then, to share the books I had at home with my brothers and sisters at church. With this, our lending library was born. The lending library began when we planted the Malawi church, and we maintained it for two years.

I brought approximately twenty to thirty titles to the church. Some were particularly accessible tracts or small paperbacks. I also brought devotional titles that were small, unintimidating books, perfect for a culture that is not well read. The more books I brought, the more our people hungered for more books.

In addition to devotional titles, I added books about ecclesiology that I read and determined to be biblically faithful. These resources benefited the church. For some of our church members, these were the first theologically rich books they had ever read. About 60 percent of our members read at least one of the books. Some read all the books on the shelf. We required members to submit a reading report before they were allowed to take another book. Sometimes the report was oral. I would ask them to explain the gist of the book they had finished. This helped me understand how much content each person was able to absorb. Overall, I was very encouraged with our church's hunger and ability to learn from books.

Two factors led to closing the lending library. First, we did not have any new books, and due to our geographical context, it was difficult to maintain the books we had. They always accrued damage from dust. Malawi is one of the dustiest places in the world, and only a few church members have spaces to keep a book for a prolonged period of time. Second, our church demolished the room that stored the bookshelf in order to expand the sanctuary and accommodate more attendees. As the church grew, there was no longer a place to put the books on display.

Bookstore

The building renovation gave us the opportunity to evaluate our book ministry. In addition to expanding the sanctuary, we added auxiliary rooms and designated one room as the bookshop. Rather than worrying about the returned books' quality, we sold books at modest prices. With the income from book sales, we purchased new titles and more copies of the most useful volumes.

The bookstore also became a resource for other churches around us. The transition from a lending library to a bookstore was important for at least four reasons. First, it expanded our book ministry's reach. We did not permit nonmembers to use the lending library. The store allowed other church pastors and members to access and purchase books for their churches.

Second, the bookshop in our congregation allowed us to showcase the doctrinal distinctives and conservative evangelical doctrines that we preach from our pulpit and teach in our classes. Third—and related—our bookshop is an alternative to the bookstores in our city that promote prosperity gospel titles that Christians buy out of ignorance and zeal for Christian learning. Prosperity authors are quite aggressive and are making their "wind" easily accessible here in Malawi (cf. 2 Pet 2:17; Jude 12). A bookshop with sound content provides the opportunity for Christians to access and be exposed to solid material from which they can learn the truth, put it on their own bookshelves in homes and congregations, lend it to others, and glorify God.

Fourth, since Malawi has a scarcity of materials written for Malawians and by Malawians, our bookstore could be an encouragement to believers by showcasing reliable resources that Malawians or other Africans are writing to God's glory.

Conclusion

Personally, I have been blessed to be discipled by a few intentional men. But I have been impacted and discipled by many more through the influence of their books. Good books make good disciplers. This creates a culture of robust readers who are studious in the things of God. We desire to cultivate that culture all the more for the good of our church, the good of the greater church in Malawi, and the glory of our Lord Jesus Christ.

PART 3

PRACTICES

Editors' Note

Part 3 exposes readers to several of the contemporary cross-cultural ministries commonly carried out by missionaries, missions agencies, and sending churches today. Only with a firm biblical and theological understanding of missions and the priority of the local church is it possible to set the parameters and guardrails for biblically faithful practices.

The arrangement of the topics breaks away from the dichotomized local-international ministry framework, which assumes ministries at home are not cross-cultural. Today the interconnectedness of nations and peoples affords many local churches the opportunity to reach different cultures and peoples who are within arm's length with less resourcing than typical of foreign-field ministry. Believers everywhere need to be encouraged by their church leaders to engage the nations both at home and abroad in realistic and achievable ways. The practices labeled "international" address some of the foreign-field challenges that missionaries encounter when they go from "here" to "there"—wherever "here" or "there" might be.

SECTION 1

LOCAL CROSS-CULTURAL PRACTICES

CHAPTER 54

Compassion and Commission: Proclaiming the Gospel to "the Poor"

Mark Tatlock

As those who have received God's extensive compassion, Christians should be compassionate toward their fellow man in tangible ways (cf. Matt 5:7; 18:33). As those who have received God's forgiveness, Christians are commissioned to proclaim the gospel of grace to their fellow man (Luke 24:46–48; John 20:21–23). But many missionaries and local church leaders fail to model to local believers how to extend compassion to the most hopeless among them—the poor.

Christ showed mercy to the poor while preaching to the poor, but His priority was gospel proclamation. That same priority should be emulated today—coupling the commission to evangelize with a compassion to help those who need it desperately. Scripture speaks about the poor categorically and about doing ministry to them with the heart of Christ. This chapter calls churches and missionaries back toward the biblical pairing of proclamation and mercy in their ministries through

their local churches. It does so by considering Christ's compassion for the poor, God's choosing of the poor, and, by way of application, the believer's commission to the poor.

Christ's Compassion for the Poor

The ministry and teaching of Jesus regarding the needy assumed the compassion commanded by God in the Old Testament, based on His own character (e.g., Deut 10:18–19; 15:11 [cf. John 12:8]; 24:17–22; Pss 41:1–3; 68:5–6; 72:12–15; 146:9; Prov 22:22–23). Jesus both taught and did tangible mercy ministry. But the social category of "the poor" also served in His teaching to figuratively illustrate the spiritual realities of every individual's identity apart from grace. The significance of that motif is seen when Christ first revealed Himself as the fulfillment of the messianic promises of Isaiah 61:1–2 in the synagogue of His hometown, Nazareth, in Luke 4:18–21:

"The Spirit of the Lord is upon me,
Because He anointed me to preach the
gospel to the poor.
He has sent me to proclaim release to
the captives,
And recovery of sight to the blind,
To set free those who are oppressed,
To proclaim the favorable year of
the Lord."

And He closed the scroll, gave it back to the attendant and sat down, and the eyes of all in the synagogue were fixed on Him. And He began to say to them, "Today this Scripture has been fulfilled in your hearing."

It is, first of all, important to notice that Jesus' Spirit-empowered ministry was thoroughly proclamational: "to preach the gospel to the poor" (v. 18). Second, Jesus paralleled "the poor" with the captive, the blind, and the oppressed as all being recipients of the good news of God's favor. He made a similar parallel in Luke 7:22 as evidence that He was the Christ: "The blind receive sight, the lame walk, the lepers are cleansed, and the deaf hear, the dead are raised up, the poor have the gospel preached to them" (Luke 7:22). "The poor" as audience of the gospel, according to Jesus' teaching, was a generalization encompassing all who were spiritually blind (John 3:3; 9:39–41), spiritually deaf (Matt 13:13), spiritually captive (Luke 13:16; John 8:34), and spiritually dead (John 5:25) but who confessed their spiritual neediness and received mercy (Matt 5:3; Luke 6:20). Jesus was communicating in all of these

instances that He was the One to meet the spiritual needs that the earthly categories of poverty illustrated.

Christ came "to seek and to save the lost" (Luke 19:10). He chose not to establish Himself in a comfortable location, requiring those interested to come and sit at His feet. Rather, in a style dramatically different from the Pharisees, who loved the places of honor at banquets and the respectable seats in the synagogues (Matt 23:6–7), Jesus chose to live simply and to associate with the poor, the lowly, the outcast, and the weary, heavy-laden (Matt 8:20; 11:28–30; 19:21; Luke 5:29–32; 7:36–50; 14:12–14; 15:1–7; 19:5–10). From the temple courts to the homes of tax collectors and sinners, from open-air preaching to the dusty pilgrim highways, Jesus ministered in person to those who were both physically and spiritually impoverished.

The Lord was often "moved with compassion" at the sight of needy people (Matt 14:14; 15:32; 20:34; Mark 1:41; Luke 7:13). But His compassion for their physically impoverished condition always extended to their spiritual impoverishment too. On one such occasion in Galilee, while busy teaching in synagogues, preaching the gospel, and healing every kind of malady, Jesus, upon seeing the crowds, "felt compassion for them" (Matt 9:36). As they continued bringing Him the sick, He turned to His disciples, and said, "The harvest is plentiful, but the workers are few. Therefore pray earnestly to the Lord of the harvest to send out workers into His harvest" (Matt 9:37–38). By "harvest," Jesus meant nothing less than the conversion of souls to faith in Him for eternal life (cf. Luke

10:1–2, 9, 16; John 4:35–36). Thus, His compassion for the plight of the "distressed and downcast" in Matthew 9 elicited compassion for their spiritual condition too, resulting in a prayer for commission obedience, the proclamation of the gospel.

In all this, Jesus prioritized proclaiming the gospel, and showed mercy while doing so. His acts of compassion were the living illustrations of the compassion that He preached in His sermons (e.g., Matt 5:7; 6:2–4; 10:7–8; 23:23; 25:35–36; Luke 6:27–36; 11:39–42; 12:33–34; 15:17–24). Though, beyond that, His life, death, and resurrection were the very substance of God's greatest compassion toward sinners; for, "though being rich, yet for [their] sake He became poor, so that [they] through His poverty might become rich" (2 Cor 8:9). Missionaries who follow Jesus' compassionate example and who keep His commission to proclaim Him, though perhaps being poor, will also be "making many rich" (2 Cor 6:10).

God's Choosing of the Poor

How the local church should treat the poor is given explicitly in the epistle of Jesus' half brother James. There again, the gospel and the poor are correlated, and that with profound insight for missions today. The category of the poor recurs multiple times in the book (e.g., Jas 1:9–11; 1:27–2:13; 5:1–6). Of interest for this chapter is its occurrence in 1:27: "Pure and

undefiled religion before our God and Father is this: to visit orphans and widows in their affliction, and to keep oneself unstained by the world."

James' audience, being primarily Jewish converts to Christianity (cf. 1:1),[1] needed only to hear the phrase "orphans and widows" to be reminded of Old Testament instructions for the larger category of the poor.[2] The verse is also a twofold statement describing both the love of God and the holiness of God. Both perfections work in harmony and are expected to become characteristic of all who confess the true God and "faith in our glorious Lord Jesus Christ" (2:1). "Visiting" the poor in times of distress means meeting their needs, whatever they may be.[3]

The category having been so introduced, James elaborates in 2:1–13. He admonishes the believers not to show favoritism to visitors in their midst who appear wealthy over against those who appear poor, nor to make such distinctions among themselves, which is the sin of partiality (vv. 1–4, 9; cf. Deut 10:17; Acts 10:34; Rom 2:11). Verse 5, then, is the crux for missions, saying, "Listen, my beloved brothers: did not God choose the poor of this world to be rich in faith and heirs of the kingdom which He promised to those who love Him?"

God has chosen that many from the poor would be saved. James' theology of election here correlates to Paul's in Ephesians 1:4–6, that God from eternity past elected those who

---

1. Cf. "the twelve tribes of the Dispersion" with John 7:35. Craig L. Blomberg and Miriam J. Kamell, *James*, ZECNT 16 (Grand Rapids: Zondervan, 2008), 28–29; Ralph P. Martin, *James*, WBC 48 (Dallas, TX: Word, 1988), 8.

2. Cf. Blomberg and Kamell, *James*, 94–95; D. Edmond Hiebert, *James*, rev. ed. (Winona Lake, IN: BMH, 1997), 127.

3. "ἐπισκέπτομαι," BDAG, 378; Hiebert, *James*, 126–27.

would be beneficiaries of the gospel. In God's sovereignty, James says, God has predestined for faith many whom He has also decreed would be poor. It is God who "makes poor and rich" (1 Sam 2:7–8; cf. Job 31:13–15; Prov 14:31; 22:2), and, profoundly, He uses that prerogative in concert with His prerogative to grant faith. Thus, "the poor of this world" (or poor in the eyes of the world),[4] more often than the rich, are beloved in God's eyes, the objects of His kindness and favor. He has chosen that they be "rich in faith," that they possess the precious treasure of faith that God Himself grants from above (Jas 1:17–18; cf. Acts 11:18; Eph 2:8–9). Thus, the poor believer's material poverty and spiritual riches are inversely related.

James does not imply that all the poor will be saved, nor that there is any moral merit in being poor. Rather, poverty is a picture of one's total lack of merit, highlighting his inability to purchase God's forgiveness (Isa 55:1–7; 2 Cor 8:9; cf. 1 Cor 1:26–29).[5] No, James means that the worldly poverty of the poor, rather than placing them at a spiritual disadvantage to the rich, more often prepares them for faith. Practically speaking, the poor are usually conscious of their material want, often reduced to begging for mercy to relieve their circumstances. They lack the earthly possessions that, by the world's estimation, can make a person happy. From a spiritual perspective, however,

the poor are in the better position to receive eternal joy, to understand God's saving provision, and to be drawn to Him.[6]

Thus, the viewpoint of God's kingdom is often countercultural. The world, seeking wealth, power, and prosperity, rejects the greatest treasure of knowing God (Jer 9:23–24). Those who have great personal wealth can more easily attempt to live without acknowledging the God on whom they are actually dependent and to whom they are accountable (Deut 8:16–18; Prov 10:15; Luke 12:13–21). They are distracted by their riches or deceived by them into false feelings of security (Matt 13:22; 19:23–26; Luke 12:13–21; cf. Rev 3:17). Dependence on God is most often experienced when one reaches the end of his own ability to meet the needs he faces. It is only then that he turns to God in faith and receives the boundless "riches of His grace" (Eph 1:7; 3:8; cf. Rom 10:12).

Again, the notion of the poor's salvation is predicated on genuine "faith in our glorious Lord Jesus Christ" (Jas 2:1). But since the poor do not have the material means to mask the pain of living in a fallen world, as the wealthy do, they are oftentimes more aware of their broken, needy, desperate spiritual condition, which can lead them to consider the gospel call to faith and repentance (Matt 5:3). The missionary and local church leader should reflect on the fact that, in reality, every human being

---

4. Grant R. Osborne, *James: Verse by Verse*, Osborne New Testament Commentaries (Bellingham, WA: Lexham, 2019), 68.

5. By this is meant simply that poverty is an object lesson, an illustration, not that poverty and wealth are expressions of *retribution theology*, the notion that all suffering is the direct result of a one's own sin (cf. John 9:2–3). On the latter, see the explanation in Tremper Longman III, "Retribution Theology in a Nutshell," in *Job*, Baker Commentary on the Old Testament: Wisdom and Psalms (Grand Rapids: Baker Academic, 2012), 159–61.

6. Blomberg and Kamell, *James*, 112.

is spiritually destitute in God's eyes, incapable of reciprocating His grace in any manner. Therefore, when ministering the gospel to the world's poor, the principles of the gospel of grace can be powerfully illustrated by how the missionary or church leader conducts his ministry (Matt 5:16; Jas 2:18).

The spiritual wealth of the poor is also expressed in what results from their precious faith—they are "heirs of the kingdom" (Jas 2:5). That phrase focuses not on immediate blessing but on the future, eschatological hope. The redeemed possess the glorious prospect of inheriting the kingdom with their sovereign Lord, Jesus Christ (Matt 5:3; 25:34; Luke 12:32). Therefore, the poor are also rich materially with a home and treasures in the present heaven (Matt 6:19–21; John 14:1–3), a future glorified body (Rom 8:23; 1 Cor 15:35–57), a crown of life (1 Cor 9:25; Jas 1:12; Rev 2:10), and an inheritance in the new heavens and new earth (1 Pet 1:4–5; 2 Pet 3:13). The kingdom, James says, and all its benefits, God "promised to those who love Him" (2:5; cf. 1:12). Notably, the verb is past tense, looking back to the fact that God made the promise to those whom He elected in ages long past.[7]

The Believer's Commission to the Poor

The opportunities are limitless for missionaries and church leaders to bring their disciples with them to extend the compassion of Christ to the neediest around them and gain a hearing for the gospel in their contexts. Yet it can also be that their search for an audience extends everywhere but among the poor in their community, that they are simply looking for a different kind of audience. It is a terrible incongruity when God's ministers of compassion, grace, and mercy refuse to extend those very gifts to the destitute in their midst. The age-old accusation of hypocrisy—well known to anyone who has attempted to regularly spread the gospel—is not unwarranted in this case. Unwillingness or disinterest characterizes such local churches in the eyes of their neighbors, who see the physically impoverished in front of them being ignored. The hope of the gospel then becomes difficult for people to hear when so many obvious needs on the ground go unmet (cf. 1 John 3:17; 4:20). The missionary or church leader is to blame for the local church being a poor model of Christ in the community.[8]

Self-denial characterized the leadership and the laity of the primitive church in Jerusalem. In Acts 2 the church was quick to share what they possessed to meet the needs of those who were in great physical need (vv. 44–45). The self-love, sinful pride, and callous disregard for others that characterized them before their conversion (cf. Titus 3:3) was affected by their true repentance so that they were characterized

---

7. Hiebert, *James*, 141.

8. "Verbal witness to the gospel cannot be separated from practical demonstrations of love and action addressing human need. To do so would be to undermine the credibility of the gospel and to be a living denial of the very message we proclaim." Craig Ott and Stephen J. Strauss, *Encountering Theology of Mission: Biblical Foundations, Historical Developments, and Contemporary Issues*, Encountering Mission (Grand Rapids: Baker, 2010), 145.

by self-denial and a love for others that sought their practical good.

Christ's invitation to His disciples to deny themselves, take up their cross, and follow Him (Mark 8:34–35) is an invitation to imitate Christ by pursuing the broken and needy with the gospel message and with practical help. Missionaries and church leaders should purposefully and prayerfully lead the believers in their ministries toward those populations that Scripture teaches are the most ready and receptive to hear the message of life and hope. In so doing, compassion for the poor might, in fact, lead to a fulfilled commission, as disciples in the local church evangelize and make new disciples of those that were, until that moment, simply ignored. By preaching of the gospel to all kinds of people, more sinners will have the chance to experience the greater riches of the mercy and grace of God, who alone can satisfy and restore the soul. Feeding the hungry, ministering to the sick, and serving the poor is not an end unto itself but a means through which some sinners, who are acutely aware of their spiritual need, will look up and see Christ radiating through the messenger.

INSERT 54.1

Three Approaches to Compassion Ministries: Maintaining a Biblical Approach

Brian Biedebach

A shift in missions over the past fifty years has resulted in fewer missionaries doing gospel proclamation, church strengthening, or church planting. Instead, many are active in social action, medical missions, social justice for child trafficking, legal teams, orphanages, and well drilling. This more "holistic" approach to missions work represents a shift where church planting and church strengthening have taken a backseat to social action. However, there needs to be a biblical approach to social issues that maintains the proper balance between focusing on gospel proclamation and maintaining the ability to show compassion and mercy to those suffering. This insert will briefly overview three main approaches to missions and argue that the biblical approach to compassion ministries is a mature church that shows mercy to those around them as a fruit of their spiritual maturity.

The First Approach: Holistic Missions

The first approach to compassion ministries can be called "holistic missions." This view became popular in the 1980s out of the Lausanne movement, and the idea is that spiritual renewal comes through preaching and social action together. The argument is that since Jesus not only preached the gospel but fed the hungry and healed the sick, missions today should take a similarly holistic approach to outreach. Promoters of this approach wrote in 1982, "In [Jesus'] ministry, *kerygma* (proclamation) and *diakonia* (service) went hand in hand. . . . Both were expressions of his compassion for people, and both should be ours."[9]

One of the main downsides of this approach, however, is that missionaries often get sidetracked from the essential work of preaching the gospel and teaching disciples.[10] In one of my first missionary assignments in Central Africa, I filled in for a missionary on furlough who had many business and agricultural programs underway. We were practicing a form of holistic missions, doing just about everything one can imagine a missionary doing. In addition to evangelism and teaching, there were chickens, goats, the building of an orphanage, well drilling, and more. The problem was that the local church was very weak in the area. The looming question was, who was going to disciple those who had come to faith in Christ? Oftentimes the daily work of protecting, maintaining, and operating the land that we owned took up almost all our time. A better situation would have been for us to focus solely on discipling people in the Scriptures, and possibly to have partnered with a separate school, led by someone else, that focused on training farmers or giving people practical skills.

The Second Approach: Extreme Holism

A second approach to compassion ministries is extreme holism, sometimes called "revisionist holism" by analysts,[11] wherein human welfare is the goal, and it is accomplished

---

9. John R. W. Stott, ed., "Evangelism and Social Responsibility: An Evangelical Commitment," Lausanne Occasional Paper 21, presented at the International Consultation on the Relationship between Evangelism and Social Responsibility, June 19–25, 1982 (Grand Rapids: Lausanne Committee for World Evangelism; World Evangelical Fellowship, 1982); https://lausanne.org/content/lop/lop-21.

10. John Stott acknowledged this potential in John R. W. Stott, *The Contemporary Christian: Applying God's Word to Today's World* (Downers Grove, IL: InterVarsity, 1992), 409. D. A. Carson's later critique is poignant: "At one time, 'holistic ministry' was an expression intended to move Christians beyond proclamation to include deeds of mercy. Increasingly, however, 'holistic ministry' refers to deeds of mercy without any proclamation of the gospel—and that is not holistic. It is not even halfistic, since the deeds of mercy are not the gospel. . . . The biggest hole in our gospel is the gospel itself." D. A. Carson, "The Hole in the Gospel," *Them* 38 (2013): 357.

11. The "revisionist" terminology comes from David J. Hesselgrave (*Paradigms in Conflict: 10 Key Questions in Christian Missions Today* [Grand Rapid: Kregel, 2005], 120–22), who recognizes this form of holism as a revision of liberation theology,

either through gospel proclamation or social action. Whereas holism is a "both/and" approach, in which proclaiming the gospel is essential, extreme holism is an "either/or" approach, in which proclaiming the gospel is nonessential. Missions could be anything that uplifts a community.

Extreme holism rejects "the dichotomy between material and spiritual, between evangelism and social action, between loving God and loving neighbor."[12] It focuses on the well-being and completeness of the target population. Its key term is often biblical *shalom*, defined by proponents as being essentially "rooted in justice and compassion."[13] Extreme holism views the Great Commission as a passage that emphasizes but one option among others that a Christian has in missions. In this vein, influential missiologist David Bosch wrote that the "missionary nature" of Jesus' ministry shows that "God's reign [or kingdom] arrives wherever Jesus overcomes the power of evil."[14] This can be in the Church or in society. Thus, the duties of gospel proclamation and discipling believers become even more diluted amid extreme holism's broad

aims of peace and prosperity than they were with the aims of moderate holism.

The Third Approach: The Priority of Preaching

The third and most biblical approach to compassion ministries is the priority of preaching. Herein the goal of spiritual renewal comes through the proclamation of the gospel, with social action being a by-product of changed hearts. Thus, the center of ministry necessarily remains the local church. When a church is planted, it will reach out to the community when it is mature and marked by inward change in its members. Social action is still present but as the fruit of believers reaching outward evangelistically.

In the words of Kevin DeYoung and Greg Gilbert, "It simply was not Jesus' driving ambition to heal the sick and meet the needs of the poor, as much as he cared for them. He was sent into the world to save people from condemnation (John 3:17), that he might be lifted up so believers could have eternal life (3:14–15)."[15] It profits sinners nothing if their lives are improved

---

the mission of which is to "promote justice in society and to establish *shalom* on the earth" (cf. Hesselgrave, 122, fig. 4).

12. Bryant L. Myers, *Walking with the Poor: Principles and Practices of Transformational Development* (Maryknoll, NY: Orbis, 1999), 327.

13. James F. Engel and William A. Dyrness, *Changing the Mind of Missions: Where Have We Gone Wrong?* (Downers Grove, IL: InterVarsity, 2000), 93.

14. David J. Bosch, *Transforming Mission: Paradigm Shifts in the Theology of Mission*, American Society of Missiology 16 (Maryknoll, NY: Orbis, 1991), 32.

15. Kevin DeYoung and Greg Gilbert, *What Is the Mission of the Church? Making Sense of Social Justice, Shalom, and the Great Commission* (Wheaton, IL: Crossway, 2011), 55. Also see Köstenberger's critique of the "incarnational model"

only to enter hell for eternity, if they gain the world but lose their souls (Matt 16:26). Therefore, the priority in missions must be the preaching of the gospel.

Conclusion

Over the span of nineteen years as a missionary in Africa, I noticed a growing trend in social action in our area and throughout the continent, as far as I could see. It seemed as if foreign churches continued pumping in social action missionaries, while missionaries involved in church-planting and church-strengthening ministries, like ours, dwindled in number. When we lost church-planting missionaries, they seemed not to be replaced, leaving a sense of imbalance. It was like the churches in the West left a garden hose on, and the end of the hose was in Africa—the water was pouring out in a wasteful way that was not accomplishing much. The message must get out to Western churches to turn off the tap and focus on "cultivating the kingdom" God's way. There are many things churches can be doing to alleviate poverty and injustice in the world. However, there are certain responsibilities they must do to fulfill the Great Commission, namely, teaching and baptizing. If we neglect the things we *must* do in order to do the things we *can* do, then we are failing to be faithful in our focus.

All missionary-sending churches need to determine if their missionaries are focused on gospel proclamation or on social action. The latter neither saves the lost nor builds up those who come to Christ. To be sure, there is a need for social support ministries. However, if compassion ministries are all that the churches are resourcing and running, then those churches are imbalanced and will lose sight of their true mission to proclaim the good news of eternal life and to make disciples. Balance begins when churches determine what percentage of its missionaries will be sent for the Great Commission/gospel proclamation ministry and what percentage will be sent for supportive compassion ministries. There is no lack of funds, only a lack of focus—so it is time for mission committees to evaluate where their focus lies. If they are not intentional about focusing their efforts on proclamation ministry, they will be at risk of becoming merely a social organization, dealing only with people's physical needs.

---

advocated by proponents of holism based on John 20:21. Andreas J. Köstenberger, *The Mission of Jesus and the Disciples according to the Fourth Gospel: With Implications for the Fourth Gospel's Purpose and the Mission of the Contemporary Church* (Grand Rapids: Eerdmans, 1998), 217.

Compassionate Evangelism: Toward Best Practices

Shannon Hurley

Outlook on life is greatly impacted by surroundings. For those living with advanced medical services, financial means, a strong justice system, and a government that fills in necessary social services, their outlook on life can fail to perceive the significance of their basic necessities. But for those living in a world with poor medical services, meager financial resources, a corrupt justice system, and a government disinterested in caring for its people, their perspective on life can be dominated by the scarcity of their basic necessities. This is often the case in the majority world. Missionaries in many majority world countries find themselves caught between these two outlooks on life, having grown up taking many things for granted but now serving people who struggle to find food, water, shelter, health, and security. That is why accompanying evangelism, which addresses the spiritual problem, with compassionate deeds toward physical problems is an important component of missions in so many contexts. Compassion is not itself evangelism, but evangelism should be compassionate.

The Rationale for Compassionate Evangelism

How should the Church respond evangelistically toward the hurting? To state the obvious: the Church should seek a way to help. How should a believer respond to hundreds of abandoned children on the streets or to an unattended person bleeding to death after a motorcycle accident? How should a Christian respond to a woman whose husband unexpectedly dies, leaving her with no income and six children? What is the proper Christian response to victims of war who are starving? Should a missionary in a village preach the Word without teaching the people to read? Or should a pastor preach to starving people and do nothing to try to satisfy their hunger?

These questions are daily realities around the world. Since faith without works is dead (Jas 2:14–26), the Church should demonstrate its faith in deeds of mercy as the Lord allows. Rather than merely praying for those in need, believers should pray to be God's agents of bringing solutions to the problems. Serving orphans, widows, prisoners, and other underresourced or marginalized groups embodies pure and undefiled religion (Jas 1:27). For this reason, the evangelistic efforts of missionaries and local churches should strive to be compassionate in nature—preaching the Word and looking to help the needy in physical ways that demonstrate the love of Christ practically.

Suggested Best Practices for Compassionate Evangelism

What are the best practices for compassionate evangelism? There are at least three. First, remember that compassionate evangelism seeks to constructively apply biblical commands to the real-life circumstances of hurting people. Because God calls for justice and mercy in the lives of His people (Mic 6:8; Prov 21:3; Isa 1:16–17; 2 Pet 1:5–8), the Church should be motivated to extend justice and mercy to sinners, who need the Savior. Jesus Christ's response to the suffering around Him exemplifies the mercy the Church is called to offer. Acts of mercy, in biblical terms, fall under the command to "love your neighbor" (Mark 12:31; Jas 2:8, 14–17). Therefore, planning activities of practical compassion alongside your evangelism strategy is a tangible way to be

Christlike. Mercy ministries are a valuable tool in a well-rounded approach to ministering to those around us.

Bible-preaching churches can be criticized as loveless, though developing a strategy for mercy ministry would change this narrative. Paul says, "If I speak with the tongues of men and of angels, but do not have love, I have become a noisy gong or a clanging cymbal" (1 Cor 13:1). Yet mercy ministry must remain within the context of proclamation ministry, for Paul also cautions, "If I give all my possessions to feed the poor, and if I surrender my body to be burned, but do not have love, it profits me nothing" (13:3). Compassionate evangelism is biblically loving and glorifies God because it powerfully displays God's love in word and in deed (1 John 3:18).

The second best practice for compassionate ministry to the needy is to remember that preaching the gospel is the only means of true and lasting transformation. In an effort to feed the hungry, educate the unlearned, comfort the brokenhearted, and mend the sick, one's eyes of compassion must remain fixated on treating the sick spiritual condition. What does it profit a man to gain the whole world but to forfeit his soul (Mark 8:36–37)? The proclaimed gospel is the Holy Spirit's tool for releasing a person from sin's power. Because God grows His Church through proclamation of the truth, love cannot replace truth, for mercy ministry without evangelism is simply humanitarian aid; it is not missions. The mercy part of the ministry must stay in its proper place: it is a servant to gospel proclamation rather than an equally ultimate goal of the mission.

As a third best practice, compassionate evangelism should be centered around the local church. Gospel workers must always direct the people they reach toward a church family. Mercy ministry and evangelism without a local church is like swimming without water. Will Christ build His Church without building up local churches? A new believer can learn to share Christ and care for the lost with the help of a parachurch organization or even on his own, but without being attached to a local church body, he has nowhere to grow and be discipled. Therefore, compassionate evangelism should be carried out alongside a local church in order to fulfill the Great Commission command to raise up new disciples who will mature in faithful obedience to the Lord in the body of Christ (Eph 4:12–13).

Conclusion

Jesus told His disciples in Matthew 5:16, "Let your light shine before men in such a way that they may see your good works, and glorify your Father who is in heaven." If a missionary moves from privileged contexts to less-resourced parts of the world, opportunities to do good deeds will be easily identifiable. They are natural Christlike responses to the hurting world around him. This response will not only satisfy the temporal with much-needed mercy; it will impact the eternal with God-glorifying truth.

CHAPTER 55

Thinking Biblically about Poverty and Spirituality

Faly Ravoahangy

Poverty is a personal reality for many around the globe. Over one billion people fall into the category of "extreme poverty," with immediate threats of starvation, chronic hunger, deprivation of basic shelter, safe drinking water, sanitation, sufficient clothing, health care, and education.[1] A third of those in extreme poverty live on the African continent. Economic reports indicate that the twelve poorest countries in the world in 2020 were all located in Africa. Madagascar, my native country and context of ministry, is ninth on that list.[2]

The word *poor* is used nearly two hundred times in the Bible, with the majority of occurrences pointing to material poverty.[3] The Bible does not spiritualize poverty away; it describes and addresses it as a reality (John 12:8). Believers, whether in urban or rural settings, must hold to a biblical framework about all things, including poverty, the Lord's providence, and individual responsibilities toward one another.

This chapter will seek to equip missionaries and congregations worldwide by shaping their thinking about material possessions and their responsibility toward the poor accordingly so that they will be equipped to faithfully display God's mercy. It first examines the spiritual pitfalls related to the acquisition and handling of money that both rich and poor must avoid. It then sets forward practices to embrace.

---

1. "Poverty," *The World Bank Group*, May 11, 2015, https://www.worldbank.org/en/topic/poverty.

2. In Madagascar 75 percent of the population is estimated to live below the international poverty line. See Luca Ventura, "Poorest Countries in the World 2024," *Global Finance Magazine*, May 6, 2024, https://www.gfmag.com/global-data/economic-data/the-poorest-countries-in-the-world.

3. William D. Mounce, ed., "poor," *Mounce's Complete Expository Dictionary of Old and New Testament Words* (Grand Rapids: Zondervan, 2006), 521–22; cf. the definition "being economically disadvantaged" or "dependent on others for support," in "πτωχός," BDAG, 896.

Pitfalls to Avoid

The global church is exposed to many spiritual snares in its stand against "the lust of the flesh and the lust of the eyes and the boastful pride of life" (1 John 2:16). Missionaries and church workers must endeavor to draw the believers' attention to three dangers related to one's view of earthly possessions: a faulty view of truth, a faulty view of money, and a faulty view of self and others.

Faulty View of Truth

When Paul reached the end of his first letter to Timothy, he went back to the theme with which he began. He was concerned with the increasing influence of false teachers in the church (1 Tim 1:3–20; 6:3–5). He asserted that false teachers are recognizable by their corrupt talk as they promote false doctrines aloof from sound biblical teaching (6:3), by their corrupt walk as they spew false rumors and controversies to cause strife (6:4), and by their corrupt hearts, which are motivated solely by financial gain (6:5).

False teaching often promotes the social needs of the poor and political liberation for oppressed peoples as the priority and *raison d'être* for the church. False teachers want people to focus on material resources, labeling possessions as a sign of God's approval on one's life. But in wealth or poverty, God's Word remains the sure and steady compass to guide every disciple through the difficulties of life. As the pillar and foundation of the truth (1 Tim 3:15), the local church must be a shield from the pervasive spread of false teaching.

Faulty View of Money

Paul's first-century instruction about material possessions and contentment are still needed today. Paul explained to Timothy that Christians should live godly lives of contentment (1 Tim 6:6–8). Twin stumbling blocks to living this way include being constantly dissatisfied or looking for satisfaction in the wrong places. Discontentment leads to spiritual apathy because it directs one's focus to what is lacking. It distorts one's view of the past, destroys the present, and ultimately assaults God's character.

Paul gave three keys to being content. First, Christians need to know what is truly valuable (1 Tim 6:6). For Paul, the goal for the Christian is to find satisfaction in a growth in godliness, a genuine relationship with God, and a healthy detachment from material things. "Gain" here is measured according to spiritual character rather than material value. Second, Christians need to ground their contentment in their knowledge of what will last (6:7). Material things belong only to this world and provide no eternal advantage. Christian hope takes the believer beyond the limits of the physical realm to a boundless eternity.

Third, Paul defines poverty and wealth to help his readers ascertain what is enough. To be biblically poor is to lack food or clothing (6:8). For the believer, however, real contentment and material prosperity have nothing to do with one another. The trap here, for both rich and poor, is attaching satisfaction to material possession (Luke 12:15). In the Malagasy culture of Madagascar, for example, both the rich and the poor operate from a worldview of defeatism, which believes that poverty or prosperity result from a predetermined fate, an ounce of good or bad fortune based on one's ability to please or not please one's ancestors, and some sort of accumulated providence based on past bad deeds. But the believer knows far better (Jas 1:9–11).

Next, in 1 Timothy 6:9–10, Paul speaks of the trap of the insatiable pursuit of money. The lust for money quickly becomes a heart demand and irrevocably leads to physical and spiritual destruction. Acquiring material wealth can quickly become a burning passion and cause people to wander away from the faith (1 Tim 1:19–20; 6:21). Paul therefore warns the believer against covetousness (1 Tim 6:11–12). Greed is a sin that afflicts both the rich and poor. It involves a shift of one's hope from God to money. This outlook pollutes the Christian's worldview and priorities. When one is rich, there can be extravagance, misspending, greed, neglect of the poor, pride, or forgetfulness of God. On the other hand, believers who live in poverty can likewise be focused more on the physical than the spiritual, leaving themselves prone to jealousy, covetousness, partiality, and again, forgetfulness of God.

Faulty View of Self and Others

Earthly possessions or lack thereof can affect one's view of his own circumstances. People in deep poverty need hope. They seek something to hold on to. Amid their preoccupations for the next meal or shelter, they need to hold on to the promises of God (Matt 6:25–31), all the while keeping in mind the coming day when God will dispense justice and reward. They must believe that the blessedness of life here does not consist in what a man has, but in who he is (Prov 10:16–17). Both wealth and poverty can be either blessings or curses, but a good conscience and godly character are a continual feast (Ps 112:1–2; Prov 22:4; Jas 2:5). The wealthy believer must resolve not to be preoccupied by amassing possessions, nor must he put his trust in them. Rather, he must strive to be generous, abound in kindness, and put the physical and spiritual benefit of others before his own (1 Tim 6:17–19). Scripture does not encourage Christians to accumulate possessions. Instead, it prioritizes the acquisition of wisdom (Prov 3:13–15; 10:22; 16:16).

Another danger to avoid is allowing financial status to shape one's view of relationships with others, especially within the church. At times the poor can feel like second-class citizens within the kingdom of God (Jas 2:1–9). They also can develop resentment at how the rich flaunt and use their resources, and harbor silent expectations that those they deem to have apparent wealth would be generous toward them.

Relationships within the church must be oriented around serving the same Lord and Savior, not on faulty perceptions, beliefs, or status. The poor must learn to focus their attention on God, not on their felt needs or on what they observe of fellow believers. In the same way, the rich must learn not to see their brother or sister in need as one who seeks to take advantage of their resources. God wants His people to display His generous and compassionate nature (Deut 15:7–11), thus believers are called to love and to give. Those with resources must guard their hearts and minds from imputing motives to fellow believers but believe the best of others (1 Cor 13:6–7) as they fully rely on God to exercise His justice on those who take advantage of their magnanimity.

When engaging in global missions, the church leadership must be equipped to train their congregants to avoid these spiritual pitfalls and hold to the biblical mindset toward money and possessions. The poor believer must transcend the local worldview and culture, and work hard, trust God, and grow in godliness. Those with means must become an example of detachment from material things and generosity. A set of practices are to be adopted in order to build a healthy biblical worldview.

Practices to Embrace

To grow in Christlikeness and to gain a healthy detachment from money and possessions, believers in the local church must be trained by the missionary and/or their leaders to implement self-restraints in their lives, minds, and hearts. Every Christian should strive to implement these four disciplines in that regard: righteous and diligent labor, wise and educated focus, purposeful and sacrificial giving, as well as tangible and impartial love. The missionary and/or church leader can help instill these disciplines in the church so that evangelism and discipleship are done with the right priorities and biblical approaches.

Righteous and Diligent Labor

Biblical wisdom and discipline lead the believer to accumulate wealth only in legitimate ways

(Prov 10:2, 16). Ill-gotten gains include wealth acquired by dubious methods, such as unhallowed or forbidden purposes, which is to say wealth that bears no relation to the command and will of God, such as thievery or dishonesty (Prov 19:1). Every follower of Christ ought to be marked by integrity, since God is not indifferent to the way one obtains money (Prov 16:11; 20:17). Dishonest gain reveals an inner love of money (1 Tim 6:10; Heb 13:5), which in turn points to a love of self (Prov 28:22; 2 Tim 3:2–5). Often it originates from being led astray by bad company (Prov 12:26, 13:20; 1 Cor 15:33). These bad influences can come from within the church as well as outside it. Christians need to be careful who they listen to and partner with financially because the Lord's money is a matter of stewardship.

Biblical wisdom and discipline lead the believer to labor with diligence to acquire wealth (Prov 10:4). Christians are called to be productive and persevere in their work (Prov 12:11, 24, 27; 13:4; 14:23–24). Industrious labor has been part of God's design for mankind since the beginning (Gen 2:15). The wise man also plans and thinks long term (Prov 6:6–11; 10:5; 21:5), knowing how to delay gratification (Prov 10:5; 21:17, 20). He who wastes what Providence gives him is unable to gather resources for the future. Wisdom leads one to refrain from unnecessary expenditures so that he will one day reap the fruits of his labor, trusting that God will bless his efforts. The reason the wise man accumulates wealth with diligence is because he wants to give more to God. His dependence on God is absolute and imperative; so is his obedience.

The missionaries and church leaders must adorn and transmit these truths to preserve themselves from hypocrisy and seek the true spiritual welfare of the people. This will often lead people to increased material welfare and dignity as image-bearers.

Wise and Educated Focus

Biblical wisdom and discipline lead the believer to value the knowledge of God over wealth (Prov 10:14). The believer's relationship with God is his source of happiness and his primary focus because he has the conviction that wisdom and knowledge have a greater intrinsic and eternal value (Prov 3:13–15; 16:16). Riches disappoint and do not last (Prov 10:15; 15:17; 23:4–5; Jer 9:23). They can lead a person to be prideful and self-reliant (Prov 18:23; 28:11, 17–18). But wisdom leads one to consider God's favor as the greatest wealth. Some people grow rich without God's blessing, and some grow rich because of it. Whichever the case may be, the focus must remain on the Giver, not the gifts.

Missionaries and church leaders must help the local church members to grow in wisdom and to continually choose to trust the Lord, not falling into despair or fear when He gives less than their "daily bread" (Matt 6:11, 25; cf. Ps 37:25; Prov 30:8).[4] The poor and rich alike are to be reminded about the principles of stewardship and accountability to God in the acquisition of, use of, and attitude toward money.

Purposeful and Sacrificial Giving

The Bible is replete with instructions on giving, and yet it is seldom taught in the global church, especially in third world countries. The missionary must faithfully point to the biblical guidance on this area of worship. In 2 Corinthians 8 and 9, Paul gives eight principles for sacrificial giving that every believer ought to live by, both individually and corporately.

First, sacrificial giving is a result of one's grasp of God's grace. The word for "grace," *charis*, appears ten times in the two chapters and expresses God's passion to share His goodness with those created in His image. Saving and sanctifying grace cause believers to set their affections on things above. It motivates them to abound in generosity in response to God's abundant gifts.

Second, sacrificial giving is subject to the disposition of the heart, not one's financial situation (2 Cor 8:2). The Macedonian believers Paul wrote about gave out of an abundance of joy, seeing it as a privilege to help their brothers and sisters in the Lord. Giving is a matter of mindset rather than income. As a Malagasy proverb says, "Even one grasshopper can be shared."[5]

Third, sacrificial giving is a measure of spiritual maturity (8:3). The Macedonians' giving was costly to them. It put them in a situation in which they had to trust God's provision. Paul shows that the measure of the

---

4. "To ask for such bread 'today' is to acknowledge our dependence on God for routine provision. . . . Jesus himself had to depend on God for food rather than taking the matter into his own hands ([Matt] 4:3–4)." R. T. France, *The Gospel of Matthew*, NICNT (Grand Rapids: Eerdmans, 2007), 248–49.

5. In Malagasy it is, "*Valala iray aza hifampizarana.*"

growth of a church is not its size but its giving. One's faithfulness to give is a proof of spiritual maturity.[6]

Fourth, sacrificial giving is done voluntarily and with joy; it is not coerced (2 Cor 8:3–4; 9:7). Paul did not have to beg the churches in Macedonia to give. Instead, they pleaded "with much urging for the grace of sharing in the ministry to the saints" (2 Cor 8:4).[7] Financial giving for the people of God is both mandatory and voluntary (Exod 36:3).

Fifth, sacrificial giving follows the example Christ Himself set (2 Cor 8:9). God is a giving God. He gave the most astounding gift imaginable when the Lord Jesus Christ, the eternal second person of the Trinity, gave up the splendor of heaven and came to earth, took on human flesh, and bore the sins of His people on the cross (cf. Phil 2:5–8). Christ's self-giving becomes the standard for His disciples' generosity.

Sixth, sacrificial giving is to be proportional to what the Lord has given (2 Cor 8:12). The Lord never asks His people to give what they do not have or to contribute beyond their means. Giving is an act of worship in accordance with His Word (1 Cor 16:2).

Seventh, sacrificial giving is meant to reduce the gap between members of the body (cf. "equality" in 2 Cor 8:13–15). Paul presents an equalizing principle, whereby those who have excess help those who lack. For believers, political or economic power should be employed for the good of those who are weak and defenseless. Those who have an above-average income in the church have the duty and privilege of being more generous.[8]

Finally, God rewards sacrificial giving with abounding blessings (2 Cor 9:6; see also Prov 3:9–10, 11:24–25; Mal 3:8–12; Matt 10:8; Luke 6:38). Those who sow generously reap far more than monetary gain (2 Cor 9:10–14). Giving is certainly intended to be a blessing to the recipient, but it is also to be a blessing for the donor. Sacrificial giving is a command for every follower of Christ. It has a cost, but it will be met with heavenly blessings, and it is part of one's testimony before a watching world.

Tangible and Impartial Love

Galatians 6:1–10 deals with Spirit-enabled Christian beneficence. A love for God and others is the basis for this beneficence; because of his desire to fulfill the law of Christ (v. 2), the believer keeps on "doing good" (vv. 9–10). The Christian church labors in direct correlation with its hope of a harvest in due time. "Doing good" requires effort, selflessness, and

---

6. Belleville points out that generosity is connected to having set Jesus as one's true Lord: "Their [the Macedonians'] preeminent concern was how best to serve Christ. It is here that they exceeded Paul's expectations. They gave out of their poverty because of the sincerity of their commitment to Christ as *Lord* (*tō kyriō*)." Linda L. Belleville, *2 Corinthians*, IVP New Testament Commentary 8 (Westmont, IL: IVP Academic, 1996), 2 Cor 8:1–5 (emphasis original).

7. Here *charis* ("grace") is used as of "the privilege of giving." A. T. Robertson, *Word Pictures in the New Testament*, vol. 4, *The Epistles of Paul* (Nashville: Broadman, 1931), 243.

8. Cf. "equality" in vv. 13, 14. Simon J. Kistemaker, *Exposition of the Second Epistle to the Corinthians*, New Testament Commentary 19 (Grand Rapids: Baker, 1997), 289.

conviction. The believer must see himself as a servant of the Master and faithfully work for Him no matter the cost. As the believer walks in faithful dependence and obedience to the Holy Spirit (Gal 5:16), his submission to the Spirit will be made evident by his good character and works (5:22–23). He will seek the welfare of others, both physically and spiritually in every circumstance, as a manifestation of his new nature in Christ.

The duration of the "doing good" (Gal 6:10) is indeterminate but with a clear termination point (v. 9). God has set birth and death as boundaries to the human life; any good service to the Lord must be performed within that limited time frame.[9] The follower of Christ must be attentive to the opportunities as they arise in God's sovereignly orchestrated plan. The one who walks in the Spirit will be alert to those openings and make the most out of them.

Galatians 6:10 also defines the beneficiaries of Christian generosity. Believers are called to do good to everyone, whether they are Christians or not, regardless of the typical social boundaries of gender, race, ethnicity, and class. Nonetheless, there is a clear order of priority. The primacy must be to serve the family of believers, those belonging to "the household of the faith."[10] That encompasses both the visible household, the local church, as well as all believers globally.[11]

By stepping in and meeting the needs of their brothers and sisters in Christ, Christians affirm the indestructible supernatural bond they have with one another. Paul uses the imagery of a "household" to speak of the church (cf. 1 Tim 3:15),[12] with love as the trademark of interpersonal relationships. From its inception, the church was a close-knit community within which each understood they had their identity and their activity connected to that of the group. As individuals were transformed by the gospel, their understanding of their duty toward their fellow men also evolved. Early in the book of Acts (2:42–45; 4:34–35), fellowship and mutual assistance were the habitual practices, the way of life in the community. Unity was evident as each church lived out in their ethos the identity of the body of Christ. Jesus' mandate to deny self and care for one another's practical needs was being fully fleshed out in the church.[13] The Holy Spirit works to

---

9. Ronald Y. K. Fung, *The Epistle to the Galatians*, NICNT (Grand Rapids: Eerdmans, 1988), 297–98.

10. The term "household of faith" refers to "persons who are related by kinship or circumstances and form a closely knit group . . . with focus on association in common cause or belief." "οἰκεῖος," BDAG, 694. A similar term is used in Ephesians 2:19 as believers are called "God's household" (cf. 1 Tim 3:15; 1 Pet 4:17).

11. The idea is that of togetherness around the common Christian faith. Both the universal and the local church enjoy that togetherness. Timothy George writes of Galatians 6:10, "This is not merely a recognition of the general maxim that 'charity begins at home' but rather an affirmation of the supernatural bond that obtains among all those who belong to the household of faith." Timothy George, *Galatians*, NAC 30 (Nashville: B&H, 1994), 428.

12. John MacArthur and Richard Mayhue, eds., *Biblical Doctrine: A Systematic Summary of Bible Truth* (Wheaton, IL: Crossway, 2017), 749.

13. See Bruce W. Winter, "Acts and Food Shortages," in *The Book of Acts in Its Graeco-Roman Setting*, ed. David W. J. Gill and Conrad Gempf (Grand Rapids: Eerdmans, 1994), 63–64.

establish spiritual union among the members of the community.[14]

Conclusion

Poverty is to be understood as an element of God's sovereign design. God is a bountiful God (1 Tim 6:17), and He sees the poor and has a heart for them. Christ even partook of their poverty in order to make those who confess their spiritual poverty rich with salvation and all its benefits (2 Cor 8:9; Phil 2:5–8), to give them the riches of His grace (Eph 2:4–7), to make them heirs of His promised kingdom (Matt 5:3; Jas 2:5). That is the good news that missionaries carry.

The Great Commission also includes a mandate to teach disciples of Christ to obey all that He has commanded. It is necessary for missionaries and church leaders to faithfully fulfill their God-given mandate by teaching believers worldwide, whether in an affluent or deprived context, by building up a scriptural worldview of poverty and wealth. The theological basis for the comportment of Christians toward one another, beyond considerations of ethnicity or socioeconomic status, is centered around the reality of being united in Christ and the mandate to represent the bountiful God. Until the Lord returns, the people of God are called to demonstrate that they are disciples of Christ by loving one another (John 13:35).

Both poor and rich will have to give an account of how their lives reflected Jesus' selfless love. The Spirit-led community must stand out by tangible and genuine love for one another, sacrificial giving, and corporate growth in the likeness of the Lord Jesus Christ. That is the Christian life. That is the Church's testimony in this broken world, in all places for all time. Charity is at the heart of Christian living. Thus, may the Church's missionary endeavors and teaching concerning poverty and wealth reflect the transforming power and the hope of the gospel.

---

14. One study on wealth in the community or fellowship (κοινωνία, *koinōnia*) that is the church, concluded about Acts 2:42, "Perhaps the best understanding of κοινωνία is the synthesis by the Holy Spirit of the new covenant members into a united group of people." Seth C. Washeck, "The Mission of Money: Luke's Ethical Mandate for Wealth in Community" (MA thesis, Denver Seminary, 2012), 73; cf. George Panikulam, *Koinōnia in the New Testament: A Dynamic Expression of Christian Life*, Analecta Biblica (Rome: Biblical Institute, 1979), 129.

Helping without Hurting: Turning Challenges into Opportunities When Showing Mercy

Lisa LaGeorge and Dave Phillips[15]

Mercy ministry is the work that churches do to meet the physical and relational needs of people around them, while introducing them to God's love through a relationship with Jesus. The end goal of mercy ministry in the local church is demonstrating the gospel message in word and deed to those being served (1 John 3:18). Parachurch ministries simply come alongside to help.

Serving those in need can beautifully display God's mercy and Christ's work, but challenges often come with it. Doing ministry in a fallen world is rarely simple. Our desire to help can backfire, causing more harm than good to those we serve. It is important, then, to recognize the opportunities and how to respond. Whether you are currently engaged in mercy ministry or just beginning, this insert aims to help you evaluate existing ministries and provides realistic considerations for new ministries.

The following challenges may speak to your cultural, geographical situation more than others, so take time to consider them as they relate to your context.

Challenge One: Finding People Who Need Help

One challenge that churches encounter is finding recipients who really need help. Conversely, other churches will know of so many needy families in the community that they will need to prioritize who to help and when. Accurately diagnosing a family's situation is a large part of this challenge as various situations call for different responses.

1. **Relief.** Relief provides temporary physical help for urgent situations, whether because of natural disasters, man-made crises, or significant generational poverty.

---

15. Adapted in part from Children's Hunger Fund training for network churches, "Rethink Mercy Foundation" (2024). Used by permission.

Relief delivers resources for someone who is in immediate need of the basics of food, clothing, or housing.

2. **Rehabilitation.** Rehabilitation seeks to help people in crisis acquire and utilize the skills and tools needed to step away from the crisis and again become functioning members of the community. Examples of rehabilitation may include counseling, job training, or literacy instruction. Relief resources can open the door for rehabilitation while the church navigates how best to serve the family.

3. **Development.** Development is the ongoing process of both helpers and the "helped" to grow in spiritual and relational health. Biblical development is essentially discipleship, the ultimate outworking of believers walking together in the church toward Christlikeness.

Paul charges the churches in Galatia, "So then, while we have opportunity, let us do good to all people, and especially to those who are of the household of the faith" (Gal 6:10). As you, then, consider who might need help, these questions may serve as a starting point:

- Are you aware of needy families within your church?
- Does your church have existing ministries that serve families in need?
- Can your church members identify neighbors in need?
- Are there particular areas of your community that are impacted by poverty?

Food may be your first means of addressing needs, but your church may also consider additional forms of aid available in your community to help you walk with a family from relief to development. Aid might include a resource pantry, low-income rental properties, and employment assistance, to name a few.

Challenge Two: Helping without Hurting

Another challenge of providing physical assistance can be the tension between truly helping someone and making their situation worse. Mercy ministry is not intended to create a situation of long-term physical dependency, and your ministry should be carefully structured to avoid this. Below are some examples of practices that should be avoided:

- Making food or other resources available in such a way that promotes long-term dependency on the assistance
- Providing cash, which could contribute to harmful behaviors
- Offering help that is focused on the charitable feelings of the giver rather than on meeting the needs of the recipient

- Misunderstanding the cultural context of the recipient when offering assistance

Avoiding these common practices can diminish the potential for harming mercy ministry recipients. The church can also begin to provide situations for people to become self-sufficient. Mercy ministry might be able to provide physical resources temporarily, but a consistent ministry should strive to help people become self-sufficient.

Careful study reveals that the Epistles say a great deal about work, need, contentment, and generosity. The apostle Paul instructed the church in Thessalonica that work was essential and honorable (2 Thess 3:6–9). To the church in Ephesus he taught that everyone who could work should work, so that those formerly in need could themselves become generous (Eph 4:28).

Challenge Three: Recipients May Take Advantage of Churches

Some churches and volunteers worry about being taken advantage of by ministry recipients. Every outreach pastor has experienced people who go from church to church seeking assistance, who seem to be just looking for handouts. The recipients may also levy demands for other assistance that is outside of the church's focus or capacity.

One way that churches have answered this challenge is to engage with other churches in the community to strategize together about how best to coordinate efforts. This can begin to address the concerns about recipients trying to misuse church resources. While every relationship is unique and requires wisdom to respond, the ministry is not ultimately responsible for the motives of recipients. Instead, volunteers must recognize that they are ultimately serving Jesus (Prov 19:17; Matt 10:42; 25:40; Heb 6:10). Maintaining a proper perspective of faithfulness will bless the hearts of the leaders and volunteers. As His servants, we can be faithful to address needs even while trusting Him when we don't see the results we hope for.

Churches and volunteers also need to recognize that they are not responsible to meet every need that emerges. Leaders and volunteers should be reminded that the main goal of mercy ministry is to meet a specific need of a suffering family while providing hope in the gospel. Volunteers should engage with their church leadership for counsel as these situations arise.

Conclusion

Helping others can beautifully display the character of God, and yet it can also bring challenges both to those being helped and to those helping. The results of faithful ministry may not be seen in this lifetime. The apostle Paul was motivated by his future appearance before Christ, and he provides great encouragement when he writes that he made it his ambition to be counted a trust-worthy steward on the day he would give an account for his life (2 Cor 5:9–10; cf. 1 Cor 4). We are called by the same Master, who rewards His "good and faithful" servants (Matt 25:21).

Whether you are the recipient of mercy or the one giving mercy, the goal is to see lives changed by the gospel. Christians long to grow in "love from a pure heart and a good conscience and an unhypocritical faith" (1 Tim 1:5), so that we may all be like Christ, our Savior. In spite of the challenges discussed here, we know there is a great opportunity to see families encouraged by timely help, to witness the transformational work of the gospel, to invoke gratitude and praise to God, and to see the growth of both volunteers and recipients as they are conformed to Christ—all through mercy ministry.

CHAPTER 56

Reaching the Global City

John Freiberg

Missiologists today have argued that a new era of missions focus has begun.[1] One church-planting network leader in Dubai has stated, "We are now transitioning into a fourth era of the modern missionary movement. In this new era, the focus is urban, and the leadership is both global and not bound by vocation."[2] The many urban areas capturing such missionary focus are only projected to grow. In 2013 economic data analysts pointed out, "One hundred years ago only two out of ten of the world's population were living in urban areas. By the middle of the twenty-first century, seven out of ten people will be living in cities. . . . Standard population projections show that virtually all global growth over the next 30 years will be in urban areas."[3]

Urban growth matters for missions because Jesus' call to make disciples moves His followers toward unreached peoples, and most of the world's unreached peoples are moving to cities that are devoid of a viable gospel witness. Therefore, this chapter aims to clarify the biblical significance of the city and to suggest some approaches for faithfully engaging urban dwellers with the good news of Jesus Christ.

The City in Scripture

For some the idea of the city conjures up notions of excitement, opportunity, and culture. For many others, the mere mention of a city may cause stress and thoughts only of negative realities such as crime, traffic, and pollution. Ultimately, Christians must seek to discern how God views the city through the lens of His Word. A person's theological vision

1. I am deeply grateful for the help of Michael Crane and Scott Yetter for their assistance in preparing this chapter.

2. Scott Zeller, "A New Era of Global Mission: Cities, the Least Reached, and Marketplace Work" (DMin diss., Southern Baptist Theological Seminary, 2015), 40.

3. "Hot Spots 2025: Benchmarking the Future Competitiveness of Cities," The Economist Intelligence Unit, research report, June 4, 2013.

of the city will have a direct influence on one's ministry methodology, expectations, and goals.

The Bible has a lot to say about cities. It is often said that Scripture starts in a garden and ends in a city. Roger Greenway and Timothy Monsma helpfully observe that three types of cities emerge in the Bible: the city that might have been, the city that will be, and the city that is.[4]

The City That Might Have Been

Some theologians assert that the cultural mandate given to Adam and Eve by God in Genesis 1:28—"Be fruitful and multiply, and fill the earth, and subdue it; and have dominion"—implicitly required the building of cities.[5] Certainly, faithfully fulfilling the creation mandate would involve the ordering of God's creation, the creating of culture, and the expansion of civilization. It is mind-boggling to consider what a sinless humanity could have accomplished with the abilities and resources our first parents were given. Without sin, death, and cultural-linguistic barriers, cities would have been places of unimaginable peace, beauty, worship, creativity, culture, power, thriving, knowledge, community, safety, joy, communion with and glory to God. Yet alas, due to the fall of mankind into sin, today "the

city stands out as both an aggregator of evil as well as a point of hope."[6]

The City That Will Be

Scripture also speaks of an eschatological city that is to come. Revelation 21 gives us a picture of this temple city coming down to the new earth and becoming the place where God once again dwells with His creation. Revelation 22:1–2 goes on to show that at the center of this city is the "river of the water of life, bright as crystal, coming from the throne of God and of the Lamb, in the middle of its street. On either side of the river was the tree of life, bearing twelve kinds of fruit, yielding its fruit every month; and the leaves of the tree were for the healing of the nations."

Here we see not only the intention of Eden realized, but we see it amplified and improved. The tree is bigger, the family (forever in nations) is bigger, and the glory is brighter. The center of gravity for this great city is the full presence of God Himself.[7] In this city God will dwell with His people, and they will enjoy Him forever. It will be everything that a city could have been without the fall, with one important distinction: it will not be filled with merely sinless creatures, but with citizens who were sinners and have been redeemed, washed clean by the

---

4. Roger S. Greenway and Timothy M. Monsma, *Cities: Missions' New Frontier* (Grand Rapids: Baker, 2000), 26–29.

5. Greenway and Monsma, 26.

6. Linda Bergquist and Michael D. Crane, *City Shaped Churches: Planting Churches in the Global Era* (Skyforest, CA: Urban Loft, 2018), 31.

7. As commentator Wes Van Fleet remarks, "To understand all these beautiful images in Revelation 21–22, we are reminded constantly that the images represent reality. Will there be streets of gold? Maybe. Will there literally be no sun? Maybe. Wherever we land, the reality is that God is present with His people and His glory is the superlative experience. This is because the great and glorious shekinah glory fills the entire city of God and no physical light sources, even the sun, could be seen with God's glory as the radiating backdrop." Wes Van Fleet, *Revelation: Worthy Is the Lamb* (Memphis: Teleios Academy, 2018), 271.

blood of the Lamb, and adopted into God's family (1 Pet 1:18–21).[8]

The City That Is

While there may be a lament over the unrealized potential of the city that could have been and there is hope for the city that will be, believers must reckon with the city that is today. Like everything in this world since the day humanity rebelled against God, the potential of the city has been perverted and poisoned by sin. Genesis 4–6 shows that within only a few generations, technology, culture, industry, music, depravity, and warfare had developed, mainly in urban centers. These marks of culture and civilization are products of sinful people, but people, nonetheless, made in the image of God. When people gather in higher density areas (i.e., cities), they tend to have an increased influence on the wider society and culture. To hide from or ignore the city is to forfeit the cultural, political, and economic high ground of society. God's people, then, must think about the city today.

A place to start is to define the term *city* as a concentrated grouping of sinful image-bearers. When one looks at the city as a faceless mass of pollution, traffic, crime, and problems, it is easy to feel discouraged, angry, and possibly indifferent. Yet, despite the nonstop demands and discouragements of ministry, Jesus did not grow bitter toward the crowds (Matt 9:35–38). Jesus was able to see through the surface-level obstacles and challenges that come with any large group of people and instead feel compassion for them. Seeing their physical and spiritual needs, He saw them as "sheep without a shepherd" (9:36). Sheep without a shepherd are unprotected, unfed, and unled. Christians must seek to view the city not just as a faceless monster but as a place where many lost individuals are living in pain and rebellion, heading toward a Christ-less eternity. Those who see urban dwellers in this way may find, as Paul did in Corinth, that God has many who are waiting to hear the good news and be counted among "His people" in the city (Acts 18:10). While there is debate about the degree to which Christians should seek to "redeem" the city,[9] there should be no doubt about the mission to redeem the souls in it.

Engaging the Global City Today

"Global cities" refers to "urban areas that impact the world far beyond their city limits through a combination of economic services and trade, political influence, and cultural dissemination."[10] The growing interconnectedness of cities brings many unique challenges as well as a great potential for the gospel. While every city is unique, ministry in almost any urban context will share in some of the obstacles, opportunities, and best practices outlined below.

Obstacles of Engaging

Urban settings present significant obstacles to potential ministry opportunities. One of

---

8. Greenway and Monsma, *Cities*, 27.

9. See, e.g, Tim Keller, *Center Church: Doing Balanced, Gospel-Centered Ministry in Your City* (Grand Rapids: Zondervan, 2012).

10. Michael Crane, *Sowing Seeds of Change: Cultivating Transformation in the City* (Portland, OR: Urban Loft, 2015), 24.

the most common and most significant is the reality of heavy traffic and busy work schedules. In much of the world, these obstacles are exacerbated by the realities of living in a dense, poorly planned, and often flooded but economically booming context. In crowded cities such as Bangkok or Jakarta, average daily commute times of multiple hours each way take a toll on family and church life. A recent study revealed that on average, Jakartans spend four hundred hours a year in traffic.[11] These types of logistical challenges are real and relevant.

There is, however, a more critical obstacle. Individual sin and systemic rebellion and brokenness entice people into destructive identities and behaviors by offering an alternative sense of belonging. This can become a massive barrier to gospel ministry. Frequently, those coming to the city seeking a better life, such as through school or work, embrace a sense of belonging in sinful identities that promote drugs, sexual rebellion, or criminal gang activity. Often urban refugees lack the institutional support of official refugee camps and only have minimal legal employment or educational options in their host cities. Many urban churches that have embraced and intentionally helped these large refugee populations have seen amazingly fruitful results.[12]

The gospel message is simple. Yet the cross-cultural proclamation of that message is rarely a simple task. Inextricably connected to culture is language. As veteran missionary and missiologist Brad Buser states, "Undergirding any serious approach to sharing the gospel cross-culturally is the ability to think and communicate at a serious level of understanding in the language and culture of the person you are reaching."[13] Not only must the missionary learn a new language with new vocabulary, but he must also learn the theological, cultural, and worldview implications that the vocabulary carries with it in his ministry context. For instance, an Islamic or Buddhist concept of sin is vastly different from a biblical one, so just using the word for "sin" without a biblical explanation will not communicate the intended meaning. Urban missionaries must be committed to taking the time to ensure that their gospel presentations are being understood clearly by the people they are trying to reach. Almost always this will require formal study of language and culture, and perhaps more importantly, long, careful, and repeated conversations with the local people.

Opportunities for Engaging

Obstacles to ministry can become powerful opportunities when viewed through a gospel lens. For instance, a sinner's hunger for community points to an opportunity to meet the need

---

11. "Jakartans Spend 400 Hours a Year in Traffic, Says Survey," *Jakarta Post*, February 9, 2015, https://www.thejakartapost.com/news/2015/02/09/jakartans-spend-400-hours-a-year-traffic-says-survey.html.

12. See Michael Crane, "The Vital Role of Faith Communities in the Lives of Urban Refugees: A Case Study of Christian Response to Refugee Populations in Kuala Lumpur, Malaysia," *International Journal of Interreligious and Intercultural Studies* 3, no. 2 (October 2020): 25–37.

13. Brad Buser, "Why Getting Fluent Today Is Harder Than Ever," *Radius Report*, May 9, 2018, http://radiusinternational.org/why-getting-fluent-today-is-harder-than-ever/.

for true Christ-centered community. Traffic and long commutes can lead to intentional and missional proximity among disciples and to a more robust ecclesiology, and the challenges of urban diversity can be met as the gospel forms people from every tribe, tongue, and nation into one new Christ-treasuring family.

OPPORTUNITIES FOR GOSPEL EXPOSURE

In the city, there is a much stronger likelihood that individuals will have to wrestle with a variety of unfamiliar truth claims and come to their own decisions as to what they will believe and practice. There are often many "neutral territories" in the city, where the open exchange of ideas can be had without the restrictions found in a smaller closed community. This sets the table for the wise urban missionary to engage in gospel conversations. Regardless of what evangelistic approach is used, the fact remains that the diversity of the city, the accessibility to peoples from unreached areas, and the melting pot of ideas that the urban environment facilitates all make the city a ripe field for spiritual harvest.

It may be a temptation to think that since there are often established churches in cities, urban ministry is not concerned with the unreached peoples of the world. But this assumes that there are no unreached people groups represented in the city.[14] Not only do unreached people groups (UPGs) come to the city for work and school, but so also do "city tribals." City tribals are "people from a tribe who move to the city and live with others from their own people . . . [but] return to their hometowns regularly and maintain ties with their tribal relatives."[15] In the city, UPG clusters are usually divided by cultural and socioeconomic divisions. For them to be meaningfully exposed to the good news requires an intentional cross-cultural initiative.[16] A well-resourced Christian community is a prime environment for mobilizing UPG believers for missions back into their native regions, some of which may be virtually inaccessible to foreigners.

OPPORTUNITY FOR GOSPEL REVITALIZATION

Although churches may already be present in the city, this does not necessarily mean that the gospel is heard in them. To the contrary, often the greatest obstacle to the spread of the gospel in a city is the bankrupt theology and nominalism of the local churches. There is a great need and therefore a great opportunity for revitalization and gospel renewal among the churches of many cities.[17] Church revitalization is a worthwhile investment alongside church planting

---

14. For a great example of reaching into an unreached people group in West Africa through a contact in New York, see Chris Clayman, "Reaching the Nations through Our Cities," *Great Commission Research Journal* 6, no. 1 (Summer 2014): 6–21.

15. Paul G. Hiebert and Eloise Hiebert Meneses, *Incarnational Ministry: Planting Churches in Band, Tribal, Peasant, and Urban Societies* (Grand Rapids: Baker Academic, 1995), 269.

16. Missiologist Timothy Monsma states, "Attention to people groups living in cities will in many cases be the key to the evangelization of these cities. There is no conflict between the challenge of the cities and the challenge of the unreached peoples. It is substantially the same challenge." Timothy Monsma, "Unreached Peoples in Cities," *Mission Frontiers*, March 1, 1991, http://www.missionfrontiers.org/issue/article/unreached-peoples-in-cities.

17. For examples of urban church revitalization, see John Folmar, "What Makes a Church Reform Possible?" *9Marks Journal*,

because the needs and challenges of the city are far too large for any one church alone to meet.

Gospel-Shaped Community

Gospel-centered churches have the opportunity to provide community to people who crave it by building a community around the only tie that lasts: union with Christ. A Christ-centered community creates identity around the very originator of community, the triune God. The only community that can truly satisfy the needs of those created in God's image is the community that finds its life in Him, namely, the Church. The weekly preaching of the Word should not be neglected, but just as important is the regular meeting of small groups or one-on-one meetings where sin can be confronted, sorrows can be shared, and precise gospel encouragement can be given and received. Especially in persecuted contexts, new believers will often lose their families and their livelihoods in exchange for embracing Christ. The local church must be there to embrace and walk alongside these new spiritual family members.

As the Holy Spirit begins to draw God's lost sheep together and people are transformed by the reconciling power of the gospel, the problems of partiality so common in the city are broken down and the stranger and sojourner are formed into "God's household" (Eph 2:11–22). This puts on display the transforming power of God that transcends barriers and creates a family among people that, apart from Christ Jesus, might be hostile not just to God but to

one another (Gal 3:28; Col 3:11). This kind of diverse, Christ-treasuring church body is a powerful gospel apologetic in urban contexts.

Best Practices for Engagement

The child of God, equipped with the Word of God and empowered by the Spirit of God has everything needed to face the challenges of urban ministry. That said, there are some specific ministry practices that have proven especially fruitful in urban contexts. These include prayer, an emphasis on the Word of God, a discipleship plan, and a robust ecclesiology.

Prayer

Scripture and church history attest to the fact that all great movements of God were soaked in fervent prayer. God has ordained in His sovereignty that He responds to the intercessory prayer of His people. When confronted with the enormity of the task of evangelism, Christ directs His disciples first to pray (Matt 9:38). The faithful urban missionary understands that only God can bring about light in the darkness of the city, and so will cultivate a lifestyle of regular prayer out of necessity.

A High View of the Word of God

To preach competently, compellingly, and faithfully, the urban minister must have a rock-solid confidence in the sufficiency of the Word of God. Often urban congregations have people with at least some education and tools to verify the pastor's claims. He must therefore not

---

October 27, 2011, https://www.9marks.org/article/journalwhat-makes-church-reform-possible/.

bring scorn or doubt upon Scripture by speaking of what he does not know, but should lead the people to greater trust in the authoritative truths of the Word. He must teach new believers how to navigate the many complexities of urban life with a biblical worldview. The role of teaching and preaching in urban discipleship, despite some current missiological "wisdom" that seeks to minimize it, is nonnegotiable.

A Discipleship Plan

Fruitful cross-cultural urban ministry usually does not happen by accident. Discipleship training that is biblically well thought out plays an important part in any church's strategy for evangelism and discipleship. Crucial to the Bible-teaching element of disciple-making is instilling in new disciples the reality that reading God's Word is not merely an intellectual exercise; it is a call to obedience. This is a delicate task, however; calling people to obey Christ in their own strength prior to regeneration can short-circuit discipleship before it even starts. On the other hand, a call to follow Christ that does not involve submission to the lordship of Christ in every area of life is also deficient. Obedience to Christ is a lifelong process of growth (2 Pet 3:18), and great care must be taken to explain that while God saves us from our sins, He saves us for good works (Eph 2:8–10). The order and inclusion of both aspects matters. Keeping the gospel central as both the grace that saves us (Titus 2:11) and the power that trains us to live righteously (2:12), will help us avoid the equally dangerous pitfalls of legalism and licentiousness.

Faithful ministry in the city also draws a line from gospel proclamation to the Christlike compassion that moves followers of Jesus to love their neighbors in tangible ways. Ministry in any context must involve sacrificial love and practical burden-bearing as believers seek to walk in repentance. In an urban context where people often live in close proximity, the life of the minister will often be the measure by which the authenticity of His message is judged.

Robust Ecclesiology

The urban missionary must know what a church is and what a church does. He must put a high value not only on leadership development and growth but also on church membership. The most fruitful urban churches are the ones that take church membership and discipline seriously as they help believers see their identity as a family united in Christ (Eph 5:23; Col 2:19). The goal of all missions is the planting of churches that are rooted in a rock-solid understanding of who God is, what He has done through the person and work of Jesus Christ, and who believers are as a result. This God-centered theology produces a zeal to see God exalted, especially in places where His good news has not yet been proclaimed. All too many missionaries go to the field without ever experiencing a healthy church back home and without having sorted out their biblical convictions regarding ecclesiology. This all too often results in their understanding of church being shaped more by the demands of their context and culture than by Scripture. Being connected to, mentored by, and held accountable to a healthy sending church is therefore essential for any church planter.

Conclusion

The world is undeniably urbanizing at a rapid pace. Christ's church must respond to this global phenomenon in a way that faithfully stewards the Great Commission potential of urban ministry. This includes, first, forming a firm theology of the city and its accompanying challenges as well as, second, forming biblically consistent strategies for engagement that are unique to the city. Cities hold much potential for reaching historically hard-to-reach people groups with the gospel.

When the apostle Paul wrote to the church at Rome—the largest city in the world at the time, he expounded the wonders of the gospel of Jesus Christ (Rom 1–11) and he exhorted the Roman believers to walk in step with that gospel so that they would "let love be without hypocrisy" (Rom 12:9; see chs. 12–16). In the same way, to reach global cities today, the global Church needs both a deep theology and deep commitment by each believer to live a life of sacrificial, gospel-driven authenticity. When God's people walk joyfully in gospel-informed and gospel-motivated obedience, they will shine brightly for His glory in dark places until they receive that new city He is preparing for them.

CHAPTER 57

Portraits of Urban Ministry Past and Present

John Freiberg

The Lord Jesus and His disciples prioritized cities as part of their strategic ministry in Israel (Matt 4:12–17; 9:35; 11:1; Luke 4:43; 8:1; 10:1; 13:22). As for Paul, it cannot be disputed that his "efforts were concentrated in cities" also.[1] For example, by the late AD 50s, he wrote to the church in Rome[2] that he had "fully preached the gospel" from Jerusalem as far as Illyricum, leaving "no further place for [him] in these regions" (Rom 15:18–23). He could make this claim because, though the majority of this vast region's land area was untouched by the gospel, he had planted churches in all of its major cities.

The pattern of the gospel first reaching the regional city and then emanating outward continued into the first centuries of church history,

and it is still effective in missions today. This chapter collects portraits of urban ministries that followed closely after the New Testament period as well as some from the present day that demonstrate the biblical model set forth in the previous chapter. These examples are intended to encourage missionaries, church planters, and pastors who are already in urban contexts, as well as inspire missionary candidates who are considering engaging in urban ministry.

Early Church Examples of Urban Ministry

The early church was in large part an urban church.[3] Two brief examples from influential leaders of the patristic period (until ca. AD

---

1. Michael Crane, "To the Ends of the Earth through Strategic Urban Centers: Reexamining the Missions Mandate in Light of the New Testament's Use of the Old Testament," in *Advancing Models of Mission: Evaluating the Past and Looking to the Future*, ed. Kenneth Nehrbass, Aminta Arrington, and Narry Santos, EMSS 29 (Littleton, CO: William Carey, 2021), 11.

2. On the date of Romans, see D. A. Carson and Douglas J. Moo, "Romans," *An Introduction to the New Testament*, 2nd ed. (Grand Rapids: Zondervan, 2005), 393–94.

3. For more on this, see Crane, "To the Ends of the Earth," passim, which builds on such works as: Ervin E. Hastey, "Reaching the Cities First: A Biblical Model of World Evangelization," in *An Urban World: Churches Face the Future*, ed. Larry L. Rose and C. Kirk Hadaway (Nashville: Broadman, 1984); Walter Kaiser, "A Biblical Theology of the City," *Urban Mission* 7, no. 1 (September 1989); Roland Allen, *Missionary Methods: St. Paul's or Ours?* (Grand Rapids: Eerdmans, 1962); Wayne A. Meeks, *The*

600/750)[4] will illustrate this: Irenaeus of Lyons and Basil of Caesarea. What is known of their ministries provides exemplary manifestation of a biblical model of urban missions.

Irenaeus of Lyons

Born in the early second century,[5] Irenaeus had been a young disciple of the early church father Polycarp of Smyrna.[6] That relationship provided a strong link to the apostles, as Polycarp was a personal disciple of the apostle John. At some point, Irenaeus was ordained a pastor and sent across the Roman Empire from Asia Minor to Lugdunum, modern-day Lyons, France. After the previous bishop was martyred (AD 177), Irenaeus was appointed bishop in his place. It is from this office that the majority of his ministry emerged.

While history remembers Irenaeus primarily for his prolific writing, which systematically and comprehensively stood against the heresies of his day, in his pastorate he was also active in gospel ministry, in his city as well as in the surrounding region. Historians Alexander Roberts and James Donaldson note, "The Episcopate of Irenaeus was distinguished by labours 'in season and out of season,' for the evangelization of Southern Gaul; and he seems to have sent missionaries into other regions of what we now call France. In spite of paganism and heresy, he rendered Lyons a Christian city."[7]

The city in which Irenaeus lived and ministered had many striking similarities to today's global metropolises. Being the capital of the region, Lyons was a center for manufacturing, trade, military, and political power.[8] This prominence brought immigrants and merchants from all over the known world. Potters from Italy,[9] marble traders from Africa,[10] missionaries from the Near East, retired military officers, and slaves from around the empire all passed through this megacity in ancient Gaul.

On one hand, as a "native of Asia Minor, steeped in the Hellenistic philosophical and rhetorical culture, Irenaeus was an outsider to the mostly Latin-speaking populace of Gaul."[11]

First Urban Christians: The Social World of the Apostle Paul (New Haven, CT: Yale University Press, 1982); Volker Rabens, "Paul's Mission Strategy in the Urban Landscape of the First-Century Roman Empire," in *The Urban World and the First Christians*, ed. Steve Walton, Paul Trebilco, and David Gills (Grand Rapids: Eerdmans, 2017).

4. On periodization see Phillip Schaff and David Schley Schaff, *History of the Christian Church*, vol. 1, *Apostolic Christianity* (1910; repr., Grand Rapids: Eerdmans, 1994), 14–15; G. W. Bromiley, "Fathers, Church," *Evangelical Dictionary of Theology*, ed. Daniel J. Treier and Walter A. Elwell (Grand Rapids: Baker Academic, 2017), 308–9.

5. J. van der Straeten, "Saint-Irénée fut-il martyre?," in *Les martyrs de Lyon*, ed. Jean Rougé and Robert Turcan (Paris: CNRS, 1978), 145–52.

6. Irenaeus, *Against Heresies* 3.4 (*ANF* 1:416–17); Eusebius, *Ecclesiastical History* 5.20.4–8 (*NPNF*[2] 1:238–39); Jerome, *De viris illustribus* 35 (*NPNF*[2] 3:370).

7. ANF 1:310. Indeed, writes McNeill, "Irenaeus exemplified the type of Christian scholar who is also animated by apostolic pastoral and missionary zeal." John T. McNeill, *The Celtic Churches, A History 200 to 1200* (Chicago: University of Chicago Press, 1974), 11–12.

8. Michael Rostovtzeff, *Social Economic History of the Roman Empire* (Oxford: Clarendon, 1957), 166.

9. Philippe Leveau, "The Western Provinces," in *The Cambridge Economic History of the Greco-Roman World*, ed. Walter Scheidel, Ian Morris, and Richard P. Saller (Cambridge: Cambridge University Press, 2007), 622.

10. Leveau, 660.

11. Jacob Rodriguez, "Irenaeus's Missional Theology: Global Christian Perspectives from an Ancient Missionary and Theologian,"

On the other hand, he was not alone in his immigrant status. As with most cities throughout history, many residents of Lyons were not natives. Irenaeus "lived in a situation of linguistic as well as religious pluralism."[12] It is probable that the demographic composition of Irenaeus's congregation reflected the diversity of the city. As Jacob Rodriguez observed, "Immigration, diaspora, cross-cultural interaction, persecution, and empire characterized Irenaeus's world and ministry. Against this historical backdrop, Irenaeus's reflections on the gospel in a multicultural world prove particularly relevant to the current situation of the global church."[13]

Such gospel reflections include the fact that Irenaeus gave "dignity and common identity to the barbarian 'other' in a way that is foreign to his Greek contemporaries" (cf. Gal 3:28; Col 3:10–11).[14] He devoted himself to dwelling among and learning the language of the locals to such an extent that he later had to apologize for his Greek being rusty (1 Cor 9:19–23).[15] Moreover, he devoted his life to sacrificially loving and shepherding a flock in one of the most persecuted regions of the Roman world (Heb 10:32–34). Persecution was not merely theory for Irenaeus; his predecessor in Lyons had died in prison for his faith.

It is no coincidence that one of the main doctrines that Irenaeus articulated in his works was the incarnation of Christ. The bishop of Lyons seemed to understand not just the theological, apologetic implications of the incarnation for salvation but also the missiological, evangelistic applications as well. He had this very attitude of the humility of Christ in himself (Phil 2:5). Irenaeus's example of participating in the culture and community life of the mission field is instructive for the missionary, urban or otherwise. As much as possible, the missionary must seek to adopt the sacrificial attitude that Irenaeus had, which was most excellently portrayed in Christ, "who, although existing in the form of God, did not regard equality with God a thing to be grasped, but emptied Himself, by taking the form of a slave, by being made in the likeness of men. Being found in appearance as a man, He humbled Himself by becoming obedient to the point of death, even death on a cross" (Phil 2:7–8).

The Christian disciple-maker must think through which of his rights and privileges are actually obstacles to service and how to lay them aside and identify as much as possible with those he is called to serve, all without compromising fidelity to the truth. As the community observes this sacrificial lifestyle, they will see the missionary facing many of the same daily struggles they face. But they will see that there is something different about the way the missionary suffers, hopes, and endures. This will create trust, respect, and, Lord willing, gospel opportunities.

JETS 59, no. 1 (March 2016): 133.

12. C. Philip Slate, "Two Features of Irenaeus' Missiology," *Missiology* 23, no. 4 (October 1, 1995): 433.

13. Rodriguez, "Irenaeus's Missional Theology," 133.

14. Rodriguez, 137.

15. Irenaeus, *Against Heresies* 1.Pref.3 (*ANF* 1:316).

Basil of Caesarea

Living two centuries after Irenaeus, Basil was bishop of Cappadocian Caesarea from AD 370 until his death in 379. He is remembered primarily for his faithful defense and articulation of Trinitarian theology against the Arian heresy. Yet his contribution to urban missiology is significant also. Originally content to live as an ascetic monk, Basil obtained a burden for public ministry as Arianism spread through the churches of Asia Minor. Like Irenaeus, his zeal for truth was not only directed in a polemical way toward false teachers and doctrines but also in a positive expression of loving instruction and care for those in his city. As historian Edward Smither states, "Unlike many monks in his day, Basil regarded the city as both his context for monastic living and Christian mission."[16]

By the time Basil was appointed bishop of Caesarea, many serious threats to the survival of the church in that city were present. Being the capital of the Roman province of Cappadocia, Caesarea owed its prominence to its location at an intersection of strategic military and trade routes. Moreover, there had been a church extant there since the first century AD, but when Basil was appointed bishop, Caesarea faced intense persecution from the Arian emperor Valens.[17] Basil's friend and contemporary Gregory of Nazianzus recounted the nature of the harassment:

> Exiles, banishments, confiscations, open and secret plots, persuasion, where time allowed, violence, where persuasion was impossible. Those who clung to the orthodox faith, as we did, were extruded [expelled] from their churches; others were intruded [imposed upon], who agreed with the Imperial soul-destroying doctrines, and begged for testimonials of impiety [i.e., testimonies of recanting their faith in Christ].[18]

In the face of such persecution, Basil not only maintained his theological commitments but also courageously and publicly chastised the emperor and his supporters.[19]

As profound as the challenge from political and religious persecution was, so was the menace of poverty and starvation. A severe famine hit the region in AD 368. Smither writes, "It is impossible to understand Basil's ministry without describing this period of tragedy."[20] Historian Susan Holman notes that Basil's famous sermon[21] of that same year,

> refers back to an extremely cold, dry winter that had been followed by an unusually

---

16. Edward L. Smither, "Basil of Caesarea: An Early Christian Model of Urban Mission," in *Reaching the City: Reflections on Mission for the Twenty-First Century*, ed. Gary Fujino, Timothy R. Sisk, and Tereso C. Casino, EMSS 20 (Pasadena, CA: William Carey Library, 2012), 60.
17. Gregory of Nazianzus, *Oratio in laudem Basilii* 43.30, 46 (*NPNF*² 7:405–6, 410).
18. Gregory of Nazianzus, *Oratio in laudem Basilii* 43.46 (*NPNF*² 7:410).
19. Gregory of Nazianzus, *Oratio in laudem Basilii* 43.48–50 (*NPNF*² 7:411).
20. Smither, "Basil of Caesarea," 63.
21. Its title is translated "In Times of Famine and Drought." Basil the Great, *Homily* 8 (PG 31:303–28).

hot, dry spring, and this led to catastrophic agricultural crisis as wells and rivers dried up and crops failed. Those able to hoard grain increased their vigilance and the market prices. Laborers began to starve. Schools closed down. The populace came to church to pray for rain. The poor who worked in the fields and wandered along the roads took on the appearance of living cadavers. Possibly the poor resorted to exposing their children, or selling them, while the rich haggled with them over the purchase price. Gregory of Nazianzus implied that the situation was heightened by the difficulty of importing emergency food supplies to a landlocked region.[22]

Basil was called to pastor faithfully in the middle of all this. Gregory testifies that even though Basil was indeed a "supplier of grain and abundant riches [and was] the poorest and most needy [person] I have known," by his sermons also he "provided, not for a famine of bread or a thirst for water, but a longing for the truly life-giving and nourishing Word."[23] For Basil, the supremacy of the Word did not result in the false dichotomy—between caring for spiritual needs and caring for physical needs—that has trapped so many (cf. Titus 3:14).

Basil did not shy away from addressing social issues from the pulpit. Smither notes,

"For Basil, authentic faith should transform Caesarea's economic system as generosity overcame greed while rich and poor worshiped together in Christian community."[24] By AD 370, a stark gap between rich and poor had developed. Yet both wealthy Christians who exploited the famine and impoverished Christians who blamed the famine to excuse certain sins were met with biblical correction from the pulpit.

Basil also initiated projects that addressed the many social and material needs of his city. Perhaps most well-known was his establishment of the *basileas* or "new city."[25] This community included a home for the poor and orphaned, had a renowned hospital (the first of its kind in recorded world history), provided skill training and opportunities for work, housed a stockpile of food that was distributed to the neediest, and also served as a hostel for weary travelers. The ethos of this society was guided by Basil's teaching on biblical hospitality:

Has a guest arrived? If he is a brother . . . he will recognize the fare we provide as properly his own. What he has left at home, he will find with us. Suppose he is weary after his journey. We then provide as much nourishment as is required to relieve his weariness. Is it a secular person who has arrived? Let him learn through actual experience . . . and let

---

22. Susan R. Holman *The Hungry Are Dying: Beggars and Bishops in Roman Cappadocia* (New York: Oxford University Press, 2001), 68–69.

23. Gregory of Nazianzus, *Oratio in laudem Basilii* 43.36 (*NPNF*[2] 7:407–8).

24. Smither, "Basil of Caesarea," 67.

25. A. Sterk, *Renouncing the World yet Leading the Church: The Monk-Bishop in Late Antiquity* (Cambridge, MA: Harvard University Press, 2004), 69.

him be given a model and pattern of frugal sufficiency in matters of food. . . . In every case, care must be taken for a good table, yet without overstepping the limits of the actual need. This should be our aim in hospitality— that the individual requirements of our guests may be cared for.[26]

Thus, for Basil, hospitality was a powerful missionary platform, a model of Christian love. Basil's life was relatively short—forty-nine years. Yet his gospel boldness, theological vigilance, and practical concern for the souls of his city have left a lasting legacy, one that is especially instructive to the modern-day urban missionary. Like Irenaeus, Basil's ministry highlights the need for both the proclamation and demonstration of the gospel in word and deed.

Current Examples of Urban Ministry

In line with the examples from the early church, there are many present-day accounts that follow the early church's example, even as they followed the example of Christ (1 Cor 11:1).[27] These examples illustrate that while there have been many changes to the makeup of the urban context over millennia, the basic needs, unique challenges, and essential elements of gospel ministry in the city have remained unchanged. Here are just a few examples.

David

As an infant, David was brought to the United States illegally. His father was a violent gang member who beat him and his mother regularly. One of his earliest and most vivid memories was getting cut by the broken glass that shattered upon him when the police broke through the window over his bed. They had come to arrest his father for murder. David lived in a one-bedroom apartment with his mother, who was the neighborhood witch doctor, and his younger brother, but he rarely came out because his face was so disfigured from the beatings he had suffered. He struggled to talk, and when he did talk, he could not keep saliva from pouring out from the side of his mouth.

Around the time that David was five, God called a Christian public school teacher to move to the inner-city neighborhood where David lived and to start working with the local church there. Partnering with some parachurch ministries, this teacher and his wife initiated an afterschool program that combined basic educational mentorship with long-term, life-on-life discipleship. They also spearheaded an internship house that hosted students from local Christian colleges and other young adult Christians desiring to be on mission together for Christ in the neighborhood. Here, as with Basil and Irenaeus, hospitality and generosity were tools for the gospel (cf. Luke 14:13–14; 16:9; 19:5–10).

The teacher, along with others from the

---

26. Basil of Caesarea, *Long Rules* 20.1–2 (PG 31:972b–c, 975a). English translation from M. Monica Wagner, *Saint Basil's Ascetical Works* (Washington, DC: Catholic University Press, 1962), 278–80; Smither, "Basil of Caesarea," 71.

27. While the names and details have been changed for security purposes, the following are real accounts of real people.

church, kept inviting David to come to Bible study or just to hang out, but for years he never wanted to go. By God's grace, one day David finally ventured out of his apartment and showed up at the high school youth group. He shared with the leaders that he wanted to start reading the Bible but could not read well. In response, the church bought him an audio Bible CD (this was before smartphones), and David began to walk around the neighborhood wearing his headphones, listening to the Word, with a big smile on his face. He came to understand that even though his earthly father had forsaken him, His heavenly Father loved him (Ps 27:10). His heavenly Father loved him with an unshakable love, a love by which Jesus Christ was willing to die for David's sins to make him a new creation in Christ (Rom 5:8; 2 Cor 5:17).

Almost twenty years have passed since David walked through those church doors. He is still there, faithfully serving and now leading the youth group. Over the years, God has provided, through generous donations by God's people, opportunities for David to have the much needed oral and facial reconstruction surgeries. But even more importantly, God brought restoration to David's family by bringing both his brother and his mother to saving faith in Christ after they witnessed the change in David's life and the love of the Christian community for their family.

David himself experienced the love of the church community. He came to know the power of a church that not only preaches orthodox gospel doctrine but produces a gospel culture, loving people compassionately. As that gospel message and culture continued to pour out of the walls of the church building through word and deed (1 John 3:18), it was received by many in the neighborhood, and it continues to have a transformative effect on the ecosystem of the community. This neighborhood, once ranked one of the most violent in the country, is now one of the safest in its city. For, as people began to follow Christ, they also began to love their neighbors, to speak out for the overlooked, to renounce violence, to value education, and to seek to live as families united by the Spirit of Christ.

Ahmed

Ahmed was born into a prominent Muslim family in East Asia, but he was raised in the United States. His father had relocated the family for better opportunities. Yet when Ahmed got into trouble with the law as a young man, he was deported back to his home country. There he married a Muslim woman and continued a lawless life, becoming a midlevel drug dealer. His family connections enabled him both to use and to traffic illegal drugs without restraint.

When Ahmed's life came crashing down, God graciously brought him a friend to tell him the gospel. He put his faith in Christ and started attending church with that friend. But when his wife and her family found out, they were strongly opposed. Eventually his wife divorced him and restricted contact with their son. As the years passed, Ahmed continued faithfully attending his church and even came to lead some of its ministries.

The church, however, was influenced by pragmatism and prosperity theology, and Ahmed's growth in Christlikeness was seriously hindered by false teaching. When the global pandemic of 2020 hit, all the churches in Ahmed's city were shut down. Forced to watch sermons online, he was providentially exposed to better preaching from around the world. A hunger started to grow in his soul for robust, biblically faithful preaching, and he began searching for a church where he could be fed from God's Word. Like the nourishment preached from Basil's pulpit in time of famine, the healing power of the Word sent out through faithful preachers had great effect during the pandemic.

In God's providence again, Ahmed's search led to a missionary in the process of planting a church, which Ahmed joined. It was even closer to his house than his former church had been. His new proximity to a faithful pastor has allowed Ahmed to dig into the Word deeply and to be discipled through formal academic study as well as life-on-life mentorship. Now he has a heart for being a bridge and a voice for gospel clarity both to the Muslim community and to the anemic church in his nation.

Putri

Putri was born into one of the Christian tribes of her country. Although the tribe claimed a Christian identity, animistic syncretism was a hallmark of its belief system. She had been raised in the city most of her life and came from a fairly wealthy, well-educated background. Still, the traditional beliefs of her culture shaped much of her worldview. Even when she landed a well-paying job in the technology industry, her unbiblical beliefs controlled her. Their grip only increased when she married a man from another Christian tribe.

The enslaving power of Putri's beliefs came to a head when her husband cheated on her. His family blamed her for his infidelity, due to her tribal background. They accused her of putting a curse on him that caused him to be unfaithful. They demanded that she perform an animistic ritual in their own tribal "church" with their "pastor" overseeing it as an act of penance. When she refused, she was cast out of the marriage.

From that time, Putri lived broken, alone, and confused about why God would let this happen to her. Then, one day she came with a friend to a Bible study hosted in a missionary's home in her city. While she normally would not associate with churches made up of people outside of her tribe, her location within this global, diverse city exposed her to the broader family of God. It was here that she heard the gospel of Jesus Christ clearly for the first time, and she saw that it was indeed "good news" (*euangelion*, gospel). She began putting off her old ways of thinking, of spiritism, of ritualism, of seeking self-worth in the opinions of others, and she started seeing herself through the lens of the gospel. She began to be a regular and welcomed guest at the missionaries' house for formal and informal discipleship. Putri began to understand her identity in Christ as she was welcomed not only into the family of God but literally into this missionary family. Once more, as with the church fathers, the consistent teaching of a hospitable pastor, confronting heresy while comforting the suffering, had life-changing effects.

The Roberts Family

After studying language and culture in a small town, the Roberts family moved to a large Muslim majority city. While there are some churches in this city, many of them are theologically weak, and virtually none of them are taking meaningful steps to reach the Muslim majority peoples of the city. But like Irenaeus, the Roberts felt burdened to participate in the culture and community for the sake of the gospel.

They decided to move near a large slum, despite being advised by local Christians that the people there would be hostile to the gospel. They had not originally intended to establish house churches, but when the COVID-19 lockdowns closed all church gatherings, the Roberts began inviting friends over for a meal and a Bible study. Most of the first attenders of these meetings were nominal Christians who had not been connected to a church previously. But the reality of the pandemic woke them up to their need for eternal hope. As they attended these Bible studies, the gospel took root in their hearts and began to bear fruit in their lives. They began believing the truth, and then they invited their unbelieving friends to come. They began seeing their Muslim neighbors not as threats to their safety but as lost sheep without a shepherd (Isa 53:6; Matt 9:36; 18:12).

Many Muslim neighbors began coming to the home Bible studies, and a few former Muslims even expressed faith in Christ. The house fellowship grew so much that it multiplied into three groups. In 2023 these house fellowships began gathering as a recognized church. In addition to navigating the challenges of getting community and government approval for meeting publicly, this phase also involved teaching and modeling for the new believers what being a gospel-formed, Christ-treasuring, mission-fulfilling family of disciples looks like.

It Began in a City

The book of Acts records the beginning of the Church, and it began in a city, Jerusalem (Acts 1:4, 8, 12; 2:1). Later, due to persecution, the gospel began spilling out to other regions through refugees viewed more in retrospect as missionaries.[28] The first recorded place where the Word was preached was another city, Samaria (8:1, 5). The first recorded missionary, Philip, was not deterred by his status as a displaced and despised outsider, but boldly "began preaching Christ to them" (8:5). The result was that many believed and "there was great joy in that city" (8:8). Then, in a short time, the church multiplied throughout the Samaritan region (9:31; 15:3).

This pattern continued through the book

---

28. Cf. Everett F. Harrison, *Interpreting Acts: The Expanding Church* (Grand Rapids: Zondervan, 1986), 139; Ajith Fernando, *Acts*, NIVAC (Grand Rapids: Zondervan, 1998), 263.

of Acts. It continued in the postbiblical early church, and it continues today. God is still offering great joy to the cities of the world through the proclamation of the same powerful Savior.

These accounts from the past and present are merely glimpses of what God is doing and is able to do in global cities. Everything He does is for His glory and for the joy of His people.

CHAPTER 58

Pursuing Justice: Representing God, the Defender of the Helpless in Cruel and Unjust Societies

George A. Crawford

It was the spring of 1799. At thirty-seven years of age and having been in India for more than five years, missionary William Carey witnessed something that shook him to the core. In his own words:

> We saw a number of people assembled on the river-side. I asked for what they were meeting, and they told me to burn the body of a dead man. I enquired if his wife would die with him; they answered yes, and pointed to her. She was standing by the pile of large billets of wood, on the top of which lay her husband's dead body. Her nearest relative stood by her; and near her was a basket of sweetmeats. I asked if this was her choice, or if she were brought to it by any improper influence. They answered that it was perfectly voluntary. I talked till reasoning was of no use, and then began to exclaim with all my might against what they were doing, telling them it was shocking murder. They told me it was a great act of holiness, and added in a very surly manner, that if I did not like to see it, I might go further off, and desired me to do so. I told them that I would not go, that I was determined to stay and see the murder, against which I should certainly bear witness at the tribunal of God. I exhorted the widow not to throw away her life; to fear nothing, for no evil would follow her refusal to be burned. But in the most calm manner she mounted the pile, and danced on it with her hands extended, as if in the utmost tranquility of spirit. Previous to this, the relative, whose office it was to set fire to the pile, led her six times round it—thrice at a time. As she went round, she scattered the sweetmeats amongst the people, who ate them as a very holy thing. This being ended, she lay down beside the corpse, and put one arm under its neck and the other over it,

when a quantity of dry cocoa-leaves and other substances were heaped over them to a considerable height, and then *ghi* was poured on the top. Two bamboos were then put over them, and held fast down, and the fire put to the pile, which immediately blazed very fiercely, owing to the dry and combustible materials of which it was composed. No sooner was the fire kindled than all the people set up a great shout of joy, invoking Siva. It was impossible to have heard the woman, had she groaned, or even cried aloud, on account of the shoutings of the people, and again it was impossible for her to stir or struggle, by reason of the bamboos held down on her, like the levers of a press. We made much objection to their use of these, insisting that it was undue force, to prevent her getting up when the fire burned. But they declared it was only to keep the fire from falling down. We could not bear to see more, but left them, exclaiming loudly against the murder, and filled with horror at what we had seen.[1]

Years later, S. Pearce Carey, William Carey's biographer and great-grandson, wrote that "his spirit was in anguish in that flame. His brain burned with her body. He vowed . . . 'to hit this accursed thing hard, if God should spare him.' For the cruelty was done in the name of religion. Such criminal ignorance of God on the part of India's priests made him sigh for more colleagues."[2]

Known as *sati* or *suttee*, the practice of widow burning had reportedly been practiced in India since at least the time of Alexander the Great.[3] The practice was believed to lead to eternal blessing, as were infanticide and the forced drowning or burning of lepers.[4] Carey and his missionary colleagues fought these murderous practices with much success, but their battle against *sati* was the longest, lasting nearly thirty years.[5] On December 4, 1829, the British governor of India and his council declared the practice both illegal and criminal.

Throughout the decades leading up to victory over *sati*, Carey and his fellow missionaries repeatedly petitioned the government. Additionally, in 1804 Carey commissioned an investigation into the number of widows murdered within thirty miles of Calcutta over the previous year and found that there had been

---

1. S. Pearce Carey, *William Carey*, 8th ed., rev. and enlarged (London: Carey Press, 1934), 182–83.

2. Carey, 183.

3. See historical tracing in Przemysław Szczurek, "Source or Sources of Diodorus' Account of Indian *sati*/Suttee (Dio. Dic. 19.33–34.6)?," in *The Children of Herodotus: Greek and Roman Historiography and Related Genres*, ed. Jakub Pigoń (Newcastle upon Tyne, UK: Cambridge Scholars, 2008), 119–43; A. B. Bosworth, *The Legacy of Alexander: Politics, Warfare, and Propaganda under the Successors* (Oxford: Oxford University Press, 2002), 173–87.

4. Wendy Doniger states other possible motives: "The larger incidence of suttee among the Brahmans of Bengal was indirectly due to the *Dayabhaga* system of law (c. 1100), which prevailed in Bengal and which gave inheritance to widows; such women were encouraged to commit suttee in order to make their inheritance available to other relatives." It should also be noted that relatives of the immolated widow would have been spared the economic burden of having to provide for her material sustenance for a prolonged period of time. Wendy Doniger, "Suttee," in *Encyclopedia Britannica*, accessed June 18, 2024, https://www.britannica.com/topic /suttee.

5. Evangeline Anderson-Rajkumar, "Ministry in the Killing Fields," *Christian History* 36 (1992): 35–37.

438 victims.[6] Carey continued to publish such death rolls for the next quarter century. By the time the practice was finally outlawed, Carey's team had reported the burnings of approximately six thousand widows over ten years in just one province. Considering that the practice had been prevalent across India for more than 2,300 years before it was outlawed, the historical total of the victims is inconceivable.[7]

In ending *satī*, William Carey reflected on the biblical call of Proverbs 24:11–12:

> Deliver those who are being taken away
> to death,
> And those who are stumbling to the
> slaughter, Oh hold them back.
> If you say, "Behold, we did not
> know this,"
> Does not He who weighs the hearts
> understand?
> And does not He who guards your
> soul know?
> And will not He render to man
> according to his work?[8]

Carey's example provides missionaries today a model of combating biblical injustice while wisely maintaining biblical priorities and credibility on the mission field.

The Biblical Definitions of Justice and Injustice

William Carey rose up against society because he knew that the evil practices he witnessed grew out of a deficient and defective knowledge of God and His righteousness. To speak of the "justice" of God is to speak of His perfect, absolute righteous essence, as well as His acts, through which He reveals His righteous essence to mankind. Because God has a perfect nature, He has established standards with which all people must comply (Deut 4:8; 2 Sam 23:3; Pss 9:4; 99:4; 119:7). Therefore, the pursuit of justice by all who are being sanctified into the image of Christ is the pursuit of the practical, experiential outworking and demonstration of God's righteousness and holiness in specific situations. It is to represent God, the Defender of the helpless (Deut 10:18; Pss 10:14; 68:5–6; 146:9; Isa 25:4).

Different Hebrew words are used in the Old Testament to describe the pursuit of godly justice. *Mishpat* most often refers to a right and proper adjudication of individual claims, of rights and wrongs, while the plural form, *mishpatim*, refers to specific adjudications or case law, similar to appellate law.[9] *Tsedaqah* tends to be more abstract in reference to community loyalty and to specific deeds of justice, taking on in postbiblical Judaism the specific sense of

---

6. Carey, *William Carey*, 221–22.

7. Carey, 364. Using the alternative spelling "suttee," Doniger states, "The first explicit reference to the practice in Sanskrit appears in the great epic Mahabharata (compiled in its present form about 400 CE). It is also mentioned by Diodorus Siculus, a Greek author of the 1st century BCE, in his account of the Punjab in the 4th century BCE. Numerous suttee stones, memorials to the wives who died in this way, are found all over India, the earliest dated 510 CE." Doniger, "Suttee."

8. Carey, *William Carey*, 364.

9. "טִפְשֵׁמ," *HALOT*, 2:652.

charitable alms.[10] The terms are coupled in some of the most significant passages on the topic of divine justice, including Isaiah 5:16, Amos 5:24, and Jeremiah 9:24. Some of the practical demonstrations of human compliance with God's justice can be seen in the context of the allocation of government services, the proper treatment of vulnerable groups within society, the proper punishment of the sins of men, and the right and proper adjudication of specific disputes.

The New Testament Greek terms for "justice" build on the *dik-* root and add the "*alpha* prefix" for negation, to show that "injustice" is the absence, lack, or the perversion of justice.[11] Passages such as Luke 18:1–8 build on the concepts of Deuteronomy 1:16–17 and 16:18–20 to depict injustice as the perversion of the moral rules and laws that God has imposed. Injustice results from unbiblical attitudes, such as fearing man while lacking the fear of God, disregarding man's dignity as an image-bearer of God, and evil actions, such as treating others with partiality, based on differences in ethnic, social, or economic status. "Injustice" is therefore a broad concept that refers to societal practices fomented by unbiblical doctrines and evil

motivations toward those who are vulnerable, in need, and without protection.

Criteria for Fighting Injustice

William Carey's fight against the murderous customs of his mission field illustrates the fight against injustice that missionaries must often undertake in their contexts. Carey acted because he wished to avoid guilt for a sin of omission in the face of overt evil.[12] There is a certain culpability for knowledgeable inaction without a good cause (Jas 4:17). Missionaries today face similar challenges. How should they respond when confronted with the reality of near and ongoing injustice? What should missionaries do concerning systemic, widespread injustices such as human trafficking?[13] Can work to address these issues be reconciled with a priority on preaching and prayer?[14] The missionary needs to align his or her thinking to key criteria, related to Scripture, the circumstances, one's integrity, and the available resources.

Consult Pertinent Scriptures

As 2 Timothy 3:16–17 states, "All Scripture is God-breathed and profitable for teaching, for

---

10. "הִקְדִּישׁ," *HALOT*, 3:1005–6.

11. E.g., "ἀδικία," BDAG, 20; "δίκαιος," BDAG, 246.

12. Carey, *William Carey*, 182–83, 221–22, 364.

13. In some regions, missionaries may encounter the widespread seizure of the real estate and other property belonging to a recently widowed woman. See International Justice Mission, *An Endline Study of the Prevalence of Property Grabbing among Widows and the Response of the Justice System in Mukono County, Uganda*, International Justice Mission, 2018, https://ijmstoragelive.blob.core .windows.net/ijmna/documents/studies/Uganda-Property-Grabbing-Prevalence.pdf.

14. While in this years-long pursuit, Carey did not neglect his primary responsibility of the ministry of the Word. Nor did he abandon it when he arranged for a preaching substitute on one particular, isolated occasion, so that he could immediately translate the text of the government mandate outlawing *sati* and prevent further loss of life. Self-trained in Greek and Hebrew while working as a cobbler, he translated Scripture into thirty-five languages of India during his years of missionary service, with the whole Bible completed in six languages, the whole New Testament into twenty-four others, and at least one gospel into five more. Carey, *William Carey*, 389–96.

reproof, for correction, for training in righteousness, so that the man of God may be equipped, having been thoroughly equipped for every good work." The most important criteria in deciding how to act against injustice is to consider whether Scripture speaks relevantly to the question. Does the historical-grammatical exegesis of any passage provide an application that directly addresses the injustice? Carey recognized that the practice of *satī* directly contradicted biblical teaching about widows,[15] and that the Bible calls for actions in similar situations (Obad 11; Luke 12:47–48; Jas 4:17).[16] Scripture is the primary lens through which the missionary evaluates all circumstances.

Consider Problems Case by Case

Some specific situations or conditions are not directly addressed by Scripture but must be analyzed carefully on an individual, case-by-case basis. Proverbs 18:13 instructs believers to be sure they understand the problem at hand before rendering a judgment: "He who responds with a word before he hears, it is folly and shame to him." According to Proverbs 19:2, "It is not good for a person to be without knowledge, and he who hurries his footsteps sins." Therefore, it is important for the missionary to evaluate the central facts of a particular situation before taking action. Prolonged investigation may not be necessary, but if a situation evolves over time, the missionary must modify his or her response as necessary.

Conserve Credibility in the Local Context

In 1 Timothy 1:5, Paul describes that the goal of proclaiming sound doctrine "is love from a pure heart and a good conscience and an unhypocritical faith." In 2 Corinthians 5:10, he reveals that "we must all appear before the judgment seat of Christ, so that each one may be recompensed for his deeds in the body, according to what he has done, whether good or bad." Therefore, a salient question that the missionary must ask is whether a gospel worker can, in good conscience, do nothing to fight injustice.

Action or inaction impacts the credibility of a missionary's character and reputation, and the missionary's deeds will either adorn or stain him or her as a minister of the gospel (2 Cor 5:18–20). It is not difficult to find contemporary examples of well-intentioned servants who prioritize social justice activities with little focus on proclaiming the gospel. Good deeds without the good news are, ultimately, of no good use. Yet a missionary's testimony is also severely damaged if he or she proclaims God's concern for the oppressed while taking no steps

---

15. Such passages include Exodus 22:22; Deuteronomy 10:18–20; Job 29:13, 31:16–17; Psalm 68:5; Proverbs 31:8–9; Jeremiah 7:6–7; Acts 6:1–6; 1 Timothy 5:3; and James 1:27. Significantly, in Isaiah 1:17, the prophet challenges the people of Israel to "seek justice, reprove the ruthless [i.e., the oppressor], execute justice for the orphan, plead [i.e., strive or contend] for the widow."

16. Irvin Busenitz connects the historical situation behind Obadiah with these passages: "Edom was not without guilt. They were fully cognizant of their brotherly duty and responsibility [when Judah was under brutal attack] but they had chosen to 'pass by on the other side' (Luke 10:31–32). Out of a spirit of arrogance, they were guilty of the sin of omission (cf. Jas 4:16–17)." Irvin A. Busenitz, *Joel and Obadiah*, Mentor Commentary (Fearn, Ross-shire, UK: Christian Focus, 2003), 256.

to implement a solution with the participation of the local church (cf. 1 Tim 5:3–16).

Conduct Cautious First Steps

If the missionary determines that action is warranted to counteract a particular evil on the field, then it is right to consider what specific response might be the most effective and the best use of the resources available. If it is determined that public action must be taken, the missionary must determine whether to address the situation directly under the sending agency or church or to partner in some respects with other individuals or organizations that could address the situation more comprehensively.

Direct response may be possible if the sending church or agency supports it. For the missionary to directly address the situation and remain "above reproach" (Titus 1:7; 1 Tim 3:2), he or she must fulfill the expectations of the role as defined by the sending church or agency. Therefore, it is essential to conduct earnest and thorough discussions with the missionary's leaders and coworkers in the gospel at the outset of any response activity. In many unjust situations around the world, one or more likeminded local churches may have already taken action to deal with the issue, perhaps alongside local *pro bono* law offices, nongovernmental organizations (NGOs), or local governments.[17] Partnering is an efficient solution to addressing the need. Caution would be needed when seeking the assistance of secular workers, since any collaboration can appear to be a spiritual alliance.

Priorities for Establishing Biblical Justice

When undertaking the fight against injustice, the missionary must keep two priorities in mind so that every action against the evil deeds of darkness shines the light of Christ. Specifically, proclamation and prayer in the context of the local church and the regular evangelistic appeal to sinners outside the church will ensure that all social actions fit within God's design for His spiritual kingdom in the Church age. Since the gospel is the instrument of true justice, the top priorities for establishing biblical justice center around the preaching and teaching of the gospel message.

The Priority of Local Church Proclamation and Prayer

The first priority for ensuring the establishment of biblical justice is preaching, teaching, and praying within the local church context. In Acts 6:1–7, the young church of Jerusalem faced a crisis concerning Greek-speaking Jewish widows. Grumbling among the Hellenists exposed the concern that the church showed partiality toward the native Palestinian Jews (v. 1). The twelve apostles summoned the congregation and stated that their priority—not to be forsaken—was the ministry of the Word and of prayer (v. 2).[18] Rather than ignore the

---

17. Some NGOs are evangelical in mission and practice, such as the International Justice Mission, which has offices in several countries to combat injustice alongside local churches (www.ijm.org).

18. Luke uses the term *kataleipō*, which refers to an intentional choice to leave something behind ("καταλείπω," BDAG, 520–21),

problem, the apostles instructed the church to select seven godly men to solve the crisis (v. 3).

In contemporary field contexts, the missionary must prioritize the work of prayer and the proclamation of the Word of God. Only once prayer and proclamation are established as the regular practices of the missionary is there room to work against injustice. Fighting injustice must be a support ministry to prayer and proclamation, not a hindrance, serving as a reinforcement of the ministry of the Word by applying biblical truth to the local context.

The Priority of Repentance and Belief

Closely related to the ministry of prayer and the Word is the ongoing priority of calling all people to saving faith in Jesus Christ. Missionaries must focus on the message of repentance and belief in the gospel as they attempt to respond to injustice of all kinds. The unbelieving world can accomplish much social good, but the real value of secular action is limited without the gospel. Christians everywhere, no matter how surrounded by oppression, abuses, and societal ills they may be, must engage their context with the biblical perspective that the world's problems are temporal and ultimate justice awaits the return of Christ (Isa 2:2–4; Mic 4:1–5). Only conversion spares from eternal suffering and addresses cosmic injustice.

Christians by their salvation are equipped to right wrongs in this world (Titus 2:1–15; 3:1–7).

Jeremiah 38 exemplifies how eternal perspective motivates an appropriate pursuit of temporal justice. When Jeremiah had been cast into a cistern under a death sentence at the request of a group of nobles,[19] help came from Ebed-melech, a servant of King Zedekiah. Ebed-melech stood before the king and argued against the injustice done to Jeremiah (vv. 7–9). His action was comparable to a modern petition in court for a writ of *habeas corpus*, challenging the detainment of a prisoner. With substantial risk to his own safety, the servant obtained an order from the king to rescue Jeremiah (vv. 10–13). This is the only instance recorded in the Old Testament of anyone speaking as an advocate for a Hebrew prophet to a sitting monarch.[20] Although Ebed-melech was a court official, he was an unlikely candidate to save Jeremiah since he was an Ethiopian foreigner. Either Ebed-melech or his ancestors had likely been trafficked, since he was a eunuch (v. 7).[21]

Why would this foreign servant pursue justice for the prophet when Jeremiah's own people had turned on him? Jeremiah 39:15–18 explains. God directed Jeremiah to seek out Ebed-melech, stating that his motivation for fighting against injustice was his trust in the one true God—that is, a regenerate servant fought injustice in this world with God's strength.

---

in contrast to *ameleō*, which refers to being careless with something, as is used in 1 Timothy 4:14 ("ἀμελέω," BDAG, 20).

19. Josephus's tradition (*Ant.* 10.7.5) claims that the mud was neck high, indicating that Jeremiah's life was in danger; he was intended to suffocate.

20. Queen Esther's petition to King Ahasuerus for her relative Mordecai and the Hebrew people is also noteworthy (Esth 7:1–6).

21. F. B. Huey, *Jeremiah, Lamentations*, NAC 16 (Nashville: Broadman and Holman, 1993), 335; H. D. M. Spence-Jones, ed., *Jeremiah*, Pulpit Commentary 2 (London: Funk and Wagnalls, 1909), 131.

Genuine and prolonged concern for justice will characterize a person who has embraced true saving faith. When God's servants prioritize spiritual transformation before temporal justice, they are pursuing true, biblical justice. That ethos guided William Carey in his work on behalf of Satan's spiritual captives.

Conclusion

William Carey, one of the earliest and most influential of modern missionaries, was able to faithfully proclaim and translate the Word of God while successfully opposing *satī*, infanticide, and other abuses. Other missionaries have faced, and will continue to face, similar challenges. They would do well to mark the statement Carey is noted for: "Expect great things from God; attempt great things for God."[22] As his life has demonstrated, with the proper prioritization and balance, those "great things" can include the proclamation of the Word, the call of men and women to repentance and saving faith in Christ, and, when necessary, the seeking of temporal justice.

Missionaries fulfill the law of Christ when they love their neighbor as themselves (Matt 22:36–40). A challenge on the field, when facing an endless horizon of desperation and need, is how to respond to the atrocities committed by lawless sinners. Missionaries need a clear framework for extending genuine, biblical love to the most unloved. The criteria set forth in this chapter for deciding how to fight injustice, as well as the priorities that inform their actions, will guide gospel workers to respond wisely in their situations.

It is imperative that missionaries respond to the brokenness around them with the core conviction that true freedom will come only through spiritual reconciliation to God, through the precious blood of the Lord Jesus Christ (1 Pet 1:17–19). It should be the prayer of every believer that Christ's light would shine brightly through them in the midst of their crooked and perverse generation (Phil 2:15). Let many missionaries who labor long for biblical justice receive their reward in heaven, just as did William Carey, hearing the righteous Judge declare to them, "Well done, good and faithful slave. . . . Enter into the joy of your master" (Matt 25:21, 23; Luke 19:17).

---

22. J. W. Morris, "Narrative of the First Establishment of This Society," in *Periodical Accounts Relative to the Baptist Missionary Society* 1 (London: J. W. Morris, 1800): 2–3.

CHAPTER 59

At-Risk Children and How Adoption Displays the Gospel

Mark Tatlock

Though adoption may sound overwhelming to many, it is a beautiful way to offer one's life in service to the gospel. Orphan care, including adoption, foster parenting, legal advocacy, and other volunteering display God's love for children, and adoption especially enacts God's own bringing of the sinners that He saves in Christ into His eternal family. Many adoptions are international, giving Christian parents the opportunity to participate in reaching the nations for Christ. Though it is not the equivalent of missions, in God's providence, Christian adoption and foster care have been a means of God's reaching souls with the good news who otherwise would never have heard—besides the children, their parents and relatives, social workers, and even outside observers.

Books have been written on the adoption process,[1] and even they do not cover every circumstance. This chapter merely serves as a high-level introduction to the topic with the hope of encouraging missions-minded Christians to consider whether God is leading them to this high calling. The chapter provides an overview of at-risk kids, followed by a closer look at orphan care internationally, and ending with an exhortation to consider adoption in a biblical and missional perspective.

A Global Picture of At-Risk Kids

A serious and critical need the Church faces today is to understand the perils of at-risk kids around the world. At-risk kids are those children who are not under the protection and care of one or two parents and who are thus vulnerable to being neglected, harmed, or

---

1. E.g., see Dan Cruver, ed., *Reclaiming Adoption: Missional Living through the Rediscovery of Abba Father* (Adelphi, MD: Cruciform, 2010); Daniel Bennett, *A Passion for the Fatherless: Developing a God-Centered Ministry to Orphans* (Grand Rapids: Kregel, 2011).

exploited in some manner. Some perils include forced labor or military service; untreated disabilities, special needs, or diseases; homelessness; and incarceration. These are elaborated below in turn.

Child labor is all too common in the world. Twenty percent of all trafficking victims worldwide are children.[2] Many are either adopted, abducted, or purchased outright for the sole purpose of serving a horrific lifestyle of forced labor, which is nothing less than slavery. Trafficking and slavery are an international phenomena—they exist in cities of the West and of Southeast Asia alike. For example, in recent years in the United States, international sporting events have been known hubs for the exchange of trafficking victims, especially of a sexual nature.

Internationally, one in every six children ages five to fourteen are involved in slavery, doing menial labor such as rolling cigarettes or making bricks. That often comes about because the children's parents incur a debt they cannot pay. For example, a father might get sick, have no money for the surgery, and unsuspectingly borrow money from a lender. After the surgery, the money lender comes and exacts the payment. When the family cannot repay it at the exorbitant interest rate, the lender makes a deal to take their children as workers in the brickyard. Then he continues to increase the interest rate so that the family can never pay off the

debt. It is not uncommon for these children, after spending their entire lives in forced labor, to become indebted as well, their parents never having paid off the original sum. Slavery of the first child turns into generational slavery, even of entire families on account of one debt.

Another risk facing many kids is exploitation as child soldiers. Refugee minors are a disastrous aftermath of war. Currently, more than 40 million children are displaced in the world, mostly due to conflict and violence.[3] Everything they have known in terms of security, stability, health care, and education has been disrupted. And the potential risk for the kids' exploitation is great. Though not all are orphans, all are affected. They have seen atrocities and experienced violence. Many of them have lost parents. It is not uncommon in a conflict area to find houses headed by a child, a fourteen- or fifteen-year-old caring for three or four younger siblings, even infants. Even when their parents are not killed, the children in conflict areas may be abducted, drugged, and forced under the influence to kill others, or be carried off to be sexually abused in the service of soldiers. It is a horrific reality.

A third risk facing kids relates to disabilities, special needs, and diseases untreated. In the developing world, disabilities such as cleft palates, heart conditions, and clubbed feet are common. A prominent threat of disease is HIV/

---

2. United Nations Office on Drugs and Crime, Policy and Research Branch, *Global Report on Trafficking in Persons*, prepared under the supervision of Sandeep Chawla, Angela Me, and Thibault le Pichon, February 2009, 48–49, https://www.unodc.org/unodc/en/human-trafficking/global-report-on-trafficking-in-persons.html.

3. "Number of Displaced Children Reaches New High of 43.3 Million," UNICEF, June 13, 2023, https://www.unicef.org/press-releases/number-displaced-children-reaches-new-high-433-million.

AIDS. But what is treatable in some parts of the world and can often be mitigated or even remedied is untreatable in other parts. Many children with disabilities or diseases suffer physically more than they need to, whether due to lack of adequate local health care or to a lack of money for treatment. Many also suffer rejection and abuse.

A fourth risk arises for the myriad children living in difficult circumstances—such as living under physical abuse or with parents who are unable to provide for them—that they run away and live on the streets. Sadly, many then turn to drugs or sniffing glue or inhalants in an attempt to escape their troubles. These kids are particularly vulnerable to the exploits of organized crime. In many places, the drug cartels and gang members actively recruit kids to sell and carry their drugs across borders, security checkpoints, and rival territories.

One final risk to many children is incarceration. Over one million kids a year are denied their liberty,[4] which in many countries occurs because children are easy victims to be exploited. For instance, a dishonest person might file a false claim with the police (or threaten to file one) to try to force the child's parents to pay them a bribe or a ransom. When the parents cannot come up with the money, the accuser reports the case and the kids go to prison. They may or may not have been guilty of a crime, but now they are locked away and almost impossible to free or even to contact.

Related to that, millions of children have at least one parent in prison. In such cases, particularly when the father is in prison, the children can become functional orphans or children of functional widows when the vulnerable children and/or mother are left to fend for themselves. Thus, even when children are free, incarceration can still be devastating for them, leading to the other risks already mentioned, to drugs, to living on the streets, and to prostitution. Into this darkness, the light of the gospel must shine. Children must be told of the love of a heavenly Father who will never leave them nor forsake them (Ps 27:10; Heb 13:5), who hears their every cry (Ps 56:8; 1 Pet 5:7), who promises to wipe away every tear (Rev 21:4), who is willing to forgive their every sin (Ps 103:13; Luke 23:34), and who runs to embrace them with open arms (Luke 15:20).

International Orphan Care

Recognizing the above risks, many countries have varying degrees of governmental and community solutions. Some countries, like the United States, facilitate foster care, the temporary, nonadoptive placement of children in a safe and stable home. Many, however, rely exclusively on nonprofit and faith-based ministries to serve this function. These are funded by local or international donors concerned about the safety and welfare of children. Where these ministries do exist, it is important for the local church to recognize the opportunities for

---

4. United Nations Committee on the Rights of the Child, *Global Study on Children Deprived of Liberty*, 74th General Assembly, July 11, 2019, https://www.ohchr.org/en/treaty-bodies/crc/united-nations-global-study-children-deprived-liberty.

Christians to be actively involved in not only serving in and supporting these ministries but also in fostering and adopting the children.

The laws of each country vary greatly, but there is an increasing pressure on nations, either due to shame or nationalism, to address the needs of at-risk children. In other countries, often due to religious and nonbiblical worldviews, children are institutionalized without access to good health care, education, or living environments.

Though foster care systems take children out of dangerous situations, the system itself also brings problems for kids. In the United States, over six hundred thousand kids enter or exit foster care in a given year.[5] None are adoptable until both parents' rights are terminated by the courts. Therefore, a lot of children in the foster system are unadoptable. Many are "repeat" foster kids (having exited and reentered), many are separated from their siblings (placed in separate homes), and many, because of the physical, developmental, or behavioral problems they bring into the home, are moved from place to place in search of someone who can handle them.

Being a foster parent does come at personal cost—time, training, trouble, personal risk, emotional investment, and saying goodbye when the children transition out. But it is filled with the joys of touching many lives over the years. A Christian couple can exhibit great faithfulness by giving themselves first to the Lord and then to these needy children. For those not led to adopt or able to foster, they can still join the work by providing short-term "respite care" for children, allowing foster parents to have an approved babysitter, even for overnight stays. In whatever capacity, Christians can provide a safe living environment where vulnerable children can hear the gospel.

However, foster care is not always available throughout the world. In countries that do not recognize fostering as an option, the common solution has been to build orphanages. Although well-meaning, the act of building better orphanages can unintentionally aggravate the problems of orphans. For instance, a widow living in an impoverished country with two young children for whom she cannot provide may find the beautiful orphanage down the road a compelling reason to give her children up as orphans. Thus, those good orphanage ministries can inadvertently contribute to more children being orphaned.

As an alternative, ministries today are attempting not to take children from widows but to come alongside them and provide job training and other legal advocacy. That does not mean that orphanages are not still the right option in some cases. There is, indeed, a need for them, for there truly are children who have no parents and no shelter. However, the breadth of services provided for the orphanages are expanding to keep families intact whenever possible by not creating an incentive for struggling parents to give up their children.

---

5. U.S. Department of Health and Human Services, Administration for Children and Families, Administration on Children, Youth and Families, Children's Bureau, *The AFCARS Report* 29 (2021), June 28, 2022, https://www.acf.hhs.gov/cb/report/afcars-report-29.

Kids who come from orphanages or through the foster system certainly have a great need for counseling. Their situations and losses are unique, even heart-wrenching. Beyond emotional trauma, it is not uncommon for them also to have physiologically driven developmental setbacks. Even children who appear fine early on may later exhibit both kinds of problems. For example, a child may have come from a good orphanage, but still she did not get the same personal attachment and stimulation as from a parent. Without them, she would be less inclined to crawl and do other activities that would build her motor functions. Thus, she may be developmentally behind other kids of her age group. Adoptive parents should be prepared for and unsurprised by such issues.

A Missional Perspective on Adoption

One should think about adoption from a missional perspective by gleaning from Scripture. Orphan care permeates both Old and New Testaments. The predominant concept of adoption in the ancient world was that of a slave being given the full rights of one's biological child. God, as He brought the nation of Israel out of slavery in Egypt, began to call them His children (Exod 4:22–23; 19:5; Deut 4:20). Israel's identity as the children of God thereafter (Isa 1:2; 63:16; 64:8; Jer 31:9; Hos 11:1) or of God as Father (Deut 8:5; Prov 3:11–12; Jer 3:19) was understood in the New Testament era

as the language of adoption (Rom 9:4). God also depicts Himself as a father to the fatherless and a defender of the helpless (Deut 10:18; Pss 10:14; 27:10; 68:5; 146:9), and He commanded Israel to be the same (Deut 24:17–18; cf. 14:29; 26:12). As for the New Testament, Ted Johnson summarizes the concept well:

> In the Greco-Roman culture of Paul's day, adoption was common, particularly among the upper class, where it was often used to gain political and/or economic advantage. Several Roman emperors adopted men who were not blood relatives for the purpose of conferring upon them certain authority and other privileges. The law of adoption held as its basic premise that a father had near absolute legal authority over his child (*patria potestas*). That authority extended to the power of life and death and continued as long as the father was alive, no matter the age of the child. Thus children were viewed in law as the possession of and under the absolute power of the father.[6]

In light of this, Scripture says that all believers are adopted into God's family. As sinners, they were "by nature children of wrath" (Eph 2:3), "accursed children" (2 Pet 2:14), even sons of the devil (John 8:44; 1 John 3:8), and slaves of sin (John 8:34–36). Yet to all who believe in Jesus' name, God gives the legal right to become His children (John 1:12; Gal

---

6. Ted Johnson, "The Message of Jesus: Our Adoption as God's Children," Grace Communion International, accessed June 18, 2024, https://www.gci.org/articles/our-adoption-as-gods-children.

3:26; 1 John 3:1). In reality, God chose such children for adoption before the foundation of the earth (Eph 1:4–6). But at a point in time, the believer was converted, set free, and given the full privileges of God's own firstborn Son, Jesus Christ (Rom 8:29), who calls the believer "brother" (Heb 2:10–18). Through the atoning death of Christ, God is making one new family from among all the families of the earth (John 11:51–52; cf. Gen 12:3). And when sinners are converted and adopted, God sends forth His Spirit to secure and assure them that they are sons of God and co-heirs with Christ to all His good gifts forever (Rom 8:15–17; Gal 4:6–7; cf. Matt 7:11; Luke 11:13). Therefore, they address God as Father (Matt 6:9; 1 Pet 1:17).

Thus, the doctrine of the believer's adoption in Christ is one the Church has always treasured.[7] The believer's adoption into God's family is the apex of all privilege. God could have done all other gracious works—predestination, regeneration, justification, sanctification, glorification—without granting the ability to enjoy fellowship with Him as a Father. But He didn't. He adopted sons and daughters. J. I. Packer observed. "Adoption is a family idea, conceived in terms of love. . . . Closeness, affection and generosity are at the heart of the relationship. To be right with God the judge is a great thing, but to be loved and cared for by God the Father is greater."[8]

Moreover, adoption represents a spiritual truth that believers can illustrate for the lost when adopting children who are estranged, abandoned, and vulnerable, for every Christian was in that condition spiritually before God adopted him or her. Christians who adopt not only give a child a gift of grace but also give the world a picture of grace. They are imitating the One they call Father (Eph 5:1). God chooses sinners to make His children; adoptive parents choose an orphan to become their child. God legally changes the sinner's status to loved, redeemed, and secured; adoptive parents legally change the orphan's status to the same—loved, redeemed, and secured.

Christians who are adoptive and foster parents should never hide their motives for serving children as they do. Not only is the parent's adoption into God's family the basis for their Christian conduct, but it is a powerful apologetic for the gospel of God their Savior. The children are exposed to the unconditional, sacrificial, electing love of God in Christ in the most tangible way this world can know—as are the children's biological parents, the adoption and foster care agents, and the Christian parents' family and neighbors.

In reality, most adoption and foster care agencies who receive government aid, even those agencies with a Christian name, will at some point disappoint Christian parents. Some agencies, to the parents' horror, have even been exposed as child traffickers themselves. Others, though well-meaning, have adopted worldly psychology and sociology to such an

---

7. A concise treatment of the doctrine is in the 1689 London Baptist Confession of Faith, § 12, accessed June 18, 2024, https://www.the1689confession.com/1689/chapter-12.

8. J. I. Packer, *Knowing God* (1973; repr., Downers Grove, IL: InterVarsity, 2021), 207.

extent that biblical morals and gospel witness are suppressed. Missions-minded parents must do their homework to choose with whom they want to partner, but then they must still expect to navigate the required training, interviews, licensing, inspections, legal proceedings, and continuing relationships with at least some personnel and co-volunteers who are either hostile to or confused about the gospel.

The Christian must be resolved that loving wounded children and the social workers who serve them does not mean passively accepting the government-approved anthropology. Believers must affirm, rather, all that the Bible says about the value of children made in God's image, the equality of all people from every tribe and tongue, and the need for patience with and sympathy toward those who have been abused and who struggle with certain sins as a result. These doctrines are usually acceptable to the unbelieving administrator. But, at the same time, believers must affirm the sinner's miserable slavery to sin, accountability before God, and desperate need for a Savior, as well as God's providence of salvation through the sinner's repentance and faith in Jesus Christ. Graciously speaking and demonstrating these truths will take time, prayer, discernment, and endurance.

To prize the gospel witness of adoption and foster care is by no means to assume that the children cared for will become Christians themselves. Only God has the power to save. But inasmuch as Christian missions are concerned with faithfully proclaiming the gospel and leaving the result in God's hands, so, too,

does gospel-driven orphan care entrust the ultimate results to God's sovereignty. The parents and children alike will face harsh realities. But the greater reality is that God often uses orphan care to bring the gospel to boys, girls, and adults who otherwise would not hear it. By it children receive the privilege of knowing that God not only desired and chose to bring them into a new home, but He chose to make Himself found by them too.

Conclusion

Much sorrow and evil in the world are experienced by at-risk boys and girls. From slaves to soldiers, with disabilities or diseases, running away or incarcerated, children in every corner of the world are suffering, abused, and on the brink of destruction. Even unbelievers in the world recognize the atrocity that this is, and their governments attempt to deal with it. God should be praised for His common grace that, imperfect though they are, some public structures and private agencies exist to alleviate childhood suffering. But foremost of all, missions-minded Christians and churches should be passionate about loving the children of the world by sacrificially meeting urgent needs in the name of Jesus Christ who makes adoption into God's family possible.

Though the process of adoption may be daunting, for missions-minded Christians it is a service of joy, a way to imitate their own adoptive Father, and one of the most realistic and tactile pictures of His grace that one could give to the world. A boy who has no hope today can have a bright future tomorrow, free from slavery. A girl suffering abuse today can be protected tomorrow and hear of the great God who saves. A social worker wrestling today with how a good God could allow such suffering can tomorrow witness His compassion through His people, if they will care for the orphan in whatever ways they are able. Moreover, Christians who take this step of faith also receive great reward as they grow in reliance upon God and see His sovereign arm move mountains to bring children into their lives. Praise be to God that He adopts into His family, and praise be to God that He allows His children to extend that same joy!

INSERT 59.1

A Street Kid Named Handsome

David Beakley

On a brisk fall afternoon in Polokwane, my wife and I encountered two young boys—"street kids"—looking for money. It was March 2007. As I spoke to them at the gate, I could see that they were from Zimbabwe. At that time, elections were happening in Zimbabwe, and that meant lots of sudden random violence, and, sadly, increased orphans. As the sun began to set (when we were looking forward to a family barbecue), it was as if the Lord spoke to me in a still small voice, *What are you doing here, David?* (1 Kgs 19:9, 13). At that moment, looking into the faces of these two children, I felt the sting of the words "Physician, heal yourself!" (Luke 4:23). Would I practice what I preached? Without further thought or consideration, I committed. From that point on, we took two African "street kids" into our house, and our children and home would be forever changed. What transpired was ten years of tears, frustration, joy, and blessing.

Life with Handsome

Within the first month, one of the boys, Brian, left us to return to the street. The second boy, Handsome, wanted to stay with our family. We discovered that Handsome left home in Zimbabwe at about age seven or eight because he was starving, had no shoes, no clothes, and no hope. When Handsome joined us, we tried homeschooling and putting him in public school. With lots of community support, Handsome was admitted to a private Christian school, even though he was an "illegal," without a visa. The rigors of education were tough, and we were consistent with discipline at home. Handsome was always included with the family and was treated as one of us. He had the opportunities of youth group, church camp, and consistent gospel teaching.

Our local church, along with our supporters, were very involved in his life, and God's grace was abundantly seen. Through a connection I had at a local gym, the compassionate owner gave Handsome a job as an associate there. He then went on to secure an international fitness trainer's qualification. For the next five years or so, Handsome excelled in training, bodybuilding, and gaining clients. As he got older, however, Handsome began to grow distant from our family and to acquire not-so-good friends. Getting him to church became a serious effort, and there were many difficult days as we tried to help him and hold him accountable. But we continued to pray.

A Tragic Day

One Saturday morning in October 2017, I received a phone call. The call was from David, the owner of the gym where Handsome was employed. He said just one sentence: "Handsome was killed in a motorcar accident last night." We were in shock and disbelief. But at 5:20 a.m. that Saturday, Handsome was gone, taken from this earth by the hand of God through a needless traffic accident that killed four souls. Handsome is now experiencing

100 percent biblical truth and biblical reality. He is either being held fully accountable before a righteous Judge or embraced by a loving heavenly Father. The difficulty for my wife and me is that all our theological background will not give us any assurance regarding Handsome's relationship with the Lord. Handsome had been given grace upon grace and often rejected or presumed upon that grace. Yet Handsome also understood and verbally embraced the biblical truth that he was given.

An Unexpected Meeting

The following Monday evening at about 8:30, after a draining Saturday and an emotionally exhausting Sunday, our doorbell rang. To my surprise, it was a man named Zion—the driver of the car in which Handsome had been riding. Then his wife, Whitney, walked up and introduced herself. After some moments at the gate, we discussed the situation. Zion had just been temporarily released from the hospital and was out of jail on bail. Charges of culpable homicide for four needless deaths were coming. Again I felt the conviction of that question, *What are you doing here, David?* and of the proverb "Physician, heal yourself." In God's sovereignty, I made a choice. I pushed the button for the gate remote and said, "Come in."

With heads hung down below their shoulders, Zion and Whitney both came into the house, where I directed them to the sofas. I then brought in Pastor Joseph Mahlaola, who lived with us. Slowly, carefully, and with as much compassion as I could muster, I explained to them the availability of God's grace. Handsome was gone. I could help him and encourage him no more. He was now in the hands of either a Judge or a Father; it was not mine to say. But here before us were Zion and his wife—people in desperate need of forgiveness.

As time stood still, we spoke of a loving God who gave His beloved Son for people such as them. If not for God's providential grace to us, we could easily have been sitting where they were sitting. The necessary words also came out. "I forgive you, because I have been forgiven myself." This is all that matters. Horizontal forgiveness is good, but the implications of that earthly contract ends at death. It is our vertical forgiveness that is critical, because it is a terrible thing to fall into the hands of the living God (Heb 10:31). After about forty-five minutes of preaching, imploring, and encouraging, we bid Zion and Whitney on their way. Neither Joseph nor I have the insight to know if they embraced Christ after our conversation. But we do know that they heard the truth about divine forgiveness, as well as the words of our forgiveness.

Lessons Learned

I want other missionaries to learn from how God used Handsome in our lives. For one thing, when they take an orphan into their home—whether by foster care, adoption, or even in the shadowlands, like in the case of Handsome—they must embrace the child as their own. Perfect love casts out fear (1 John 4:18). Acceptance and love involve the church too. Orphan care should involve the broader body of Christ, which the missionary must encourage. But all Christian parents must persist through challenges. Although parenting Handsome had considerable difficulties, striving for consistency and not giving up bore fruit in his life for a time. Perseverance is key with at-risk kids.

Of all our difficulties, the most difficult day is when God shows us that we must diligently, willingly, and eagerly apply what our Savior has taught us. The day I met Handsome, I heard God's voice through remembrance of Scripture and reasoning. The sermon I had preached on the previous Lord's Day was "The Good Samaritan"—nothing short of providential. It was this prompting that brought conviction to take a risk on Handsome for the long haul and to answer God's call to live out my faith.

We are called to love one another no less than how Christ has loved us (John 13:34; 15:12). Not only is the ground level at the foot of the cross, but all heads are level at the foot of the cross. There is not one slightly more righteous or slightly more deserving than another, including missionaries. This is not just missions—this is living for Christ.

CHAPTER 60

Health Care Missions as a Discipleship Strategy

Carlan Wendler

The Bible is the special revelation of the Creator and giver of life. It is no surprise therefore that its pages give ample attention to issues of suffering, sickness, and care for the ill. This chapter gives a biblical and historical context for health care missions, sketches principles that mark health care's strategic place in discipleship, and then offers a few cautions for how this approach can risk failing to execute the Great Commission.

While *missions* is the commissioning and sending out of individuals and teams across cultural and geographical divides to proclaim Christ, win converts, and establish churches that will carry on the ministry,[1] *health care missions* (HCM) is the use of clinical and/or public health activities as a context for missions to take place in a given community. HCM will look different from community to community, though its principles transcend cultural differences.[2] Historically, HCM has been comprised largely of nurses and physicians, but more recently it has grown to include dentists, pharmacists, therapists, public health workers, and a host of others. There is also a rising expectation among postcolonial nations that they should provide for the primary care needs of their own populations, as expressed in the Alma-Ata Declaration of 1978,[3] which has created an opportunity for many health care professionals to train and mentor others cross-culturally. If health care work provides the context for the gospel to penetrate and transform individuals within a community, it is classed here as HCM.

---

1. This definition is largely built upon the work of George W. Peters, *A Biblical Theology of Missions* (Chicago: Moody, 1972), 2.

2. Cf. John Lowe, *Medical Missions: Their Place and Power* (London: T. Fisher Unwin, 1887).

3. World Health Organization Regional Office for Europe, *Declaration of Alma-Ata* (Alma-Ata, USSR: International Conference on Primary Health Care, 1978), October 8, 2019, https://www.who.int/publications/i/item/WHO-EURO-1978-3938-43697-61471; cf. Carlan Wendler, Doug Lindberg, Greg Sund, "Research as Mission: Experiences and Expectations of Mission Agency Leadership regarding the Ministry Role of Clinical and Public Health Research," *Christian Journal of Global Health* 9, no. 1 (June 2022): 68–76, https://doi.org/10.15566/cjgh.v9i1.647.

While evangelism often takes place between a health care provider and recipient or between a provider and host, proper HCM strategy also focuses on the discipleship of health care coworkers.

Precedents and Context

The context that is essential to developing biblical HCM can be gleaned from a chronological overview of redemptive history: Old Testament precedents, New Testament illustrations and instructions, early and medieval Christian experience, and Protestant medicine and missions.

Old Testament Precedents

Adam's fall into sin introduced disease and decay into the human experience (Gen 2:17; 3:16–19). God's subsequent curse on mankind made the development of medicine necessary. But in reality, the Old Testament clearly shows God in the role of healer, manifesting His preserving care of His creatures as He intervenes in their frailties. The patriarchs understood this and regularly displayed their dependence on God for healing and overcoming barrenness by their prayers (Gen 20:17; 25:21; 30:22). Perhaps Eliphaz best summarizes God's active healing role in his first discourse with Job: "For He inflicts pain and gives relief; He wounds, and His hands also heal" (Job 5:18).

Healing therefore is ultimately God's work. As believers participate in the process of healing, they act as His agents. Furthermore, when God does not heal, believers are uniquely positioned to offer consolation, as they know that suffering sometimes results from God's favor rather than displeasure (Gen 32:24–32; Job 2:1–8), and that He is near to those who suffer (Ps 34:18).

Ministering to the ill and injured has been part of God's call on His people from the earliest times. God codified care for the sick into the priestly duties of His people (Lev 13–14) and brought condemnation upon Israel's leaders when they failed to comply (e.g., Isa 58; Ezek 34). This kind of care is a key aspect of the law of love that defines God's family (John 13:34; 1 John 2:7–8). Further, physical malady serves to powerfully illustrate the reality of the ailment of sin (Ps 103:1–3). Numbers 21 links sickness and sin in a visceral way. After God sent fiery serpents as judgment for Israel's complaining, "Moses made a bronze serpent . . . and it happened, that if a serpent bit any man, when he looked to the bronze serpent, he lived" (Num 21:9).[4]

New Testament Illustrations and Instructions

The ministry of the Messiah was often summarized as teaching and healing (Matt 4:23;

---

4. This episode is one of the most commonly held origins of the rod of Asclepius, a pole or staff wrapped in a snake, symbolizing the healing arts (cf. the caduceus). See Christopher Eames, "Does the Serpentine Symbol of Healing Have a Biblical Origin?" Armstrong Institute for Biblical Archaeology, February 15, 2019, https://armstronginstitute.org/144-does-the-serpentine-symbol-of -healing-have-a-biblical-origin. For other parallels between spiritual and physical ailment, see Psalms 32:3–4; 38:3–4; Proverbs 7:23; Daniel 4; Luke 5:17–26; John 9:41; Ephesians 2:1–3.

9:35). Christ performed most of His miracles in the context of human suffering or need. When Jesus delegated His mission to the Twelve and then to the Seventy, He gave the same twofold instruction: proclaim and heal (Luke 9:2; 10:9). For Jesus, teaching and healing were the ideal pairing for ministry that pointed to salvation in Him (Matt 11:2–6; cf. Isa 35:5–6; 61:1–2; Mal 4:2).

Following Jesus' earthly ministry and the earliest years of the Church, miraculous healings receded and a new pattern arose, especially as medical professionals began working in cosmopolitan communities. James wrote of elders praying and anointing with oil (Jas 5:14), and Paul advised Timothy to use a contemporary remedy for his stomach ailments (1 Tim 5:23). God's choice of a Gentile physician, Luke, as a New Testament author cemented both the multiethnic and compassion-oriented character of the nascent Christian faith (Col 4:14).

Early and Medieval Christian Experience

The early Christians were indeed known for their care of the ill and outcast. Their concept of all people bearing the image of God (Gen 1:26–27) compelled them to care for the suffering, sometimes at great personal cost.[5] Though it is impossible to know the number of people who came to faith in the context of receiving or observing Christian benevolence, health care clearly formed part of the early church's evangelism.[6]

After the Church received official state sanction and formalized its hierarchy in the fourth century, it became more deliberative with missionary outreach. Christians established outposts, blending spiritual discipline and practical helps for the surrounding communities. Some already-established churches served as infirmaries, as was the case in Caesarea under Basil in the fourth century.[7] In later centuries, convents and monasteries became centers of health care as well as theological education. To a large extent, monasteries in the Holy Roman Empire were the closest approximation to a hospital for those in medieval Europe. The rhythms of work and prayer wove through garden and kitchen, closet and chapel, clinic and courtyard.

Protestant Medicine and Missions

The Reformation of the sixteenth century left this model of ministry largely unchallenged. For example, John Calvin organized hospitals for the poor in plague-stricken Geneva and started many public health practices.[8] A burning passion for biblical doctrine seemed to fuel rather than extinguish the energy of the Reformers in general for caring for the ill.

When God raised up William Carey and

---

5. Gary B. Ferngren, *Medicine and Health Care in Early Christianity* (Baltimore: Johns Hopkins Press, 2009), 103.

6. E.g., Eusebius, *Ecclesiastical History* 7.32.23 (*NPNF*[2] 1:320).

7. Gregory of Nazianzus, *Oratio in laudem Basilii* 43.35–36, 43.63 (*NPNF*[2] 7:407–8, 416). See also Charles Schmidt, *The Social Results of Early Christianity* (London: William Isbister, 1889), 267.

8. Merle d'Aubigné and Jean Henri, *History of the Reformation in Europe in the Time of Calvin* (New York: R. Carter and Brothers, 1877), 69.

the Baptist Missionary Society at the end of the eighteenth century, the same elements were present: his society took up a tripartite model of church, classroom, and clinic.[9] In the nineteenth century, John Scudder, the first medical missionary from the United States, wrote in a letter to his parents, "Through the means of medicine I hope to do much good, as many hear the gospel by this means who, in all probability, would never hear it in any other way."[10] Simply put, health care opens a door for evangelism and provides a rich context for discipleship.

Principles and Practices

In forming Christ followers into evangelists and disciple-makers themselves, HCM employs three principles and practices in its strategy to evangelize patients and disciple coworkers. It is necessary to explore each of these to understand the outworking of HCM in the world today as it seeks to follow Christ's example in the Gospels.

Time Together

In the transmission of character and mission, there is no substitute for passing hours in close company with a disciple. The Lord chose men to "be with Him" (Mark 3:14), observing His patterns of work and rest, learning his practices of private and corporate worship, hearing His teaching and watching Him interact with people from all walks of life, Pharisees and prostitutes alike. The disciples accompanied Christ in routine and extraordinary events during His years of ministry. Though the Master reserved special secluded sessions for prayer and communion with the Father, Jesus' disciples had near total access to Him.

In discipling coworkers, clinical interactions with patients provide ample context for the display of compassion, diligence, and faith. Following up on laboratory results, making phone calls or home visits, talking with family members, and giving advice to neighbors all afford opportunities to demonstrate Christian character. Even the hours spent on paperwork and continuing education can demonstrate the kinds of quiet discipline and devotion that marked the Great Physician.

In patient care, moments of service and sacrifice come with occasions to speak truth. Relationships that develop over days of hospitalization or months of outpatient care give the provider repeated occasions to show love and proclaim Christ. Time is the great ally of love. And without love, proclamation is a mere cacophony (1 Cor 13:1).

Clinical instruction, which has become more prominent in the last fifty years of HCM,[11] also brings disciple-makers and disciples into

---

9. George Smith, *Life of William Carey* (London: R. R. Clarke., 1885), 292.

10. J. B. Waterbury, *Memoirs of the Rev John Scudder, MD: Thirty-Six Years Missionary in India* (New York: Harper and Brothers, 1870), 24.

11. A detailed history is beyond the scope of this chapter. It will suffice to say that the confluence of three currents in the 1960s and 1970s resulted in a renewed push toward health care missions with education as a major component: (1) the explosion of Christian nonprofit (parachurch) organizations after World War II (cf. Eva Pascal, "Do-It-Yourself Missions: The Rise of Independent Faith-Based Organizations and the Changing Contours of Missions," in *2010Boston: The Changing Contours of World Mission and*

long-term, close contact. In addition to the time together described above, the natural flow of authority and instruction between teacher and student facilitates the transmission of practical and theological understanding. Because HCM settings are so varied, the disciple can observe the missionary in both stressful and calm times. It is not uncommon for medical missionaries to quickly shift from routine interactions with colleagues to emergency counseling sessions with devastated parents. Further, as most HCM contexts are underresourced, the evangelistic urgency of reaching patients with the gospel before they expire means there is a steady flow of opportunities to witness and pray. Few missions arrangements generate such intense and prolonged opportunities for life-on-life discipleship with believing students and evangelism of suffering or dying souls.

Responsibility

The second hallmark of discipleship is responsibility. As observation gives way to imitation, the disciple-maker begins to stand back and allow the protégé to lead. The pupil will at times err, like when some disciples tried to keep the little children from coming to Jesus for a blessing (Mark 10:13–16). They needed correction. Many times the disciple will pick up the wrong lesson or interject an old prejudice, like assuming congenital blindness must have

been a result of a particular sin (John 9:1–3), or when James and John were ready to call down lightning on unrepentant towns (Luke 9:51–56). They needed proportionate rebuke. Yet the overall tone of Christ's ministry in making disciples, and thus the model for missionaries to replicate, is one of encouragement to engage in kingdom work. Once oriented by the Master, the disciples needed to feel the weight of responsibility for the valuable mission with which they had been entrusted.

In HCM the disciple-maker first asks the coworker or student to take a spiritual history of the patient, finding out what the patient believes about their ailment, and if applicable, reflect on how their decisions might have contributed to the disease. Every patient has some belief about what caused their ailments. Even if it is not always a demon or a witch's spell cast upon them, such things as believing that they let their child's feet get too cold or that their marital infidelity has led to infertility have an impact on how the patient will interact with the Christian clinician. The conversation that reveals this naturally leads to a discussion of God and His plan for His creation. The disciple-maker can assign a few targeted verses to memorize in the local language, better equipping the disciple for ministry. The disciple then learns to pray for and with patients— initially with those in the throes of pain or

---

Christianity, ed. Todd M. Johnson, Rodney L. Petersen, Gina A. Bellofatto, and Travis L. Myers [Eugene, OR: Pickwick, 2012], 193); (2) the emphasis on holistic or integral mission coming from theologians like John Stott and René Padilla (e.g., C. René Padilla, "Holistic Mission," Lausanne Occasional Paper 33, produced at the 2004 Forum for World Evangelism, September 29 to October 5, 2004, https://lausanne.org/content/holistic-mission-lop-33); and (3) the rising expectation among postcolonial nations that they should provide for the primary care needs of their own populations, as mentioned above.

loss (compassion prayers), then with those facing fear or imminent death (comfort prayers), and finally with those who are focused on the physical to the neglect of the spiritual (conviction prayers). After listening, memorizing, and praying, the disciple is ready to evangelize, teach, and counsel.

Health care teams tend to form slowly and endure for extended periods in their communities. Medical and nursing licenses require a significant investment of time and money, so health care professionals usually stay put in a place where they can earn a living. This means there is enough time for the disciple to assume graduated responsibility while being supervised. In training programs, the months and years necessary to develop minimum competencies in clinical care mean that the disciple-maker and disciple can cover a lot of ministry training together before program completion. Therefore, in addition to observation, the disciple-maker can add a ballast of practical responsibility so that he better equips his disciple to endure.

Reward

A fully trained disciple becomes like his master. As he starts exercising his faith, he begins to accumulate experiences of God's grace in his life and the lives of his patients. A sick child gets well and goes home with her family. A terrified father learns to rest in the goodness of divine providence. A rebel repents in the face of her sin and its consequences.

Having experienced such fruit, the disciple, in time, turns toward others less experienced than himself and joyfully begins to pass on the lessons he has learned. He becomes a disciple-maker in his own right and now shares in the fellowship of faithful servants. He begins to relate with his mentor more like a peer than a pupil. His discipler becomes a friend and a brother (John 13:16; 15:15; 20:17). For those who respond well to correction and are willing to invest their time, the reward of fruitfulness and fellowship is all but guaranteed.

In addition to the long-term nature of the relationships formed, HCM is well-suited for multiplication and growth. Health care missionaries typically situate themselves in needy places. That need means that those they have trained are often deployed into the same community or nation. This permits replication of the ministry to occur without the need for slow and burdensome adaptation to a divergent local context. Ideally the disciples spread far away enough to learn dependency on the Spirit but close enough to call for help when needed. Further, as health care professionals tend to enjoy a high degree of trust in society, the influence and impact disciples can have on their communities are often amplified.

Pitfalls to Avoid

There are at least three obstacles to fruitfulness in HCM. The first is a shallow integration of witness and work in the heart of the missionary. Most professional training programs in developed countries are firmly entrenched in a secular, materialist worldview. This means the models of health care instruction in which most missionaries trained will not have encouraged (and may directly oppose) the integration of faith and practice. Christian nurses might never have prayed with a patient during training. After more than a decade in training, a Christian physician may still be a novice in diagnosing and addressing a patient's spiritual needs. Churches and sending agencies must faithfully screen applicants for evidence of witness-work integration and provide needed resources like mentorships to overcome this deficiency.

The best time to invest in this kind of integration is often before deployment, because the crushing clinical needs in most HCM contexts demand constant attention. Just meeting minimum safety and quality standards on the field requires enormous effort and time. Added to that, the paucity of health care professionals who are willing to live in remote areas means there are more needy patients than the staff can adequately address.

The medical missionary must resolve in his heart that the clinical cannot automatically trump the spiritual. He must structure his time in such a way as to facilitate nonclinical activities as well. There has to be room for Bible study with coworkers and students, context-appropriate preaching, and active ministry in the local church. The Master did not heal every sick person He encountered (John 5:2–17). And when He did exhaust Himself in care for the sick and oppressed, He sought spiritual solitude and renewal (Mark 1:32–35). The demands on Christ during His earthly ministry were greater than the demands any missionary has ever faced, yet He always responded with grace, looking beyond the physiological and making time for whole-person care (Luke 8:40–55).

A second pitfall is the neglect of the local church. Health care missionaries often engage in ministries that draw their attention and effort toward nonchurch institutions. The missionary may easily be pulled into well-intentioned projects that prioritize health care over spiritual ministry. Donors are often eager to help build obstetrics wards in missions hospitals or operating rooms for children. Secular sponsors willingly endorse projects that do not conflict with their humanist worldview. Nursing and medical schools are likewise favored funding projects for high-income donors, as the promise of "force multipliers" and "return on investment" is a strong lure in educational endeavors. HCM without clear strategies to prioritize the development of the local church and its leadership will almost inevitably digress into a "follow the funding" model, whereby donors dictate the priorities and the hospital stands in grandeur while the church is left in disrepair. The Church is the only institution that Christ promised to build (Matt 16:18), and His disciples never err in prioritizing attention to its health.

A final pitfall involves misunderstanding the nature of poverty and human suffering. A mistaken diagnosis always results in a mistaken treatment plan. Christians have a role to play in physical relief efforts (1 Cor 16:1–4). Yet relief work cannot be the final expression of the gospel. It is true that Christ occasionally healed without preaching. However, in three years of public ministry He usually combined the two, and He taught His disciples to do the same. He left His men behind to replicate and multiply

His impact on the world. Any methodology therefore that purports to follow the Master's pattern will necessarily emphasize the deliberate training of people who will faithfully declare the truth of God and demonstrate the love of God.

Conclusion

The care of the sick was a part of God's call on His people from the very beginning. Though the Master's combination of teaching and healing was remarkable for its volume and intensity, it was also in perfect continuity with His priestly and prophetic predecessors. This concern for bodies and souls continued via His apostles and disciples in various ways throughout church history, with a particular emphasis in the last half century on the clinical training of nationals.

As a methodology, HCM provides unparalleled opportunity for disciple-maker and disciple to spend time together, grow in responsibility, and benefit from the rewards of fruitfulness and fellowship. Though by no means the only biblical methodology of discipleship, properly conceived and executed HCM closely imitates Christ's own strategy. For us, whose missionary vision is "the gospel for every person, a church for every believer, a pastor for every church, and training for every pastor," HCM has a key role to play at every link of that chain. Patients and coworkers learn of Christ and are connected to local bodies of believers. Responsible men are identified, instructed, and installed in positions of church leadership. Small wonder, then, that health care missions are a choice instrument of grace in God's symphony of love in deed and in truth (1 John 3:18).[12]

---

12. For further reading, see Robert Coleman, *The Master Plan of Evangelism* (Grand Rapids: Baker, 2006); Lowe,; Peters, *Biblical Theology of Missions*.

INSERT 60.1

Medical and Urban Ministry in a Muslim Majority City

Ava Flores

Before my husband and I were married, we both knew that we wanted to serve overseas. We were reluctant to start dating because we thought God had called us to hard places and that we would likely be single our whole lives. But the Lord helped us to see how we could serve Him better together. This happened in the context of urban ministry, with my husband focused on church planting and me on medical ministry.

Neither of us is particularly fond of urban life. Yet we recognized the Lord working in us and teaching us to have a heart for being wherever people live. After praying about it, we were drawn to big cities in the Muslim world. We also became more aware of the concept of unreached people groups. John Piper's books on the unreached world were instrumental.[13] Ultimately, the intersection of urban ministry, the Muslim world, and unreached ethnic groups brought us to our city—which, to avoid jeopardizing the open doors we have there now, I will leave unnamed.

Today our primary focus is church planting among several unreached people groups in the city. We are gathering small groups into church plants and are also trying to strengthen churches that already exist, specifically those with hearts for reaching Muslims around them.

Medical Ministry

The Lord opened up another aspect of ministry for us, a medical ministry to our Muslim neighbors. In our host country, the medical system is lacking and difficult to navigate, especially for the most vulnerable of the population such as women and children. This reality weighed heavily on us when we realized that we were attending neighbors' funerals nearly every week. The deaths appeared to be preventable or caused by curable diseases. Yet foreigners cannot practice medicine here, and for me—being a licensed physician associate from the United States and seeing all these needs while feeling unable to help—was very hard. I realized how much pride I had in my identity as a medical professional and how much weight I had laid on modern medicine, which led me back to the feet of our Great Physician. Not being able to practice openly was humbling and frustrating, but by God's grace, He eventually made a way for me to use my skills. I saw how strategic and helpful my skills could be for the spread of the gospel.

I began making house visits, offering neighbors medical advice, and consulting on medical needs. Neighbors would eagerly agree to these visits and to medical advice. And that led to starting a medical consultancy business with an office in the heart of our unreached neighborhood. In addition to consulting, we also provide CPR and first aid training. We aim to equip community members in emergency care for their friends and family and to help prevent accidental

---

13. For example, the 1993 title that has been republished three times since, most recently as John Piper, *Let the Nations Be Glad! The Supremacy of God in Missions*, 30th anniversary ed. (Grand Rapids: Baker Academic, 2022).

deaths and delayed treatment of serious diseases. Not only is this work meaningful and exciting, but we were able to keep our work visas to remain in the country.

Our medical consulting is more than just a service to the community; it is a doorway for ministry. For an expat like me (who clearly sticks out as a foreigner), visiting the homes of community members in our surrounding unreached neighborhood can draw unwanted attention. However, it is especially suspicious for nationals who are known to be Christians to go into a Muslim home. This can cut off inroads for the gospel quickly. But as a known member of the community and medical consultant, onlooking neighbors are much less suspicious seeing my team and I enter Muslim homes. No backlash is brought against the family, because neighbors understand the family is simply welcoming a foreigner or needs medical advice, and many opportunities for both physical and spiritual needs can be met.

This business also allows us to help believing nationals stay in the city to do ministry. Jobs in huge cities can be transient. Providing good jobs is a huge need, especially when the job allows time for ministry and discipleship. I have three national employees working with me who otherwise would have relocated far from their church community and ministry. It is exciting to see them grow in their boldness in sharing their faith through our business.

Students considering useful vocations for the Lord, missionaries in training, and medical professionals considering the mission field should know how fruitful this platform can be. It is genuine, trustworthy, and a gateway into homes and relationships. The more capable the professional, the more open the gateway.

Building Bridges

Let me share one example about how our medical ministry supports our church-planting focus. One day when my husband was talking to the street-food sellers around our house, he learned that one of the men's wives had cancer. This Muslim mother of four, unable to receive adequate care for her illness, was in an advanced stage. But my coworker, an Indonesian nurse, and I were welcomed into their home to provide care in her final days. We alleviated some of her pain but also shared the gospel and prayed. She soon passed away, but we have hopes that her faith and prayers were genuine. It was only after her passing that we discovered that her father-in-law was the newly elected leader of the district in which our house and ministry reside. This devout Muslim man was so touched by our service to his daughter-in-law that he opened up the entire community to our ministry. In fact, when our church began the process of gathering publicly, he provided the legal documentation and signatures to make it official.

Our medical ministry builds bridges between national believers (my employees and colleagues) and national unbelievers (my patients and their families). The believers' lives—their compassion, their integrity, their love for Jesus Christ—are put on display to back up the words they speak, bringing the gospel into otherwise impenetrable homes. Medical systems are broken. Urban centers are broken. But at this intersection there are powerful ways to put the healing power of the gospel on display to lost people in great numbers. This is one of the many ways that Christ is building His church in our city.

Evangelism in a Burundi Hospital

Carlan Wendler

Fantine[14] was admitted to a mission hospital in rural Burundi with a poor prognosis. She was twenty-seven years old, a single mother with a five-year-old son, and dying of AIDS. In her despair, she had abandoned her son and abandoned the medication regimen that had been holding the HIV virus at bay, leading then to multiple infections. She was already dead in her own mind and soul.

Arlene was a senior medical student rotating on the internal medicine service when Fantine was admitted. While she presented her patient during morning rounds, the discussion turned, as usual, to the "problem list": opportunistic infections, sexually transmitted diseases, HIV/AIDS, depression. While her professor posed questions about the origin of Fantine's numerous physical problems, Arlene oriented the team toward her spiritual state: "Her main problem is her sin and separation from God."

"And what do you propose as treatment?" asked the professor.

---

14. Fantine is a pseudonym for the woman whose identity here has been protected.

"She needs to hear and believe the gospel," Arlene replied confidently.

Arlene had correctly diagnosed the true origin of Fantine's multiple maladies. Her prescription was perfect. After declining her professor's well-intentioned offer of help in presenting the gospel ("Thank you professor, but my Kirundi is a little bit more fluent than yours"), Arlene spent an hour sharing the good news of Christ's atoning work and His offer of forgiveness. Fantine responded in faith. There were immediate results. The peace that replaced the fear and despondency in her heart was so evident that a patient in a neighboring bed, a thirty-three-year-old woman with terminal stomach cancer, asked Arlene if she could share that same message one more time. Two women got saved that afternoon. One was discharged the next day on palliative care to spend her remaining days at home with family. The other started taking her antiretroviral medications, caring for her son, and smiling again.

Arlene found her professor. "What do I do next? How do I help her in her new faith?" This started a process whereby Arlene prayed with Fantine, memorized Scripture with her, and helped her plug into a church in her village. She was discharged after about two weeks, having been completely transformed. Arlene followed up with Fantine for almost two years when she would come back for follow-up outpatient visits. Fantine even made a special trip to the hospital to check on that professor when she heard he had fallen ill briefly. Both Fantine, the patient, and Arlene, the student, were changed by the whole process. Both found new energy for knowing Christ and making Him known.

CHAPTER 61

Global Opportunities through Education: Advantages, Trends, and Issues

Mark D. Rentz

A growing worldwide demand for education and specialized skill training has created a wave of opportunities for Christian educators to integrate their work and witness for the purpose of world evangelism. A leader in one of the largest and oldest international missions organizations recently said that education is the sphere that always has the most opportunities. Concerning what profession would help someone most in serving overseas, he said, "Get a qualification in education."[1] Indeed, educators are needed in a wide variety of fields. These reflect global job markets as well as development priorities and economic growth opportunities in any given nation. In fact, education itself is one of the world's largest industries, with expenditures soon to reach ten trillion dollars per year worldwide.[2]

Such growth highlights the potential for Christians to use the teaching profession for the Great Commission. However, it also highlights the need to strategize wisely. When one considers the great missionary Paul as an example, the many advantages that professionalism offers to missional living become clear. To properly harness these, the current trends in the world of global education must also be observed. Finally, a proper accounting of the challenges in this field will help prepare those who are gifted for it. This chapter outlines those three aspects—advantages, trends, and challenges—so that the educator may go and make disciples of all nations (Matt 28:19).

1. Personal correspondence (January 5, 2023) with Chris Binder, Interserve regional director from the United Kingdom and Ireland for the work of Interserve in Europe and West and Central Africa.

2. "$10 Trillion Global Education Market in 2030," *HolonIQ,* June 2, 2018, https://www.holoniq.com/notes/10-trillion-global-education-market-in-2030.

Advantages

Though the apostle Paul was not a formal educator in today's sense of the word, wisdom can be gleaned from his ministry for those in the education field. In particular, he made use of six advantages of his profession and professionalism in order to proclaim the gospel to the Gentiles. Those six advantages have analogies in the world today.

Paul's first advantage was his knowledge of language in the first century AD. Though Paul's native tongue, often called a "heart language," was probably Aramaic,[3] he spoke in Greek to Gentiles throughout the Roman world. The latter was the *lingua franca*, the international trade language, of his day. Thus, it was spoken in political, philosophical, educational, religious, and mundane settings too. It was the language in which Paul conducted business.

Second, Paul had a global marketplace kind of job, allowing him to trade internationally. His skill of tent making (Acts 18:3) was in demand wherever people lived and worked, and it was highly portable.

Third, and related to his tent-making occupation, Paul was an independent contractor. Like millions of people today, he worked in a "gig" economy. He paid for his food, bare necessities, and rent (Acts 28:30), all by taking ample jobs or selling the ample inventory of his craft. His trade also allowed him to self-fund most of his missionary enterprise, but it still afforded him the time to teach disciples (19:9) and to evangelize in the synagogues and marketplaces (17:17).

Fourth, Paul's tent-making skill was culturally acceptable. It was understood and appreciated. Not only was it practical, but it could even be valued as artisanal.[4] Making tents never raised the suspicions of anyone to whom he preached, and his job was never questioned by the authorities as an illegitimate front.[5]

As a fifth advantage, Paul could travel widely, and he did—more widely than many Christians do today. He journeyed by land and sea, from Israel to Arabia to Asia Minor to Europe (Acts 16:9ff.; Gal 1:17). The maps of his missionary journeys in the back of many Bibles show that he covered quite a lot of territory and established many churches. This was possible because of the international thoroughfares maintained by the Roman Empire.

Sixth and last, Paul had Roman citizenship, which opened up access to every place God called him to go. Of course not everyone loved Roman hegemony, but Roman citizenship was prestigious and usually provided respectable, sometimes even preferential, treatment (Acts 21:39; 22:28). Paul made use of such freedoms and advantages for the kingdom of God.

---

3. William R. Stegner, "Jew, Paul the," *Dictionary of Paul and His Letters*, ed. Gerald F. Hawthorne, Ralph P. Martin, and Daniel G. Reid (Downers Grove, IL: InterVarsity, 1993), 504.

4. Most likely the term *tentmaker* (Gk. *skēnopoios*) meant "leather-worker," including but not limited to tents. Wilhelm Michaelis, "σκηνοποιός," *TDNT*, 7:393–94; P. W. Barnett, "Tentmaking," *Dictionary of Paul and His Letters*, ed. Gerald F. Hawthorne, Ralph P. Martin, and Daniel G. Reid (Downers Grove, IL: Inter-Varsity, 1993), 925–26.

5. See the enlightening discussion Eckhard J. Schnabel, *Paul the Missionary: Realities, Strategies and Methods* (Downers Grove, IL: Inter-Varsity, 2008), 297–300.

Analogies to these six advantages are available for educators who love Jesus today. In fact, with globalization, the advantages are bigger than ever. The use of English is more pervasive than Greek ever was, and education—often given in English—is an international business. Educators are mobile, visiting, moving to, and working in large and small cities of the world,[6] whether they be in countries of restricted or open access toward the gospel. Being an educator overseas allows one to be self-sufficient and to self-fund ministry efforts. Plus, the role of a teacher is universally understood and respected by citizens and by governments. Travel on a passport is easier and faster than ever, and citizenship in a few nations of the world facilitates gateways into many others.

Using these advantages, educators can integrate work and witness through direct contact with a host of people groups around the world. They can also bless the nations with their ministries and witness outside of work hours, just as the apostle Paul did. All of the above freedoms can be creatively and strategically used by educators "as slaves of God" (1 Pet 2:16).

Trends

To harness the above advantages of a profession on the mission field, the trends in the education field in particular must now be examined more closely. Certain current trends present opportunities for the missions-minded educator. These may be long- or short-lived; only the Lord knows. But while they persist, Christians can lay hold of and use them to great advantage for the gospel.

International Enrollment

One emerging trend is that universities around the world are attracting international enrollment. It is normal now for them to hire faculty internationally, to actively recruit international students, and to make partnerships across borders for research collaboration and study abroad programs. This makes the occasions plentiful for host country evangelism (toward students coming from abroad), second-country evangelism (going to students abroad), and even third-country evangelism (where both educators and students meet abroad). Plus, simultaneous outreach to multiple unreached people groups is possible. One missions strategist reported,

> Ministry to international students remains very strategic and happens around the world. We have Indian partners who have had a very fruitful ministry to international students from central Asia and the Middle East, coming to India to study. Expatriate partners in southeast Asia have been instrumental in setting up a national ministry to international students. Envisioning the national church in countries around the world where there is a significant international student population is likely to remain a strategic role for mission workers.[7]

---

6. In 1981 I went to the relatively small Japanese city of Asahikawa, Hokkaido, and taught in two prestigious high schools and one technical college for three years. Educational opportunities abroad exist in cities of every size.

7. Personal correspondence (January 5, 2023) with Chris Binder.

One student from Taiwan shared with me that he became a Christian, along with his wife, while studying for a PhD in electrical engineering at an American university. After being discipled by a welcoming church—one with an international Bible study and student outreach—he decided to become a professor. He now teaches at a university in Singapore that attracts students from China. He and his wife joined a predominantly Chinese church in Singapore, and they began an international student ministry to reach and disciple Chinese students. Although he had job opportunities back home in Taiwan, he decided to strategically blend work as a professor with witness as a Christian among Chinese people groups and other nations in a third country.

English Education

International educators are in demand in many disciplines. Demand is highest, though, for English language teachers. For more than forty years, English has been widely perceived as a "global language," meaning that it serves a special role in every country,[8] like a *lingua franca*. Around the world, English serves in four capacities: a native language, a priority foreign language, an official language, and a language of professional, academic, and scientific discourse. In regard to the latter, David Nunan, former president of TESOL (Teachers of English to Speakers of Other Languages), wrote that "English is currently the undisputed language of science and technology," and that in specific subdisciplines English appears to be the language for communication, journals, and academia.[9]

Because of this predominance, many countries are mandating that English be taught at earlier and earlier levels in their public schools. Where it used to be taught in high schools, it is now being taught in elementary schools in countries like Vietnam, South Korea, China, and Iraq. Similar is the rise of ESP (English for Specific Purpose) courses, which are either academic or vocational in nature. Academic courses include subjects like business English, medical English, aviation English, English for computer science, English for engineering, and English for architecture. Vocational ESP courses include realms such as tourism and hospitality.

Short English courses and English-teaching camps are now also popular in many places, including English-speaking countries (e.g., for students hosted in study abroad programs). These courses or camps may last from one week to a month. They are high energy and usually involve active learning methods, sightseeing, fun and games, sports, arts and crafts, songs, and cultural exploration. Some missions agencies and churches have provided camps with an evangelistic emphasis or simply as an outreach to foreign neighbors. Lessons are highly structured and planned so that native-speaking conversation partners can provide guidance. Naturally,

---

8. David Crystal, *English as a Global Language,* 2nd ed. (Cambridge: Cambridge University Press, 2003), 3.
9. David Nunan, "The Impact of English as a Global Language on Educational Policies and Practices in the Asia-Pacific Region," *TESOL Quarterly* 37, no. 4 (Winter 2003): 589–613.

this manifestation has an intensified level of contact with people for a short period of time.

Native-speaking English teachers are in especially high demand. According to Kitty Purgason, professor emerita in the Department of Applied Linguistics and TESOL at Biola University, "Although people are learning English at a younger and younger age, there are still opportunities to work with university students around the world."[10] She suggested that those interested in teaching English abroad contact organizations such as ELIC and Teach Beyond, contact missions agencies, or look for direct hire through global universities.[11] She added, "Look at where the need for a Christian presence and witness are greatest,[12] and then look for teaching opportunities."[13]

Online Education

Another trend is online education, which has been growing for years. Then, when the COVID-19 pandemic spared no country in 2020–2021, teachers worldwide were suddenly thrust in front of a computer screen to teach their students. Added to that, many language programs and entrepreneurial companies are now hiring ESL teachers for online classes and individual tutoring for students throughout the world. As a result, private language tutoring and coaching also took off. For example, one female educator I know of had a love for the Muslim world and so began tutoring Saudi women one-on-one in English online. She charged a modest hourly fee, allowing her to develop deep friendships and to have many opportunities to share her faith and answer questions about Jesus.

As mentioned above, education itself is one of the world's largest industries. Entrepreneurs in education technology are realizing the potential for innovative ventures to create solutions. These include entire schools, training centers, coaching businesses, certificate programs, online degrees, and courses *à la carte*. Teachers are being asked to experiment with things like "flipped classrooms," blended and hybrid learning, learning management systems, augmented and virtual reality, digital books and materials, and in the near future, artificial intelligence. To wisely make use of this trend, Christian educators can and should continuously upgrade their educational and technology skills, techniques, methods, and tools through training, classes, workshops, conferences, and other professional development opportunities. It is vital to stay current in today's rapidly changing educational landscape.

Expatriate Education

Another rapidly growing opportunity is teaching overseas in international schools. First established two hundred years ago for the children of embassy staff, international schools later

---

10. Personal correspondence (December 21, 2022) with Dr. Kitty Purgason.

11. These ministries can be found at their websites: ELIC, accessed June 18, 2024, https://www.elic.org/; Teach Beyond, accessed June 18, 2024, https://teachbeyond.org/.

12. See the Joshua Project, accessed June 18, 2024, https://joshuaproject.net/.

13. Personal correspondence (December 21, 2022) with Dr. Kitty Purgason.

multiplied everywhere that multinational companies expanded their operations in the world. In just the last twenty years, in a period of rapid globalization fueled by economic, political, and technological factors, English language international schools grew from approximately one thousand to eight thousand schools, now enrolling 4.5 million students, and that number could double by 2030.[14] Many global cities have dozens of English-speaking international schools each, such as Dubai, Abu Dhabi, Beijing, Shanghai, Bangkok, Tokyo, Singapore, and Riyadh. Thus, opportunities abound for Christian educators in many restricted access countries.

Teaching in a school for missionary children is another strategic and invaluable way to be part of a larger effort to reach dozens of nations and people groups. An admissions officer at an overseas missionary academy[15] explained that their teachers care for the whole-life needs of hundreds of students as they educate and prepare them for college in their home countries. This is their sacred commitment to their students' families, who are working hard to plant churches, raise up pastors, and translate the Bible around the world. Harnessing the above trends can do great good in advancing the gospel globally.

Challenges

There are, however, important challenges for the global educator today. These ought to be appreciated for the sake of the gospel, lest those who proclaim the gospel inadvertently "unpreach" it with their lives. Like every missions strategy, one must count the cost (Luke 14:28–33).

Mission Clarity

With education as a missions strategy, maintaining clarity of objectives can be a real challenge. Though Paul was a tentmaker, he aligned his work with the priority of his missionary service. Having a biblically accurate view of one's end goal and the means for achieving it is likewise important for the global educator today. How one will bring glory to God in his or her endeavors—such as planting a church or serving in one already established—is a goal that must be settled before departing. If not, the goer may suffer severely discouraging setbacks, especially if in a foreign field.

The missional educator should always emphasize the church in his or her going. If healthy, biblical churches already exist in the educator's area of service, then he or she should partner with leaders of the particular church that they will join in order to know how best to support and build up the body of Christ there. Students or colleagues whom the educator disciples must then be pointed to this church or to a like-minded sister church.

Thus, although most educators are financially self-sufficient, if they are purposefully

---

14. Alan Wechsler, "The International School Surge," *The Atlantic*, June 5, 2017, https://www.theatlantic.com/education/archive/2017/06/the-international-school-surge/528792/.

15. Black Forest Academy, an international Christian school in Kandern, Germany, partners with global Christian workers and has provided affordable education since 1956.

leaving their homelands as gospel emissaries, they ought still to be sent out and connected to a home church that has confirmed their preparedness and qualification. Educators should be active in leadership at their sending churches, as Paul was in his, and active in evangelism before they cross national borders. One missions leader put it this way:

> There are people with medical and educational skill sets who want to serve abroad, and they should prepare themselves by serving the local church in their home country. A practical step would be to teach God's Word in one's native language before trying to teach it in another. Serving the local church will help the local sending church assess the spiritual maturity, ministry experience, and confirmation of calling of the global educator before the educator goes abroad.[16]

The educator must thoroughly think through these details and prepare in order to maintain mission clarity and biblical priorities.

Language Learning

Another challenge is that educators, especially language teachers, ironically, may have a hard time learning a second language. But like Paul, educators should be able to use the target language of the people group where they live and serve for communicating the gospel. Learning the people's heart language especially—not only the *lingua franca*—takes time and effort. The missions leader above also underscored the importance of language learning for effective ministry:

> Language fluency is vital for a global educator. For many trainers, ESL [English as a Second Language] teachers, and professors, there is an increased need for them to be diligent students of their host countries' language. Without clear communication, can the gospel truly be understood? Therefore, having clear parameters to study language and to check fluency is needed.[17]

Plus, by learning the heart language of the people, the educator will grow a deeper love for the people and a deeper understanding of them and of how to communicate the gospel.

Humility and Listening

Teachers are given a "sage on the stage" reverence in many cultures, making some of the biggest challenges for global educators humility and listening skills. Teachers coming from the West in particular may need to listen to their hosts most of all. It is not the teachers' fault that their homeland has accrued stereotypes for its past or present sins, although often they do not realize how much they in fact conform to those stereotypes. In any case, for the love of souls and of Christ, Christians must be sympathetic to those who suspect them.

---

16. Personal correspondence (January 4, 2023) with a missions leader who prefers to remain anonymous because his agency sends workers to highly restrictive areas among unreached language groups.

17. Anonymous personal correspondence (January 4, 2023).

Gaining a heart of cross-cultural wisdom often leads to a deeper understanding of one's own culture (back home) as well as his or her new culture (where God has called the person to minister), with students and new friends to serve as informal guides. Donald N. Larson, former anthropology and linguistics professor at Bethel College, suggested that the three roles every missionary should develop are learner, trader, and storyteller, progressing one role in that order every three months.[18] He suggested that as a learner, the person put major emphasis on language, which "is the primary symbol of identification in [a] host community."[19] Educators need to listen a lot and not just speak. Language teachers who learn a second language are often transformed by the humbling experience.

Over time God can cultivate in educators a spirit of humility, as they depend on Him to show them any attitudes of superiority they may have based on their national identity, occupation, or cultural biases. Thomas Hale III spent time as an educator in a restricted access country. He wrote that in some areas, "the impulse behind this [missional] education, as well as 'democratization' and 'development,' is similar to the one behind the 'civilizing' mission of colonialism. It is the notion that we know best, and that we are duty bound to help others to reach our advanced level."[20]

Let missionaries pattern their lives, rather, on Paul's kind of diplomacy. He separated out man-made customs and traditions, his national and ethnic identity, any supposed traditional superiority (e.g., based on circumcision), and cultural biases from the message of the gospel (1 Cor 9:20–22). He said, "I have become all things to all men, so that I may by all means save some. So, I do all things for the sake of the gospel" (9:22–23).

Outsider Suspicion

Even as they walk humbly before God and man, one of the challenges facing Christian educators from the West is the increasing suspicion of them in many parts of the world. This comes primarily from governments, but it also comes in some cases from students, academic colleagues, and people on the street. Thomas Hale III, who worked nineteen years in the former Soviet Union, ten of those in nongovernmental organization leadership, relates a story about how prevalent this mindset of suspicion can be, even in the church where one is attending:

I had regularly attended the church for over a year when I was asked to give my testimony in a morning service. The person who introduced me had known me for many months and had always been pleasant and kind to me. So, I was shocked when she told everyone she had been certain I was a spy when I had first

---

18. Donald N. Larson, "The Viable Missionary: Learner, Trader, Story Teller," *Missiology* 6, no. 2 (April 1978): 155–63.

19. Larson, 159.

20. Thomas Hale III, *Authentic Lives: Overcoming the Problem of Hidden Identity in Outreach to Restrictive Nations* (Pasadena, CA: William Carey Library, 2016), 127.

arrived. She assured the congregation that she now knew she had been mistaken, and I was harmless.[21]

Toward educators coming from the Global South there might be less suspicion. The irony is that, given the relative power and wealth of the West in contrast to southern nations, demand is still highest for Western education and in English. The Western educator may be more carefully watched and yet still more coveted. Hence, educators from the Global South, being under less scrutiny, may be more effective in restricted-access countries for the gospel. Educators must be wise, then, from wherever they come, in choosing a host country and navigating its suspicions. They must integrate work and witness, being as wise as serpents and as harmless as doves (Matt 10:16) to teach minds and reach hearts.

Conclusion

Christian educators, missions agencies, and sending churches need to size up the growing global wave of educational opportunities. They should consider the times in which they live and how best to use educational gifts, experience, training, tools, skills, and degrees overseas. They can utilize global trends in language, citizenship, passports, and travel to serve the Lord as Paul did, to bring the hope of Christ to the nations. These are tremendous advantages.

A great number of countries want, need, and welcome teachers and professors who possess valuable knowledge and transferrable skills. Therefore, missions-minded educators can start by researching where the need for a Christian presence and witness are greatest and by looking for teaching opportunities there. Then—whether going globally long-term or short-term, in-person or online, at a university, an international school, a mission school academy, or a public or private institution—let them establish the same priority as Paul's missionary service, to bring glory to God. And like Paul, let them start and end with the church, being sent out by a church to help plant or build up a church.

For global educators, integrating work and witness will entail mission clarity, language learning, a humble posture of listening, learning, and diplomacy, and cross-cultural sensitivity. Challenges though these may be, with preparation and prayer they can be met well for the sake of the gospel. And all should pray the Lord of the harvest to send out more Christian educators into His fields, for the global opportunities for missions through education are plentiful!

---

21. Hale, 16.

Seeking the Educational Well-Being of the City

Peter Olivetan

Through the pen of Jeremiah, Yahweh instructed the newly arrived exiles in Babylon to seek the well-being of the city (Jer. 29:1–14). He commanded them, "Seek the peace of the city where I have sent you into exile, and pray to Yahweh on its behalf; for in its peace you will have peace" (29:7). While the imperatives of that letter were uniquely given to the Jewish exiles, they provide guidance and instruction for God's people of all time on how they should live and function within the societies where the Lord sends them.

One contemporary initiative for seeking the well-being of the city where faithful sojourners reside (1 Pet 2:11) is education. Education is one of the most crucial and impactful arenas for improving the well-being of a city or a people for it focuses on the all-important development of its youth. This insert identifies at least four general ways that engagement in education enables Christians in their evangelistic and disciple-making endeavors. It also particularly considers the strategic impact of establishing Christian-led universities in contexts where the majority of the population identify as non-Christian.

The Benefits of Educational Engagement

First, pursuing educational well-being enables Christians to love their neighbors as they love themselves (Matt 5:43; 22:39). Such love puts the learning needs of students and their families first, as there is no better way to love families than to selflessly invest in their children of any age with excellence. The best educators always put the learning needs of others first, and Christians have proven to be the best and most sought-after educators historically and globally. Those who have been born again by the Holy Spirit (John 3:3–8) are new people (2 Cor 5:17) and are able to love others in supernatural ways unknown by those in the world (1 John 4:7–19). Because of the love of Christ, believing teachers are uniquely able to shape and impact lives.

Second, pursuing educational well-being enables Christians to make Jesus known and to authenticate the gospel message. Christian educators have natural opportunities to present the life-saving gospel with those in their sphere of influence. Sometimes those opportunities are in their classrooms, and sometimes they are in private out-of-class conversations. Often they are with those outside the institution who respect them. In every country, being an outstanding educator gives one a special platform in the community. The testimony of their lives speaks volumes to the watching world. They have the chance to show who Jesus is and what the transformed life (and family) looks like.

In most countries and cultures today, the genuine Christian life (and especially a genuine Christian family) remains a rare commodity. Locals watch and talk among themselves about the remarkable Christians they know. Godly Christian educators also give credibility to the church of Jesus Christ in their communities. When they live as His people in the world, their lives enhance the testimony of known local churches. They put the grace and mercy of Jesus on display.

Third, pursuing educational well-being enables Christians to teach and model truth. Essential to disciple-making is advancing truth, which true Christian educators do by teaching from a biblical worldview, as authority figures who acknowledge God as Creator and Sovereign, and the Bible as the source of truth. They do not syncretize worldviews, as that would violate their

conscience and undermine their integrity. If the system requires them to teach something contrary to biblical truth, they creatively find another way or graciously object.

As a support to the propositions of the truth they proclaim, Christian educators have the opportunity to model biblical values inside and outside the classroom. After parents, the most influential people in children's lives are their teachers. Teachers who are strong on biblical values have the greatest impact in the majority of the world today, where those values are not taught and are therefore unknown, such as integrity, telling the truth, sacrificially serving others, and working hard, among many others.

Also, Christian education, done properly, clarifies and models biblical missions, instructing on the purpose of humans to live for God's glory. It answers the questions of why humans are on the planet and what God's mandates are for them. While Christian teachers may not be permitted to articulate these truths in the classroom, they can find ways to do so in personal conversation and by the testimony of their lives.

Fourth, pursuing educational well-being enables Christians to build and strengthen local churches. Every Christian educator, by biblical mandate, also needs to play an active part in a local assembly of believers. Where there is no local church, Christian educators have the opportunity (and responsibility) to be part of planting it. Where there is an existing church, they should join and be active in strengthening it. Serving in another land as a Christian educator opens unique doors, leading, as God directs, to opportunities to make new disciples. The Christian teacher must be part of a local church into which to integrate students who come to true faith.

In summary, ways to seek the well-being of the city via educational initiatives are essentially without end, ranging from starting and operating schools and universities, to teaching in existing schools, to being a teacher's assistant, to offering high-impact after-school programs, including foreign language instruction and tutoring. Christian engagement in education opens up immense opportunities for believers to steward their vocations as conduits for God's grace as people who love and serve God as proclaimers of the truth in word and deed. The goal is that their impact would resonate across generations and lands as students pass on the light of Christ they gain through their godly teachers.

The Impact of Christian-Led Universities in Non-Christian Contexts

Natural next questions include how missionaries and local churches might pursue the well-being of their city through education. A specific question to ask is whether forming institutions of higher education, particularly Christian universities, is a wise evangelistic and disciple-making strategy in non-Christian majority contexts. Missions-oriented educational entrepreneurs must consider the many opportunities and potential pitfalls.

Remarkable Opportunities

In most parts of the non-Christian majority world, opportunities in higher education, while existent, are often inferior. Universities lack funding, are not committed to educational excellence, and employ professors and administrators who are at times easily bribed. In contrast, institutes of higher learning organized and led by Christians are marked by a fundamentally different philosophy and a greater level of intrinsic motivation—namely, serving Jesus Christ (Col 3:23–24). In light of such motivation, Christian education presents at least five opportunities.

1. **The opportunity to model commitment to Jesus.** Everything Christians do must flow from the central focus of making disciples (Matt 28:19–20). Engagement inside and outside the classroom provides opportunities to share and live the saving gospel of Jesus with this evangelistic aim in mind.
2. **The opportunity to offer quality education.** Christian professors are

motivated intrinsically to glorify God[22] as they seek the academic success of their students. They are not striving to build their own notoriety. Their emphasis is on quality and student results.

3. **The opportunity to offer an honest education.** Christian professors do not accept bribes or expect unrighteous compensation for their service. They help parents and students learn that legitimate success will follow their diligent labors.

4. **The opportunity to shape young minds.** Professors have the priceless opportunity to influence and mold the minds of eager learners. Christian professors can develop a truly Christian worldview in their students as they ground them in biblical truth in all disciplines.

5. **The opportunity to influence future leaders and, potentially, a nation's direction.** Again, after parents, the most influential people in the lives of the youth are their teachers and coaches. Christian professors have the singular opportunity to invest in the future leaders of nations and, therefore, have an opportunity to impact the eventual decisions they may make.

Others have noted how the application of biblical Christianity brings human flourishing.[23] Wherever the gospel has been fully preached and biblical churches established, the by-product has been personal and national development. Bringing the Word of God to people is equivalent to bringing light into darkness (Ps 119:130). Christian missionaries have been instrumental in establishing democratic governments in non-Western countries, through their labors to provide education, do local and national publishing, and establish volunteer organizations. Positive changes to foreign governments was not their mission but was their eventual by-product, especially through those missionaries involved in education.[24]

Ever-Present Challenges

Modeling the Christian faith and making disciples through higher education is easier said than done. Following are some ever-present challenges to consider—universal

---

22. Every Christian educator needs to have read Andreas J. Köstenberger, *Excellence: The Character of God and the Pursuit of Scholarly Virtue* (Wheaton, IL: Crossway, 2011). His book lays the foundation for truly outstanding schools.

23. E.g., Alvin J. Schmidt, *How Christianity Changed the World* (Grand Rapids: Zondervan, 2001); D. James Kennedy and Jerry Newcombe, *What If Jesus Had Never Been Born?* (Nashville: Thomas Nelson, 1994).

24. Robert D. Woodberry, "The Missionary Roots of Liberal Democracy," *American Political Science Review* 106, no. 2 (May 2012): 244–74; Rodney Stark, *How the West Won: The Neglected Story of the Triumph of Modernity* (Wilmington, DE: ISI Books, 2015), 367; Andrea Palpant Dilley, "The Surprising Discovery about Those Colonialist, Proselytizing Missionaries," *Christianity Today*, January 8, 2014, https://www.christianitytoday.com/ct/2014/january-february/world-missionaries-made.html.

challenges that educators in non-Christian majority world nations face.

1. **Local government regulations.** Local laws are not always favorable to faith-based educational programs. Sometimes, while endeavoring to squelch political or social opposition, governments crush constitutionally protected religious freedoms. Because of this, teaching biblical Christianity is increasingly considered "hate speech" in many nations.[25]

2. **Local pushback against competitive startups**. Breaking into the educational marketplace can pose an apparent threat to the self-protective educational establishment. The more excellent the program one seeks to introduce, the more likely some pushback will come.

3. **Finding and maintaining qualified faculty members**. In addition to finding faculty who are skilled in their fields, missions-driven administrators are committed to finding those who are faithful church men and women. Such staffing undergirds the missions focus of the university and is essential for long-term success.

4. **Religiously diverse student body.** In non-Christian majority nations, one cannot expect every student to sign a statement of faith as a believer. When enrolling, each student (and parent) must understand that the education will be based on the Bible, and student life will be governed by the Scriptures. While such transparency can eliminate much conflict, it can never fully solve the clash of worldviews that may occur in the classroom.

5. **Self-sustainability while competing with state-subsidized schools.** From the outset, the goal of self-sustainability will be challenging. It will be a mammoth undertaking to compete with state-subsidized institutions. Tuition fees will necessarily be higher than that of local schools. To go with the higher student cost, Christian institutions must ensure the offered services and results are exceptionally good and continually improving.

6. **There is always the additional danger of "mission drift."** Few schools maintain the vision of their founders for more than two generations. The constant battle for fidelity must be vigorously fought at the board level. When faculty and staff understand that the university is not a replacement for a local church, it helps them keep their perspective straight.

---

25. Alex Anhalt, "Is the Bible Hate Speech?," January 31, 2024, https://www.mnnonline.org/news/is-the-bible-hate-speech/.

Conclusion

Higher education is one of the unique and strategic ways for men and women to use their gifts and experience to make disciples and influence lives for the glory of God and, if He wills, to change nations. There are opportunities in every country to develop or improve Christian education. Some particular recommendations for modern missionaries and church leaders, who are also educational entrepreneurs, include the following:

1. Strive to understand the educational needs of a nation, cultural context, or a particular educational niche that will benefit the development of local students. Endeavor to build an innovative and practical curriculum for them that meets best standards and practices in the country.
2. Aim to be self-sustaining. This will force the school to stay on top of local market needs and take steps toward financial independence. While this may not be possible in developing economies, it needs to be the objective of the institution.
3. Most importantly, have an oversight board govern the school to help prevent mission and theological drift.

When following the guidance of God to actively seek the well-being of others via education, the opportunities to do so are virtually unlimited. So the reason to engage in educational well-being as a Christian is to impact lives for God's glory—students, first and foremost, followed by parents, as well as staff and coworkers. There are few arenas or professions more suited to add to the well-being of a people as one strives to make disciples of Jesus.

From Book Tables to Church Pews: Effective Campus Ministry in Lilongwe, Malawi

Chisomo Masambuka

The Foundations of Campus Ministry in Lilongwe

In 2015 Reformation Bible Church began in a high-density district of Lilongwe, Malawi, called Area 25. Among the wonders of the small local congregation was the clear teaching and preaching of God's Word and its dedication to upholding a sound ecclesiology. Soon the new church attracted a younger congregation. Growth in a high-density area came through persistent evangelism. As the church faithfully evangelized, God graciously provided the fruit. As the church grew, it most attracted a particular demographic: college students and new college graduates. Many of the church members are still students or are freshly out of college. The hearts of these members were set on taking the gospel to their campuses.

Another local campus ministry had already started with book tables. Most of the books were Puritan writings—authors and works that most students had never heard of. These books appealed to students, not because of a fascination with rare books, but because they clearly explained God's holiness, man's depravity, and Christ's redemption. Unlike some other Christian teachings that are imported into Africa, the Puritan books were neither entertaining nor beautifully designed. They taught students that preaching, discipleship, and accountability in the body of Christ are the primary means of gospel grace and the basis of Christian ministry. Other ministry methods managed to get college students excited about Christ, but only sound doctrine got them committed to local churches.

Campus ministry in Malawi has generally revolved around student leadership to the exclusion of the role of the local church. The main problem is that when believing college students are committed to a movement but not to a local church, their movements are dominated by immaturity, sin, and showmanship. However, the failure of most campus ministries in Malawi is not viewed by them as a failure. This reality further epitomizes the deviation of many of the leaders from biblical thinking and living.

The Work

Campus ministry is only a part of the outreach work at Reformation Bible Church in Lilongwe. The church conducts evangelism training weekly, which has created a culture of habitual evangelism. Those trained in evangelism looked for ways to serve and began a ministry at a teacher training college nearby. Around that time, the campus outreach program underwent a paradigm shift; whereas, previously, evangelism teams would come to share the gospel, now the church aimed to create a Christian community on the campus. Developing a core presence necessitated developing a philosophy of ministry to match the nature of the campus work and to help lay a structure of discipleship that would facilitate ongoing church involvement.

Because there is no such thing as a "Campus Ministry for Dummies" book, the church developed their philosophy of campus ministry by searching the Scriptures, praying regularly, and seeking godly counsel. It became apparent that the campus ministry must rely heavily on the sufficiency of Scripture, expository preaching, and active accountability in the local church. Campus ministry is not about increasing the attendance and membership of a local church, although that often follows as fruit. The temporary nature of student life means the work of campus ministry should focus on equipping men and women to live as faithful Christians in whatever path of life God places them on after graduation.

As the believers of Reformation Bible Church navigated their call to campuses around the city, they set about the work of establishing the basic tenets of the Christian faith in the simplest yet most practical ways to help both students and the church understand their biblical obligations:

1. Getting the gospel right: evangelism
2. Getting the Bible right: Bible study
3. Getting church right: church membership
4. Getting missions right: life and practice

The Fruit

It stands as a testimony of God's providential grace that the activities of weak and feeble people in a local church has borne fruit for His kingdom. The Lord's work in campuses around the city should not be measured by numerical growth of the ministries themselves, because numbers do not give a full picture of fruit and maturity. The increasing number of these graduates who are now faithful members in local churches stands as the greatest impact of the work of campus ministry.

The call of 2 Timothy 2:2 is to entrust the teaching of the faith to faithful men who will entrust it to other faithful men. The church's discipleship efforts to raise up future elders and deacons experienced incredible growth as more and more younger men have grown in their knowledge of God. The increasing number of deacons and elders in Reformation Bible Church are men who have come from campus ministry. These men have come to love and cherish the mission of the church in Malawi.

The Calling

The church's calling to make disciples of all nations means that the local church is called to bring the gospel to the community outside its doors where the nations' citizens live. The college campus is not excluded from the sphere of the Great Commission but is a strategic center, since the collective morality of the nation is cultivated in institutions of higher learning. As hundreds of university students respond to the gospel call in Malawi and across Africa, and even more respond in faith around the world, may each in turn preach the gospel and make disciples of Christ.

CHAPTER 62

Imitating God's Gracious Invitation: Biblical Hospitality and the Gospel

Mark Tatlock

One of the most impactful and loving things an individual can do is extend a welcoming invitation. Biblical hospitality is the demonstration of the spiritual reality that God welcomes and serves those who have no ability to reciprocate His mercy and kindness. Missionaries and church leaders preach the gospel as God's invitation to man. Thus, they should practice hospitality as a regular and active component of their ministry because it is the means by which they both model God's invitation and create opportunities to present the gospel to those they host.

This chapter will briefly address some misnomers about hospitality before defining it from Scripture. Hospitality is neither about self-promotion—which is an easy temptation for missionaries, who seek to gain an audience—nor primarily about fellowshipping with believers. Instead, biblical hospitality is the extension of care and compassion for strangers, illustrating God's heart, as communicated in

both the Old and New Testaments. Believers in cross-cultural settings have ample opportunities to practice biblical hospitality and thus participate in biblical missions, especially missionaries and church leaders who are already attempting to advance the Great Commission.

What Biblical Hospitality Is Not

Before understanding what biblical hospitality is, three common misnomers must be addressed. The first is that hospitality is defined as having fellow believers over for a meal. Though entertaining Christians is not wrong, it does not capture the Bible's intention behind the commands for hospitality and can set missionary wives, particularly, against frustrating expectations. To be sure, being hospitable is a "one another" command for the Church (1 Pet 4:9; cf. Rom 12:13 below). But Scripture indicates that hospitality is usually demonstrating kindness toward strangers who are unable to reciprocate (1 Tim 5:10;

Heb 13:2). It exemplifies God's own character (Deut 10:18–19) and His greatest demonstration of unmerited kindness: the love of Christ in coming, living, dying, and rising again to pardon sinners (spiritual strangers) who had no ability to repay Him (2 Cor 8:9; cf. Matt 18:21–35). Hospitality should illustrate the gospel's one-sidedness.

Another improper view of hospitality is the need for "picture perfect" table spreads. Besides placing burdens on those who are not artistic, this idea, influenced by popular social media sites and commercial marketing campaigns, tends toward impressing others. While some forms of hospitality may be aesthetically pleasing, humble service and generosity, not a meal's presentation, is the core to biblical hospitality. Missionaries and church leaders who associate their effectiveness with all that involves a "successful" hosting event might limit the opportunities they take to practice hospitality, or they might cause church members to wrongly associate hospitality with a given financial cost or style.

The final deficient view to be discussed is that hospitality is the domain of women. In part, that idea arises because of wives' good and significant preparatory role in the home, and, again, because of social and commercial media. However, though women are involved, Scripture says that men are the ones to lead the household, which means they must lead the family in obedience to this command for all Christians. Missionaries and church leaders who pass the hosting responsibility to their wives are abdicating their God-given responsibility to minister through hospitality.

What Biblical Hospitality Is

Having addressed improper conceptions of hospitality, the rest of this chapter will show how Scripture defines it. God's Word explains that biblical hospitality is an act largely conducted to benefit strangers and by those who are themselves sojourners in this world. Several passages also state that men, as leaders, must initiate biblical hospitality, that it has no expectation of return, and that it shows no favoritism in those it serves. Underlying each section will be the exhortation that hospitality should be a picture of the gospel. It should be a natural component of the missionary and church leader's regular ministry toward those outside of his home.

Strangers as Recipients of Hospitality

The Greek word used for "hospitality" in the New Testament is *philoxenia*. It is a compound word from *philos* ("lover of [something]; friend")[1] and *xenos* ("strange; stranger, foreigner").[2] The usage of *philoxenia* (and the adjective *philoxenos*, "hospitable") in Greek literature regularly corresponds to that compound meaning of "love to strangers," treating the unfamiliar as a guest.[3]

Hospitality was a necessity for travelers in the ancient world to survive. The *Evangelical Dictionary of Biblical Theology* concisely explains this background:

---

1. "φίλος," BDAG, 1058–59.
2. "ξένος," BDAG, 684.
3. "ξένος," *NIDNTTE*, 3:442–46.

The plight of aliens was desperate. They lacked membership in the community, be it tribe, city, state, or nation. As an alienated person, the traveler often needed immediate food and lodging. Widows, orphans, the poor, or sojourners from other lands lacked the familial or community status that provided a landed inheritance, the means of making a living, and protection. In the ancient world the practice of hospitality meant graciously receiving an alienated person into one's land, home, or community and providing directly for that person's needs.[4]

One New Testament example is Gaius's reception of the traveling brothers in 3 John 5–6.

However, Christian hospitality is not limited to Christian strangers, nor even to strangers in general; it extends to enemy strangers in particular. In Paul's letter to the Romans, the first eleven chapters explain the gospel that Paul preached (cf. Rom 1:16). Then, chapter 12 begins with the familiar passage, "Therefore I exhort you, brothers, by the mercies of God, to present your bodies as a sacrifice—living, holy, and pleasing to God" (12:1). As the chapter continues, Paul explains what a "living sacrifice" looks like in the Romans' hostile context:

> rejoicing in hope, persevering in affliction, being devoted to prayer, contributing to the needs of the saints, pursuing hospitality (*philoxenian*). Bless those who persecute you; bless, and do not curse. Rejoice with those who rejoice; weep with those who weep, by being of the same mind toward one another, not being haughty in mind, but associating with the humble. Do not be wise in your own mind. Never paying back evil for evil to anyone, respecting what is good in the sight of all men, if possible, so far as it depends on you, being at peace with all men, never taking your own revenge, beloved—instead leave room for the wrath of God. For it is written, "Vengeance is Mine, I will repay," says the Lord. "But if your enemy is hungry, feed him, and if he is thirsty, give him a drink; for in so doing you will heap burning coals on his head." Do not be overcome by evil, but overcome evil with good. (Rom 12:12–21)

Paul's command to "pursue hospitality" (v. 13) is wedged right between "the needs of the saints" and "bless those who persecute you." Believers in Rome were experiencing "affliction," personal evils done against them by pagan neighbors. But quite the opposite of repaying "evil for evil," believers were to open their homes, share their food, empathize with their neighbors, and so overcome evil with good. Unlike the world—which demonstrates love only to those who love in return but hatred toward enemies (Matt 5:43)—Christians are to practice hospitality even to their enemies (5:44–45; cf. Luke 6:32–36). This was the radical nature of God's love that was demonstrated

---

4. Rodney Duke, "Hospitality," in *Evangelical Dictionary of Biblical Theology*, ed. Water A. Elwell, (Grand Rapids: Baker, 1996), 359.

in Christ's death for His people "while we were yet sinners," Paul says, even "while we were enemies" (Rom 5:8–10). What a picture of the gospel!

Sojourners as Givers of Hospitality

When Peter wrote his first letter, probably from hostile Rome (1 Pet 5:13),[5] he viewed the churches of Asia Minor as "scattered" throughout the Roman Empire, just as Israel had been scattered in their exile (1:1; cf. Jas 1:1). The Church, like Israel, consisted of God's children and people (1 Pet 1:14–16; 2:9–10). Echoing Paul's theme of the "citizen of heaven" (cf. Phil 3:20), Peter encouraged them to no longer call this world home. Their identity, rather, as the children and people of God, was that of the sojourner and the exile (1:17; 2:11; cf. 2 Pet 1:13–14). In the world around them, they faced persecution (1 Pet 4:12–19). It was in that context that Peter commanded, "Be hospitable to one another" (4:9).

Biblical hospitality is therefore showing kindness to strangers as a stranger oneself in this world. Believers do have a home, an inheritance laid up for them in heaven, into which they have been welcomed and which cannot be taken away (1 Pet 1:4–5; cf. John 14:1–3; Heb 11:8–10, 13–16). But that inheritance is theirs not because they deserve it; it is because of God's "great mercy" in Christ (1 Pet 1:3). In gratitude, then, the believer is to turn around and treat other aliens and sojourners just like God has treated him: mercifully, generously, hospitably.

Local Church Elders as Leaders in Hospitality

Alexander Strauch, who spent the majority of his ministry training elders, wrote a book titled *The Hospitality Commands* fueled by his conviction that hospitality is neglected among elders. In it he notes the fact that men, particularly leaders, are to be leading the charge on hospitality as seen in the key "elder qualification" verses in 1 Timothy 3 and Titus 1.[6] In the first of these, Paul writes, "An overseer, then, must be above reproach, the husband of one wife, temperate, sensible, respectable, hospitable" (1 Tim 3:2). Before a man is entrusted with leading God's household, he must demonstrate, among other things, that he manages his own home well (3:4), and that includes the welcoming of strangers into it.

Likewise, Paul tells Titus that an overseer "must be beyond reproach as God's steward, not self-willed, not quick-tempered, not addicted to wine, not pugnacious, not fond of dishonest gain, but hospitable, loving what is good" (Titus 1:7–8). Here, again, spiritual leaders must be hospitable, which, according to the context, is also colored by humility and generosity (the opposites of "self-willed" and "fond of dishonest gain"). These two key texts show

---

5. Edwin A. Blum, "1 Peter," in *EBC*, vol. 12, *Hebrews through Revelation*, ed. Frank E. Gaebelein (Grand Rapids: Zondervan, 1981), 212, 253.

6. Alexander Strauch, *The Hospitality Commands: Building Loving Christian Community* (Littleton, CO: Lewis and Roth, 1993), 43–44.

that hospitality is not only, nor even primarily, commanded to women. Indeed, the letters to Timothy and Titus indicate that it is men who are to provide leadership in obeying this command.

Given Freely

John Calvin, mourning the demise of the ancient practice of hospitality, wrote, "This office of humanity has also nearly ceased to be properly observed among men; for the ancient hospitality, celebrated in histories, is unknown to us, and Inns now supply the place of accommodations for strangers."[7] Calvin refers to the introduction of a secular industry that provided for the needs of travelers, and to the Church's reliance on public lodgings rather than opening their homes to one another (cf. Phlm 22). Today, five hundred years after Calvin, travel has become recreational, and the global "hospitality industry" is lucrative, involving hotels, conference centers, tourism, dining, and entertainment. The industry's existence is not wrong, but doubtless, Calvin's words ring true today, that the Church is in many places out of practice and unable to match the world's forms of hospitality.

Jesus commands His disciples to open up their homes, specifically, to those who "do not have the means to repay" (Luke 14:12–14). Their reward will come from God at the resurrection (14:14). The Good Samaritan in Luke 10 is an excellent example of being hospitable, even when away from home, to those who cannot return the favor. A Jewish traveler beaten and left for dead could not care for himself, and though several of his countrymen passed by him on the road, it was a despised Samaritan who loved his neighbor as himself (Luke 10:27–29, 36–37; cf. Lev 19:18). The Samaritan bandaged the man's wounds, took him to an inn, personally tended to him there, left money and instructions for his continued care, and pledged to return and pay any excess cost later on (Luke 10:33–35). Though global missions inevitably involves ministry in the home, believers ought to be prepared to show compassion on the road like the Samaritan did, to "welcome" the needy stranger at inconvenient times and places (Luke 9:11), without repayment.

As to hospitality shown between Christians, the apostle Peter's instruction is likewise poignant. He commands the churches of Asia Minor, "Be hospitable to one another without grumbling [or complaining]" (1 Pet 4:9). The qualification "without grumbling" indicates that hospitality was not primarily about having a good time with one's friends; rather, it required sacrifice, service, and "expecting nothing in return" (Luke 6:35). In place of a begrudging heart, Christians of all times are to be eager to share and meet others' needs (Titus 3:14; Heb 13:16). This is not an easy command to follow; after all, it imitates Christ. But, for the Christian, that is its own reward too.

Biblical hospitality surely has as its highest

---

7. John Calvin, *Commentaries on the Epistle of Paul the Apostle to the Hebrews*, trans. John Owen, (Edinburgh: Calvin Translation Society, 1852), 340.

goal the outward reach to the spiritually battered stranger, physically extending a welcoming and helping hand, while verbally pointing to the free gift of grace and mercy at the cross. This is already the message that missionaries and church leaders preach in words. They ought therefore to practice it in deeds also.

Without Favoritism

Biblical hospitality should also be exercised by congregations, not just individuals, and missionaries and church leaders need to provide instruction. In the letter of the apostle James, he confronts an unbiblical form of hospitality occurring within the walls of the church. Some were apparently holding an attitude of favoritism for the wealthy over the poor (Jas 2:1–7), a form of the broader sin of "partiality" (2:9; cf. Deut 10:17; Act 10:34; Rom 2:11), which disobeys the biblical command to "love your neighbor as yourself" (Jas 2:8). "For," he writes,

> if a man comes into your assembly with a gold ring and dressed in bright clothes, and there also comes in a poor man in dirty clothes, and you pay special attention to the one who is wearing the bright clothes, and say, "You sit here in a good place," and you say to the poor man, "You stand over there, or sit down by my footstool," have you not made distinctions among yourselves, and become judges with evil thoughts? . . . You have dishonored the poor man. (Jas 2:2–4, 6)

That is not biblical hospitality. Nor is favoritism acceptable in an individual's selection of

whom to show hospitality. "If a brother or sister is without clothing and in need of daily food, and one of you says to them, 'Go in peace, be warmed and be filled,' and yet you do not give them what is necessary for their body, what use is that?" (Jas 2:15–16).

The act of sharing food and clothing was the testimony of the early church. Acts 2 records that on the day of Pentecost, "about three thousand souls" came to faith in Christ (v. 41). Many Jews of the Dispersion as well as Gentile proselytes had come to Jerusalem only for the Feast of Weeks ("Pentecost"; vv. 5, 8–11; cf. Lev 23:15–25; Deut 16:16). That meant practically, then, that there were many literal sojourners and aliens in the Church on the day of its birth. Though these were not in their home country, many stayed after their conversion to receive the apostles' teaching (Acts 2:41–42, 46–47), which meant that they did not have a livelihood. Yet, "all those who had believed were together and had all things in common; and they began selling their property and possessions and were dividing them up with all, as anyone might have need" (2:44–45). The early church demonstrated biblical hospitality in a way that should be emulated!

In time the apostle James, elder at the church in Jerusalem (Acts 15:13, 22; 21:18; Gal 2:9), needed to confront believers in the Dispersion, likely including some of those Pentecost converts who had returned to their homelands (Jas 1:1). They had fallen into favoritism rather than having all things in common. But God is no respecter of persons (Acts 10:34). All believers have come to Him equally through

Christ, humbling themselves, confessing their spiritual bankruptcy, casting themselves upon the beneficent mercy of God. Hospitality with partiality is unbiblical, secular, and entirely unfitting for missionaries and church leaders who are called to model the gospel through their actions, not just their words.

Conclusion

The key example of biblical hospitality is found in the compassionate heart of Jesus. He modeled what every believer is to exemplify in hospitality, starting with the missionaries and church leaders, who are tasked with bringing the local church to maturity in Christ (Eph 4:12–13). Men, whether they are leaders of the church or just leaders of their home, are to lead in the activities of hospitality. This means that they must live counterculturally, such as welcoming a broken stranger. By doing so, they show him, through an act of biblical hospitality, the great compassion of Christ who heals the broken and saves the lost. Furthermore, their countercultural ministry will prove to be among the greatest means of communicating the gospel cross-culturally. That should add even greater motivation to all missionaries and church leaders as they strive to advance the Great Commission.

INSERT 62.1

The Missionary Wife and Hospitality

Shelbi Cullen

Ava from Southeast Asia and Nina from Eastern Europe are two missionary wives and mothers who strive to live out the biblical command to practice hospitality within the constraints of their different field contexts. They discussed what it means to pursue "contributing to the needs of the saints" (Rom 12:13) out of an ongoing "love of the brothers"—even those who are to them "strangers" (Heb 13:1–2)— so that they live out from the heart the biblical command to "be hospitable to one another without grumbling" (1 Pet 4:9).

Ava

I believe hospitality is a vital ministry. Missionary candidates often wonder what they should do at home now if they want to serve on the field later. The truth is, if you're unwilling to converse with strangers, invest in difficult relationships, or open your home now, you won't magically become willing to do those things overseas. Missions work will likely prove even more challenging without that foundation. My advice is to embrace opportunities to serve however the Lord has gifted you, meet new people, and get involved in whatever ministries are available now, rather than "save" that energy or that time for later on. Your local church might not be engaged in the exact ministry you envision plugging into later, but there are always ways to do significant ministry now that will train you for a hospitality ministry later—open your heart and home, build relationships, and serve people with gladness. The preparation you put in today will pave the way for future service if you are open, and I'm confident it will lead to a robust hospitality ministry in whatever context you live and serve.

Nina

Hospitality might be the greatest ministry the Lord can give to a missionary wife. I never thought that cooking and hosting would unlock doors to gospel ministry, but God grew skills in me on the mission field, right in my own home. I was never a cook; I didn't learn how to cook till I was in college—and that was survival-mode cooking at best. Once you're on the mission field, you start missing familiar flavors and recipes, which can lead to improvising in the kitchen in ways that will fascinate your family and eventually your guests. Now I cook a lot for people all the time! Sunday meals, pastoral training students who sometimes come over twice a week, and even uninvited drop-in guests—they all keep me ready to whip up a quick meal at a moment's notice. I figured out the value of always having a dessert on hand, especially homemade baked goods, because they make every visit inviting and they complete a meal with no extra preparation—and I never need to expect that a guest will bring a dessert or treat. There are challenges to this kind of flexibility—consider all of the reconfigurations of a meal, a table, a home, and a family that come with special events ranging from large Christmas dinners to intimate birthday meals. Now I have learned not only to embrace these little reconfigurations, but I welcome them as God's providence of ministry to me and through me.

The World in Our Backyard: Local Outreach to International Student Communities

Mark D. Rentz

People move all over the globe because God sovereignly causes, commands, or allows it. For example, God confused human languages at Babel to cause people to spread out over the earth (Gen 11:1–9). God commanded Abraham, "Go forth from your land, and from your kin and from your father's house, to a land which I will show you" (12:1). It was then that He began to unfold His sovereign plan to save and bless a people from among all nations (12:2–3). Later Abraham's nephew Lot saw the well-watered plain of the Jordan, and God allowed him to live there temporarily (13:10–11; cf. 19:1ff.).

Throughout Scripture, geographic mobility is seen occurring for many apparent reasons: disaster, war, hostility, crime, slavery, marriage, family strife, economic opportunity, natural resources, religious pilgrimage, and persecution. Yet the earth is the Lord's and all it contains (Ps 24:1). He decrees of nations "their appointed times and the boundaries of their habitation" (Acts 17:26; cf. 14:16–17; Deut 32:8; Ezek 5:5). He uses such forces as the means to His ends.

Scripture also shows that when God "came down" and interacted with people, He frequently met them in motion, when and where they least expected. Jesus, for example, had many evangelistic encounters on the way as He moved from town to town (e.g., Mark 5:21–43; 7:24–30; 10:46–52; Luke 19:1–10; John 4:7–43). Others God met while they were in hiding (Judg 6:11) or in exile (Gen 21:14–21), in flight (Gen 28:10–17; 1 Kgs 19:9) or in pursuit (Acts 9:1–19), in the act of obedience (Josh 5:13–15) or in disobedience (Num 22:22–35). From a human perspective, they were unplanned, and yet they were divine appointments.

Christ has commanded His Church to be in motion also. For one thing, believers are "sojourners and exiles" in this world like

Abraham (Heb 11:9, 10; 1 Pet 1:17; 2:11). Their citizenship is in heaven (Phil 3:20). But they are also Christ's ambassadors. As such, not only are Christians sent and sending others to the nations (Matt 28:19–20; John 20:21; Acts 13:1–3; 3 John 7–8), but they are called to welcome and receive strangers from every nation (cf. Rom 12:13; 1 Tim 5:10; Heb 13:2), just as God welcomes them to Himself (Acts 10:34–35). Indeed, God has determined the times and locations of individual churches just as he has for the nations and people in them. He has placed churches in strategic cities for reaching the nations that come to them, that are in their backyard.

This strategy of reaching geographically transplanted people often occurs in university cities. One example is drawn from Tempe, Arizona, USA, a suburb of Phoenix and home to a small teachers college, whose total population was 2,495 people in the year 1930.[8] By 1995 the college had become a major university (Arizona State University) with 2,496 enrolled international students from 132 countries.[9] Twenty-five years later, by 2020, the university enrolled more than 13,000 international students, the majority of whom came from what is considered the most unevangelized region of the world, the so-called "10/40 window."[10] Students from some of the most restricted-access countries in the world have come to this university city, many of them at great expense with urgent needs (cf. Titus 3:14).

The local church was present throughout the decades of growth of the international communities in its neighborhood. A growing network of believers welcomed, witnessed to, and showed Christ's love to the students who arrived from overseas. One evangelistic initiative involved a couple in 1973 who moved from another state to open a Christian bookstore across from the university campus. They began arranging airport pickups for newly arrived international students and organizing fun trips, retreats, dinners, holiday celebrations, and international Bible studies for them. The couple recruited other believers to join them in full-time outreach on campus, and they established an international student club recognized by the university.

Other Christian clubs on campus began reaching out to students as well. Bibles and Christian literature in different languages were given away. Two retired professors

---

8. Bureau of the Census, *1930 Census: Volume 1: Population, Number and Distribution of Inhabitants*, under the supervision of Leon E. Truesdell (U.S. Department of Commerce, 1930), 96 ("Population–Arizona," Table 4), https://www2.census.gov/library/publications/decennial/1930/population-volume-1/03815512v1ch03.pdf.

9. "Semester Report," International Student Office, Arizona State University, Fall 1995.

10. IIE Open Doors "Leading Institutions," from the 2023 Open Doors Report, https://opendoorsdata.org/data/international-students/leading-institutions/.

from the university began both a weekly international wives' program and an international Sunday morning Bible class at the local church. Trained volunteers taught a free English class for the wives and provided them with transportation and childcare. A friendship program was started for volunteer families to welcome international students once a month into their homes through the university's International Student Office. Many of the local churches promoted the latter and used it as a door for the gospel. I, then an ESL (English as a Second Language) instructor on campus, created a conversation partner program in 1986 for hundreds of ESL students, meeting weekly with American students for friendly conversation. Many, though not all, of the Americans were believing university students belonging to local churches. That teacher also spearheaded a homestay family program for students to live with American host families. By the late 1980s, a small student and faculty prayer group began meeting weekly on campus to pray for world evangelism and for the international students coming to the university. They met early every Monday morning for seven years in faithful prayer.

The network of believers involved in welcoming international students continued to grow as God multiplied the number of Christians at the school—whether students, faculty, or administrators. Together they sought creative ways to befriend and serve international students. Some believers with a heart for Turkey moved into the apartments near campus where many Turkish students had taken up residence. Some began playing soccer with Muslim students, shopping at Middle Eastern grocery stores, and eating at Middle Eastern restaurants. Churches with increasingly mixed memberships began offering Bible studies in Korean, Japanese, and Chinese on or near campus. Semester-long missions courses were offered for more than twenty years in the local churches, wherein engagement with and service to international students was a key component.

Huge waves of internationals have landed on the shores of university cities. The United States experienced the great influx of Iranians in the 1970s, Japanese in the 1980s, and Koreans in the 1990s.[11] More recent waves have included Saudi, Chinese, Indian, Brazilian, and African students. Small movements of students have also come from a hundred other countries, some with scholarships but most on personal funds. Likewise, international students have

---

11. For past trends and current international students' statistics, check out the Open Doors Report, the annual report from the Institute for International Education (IIE), available for order online at https://www.iie.org/research-initiatives /open-doors/; or access their annual data free at "Annual Release," Open Doors, https://opendoorsdata.org/annual-release /international-students/.

been attracted to a dozen other countries leading the world in higher education.

There are other outlets for welcoming the nations in one's backyard. Population centers are always mixed, especially with today's increasing globalization of markets and cultures. Missions-minded churches and believers need only to heed Jesus' words to His disciples: "Lift up your eyes and look on the fields, that they are white for harvest" (John 4:35).

INSERT 62.3

Evangelism to Indian Medical Students in the Philippines

Devraj Urs

Students Far from Home

Davao City, Philippines, is home to the Davao Medical School Foundation, hosting around five thousand students ranging from ages seventeen to twenty-four. In recent years, its intake of Indian students in particular has exploded. Most of these young people have never been outside their home cities in India, and now they are in a different country altogether. They are ripe for a church invitation and hungry for hospitality—especially Indian food.

When I came to Davao City in May 2018, my friend Philip was already pastoring in the city. Philip invited me to join his newly started Bible study to reach these hungry students. About twenty to thirty people would show up on a Saturday, mostly teenagers, many of them with a non-Christian background. They had come simply because they loved the company of other Indians and because there was another Indian (me) who was going to teach them. I knew their national language, and Philip allowed me to teach this Bible study as a ministry of his church.

Starting that Bible study began a years-long roller-coaster journey of evangelism and teaching. God opened doors for preaching at a youth conference, for discipleship and lasting friendships, and for salvation of several of these Indian students. My family's inviting them into our home also opened up counseling opportunities. God even opened the doors for a radio ministry at a local Christian station, which granted me a slot to speak to Indians by broadcast.

The Fruit of Our Labors

The aim Philip and I had with the above ministries was to proclaim the Word and build friendships. But we also wanted to build the bridge between campus ministry and the local church, with the conviction that such was the local church's responsibility. We wanted other churches in our cities to start seeing the need also—that they had an abundance of international students at their doorstep. Therefore, we were intentional, too, in helping Christian students get plugged into local churches instead of remaining lifelong members of a campus ministry only.

However, a long-term challenge for our students has been that when they go back to India, it is quite difficult to find a good, strong, local church. In the students' hometowns, there are often either no churches at all or only charismatic, pragmatic churches. One student has attended a church of 130,000 people in Hyderabad, because even though they preach a weak gospel, he said it was the best he could find. This fact saddens students who are awakened to it.

I have had some literally cry on the phone with me, saying that they missed the fellowship back in Davao. These young believers have grown discernment skills to recognize poor and false doctrine from their time of discipleship in the Bible study and in Philip's church.

The students also began leaving, convinced that as disciples of Christ, they needed to share the gospel in their capacity as doctors. In India, doctors are pushed up the social ladder straight to the top, and they are able to minister to people of all religions. Patients are often open to hearing the gospel because the doctor has helped them physically. Some of the students who lack a strong local church are also seeking to be trained for elder qualification. One student wanted to be both a pastor and a doctor, so we spent some time equipping him for ministry, and now he is back in India. For all of this fruit of our labors, we give thanks to God and rejoice in His gracious providence.

Needs and Lessons

There are needs remaining and lessons to be learned. First, Christians should realize that to reach non-Christian university students, any believer can meet them on campus. I advise bringing a friend along from church and being prayerful together. When the gospel cannot directly be shared on campus, the opportunities of friendship, Bible studies, and family hospitality can be.

Someone simply has to go out to the students and then invite them into the context of the local church. When inviting students into the home, Christians should invite other church members to build friendships around these people also. Friendship evangelism works—but it must be remembered that the goal is evangelism with friendship affirming it. The goal is a friendship that leads the student to Christ so that the disciple-making process can begin. Students will soon be gone to some other place, so the opportunity to actually speak the gospel should not be missed.

Once the body of Christ is involved in their lives, international students find a place of refuge; there are people who care for them, and they talk about this God who cares for them too, enough to send His Son to save them. University environments tend to be hard on students because the students are busy trying to reach academic goals and are bombarded with information and ideas. Yet, once students are in a safe environment with caring people, their hearts tend to soften, to be more open to the gospel.

Ethnicity makes no difference. We have had Filipinos at our church who thought that because they were not Indian, they could not reach Indian students. But there have been Filipinos in our church who are doctors and have had fruitful Bible studies with Indian medical students. Any believer in the Lord Jesus can go and make disciples as well as any other. In our context, it can be as simple as seeing a student on the street and inviting that person home for a meal. Students love free meals, and meals allow Christians to show love, compassion, and the gospel to a stranger. The Lord blesses bold efforts like these.

Finally, we must pray—especially for the students. Many go back to India, but when they cannot find a good church nearby, they become depressed. We pray that the Lord continues to sustain their faith, and we pray for good churches to be established in India to meet such a need. We must also pray for Indian training centers, that many more men would be trained to plant churches. Ideally, even our students interested in pastoral ministry would go from the Philippines back to the seminary in India, where internships would be created for them and they would be sent out to make disciples of our Lord in India.

CHAPTER 63

The Marketplace Believer: Ambassadors for Christ on the Clock

Eric Weathers

The Great Commission primarily entails Christians serving cross-culturally to preach the gospel and make disciples. However, not all believers are gifted with that opportunity. Many are called to be disciple-makers and evangelists at home. Whatever the case, all Christians are called to be Jesus' witnesses to the souls around them. They are to be the salt of the earth (Matt 5:13), a city on a hill (5:14–16), stars in the universe (Phil 2:15), and the aroma of Christ in the world (2 Cor 2:14). For many Christians, the forum in which they will be witnesses the most is their workplace.

In Paul's epistle to the Ephesians, he instructs Christians how to be salt and light in the slave-master relationship, and that instruction is useful for the workplace today.

Slaves, be obedient to those who are your masters according to the flesh, with fear and trembling, in the integrity of your heart, as to Christ; not by way of eyeservice, as men-pleasers, but as slaves of Christ, doing the will of God from the heart, serving with good will as to the Lord, and not to men, knowing that whatever good thing each one does, this he will receive back from the Lord, whether slave or free. And masters, do the same things to them, giving up threatening, knowing that both their Master and yours is in heaven, and there is no partiality with Him. (Eph 6:5–9)

Parallel instructions are found in Colossians 3:22–25; 1 Timothy 6:1–2; and Titus 2:9–10. While Paul is mindful in these passages of Christian ethics, he is also concerned with Christian witness. For, when Christians serve Christ boldly in their work, their behavior will adorn the doctrine of the Savior whom they represent (Titus 2:9; cf. 1 Tim 6:1).

Such workplace witnesses are fulfilling the Great Commission, not only as links in the "supply chain" of financial support for missionaries abroad but also as being evangelists themselves locally (cf. 2 Tim 4:5). They use their vocation to reach marketplace circles with the gospel of Jesus Christ. This chapter is for them. It uses Ephesians 6 and its context as a template and examines three ways in which Paul instructs the workplace witness: being filled with the Spirit, doing Spirit-filled work, and being a Spirit-filled leader.

Being Filled with the Spirit

Fundamental to a workplace witness for Jesus is Paul's command to "be filled with the Spirit" (Eph 5:18). This should be seen in context. Whereas the first three chapters of Ephesians inform Christians about their identity in Christ, the last three chapters instruct them how to behave like faithful saints.[1] In chapter 5 specifically, Paul implores Christians to imitate (or image) God to the world (v. 1). As part of this, he urges that they "look carefully how [they] walk, not as unwise but as wise, redeeming the time, because the days are evil" (vv. 15–16). Following this comes Paul's command to be "filled with the Spirit" (5:18).

In Paul's mind, being Spirit-filled very much has an apologetic, evangelistic purpose for the Christian walk; it enables one to be salt and light in the world. It is part of redeeming the time and walking wisely before outsiders who observe the Christian's conduct in any and every aspect of life (Col 4:5–6). The Christian's time on the clock matters for Christ. Therefore, the Christian must be filled with the Spirit while working.

All believers are indwelt by the Holy Spirit at their conversion (Rom 8:9). However, Paul's command is that believers "be filled" with the Spirit also, that is, that they continually submit themselves to His control (cf. Rom 8:11–14; Gal 5:16, 25).[2] The degree to which faithful saints do that will become manifest as a church in speech, in song, and in "being subject to one another in the fear of Christ" (Eph 5:18–21). This last fruit of mutual submission is of special significance to Paul, for he further applies it in various relationships of the Christian life: wives and husbands, children and parents, slaves and masters, and each one to the Lord.

As was typical in the first-century church, there were both slaves and masters among the saints in Ephesus. Since slavery was a common institution in the ancient Near East,[3] Paul was familiar with it. It was wide-ranging; the slave-master relationship could be miserable and inhumane, or it could be mutually beneficial and loyal. In fact, as a Christian Paul identified

---

1. Harold Hoehner, *Ephesians: An Exegetical Commentary* (Grand Rapids: Baker, 2002), 67.

2. John MacArthur and Richard Mayhue, *Biblical Doctrine: A Systematic Summary of Bible Truth* (Wheaton, IL: Crossway, 2018), 369–74. Harold Hoehner (*Ephesians*, 500) says that the present imperative passive "be filled" (from *plēroō*) "probably indicates an iterative force, a repeated action of filling by the Spirit. The imperative mood places the responsibility on the believers. The passive voice suggests that believers cannot fill themselves. Rather, believers are to be filled by the Spirit. Thus, believers are exhorted to be filled repeatedly by the Holy Spirit no matter where they are or what they are doing." In other words, "the Holy Spirit is the means [or Agent] by which believers are filled with Christ and His will." Hoehner, *Ephesians*, 499.

3. In the Roman Empire of Paul's age, slavery was a way of life. Over one-third of the empire's population were slaves, including Christians. They were doctors, lawyers, teachers, cooks, craftsmen, farmers, and foreign prisoners of war. Many, to feed their families, voluntarily became slaves until they could support themselves. Clinton E. Arnold, *Ephesians*, ZECNT (Grand Rapids: Zondervan, 2010), 420–21.

himself deeply with the latter kind of slavery, writing in Titus 1:1 that he was God's slave and Jesus' apostle.[4] In reality, every Christian, regardless of their social standing, is purchased by Christ out of their slavery to sin, and Christ has become their beneficent owner and Master (John 8:34–36; 15:14–15; Rom 6:16–18; 1 Cor 6:20; Eph 1:7; 1 Pet 1:18–19; Rev 1:5).[5] So too, all believers are baptized into the same Spirit, regardless of their socioeconomic standing in slavery or freedom (1 Cor 12:13).

Thus, Paul's message in Ephesians 6 is not about the human institution of slavery itself. Rather, it is about how Spirit-filled believers ought to work, "whether slave or free" (6:8) yet as "slaves of Christ" (6:6). Those who work this way, under the Spirit's control, will walk wisely, redeem the time, and confess to a watching world the gospel truth that Christians have been set free from their sins to serve a new and loving Master, their Savior Jesus Christ.

Working as unto Christ

Paul exhorts the Ephesians that Spirit-filled workers redeem the time in three ways: following instructions, doing God's will from the heart, and looking to the Lord for their reward.

Being Obedient

Paul's opening command for the work relationship is straightforward: "Slaves, be obedient to those who are your masters according to the flesh" (Eph 6:5). Such an unqualified expectation assumes that all legitimate authority is given by God (Rom 13:1). But it also assumes the consequence of being Spirit-filled—voluntarily preferring one another in the fear of Christ (Eph 5:21; cf. Rom 12:20; Phil 2:3–4). The command, then, has to do with both ordained authority and love for one's neighbor. By contrast, one who in the workplace is not being Spirit-filled will have no ability to obey Scripture's instructions on either basis. This will inevitably come out in a lack of obedience to employer directives. Such a worker cannot rightly witness for Christ in the workplace because a lack of honor toward others betrays a lack of honor toward Christ, his ultimate Master (Eph 6:5, 9).

Thus, Paul underscores the seriousness of the Christian's duty to obey his leaders with a series of explanatory descriptions. The first of these is "with fear and trembling" (Eph 6:5). Paul uses the same word pair in Philippians when calling believers to "work out your salvation with fear and trembling" (Phil 2:12). The phrase draws on the "household code" of slavery in the first century, expressing that a subordinate honors the social position of their superordinate, not that one is intimidated by the other.[6] In Ephesians 6:5, then, it means "a deep and reverential sense of accountability to God or Christ."[7] Thus, Spirit-filled workers are

---

4. Every author of the New Testament Epistles identifies himself as a "slave" of Jesus Christ: Paul (Rom 1:1; Phil 1:1), James (Jas 1:1), Peter (2 Pet 1:1), Jude (Jude 1), and John (Rev 1:1).

5. See the treatment of this subject in John MacArthur, *Slave: The Hidden Truth about Your Identity in Christ* (Nashville: Thomas Nelson, 2010).

6. Lynn H. Cohick, *The Letter to the Ephesians*, NICNT (Grand Rapids, Eerdmans, 2020), 401.

7. Spiros Zodhiates, "φόβος," *The Complete Word Study Dictionary* (Chattanooga, TN: AMG, 1992), 1450.

to undertake the directives of their employers respectfully and deferentially, as if obeying God Himself.

Second, obedience is to be "in the integrity of your heart," Paul writes (Eph 6:5). Sincere obedience is active obedience that lacks a hidden agenda. The employee must not pretend to be laboring when he is loitering, or as it is put in verse 6, he must not render "eyeservice" (*ophthalmodoulia*). Paul likely invented that term, as it does not appear to be used in other Greek writings prior to this text and Colossians 3:22.[8] It can be translated as "eye-slavery," describing the way that some employees work with diligence only while being watched by their employer. Paul repudiates any form of service done only for being seen.[9] Most employers (as well as sixth-grade school teachers) have witnessed that kind of behavior countless times. When the boss is present, idleness and misbehavior are absent; but, as the adage goes, "when the cat is away, the mice are at play."

To the contrary, Christians must work with integrity or sincerity. They must not vacillate in their effort or productivity depending on their audience. They are to labor just as hard or harder at home than when under the boss's nose. They are, in fact, working for Jesus Himself (cf. Col 3:17, 23). It has been said that the least reached people group is that of coworkers. But one's diligence to serve Christ well can be a powerful witness to unbelieving associates, colleagues, and office mates.

Doing God's Will from the Heart

Being Spirit-filled means that believers must "not be foolish, but understand what the will of the Lord is" (Eph 5:17). This implies that those who are ambivalent toward knowing God's will are fools. Spirit-filled workers, on the other hand, are commanded to be "doing the will of God from the heart" (6:6). They must know His will with full confidence. Though God's will can be mined from many places in Scripture (e.g., 1 Thess 4:3; 5:18; 1 Tim 2:4; 2 Pet 3:9), here Paul makes clear what the Lord's will is in the context of work: God expects integrity. This is a point Paul has already driven home in verse 6. Now he makes it more explicit in what follows.

The "doing" of God's will is presented both positively and negatively in verse 7. Positively, doing God's will is "serving [one's master] with good will as to the Lord." Negatively, it is serving as "not to men" (Eph 6:7). The verb for "serve" here (*douleuō*) literally means "performing the duties of a slave,"[10] a readily understood image. But the "slaving" that Paul commands would stand out in the first-century world because it would be done "with good will" (*eunoias*). A prime example is the once unprofitable, rebellious, runaway slave Onesimus, who, after he became a Christian, willingly returned to his

---

8. Francis Foulkes, *Ephesians: An Introduction and Commentary*, TNTC 10 (Downers Grove, IL: InterVarsity, 1989), 172; Andrew T. Lincoln, *Ephesians*, WBC 42 (Dallas: Word, 1990), 421.

9. Arnold, *Ephesians*, 423.

10. "δουλεύω," BDAG, 259.

believing master (Phlm 10–21). Today, as in the first century, right serving is done in an attitude of favorable willingness, even enthusiasm.[11]

The Christian demonstrates that good attitude, again, by rendering service to his employer as if to Jesus Himself. Christians are "slaves (*douloi*) of Christ," bondservants in the household of God (Eph 6:6). [12] When things are falling apart on the job and the boss is an unbearable tyrant, the believer must be wise and remember what God's will for him is: "serving with good will as to the Lord, and not to men" (6:7). As believers labor for and alongside people who are dead in sins and transgressions, as all believers once were, they are encouraged to ask the Lord to turn an agonizing situation into an opportunity for their coworkers to see the gospel of peace active in the believer's life (Eph 2:1–16).

Believers face other temptations to abandon God's will in the marketplace. Two of the most common involve greed and sexual immorality. As for greed, the temptation to deceitfully manipulate time cards, expense reports, sales projections, or financial statements can be great. But God's economy is one of truth and righteousness (Prov 20:10). Though a misrepresentation of numbers may bring a short-term financial gain, it insults God and its end is destruction. Believers ought to demonstrate contentment, rather, that they have surpassing riches in Christ of which the world knows nothing (Phil 3:8–11). And whatever scorn the world may have for Christian integrity, to be identified with Christ is more rewarding to the believer than all the "treasures of Egypt" (Heb 11:26). That speaks volumes to attentive coworkers and managers.

Second, the Christian in the workplace must be wary of sexual temptation. As with elders in a church, a Christian who would be a witness in the workplace must be "above reproach" (1 Tim 3:2). This means more than avoiding overt immorality. It means taking due caution against the appearance of impropriety. In accusatory cultural climates, this is especially important. Something like dining alone with a coworker of the opposite sex can place a Christian testimony in jeopardy. But sexual and romantic integrity leaves a mark on unbelieving coworkers. Oftentimes, writes Peter, "They are surprised that you do not run with them into the same excesses of dissipation" (which, in context, meant sexual sin), and they may malign the believer for it (1 Pet 4:3–4). But they will also remember his or her excellent conduct and be convicted and warned of the justice and holiness of God, who sees everything (2:12). Such a testimony also provides opportunities to speak of the transformation of life that salvation brings.

Looking to the Lord for Reward

The third way in which Spirit-filled workers walk wisely is by looking to the Lord for their

---

11. "εὔνοια," BDAG, 409.

12. Peter O'Brien writes, "God's will is to be performed by 'slaves of Christ' within everyday life of the household. They are to serve their masters 'wholeheartedly' (lit. 'from the soul'), an expression which is virtually synonymous with 'sincerity of heart' [in v. 5]." Peter Thomas O'Brien, *The Letter to the Ephesians*, PNTC (Grand Rapids: Eerdmans, 1999), 451.

reward: "knowing that whatever good thing each one does, this he will receive back from the Lord, whether slave or free" (Eph 6:8). The words "receive back" mean nothing less than a reward from Jesus Christ (cf. Rom 2:6; 1 Pet 5:4),[13] but they are conditioned on the "good" that workers do (defined as serving Christ). The consequences of doing wrong are an equal and opposite warning that Paul issues to slaves and masters in Colossians 3:24–25.

Reward motivates good behavior; it motivates Godward obedience and integrity in the workplace. It also comforts believers who are not recognized or rewarded as they should be by their earthly employers. Significantly, the word for "master" in Ephesians 6:5 and "Lord" in verses 7–8 is identical in the Greek: *kyrios*. The significance of that for "slaves of Christ" is their knowing that Christ will hold all earthly masters accountable (Luke 12:42–46). The latter do not have the final word.

Christians in the workplace may be tempted into silence by workplace censorship and persecution for the name of Christ. Rare are the employers who hire Christian employees to evangelize their coworkers and customers. In reality, companies in developed countries are more and more excluding or penalizing Christian voices from workplace forums. In recent years, global corporations have been racing to require their own employees and business partners to prove implementation of fashionable social agendas that war against God, related to gender, sexuality, and ethnicity, so as to show themselves relevant to the spirit of the age. The hiring process and employee training are sometimes even designed to shame employees who do not conform to progressive social and political views.

Yet, when Christians suffer for the sake of righteousness and when they fearlessly, gently, and respectfully stand for truth by sanctifying Christ as Lord in their hearts, always ready to make a defense to everyone, without exception, who asks them why they have such great hope, they will answer with gentleness and with a good conscience (1 Pet 3:13–17), and they will not be silent, because they are looking to Christ for their reward. Enduring insult for His name is a fruit of being Spirit-filled and a cause for rejoicing (1 Pet 4:14–16). Some coworkers will wonder about how these Christians manage it all, what gives them their joy, or how their personal lives can be so filled with hope, and the Christian will respond: "Jesus Christ."[14] That alone is sufficient reason for Christians not to succumb to censorship temptations.

The evangelistic conversations that arise need always to be tactful and gracious. They will often start at work and finish after hours, or they may need to come outside of work hours altogether. But the life of Christian integrity

---

13. Benjamin L. Merkle, *Exegetical Guide to the Greek New Testament: Ephesians* (Nashville: B&H Academic, 2016), 204.

14. In workplace evangelism, it is prudent to keep a record of the name of the person posing the question, what specifically was discussed, and how the Christian's input was elicited or welcomed. In the current "cancel culture"—in which the memory or voice of anyone considered offensive must be removed—one has to be ready to present details in self-defense, if ever required, to testify about spiritual and moral conversations conducted honorably.

and gracious suffering will prompt the opportunities to proclaim the gospel in the workplace. Let Christians be encouraged; faithful proclamation will be rewarded in eternity (Luke 16:9; John 4:36).

Leading as unto Christ

Finally, Paul does not limit his exhortations to slaves only, but also to masters. Therefore, being filled with the Spirit has implications for leaders in the workplace. In Ephesians 6:9 he writes, "Masters, do the same things to them," that is, to their slaves. One might ask, "What things are these? Is the master to be obedient to the slave?" However, the verb "do" (*poieō*) indicates the answer, being used twice already in these verses. The last time was in verse 8, expressing that the Lord will reward "whatever good thing each one does (*poiēsē*)," and before that was verse 6, commanding that slaves of Christ be "doing (*poiountes*) the will of God from the heart." Leaders and managers therefore are to do exactly those things too. They are to do good to their workers, do God's will with integrity, and in general be leaders "as slaves of Christ."

Paul applied this first with a negative prohibition for leaders: "giving up threatening" (Eph 6:9). Paul knew what it meant to threaten, for, before his conversion, he menaced and intimidated Christians with the promise to harm them (cf. Acts 9:1). Holding employees accountable is different. Managers should recognize that their employees' submission is entirely voluntary. Scripture never condones capricious leadership that keeps subordinates awake at night in fear of losing their jobs. It condemns leadership that withholds earned pay, promotion, or benefits when the leader has the means to bestow them (Lev 19:13; Deut 24:15; Prov 3:27; Jas 5:4).

On the contrary, Scripture calls for servant leadership, leaders who are Spirit-filled and so are "subject to one another in the fear of Christ" (Eph 5:21). That is to say, they are forgiving (Phlm 15–18), looking out for their employees' interests (Phil 2:4), honoring them (Rom 12:10), and managing them as if they were fellow slaves of Christ with them (Eph 6:9). They look to the same Lord for their reward and are accountable to the same Lord for any wrongdoing. In Paul's words "there is no partiality with Him" (6:9). As Jesus' slave, the Christian boss is to do God's will from the heart, blessing subordinates, for they report to the same ultimate Master. A leader that serves Christ well is perfectly situated to answer everyone who asks him or her to give an account for the hope that is in them, so that the name of Christ will be exalted even in the office (1 Pet 3:15–16).

Conclusion

Christians, whether in their own culture or across cultures, are witnesses for Christ. That means they must redeem their time at work. For them, Paul's message from Ephesians 6:5–9 and context is as applicable today as it was in its first-century Roman context. Those who have been redeemed by Christ are happy to call Him their Master. That being so, their work as unto Christ is a testimony to adorn the gospel that proclaims Him their Savior, which gospel they also open their mouths to proclaim.

Faithful workplace witnesses are filled with the Spirit, do Spirit-filled work, and are Spirit-filled leaders. As they submit their lives to the Spirit's control, the fruit of obedience, integrity, and looking to Christ for their reward is an apologetic for the gospel. They use their marketplace opportunities and circles of influence to reach others for Christ, whom missionaries and pastors do not have opportunities to reach. In so doing, their labors bear fruit that not only supports the Great Commission on a global scale but fulfills it on the local level. Let Christians go therefore and witness for Christ on the clock.

INSERT 63.1

Building a Corporation in Ethiopia to Reach the Nations

Abera Ajula

Ethiopia is well-known for coffee exporting. But there is a little-known connection between the coffee exporting business in Ethiopia and the Great Commission. This essay tells the story of one missions-minded business owner and draws applications for others like him around the world.

A Coffee Company and a Mission

An export company well-known in the capital city, Addis Ababa, is owned by a local man who loves the Lord Jesus Christ. Through his business, he wanted to donate to something that would produce spiritual fruit, so he decided to establish a ministry for church planting and the revitalization of existing churches throughout his home country of Ethiopia. He began to set aside his profits to fund evangelistic endeavors, specifically sending missionaries to different parts of the country where unreached people groups had never heard the gospel. And there are many such groups still today!

When I met this businessman, he told me, "The money that I have, it is not my money." He meant that all he possessed belonged to God. He continued, "I want to invest God's money into missions." That is precisely what he did. Today he supports more than thirty-six missionaries who plant churches and shepherd the believers. He has big plans to add more missionaries, as the Lord will allow.

However, the owner's missions ministry does much more than donate profits. It also promotes active evangelism within his corporation. Of his more than six hundred permanent employees, from the head office in Addis to the districts of the country, and thousands of seasonal workers, a few are Muslim, some are Ethiopian Orthodox, a few are Roman Catholic, and the majority are Protestants. His goal from the beginning has been to show his employees the light of the gospel by creating opportunities for them to interact with faithful, Bible-practicing believers. Therefore, believers work among nonbelievers regularly, and he often invites local pastors to preach the gospel in a chapel-like service to all of his employees who are willing to attend (and most of them do!). Recently he held a reception for his newly married son and invited all of his employees to attend as his honored guests. At the party, they all heard the proclamation of the gospel and his son's testimony of faith. His prayer was that this reception event would lead to the reception of the gospel in the hearts of his workers.

Lessons for Businesspeople Globally

The story from my country is just one of many surprising examples of the unique missions path that is commonly called "business as missions." Like the others, it is surprising for several good reasons, which are listed below.

- The source of missions funding coming from business profits rather than church donations makes for an unusual and creative way to support the work of the Lord.
- Because the Lord has blessed this owner's donation model with a successful company, the scale of one man's missions impact continues to increase significantly.
- Evangelism within a secular business context is rare and, in many places, unlawful. But as the head of his company, this man has found ways to be intentional with evangelism.
- The attitude of the businessman to see his profits as God's money is uncommon and inspiring. His biblical perspective has helped him value the Lord's harvest and support seed sowers with urgency.
- The strategic nature of sending missionaries to unreached people groups demonstrates thoughtful intentionality. Not only does the believing business owner care for the souls of his employees, but he gladly gives for people in far-off places whom he will never meet.

For the Christian businessperson or company leader considering doing "business and missions," our Ethiopian brother should be noted in at least the following ways. First, the businessperson's greatest concern is not profits but the proclamation and propagation of the gospel. He or she must believe that the business exists for the Lord's kingdom, because Jesus Christ is King of kings, Lord of lords, and Boss of bosses.

Second, the owner must consider finances and resources as a stewardship for the cause of Christ. The Lord of the harvest desires to involve each person and their resources to raise up workers for His ready field. Business owners would do well, even now, to look for specific ways that their business can help support faithful missionaries as well as preach the gospel message to those in the company and in its sphere of operations.

Third, owners must recognize that they are witnesses for Christ in all that they say and do. They represent Christ as His ambassadors with their work integrity, company policies, employee interactions, and dealings with outside agencies and local government.

Finally, let us all praise God for examples of other faithful brothers and sisters who do "business as missions" to the glory of the Father. They are inspiring people to follow on the path to true success. The greatest profit, beyond participating in the gospel's expansion through one's business efforts, is something that is only realized at the end of this age. It comes once all investments have been made, and the Lord calls us each forward and proclaims with His favor, "Well done, good and faithful slave. You were faithful with a few things, I will put you in charge of many things; enter into the joy of your master" (Matt 25:23).

INSERT 63.2

The Call to Local Cross-Cultural Outreach

Mark Tatlock

Today, due to the globalization of industries and the immigration patterns of countries near and far, the nations have more access to the gospel—and are therefore more accessible to gospel proclaimers—than at any time in history. Most cities and towns (and even many villages and neighbor-hoods) around the world are increasingly ethnically diverse. This means that while many developing countries remain closed to missionary activity through governmental policies and social prohibitions, their unreached populations are now within arm's reach of everyday believers in evangelical churches. So, while the mass media is focused on geopolitical and multilateral diplomacy, God is doing the more important work of reconciling to Himself people from many tribes and tongues, and nations through the ambassadors He has already established in globalized locations across the world.

Church leaders should help their local church members understand this ever-expanding opportunity for cross-cultural ministry where they live and work. What follows are four ways the church leader can play a central role in imparting a vision for local cross-cultural outreach.

Help Them Identify a Starting Place for Service

Local church leaders should be the first in their congregations to research and understand the cross-cultural reality of their community. Armed with real knowledge, they can help their people to appreciate the opportunities before them for local cross-cultural outreach. A straightforward starting place is to look at the labor market in the area, for example. Because of globalization, there is no industry that doesn't have an international connection or dynamic. Therefore, it is likely that businesses near a local church have brought internationals locally for work. Cross-cultural ministry no longer requires travel or relocation—the developing nations have come to them. There has never been as critical a time for churches to strategize about how to proclaim the gospel to the immigrants, refugees, and foreigners around them. If church leaders help their people to see their point on the map as a growing multiethnic center, then they can begin to think strategically about how to reach the nations among them through their ministries.

Help Them Find the Opportunities in the Church

Every believer can be involved in local cross-cultural ministry in natural ways that spring from the congregation itself. For example, the youth ministry might be the most culturally integrated population in the church. School-aged children of foreigners are perhaps already involved in church programs or are being actively evangelized through student outreach ministries. Many such students were born and raised in the new country and might not actively demonstrate the norms, language, and appearance of their parents' culture. However, the reality of a different culture at home creates an opportunity for pastors and leaders to be intentional to bring the gospel to the families, rather than being oblivious to or disinterested in the cultural and even socioeconomic realities of those to whom they are already connected.

Instill in Them a Zeal to Engage with the Truth

The call to biblical missions at home should not be a radical call, but it often seems to be, as many churches go about their business as usual without a concerted effort to reach the nations around them. Apathy is not the only cause of stalled outreach, however. The local evangelical believers in many villages, towns, cities, states, and nations watch the theologically liberal churches, false religions, and local governments around them run social gospel programs to meet the influx of needs that many foreigners have. Ceding the work of reaching the nations to those with a compromised, false, or nonexistent gospel is a pragmatic response that is nevertheless apathy. The primary voice of the gospel in the real-life sphere of the foreigner should be from the conservative evangelical church above all others. True believers should be encouraged by their leaders to be intentional to learn the reasons why people have immigrated to them. They should be alert to routine, casual opportunities to talk to foreigners personally, to ask them questions and hear their answers, and to care about the stories they tell and the situations they relay.

Encourage Them to Be Innovative and Intentional

To help the local believers consider their role in biblical missions to their community, church leaders need to help them see how they can actually reach the foreigners around them. Both the leadership and their people should adopt the attitude of willingness to "just try something" within their power to do. A simple, personal approach is the best way for everyday believers to do what the well-resourced social help programs cannot do—engage the lost with the gospel of Jesus Christ (Acts 3:6). Stemming from gospel proclamation, local churches will often come to realize that they can provide a variety of types of care and resources for foreigners with material needs, such as to immigrant and refugee families, their widows and orphans, their single mothers, and their newly homeless.

Some intentional ways local churches can conduct ministry among the foreign populations around them with minimal expense include these:

- Creating ethnic ministry teams for evangelism and early discipling

- Teaching the local language as a free program for foreigners
- Inviting stay-at-home mothers to women's events that teach practical matters for families
- Providing tutoring for those taking courses for work advancement
- Befriending international students and offering regular hospitality
- Learning a locally spoken foreign language
- Going to ethnic restaurants and befriending the owners
- Praying for the nations from the pulpit and in groups

Conclusion

Believers are called to function as priests of God who "proclaim the excellencies of Him who has called [them] out of darkness into His marvelous light," because of His mercy (1 Pet 2:9–10). Some local churches are awakening to the great harvest God has brought to them (John 4:35), reaching the lost from the nations and becoming multiethnic churches to the glory of Christ. May they excel still more (1 Thess 4:1), and may others join them! It is time for the evangelical church everywhere to faithfully pursue this God-given responsibility.

SECTION 2

INTERNATIONAL PRACTICES

SUB-SECTION 1:
SHORT-TERM MINISTRY

CHAPTER 64

Short-Term Ministries, Not Short-Term Missions

Rodney Andersen

Short-term ministries (STMs) have been common in the United States for decades and are even growing in popularity in other countries. While it is hard to estimate the amount of money spent on them, their growth has been well documented.[1] Many have questions about whether STMs are a good use of time and money, are effective, and most importantly, are biblical.

Short-term ministries, often called "short-term missions," refer to the practice of sending church members to another location for one to six weeks to perform ministry tasks. It is preferable to label these efforts as *ministries* rather than missions so that participants do not mistakenly conclude that spending a few weeks in another country makes one a missionary.

It is common for churches to send teenagers on STMs because teenagers often have time for missions trips and the adults hope that such trips will encourage young people to get excited about God as they fulfill their church's need to participate in missions. The benefit that many young people can find others outside the church to help pay for these trips only adds to their appeal. It is no surprise that such trips have gained in popularity. This chapter, then, examines STMs from several angles: their potential dangers, their biblical support, their benefits, and their effective implementation.

---

1. Steve Corbett and Brian Fikkert, *When Helping Hurts: Alleviating Poverty without Hurting the Poor . . . and Ourselves* (Chicago: Moody, 2012); Don Fanning, "Short Term Missions: A Trend That Is Growing Exponentially," Liberty University Center for Global Ministries, Trends and Issues in Missions 4 (2009), https://digitalcommons.liberty.edu/cgi/viewcontent.cgi?httpsredir=1&article=1003&context=cgm_missions.

Potential Dangers

As STMs have grown in popularity, so have concerns about the cost, effectiveness, and even the potential harm that STM teams may be causing.[2] These concerns cannot be overlooked.

Concerns about the Cost: Are STMs a Good Stewardship of Time and Money?

STM trips require planning and expense—time and effort that could be spent elsewhere. Teams need to be selected, money raised, preparations made, activities planned, travel and lodging arranged, and food purchased and prepared. Many of these tasks must be done by the full-time missionary, who is then necessarily taken away from his other ministry responsibilities. Added to the time required to have an STM is the high financial cost of sending, lodging, and feeding a team of foreigners. The cost to send a team usually far exceeds what it would have cost for locals to perform the same tasks.

Concerns about Effectiveness: Are STMs Effective?

Many teams who are sent cross-culturally can have only minimal interaction with locals due to an inability to speak the local language. Even when team members have local language fluency or a translator is available, evangelistic efforts are often haphazard, approaching people randomly and with little success at even maintaining a conversation. To this can be added the many building projects done that are only later to be unused or torn down. Relationships between the STM team members and locals quickly disappear in the days and weeks after the trip.

Concerns about Potential Harm: Are STMs Actually Harming Those They Seek to Help?

Evangelistic efforts often seek a "decision" for Christ with no follow-up to disciple the individual or even verify that there is spiritual fruit in that person's life confirming their salvation. That individual is left with the "comfort" of believing he is saved when he has never really given his life to Christ. Future efforts to reach this person may be met with the response "I already tried that." To this can be added concerns about offending locals due to cultural differences, hurting local industry by giving handouts, perpetuating a faulty view of Western superiority, and imparting an incorrect view of missions to participants and locals.

With all these concerns, it is right to question whether the benefits of an STM can outweigh the costs and avoid these potential dangers. More important is the question of whether Scripture gives any indication that STMs can be of any benefit.

---

2. Corbett and Fikkert, *When Helping Hurts*, 151; Darren Carlson, "Why You Should Consider Canceling Your Short-Term Mission Trips," The Gospel Coalition, June 18, 2012, https://www.thegospelcoalition.org/article/why-you-should-consider-cancelling-your-short-term-mission-trips/; Daniel Threlfall, "Five Reasons Your Short-Term Mission Trip Might Do More Harm Than Good," *Share Faith*, February 2014, https://www.sharefaith.com/blog/2014/02/reasons-short-term-mission-trip-harm-good/.

Biblical Support for STMs

The apostles and the early church lived out the Great Commission in the book of Acts and the Epistles through the planting of local churches.

Some STMs were also practiced by the early church. Examples include Paul and Barnabas or Paul and Silas, whenever they went to "strengthen the churches" they had already planted (Acts 14:22; 15:36, 41; 16:5; 18:23). These were STMs from the point of view of those fledgling churches. To this can be added Epaphroditus being sent from the church in Philippi to minister to the needs of missionary Paul on the field and to provide him with funds (Phil 2:25–30; 4:18). Likewise, the collection of funds sent by a delegation from the churches of Achaia, Macedonia, and Galatia to the church at Jerusalem during its famine can be considered an STM (Acts 24:17; Rom 15:25–26; 1 Cor 16:1–4; 2 Cor 8:18–23; cf. Acts 11:28).

It is critical to recognize that these accounts in Acts and the Epistles are descriptive; they are not commands to the church. At the same time, the book of Acts is intended not merely to recount history but to show the work of God through the early church and to provide examples of how the early church supported the spread of the gospel in other regions. In the examples above, we see that the STM trips of the early church were gospel-focused and included both evangelism and the strengthening of the missionaries and the church.

While STMs may not always include personal evangelism, they should always be supporting the ongoing ministry of a missionary or church. STMs are not an end in themselves. They must support God's program, the local church. All STMs must support the existing efforts of God's churches in the regions to which they are sent.

Benefits of an STM Team

While recognizing the biblical mandate to make disciples of all the nations and the biblical examples of STMs in Scripture, there is no biblical command to send STM teams. This decision must be made by each church after carefully evaluating the benefits of these teams against the associated costs. When STMs are done well, they can provide benefits to gospel ministry, the missionary, the receiving church, the sending church, and to each individual who is sent.

Benefit to the Ministry

The primary reason that STM teams are sent is for the advancement of the gospel. This may involve direct evangelism, partnership in evangelistic activities or church ministry, construction of ministry facilities, or a variety of other gospel ministries. While humanitarian efforts can be a demonstration of love to the world, these types of activities should be done by the local church where long-lasting relationships can be built. STMs, as modeled by the early church, were focused on gospel ministry, strengthening the church, and encouraging the long-term missionaries. Clint Archer correctly states,

> Everything in missions must undergird the goal of propagating the gospel. This pattern

should inform the path our STM planning takes. The spread of the gospel is what brings lasting change to individuals and societies. STM trips must serve this cause, . . . supporting the work that is being done by missionaries the world over.[3]

All STM activities should be done in partnership with the ongoing ministry of a full-time missionary or established church. The activities performed by an STM team without the ongoing discipleship of a local church will either be ineffective or leave immature believers needing strengthening.

Benefit to the Missionary

The second great benefit of an STM is the support and encouragement of missionary families. The team's visit provides a visible reminder to the missionaries that they are not alone in their desire to see Christ exalted among the nations. The fellowship, counsel, and prayer that an STM team provides to the missionary can be a huge boost to a weary missionary's spirits.

In addition, the missionary is benefited when an STM member becomes excited about the ministry in that country. When a member sees the ministry that is happening abroad and participates in it, he or she is much more likely to financially support that ministry through ongoing giving. This excitement is multiplied as the STM member tells family and friends about the ministry they witnessed abroad.

Benefit to the Church Abroad

One of the greatest beneficiaries of an STM team often goes unnoticed—the believers serving alongside the missionary. The encouragement of like-minded believers from the sending church can energize the church where the missionary serves. Although the church sees the missionary on a regular basis, they do not always have the opportunity to see many lay believers proclaim the gospel. The willingness of an STM team to raise support, use vacation time, and prepare for the ministry can have a great impact on those in the missionary's church.

Benefit to the Sending Church

When the teams are both preparing for a trip and when they return, they create an infectious enthusiasm for missions and evangelism that will spread to others. STM members should have the opportunity to share what God is doing through ministries around the world. By doing so, their passion for ministry stimulates individuals from the sending church to have a greater passion for missions.

Benefit to the STM Member

Although the value of the experience to the STM members should not be the primary reason for sending an STM team, the members derive significant benefit from the opportunity to serve. It is a life-changing experience to travel to a different part of the world and minister in a new context. Some STM members

---

3. Clint Archer, *Holding the Rope: Short-Term Missions, Long-Term Impact* (Pasadena, CA: William Carey Library, 2014), 19.

come to appreciate God's work across the globe for the first time, while others come to appreciate God's goodness to them as never before. For some STM members, the experience of evangelism in a different region causes them to consider becoming a missionary themselves one day. Although there are many benefits to the STM member, their spiritual growth should never be the primary purpose for the STM. The STM member gains the most spiritual benefits when she or he recognizes that the progress of the gospel is more important than personal enrichment.

Recognizing these potential benefits does not negate the potential for ineffectiveness or harm that STMs can cause. Therefore, guiding principles must be followed in the implementation of an STM program as discussed below.

Implementation of an STM Program

Before determining to send out an STM team from a church, it is critical that the church understands that short-term ministries are not a substitute for missions or missionaries. The work of missions is the planting of churches, and this cannot be accomplished by a group of young people in the period of a few weeks. Planting churches requires an elder-qualified missionary who has been theologically trained and is fluent in the local language, one who can proclaim Christ, disciple believers, and appoint elders who can lead the local church. STMs are valuable in coming alongside these efforts, but they do not replace them. The following principles in the creation, preparation, execution,

and evaluation of STM teams should help to implement an effective program.

Creation of STM Teams

The method of choosing a place to send an STM team and a ministry it will perform is simple: let the missionaries do it for you. Rather than determining to send a team based on the desires of those in the local church, elders should determine to send a team based on the needs of the mission field. They should ask the missionaries whom their church supports if they would like an STM to help them with any ministry. If the answer is no, then a team should not be sent! If the missionary does request a team, the elders must be sure to ask what ministry they want the team to accomplish, what dates they want the team present, how many people to include on the team, and what skills the team members should possess. This first step—letting the long-term missionary drive the decision on whether to send an STM team and the specifics about the team—is the most fundamental and critical step in the process. It must not be neglected.

The second most important element is the selection of individuals who will participate on the team. Composing an STM team is not an opportunity to engage individuals in your church who are struggling in their walk with the Lord and need a "jump-start" to their spiritual lives. Sending a half-hearted or spiritually lethargic student for gospel ministry will disrupt the team itself and may cause harm to the ministry the church is endeavoring to support. Instead, select STM participants who have shown themselves to be consistent in their devotion to Christ and faithful in church ministry. Each participant should already be a member of the church and have the recommendation of the pastor to serve in this way. Additionally, the team leader must be a man of proven character and leadership. He will be functioning as the shepherd of the team and will be called to provide both logistical and spiritual leadership. Team selection—especially of the team leader—is critical to an effective STM team.

Preparation of STM Teams

After selection of the STM team, the team must faithfully prepare prior to their departure. If a team is properly prepared, the trip will be a joy as they implement their plans and watch God work in each of the lives involved. On the other hand, an unprepared team often results in frustration, ineffectiveness, and conflict. To prepare properly, the team leader should talk to the missionary host with whom the team will be serving in order to discuss the different aspects of the ministry to be performed. Whatever ministry the team will accomplish, they should have all aspects of that ministry ready to go prior to departure for the field. Recognizing that unexpected circumstances may alter the precise plans of the ministry, teams should be doubly prepared. If the expected ministry is two sermons, four sermons should be prepared. If the ministry includes presenting the gospel through English lessons, the team should be prepared for students being at different English levels than expected. If the team is not overly prepared, then it is unprepared.

A well-prepared STM team will have all aspects of the trip, including passports, visas, ministry supplies, and a myriad of other items figured out long before departure. Delegating tasks to different team members is often wise. A team can have a financial coordinator for expenditures, a designated photographer, a shopper of gifts for host families, and other task leaders. It is usually wise to have an alternate team leader in case an emergency occurs and the regular team leader cannot fulfill his role. It is also wise to designate a female leader for the team whom the other women on the team can approach if needed.

While all preparation is important, none is as critical as spiritual preparation. The team leader should lead the team in times of prayer during every team meeting and encourage private prayer leading up to the trip. Unity should be fostered among team members prior to departure through activities such as discussions of past cross-cultural experiences and team-building activities like hiking or game nights. A crucial aspect of that, which must not be overlooked, is thoughtful preparation of salvation testimonies by each person on the team. The team leader should lead the team on how to present the gospel clearly through their testimonies, making sure the focus is on the work of Christ. In addition, the team should prepare for evangelistic opportunities, including memorization of key Scriptures to explain the gospel.[4]

---

4. A useful resource for testimony and evangelism preparation is by Will Metzger, *Tell the Truth: The Whole Gospel Wholly by*

Finally, a team leader should prepare the team spiritually by reminding them that they must demonstrate Christlike attitudes during the trip, including humility, a servant's heart, and sacrificial love (John 13:1, 34; Phil 2:3–8; e.g., John 13:5–15). Various difficulties and a temptation to complain and argue will arise while doing ministry. Meditating on the example of Christ and seeking to be like Him through the power of the Spirit will prepare the team to respond to challenges in a godly way.

Performance of STM Teams

When the team arrives in the country, they must be prepared to be flexible. Unexpected challenges in ministry, transportation, or living conditions are almost certain. The team leader's attitude toward those changes will be watched by the rest of the team. If he complains or demonstrates frustration, they will follow his lead. "Consider it all joy, my brothers, when you encounter various trials" (Jas 1:2)—not "if" but "when." Therefore, the leader must set an example of joy in the midst of challenging circumstances.

For some of the team members, the conditions on the STM may be more challenging than they were expecting or, perhaps, more than they have ever experienced in the past. Therefore, the team leader must faithfully provide biblical counsel and encouragement throughout the trip. Team members should be reminded of their Savior who sacrificed heavenly riches to come to earth as a servant (Mark 10:45; 2 Cor 8:9). The STM team should press on in faithful service, "abounding in the work of the Lord, knowing that [their] labor is not in vain in the Lord" (1 Cor 15:58).

Evaluation of STM Teams

Once the team arrives back home from the STM trip, they will likely be exhausted. They have spent all of their energy serving others and will need some rest. However, there are some final tasks to complete before "closing the books" on the STM experience. First, STM team leaders should have a debrief time with the STM team members, ideally before arriving back in the home country. While the experience is still fresh in their minds, the team members will be better able to evaluate the trip. Second, there should be a debrief time between the missionary host and a leader from the sending church. All may have gone well in the view of the team leader, but the missionary or local church leader will have a unique perspective on the benefits of the team. Third, there should be a time for the STM team to report back to the sending church what God has accomplished on the STM trip. If preparation was done properly, the church has been praying for the team and helped to financially support the team. Reporting back to the church follows the example of Paul, who reported back to the church what God had done (Acts 14:27–28). This reporting should focus on the ministry, the ongoing work in the country of ministry, and, above all, give glory

---

Grace Communicated Truthfully and Lovingly, 4th ed. (Downers Grove, IL: InterVarsity, 2012).

to God. Finally, the team must not neglect to give thanks to all of those who sacrificially donated to make the trip possible. The STM trip was a joint effort of the givers and the goers, and it is appropriate for gratitude to be expressed to the ones unable to go.

Conclusion

Although STMs are not a replacement for the work of missionaries, they can complement the work that is being done by those missionaries.

This starts with seeing the ministry and the ongoing work of the missionary as the main beneficiary of these STM teams rather than the participants themselves. Effective STMs will provide an opportunity for those who are already faithfully serving in their local church to support the spread of the gospel elsewhere. When the focus is on what God is doing in the lives of other people, the STM member will be blessed in the process. Most of all, God will be glorified in the advance of His gospel.

Anatomy of a Short-Term Ministry Trip: Purpose, Impact, Planning, and Training

David E. Bosworth

Paul's short-term ministry trips around the Roman Empire are referred to as missionary journeys. The term implicitly recognizes that more than mere travel occurred. Though we retain the phrase short-term ministry trip (STM) for pragmatic reasons, we would drastically improve such experiences by approaching them with the controlling metaphor of a journey. By God's grace and the Holy Spirit's enablement, STMs evince change in the lives of the participants, the missionary hosts, the nationals, and the unbelievers touched by

the outreach. Planning such an undertaking is complex. Paul's journeys provide us a model for our own planning. The following should be considered when planning and leading an STM.

Determine a Specific Vision for the Trip

Every STM has the purpose of making Christ known among the lost, though not every STM has an identical vision for bringing about this purpose. For example, some STMs might bring medical relief amid human suffering. Others might assist with construction, administration, or other practical needs. Still others might seek to equip or teach. It is best to clarify how the trip aims to accomplish the purpose of proclaiming Christ's redemption.

Luke gives us insight into Paul's vision for traveling to southern Galatia when he indicates that Paul returned to Lystra, Iconium, and Antioch for a second time to establish leadership in the new churches (Acts 14:21–23). He visited these cities at least twice more in the coming years (16:1–2; 18:23) and corresponded with the believers there as well (Gal 4:12–14), all with the specific intent of raising up strong leadership.

Develop a Process for Screening and Assimilating a Team

Developing a specific vision for a trip helps planners decide which applicants to invite into the team. Trips with a vision require specific skills. Once those skills are identified, it becomes easier to select participants. Paul chose Timothy to accompany him on his second missionary journey (Acts 16:1–3). Timothy was selected because Paul noticed him and because the believers in Derbe and Lystra commended him to Paul. In contrast, John Mark was not selected by Paul based on his abandonment of the team on the previous journey (12:25; 15:36–38), though Paul later affirmed that he was

useful to him (2 Tim 4:11; Phlm 24). The biblical examples illustrate that character matters when considering team members.

Set Up Appropriate Methods for Soliciting and Receiving Funds

Collecting and distributing funds according to ability and need is a longstanding practice within the Church (Acts 4:32–35; 11:27–30). Paul collected funds for his own ministry as well as to help other churches (Phil 4:10–14; 2 Cor 8:1–15). Inviting others to partner in the ministry is a way of engaging a broader group to join the mission itself; in addition it is a practical means to fund STMs. Funds should be collected in a practical way that is accessible to both the giver and the administrator of the gift. Most importantly, the way in which the funds are collected should have transparent integrity (2 Cor 8:18–21).

Arrange All Aspects of Transportation

Short-term ministries transportation requires spiritual dependence. Paul traveled over ten thousand miles on foot and by sea. Though he had to give attention to the practical aspects of getting from one place to another, Paul remained sensitive to the Lord's leading in his planning process. When in Phrygia, he attempted to get to Asia, but the Holy Spirit forbade him (Acts 16:7). When in Mysia, he could not go to Bithynia (16:8).

And in Troas, the Lord sent him a vision of the Macedonian man directing him onward to Europe (16:9). Transportation should be planned carefully with consideration for safety (27:4) but ultimately with the attitude that God determines where we go and how we get there (Jas 4:13–15).

Perform Risk Assessment and Mitigation

At times Paul moved into dangerous situations with trust in the Lord (2 Cor 11:23–27). On other occasions, he carefully avoided the risk of personal harm (Acts 9:23–25). In still other situations, he submitted to the advice of others who encouraged him to avoid unnecessary exposure to danger (17:10–15). Understanding when to take risks and when to avoid them involves discernment when you are on a trip. Some questions to ask include: What are the legal implications? How does the risk align with the vision for the trip? What resources does the church or sending organization possess to respond in a worst-case scenario? What is the potential impact on others in a worst-case scenario?

Plan Out the Discipleship Components of the STM

While there are certainly outward-facing benefits to the recipients of an STM, inward spiritual benefits also come to participants. Paul rarely traveled alone. He consistently brought others along and trained them in the process (Acts 13:2; 15:25; 16:3; 18:18; 19:22; 20:4). STM planning should consider how to prepare participants beforehand and how to engage in meaningful discipleship as they go. After trips it is necessary to debrief and assess spiritual changes in the participants. These plans will look different based on the participants and the vision of the trip, but what is important is intentional discipleship; nothing happens by accident.

Collect All Necessary Documentation for the Trip

The apostles did not have passports or legal documents like ours today, but that doesn't mean that access was unlimited. Paul relied on his Roman citizenship twice for his own preservation and the advancement of the gospel (Acts 16:37–39; 22:23–29). It is wise and prudent to make sure that all documentation is in good order. What needs to be reviewed, signed, or obtained will differ widely from context to context, and having the right information at the right time may save a life and prevent legal issues from ending missionary endeavors.

Conclusion

Spending a lengthy period of time in a location as a career missionary affords opportunities for language learning and acculturation, both of which are critical to effective communication of the gospel.

Nevertheless, Paul accomplished valuable ministry even on short visits to many places in the Roman Empire. When well-planned and rightly focused, short-term ministry trips play important roles in the fulfillment of the Great Commission.

CHAPTER 65

Examining Short-Term Missions in Modern Church History

Lisa LaGeorge

Short volunteer trips may be a form of ministry, but by their temporary nature, they are not the same type of vocation as missions. The investment of biblical missions is a long-term, cross-cultural, and often transnational lifestyle for the purpose of gospel proclamation and disciple-making. Elsewhere in this textbook, "STM" is used to identify a volunteer "short-term ministry" trip. Nevertheless, as the common nomenclature of "STM" in missiological research is "short-term missions," that definition is retained in this chapter so as not to misrepresent the researchers cited below.

The increase of short-term missions projects or trips (STMs) over the past three decades has become a force to be reckoned with. It has been called an "industry,"[1] a "giant,"[2] and a "God-commanded, repetitive deployment of swift, temporary non-professional missionaries."[3] Some consider STMs fabulous opportunities, and others classify them as colossal missiological mistakes. While the numbers of worldwide STM participants are difficult to ascertain, studies in the number of North American STM travelers showed an explosion of participants from 22,000 in 1979 to 1.6 million in 2005.[4] Another study suggests that some 8 million adults from the United States have participated in at least one STM trip between 2003 and

---

1. David Livermore, *Serving with Eyes Wide Open: Doing Short-Term Missions with Cultural Intelligence* (Grand Rapids: Baker, 2006), 12.

2. Roger Peterson, Gordon Aeschliman, and R. Wayne Sneed, *Maximum Impact Short-Term Mission: The God-Commanded, Repetitive Deployment of Swift, Temporary, Non-Professional Missionaries* (Minneapolis: Short Term Evangelical Missions Ministries, 2003), 242.

3. Peterson, Aeschliman, and Sneed, 117.

4. Stan Guthrie, *Missions in the Third Millennium: 21 Key Trends for the 21st Century*, rev. and exp. ed. (Waynesboro, GA: Authentic Media, 2001), 109; Robert Wuthnow, *Boundless Faith: The Global Outreach of American Churches* (Los Angeles: University of California Press, 2009), 170.

2008.[5] Those numbers diminished in the following decade and were brought to a screeching halt by COVID-19 in 2020.

However, as people have begun traveling again, churches, schools, and agencies are reevaluating STM structures and motivations. Given that renewed interest, this chapter examines the practical bases that are claimed by proponents for the STM phenomenon. It does so by examining certain historical trends in, motivations behind, benefits from, and critiques of STMs. Finally, a conclusion is drawn as to whether STMs are useful in the Church's mission.

Historical Trends in Short-Term Missions

Prior to 1950, few people traveled under the banner of missions unless they were moving to a new location for life. A few examples of short ministry trips do exist prior to this date but are rare in church history. One such example is Robert Cleaver Chapman (1803–1902), a pastor from Barnstaple, England, who took his sabbatical periods to travel to Ireland and Spain for intentional seasons of gospel proclamation.[6] Lilias Trotter (1853–1928), a missionary to Algeria, encouraged self-funded young women from her native England to volunteer as "short-servicers" in the early 1900s to temporarily assist the missionaries in their homes.[7]

In the 1960s, STMs involvement started to gain momentum. Entire agencies were founded that focused exclusively on the mobilization and facilitation of young adults to go short term on the mission field. Youth With A Mission (YWAM) began in 1960, Yugo Ministries in 1964, and Teen Missions International in 1970.[8] These agencies sent many thousands of participants to the field.

Although the trend started with missions agencies, whether traditional or exclusively short term, as in the examples above, churches and denominations have become increasingly involved as well. A 2009 examination of STM stated that the Southern Baptist Convention was sending 150,000 of its members abroad annually as STM team members, while the United Methodist Church was sending more than 100,000.[9]

While the earlier STMs focused on adult participants with identifiable technical skills, a noticeable trend in the past fifty years has been the exponential involvement of teenagers and young adults, who are nearly twice as likely to go on a trip as are middle-aged adults.[10] By the first decade of the twenty-first century, STMs became an expected part of almost every church high school youth group. Another recent study observed,

In addition to high schoolers, undergraduate college students began to be heavily involved

---

5. Barna Group, "Despite Benefits, Few Americans Have Experienced Short-Term Mission Trips," Barna, October 6, 2008, https://www.barna.com/research/despite-benefits-few-americans-have-experienced-short-term-mission-trips/, para. 4.

6. William Henry Bennet, *Robert Cleaver Chapman of Barnstaple* (Whitefish, MT: Kessinger, 2007), 55, 96.

7. Miriam H. Rockness, *A Passion for the Impossible: The Life of Lilias Trotter* (Grand Rapids: Discovery House, 2003), 241.

8. Peterson, Aeschliman, and Sneed, *Maximum Impact Short-Term Mission*, 241.

9. Wuthnow, *Boundless Faith*, 167.

10. Wuthnow, 172.

in STMs. The participation of college-age students in missions is a part of the fabric of mission history—but historically, these movements were focused on sending long-term workers. STM has created a new paradigm. While many schools in Higher Christian Education offer multiple study-abroad programs, few sponsor any mission trip that lasts more than a month. One week trips over Spring Break are the most common length for an STM.[11]

Despite their relatively short history, STMs are now practiced by a diverse set of institutions, ages, and vocations.

Motivations behind Short-Term Missions

While it is difficult to fully understand an individual's motivations for participation in an STM trip, many missiologists, youth pastors, educators, and STM marketers have compiled lists of reasons why students participate. In his excellent critique of STMs, David Livermore observed that participants often provide multiple reasons.[12] Their biblical motivations include obedience to the Great Commission. However, Livermore also states that STMs appeal to participants' sense of adventure. He points to the personal tension involved in this combination and, correspondingly, to the differences that often arise between, on the one hand, reports given by participants to their sending churches and, on the other hand, their personal conversations: "Such conversations are filled with stories about who got stopped going through customs, what it was like to eat the food, bartering the shopkeeper down to a ridiculous price, and experiencing the driving habits of the locals."[13]

Some missions agencies emphasize and even advertise the "fun" nature of missions. Other motivations cited include the student's seeing the STM opportunity as a time to mature personally and to prove themselves worthy of respect and responsibility.[14] Still others have an "eclectic lifestyle and diversity," and are globally aware and cause-oriented.[15] Related to the latter, Edwin Zehner's assessment of STMs from North Americans examines the opportunities' rhetorical appeal to participants. He notes that motivations for missions in general and STMs in particular among the evangelical community have shifted dramatically in the past half century, away from a focus on the proclamation of the gospel and toward humanitarian work.[16]

---

11. Robert J. Priest and Joseph Paul Priest, "They See Everything and Understand Nothing: Short-Term Mission and Service Learning" (paper presented at the meeting of the Evangelical Missiological Society, Minneapolis, September 2007), 4; cf. Robert J. Priest and Joseph Paul Priest. "They See Everything and Understand Nothing: Short-Term Mission and Service Learning," *Missiology* 36, no. 1 (2008): 53–73.

12. Livermore, *Serving with Eyes Wide Open*, 49.

13. Livermore, 50.

14. Robert J. Priest, Terry Dischinger, Steve Rassmussen, and C. M. Brown, "Researching the Short-Term Missionary Movement," *Missiology* 34, no. 4 (2006): 433–34.

15. Barna Group, "Despite Benefits, Few Americans Have Experienced Short-Term Mission Trips."

16. Edwin Zehner, "On the Rhetoric of Short-Term Missions Appeals, with Suggestions for Team Leaders," in *Effective*

Benefits from Short-Term Missions

Advocates of STMs suggest multiple benefits for those who participate. These benefits range from personal spiritual development to church growth to evangelism. But perhaps one of the most often publicized benefits of STMs is the personal social development of team members, including worldview expansion. A summary of a report by the Barna Group states, "Most people who embark on service adventure describe the trips as life-changing. In fact, three-quarters of trip goers report that the experience changed their life in some way."[17] Similarly, Chris Eaton and Kim Hurst in their book *Vacations with a Purpose* suggest that the participant is personally stretched, exposed to spiritual and human needs, enlightened by learning firsthand about the world, and encounters God through the experience of change and trust.[18]

Others suggest that a benefit of STMs is participants' discovery of their spiritual gifts, receiving ministry training, or growing spiritually. The expansion of participants' understanding of the global Church also increases enthusiasm for the so-called *missio Dei* ("mission of God"), both in the participant and the sending entity.[19] All in all, participants may be able to provide their sending church with a clearer understanding of the spiritual and physical needs of their fellow Christians around the world.

Another benefit of STMs is that they may be the means for individuals from a variety of underrepresented socioeconomic and ethnic backgrounds to experience other cultures. One survey of Christian college and graduate school students concluded that "compared to international tourism expenditures, or to study abroad, short-term missions is relatively inexpensive."[20]

Student participants may also be persuaded by their involvement in STMs to focus their studies toward vocational missions. For them, an STM experience can become a milestone in their preparation toward a life of service. While critiquing many STM practices, elder missionary statesman Robertson McQuilkin suggested that STMs may propel some participants to return long term to the mission field.[21] The question of translating STM participants into career missionaries has remained at the forefront of serious discussions over STMs, and it has been noted as a common factor in increasing both full-time and part-time missions staff.

Participants are not the only beneficiaries of STMs. Host missionaries, churches, and communities may also profit from their interaction with STM participants. McQuilkin suggests that thoughtful STM teams can serve to reinforce the work of career missionaries.[22] That reinforcement may come in the form of

---

Engagement in Short-Term Missions: Doing It Right!, ed. Robert J. Priest, EMSS 16 (Pasadena, CA: William Carey Library, 2008), 187.

17. Barna Group, "Despite Benefits, Few Americans Have Experienced Short-Term Mission Trips."

18. Chris Eaton and Kim Hurst, *Vacations with a Purpose* (Elgin, IL: David C. Cook, 1994), 24–26.

19. Peterson, Aeschliman, and Sneed, *Maximum Impact Short-Term Mission*, 233–36.

20. Priest and Priest, "They See Everything and Understand Nothing," 3.

21. Robertson McQuilkin, "Six Inflammatory Questions: Part Two," *EMQ* 30 (July 1994): 259–60.

22. McQuilkin, 259.

physical assistance such as building projects or literature distribution, personal encouragement through spiritual fellowship and prayer, professional development, and community engagement.

From their interviews with missionaries around the world, Enoch Wan and Geoffrey Hartt collected an extensive list of benefits. Some of the benefits delivered by STM participants are as follows:

- Delivering resources to the field
- Extending a long-term missionary reach
- Providing access to areas restricted to missionaries
- Providing encouragement to the long-term missionary staff
- Providing support for the missionary kids
- Meeting physical needs
- Providing administrative support
- Enabling evangelism at public events closed to missionaries
- Contributing to the formation of new groups and sending networks[23]

Visiting STM teams may benefit host congregations in many ways, including helping them to build relationships with those from other cultures, affirming newer believers or congregations in their faith and ministry, and bringing them financial support and resources.[24]

Thus, STM has many positive benefits for participants to become involved, including self-reported personal and spiritual growth, worldview expansion, and greater involvement in the church, both local and global.

Critiques of Short-Term Missions

While admirable motivations and benefits in STM may exist, anyone involved should be able to identify the dangers and difficulties that affect participants, host missionaries, and host communities. STM cannot guarantee risk-free involvement, and it is possible to cause more harm than help via STM. Hosts, senders, and participants must weigh the drawbacks. The shortcomings can be found in critical appraisals from proponents of STMs, missionaries, and sociologists alike. The majority of the critiques below focus on the difficulties encountered by and because of participants.

General STM Shortcomings

One example of a comprehensive critique of STM comes from Richard Slimbach, a sociology professor who has long been an advocate of cross-cultural learning. At a gathering of missions practitioners in the United States, Slimbach summarized the concerns of multiple researchers. Among his concerns was that a trip of less than two weeks "allows participants to have only transitory and nonrepetitive

---

23. Enoch Wan and Geoffrey Hartt, "Complementary Aspects of Short-Term Missions and Long-Term Missions: Case Studies for a Win-Win Situation," in *Effective Engagement in Short-Term Missions: Doing It Right!*, ed. Robert J. Priest, EMSS 16 (Pasadena, CA: William Carey Library, 2008), 96.

24. See, e.g., Robert J. Priest, "Peruvian Protestant Churches Acquire 'Linking Social Capital' through STM Partnerships," *Journal of Latin American Theology* 2, no. 2 (2007): 181–87.

encounters with locals, and to acquire only a superficial and usually stereotypic view of community culture."[25] Large teams, majority white participants, lack of cultural training, and participants' egoistic expectations were other concerns that Slimbach raised.

While applauding STMs for their strong spiritual impact on the participants, Robertson McQuilkin focuses on where the philosophy of STM may be weak. Because of its temporary nature, STM is not valid, he says, for finishing the task of world evangelism or for fulfilling one's call to missionary service.[26]

Another censure of STMs is the extensive financial cost involved in sending teams. Some have stated that STMs are guilty of jeopardizing the funding of long-term missions. One study cited a missionary host as saying, "If participants are not 'properly and thoroughly prepared and trained,' STM is a waste of time and money and may cause serious harm to all."[27] Another study noted the critique of a Peruvian pastor about the cost of sending an STM team to Peru: "If they sent us the money they spend on their international travel, we could build more churches, feed more children, train more pastors."[28]

Shortcomings of STM for Participants

One especially potent critique of short-term missions is that the motivation of many participants is solely to derive the personal benefit of the experience, with little or no consideration of the impact on the receiving community or the ultimate purpose of missions. STM structures often permit participants to go to the field in spite of egocentric motivations, negligible culture and language skills, or incompetent leadership. For some participants, trips result in little more than braided hair, souvenirs, pictures with dark-skinned children, and stories of strange foods and bathroom facilities.[29]

Participants may view these STMs as an opportunity to travel and fill some sort of void in their lives. Slimbach, in his paper "The Mindful Missioner," concludes that the high volume of STMs is due to the rise of the simplified tourism industry, increased wealth in the Church, more awareness of the world's pain, and the West's shift from a production to a consumer society. The latter contributes to an expanding craving for "peak experiences."[30] For some participants, STM trips are an adventurous alternative vacation, and they are even advertised as such.

---

25. Richard Slimbach, "Short-Term Missions by Many Other Names" (paper presented at the meeting of the Evangelical Missiological Society, Minneapolis, September 2007).

26. McQuilkin, "Six Inflammatory Questions," 258–59.

27. (Paul) Kim Doosik, "Intercultural Short-Term Missions' Influence on Participants, Local Churches, Career Missionaries, and Mission Agencies in the Presbyterian Church of Korea (Kosin)" (PhD diss., Reformed Theological Seminary, 2001), 136.

28. Hunter Farrell, "Short-Term Missions: Paratrooper Incursion or 'Zaccheus Encounter'?" *Journal of Latin American Theology* 1, no. 2 (2007): 72.

29. Christopher Heuertz, "A Community of the Broken," *Christianity Today*, September 5, 2007, https://www.christianitytoday.com/biblestudies/articles/evangelism/070905.html, para. 10–11.

30. Richard Slimbach, "The Mindful Missioner," in *Effective Engagement in Short-Term Missions: Doing It Right!*, ed. Robert J. Priest, EMSS 16 (Pasadena, CA: William Carey Library, 2008), 158.

Even if their own personal growth is the purpose behind participation, some research indicates that mere weeks post-trip, many participants experience little or no significant change following their STM. Through his study of two hundred North Americans who participated in a weeklong building project in Honduras, sociologist and former missionary Kurt Ver Beek challenged the concept of any tangible or intangible impact on the participant.[31] Likewise, Cultural Intelligence researcher David Livermore has demonstrated that short trips leave little long-term impact on participants.[32]

Perhaps such quick degeneration of the STM impact is a result of poor training and inadequate leadership. Miriam Adeney cautions that training is essential because many short-term workers may "have a heart for the Lord, but only a sketchy knowledge of Scripture, little experience in evangelism or apologetics, and a lackadaisical practice of spiritual disciplines."[33] Echoing Adeney's concerns, Robert Priest examine a failure to adequately train leaders: "While youth pastors are typically expected to lead STM, sometimes on an annual basis, nothing in the curriculum of most seminaries is oriented toward instructing youth pastors in what is needed for STM."[34]

Finally, by way of summarizing some of the negative impacts of STMs on participants, Alex Smith provides an excellent list of the "concerns, dangers, and warnings for the future" of STMs:[35]

1. Short-sighted convenience without long-term commitment—inadequate personal vision
2. Self-centered individualism without deep altruistic concern for others—false focus
3. Instant gratification without distant responsibility—questionable motivation
4. Intense activity without deliberate purpose—lacking significant eternal goals
5. Social service participation without evangelistic proclamation—short-circuited outcomes in spiritual duty
6. Immediate satisfaction without eternal consequences—fuzzy ultimate expectations
7. Humanistic self-sufficiency without theological reflection and analysis—unevaluated self-dependency

Shortcomings of STM for Hosts

Another critique of STMs is the negative impact that a team's presence and performance may have on the life and ministry of the host missionary. The STM team will definitely cause a disruption in the normal flow of life and ministry for the missionary, and it may,

---

31. Kurt Ver Beek, "Lessons from a Sapling: Review of Quantitative Research on Short-Term Missions," in *Effective Engagement in Short-Term Missions: Doing It Right!*, ed. Robert J. Priest, EMSS 16 (Pasadena, CA: William Carey Library, 2008), 408–74.

32. Livermore, *Serving with Eyes Wide Open*, 70.

33. Miriam Adeney, "McMissions," *Christianity Today* 40 (November 11, 1996): 14–15.

34. Priest, "Peruvian Protestant Churches," 9.

35. List reproduced from Alex Smith, "Evaluating Short-Term Missions: Missiological Questions," in *Effective Engagement in Short-Term Missions: Doing It Right!*, ed. Robert J. Priest, EMSS 16 (Pasadena, CA: William Carey Library, 2008), 56–57.

in fact, through cultural or political blunders, actually damage the reputation and status of the missionary. Likewise, team complaints and conflicts may discourage the hosts. Without proper planning, team orientation, and adequate leadership, the strength of the host missionary can be depleted by caring for a group of short-term workers.[36] I am a missionary myself, who at one time hosted STM teams in a remote location. I can attest to the sense of physical relief occasionally brought about by watching the last boat of STM workers pull away from the beach.

The missionaries are not the only ones affected by STM participants. The entire host church may find that the planning and hosting that STM groups require distract from their true mission.[37] STMs can also create financial dependency within the national church by an influx of foreign money.[38]

The STM team can have a negative impact on the host community. Confusing religious communication is only the beginning of possible challenges presented by an influx of temporary foreign workers. Host churches and communities in the developing world may also struggle with residual financial dependency, visitors' paternalistic attitudes, and displaced local labor. In addition, the short duration of STMs may create a spiritual vacuum if no follow-through discipleship is provided.[39]

Conclusion

The world needs to know Jesus, and He has chosen to use His people as one of His primary instruments of making Himself known. Although short-term ministries have not been commonly deployed until the latter half of the twentieth century, the rapid growth and challenges of these trips requires careful attention. As those who travel under the Christian banner, and thus represent Christ in their activities, participants must be especially alert to their motivations for and the dangers of short-term missions. Millions of people are physically, emotionally, and spiritually impacted annually—for better or for worse—by participating on a team, sending a team, or hosting a team. The literature on STMs, at both the popular and scholarly level, must continue to caution and inform participation, as well as encourage proper training of teams to minimize their negative impact and to have more positive interactions with the world that needs to know Jesus.

---

36. Robert Yackley, "When the Saints Go Marching In," *EMQ* 30, no. 3 (1994): 302–7; JoAnn Van-Engen, "The Cost of Short-Term Missions," *The Other Side* 36 (January–February, 2000): 22.

37. Farrell, "Short-Term Missions," 72.

38. Farrell, 73; Adeney, "McMissions," 14–15.

39. Rolando Cuellar, "Short-Term Missions Are Bigger Than You Think: Implications for the Local Church," in *Effective Engagement in Short-Term Missions: Doing It Right!*, ed. Robert J. Priest, EMSS 16 (Pasadena, CA: William Carey Library, 2008), 282.

CHAPTER 66

Difficult-to-Access Ministry Trips: Principles from the Alaskan Bush

Nathan Schneider, with Jeff Crotts and Randy Karlberg

Alaska, the "Land of the Midnight Sun," presents unique challenges for churches endeavoring to engage in missionary efforts to the region. Despite Alaska's rugged mountains, pristine lakes, and trophy hunting and fishing, arctic living is not easy. The long, cold, dark winters take their toll on even the most resilient in spirit and often lead to a sense of isolation and depression. Despite nearly two centuries of attempts, the vast arctic wilderness known as the Alaskan bush remains largely an unreached mission field.

Around two-hundred fifty villages dot the remote wilderness. Each village is distinct, influenced by geography, climate, and a variety of indigenous cultural heritages. A strong relational network transcends layers of indigenous differences, making the bush "a very big small place." Grace Christian School (GCS) in Anchorage, Alaska, has engaged the indigenous populations of Alaska for more than twenty years by sending teams of students and faculty to interact evangelistically with children in remote village schools by bush plane. Most of Alaska has no road access, so the challenges of reaching these isolated communities mirror difficulties missionaries face globally when trying to reach difficult-to-access locations.

Nearly twenty-five years ago, a GCS teacher received a distressing call that three teenagers had committed suicide in a remote village that was already facing endemic issues like alcohol abuse,[1] domestic violence,[2] and depression among its youth. The remoteness of

1. In fact, a 2008 report published by the CDC found that roughly 11.7 percent of Native American and Alaska Native deaths could be tied to alcohol use, a figure nearly three times that of the US in general. T. S. Naimi, et al., "Alcohol-Attributable Deaths and Years of Potential Life Lost Among American Indians and Alaska Natives—United States, 2001–2005," *Morbidity and Mortality Weekly Report* 57, no. 34 (August 29, 2008): 938–41, https://www.cdc.gov/mmwr/preview/mmwrhtml/mm5734a3.htm.

2. According to a 2016 study by the Department of Public Safety, 54% of sexual assault victims in the state were Alaska Native, an astounding figure considering only 20% of the state population is native. Of these assaults, 47% of the alleged attackers were

the village and its small size and close familial relationships compounded the acute impact felt by each village member. The caller asked if GCS could come give the children of the village hope. A couple of teachers and several students quickly took two small bush planes to the village. This early journey knit a deep, trusting, and long-lasting relationship that has spread to a network of ministry opportunities in more than ten Alaskan villages. Now the student missions ministry sends teams to as many as six villages in a season. The principles gleaned have wider implications beyond Alaska.

Building and Gauging Trust

Several factors contribute to building trust among populations and gaining a hearing for the gospel. First, the teammates' steadfast commitment to visit the villages has led to strong bonds of trust with the local people, especially for those residents who remember teams coming as far back as their childhood. The ongoing regularity of the visits have fostered deep, trusting relationships. Second, the teammates' willingness to perform practical tasks like tutoring students, organizing the village school library, and playing with the children at recess continues to break down barriers of foreignness and benefits the village, which endears the team to the residents. When suspicious or cynical residents see a team of outsiders working together for the betterment of the village and

especially of the children of that village, they soften and relational equity is built. The path toward gospel evangelism involves a willingness to serve, meet needs, and offer hope.

Trust exists on a continuum, built slowly, broken quickly—particularly in cross-cultural missions. Twenty years of GCS's ministry to rural Alaska villages has given some key indicators of when a threshold of trust has been reached with the local people. Across cultures, one thing that all parents have in common is protecting their children, so one sign of trust is when people allow their children to be in the care of teammates, particularly for personal and group interaction. Many government-funded village schools allow the team to speak at secular assemblies during school hours on themes such as social media and cyber-bullying, the dangers of drugs and alcohol, and the importance of friendship. After school hours, village leaders allow the team to invite students and the community back to the school for a time of open gym, games, crafts, and skits that weave in the gospel message and related themes. Students from the team share their salvation testimony each night during their stay in the village, often resulting in vulnerable and honest conversations and the gifting of Bibles to students who are interested in receiving one of their own.

A second indicator that a threshold has been reached in building relational trust is when

Alaska Native as well. It's generally accepted as fact that these crimes are grossly underreported. In rural Alaska, the victims are frequently younger in age, with 14-year-old girls being the most common victim, and the assailant most likely someone she knows. Alaska Criminal Records and Identification Bureau, *Felony Level Sex Offenses 2016: Crime in Alaska Supplemental Report*, October 26, 2017, https://dps.alaska.gov/getmedia/0637d6db-11f0-4d61-88a9-2d94a8e48547/Felony-Level-Sex-Offenses-2016.

invitations arise to participate in those activities the villages deem most significant and intimate for community life. A GCS team was invited on one occasion to participate in a funeral and subsequent meal celebration, reflecting the honor and respect the village leadership gave to their visitors. On another occasion, one team leader was invited to join the community in a whale hunt, a centuries-old tradition among coastal native communities that only Native Alaskans are legally allowed to undertake. The hunt was a success, and the joy of the village was palpable as they shared the plentiful meat with the whole community and the team. Such invitations are rare privileges for outsiders that evidence real relationships and signify the kind of earned trust that will facilitate gospel conversations.

Principles Learned

Grace Christian School has found great success using teams of students and faculty to reach cross-culturally into rural Alaska Native communities, with the student-to-student ministry being the central feature of this outreach. Not all ministries face the same circumstances and challenges when attempting to establish relationships for the gospel with difficult-to-access indigenous communities across cultures, languages, and people groups. Nevertheless, some transcultural principles warrant consideration.

First, teams need to understand there is no substitute for developing long-term relationships. People, not activities, are the focus of ministry. Given how difficult it can be to access rural communities, future trips aren't guaranteed. Repeated visits give village leaders confidence in the team's care and trustworthiness and help the team sense the "long game" of gospel ministry—building trust with the local people as the Lord opens doors for the clear proclamation of salvation in Jesus Christ.

Second, teams should be willing to embrace creative means of gospel outreach. Each member of the team must be willing to address physical and spiritual needs with innovative, flexible methods. No two villages share the same needs, so there are often an array of opportunities to provide some kind of teaching, whether through dramas, sports, counseling, tutoring, or cooking and providing maintenance services for the villagers. With an adventuresome spirit, the teammates will discern the needs on the ground and consider how to address them and leverage them for displaying and discussing the gospel message of Christ, the ultimate Helper.

Third, teams must resist one-size-fits-all approaches to missions. Each local community has its own cultural values, traditions and practices, ethnic and tribal roots, and lifestyle factors that are influenced by the social and natural environment in which they live. Thus, each ministry target needs a specially tailored ministry plan so that the team can engage the people distinctly and meaningfully. Teams might find, however, that there are cultural and social elements that transcend local differences and bind the larger native peoples of a geographic area together in a way that will help to develop a larger village missions strategy. Some examples of commonalities include the value placed on family and children, and the pride taken in upholding and passing down native traditions. Similarly, many share features of nature and ancestral worship found in traditional spiritism; some might have syncretized with foreign works-oriented religions, such as the Roman Catholic and Russian Orthodox churches that pepper the Alaskan bush; and still others might have succumbed to the sweeping dangers of prosperity gospel movements.

The Future of Successful Short-Term Ministry Trips

After laying the years-long groundwork to build trusting relationships with rural communities for the sake of the gospel, short-term ministry teams to the Native Alaskans have asked the question that faithful pioneer missionaries have always come to ask: "What now?" The answer today is the same as it has always been: raise up an indigenous expositor of the Word of God in every village. The faithful pastoral ministry of a trained biblical expositor is the one solution that promises long-lasting and deep-impacting results. The power for true gospel transformation and long-term impact comes when an indigenous man is trained to rightly and accurately explain the Scriptures to his own people and shepherd them in the knowledge of Jesus Christ by the word of truth.

Short-term ministry teams, like those to the remote Alaskan bush, recognize that there is no overarching, surefire strategy to winning people from their native communities to Christ. Salvation is an individual, independent work of the Holy Spirit, which happens in the Lord's time, in the Lord's way. Yet, as God opens up opportunities to build relationships and people are saved through gospel proclamation, the activity of the short-term team shifts to working with long-term missionaries to identify a man from the local village who can be trained and equipped to handle God's Word for gospel ministry in his community over the long term.

The challenge before Christ's churches in Alaska is to find a pathway for equipping the man they identify so that he is trained in expository preaching and instructed in sound doctrine and able to minister in an existent church or plant a new one. Short-term ministers and the churches that send them must pray that the light of the gospel will shine in each individual village like a single pinprick of light on the map until the landscape is alight with the preaching of God's Word. As the authority of Scripture takes root, the Lord will bring His mission to completion in "the Last Frontier" of Alaska and all other difficult-to-access locations worldwide.

SUB-SECTION 2: MISSIONS PARTNERSHIP STRATEGIES

CHAPTER 67

Can We Work Together? A Biblical Theology of Collaboration

James Harmeling

In 1997 the World Evangelical Fellowship Missions Commission published the results of an extensive research project on the growing rate of missionary attrition. While factors differed with missionaries sent out from different nations, it was clear that unresolved conflicts between missionaries was the leading cause of their departure from the field, especially those sent from the United States.[1] Human depravity inevitably causes dissension among fellow believers working together on the field. Paul Akin, working with the International Mission Board of the Southern Baptist Convention, illustrates missionary dissension with a math equation: "Sinful people + work with other sinful people + those people trying to witness to and reach other sinful people = lots of sinful people and potential for conflict."[2]

"Collaboration," in Scripture, relates God's work of redemption to His commission for His people. People "co-labor," or work together, to accomplish something, which is why the apostle Paul describes Epaphroditus as a "fellow worker" (*synergos*) in the gospel (Phil 2:25). Effective collaboration requires human relationships, not merely mechanical methodologies.

---

1. Peter W. Brierly, "Missionary Attrition: The ReMAP Research Project," in *Too Valuable to Lose: Exploring the Causes and Cures of Missionary Attrition*, ed. William D. Taylor (Pasadena, CA: William Carey Library, 1997), 85–103.

2. Paul Akin, "The Number One Reason Missionaries Go Home," IMB, May 25, 2017, https://www.imb.org/2017/05/25/number-one-reason-missionaries-go-home/.

Therefore, the application steps highlighted in this chapter for building strong working relationships in ministry and mission endeavors should be viewed as practical wisdom that is recommended but not commanded for use.

The Biblical Basis for Collaboration

The Bible depicts the triune God—Father, Son, and Holy Spirit—as acting according to the single divine nature (Deut 6:4; Isa 46:9). Those whom God redeems must seek to be aligned in unity of will and purpose to bring Him glory. Collaboration happens when the people redeemed by God's Son work together to accomplish the will of God the Father through the power of God's Spirit. Therefore, the foundation of a biblical theology of human collaboration is the will and work of God.

Human involvement in fulfilling God's Great Commission reflects the work of the triune God in revelation, creation, redemption, and sanctification. The Christian continuance of God's work to glorify Himself in His revelation, creation, redemption, and sanctification requires partnership and collaboration. God works through redeemed humans to operate in union to accomplish His purpose of unfolding and fulfilling His plan of redemption across the world. This purpose may incorporate specific areas of ministry, such as foreign missions, theological training, and leadership development, but the result of collaboration is always that God receives the glory.

Revelation

God's revelation to humanity came progressively over time, as revealed in the Old and New Testaments. He chose to make Scripture a collaborative effort of various men prepared and inspired by His Spirit to write down His eternal truth, utilizing their personalities and language abilities. Second Peter 1:20–21 makes it clear that the Bible was not merely an invention of one man's imagination or some fabricated narrative through a single human editor. Multiple men contributed to the writing of the completed canon, sovereignly superintended in the writing process by the Holy Spirit, the divine author of Scripture. Even some books like Psalms and Proverbs are collaborative works with multiple human authors, by the Holy Spirit's design. Furthermore, God continues to require collaboration in bringing His written revelation to bear today, specifically through a plurality of elders who minister to the local churches, so that the flock of God obeys the commands of Scripture (1 Tim 3:2).

Creation

God created everything, and His first words to humanity involved overseeing and perpetuating His creative work (Gen 1:26–28; 2:15). The man and the woman were to reproduce more humans and nurture the creation around them. God reiterated His creation mandate later to Noah after the flood (Gen 9:1, 7). God created life and calls humans to work together as His conduits to further its growth and diversity.

Redemption

God is the One who redeems. Humans cannot grant eternal life or provide adequate payment for sin. Nonetheless, God commissions humans to actively participate in His work of redemption by proclaiming the gospel. Jesus commissioned His followers to make disciples of all nations, who were to go out together and proclaim the truth of the gospel message, win converts, and teach them to obey Christ's commands (Matt 28:19–20). While the Holy Spirit empowers these ambassadors to accomplish this task successfully (Acts 13:1–4; 16:14; Rom 15:18–19; 1 Cor 2:3–5; 2 Cor 3:4–6), they were still called to perform it (Acts 1:8; Rom 10:14–15). The four Gospels and the book of Acts reveal that the ministries of the apostles and disciples, from evangelism to church planting, were team efforts. Ministry to and through the local church continues to require collaborative work today.

Sanctification

Sanctification is a work of Father, Son, and Spirit (John 17:17; 1 Cor 1:30; Eph 5:25–27; 1 Thess 5:23; 2 Thess 2:13; 1 Pet 1:2). The Holy Spirit inhabits and gifts the redeemed people of God so that they build up the body of Christ to mature manhood (Eph 4:4–13). The saints of God, empowered by the Holy Spirit, interact with one another and stimulate growth in Christ (Heb 10:24). Therefore, ministry in the local church is a collaborative work divinely designed to produce maturity in faith. Within the body of believers, the Spirit gifts men to form a leadership unit to oversee, model, and guide this sanctifying work (Phil 1:1; 1 Tim 3:1–13; Titus 1:5; Jas 5:14; 1 Pet 5:1–3).

How to Build Strong Collaborative Relationships

Strong, unified collaboration does not happen automatically. It requires constant effort. Paul challenges the church in Ephesus to be "diligent to keep the unity of the Spirit in the bond of peace" (Eph 4:3). The Holy Spirit unifies the redeemed in Christ, but because regeneration has not yet erased all sinful tendencies, believers must pursue the things that cultivate peace and edify the church (Rom 14:19). There are at least five categories to consider for maintaining spiritual unity in collaboration: conviction, character, communication, commitment, and care.

Conviction

Healthy collaborative efforts spring from proper mutual conviction. This includes conviction of the gospel's truth and the mission's importance. Working together is difficult if there is a question of conviction on central doctrinal truths and the importance of the work at hand. John begins his first epistle in memorable fashion: "What was from the beginning, what we have heard, what we have seen with our eyes, what we beheld and touched with our hands, concerning the Word of Life—and the life was manifested, and we have seen and bear witness and proclaim to you the eternal life, which was with the Father and was manifested to us" (1 John 1:1–2).

The apostle is about to write out a conviction that he shares with the other apostles. Each apostle was willing to die for the Word of Life, Jesus Christ. Such conviction that eternal life is found in Jesus bonds believers together. They work together on a shared mission because they must. God's revelation convinces them that to proclaim the gospel is God's will. Several questions about the conviction of co-laborers should be asked at the outset of working together with others in gospel endeavors.

1. Are those I am considering working with committed to God's glory, or do they seek their own agenda and promotion?
2. Do we agree on essential points of doctrine? Do we agree on our definition of the gospel? Are there areas of disagreement on any theological point that causes concern?
3. Are the disagreements of doctrinal conviction in some areas significant enough to prevent collaboration on ministry efforts?
4. Do we agree on the direction and goal of the mission?
5. Do we agree on the methods, timing, and values used to accomplish the goal?
6. Do we agree on the roles each person or ministry plays in the project or in ongoing ministry endeavors?

Leaders work together best when they take the time to examine and understand one another's convictions and calling from God. Paul and Barnabas agreed on the central mission of gospel proclamation, but they parted ways when it came to how they would execute that mission. Barnabas wanted to include his cousin John Mark, but Paul refused to consider him (Acts 15:36–40). This ended their working relationship even as they shared the same mission.

The grand collaborative effort of the twelve tribes of Israel sending a representative to jointly spy out the land of Canaan was ruined by a division of conviction. Ten tribal representatives did not believe God would help them overpower their enemies. Joshua and Caleb had confidence that God would deliver stronger foes into their hands (Num 13:1–14:10). This was a pivotal moment in that generation's existence. They were doomed to remain in the wilderness because of a lack of unified conviction of God's promise and power.

Ministry teams will be only as effective as the convictions they share and upon which they act. Leaders of collaborative efforts must focus on what they believe the Scriptures indicate as essential for sound gospel ministry.

Character

It is difficult to work with people if they cannot be trusted. Trust is built on standards of conduct as prescribed in Scripture. This is why Paul emphasizes the spiritual maturity of elder and deacon candidates (1 Tim 3:1–13; Titus 1:5–9). Their character sets the tone for local church purity and unity. There can be no harmony in a ministry or mission endeavor if the leaders are untrustworthy and suspect in their pursuit of godliness. Ephesians 4:1–2 highlights how the believer is to walk in a manner worthy of his calling in Christ, displaying humility, gentleness, patience, and forbearance.

Jesus constantly confronted the disciples' competitive spirit among themselves. He told them not to lord over one another like the pagan politicians of Rome, but to act like servants instead (Mark 9:33–37; 10:35–45; Luke 22:24–27). Their servant leadership set them apart as a group of apostles working together to proclaim the gospel (John 13:12–17, 34–35; cf. Acts 11:1–3ff.; 15:4–6ff.). When the consideration of the minister's character is minimized, selfish motives take over and teamwork suffers. Divisions and factions result.

The Corinthian church was a classic example of failed collaboration due to spiritual immaturity (1 Cor 3:1–7). The believers divided needlessly into factions, conforming more to the sinful world than to Christ. Paul called them to unity by denying themselves preeminence and lawful rights (6:1–8; 8:9; 9:1–23) and by pursuing one another's well-being (10:23–33; 12:4–7, 12–26; 13:1–13)—and they responded with repentance and obedience (2 Cor 7:5–13). In contrast, Paul commended the character of the Philippian believers and called them to further mimic Christ's humility (Phil 2:5–11) with selfless spirits that were concerned for others' welfare (vv. 19–24), demonstrating the willingness to sacrifice for the sake of another (vv. 25–30). For Paul, character was a key factor for ministry collaboration.

Noting Jesus' example of humility is critical when developing collaborative ministry efforts.

Humility is especially relevant when attempting cross-cultural cooperation.[3] Missionaries must make deliberate efforts to consider another's culture as valuable as their own. Western missionaries, who tend to have an aggressive task-oriented approach to ministry, find it a common struggle to value other cultures and priorities to the degree that they will partner equally with the redeemed people there. Conversely, those working with Western missionaries can struggle to appreciate the value of task focus that is brought to the team. Fruitful ministry relationships happen only when all involved humbly prioritize their partnership relationship and seek to be Christlike to one another.

Communication

Another essential for mission unity is clear and continuous communication. Since collaboration requires developing trusting relationships, communication is critical for each party to understand the other and to reinforce the value of each person's contribution. In Philippians 4:2–3, Paul charges the congregation to work together to resolve a conflict that had arisen between two women, Euodia and Syntyche, who were his former coworkers. While Scripture does not state the nature of their dispute, Paul does not remain silent on the issue. There was

---

3. See Mary Lederleitner, *Cross-Cultural Partnerships: Navigating the Complexities of Money and Mission* (Downers Grove, IL: InterVarsity, 2010), 34. She emphasized the importance of humility in listening to other believers from different nations and cultures instead of automatically criticizing them for their differences: "In order to work together well we need to listen to one another. We need to not only deeply grasp how our partners feel and what they believe but also take the additional step to understand why such feelings and beliefs are wholly logical within a given context. . . . If we never take that step, at some level within our hearts we will continue to demean how others think and function in the world. When it comes to money and cross-cultural ministry partnerships, a misunderstanding of individualistic and collectivistic worldviews is often at the heart of our most destructive ministry conflicts."

tension in their relationship, and everyone who interacted with them needed to address the communication problem and work through it. Paul does not passively hope the Philippian church would notice and deal with this divisive issue. Nor does he ignore it and hope that time would lessen its impact. He points it out publicly so that the congregation will solve the interpersonal conflict and advance together in gospel work, and so that future audiences will value peace-making communication.

Good interpersonal communication requires sensitivity to others and a selfless consideration of their preferences and needs. It is worth taking the time and making the effort to clarify any matters that might lead to interpersonal problems, whether that means providing instructions about how to communicate effectively as a team or voicing frustrations as they surface. Generally, it is better to overcommunicate about the relationship dynamics that might affect the team than to neglect the reality of communication breakdowns.

The following questions can help a team to define the collaborative relationship:

1. Do we agree on the end goal?
2. Do we agree on the path and process of achieving the end goal?
3. Have we clarified each party's roles in accomplishing the end goal?
4. Have we communicated which steps each party believes to be most vital in order to make progress?
5. Are we faithfully meeting our responsibilities and finishing our portion of the work? Are we faithfully staying in communication when other parties rely on us for next steps?
6. Have we identified and resolved potential disagreements or divisions?
7. Do we understand significant cultural expressions, both verbal and nonverbal, that communicate caution, disagreement, confusion, or frustration?
8. Have we consistently restated positively the worth of what each person brings to the collaborative effort?

As Paul calls for patience among the saints ministering together (Eph 4:1–3; 1 Thess 5:14; 2 Tim 4:1–2), so also mission work requires patience and perseverance. Missionaries tend to have strong personalities. Their toughness helps them adapt to foreign cultures and rebound from traumatic setbacks. This strength can also turn into a liability. It can create stubbornness of will and inflexibility in process, especially between fellow missionaries. Since frustrating conflicts often arise on the mission field, God's workers must manifest supernatural patience. Well-functioning team dynamics require time, forgiveness, and bearing with one another for the sake of peace (Col 3:12–15).

Commitment

Collaboration is difficult because of human weaknesses and sinful habits. Communication often misfires, or one party may neglect communicating entirely. Proverbs 10:26 presents a double comparison that emphasizes how damaging lazy and unreliable workers are to those who rely on them: "Like vinegar to the teeth and like smoke to the eyes, so is the sluggard to those who send him." They irritate others like smoke to the eyes and generate bitterness like vinegar on teeth. Collaboration is a tender garden of relational trust that requires tending, watering, and weeding. Collaboration implies hard work—it requires commitment, including encouraging sacrificial labor, setting realistic goals, and affirming effort even if there appears to be less giftedness on someone's part. All missionary enterprises are difficult projects that few can accomplish alone, so excelling in communicating with the team is essential to reach the agreed-upon goal.

Care

While ministry tasks are important, relationships are more important. Effective missionary teamwork must not only move forward to accomplish a worthy goal, but it must do so without sacrificing relationships in the process. Thus, co-laborers must care for one another both in heart and action. Care involves conflict resolution. Believers should nurture relationships over time and consider deeper heart issues that repeatedly provoke anger.[4]

The following questions should be regularly reviewed by the collaborators on a team:

1. Are we currently displaying a servant spirit and humble deference to one another?
2. Do we value our partners' priorities?
3. Do we value all contributions?
4. Are we keeping in contact after a project is complete? Does the relationship matter outside of accomplishing goals?

Conclusion

Christian relational harmony requires diligent effort, but the Holy Spirit has already made unity possible (Eph 4:3). Failed attempts at collaboration should not cause believers to despair of ever finding any fruitful co-laboring in the fields of harvest. God calls believers to work together. Therefore, with careful, hopeful partnerships, believers can accomplish God's will by His power for His glory.

In Ephesians 3, Paul reveals the "mystery" of Christ that confounds all human wisdom—unity in the body of Christ. Part of the mystery is that people can get along with one another who have no earthly reason to do so. In Christ both Jew and Gentile are bonded in a positive working relationship through the transforming power of the Spirit of Christ (3:1–6). No human power can accomplish this level of collaboration. This is why Paul concludes the chapter by bowing his knees before God in joyous praise. In verses 20–21 he proclaims, "Now to Him who is able to do far more abundantly beyond all that we ask or understand, according to the power that works within us, to Him be the glory in the church and in Christ Jesus to all generations forever and ever. Amen."

---

4. The opposite approach is the law court model of conflict resolution, which exposes believers to open shame and dishonors Christ. Alfred Poirier, *The Peacemaking Pastor: A Biblical Guide to Resolving Church Conflict* (Grand Rapids: Baker, 2006), 12–13; cf. Ken Sande, *The Peacemaker: A Biblical Guide to Resolving Personal Conflict*, 3rd ed. (Grand Rapids: Baker, 2004), 53–56.

The Partnership Strategies of Paul, Apostle to the Outskirts

Chris Burnett

Missionaries like Paul long to proclaim the gospel of God's grace to sinners who have never heard it before (Rom 15:20–21). Paul's letter to the Romans not only unfolds the precious truths of the gospel, but it reveals Paul's heart for proclamation ministry to the outer limits of the known world. This insert will survey the ministry partnership strategies that Paul describes in Romans 15:14–16:27 that are necessary for pushing the gospel into farther territories of the Roman Empire. Paul's partnership strategies reflect the power of the gospel to unite people of different cultures and employ their gifts in collaborative service. These same strategies remain foundational to missionary partnerships today as the gospel moves to the outskirts.

The Foundation of Partnerships: Gospel Unity

The righteousness of God in the gospel applies to daily life. Paul argues from Romans 12 onward that in practical terms the gospel encourages believers to possess a unifying love that serves the body of Christ (12:3–21), it compels believers to extend love to those outside of the household of faith (13:8–10), and it motivates believers to remove stumbling blocks to fellowship and peace (14:13). Unity is both possible and expected because Christ has become the servant of both the circumcised and the uncircumcised, of the Jewish people, according to promise, and of the Gentiles, according to mercy (15:7–13).

In 15:14 and following, Paul applies the gospel principle of unity to his strategies for involving ministry partners in global missions to reach Gentiles farther out. He expects that the Holy Spirit is leading him to go to Spain (15:24). For Paul, pioneering missionary work is a biblical ideal and a personal ambition (15:20–21). Though he eagerly desires to travel such a distance with the gospel, along the way he hopes to enjoy some refreshing fellowship, finally in person, with the Roman believers to whom he writes, who can also assist him with missionary support for Spain (15:22–24).

The Substance of Partnerships: Gospel Unity on Display

First, however, Paul has to complete some unfinished business—bringing material aid to the Jerusalem church from the churches in Macedonia and Achaia (15:25–27). During a time of need due to a famine in Palestine, Gentile believers on one end of the cultural and salvation-historical spectrum took the opportunity to serve with their resources some believers on the other end of the spectrum and in a different region. A gift given and a gift received are clear, practical demonstrations of gospel unity between Gentile and Jewish believers that churches and nonbelievers can see with their own eyes. Paul needed to "put [his] seal on this fruit of theirs" (15:28) by delivering the gift, after which time he planned to come to Rome. The Roman church was invited to pray to God for this delivery as well as his deliverance from evil men (15:30–31). As they prayed, they were to consider how to be similarly fruitful for the sake of gospel witness by partnering with Paul to advance the Great Commission in

Spain. From Paul's perspective, money was not the issue—gospel partnership was.

The People of Partnerships: Gospel Unity in Action

In Romans 16, Paul gives a list of greetings to more than two dozen brothers and sisters who are partners with him for the sake of the gospel (vv. 1–16, 21–23). Every name in the list is a member of one of the house churches in Rome. Paul knows about half of them personally and is well acquainted with several others, either through brief interactions or by reputation—all before he has even set foot in the capital city.[5] Most of these believers are Gentiles and either slaves or freed slaves, or descendants of them.[6] Therefore, their names reveal a dynamic, multicultural, and socioeconomically diverse group of sinners who had individually been united with Christ and collectively united to one another in God's family.

An overarching logic to the list demonstrates the variety of Paul's gospel-centered partnerships.[7] In verses 3–7, Paul sends his greetings to his missionary coworkers who are currently in Rome and would have heard this letter read to them, legitimizing their

---

5. Thomas R. Schreiner, *Romans*, BECNT (Grand Rapids: Baker, 1998), 786–97; Douglas J. Moo, *The Letter to the Romans*, 2nd ed., NICNT (Grand Rapids: Eerdmans, 2018), 933–34.

6. James D. G. Dunn, *Romans 9–16*, vol. 38B, WBC (Nashville: Thomas Nelson, 1988), 900; Moo, *Romans*, 934–35.

7. The segments are stated in Schreiner, *Romans*, 789, and treated from 789–98.

role as co-ministers. In verses 8–15, Paul sends greetings to other believers whom he either knows personally or are friends of friends. In verse 16, he extends his greetings to everyone in the Roman churches as well as from the churches in the eastern Mediterranean region, which shows corporate solidarity with local churches wherever he has ministered.[8]

Paul's list bears witness to the gospel he preaches. By sending these greetings, and doing so in this order, Paul exhibits the spirit of unity that he has been instructing in the prior chapters of the letter. He even gives the common instruction that all who hear his words "greet one another with a holy kiss" (16:16; cf. 1 Cor 16:20; 2 Cor 13:12; 1Thess 5:26). In this way, believers everywhere must also practically demonstrate gospel unity and committed love to brothers and sisters in the faith who might come from very different social, cultural, and economic realities.

To Paul, gospel unity is practical, not theoretical—those who have been loved by God will show love in tangible, visible, reproducible ways, starting with meaningful greetings with words and actions, as demonstrated in Paul's warm greetings. They highlight the proper application of the gospel to real life: spiritual fellowship in the body of Christ is visible, beginning with intentional relationships and leading to productive partnerships for the gospel out in the world.

Nevertheless, Romans 16:17–20 shows that Christian affection is not to be extended or offered to those who work to undo the ministry of the gospel. Where there is no true gospel unity, there can be no true, effective partnership in missions. The danger of sin disrupting gospel unity is also why Paul exhorts the Romans in 16:19 to "be wise in what is good and innocent in what is evil." The more the gospel takes root in the body, the more Satan will try to strike against the heel of the Lord of the Church. So, to preserve their righteousness and gospel unity, Paul calls the Roman church not to be so simple-minded about evil that they do not know it when they see it. Regardless, "the God of peace will soon crush Satan under [their] feet" (v. 20).

Lessons from Paul's Partnership Strategies

Romans 15:14–16:27 reveals several lessons for ministry partnerships between local churches and missionaries with sending churches. First, biblical partnership strategies must be rooted in gospel unity, requiring discernment and protection from false and destructive partnerships. Second, to model gospel unity, biblical partnerships

---

8. Dunn, *Romans 9–16*, 899; Schreiner, *Romans*, 798.

must be practical, beginning with tangible expressions of mutual love and meeting material needs as they arise. Third, biblical partnerships should be sought after, because they will be used by God to demonstrate the power of the gospel before the onlooking world that only understands selfish desires and disunity.

Paul's letter depicts the real-world application of the gospel in reproducible ways: through public demonstrations of fellowship, by providing missionary support, and by meeting material needs in a timely fashion. What is needed to take the gospel to the outskirts is not a novel business or political partnership—it is unity in the gospel of Jesus Christ, shown in a willingness to welcome diverse believers in Christ, to support other churches, and to partner with missionaries for the furtherance of the gospel. With this paradigm for ministry partnership operative, the gospel will strengthen churches in different parts of the world (Rom 16:25), sinners in the outskirts will be led to the "obedience of faith" (16:26), and all the glory forever will go "to the only wise God, through Jesus Christ" (16:27).

CHAPTER 68

Cooperation and Separation: Partnership in the Gospel Strategically and Selectively

Tim Cantrell

One rightly wonders where global Christianity would be today were it not for gospel partnerships. The modern missions movement exemplifies the fruit of strategic ministry partnerships for the sake of the gospel.[1] Yet God's gift of cooperation has also been hijacked by Satan to cause untold harm, heresy, and ruin around the world. In the Old Testament, unholy alliances almost always ended badly for Israel and Judah (Exod 34:16; Num 25:6–9; Deut 7:1–8; Josh 9; 1 Kgs 11:2; 1 Kgs 22; Mal 2:10–16). In recent church history, ecumenical partnerships like Evangelicals and Catholics Together have weakened the gospel witness of the church.[2] In this age between

creation and new creation, partnerships will never be perfect, but they are necessary to fulfill the mission of the church effectively.

This chapter deals with ministry partnerships. These include interorganizational and interpersonal collaborations, particularly on joint ventures with the purposes of evangelism and discipleship, as well as other strongly related Christian projects, such as mercy ministry and education, to name a few. This chapter presents a biblical doctrine of separation and a model for classifying different categories of ministry cooperation so that partnerships will be God-honoring, lasting, and fruitful.[3]

---

1. Historically, entities like the London Missionary Society, the Church Missionary Society, and China Inland Mission primarily operated through the partnership of many local churches supporting them. Less formal partnerships like the Cambridge Seven, the Saint Andrews Seven, the Auca Five, and others demonstrate the power of partnerships between individuals as well.

2. Prominent American ministry leaders Charles Colson and Richard John Neuhaus cosigned the ecumenical document "Evangelicals and Catholics Together: The Christian Mission in the Third Millennium," as published in *First Things* 43 (March 1994): 15–22. For its recounting from a conservative evangelical perspective, see Iain H. Murray, *Evangelicalism Divided: A Record of Crucial Change in the Years 1950 to 2000* (Carlisle, PA: Banner of Truth, 2000), 215–49.

3. For a helpful treatment of the levels of separation and unity needed for Christian collaboration, see Richard I. Gregory and Richard W. Gregory, *On the Level: Discovering the Levels of Biblical Relationships among Believers* (Grandville, MI: IFCA, 2005).

The Doctrine of Separation

In John 17, in His High Priestly Prayer on the eve of His crucifixion, Jesus prayed for purity (vv. 6–19) before He prayed for unity (vv. 20–24). Separation from the world is a prerequisite for genuine unity in the body of Christ. Jesus' half brother James did the same, showing that unity is a fruit of purity and not vice versa: "But the wisdom from above is first pure, then peaceable" (Jas 3:17). The doctrine of separation and the doctrine of Christian unity are intertwined, since both involve defining Christian identity in Christ through unity around the truth of the gospel.

The biblical doctrine of separation arises exegetically from three categories of biblical imperatives: separation in the personal lives of believers, separation of the church from false teachers, and separation of the church from disobedient brethren. Separation at the personal level—fleeing from sin, temptation, and worldliness of all kinds in order to strive for Christlikeness (Rom 12:1–2; Eph 4:17–32; Phil 3:11–14; Col 3:5–10)—reflects the transforming power of the gospel in the life of each believer. That gospel-driven separation extends to the ecclesial level. Scripture calls the church to separate from false teachers because their lives and doctrines distort the gospel (Rom 16:17–19; Titus 1:10–14; 3:9–11; 2 John 1:9–11). Likewise, God's Word calls the church to separate from unrepentant members living in sin or willful error, denying the transformative power of the gospel in their lives and misrepresenting God's church to the watching world (Matt 18:15–20; 1 Cor 5:5–11; 2 Thess 3:6, 14–15). In each of these imperative applications, the gospel is the primary boundary issue driving the need for separation.

Beginning with a doctrine of separation can seem counterintuitive in the context of missions. Veteran missionary and missiologist William Smallman notes that "the high priority given to evangelism," especially in missions, often seems to push toward a minimization of biblical truth.[4] Alternatively, as David Doran has said, "Every great revival has drawn a line between truth and error. . . . Genuine gospel unity flows from genuine gospel separation."[5] Missions requires gospel unity over the content of the message preached. The proclamation of the truth necessarily entails a separation from doctrinal error.

A Model for Cooperation

God's Word gives His servants many reasons for effectively partnering together in the Great Commission. The New Testament Epistles attest to various levels of cooperation between local churches: financial cooperation for the sake of supporting Christians in need elsewhere (1 Cor 16:1; 2 Cor 8:1–7), theological cooperation to address emergent doctrinal issues that

---

4. W. Edward Glenny and William H. Smallman, *Missions in a New Millennium: Change and Challenges in World Missions* (Grand Rapids: Kregel, 2000), 216–17. A recent example of a popular book that turns the biblical option of collaboration into a moral requirement at the expense of doctrinal discernment is Neil Powell and John James, *Together for the City: How Collaborative Church Planting Leads to Citywide Movements* (Downers Grove, IL: InterVarsity, 2019).

5. David Doran, "Potential Pitfalls of Together for the Gospel," *9Marks Journal: Cooperation* (March–April 2008), republished on *Life Together*, February 25, 2010, https://www.9marks.org/article/potential-and-pitfalls-together-gospel/.

needed apostolic input (Acts 15:1–35), and missionary cooperation for the spread of the gospel (2 Cor 8:19).[6] Scripture therefore provides a framework for wisely thinking through ministry partnerships for different purposes.[7]

A model of cooperation built on Scripture's framework will represent levels of cooperation between churches, ministries, and individuals. It must above all keep ministry Christ-centered by requiring unity of belief in the gospel (Rom 1:16–17; 1 Cor 2:2; 15:3–4). In this way, the gospel itself has an initial, primary role in separation, ensuring that cooperation is gospel-bounded. Once this unity defines the boundary of all collaboration, the doctrine of separation can begin to emerge with regard to specific types of partnerships. Not all ministry partnerships require consensus on the array of potential ministry roles and responsibilities; partnerships such as Christian education, church planting and missions, church membership and deacons, pastoral training, and eldership. However, deep agreement on ministry matters makes for the strongest partnerships (Acts 20:27; Eph 4:13).[8]

The components of a gospel-bounded model of cooperation form concentric rings, much like a "bull's-eye" target. All biblical partnerships begin at the outermost ring of the bull's-eye, the boundary. But here it is suggested there are at least seven rings total of ministry cooperation that move toward the center.

Ministries more inward toward the center represent the deepening levels of commitment and collaboration required to accomplish their task. These seven rings can further be broken down into two segments. The outermost three levels represent cooperative ministries with parachurch and interdenominational church groups. The remaining four rings move further inward toward the center of the bull's-eye, representing partnership activities with groups of closely associated, like-minded churches, or within the local church itself. This gospel-bounded, Christ-centered model of cooperation is described below, beginning at the boundary and then moving inward according to the two segments of partnership.

The Outer Boundary

The line of demarcation that separates the ministries affiliated with the Church from the activities of the world is "the truth," which is "the faith" that has been "once for all handed down" to believers in Christ and in His Word (Jude 3). The content of the gospel forms a God-given barrier, a biblically established fence (Jude 3–4; 1 Tim 3:15; 2 Tim 2:15; 4:4). The Bible forbids Christians from "greeting" or "receiving" false teachers who deny the biblical gospel; such teachers are "to be accursed" (2 John 9–11; Gal 1:6–9). This necessarily precludes ministry cooperation with religious groups wanting to be

---

6. Tom Ascol, "Pastor's Forum: Are Denominations Worth It?," *9Marks Journal: Church and Churches* (March–April 2013), republished on *Life Together*, May 10, 2013, https://www.9marks.org/article/journalpastors-forum-are-denominations-worth-it-0/.

7. This section draws from the work of Scott Aniol, "Is It Wrong to Separate from other Christians?," *By the Waters of Babylon*, October 24, 2022, https://g3min.org/is-it-wrong-to-separate-from-other-christians/.

8. The "gospel-centered" paradigm has been very popular of late, but Scott Aniol gives a helpful caution. See Scott Aniol, "Unity and Separation," *By the Waters of Babylon*, November 5, 2021, https://g3min.org/unity-and-separation/.

identified as Christian, such as Mormons and Roman Catholics.[9] Outside of the biblical gospel, there is no Christian fellowship, unity, or ministry partnership (2 Cor 6:14–18).

All Christians will have non-Christian friends, neighbors, and fellow citizens of earthly nations whom they care for and want to reach for Christ (1 Cor 5:10; 10:27). Christians will also collaborate with them often in all kinds of temporal causes, such as pro-life advocacy or other good local, moral, or political causes (cf. Jer 29:5–7). However, partnering with unbelievers in ministry efforts, especially those who profess another gospel, ultimately only harms the work itself. Creeds, confessions, and catechisms have been written to explicitly define the faith and to defend gospel clarity from confusion with other gospels. Wise collaboration in ministry always starts with "guarding the gospel" (1 Tim 6:20–21; 2 Tim 1:12–14).

Segment 1, Rings 1–3: Parachurch and Interdenominational Relationships

Because believers have various opinions about different points of doctrine and the teaching of Scripture, unity can vary among believers who equally hold to the biblical gospel. In determining the appropriate level of cooperation between different Christians or different

ministries, understanding the purpose of the partnership helps classify whether disagreements on certain doctrinal or practical matters will affect the partnership. Of the seven rings that lead to the center of the partnership model, the first three rings are described below.

THE OUTERMOST RING: CHRISTIAN FELLOWSHIP

Anyone within the bounds of the gospel shares true unity with every brother and sister united to Christ by grace through faith (Eph 4:4–6). Amid this lost and lonely world of unbelievers, few joys light up the darkness like meeting other Christians. Relationships at the level of Christian fellowship are governed by the well-known phrase "In essentials, unity; in nonessentials, liberty; in all things, charity."[10] Since the goal of Christian fellowship is mutual encouragement, the degree of unity required to achieve it is low, as long as it is indeed grounded in the biblical gospel. Christian choirs, music and radio ministries, camps, and conference centers are examples of cooperatives in ring one.

THE SECOND RING: EVANGELISM AND MERCY MINISTRY

Christians from various denominations and doctrinal convictions may come together, convinced they can be more effective together

---

9. Regarding the false gospel of the so-called "Church of Jesus Christ of Latter-day Saints" (Mormonism), see Anthony Hoekema, "Mormonism," in *The Four Major Cults: Christian Science, Jehovah's Witnesses, Mormonism, and Seventh-day Adventism* (Grand Rapids: Eerdmans, 1963), 33–62; Walter Martin, "Mormonism—The Latter-day Saints," in *The Kingdom of the Cults*, 6th ed. (Minneapolis: Bethany House, 2019), 217–302. Regarding the false gospel of the Roman Catholic religion, see R. C. Sproul, "Justification," in *Are We Together? A Protestant Analyzes Roman Catholicism* (Sanford, FL: Ligonier, 2012), 29–50.

10. Attributed to Rupertus Meldenius (AD 1582–1651), with discussion in Schaff, Phillip, *History of the Christian Church* (Grand Rapids: Eerdmans, 1910), 7:650–53.

than separately, to help cases of urgent physical want. Missions history is filled with fruitful examples of Christian hospitals, orphanages, rescue missions, crisis pregnancy centers, emergency aid and relief, rehabilitation centers, and transitional living environments. All of these ministries were started because fellow believers shared a burden to "meet pressing needs" for the sake of gospel witness (Titus 3:14). Whether run under a denominational, associational, or parachurch structure, these endeavors should always direct new converts to faithful local churches (Acts 2:41–47).

THE THIRD RING: CHRISTIAN EDUCATION

In the face of increasingly aggressive, anti-Christian societies, the need is urgent for Christian families to unite for educating the next generation. This third ring of cooperation is largely concerned with worldview training and a foundational level of theological knowledge within a broader context of preparing young people to live lives that are pleasing to God and to be salt and light in the world (Matt 5:13–14). It may include topic-specific camps, seminars, and conferences, and formal studies that support the global advance of the gospel and its ministry in the local church, such as Bible colleges, seminaries, and divinity schools. However, while this level of cooperation supports Great Commission ministry, it does not require participants to agree fully on how local church ministry must be conducted.

Some churches and denominations can establish and govern their own grade schools or universities within their home states.[11] Yet, where that is not possible, Christians might find benefit in parachurch or para-denominational institutions with faculties unified around an orthodox statement of faith and with administrations holding to God-honoring organizational objectives. Many schools formally and closely ally themselves with like-minded churches through their board members, doctrinal statements, and bylaws. Others ally informally by sourcing their teachers and students from specific churches.

Besides schools, cooperation applies to other parachurch Christian educational ministries that bear fruit for the kingdom. Some examples may include publishing houses, Bible societies, Bible translation agencies, and certification and accreditation bodies. However, since missions is the job of the church, the ability of parachurch efforts to fulfill the Great Commission is limited to a supporting role. The local church is the only body that can baptize new converts, admit them to the Lord's Table, or remove them from Christian fellowship if unrepentant (Matt 16:13–20; 18:15–20; John 20:23; Acts 2:41–47). Parachurch ministries are intended to assist churches, but they can never replace the church or fulfill the church's God-given mission.[12]

---

11. For a helpful summary on the role of Christian education in the mission of the church and under the church's oversight, see Andy Chambers, "Christian Colleges—Accountable, Not Autonomous," *SBC Life*, September 1, 2002, https://www.baptistpress.com/resource-library/sbc-life-articles/christian-colleges-accountable-not-autonomous/. African Christian University, located in Zambia, is an active example; cf. "ACU Background," African Christian University, accessed June 18, 2024, http://acu-zambia.com/.

12. For a brief biblical defense of parachurch mission agencies, recognized as Christian "societies" with "committees," see William Carey, *Enquiry into the Obligations of Christians to Use Means for the Conversion of the Heathens in Which the Religious*

Segment 2, Rings 4–7: Local Churches and Closely Associated Churches

Beyond parachurch and interdenominational cooperation, four rings move further inward toward the center of the bull's-eye with increasing doctrinal unity. Because of the need for greater doctrinal and practical alignment to accomplish partnership activities at this level, local churches must collaborate with like-minded churches with whom they are closely associated.

THE FOURTH RING: CHURCH-PLANTING MISSIONS

The missionary heartbeat of any church starts with a passion for Christ and a compassion for lost souls—that is, a soul-winning focus on personal evangelism (Matt 4:19; 28:19; Acts 1:8; 8:4). But beyond evangelism, the Lord's Great Commission requires sustained discipleship in Him. Thus, in the book of Acts, the Holy Spirit's pattern for how the Great Commission would be fulfilled was made clear: churches planting churches. The Spirit directed the church at Antioch to send out Paul and others on at least three successive church-planting missions (Acts 13–20; esp. 13:2, 4). This shows that the church-planting mission penetrates beyond Christians and parachurch ministries partnering for evangelism and mercy (ring two) into the tighter, closer unity of partnerships within and between doctrinally aligned local churches (ring four).

While the preceding efforts in rings one through three are all important tasks for supporting Christ's commission or being an extension of His mercy to a watching world, biblically speaking they all take second place to planting churches. Establishing new local churches in new contexts is the most direct fulfillment of the Great Commission. Partnerships in this effort may come through more formal denominations and associations or through informal networks and interchurch relationships, and they will be voluntary partnerships.[13] For example, the church that sends out a church-planting team can often refer their missionaries to other like-minded congregations to partner with their mission through prayer, personnel, finances, and other resources too.

THE FIFTH RING: LOCAL CHURCH MEMBERSHIP AND DEACONS

Spiritual unity in the gospel is an awesome, unseen reality in which the Holy Spirit joins believers to Christ's Church worldwide by faith (Eph 4:4–6). That unity becomes visible only through full-immersion water baptism in the context of a local church (1 Cor 12:12–13, 27). New converts testify to the lordship of Christ in the waters of baptism and join the local congregation to labor side by side in the work of the

---

State of the Different Nations of the World, the Success of Former Undertakings, and the Practicability of Further Undertakings, Are Considered (Leicester: Ann Ireland, 1792), 82–84.

13. The biblical principle of local church autonomy requires that church partnerships in planting new churches not be forced. See treatment by Kevin Bauder, "Thoughts on Baptists and Independence," Central Baptist Theological Seminary, September 25, 2015, https://centralseminary.edu/thoughts-on-baptists-and-independence/.

gospel and discipleship. Elders should receive into membership only those believers with a credible profession of faith.

For Christians to closely join with one another in the ministry of the local church, they must make a robust commitment to the church's doctrine and to brotherly affection, including biblical peacemaking (Rom 12:10, 18). Jesus said the world will recognize Christ's disciples by their love for one another (John 13:34–35), which is radically different from how the world's cutthroat business partnerships operate (cf. Rom 12:1–2). A statement of faith, doctrinal distinctives, and historic confessions are helpful, biblical tools to guard the church's orthodoxy, and a church covenant can be a regular reminder of specific ways that Christ calls a church's members to love one another.[14]

The service ministries of local church deacons are designed to exemplify the impact that a blameless character and a consistent Christian example can make in the life of the local church (1 Tim 3:8–13). Because deacons can affect the unity of the congregation more widely than most members, a high degree of doctrinal agreement with the elders should be prioritized and expected. Some church leaders may appoint a man as deacon who could not serve as an elder, due to minor differences in doctrine. Yet because of his proven character as one who guards the unity of the church, he can still serve fruitfully.

THE SIXTH RING: PASTORAL TRAINING

Believers everywhere should praise God for the pastoral training institutions that have been bastions of biblical orthodoxy, such as Bible schools and theological seminaries.[15] Many academic programs worldwide have proven to be a powerful tool the Lord has used to train His chosen church leaders for the next generation. Nonetheless, God gave local churches the job of training the future leaders of the church (2 Tim 2:2; Titus 1:5), and training pastors requires a high degree of agreement and practical unity for the church leaders who train them. For this reason, seminaries best serve the church when they are under the close oversight, leadership, and accountability of partnering local churches with a high degree of doctrinal unity.

When it comes to nonacademic, church-based pastoral training, it is again wise for a training program to involve a network of churches and leaders with the combined total of many years of experience. To cooperate well in the training, each church can willingly donate their pastor's time, as part of his biblical calling to raise up the next generation of pastors (cf. 1 Tim 4:14; 5:22; 2 Tim. 2:2). The churches must also identify a number of biblically qualified, gifted men evidencing God's call into pastoral ministry. The ecclesial emphasis of pastoral training is itself an expression of hopeful cooperation: local churches make the effort

---

14. For an example from a local church in South Africa, see "Our Church Covenant," Antioch Bible Church, accessed June 18, 2024, https://www.antiochbiblechurch.org.za/our-church-covenant/.

15. On how these institutions advance the cause of missions, see Sunny Tan and Will Brooks, "Theological Education as Integral Component of World Mission Strategy," in *World Mission: Theology, Strategy, and Current Issues*, ed. Scott N. Callaham and Will Brooks (Bellingham, WA: Lexham, 2019), 184–90.

to raise up the future leaders of other local churches.

THE CLOSEST RING: ELDERS

When it comes to participation in ministry, the deepest level of spiritual unity must be found among fellow overseers in the local church. Elders are pastors, who are tasked with teaching and defending sound doctrine as a primary means of shepherding the blood-bought flock of Christ. To harm a church, Satan's first target is always its leaders. Because of the weight of spiritual responsibility entrusted to them, God holds elders to the highest standard in life and doctrine (Acts 20:28–31; 1 Tim 3:1–7; 4:6–16; 5:17–25; Titus 1:5–9; Jas 3:1; 1 Peter 5:1–3).

Churches that desire unity among their elders are often helped by a structured, formal ordination process, because through it their leaders can be trained for the role and then publicly recognized as qualified elders. The training and recognition process helps the church hold their leaders accountable to their solemn vow of shepherding the flock of God as a plurality of elders (1 Pet 5:1–4; cf. Acts 11:30; 20:17, 28; Jas 5:14). After marriage, the deepest level of human partnership known to Scripture is that of God's chosen men modeling Christian love and unity amongst themselves for the sake of the local church body.

Conclusion

The evangelical church is fragmented today by divisions of all kinds, biblical and unbiblical. Some separation can be avoided, but still a retrieval of the doctrine of separation is desperately needed for the sake of the gospel's clarity. This separation provides the foundation upon which fruitful ministry partnerships can be built, level by level, from a basic agreement on the biblical gospel to the deepest commitments in doctrine and practice. May the risen Lord equip His church in these dark days with heavenly wisdom and strength, so that it might shine the gospel's light to perishing souls as believers dwell together in unity (Ps 133:1).

The Conflicting Mission of the Church and Parachurch in India

Sammy Williams

The relationship between parachurch organizations and churches in India reveal missions that are too often in conflict. Despite the significant service to the church's mission worldwide, tendencies for the parachurch to diminish and eclipse the church's role in India have arisen. The following brief historical survey offers warnings about certain challenges along with biblical correctives.

Growth of the Indian Parachurch

Due to the vast number of groups and ideologies involved, it is difficult to summarize the parachurch in India. Yet, for simplicity, three strong trends are notable from the 1900s onward. The first is social movements. "To visit orphans and widows in their affliction" (Jas 1:27) has been integrated into most missionary efforts in India.

This was motivated by legitimate needs, as demonstrated by the abysmal life expectancy rate of just twenty-three years in 1901 nationwide.[16] The premier Christian medical college was founded in 1900, and now multiple missions hospitals and medical training centers exist, which have changed the lives of countless Indians throughout the years.[17] By 1947 there were more than 400 such hospitals and institutions in India, and in 1988 the number crossed 2,500.[18]

Other focuses in Indian social movements included the development of Christian schools and orphanages. Missionary schools helped to uplift the tribal and lower strata of society, and even contributed to the independence movement of India in the first half of the twentieth century.[19] Christian schools enroll 74 percent of the non-Christian Indian

16. Bhagawati Bagsmrita, Choudhury Labananda, "Generation Life Table for India, 1901–1951," *Middle East Journal of Age and Ageing* 12, no. 3 (October 2015), http://www.me-jaa.com/October2015/LifeTable.pdf.

17. "The CMC Story," Christian Medical College Vellore, accessed June 18, 2024, https://www.cmch-vellore.edu/content.aspx?Pid=P171127016.

18. Rama Baru, "Missionaries in Medical Care," *Economic and Political Weekly* 34, no. 9 (February 27–March 5, 1999): 523.

19. Rudolf C. Heredia, "Education and Mission: School as Agent of Evangelisation," *Economic and Political Weekly* 30, no. 37 (September 16, 1995): 2338.

student population and are still preferred for their academic standards today.[20]

A second trend involves social movements. The twentieth century saw many missions organizations focus on evangelism among college and university campuses. Only a few organizations were Western in origin, while Indian-led organizations have spread to all the urban college campuses of India.

A third trend is missionary movements.[21] In the 1950s a fresh breath of missionary interest blew through the Indian church, especially in the south. In 1954 the Indian Evangelical Overseas Mission was formed to encourage indigenous and international missions among Indian believers, sending its first missionary to Kenya. The effort was reborn in 1965 as the Indian Evangelical Mission. In 1954 young people involved in prayer cell groups became the nucleus of the Friends Missionary Prayer Band. They sent their first missionary in 1967. Then, in 1972 the group started a project to send missionaries to the eleven neediest states of North India.

Over the next two decades, vast growth took place in the number of interdenominational missions groups. New groups to arrive included the Church Growth Missionary Movement, the Fellowship of Evangelical Friends, the missionary arm of the Full Gospel Young Men's Association, the India Church Growth Mission, the Kashmir Evangelical Fellowship, and the Voice of the Gospel.

Some Challenges Arising from the Parachurch

In light of India's historical situation, challenges to the church-parachurch relationship that need to be addressed include social justice, ecumenism, and the church's prerogative to send missionaries rather than organizations. As for social justice, World Vision is among the top fifteen largest parachurch ministries in India in terms of annual revenue.[22] The purpose statement for their work in India reads: "Through development, relief and advocacy, we pursue fullness of life for every child by serving the poor and oppressed regardless of religion, race, ethnicity or gender as a demonstration

20. "Muslim Minority Schools Account for 22.75 Pc of Religious Minority Schools, Christian Community Schools at 72 Pc: NCPCR," *Times of India*, August 10, 2021, https://timesofindia.indiatimes.com/education/news/muslim-minority -schools-account-for-22-75-pc-of-religious-minority-christian-community-schools-at-72-pc-ncpcr/articleshow /85213596.cms.

21. The following information is drawn from a comprehensive list of missions, along with some articles on indigenous missions, in *Indigenous Missions of India*, ed. Roger E. Hedlund and F. Hrangkhuma (Madras: Church Growth Research Centre, 1980).

22. Cf. India Ministry of Home Affairs, *FCRA Annual Report 2009–2010: Receipt and Utilization of Foreign Contribution by Voluntary Associations* (New Delhi, 2012), 20, https://fcraonline.nic.in/home/PDF_Doc/annual/ar2009-10.pdf.

of God's unconditional love for all people."[23] Thus, the main priority in their projects is social welfare and upliftment.[24] This is representative of much of the parachurch work going on in the country. It is troubling that a large number of parachurch organizations pursue social justice work without at least stating a clear gospel-oriented purpose.

Another challenge that must be addressed is the dual priority of ecumenism and numerical growth. The early movements of the parachurch in India focused on developing unity across denominational lines. Bishop Azariah went to Edinburgh in 1910 to develop strategies for indigenization with Western ecumenical leaders Sherwood Eddy and John Mott. Dr. Mott formed the National Christian Council, which resulted in the historic creation of the Church of South India in 1947, the first unification of an episcopal church (Anglican) with nonepiscopal churches (Congregational and Presbyterian) since the Reformation.[25] One of the founding fathers of the likewise ecumenical Church Growth Movement, Donald McGavran, developed his principles through thirty years of service in India. He has influenced much of the emphasis on mass movements, people groups, and contextualization in modern missiology.[26]

A final challenge in India is the divorce of missions from the Church. In their desire to speed the process of sending out missionaries, most parachurch organizations mentioned above developed their own schools and reduced the emphasis on Bible training. Connected to less Bible training, the idea of a "sending church" was rare. The majority of the workers and missionaries were recruited directly by and were "sent" from the parachurch organization alone.

Biblical Correctives

The challenges raised above are not fatal. To fulfill the mandate given to the Church by Jesus Christ, the Indian church and its relationship to the parachurch can and should reform. Most fundamentally the Indian church should recognize that when the parachurch is at its best, it functions as a servant of the church. The word *parachurch*, though not a biblical term, comes from the Greek word *para* ("alongside") combined with "church." Thus, by name at least, such

---

23. "Who We Are?" World Vision India, accessed June 18, 2024, https://www.worldvision.in/AboutUs/who-we-are.aspx.

24. This is evident in their *World Vision India: Annual Report 2020–21* (Kodambakkam, 2022), https://www.worldvision.in/CMSAdmin/Uploads/WV_India-Annual%20Report-2020_2021.pdf.

25. C. B. Firth, *An Introduction to Indian Church History*, Christian Student's Library (Serampore, India: Christian Literature Society, 1961), 240.

26. See the full statement of McGavran's thesis in Donald McGavran, *The Bridges of God* (1955; repr., Eugene, OR: Wipf and Stock, 2005), 109.

ministries should only exist to enhance and highlight the ministry and primacy of the local church. Missions agencies are essential to facilitating the logistics of administration and finances of overseas work. But the benefit of the primary relationship of a missionary to his or her sending church(es) cannot be replaced (cf. Acts 13:2–4; 14:26–28).

Paul's methodology in Ephesus is instructive. He chose this major city center and established a church there over two years, focused on discipleship (Acts 19:1–9). He could then state that "all who lived in Asia" were reached with the gospel (19:10). What a powerful contrast from today's approach to missions! Paul saw the church as the primary missions center, and therefore the church's goal should always be to establish churches in key unreached cities through the deep, sustained, long-lasting work of discipleship.

Also, we must not let our hearts be enamored by the greater size or financial potential of parachurch ministries. The lesson of history is that they will all fade away after a season of usefulness, for only the church endures. Christ has promised to build His church (Matt 16:18), not the parachurch. A biblically minded missions philosophy must focus on the primacy of the local church both on the home front and in the field. Therefore, we must give the firstfruits of our resources and of our people to the work of missions that is committed to building the church of Jesus Christ.

Conclusion

Much work is left to be done in the Lord's vineyard of India. Parachurch organizations must come alongside local churches and church-sent missionaries to promote the proclamation of the gospel and the discipleship of believers. However, the history of these organizations in India warns of the dangerous trends of social justice, ecumenism, and misled missiologies challenging the church's mission rather than supporting it. Those involved in parachurch organizations must seek to employ the biblical correctives to these challenges so that they will be faithful to obey Jesus Christ in His mission of building the church.

The Strategic Role of On-Air Preaching in Hostile Contexts

Edward W. Cannon

The Far East Broadcasting Company (FEBC)[27] began in 1945 with the goal of taking the gospel to unreached peoples through radio waves. In their wartime experiences, the ministry founders saw the power of radio firsthand as it aided military efforts against an allied enemy. In the late 1940s, when the Chinese revolution expelled foreign missionaries and began persecuting Christians, delivering the gospel by radio quickly became the singular focus of FEBC. The company viewed each radio as a "portable missionary." FEBC erected powerful shortwave towers and began broadcasting. Soon millions were responding to God's Word as it was taught. Listeners were experiencing the life-transforming power of the gospel through radio. Over the years, the ministry expanded to the Philippines, Korea, Indonesia, and all across Asia. Today the network broadcasts in more than 150 languages in nearly fifty countries, all with the primary purpose of teaching the Word of God to the least reached.

Reasons for Preaching in Hostile Contexts

It is hard for many people to understand what it is like to live in countries that have no churches, no pastors, and no Bibles. But in the majority world, Christianity is either unknown, oppressed by other faiths, or even illegal. It is very dangerous to openly evangelize in many places. Even so, Jesus commanded His followers to make disciples of all nations, not just the ones that are easiest to reach (Matt 28:18–20). Radio signals are vital, as they can transcend government borders, radical opposition, and even difficult terrain.

The media that people use to listen to content varies from country to country and from culture to culture. The preferred platform in some places might be local FM

---

27. See "Great God, Great Mission: The Story of FEBC," FEBC, accessed June 18, 2024, https://www.febc.org/about/history/.

radio, whereas in others, short- or medium-wave broadcasts are needed. With the recent and ever-changing developments of social media platforms, understanding how to reach listeners is even more challenging. But broadcasting content into these difficult regions is only a small part of the challenge. The larger question centers upon what content to broadcast and how to do that most effectively.

Broadcasters around the world know what makes for exceptional radio. The most important thing is not the clarity of the signal, the quality of the voice, or even the platform of the broadcast. Those are all important aspects of radio, but successful broadcasters know that "content is king." FEBC has appropriated and customized that phrase: "Content is King when the King is the Content." With this approach, the goal is not just to have many listeners, or to broadcast programs people enjoy. Rather, the goal is to inspire listeners to follow Christ. Romans 10:14 is especially instructive for Christian broadcasters: "How then will they call on Him in whom they have not believed? How will they believe in Him whom they have not heard? And how will they hear without a preacher?" The task is clearly laid out. Jesus commands His followers to make disciples by "teaching them to keep all that I commanded you" (Matt 28:20). A broadcasting ministry therefore must endeavor to use all its expertise to produce faithful preaching of God's Word over a signal that people can hear.

Strategies for Preaching in Hostile Contexts

Broadcasters need to consider several important points to ensure that people in hostile environments can hear and understand the broadcasts. As noted, the message itself is the highest priority. People may not listen, however, if they do not trust the broadcaster, cannot clearly understand the speaker, or have no way to ask questions. In light of these obstacles, a broadcasting ministry would do well to establish three strategic pillars to enhance the ability to preach effectively into the most challenging settings.

First, the broadcast voice must be an indigenous one, speaking the local language in the local dialect. Many cultures are suspicious of foreign influences, so hearing someone from one's own culture engenders trust. Second, the broadcast must speak from a position of local awareness. Ministries that transmit widely will have Hindus, Muslims, Buddhists, and animists as their audience. Acknowledging what local people already believe about God and about the world is a critical element for effective on-air preaching.

Third, giving listeners the opportunity to ask questions and seek a better understanding is especially important in places of spiritual darkness. The ministry should be, in FEBC's terms, "close to the listener." When staff members are in local communities and networked with the local church, the broadcasters enhance their understanding of the culture. Encouraging and engaging with listener feedback through letters, phone calls, emails, texts, and social media will help prevent the broadcasts from falling on deaf ears.

Measuring Success

During its many decades of ministry, FEBC has diligently sought to evaluate the effectiveness of its programming. For many years the metrics were tracked through millions of handwritten letters from listeners in China,

Russia, and Southeast Asia. Current feedback comes from online apps and social media. It is helpful to sort the feedback by program type, whether music, devotional, or other programming related to the Christian life. Throughout the company's broadcasting tenure, people have responded consistently and overwhelmingly to the Bible teaching programs more than any other type. Thousands upon thousands have reached out to ask for more preaching. Such a spiritually hungry response is the mark of success that an evangelistic ministry should value the most. May broadcast ministries of all forms and ranges, for the sake of the Lord's commission, remain faithful to the goal of preaching God's Word until all have heard.

INSERT 68.3

Can You Find Me in the Forest? A Testimony of Media's Reach for the Gospel

Nathan Giesbrecht

More than a decade ago, I was in a state of absolute grief from a recent divorce and from the death of my father. To cope, I drank whiskey daily. I went to a psychiatrist,

who prescribed six different antidepressants, which never helped. I eventually stopped seeing my kids, and I moved in with a woman with a background in witchcraft. Since the antidepressants didn't work, I started adding narcotics and sedatives. The shame of abandoning my kids overtook me amid my self-pity, and after three years of neglecting them, I walked to the edge of a high cliff to jump off. However, I simply could not go through with it because I wanted my children to know that I never stopped loving them.

I got fired from my career as a speech and language pathologist because I was drunk and stoned almost every day. I took a job cutting fence posts on the overnight shift in the middle of the forest in British Columbia, Canada. I found an old cassette player and radio with no numbers left on the dial, and spent eight hours wiring up coat hangers to get some reception and keep myself awake at the saw. The only station I could get to play was some guy whom the broadcast announced as "unleashing God's truth one verse at a time." It was *Grace to You* with Pastor John MacArthur.

I had never heard anyone talk about sin before. I had known about hell but never that I deserved to go there—because God is holy and He demands perfect obedience from me. When the radio producer said, "We would like to send you a free resource," I grabbed a lumber crayon and scribbled the address on a cardboard box lid. Later that month, I was on drugs and fell asleep at the wheel, but in God's mercy, I passed out in the one spot in the forest where there were no trees. I woke up unharmed, and one of *Grace to You*'s free CDs that was sent to me had fallen out of the visor pocket, landing in my lap: "The Believer's Comfort in Christ's Return."[28] Amid my outright rebellion, the truth was falling into my lap.

One day the pastor was preaching from Ephesians 5:1–2: "Therefore be imitators of God, as beloved children, and walk in love, just as Christ also loved us and gave Himself up for us." He explained the atonement and that real love was sacrificial. On the other hand, I had only been selfish. I saw from this passage that I was guilty before God for forty years of sin—especially the sin of abandoning my children. Children who are loved by a good Father walk in that love because they imitate Him. But I could not imitate God. I needed rescue from my sin, and Ephesians 5:2 showed me the remedy for my problem. Jesus lived the perfect life that I had failed to live, and then He died in my place the death that I could not survive. The love of Christ overwhelmed me, and I fell to my knees, begged God to forgive me, and trusted Jesus to save me.

Immediately I sensed a need to make things right, especially toward my children.

---

28. The sermon has since changed titles in the *Grace to You* archives: John MacArthur, "The End of the Universe, Part 3," sermon 90-362, preached September 28, 2008, https://www.gty.org/library/sermons-library/90-362/the-end-of -the-universe-part-3.

I left the woman with whom I was living, telling her, "I'm going to get my boys." As I was running out the door, I also went to get my drugs, but instead I slammed the drawer shut and have never wanted another drug since. I told my ex-wife what Jesus had done for me, and I asked her forgiveness. She was not interested in reconciling, but she agreed to share custody of my sons. I eventually got my career back, and a year later I led a coworker to salvation in Christ. A year after that, she became my wife.

Soon I realized that the churches I was attending were not handling the Word of God and preaching the gospel like the radio preacher did. I became frustrated and wanted to become a part of the solution, so I contacted a theological seminary I knew I could trust. A few years later, I got to personally thank Pastor MacArthur for his faithfulness to preach Christ. He encouraged me to start seminary online in Canada. Within a few more years, my wife and I sold all our belongings to raise the finances for moving to The Master's Seminary in Los Angeles, California. The Lord provided all our needs through the undeserved love and support of His church. We have since moved back to British Columbia, Canada, to plant a church on Vancouver Island. Hallelujah, what a Savior!

There are at least two important lessons from my story for believers who desire to partner in strategic ways for the gospel,

as was the case with the sermon-recording ministry through which I was saved. First, when missionaries and church planters consider their strategies, they must consider that God often uses unorthodox and unpredictable ways to call His chosen lambs to Himself. No one could have imagined an old radio with no antenna, a lumber crayon, and a cardboard box lid to be some of God's means to bring the gospel to a lost sinner in the Canadian forest. Also, very often, people who are depressed, suicidal, and financially down-and-out are also "technologically impoverished." They cannot afford an internet-connecting cell phone or a service plan. Additionally, while the internet may go just about everywhere, its videos certainly do not reach the person who prefers a daily dose of drugs to a daily dose of social media. Only God can overcome these challenges, which is a reminder that God has strategies hidden from view, and they always turn out gloriously.

Second, there was no intentional strategy here by the radio ministry in my case. The preacher did not plan to reach a suicidal sinner in the forest of British Columbia—but God did. The preacher was faithful, and that is our call as ministers of the gospel: we preach Christ (1 Cor 1:23). Yet the reality is that God used many nameless ministry partners in my conversion, whom I hope to thank one day in heaven. Those involved in the sermon recording, the radio uploading and programming, the delivery of the CDs, and the donors who covered the international mailing expense, and so many more—they sought to be useful to Christ and faithful in the process. These many years later, I now join these faceless brothers and sisters as their partner, proclaiming the glorious gospel far away.

CHAPTER 69

Partnership Strategies in Africa with Local Leaders and Rural Communities

Thomas Hodzi

A rural community in an African context is like a family. Everyone knows everyone and shares most things, especially when facing hardship and challenge. Economically, most people struggle and rely on subsistence farming because jobs are scarce. In Zimbabwe, like many other African nations, most of the population lives in such rural areas. Most villages are difficult to reach and difficult to inhabit. Traditional pagan religions and poverty are prevalent. Thus, although "the laborers are few," there is potential for a plentiful harvest for the gospel (Luke 10:1–2; cf. John 4:34–36).

To gain inroads for the gospel in these contexts, outside ministries must first be accepted as a member of the rural community family. Every village is led by a village head, considered the father of that community. The authority of the village head extends to solving disputes, distributing land, and organizing any work that benefits the community. Above the village head is the village headman who reports to the chief. These traditional leaders are the custodians of their people, culture, and religion. Thus, a community's acceptance of an outsider is determined by whether their local leaders give approval. But missionaries must also diligently maintain and strengthen that familial relationship once gained. This includes strategically partnering with these leaders, sharing resources, and being present and available in time of need.

A ministry entering a cultural family in the above way can see it transformed into the family of God (John 1:12; 11:52; Eph 2:19; 1 Pet 2:9–10). The ministry does not enter to commandeer headship for itself, nor to provide it with material mercies only to leave it spiritually unchanged. But wisdom is needed for this. The present chapter, then, outlines partnering strategies for the missionary's engagement with local leaders and with mercy ministries in a way that truly advances the gospel and honors the Lord of the harvest.

Partnering Strategies with Local Leaders

Support of a community's leaders are essential for any ministry to remain long-term in the typical rural African village. A major challenge is that the local leaders are almost always unbelievers. Worldviews will inevitably clash when a missionary enters and remains. There will be a tension for the missionary between showing the leaders respect and remaining faithful in the gospel and in his testimony before the Lord Jesus Christ. Below are eleven strategies, learned over years of ministry in a Zimbabwean rural context, for engaging and maintaining partnerships with local leaders. These should be informed by a fear of the Lord and an effort to find favor in the sight of God and man (Prov 3:4; Luke 2:52).

1. Having a Local Contact

To gain access to a rural community, the missionary or ministry must be introduced to the leaders by a person of integrity within the village. Great care must be taken in selecting such a person, as their reputation may affect the ministry's future. This person can also serve as a sounding board to help the missionary detect undertones that he might miss in his communication, for the local contact is from the village and understands its dynamics.

2. Understanding Protocol and Relationship Dynamics

Due diligence in understanding the authority structure in the village is vital. The chief cannot be approached without showing honor to the village head, who reserves the right of making introductions up the chain to the chief. The local contact is also important to helping the missionary understand this and other protocols with traditional leaders before the first meeting. It is not uncommon for missionaries to be caught in a power struggle, since some leaders do not get along and already fight for power and recognition before he arrives. Missionaries ought not to go blindly into this dynamic.

There are two systems of authority: the cultural traditional authority, run by the chiefs, and the governmental authority, represented by councillors, members of Parliament, and other national officials. In theory these two systems are supposed to work together, but in reality they have separate demands. The missionary will have to appease both—for God gave them both authority—without compromising biblical teaching (Rom 13:1–5; 1 Tim 2:1–4; 1 Pet 2:13–17).

3. Managing Expectations

People not from the village are often met with suspicion and presumptuous expectations. Regarding the former, leaders have a commendable sense of responsibility to protect their village. Any history of previous visitors taking advantage of their village for personal gain may affect the leader-to-missionary dynamics. Others may have come in the past and benefited financially from the poverty of the village, that is, through gaining foreign support that never reached the villagers themselves. Therefore, ministers need to beware of seemingly simple things, like taking pictures of those in need, until a strong relationship of trust has been established with leaders. An evident love for the village's people and a desire to see its community develop are necessary.

Furthermore, there is the shadow of complicated race relations that often goes along with the politics of a country. The colonial past is not a distant memory, and it is imperative to steer away from political talk that might unnecessarily fuel the fear of colonialism's return. If one is not of the indigenous descent, more work will be needed to communicate mutual respect.

Yet presumptuous expectations are often present also. These are usually in the sphere of the local leader's personal and communal financial benefit. First impressions, such as the missionary's dress or cars driven, can be decisive. The missionary ought to be careful not to make concrete promises of gifts or aid. These will be remembered and will destroy trust when left unfulfilled. Even when plans seem certain, they must be communicated in such a way as to point leaders to rely on the sovereignty and faithfulness of God to fulfill them (Ps 146:5; Jas 1:16–17).

4. Emphasizing Areas of Agreement

In the past, missionaries have faced challenges when introducing local leaders to the church or to a pastoral training ministry. Two reasons for this have been observed. The first is that the Bible is sometimes associated with the colonial past. The second is that the gospel is a direct contradiction to African traditional religions.

In both of these scenarios, missionaries need wisdom from the Lord to find common ground with leaders. And like the apostles, modern-day missionaries, though they do not utter inspired speech, should rely on the Holy Spirit's grace to speak wisely before leaders (Matt 10:16–20; Col 4:6).[1] For example, in one situation, a certain local leader posed both of the above two challenges until the missions team emphasized that the instruction they intended to give would be in the local language and not English—which the leader had associated with colonialism. This simple commonality of the indigenous language gained ground for the gospel.

5. Practically Caring for Leaders

Knowing the leaders personally and showing genuine care for them and for their families is important. A helpful Shona proverb translates, "A relationship is strengthened by sharing food." Plus, in meeting physical needs, gospel opportunities are created (Gal 6:9–10). Leaders often struggle privately from a lack of food, but they keep a strong face for their community. Blessing the leader with food is a loving act so that he can reciprocate by sharing the little that he has for strengthening the relationship also.

6. Communicating Intentionally

Key to maintaining good relationships with local leaders is good, respectful, and gracious communication that builds trust (Prov 16:13).

---

1. William Hendriksen, *Matthew*, New Testament Commentary 9 (Grand Rapids: Baker, 1973), 464; Leon Morris, *The Gospel according to Matthew*, PNTC (Grand Rapids: Eerdmans, 1992), 254–55; Craig L. Blomberg, *Matthew*, NAC 22 (Nashville: Broadman and Holman, 1992), 175.

It is wise to make a regular, scheduled visit to leaders at least once a month to communicate present happenings and any plans the ministry may have. The village head is like the father of the local community and will feel that he needs to know what is afoot.

7. Honoring Leaders before Their People

Whenever the missionary has an opportunity, he should honor leaders in front of their people. This does not always translate to giving them a platform to speak; they could use it to give false teaching. Thus, depending on the context, though especially in a church setting, it may be wiser merely to acknowledge their presence and to express appreciation for them. It is common for leaders in public to attribute all success to themselves. Rather than trying to correct the narrative, missionaries do well to honor and thank the leader while giving all praise to the Lord (Pss 29:2; 115:1). To do so is not compromising but wise.

8. Including Leaders in Community Development

When doing any development work with the village, leaders should be included as beneficiaries. For example, when agricultural training was provided in one village, the village head was included in the leadership so as to remove any suspicions of political underhandedness or ulterior motives. While donors and mercy ministries want to serve "the poorest of the poor," they need to be convinced of the necessity of winning over leaders, because the community listens to their leaders as heads of the village family.

9. Praying for Leaders

Related to the last strategy is 1 Timothy 2:1–4, which compels Christians to pray for "all who are in authority." When village leaders are not only honored and included but also prayed for, this contributes to believers living "a tranquil and quiet life in all godliness and dignity" (2:2). It also maintains the godly goal of exposing the leaders to the gospel in every possible way so that they, too, might come to a full knowledge of the truth (2:4). The missionary's hope is to become fellow partakers of grace with them as he proclaims grace to others (Phil 1:7).

10. Guarding against Compromise

The missionary must be firm in certain matters, such as not collaborating with or contributing to ceremonies held by local leaders that have religious meaning. Nor can he become involved in political rallies that may close off gospel opportunities within the community. Opposition to these reservations will come, but the Lord's people must have a determination to remain steadfast as they look to Christ's coming (2 Pet 3:17–18) and boldness to speak truthfully in love (Eph 4:15).

11. Walking in Wisdom

Finally, the missionary must pray for wisdom from the Lord in all interactions with leaders. The unexpected and the unclear will occur. Bribes to permit work will be elicited, but the missionary must remain above reproach (1 Tim

3:2; Titus 1:6) and trust the Lord to establish His will in His time. One should always take a fellow believer to official meetings for accountability, a guard against corruption, and a help in prayer (Col 4:5–6). Likewise, it is imperative that agreements regarding the exchange of money be made in writing.

Summary

A ministry needs a community to serve in, and the community follows its leaders. These eleven strategies will assist the missionary to walk in favor with God and men, and to communicate genuine care for leaders and their communities without compromising gospel integrity. Missionaries have made mistakes over the years, but God has been gracious to cause His work to progress through weak vessels.

Partnership Strategies with Mercy Ministries

Given the typical rural scene, where villagers are often in genuine need, mercy ministry is an essential and inevitable part of the missions task. This does not mean that the gospel cannot reach people without mercy outlets (Rom 1:16–17). However, teams will find it difficult to proclaim the gospel to hungry people if they are loving them in word only and not "in deed and truth" (1 John 3:17–18). Mercy ministry boils down to that principle.

Partnering with such ministry outlets and providers can take different forms, like supplying food, equipping communities through self-sustaining projects, or providing medical assistance. Practically, these should make for the longevity of the greater ministry of the local church and of pastoral training. Mercy is not to be a distraction from the gospel but a tool to reach people with the gospel. Maintaining this balance will inevitably present challenges. Thus, below are six additional principles of wisdom, learned over the years in Zimbabwe, to help missionaries wisely use mercy ministry for the gospel in Africa.

1. Working through a Healthy Church

The manifold wisdom of God is made known through the church (Eph 3:8–10). Therefore, a healthy church should be the foundation, emphasis, and immediate goal of any missions work for God's glory. The church is the center of evangelism, discipleship, and equipping, so, then, if there is no existing healthy church in a community, it is imperative that one first be planted before mercy ministries "move in." These ministries may arise concurrently, but this requires exceptional intentionality on the part of the missionary to maintain priorities.

Introducing mercy ministry too soon can pose a danger. In the case of a church plant, false conversions become common as people are attracted for temporal rather than eternal benefit. To guard against this temptation, it is often wise to start a church plant without a building, letting a healthy membership be established first. Finding church buildings empty when the mercy ministry stops is all too common. Patience is necessary for establishing a healthy church, one that is a witnessing community of members (1 Pet 3:15–16), has biblical leadership (1 Tim 3:1–7), and practices expository preaching (2 Tim 4:1–5). Yet this platform is where mercy starts and extends to unbelievers in a sustained, Great Commission–supporting manner.

2. Building Relationships around the Gospel

Mercy ministry fosters the building of relationships as open doors for the gospel in rural families. It means showing a picture of love unlike the world, visiting people, getting to know and understand them, and pointing them to Christ. But mercy ministry is not just a tool for evangelism (cf. Matt 5:16; Titus 3:8, 14; 1 Pet 2:12); it is also a means of mutual love in the church (Gal 6:10; Heb 10:24) and a tool for discipleship (1 Thess 2:7–12). By it, believers teach other believers what it means to be content in Christ with little or with much, and to show it by generosity toward one's neighbor (Phil 4:11–13). Then, when one shares with his unbelieving neighbor, he can use that as an opportunity to share the gospel too. If mercy does not connect to the gospel, it should not be a ministry of the church; it is a distraction from its mission.

3. Exemplifying Excellence with Wisdom

There is a danger in neglecting excellence in rural ministry. For example, by giving away "hand-me-downs" (unwanted or soiled goods) or by doing acts of mercy in a substandard way, the gospel is not adorned (Prov 3:27–28; 1 Tim 2:9–10; cf. Jas 1:15–17). On the other hand, building a school with excellence communicates something about one's worship of God and respect for people. Jesus Christ is worth excellence in everything. Still, the ministry must practice balance in giving what is excellent with what fits a given context. It would not be best, for example, that an orphan stand out by wearing the latest designer label shoes. Mercy is not frivolity but a responsible sharing of God's gracious gifts (1 Tim 6:7–10, 17–19).

4. Promoting What Gives Dignity

Scripture speaks much about what gives dignity to men and women. Their inherent dignity derives from their being made in God's image and likeness (Gen 1:26, 27; Jas 3:9–10), and though that image is marred by sin, it is restored in Christ (Eph 4:24; Col 3:10). Thus, when a person chooses to live a godly, obedient life, it is "dignified" (*semnos*), meaning "worthy of respect" (1 Tim 2:2; 3:8, 11; Titus 2:2).[2]

Mercy ministry should promote the above truths; it should seek to maintain and to restore dignity to one's fellow man. Practically, a father would have more dignity before his neighbor, wife, and children if he brought home things for which he had worked rather than things he had simply been given. But diligent work is also obedience to God's command, a means toward loving one's neighbor, and a reflection of the gospel's life-changing power (Eph 4:28; 2 Thess 3:6–13). This is where self-sustaining projects, as a component of mercy ministry, are useful in that they allow believers an outlet of

---

2. "σεμνός," BDAG, 919.

obedience to God, testimony to their neighbors, and provision for their families. In one example, a peanut-growing project allowed parents to pay for the children's school fees, share food with their neighbor, and give more generously to the expansion of the Lord's work in the church.

The principle of dignity can be applied on a community level. Tasks such as fixing roads are already communal, because the resource is continually used by all. But the labor can also be communal. The same is true for ministry projects. When a Bible school was built in one Zimbabwean village, the community molded the bricks with cement and did most of the construction. Such an arrangement comes at a cost to the mission; the missionary must be firm with donors, insisting that their money is better spent invested in the gifts already found in the community rather than in things imported. But then, instead of a mentality that says, "This school was built for us," the locals can say, "We built our school with the help of others."

5. Graciously Saying No

There will always be need in the world (Mark 14:7). However, the missionary is not called to meet every need. It is not that some needs are unimportant, but that other people may be more equipped to meet them (e.g., Acts 6:1–6). Mercy ministries can end up demanding so much time and energy that it distracts from the missionary's purpose on the field. A team must always ask, "Do we have the time and resources to add another project and to do it effectively without detracting from the ministry of the church or from training leaders?"

The ministry must also ask itself critical questions regarding outside help: "Are people being empowered or made dependent by it, and is it effective for gospel witness?" People can be hindered by "help" in the long run. For a ministry to show the goodness of God, it must seek the good of the person being helped— not of the helper—and ultimately that good is found in the gospel. But humanist, feel-good philanthropy and ecumenical ministries that cloud the gospel will rob a project of the missionary's original purpose in it. This means that sometimes the missionary will have to say no to outside help or to entire projects and must trust the Lord for other means in His good time.

6. Living and Working by Example

It is important to be an example of what one's ministry expects other people to do (e.g., 1 Thess 1:9; 4:9–12). This is especially so when it comes to self-sustaining projects and hard work. It might mean having a small field in the village where people can see the missionary doing work they can emulate. A missionary telling people to work hard while he sits all week, preaches, and receives funds from outside makes his testimony lose impact in rural places. Moreover, physically laboring will serve as a visible counter to the prosperity gospel, now so prevalent in Africa, by displacing it with a practical theology of work.

Conclusion

The typical African rural community is a family, and the missionary truly seeks to become a part of that family for its good and God's glory.

Thus, partnerships with local leaders and mercy ministry outlets are unavoidable. Yet, in God's providence, they are also useful for fulfilling the Great Commission.

To seek strategic partnerships with local leaders is to recognize that God is the One who placed them in authority and to look for opportunities to expose them to the gospel. The eleven strategies listed above should help guide the missionary to use these relationships for evangelism, church planting, and everything flowing from them. Then, because rural ministry in Africa demands strategic partnerships that understand the community's fabric, mercy ministries must also be done wisely. The gospel and ministry of the church must be in the forefront, not distracted or detracted from by mercy outlets. The six strategies observed in this regard should help one navigate the pitfalls.

The potential harvest for eternal life in rural Africa is great, but the laborers are few. Therefore, in all things, let the gospel-bearer who goes there wisely seek fruitful partnerships to advance his true mission, without compromise, without distraction. Then he will be able to praise the Lord of the harvest that the one who sows and the one who reaps do, in fact, rejoice together (John 4:36).

SUB-SECTION 3: CULTURAL ENGAGEMENT

CHAPTER 70

Fighting through the Fog: Exercising Discernment as a Missions Leader

Mark Tatlock

"The fog of war" is a phenomenon well captured by nineteenth-century Prussian general Carl von Clausewitz. In his book *On War*, he wrote, "War is the realm of uncertainty; three quarters of the factors on which action in war is based are wrapped in a fog of greater or lesser uncertainty. A sensitive and discriminating judgment is called for; a skilled intelligence to scent out the truth."[1] Fog is the experience of strategist and soldier alike. The latter have often recalled the confusion of direction, location, and perspective on the battlefield. Their officers' orders become tangled and revised with poor communication. Their hearing and vision are at times impaired with no hope of improvement. All this creates a constant perceptual fog surrounding the battle. Because of it, there are more casualties, and not just of lives but of battles and wars.

The same discriminating judgment called for by the fog of war is essential in missions today. Missionaries are engaged in a spiritual battle for the souls of men. Their offensive weapon is the Word of God, the sword of the Spirit (Eph 6:17; Heb 4:12), and they wield it to proclaim the gospel, fight back the spiritual forces, and break the bondage of sin in peoples' lives. But the spiritual battlefield is made perilous by unbiblical philosophies that cloud and confuse modern-day missions, philosophies

---

1. Carl von Clausewitz, *On War*, ed. and trans. Michael Howard and Peter Paret, indexed ed. (1832; repr., Princeton, NJ: Princeton University Press, 1984), 101.

that ultimately inhibit the missionary's ability to achieve the missional obligations of the New Testament. Therefore, those going into the battle must cultivate biblical discernment in order to fight through the fog of extrabiblical philosophies and not be taken captive. Missions pastors and leaders must take this responsibility more seriously than ever before. Four essential considerations are needed: first, the meaning of discernment; second, the tools of discernment; third, the obligation of discernment; and finally, the exercise of discernment.

The Meaning of Discernment

A key text for defining discernment in missions is 1 Corinthians 2. There Paul underscores the importance of clarity in gospel preaching. For it is truth that confronts the false teachers of every era. The truth confronts fake gospels, heresies, ideologies, and worldviews that hold sinners captive. It was the truth Corinth recognized in the first century AD, and it is true in Jakarta, Cairo, Brussels, Washington, DC, and Mexico City in the twenty-first century. This generation of missionaries faces the same battle.

On one side of the confrontation is "the wisdom of men." By it, men intend to impress and persuade one another with words of superiority (1 Cor 2:1–5). They seek to find meaning and reason for their lives, and so create systems of thought, "principles of this world," that seem to justify their existence (cf. Gal 4:3; Col 2:8). But these systems inevitably align with their evil desires, which are diametrically opposed to the truth of God, His purposes, and His kingdom. Their wisdom is but empty words (Eph 5:6), fleshly (2 Cor 1:12), ultimately demonic (Jas 3:15), and unable to lead sinners to God (1 Cor 1:21). It only blinds and condemns them (2 Cor 4:4).

On the other side of this conflict is the wisdom of God, which is revealed to sinners first in the person and work of Jesus Christ (1 Cor 2:7–9). The gospel of Christ cuts through the confusion of their worldly, futile, and darkened thinking (Rom 1:21; Eph 4:17–18); it brings them to see the glory of Christ and to believe in Him (2 Cor 4:4); and then it endows them with the mind of Christ Himself (1 Cor 2:10–16). Once illumined by the gospel, the Christian then uses the entirety of God's Word to cut through the fog of worldviews and to combat every ideology and speculation that opposes God (cf. 2 Cor 10:3–6). This is wisdom "from above" (Jas 3:17), and God delights to give it to His children (Prov 2:7; Eph 1:17; Jas 1:5).

First Corinthians 2:14–15 says, "A natural man does not accept the depths of the Spirit of God, for they are foolishness to him, and he cannot understand them, because they are spiritually examined. But he who is spiritual examines all things." The word for "examine" here is in Greek *anakrinō*, which in some contexts is translated "discern."[2] A closely related verb, which Paul also used in his letters, is *diakrinō* (e.g., 1 Cor 4:7; 6:5; 11:31; 14:29), the noun form of which is *diakrisis*,

---

2. "ἀνακρίνω," BDAG, 66.

"distinguishing" or "discernment" (1 Cor 12:10).[3] All three are compounds of the root word *krinō*, which means to make a judgment based on facts.[4] All are used in the New Testament to express the ability or act of evaluating by careful distinction; a close study or examination of what is said or taught in order to judge right from wrong, truth from error, that which is of God from that which is of man (e.g., Acts 17:11; 1 Cor 14:24, 29; Heb 5:14).[5] That is what biblical discernment means.

The Tools of Discernment

According to 1 Corinthians 2, God has also given the believer tools for the practice of discernment. Christians are able to assess the ideas of men—their so-called "wisdom" in light of God's wisdom—because God has given them "the mind of Christ" through His indwelling Spirit and His inspired Word (2:12–16). They can know how God evaluates any spiritual thing inasmuch as Christ Himself knows it; not exhaustively as He does, of course, but truly as He does. Moreover, when it comes to spiritual things, those with the mind of Christ—through His Spirit illuminating His Word—are *not* subject to the judgment of those without it (2:15).[6]

B. B. Warfield expressed the latter well. In the 1890s, he preached a sermon at Princeton Seminary titled "Incarnate Truth." The text for his sermon to the divinity students there was John 1:14, "And the Word became flesh, and dwelt among us . . . full of grace and truth." Since Jesus was the highest manifestation, the very incarnation of truth, and its source, Warfield said, no truth could be antagonistic to the faith that Jesus founded (cf. John 14:6).[7] That being so, he exhorted his students:

Let us, then, cultivate an attitude of courage as over against the investigations of the day [in philosophy, science, and history]. None should be more zealous in them than we. None should be more quick to discern truth in every field, more hospitable to receive it, more loyal to follow it whithersoever it leads. . . . The curse of the Church has been her apathy to truth, in which she has too often left to her enemies that study of nature and of history and philosophy, and even that investigation of her own peculiar treasures, the Scriptures of God, which should have been her chief concern. Thus she has often been forced to learn from the inadvertent or unwilling testimony of her foes the facts she has needed to protect herself from their assaults. And thus she has been led to borrow from them false theories in philosophy, science, and criticism, to make unnecessary concessions to them, and to expose herself, as they changed their positions from time to time, to unnecessary disgrace. . . . All the truth belongs to us as

---

3. "ἀνακρίνω; διακρίνω," L&N, 1:363 (30.109), esp. n. 22; cf. the translators' note in the LSB at 1 Cor 12:10.

4. "κρίνω," BDAG, 568.

5. "διακρίνω," BDAG, 231.

6. W. Harold Mare, "1 Corinthians," in *EBC*, vol. 10, *Romans through Galatians*, ed. Frank E. Gaebelein (Grand Rapids: Zondervan, 1976), 203.

7. B. B. Warfield, "Incarnate Truth," in *Princeton Sermons* (New York: Fleming H. Revell, 1893), 107.

followers of Christ, the Truth; let us at length enter into our inheritance.[8]

Warfield knew that the only unchanging and certain foundation for ministry—and, for that matter, knowledge—was the Word of God, the deposit of truth. He also knew that courage was critical for the pastors and theologians of his tomorrow, for they needed to rightly examine and critique the popular theories of their day by bringing Scripture to bear upon them. The reverse, to shape their view of Scripture based on those popular, changing theories, would be to dishonor Jesus Christ.

Bringing Scripture to bear on contemporary ideas—this is what pastors do week in and week out in the pulpit. They know the things to which their congregations are daily exposed; things in the media and in pop culture, things in the classroom and in the boardroom. By expositing the Word and then applying it, pastors bring God's truth to bear on science, history, philosophy, and so on, and help their flocks to edit out the lies that are fed to them by the world. They bring clarity from the Bible to the fog of battle that is the Christian life. They teach their flocks to discern truth from error.

The task is no different concerning global missions. Besides training missionaries in evangelism, apologetics, and discipleship, pastors must also enable their missionaries to confront misleading ideologies that threaten these things, such ideologies as arise from partnerships, misunderstandings in their congregation, poor

Bible translations and other resources. In this area, fog of corrupt philosophies abound. But the tools they need for discernment in missions are the same as those for living the Christian life: God's Word, God's Spirit to illumine it, and God's people to admonish one another in it (Rom 15:14; Col 1:28; 3:16).

The Obligation of Discernment

The Greek words for discernment in Scripture are also used literally and figuratively of courtroom settings. They depict a trial set before an examining judge (Luke 23:14; Acts 4:9; 1 Cor 4:3; 9:3). The judge is responsible to execute justice based on the facts of the case in light of the law. He cannot merely acknowledge what the proper ruling would be; he must decide for it also. He must pronounce it and see that it is executed. So, too, Christians must scrutinize in light of Scripture the details of the missionary practices and cultures they encounter, and then they must take action to live accordingly. This is the obligation of exercising discernment in missions.

Throughout Scripture we see that it is not enough simply to align one's theology with the truth; one must practice the truth also (John 3:21; 1 John 1:6). Psalm 1 teaches that when a man meditates on the Word, it informs how he walks in this world. Proverbs 2 teaches that when a man gets wisdom into his heart, it guides his choice of path and of the company he keeps. This is the principle that orthodoxy ("right doctrine"), if it is truly orthodox,

---

8. Warfield, 109–10.

produces orthopraxy ("right practice"). On the other hand, heterodoxy ("errant doctrine") inevitably leads to heteropraxy ("errant practice"). A great deal of missions literature today uses the terms *orthodoxy* and *orthopraxy*. That is, however, no guarantee of accuracy. The Church needs discernment even about discernment, so to speak. Christians must examine the Scriptures diligently to see if the practices being extrapolated from the Scriptures are right (cf. Acts 17:11).

Inescapably, an orthopraxy of the Great Commission requires missionaries and their sending churches to examine the contemporary landscape. They must discern what in modern missiology is divine wisdom and what is worldly wisdom. Then they must choose the wisdom that is of Christ for their own course of action, and they must hold one another accountable to it. Only then will they succeed in the commission God has given His people. Too many churches today—though being faithful, Bible-teaching churches—are engaged from a distance in missionary enterprises that are not aligned with their ministry philosophy at home. There is an inconsistency between doctrine and practice. Some practical exhortations to exercise discernment are needed. Just as a local church wants to maintain a biblical philosophy of music in worship, youth ministry, and so on, what they do and what they support in missions should also align with a biblical philosophy of ministry.

The Exercise of Discernment

The "tip of the spear" in this battle of missions has to do especially with culture, then the classroom, and finally commitment. Culture is the dominant note in missions talk today, how missionaries are to live and minister in cultures foreign to them, cultures different from the contexts in which they first learned Christ. This discussion pervades the missions classroom and presses the issue of commitment. To exercise discernment amid all this talk, then, missionaries and their churches need to rightly define culture, discern what is taught in the classroom, and commit to the truth.

Defining Culture

Many models exist for understanding culture.[9] The model that reflects the biblical appraisal of culture is one of concentric circles. A worldview is at the culture's core, and then its values, institutions, and observable behaviors are constructed around it.[10] *Worldview* means just

---

9. For example, one model maps culture as a power-centric triangle of people, places, and practices in competition (José M. Causadias, "What Is Culture? Systems of People, Places, and Practices," *Applied Developmental Science* 24, no. 4 [2020]: 310–22). Another visualizes culture as a Venn diagram in three overlapping circles of artifacts, society, and logic (Richard H. Reeves-Ellington and Francis J. Yammarino, *What Is Culture? Generating and Applying Cultural Knowledge* (Lewiston, NY: Mellen, 2010), 25. A third, widely used model approximates culture as a product of six conceptual "dimensions" that are measured nation by nation across the globe (Geert Hofstede, "Dimensionalizing Cultures: The Hofstede Model in Context," *Online Readings in Psychology and Culture* 2, no. 1 [2011]: art. 8, https://doi.org/10.9707/2307-0919.1014).

10. This model was first developed and published by G. Linwood Barney, "The Supracultural and the Cultural," in *The Gospel and Frontier Peoples*, ed. R. Pierce Beaver (Pasadena, CA: William Carey Library, 1973), 45–57. A more complex development of this, the "cultural onion" model, was given by Eugene W. Bunkowske, "THY573: Outreach Ministry in Context" (course notes,

what it sounds like; one's view of the world, that is, a pattern of ideas and beliefs that attempt to make sense of God, the world, and man's relationship to God and the world.[11] This is at the center or core of every culture. Conceivably a worldview takes two forms: religious and nonreligious. It might be a formal religion like Islam or an informal religion pretending not to be, like secularism.

But it is the outermost layer or circle that is most observable in a culture. It might be called the aesthetics. It includes things like a society's architecture, music, arts, and dress; its literature, television, and entertainment industry; its social media, "pop culture," and behavior. All these are the first things encountered when one moves and lives cross-culturally. They are exposing layers of deeply held convictions layered upon underlying institutions and values, which themselves are collected experiences of fundamental worldview.

Some missions endeavors start with the outermost layer and try to effect change there. That misses the core issue and is misguided. After all, Scripture says, "Man looks at the outward appearance, but Yahweh looks at the heart" (1 Sam 16:7). The heart of a culture must be transformed before its behavior is affected. Of course, cultures and societies have no such "hearts" in themselves; they are simply composed of people who do. It is the hearts of *people* that must be changed, and fundamentally so, in their worldview. That is what the Great Commission is after—redeeming people, not cultures. It is true that when people are changed, they organize with other changed people, and *then* institutions are approached with biblical values and cultural behaviors are affected. Certainly, Christians should do this (Matt 5:13–16), and yes, cultures do change as a result of the gospel. But cultural change is *not* the gospel, and so it is not the Church's mission.[12] Missionaries must discern where this idea encroaches on their proclamation of salvation to lost sinners. They are after worldview, not aesthetics; hearts, not behaviors.

Discerning Worldview in the Classroom

Every person, like every culture, has a fundamental worldview, and there are many worldviews in currency today. The dominant ones are propagated in the education of young people.[13] Students, particularly, must be skilled at recognizing the worldviews that underlie the ideas they encounter (Heb 5:14). Parents must recognize that in their alma maters, even in many Christian institutions, the philosophies, traditions, and widely accepted principles of the world have crept in.

Concordia Theological Seminary, 2002), 1.

11. Jeff Myers and David A. Noebel, *Understanding the Times: A Survey of Competing Worldviews* (Manitou Springs, CO; Colorado Springs, CO: Summit Ministries; David C. Cook, 2015), 5–6.

12. This is the subject of Kevin DeYoung and Greg Gilbert, *What Is the Mission of the Church? Making Sense of Social Justice, Shalom, and the Great Commission* (Wheaton, IL: Crossway, 2011).

13. See discussion and analysis in David A. Noebel, *Understanding the Times: The Story of the Biblical Christian, Marxist/Leninist and Secular Humanist Worldviews* (Colorado Springs, CO: Summit Ministries, 1991), 7–28, esp. 1–5.

The field of global missions has not been immune. The same ideas influence undergraduate and graduate ministry degrees in the United States and then are exported to the world. Christian universities, Bible colleges, and seminaries have altered or accommodated their missions curricula based on humanitarian theories and Christian teaching that integrates, if not prioritizes, secular sociology, cultural studies, and anthropology. Their students, in due time, produce the majority of written works on missions, which then become the textbooks fed back into the universities. International students also imbibe their teaching, for many are raised up by missionaries abroad and sent to the missionaries' trusted alma maters. Some are supported by their conservative churches back home, intending them to get advanced training in the United States. But then the students return to their home context and ministry, are entrusted with leadership, and introduce the harmful theories and methods of their professors and Bible colleges. Thus, theological drift occurs in what were once sound institutions, and adherence to historic doctrinal statements is replaced in the areas of evangelism, discipleship, church planting, Bible translation, leadership training, and mercy ministries. All this is due to a failure to discern worldviews in the classroom.

Therefore pastors must help those they send to the mission field to beware of those trends. They must shepherd their missionaries in selecting schools, books, and agencies consistent in principle with what they themselves teach. It is not that pastors must be experts in missiology; though, those that are specially given oversight of missions should be diligent students of the field. But all pastors must accept the duty and responsibility to be informed and to guide those they train and support. They must teach them discernment and provide them with resources that do likewise.

Committing to the Truth

The point of all this is how one is to effectively bring truth into another culture. One might recognize the origins of an idea as being an anti-Christian worldview but then still think it harmless to adopt the idea into one's anthropology and missiology. Yet, insofar as the idea arises from that worldview's assumptions and not from general truths revealed in creation, it is theologically and morally bankrupt, contradictory of biblical anthropology, and must be rejected from missions strategy. It has no place in evangelism except as a foil to show man's rebellion against God in the mind (Rom 8:7; 1 Cor 2:14). Pastors and missionaries must singularly commit to the truth that is the Church's treasure and only weapon, the Word of God.

Another example will illustrate this well. The biblical counseling movement arose in the last decades of the twentieth century to confront the increasing integration of secular psychology and sociology within "Christian counseling."[14] The institutions of psychology

---

14. See the introduction in the book that started the movement: Jay E. Adams, *Competent to Counsel: Introduction to Nouthetic Counseling* (Grand Rapids: Zondervan, 1970), esp. xviii–xxii and 17–19. For a brief history of the movement and further resources, see the organization Adams founded, "Beliefs and History," Christian Counseling and Education Foundation, accessed June 18,

had embraced views of man that assumed him to be an evolved animal and his spiritual problems to be physical, "mental," or socially conditioned. When their diagnoses and prognoses, though fundamentally based on these antibiblical assumptions, were integrated into the teaching of Christian universities and seminaries, trickling down into Christian clinics and churches, a need for biblical reform arose. That reform has now produced a load of resources, all grounded in the authority and sufficiency of Scripture for dealing with spiritual problems.

In a similar way, missiology has seen a proliferation of this integrationist approach. In the same way, missiology needs a biblical reform. Christian higher education at large has been revising its approaches according to secular humanism and sociology, rather than to Scripture as sufficient (Pss 19:7–11; 119:9; 2 Tim 3:16; 2 Pet 1:3–4). It is embracing secular criticisms of Scripture that minimize it as authoritative, just as Warfield lamented a century and a half ago. This is not unlike religious syncretism, the wedding of the Christian faith to a person's former belief systems; only now the church is effectively doing this for the unbeliever and wedding the Christian worldview to secular humanism. When the Bible is undermined and put on a level with other authorities, there is already a failure to teach Scripture as Jesus commanded in the Great Commission (Matt 28:20). And that failure will only increase, both at home in missions training and abroad on the mission field.

This approach has very practical effects. First, those evangelized are not taught a confident bibliology (the doctrine of the Bible as God's Word) nor, thus, how to study their Bibles. Then a lack of teaching concerning inspiration, authorial intent, inerrancy, and sufficiency leaves the Bible open to subjective interpretations, which will rule in the convert's life and church. Cultural ideas are inevitably imported into the reading of Scripture with no controls. Subjective reading methods, such as "reader response hermeneutics," "trajectory hermeneutics," or "queer hermeneutics," in which the transient personal and cultural values are more authoritative than the text, are bound to continue. While those are strongest in cultures that embrace secularism, mystical and syncretistic readings will abound in other, more formally religious contexts. But all will obstruct the only gospel that saves.

Scripture warns against this. "See to it that no one takes you captive through philosophy and empty deception" (Col 2:8). "Guard what has been entrusted to you, turning aside from godless and empty chatter and the opposing arguments of what is falsely called knowledge" (1 Tim 6:20). "For our struggle is not against flesh and blood, but against the rulers, against the authorities, against the world forces of this darkness, against the spiritual forces of wickedness in the heavenly places. Therefore, take up the full armor of God . . . and the sword of the Spirit, which is the word of God" (Eph 6:12–17). The Church has one gospel to preach and only

---

2024, https://www.ccef.org/about/beliefs-and-history.

one worldview to teach, that of Jesus Christ in the Scriptures. The Church must commit to the truth as sufficient and authoritative for completing her task. This is the exercise of discernment.

Conclusion

In the words of General von Clausewitz, the fog of war calls for "a skilled intelligence to scent out the truth."[15] Missionaries must be men and women of biblical discernment. They must make good use of the tools for discernment God has given, His Word, illumined by His Spirit, with the help of His people. They must themselves be discipled so that their senses are trained to discern good and evil, truth and error, the wisdom of God and the wisdom of men when they go to disciple others. They must be committed to following through on right doctrine with right practice and to holding one another accountable in them. They must not be dissuaded by contemporary ideas of engagement, but rightly define culture, discern worldview, and commit to the truth.

Pastors are raising up generals for the battle of missions. It is a battle for the souls of men, and the stakes are high. It is a battle wrapped in the fog of worldly philosophies that diminish and shroud the only gospel that saves. But God has not only commissioned His people to fight; He has equipped them for the fight as well. May missions leaders honor their Lord, then, and fight faithfully through the fog.

15. Von Clausewitz, *On War*, 101.

Missionary Challenges in the MENA Region

Hanna Shahin

The MENA (Middle East and North Africa) region is predominantly Muslim, with individuals exercising varying degrees of adherence to Islam's tenets, depending on the school of thought to which they belong.[16] Since each MENA country has adopted one theological school over another, it follows that the severity and scope of the challenges differ accordingly. Thus the challenges to missionaries in Saudi Arabia, which follows the strict Hanbali school of jurisprudence may be more dangerous

16. "The Historical Development of Sharia Law," *Britannica*, accessed June 18, 2024, https://www.britannica.com /topic/Shariah/Development-of-different-schools-of-law.

than those met in a country like Morocco, which adheres to the more lenient Maliki school. Yet many challenges are common to the entire region. Identifying and naming such challenges should serve not as a discouragement but as a catalyst for prayerful dependence on God's sovereign grace and power as the Church seeks to make wise decisions and boldly honor Christ in obedience to His Great Commission.

Religious Opposition

In 1928 Egyptian schoolteacher Hassan Al-Banna founded a group that became known as the Muslim Brotherhood. In subsequent decades, the Muslim Brotherhood gave birth to terrorist groups such as Al Qaeda, Al Shabab, and ISIS, as well as others across the region, extending even into sub-Saharan Africa.[17] The group's aim was to bring back the "Islamic Golden Age," which extended from the seventh to the thirteenth century.[18] Each sect aspires to see the day when the Umma, or the universal community of Islam, dominates the world stage.

In the Islamic world, citizens are first and foremost Muslim, whether they are ethnically Arab, Turkish, or Persian. Following Islam is not a choice the person makes but is seen to be a distinct part of one's identity. Challenging the faith of a Muslim therefore is punishable by law. In a country like Morocco, which follows the more lenient Maliki school of jurisprudence, such a "crime" is met with a six-month jail sentence.[19]

Straying from Islam constitutes a crime for the Muslim as well. In this case, however, the punishment can be much more severe. In countries under Hanbali jurisprudence, such an act can bring years of imprisonment, torture, or even death.[20] Thus, the missionary will encounter Muslims who are understandably hesitant to honestly consider opposing religious viewpoints. As a result, people are, in a real sense, deprived of their will to think. They become prisoners of conscience, walled in by fear of the temporal consequences of turning from Islam.

Christian missionaries in MENA countries frequently find opposition from the visible Christian church as well. Between 5 and 10 percent of the MENA population belong to one of several traditional nominally Christian sects. Among these are

---

17. Zachary Laub, "Egypt's Muslim Brotherhood," Council on Foreign Relations, August 15, 2019, https://www.cfr.org/backgrounder/egypts-muslim-brotherhood.

18. "Islamic Golden Age," Islamic History, accessed June 18, 2024, https://islamichistory.org/islamic-golden-age/.

19. "Religious Freedom in Morocco," European Centre for Law and Justice, March 1, 2021, http://media.aclj.org/pdf/Religious-Freedom-in-Morocco-ECLJ-Report-March-2021.pdf.

20. See the U.S. Department of State, *Saudi Arabia 2022 International Religious Freedom Report*, https://www.state.gov/wp-content/uploads/2023/05/441219-SAUDI-ARABIA-2022-INTERNATIONAL-RELIGIOUS-FREEDOM-REPORT.pdf.

the Copts of Egypt and Sudan, the Greek Orthodox, and Roman Catholics. Like the Muslims, many of these groups perceive evangelical missionaries as a foreign threat. They accuse the missionaries of being "sheep-stealers," since the evangelical ministries typically reach more nominal Christians than Muslims.

Cultural Opposition

Along with the fear of punishment for going against the broader Islamic establishment, Muslims must also grapple with the notion of shame. Like many African countries, the MENA region is made up of "honor and shame" societies. Though most of the region has been urbanized, the clan mindset has not evolved much throughout the previous centuries. One's identity is tightly knit to that of his family. A person's family name therefore is much more important than his own first name. Bringing shame to the family name causes serious problems. When the community finds one of its members to be shameful, that person's marriage, home, job, and life are at risk. The danger in this instance does not come from the state or the mosque but from the individual's own family and neighbors.

There are several ways one might bring shame upon himself or his family, but forsaking Islam for another faith is one of the primary catalysts. Western individualism and breaking from cultural norms are simply not tolerated. Coupled with generally low literacy rates and the limited opportunities women have for education, employment, and independence, these cultural factors call for special persistence and wisdom on the part of Christian missionaries in the MENA region.

Conclusion

Opposition to gospel progress should not surprise the Bible-reading Christian (Matt 13:19; 2 Cor 4:4; 1 Pet 5:8–9). The kinds of hurdles the Christian missionary faces in the MENA region, whether formal or informal, religious or cultural, are manifestations of a world system that is defiant against its Creator. Identifying the obstacles helps the church and its missionaries develop wise strategies for the work. And placing those obstacles in their proper theological context reminds the faithful MENA missionary that his duty is the same as that of every pastor and evangelist—to rest in the saving power of the Word of Christ and to proclaim Him confidently and boldly as the risen Lord.

An Open Letter to Hindu Christ Followers

Daniel Surya Avula

I am a convert from Hinduism. After completing my pastoral training, the Lord allowed me to plant a local church in a predominantly Hindu neighborhood. The church is in one of the thriving cities in India, and our gatherings and fellowship reflect the local culture. The Lord caused the growth, as everyone in the congregation is committed to worship, discipleship, and evangelism. The Lord is also making this church and its ministry a blessing to other churches. In addition, the church has been praying and planning to launch a seminary to train pastors and plant more faithful Bible teaching churches in India to reach the unreached people for God's glory.

When churches and missionary organizations deploy biblical evangelistic methods and ecclesiological approaches, they see enduring fruit. On the contrary, pragmatic missiological methods are ineffective and often counterproductive. Such is the sad case with some efforts in India. This insert seeks to expose the failings of these groups and call them to biblical fidelity.

Indian Insider Movements

The groups of particular concern in India include "Hindu Christ followers," "churchless Christians," and "unbaptized believers in Christ."[21] These titles are sometimes used synonymously within the broader category of Indian insider movements.[22] The movements' members claim to have embraced Jesus for salvation, but they refuse to publicly identify as Christians or associate with Christian churches. They emphasize the importance of a change of heart, not

---

21. Matt Bennett, "Unveiling the Muslim Insider Movement (Part 2): Root Inspection," ABWE, October 22, 2019, https://www.abwe.org/blog/unveiling-muslim-insider-movement-part-2-root-inspection.

22. The fundamental tenet of the insider movements (IM) in India is that new believers must secretly adapt Christianity to their Hindu/Sikh worship, prayers, fasts, rituals, and customs. H. Talman and J. J. Travis, eds., *Understanding Insider Movements: Disciples of Jesus within Diverse Religious Communities* (Pasadena, CA: William Carey Library, 2015), 159–60. Hindu Christ followers also rely on Hindu scriptures for guidance and evangelism. Often they argue that Jesus Christ is in the Vedas, their ancient scriptures.

religion.[23] In other words, they refuse to break from their Hindu environment.[24]

Hindu Christ followers believe their covert approach is the best way to reach people lost in Hinduism. Their intentions may be noble, but their methods are wrong and ineffective for the following reasons.

The Flawed Approach

First, Hindu Christ followers fail to understand and serve the one true God. Hindus believe in a pantheon of gods (330 million), obey numerous gurus, and concede many ways of salvation, from *Astika* (theism) to *Nastika* (atheism).[25] The Hindu Christ followers approach leads people to the notion that the God of the Bible is one among many gods. It is impossible, however, to worship Yahweh while yoking to false gods (Ps 106:28). Jesus is the Way, the Truth, and the Life (John 14:6). A proper understanding of the triune God demands that Christians leave false religious systems like Hinduism and worship and serve Him alongside other believers.

Second, the approach of Hindu Christ followers is misaligned with the gospel. The gospel demands a clear separation from the darkness of paganism (Eph 4:17–19). The Lord delivers His people from that domain and transfers them to the kingdom of His Son (Col 1:13). It is wrong therefore to continue visiting Hindu temples, reading Hindu scriptures, practicing Hindu rituals, and calling oneself a Hindu after conversion to Christ. The authentic gospel leads to authentic conversion, involving repentance from sin and devotion to the true and living God (1 Thess 1:9).

Third, Hindu Christ followers do not understand the meaning and purpose of the church. The church is the one human institution Jesus promised to build (Matt 16:18). It is the assembly of believers who have been called out from the world, redeemed by the blood of Christ (Eph 1:22–23; Heb 12:23; 2 Tim 1:9).[26] The church is "a chosen race, a royal priesthood, a holy nation, a people for God's own possession" (1 Pet 2:9). It is shocking and highly problematic that some would consider themselves a part of this unique, spiritual fellowship, and yet refuse to participate with its corporate gatherings or be identified with its members.

Fourth, Hindu Christ followers do not devote themselves to the teaching of God's

---

23. Talman and Travis, 160.

24. John and Anna Travis, "Contextualization among Hindus, Muslims, and Buddhists," *Mission Frontiers* 27, no. 5 (September–October 2005), https://www.missionfrontiers.org/issue/article/contextualization-among-hindus-muslims-and-buddhists.

25. Sashi Tharoor, *The Hindu Way: An Introduction to Hinduism* (New Delhi: Aleph, 2019), 9.

26. John MacArthur and Richard Mayhue, *Biblical Doctrine: A Systematic Summary of Bible Truth* (Wheaton, IL: Crossway, 2017), 740.

Word, fellowship, breaking of bread, and prayer (Acts 2:42). These activities are to mark true believers. In addition, Christ has given baptism and the Lord's Supper as ordinances to be observed in the context of a local congregation (Matt 28:19; 1 Cor 11:23–26). Since they refuse to join a local church, Hindu Christ followers cannot observe these ordinances. In doing so, they forfeit the Lord's gifts of grace to His people and lead others to a stunted understanding of Christ's Church.

Conclusion

Hindu Christ followers often have a tremendous desire to see their families, friends, and communities come to Christ. However, the methods they employ are unbiblical, ungodly, and deceptive. Ultimately, if someone continues to call themselves a Hindu after conversion, Hindus will genuinely think the person is a practicing Hindu. This is intentional deception. Believers must never act fraudulently (2 Cor 4:2).

Jesus' followers, on the other hand, reveal their true identity (Acts 11:26; 1 Pet 4:16). The very name Christian reflects the believer's identity in Christ. In the New Testament, Christians always confronted the lost with the gospel, even in the face of humiliation, persecution, suffering, and death. As lights in the world, Christians must shine before others so they may see the believer's good works and give glory to God (Matt 5:14–16). Christ's church must always be conducted Christ's way. May the Lord help Christians in India reach their neighbors and honor their Savior in the way He has prescribed.

CHAPTER 71

Toward a Biblical Model of Cultural Engagement

Chris Burnett

Some missionaries who highly prioritize theological precision minimally acknowledge the cultural differences between them and the people they serve. After many years of interpersonal distance, they wonder why the locals identify the missionaries more by their foreignness than by their faith and why Jesus Christ seems to remain strangely superfluous to them. Other missionaries so greatly value becoming one with the people that they risk losing sight of the reason they were sent to them in the first place. Over time, in the lifestyle of the adoptive culture, they risk downplaying the urgency of the gospel and can slip into a blithe apathy. Both missionary extremes are marked by a degree of indifference toward the people they serve.

The goal of this chapter is to present a model of cultural engagement for missionaries and all believers to follow that balances the desire to proclaim the gospel in new cultures and the desire to do so in culturally appropriate ways. The model can simply be called the "biblical missions model" of cultural engagement. A brief discussion of the need for the model for both evangelism and disciplemaking precedes the descriptions and details of the model.

Cultural Engagement, Cross-Cultural Communication, and the Missionary

"Cultural engagement," from the standpoint of the Great Commission, and therefore biblical missions, represents the broad range of missionary activities that aim to faithfully deliver the meaning of the text of Scripture to new audiences so that they can apply what they learn to their local situations. True connection with the local people is forged through the ministry of the Word, namely, preaching, teaching, and Bible translation—proclamation ministries that might be called "cross-cultural communication," which are at the heart of all biblical cultural engagement. However, how cultural engagement is applied is as dynamic as the cultures themselves, even though the biblical principles are unchanging. Ultimately, the goal of being present with the local people is to get them to understand the message of Scripture and respond in faith. Biblical cultural engagement therefore rejects practices of cultural accommodation that in any way might lead the audience to misconstrue the message of the biblical text that is being proclaimed.

The principle of engaging culturally is guided by Paul's teaching in 1 Corinthians 9:19–23 and modeled by all of the apostles' ministries.

> For though I am free from all, I have made myself a slave to all, so that I may win more. And to the Jews I became as a Jew, so that I might win Jews. To those who are under the Law, as under the Law though not being myself under the Law, so that I might win those who are under the Law. To those who are without law, as without law, though not being without the law of God but under the law of Christ, so that I might win those who are without law. To the weak I became weak, that I might win the weak. I have become all things to all men, so that I may by all means save some. So I do all things for the sake of the gospel, so that I may become a fellow partaker of it. (1 Cor 9:19–23)

The method of Paul's engagement was not to alter the gospel by capitulating to the common concepts and practices of his audience that could dilute the truth or syncretize it with false beliefs. It was, rather, to adapt his lifestyle to the morally neutral ways of the local people in service to the gospel. He so prioritized the objective, urgent message that he sacrificially altered his way of life—his customs, his comforts, his freedoms, his safety—in order to identify with those who needed to hear the good news with which he was entrusted. Nothing was inviolable except obedience to Christ. In the same way, the faithful missionary must be willing to sacrifice all areas of lifestyle that do not compromise his gospel witness in order to become a better communicant of Christ and His saving gospel.

Biblical engagement with the culture includes such things as speaking the local language (Acts 21:40; cf. 1 Cor 13:1), working in the local market (Acts 18:1–3), receiving local hospitality (Acts 28:1–2, 7; 1 Cor 10:27), observing local codes of honor (Rom 12:17; 2 Cor 8:21), adapting to local clothing conventions (1 Cor 11:4–16), submitting to local authorities (Rom 13:7; 1 Pet 2:13, 17), and exercising one's legal liberties (Acts 22:25–29; 25:11; 1 Pet 2:16)—yet always honoring and obeying the Lord above all (Acts 5:29; 1 Cor 9:21). By these means, the missionary today, like the apostles, can make himself "a slave to all" (1 Cor 9:19) and become "all things to all men" (9:22) in order to gain the clearest hearing possible for cross-cultural communication of the gospel.

Cross-cultural communication remains central to the effectiveness of biblical missions. Cultural anthropologists recognize that successful communication between people from different cultural backgrounds and languages requires nuanced interaction, since "cultural perceptions and symbol systems differ enough to alter the communication event."[1] Evangelical missiologists urge practitioners to learn deeply about the local culture and take care to eliminate misunderstandings that arise from underlying cultural assumptions as much as possible when proclaiming the gospel and teaching Christian theology. They encourage missionaries to achieve a high degree of cultural awareness, beginning by entering the target culture as a learner to "study the local culture phenomenologically."[2]

Cultural learning, while important, does not fill all the gaps the missionary encounters in his new context. Many of the missionary's problems are not on the street but in the pews. Of all the "labor and hardship" the apostle Paul faced in gospel ministry, which he labeled in 2 Corinthians 11:23–33 as his journeys, opposition, and physical sufferings, he wanted his fellow believers to understand: "Apart from such external things, there is the daily pressure on me of concern for all the churches" (v. 28). Missions scholars and practitioners must pay close, daily attention to how they communicate the Word of God to believers, rather than consider the "external things" that regularly affect the missionary to be the bulk of their work. Therefore, cross-cultural communication, in the framework of biblical missions, refers to cultural engagement that involves proclaiming God's Word in the local church, equipping the members, and raising up elders, so that the church will foster a new Christian culture and advance the gospel outward in the world.

Substantial development occurs in the life of the believer between spiritual birth and spiritual maturity, according to God's design (Phil 1:6). The spiritual growth of the body must be cultivated tenderly, first by the missionary and then by the men who replace him as the local pastors. New Christians do not automatically understand the full impact of the theology in their Bible, so they need teachers to patiently train them first in the "elementary principles of the oracles of God" until they themselves become the teachers (Heb 5:12).

However, some missionaries can become so consumed with evangelistic (even pre-evangelistic) activities outside of the church that they have little time to prepare themselves for the pulpit. When they do not deepen the biblical understanding of their members through exegetical study and careful preaching and teaching, they fail to give them the "pure milk of the word" that they need in order to grow to spiritual adulthood (1 Pet 2:2). In practice they have deemphasized the cross-cultural communication needed within the local body that facilitates the transformation of the believers from their worldly culture to a biblically aligned culture as fellow "strangers and exiles on the earth" (Heb 11:13; cf. 1 Pet 1:1; 2:11).

Such ministry emphases are lopsided, focusing so much cultural engagement outside of the church that they risk never producing

---

1. As quoted and used interchangeably with "intercultural communication" in Larry A. Samovar, Edwin R. McDaniel, Richard E. Porter, and Carolyn S. Roy, *Communication between Cultures*, 8th ed. (Boston: Wadsworth, Cengage Learning, 2007), 9.
2. Paul G. Hiebert, *Anthropological Reflections on Missiological Issues* (Grand Rapids: Baker, 1994), 88.

healthy disciples inside the church. Over time, their churches fill up with sluggish children, who have become "dull of hearing," who need "milk and not solid food" (Heb 5:11–12). Such believers cower under opposition from the outside world and suffer few pains to plead for sinners to receive Christ. Ironically, the same leaders may wonder why their men poorly manage their homes and do not aspire to eldership, while women participate more eagerly in church ministries.

Missionaries in situations like these err with regard to the biblical basics of the Great Commission. Those with a weak gospel proclamation on the street turn nonbelievers into local church members, reinforcing their self-righteousness and profaning the worship of God. Those with weak teaching in the pulpit make disobedient disciples who are perpetually dependent on the missionary, keeping the church at arm's length from indigenization and expansion. In the end, they spend many years and copious resources never planting a biblically transformed, missions-sending church.

These broad categories of problems do not mean that missionaries have no concern for the churches like Paul, but they need to refocus their attention on the kinds of cultural investments that will directly impact their ability to proclaim the gospel with clarity and train believers with conviction. For this reason, the biblical missions model of cultural engagement is set forth.

Description of the Biblical Missions Model

A missionary who employs the grammatical-historical hermeneutic and a conservative exegetical method has the tools and the determination to understand the meaning and significance of the text he desires to communicate in the new context. Yet he must approach the target audience with cultural awareness and sensitivity, to ensure that his words and actions move toward the ultimate goal of making theologically sound local disciples. The proclamation activities that accord with biblical missions are confrontational in nature and buttressed by ideological and practical parameters.

The Confrontational Character of Cross-Cultural Communication

Contrary to contemporary proposals for inter-religious dialogue and ecumenical outreach, the missionary who follows the biblical missions model is called to the ministry of "assertion." This technical term indicates that cross-cultural communication is not a morally neutral spiritual knowledge transfer but a confrontational act. Assertion refers to the declarative, verbal proclamation of the biblical propositions that the missionary desires for the audience to adopt as true for themselves.[3] An assertion is only possible when the speaker is certain that the knowledge he verbally imparts to his audience is true and neither acknowledged nor understood by his hearers.[4]

---

3. Marc Cortez, "Context and Concept: Contextual Theology and the Nature of Theological Discourse," *WTJ* 67, no. 2 (2005): 94.

4. John Turri, *Knowledge and the Norm of Assertion: An Essay in Philosophical Science* (Cambridge, UK: Open Book, 2016), 2.

The missionary, who is convinced that biblical doctrine needs to reach the minds and hearts of the people in order for them to be spiritually transformed, provokes his audience to abandon their prior spiritual knowledge and adopt the new content that is communicated to them as the Word of God (1 Thess 2:13). The goal, as described by missiologist and practitioner E. D. Burns, is "to create a tension in the unbeliever's interpretation of reality and existence. We want them to doubt the source and authority of their belief and value system. . . . We must expose that they don't have all the answers and that even some of their answers are dissatisfying."[5] Therefore, missionaries must be culturally aware enough to know which unbiblical beliefs and customs of the audience need disrupting.

The missionary is not called to be a provocateur, however; he is a biblical expositor. In a winsome way, the missionary must assess the best methods of communicating the biblical propositions in the target culture, taking care to avoid unnecessarily offending his audience. His confrontation comes by "speaking the truth in love" (Eph 4:15), always using words "with grace, seasoned with salt" (Col 4:6), so that he is "ready to make a defense to everyone who asks [him] to give an account for the hope that is in [him], yet with gentleness and fear" (1 Pet 3:15), "having a good conscience" as he speaks and acts with "good conduct" (3:16). While each culture has its own rules for social engagement, these biblical descriptions are the goal of every proclaimer who has a message for the people outside and inside the church.

The Parameters of Cultural Engagement

Three parameters circumscribe the missionary's cultural engagement so that he communicates the truths of Scripture with theological clarity, textual confidence, biblical fidelity, and eagerness for spiritual transformation. The parameters are theological, linguistic, and transformational.

THE THEOLOGICAL PARAMETER

The first parameter sets up theological guardrails so that the missionary does not forget that when he speaks to people who do not know Christ savingly, he is speaking to sinners who live in sin and perpetuate corrupted cultures and have no innate ability to produce God-pleasing spiritual fruit individually or as a culture (Eph 2:1–3). The recognition of the fallenness of man in society is an important reminder that the missionary's immediate redemptive mission is not society-wide but a ministry of reconciliation to each person (2 Cor 5:17–21): God is at work "in Christ reconciling the world to Himself" (v. 19) by making a new creation of individual sinners (v. 17) through the apostolic ministry of begging and pleading for them to "be reconciled to God" (v. 20). Labeling any cultural activity as missiological

---

5. Affirmed in E. D. Burns, *The Transcultural Gospel: Jesus Is Enough for Sinners in Cultures of Shame, Fear, Bondage, and Weakness* (Cape Coral, FL: Founders, 2021), 7; Daniel Strange, *Their Rock Is Not Like Our Rock* (Grand Rapids: Zondervan, 2015), 28.

engagement can distract the practitioner from preaching and teaching the gospel, which constitute the ministry of reconciliation explicitly.

Proclamation ministry must be conducted with the conviction that only the biblical worldview is true to reality, that only God can make sinners spiritually alive (Eph 2:4–10), and that "God is now commanding men that everyone everywhere should repent" (Acts 17:30). Any secondary missionary activity is only a kingdom-oriented effort if it contributes to the proclamation of Scripture to unrepentant sinners for their salvation and to regenerate believers for their maturity as disciples of Christ.

THE LINGUISTIC PARAMETER

The second parameter for cultural engagement according to the biblical missions model is linguistic. One reason for missionaries to be bold in their proclamation is that all languages operate according to established grammatical rules and are therefore able to accurately express the meaning of Scripture in their contexts. When the proclaimer uses understandable language, audiences perceive an accurate meaning and can be expected to apply it responsibly.

The original and the target language are culture-bound, which might complicate Bible translation and exposition, but the differences in background contexts neither block the discovery of the original meaning nor distort the message, nor hinder its application by the contemporary audience. It does not matter how diverse the target language is from the original biblical language or how culturally particular and complex it is, because most human languages share simple concepts with words that function similarly and lead to stable meanings that are commonly recognized.[6] However, the reality of language universals does not release the missionary from his responsibility to express the biblical propositions in a culturally understandable way. He must possess at least a basic awareness of the local culture and worldview if he is going to pursue pre-evangelistic encounters that will lead to confrontational evangelism.

THE TRANSFORMATIONAL PARAMETER

The third parameter of biblical cultural engagement, the transformational parameter, drives the biblical missions model forward with a well-defined goal: the conversion of individual sinners who become biblical disciples of Christ within the context of the local church. "Transformation" reflects that at conversion the believer pursues obedience to the authoritative Word of God (Rom 6:17–18, 22) and embarks on a path of worldview and lifestyle change within the context of his local culture, living in an increasingly sanctifying conformity to the Scriptures that the missionary has proclaimed (Rom 10:9–10; 1 Cor 6:11). The

---

6. Cliff Goddard and Anna Wierzbicka, *Words and Meanings: Lexical Semantics across Domains, Languages, and Cultures* (Oxford: Oxford University Press, 2014), 10–20. Also see Edith A. Moravcsik, "Explaining Language Universals," in *The Oxford Handbook of Language Typology*, ed. Jae Jung Song (Oxford: Oxford University Press, 2011), 69; also see her explanation in Edith A. Moravcsik, *Explaining Language Typology* (Cambridge: Cambridge University Press, 2013), 5–9.

hope of widespread gospel transformation of the culture and society is not the missionary's goal directly, but as the Lord saves sinners individually and matures them by the power of the Spirit, they live as God-glorifying influences in the world and may contribute to the good of society with increasing notice (Eph 4:11–16; Phil 2:15; 1 Pet 2:17; 3:15).

The transformational parameter intersects with the linguistic parameter in the following way: when an individual comprehends that the original meaning of a text is relatable to his life and his culture and applies it in obedience to Christ, the proclaimed message has become "indigenized" for him.[7] The hopeful endpoint of scriptural indigenization makes it advantageous for the missionary to observe and understand the dynamic beliefs, traditions, and customs of the receptor culture. Indigenization is always the goal: to bring out the significance of the text in ever-changing ways that are appropriate to the situation, so that hearers apply the text by the power of the Spirit, beginning with repenting and repudiating all pagan spiritual knowledge and growing in the grace and knowledge of the Lord Jesus Christ.

Transformation (and scriptural indigenization) is evident when true believers reject their prior idolatry and worship the true and living God (John 17:14–17; 1 John 2:15; cf. 1 Thess 1:9). They worship Christ with a new,

transcultural identity of faith that they exercise in the ways all generations of believers have done before. Ironically, the more the local believer understands and applies Scripture to his life, the more he will identify with believers of all time and across many cultures, because they are united by a common biblical worldview and lifestyle of faith with all who are united to Christ.[8]

Step-by-Step Guide to the Biblical Missions Model

The descriptions above of the biblical missions model of cultural engagement must move from theory to real-life implementation. A synthetic list of missionary activities is now presented to reinforce the value of proclamation ministries in practice that faithful missionaries employ. The list serves as a step-by-step guide to conducting biblically faithful cultural engagement.

It is useful to note that most of the steps listed will be ongoing missions activities, even though they will only be listed at their starting point. The time required to advance to the next step in the sequence is a matter of divine providence and cannot be estimated here. Activities listed with bullet points rather than sequential numbering reflect some flexibility in the order in which they might occur, depending on the context.

---

7. The use of the term *indigenization* here is specifically linked to Scripture and does not encompass the range of sociocultural components that might be intended by the use of the term elsewhere. In missiological use, conservative evangelical missiologist George Peters remarked that by 1989 indigenization was both subjective and variable depending on who used it. George W. Peters, "Foreword," in *Contextualization: Meanings, Methods, and Models* (Pasadena, CA: William Carey Library, 1989), ix.

8. Recognized by Hiebert, *Anthropological Reflections*, 85; Iain N. Murray, *Evangelicalism Divided: A Record of Crucial Change in the Years 1950 to 2000* (Carlisle, PA: Banner of Truth, 2000), 166.

Outline of the Biblical Missions Model

I. Preparation
  A. Learn.
    1. Learn conservative evangelical doctrine.
    2. Learn original language exegesis.
    3. Learn text-driven exegetical theological method.
    4. Learn target language.
  B. Practice.
    1. Practice historical, grammatical hermeneutics.
    2. Practice text-driven exegetical theological method.
    3. Practice expository preaching.
  C. Observe.
    • Observe cultural customs and practices.
    • Seek to understand worldview and beliefs.
    • Seek to understand customs and practices.

II. Proclamation
  A. Evangelize the people.
    • Involve an interpreter until language proficiency.
    • Translate Scripture if needed.
    • Confront sins and false beliefs.
    • Preach the gospel.
  B. Preach expository sermons.
    1. Regularly assemble believers for the preaching event.
    2. Prefer Bible books to topics.
  C. Teach expositionally in the local church.
    1. Regularly assemble believers for Bible study.
    2. Instill regular Bible reading behaviors.
    3. Train believers in hermeneutics, including basic native linguistic analysis.
    4. Guide to determine text's meaning and intentions (implications).
    5. Guide to propose possible applications.
    6. Guide to evaluate customs and practices of the church.
  D. Identify maturing disciples in the local church.
    1. Conduct full-immersion water baptism.
    2. Encourage formal church membership.
    3. Observe responsiveness to teaching and progressive sanctification.
    4. Encourage ministry participation.
  E. Train leaders for the local church.
    1. Train in biblical exposition.
    2. Train in expository preaching.
    3. Train in pastoral ministry.
    4. Train to apply Scripture in order to mature in holiness and avoid syncretism.
      a. In the life of the believers (personal, family, daily life)
      b. In the life of the church (worship, ministries)
      c. In the witness of the church to the world (evangelism, outreach)
    5. Train to plant new local churches.

Explanation of Major Features

The presentation of the biblical missions model of cultural engagement demonstrates the core distinctives of proclamation ministry. Five explanations are offered for understanding the model's structure. First, the model identifies that God's agent for accomplishing most of the steps is the biblically trained missionary. Active participation by local believers will begin to bear fruit for scriptural indigenization at step II.C.5.

Second, the model recognizes only two major groupings of missionary activities: those that prepare the missionary for verbal proclamation in the new culture (step I) and those that accomplish it to some degree (step II). The missionary's preparation phase includes the pre-evangelistic activities of step I.C because they are essential for missionary work but are not directly the work of proclamation. While the preparations might be heavily cultural-missiological (step I.C) and biblical-theological (steps I.A and B), the activities are not yet assertive in the sense of the cultural engagement indicated by the model.

Third, evangelistic proclamation is paramount to establishing the local church, which is why it is reflected first in step II.A and again in the maturing congregation at II.E.4.c. As the church begins to reproduce in step II.E.5, the proclamation phase will begin its sequence again, this time with indigenous leaders planting new local churches in their culture and conducting missionary outreach in new contexts.

Fourth, the proclamation phase is constructed to show that discipleship is the central thrust of the Great Commission. By step II.D the missionary should be able to identify the role that the proclamation activities of II.A, B,

and C have played in transforming regenerate believers by the power of the Word of God. Only maturing men who meet the biblical qualifications of an elder (1 Tim 3:1–7; Titus 1:5–9) will be entrusted with the work of proclamation ministry in and through the local church, according to II.E, though qualified women can undertake the ministries of II.E.4 to train women and children.

Fifth, even though the model outlines a sequence of steps by phase, a certain flexibility is to be expected (as the bulleted items of I.C and II.A most reflect), depending on the dynamics of the situation in which the missionary finds himself at a given time. The Great Commission itself, while principally outlining a logical and chronological sequence for missionary activity, is controlled by the Holy Spirit and thus allows for a rich variety of approaches within the preparation and proclamation phases. When following the biblical missions model, as in everything, the missionary must consult the Lord and experienced partners for practical wisdom on how to proceed.

Conclusion

The mission of the Church in the world is clear: biblically trained believers must go and confront the false beliefs and evil practices of every culture. They do this by confrontationally asserting the content of Scripture and discipling all regenerate believers toward God-glorifying maturity. The kind of cultural engagement that delivers the truth and brings it to bear in a foreign context is described by the "biblical missions model." The model synthesizes key linguistic, theological, and missiological discussions with the goal of ensuring that proclamation ministry (cross-cultural communication) is not sidelined by distractions, so that God's Great Commission task is accomplished to the praise and glory of the Son.

The presentation of the biblical missions model demonstrates at least four core distinctives. First, the model reveals God's gracious design to use human agents who are faithfully trained as his mouthpieces in the world. Second, it indicates that every activity missionaries undertake either prepares for or actively involves the verbal assertion of the biblical content. Third, the model recognizes the life cycle of evangelism and discipleship in the context of the local church, wherein all activities either feed into or flow out of the local church, according to God's design. Finally, the flexibility inherent in the model requires biblical humility in prayer and wise counsel to spiritually discern in a world of many missiological distractions how to "do the next thing" that God will bless.[9]

---

9. The phrase "Do the next thing" was popularized by Elisabeth Elliot, wife of missionary martyr Jim Elliot. The original source was in a poem by Mrs. George A. Paull, *Ye Nexte Thynge*, published by Eleanor Amerman Sutphen (New York: Fleming H. Revell, 1897), 1.

Too Cultured? Hyper-Contextualization in Asia Today

E. D. Burns

Christ said He would build His church (Matt 16:18). Though He is indeed doing that, His church still faces a blitz from the enemy on multiple fronts. For the local churches in Asia, the attack often comes in the form of false teaching. As in the rest of the world, the prosperity gospel is highly visible and destructive in Asia. But there are less obvious threats as well. Local Asian churches face an insidious form of false teaching disguised as one type of missiological contextualization or another. Such errors of contextualization creep in unnoticed through pragmatic suggestions about how to make biblical teaching more culturally relevant. These kinds of suggestions are often received without scrutiny because they are "useful" and "proven to work," or the missionaries who promote them appear to "have good hearts." These methods, however, emerge from aberrant theology and can prove more useful to the enemy than to the Lord. Though not restricted to Asia, the trends that follow are quite problematic.

Honor-Shame Gospel

The heart of the gospel hinges on the imputation of Christ's righteousness through faith alone (Rom 4–5; Gal 2:20–21; 3:10–14). Yet it is not uncommon to read missions literature promoting the honor-shame gospel,[10] explicitly suggesting that the doctrine of justification is a Western concept imposed upon Scripture. In contrast, they teach that "faith" means "faithfulness." The good news these missiologists promote throughout Asia therefore is that people can honor God through faithfulness and allegiance to Him. Insofar as one honors God, God will return the honor by adopting the faithful into His family. In other words, salvation depends on a life of loyalty to God. This is a fundamentally different gospel, much

like what Paul raged against in Galatians, which said that to achieve the blessings of the promise to Abraham, Christians must follow the law of Moses (Gal 2:11–21), and like what Luther battled against in the Reformation, both the works-righteousness system of Roman Catholicism and the meritorious asceticism of mysticism. Sinners are indeed justified by faithfulness—the faithfulness of another, the Lord Jesus Christ. Salvation comes through faith alone as the repentant sinner receives the righteousness of the Faithful One (Gal 2:17–21).

Rapid-Cycle Church-Planting and Disciple-Making Movements

The push for speed has captivated the evangelical missions world. What could be more motivating than the notion that believers can hasten the return of Christ by taking the gospel to every people group (Matt 24:14)? Whether from naive or pragmatic motives, many peddlers of multiplicative ministry approaches, such as rapid-cycle church-planting and disciple-making movements,[11]

---

10. The honor-shame gospel is commonly used to reframe the ancient gospel for non-Western cultures that value honor and (avoid) shame over any other set of values. Instead of framing the gospel as the good news of objective righteousness in Christ through faith alone, the honor-shame perspective claims that the original problem is shame (not original sin in Adam) and that the solution to the problem is honor. The way of finding honor is through faithfulness (not faith alone). In other words, it is an emphasis on expiation and sanctification, not propitiation and justification. For an argument for the centrality of receiving Christ's righteousness through faith alone over against achieving God's approval and honor through faithfulness, see E. D. Burns, *Ancient Gospel, Brave New World: Jesus Still Saves Sinners in Cultures of Shame, Fear, Bondage, and Weakness* (Cape Coral, FL: Founders, 2021), 205–76.

11. The seminal book promoting disciple-making movements was David Watson and Paul Watson, *Contagious Disciple Making: Leading Others on a Journey of Discovery* (Nashville: Thomas Nelson, 2014). A good review of it can be found in Ed Roberts, "Book Review: Contagious Disciple Making, by David and Paul Watson," 9Marks, July 16, 2015, https://www.9marks.org/review/book-review-contagious-disciple-making-by-david-and-paul-watson/.

promise that their methods will generate multiple churches monthly or even weekly. Such strategies, however, disregard the clear biblical prohibition against appointing new converts as elders (1 Tim 3:6). To be fair, when many borrow ideas and language from popular missions methods like these, they are not being devious, but gullible. There are, however, others who intentionally compromise the biblical mandates to teach the Word and train other men who will unknowingly do the same.

Egalitarian Leadership

Many macro- and micro-level cultures within Asia are traditionally matriarchal, with the mothers and wives holding social control. In such settings, it is common for men in the highest positions of power, whether corporately or politically, to listen to their mothers and fear displeasing them over their business partners or political advisers. It is also assumed that many men have mistresses who sexually manipulate them. This is not the case for every macro and micro culture in Asia, and it is certainly not the case for every individual. But the issue gets discussed in varying degrees across many cultures in Asia. With this cultural background of

pre-evangelized and pre-discipled gender-role dysfunction, the local church tends to struggle with the roles of men and women in the church. Missionaries who are themselves egalitarian encourage men and women alike to be elders and pastors.

The proponents of egalitarianism evade Paul's prohibition of women in church leadership (e.g., 1 Tim 2:8–14; 1 Cor 14:34) with the use of two hermeneutical arguments.[12] First, they argue that Paul was not writing about the universal church but about certain unqualified women in the first-century contexts of Ephesus and Corinth. Second, they claim that Paul's letters are not binding. Rather, he was making wise recommendations that, though worthy to consider, are not immediately realistic in the Asian matriarchal context. The latter idea, though ubiquitous, is not often in print; rather, it comes from millennia of ingrained tradition in a context where people strongly follow tradition, custom, and sociofamilial expectations.

Insider Movements

There is a strain of missiological debate about how quickly Muslims and Hindus who turn to Jesus in faith should publicly withdraw from Islamic or Hindu customs

---

12. For this occurrence in cross-cultural discussions, see Loren Cunningham and David Hamilton, *Why Not Women?* (Seattle, WA: YWAM, 2000); E. Randolph Richards and Brandon J. O'Brien, *Misreading Scripture with Western Eyes: Removing Cultural Blinders to Better Understand the Bible* (Downers Grove, IL: InterVarsity, 2012), 169–70. For the more general arguments from egalitarians, see Janet George, *Still Side by Side* (Christians for Biblical Equality, 2013); William J. Webb, *Slaves, Women, and Homosexuals* (Downers Grove, IL: InterVarsity, 2001); Rebecca Groothuis, *Good News for Women: A Biblical Picture of Gender Equality* (Grand Rapids: Baker, 1997).

to follow Christ.[13] Conversion from Islam to Christianity is rare in Asia, and it can be dangerous for the new convert to make his new allegiance known. It is wise, some missiologists argue, to secretly worship "Isa" (Jesus in Arabic) in the mosque and to change nothing externally with regard to Islamic customs—in other words, to be an "insider." This is an extreme position and not equally shared by all missiologists. Many missiologists, probably even the majority, would suggest maintaining some customs that are redeemable while separating from old traditions that conflict with essential Christian doctrine. Nevertheless, it seems that arguments for radical positions are what gradually shift the window of tolerable and acceptable praxis. And because of social pressure to avoid being close-minded, new passionate proposals based on unique standpoints and experiences can quickly shift opinions without much deliberation and debate. Such proposals hardly fit the call to discipleship that Jesus gave.

To the chagrin of some Western missionaries who promote insider movement strategies, many local Asian Christians often insist on suffering for Christ and breaking free of the chains of Islam even in the face of martyrdom. Nevertheless, a strong spirit of compromise exists throughout Asia wherever easy-believism and the gospel of "safety-ism" is promoted by Western missionaries. The challenge here is not so much to convince local believers to be bold in their faith, but to deal with the obstacles that come from Western missionaries who insist on creating an insider movement of secret followers of Isa.

In all of the challenges missionaries face in the Great Commission, let us not forget the duty of the Word-driven missionary. We should stand courageously against the temptation to hesitantly discuss the Word as helpful advice for cultural flourishing. No. Rather, we should humbly declare the Word as a heavenly announcement for eternal salvation. We must devote ourselves with surgeon-like precision and sniper-like accuracy to communicating the gospel rightly, not contextualizing the gospel "relevantly."

---

13. For a survey on the topic of insider movements, see Harley Talman and John Jay Travis, eds., *Understanding Insider Movements: Disciples of Jesus within Diverse Religious Communities* (Pasadena, CA: William Carey Library, 2015). For books expressing concerns, see Joshua Lingel, Jeff Morton, and Bill Nikides, *Chrislam: How Missionaries Are Promoting an Islamicized Gospel* (Garden Grove, CA: i2 Ministries, 2011); Ayman Ibrahim and Ant Greenham, eds., *Muslim Conversions to Christ* (New York: Peter Lang, 2018); Derek Brotherson, *Contextualization or Syncretism? The Use of Other-Faith Worship Forms in the Bible and in Insider Movements*, Evangelical Missiological Society Monograph Series 10 (Eugene, OR: Pickwick, 2021).

Marketplace Ministry: A Natural Approach to Disciple-Making

Peter Olivetan

"Marketplace ministry" refers to a missions approach that involves actively, intentionally engaging with nonbelievers through marketplace relationships or social networks. It is alternatively referred to as "tentmaking," "business as missions," "business for transformation," and "business for blessing." It is one of the most natural approaches to making disciples, which makes it an effective avenue for global missions. Below is a summary of the effectiveness that it seeks, the advantages it has, and the challenges it faces.

The Effectiveness It Seeks

When missionaries are rightly taught not to be numbers-oriented, they may find it easy to rationalize nonproductive ministries and focus broadly on faithfulness only. By contrast, each potential missionary should be asking deep-level strategic questions. Their goal ought to be employing the most effective way to fulfill Jesus' mandate in the particular country or region they are considering. Answers will vary. In some

situations, sending a traditional missionary is the legal, most appropriate, and wisest option. In other contexts, this would be legally possible but culturally ineffective and therefore unwise. In still other situations, it would be both illegal and culturally ineffective and therefore simply foolish. Each situation must be carefully and prayerfully evaluated. In the latter two cases, marketplace ministry is highly advisable.

That said, marketplace ministers must also be held accountable for effectiveness. They are often (and rightly) challenged by their sending churches as to whether they are "keeping the main thing the main thing." Biblically speaking, "the main thing" of the Great Commission—in other words, its central mandate—is not faithfulness in the marketplace but making disciples (Matt 28:18–20). Still, making disciples requires intentional relationships with people, and that is something marketplace ministry affords well. This leads to its advantages.

The Advantages It Has

Four main advantages of marketplace ministry are worth mentioning. First, this approach provides natural relationships. Building relationships in a foreign land is not easy and takes time. On the other hand, marketplace ministers—whether teachers, coaches, medical professionals, engineers, or businesspeople—have genuine, natural opportunities. What they do occupationally makes sense to the locals and therefore opens doors. Careers in the service sector typically provide the most relationships, but God can use (and has used) virtually any profession to make disciples.

Second, marketplace ministry provides the disciple-maker with the most important element, time with those relationships. A few years ago, a large international agency surveyed all of their missionaries in the Muslim world, asking them how many hours on average they spent with Muslims weekly. The collective average was only six hours.[14] Since virtually all people work for a living, that low number makes sense. Traditional missionaries see people only outside of work hours. In contrast, marketplace ministers spend up to ten times that amount of time with the people they are trying to reach. At a minimum, they are engaged for thirty to fifty hours per week with unbelievers just through their profession.

Third, marketplace ministry provides access to those who have never heard the gospel. Roughly 80 percent of the unreached people on the planet live in the so-called 10/40 Window, the area between 10° N latitude and 40° N latitude.[15] In most of that area's countries, it is illegal to go as a traditional missionary. However, going in as a marketplace professional provides access. Now this requires an honorable, legitimate occupation, as opposed to "tent-faking," the setting up of a false business platform. Plus, those who view their work as a way to glorify God will work with more excellence than their colleagues or competitors (Eph 6:7; Col 3:23). Such commitment can even open doors to civil leaders (Prov 22:29).

Finally, marketplace ministers have the opportunity to authenticate the gospel. The worker shares the message as well as the testimony of his daily life. Over time his local friends begin to realize that the reason he

---

14. This information was communicated via personal conversation.

15. Luis Bush, "What Is the 10/40 Window?," Luis Bush Papers, October 22, 1996, https://luisbushpapers.com/1040window/1996/10/22/what-is-the-1040-window/. The phrase was coined by Luis Bush in 1990 following his comments at the second International Congress of World Evangelization (Lausanne II); cf. Robert T. Coote, "'AD 2000' and the '10/40 Window': A Preliminary Assessment," *International Bulletin of Missionary Research* 24, no. 4 (October 2000): 160–66. However, with the growth of the Global South since then, the "0/40 Window" would now more accurately represent the primary block of the unreached.

is different is something spiritual, not cultural. They realize they are engaging with a person who has been transformed by the power of God.

The Challenges It Faces

With increased opportunities also come challenges. Three are noteworthy. First, marketplace ministers often take on more risk than traditional workers. They often have additional legal or financial risks, plus more personal exposure to harm if they become publicly known.

Second, this ministry also requires hard work. Missional workers have the same challenges as unbelieving expatriate workers, like learning a new language and culture and dealing with the daily pressures of their jobs. For a business owner, challenges are increased; the owner must consistently add value to customers, train and lead staff, meet payroll, keep up with taxes and regulations, and walk with integrity in corrupt societies. This role is only for dedicated persons.

Third, marketplace ministers need encouragement and accountability to stay on target. Because the best of them are committed to honoring God and serving people with their work, they can find themselves left with little time for spiritual ministry. This is why true ministers align themselves with others of like mind, to help them do both. It is why organizations like C12 Group and APEX Expats exist.[16]

Thus, there are at once many advantages and challenges to a marketplace ministry approach to missions. The challenges are not insurmountable, and as the advantages outweigh the challenges, every modern sending church needs to seriously consider the marketplace approach. They need to consider how to mobilize and leverage the professional resources of their congregation to fulfill Christ's mandate to make disciples of all nations.

---

16. "About," C12 Group, accessed June 18, 2024, https://www.joinc12.com/about/; "About," APEX Expats, accessed June 18, 2024, https://apexexpats.net. A somewhat similar organization is Christian Business Men's Connection (CBMC); see "Mission," CBMC, accessed June 18, 2024, https://www.cbmc.com.

Marketplace Ministry: The "10x" Factor

L. C. Ridley

Missionaries in many contexts follow what can be considered the Full-Time Ministry Model, where full-time religious work on the field is the goal. Many missionaries in the Middle East desire to achieve this goal, but the reality is there is no legal permission to do full-time religious work. Hence, missionaries need some other reason for being in the community. This is where marketplace ministry comes into play. Marketplace ministry is called the "10x factor." It gives the missionary ten times more effectiveness in the Middle East than the traditional full-time missionary approach. This insert explains the difference between marketplace ministry and other ministry models.

The biblical precedent for marketplace ministry comes from the description of Paul in Acts 18:1–4 as a tentmaker. Provisions from tentmaking supported Paul's missions work. In countries that do not give legal permission or legal recognition to be a member of the clergy or a minister, tentmaking is a popular route. However, within tentmaking there is variety. The primary alternatives are the Platform Model and the Marketplace Ministry Model. Each has a particular philosophy of ministry.

In the Platform Model, the missionary's occupation or business is a secondary consideration—a platform to remain in the country. Neighbors ask questions about the foreign believer's business, and when the missionary, who desires to serve primarily in an evangelistic capacity, stumbles to explain what his recognized occupation is, the locals naturally conclude he is hiding something from them and is a suspicious character. In this way, the missionary might appear to operate a drug front in an empty store, for example. Thus, from the standpoint of public perception, the Platform Model is self-defeating for evangelism.

There is another problem with the Platform Model: missionaries employing it often struggle to fulfill their platform occupations well. They might lack the skill sets, qualifications, and even interest in their secular employments. Their struggles with their jobs might become apparent to themselves and to those who work with them. The struggles are legitimate: they tell people in their home country they are missionaries, but they struggle in ministry, and they tell locals they are professionals, yet they struggle in their professions. Many who undertake the Platform Model suffer health issues from these tensions and end up leaving the field altogether.

The alternative to the Platform Model is the Marketplace Ministry Model. The first principle of Marketplace Ministry is that the chosen profession has to fit both the missionary and the community. The missionary must do the kind of work that he has an ability, natural interest, and excitement to get up in the morning to do. As the neighbors observe his work, the profession must be useful in their context. Following the Marketplace Ministry Model involves true integration into the community. Some of the benefits of getting a real job or starting a real business in the country is that the missionary never feels a need to bend the truth regarding the reason for being there. There will be real work, real stressors, real timelines, and real deadlines. Often these missionaries will undertake their marketplace position while learning the language and culture, which multiplies the missionary's real-life challenges.

Marketplace ministry in the Middle East is a difficult path, yet it is a rewarding one for at least two reasons. First, missionaries who embrace the Marketplace Ministry Model are totally immersed in the culture and often display exceptional maturity as they work in the culture. They are on the best and quickest path to learn the language and culture and to build meaningful relationships with locals in the work environment. Friendships blossom when people see one another in challenging situations like the workplace.

Second, the most important positive outcome of the Marketplace Ministry Model is the amount of time spent with local people. The missionary joins the community, for example, by taking public transport to work, rising early in the morning and returning home late in the evening, and leading a very busy life during the workweek around many other similar workers. Social activity is generally reserved for the weekend, as most local citizens who are well integrated into society often work fifty hours each week and are simply too busy to spend interpersonal time on weekdays. Yet missionaries who do marketplace ministry spend every day of the week with the locals, multiplying the time they are present with them from what might otherwise be perhaps six hours on the weekend to upward of sixty hours across the week.

In terms of time spent, the Marketplace Ministry Model is considered the "10x factor," since it garners ten times the amount of missionary presence with the local people than most missionaries in the Full-Time Ministry Model are privileged to enjoy. The sheer quantity of hours spent working among locals can lead to enjoying better quality time with them as relationships develop. While spending time at work could be viewed as taking time away from ministry, these Marketplace Ministry missionaries spend all their time with people at work, and by being with people, they spend all their time doing ministry.

Therefore, not only does the Marketplace Ministry Model shorten the learning curve for those who are trying to fulfill the Great Commission, but it embeds the missionary in the mission, leading to opportunities for evangelism and discipleship, according to God's plan and purposes. A lot of resources of time, money and people have been invested in taking the gospel to the Middle East. The Marketplace Ministry Model may be the most efficient way to continue this work for most missionaries today.

CHAPTER 72

Ten Mistakes Missionaries Make

Cecil Stalnaker

In cross-cultural ministry, all missionaries make mistakes. Sometimes they are innocent, like mistaking two similar words while preaching in a foreign language.[1] However, some mistakes are much worse. Certain errors can be critical because they negatively impact the ministry of the missionary or the reputation of God, the local church, or the gospel itself. This chapter identifies ten mistakes that new ministers should avoid to become more effective.

Mistake 1: Failure to Prepare Theologically for Cross-Cultural Ministry

Teaching at an internationally oriented seminary in Europe, I had numerous students fresh off the mission field coming to take up their studies. They planned to take a break from their cross-cultural ministry, study at the seminary, and then return to missionary work. The reason behind this for several students was their realization that they were over their heads theologically in their cross-cultural ministry. They needed further theological education.

Being adept theologically is essential because missionaries have all kinds of theological encounters on the mission field. Many encounters arise with unbelievers, such as in Paul's case in Athens (Acts 17:19, 24–29). But many come from young or seasoned believers, and some even from fellow missionaries. All missionaries will have to face, at one time or another, false theological ideas related to an understanding of God, Jesus Christ, Scripture, and human nature. Missionaries must therefore work at being good theologians. This does not necessarily mean that all will have a Bible college or seminary education. However, the missions world is a theological one; whether a missionary is a church planter, evangelist,

---

1. For example, I am a nonnative French speaker who ministered south of Brussels, Belgium. Early on after learning the language, I served the Lord's Supper to a congregation, reading 1 Corinthians 11:23–26. Then, to the amusement of my listeners, I took the bread (in French, *le pain*) and said, "This piece of rabbit (*lapin*) represents the body of our Lord." After the service, I learned of my mistake from the generous church family.

trainer of pastors, support worker, or refugee worker, all missionaries will be involved in theology.

Moreover, theological preparation is needed because Satan's goal is to create a counterfeit kingdom rivaling and replacing God's kingdom. Satan's goal is to "make [himself] like the Most High" (Isa 14:14). He will promote his kingdom through lies, "for he is a liar and the father of lies" (John 8:44). Scripture warns that his counterfeit strategy is to establish false Christs (Matt 24:5, 24), false prophets (Matt 7:15), false apostles (2 Cor 11:13), false teachers (2 Pet 2:1), and false gospels (Gal 1:6–7). Such threats will even infiltrate unsuspecting churches (Acts 20:29–30). Those without solid theological knowledge and understanding can be easily duped.

Mistake 2: Failure to Enter the Culture with Humility

Missionary work requires humility, for which Jesus is the model. Having been sent by the Father into the world, Jesus entered upon His mission with humility. He did nothing out of selfish ambition but looked out for the interests of others rather than his own (Phil 2:3–6). The book of Acts records that Paul likewise learned to serve the Lord "with all humility" and even tears (Acts 20:19). Such humility is critical to missions for at least two reasons.

For one, adapting to a culture and truly becoming the servant of the people being reached takes unnatural humility (cf. 1 Cor 9:19–23). This attitude is often difficult for highly educated missionaries or those who come from upper-class families. Even being proud of one's country or customs can be obstacles, for example, when a missionary says to his audience, "Back home, we do it this way." Most missionaries naturally believe they are doing things rightly, so it takes humility for them to ask themselves, *Am I importing my own cultural traditions into this new culture, or is what I am doing a true biblical principle that should be applied across cultures?* It takes humility to sit at the feet of an indigenous people to understand and learn their language and customs. Yet humble missionaries will be diligent students, regarding their people as more important than themselves (Phil 2:3).

It also takes humility for a missionary to step aside and let indigenous churchmen take on leadership roles, including preaching and teaching. This requires him to recognize when other, newer believers have been given the necessary spiritual gifts and talents from God, which, given the proper training, would enable them to do an even better job than the missionary himself. Humility is required from the very start if the missionary would lay a foundation for the success of national laborers. No humble missionary holds on to a ministry post that national believers should take up (cf. Acts 14:23).

Mistake 3: Failure to Take the Culture Seriously

Like fish in water, people are immersed in their own culture more than they ever know. Missiologist Paul Hiebert defines culture as "the more or less integrated system of ideas, feelings, and values and their associated patterns of behavior and products shared by a group of people who organize and regulate what they think, feel and do."[2] Otherwise stated, each culture is a pattern of living or a road map by which its members interact.

The missionary must take the culture seriously because the gospel's message has to be communicated within that cultural context. Thus, a missionary must know how indigenous people think and behave, what they value, and what they assume. If he does not take the time to learn and understand the culture, unnecessary offenses may be given as buffers to the gospel and misunderstandings will certainly occur, including misunderstandings of the gospel.

A lack of cultural concern could appear in several ways. One example is that a missionary could spend more time with fellow missionaries than he does with the local people. A second example might be remaining on the field only for abbreviated terms. As a third example, one could view the indigenous people as "pet projects"—which is not biblical missions—rather than seriously engaging with them as equals created in the image of God (Gen 1:26). Conversely, missionaries could gain a sinful, critical spirit; they might become increasingly paternalistic, ethnocentric, or even reject the people out of growing prejudice. Finally, a missionary might allow for little credibility in the eyes of the indigenous people, which

significantly lowers his ability to influence them for the kingdom of God (see above on humility). Missionaries must beware; the culture into which they go matters for their mission.

Mistake 4: Failure to Understand and Interact with the Worldview

Understanding the worldview of the target culture is also crucial for the kingdom of God to advance. Worldview is best defined as "the basic assumption about reality which lies behind the beliefs and behavior of a culture."[3] These are assumptions about life and the world that the people in a culture share. Worldview concerns these factors:

- God—what is believed about God or false gods
- Man—what it means to be human and what the human condition is
- Afterlife—what happens when a person dies and why it happens
- Knowledge/truth—what can be known about the above matters and how
- Morality—what is right, what is wrong, and on what basis this is determined
- History—how one should interpret and relate to the past

Understanding each of the above aspects of a worldview helps the missionary to effectively engage people in the culture that holds to it. Missionaries will, for instance, want to

---

2. Paul Heibert, *Anthropological Insights for Missionaries* (Grand Rapids: Baker, 1985), 30.

3. Heibert, 45.

know if a supreme god exists in the people's worldview or if they have a plethora of gods. For the true God must not be inadvertently added to the people's pantheon nor identified with any false god (cf. Acts 17:23). Missionaries must investigate how a culture views mankind, whether sinful or good by condition, so as to correct false appraisals of man's worth or ability, to proclaim the bad news of condemnation, and to make way for the good news of salvation. Missionaries must also discern a culture's assumptions about truth and knowledge, for God's direct, special revelation in the Bible is the basis for the gospel's authority and validity in all times and in all places, and it will come into direct conflict with traditions. Knowing the people's view of God, man, sin, and truth will guide how best to proclaim the gospel.

Mistake 5: Failure to Take Language Learning Seriously

It is God's design for people to hear the gospel in their mother tongue (Acts 2:1–11). No doubt, many or most of the individuals in Jerusalem on Pentecost could have understood the apostles in the contemporary trade language (Greek) or even the prominent local language (Aramaic). Yet the Holy Spirit chose to impress the truth upon the heart of each hearer "in [their] own language in which [they] were born" (2:8). Notwithstanding the other purposes of this miracle—such as the validation of the messenger (1 Cor 14:22) and the signaling of a change in dispensations (Acts 2:16ff.)—it affirms the global reach of the gospel that was always intended by God (Gen 12:3; 22:18; 26:4; Isa 42:6; 49:6; 60;1–3; Gal 3:8). In fact, diverse languages may continue to be spoken and recognized in Christ's kingdom and the eternal state, no longer frustrating communication but simply adding to the rich glory of God's dominion (cf. Dan 7:13–14; Rev 5:9; 7:9; 21:24, 26; 22:2).[4]

The use of translators is helpful and sometimes necessary in advancing the gospel. But they cannot be the long-term solution. The missionary cannot gauge whether his translator correctly communicated the truth. Nor is the missionary able to gauge whether what was translated accurately was understood by the hearer. There can be inaccuracies, even perversions of the gospel in the process. So, translators should not be relied upon as a missions strategy. Other missionaries never become proficient in their target language because they get sidetracked from language study. They permit other ministry activities to overrule it, especially those where their mother tongue can be employed.

Yet, besides God's designs at Pentecost and possibly in eternity, and besides gospel clarity, language learning is critical to missionary effectiveness in other ways. Learning the people's tongue establishes the missionary's credibility. Missionaries who diligently learn the tongue tend to be taken more seriously than those who have not. It often brings respect and authority. Moreover, language learning demonstrates to

---

4. Cf. Randy Alcorn, *Heaven* (Wheaton, IL: Tyndale, 2004), 363–65, 380.

the indigenous people that they matter to God (Isa 49:6). It is one of the clearest testimonies that one's mission is a labor of love.

Mistake 6: Failure to Focus on Disciple-Making

Some missionaries err by focusing on success, defined as large numbers of converts. Practically, numbers can be a sign of something healthy (e.g., Acts 2:41; 4:4). However, focusing on numbers is misleading. The Great Commission is concerned not with professions of faith only but with repentant, believing disciples of Jesus Christ, forgiven of their sins and walking in His commandments (Matt 28:19–20; Luke 24:46–48; John 20:21–23). Conversely, when numbers are thought to be the marker of success, the missionary's endurance is highly weakened. Missionaries who do not feel successful often leave the mission field and either head home or go to a field with better prospects for large numbers to respond. They will lack the faithfulness that Christ requires of His servants (Matt 25:21; 1 Cor 4:2), and they will not see Christ formed in any of those they leave behind (Gal 4:19). Disciple-making, not professed conversions, should be the focus.

Mistake 7: Failure to Recognize the Sovereignty of God in Evangelism

Looking for success is nothing new in missiology. The alleged keys to success have been many:

power evangelism, incarnational evangelism, apostolic leadership, finding a "person of peace," discovering territorial spirits, culturally accommodating contextualization methods, insider movements, discovery Bible studies, obedience-oriented discipleship, and more. Many believe that if they can just find the correct method, numbers will surely turn to the Lord.

However, both the quality and the quantity of missions success come from God. It is Christ who builds His church (Matt 16:18; Acts 2:47).[5] It is God who produces all spiritual fruit (Col 2:19). He "opened a door of faith to the Gentiles" (Acts 14:27), and He opens the hearts of unbelievers to receive the truth (Acts 16:14). Scripture never attributes any human method as the key, the "silver bullet," to anyone's conversion. Preachers can till the ground, sow the seed, and water the sprout, but it is always God who gives the growth (1 Cor 3:6–7). That being so, the preacher must rely on the Holy Spirit working through the preaching of His Word to convert all those whom God has sovereignly chosen to draw by faith to His Son (1 Cor 2:1–5; 2 Cor 4:1–10).

Mistake 8: Failure to Recognize the Demonic Dimension

Missionaries must recognize that missions work is more than a human endeavor. A blind spot has been noted, in Westerners in particular, regarding the spirit world.[6] Their cultural

---

5. According to Longenecker, that "the Lord" (*ho kyrios*), that is, Jesus, was adding to His church is emphasized in Acts 2:47. Richard N. Longenecker, "The Acts of the Apostles," in *EBC*, vol. 9, *John and Acts*, ed. Frank E. Gaebelein (Grand Rapids: Zondervan, 1981), 291.

6. Paul Hiebert, "The Flaw of the Excluded Middle," *Missiology: An International Review* 10, no. 1 (January 1982): 35–47.

background, the worldview of which is tainted by secularism, often makes it difficult for them to comprehend the reality of demonic opposition in the battle that evangelism is. The apostle Paul, however, described how Satan "has blinded the minds of the unbelieving" (2 Cor 4:4). He knew that the missionary's battle was not with flesh and blood but with "the schemes of the devil" and his "spiritual forces of wickedness" (Eph 6:11–12). Therefore, spiritual warfare is a reality to be faced with awareness, prayer, and preparation (2 Cor 10:3–5).

Most of the devil's work is deceptive. He seeks to create a counterfeit kingdom (see above under Mistake 1). "Satan disguises himself as an angel of light," as do his ministers (2 Cor 11:14). He opposes the kingdom of God by distorting, altering, and contradicting God's truth. Missionaries will encounter savage wolves (Matt 10:16; Acts 20:19), who attempt to prey upon God's people (e.g., 2 Cor 11:3–4). Thus, the missionary Paul was deeply concerned that the believers he left behind not be led astray through "doctrines of demons" (1 Tim 4:1). So, too, ought missionaries today, who would be like him.

Mistake 9: Failure to Communicate Effectively with People Back Home

The people back home are sometimes left in the dark regarding their missionaries. Many communicate with their supporting churches, but others fail them through silence from the field. This should not be. Sending and supporting churches have made an essential investment in the kingdom. The elders have rightly seen their responsibility to make disciples of Christ both near and far. Many brothers and sisters in these churches have also made financial sacrifices to support their missionaries. It is only right that they should be informed of the work, its progress, its obstacles, and its prayer needs.

Missionary Paul was a communicator. Despite the lack of speed and technology in his day, correspondence was a priority for him. Even in prison, he sent to churches that were part of his life (Phil 1:12–14; Col 4:3, 4). He frequently called them his "fellow partakers," and "fellow workers," and "partners," in the gospel (Phil 1:7; 4:3; Col 4:11; Phlm 17). Missionaries today must likewise remember that people back home are not mere supporters or spectators; they are ministry partners (3 John 8). Not only, then, should partners communicate out of responsibility and accountability but also out of encouragement, to elevate a vision in the local church for global evangelism and disciple-making.

Mistake 10: Failure to Recognize Mission Drift

Harvard University, founded as Harvard College in 1636, had as its most basic purpose to leave a literate clergy for the Puritan churches of New England.[7] Almost four hundred years later, the university has a humanist chief chaplain professing no faith in God.[8] Mission drift

---

7. Samuel Eliot Morison, *Three Centuries of Harvard: 1636–1936* (Cambridge, MA: Harvard University Press, 1936), 23.

8. Emma Goldberg, "The New Chief Chaplain at Harvard? An Atheist," *New York Times*, August 26, 2021, https://www.nytimes.com/2021/08/26/us/harvard-chaplain-greg-epstein.html.

on the part of Harvard is dramatic, from a God-shaped founding faculty to a secular modern one.[9] But other Christian organizations, including missions agencies and even churches, have started out with a pure gospel and a Great Commission philosophy, and then in time have slowly drifted away. Other goals and values crowded out Christ and disciple-making.

Christians in general and missionaries in particular can engage in many worthwhile activities. Yet the missions model of the apostles must always be kept central. This is seen succinctly in Acts 14:21–23, when Paul and Barnabas were in the cities of Derbe, Lystra, Iconium, and Pisidian Antioch. Their tasks were summarized as the following: (1) proclaiming the gospel, (2) making new disciples, (3) strengthening the souls of maturing disciples, and (4) appointing indigenous elders, which is to say, planting churches.[10]

Missional drift occurs when missionaries, churches, or agencies lose focus on the above mentioned four activities. It most often occurs when activity goals are set too broadly. This does not mean that medical missions, digging wells, or caring for orphans, for example, cannot be a part of missions work. They are indeed missions if they are simultaneously proclaiming the gospel, making disciples, strengthening the souls of believers, or playing a role in planting new churches. But if not, mission drift has set in, and responsible churchmen and missionaries must redirect their efforts toward the apostolic model.

Conclusion

The above missionary mistakes need to be avoided as much as possible. More could be added, but a complete list is impossible. Missionaries will inevitably make mistakes. Some will be harmless. Yet for those that are hurtful, repentance is needed as well as confidence that God's grace abounds all the more. Christ will build His Church despite any Christian's failures. He knows our frame (Ps 103:14; Heb 4:15), that all missionaries are human and therefore weak and sinful. None will cross the finish line mistake-free. Still, God uses those who are simply available, prepared, faithful, and teachable. By His grace, the kingdom of God advances and His servants are welcomed home with comforting words, "Well done, good and faithful slave" (Matt 25:21).

---

9. The divinity school's "About" page reads, "Now, two centuries later, the concerns of the founders of Harvard continue to guide the Divinity School, but within a much enlarged and broadened sense of mission." "History and Mission," Harvard Divinity School, accessed June 18, 2024, https://hds.harvard.edu/about/history-and-mission.

10. See Eckhard J. Schnabel, *Paul the Missionary* (Downers Grove, IL: IVP Academic, 2008), 28.

Building Cultural Intelligence in Pre-Field Missions Training

Lisa LaGeorge

In the beginning of the millennium, social researchers in Singapore began to investigate geographically mobile employees at multinational companies, asking the question, "How do we know if employees who move cross-culturally for work will be successful?"[11] The resulting field of study led to the concept of cultural intelligence (CQ):[12] the ability to learn, adapt, relate, and function successfully across various cultural settings. Researchers discovered that strong CQ among employees contributes substantial cost benefits to the international business community, especially in the realm of employee retention.

Effective CQ is an essential skill for any Christian for three primary reasons: each individual comes from a culture, the Church is multicultural, and reading the Scriptures is a cross-cultural activity. First, everyone is born into a culture, including various regional, national, or religious settings. Second, the family of God is multicultural. How beautiful are the passages in Revelation that reveal men and women from every tongue, tribe, and nation worshiping at the feet of God! Learning to engage together in this life can be challenging, but such harmony provides a signpost for a watching world to see how God's kingdom truly functions. Finally, reading the Bible is a cross-cultural activity; the Scriptures cross boundaries of history, linguistics, and ethnic and national realities. Consider, for example, the differences between the Gospels. Matthew contains more Jewish culture; and Luke explains Jesus' life to Greek readers. CQ can caution the believer to study the Scriptures more carefully and to question faulty interpretations that may arise out of our own cultural experience. A greater knowledge of our own cross-cultural awareness and strategies can

---

11. See, e.g., the work in the various essays of Soon Ang and Linn van Dyne, eds., *Handbook of Cultural Intelligence: Theory, Measurement, and Application* (New York: Routledge, 2008).

12. The Q refers to *quotient*, as in the familiar abbreviation IQ (intellectual quotient) and the nickname EQ (emotional intelligence).

provide a clearer understanding of God's Word. Every Christian needs growing cultural intelligence.

Developing cultural intelligence is also an essential skill for any Christian preparing for cross-cultural missions. For the person considering long-term or even short-term missions, developing this intelligence is a significant factor in both predicting and assisting the development of effective relationships in a cross-cultural setting. Multicultural teams and church settings bring relational and leadership challenges that can be eased with active CQ.

Each activity within ministry also requires cultural awareness. Consider the conversation Jesus had with the Samaritan woman at Jacob's well in John 4 or Paul's address of the Areopagus in Acts 17. Both utilized their understanding of the erroneous beliefs in the culture to clarify the message of the gospel to their hearers. Cross-cultural workers need to recognize their own cultural influences, be alert to the cross-cultural nature of the Scriptures, and be able to clearly communicate through both into the target culture.

Adapting to a culture is, additionally, an incarnational means of serving the gospel in that location. The hard work of learning a new language, moving to a new location,

and setting aside familiar comforts and preferences demonstrates a love for the new culture and people. In a small way, cultural adaptation demonstrates Jesus' incarnation of leaving His heavenly home to walk the dusty roads of Israel.

Intentional cultural adjustment further demonstrates that the gospel is greater than any one culture—it is not a "Western religion." Instead, Jesus is Lord of all, and He intends to call His church from all of humanity.

In addition to the biblical, theological, and ecclesiastical education often undertaken, cultural preparation in missions training is frequently focused on building a base of knowledge about a target country. While cultural knowledge is one element of CQ, three additional components point to effective adaptability: exploring personal motivation for cross-cultural interaction, developing strategies for continuing observation, and behaving appropriately in various cultural situations.

Effective training situations must occur in active, relational scenarios that include reflection for applying the acquired CQ skills. Such experiences will provide participants with opportunities to improve their learning methods and to process what they learn about God, themselves, others, and cultural engagement.[13] The following is a short description of each of the four CQ

---

13. For more of this type of training, see Lisa LaGeorge, "Short-Term Missions at The Master's College: An Experimental Education" (PhD diss., Biola University, 2009).

factors with suggestions for individual and team activities that will build growing cultural intelligence.[14]

CQ Drive: Exploring Motivation

Why is this person engaging in missions? Is the person motivated by guilt or adventure or God's glory? Appropriate motivation will provide determination and confidence to keep going even through the discomfort of cross-cultural adaptation.

- Consider motivation in previous travel experiences. What might be different this time?
- Take a long hike as a team or do some extensive physical labor together. How do you and team members respond when the activity is hard enough to make you want to quit?
- Spend some time journaling to reflect on what failure in this process might look like and how that relates to your motivation in participation.

CQ Knowledge: Building Information

What do you know about the country you are going to—particularly its culture, language, and history? Gathering facts about a country may be simple, but that knowledge must be applied for successful engagement.

- Take time to research the target country. Include a brief history, ethnic composition, political structure, church history, economic realities, etc.
- Read a novel or watch a movie from the country. Works of fiction may not be entirely accurate, but they do provide practice in asking good questions about worldview.
- Pray through information from news sources, *Operation World*,[15] or host missionaries.

CQ Strategy: Planning Adjustment

How do you handle confusion? Are you able to observe and understand various cultural activities? CQ strategy is applying appropriate curiosity to discern what is happening around you.

- Do your grocery shopping or eat your dinner in an unfamiliar, culturally diverse part of town.
- Watch a foreign movie with characters from foreign cultures, and practice

---

14. For additional resources, see David Livermore, *Expand Your Borders: Discover 10 Cultural Clusters* (East Lansing, MI: Cultural Intelligence Center, 2013). Also, "Assessments," The Center for Cultural Intelligence, accessed June 18, 2024, https://culturalq.com/products-services/assessments/.

15. For various prayer calendars and topics, see the Operation World website (https://operationworld.org/).

asking questions about the characters' worldview. Where did they ultimately come from? What is their purpose in life? What's wrong with the world? What's the solution to the problems?

- Take a class that teaches you a new skill, and journal your reflection on the process.
- Interview a teacher or professor who knows you well, asking what they have observed about your learning process.

CQ Action: Behaving Appropriately

Can you put all your knowledge and strategies together to engage people in a situation in a way that is thoughtful and appropriate? CQ action describes a person's verbal and nonverbal response in a cross-cultural setting.

- Study how various cultural patterns such as greetings and leave-takings are conducted, and then practice with team members.
- Interview someone from your target culture.
- Play a group game with your team and assign different behaviors to each team member (one person talks all the time, one person only speaks in single syllables, one only asks the question "why" etc.). Debrief the team's responses, frustrations, and successes.

The Christian life is a pilgrimage. Consider Hebrews 11:8–10: "By faith Abraham, when he was called, obeyed by going out to a place which he was to receive for an inheritance; and he went out, not knowing where he was going . . . for he was looking for the city which has foundations, whose architect and builder is God." As His people journey near and far for the sake of making Him known, may God find His people faithful.

A Biblical Framework for Shalom Today

William D. Barrick

The Hebrew noun *shalom* and its related words possess a wide semantic range, including "peace," "friendship," "well-being," "prosperity," "health," "wholeness," "completeness," and "soundness."[16] The prophet Jeremiah employed the word several times in his message to the exiles in Babylon when he explained that the Lord wanted them to settle down and live among their captors (Jer 29:4–6). In other words, they were to blossom where they had been sent. They were to actively seek the shalom of the city, and simultaneously pray to Yahweh for its inhabitants to experience shalom (29:7). Jeremiah furthermore revealed that God had plans of shalom for His exiled people (29:11).

Imposing the commonly understood meaning of "peace" upon all occurrences of this multifaceted word abuses its meaning and ignores the biblical context. In fact, though it was usually translated in the Septuagint via the Greek term *eirēnē*, this alongside the New Testament's quotations and teachings shows that the Greek term came to acquire a similarly broad range of applications as had shalom.[17] How then are ministers, missionaries, and servants of God to understand and live shalom?

Living Shalom Socially

Friendly alliances can express an attitude of shalom. Jacob showed shalom to the Hivites in Canaan (Gen 34:21), but his disobedient sons turned shalom on its head (34:25–31). Years later Joshua made shalom with the Gibeonites (Josh 10:1–4). That shalom came about through Gibeonite subterfuge and entailed a mutual threat toward others in the region. Joshua's intention was good, but the alliance suffered because he did not first seek the Lord's will. Indeed, living shalom can be a challenging and dangerous path to follow.

In the New Testament, Paul instructs believers, "If possible, so far as it depends on you, be at peace with all men" (Rom 12:18; cf. Heb 12:14). Shalom here involves a mutual commitment for well-being in which the

---

16. "שׁוֹלַם," *HALOT*, 1506–10.
17. "εἰρήνη," *NIDNTTE*, 2:112–13.

obedient believer takes the lead role (1 Cor 7:15). As in the Gibeonite conspiracy, shalom might threaten others, believer and unbeliever alike, especially when one party has ulterior motives. In that sense, disobedience nullifies shalom. However, wise behavior produces shalom even in hostile environments that are not characterized by peace.

Living Shalom Salvifically

The Lord seeks shalom for His people by graciously forgiving the sins of the rebellious (Ps 85:1–3; cf. Rom 5:1). In His steadfast loyal love and mercy, He delights to save and restore objects of His wrath (Ps 85:4–7). He speaks shalom to His people, and His glory dwells among them (vv. 8–9). When the Lord's righteousness and shalom "kiss each other," His people experience the fullest truth, justice, and good (vv. 10–13).

Ecclesiastically, the Lord's gracious blessing upon His priestly servants brings shalom (Num 6:22–27; cf. 1 Pet 2:4–12). Aaron and his sons were to bless the people by conveying His blessing. The Lord Himself gives shalom and He blesses His servants for being active in producing shalom (Num 6:26–27).

Messiah bears the title *Sar Shalom*, or "Prince of Peace" (Isa 9:6). He paid the full sacrificial price for the shalom of His people (Isa 53:5; cf. John 14:27). Indeed, He Himself is that shalom for "aliens and strangers" whom He now brings into one household (Eph 2:14–22). He sends preachers of the gospel of shalom (Isa 52:7; Eph 6:15) and by His own example guides in the way of shalom (Luke 1:74–79).

Eschatologically, shalom is an essential element in God's kingdom plan (Mic 4:1–5). The community of believers will join together to obey the Lord's Word and worship Him (vv. 1–2). His righteous judgment will bring shalom and abolish conflict so that His kingdom will be a time of satisfaction and security (vv. 3–4). The kingdom therefore will be characterized by His people's commitment to exhibit His character (v. 5).

Living Shalom Sagaciously

Living wisely according to God's instructions brings shalom (Prov 3:13–18). Blessing attends the acquisition of godly wisdom, a wisdom producing longevity, riches, honor, and happiness, and a wisdom that results in shalom (Jas 3:17–18).

As with the famous double proverb about the proper response to fools (Prov 26:4–5), God's people are not always to seek shalom. For instance, "You shall never seek their peace [shalom] or their prosperity all your days" (Deut 23:6). In the end, no matter how much shalom believers exemplify, the wicked will not experience true shalom (Isa 48:22). Discerning when to seek and when not to seek shalom requires God-given, Word-driven wisdom. Jesus personally instructed His seventy disciples about this difficult matter as they set out on their ministry campaign (Luke 10:1–16).

Living Shalom Strategically

As priests of God (1 Pet 2:9–10), Christians must undertake a mission of shalom to all peoples. Serving the Prince of Shalom, they are to seek the shalom of the people where they live (socially, salvifically, and sagaciously), despite the hostility to Christ and His gospel they are sure to encounter. Christians are to pray earnestly for their neighbors' shalom—especially their salvation, but also for their overall welfare. The places in which Christians live ought to be better because of their presence. As Christ followers love those around them without expectation of any reward, they will experience shalom to its fullest extent this side of heaven. "Therefore, beloved, since you look for these things, be diligent to be found by Him in peace [*eirēnē*], spotless and blameless" (2 Pet 3:14).

For the missionary, such living might involve a number of strategic choices of which the following serve merely as examples:

- Adopt carefully chosen culturally appropriate clothing. Make the choices with advice from wise national believers who recognize the difference between sensible dress and extreme dress (overculturalization). Clothing can create shalom or inflame lust.

- Select housing that recognizes the missionary family's needs as well as what is most acceptable to national believers. Avoid flaunting American/missionary wealth and possessions. Housing can promote shalom or signal materialism and pride.

- Behave as a guest within the adopted country and its culture. A guest's behavior can be a stumbling block to shalom when one acts more like a colonizer than an evangelist. Example: Applying an American standard to what a church building or church service should be rather than making appropriate cultural adaptations. Only a few hymns or spiritual songs should use American (or British/Irish/Welsh) melodies rather than melodies originating within the national culture.

Ethos Before *Logos*:
Acts 18 as a Case Study

David Beakley

If content alone is the means that God uses to save people, then missions would be all about a medium. If this were so, the apostle Paul would find a way to tap into the Roman communication system and blindly broadcast the gospel on every public forum. He would not care at all about cultural differences and how Jews and Gentiles would understand the gospel given their different backgrounds. Instead, we see the apostle Paul incorporate aspects of persuasion to reach the human heart that were commonly known in his day. They are:[18]

- *Logos* (the Greek word for "word") is an appeal to the logic and internal consistency of the argument or message.
- *Ethos* (the Greek word for "character") is an appeal to the trustworthiness and credibility of the writer or the speaker.
- *Pathos* (the Greek word for "passion,"

"suffering," or "experience") is an emotional appeal to the audience's sympathies and passions.

A glimpse into Paul's ministry reveals the presence of all three and provides a good reminder for modern mission efforts.

A Common Mistake

In Acts 9:19–20 we see Paul's newfound missions strategy unfold. As a rookie missionary to the Gentiles, Paul certainly had an abundance of *pathos* (zeal) and biblical doctrine in his *logos* (message), yet he lacked *ethos* (credibility) among his audiences. Paul was previously known as the Jewish Attila the Hun to his compatriots (Acts 9:13–14, 21). It might be that when he entered the scene, they were busy trying to find a quick exit, making it difficult for those who knew about his past to process what he was saying

---

18. These terms are in common use today, sourced originally in Aristotle's book *Rhetoric* (1.2.3) and having been commonly used in the New Testament era, such as by the apostle Paul. See, e.g., David A. deSilva, "Appeals to *Logos, Pathos,* and *Ethos* in Galatians 5:1–12: An Investigation of Paul's *Inventio,*" in *Paul and Ancient Rhetoric: Theory and Practice in the Hellenistic Context*, ed. Stanley E. Porter and Bryan R. Dyer (Cambridge: Cambridge University Press, 2016), 245–64.

in the present (cf. 9:26). While Paul is to be commended for his boldness, his effectiveness would have proved to be futile if he did not establish his *ethos*.

Unfortunately, many missionaries in a cross-cultural context fall into the trap of neglecting to establish *ethos* and simply unleash the gospel on a completely foreign people group. In the same way that Greek and Roman audiences did not give credibility to a Jewish speaker automatically, many people in a cross-cultural setting are not naturally attracted to a Western preacher. Everyone has their presuppositions, and it is fair to conclude that people in a cross-cultural context would most likely have stronger and more entrenched presuppositions. For example, the centuries of colonialism and colonial expansion by Europe in India, Asia, and Africa as well as geopolitical influence by the United States of America in Indonesia, China, Central America, South America, Africa, and the Middle East will easily create a multiplex of presuppositions about European and American preachers and missionaries. This is especially true for countries that experienced the advancement of the gospel concurrent with military conquest of their countries.

Because the apostle Paul believed that the gospel was an obligation that he had toward all unbelievers (Rom 1:14), his time on the field caused him to focus on establishing character credibility (*ethos*) while proclaiming the gospel (*logos*).

Leading with *Ethos* and *Pathos*

Paul retained an important shepherding role among the immature Christians in Corinth, even though he had been absent while on his missionary journeys. In his first letter to the Corinthians, he had many difficult words to deliver, but before Paul launched into a stern but sound response (*logos*) to this Gentile church, he first addressed them with appropriate *ethos* and *pathos*, as can be seen in 1 Corinthians 4:1–7. In this passage, the apostle asserted the reasons the believers could trust him, as a means of appealing to their hearts, in order to admonish them for their sins.

First, Paul confirmed to his readers that his identity was not rooted in his Jewishness, nor even in his apostleship—he was a servant of Christ and steward of the mysteries of God (1 Cor 4:1). Paul not only established his own credibility, but the trustworthiness of the message, since it is inextricably tied to the messenger. Paul and Apollos could only explain the gospel to others when their full embrace of its life-changing power was evident to all.

Second, Paul identified with his Gentile brothers and sisters when he spoke a shocking, countercultural truth: Paul declared that no person can claim superiority over another in any way (1 Cor 4:7). He did this by proclaiming that all people are where they are and have what they have as a gift from God. No one can lay claim to their ethnicity, language, or culture as something they developed in a way that would be profitable for others to emulate. In application to today, before Western missionaries can begin to convince their cross-cultural congregations to leave their cultural roots and embrace biblical teaching, they must first convince those same congregants that they themselves have left their own Western culture as well. Without being careful, a Western missionary could unintentionally leave the impression that the way to heaven is first through adopting Western cultural practices.

After establishing his own legitimacy and the trustworthiness of the gospel, Paul then moved to *pathos*, giving an emotional appeal to establish a connection with the people he loved. In 1 Corinthians 4:8–13, Paul explained his toil and suffering on behalf of his audience. While the young Corinthian church members all acted like kings and spiritual giants (4:8), Paul pointed out that he and Apollos were actually fools for Christ (4:9–10). They experienced hunger, thirst, rough treatment, homelessness, persecution, slander, and were seen as the scum of the world (4:11–13). He spoke this way not only for Christ's sake, but for the sake of these Gentile believers. Paul established *pathos* to build his own credibility before he delivered the *logos* in the rest of the letter—the gospel truth for holiness and Christian living to these materialistic, hedonistic, and formerly polytheistic young Greek believers.

Conclusion

As a missionary prepares to launch an impassioned appeal (*pathos*) for the target audience to believe and apply the revealed Word of God (*logos*), it is critical to understand as much as possible whether the listeners have any unseen barriers to receiving the message. It is important that all missionaries learn to accurately read the people well and search for hindrances of any type that might arise from a lack of understanding the negative influence from their local culture and worldview, history, habits, and impressions of the stranger among them. Missionaries would do well to establish their *ethos* by observing the target culture with great eagerness so that their *pathos* will be most fruitful in helping their cross-cultural audiences embrace the *logos* of the true knowledge of God soundly. If the apostle Paul had to learn this lesson, then so must all who follow his example.

CONCLUSION

Closing a textbook on any subject is easier for the reader than for the editors, especially when more topics could be covered and those that have been covered could have been expanded. However, we pray that the selections provided are sufficient to make the case that Christ is worthy in every context and in all circumstances of our faithful pursuit of a biblical approach to missions. We conclude with a summary of the major lessons of the textbook and reflection questions that further guide the discussion of biblical missions for our readers.

A Final Summary

A significant number of writings from all global regions in *Biblical Missions: Principles, Priorities, and Practices* have advanced one main idea: that Christ has commanded believers to proclaim His gospel to sinners and make disciples, according to the authoritative and sufficient Word of God. When believers carry out the Great Commission to the nations in a new context, whether at home or abroad, they are participating in missions. There are many ways to practice cultural engagement and many obstacles to doing it biblically, several of which the authors have addressed directly. The sociocultural complexities of a globalized world are only increasing, and they can affect the work of cross-cultural proclamation. Yet it seems that many missions-minded believers need to be reminded of the simplicity of Christ's Great Commission. This textbook has attempted to expose believers to the accessible and achievable design of the mission of the Church given by Christ.

Part 1 taught that God's heart for the nations is prevalent throughout the Old Testament, yet the outward strategy to reach them is revealed in the New Testament Great Commission. Ministries that are centered on delivering the content of Scripture verbally have always been God's powerful means of redeeming people from every tribe and tongue, even in the face of opposition and distortion. Compromising this strategy has hindered the Church at various points of history—particularly in the last half century—as many cross-cultural ministries have yielded to unbiblical worldviews with methods that risk syncretizing the truth with error.

Nevertheless, God continues to bless those who remain faithful to proclaim the Word with boldness and accuracy, who challenge false beliefs and make disciples through local churches. Biblical missions results in local believers ministering among their people in culturally appropriate ways and yet counter-culturally because of their spiritual transformation. Faithful ministry in new locations is always costly, yet the end is near. Knowing God's future plans for His kingdom instills in believers a blessed hope and reminds all people—not just missionaries—to labor in biblical missions with urgency.

Part 2 celebrated the local church's indispensable, multifaceted role of raising, sending, and supporting missionaries who will train, support, and care for indigenous leaders from every tribe and tongue. Ministry in, to, and through the local church must therefore be the priority of biblical missions, starting with the sending church. Sending churches play a critical role in providing spiritual oversight, practical help, encouraging communication, and intercessory prayer for their brothers and sisters who labor in the field for the sake of Christ's name—both for their missionaries and for the indigenous church leaders they are raising up to serve the local people.

The priority of indigenous church planting is an arduous missionary task, as only the sovereign Lord can raise up qualified local men to preach, teach, and shepherd souls under the authority of Scripture. Laboring for local discipleship despite opposition requires actively trusting that God will use His Word to foster unity, maturity, and restoration in the face of sin's disruptions. Respecting indigenous leadership anticipates that missionaries will transition leadership roles to them. So, it is imperative that local men are equipped biblically, theologically, and pastorally to govern, sustain, and expand the witness of their local churches. Given Christ's promise to build His church, all ministry activities must connect to the ministries of the local church. For this reason, biblical missions requires the accuracy in Bible translation and the publishing of theologically rich, supportive literature to increase biblical literacy and train church leaders. Equipping national worship leaders serves to help the local church worship and evangelize in theologically sound ways, bringing biblical fidelity to both sermon and song. Every priority aims for Christ to be glorified as He builds His church.

Part 3 connected the principles and priorities of biblical missions to several of the contemporary cross-cultural ministries at home and abroad that the Lord has used to impact the nations with the gospel. Yet when local and international ministries are conducted apart from sound doctrine and sound practice, they distort the gospel and distract their audiences from hearing the Word and see-ing it lived out. With a biblical focus, Christ's followers must understand both the urgent needs and strategic opportunities around them in order to compassionately communicate and demonstrate the unchanging gospel with clarity and courage wherever God has placed them.

Opportunities for local and international cultural engagement are vast and require creativity and teamwork with local church leadership to advance the Great Commission. Major spheres of influence include the workplace as an integrity-driven platform for gospel witness and neighbor-hoods as locations ready to receive practical help and Word-centered compassion. Doors for the gospel open among the vulnerable and the suffering, where the message of hope in Christ is accompanied by compassionate and skillful help. Believers should consider cross-cultural openings in education and business, and on university campuses, which provide channels for making disciples.

As the maturing global church participates even more in sending missionaries out from their local churches, their international efforts will bring new challenges. Short-term ministries, when focused on proclaiming Christ and supporting long-term workers, can benefit home and foreign fields, unlike self-focused trips that leave little lasting benefit to the field. Likewise, ministry partnerships, when biblically grounded, can accomplish much. Missionaries must exercise courage, character, and conviction as they navigate cultural and linguistic pitfalls to communicating the gospel message with clarity in their new context. The biblical model of missions is both understandable and achievable, although it is not simple to accomplish and often entails a lifelong pursuit of it. Because biblical missions is God's heart and Christ's plan, the missionary and church leader, led by the Holy Spirit through His Word, can prove faithful. By the definition of biblical missions, they are to be deemed successful.

A Final Challenge

Biblical Missions: Principles, Priorities, and Practices has presented a solid biblical foundation for understanding God's design for missions today, providing you a range of effective ministry strategies with examples of how they are employed by faithful workers around the world. Our prayer is that you will have the settled confidence that you can fulfill your role in the Great Commission by the power of the Holy Spirit who works in you through His authoritative and sufficient Word. We trust that this resource has helped you to gain a greater cross-cultural perspective on God's work in the world and to be more discerning about missions teaching and activities so that you are better equipped to carry out biblical missions for the cause of Christ's kingdom.

Where will you go from here once you close this book? Our hope is that your next action is to "go therefore and make disciples of all the nations" (Matt 28:19) near and far for the glory and honor of the Lord Jesus Christ. For those of you already active in advancing the Great Commission, we encourage you to "excel still more" (1 Thess 4:1). However, with all that you have now contemplated about biblical missions, even the most seasoned missionary might benefit from reflection on their approach. As you prayerfully prepare your next steps of cultural engagement, we encourage you to ask yourself the following questions to help you adhere to the ultimate aims and alignment of biblical missions:

1. What is your standard for evaluating if you are working faithfully and effectively to advance the Great Commission? How has your standard changed with this study of biblical missions?
2. Overall, do these practices you implement seem to flow from and serve the earlier principles

and priorities grounded in God's Word? Or do they subordinate scriptural authority to contemporary cultural values?

3. Do your methods of discipling believers focus on teaching obedience to all of Jesus' commands? How exactly do you help new believers grow into maturity?

4. Do your top priorities in missions include church planting, local church strengthening, and the training of indigenous pastors and church leaders? If not, which of your priorities need reordering, and how might you do that practically?

5. In what ways might your cross-cultural practices not align with and apply the principles and priorities of biblical missions? What will it take to change that?

6. What guardrails and parameters for cultural engagement do you still need to establish? How will you set them up?

7. In practice, how do you prioritize proclaiming an exclusive gospel that calls for repentance and belief in Christ's atoning work?

8. What steps can you take to regularly assess your adherence to biblical missions and correct for any subtle drift over time?

9. In what specific ways has your understanding of "indigenous leadership training" sharpened, and how might you be more involved in it practically?

10. What understanding do you now have of the global church, and how has your understanding changed?

Finally, we encourage you to transition from a reader of missions to a student by following up with the companion volume, the *Biblical Missions: Principles, Priorities, and Practices Workbook*. The workbook turns the textbook's wise instruction and insights into application and action through twenty-four lessons with questions and projects. These workbook lessons will help you translate your maturing biblical convictions into scripturally aligned conduct on every topic discussed in the textbook. We trust that as you utilize the workbook, you will be further challenged and assisted in developing a perspective on missions that is faithful to God's Word. Christ exhorted His disciples this way: "The harvest is plentiful, but the workers are few. Therefore pray earnestly to the Lord of the harvest to send out workers into His harvest" (Matt 9:37–38). Our prayer is that this study has better equipped you to go into the harvest field and be faithful to biblical missions.

Contributors

Abera Ajula (ThM): Director of Pastoral Leadership Training, the Ethiopian Kale Heywet Church; former Dean of Students, campus pastor, and professor, Evangelical Theological College (Ethiopia)

Astrit Allushi (ThM): Dean and professor, Southeastern Europe Theological Seminary, Albania; local church minister in Tirana, Albania

Rodney Andersen (MDiv): Director, Grace Ministries International; faculty, The Master's Seminary (USA); former missionary to China; local church minister in Los Angeles, California

Santiago Armel (ThM): Vice President and professor, Expositors Seminary (Colombia); local church minister in Cali, Colombia

William Barrick (ThD): Emeritus Professor of Old Testament, The Master's Seminary; faculty, Asia Biblical Theological Seminary (Thailand); former Bible translator in Bangladesh

Marco Bartholomae (MDiv, ThM in progress): Director of Membership and Field Development, The Master's Academy International; former MDiv director, European Bible Training Center (Germany); former minister in Germany; local church minister in Los Angeles, California

David Beakley (PhD): Former Academic Dean and professor, Christ Seminary (South Africa); former Regional Director for Africa, The Master's Academy International; former Africa Regional Shepherd, Grace Ministries International; former missionary to South Africa; local church minister in Peoria, Illinois

Brian Biedebach (PhD): Dean of Students and professor, The Master's Seminary; former missionary to Malawi and South Africa; local church minister in Los Angeles, California

Mark Borisuk (PhD): Translation and publishing consultant; missionary in a discreet location in Asia

David E. Bosworth (PhD): Faculty, Colorado Christian University; educational travel consultant, Greek Bible Tours; former Executive Director, Short Term Mission Toolbox; former Director of International Ministries, The Master's University

Maurice Boutros (MDiv in progress): Faculty at a pastoral training institute in the Middle East; missionary candidate to Egypt

Kristian Brackett (ThM, DMin): MDiv director and professor, European Bible Training Center (Germany); former Assistant Dean, Teološka Biblijska Akademija (Croatia); former missionary to Croatia

Lauren Brown: Director of Women's Ministries and missionary wives liaison in a local church in Los Angeles, California

Chris Burnett (PhD): Associate Director of Academics, The Master's Academy International; faculty, The Master's Seminary; former missionary to Italy; local church minister in Los Angeles, California

E. D. Burns (PhD): International Director of Frontier Dispatch; faculty, Asia Biblical Theological Seminary (Thailand); missionary in Southeast Asia; former missionary in Alaska and in the Middle East

Nathan Busenitz (PhD): Executive Vice President, Provost, and professor, The Master's Seminary; local church minister in Los Angeles, California

Brooks Buser (PhD): President and training campus leader, Radius International; former missionary and lead translator to the Yembiyembi people of Papua New Guinea

Scott N. Callaham (PhD): Dean and faculty, The Institute of Public Theology; host of the Daily Dose of Aramaic podcast; composer of Chinese worship music; former missionary to Singapore

Edward W. Cannon (MBA): President and CEO of Far East Broadcasting Company; board member, Revive Our Hearts ministries and National Religious Broadcasters; former Executive Vice President, Moody Bible Institute

Tim Cantrell (PhD): President and professor, Shepherds' Seminary Africa (South Africa); local church minister in Johannesburg, South Africa

Newton Chilingulo (MA, DMin in progress): Professor and Director of Advancement at Central African Preaching Academy (Malawi); local church minister in Lilongwe, Malawi

Jung-Ui Cho (ThM): Local church minister in Yongin City, South Korea

Abner Chou (PhD): President and professor, The Master's University and Seminary; head translator of the Legacy Standard Bible; local church minister in Los Angeles, California

Mark Christopher (ThM, PhD in progress): Academic Dean of the Berean Bible Institute (South Africa); faculty, Christ Seminary, Cape Town (South Africa); local church minister in Cape Town, South Africa

Luis Contreras (ThM, DMin): Translation and Production Voice for *Gracia a vosotros* media ministry; faculty, The Master's Seminary in Spanish, Seminario Berea (Spain), and Seminario para la Predicación Expositiva (Honduras); former missionary to Mexico; local church minister in Los Angeles, California

George A. Crawford (JD): Retired Administrative Law Judge; former Enforcement Attorney; faculty, The Master's University; local church minister in Los Angeles, California

Jeff Crotts (MDiv, DMin): Administrator and professor, The Master's Seminary, Anchorage, Alaska Distance Location; local church minister in Anchorage, Alaska

Shelbi Cullen (DEdMin): Faculty, The Master's University; cohost of The Women's Hope podcast; local church biblical counselor, women's ministry leader in Los Angeles, California

Kellie Cunningham (MME, DMA in progress): Faculty, The Master's University; Nationally Certified Teacher of Music (USA); local church children's choir program director in Los Angeles, California

Kyle Davis (ThM, PhD in progress): Translation Consultant, Bible Translation Fellowship; missionary in South Africa

Dave Deuel (PhD): Senior Research Fellow Emeritus, the Joni Eareckson Tada Disability Research Center; Academic Dean Emeritus, The Master's Academy International; Catalyst for the Disability Concerns Issue Network, the Lausanne Movement; Chairperson, New York State Council on Developmental Disabilities

Todd Dick (MDiv, DMin): Faculty, Teološka Biblijska Akademija (Croatia) and the European Bible Training Center (Germany); missionary and local church minister in Mursko Središće, Croatia

David M. Doran (ThM, DMin): President and professor, Detroit Baptist Theological Seminary; President of Grace Baptist Mission; local church minister in Allen Park, Michigan

Talgat Dossayev (MDiv in progress): Translation Coordinator, The Master's Academy International; local church minister in Kazakhstan

Kyle C. Dunham (ThD): Faculty, Detroit Baptist Theological Seminary; former local church minister in New York; former missionary to Ecuador

Kevin Edwards (DDiv): Former missionary in a discreet location; local church minister in Atlanta, Georgia

Ava Flores [pseudonym] (MSPA): CEO of an overseas community healthcare business; wife of a church planter in Southeast Asia

Philip F. Foley (DEdMin): Faculty, The Cornerstone Bible College and Seminary (USA); local church minister in Vallejo, California

John Freiberg (DMin): Church planter and missions team leader in Southeast Asia

Nathan Giesbrecht (MDiv): Church planter, Vancouver Island, Canada

John Glass (MDiv, DMin): Church planter in France and Switzerland; founder of Calvin Tours, Geneva; France Field Director and member of European Field Council for Grace Ministries International

Michael A. Grisanti (PhD): Distinguished Research Professor of Old Testament, Chair of the Old Testament Department, and Director of the TMS Israel Study Trip, The Master's Seminary; local church minister in Los Angeles, California

Carl A. Hargrove (ThM, DMin): Co-founder, African Revitalization Centre; Director, Grace Advance; faculty, The Master's Seminary; local church minister in Los Angeles, California

James Harmeling (PhD): Director, Shepherds International Training Academy; local church minister and missionary in Singapore

Walter Heaton (MDiv): Chief Editor of Publications and General Secretary for the Udruga za Teološko i Biblijsko Proučavanje (Croatia); Assistant Dean, registrar, and faculty, Teološka Biblijska Akademija (Croatia); missionary to Croatia

Thomas Hochstetter (BTh): Faculty, Europäisches Bibel Trainings Centrum (Germany); songwriter; local church minister in Berlin, Germany

Thomas Hodzi (MDiv): Director, Christ of First Importance Ministries (Zimbabwe); Principal and professor, Shona Bible Institute (Zimbabwe); local church minister in Harare, Zimbabwe

Philip S. Hunt (DD): President and Vice Chancellor, Central Africa Baptist University (Zambia); local church minister and missionary in Kitwe, Zambia

Shannon Hurley (MDiv, DMin): Founder of Sufficiency of Scripture Ministries (Uganda); founder and professor at Shepherds Training College (Uganda); missionary in Luwero, Uganda

Eduardo Izquierdo (ThM): Faculty, Instituto Universitario Cristiano de las Americas and Seminario Bíblico Palabra de Gracia (Mexico); local church minister in Monterrey, Mexico

Mark Jeffries (PhD): President and professor of theology at a pastoral training institute in the Middle East; missionary and local church minister in a discreet location in the Middle East

Oleg Kalyn (ThM): Dean of the MDiv program and professor, Grace Bible Seminary (Ukraine); local church minister in Kyiv, Ukraine

Randy Karlberg (MDiv): Superintendent, Grace Christian School, Anchorage, Alaska; former teacher and minister in rural Alaska; local church minister in Anchorage, Alaska

Brad Klassen (PhD): Director of ThM Studies and professor, The Master's Seminary; former missionary to the Soviet Union; local church minister in Los Angeles, California

Rick Kress (MDiv): Director of Global Publications, The Master's Academy International; founder and publisher of Kress Biblical Resources

Lisa LaGeorge (PhD): Senior Director, CHF Academy at Children's Hunger Fund; former administrator and faculty, The Master's University; former missionary to Alaska; local women's Bible teacher

Jenuan Lira (MABC): Executive Secretary and Soul Care Minister of Maranatha Multicultural Ministries (Brazil); local church minister in Fortaleza, Brazil

Stephen Lonetti (DMin): President of LifeGate Worldwide; former faculty, The Master's Seminary; former missionary to the Taliabo people, Indonesia; local church minister in St. Paul, Minnesota

John MacArthur (DD, LittD): Pastor-Teacher, Grace Community Church; Chancellor Emeritus, The Master's University and Seminary; author; featured teacher, *Grace to You* media ministry

Chisomo Masambuka (MDiv in progress): Former business director of Central African Preaching Academy (Malawi); local church minister in Lilongwe, Malawi

Conrad Mbewe (PhD): Director of Advancement and Faculty and professor, African Christian University (Zambia); local church minister in Lusaka, Zambia

Massimo Mollica (MDiv): Faculty, Accademia Teologica Italiana (Italy); missionary in Genova, Italy

Juan Moncayo (MDiv, PhD in progress): Founder, Centro de Consejería Bíblica La Fuente (Ecuador); certified biblical counselor, Association of Certified Biblical Counselors; council member, Biblical Counseling Coalition; faculty, The Master's Seminary; local church minister in Quito, Ecuador

Nathan Odede (MA[Ed], MA[OT], PhD in progress): Africa Coordinator for an undisclosed international Christian charity; higher education quality assurance consultant; former faculty, Christ Seminary (South Africa)

Peter Olivetan [pseudonym] (MDiv): founder and coordinator, APEX International Expatriates; founder and chairman of an education not-for-profit organization; church planter, marketplace minister, and seminary leader in Europe and West Asia

Alejandro Peluffo (ThM): Dean and professor, Instituto de Expositores (Argentina); local church minister in Buenos Aires, Argentina

Tom Pennington (MA, DD): Administrator and professor, The Master's Seminary, Dallas Distance Location; former Managing Director, *Grace to You* media ministry; local church minister in Southlake, Texas

David Perez (MDiv): Faculty, Instituto Universitario Cristiano de las Americas and Seminario Bíblico Palabra de Gracia (Mexico); church planter in Monterrey, Mexico

Dave Phillips: Founder and President, Children's Hunger Fund (USA)

Josué Pineda Dale (ThM, PhD in progress): Director of men's ministry, *Volvamos al evangelio* publication ministry; author and editor; former Administrative Coordinator of Spanish Education and instructor, The Master's Seminary; local church minister in Hutchinson, Kansas

Paul T. Plew (EdD): Faculty Emeritus and Former Music Dean and Chairman of Choral Activities, The Master's University; local church minister in Santa Clarita, California

Betty Price (MA): Faculty and missions team leader, former Associate Dean of Students, The Master's University; former local church Director of Women's Ministries in Los Angeles, California

Robert Provost (MDiv, DD): Former Executive Vice President, The Master's University and Seminary; former Director of Europe and Soviet Union, SEND International; former President, Slavic Gospel Association; local church minister in Rockford, Illinois

Charlie Rampfumedzi (MA, DMin): President and professor, Christ Seminary (South Africa); local church minister in Polokwane, South Africa

Sean Ransom (MDiv, DMin): President and professor, The Expositor's Academy (the Philippines); Regional Director for Asia, The Master's Academy International; Asia Regional Shepherd, Grace Ministries International

Faly Ravoahangy (MDiv, DMin): Founder and President, Madagascar 3M; Dean, 3M Preaching Institute; local church minister and denomination board vice-president in Antananarivo, Madagascar

Mark D. Rentz (MA): International Higher Education teacher, trainer, author; former Associate Vice Provost for International Education, University at Albany, SUNY; former Executive Director, Intensive ESL program, Arizona State University; former local church missions director; former missionary and teacher in Japan

Michael Riccardi (PhD): Faculty, The Master's Seminary; local church minister in Los Angeles, California

L. C. Ridley [pseudonym] (MDiv, MBA): Marketplace minister in a discreet location in the Middle East

Nathan Schneider (ThM): Administrator and professor, The Master's Seminary, Anchorage, Alaska Distance Location; local church minister in Anchorage, Alaska

Hanna Shahin (PhD): Founder and President, Endure International; author; educator in the Middle East

Bill Shannon (MDiv, DMin): local church minister, overseeing biblical counseling, in Los Angeles, California

Aaron Shryock (PhD): Bible translator in Cameroon and Chad, Horizons International; former missionary to Cameroon; former Director and professor, Tyndale Center for Bible Translation at The Master's Seminary

Billy C. Sichone (PhD): Deputy Vice Chancellor of Academics and Research Affairs, Central Africa Baptist University (Zambia)

Cecil Stalnaker (PhD): Professor Emeritus of Intercultural Studies and Practical Theology, Tyndale Theological Seminary (the Netherlands); missionary trainer, Greater European Mission; former missionary to Belgium and the Netherlands; equipper in missions and evangelism for local churches in California

Benjamin Straub (ThM, MEd in progress): Dean of the School of Bible, Central Africa Baptist University (Zambia); missionary to Zambia

Daniel Surya Avula (ThM): President, Fullness of Joy Ministries (India); faculty, Grace Life Theological Seminary (India); local church minister in Visakhapatnam, India

Jimmy Tan (MDiv, DBA): Vice President, Asia-Pacific, The Master's Academy International; Executive Board Member of Grace to Asia media ministry; faculty, Singapore University of Social Sciences; local church missions committee member in Singapore

Mark Tatlock (EdD): President, The Master's Academy International; faculty, The Master's University and Seminary; former Executive Vice President and Provost, The Master's University; local church minister in Los Angeles, California

Devraj Urs (ThM): Director and professor, The Expositor's Academy (the Philippines); local church minister in Davao City, the Philippines

Silas Van Duh Hmung (ThM): Professor and Dean of Students, Expository Preaching and Teaching Academy (Myanmar); local church minister in Yangon, Myanmar

Rubén Videira-Soengas (ThM): Academic Dean and professor, Seminario Berea (Spain and Portugal); local church minister in León, Spain

Philippe Viguier (MDiv): Faculty, Faculté Théologique Scriptura (France); music producer; local church minister in Lyon, France

Michael J. Vlach (PhD): Faculty, Shepherds Theological Seminary (USA); former faculty, The Master's Seminary

Paul Washer (MDiv): Founder and Missions Director, HeartCry Missionary Society; former missionary to Peru

Eric Weathers (MDiv, DMin): Senior Vice President of Strategic Partnerships, The Master's Academy International; former sales manager in a globally recognized logistics corporation

Carlan Wendler (MD, MDiv in progress): Faculty, Hope Africa University (Burundi); Chief Medical Officer, Kibuye Hope Hospital (Burundi); Cofounder and President, African Medical Education Fund; missionary to Burundi

Sammy Williams (MDiv): Dean and professor, Pastoral Training Seminary (India); local church minister in Goa, India

Marty Wolf: Missionary with Friends of Israel Gospel Ministry, based in Los Angeles, California; former missionary in Canada

David Zadok (MA, DMin): Director of HaGefen Publishing; retired Major of the Israel Defense Forces; local church minister in Neve Mivtah, Israel

GLOSSARY

angelology: The doctrine of spiritual beings that covers what can be known from Scripture about angels, demons, and Satan.

anthropology: The study of mankind and culture; theologically it studies man as image-bearer of his Creator, who bears spiritual responsibility toward God and must model the perfect Son of God's ethic toward creation and fellow humans.

authority of Scripture: The quality of Scripture that derives from the character of God as the objective arbiter of truth, who has revealed His knowledge clearly and adequately in human language by His Holy Spirit, who effectually illuminates and enables a person to appraise Scripture spiritually as the wisdom and power of God.

biblical counseling: A function of Great Commission disciple-making, focusing on the personal, obedient implementation of the Word, which is the sufficient means of spiritual reconciliation and healing from disorders caused by sin and suffering.

biblical missions: The Great Commission task of proclaiming the excellencies of Christ to sinners cross-culturally and applying the authority and sufficiency of Scripture to every activity of disciple-making in all contexts.

bibliology: The doctrines that include the revelation, inspiration, illumination, clarity, authority, inerrancy, sufficiency, canonicity, and preservation of Scripture; these doctrines reinforce that the sixty-six books of the Bible are the authoritative and sufficient source of divine spiritual knowledge by which sinners obey God, are saved, and grow as disciples in every place.

business as missions (BAM): The category of local and international cross-cultural ministry, whereby a believer undertakes a commercial business venture to gain opportunities for evangelism and discipleship.

canonicity of Scripture: The completed, divine authorship of the sixty-six books of the Bible by means of verbal, plenary inspiration, by which all "truth" is tested.

centrifugal: The active idea of gospel witness, spreading the gospel outward from one location and cultural context to other locations and cultural contexts.

centripetal: The passive idea of gospel witness, drawing participants from other locations and cultural contexts toward the center of existing gospel witness.

Christology: The study of the person and work of the Lord Jesus Christ, who is the glorious, preexistent Son of God, coeternal and coequal to the Father and the Holy Spirit.

church, the: The New Testament term used universally for believers in Christ who have been regenerated by the Holy Spirit, and locally for believers who gather for worship, discipleship, and service in one location and context.

church planting: The founding of an assembly of believers in a new location, with the goal of establishing and organizing a self-governing, self-supporting, and self-propagating church that will live out the discipleship model of the Great Commission.

church strengthening: A broader term than church planting that represents a range of ministries in the local church that support the elders in providing spiritual oversight of the flock.

contextual theology: The subjective expressions of theology that are particularly developed in the non-Western global church, which might be built on a biblical hermeneutic and exegetical method or on nonconservative contextual hermeneutics.

contextualization: In nonconservative, ecumenical circles, the term expands to matters of cultural accommodation, but it is used by many conservative evangelicals to represent personal cultural adaptations as well as the process of articulating and appropriating the content of biblical truth in a new context. *See* linguistic accommodation.

Counter-Reformation: The Reformation-era movement by Roman Catholic and Eastern Orthodox clerical orders to supplant the propagation of Protestant missionary biblical proclamation in and outside of Europe with strategic, culturally accommodating activities designed to advance a false gospel.

cross-cultural communication: At the core of biblical cultural engagement, it is the general term for the proclamation of biblical truth through verbal assertions between members of different cultures, and is used synonymously with intercultural communication.

cultural accommodation: Strategies that adapt the biblical and theological content of Scripture to the assumptions and values of the recipient culture in some way that compromises the biblical writer's intent for the text and its theology.

cultural engagement: The broad range of missionary activities that aim to faithfully deliver the meaning of the text of Scripture to new audiences so they apply what they learn to their local situations.

culture: Reflects the complex contextual and generational worldviews, values, and ways of living of dynamic people groups and ideological communities, but it is not a morally neutral term, since all cultures are composed of people who are marred by the noetic effects of sin.

decisionism: The practice by some missionaries to pursue individuals to make "decisions for Christ" through altar calls or leading people to recite "the sinner's prayer," including "rededication."

developing world: Synonymous with *third world, two-thirds world, Global South*, and *majority world* to reflect the historic demographic shift in the global church population predominantly from Europe and North America to the regions of Latin America, Africa, the Middle East, and Asia.

discipleship: The intentional function of the local church to "go," "baptize," and "teach," according to the Great Commission, in order to reproduce regenerate believers who know and obey all that Christ commands, as contained in the entire canon of Scripture, under the shepherding oversight of local church elders.

discipleship making movement (DMM): A strategic, rapid church growth model that is designed for use in unreached foreign contexts, also called the "church planting movement" (CPM).

ecclesiology: The study of the church, the universal assembly of the redeemed, with application to the governance, public worship, and ministries of the local church.

ecumenism: Represents formal or informal cross-denominational alliances (including Roman Catholicism and Eastern Orthodoxy) that seek unity through doctrinal flexibility so that they cooperate practically in political, social, and cultural engagement activities.

education, formal, informal: *Formal* refers to structured learning in an institutional setting that results in a certificate or degree; *informal* is limited to learning in the context of the local church, whether from the pulpit, Bible studies, Sunday school classes, or discipleship.

epistemology: The study of the nature of knowledge and rational belief relative to a comprehensive way of understanding reality and transcendent truth claims by a person or society.

eschatology: The doctrine of end-times events, or the "last things" (Gk. *eschaton*), is the study of how God will bring history to completion through the Lord Jesus Christ—who will reign over a restored earth as the last Adam and the ultimate Davidic King and then usher in the eternal state of His kingdom on the new earth.

eschaton: *See* eschatology.

ethnodoxology: An approach to worship music that reflects the creativity and the musical idioms of individual cultures as local songwriters and missionaries collaborate to write scriptural content into songs for personal and congregational worship.

euangelion. *See* gospel.

evangelicalism: The broad, contemporary term for the orthodox Christian faith, grounded in biblical doctrine and recognized by the creeds of the historic ecumenical councils (AD 325–681).

evangelism: The Great Commission task of verbally proclaiming the gospel message to the unbeliever, to bring individual sinners from all nations and worldviews to the saving knowledge of the King of kings, that they might worship Him as the only God.

expatriate, expatriate families: Individuals and families who reside outside their country of citizenship who are immersed in the international community of their location, and are generally less integrated with the local people, often in terms of language, culture, and lifestyle.

exposition, expositional, expository preaching: Biblical interpretation and explanation of a biblical text, accompanied by contemporary, context-specific application when preaching sermons and teaching lessons from the text.

frontier missions: Related to pioneer missions, it is activity of church planting among unreached people groups, who are in cultures that have not yet been exposed to the gospel message.

global city: As defined by Michael Crane, global cities are "urban areas that impact the world far beyond their city limits through a combination of economic services and trade, political influence, and cultural dissemination."

global church: The missiological term for the universal church, which is the worldwide community of regenerate believers, which often references churches in non-Western regions.

Global South: *See* developing world.

global theologies: *See* contextual theology.

gospel: God's powerful message of salvation in the Bible through the person and work of the Lord Jesus Christ, freely offered to sinners; used lowercase to distinguish from the Gospels, the New Testament books of Matthew, Mark, Luke, and John.

grammatical-historical hermeneutic: The method of determining the sense of a biblical text according to the rules of grammar and the facts of history, according to the author's original intent for the inspired text.

Great Commission: The singular mission of the church given by the risen Christ to His disciples in the Gospels and Acts, according to which He commands them and all disciples to go to the nations to preach and teach the exclusive gospel of God from the content of Scripture, baptize new disciples, and establish local churches.

hamartiology: The biblical doctrine of sin, which is foundational to biblical anthropology, as every aspect of an unregenerate person's being is totally contaminated by sin, affecting the individual and his or her society.

hermeneutics: The science of interpretation, which generally aims to establish the foundational principles, methods, and rules whereby all languages and writings can be exegetically analyzed and accurately interpreted, particularly the writings of the biblical canon.

holistic evangelism, holistic mission: The term used to include social action as part of the mission of the church, which may be disconnected from the proclamation ministries of preaching and teaching, disciple-making, or the priority of establishing and maturing believers in the local church.

hospitality: A practical ministry that demonstrates the spiritual reality that God welcomes and serves those who have no ability to reciprocate His mercy and kindness.

inculturation, inculturists: Roman Catholic mission theory and theorists who have modernized the Counter-Reformation cultural accommodation practices similarly to evangelical contextualization.

indigenization: Refers to the subjective quality of Scripture that results when an individual comprehends that the original meaning of a text is relatable to his or her life and culture and applies it in obedience to Christ.

indigenous: A description of people originating from their traditional land, generally maintaining local beliefs, worldviews, and cultural customs before Christ, yet, as the redeemed, retaining cultural elements that do not contradict the gospel or promote sin.

indigenous missions: The process of recognizing men, native and local in another country, who are qualified to preach and to shepherd churches as elders, followed by the equipping and commissioning of those men for ministry to the local people.

inerrancy of Scripture: This doctrine is defined by Scripture's self-attestation that the words and syntax of the Bible in the original autographs are absolutely true when interpreted in their historical, grammatical, literary, and moral settings for all of the content and any topic or concept therein presented.

insider movement: The missionary-promoted strategy of encouraging Christian converts to remain within their original contextual community, primarily to practice faith in Christ inwardly, while demonstrating some degree of adherence to the false faith of origin.

inspiration of Scripture: The doctrine that every word of Scripture was penned by men with distinct personalities, styles, intellects, and wills, through the supernatural moving of the Holy Spirit.

kingdom of God: The central and unifying theme of Scripture, defined as the rule of God over His creation, which is spiritually present in and through believers in the church age, but will be manifested in the future, when the Lord Jesus Christ comes to reign on the earth in the millennium, followed by the Eternal State of the new heavens and new earth.

liberation theology: Roman Catholic and ecumenical political theology with Marxist ideologies that encompasses a range of sociopolitical contextual theologies worldwide, including feminist theology, queer theology, and critical race theory, among other emerging contextual theologies.

linguistic accommodation: Articulating the content of biblical truth according to the rules of grammar and the implications of culturally shaped terminology, such as idioms, expressions, and certain word choices, which is necessary to cross-cultural communication. *See* contextualization.

majority world: *See* developing world.

mercy ministry: Acts of compassion toward those in need, integrated with the proclamation of the gospel, balancing immediate relief, rehabilitation, and long-term development and discipleship through the local church.

missio Dei: The "mission of God" theological paradigm requires a uniformly missiological reading of Scripture that sees the church as playing a part in God's mission, whether or not proclamation is involved.

missiology: The study of Christian missions, which may include studies of biblical and theological themes, missions history, and theories and concepts from the intercultural, sociocultural, ethnographic, and anthropological disciplines.

mission(s) agency, missions sending agency: A parachurch organization that comes alongside the church to provide administrative and strategic support for missionaries or missionary projects without taking over the spiritual responsibilities of the sending or local church.

missional hermeneutic: *See missio Dei.*

missionary: A biblically qualified believer who is sent out from his or her local church to fulfill the Great Commission tasks of missions, especially in a foreign context with a different culture. *See* missions.

missions: The Great Commission task of proclaiming the excellencies of Christ to sinners cross-culturally and applying the authority and sufficiency of Scripture to every activity of disciple-making in all contexts.

nation: Refers to geopolitical nation-states, while sociologically it is an ethnic group of people (or people group) united by family heritage, culture, and traditions, which, together, accentuate the foreignness of the missionary who is commanded to "go" to the foreign environment of "the nations."

obedience-based discipleship: A recent trend of encouraging unregenerate participants in Christian ministries to pursue obedience before conversion.

orthodoxy: Refers to sound doctrine, exegetically harnessed and circumscribed from the biblical canon.

orthopraxy: The biblically faithful practices that follow from applying sound doctrine to life and ministry.

parachurch organization: *See* mission agency, missions sending agency.

people group: *See* nation.

pioneer missions: *See* frontier missions.

pneumatology: The doctrine of God the Holy Spirit, who is coeternal and coequal to the Father and the Son.

pragmatism: As a missions paradigm, it represents the success-oriented view that Great Commission service must focus on activities that are perceived as useful and can achieve measurable results.

proclamation: Cultural engagement activities that affirm and apply the authority and sufficiency of Scripture, including preaching, teaching, Bible translation, Christian publication, and theological and pastoral education.

propositional assertion: Words, arranged syntactically to provide meaning, whether imperatives, exclamations, or any descriptive text in declarative sentences or indicative statements, encompassing all genres, such as narrative, history, poetry, prophecy, and apocalyptic literature, which accurately reveal a truth claim.

prosperity gospel: A movement by false teachers, usually in Pentecostal and charismatic circles, to gain spiritual authority over people by convincing them that God's will is their physical well-being and financial success, which can be secured through donations and submission.

regeneration: The doctrine that signifies the creation of new life in the soul of a person by the Holy Spirit, leading to repentance from sin and belief in the gospel.

revelation: General revelation is the nonverbal yet universally accessible witness of the Creator's wisdom, power, and moral superiority that serves to condemn fallen man; particular or special revelation is the verbal revelation in the canon of Scripture about God's will, purposes, and promises that He reveals to all whom He is saving, which includes the gospel.

scriptural indigenization: The subjective quality of Scripture that results when an individual in his or her cultural context comprehends that the original meaning of a biblical text is relatable to his or her life and culture and applies it in obedience to Christ by faith.

short-term ministries: Refers to the practice of sending out church members to another location for a limited time to perform ministry tasks, such as lending support and encouragement to missionaries, helping accomplish special ministry projects, and serving local churches at the invitation of the local church elders.

social gospel: The term for the ministry priority of conducting social welfare and educational programs as cultural engagement over evangelistic proclamation, prominent in theologically liberal and ecumenical circles, dating back to the early twentieth century.

soteriology: The doctrine at the core of the gospel that defines salvation as a divine work of grace on the basis of the righteousness of Jesus Christ, so that the sinner may be undeservedly imputed Christ's righteousness and acquitted of guilt, granted by faith a new nature that is progressively sanctified and preserved for final justification in paradise with God.

sufficiency of Scripture: The doctrine that affirms that the Bible provides all the necessary content for finite man to know God and to adequately perceive His will for salvation.

syncretism: Describes the admixture of uniquely Christian content with primal, pagan, or secular realities, including concepts, symbols, beliefs, or practices that lead to the spiritual and theological contamination of the gospel, undermining its integrity and distracting from the call to salvation and maturity in Christ.

third world: *See* developing world.

transformation: An increasingly sanctifying conformity to the Scriptures that begins at conversion to Christ, when the believer, by faith, pursues obedience to the authoritative Word of God and embarks on a path of worldview and lifestyle change within the context of his or her local culture.

two-thirds world: *See* developing world.

universal church: *See* global church.

unreached people group: *See* frontier missions, nation.

worldview: A distinct understanding of life in all its components and cohesion that becomes a person's framework for understanding the world and everything in it, which most commonly includes beliefs about divinity, truth, morality, aesthetics, the purpose of humanity on the plane of existence, human problems and solutions, community, and the afterlife.

SCRIPTURE INDEX

Nehemiah

Esther

Job

Psalms

Proverbs

Mark

Romans

1 Corinthians

Subject Index

Page numbers with a t indicate tables.

Chilingulo, Newton, 252, 643–45
Cho, Jung-Ui, 441–44
Chou, Abner, 7–15, 205–7
Christ
    authority 22–23, 94, 107–8
    Christology, 210, 275–76, 502, 518, 555, 898
    compassion, 67–68, 653–55, 749
    cornerstone of missions, 7, 38, 94, 411–12
    exclusivity 31, 95–96
    Great Commission and, 93–103, 107–8, 111, 210, 261,
        577–78
    kingdom of God and, 90–91. See also kingdom of God
    life: birth, 63, 73, 120; crucifixion and death, 120–21, 210–
        11, 280–81, 418–19, 423; dedication, 63–64; genealogy,
        55, 62–63
    miracles, 66, 67–68, 714–15
    nonexclusively, 62–69
    prophecies, 74, 213
    return, 198–204. See also Christ's return
    salvation, 62, 84, 120–21, 122–25, 180–81, 210, 417–18
    Samaritan woman and, 66–67
    sermons: clearing of temple and, 68–69; first sermon, 64;
        good Samaritan, 64–65
    supremacy 305, 424
    unbelief toward, 65–66
Christ's return. See also last days
    eschatology: evangelization, 210–12; future hope, 210; godly
        living, 209–12, 427; imminency, 208–13; models, 215–16;
        "pan-millennialism," 212–13; rapture, 209, 212; world
        events, 211
    ministry toward, 209, 210, 211–12, 213
    parousia, 211, 213
Christian, the
    example, 91, 353–56, 424–25
    faith, 19, 203–4
    God's Word, 10, 587–89
    opposition to, 18, 199–200, 255–57, 843–45
Christopher, Mark, 481–83
Chrysostom, John, 161, 511
church, the. See also local church; home church; sending church
    commands, 10, 57–59, 84–86, 207, 397, 424. See also Great
        Commission
    definition, 898
    discipleship: in, 112–13; growth, 72–73, 78–79; outside, 113.
        See also Acts, book of
    early, 176–77, 715
    elders, 263–71, 389. See also elders
    endtimes, 198–204. See also Christ's return
    global. See global church
    missions and, 39–40, 111–12, 234–41, 733
    priorities, 219
    types: home, 290; sending, 234; supporting, 234. See also
        missionaries; missions

church planting. See also missionaries; planted church
    challenges: authority, 390–91; discipline and, 435; division,
        425; final phase, 486; financial, 409–10; focus, 409;
        models, 408–9; moral relativism, 389, 391
    cooperatively, 813
    defined, 263–64, 388
    parameters: application, 415–16; disciple-makers, 386–89;
        joys, 407–13; local church and, 266, 386–87, 401–2;
        redemptive narratives, 391–92
    principles: biblical view, 40, 90, 393–94, 397–99, 411; core
        values, 400–401, 410–13; cross-cultural adaptation, 403,
        847–48; fervent prayer, 403–4, 412–13; qualified leader, 389,
        441–44; strengthening, 263–64, 611–12, 614, 658, 898
    strategy: development, 388–89; movements, 196–97, 385–86;
        partnering, 394–96; theological, 194–95, 231–32, 270
Clement of Alexandria, 159
collaboration
    biblical: command, 798–99; defined, 797; Great Commission,
        798, 799; separation, 809
    challenges, 797, 803, 808
    cooperation: biblical, 809–10; Christian fellowship, 811;
        church planting, 813; education, 812; gospel centered,
        810–11; leadership, 813–15; mercy ministries, 811–12,
        830–33
    parachurch, 811–12, 816–19. See also parachurch
    preparation: care, 803; character, 800–802; commitment,
        802–3; communication, 801–2; conviction, 799–800
    strategies: affection, 805–6; hospitality, 804–5; support, 805,
        806
Columbia, missionary to, 361–63
Commonwealth of Independent States (CIS), 171–73
compassion missions. See also health care missions (HCM);
    injustice
    approaches: biblical, 663; extreme holism, 659–60; holistic,
        40, 659, 901; local, 664
    challenges: dependency, 674–75; discernment, 675–76;
        diagnosis, 673–74
    mercy ministries, 830–33
    preaching priority, 660–61, 663–64
    rationale, 658, 661, 662–63
communication
    cross-cultural: 132–40
    history, 574–76, 598–600
conflict resolution
    biblical confrontation, 439–41, 448, 797
    forgiveness, 432–33
    harboring bitterness, 431
    reconciliation, 435–36
    willingness to forgive, 431–32
Conservative Judaism, 149
Constantine, Emperor, 160–61
contextualization
    cultural accommodation, 20–21, 36, 167, 195, 898

education. *See also* global, educators; marketplace ministry; missionaries, training
    campus ministry, 740–42
    college, 409, 727–28, 736–37, 739, 751–55, 812, 841
    Holy Spirit, 528–29, 554, 589–90
    local church: benefit, 526–27; members, 421–22; neglect, 514–15, 544; school, 525, 812, 840–41
Edwards, Jonathan, 252, 254–55, 431. *See also* Brainerd, David
Edwards, Kevin, 255–57
elders
    biblical definition, 285–86, 304–11, 312–18, 389, 441–44, 487
    developing: candidates, 511–12, 814, 815; philosophy, 289–90, 300–301
    hospitality, 746–77
    missions: church planting, 263–64; evaluating, 287–88, 351–52; grid, 290–92; leadership team (MLT), 287–88, 288–89, 302; strategy, 289–92, 421–22, 470–71
    missionaries: evaluating 286–66, 334–35, 399; shepherding, 333–35, 337, 421–22
elder-qualified, 263–67
    church strengthening, 263–64, 281, 611–12, 614, 658, 766–69, 898
    New Testament pattern, 264–67, 329
    reason for, 263–64, 285–86
election
    covenant people, 53–54, 55–56
    gentile, 54–55
eschatology
    last days and, 90–91, 198–99, 204–7, 281–83. *See also* Christ's return
    missions: faithful, 203–4; fervency, 200–201; focus, 201–3; fortitude, 199–200
    models: new creation, 214–16; spiritual vision, 214
    viewpoints: amillennial, 214; millennial 42–43, 88–91; postmillennial, 85; premillennial, 90–91; scriptural, 90, 206–8
ethnicity
    church and, 52–60, 421–22
    covenant people, 53–56. *See also* Israel
    definition 53, 57, 417
    gentiles, 54, 55–57
    leadership and, 421–22, 441–44
    nationality and, 418–19
    unity, 418–19
ethnocentrism, 59–60
Evangelical Alliance, 191
evangelicalism, 35, 505, 508, 625, 899
evangelism, 900
    arts in. *See* media; music
    biblical. *See* Great Commission
    compassion, 653–58, 672, 688–89. *See also* compassion missions
    history: biblical proclamation and, 163–64; ecumenism,

166–68; fourth century, 160–62; modern era developments, 165–66; overview, 157; paradigm shift, 162–64; reformation-era, 164–65; subapostolic age, 157–58; third-century fathers, 159–60
    Jewish, 149–50, 151–54, 418–19
evangelists. *See also* pastors
    preach the Word, 404–5
    train leaders, 295–96, 405, 456–57
expatritate, 729–30, 900

faith
    biblical, 19, 127
    last days, 203–4
    missionary message, 133–34
    obedience-based, 126–27, 902
false teachers, 11–13, 29, 33–34, 275
family, missionary's
    culture, 361–63, 366, 445–52, 455–65, 461–63
    decision making, 359–60
    roles: biblical, 353–54, 362–63; children, 355–56, 357–58, 359–60, 364–65, 458; marriage 354–55, 364, 457, 464–65; parental, 355–56
    preparation, 356–58, 456–58, 693
    support, 339, 365, 366–67, 458–59, 460–61
    temptations, 358–59, 364–66, 463–64
financial support
    church planting, 409–10
    global investment, 324–25
    investment, 319–24
    letters, 328–31
    missions, 345, 347–51, 366–67, 521
flawed thinking
    focusing on: men, 36; success, 36, 38. *See also* number-based conversions
    forgetting God, 36–37, 61–62
    weak ecclesiology, 35–41
Flores, Ava, 720–23
Foley, Phillip F., 115–17
forgive(ness)
    believer's responsibility, 431–33, 435–36
    conditional, 433–34
    cultural differences, 430–32
    God's, 432–34
    withholding, 434–35
Freiberg, John, 677–84, 685–94
frontier missions, 388, 900
Fuller, Andrew, 300–303
furlough, 228, 338–39, 341, 369, 460–61

Giesbrecht, Nathan, 822–25
Glass, John, 312–18, 413–16
global
    church: definition, 900; music, 563–69

LaGeorge, Lisa, 452–54, 673–76, 784–91, 875–78
language
    benefit of English, 726, 728–29
    challenges, 731–32
    learning, 18, 165, 357, 359, 388, 403, 490
    missions, 854–55
larger mission, 40
Larson, Donald N., 732
last days. *See also* Christ's return
    described, 198–99
    eschatology and, 205–7
    faithfulness during, 203–4
    fervency, 200–201
    fortitude during, 199–200
    perseverance during, 204
Lausanne Movement, 40, 192–94
leadership
    cross-cultural, 441–44
    local church, 342–44
Lenski, R. C. H., 503
liberation theology, 194, 902
linguistic accommodation, 20, 21, 160, 161, 167, 902
Lira, Jenuan, 479–81
Livermore, David, 786, 790
local church
    education: benefit, 526–27; neglect, 514–15, 544; members, 421–22; school, 525
    hospitality, 748–49
    leadership: responsibility, 524–25, training, 524–26, 766–69
    missionaries: care, 298–99, 302–3, 333–34, 337, 340–42; evaluate, 294–95, 296; oversight, 297–98; pray, 226–27, 296, 302, 304–11, 312–18, 403–4; training, 295–96, 456–57
    preach: God's glory, 224–25, 264–65, 397–98; man's sinfulness, 225–26; missions, 226, 401–2, 766–69. *See also* short-term ministries
    prioritize: missions financially, 224, 291–92; missions personally, 223–24, 766–69
    promote: lost, the, 229, 405–6; missionaries, 227–28, 293–94, 298
Lonetti, Stephen, 140–43, 385–94
Luther, Martin, 151, 174–75
Lystra, preaching in, 137–38

MacArthur, John, xix–xxi, 198–204, 262, 320, 321, 405–6, 823, 824
Manasseh, King, 177–78
mankind
    destruction 417–18
    ethnicity. *See* ethnicity
    race, 417
    redemption, 120–21, 575–78
    response, 121–22

sinful, 119–20
    unity for, 417–22
man's rebellion, 44–45, 119–20
marketplace ministry
    advantages, 726, 863–64
    challenges, 864
    educators, 728–30, 739
    for Christ: God's will, 760–61, 862, 865; obedience, 759–60; reward, 761–62
    leaders, 763–64; 765–66
    medical. *See* compassion ministries
    mission driven, 764–66
    models: Marketplace, 866–67; Platform, 865–66
    spirit-filled, 758–59
    temptations, 761
    witnesses, 757–58, 763–64
Marshall, I. Howard, 319–20, 348–49
martyrs, 175–76, 255–57, 257–59
Masambuka, Chisomo, 740–42
Maxwell, John, 322–23
Mbewe, Conrad, 407–13
McQuilkin, Robertson, 787, 789
media
    biblical mandate, 619–20, 625, 626
    challenges, 113, 638–39
    company, 627–29, 632–35
    examples: bookstore, 644–45; library, 643–44; New Testament , 621–22; Old Testament, 620–21
    foundation: biblical, 622, 623; discernment, 624–25, 627; resources, 623–24;
    need, 626–27, 635–39
    platforms: audio, 622, 820–22; digital, 113, 628; film, 623; print, 620–22, 822–25; visual, 623
medical missions. *See* health care missions (HCM)
mercy ministry. *See* compassion missions
merism, 107
Messiah. *See* Christ
ministries
    God-ordained, 37–38
    marketplace, 345–46, 349, 726. *See also* marketplace ministry
    parachurch: benefits, 111, 293–94, 334, 402, 543, 673; challenges, 39, 817–18; collaboration, 811–12, 816–19; definition, 818–19
    short-term. *See* short-term ministries (STMs)
    unqualified, 526
    urban. *See* urban ministry
Minucius Felix, 159
missiology
    authority: God-ordained, 28–29; sending church, 29–30, 264
    challenges: church role, 264, 719, 733; ecumenism, 166–67, 188, 190–94; pride, 36–37, 731–32; tensions, 19–22; worldview, 37–38, 839–40
    developments, 165–66

effect, 774, 789–90; help versus harm, 774, 786, 788–89;
     missionary, 790–91; training, 789–90
  definition, 773, 780, 784
  implementation: cost, 781; evaluation, 779–80, 782–83;
     performance, 779; preparation, 778–79, 781–82, 789–90;
     selection, 777–78, 781, vision, 780–81
  participants, 773, 784–85
  trends, 785–86
Shryock, Aaron, 582–90
Sichone, Billy C., 543–47
Sills, David, 508–9
single missionaries, 452–54
sinners
  believer's responsibility, 242–44, 421–25, 431
  church responsibility, 88–89, 279–80, 427
  reformation 174, 180–81
  regeneration, 96, 126, 177, 251–52, 298, 708, 903
  repentance 122–25, 173, 433–34
  and Scripture, 27, 95–96, 278–79
  worldview 391, 420, 839–40
Slavic nations, 171–73
Slimbach, Richard, 788–89
social justice, 192–93
sola fide, 180
sola gratia, 180
sola Scriptura, 165, 176, 189
soli Deo gloria, 180
solus Christus, 180
soteriology, 127, 279–80, 473, 904
spiritual fruit, 123–25
spiritual understanding, 25, 835–43. *See also* discernment
Spurgeon, Charles, 223, 237, 393–94, 428, 499–500
Stalnaker, Cecil, 234–41, 868–74
strategies
  discipleship, 115. *See also* discipleship
  missions, 19–22, 26–28, 115–17, 235. *See also* missions
  Paul's, 136–37
Straub, Benjamin, 543–47
Strauch, Alexander, 746
Strauss, Stephen J., 43, 225
Stott, George, 260
Stott, John, 192–93
students. *See also* education
  college, 18, 740, 185
  high school, 691, 728, 785
  medical, 723, 754–56
subapostolic age, 157–58
Sun, Wendel, 514
support
  church and, 234–35, 290–91, 333–40, 366–67
  elder, 300–301
  letters, 328–31
  member, 302–3

for missionaries, 300–303, 333–40, 409–10
  mission support teams (MLT), 302
Surya, Daniel Avula, 846–48
syncretism, 31, 163, 190, 435, 904

Tan, Jimmy, 520–22
Tan, Sunny, 510, 515
Tatlock, Mark, 28–30, 61–69, 304–11, 423–25, 573–81, 629–32,
  653–58, 703–10, 743–49, 766–69, 835–43
Taylor, Hudson, 21, 486
teaching. *See* disciple-making
temptations
  missionaries: deceit, 358–59, 375–76; destructive nature,
     371–72; discipline, 376; finances, 370–71
  Word of God and, 372–75
Tertullian, 160
theological
  education: benefits, 526–27, 544–45; differences, 527–59;
     errors 544; maturity, 526–27; mentorship, 540–42;
     method, 503–4, 529–31; necessity, 523–25; philosophy,
     531, 543; schools, 500–503, 516–20
  injustice, 29, 508–9
  strategy: biblical view, 510, contextual, 160, 898
  support, 26–28, 300–303
  training: impact, 502–4, 513–14, 529; intentional, 504–7,
     509–510; missionaries, 28–29, 295–96, 456–57, 504–7 (*see
     also* indigenous, training); neglectful, 508–9, 514–15, 544;
     pastors, 28–30, 89–90, 500–502, 526
translation
  publishing: discernment, 633; translators, 634. *See also* media
  software, 603–4
  step-by-step, 605–7. *See also* Bible, translation
  theories: dynamic equivalence, 602–3; evaluating, 601; formal
     equivalence, 601–2; linguistic accommodation, 161; reader-
     oriented, 603; relevance, 604–5
Tyndale, William, 165, 176, 179, 585

Ukraine, 380–82
urban ministry
  biblical model, 686–90, 693–94
  early church, 685–86
  present-day, 690–93, 720–23
Urs, Devraj, 754–56

Van Duh Hmung, Silas, 185–87
Vatican, preaching near the, 143–46
Venn, Henry, 476–78, 489
Verr Beek, Kurt, 790
Videira-Soengas, Rubén, 523–31
Viguier, Philippe, 560–62
Vlach, Michael, 214–16
von Clausewitz, Carl, 835, 843

THE CENTER FOR
BIBLICAL MISSIONS
at TMAI

Equipping the global church
for effective biblical missions

The Center for Biblical Missions at TMAI seeks to produce and house scripturally based resources to equip believers for global missions in every region of the world.

CONTENT

Access biblical resources for your ongoing education

- Videos from the authors
- Field documentaries
- Online courses
- Downloadable articles & study guides

CONSULTING

Engage with missions leaders to shape your strategy

- Expert guidance from trusted ministry partners in our network
- Personalized consultations
- Missions strategy development

CONNECTING

Network with our missions-minded community

- Supportive relationships for local churches & missions leaders
- Missions conferences
- Short-term opportunities & internships

THE **MASTER'S ACADEMY INTERNATIONAL**

Training
Church Leaders
Worldwide

The Master's Academy International (TMAI) is a non-profit organization that has been committed to fulfilling the Great Commission by training indigenous church leaders to be approved pastor-teachers, able to equip their churches to make biblically sound disciples.

Partner With Us

INTERCEDE

Prayer is still our greatest need today. We invite you to join us in praying for the Lord's work through TMAI around the world. Sign up for prayer updates at *tmai.org/subscribe*.

INVEST

Our ministry would not be possible without the generosity of our donors. If you are interested in financially supporting this exciting global work, visit *tmai.org/donate*.

INTRODUCE

You can play a significant role in TMAI's ministry by introducing us to others who share a passion to see Christ's name exalted among the nations. Email us at *info@tmai.org*.

Our Schools

Albania | Argentina | Croatia | Czech Republic | Germany | Honduras | India
Italy | Japan | Malawi | Mexico | Myanmar | Middle East | Russia | South Africa
Spain | The Philippines | Ukraine | United States (Russian-Speakers)

Learn More

TMAI.ORG · 818.909.5570 · INFO@TMAI.ORG